POCKET
CRIMINAL
CODE

2001

POCKET CRIMINAL CODE

2001

With Forms of Charges from
The Police Officers Manual
by Gary P. Rodrigues, B.A., LL.B.,
of the Ontario Bar

*Incorporating R.S.C. 1985
and subsequent amendments*

CARSWELL
Thomson Professional Publishing

This publication is not engaged in rendering legal, accounting or other professional advice. If legal advice or other expert assistance is required, the services of a competent professional should be sought. The analysis contained herein represents the opinions of the authors and should in no way be construed as being either official or unofficial policy of any governmental body.

The work reproduces official English language versions of federal statutes and/or regulations. As this material also exists in official French language from, the reader is advised that reference to the official French language version may be warranted in appropriate circumstances.

⊖ The paper used in this publication meets the minimum requirements of American National Standard for Information Sciences — Permanence of Paper for Printed Library Materials, ANSI Z39.48-1984.

Canadian Cataloguing in Publication Data

The National Library of Canada has catalogued this publication as follows:

Canada. Criminal Code
    Pocket Criminal Code and . . .

1988

Title includes titles of several individual statutes, 1988-1994?; issues for 1995
have title: Pocket criminal code.

"The companion volume to the Police officers manual".

Continues: Canada. Criminal Code. Pocket Criminal Code and
miscellaneous statutes, ISSN 0702-7680.

ISSN 0841-6214

ISBN 0-459-26053-7 (2001)

1. Criminal Law — Canada — Handbooks, manuals, etc. I. Title.

KE8803.7.A29   345.71'002632   C89-030281-2 rev
KF9219.C2

CARSWELL
Thomson Professional Publishing

One Corporate Plaza   Customer Relations
2075 Kennedy Road   Toronto 1-416-609-3800
Scarborough, Ontario   Elsewhere in Canada/U.S. 1-800-387-5164
M1T 3V4   Fax 1-416-298-5094
                               World Wide Web: http://www.carswell.com
                                   E-mail: orders@carswell.com

PREFACE

The 2001 *Pocket Criminal Code* features twelve major statutory developments occurring in the year 2000 and late 1999. Where amendments have not yet been proclaimed in force at the time of publication, they appear as shaded text. The following are highlights of the said statutory developments:

1) *An Act to amend the Criminal Code (flight)* (S.C. 2000, c. 2, in force on Royal Assent date March 30, 2000): The Act makes it a *Criminal Code* offence to flee police in a motor vehicle. The offence *simpliciter* is a hybrid offence with a maximum sentence of five years imprisonment in proceedings by indictment. The new offences of flight causing bodily harm and flight causing death are indictable and punishable by maximum sentences of 14 years and life respectively. Pursuant to these amendments, where an accused is charged with criminal negligence causing death, criminal negligence causing bodily harm, or manslaughter arising out of the operation of a motor vehicle or the navigation or operation of a vessel or aircraft, and the evidence does not prove such offence but does prove flight causing bodily harm or flight causing death, an accused may be convicted of such lesser offence, as the case may be. An accused convicted of any of the new offences may also be subject to a discretionary driving prohibition order under s. 259(2) of the *Code*.

2) *An Act to amend the Customs Act and the Criminal Code* (S.C. 1998, c. 7, proclaimed in force May 1, 2000): Its amendments to the *Criminal Code* and the *Customs Act* allow the Minister of National Revenue to designate customs officers who will be permitted to exercise the powers and obligations of peace officers under ss. 254, 256, and 495 to 497 of the *Code*. Designated officers will be able to exercise the powers set out in ss. 495 to 497 of the *Code* in relation to a criminal offence under any act of Parliament. They will also have the authority to demand the necessary breath samples from impaired drivers. Section 498 of the *Code* has been amended to authorize peace officers to release persons who have been placed in their custody by designated customs officers in the circumstances set out in that section. Section 503 of the *Criminal Code* has also been amended to authorize peace officers to bring before a justice persons who have been placed in their custody by designated customs officers.

3) The *Personal Electronic Information Protection and Electronic Documents Act* (S.C. 2000, c. 5, Part 3 proclaimed in force May 1, 2000): Part 3 of the Act amends the *Canada Evidence Act* to give notices and Acts published electronically by the Queen's Printer the same legal authority as notices and Acts published on paper. Part 3 also contains provisions designed to clarify the assessment by courts of the integrity of electronic documents introduced as evidence.

Preface

4) The *Civil International Space Station Agreement Implementation Act* (S.C. 1999, c. 35, proclaimed in force May 1, 2000): Section 11 of the Act amends s. 7 of the *Criminal Code* to make Canadian and Partner state crew members of space stations amenable to criminal prosecution in Canada for specified acts and omissions which, if committed in Canada, would constitute indictable offences.

5) *An Act to amend the Criminal Records Act and to amend another Act in consequence* (S.C. 2000, c. 1, Royal Assent March 30, 2000 but not in force as at June 30, 2000; incorporated as shaded text): The Act would amend the *Criminal Records Act* with respect to pardons. Proposed amendments to the Act include those which provide for the clarification of refusal and revocation procedures, imposition of a one-year waiting period for persons reapplying for a pardon after one has been denied, the automatic revocation of a pardon upon a subsequent conviction for a hybrid offence, subject to certain exceptions, and for indicating in the national automated criminal records retrieval system the existence of certain pardoned records so as to allow for such records to be disclosed in order to be used in screening individuals for positions of trust or authority in relation to children or other vulnerable persons. The act would also amend s. 750(4) of the *Criminal Code* in order to add references to "issued" as well as "granted" pardons.

6) *An Act to amend the Criminal Code (victims of crime) and another Act in consequence* (S.C. 1999, c. 25, proclaimed in force December 1, 1999): Included in shaded text in the 2000 Edition and fully incorporated into this edition, this Act amends the *Code* to afford greater protection to victims and witnesses in the criminal justice system. It addresses such matters as limits on cross-examination by self-represented accused persons, publication bans, considerations of victims' safety in the context of judicial interim release decisions, procedures for notifying victims of the right to give impact statements and governing the presentation of such statements, minimum victim fine surcharges and the rights of victims to be notified of the operation of provisions governing judicial review of parole eligibility of accused persons sentenced to life imprisonment.

7) *An Act to modernize the Statues of Canada in relation to benefits and obligations* (S.C. 2000, c. 12, Royal Assent, June 29, 2000, but not in force as at June 30, 2000; amendments to the *Criminal Code* and *Firearms Act* incorporated as shaded text): This Act would amend the *Code* and the *Firearms Act* to extend to common-law partners of the same or opposite sex the same rights and obligations in specified circumstances as those accorded to married couples. It defines "common-law partner" for the purposes of both acts as a person who is cohabiting with an individual in a conjugal relationship, having so cohabited for a period of at least one year. It would repeal s. 23(2) of the *Code* which exempts married spouses from being accessories after the fact where they have received, comforted or assisted a spouse who is party to an offence for the purposes of enabling the spouse to escape. It would amend s. 215(2) of the *Code* by imposing a mutual obligation on common-law couples to provide one another the necessaries of life and making them criminally responsible for failing to do so, and by making consequential changes to the presumptions prescribed by s. 215(4). Finally, the Act would repeal s. 329 of the *Code* which creates specific offences of theft between spouses. Proposed

amendments to the Firearms Act include those which would add common-law partners of grandfathered individuals to the next of kin eligible under s. 12 to hold licences authorizing possession of specified handguns, and those which would include common-law partners and former common-law partners among those whom a chief firearms officer is authorized by s. 55 to interview for the purpose of investigating an individual's eligibility to hold a licence.

8) *An Act to amend the National Defence Act, the DNA Identification Act and the Criminal Code* (S.C. 2000, c. 10, proclaimed in force June 30, 2000): Amendments to the *Code* made by this Act include those which extend the prohibition against unauthorized use of bodily substances and the results of forensic DNA analysis to include those now authorized to be obtained by order of a military judge under the *National Defence Act* and those designed to clarify and strengthen the existing regime concerning the taking of bodily substances for the purpose of forensic DNA analysis.

9) *An Act to amend the Criminal Code (impaired driving causing death and other matters)* (S.C. 2000, c. 25, Royal Assent, June 29, 2000, but not in force as at June 30, 2000; amendments to the *Code* incorporated as shaded text): This Act would amend the *Code* by increasing the maximum penalty for impaired driving causing death from fourteen years to life and by providing for issuance of warrants for the taking of blood samples for the purpose of testing for the presence of drugs.

10) The new *Proceeds of Crime (Money Laundering) Act* (S.C. 2000, c. 17, Royal Assent June 29, 2000; consequential amendment to the *Criminal Code* not in force as at June 30, 2000; incorporated as shaded text): This Act would repeal and replace the *Proceeds of Crime (Money Laundering) Act*, S.C. 1991, c. 26. It would consequentially amend s. 488.1 (11) to exempt claims of solicitor-client privilege under the *Proceeds of Crime Money Laundering Act* from the *Code*'s procedure to determine claims of solicitor-client privilege.

11) The *Crimes Against Humanity and War Crimes Act* (S.C. 2000, c. 24, Royal Assent, June 29, 2000, but not in force as at June 30, 2000; amendments to the *Code* and the *Extradition Act* incorporated as shaded text): This Act is designed to implement Canada's obligations under the *Rome Statute of the International Criminal Court*. It would repeal and replace ss. 7(3.71) to (3.77) of the *Criminal Code*, creating a new Act under which Canada would have the jurisdiction to prosecute persons directly for the international crimes of genocide, crimes against humanity, and war crimes, rather than for corresponding domestic crimes. It would amend s. 183 of the *Code* by adding the offences which the new Act would create to those subject to the electronic surveillance techniques authorized by Part VI. Proposed amendments to s. 469 would require that offences under ss. 4 to 7 of the new Act (genocide, crimes against humanity, war crimes, breach of command/superior responsibility) be tried in the superior courts. Amendments to s. 607(6) would extend the exception to the special plea of *autrefois convict* for foreign trials *in absenta* to acts and omissions committed outside Canada that would be offences under the new Act. Finally, proposed amendments to s. 745 would require persons convicted of second degree murder and who have prior convictions for specified offences under the new Act to serve a mandatory sentence of life imprisonment without eligibility for parole for twenty-five years. The Act

would amend the *Extradition Act* by creating a new section 6.1 to prevent any person whose surrender is sought by the International Criminal Court (ICC) from claiming immunity from arrest or extradition under Canadian law. Proposed amendments to s. 14 of the *Extradition Act* would provide additional time for the ICC to make a formal request for extradition and to forward the necessary supporting documents after the provisional arrest of a suspect. Other amendments to the *Extradition Act* include those which would make special provision for judicial interim release and detention of persons sought by the ICC (including reverse onus provisions), those which would allow the Minister of Justice to delay making a surrender order pending post-committal challenges by an accused to the jurisdiction of the ICC and the admissibility of a case, those which would preclude, in ICC cases, the application of the various grounds for refusing surrender of a person by the Minister, and those which would authorize peace officers to detain accused persons making unscheduled landings in Canada while in transit to the ICC pending transmission of a request for consent to transfer to the minister from the requesting jurisdiction.

12) *An Act Respecting DNA Identification and to make consequential amendments to the Criminal Code and other Acts* (S.C. 1998, c. 37, ss. 15 to 24 amending the *Criminal Code*, and s. 25 amending the *Criminal Records Act*, proclaimed in force June 30, 2000): Amendments to the *Criminal Code* provide for orders authorizing the collection of bodily substances from which DNA profiles can be derived for inclusion in the DNA data bank established by the Act. The amendments further provide that such substances may be collected from offenders under sentence who meet specified criteria. Amendments to the *Criminal Records Act* are designed to clarify that forensic DNA analysis results contained in the convicted offenders index of the National DNA Data Bank are to be considered "a judicial record of conviction" for the purposes of s. 6 of the *Criminal Records Act* governing custody of records.

The forms of charges have also been fully revised and updated.

SUMMARY TABLE OF CONTENTS

(As amended to June 30, 2000)

TABLE OF CONTENTS

xi

Table of Contents

Table of Contents

Table of Contents

Table of Contents

PART IV — OFFENCES AGAINST THE ADMINISTRATION OF LAW AND JUSTICE

Interpretation

Corruption and Disobedience

Misleading Justice

Escapes and Rescues

Table of Contents

Table of Contents

Bodily Harm and Acts and Omissions Causing Danger to the Person

Motor Vehicles, Vessels and Aircraft

Assaults

Table of Contents

Kidnapping, Hostage Taking and Abduction

Abortion

Venereal Diseases

Offences Against Conjugal Rights

Unlawful Solemnization of Marriage

Blasphemous Libel

Defamatory Libel

Table of Contents

Table of Contents

Table of Contents

Table of Contents

Offence

Table of Contents

PART XV — SPECIAL PROCEDURE AND POWERS

General Powers of Certain Officials

Forensic DNA Analysis

Table of Contents

PART XVI — COMPELLING APPEARANCE OF AN ACCUSED BEFORE A JUSTICE AND INTERIM RELEASE

Interpretation

Arrest without Warrant and Release from Custody

Appearance of Accused before Justice

Table of Contents

Table of Contents

Table of Contents

Jurisdiction of Judges
Judge's Jurisdiction with Consent

Election

Trial

General

PART XIX.1 — NUNAVUT COURT OF JUSTICE

PART XX — PROCEDURE IN JURY TRIALS AND GENERAL PROVISIONS
Preferring Indictment

General Provisions respecting Counts

Table of Contents

Special Provisions Respecting Counts

Particulars

Ownership of Property

Joinder or Severance of Counts

Joinder of Accused in Certain Cases

Proceedings when Person Indicted is at Large

Change of Venue

Amendment

Inspection and Copies of Documents

Pleas

Table of Contents

Corporations

Record of Proceedings

Pre-hearing Conference

Juries

Empanelling Jury

Trial

Evidence on Trial

Table of Contents

Table of Contents

Table of Contents

Table of Contents

Table of Contents

Table of Contents

Table of Contents

Table of Contents

Table of Contents

Sureties to Keep the Peace

Appeal

Interim Release of Appellant

Procedure on Appeal

Summary Appeal on Transcript or Agreed Statement of Facts

Appeals to Court of Appeal

Fees and Allowances

PART XXVIII — FORMS

Table of Contents

CANADA EVIDENCE ACT

PART I — APPLICATION

Witnesses

Table of Contents

Table of Contents

Table of Contents

Table of Contents

Citation

CONTROLLED DRUGS AND SUBSTANCES ACT
Short Title

Interpretation

PART I — OFFENCES AND PUNISHMENT
Particular Offences

Sentencing

PART II — ENFORCEMENT
Search, Seizure and Detention

Restraint Orders

Forfeiture of Offence-related Property

Forfeiture of Proceeds of Crime

PART III — DISPOSAL OF CONTROLLED SUBSTANCES

Table of Contents

1

Table of Contents

Table of Contents

Table of Contents

Table of Contents

Table of Contents

Table of Contents

Extradition from a Foreign State

Schedule I

PART II — EXTRADITION IRRESPECTIVE OF TREATY

SCHEDULE I — LIST OF CRIMES

SCHEDULE II

Table of Contents

Table of Contents

Licences, Registration Certificates and Authorizations
Applications

Issuance

Term

Refusal to Issue and Revocation

International and Interprovincial Carriers

References to Provincial Court Judge

Appeals to Superior Court and Court of Appeal

Canadian Firearms Registration System
Registrar of Firearms

Records of the Registrar

Table of Contents

Transitional Provisions
Licences

Registration Certificates

Authorized Transportation of Firearms

Conditional Amendments to this Act

IDENTIFICATION OF CRIMINALS ACT
Short Title

Her Majesty

Identification of Criminals

Destruction of Fingerprints and Photographs

INTERPRETATION ACT
Short Title

Table of Contents

Table of Contents

Table of Contents

Repeal

Annual Report

YOUNG OFFENDERS ACT

SHORT TITLE

INTERPRETATION

DECLARATION OF PRINCIPLE

ALTERNATIVE MEASURES

JURISDICTION

DETENTION PRIOR TO DISPOSITION

NOTICES TO PARENTS

RIGHT TO COUNSEL

APPEARANCE

MEDICAL AND PSYCHOLOGICAL REPORTS

APPLICATION OF PART XX.1 OF THE CRIMINAL CODE (MENTAL DISORDER)

PRE-DISPOSITION REPORT

DISQUALIFICATION OF JUDGE

TRANSFER

Table of Contents

Table of Contents

Table of Contents

TABLE OF CONCORDANCE

Table of Concordance

R.S.C. 1970, c. C-34	R.S.C. 1985, c. C-46	R.S.C. 1970, c. C-34	R.S.C. 1985, c. C-46
7(1)(b)	8(1)(a)	41	41
8	9	42	42
9	10	43	43
10	11	44	44
11	12	45	45
12	13	Part II	Part II
13	—	46	46
14	14	47	47
15	15	48	48
16	16	49	49
17	17	50	50
18	18	51	51
19	19	52	52
20	20	53	53
21	21	54	54
22	22	55	55
23	23	56	—
23.1	23.1 [en. R.S. 1985, c. 24 (2nd Supp.), s. 45]	57	56
		58	57
		59	58
		60	59
24	24	61	60
25	25	62	61
26	26	63	62
27	27	64	63
28	28	65	64
29	29	66	65
30	30	67	66
31	31	68	67
32	32	69	68
33	33	70	69
—	33.1 [en. 1995, c. 32, s. 1]	71	70
		72	71
34	34	73	72
35	35	74	73
36	36	75	74
37	37	76	75
38	38	76.1	76
39	39	76.2	77
40	40	76.3	78

R.S.C. 1970, c. C-34	R.S.C. 1985, c. C-46	R.S.C. 1970, c. C-34	R.S.C. 1985, c. C-46
106.2	110	133(7)	145(7) [rep. 1985, c. 27 (1st Supp.), s. 20(2)]
106.3	111		
106.4	112		
106.5	113		
106.6	114	134	146
106.7	115	135	147
106.8	116	136	148
106.9	117	137	149
Part III	Part IV	Part IV	Part V
107	118	138	150
108	119	139	150.1
109	120	140	150.1(1) [en. R.S. 1985, c. 19 (3rd Supp.), s. 1]
110	121		
111	122		
112	123	113	124	—	150.1(2)
113	124	—	150.1(3)
114	125	—	150.4
115	126	—	150.5
116	127	—	151
117	128	—	152
118	129	142–145	—
119	130	—	153
120	131	147	154 [rep. R.S. 1985, c. 19 (3rd Supp.), s. 1]
121	132		
122	133		
122.1	134		
123	135 [rep. R.S. 1985, c. 27 (1st. Supp.), s. 17]	148–149	—
		150	155
124	136	151–153	156–158 [rep. 1985, c. 19 (3rd Supp.), s. 2]
125	137		
126	138	154	159
127	139	155	160
128	140	156	—
129	141	157–158	161–162 [rep. 1985, c. 19 (3rd Supp.), s. 4]
130	142		
131	143		
132	144	—	161 [en. 1993, c. 45, s. 1]
133	145		

Table of Concordance

Table of Concordance

R.S.C. 1970, c. C-34	R.S.C. 1985, c. C-46	R.S.C. 1970, c. C-34	R.S.C. 1985, c. C-46
237	253	—	273.1 [en. 1992, c. 38, s.1]
238	254		
238(2)	254(2)	—	273.2 [en. 1992, c. 38, s.1]
238(6)	254(6)		
239	255	—	273.3 [en. 1992, c. 38, s.1]
240	256		
240.1	257		
241	258	246.4	274
241(1)(a)	258(1)(a)	246.5	275
242	259	246.6	276
242(1)	259(1)	246.6(1)	276(1)
242(2)	259(2)	—	276.1 [en. 1992, c. 38, s.2]
242(4)	259(4)		
242(5)(a)	259(5)(a)	—	276.2 [en. 1992, c. 38, s.2]
243	260		
243.1	261	—	276.3 [en. 1992, c. 38, s.2]
243.2	262		
243.3	263	—	276.4 [en. 1992, c. 38, s.2]
—	264 [rep. R.S. 1985, c. 27 (1st Supp.), s. 37]		
	264 [en. 1993, c. 45, s. 2]	—	276.5 [en. 1992, c. 38, s.2]
243.4	264.1		
244	265		
245	266	246.7	277
245.1	267	246.8	278
245.2	268	247	279
245.3	269	247.1	279.1 [en. R.S. 1985, c. 27 (1st Supp.), s. 40]
245.4	269.1		
246	270		
246.1	271	248	—
246.1(1)	271(1)	249	280
246.1(2)	271(2) [rep. R.S. 1985, c. 19 (3rd Supp.), s. 10]	250	281
		250.1	282
		250.2	283
		250.3	284
246.2	272	250.4	285
246.3	273	250.5	286

R.S.C. 1970, c. C-34	R.S.C. 1985, c. C-46	R.S.C. 1970, c. C-34	R.S.C. 1985, c. C-46
301.1(2)	342(2)	328	370
301.1(3)	342(3) [rep. R.S. 1985, c. 27 (1st Supp.), s. 44]	329	371
		330	372
		331	373 [rep. R.S. 1985, c. 27 (1st Supp.), s. 53]
301.2	342.1 [en. R.S. 1985, c. 27 (1st Supp.), s. 45]	332	374
		333	375
302	343	334	376
303	344	335	377
304	345	336	378
305	346	Part VIII	Part X
305.1	347	337	379
306	348	338	380
306(3)	—	339	381
306(4)	348(3)	340	382
307	349	341	383
308	350	342	384
309	351	343	385
310	352	344	386
311	353	345	387
312	354	346	388
313	355	347	389
314	356	348	390
315	357	349	391
316	358	350	392
317	359	351	393
318	360	352	394
319	361	353	395
320	362	354	396
321	363	355	397
322	364	356	398
323	365	357	399
324	366	358	400
325	367	359	401
325(1)	367(1)	360	402
325(2)	367(2) [rep. 1994, c. 44, s. 24]	361	403
		362	404
326	368	363	405
327	369	364	406

R.S.C. 1970, c. C-34	R.S.C. 1985, c. C-46	R.S.C. 1970, c. C-34	R.S.C. 1985, c. C-46
420.11	462.31 [en. R.S. 1985, c. 42 (4th Supp.), s.2]	420.22	462.42 [en. R.S. 1985, c. 42 (4th Supp.), s.2]
420.12	462.32 [en. R.S. 1985, c. 42 (4th Supp.), s.2]	420.23	462.43 [en. R.S. 1985, c. 42 (4th Supp.), s.2]
420.13	462.33 [en. R.S. 1985, c. 42 (4th Supp.), s.2]	420.24	462.44 [en. R.S. 1985, c. 42 (4th Supp.), s.2]
420.14	462.34 [en. R.S. 1985, c. 42 (4th Supp.), s.2]	420.25	462.45 [en. R.S. 1985, c. 42 (4th Supp.), s.2]
420.15	462.35 [en. R.S. 1985, c. 42 (4th Supp.), s.2]	420.26	462.46 [en. R.S. 1985, c. 42 (4th Supp.), s.2]
420.16	462.36 [en. R.S. 1985, c. 42 (4th Supp.), s.2]	420.27	462.47 [en. R.S. 1985, c. 42 (4th Supp.), s.2]
420.17	462.37 [en. R.S. 1985, c. 42 (4th Supp.), s.2]	420.28	462.48 [en. R.S. 1985, c. 42 (4th Supp.), s.2]
420.18	462.38 [en. R.S. 1985, c. 42 (4th Supp.), s.2]	420.29	462.49 [en. R.S. 1985, c. 42 (4th Supp.), s.2]
420.19	462.39 [en. R.S. 1985, c. 42 (4th Supp.), s.2]	420.3	462.5 [en. R.S. 1985, c. 42 (4th Supp.), s.2]
420.2	462.4 [en. R.S. 1985, c. 42 (4th Supp.), s.2]	Part XI	Part XIII
		421	463
		422	464
		423	465
420.21	462.41 [en. R.S. 1985, c. 42 (4th Supp.), s.2]	423(1)(c)	—
		423(1)(d)	465(1)(c)
		423(1)(e)	465(1)(d)

Table of Concordance

R.S.C. 1970, c. C-34	R.S.C. 1985, c. C-46	R.S.C. 1970, c. C-34	R.S.C. 1985, c. C-46
423(2)	465(2) [rep. R.S. 1985, c. 27 (1st Supp.), s. 61(3)]	440	484
		440.1	485
		440.2	485.1 [en. R.S. 1985, c. 27 (1st Supp.), s. 67]
423(3)	465(3)		
423(4)	465(4)		
423(5)	465(5)	442	486
—	465(6)	442(1)	486(1)
423(6)	465(7)	—	486(1.1) [en. 1993, c. 45, s. 7]
424	466		
425	467	—	486(1.2) [en. 1993, c. 45, s. 7]
Part XII	Part XIV		
426	468	—	486(1.3) [en. 1993, c. 45, s. 7]
427	469		
428	470	—	486(1.4) [en. 1993, c. 45, s. 7]
429	471		
429.1	472 [rep. 1985, c. 27 (1st Supp.), s. 63]		
430	473	442(2.1)	486(2.1)
431	474	442(2.2)	486(2.2)
431.1	475	442(3)	486(3)
432	476	442(3.1)	486(4)
433	477	442(4)	486(5)
—	477.1	442(5)	486(6) [rep. R.S. 1985, c. 19 (3rd Supp.), s. 14(2)]
—	477.2		
—	477.3		
—	477.4		
434	478	443	487
435	479	—	487.01 [en. 1993, c. 40, s. 15]
436	480		
437	481	—	487.02 [en. 1993, c. 40, s. 15]
438	482		
438(1.1)	482(2)	—	487.03 [en. 1993, c. 40, s. 15]
438(2)	482(3)		
438(3)	–	—	487.04 [en. 1995, c. 27, s. 1]
438(4)	482(4)		
438(5)	482(5)		
Part XIII	Part XV		
439	483		

Table of Concordance

R.S.C. 1970, c. C-34	R.S.C. 1985, c. C-46	R.S.C. 1970, c. C-34	R.S.C. 1985, c. C-46
508	579	533.1	625.1 [en. R.S. 1985, c. 27 (1st Supp.), s. 127]
—	579.1 [en. 1994, c. 44, s. 60]		
		534	606
509	580	535	607
510	581	535(6)	607(6)
511	582	536	608
512	583	537	609
513	584	538	610
514	585	539	611
515	586	540	612
516	587	541	613
517	588	542–547	614–619 [rep. 1991, c. 43, s. 3]
518	589		
519	590		
520	591	549	621
521	592	550	622
522	593	551	623
523–525	594–596 [rep. R.S. 1985, c. 27 (1st Supp.), s. 120]	552	624
		553	625
		553.1	625.1
		554	626
526	597	555	627 [rep. R.S. 1985, c. 2 (1st Supp.), ss. 1 and 3]
526.1	598		
527	599		
527(1)	599(1)		
527(1.1)	599(2) [rep. R.S. 1985, c. 1 (4th Supp.), s. 16]	556	—
		557	628 [rep. R.S. 1985, c. 27 (1st Supp.), s. 129]
527(2)	599(3)	558	629
527(3)	599(4)	559	630
527(4)	599(5)	560	631
528	600	561	632
529	601	562	633
530	602 [rep. R.S. 1985, c. 27 (1st Supp.), s. 124]	563	634
		564 [rep. 1977–78, c. 36, s. 4]	635 [rep. R.S. 1985, c. 2 (1st Supp.), s. 2]
531	603		
532	604	—	635 [en. 1992, c. 41, s. 2]
533	605		

R.S.C. 1970, c. C-34	R.S.C. 1985, c. C-46	R.S.C. 1970, c. C-34	R.S.C. 1985, c. C-46
565	636 [rep. 1992, c. 41, s. 2]	593	666
		594	667
566	637 [rep. 1992, c. 41, s. 2]	594(3.1)	667(4)
		594(4)	667(5)
567	638	595	668
568	639	596	669
569	640	597	669.1 [en. R.S. 1985, c. 27 (1st Supp.), s. 137]
570	641		
571	642		
572	643	597.1	669.2 [en. R.S. 1985, c. 27 (1st Supp.), s. 137]
573	644		
574	645		
575	646	—	669.3 [en. 1994, c. 44, s. 66]
576	647		
576.1	648		
576.2	649	598	670
577	650	599	671
578	651	600	672
579	652	—	Part XX.1 [en. 1991, c. 43, s. 4]
580	653		
581	654	—	672.1–672.95 [en. 1991, c. 43, s. 4]
582	655		
583	656		
584	657	Part XVIII	Part XXI
584.1	657.1 [en. R.S. 1985, c. 23 (4th Supp.), s. 3]	601	673
		601 "sentence"	673 "sentence"
		602	674
585	658	603	675
586	659 [rep. R.S. 1985, c. 19 (3rd Supp.), s. 15]	603(1.1)	675(2)
		603(2)	675(3)
		603(3)	675(4)
—	659 [en. 1993, c. 45, s. 9]	604	—
		605	676
		606	677
587	660	607	678
588	661	607.1	678.1 [en. R.S. 1985, c. 27 (1st Supp.), s. 140]
589	662		
590	663		
591	664	608	679
592	665	608.1	680

R.S.C. 1970, c. C-34	R.S.C. 1985, c. C-46	R.S.C. 1970, c. C-34	R.S.C. 1985, c. C-46
608.2	681 [rep. 1991, c. 43, s. 9, Sch., item 7]	631.1	703.1 [en. R.S. 1985, c. 27 (1st Supp.), s. 149]
609	682	631.2	703.2 [en. R.S. 1985, c. 27 (1st Supp.), s. 149]
610	683		
610(5)	683(5)	632	704
611	684	633	705
612	685	634	706
613	686	635	707
614	687	636	708
615	688	637	709
616	689	638	710
616(1)	689(1)	639	711
617	690	640	712
618	691	640(1)	712(1)
618(1)(b)	691(1)(b)	640(2)	712(2)
619	—	640(3)	712(3) [rep. R.S. 1985, c. 27 (1st Supp.), s. 153]
620	692		
620(3)(b)	692(3)(b)		
621	693		
621(1)	693(1)	641	713
622	694	—	713.1 [en. 1994, c. 44, s.76]
622.1	694.1 [en. R.S. 1985, c. 34 (3rd Supp.), s. 13]	642	714
		643	715
622.2	694.2 [en. R.S. 1985, c. 34 (3rd Supp.), s. 13]	643.1	715.1 [en. R.S. 1985, c. 19 (3rd Supp.), s. 16]
623	695	Part XX	Part XXIII
624	696	(Note: Part XXIII, R.S.C. 1985, c. 46 replaced by S.C. 1995, c. 22. See the end of this Table for a Table of Equivalent Sections.)	
Part XIX	Part XXII		
625	697		
626	698	644	716
627	699	645	717
628	700	646	718
629	701	646.1	718.1 [en. R.S. 1985, c. 27 (1st Supp.), s. 156]
630	702		
631	703		

R.S.C. 1970, c. C-34	R.S.C. 1985, c. C-46	R.S.C. 1970, c. C-34	R.S.C. 1985, c. C-46
683	749	717	783
685	750	718	—
686	751	719	784
Part XXI	Part XXIV	Part XXIV	Part XXVII
687	752	720	785
688	753	721	786
689	754	722	787
690	755	722(1)	787(1)
691	756	722(2)	787(2)
692	757	722(3)–(11)	787(3)–(11) [rep. R.S. 1985, c. 27 (1st Supp.), s. 171]
693	758		
694	759		
695	760		
695.1	761	723	788
Part XXII	Part XXV	724	789
696	762	725	790
697	763	725(1)	790(1)
698	764	725(2)	790(2)
699	765	725(3)	790(3) [rep. R.S. 1985, c. 27 (1st Supp.), s. 172]
700	766		
701	767		
701.1	767.1 [en. R.S. 1985, c. 27 (1st Supp.), s. 167]	725(4)	790(4) [rep. R.S. 1985, c. 27 (1st Supp.), s. 172]
702	768		
703	769	725(5)	—
704	770	726	791 [rep. R.S. 1985, c. 27 (1st Supp.), s. 173]
705	771		
706	772		
707	773	727	—
Part XXIII	Part XXVI	728	792 [rep. 1985, c. 27 (1st Supp.), s. 174]
708	774		
709	775	729	793 [rep. 1985, c. 27 (1st Supp.), s. 175]
710	776		
711	777		
712	778	730	794
713	779	731	795
714	780	732	796 [rep. 1985, c. 27 (1st Supp.), s. 176]
715	781		
716	782		

R.S.C. 1970, c. C-34	R.S.C. 1985, c. C-46	R.S.C. 1970, c. C-34	R.S.C. 1985, c. C-46
732.1	797 [rep. 1985, c. 27 (1st Supp.), s. 176]	747 "appeal court"	812 "appeal court"
		747(a)	812(f)
733	798	747(b)	812(g)
734	799	747(c)	812(c)
735	800	747(d)	812(b)
736	801	747(e)	812(a)
736(1)	801(1)	747(f)	812(d)
736(2)	801(2)	747(g)	—
736(3)	801(3)	747(h)	812(e) [rep. 1992, c. 51, s. 43(2)]
736(4)	801(4) [rep. R.S. 1985, c. 27 (1st Supp.), s. 177(2)]	747(i)	812(h)
		748	813
736(5)	801(5) [rep. R.S. 1985, c. 27 (1st Supp.), s. 177(2)	749	814
		750	815
		751	—
737	802	752	816
738	803	752.1	817
738(2)	—	752.2	818
738(3)	803(2)	752.3	819
738(3.1)	803(3)	753	820
738(4)	803(4)	754	821
738(5)–(8)	803(5)–(8) [rep. 1991, c. 43, s. 9, Sch., item 11]	755	822
		755.1	823 [rep. 1991, c. 43, s. 9, Sch., item 14]
739	804	756	824
740	805 [rep. R.S. 1985, c. 27 (1st Supp.), s. 179]	757	825
		758	826
741	806	759	827
742	807	760	828
743	808	761	829
744	809	762	830
745	810	763	831
—	810.1 [en. 1993, c. 45, s. 11]	764	832
		765	833
		766	834
746	811	767	835
747	812	768	836

R.S.C. 1970, c. C-34	R.S.C. 1985, c. C-46	R.S.C. 1970, c. C-34	R.S.C. 1985, c. C-46
—	Form 50 [en. 1991, c. 43, s. 8]	774	—
—	Form 51 [en. 1991, c. 43, s. 8]		

Part III: Firearms and Other Weapons

Table of Equivalent Sections

The *Firearms Act*, S.C. 1995, c. 39 repeals and replaces Part III of the *Criminal Code*. What follows is a table of equivalent sections and subsections which identify, insofar as possible, the substantive correspondence between sections and subsections of the new and old Part III. Note that certain of the provisions of the old Part III also correspond to the provisions of the *Firearms Act* itself.

Part III S.C. 1995, c. 39	Part III R.S.C. 1985, c. C-46 (prior to enactment of S.C. 1995, c. 39)	Part III S.C. 1995, c. 39	Part III R.S.C. 1985, c. C-46 (prior to enactment of S.C. 1995, c. 39)
84(1)	84(1)	92(2), (3)	91(1)
84(2)	84(1.1)	92(4)	91(4)
84(3)	84(2)	92(5), (6)	—
84(3.1)	—	93	91(2)
84(4)	—	94(1), (2)	90(2); 91(3)
85	85	94(3)	—
86(1)	86(2)	94(4)	90(4); 91(5)
86(2)	86(3)	94(5)	—
86(3)	86(2), (3)	95	—
87	86(1)	96	—
88	87	97	—
89	88	98	—
90	89	99	93; 94; 95; 96; 97
91(1)	—	100	—
91(2), (3)	90(1); 91(1)	101	93(1); 94; 95; 96; 97
91(4)(a)	90(3.1); 91(4)(b)	102	95.1
91(4)(b)	91(4)(c)	103	95(1)
91(5)	—	104	95(1); 96(3); 97(3)
92(1)	—		

Part III S.C. 1995, c. 39	Part III R.S.C. 1985, c. C-46 (prior to enactment of S.C. 1995, c. 39)	Part III S.C. 1995, c. 39	Part III R.S.C. 1985, c. C-46 (prior to enactment of S.C. 1995, c. 39)
105(1)	104(1), (2); 105(2), (8)	117.03	102
105(2)	104(5); 105(8)	117.04	103(1), (2), (3), (3.1)
106	105(2); 105(8)	117.05(1)	103(4)
107	—	117.05(2)	103(4.1)
108	104(3), (3.1), (4), (5)	117.05(3)	103(5)
109	100(1), (1.1), (1.3)	117.05(4)	103(6)
110	100(2), (2.1), (3)	117.05(5)	—
111(1)	100(4)	117.05(6)	—
111(2)	100(5)	117.05(7)-(9)	103(8)
111(3)	100(6)	117.06(1)	103(7)
111(4)	100(9)	117.06(2)	103(7.1)
111(5)	100(7)	117.07	92; 98(1), (3)
111(7)	—	117.08	92; 98(2)
111(8)-(10)	100(10)	117.09(1), (2)	91(6); 99
111(11)	100(11)	117.09(3)	–
112	—	117.09(4), (5), (6), (7)	92(2); 98(3)
113	100(1.1), (1.2)	117.1	–
114	—	117.11	115(1)
115	100(13)	117.12	115(2)
116	100(7.1)	117.13	–
117	—	117.14	91.1
117.01	100(12); 103(10)	117.15	116; 84(1) "prohibited weapon"; "restrictred weapon"
117.011	—		
117.012	—		
117.02	101		

Part XXIII: Sentencing

Table of Equivalent Sections

Bill C-41 (1995, c. 22) repealed and replaced the whole of Part XXIII of the *Criminal Code*, R.S.C. 1985, c. C-46. The substance of many of the sections of Part XXIII as it existed prior to the proclamation of Bill C-41 (1995, c. 22) was carried over into the new Part XXIII, but because many new sections were introduced, a complete renumbering of sections was required. What follows is a table of equivalent sections and subsections, which identifies, insofar as possible, the substantive correspondence between sections and subsections, of the "new" and "old" Part XXIII.

Part XXIII S.C. 1995, c. 22 "New" section	Part XXIII R.S.C. 1985, c. C-46 Prior equivalent section/subsection	Part XXIII S.C. 1995, c. 22 "New" section	Part XXIII R.S.C. 1985, c. C-46 Prior equivalent section/subsection
716	716	726	—
717	—	726.1	—
717.1	—	726.2	—
717.2	—	727	—
717.3	—	728	—
717.4	—	729	—
718	—	730	736
718.1	—	731	737
718.2	—	731(1)(a)	737(1)(a)
718.3	717	731(2)	—
718.3(1)	717(1)	731.1	—
718.3(2)	717(2)	732	737
718.3(3)	717(3)	732(1)	737(1)(c)
718.3(4)	717(4)	732(2)	—
718.3(5)(not in force at date of publication)	—	732(3)	—
		732.1	737
		732.1(1)	—
719	721	732.1(2)(a)	737(2)
720	—	732.1(2)(b)	737(2)
721	735	732.1(2)(c)	— [cf. 737(2)(f)]
721(1)	735(1)		
721(2)	—	732.1(3)(a)	737(2)(a)
721(3)	—	732.1(3)(b)	737(2)(f)
721(4)	—	732.1(3)(c)(i)	737(2)(c)
722	735	732.1(3)(c)(ii)	—
722(1)	735(1.1)	732.1(3)(d)	737(2)(d)
722(2)	735(1.2)	732.1(3)(e)	737(2)(b)
722(3)	735(1.3)	732.1(3)(f)	—
722(4)	735(1.4)	732.1(3)(g)	—
722.1	735(2)	732.1(3)(h)	737(2)(h)
723	—	732.1(4)	737(3)
724	—	732.1(5)(a)(i)	737(4)(b)
725	—	732.1(5)(a)(ii)	—

Part XXIII S.C. 1995, c. 22 "New" section	Part XXIII R.S.C. 1985, c. C-46 Prior equivalent section/subsection	Part XXIII S.C. 1995, c. 22 "New" section	Part XXIII R.S.C. 1985, c. C-46 Prior equivalent section/subsection
732.1(5)(a)(iii)	—	734.4	723
732.1(5)(b)	—	734.5	—
732.2	738	734.6	724
732.2(1)(a)	738(1)(a)	734.6(1)(a) [default of payment of fine]	724(1) [fine]
732.2(1)(b)	738(1)(b)		
732.3(1)(c)	—		
732.2(2)(a)	738(2)(a)	734.6(1)(b) [forfeiture not paid; any other method provided by law]	724(1) [forfeiture; civil proceedings]
732.2(2)(b)	738(2)(b)		
732.2(3)	738(3)		
732.2(4)	—		
732.2(5)	738(4)	734.6(1)(c) [A.G. of province]	724(1) [Her Majesty]
732.2(6)	738(5)		
733	739		
733(1)(a) [probation officer]	739(1) [prosecutor]	734.6(1)(d) [A.G. of Canada]	724(1) [Her Majesty]
733(1)(b)	739(1)(b)		
733(2)	739(2)	734.6(1) [filing of order in civil court with jurisdiction]	—
733.1	740		
733.1(1)(a)	—		
733.1(1)(b)	740(1)		
733.1(2)	740(2)	734.6(2)	—
734	718	734.7	718
734(1) [offence]	718(1) [indictable offence, five years or less]	734.7(1)(a)	718(7)
		734.7(1)(b)	—
		734.7(2)	718(8)
734(2)	—	734.7(3)	—
734(3)	—	734.7(4)	—
734(4)	—	734.8	722
734(5)	—	734.8(1)	722(5)
734(6)	— [cf. 725(3); 726(3)]	734.8(2)	722(1)
		734.8(3)	722(2)
734(7)	—	734.8(4)	722(3)
734.1	—	734.8(5)	722(4)
734.2	—	735	719
734.3	— [cf. 718(11)]	735(1)	719

Table of Concordance

Part XXIII S.C. 1995, c. 22 "New" section	Part XXIII R.S.C. 1985, c. C-46 Prior equivalent section/subsection	Part XXIII S.C. 1995, c. 22 "New" section	Part XXIII R.S.C. 1985, c. C-46 Prior equivalent section/subsection
735(2) [civil court with jurisdiction]	720 [superior court]	743.1(6)	731(8)
		743.2	731.1
		743.3	732(1)
736	718.1	743.4	733
737	727.9	743.5	741.1
738	725	743.6	741.2
738(1)(a)	725(1)	743.6(1)	741.2
738(1)(b)	—	743.6(2)	—
738(1)(c)	—	744	734
738(2)	—	745	742
739	726	745(a)	742(a)
739(a)	726(1)	745(b)	742(a.1)
739(b)	—	745(c)	742(b)
740	—	745(d)	742(c)
741	726	745.1	742.1
741(1) [civil court with jurisdiction]	726(2) [superior court]	745.2	743
		745.3	743.1
741(2)	726(3); 725(3)	745.4	744
741.1	—	745.5	744.1
741.2	—	745.6	745
742	—	745.6(2)(a)	745(2)
742.1	—	745.6(2)(b)	745(2)
742.2	—	745.6(2)(c)	745(2)
742.3	—	745.6(2)(d)	—
742.4	—	745.6(2)(e)	745(2)
742.5	—	745.6(3)	—
742.6	—	745.6(4)	745(3)
742.7	—	745.6(5)	745(4)
743	730	745.6(6)	745(5)
743.1	731	745.6(7)	745(6)
743.1(1)	731(1)	745.6(8)	745(7)
743.1(2)	731(2)	746	746
743.1(3)	731(3)	746.1	747
743.1(4)	731(4)	746.1(1)	747(1)
743.1(5)	731(5)	746.1(2)	747(2)
		746.1(3)	747(2.1)

c

Table of Concordance

Part XXIII S.C. 1995, c. 22 "New" section	Part XXIII R.S.C. 1985, c. C-46 Prior equivalent section/subsection	Part XXIII S.C. 1995, c. 22 "New" section	Part XXIII R.S.C. 1985, c. C-46 Prior equivalent section/subsection
(Note: ss. 747 to 747.8 not in force at date of publication.)		750(4)	748(4)
748	749	750(5)	748(5)
748.1	750		
749	751	750(6)	748(6)
750	748		
750(1) [two years or more]	748(1) [exceeding five years]	751	728
750(2)	748(2)	751.1	729
750(3)	748(3)		

CRIMINAL CODE

An Act respecting the criminal law

Revised Statutes of Canada, 1985
Chapter C–46
and Amendments

An Act respecting the criminal law

R.S.C. 1985, c. C-46, as am. R.S.C. 1985, c. 2 (1st Supp.), ss. 1–3; R.S.C. 1985, c. 11 (1st Supp.), s. 2; R.S.C. 1985, c. 27 (1st Supp.), ss. 1–187, 203; R.S.C. 1985, c. 31 (1st Supp.), s. 61; R.S.C. 1985, c. 47 (1st Supp.), s. 1; R.S.C. 1985, c. 51 (1st Supp.), s. 1; R.S.C. 1985, c. 52 (1st Supp.), ss. 1–3; R.S.C. 1985, c. 1 (2nd Supp.), s. 213; R.S.C. 1985, c. 24 (2nd Supp.), ss. 45–47; R.S.C. 1985, c. 27 (2nd Supp.), s. 10; R.S.C. 1985, c. 35 (2nd Supp.), s. 34; R.S.C. 1985, c. 10 (3rd Supp.), ss. 1, 2; R.S.C. 1985, c. 19 (3rd Supp.), ss. 1–16; R.S.C. 1985, c. 30 (3rd Supp.), ss. 1, 2; R.S.C. 1985, c. 34 (3rd Supp.), ss. 9–13; R.S.C. 1985, c. 1 (4th Supp.), ss. 13–18, 45; R.S.C. 1985, c. 23 (4th Supp.), ss. 1–8; R.S.C. 1985, c. 29 (4th Supp.), s. 17; R.S.C. 1985, c. 30 (4th Supp.), s. 45; R.S.C. 1985, c. 31 (4th Supp.), ss. 94–97; R.S.C. 1985, c. 32 (4th Supp.), ss. 55–62; R.S.C. 1985, c. 40 (4th Supp.), s. 2; R.S.C. 1985, c. 42 (4th Supp.), ss. 1–8; R.S.C. 1985, c. 50 (4th Supp.), s. 1; S.C. 1989, c. 2, s. 1; 1990, c. 15, s. 1; 1990, c. 16, ss. 2–7; 1990, c. 17, ss. 7–15; 1990, c. 44, s. 15; 1991, c. 1, s. 28; 1991, c. 4, ss. 1, 2; 1991, c. 28, ss. 6–12; 1991, c. 40, ss. 1–41; 1991, c. 43, ss. 1–10 [s. 10(8) not in force at date of publication.]; 1992, c. 1, s. 58; 1992, c. 11, ss. 14–18; 1992, c. 20, ss. 199–204, 215, 216, 228, 229; 1992, c. 21, s. 9; 1992, c. 22, s. 12; 1992, c. 27, s. 90; 1992, c. 38; 1992, c. 41; 1992, c. 47, ss. 68–72; 1992, c. 51, ss. 32–43, 67; 1993, c. 7; 1993, c. 25, ss. 93–96; 1993, c. 28, s. 78 (Sched. III, items 25–37); 1993, c. 34, s. 59(1); 1993, c. 37; 1993, c. 40; 1993, c. 45; 1993, c. 46; 1994, c. 12, s. 1; 1994, c. 13, s. 7; 1994, c. 38, ss. 14, 25; 1994, c. 44, ss. 1–84; 1995, c. 5, s. 25(1)(g); 1995, c. 19, ss. 37–41; 1995, c. 22, ss. 1–12, 14, 15, 19–24 [s. 6 (as it enacts ss. 718.3(5), 747–747.8 of the *Criminal Code*) not in force at date of publication.]; 1995, c. 27, ss. 1, 3; 1995, c. 29, ss. 39, 40; 1995, c. 32, s. 33; 1995, c. 39, ss. 138–157, 188–190 [s. 139 (as it amends s. 97 of the *Criminal Code*) to come into force January 1, 2003 if not proclaimed in force sooner.]; 1995, c. 42, ss. 73–78, 86, 87; 1996, c. 8, s. 32; 1996, c. 16, s. 60; 1996, c. 19, ss. 65–76, 93.3; 1996, c. 31, ss. 68–72; 1996, c. 34, ss. 1–8 [ss. 1, 2(1), 3–5 not in force at date of publication.]; 1997, c. 2; 1997, c. 9, s. 124 [Not in force at date of publication.]; 1997, c. 16, ss. 1–7; 1997, c. 17, ss. 1–10; 1997, c. 18, ss. 2–115, 139.1, 140, 141 [ss. 106, 107 not in force at date of publication.]; 1997, c. 17, ss. 1–10; 1997, c. 23, ss. 1–20, 26, 27; 1997, c. 30, ss. 1–3; 1997, c. 39, ss. 1–3; 1998, c. 7, ss. 2, 3; 1998, c. 9, ss. 2–8; 1998, s. 15, s. 20; 1998, c.

30, ss. 14, 16; 1998, c. 34, ss. 8, 9, 11; 1998, c. 35, ss. 119–121; 1998, c. 37, ss. 15–24; 1999, c. 2, s. 47; 1999, c. 3, ss. 25–58; 1999, c. 5, ss. 1–47, 51, 52; 1999, c. 17, s. 120; 1999, c. 18, ss. 92–95; 1999, c. 25; 1999, c. 28, ss. 155, 156; 1999, c. 31, ss. 67–69; 1999, c. 32, ss. 1–6; 1999, c. 33, s. 346; 1999, c. 35, s. 11; 2000, c. 1, s. 9 [Not in force at date of publication.]; 2000, c. 2; 2000, c. 10, ss. 13–24; 2000, c. 12, ss. 91–95 [Not in force at date of publication.]; 2000, c. 17, s. 89 [Not in force at date of publication.]; 2000, c. 24, ss. 42–46 [Not in force at date of publication.]; 2000, c. 25 [Not in force at date of publication.].

Short Title

1. Short title — This Act may be cited as the *Criminal Code*.

Interpretation

2. Definitions — In this Act,

"Act" includes

    (a) an Act of Parliament,

    (b) an Act of the legislature of the former Province of Canada,

    (c) an Act of the legislature of a province, and

    (d) an Act or ordinance of the legislature of a province, territory or place in force at the time that province, territory or placebecame a province of Canada;

"Attorney General"

    (a) with respect to proceedings to which this Act applies, means the Attorney General or Solicitor General of the province in which those proceedings are taken and includes his lawful deputy, and

    (b) with respect to

        (i) the Yukon Territory, the Northwest Territories and Nunavut, or

        (ii) proceedings commenced at the instance of the Government of Canada and conducted by or on behalf of that Government in respect of a contravention of, a conspiracy or attempt to contravene or counselling the contravention of any Act of Parliament other than this Act or any regulation made under any such Act,

means the Attorney General of Canada and includes his lawful deputy;

"bank-note" includes any negotiable instrument

    (a) issued by or on behalf of a person carrying on the business of banking in or out of Canada, and

    (b) issued under the authority of Parliament or under the lawful authority of the government of a state other than Canada, intended to be used as money or as the equivalent of money, immediately on issue or at some time subsequent thereto, and includes bank bills and bank post bills;

"bodily harm" means any hurt or injury to a person that interferes with the health or comfort of the person and that is more than merely transient or trifling in nature;

"Canadian Forces" means the armed forces of Her Majesty raised by Canada;

"cattle" means neat cattle or an animal of the bovine species by whatever technical or familiar name it is known, and includes any horse, mule, ass, pig, sheep or goat;

"clerk of the court" includes a person, by whatever name or title he may be designated, who from time to time performs the duties of a clerk of the court;

Proposed Addition — 2 "common-law partner"

"common-law partner", in relation to an individual, means a person who is cohabiting with the individual in a conjugal relationship, having so cohabited for a period of at least one year;

2000, c. 12, s. 91 [Not in force at date of publication.]

"complainant" means the victim of an alleged offence;

"counsel" means a barrister or solicitor, in respect of the matters or things that barristers and solicitors, respectively, are authorized by the law of a province to do or perform in relation to legal proceedings;

"count" means a charge in an information or indictment;

"court of appeal" means

    (a) in the Province of Prince Edward Island, the Appeal Division of the Supreme Court, and

    (b) in all other provinces, the Court of Appeal;

"court of criminal jurisdiction" means

    (a) a court of general or quarter sessions of the peace, when presided over by a Superior Court judge,

    (a.1) in the Province of Quebec, the Court of Quebec, the municipal court of Montreal and the municipal court of Quebec;

    (b) a provincial court judge or judge acting under Part XIX, and

    (c) in the Province of Ontario, the Ontario Court of Justice;

"criminal organization" means any group, association or other body consisting of five or more persons, whether formally or informally organized,

    (a) having as one of its primary activities the commission of an indictable offence under this or any other Act of Parliament for which the maximum punishment is imprisonment for five years or more, and

    (b) any or all of the members of which engage in or have, within the preceding five years, engaged in the commission of a series of such offences;

"criminal organization offence" means

(a) an offence under sectiion 467.1 or an indictable offence under this or any other Act of Parliament committed for the benefit of, at the direction of or in association with a criminal organization for which the maximum punishment is imprisonment for five years or more, or

(b) a conspiracy or an attempt to commit, being an accessory after the fact in relation to, or any counselling in relation to, an offence referred to in paragraph (a);

"day" means the period between six o'clock in the forenoon and nine o'clock in the afternoon of the same day;

"document of title to goods" includes a bought and sold note, bill of lading, warrant, certificate or order for the delivery or transfer of goods or any other valuable thing, and any other document used in the ordinary course of business as evidence of the possession or control of goods, authorizing or purporting to authorize, by endorsement or by delivery, the person in possession of the document to transfer or receive any goods thereby represented or therein mentioned or referred to;

"document of title to lands" includes any writing that is or contains evidence of the title, or any part of the title, to real property or to any interest in real property, and any notarial or registrar's copy thereof and any duplicate instrument, memorial, certificate or document authorized or required by any law in force in any part of Canada with respect to registration of titles that relates to title to real property or to any interest in real property;

"dwelling-house" means the whole or any part of a building or structure that is kept or occupied as a permanent or temporary residence, and includes

(a) a building within the curtilage of a dwelling-house that is connected to it by a doorway or by a covered and enclosed passage-way, and

(b) a unit that is designed to be mobile and to be used as a permanent or temporary residence and that is being used as such a residence;

"every one", **"person"**, **"owner"**, and similar expressions include Her Majesty and public bodies, bodies corporate, societies, companies and inhabitants of counties, parishes, municipalities or other districts in relation to the acts and things that they are capable of doing and owning respectively;

"explosive substance" includes

(a) anything intended to be used to make an explosive substance,

(b) anything, or any part thereof, used or intended to be used, or adapted to cause, or to aid in causing an explosion in or with an explosive substance, and

(c) an incendiary grenade, fire bomb, molotov cocktail or other similar incendiary substance or device and a delaying mechanism or other thing intended for use in connection with such a substance or device;

"firearm" means a barrelled weapon from which any shot, bullet or other projectile can be discharged and that is capable of causing serious bodily injury or death to a person, and includes any frame or receiver of such a barrelled weapon and anything that can be adapted for use as a firearm;

"Her Majesty's Forces" means the naval, army and air forces of Her Majesty wherever raised, and includes the Canadian Forces;

"highway" means a road to which the public has the right of access, and includes bridges over which or tunnels through which a road passes;

"indictment" includes

(a) information or a count therein,

(b) a plea, replication or other pleading, and

(c) any record;

"internationally protected person" means

(a) a head of state, including any member of a collegial body that performs the functions of a head of state under the constitution of the state concerned, a head of a government or a minister of foreign affairs, whenever that person is in a state other than the state in which he holds that position or office,

(b) a member of the family of a person described in paragraph (*a*) who accompanies that person in a state other than the state in which that person holds that position or office,

(c) a representative or an official of a state or an official or agent of an international organization of an intergovernmental character who, at the time when and at the place where an offence referred to in subsection 7(3) is committed against his person or any property referred to in section 431 that is used by him, is entitled, pursuant to international law, to special protection from any attack on his person, freedom or dignity, or

(d) a member of the family of a representative, official or agent described in paragraph (*c*) who forms part of his household, if the representative, official or agent, at the time when and at the place where any offence referred to in subsection 7(3) is committed against the member of his family or any property referred to in section 431 that is used by that member, is entitled, pursuant to international law, to special protection from any attack on his person, freedom or dignity;

"justice" means a justice of the peace or a provincial court judge, and includes two or more justices where two or more justices are, by law, required to act or, by law, act or have jurisdiction;

"mental disorder" means a disease of the mind;

"military" shall be construed as relating to all or any of the Canadian Forces;

"military law" includes all laws, regulations or orders relating to the Canadian Forces;

"motor vehicle" means a vehicle that is drawn, propelled or driven by any means other than muscular power, but does not include railway equipment;

"municipality" includes the corporation of a city, town, village, county, township, parish or other territorial or local division of a province, the inhabitants of which are incorporated or are entitled to hold property collectively for a public purpose;

"newly-born child" means a person under the age of one year;

"night" means the period between nine o'clock in the afternoon and six o'clock in the forenoon of the following day;

"offence-related property" means any property, within or outside Canada,

(a) by means of or in respect of which a criminal organization offence is committed,

(b) that is used any manner in connection with the commission of a criminal organization offence, or

(c) that is intended for use for the purpose of committing a criminal organization offence,

but does not include real property, other than real property built or significantly modified for the purpose of facilitating the commission of a criminal organization offence;

"offender" means a person who has been determined by a court to be guilty of an offence, whether on acceptance of a plea of guilty or on a finding of guilt;

"offensive weapon" has the same meaning as "weapon";

"peace officer" includes

(a) a mayor, warden, reeve, sheriff, deputy sheriff, sheriff's officer and justice of the peace,

(b) a member of the Correctional Service of Canada who is designated as a peace officer pursuant to Part I of the *Corrections and Conditional Release Act*, and a warden, deputy warden, instructor, keeper, jailer, guard and any other officer or permanent employee of a prison other than a penitentiary as defined in Part I of the *Corrections and Conditional Release Act*,

(c) a police officer, police constable, bailiff, constable, or other person employed for the preservation and maintenance of the public peace or for the service or execution of civil process,

(d) an officer or a person having the powers of a customs or excise officer when performing any duty in the administration of the *Customs Act* or the *Excise Act*,

(e) a person designated as a fishery guardian under the *Fisheries Act* when performing any duties or functions under that Act and a person designated as a fishery officer under the *Fisheries Act* when performing any duties or functions under that Act or the *Coastal Fisheries Protection Act*,

(f) the pilot in command of an aircraft

(i) registered in Canada under regulations made under the *Aeronautics Act*, or

(ii) leased without crew and operated by a person who is qualified under regulations made under the *Aeronautics Act* to be registered as owner of an aircraft registered in Canada under those regulations,

while the aircraft is in flight, and

(g) officers and non-commissioned members of the Canadian Forces who are

 (i) appointed for the purposes of section 156 of the *National Defence Act*, or

 (ii) employed on duties that the Governor in Council, in regulations made under the *National Defence Act* for the purposes of this paragraph, has prescribed to be of such a kind as to necessitate that the officers and non-commissioned members performing them have the powers of peace officers;

"prison" includes a penitentiary, common jail, public or reformatory prison, lock-up, guard-room or other place in which persons who are charged with or convicted of offences are usually kept in custody;

"property" includes

 (a) real and personal property of every description and deeds and instruments relating to or evidencing the title or right to property, or giving a right to recover or receive money or goods,

 (b) property originally in the possession or under the control of any person, and any property into or for which it has been converted or exchanged and anything acquired at any time by the conversion or exchange, and

 (c) any postal card, postage stamp or other stamp issued or prepared for issue under the authority of Parliament or the legislature of a province for the payment to the Crown or a corporate body of any fee, rate or duty, whether or not it is in the possession of the Crown or of any person;

"prosecutor" means the Attorney General or, where the Attorney General does not intervene, means the person who institutes proceedings to which this Act applies, and includes counsel acting on behalf of either of them;

"provincial court judge" means a person appointed or authorized to act by or pursuant to an Act of the legislature of a province, by whatever title that person may be designated, who has the power and authority of two or more justices of the peace and includes the lawful deputy of that person;

"public department" means a department of the Government of Canada or a branch thereof or a board, commission, corporation or other body that is an agent of Her Majesty in right of Canada;

"public officer" includes

 (a) an officer of customs or excise,

 (b) an officer of the Canadian Forces,

 (c) an officer of the Royal Canadian Mounted Police, and

 (d) any officer while the officer is engaged in enforcing the laws of Canada relating to revenue, customs, excise, trade or navigation;

"public stores" includes any personal property that is under the care, supervision, administration or control of a public department or of any person in the service of a public department;

"railway equipment" means

>   (a) any machine that is constructed for movement exclusively on lines of railway, whether or not the machine is capable of independent motion, or
>
>   (b) any vehicle that is constructed for movement both on and off lines of railway while the adaptations of that vehicle for movement on lines of railway are in use;

"steal" means to commit theft;

"superior court of criminal jurisdiction" means

>   (a) in the Province of Ontario, the Court of Appeal or the Superior Court of Justice,
>
>   (b) in the Province of Quebec, the Superior Court,
>
>   (c) in the Province of Prince Edward Island, the Supreme Court,
>
>   (d) in the Provinces of New Brunswick, Manitoba, Saskatchewan and Alberta, the Court of Appeal or the Court of Queen's Bench,
>
>   (e) in the Provinces of Nova Scotia, British Columbia and Newfoundland, the Supreme Court or the Court of Appeal,
>
>   (f) in the Yukon Territory, the Supreme Court,
>
>   (g) in the Northwest Territories, the Supreme Court, and
>
>   (h) in Nunavut, the Nunavut Court of Justice;

"territorial division" includes any province, county, union of counties, township, city, town, parish or other judicial division or place to which the context applies;

"testamentary instrument" includes any will, codicil or other testamentary writing or appointment, during the life of the testator whose testamentary disposition it purports to be and after his death, whether it relates to real or personal property or to both;

"trustee" means a person who is declared by any Act to be a trustee or is, by the law of a province, a trustee, and, without restricting the generality of the foregoing, includes a trustee on an express trust created by deed, will or instrument in writing, or by parol;

"unfit to stand trial" means unable on account of mental disorder to conduct a defence at any stage of the proceedings before a verdict is rendered or to instruct counsel to do so, and, in particular, unable on account of mental disorder to

>   (a) understand the nature or object of the proceedings
>
>   (b) understand the possible consequences of the proceedings, or
>
>   (c) communicate with counsel;

"valuable mineral" means a mineral of a value of at least $100 per kilogram, and includes precious metals, diamonds and other gemstones and any rock or ore that contains those minerals;

"valuable security" includes

> (a) an order, exchequer acquittance or other security that entitles or evidences the title of any person
>
>> (i) to a share or interest in a public stock or fund or in any fund of a body corporate, company or society, or
>>
>> (ii) to a deposit in a financial institution,
>
> (b) any debenture, deed, bond, bill, note, warrant, order or other security for money or for payment of money,
>
> (c) a document of title to lands or goods wherever situated,
>
> (d) a stamp or writing that secures or evidences title to or an interest in a chattel personal, or that evidences delivery of a chattel personal, and
>
> (e) a release, receipt, discharge or other instrument evidencing payment of money;

"victim" includes the victim of an alleged offence;

"weapon" means any thing used, designed to be used or intended for use

> (a) in causing death or injury to any person, or
>
> (b) for the purpose of threatening or intimidating any person

and, without restricting the generality of the foregoing, includes a firearm;

"wreck" includes the cargo, stores and tackle of a vessel and all parts of a vessel separated from the vessel, and the property of persons who belong to, are on board or have quitted a vessel that is wrecked, stranded or in distress at any place in Canada;

"writing" includes a document of any kind and any mode in which, and any material on which, words or figures, whether at length or abridged, are written, printed or otherwise expressed, or a map or plan is inscribed.

R.S. 1985, c. 11 (1st Supp.), s. 2; c. 27 (1st Supp.), ss. 2, 203; c. 31 (1st Supp.), s. 61; c. 1 (2d Supp.), Sched. IV; c. 27 (2d Supp.), Sched.; c. 35 (2d Supp.), s. 34; c. 28 (4th Supp.), s. 34; c. 32 (4th Supp.), s. 55; c. 40 (4th Supp.), s. 2; 1990, c. 17, s. 7; 1991, c. 1, s. 28; 1991, c. 40, s. 1; 1991, c. 43, ss. 1, 9; 1992, c. 20, s. 216(1)(a); 1992, c. 51, s. 32; 1993, c. 28, s. 78 (Sched. III, item 25) [Repealed in part 1999, c. 3, (Sched., item 5).]; 1993, c. 34, s. 59(1); 1994, c. 44, s. 2; 1995, c. 29, ss. 39, 40; 1995, c. 39, s. 138; 1997, c. 23, s.1; 1998, c. 30, s. 14(d); 1999, c. 3, s. 25; 1999, c. 5, s. 1; 1999, c. 28, s. 155; 1999, c. 25, s. 1

3. Descriptive cross references — Where, in any provision of this Act, a reference to another provision of this Act or a provision of any other Act is followed by words in parenthesis that are or purport to be descriptive of the subject-matter of the provision referred to, the words in parenthesis form no part of the provision in which they occur but shall be deemed to have been inserted for convenience of reference only.

PART I

General

4. (1) Postcard a chattel, value — For the purposes of this Act, a postal card or stamp referred to in paragraph (*c*) of the definition "property" in section 2 shall be deemed to be a chattel and to be equal in value to the amount of the postage, rate or duty expressed on its face.

(2) Value of valuable security — For the purposes of this Act, the following rules apply for the purpose of determining the value of a valuable security where value is material:

(a) where the valuable security is one mentioned in paragraph (*a*) or (*b*) of the definition "valuable security" in section 2, the value is the value of the share, interest, deposit or unpaid money, as the case may be, that is secured by the valuable security;

(b) where the valuable security is one mentioned in paragraph (*c*) or (*d*) of the definition "valuable security" in section 2, the value is the value of the lands, goods, chattel personal or interest in the chattel personal, as the case may be; and

(c) where the valuable security is one mentioned in paragraph (*e*) of the definition "valuable security" in section 2, the value is the amount of money that has been paid.

(3) Possession — For the purposes of this Act,

(a) a person has anything in **"possession"** when he has it in his personal possession or knowingly

(i) has it in the actual possession or custody of another person, or

(ii) has it in any place, whether or not that place belongs to or is occupied by him, for the use or benefit of himself or of another person; and

(b) where one of two or more persons, with the knowledge and consent of the rest, has anything in his custody or possession, it shall be deemed to be in the custody and possession of each and all of them.

(4) Expressions taken from other acts — Where an offence that is dealt with in this Act relates to a subject that is dealt with in another Act, the words and expressions used in this Act with respect to that offence have, subject to this Act, the meaning assigned to them in that other Act.

(5) Sexual intercourse — For the purposes of this Act, sexual intercourse is complete on penetration to even the slightest degree, notwithstanding that seed is not emitted.

(6) Proof of notifications and service of documents — For the purposes of this Act, the service of any document and the giving or sending of any notice may be proved

(a) by oral evidence given under oath by, or by the affidavit or solemn declaration of, the person claiming to have served, given, or sent it; or

(b) in the case of a peace office, by a statement in writing certifying that the document was served or the notice was given or sent by the peace officer, and such a statement is deemed to be a statement made under oath.

(7) Attendance for examination — Notwithstanding subsection (6), the court may require the person who appears to have signed an affidavit, solemn declaration or statement referred to in that subsection to appear before it for examination or cross-examination in respect of the issue of proof of service or the giving or sending of any notice.

R.S. 1985, c. 27 (1st Supp.), s. 3; 1994, c. 44, s. 3; 1997, c. 18, s. 2.

5. Canadian Forces not affected — Nothing in this Act affects any law relating to the government of the Canadian Forces.

6. (1) Presumption of innocence — Where an enactment creates an offence and authorizes a punishment to be imposed in respect of that offence,

(a) a person shall be deemed not to be guilty of the offence until he is convicted or discharged under section 730 of the offence; and

(b) a person who is convicted or discharged under section 730 of the offence is not liable to any punishment in respect thereof other than the punishment prescribed by this Act or by the enactment that creates the offence.

(2) Offences outside Canada — Subject to this Act or any other Act of Parliament, no person shall be convicted or discharged under section 730 of an offence committed outside Canada.

(3) Definition of "enactment" — In this section **"enactment"** means

(a) an Act of Parliament, or

(b) an Act of the legislature of a province that creates an offence to which Part XXVII applies,

or any regulation made thereunder.

R.S. 1985, c. 27 (1st Supp.), s. 4; 1995, c. 22, ss. 10, 18.

7. (1) Offences committed on aircraft — Notwithstanding anything in this Act or any other Act, every one who

(a) on or in respect of an aircraft

(i) registered in Canada under regulations made under the *Aeronautics Act*, or

(ii) leased without crew and operated by a person who is qualified under regulations made under the *Aeronautics Act* to be registered as owner of an aircraft registered in Canada under those regulations, while the aircraft is in flight, or

(b) on any aircraft, while the aircraft is in flight if the flight terminated in Canada,

commits an act or omission in or outside Canada that if committed in Canada would be an offence punishable by indictment shall be deemed to have committed that act or omission in Canada.

(2) Idem — Notwithstanding this Act or any other Act, every one who

(a) on an aircraft, while the aircraft is in flight, commits an act or omission outside Canada that if committed in Canada or on an aircraft registered in Canada under regulations made under the *Aeronautics Act* would be an offence against section 76 or paragraph 77(a),

(b) in relation to an aircraft in service, commits an act or omission outside Canada that if committed in Canada would be an offence against any of paragraphs 77(b), (c) or (e),

(c) in relation to an air navigation facility used in international air navigation, commits an act or omission outside Canada that if committed in Canada would be an offence against paragraph 77(d)

(d) at or in relation to an airport serving international civil aviation, commits an act or omission outside Canada that if committed in Canada would be an offence against paragraph 77(b) or (f), or

(e) commits an act or omission outside Canada that if committed in Canada would constitute a conspiracy or an attempt to commit an offence referred to in this subsection, or being an accessory after the fact or counselling in relation to such an offence,

shall be deemed to have committed that act or omission in Canada if the person is, after the commission thereof, present in Canada.

(2.1) Offences against fixed platforms or international maritime navigation — Notwithstanding anything in this Act or any other Act, every one who commits an act or omission outside Canada against or on board a fixed platform attached to the continental shelf of any state or against or on board a ship navigating or scheduled to navigate beyond the territorial sea of any state, that if committed in Canada would constitute an offence against, a conspiracy or an attempt to commit an offence against, or being an accessory after the fact or counselling in relation to an offence against, section 78.1, shall be deemed to commit that act or omission in Canada if it is committed

(a) against or on board a fixed platform attached to the continental shelf of Canada;

(b) against or on board a ship registered or licensed, or for which an identification number has been issued, pursuant to any Act of Parliament;

(c) by a Canadian citizen;

(d) by a person who is not a citizen of any state and who ordinarily resides in Canada;

(e) by a person who is, after the commission of the offence, present in Canada;

(f) in such a way as to seize, injure or kill, or threaten to injure or kill, a Canadian citizen; or

(g) in an attempt to compel the Government of Canada to do or refrain from doing any act.

(2.2) Offences against fixed platforms or navigation in the internal waters or territorial sea of another state — Notwithstanding anything in this Act or any other Act, every one who commits an act or omission outside Canada against or on board a fixed platform not attached to the continental shelf of any state or against or on board a ship not navigating or scheduled to navigate beyond the territorial sea of any state, that if committed in Canada would constitute an offence against, a conspiracy or an attempt to commit an offence against, or being an accessory after the fact or counselling in relation to an offence against, section 78.1, shall be deemed to commit that act or omission in Canada

(a) if it is committed as described in any of paragraphs (2.1)(b) to (g); and

(b) if the offender is found in the territory of a state, other than the state in which the act or omission was committed, that is

(i) a party to the Convention for the Suppression of Unlawful Acts against the Safety of Maritime Navigation, done at Rome on March 10, 1988, in respect of an offence committed against or on board a ship, or

(ii) a party to the Protocol for the Suppression of Unlawful Acts against the Safety of Fixed Platforms Located on the Continental Shelf, done at Rome on March 10, 1988, in respect of an offence committed against or on board a fixed platform.

(2.3) Space Station — Canadian crew members — Despite anything in this Act or any other Act, a Canadian crew member who, during a space flight, commits an act or omission outside Canada that if committed in Canada would constitute an indictable offence is deemed to have committed that act or omission in Canada, if that act or omission is committed

(a) on, or in relation to, a flight element of the Space Station; or

(b) on any means of transportation to or from the Space Station.

(2.31) Space Station — crew members of Partner States — Despite anything in this Act or any other Act, a crew member of a Partner State who commits an act or omission outside Canada during a space flight on, or in relation to, a flight element of the Space Station or on any means of transportation to and from the Space Station that if committed in Canada would constitute an indictable offence is deemed to have committed that act or omission in Canada, if that act or omission

(a) threatens the life or security of a Canadian crew member; or

(b) is committed on, or in relation to, a flight element provided by Canada or damages a Canadian flight element.

(2.32) Proceedings by Attorney General of Canada — Despite the definition "Attorney General" in section 2, the Attorney General of Canada may conduct proceedings in relation to an offence referred to in subsection (2.3) or (2.31). For that purpose, the Attorney General of Canada may exercise all the powers and perform all the duties and functions assigned to the Attorney General by or under this Act.

(2.33) Consent of Attorney General of Canada — No proceedings in relation to an offence referred to in subsection (2.3) or (2.31) may be instituted without the consent of the Attorney General of Canada.

(2.34) Definitions — The definitions in this subsection apply in this subsection and in subsections (2.3) and (2.31).

"Agreement" has the same meaning as in section 2 of the *Civil International Space Station Agreement Implementation Act*.

"Canadian crew member" means a crew member of the Space Station who is

(a) a Canadian citizen; or

(b) a citizen of a foreign state, other than a Partner State, who is authorized by Canada to act as a crew member for a space flight on, or in relation to, a flight element.

"crew member of a Partner State" means a crew member of the Space Station who is

(a) a citizen of a Partner State; or

(b) a citizen of a state, other than that Partner State, who is authorized by that Partner State to act as a crew member for a space flight on, or in relation to, a flight element.

"flight element" means a Space Station element provided by Canada or by a Partner State under the Agreement and under any memorandum of understanding or other implementing arrangement entered into to carry out the Agreement.

"Partner State" means a State, other than Canada, who contracted to enter into the Agreement and for which the Agreement has entered into force in accordance with article 25 of the Agreement.

"space flight" means the period that begins with the launching of a crew member of the Space Station, continues during their stay in orbit and ends with their landing on earth.

"Space Station" means the civil international Space Station that is a multi-use facility in low-earth orbit, with flight elements and dedicated ground elements provided by, or on behalf of, the Partner States.

(3) Offence against internationally protected person — Notwithstanding anything in this Act or any other Act, every one who, outside Canada, commits an act or omission against the person of an internationally protected person or against any property referred to in section 431 used by that person that if committed in Canada would be an offence against section 235, 236, 266, 267, 268, 269, 271, 272, 273, 279, 279.1, 280 to 283, 424 or 431 shall be deemed to commit that act or omission in Canada if

(a) the act or omission is committed on a ship that is registered or licensed, or for which an identification number has been issued, pursuant to any Act of Parliament;

(b) the act or omission is committed on an aircraft

    (i) registered in Canada under regulations made under the *Aeronautics Act*, or

    (ii) leased without crew and operated by a person who is qualified under regulations made under the *Aeronautics Act* to be registered as owner of an aircraft in Canada under those regulations;

(c) the person who commits the act or omission is a Canadian citizen or is, after the act or omission has been committed, present in Canada; or

(d) the act or omission is against

    (i) a person who enjoys the status of an internationally protected person by virtue of the functions that person performs on behalf of Canada, or

    (ii) a member of the family of a person described in subparagraph (i) who qualifies under paragraph (*b*) or (*d*) of the definition "internationally protected person" in section 2.

(3.1) Offence of hostage taking — Notwithstanding anything in this Act or any other Act, every one who, outside Canada, commits an act or omission that if committed in Canada would be an offence against section 279.1 shall be deemed to commit that act or omission in Canada if

(a) the act or omission is committed on a ship that is registered or licensed, or for which an identification number has been issued, pursuant to any Act of Parliament;

(b) the act or omission is committed on an aircraft

    (i) registered in Canada under regulations made under the *Aeronautics Act*, or

    (ii) leased without crew and operated by a person who is qualified under regulations made under the *Aeronautics Act* to be registered as owner of an aircraft in Canada under such regulations;

(c) the person who commits the act or omission

    (i) is a Canadian citizen, or

    (ii) is not a citizen of any state and ordinarily resides in Canada;

(d) the act or omission is committed with intent to induce Her Majesty in right of Canada or of a province to commit or cause to be committed any act or omission;

(e) a person taken hostage by the act or omission is a Canadian citizen; or

(f) the person who commits the act or omission is, after the commission thereof, present in Canada.

(3.2) Offences involving nuclear material — Notwithstanding anything in this Act or any other Act, where

>(a) a person, outside Canada, receives, has in his possession, uses, transfers the possession of, sends or delivers to any person, transports, alters, disposes of, disperses or abandons nuclear material and thereby
>
>>(i) causes or is likely to cause the death of, or serious bodily harm to, any person, or
>>
>>(ii) causes or is likely to cause serious damage to, or destruction of, property, and
>
>(b) the act or omission described in paragraph (a) would, if committed in Canada, be an offence against this Act,

that person shall be deemed to commit that act or omission in Canada if paragraph (3.5)(a), (b) or (c) applies in respect of the act or omission.

(3.3) Idem — Notwithstanding anything in this Act or any other Act, every one who, outside Canada, commits an act or omission that if committed in Canada would constitute

>(a) a conspiracy or an attempt to commit,
>
>(b) being an accessory after the fact in relation to, or
>
>(c) counselling in relation to,

an act or omission that is an offence by virtue of subsection (3.2) shall be deemed to commit the act or omission in Canada if paragraph (3.5)(a), (b) or (c) applies in respect of the act or omission.

(3.4) Idem — Notwithstanding anything in this Act or any other Act, every one who, outside Canada, commits an act or omission that if committed in Canada would constitute an offence against, a conspiracy or an attempt to commit or being an accessory after the fact in relation to an offence against, or any counselling in relation to an offence against,

>(a) section 334, 341, 344 or 380 or paragraph 362(1)(a) in relation to nuclear material,
>
>(b) section 346 in respect of a threat to commit an offence against section 334 or 344 in relation to nuclear material,
>
>(c) section 423 in relation to a demand for nuclear material, or
>
>(d) paragraph 264.1(1)(a) or (b) in respect of a threat to use nuclear material

shall be deemed to commit that act or omission in Canada if paragraph (3.5)(a), (b) or (c) applies in respect of the act or omission.

(3.5) Idem — For the purposes of subsections (3.2) to (3.4), a person shall be deemed to commit an act or omission in Canada if

>(a) the act or omission is committed on a ship that is registered or licensed, or for which an identification number has been issued, pursuant to any Act of Parliament;

(b) the act or omission is committed on an aircraft

   (i) registered in Canada under regulations made under the *Aeronautics Act*, or

   (ii) leased without crew and operated by a person who is qualified under regulations made under the *Aeronautics Act* to be registered as owner of an aircraft in Canada under those regulations; or

(c) the person who commits the act or omission is a Canadian citizen or is, after the act or omission has been committed, present in Canada.

(3.6) Definition of "nuclear material" — For the purposes of this section, **"nuclear material"** means

(a) plutonium, except plutonium with an isotopic concentration of plutonium-238 exceeding eighty per cent,

(b) uranium-233,

(c) uranium containing uranium-233 or uranium-235 or both in such an amount that the abundance ratio of the sum of those isotopes to the isotope uranium-238 is greater than 0.72 per cent,

(d) uranium with an isotopic concentration equal to that occurring in nature, and

(e) any substance containing anything described in paragraphs (*a*) to (*d*),

but does not include uranium in the form of ore or ore-residue.

(3.7) Jurisdiction — Notwithstanding anything in this Act or any other Act, every one who, outside Canada, commits an act or omission that, if committed in Canada, would constitute an offence against, a conspiracy or an attempt to commit an offence against, being an accessory after the fact in relation to an offence against, or any counselling in relation to an offence against, section 269.1 shall be deemed to commit that act or omission in Canada if

(a) the act or omission is committed on a ship that is registered or licensed, or for which an identification number has been issued, pursuant to any Act of Parliament;

(b) the act or omission is committed on an aircraft

   (i) registered in Canada under regulations made under the *Aeronautics Act*, or

   (ii) leased without crew and operated by a person who is qualified under regulations made under the *Aeronautics Act* to be registered as owner of an aircraft in Canada under those regulations;

(c) the person who commits the act or omission is a Canadian citizen;

(d) the complainant is a Canadian citizen; or

(e) the person who commits the act or omission is, after the commission thereof, present in Canada.

(3.71) Jurisdiction: war crimes and crimes against humanity — Notwithstanding anything in this Act or any other Act, every person who, either before or after the coming into force of this subsection, commits an act or omission outside

Canada that constitutes a war crime or a crime against humanity and that, if committed in Canada, would constitute an offence against the laws of Canada in force at the time of the act or omission shall be deemed to commit that act or omission in Canada at that time if,

> (a) at the time of the act or omission,
>
>> (i) that person is a Canadian citizen or is employed by Canada in a civilian or military capacity,
>>
>> (ii) that person is a citizen of, or is employed in a civilian or military capacity by, a state that is engaged in an armed conflict against Canada, or
>>
>> (iii) the victim of the act or omission is a Canadian citizen or a citizen of a state that is allied with Canada in an armed conflict; or
>
> (b) at the time of the act or omission, Canada could, in conformity with international law, exercise jurisdiction over the person with respect to the act or omission on the basis of the person's presence in Canada, and subsequent to the time of the act or omission the person is present in Canada.

Proposed Repeal — 7(3.71)

(3.71) [Repealed 2000, c. 24, s. 42. Not in force at date of publication.]

(3.72) Procedure and evidence — Any proceedings with respect to an act or omission referred to in subsection (3.71) shall be conducted in accordance with the laws of evidence and procedure in force at the time of the proceedings.

Proposed Repeal — 7(3.72)

(3.72) [Repealed 2000, c. 24, s. 42. Not in force at date of publication.]

(3.73) Defences — In any proceedings with respect to an act or omission referred to in subsection (3.71), notwithstanding that the act or omission is an offence under the laws of Canada in force at the time of the act or omission, the accused may, subject to subsection 607(6), rely on any justification, excuse or defence available under the laws of Canada or under international law at that time or at the time of the proceedings.

Proposed Repeal — 7(3.73)

(3.73) [Repealed 2000, c. 24, s. 42. Not in force at date of publication.]

(3.74) Conflict with internal law — Notwithstanding subsection (3.73) and section 15, a person may be convicted of an offence in respect of an act or omission referred to in subsection (3.71) even if the act or omission is committed in obedience to or in conformity with the law in force at the time and in the place of its commission.

Proposed Repeal — 7(3.74)

(3.74) [Repealed 2000, c. 24, s. 42. Not in force at date of publication.]

(3.75) Attorney General of Canada — Notwithstanding any other provision of this Act, no proceedings may be commenced with respect to an act or omission referred to in subsection (3.71) without the personal consent in writing of the Attorney General or Deputy Attorney General of Canada, and such proceedings may only be conducted by the Attorney General of Canada or counsel acting on behalf thereof.

Proposed Repeal — 7(3.75)

(3.75) [Repealed 2000, c. 24, s. 42. Not in force at date of publication.]

(3.76) Definitions — For the purposes of this section,

"conventional international law" means

   (a) any convention, treaty or other international agreement that is in force and to which Canada is a party, or

   (b) any convention, treaty or other international agreement that is in force and the provisions of which Canada has agreed to accept and apply in an armed conflict in which it is involved;

"crime against humanity" means murder, extermination, enslavement, deportation, persecution or any other inhumane act or omission that is committed against any civilian population or any identifiable group of persons, whether or not it constitutes a contravention of the law in force at the time and in the place of its commission, and that, at that time and in that place, constitutes a contravention of customary international law or conventional international law or is criminal according to the general principles of law recognized by the community of nations;

"war crime" means an act or omission that is committed during an international armed conflict, whether or not it constitutes a contravention of the law in force at the time and in the place of its commission, and that, at that time and in that place, constitutes a contravention of the customary international law or conventional international law applicable in international armed conflicts.

Proposed Repeal — 7(3.76)

(3.76) [Repealed 2000, c. 24, s. 42. Not in force at date of publication.]

(3.77) Meaning of "act or omission" — In the definitions "crime against humanity" and "war crime" in subsection (3.76), **"act or omission"** includes, for greater certainty, attempting or conspiring to commit, counselling any person to commit, aiding or abetting any person in the commission of, or being an accessory after the fact in relation to, an act or omission.

Proposed Repeal — 7(3.77)

(3.77) [Repealed 2000, c. 24, s. 42. Not in force at date of publication.]

(4) Offences by public service employees — Every one who, while employed as an employee within the meaning of the *Public Service Employment Act* in a place outside Canada, commits an act or omission in that place that is an offence under the laws of that place and that, if committed in Canada, would be an offence punishable by indictment shall be deemed to have committed that act or omission in Canada.

(4.1) Offence in relation to sexual offences against children — Notwithstanding anything in this Act or any other Act, every one who, outside Canada, commits an act or omission that if committed in Canada would be an offence against section 151, 152, 153, 155 or 159, subsection 160(2) or (3), section 163.1, 170, 171 or 173 or subsection 212(4) shall be deemed to commit that act or omission in Canada if the person who commits the act or omission is a Canadian citizen or a permanent resident within the meaning of the *Immigration Act*.

(4.2) No proceedings — Proceedings with respect to an act or omission that if committed in Canada would be an offence against section 151, 152, 153, 155 or 159, subsection 160(2) or (3) or section 163.1, 170, 171 or 173 shall be instituted in Canada only if a request to that effect to the Minister of Justice of Canada is made by

    (a) any consular officer or diplomatic agent accredited to Canada by the state where the offence has been committed; or

    (b) any minister of that state communicating with the Minister through the diplomatic representative of Canada accredited to that state.

(4.3) Consent of Attorney General — Proceedings referred to in subsection (4.2) may only be instituted with the consent of the Attorney General.

(5) Jurisdiction — Where a person is alleged to have committed an act or omission that is an offence by virtue of this section, proceedings in respect of that offence may, whether or not that person is in Canada, be commenced in any territorial division in Canada and the accused may be tried and punished in respect of that offence in the same manner as if the offence had been committed in that territorial division.

(5.1) Appearance of accused at trial — For greater certainty, the provisions of this Act relating to

    (a) requirements that an accused appear at and be present during proceedings, and

    (b) the exceptions to those requirements,

apply to proceedings commenced in any territorial division pursuant to subsection (5).

(6) Where previously tried outside Canada — Where a person is alleged to have committed an act or omission that is an offence by virtue of this section and that person has been tried and dealt with outside Canada in respect of the offence in such a manner that, if that person had been tried and dealt with in Canada, he would be able to plead *autrefois acquit, autrefois convict* or pardon, that person shall be deemed to have been so tried and dealt with in Canada.

(7) Consent — No proceedings shall be instituted under this section without the consent of the Attorney General of Canada if the accused is not a Canadian citizen.

(8) Definition of "flight" and "in flight" — For the purposes of this section, of the definition "peace officer" in section 2 and of sections 76 and 77, **"flight"** means the act of flying or moving through the air and an aircraft shall be deemed to be in flight from the time when all external doors are closed following embarkation until the later of

(a) the time at which any such door is opened for the purpose of disembarkation, and

(b) where the aircraft makes a forced landing in circumstances in which the owner or operator thereof or a person acting on behalf of either of them is not in control of the aircraft, the time at which control of the aircraft is restored to the owner or operator thereof or a person acting on behalf of either of them.

(9) Definition of "in service" — For the purposes of this section and section 77, an aircraft shall be deemed to be in service from the time when pre-flight preparation of the aircraft by ground personnel or the crew thereof begins for a specific flight until

(a) the flight is cancelled before the aircraft is in flight,

(b) twenty-four hours after the aircraft, having commenced the flight, lands, or

(c) the aircraft, having commenced the flight, ceases to be in flight,

whichever is the latest.

(10) Certificate as evidence — If in any proceedings under this Act a question arises as to whether any person is a person who is entitled, pursuant to international law, to special protection from any attack on his person, freedom or dignity, a certificate purporting to have been issued by or under the authority of the Minister of Foreign Affairs stating any fact relevant to that question is admissible in evidence in those proceedings without proof of the signature or authority of the person appearing to have signed it and, in the absence of evidence to the contrary, is proof of the facts so stated.

(11) Idem — A certificate purporting to have been issued by or under the authority of the Minister of Foreign Affairs stating

(a) that at a certain time any state was engaged in an armed conflict against Canada or was allied with Canada in an armed conflict,

(b) that at a certain time any convention, treaty or other international agreement was or was not in force and that Canada was or was not a party thereto, or

(c) that Canada agreed or did not agree to accept and apply the provisions of any convention, treaty or other international agreement in an armed conflict in which Canada was involved,

is admissible in evidence in any proceedings under this Act without proof of the signature or authority of the person appearing to have issued it, and is proof of facts so stated.

R.S. 1985, c. 27 (1st Supp.), s. 5; c. 10 (3d Supp.), s. 1; c. 30 (3d Supp.), s. 1(1), (3); 1992, c. 1, s. 58(1), Schedule I, items 1(1), (2); 1993, c. 7, s. 1; 1995, c. 5, s. 25(1)(g); 1997, c. 16, s. 1; 1999, c. 35, s. 11.

8. (1) Application to territories — The provisions of this Act apply throughout Canada except

(a) in the Yukon Territory, in so far as they are inconsistent with the *Yukon Act*;

(b) in the Northwest Territories, in so far as they are inconsistent with the *Northwest Territories Act*, and

(c) in Nunavut, in so far as they are inconsistent with the *Nunavut Act*.

(2) Application of criminal law of England — The criminal law of England that was in force in a province immediately before April 1, 1955 continues in force in the province except as altered, varied, modified or affected by this Act or any other Act of the Parliament of Canada.

(3) Common law principles continued — Every rule and principle of the common law that renders any circumstance a justification or excuse for an act or a defence to a charge continues in force and applies in respect of proceedings for an offence under this Act or any other Act of Parliament except in so far as they are altered by or are inconsistent with this Act or any other Act of Parliament.

1993, c. 28, s. 78 (Sched. III, item 26).

9. Criminal offences to be under law of Canada — Notwithstanding anything in this Act or any other Act, no person shall be convicted or discharged under section 730

(a) of an offence at common law,

(b) of an offence under an Act of the Parliament of England, or of Great Britain, or of the United Kingdom of Great Britain and Ireland, or

(c) of an offence under an Act or ordinance in force in any province, territory or place before that province, territory or place became a province of Canada,

but nothing in this section affects the power, jurisdiction or authority that a court, judge, justice or provincial court judge had, immediately before April 1, 1955, to impose punishment for contempt of court.

R.S. 1985, c. 27 (1st Supp.), s. 6; 1995, c. 22, ss. 10, 18.

10. (1) Appeal — Where a court, judge, justice or provincial court judge summarily convicts a person for a contempt of court committed in the face of the court and imposes punishment in respect thereof, that person may appeal

(a) from the conviction; or

(b) against the punishment imposed.

(2) Idem — Where a court or judge summarily convicts a person for a contempt of court not committed in the face of the court and punishment is imposed in respect thereof, that person may appeal

(a) from the conviction; or

(b) against the punishment imposed.

(3) Part XXI applies — An appeal under this section lies to the court of appeal of the province in which the proceedings take place, and, for the purposes of this section, the provisions of Part XXI apply, with such modifications as the circumstances require.

R.S. 1985, c. 27 (1st Supp.), s. 203.

11. Civil remedy not suspended — No civil remedy for an act or omission is suspended or affected by reason that the act or omission is a criminal offence.

12. Offence punishable under more than one Act — Where an act or omission is an offence under more than one Act of Parliament, whether punishable by indictment or on summary conviction, a person who does the act or makes the omission is, unless a contrary intention appears, subject to proceedings under any of those Acts, but is not liable to be punished more than once for the same offence.

13. Child under twelve — No person shall be convicted of an offence in respect of an act or omission on his part while that person was under the age of twelve years.

14. Consent to death — No person is entitled to consent to have death inflicted on him, and such consent does not affect the criminal responsibility of any person by whom death may be inflicted on the person by whom consent is given.

15. Obedience to de facto law — No person shall be convicted of an offence in respect of an act or omission in obedience to the laws for the time being made and enforced by persons in *de facto* possession of the sovereign power in and over the place where the act or omission occurs.

16. (1) Defence of mental disorder — No person is criminally responsible for an act committed or an omission made while suffering from a mental disorder that rendered the person incapable of appreciating the nature and quality of the act or omission or of knowing that it was wrong.

(2) Presumption — Every person is presumed not to suffer from a mental disorder so as to be exempt from criminal responsibility by virtue of subsection (1), until the contrary is proved on the balance of probabilities.

(3) Burden of proof — The burden of proof that an accused was suffering from a mental disorder so as to be exempt from criminal responsibility is on the party that raises the issue.

1991, c. 43, s. 2.

17. Compulsion by threats — A person who commits an offence under compulsion by threats of immediate death or bodily harm from a person who is present when the offence is committed is excused for committing the offence if the person believes that the threats will be carried out and if the person is not a party to a conspiracy or association whereby the person is subject to compulsion, but this section does not apply where the offence that is committed is high treason or treason, murder, piracy, attempted murder, sexual assault, sexual assault with a weapon, threats to a third party or causing bodily harm, aggravated sexual assault, forcible abduction, hostage taking, robbery, assault with a weapon or causing bodily harm, aggravated assault, unlawfully causing bodily harm, arson or an offence under sections 280 to 283 (abduction and detention of young persons).

R.S. 1985, c. 27 (1st Supp.), s. 40(2).

18. Compulsion of spouse — No presumption arises that a married person who commits an offence does so under compulsion by reason only that the offence is committed in the presence of the spouse of that married person.

19. Ignorance of the law — Ignorance of the law by a person who commits an offence is not an excuse for committing that offence.

20. Certain acts on holidays valid — A warrant or summons that is authorized by this Act or an appearance notice, promise to appear, undertaking or recognizance issued, given or entered into in accordance with Part XVI, XXI or XXVII may be issued, executed, given or entered into, as the case may be, on a holiday.

Parties to Offences

21. (1) Parties to offence — Every one is a party to an offence who

    (a) actually commits it;

    (b) does or omits to do anything for the purpose of aiding any person to commit it; or

    (c) abets any person in committing it.

(2) Common intention — Where two or more persons form an intention in common to carry out an unlawful purpose and to assist each other therein and any one of them, in carrying out the common purpose, commits an offence, each of them who knew or ought to have known that the commission of the offence would be a probable consequence of carrying out the common purpose is a party to that offence.

22. (1) Person counselling offence — Where a person counsels another person to be a party to an offence and that other person is afterwards a party to that offence, the person who counselled is a party to that offence, notwithstanding that the offence was committed in a way different from that which was counselled.

(2) Idem — Every one who counsels another person to be a party to an offence is a party to every offence that the other commits in consequence of the counselling that the person who counselled knew or ought to have known was likely to be committed in consequence of the counselling.

(3) Definition of "counsel" — For the purposes of this Act, **"counsel"** includes procure, solicit or incite.

R.S. 1985, c. 27 (1st Supp.), s. 7(1).

23. (1) Accessory after the fact — An accessory after the fact to an offence is one who, knowing that a person has been a party to the offence, receives, comforts or assists that person for the purpose of enabling that person to escape.

(2) Husband or wife, when not accessory — No married person whose spouse has been a party to an offence is an accessory after the fact to that offence by receiving, comforting or assisting the spouse for the purpose of enabling the spouse to escape.

Proposed Repeal — 23(2)

(2) [Repealed 2000, c. 12, s. 92. Not in force at date of publication.]

23.1 Where one party cannot be convicted — For greater certainty, sections 21 to 23 apply in respect of an accused notwithstanding the fact that the person whom the accused aids or abets, counsels or procures or receives, comforts or assists cannot be convicted of the offence.

R.S. 1985, c. 24 (2d Supp.), s. 45.

24. (1) Attempts — Every one who, having an intent to commit an offence, does or omits to do anything for the purpose of carrying out his intention is guilty of an attempt to commit the offence whether or not it was possible under the circumstances to commit the offence.

(2) Question of law — The question whether an act or omission by a person who has an intent to commit an offence is or is not mere preparation to commit the offence, and too remote to constitute an attempt to commit the offence, is a question of law.

Protection of Persons Administering and Enforcing the Law

25. (1) Protection of persons acting under authority — Every one who is required or authorized by law to do anything in the administration or enforcement of the law

    (a) as a private person,

    (b) as a peace officer or public officer,

    (c) in aid of a peace officer or public officer, or

    (d) by virtue of his office,

is, if he acts on reasonable grounds, justified in doing what he is required or authorized to do and in using as much force as is necessary for that purpose.

(2) Idem — Where a person is required or authorized by law to execute a process or to carry out a sentence, that person or any person who assists him is, if that person acts in good faith, justified in executing the process or in carrying out the sentence notwithstanding that the process or sentence is defective or that it was issued or imposed without jurisdiction or in excess of jurisdiction.

(3) When not protected — Subject to subsections (4) and (5), a person is not justified for the purposes of subsection (1) in using force that is intended or is likely to cause death or grievous bodily harm unless the person believes on reasonable grounds that it is necessary for the self-preservation of the person or the preservation of any one under that person's protection from death or grievous bodily harm.

(4) When protected — A peace officer, and every person lawfully assisting the peace officer, is justified in using force that is intended or is likely to cause death or grievous bodily harm to a person to be arrested, if

(a) the peace officer is proceeding lawfully to arrest, with or without warrant, the person to be arrested;

(b) the offence for which the person is to be arrested is one for which that person may be arrested without warrant;

(c) the person to be arrested takes flight to avoid arrest;

(d) the peace officer or other person using the force believes on reasonable grounds that the force is necessary for the purpose of protecting the peace officer, the person lawfully assisting the peace officer or any other person from imminent or future death or grievous bodily harm; and

(e) the flight cannot be prevented by reasonable means in a less violent manner.

(5) Power in case of escape from penitentiary — A peace officer is justified in using force that is intended or is likely to cause death or grievous bodily harm against an inmate who is escaping from a penitentiary within the meaning of subsection 2(1) of the *Corrections and Conditional Release Act*, if

(a) the peace officer believes on reasonable grounds that any of the inmates of the penitentiary pose a threat of death or grievous bodily harm to the peace officer or any other person; and

(b) the escape cannot be prevented by reasonable means in a less violent manner.

1994, c. 12, s. 1.

26. Excessive force — Every one who is authorized by law to use force is criminally responsible for any excess thereof according to the nature and quality of the act that constitutes the excess.

27. Use of force to prevent commission of offence — Every one is justified in using as much force as is reasonably necessary

(a) to prevent the commission of an offence

(i) for which, if it were committed, the person who committed it might be arrested without warrant, and

(ii) that would be likely to cause immediate and serious injury to the person or property of anyone, or

(b) to prevent anything being done that, on reasonable grounds, he believes would, if it were done, be an offence mentioned in paragraph (*a*).

28. (1) Arrest of wrong person — Where a person who is authorized to execute a warrant to arrest believes, in good faith and on reasonable grounds, that the person whom he arrests is the person named in the warrant, he is protected from criminal responsibility in respect thereof to the same extent as if that person were the person named in the warrant.

(2) Person assisting — Where a person is authorized to execute a warrant to arrest,

(a) every one who, being called on to assist him, believes that the person in whose arrest he is called on to assist is the person named in the warrant, and

(b) every keeper of a prison who is required to receive and detain a person who he believes has been arrested under the warrant, is protected from criminal responsibility in respect thereof to the same extent as if that person were the person named in the warrant.

29. (1) Duty of person arresting — It is the duty of every one who executes a process or warrant to have it with him, where it is feasible to do so, and to produce it when requested to do so.

(2) Notice — It is the duty of every one who arrests a person, whether with or without a warrant, to give notice to that person, where it is feasible to do so, of

(a) the process or warrant under which he makes the arrest; or

(b) the reason for the arrest.

(3) Failure to comply — Failure to comply with subsection (1) or (2) does not of itself deprive a person who executes a process or warrant, or a person who makes an arrest, or those who assist them, of protection from criminal responsibility.

30. Preventing breach of peace — Every one who witnesses a breach of the peace is justified in interfering to prevent the continuance or renewal thereof and may detain any person who commits or is about to join in or to renew the breach of the peace, for the purpose of giving him into the custody of a peace officer, if he uses no more force than is reasonably necessary to prevent the continuance or renewal of the breach of the peace or than is reasonably proportioned to the danger to be apprehended from the continuance or renewal of the breach of the peace.

31. (1) Arrest for breach of peace — Every peace officer who witnesses a breach of the peace and every one who lawfully assists the peace officer is justified in arresting any person whom he finds committing the breach of the peace or who, on reasonable grounds, the peace officer believes is about to join in or renew the breach of the peace.

(2) Giving person in charge — Every peace officer is justified in receiving into custody any person who is given into his charge as having been a party to a breach of the peace by one who has, or who on reasonable grounds the peace officer believes has, witnessed the breach of the peace.

Suppression of Riots

32. (1) Use of force to suppress riot — Every peace officer is justified in using or in ordering the use of as much force as the peace officer believes, in good faith and on reasonable grounds,

(a) is necessary to suppress a riot; and

(b) is not excessive, having regard to the danger to be apprehended from the continuance of the riot.

(2) Person bound by military law — Every one who is bound by military law to obey the command of his superior officer is justified in obeying any command given by his superior officer for the suppression of a riot unless the order is manifestly unlawful.

(3) Obeying order of peace officer — Every one is justified in obeying an order of a peace officer to use force to suppress a riot if

(a) he acts in good faith; and

(b) the order is not manifestly unlawful.

(4) Apprehension of serious mischief — Every one who, in good faith and on reasonable grounds, believes that serious mischief will result from a riot before it is possible to secure the attendance of a peace officer is justified in using as much force as he believes in good faith and on reasonable grounds,

(a) is necessary to suppress the riot; and

(b) is not excessive, having regard to the danger to be apprehended from the continuance of the riot.

(5) Question of law — For the purposes of this section, the question whether an order is manifestly unlawful or not is a question of law.

33. (1) Duty of officers if rioters do not disperse — Where the proclamation referred to in section 67 has been made or an offence against paragraph 68(*a*) or (*b*) has been committed, it is the duty of a peace officer and of a person who is lawfully required by him to assist, to disperse or to arrest persons who do not comply with the proclamation.

(2) Protection of officers — No civil or criminal proceedings lie against a peace officer or a person who is lawfully required by a peace officer to assist him in respect of any death or injury that by reason of resistance is caused as a result of the performance by the peace officer or that person of a duty that is imposed by subsection (1).

(3) Section not restrictive — Nothing in this section limits or affects any powers, duties or functions that are conferred or imposed by this Act with respect to the suppression of riots.

Self-Induced Intoxication

33.1 (1) When defence not available — It is not a defence to an offence referred to in subsection (3) that the accused, by reason of self-induced intoxication, lacked the general intent or the voluntariness required to commit the offence, where the accused departed markedly from the standard of care as described in subsection (2).

(2) Criminal fault by reason of intoxication — For the purposes of this section, a person departs markedly from the standard of reasonable care generally recognized in Canadian society and is thereby criminally at fault where the person, while in a state of self-induced intoxication that renders the person unaware of, or incapable of consciously controlling, their behaviour, voluntarily or involuntarily interferes or threatens to interfere with the bodily integrity of another person.

(3) Application — This section applies in respect of an offence under this Act or any other Act of Parliament that includes as an element an assault or any other interference or threat of interference by a person with the bodily integrity of another person.

1995, c. 32, s. 1.

Defence of Person

34. (1) Self-defence against unprovoked assault — Every one who is unlawfully assaulted without having provoked the assault is justified in repelling force by force if the force he uses is not intended to cause death or grievous bodily harm and is no more than is necessary to enable him to defend himself.

(2) Extent of justification — Every one who is unlawfully assaulted and who causes death or grievous bodily harm in repelling the assault is justified if

(a) he causes it under reasonable apprehension of death or grievous bodily harm from the violence with which the assault was originally made or with which the assailant pursues his purposes; and

(b) he believes, on reasonable grounds, that he cannot otherwise preserve himself from death or grievous bodily harm.

35. Self-defence in case of aggression — Every one who has without justification assaulted another but did not commence the assault with intent to cause death or grievous bodily harm, or has without justification provoked an assault on himself by another, may justify the use of force subsequent to the assault if

(a) he uses the force

(i) under reasonable apprehension of death or grievous bodily harm from the violence of the person whom he has assaulted or provoked, and

(ii) in the belief, on reasonable grounds, that it is necessary in order to preserve himself from death or grievous bodily harm;

(b) he did not, at any time before the necessity of preserving himself from death or grievous bodily harm arose, endeavour to cause death or grievous bodily harm; and

(c) he declined further conflict and quitted or retreated from it as far as it was feasible to do so before the necessity of preserving himself from death or grievous bodily harm arose.

36. Provocation — "Provocation" includes, for the purposes of sections 34 and 35, provocation by blows, words or gestures.

37. (1) Preventing assault — Every one is justified in using force to defend himself or any one under his protection from assault, if he uses no more force than is necessary to prevent the assault or the repetition of it.

(2) Extent of justification — Nothing in this section shall be deemed to justify the wilful infliction of any hurt or mischief that is excessive, having regard to the nature of the assault that the force used was intended to prevent.

Defence of Property

38. (1) Defence of personal property — Every one who is in peaceable possession of personal property, and every one lawfully assisting him, is justified

(a) in preventing a trespasser from taking it, or

(b) in taking it from a trespasser who has taken it,

if he does not strike or cause bodily harm to the trespasser.

(2) Assault by trespasser — Where a person who is in peaceable possession of personal property lays hands on it, a trespasser who persists in attempting to keep it or take it from him or from any one lawfully assisting him shall be deemed to commit an assault without justification or provocation.

39. (1) Defence with claim of right — Every one who is in peaceable possession of personal property under a claim of right, and every one acting under his authority, is protected from criminal responsibility for defending that possession, even against a person entitled by law to possession of it, if he uses no more force than is necessary.

(2) Defence without claim of right — Every one who is in peaceable possession of personal property, but does not claim it as of right or does not act under the authority of a person who claims it as of right, is not justified or protected from criminal responsibility for defending his possession against a person who is entitled by law to possession of it.

40. Defence of dwelling — Every one who is in peaceable possession of a dwelling-house, and every one lawfully assisting him or acting under his authority, is justified in using as much force as is necessary to prevent any person from forcibly breaking into or forcibly entering the dwelling-house without lawful authority.

41. (1) Defence of house or real property — Every one who is in peaceable possession of a dwelling-house or real property, and every one lawfully assisting him or acting under his authority, is justified in using force to prevent any person from trespassing on the dwelling-house or real property, or to remove a trespasser therefrom, if he uses no more force than is necessary.

(2) Assault by trespasser — A trespasser who resists an attempt by a person who is in peaceable possession of a dwelling-house or real property, or a person lawfully assisting him or acting under his authority to prevent his entry or to remove him, shall be deemed to commit an assault without justification or provocation.

42. (1) Assertion of right to house or real property — Every one is justified in peaceably entering a dwelling-house or real property by day to take possession of it if he, or a person under whose authority he acts, is lawfully entitled to possession of it.

(2) Assault in case of lawful entry — Where a person

    (a) not having peaceable possession of a dwelling-house or real property under a claim of right, or

    (b) not acting under the authority of a person who has peaceable possession of a dwelling-house or real property under a claim of right,

assaults a person who is lawfully entitled to possession of it and who is entering it peaceably by day to take possession of it, for the purpose of preventing him from entering, the assault shall be deemed to be without justification or provocation.

(3) Trespasser provoking assault — Where a person

    (a) having peaceable possession of a dwelling-house or real property under a claim of right, or

    (b) acting under the authority of a person who has peaceable possession of a dwelling-house or real property under a claim of right,

assaults any person who is lawfully entitled to possession of it and who is entering it peaceably by day to take possession of it, for the purpose of preventing him from entering, the assault shall be deemed to be provoked by the person who is entering.

Protection of Persons in Authority

43. Correction of child by force — Every schoolteacher, parent or person standing in the place of a parent is justified in using force by way of correction toward a pupil or child, as the case may be, who is under his care, if the force does not exceed what is reasonable under the circumstances.

44. Master of ship maintaining discipline — The master or officer in command of a vessel on a voyage is justified in using as much force as he believes, on reasonable grounds, is necessary for the purpose of maintaining good order and discipline on the vessel.

45. Surgical operations — Every one is protected from criminal responsibility for performing a surgical operation on any person for the benefit of that person if

(a) the operation is performed with reasonable care and skill; and

(b) it is reasonable to perform the operation, having regard to the state of health of the person at the time the operation is performed and to all the circumstances of the case.

PART II — OFFENCES AGAINST PUBLIC ORDER

Treason and other Offences against the Queen's Authority and Person

46. (1) High treason — Every one commits high treason who, in Canada,

(a) kills or attempts to kill Her Majesty, or does her any bodily harm tending to death or destruction, maims or wounds her, or imprisons or restrains her;

(b) levies war against Canada or does any act preparatory thereto; or

(c) assists an enemy at war with Canada, or any armed forces against whom Canadian Forces are engaged in hostilities, whether or not a state of war exists between Canada and the country whose forces they are.

(2) Treason — Every one commits treason who, in Canada,

(a) uses force or violence for the purpose of overthrowing the government of Canada or a province;

(b) without lawful authority, communicates or makes available to an agent of a state other than Canada, military or scientific information or any sketch, plan, model, article, note or document of a military or scientific character that he knows or ought to know may be used by that state for a purpose prejudicial to the safety or defence of Canada;

(c) conspires with any person to commit high treason or to do anything mentioned in paragraph (*a*);

(d) forms an intention to do anything that is high treason or that is mentioned in paragraph (*a*) and manifests that intention by an overt act; or

(e) conspires with any person to do anything mentioned in paragraph (*b*) or forms an intention to do anything mentioned in paragraph (*b*) and manifests that intention by an overt act.

(3) Canadian citizen — Notwithstanding subsection (1) or (2), a Canadian citizen or a person who owes allegiance to Her Majesty in right of Canada,

(a) commits high treason if, while in or out of Canada, he does anything mentioned in subsection (1); or

(b) commits treason if, while in or out of Canada, he does anything mentioned in subsection (2).

(4) Overt act — Where it is treason to conspire with any person, the act of conspiring is an overt act of treason.

47. (1) Punishment for high treason — Every one who commits high treason is guilty of an indictable offence and shall be sentenced to imprisonment for life.

(2) Punishment for treason — Every one who commits treason is guilty of an indictable offence and liable

(a) to be sentenced to imprisonment for life if he is guilty of an offence under paragraph 46(2)(*a*), (*c*) or (*d*);

(b) to be sentenced to imprisonment for life if he is guilty of an offence under paragraph 46(2)(*b*) or (*e*) committed while a state of war exists between Canada and another country; or

(c) to be sentenced to imprisonment for a term not exceeding fourteen years if he is guilty of an offence under paragraph 46(2)(*b*) or (*e*) committed while no state of war exists between Canada and another country.

(3) Corroboration — No person shall be convicted of high treason or treason on the evidence of only one witness, unless the evidence of that witness is corroborated in a material particular by evidence that implicates the accused.

(4) Minimum punishment — For the purposes of Part XXIII, the sentence of imprisonment for life prescribed by subsection (1) is a minimum punishment.

48. (1) Limitation — No proceedings for an offence of treason as defined by paragraph 46(2)(*a*) shall be commenced more than three years after the time when the offence is alleged to have been committed.

(2) Information for treasonable words — No proceedings shall be commenced under section 47 in respect of an overt act of treason expressed or declared by open and considered speech unless

(a) an information setting out the overt act and the words by which it was expressed or declared is laid under oath before a justice within six days after the time when the words are alleged to have been spoken; and

(b) a warrant for the arrest of the accused is issued within ten days after the time when the information is laid.

Prohibited Acts

49. Acts intended to alarm Her Majesty or break public peace — Every one who wilfully, in the presence of Her Majesty,

(a) does an act with intent to alarm Her Majesty or to break the public peace, or

(b) does an act that is intended or is likely to cause bodily harm to her Majesty,

is guilty of an indictable offence and liable to imprisonment for a term not exceeding fourteen years.

50. (1) Assisting alien enemy to leave Canada, or omitting to prevent treason — Every one commits an offence who

(a) incites or willfully assists a subject of

(i) a state that is at war with Canada, or

(ii) a state against whose forces Canadian Forces are engaged in hostilities, whether or not a state of war exists between Canada and the state whose forces they are,

to leave Canada without the consent of the Crown, unless the accused establishes that assistance to the state referred to in subparagraph (i) or the forces of the state referred to in subparagraph (ii), as the case may be, was not intended thereby; or

(b) knowing that a person is about to commit high treason or treason does not, with all reasonable dispatch, inform a justice of the peace or other peace officer thereof or make other reasonable efforts to prevent that person from committing high treason or treason.

(2) Punishment — Every one who commits an offence under subsection (1) is guilty of an indictable offence and liable to imprisonment for a term not exceeding fourteen years.

51. Intimidating Parliament or legislature — Every one who does an act of violence in order to intimidate Parliament or the legislature of a province is guilty of an indictable offence and liable to imprisonment for a term not exceeding fourteen years.

52. Sabotage — **(1)** Every one who does a prohibited act for a purpose prejudicial to

(a) the safety, security or defence of Canada, or

(b) the safety or security of the naval, army or air forces of any state other than Canada that are lawfully present in Canada,

is guilty of an indictable offence and liable to imprisonment for a term not exceeding ten years.

(2) "prohibited act" — In this section, **"prohibited act"** means an act or omission that

(a) impairs the efficiency or impedes the working of any vessel, vehicle, aircraft, machinery, apparatus or other thing; or

(b) causes property, by whomever it may be owned, to be lost, damaged or destroyed.

(3) Saving — No person does a prohibited act within the meaning of this section by reason only that

(a) he stops work as a result of the failure of his employer and himself to agree on any matter relating to his employment;

(b) he stops work as a result of the failure of his employer and a bargaining agent acting on his behalf to agree on any matter relating to his employment; or

(c) he stops work as a result of his taking part in a combination of workmen or employees for their own reasonable protection as workmen or employees.

(4) Idem — No person does a prohibited act within the meaning of this section by reason only that he attends at or near or approaches a dwelling-house or place for the purpose only of obtaining or communicating information.

53. Inciting to mutiny — Every one who

(a) attempts, for a traitorous or mutinous purpose, to seduce a member of the Canadian Forces from his duty and allegiance to Her Majesty, or

(b) attempts to incite or to induce a member of the Canadian Forces to commit a traitorous or mutinous act,

is guilty of an indictable offence and liable to imprisonment for a term not exceeding fourteen years.

54. Assisting deserter — Every one who aids, assists, harbours or conceals a person who he knows is a deserter or absentee without leave from the Canadian Forces is guilty of an offence punishable on summary conviction, but no proceedings shall be instituted under this section without the consent of the Attorney General of Canada.

55. Evidence of overt acts — In proceedings for an offence against any provision in section 47 or sections 49 to 53, no evidence is admissible of an overt act unless that overt act is set out in the indictment or unless the evidence is otherwise relevant as tending to prove an overt act that is set out therein.

56. Offences in relation to members of R.C.M.P — Every one who wilfully

(a) persuades or counsels a member of the Royal Canadian Mounted Police to desert or absent himself without leave,

(b) aids, assists, harbours or conceals a member of the Royal Canadian Mounted Police who he knows is a deserter or absentee without leave, or

(c) aids or assists a member of the Royal Canadian Mounted Police to desert or absent himself without leave, knowing that the member is about to desert or absent himself without leave,

is guilty of an offence punishable on summary conviction.

R.S. 1985, c. 27 (1st Supp.), s. 8.

Passports

57. (1) Forgery of or uttering forged passport — Every one who, while in or out of Canada,

    (a) forges a passport, or

    (b) knowing that a passport is forged

        (i) uses, deals with or acts on it, or

        (ii) causes or attempts to cause any person to use, deal with, or act on it, as if the passport were genuine,

is guilty of an indictable offence and liable to imprisonment for a term not exceeding fourteen years.

(2) False statement in relation to passport — Every one who, while in or out of Canada, for the purpose of procuring a passport for himself or any other person or for the purpose of procuring any material alteration or addition to any such passport, makes a written or an oral statement that he knows is false or misleading

    (a) is guilty of an indictable offence and liable to imprisonment for a term not exceeding two years; or

    (b) is guilty of an offence punishable on summary conviction.

(3) Possession of forged, etc., passport — Every one who without lawful excuse, the proof of which lies on him, has in his possession a forged passport or a passport in respect of which an offence under subsection (2) has been committed is guilty of an indictable offence and liable to imprisonment for a term not exceeding five years.

(4) Special provisions applicable — For the purposes of proceedings under this section,

    (a) the place where a passport was forged is not material; and

    (b) the definition "false document" in section 321, and section 366, apply with such modifications as the circumstances require.

(5) "passport" — In this section, **"passport"** means a document issued by or under the authority of the Minister of Foreign Affairs for the purpose of identifying the holder thereof.

(6) Jurisdiction — Where a person is alleged to have committed, while out of Canada, an offence under this section, proceedings in respect of that offence may, whether or not that person is in Canada, be commenced in any territorial division in Canada and the accused may be tried and punished in respect of that offence in the same manner as if the offence had been committed in that territorial division.

(7) Appearance of accused at trial — For greater certainty, the provisions of this Act relating to

    (a) requirements that an accused appear at and be present during proceedings, and

    (b) the exceptions to those requirements,

apply to proceedings commenced in any territorial division pursuant to subsection (6).

R.S. 1985, c. 27 (1st Supp.), s. 9; 1994, c. 44, s. 4; 1995, c. 5, s. 25(1)(g).

58. (1) Fraudulent use of certificate of citizenship — Every one who, while in or out of Canada,

(a) uses a certificate of citizenship or a certificate of naturalization for a fraudulent purpose, or

(b) being a person to whom a certificate of citizenship or a certificate of naturalization has been granted, knowingly parts with the possession of that certificate with intent that it should be used for a fraudulent purpose,

is guilty of an indictable offence and liable to imprisonment for a term not exceeding two years.

(2) Definition of "certificate of citizenship" and "certificate of naturalization" — In this section, **"certificate of citizenship"** and **"certificate of naturalization"** respectively, mean a certificate of citizenship and a certificate of naturalization as defined by the *Citizenship Act.*

Sedition

59. (1) Seditious words — Seditious words are words that express a seditious intention.

(2) Seditious libel — A seditious libel is a libel that expresses a seditious intention.

(3) Seditious conspiracy — A seditious conspiracy is an agreement between two or more persons to carry out a seditious intention.

(4) Seditious intention — Without limiting the generality of the meaning of the expression **"seditious intention"**, every one shall be presumed to have a seditious intention who

(a) teaches or advocates, or

(b) publishes or circulates any writing that advocates,

the use, without the authority of law, of force as a means of accomplishing a governmental change within Canada.

60. Exception — Notwithstanding subsection 59(4), no person shall be deemed to have a seditious intention by reason only that he intends, in good faith,

(a) to show that Her Majesty has been misled or mistaken in her measures;

(b) to point out errors or defects in

(i) the government or constitution of Canada or a province,

(ii) Parliament or the legislature of a province, or

(iii) the administration of justice in Canada;

(c) to procure, by lawful means, the alteration of any matter of government in Canada; or

(d) to point out, for the purpose of removal, matters that produce or tend to produce feelings of hostility and ill-will between different classes of persons in Canada.

61. Punishment of seditious offences — Every one who

(a) speaks seditious words,

(b) publishes a seditious libel, or

(c) is a party to a seditious conspiracy,

is guilty of an indictable offence and liable to imprisonment for a term not exceeding fourteen years.

62. (1) Offences in relation to military forces — Every one who wilfully

(a) interferes with, impairs or influences the loyalty or discipline of a member of a force,

(b) publishes, edits, issues, circulates or distributes a writing that advises, counsels or urges insubordination, disloyalty, mutiny or refusal of duty by a member of a force, or

(c) advises, counsels, urges or in any manner causes insubordination, disloyalty, mutiny or refusal of duty by a member of a force,

is guilty of an indictable offence and liable to imprisonment for a term not exceeding five years.

(2) "member of a force" — In this section, **"member of a force"** means a member of

(a) the Canadian Forces; or

(b) the naval, army or air forces of a state other than Canada that are lawfully present in Canada.

Unlawful Assemblies and Riots

63. (1) Unlawful assembly — An unlawful assembly is an assembly of three or more persons who, with intent to carry out any common purpose, assemble in such a manner or so conduct themselves when they are assembled as to cause persons in the neighbourhood of the assembly to fear, on reasonable grounds, that they

(a) will disturb the peace tumultuously; or

(b) will by that assembly needlessly and without reasonable cause provoke other persons to disturb the peace tumultuously.

(2) Lawful assembly becoming unlawful — Persons who are lawfully assembled may become an unlawful assembly if they conduct themselves with a common purpose in a manner that would have made the assembly unlawful if they had assembled in that manner for that purpose.

(3) Exception — Persons are not unlawfully assembled by reason only that they are assembled to protect the dwelling-house of any one of them against persons who are threatening to break and enter it for the purpose of committing an indictable offence therein.

64. Riot — A riot is an unlawful assembly that has begun to disturb the peace tumultuously.

65. Punishment of rioter — Every one who takes part in a riot is guilty of an indictable offence and liable to imprisonment for a term not exceeding two years.

66. Punishment for unlawful assembly — Every one who is a member of an unlawful assembly is guilty of an offence punishable on summary conviction.

67. Reading proclamation — A person who is

   (a) a justice, mayor or sheriff, or the lawful deputy of a mayor or sheriff,

   (b) a warden or deputy warden of a prison, or

   (c) the institutional head of a penitentiary, as those expressions are defined in subsection 2(1) of the *Corrections and Conditional Release Act*, or that person's deputy,

who receives notice that, at any place within the jurisdiction of the person, twelve or more persons are unlawfully and riotously assembled together shall go to that place and, after approaching as near as is safe, if the person is satisfied that a riot is in progress, shall command silence and thereupon make or cause to be made in a loud voice a proclamation in the following words or to the like effect:

> Her Majesty the Queen charges and commands all persons being assembled immediately to disperse and peaceably to depart to their habitations or to their lawful business on the pain of being guilty of an offence for which, on conviction, they may be sentenced to imprisonment for life. GOD SAVE THE QUEEN.

1994, c. 44, s. 5.

68. Offences related to proclamation — Every one is guilty of an indictable offence and liable to imprisonment for life who

   (a) opposes, hinders or assaults, wilfully and with force, a person who begins to make or is about to begin to make or is making the proclamation referred to in section 67 so that it is not made;

   (b) does not peaceably disperse and depart from a place where the proclamation referred to in section 67 is made within thirty minutes after it is made; or

   (c) does not depart from a place within thirty minutes when he has reasonable grounds to believe that the proclamation referred to in section 67 would have been made in that place if some person had not opposed, hindered or assaulted, wilfully and with force, a person who would have made it.

69. Neglect by peace officer — A peace officer who receives notice that there is a riot within his jurisdiction and, without reasonable excuse, fails to take all reasonable steps to suppress the riot is guilty of an indictable offence and liable to imprisonment for a term not exceeding two years.

Unlawful Drilling

70. (1) Orders by Governor in Council — The Governor in Council may by proclamation, make orders

    (a) to prohibit assemblies, without lawful authority, of persons for the purpose

        (i) of training or drilling themselves,

        (ii) of being trained or drilled to the use of arms, or

        (iii) of practising military exercises; or

    (b) to prohibit persons when assembled for any purpose from training or drilling themselves or from being trained or drilled.

(2) General or special order — An order that is made under subsection (1) may be general or may be made applicable to particular places, districts or assemblies to be specified in the order.

(3) Punishment — Every one who contravenes an order made under this section is guilty of an indictable offence and liable to imprisonment for a term not exceeding five years.

Duels

71. Duelling — Every one who

    (a) challenges or attempts by any means to provoke another person to fight a duel,

    (b) attempts to provoke a person to challenge another person to fight a duel, or

    (c) accepts a challenge to fight a duel,

is guilty of an indictable offence and liable to imprisonment for a term not exceeding two years.

Forcible Entry and Detainer

72. (1) Forcible entry — A person commits forcible entry when that person enters real property that is in the actual and peaceable possession of another in a manner that is likely to cause a breach of the peace or reasonable apprehension of a breach of the peace.

(1.1) Matters not material — For the purposes of subsection (1), it is immaterial whether or not a person is entitled to enter the real property or whether or not that person has any intention of taking possession of the real property.

(2) Forcible detainer — A person commits forcible detainer when, being in actual possession of real property without colour of right, he detains it in a manner that is likely to cause a breach of the peace or reasonable apprehension of a breach of the peace, against a person who is entitled by law to possession of it.

(3) Questions of law — The questions whether a person is in actual and peaceable possession or is in actual possession without colour of right are questions of law.

R.S. 1985, c. 27 (1st Supp.), s. 10.

73. Punishment — Every person who commits forcible entry or forcible detainer is guilty of

(a) an offence punishable on summary conviction; or

(b) an indictable offence and liable to imprisonment for a term not exceeding two years.

R.S. 1985, c. 27 (1st Supp.), s. 11; 1992, c. 1, s. 58(1), Schedule I, item 2.

Piracy

74. (1) Piracy by law of nations — Every one commits piracy who does any act that, by the law of nations, is piracy.

(2) Punishment — Every one who commits piracy while in or out of Canada is guilty of an indictable offence and liable to imprisonment for life.

75. Piratical acts — Every one who, while in or out of Canada,

(a) steals a Canadian ship,

(b) steals or without lawful authority throws overboard, damages or destroys anything that is part of the cargo, supplies or fittings in a Canadian ship,

(c) does or attempts to do a mutinous act on a Canadian ship, or

(d) counsels a person to do anything mentioned in paragraph (a), (b) or (c),

is guilty of an indictable offence and liable to imprisonment for a term not exceeding fourteen years.

R.S. 1985, c. 27 (1st Supp.) s. 7(3).

Offences Against Air or Maritime Safety

76. Hijacking — Every one who, unlawfully, by force or threat thereof, or by any other form of intimidation, seizes or exercises control of an aircraft with intent

(a) to cause any person on board the aircraft to be confined or imprisoned against his will,

(b) to cause any person on board the aircraft to be transported against his will to any place other than the next scheduled place of landing of the aircraft,

(c) to hold any person on board the aircraft for ransom or to service against his will, or

(d) to cause the aircraft to deviate in a material respect from its flight plan,

is guilty of an indictable offence and liable to imprisonment for life.

77. Endangering safety of aircraft or airport — Every one who,

(a) on board an aircraft in flight, commits an act of violence against a person that is likely to endanger the safety of the aircraft,

(b) using a weapon, commits an act of violence against a person at an airport serving international civil aviation that causes or is likely to cause serious injury or death and that endangers or is likely to endanger safety at the airport,

(c) causes damage to an aircraft in service that renders the aircraft incapable of flight or that is likely to endanger the safety of the aircraft in flight,

(d) places or causes to be placed on board an aircraft in service anything that is likely to cause damage to the aircraft, that will render it incapable of flight or that is likely to endanger the safety of the aircraft in flight,

(e) causes damage to or interferes with the operation of any air navigation facility where the damage or interference is likely to endanger the safety of an aircraft in flight,

(f) using a weapon, substance or device, destroys or causes serious damage to the facilities of an airport serving international civil aviation or to any aircraft not in service located there, or causes disruption of services of the airport, that endangers or is likely to endanger safety at the airport, or

(g) endangers the safety of an aircraft in flight by communicating to any other person any information that the person knows to be false,

is guilty of an indictable offence and liable to imprisonment for life.

1993, c. 7, s. 3.

78. (1) Offensive weapons and explosive substances — Every one, other than a peace officer engaged in the execution of his duty, who takes on board a civil aircraft an offensive weapon or any explosive substance

(a) without the consent of the owner or operator of the aircraft or of a person duly authorized by either of them to consent thereto, or

(b) with the consent referred to in paragraph (a) but without complying with all terms and conditions on which the consent was given,

is guilty of an indictable offence and liable to imprisonment for a term not exceeding fourteen years.

(2) Definition of "civil aircraft" — For the purposes of this section, **"civil aircraft"** means all aircraft other than aircraft operated by the Canadian Forces, a po-

lice force in Canada or persons engaged in the administration or enforcement of the *Customs Act* or the *Excise Act*.

R.S. 1985, c. 1 (2d Supp.), Schedule III.

78.1 (1) Seizing control of ship or fixed platform — Every one who seizes or exercises control over a ship or fixed platform by force or threat of force or by any other form of intimidation is guilty of an indictable offence and liable to imprisonment for life.

(2) Endangering safety of ship or fixed platform — Every one who

(a) commits an act of violence against a person on board a ship or fixed platform,

(b) destroys or causes damage to a ship or its cargo or to a fixed platform,

(c) destroys or causes serious damage to or interferes with the operation of any maritime navigational facility, or

(d) places or causes to be placed on board a ship or fixed platform anything that is likely to cause damage to the ship or its cargo or to the fixed platform,

where that act is likely to endanger the safe navigation of a ship or the safety of a fixed platform, is guilty of an indictable offence and liable to imprisonment for life.

(3) False communication — Every one who communicates information that endangers the safe navigation of a ship, knowing the information to be false, is guilty of an indictable offence and liable to imprisonment for life.

(4) Threats causing death or injury — Every one who threatens to commit an offence under paragraph (2)(a), (b) or (c) in order to compel a person to do or refrain from doing any act, where the threat is likely to endanger the safe navigation of a ship or the safety of a fixed platform, is guilty of an indictable offence and liable to imprisonment for life.

(5) Definitions — In this section,

"fixed platform" means an artificial island or a marine installation or structure that is permanently attached to the seabed for the purpose of exploration or exploitation of resources or for other economic purposes;

"ship" means every description of vessel not permanently attached to the seabed, other than a warship, a ship being used as a naval auxiliary or for customs or police purposes or a ship that has been withdrawn from navigation or is laid up.

1993, c. 7, s. 4.

Dangerous Substances

79. Duty of care re explosive — Every one who has an explosive substance in his possession or under his care or control is under a legal duty to use reasonable care to prevent bodily harm or death to persons or damage to property by that explosive substance.

80. Breach of duty — Every one who, being under a legal duty within the meaning of section 79, fails without lawful excuse to perform that duty, is guilty of an indictable offence and, if as a result an explosion of an explosive substance occurs that

(a) causes death or is likely to cause death to any person, is liable to imprisonment for life; or

(b) causes bodily harm or damage to property or is likely to cause bodily harm or damage to property, is liable to imprisonment for a term not exceeding fourteen years.

81. (1) Using explosives — Every one commits an offence who

(a) does anything with intent to cause an explosion of an explosive substance that is likely to cause serious bodily harm or death to persons or is likely to cause serious damage to property;

(b) with intent to do bodily harm to any person

(i) causes an explosive substance to explode,

(ii) sends or delivers to a person or causes a person to take or receive an explosive substance or any other dangerous substance or thing, or

(iii) places or throws anywhere or at or on a person a corrosive fluid, explosive substance or any other dangerous substance or thing;

(c) with intent to destroy or damage property without lawful excuse, places or throws an explosive substance anywhere; or

(d) makes or has in his possession or has under his care or control any explosive substance with intent thereby

(i) to endanger life or to cause serious damage to property, or

(ii) to enable another person to endanger life or to cause serious damage to property.

(2) Punishment — Every one who commits an offence under subsection (1) is guilty of an indictable offence and liable

(a) for an offence under paragraph (1)(a) or (b), to imprisonment for life, or

(b) for an offence under paragraph (1)(c) or (d), to imprisonment for a term not exceeding fourteen years.

82. (1) Possession without lawful excuse — Every person who, without lawful excuse, the proof of which lies on the person, makes or has in the possession or under the care or control of the person any explosive substance is guilty of an indictable offence and liable to imprisonment for a term not exceeding five years.

(2) Possession in association with criminal organization — Every person who, without lawful excuse, the proof of which lies on the person, makes or has in the possession or under the care or control of the person any explosive substance for the benefit of, at the direction of or in association with a criminal organization is guilty of an indictable offence and liable to imprisonment for a term not exceeding fourteen years.

R.S. 1985, c. 27 (1st Supp.), s. 12; 1997, c. 23, s. 2.

82.1 Sentences to be served consecutively — A sentence imposed on a person for an offence under subsection 82(2) shall be served consecutively to any other punishment imposed on the person for an offence arising out of the same event or series of events and to any other sentence to which the person is subject at the time the sentence is imposed on the person for an offence under subsection 82(2).

1997, c. 23, s. 2.

Prize Fights

83. (1) Engaging in prize fight — Every one who

(a) engages as a principal in a prize fight,

(b) advises, encourages or promotes a prize fight, or

(c) is present at a prize fight as an aid, second, surgeon, umpire, backer or reporter,

is guilty of an offence punishable on summary conviction.

(2) Definition of "prize fight" — In this section, **"prize fight"** means an encounter or fight with fists or hands between two persons who have met for that purpose by previous arrangement made by or for them, but a boxing contest between amateur sportsmen, where the contestants wear boxing gloves of not less than one hundred and forty grams each in mass, or any boxing contest held with the permission or under the authority of an athletic board or commission or similar body established by or under the authority of the legislature of a province for the control of sport within the province, shall be deemed not to be a prize fight.

R.S. 1985, c. 27 (1st Supp.), s. 186.

PART III — FIREARMS AND OTHER WEAPONS

Interpretation

84. Definitions — **(1)** In this Part and subsections 491(1), 515(4.1) and (4.11) and 810(3.1) and (3.11),

"ammunition" means a cartridge containing a projectile designed to be discharged from a firearm and, without restricting the generality of the foregoing, includes a caseless cartridge and a shot shell;

"antique firearm" means

(a) any firearm manufactured before 1898 that was not designed to discharge rim-fire or centre-fire ammunition and that has not been redesigned to discharge such ammunition, or

(b) any firearm that is prescribed to be an antique firearm;

"authorization" means an authorization issued under the *Firearms Act*;

"automatic firearm" means a firearm that is capable of, or assembled or designed and manufactured with the capability of, discharging projectiles in rapid succession during one pressure of the trigger;

"cartridge magazine" means a device or container from which ammunition may be fed into the firing chamber of a firearm;

"chief firearms officer" means a chief firearms officer as defined in subsection 2(1) of the *Firearms Act*;

"cross-bow" means a device with a bow and a bowstring mounted on a stock that is designed to propel an arrow, a bolt, a quarrel or any similar projectile on a trajectory guided by a barrel or groove and that is capable of causing serious bodily injury or death to a person;

"export" means export from Canada and, for greater certainty, includes the exportation of goods from Canada that are imported into Canada and shipped in transit through Canada;

"firearms officer" means a firearms officer as defined in subsection 2(1) of the *Firearms Act*;

"handgun" means a firearm that is designed, altered or intended to be aimed and fired by the action of one hand, whether or not it has been redesigned or subsequently altered to be aimed and fired by the action of both hands;

"imitation firearm" means any thing that imitates a firearm, and includes a replica firearm;

"import" means import into Canada and, for greater certainty, includes the importation of goods into Canada that are shipped in transit through Canada and exported from Canada;

"licence" means a licence issued under the *Firearms Act*,

"prescribed" means prescribed by the regulations;

"prohibited ammunition" means ammunition, or a projectile of any kind, that is prescribed to be prohibited ammunition;

"prohibited device" means

    (a) any component or part of a weapon, or any accessory for use with a weapon, that is prescribed to be a prohibited device,

    (b) a handgun barrel that is equal to or less than 105 mm in length, but does not include any such handgun barrel that is prescribed, where the handgun barrel is for use in international sporting competitions governed by the rules of the International Shooting Union,

    (c) a device or contrivance designed or intended to muffle or stop the sound or report of a firearm,

    (d) a cartridge magazine that is prescribed to be a prohibited device, or

    (e) a replica firearm;

"prohibited firearm" means

   (a) a handgun that

   (i) has a barrel equal to or less than 105 mm in length, or

   (ii) is designed or adapted to discharge a 25 or 32 calibre cartridge,

but does not include any such handgun that is prescribed, where the handgun is for use in international sporting competitions governed by the rules of the International Shooting Union,

   (b) a firearm that is adapted from a rifle or shotgun, whether by sawing, cutting or any other alteration, and that, as so adapted,

   (i) is less than 660 mm in length, or

   (ii) is 660 mm or greater in length and has a barrel less than 457 mm in length,

   (c) an automatic firearm, whether or not it has been altered to discharge only one projectile with one pressure of the trigger, or

   (d) any firearm that is prescribed to be a prohibited firearm;

"prohibited weapon" means

   (a) a knife that has a blade that opens automatically by gravity or centrifugal force or by hand pressure applied to a button, spring or other device in or attached to the handle of the knife, or

   (b) any weapon, other than a firearm, that is prescribed to be a prohibited weapon;

"prohibition order" means an order made under this Act or any other Act of Parliament prohibiting a person from possessing any firearm, cross-bow, prohibited weapon, restricted weapon, prohibited device, ammunition, prohibited ammunition or explosive substance, or all such things;

"Registrar" means the Registrar of Firearms appointed under section 82 of the *Firearms Act*;

"registration certificate" means a registration certificate issued under the *Firearms Act*,

"replica firearm" means any device that is designed or intended to exactly resemble, or to resemble with near precision, a firearm, and that itself is not a firearm, but does not include any such device that is designed or intended to exactly resemble, or to resemble with near precision, an antique firearm;

"restricted firearm" means

   (a) a handgun that is not a prohibited firearm,

   (b) a firearm that

   (i) is not a prohibited firearm,

   (ii) has a barrel less than 470 mm in length, and

   (iii) is capable of discharging centre-fire ammunition in a semi-automatic manner,

(c) a firearm that is designed or adapted to be fired when reduced to a length of less than 660 mm by folding, telescoping or otherwise, or

(d) a firearm of any other kind that is prescribed to be a restricted firearm;

"restricted weapon" means any weapon, other than a firearm, that is prescribed to be a restricted weapon;

"superior court" means

(a) in Ontario, the Superior Court of Justice, sitting in the region, district or county or group of counties where the relevant adjudication was made,

(b) in Quebec, the Superior Court,

(c) in New Brunswick, Manitoba, Saskatchewan and Alberta, the Court of Queen's Bench,

(d) in Nova Scotia, British Columbia and a territory, the Supreme Court, and

(e) in Prince Edward Island and Newfoundland, the Trial Division of the Supreme Court;

"transfer" means sell, provide, barter, give, lend, rent, send, transport, ship, distribute or deliver.

(2) Barrel length — For the purposes of this Part, the length of a barrel of a firearm is

(a) in the case of a revolver, the distance from the muzzle of the barrel to the breach end immediately in front of the cylinder, and

(b) in any other case, the distance from the muzzle of the barrel to and including the chamber,

but does not include the length of any component, part or accessory including any component, part or accessory designed or intended to suppress the muzzle flash or reduce recoil.

(3) Certain weapons deemed not to be firearm — For the purposes of sections 91 to 95, 99 to 101, 103 to 107 and 117.03 of this Act and the provisions of the *Firearms Act*, the following weapons are deemed not to be firearms;

(a) any antique firearm;

(b) any device that is

(i) designed exclusively for signalling, for notifying of distress, for firing blank cartridges or for firing stud cartridges, explosive-driven rivets or other industrial projectiles, and

(ii) intended by the person in possession of it to be used exclusively for the purpose for which it is designed;

(c) any shooting device that is

(i) designed exclusively for the slaughtering of domestic animals, the tranquillizing of animals or the discharging of projectiles with lines attached to them, and

(ii) intended by the person in possession of it to be used exclusively for the purpose for which it is designed; and

(d) any other barrelled weapon, where it is proved that the weapon is not designed or adapted to discharge

(i) a shot, bullet or other projectile at a muzzle velocity exceeding 152.4 m per second, or

(ii) a shot, bullet or other projectile that is designed or adapted to attain a velocity exceeding 152.4 m per second.

(3.1) Exceptions — antique firearms — Notwithstanding subsection (3), an antique firearm is a firearm for the purposes of regulations made under paragraph 117(*h*) of the *Firearms Act* and subsection 86(2) of this Act.

(4) Meaning of "holder" — For the purposes of this Part, a person is the **holder** of

(a) an authorization or a licence if the authorization or licence has been issued to the person and the person continues to hold it; and

(b) a registration certificate for a firearm if

(i) the registration certificate has been issued to the person and the person continues to hold it, or

(ii) the person possesses the registration certificate with the permission of its lawful holder.

1995, c. 39, s. 139; 1998, c. 30, s. 16.

Use Offences

85. (1) Using firearm in commission of offence — Every person commits an offence who uses a firearm

(a) while committing an indictable offence, other than an offence under section 220 (criminal negligence causing death), 236 (manslaughter), 239 (attempted murder), 244 (causing bodily harm with intent — firearm), 272 (sexual assault with a weapon), 273 (aggravated sexual assault), 279 (kidnapping), 279.1 (hostage-taking), 344 (robbery) or 346 (extortion),

(b) while attempting to commit an indictable offence, or

(c) during flight after committing or attempting to commit an indictable offence,

whether or not the person causes or means to cause bodily harm to any person as a result of using the firearm.

(2) Using imitation firearm in commission of offence — Every person commits an offence who uses an imitation firearm

(a) while committing an indictable offence,

(b) while attempting to commit an indictable offence, or

(c) during flight after committing or attempting to commit an indictable offence,

whether or not the person causes or means to cause bodily harm to any person as a result of using the imitation firearm.

(3) Punishment — Every person who commits an offence under subsection (1) or (2) is guilty of an indictable offence and liable

    (a) in the case of a first offence, except as provided in paragraph (b), to imprisonment for a term not exceeding fourteen years and to a minimum punishment of imprisonment for a term of one year;

    (b) in the case of a first offence committed by a person who, before January 1, 1978, was convicted of an indictable offence, or an attempt to commit an indictable offence, in the course of which or during flight after the commission or attempted commission of which the person used a firearm, to imprisonment for a term not exceeding fourteen years and to a minimum punishment of imprisonment for a term of three years; and

    (c) in the case of a second or subsequent offence, to imprisonment for a term not exceeding fourteen years and to a minimum punishment of imprisonment for a term of three years.

(4) Sentences to be served consecutively — A sentence imposed on a person for an offence under subsection (1) or (2) shall be served consecutively to any other punishment imposed on the person for an offence arising out of the same event or series of events and to any other sentence to which the person is subject at the time the sentence is imposed on the person for an offence under subsection (1) or (2).

1995, c. 39, s. 139.

86. (1) Careless use of firearm, etc. — Every person commits an offence who, without lawful excuse, uses, carries, handles, ships, transports or stores a firearm, a prohibited weapon, a restricted weapon, a prohibited device or any ammunition or prohibited ammunition in a careless manner or without reasonable precautions for the safety of other persons.

(2) Contravention of storage regulations, etc — Every person commits an offence who contravenes a regulation made under paragraph 117(*h*) of the *Firearms Act* respecting the storage, handling, transportation, shipping, display, advertising and mail-order sales of firearms and restricted weapons.

(3) Punishment — Every person who commits an offence under subsection (1) or (2)

    (a) is guilty of an indictable offence and liable to imprisonment

        (i) in the case of a first offence, for a term not exceeding two years, and

        (ii) in the case of a second or subsequent offence, for a term not exceeding five years; or

    (b) is guilty of an offence punishable on summary conviction.

1995, c. 39, ss. 139, 163.

87. (1) Pointing a firearm — Every person commits an offence who, without lawful excuse, points a firearm at another person, whether the firearm is loaded or unloaded.

(2) **Punishment** — Every person who commits an offence under subsection (1)

(a) is guilty of an indictable offence and liable to imprisonment for a term not exceeding five years; or

(b) is guilty of an offence punishable on summary conviction.

1995, c. 39, s. 139.

Possession Offences

88. (1) Possession of weapon for dangerous purpose — Every person commits an offence who carries or possesses a weapon, an imitation of a weapon, a prohibited device or any ammunition or prohibited ammunition for a purpose dangerous to the public peace or for the purpose of committing an offence.

(2) **Punishment** — Every person who commits an offence under subsection (1)

(a) is guilty of an indictable offence and liable to imprisonment for a term not exceeding ten years; or

(b) is guilty of an offence punishable on summary conviction.

1995, c. 39, s. 139.

89. (1) Carrying weapon while attending public meeting — Every person commits an offence who, without lawful excuse, carries a weapon, a prohibited device or any ammunition or prohibited ammunition while the person is attending or is on the way to attend a public meeting.

(2) **Punishment** — Every person who commits an offence under subsection (1) is guilty of an offence punishable on summary conviction.

1995, c. 39, s. 139.

90. (1) Carrying concealed weapon — Every person commits an offence who carries a weapon, a prohibited device or any prohibited ammunition concealed, unless the person is authorized under the *Firearms Act* to carry it concealed.

(2) **Punishment** — Every person who commits an offence under subsection (1)

(a) is guilty of an indictable offence and liable to imprisonment for a term not exceeding five years; or

(b) is guilty of an offence punishable on summary conviction.

1995, c. 39, s. 139.

91. (1) Unauthorized possession of firearm — Subject to subsections (4) and (5) and section 98, every person commits an offence who possesses a firearm, unless the person is the holder of

(a) a licence under which the person may possess it; and

(b) a registration certificate for the firearm.

(2) **Unauthorized possession of prohibited weapon or restricted weapon** — Subject to subsection (4) and section 98, every person commits an offence who possesses a prohibited weapon, a restricted weapon, a prohibited de-

vice, other than a replica firearm, or any prohibited ammunition, unless the person is the holder of a licence under which the person may possess it.

(3) Punishment — Every person who commits an offence under subsection (1) or (2)

(a) is guilty of an indictable offence and liable to imprisonment for a term not exceeding five years; or

(b) is guilty of an offence punishable on summary conviction.

(4) Exceptions — Subsections (1) and (2) do not apply to

(a) a person who possesses a firearm, a prohibited weapon, a restricted weapon, a prohibited device or any prohibited ammunition while the person is under the direct and immediate supervision of a person who may lawfully possess it, for the purpose of using it in a manner in which the supervising person may lawfully use it; or

(b) a person who comes into possession of a firearm, a prohibited weapon, a restricted weapon, a prohibited device or any prohibited ammunition by the operation of law and who, within a reasonable period after acquiring possession of it,

(i) lawfully disposes of it, or

(ii) obtains a licence under which the person may possess it and, in the case of a firearm, a registration certificate for the firearm.

(5) Borrowed firearm for sustenance — Subsection (1) does not apply to a person who possesses a firearm that is neither a prohibited firearm nor a restricted firearm and who is not the holder of a registration certificate for the firearm if the person

(a) has borrowed the firearm;

(b) is the holder of a licence under which the person may possess it; and

(c) is in possession of the firearm to hunt or trap in order to sustain the person or the person's family.

1995, c. 39, s. 139.

92. (1) Possession of firearm knowing its possession is unauthorized — Subject to subsections (4) and (5) and section 98, every person commits an offence who possesses a firearm knowing that the person is not the holder of

(a) a licence under which the person may possess it; and

(b) a registration certificate for the firearm.

(2) Possession of prohibited weapon, device or ammunition knowing its possession is unauthorized — Subject to subsection (4) and section 98, every person commits an offence who possesses a prohibited weapon, a restricted weapon, a prohibited device, other than a replica firearm, or any prohibited ammunition knowing that the person is not the holder of a licence under which the person may possess it.

(3) Punishment — Every person who commits an offence under subsection (1) or (2) is guilty of an indictable offence and liable

(a) in the case of a first offence, to imprisonment for a term not exceeding ten years;

(b) in the case of a second offence, to imprisonment for a term not exceeding ten years and to a minimum punishment of imprisonment for a term of one year; and

(c) in the case of a third or subsequent offence, to imprisonment for a term not exceeding ten years and to a minimum punishment of imprisonment for a term of two years less a day.

(4) Exceptions — Subsections (1) and (2) do not apply to

(a) a person who possesses a firearm, a prohibited weapon, a restricted weapon, a prohibited device or any prohibited ammunition while the person is under the direct and immediate supervision of a person who may lawfully possess it, for the purpose of using it in a manner in which the supervising person may lawfully use it; or

(b) a person who comes into possession of a firearm, a prohibited weapon, a restricted weapon, a prohibited device or any prohibited ammunition by the operation of law and who, within a reasonable period after acquiring possession of it,

(i) lawfully disposes of it, or

(ii) obtains a licence under which the person may possess it and, in the case of a firearm, a registration certificate for the firearm.

(5) Borrowed firearm for sustenance — Subsection (1) does not apply to a person who possesses a firearm that is neither a prohibited firearm nor a restricted firearm and who is not the holder of a registration certificate for the firearm if the person

(a) has borrowed the firearm;

(b) is the holder of a licence under which the person may possess it; and

(c) is in possession of the firearm to hunt or trap in order to sustain the person or the person's family.

(6) Evidence for previous conviction — Where a person is charged with an offence under subsection (1), evidence that the person was convicted of an offence under subsection 112(1) of the *Firearms Act* is admissible at any stage of the proceedings and may be taken into consideration for the purpose of proving that the person knew that the person was not the holder of a registration certificate for the firearm to which the offence relates.

1995, c. 39, s. 139.

93. (1) Possession at unauthorized place — Subject to subsection (3) and section 98, every person commits an offence who, being the holder of an authorization or a licence under which the person may possess a firearm, a prohibited weapon, a restricted weapon, a prohibited device or prohibited ammunition, possesses the firearm, prohibited weapon, restricted weapon, prohibited device or prohibited ammunition at a place that is

(a) indicated on the authorization or licence as being a place where the person may not possess it;

(b) other than a place indicated on the authorization or licence as being a place where the person may possess it; or

(c) other than a place where it may be possessed under the *Firearms Act*.

(2) Punishment — Every person who commits an offence under subsection (1)

(a) is guilty of an indictable offence and liable to imprisonment for a term not exceeding five years; or

(b) is guilty of an offence punishable on summary conviction.

(3) Exception — Subsection (1) does not apply to a person who possesses a replica firearm.

1995, c. 39, s. 139

94. (1) Unauthorized possession in motor vehicle — Subject to subsections (3) to (5) and section 98, every person commits an offence who is an occupant of a motor vehicle in which the person knows there is a firearm, a prohibited weapon, a restricted weapon, a prohibited device, other than a replica firearm, or any prohibited ammunition, unless

(a) in the case of a firearm,

(i) the person or any other occupant of the motor vehicle is the holder of

(A) an authorization or a licence under which the person or other occupant may possess the firearm and, in the case of a prohibited firearm or a restricted firearm, transport the prohibited firearm or restricted firearm, and

(B) a registration certificate for the firearm,

(ii) the person had reasonable grounds to believe that any other occupant of the motor vehicle was the holder of

(A) an authorization or a licence under which that other occupant may possess the firearm and, in the case of a prohibited firearm or a restricted firearm, transport the prohibited firearm or restricted firearm, and

(B) a registration certificate for the firearm, or

(iii) the person had reasonable grounds to believe that any other occupant of the motor vehicle was a person who could not be convicted of an offence under this Act by reason of sections 117.07 to 117.1 or any other Act of Parliament; and

(b) in the case of a prohibited weapon, a restricted weapon, a prohibited device or any prohibited ammunition,

(i) the person or any other occupant of the motor vehicle is the holder of an authorization or a licence under which the person or other occupant may transport the prohibited weapon, restricted weapon, prohibited device or prohibited ammunition, or

(ii) the person had reasonable grounds to believe that any other occupant of the motor vehicle was

    (A)   the holder of an authorization or a licence under which the other occupant may transport the prohibited weapon, restricted weapon, prohibited device or prohibited ammunition, or

    (B)   a person who could not be convicted of an offence under this Act by reason of sections 117.07 to 117.1 or any other Act of Parliament.

(2) Punishment — Every person who commits an offence under subsection (1)

    (a) is guilty of an indictable offence and liable to imprisonment for a term not exceeding ten years; or

    (b) is guilty of an offence punishable on summary conviction.

(3) Exception — Subsection (1) does not apply to an occupant of a motor vehicle who, on becoming aware of the presence of the firearm, prohibited weapon, restricted weapon, prohibited device or prohibited ammunition in the motor vehicle, attempted to leave the motor vehicle, to the extent that it was feasible to do so, or actually left the motor vehicle.

(4) Exception — Subsection (1) does not apply to an occupant of a motor vehicle where the occupant or any other occupant of the motor vehicle is a person who came into possession of the firearm, prohibited weapon, restricted weapon, prohibited device or prohibited ammunition by the operation of law.

(5) Borrowed firearm for sustenance — Subsection (1) does not apply to an occupant of a motor vehicle where the occupant or any other occupant of the motor vehicle is a person who possesses a firearm that is neither a prohibited firearm nor a restricted firearm and who is not the holder of a registration certificate for the firearm if the person

    (a) has borrowed the firearm;

    (b) is the holder of a licence under which the person may possess it; and

    (c) is in possession of the firearm to hunt or trap in order to sustain the person or the person's family.

1995, c. 39, s. 139.

95. (1) Possession of prohibited or restricted firearm with ammunition — Subject to subsection (3) and section 98, every person commits an offence who, in any place, possesses a loaded prohibited firearm or restricted firearm, or an unloaded prohibited firearm or restricted firearm together with readily accessible ammunition that is capable of being discharged in the firearm, unless the person is the holder of

    (a) an authorization or a licence under which the person may possess the firearm in that place; and

    (b) the registration certificate for the firearm.

(2) Punishment — Every person who commits an offence under subsection (1)

(a) is guilty of an indictable offence and liable to imprisonment for a term not exceeding ten years and to a minimum punishment of imprisonment for a term of one year, or

(b) is guilty of an offence punishable on summary conviction and liable to imprisonment for a term not exceeding one year.

(3) Exception — Subsection (1) does not apply to a person who is using the firearm under the direct and immediate supervision of another person who is lawfully entitled to possess it and is using the firearm in a manner in which that other person may lawfully use it.

1995, c. 39, s. 139.

96. (1) Possession of weapon obtained by commission of offence — Subject to subsection (3), every person commits an offence who possesses a firearm, a prohibited weapon, a restricted weapon, a prohibited device or any prohibited ammunition that the person knows was obtained by the commission in Canada of an offence or by an act or omission anywhere that, if it had occurred in Canada, would have constituted an offence.

(2) Punishment — Every person who commits an offence under subsection (1)

(a) is guilty of an indictable offence and liable to imprisonment for a term not exceeding ten years and to a minimum punishment of imprisonment for a term of one year; or

(b) is guilty of an offence punishable on summary conviction and liable to imprisonment for a term not exceeding one year.

(3) Exception — Subsection (1) does not apply to a person who comes into possession of anything referred to in that subsection by the operation of law and who lawfully disposes of it within a reasonable period after acquiring possession of it.

1995, c. 39, s. 139.

97. (1) Delivery of firearm to person without firearms acquisition certificate — Every one who sells, barters, gives, lends, transfers or delivers any firearm to a person who does not, at the time of the sale, barter, giving, lending, transfer or delivery or, in the case of a mail–order sale, within a reasonable time prior thereto, produce a firearms acquisition certificate for inspection by the person selling, bartering, giving, lending, transferring or delivering the firearm, that that person has no reason to believe is invalid or was issued to a person other than the person so producing it,

(a) is guilty of an indictable offence and liable to imprisonment for a term not exceeding two years; or

(b) is guilty of an offence punishable on summary conviction.

(2) Saving provision — Subsection (1) does not apply to a person

(a) lawfully in possession of a firearm who lends the firearm

(i) to a person for use by that person in his company and under his guidance or supervision in the same manner in which he may lawfully use it,

(ii) to a person who requires the firearm to hunt or trap in order to sustain himself or his family, or

(iii) to a person who is the holder of a permit issued under subsection 110(1), (6), or (7) permitting the lawful possession of the firearm;

(b) who returns a firearm to a person who lent it to him in circumstances described in paragraph (a);

(c) who comes into possession of a firearm in the ordinary course of a business described in paragraph 105(1)(a) and who returns the firearm to the person from whom it is received; or

(d) who is a peace officer, local registrar of firearms or firearms officer who returns a firearm to a person who had lawfully possessed the firearm and subsequently lost it or from whom it had been stolen.

(3) Acquisition of firearm without firearms acquisition certificate — Every one who imports or otherwise acquires possession in any manner whatever of a firearm while he is not the holder of a firearms acquisition certificate

(a) is guilty of an indictable offence and liable to imprisonment for a term not exceeding two years; or

(b) is guilty of an offence punishable on summary conviction.

(4) Saving provision — Subsection (3) does not apply to a person who

(a) acquires a firearm in circumstances such that, by virtue of subsection (2), subsection (1) does not apply to the person from whom he acquires the firearm;

(b) reacquires a firearm from a person to whom he lent the firearm;

(c) imports a firearm at a time when he is not a resident of Canada;

(d) comes into possession of a firearm by operation of law and thereafter, with reasonable despatch, lawfully disposes of it or obtains a firearms acquisition certificate under which he could have lawfully acquired the firearm;

(e) comes into possession of a firearm in the ordinary course of a business described in paragraph 105(1)(a) or (b) or 105(2)(a) or (b); or

(f) has lawfully possessed a firearm and has subsequently lost it, or from whom it had been stolen, and who then reacquires it from a peace officer, local registrar of firearms or firearms officer or finds it and so reports to a peace officer, local registrar of firearms or firearms officer.

1991, c. 40, ss. 10, 38.

Proposed Amendment — 97

97. (1) Sale of cross-bow to person without licence — Every person commits an offence who at any time sells, barters or gives a cross-bow to another person, unless the other person produces for inspection by the person at that time a licence that the person has no reasonable grounds to believe is invalid or was issued to anyone other than the other person.

(2) Punishment — Every person who commits an offence under subsection (1)

(a) is guilty of an indictable offence and liable to imprisonment for a term not exceeding two years; or

(b) is guilty of an offence punishable on summary conviction.

(3) Exception — Subsection (1) does not apply to a person who lends a cross-bow to another person while that other person is under the direct and immediate supervision of a person who may lawfully possess it.

1995, c. 39, s. 139 [Not in force at date of publication.]

98. (1) Transitional — licences — Every person who, immediately before the coming into force of any of subsections 91(1), 92(1), 93(1), 94(1) and 95(1), possessed a firearm without a firearm acquisition certificate because

(a) the person possessed the firearm before January 1, 1979, or

(b) the firearm acquisition certificate under which the person had acquired the firearm had expired,

shall be deemed for the purposes of that subsection to be, until January 1, 2001 or such other earlier date as is prescribed, the holder of a licence under which the person may possess the firearm.

(2) Transitional — licences — Every person who, immediately before the coming into force of any subsections 91(1), 92(1), 93(1), 94(1) and 95(1), possessed a firearm and was the holder of a firearm acquisition certificate shall be deemed for the purposes of that subsection to be, until January 1, 2001 or such other earlier date as is prescribed, the holder of a licence under which the person may possess the firearm.

(3) Transitional — registration certificates — Every person who, at any particular time between the coming into force of subsection 91(1), 92(1) or 94(1) and the later of January 1, 1998 and such other date as is prescribed, possesses a firearm that, as of that particular time, is not a prohibited firearm or a restricted firearm shall be deemed for the purposes of that subsection to be, until January 1, 2003 or such other earlier date as is prescribed, the holder of a registration certificate for that firearm.

1995, c. 39, s. 139.

99. (1) Weapons trafficking — Every person commits an offence who

(a) manufactures or transfers, whether or not for consideration, or

(b) offers to do anything referred to in paragraph (*a*) in respect of

a firearm, a prohibited weapon, a restricted weapon, a prohibited device, any ammunition or any prohibited ammunition knowing that the person is not authorized to do so under the *Firearms Act* or any other Act of Parliament or any regulations made under any Act of Parliament.

(2) Punishment — Every person who commits an offence under subsection (1) is guilty of an indictable offence and liable to imprisonment for a term not exceeding ten years and to a minimum punishment of imprisonment for a term of one year.

1995, c. 39, s. 139.

100. (1) Possession for purpose of weapons trafficking — Every person commits an offence who possesses a firearm, a prohibited weapon, a restricted weapon, a prohibited device, any ammunition or any prohibited ammunition for the purpose of

    (a) transferring it, whether or not for consideration, or

    (b) offering to transfer it,

knowing that the person is not authorized to transfer it under the *Firearms Act* or any other Act of Parliament or any regulations made under any Act of Parliament.

(2) Punishment — Every person who commits an offence under subsection (1) is guilty of an indictable offence and liable to imprisonment for a term not exceeding ten years and to a minimum punishment of imprisonment for a term of one year.

1995, c. 39, s. 139.

101. (1) Transfer without authority — Every person commits an offence who transfers a firearm, a prohibited weapon, a restricted weapon, a prohibited device, any ammunition or any prohibited ammunition to any person otherwise than under the authority of the *Firearms Act* or any other Act of Parliament or any regulations made under an Act of Parliament.

(2) Punishment — Every person who commits an offence under subsection (1)

    (a) is guilty of an indictable offence and liable to imprisonment for a term not exceeding five years; or

    (b) is guilty of an offence punishable on summary conviction.

1995, c. 39, s. 139

Assembling Offence

102. (1) Making automatic firearm — Every person commits an offence who, without lawful excuse, alters a firearm so that it is capable of, or manufactures or assembles any firearm that is capable of, discharging projectiles in rapid succession during one pressure of the trigger.

(2) Punishment — Every person who commits an offence under subsection (1)

    (a) is guilty of an indictable offence and liable to imprisonment for a term not exceeding ten years and to a minimum punishment of imprisonment for a term of one year, or

    (b) is guilty of an offence punishable on summary conviction and liable to imprisonment for a term not exceeding one year.

1995, c. 39, s. 139

Export and Import Offences

103. (1) Importing or exporting knowing it is unauthorized — Every person commits an offence who imports or exports

(a) a firearm, a prohibited weapon, a restricted weapon, a prohibited device or any prohibited ammunition, or

(b) any component or part designed exclusively for use in the manufacture of or assembly into an automatic firearm,

knowing that the person is not authorized to do so under the *Firearms Act* or any other Act of Parliament or any regulations made under an Act of Parliament.

(2) Punishment — Every person who commits an offence under subsection (1) is guilty of an indictable offence and liable to imprisonment for a term not exceeding ten years and to a minimum punishment of imprisonment for a term of one year.

(3) Attorney General of Canada may act — Any proceedings in respect of an offence under subsection (1) may be commenced at the instance of the Government of Canada and conducted by or on behalf of that government.

1995, c. 39, s. 139

104. (1) Unauthorized importing or exporting — Every person commits an offence who imports or exports

(a) a firearm, a prohibited weapon, a restricted weapon, a prohibited device or any prohibited ammunition, or

(b) any component or part designed exclusively for use in the manufacture of or assembly into an automatic firearm,

otherwise than under the authority of the *Firearms Act* or any other Act of Parliament or any regulations made under an Act of Parliament.

(2) Punishment — Every person who commits an offence under subsection (1)

(a) is guilty of an indictable offence and liable to imprisonment for a term not exceeding five years; or

(b) is guilty of an offence punishable on summary conviction.

(3) Attorney General of Canada may act — Any proceedings in respect of an offence under subsection (1) may be commenced at the instance of the Government of Canada and conducted by or on behalf of that government.

1995, c. 39, s. 139

Offences relating to Lost, Destroyed or Defaced Weapons, etc.

105. (1) Losing or finding — Every person commits an offence who

(a) having lost a firearm, a prohibited weapon, a restricted weapon, a prohibited device, any prohibited ammunition, an authorization, a licence or a registration certificate, or having had it stolen from the person's possession, does not with reasonable despatch report the loss to a peace officer, to a firearms officer or a chief firearms officer, or

(b) on finding a firearm, a prohibited weapon, a restricted weapon, a prohibited device or any prohibited ammunition that the person has reasonable grounds to believe has been lost or abandoned, does not with reasonable despatch deliver it to a peace officer, a firearms officer or a chief firearms officer or report the finding to a peace officer, a firearms officer or a chief firearms officer.

(2) Punishment — Every person who commits an offence under subsection (1)

(a) is guilty of an indictable offence and liable to imprisonment for a term not exceeding five years; or

(b) is guilty of an offence punishable on summary conviction.

1995, c. 39, s. 139

106. (1) Destroying — Every person commits an offence who

(a) after destroying any firearm, prohibited weapon, restricted weapon, prohibited device or prohibited ammunition, or

(b) on becoming aware of the destruction of any firearm, prohibited weapon, restricted weapon, prohibited device or prohibited ammunition that was in the person's possession before its destruction,

does not with reasonable despatch report the destruction to a peace officer, firearms officer or chief firearms officer.

(2) Punishment — Every person who commits an offence under subsection (1)

(a) is guilty of an indictable offence and liable to imprisonment for a term not exceeding five years; or

(b) is guilty of an offence punishable on summary conviction.

1995, c. 39, s. 139

107. (1) False statements — Every person commits an offence who knowingly makes, before a peace officer, firearms officer or chief firearms officer, a false report or statement concerning the loss, theft or destruction of a firearm, a prohibited weapon, a restricted weapon, a prohibited device, any prohibited ammunition, an authorization, a licence or a registration certificate.

(2) Punishment — Every person who commits an offence under subsection (1)

(a) is guilty of an indictable offence and liable to imprisonment for a term not exceeding five years; or

(b) is guilty of an offence punishable on summary conviction.

(3) Definition of "report" or "statement" — In this section, **"report"** or **"statement"** means an assertion of fact, opinion, belief or knowledge, whether material or not and whether admissible or not.

1995, c. 39, s. 139

108. (1) Tampering with serial number — Every person commits an offence who, without lawful excuse, the proof of which lies on the person,

(a) alters, defaces or removes a serial number on a firearm; or

(b) possesses a firearm knowing that the serial number on it has been altered, defaced or removed.

(2) Punishment — Every person who commits an offence under subsection (1)

(a) is guilty of an indictable offence and liable to imprisonment for a term not exceeding five years; or

(b) is guilty of an offence punishable on summary conviction.

(3) Exception — No person is guilty of an offence under paragraph (1)(b) by reason only of possessing a firearm the serial number on which has been altered, defaced or removed, where that serial number has been replaced and a registration certificate in respect of the firearm has been issued setting out a new serial number for the firearm.

(4) Evidence — In proceedings for an offence under subsection (1), evidence that a person possesses a firearm the serial number on which has been wholly or partially obliterated otherwise than through normal use over time is, in the absence of evidence to the contrary, proof that the person possesses the firearm knowing that the serial number on it has been altered, defaced or removed.

1995, c. 39, s. 139

109. (1) Mandatory prohibition order — Where a person is convicted, or discharged under section 730, of

(a) an indictable offence in the commission of which violence against a person was used, threatened or attempted and for which the person may be sentenced to imprisonment for ten years or more,

(b) an offence under subsection 85(1) (using firearm in commission of offence), subsection 85(2) (using imitation firearm in commission of offence), 95(1) (possession of prohibited or restricted firearm with ammunition), 99(1) (weapons trafficking), 100(1) (possession for purpose of weapons trafficking), 102(1) (making automatic firearm), 103(1) (importing or exporting knowing it is unauthorized) or section 264 (criminal harassment),

(c) an offence relating to the contravention of subsection 5(3) or (4), 6(3) or 7(2) of the *Controlled Drugs and Substances Act*, or

(d) an offence that involves, or the subject-matter of which is, a firearm, a cross-bow, a prohibited weapon, a restricted weapon, a prohibited device, any ammunition, any prohibited ammunition or an explosive substance and, at the time of the offence, the person was prohibited by any order made under this Act or any other Act of Parliament from possessing any such thing

the court that sentences the person or directs that the person be discharged, as the case may be, shall, in addition to any other punishment that may be imposed for that offence or any other condition prescribed in the order of discharge, make an order prohibiting the person from possessing any firearm, cross-bow, prohibited weapon, restricted weapon, prohibited device, ammunition, prohibited ammunition and explosive substance during the period specified in the order as determined in accordance with subsection (2) or (3), as the case may be.

(2) Duration of prohibition order — first offence — An order made under subsection (1) shall, in the case of a first conviction for or discharge from the offence to which the order relates, prohibit the person from possessing

    (a) any firearm, other than a prohibited firearm or restricted firearm, and any cross-bow, restricted weapon, ammunition and explosive substance during the period that

        (i) begins on the day on which the order is made, and

        (ii) ends not earlier than ten years after the person's release from imprisonment after conviction for the offence or, if the person is not then imprisoned or subject to imprisonment, after the person's conviction for or discharge from the offence; and

    (b) any prohibited firearm, restricted firearm, prohibited weapon, prohibited device and prohibited ammunition for life.

(3) Duration of prohibition order — subsequent offences — An order made under subsection (1) shall, in any case other than a case described in subsection (2), prohibit the person from possessing any firearm, cross-bow, restricted weapon, ammunition and explosive substance for life.

(4) Definition of "release from imprisonment" — In subparagraph (2)(a)(ii), "release from imprisonment" means release from confinement by reason of expiration of sentence, commencement of statutory release or grant of parole.

(5) Application of ss. 113 to 117 — Sections 113 to 117 apply in respect of every order made under subsection (1).

1995, c. 39, s. 190(d); 1996, c. 19, s. 65.1.

110. (1) Discretionary prohibition order — Where a person is convicted, or discharged under section 730, of

    (a) an offence, other than an offence referred to in any of paragraphs 109(1)(a), (b) and (c), in the commission of which violence against a person was used, threatened or attempted, or

    (b) an offence that involves, or the subject-matter of which is, a firearm, a cross-bow, a prohibited weapon, a restricted weapon, a prohibited device, ammunition, prohibited ammunition or an explosive substance and, at the time of the offence, the person was not prohibited by any order made under this Act or any other Act of Parliament from possessing any such thing,

the court that sentences the person or directs that the person be discharged, as the case may be, shall, in addition to any other punishment that may be imposed for that offence or any other condition prescribed in the order of discharge, consider whether it is desirable, in the interests of the safety of the person or of any other person, to make an order prohibiting the person from possessing any firearm, cross-bow, prohibited weapon, restricted weapon, prohibited device, ammunition, prohibited ammunition or explosive substance, or all such things, and where the court decides that it is so desirable, the court shall so order.

(2) Duration of prohibition order — An order made under subsection (1) against a person begins on the day on which the order is made and ends not later than ten years after the person's release from imprisonment after conviction for the offence to which the order relates or, if the person is not then imprisoned or subject to imprisonment, after the person's conviction for or discharge from the offence.

(3) Reasons — Where the court does not make an order under subsection (1), or where the court does make such an order but does not prohibit the possession of everything referred to in that subsection, the court shall include in the record a statement of the court's reasons for not doing so.

(4) Definition of "release from imprisonment" — In subsection (2), "release from imprisonment" means release from confinement by reason of expiration of sentence, commencement of statutory release or grant of parole.

(5) Application of ss. 113 to 117 — Sections 113 to 117 apply in respect of every order made under subsection (1).

1995, c. 39, ss. 139, 190(e).

111. (1) Application for prohibition order — A peace officer, firearms officer or chief firearms officer may apply to a provincial court judge for an order prohibiting a person from possessing any firearm, cross-bow, prohibited weapon, restricted weapon, prohibited device, ammunition, prohibited ammunition or explosive substance, or all such things, where the peace officer, firearms officer or chief firearms officer believes on reasonable grounds that it is not desirable in the interests of the safety of the person against whom the order is sought or of any other person that the person against whom the order is sought should possess any such thing.

(2) Date for hearing and notice — On receipt of an application made under subsection (1), the provincial court judge shall fix a date for the hearing of the application and direct that notice of the hearing be given, in such manner as the provincial court judge may specify, to the person against whom the order is sought.

(3) Hearing of application — Subject to subsection (4), at the hearing of an application made under subsection (1), the provincial court judge shall hear all relevant evidence presented by or on behalf of the applicant and the person against whom the order is sought.

(4) Where hearing may proceed *ex parte* — A provincial court judge may proceed *ex parte* to hear and determine an application made under subsection (1) in the absence of the person against whom the order is sought in the same circumstances as those in which a summary conviction court may, under Part XXVII, proceed with a trial in the absence of the defendant.

(5) Prohibition order — Where, at the conclusion of a hearing of an application made under subsection (1), the provincial court judge is satisfied that the circumstances referred to in that subsection exist, the provincial court judge shall make an order prohibiting the person from possessing any firearm, cross-bow, prohibited weapon, restricted weapon, prohibited device, ammunition, prohibited ammunition or explosive substance, or all such things, for such period, not exceeding five years, as is specified in the order, beginning on the day on which the order is made.

(6) Reasons — Where a provincial court judge does not make an order under subsection (1), or where a provincial court judge does make such an order but does not prohibit the possession of everything referred to in that subsection, the provincial court judge shall include in the record a statement of the court's reasons.

(7) Application of ss. 113 to 117 — Sections 113 to 117 apply in respect of every order made under subsection (5).

(8) Appeal by person or Attorney General — Where a provincial court judge makes an order under subsection (5), the person to whom the order relates, or the Attorney General, may appeal to the superior court against the order.

(9) Appeal by Attorney General — Where a provincial court judge does not make an order under subsection (5), the Attorney General, may appeal to the superior court against the decision not to make an order.

(10) Application of Part XXVII to appeals — The provisions of Part XXVII, except sections 785 to 812, 816 to 819 and 829 to 838, apply in respect of an appeal made under subsection (8) or (9), with such modifications as the circumstances require and as if each reference in that Part to the appeal court were a reference to the superior court.

(11) Definition of "provincial court judge" — In this section and sections 112, 117.011 and 117.012, "provincial court judge" means a provincial court judge having jurisdiction in the territorial division where the person against whom the application for an order was brought resides.

1995, c. 39, s. 139

112. Revocation of prohibition order under s. 111(5) — A provincial court judge may, on application by the person against whom an order is made under subsection 111(5), revoke the order if satisfied that the circumstances for which it was made have ceased to exist.

1995, c. 39, ss. 139, 190(e).

113. (1) Lifting of prohibition order for sustenance or employment — Where a person who is or will be a person against whom a prohibition order is made establishes to the satisfaction of a competent authority that

(a) the person needs a firearm or restricted weapon to hunt or trap in order to sustain the person or the person's family, or

(b) a prohibition order against the person would constitute a virtual prohibition against employment in the only vocation open to the person,

the competent authority may, notwithstanding that the person is or will be subject to a prohibition order, make an order authorizing a chief firearms officer or the Registrar to issue, in accordance with such terms and conditions as the competent authority considers appropriate, an authorization, a licence or a registration certificate, as the case may be, to the person for sustenance or employment purposes.

(2) Factors — A competent authority may make an order under subsection (1) only after taking the following factors into account;

(a) the criminal record, if any, of the person;

(b) the nature and circumstances of the offence, if any, in respect of which the prohibition order was or will be made; and

(c) the safety of the person and of other persons.

(3) Effect of order — Where an order is made under subsection (1),

(a) an authorization, a licence or a registration certificate may not be denied to the person in respect of whom the order was made solely on the basis of a prohibition order against the person or the commission of an offence in respect of which a prohibition order was made against the person; and

(b) an authorization and a licence may, for the duration of the order, be issued to the person in respect of whom the order was made only for sustenance or employment purposes and, where the order sets out terms and conditions, only in accordance with those terms and conditions, but, for greater certainty, the authorization or licence may also be subject to terms and conditions set by the chief firearms officer that are not inconsistent with the purpose for which it is issued and any terms and conditions set out in the order.

(4) When order can be made — For greater certainty, an order under subsection (1) may be made during proceedings for an order under subsection 109(1), 110(1), 111(5), 117.05(4) or 515(2), paragraph 732.1(3)(d) or subsection 810(3).

(5) Meaning of "competent authority" — In this section, "competent authority" means the competent authority that made or has jurisdiction to make the prohibition order.

1995, c. 39, ss. 139, 190(e).

114. Requirement to surrender — A competent authority that makes a prohibition order against a person may, in the order, require the person to surrender to a peace officer, a firearms officer or a chief firearms officer

(a) any thing the possession of which is prohibited by the order that is in the possession of the person on the commencement of the order, and

(b) every authorization, licence and registration certificate relating to any thing the possession of which is prohibited by the order that is held by the person on the commencement of the order.

and where the competent authority does so, it shall specify in the order a reasonable period for surrendering such things and documents and during which section 117.01 does not apply to that person.

1995, c. 39, s. 139.

115. (1) Forfeiture — Unless a prohibition order against a person specifies otherwise, every thing the possession of which is prohibited by the order that, on the commencement of the order, is in the possession of the person is forfeited to Her Majesty.

(2) Disposal — Every thing forfeited to Her Majesty under subsection (1) shall be disposed of or otherwise dealt with as the Attorney General directs.

1995, c. 39, s. 139

116. Authorizations revoked or amended — Every authorization, licence and registration certificate relating to any thing the possession of which is prohibited by a prohibition order and issued to a person against whom the prohibition order is made is, on the commencement of the prohibition order, revoked, or amended, as the case may be, to the extent of the prohibitions in the order.

1995, c. 39, s. 139

117. Return to owner — Where the competent authority that makes a prohibition order or that would have had jurisdiction to make the order is, on application for an order under this section, satisfied that a person, other than the person against whom a prohibition order was or will be made,

    (a) is the owner of any thing that is or may be forfeited to Her Majesty under subsection 115(1) and is lawfully entitled to possess it, and

    (b) in the case of a prohibition order under subsection 109(1) or 110(1), had no reasonable grounds to believe that the thing would or might be used in the commission of the offence in respect of which the prohibition order was made,

the competent authority shall order that the thing be returned to the owner or the proceeds of any sale of the thing be paid to that owner or, if the thing was destroyed, that an amount equal to the value of the thing be paid to the owner.

1995, c. 39, s. 139

117.01 (1) Possession contrary to order — Subject to subsection (4), every person commits an offence who possesses a firearm, a cross-bow, a prohibited weapon, a restricted weapon, a prohibited device, any ammunition, any prohibited ammunition or an explosive substance while the person is prohibited from doing so by any order made under this Act or any other Act of Parliament.

(2) Failure to surrender authorization, etc. — Every person commits an offence who wilfully fails to surrender to a peace officer, a firearms officer or a chief firearms officer any authorization, licence or registration certificate held by the person when the person is required to do so by any order made under this Act or any other Act of Parliament.

(3) Punishment — Every person who commits an offence under subsection (1) or (2)

    (a) is guilty of an indictable offence and liable to imprisonment for a term not exceeding ten years; or

    (b) is guilty of an offence punishable on summary conviction.

(4) Exception — Subsection (1) does not apply to a person who possessed a firearm in accordance with an authorization or licence issued to the person as the result of an order made under subsection 113(1).

1995, c. 39, s. 139

117.011 (1) Application for order — A peace officer, firearms officer or chief firearms officer may apply to a provincial court judge for an order under this section where the peace officer, firearms officer or chief firearms officer believes on reasonable grounds that

> (a) the person against whom the order is sought cohabits with, or is an associate of, another person who is prohibited by any order made under this Act or any other Act of Parliament from possessing any firearm, cross-bow, prohibited weapon, restricted weapon, prohibited device, ammunition, prohibited ammunition or explosive substance, or all such things; and

> (b) the other person would or might have access to any such thing that is in the possession of the person against whom the order is sought.

(2) Date for hearing and notice — On receipt of an application made under subsection (1), the provincial court judge shall fix a date for the hearing of the application and direct that notice of the hearing be given, in such manner as the provincial court judge may specify, to the person against whom the order is sought.

(3) Hearing of application — Subject to subsection (4), at the hearing of an application made under subsection (1), the provincial court judge shall hear all relevant evidence presented by or on behalf of the applicant and the person against whom the order is sought.

(4) Where hearing may proceed *ex parte* — A provincial court judge may proceed *ex parte* to hear and determine an application made under subsection (1) in the absence of the person against whom the order is sought in the same circumstances as those in which a summary conviction court may, under Part XXVII, proceed with a trial in the absence of the defendant.

(5) Order — Where, at the conclusion of a hearing of an application made under subsection (1), the provincial court judge is satisfied that the circumstances referred to in that subsection exist, the provincial court judge shall make an order in respect of the person against whom the order was sought imposing such terms and conditions on the person's use and possession of anything referred to in subsection (1) as the provincial court judge considers appropriate.

(6) Terms and conditions — In determining terms and conditions under subsection (5), the provincial court judge shall impose terms and conditions that are the least intrusive as possible, bearing in mind the purpose of the order.

(7) Appeal by person or Attorney General — Where a provincial court judge makes an order under subsection (5), the person to whom the order relates, or the Attorney General, may appeal to the superior court against the order.

(8) Appeal by Attorney General — Where a provincial court judge does not make an order under subsection (5), the Attorney General may appeal to the superior court against the decision not to make an order.

(9) Application of Part XXVII to appeals — The provisions of Part XXVII, except sections 785 to 812, 816 to 819 and 829 to 838, apply in respect of an appeal made under subsection (7) or (8), with such modifications as the circumstances require and as if each reference in that Part to the appeal court were a reference to the superior court.

1995, c. 39, s. 139.

117.012 Revocation of order under s. 117.011 — A provincial court judge may, on application by the person against whom an order is made under subsection 117.011(5), revoke the order if satisfied that the circumstances for which it was made have ceased to exist.

1995, c. 39, s. 139

Search and Seizure

117.02 (1) Search and seizure without warrant where offence committed — Where a peace officer believes on reasonable grounds

(a) that a weapon, an imitation firearm, a prohibited device, any ammunition, any prohibited ammunition or an explosive substance was used in the commission of an offence, or

(b) that an offence is being committed, or has been committed, under any provision of this Act that involves, or the subject-matter of which is, a firearm, an imitation firearm, a cross-bow, a prohibited weapon, a restricted weapon, a prohibited device, ammunition, prohibited ammunition or an explosive substance,

and evidence of the offence is likely to be found on a person, in a vehicle or in any place or premises other than a dwelling-house, the peace officer may, where the conditions for obtaining a warrant exist but, by reason of exigent circumstances, it would not be practicable to obtain a warrant, search, without warrant, the person, vehicle, place or premises, and seize any thing by means of or in relation to which that peace officer believes on reasonable grounds the offence is being committed or has been committed.

(2) Disposition of seized things — Any thing seized pursuant to subsection (1) shall be dealt with in accordance with sections 490 and 491.

1995, c. 39, s. 139.

117.03 (1) Seizure on failure to produce authorization — Notwithstanding section 117.02, a peace officer who finds

(a) a person in possession of a firearm who fails, on demand, to produce, for inspection by the peace officer, an authorization or a licence under which the person may lawfully possess the firearm and a registration certificate for the firearm, or

(b) a person in possession of a prohibited weapon, a restricted weapon, a prohibited device or any prohibited ammunition who fails, on demand, to produce, for inspection by the peace officer, an authorization or a licence under which the person may lawfully possess it,

may seize the firearm, prohibited weapon, restricted weapon, prohibited device or prohibited ammunition unless its possession by the person in the circumstances in which it is found is authorized by any provision of this Part, or the person is under the direct and immediate supervision of another person who may lawfully possess it.

(2) Return of seized thing on production of authorization — Where a person from whom any thing is seized pursuant to subsection (1) claims the thing

69

within fourteen days after the seizure and produces for inspection by the peace officer by whom it was seized, or any other peace officer having custody of it,

    (a) an authorization or a licence under which the person is lawfully entitled to possess it, and

    (b) in the case of a firearm, a registration certificate for the firearm,

the thing shall forthwith be returned to that person.

(3) Forfeiture of seized thing — Where any thing seized pursuant to subsection (1) is not claimed and returned as and when provided by subsection (2), a peace officer shall forthwith take the thing before a provincial court judge, who may, after affording the person from whom it was seized or its owner, if known, an opportunity to establish that the person is lawfully entitled to possess it, declare it to be forfeited to Her Majesty, to be disposed of or otherwise dealt with as the Attorney General directs.

1995, c. 39, s. 139.

117.04 (1) Application for warrant to search and seize — Where, pursuant to an application made by a peace officer with respect to any person, a justice is satisfied that there are reasonable grounds to believe that it is not desirable in the interests of the safety of the person, or of any other person, for the person to possess any weapon, prohibited device, ammunition, prohibited ammunition or explosive substance, the justice may issue a warrant authorizing a peace officer to search for and seize any such thing, and any authorization, licence or registration certificate relating to any such thing, that is held by or in the possession of the person.

(2) Search and seizure without warrant — Where, with respect to any person, a peace officer is satisfied that there are reasonable grounds to believe that it is not desirable, in the interests of the safety of the person or any other person, for the person to possess any weapon, prohibited device, ammunition, prohibited ammunition or explosive substance, the peace officer may, where the grounds for obtaining a warrant under subsection (1) exist but, by reason of a possible danger to the safety of that person or any other person, it would not be practicable to obtain a warrant, search for and seize any such thing, and any authorization, licence or registration certificate relating to any such thing, that is held by or in the possession of the person.

(3) Return to justice — A peace officer who executes a warrant referred to in subsection (1) or who conducts a search without a warrant under subsection (2) shall forthwith make a return to the justice who issued the warrant or, if no warrant was issued, to a justice who might otherwise have issued a warrant, showing

    (a) in the case of an execution of a warrant, the things or documents, if any, seized and the date of execution of the warrant; and

    (b) in the case of a search conducted without a warrant, the grounds on which it was concluded that the peace officer was entitled to conduct the search, and the things or documents, if any, seized.

(4) Authorizations etc., revoked — Where a peace officer who seizes any thing under subsection (1) or (2) is unable at the time of the seizure to seize an authorization or a licence under which the person from whom the thing was seized may possess the thing and, in the case of a seized firearm, a registration certificate for the firearm, every authorization, licence and registration certificate held by the person is, as at the time of the seizure, revoked.

1995, c. 39, s. 139.

117.05 (1) Application for disposition — Where any thing or document has been seized under 117.04(1) or (2), the justice who issued the warrant authorizing the seizure or, if no warrant was issued, a justice who might otherwise have issued a warrant, shall, on application for an order for the disposition of the thing or document so seized made by a peace officer within thirty days after the date of execution of the warrant or of the seizure without a warrant, as the case may be, fix a date for the hearing of the application and direct that notice of the hearing be given to such persons or in such manner as the justice may specify.

(2) Ex parte hearing — A justice may proceed *Ex parte* to hear and determine an application made under subsection (1) in the absence of the person from whom the thing or document was seized in the same circumstances as those in which a summary conviction court may, under Part XXVII, proceed with a trial in the absence of the defendant.

(3) Hearing of application — At the hearing of an application made under subsection (1), the justice shall hear all relevant evidence, including evidence respecting the value of the thing in respect of which the application was made.

(4) Forfeiture and prohibition order on finding — Where, following the hearing of an application made under subsection (1), the justice finds that it is not desirable in the interests of the safety of the person from whom the thing was seized or of any other person that the person should possess any weapon, prohibited device, ammunition, prohibited ammunition and explosive substance, or any such thing, the justice shall

> (a) order that any thing seized by forfeited to Her Majesty or be otherwise disposed of; and

> (b) where the justice is satisfied that the circumstances warrant such an action, order that the possession by that person of any weapon, prohibited device, ammunition, prohibited ammunition and explosive substance, or of any such thing, be prohibited during any period, not exceeding five years, that is specified in the order, beginning on the making of the order.

(5) Reasons — Where a justice does not make an order under subsection (4), or where a justice does make such an order but does not prohibit the possession of all of the things referred to in that subsection, the justice shall include in the record a statement of the justice's reasons.

(6) Application of ss. 113 to 117 — Sections 113 to 117 apply in respect of every order made under subsection (4).

(7) Appeal by person — Where a justice makes an order under subsection (4) in respect of a person, or in respect of any thing that was seized from a person, the person may appeal to the superior court against the order.

(8) Appeal by Attorney General — Where a justice does not make a finding as described in subsection (4) following the hearing of an application under subsection (1), or makes the finding but does not make an order to the effect described in paragraph (4)(b), the Attorney General may appeal to the superior court against the failure to make the finding or to make an order to the effect so described.

(9) Application of Part XXVII to appeals — The provisions of Part XXVII, except sections 785 to 812, 816 to 819 and 829 to 838, apply in respect of an appeal made under subsection (7) or (8) with such modifications as the circumstances require and as if each reference in that Part to the appeal court were a reference to the superior court.

1995, c. 39, s. 139.

117.06 (1) Where no finding or application — Any thing or document seized pursuant to subsection 117.04(1) or (2) shall be returned to the person from whom it was seized if

    (a) no application is made under subsection 117.05(1) within thirty days after the date of execution of the warrant or of the seizure without a warrant, as the case may be; or

    (b) an application is made under subsection 117.05(1) within the period referred to in paragraph (a), and the justice does not make a finding as described in subsection 117.05(4).

(2) Restoration of authorizations — Where, pursuant to subsection (1), any thing is returned to the person from whom it was seized and an authorization, a licence or a registration certificate, as the case may be, is revoked pursuant to subsection 117.04(4), the justice referred to in paragraph (1)(b) may order that the revocation be reversed and that the authorization, licence or registration certificate be restored.

1995, c. 39, s. 139

Exempted Persons

117.07 (1) Public officers — Notwithstanding any other provision of this Act, but subject to section 117.1, no public officer is guilty of an offence under this Act or the *Firearms Act* by reason only that the public officer

    (a) possesses a firearm, a prohibited weapon, a restricted weapon, a prohibited device, any prohibited ammunition or an explosive substance in the course of or for the purpose of the public officer's duties or employment;

    (b) manufactures or transfers, or offers to manufacture or transfer, a firearm, a prohibited weapon, a restricted weapon, a prohibited device, any ammunition or any prohibited ammunition in the course of the public officer's duties or employment;

    (c) exports or imports a firearm, a prohibited weapon, a restricted weapon, a prohibited device or any prohibited ammunition in the course of the public officer's duties or employment;

(d) exports or imports a component or part designed exclusively for use in the manufacture of or assembly into an automatic firearm in the course of the public officer's duties or employment;

(e) in the course of the public officer's duties or employment, alters a firearm so that it is capable of, or manufactures or assembles any firearm with intent to produce a firearm that is capable of, discharging projectiles in rapid succession during one pressure of the trigger;

(f) fails to report the loss, theft or finding of any firearm, prohibited weapon, restricted weapon, prohibited device, ammunition, prohibited ammunition or explosive substance that occurs in the course of the public officer's duties or employment or the destruction of any such thing in the course of the public officer's duties or employment; or

(g) alters a serial number on a firearm in the course of the public officer's duties or employment.

(2) Definition of "public officer" — In this section, **"public officer"** means

(a) a peace officer;

(b) a member of the Canadian Forces or of the armed forces of a state other than Canada who is attached or seconded to any of the Canadian Forces;

(c) an operator of a museum established by the Chief of the Defence Staff or a person employed in any such museum;

(d) a member of a cadet organization under the control and supervision of the Canadian Forces;

(e) a person training to become a police officer or a peace officer under the control and supervision of

(i) a police force, or

(ii) a police academy or similar institution designated by the Attorney General of Canada or the lieutenant governor in council of a province;

(f) a member of a visiting force, within the meaning of section 2 of the *Visiting Forces Act*, who is authorized under paragraph 14(a) of that Act to possess and carry explosives, ammunition and firearms;

(g) a person, or member of a class of persons, employed in the public service of Canada or by the government of a province or municipality who is prescribed to be a public officer; or

(h) a chief firearms officer and any firearms officer.

1995, c. 39, s. 139

117.08 Individuals acting for police force, Canadian Forces and visiting forces — Notwithstanding any other provision of this Act, but subject to section 117.1, no individual is guilty of an offence under this Act or the *Firearms Act* by reason only that the individual

(a) possesses a firearm, a prohibited weapon, a restricted weapon, a prohibited device, any prohibited ammunition or an explosive substance,

(b) manufactures or transfers, or offers to manufacture or transfer, a firearm, a prohibited weapon, a restricted weapon, a prohibited device, any ammunition or any prohibited ammunition,

(c) exports or imports a firearm, a prohibited weapon, a restricted weapon, a prohibited device or any prohibited ammunition,

(d) exports or imports a component or part designed exclusively for use in the manufacture of or assembly into an automatic firearm,

(e) alters a firearm so that it is capable of, or manufactures or assembles any firearm with intent to produce a firearm that is capable of, discharging projectiles in rapid succession during one pressure of the trigger,

(f) fails to report the loss, theft or finding of any firearm, prohibited weapon, restricted weapon, prohibited device, ammunition, prohibited ammunition or explosive substance or the destruction of any such thing, or

(g) alters a serial number on a firearm,

if the individual does so on behalf of, and under the authority of, a police force, the Canadian Forces, a visiting force, within the meaning of section 2 of the *Visiting Forces Act*, or a department of the Government of Canada or of a province.

1995, c. 39, s. 139

117.09 (1) Employees of business with licence — Notwithstanding any other provision of this Act, but subject to section 117.1, no individual who is the holder of a licence to possess and acquire restricted firearms and who is employed by a business as defined in subsection 2(1) of the *Firearms Act* that itself is the holder of a licence that authorizes the business to carry out specified activities in relation to prohibited firearms, prohibited weapons, prohibited devices or prohibited ammunition is guilty of an offence under this Act or the *Firearms Act* by reason only that the individual, in the course of the individual's duties or employment in relation to those specified activities,

(a) possesses a prohibited firearm, a prohibited weapon, a prohibited device or any prohibited ammunition;

(b) manufactures or transfers, or offers to manufacture or transfer, a prohibited weapon, a prohibited device or any prohibited ammunition;

(c) alters a firearm so that it is capable of, or manufactures or assembles any firearm with intent to produce a firearm that is capable of, discharging projectiles in rapid succession during one pressure of the trigger, or

(d) alters a serial number on a firearm.

(2) Employees of business with licence — Notwithstanding any other provision of this Act, but subject to section 117.1, no individual who is employed by a business as defined in subsection 2(1) of the *Firearms Act* that itself is the holder of a licence is guilty of an offence under this Act or the *Firearms Act* by reason only that the individual, in the course of the individual's duties or employment, possesses, manufactures or transfers, or offers to manufacture or transfer, a partially manufactured barrelled weapon that, in its unfinished state, is not a barrelled weapon from which any shot, bullet or other projectile can be discharged and that is capable of causing serious bodily injury or death to a person.

(3) Employees of carriers — Notwithstanding any other provision of this Act, but subject to section 117.1, no individual who is employed by a carrier, as defined in subsection 2(1) of the *Firearms Act*, is guilty of an offence under this Act or that Act by reason only that the individual, in the course of the individual's duties or employment, possesses any firearm, cross-bow, prohibited weapon, restricted weapon, prohibited device, ammunition or prohibited ammunition or transfers, or offers to transfer any such thing.

(4) Employees of museums handling functioning imitation antique firearm — Notwithstanding any other provision of this Act, but subject to section 117.1, no individual who is employed by a museum as defined in subsection 2(1) of the *Firearms Act* that itself is the holder of a licence is guilty of an offence under this Act or the *Firearms Act* by reason only that the individual, in the course of the individual's duties or employment, possesses or transfers a firearm that is designed or intended to exactly resemble, or to resemble with near precision, an antique firearm if the individual has been trained to handle and use such a firearm.

(5) Employees of museums handling firearms generally — Notwithstanding any other provision of this Act, but subject to section 117.1, no individual who is employed by a museum as defined in subsection 2(1) of the *Firearms Act* that itself is the holder of a licence is guilty of an offence under this Act or the *Firearms Act* by reason only that the individual possesses or transfers a firearm in the course of the individual's duties or employment if the individual is designated, by name, by a provincial minister within the meaning of subsection 2(1) of the *Firearms Act*.

(6) Public safety — A provincial minister shall not designate an individual for the purpose of subsection (4) where it is not desirable, in the interests of the safety of any person, to designate the individual.

(7) Conditions — A provincial minister may attach to a designation referred to in subsection (4) any reasonable condition that the provincial minister considers desirable in the particular circumstances and in the interests of the safety of any person.

1995, c. 39, s. 139.

117.1 Restriction — Sections 117.07 to 117.09 do not apply if the public officer or the individual is subject to a prohibition order and acts contrary to that order or to an authorization or a licence issued under the authority of an order made under subsection 113(1).

1995, c. 39, s. 139

General

117.11 Onus on the accused — Where, in any proceedings for an offence under any of sections 89, 90, 91, 93, 97, 101, 104 and 105, any question arises as to whether a person is the holder of an authorization, a licence or a registration certificate, the onus is on the accused to prove that the person is the holder of the authorization, licence or registration certificate.

1995, c. 39, s. 139.

117.12 (1) Authorizations, etc. as evidence — In any proceedings under this Act or any other Act of Parliament, a document purporting to be an authorization, a licence or a registration certificate is evidence of the statements contained therein.

(2) Certified copies — In any proceedings under this Act or any other Act of Parliament, a copy of any authorization, licence or registration certificate is, if certified as a true copy by the Registrar or a chief firearms officer, admissible in evidence and, in the absence of evidence to the contrary, has the same probative force as the authorization, licence or registration certificate would have had if it had been proved in the ordinary way.

1995, c. 39, s. 139.

117.13 (1) Certificate of analyst — A certificate purporting to be signed by an analyst stating that the analyst has analyzed any weapon, prohibited device, ammunition, prohibited ammunition or explosive substance, or any part or component of such a thing, and stating the results of the analysis is evidence in any proceedings in relation to any of those things under this Act or under section 19 of the *Export and Import Permits Act* in relation to subsection 15(2) of that Act without proof of the signature or official character of the person appearing to have signed the certificate.

(2) Attendance of analyst — The party against whom a certificate of an analyst is produced may, with leave of the court, require the attendance of the analyst for the purposes of cross-examination.

(3) Notice of intention to produce certificate — No certificate of an analyst may be admitted in evidence unless the party intending to produce it has, before the trial, given to the party against whom it is intended to be produced reasonable notice of that intention together with a copy of the certificate.

(4) Proof of service — For the purposes of this Act, service of a certificate of an analyst may be proved by oral evidence given under oath by, or by the affidavit or solemn declaration of, the person claiming to have served it.

(5) Attendance for examination — Notwithstanding subsection (4), the court may require the person who appears to have signed an affidavit or solemn declaration referred to in that subsection to appear before it for examination or cross-examination in respect of the issue of proof of service.

1995, c. 39, s. 139

117.14 (1) Amnesty period — The Governor in Council may, by order, declare for any purpose referred to in subsection (2) any period as an amnesty period with respect to any weapon, prohibited device, prohibited ammunition, explosive substance or component or part designed exclusively for use in the manufacture of or assembly into an automatic firearm.

(2) Purposes of amnesty period — An order made under subsection (1) may declare an amnesty period for the purpose of

(a) permitting any person in possession of any thing to which the order relates to do anything provided in the order, including, without restricting the generality of the foregoing, delivering the thing to a peace officer, a firearms officer or a chief firearms officer, registering it, destroying it or otherwise disposing of it; or

(b) permitting alterations to be made to any prohibited firearm, prohibited weapon, prohibited device or prohibited ammunition to which the order relates so that it no longer qualifies as a prohibited firearm, a prohibited weapon, a prohibited device or prohibited ammunition, as the case may be.

(3) Reliance on amnesty period — No person who, during an amnesty period declared by an order made under subsection (1) and for a purpose described in the order, does anything provided for in the order, is, by reason only of the fact that the person did that thing, guilty of an offence under this Part.

(4) Proceedings are a nullity — Any proceedings taken under this Part against any person for anything done by the person in reliance of this section are a nullity.

1995, c. 39, s. 139.

117.15 (1) Regulations — Subject to subsection (2), the Governor in Council may make regulations prescribing anything that by this Part is to be or may be prescribed.

(2) Restriction — In making regulations, the Governor in Council may not prescribe any thing to be a prohibited firearm, a restricted firearm, a prohibited weapon, a restricted weapon, a prohibited device or prohibited ammunition if, in the opinion of the Governor in Council, the thing to be prescribed is reasonable for use in Canada for hunting or sporting purposes.

1995, c. 39, s. 139

PART IV — OFFENCES AGAINST THE ADMINISTRATION OF LAW AND JUSTICE

Interpretation

118. Definitions — In this Part

"evidence" or **"statement"** means an assertion of fact, opinion, belief or knowledge whether material or not and whether admissible or not;

"government" means

(a) the Government of Canada,

(b) the government of a province, or

(c) Her Majesty in right of Canada or a province;

"judicial proceeding" means a proceeding

(a) in or under the authority of a court of justice

(b) before the Senate or House of Commons or a committee of the Senate or House of Commons, or before a legislative council, legislative assembly or house of assembly or a committee thereof that is authorized by law to administer an oath,

(c) before a court, judge, justice, provincial court judge or coroner,

(d) before an arbitrator or umpire, or a person or body of persons authorized by law to make an inquiry and take evidence therein under oath, or

(e) before a tribunal by which a legal right or legal liability may be established, whether or not the proceeding is invalid for want of jurisdiction or for any other reason;

"office" includes

(a) an office or appointment under the government,

(b) a civil or military commission, and

(c) a position or an employment in a public department;

"official" means a person who

(a) holds an office, or

(b) is appointed to discharge a public duty;

"witness" means a person who gives evidence orally under oath or by affidavit in a judicial proceeding, whether or not he is competent to be a witness, and includes a child of tender years who gives evidence but does not give it under oath, because, in the opinion of the person presiding, the child does not understand the nature of an oath.

R.S. 1985, c. 27 (1st Supp.), ss. 15, 203.

Corruption and Disobedience

119. (1) Bribery of judicial officers, etc. — Every one who

(a) being the holder of a judicial office, or being a member of Parliament or of the legislature of a province, corruptly

    (i) accepts or obtains,

    (ii) agrees to accept, or

    (iii) attempts to obtain,

any money, valuable consideration, office, place or employment for himself or another person in respect of anything done or omitted or to be done or omitted by him in his official capacity, or

(b) gives or offers, corruptly, to a person mentioned in paragraph (*a*) any money, valuable consideration, office, place or employment in respect of anything done or omitted or to be done or omitted by him in his official capacity for himself or another person,

is guilty of an indictable offence and liable to imprisonment for a term not exceeding fourteen years.

(2) Consent of Attorney General — No proceedings against a person who holds a judicial office shall be instituted under this section without the consent in writing of the Attorney General of Canada.

120. Bribery of officers — Every one who

(a) being a justice, police commissioner, peace officer, public officer or officer of a juvenile court, or being employed in the administration of criminal law, corruptly

(i) accepts or obtains,

(ii) agrees to accept, or

(iii) attempts to obtain,

for himself or any other person any money, valuable consideration, office, place or employment with intent

(iv) to interfere with the administration of justice,

(v) to procure or facilitate the commission of an offence, or

(vi) to protect from detection or punishment a person who has committed or who intends to commit an offence, or

(b) gives or offers, corruptly, to a person mentioned in paragraph (a) any money, valuable consideration, office, place or employment with intent that the person should do anything mentioned in subparagraph (a)(iv), (v) or (vi),

is guilty of an indictable offence and liable to imprisonment for a term not exceeding fourteen years.

121. (1) Frauds on the government — Every one commits an offence who

(a) directly or indirectly

(i) gives, offers, or agrees to give or offer to an official or to any member of his family, or to any one for the benefit of an official, or

(ii) being an official, demands, accepts or offers or agrees to accept from any person for himself or another person,

a loan, reward, advantage or benefit of any kind as consideration for cooperation, assistance, exercise of influence or an act or omission in connection with

(iii) the transaction of business with or any matter of business relating to the government, or

(iv) a claim against Her Majesty or any benefit that Her Majesty is authorized or is entitled to bestow,

whether or not, in fact, the official is able to cooperate, render assistance, exercise influence or do or omit to do what is proposed, as the case may be;

(b) having dealings of any kind with the government, pays a commission or reward to or confers an advantage or benefit of any kind on an employee or official of the government with which he deals, or to any member of his family, or to any one for the benefit of the employee or official, with respect to those dealings, unless he has the consent in writing of the head of the branch of government with which he deals, the proof of which lies on him;

(c) being an official or employee of the government, demands, accepts or offers or agrees to accept from a person who has dealings with the government a commission, reward, advantage or benefit of any kind directly or indirectly, by himself or through a member of his family or through any one for his benefit, unless he has the consent in writing of the head of the branch of government that employs him or of which he is an official, the proof of which lies on him;

(d) having or pretending to have influence with the government or with a minister of the government or an official, demands, accepts or offers or agrees to accept for himself or another person a reward, advantage or benefit of any kind as consideration for cooperation, assistance, exercise of influence or an act or omission in connection with

(i) anything mentioned in subparagraph (a)(iii) or (iv), or

(ii) the appointment of any person, including himself, to an office;

(e) gives, offers, or agrees to give or offer to a minister of the government or an official a reward, advantage or benefit of any kind as consideration for cooperation, assistance, exercise of influence or an act or omission in connection with

(i) anything mentioned in subparagraph (a)(iii) or (iv), or

(ii) the appointment of any person, including himself, to an office; or

(f) having made a tender to obtain a contract with the government

(i) gives, offers or agrees to give or offer to another person who has made a tender or to a member of his family, or to another person for the benefit of that person, a reward, advantage or benefit of any kind as consideration for the withdrawal of the tender of that person, or

(ii) demands, accepts or offers or agrees to accept from another person who has made a tender a reward, advantage or benefit of any kind as consideration for the withdrawal of his tender.

(2) Contractor subscribing to election fund — Every one commits an offence who, in order to obtain or retain a contract with the government, or as a term of any such contract, whether express or implied, directly or indirectly subscribes or gives, or agrees to subscribe or give, to any person any valuable consideration

(a) for the purpose of promoting the election of a candidate or a class or party of candidates to Parliament or the legislature of a province; or

(b) with intent to influence or affect in any way the result of an election conducted for the purpose of electing persons to serve in Parliament or the legislature of a province.

(3) Punishment — Every one who commits an offence under this section is guilty of an indictable offence and liable to imprisonment for a term not exceeding five years.

122. Breach of trust by public officer — Every official who, in connection with the duties of his office, commits fraud or a breach of trust is guilty of an indictable offence and liable to imprisonment for a term not exceeding five years, whether or not the fraud or breach of trust would be an offence if it were committed in relation to a private person.

123. (1) Municipal corruption — Every one who

(a) gives, offers or agrees to give or offer to a municipal official, or

(b) being a municipal official, demands, accepts or offers or agrees to accept from any person, a loan, reward, advantage or benefit of any kind as consideration for the official

(c) to abstain from voting at a meeting of the municipal council or a committee thereof,

(d) to vote in favour of or against a measure, motion or resolution,

(e) to aid in procuring or preventing the adoption of a measure, motion or resolution, or

(f) to perform or fail to perform an official act,

is guilty of an indictable offence and liable to imprisonment for a term not exceeding five years.

(2) Influencing municipal official — Every one who

(a) by suppression of the truth, in the case of a person who is under a duty to disclose the truth,

(b) by threats or deceit, or

(c) by any unlawful means, influences or attempts to influence a municipal official to do anything mentioned in paragraphs (1)(c) to (f)

is guilty of an indictable offence and liable to imprisonment for a term not exceeding five years.

(3) "municipal official" — In this section **"municipal official"** means a member of a municipal council or a person who holds an office under a municipal government.

R.S. 1985, c. 27 (1st Supp.), s. 16.

124. Selling or purchasing office — Every one who

(a) purports to sell or agrees to sell an appointment to or resignation from an office, or a consent to any such appointment or resignation, or receives or agrees to receive a reward or profit from the purported sale thereof, or

(b) purports to purchase or gives a reward or profit for the purported purchase of any such appointment, resignation or consent, or agrees or promises to do so,

is guilty of an indictable offence and liable to imprisonment for a term not exceeding five years.

125. Influencing or negotiating appointments or dealing in offices — Every one who

(a) receives, agrees to receive, gives or procures to be given, directly or indirectly, a reward, advantage or benefit of any kind as consideration for cooperation, assistance or exercise of influence to secure the appointment of any person to an office,

(b) solicits, recommends or negotiates in any manner with respect to an appointment to or resignation from an office, in expectation of a direct or indirect reward, advantage or benefit, or

(c) keeps without lawful authority, the proof of which lies on him, a place for transacting or negotiating any business relating to

    (i) the filling of vacancies in offices,

    (ii) the sale or purchase of offices, or

    (iii) appointments to or resignations from offices,

is guilty of an indictable offence and liable to imprisonment for a term not exceeding five years.

126. (1) Disobeying a statute — Every one who, without lawful excuse, contravenes an Act of Parliament by wilfully doing anything that it forbids or by wilfully omitting to do anything that it requires to be done is, unless a punishment is expressly provided by law, guilty of an indictable offence and liable to imprisonment for a term not exceeding two years.

(2) Attorney General of Canada may act — Any proceedings in respect of a contravention of or conspiracy to contravene an Act mentioned in subsection (1), other than this Act, may be instituted at the instance of the Government of Canada and conducted by or on behalf of that Government.

127. (1) Disobeying order of court — Every one who, without lawful excuse, disobeys a lawful order made by a court of justice or by a person or body of persons authorized by any Act to make or give the order, other than an order for the payment of money, is, unless a punishment or other mode of proceeding is expressly provided by law, guilty of an indictable offence and liable to imprisonment for a term not exceeding two years.

(2) Attorney General of Canada may act — Where the order referred to in subsection (1) was made in proceedings instituted at the instance of the Government of Canada and conducted by or on behalf of that Government, any proceedings in respect of a contravention of or conspiracy to contravene that order may be instituted and conducted in like manner.

128. Misconduct of officers executing process — Every peace officer or coroner who, being entrusted with the execution of a process, wilfully

    (a) misconducts himself in the execution of the process, or

    (b) makes a false return to the process,

is guilty of an indictable offence and liable to imprisonment for a term not exceeding two years.

129. Offences relating to public or peace officer — Every one who

(a) resists or wilfully obstructs a public officer or peace officer in the execution of his duty or any person lawfully acting in aid of such an officer,

(b) omits, without reasonable excuse, to assist a public officer or peace officer in the execution of his duty in arresting a person or in preserving the peace, after having reasonable notice that he is required to do so, or

(c) resists or wilfully obstructs any person in the lawful execution of a process against lands or goods or in making a lawful distress or seizure,

is guilty of

(d) an indictable offence and liable to imprisonment for a term not exceeding two years, or

(e) an offence punishable on summary conviction.

130. Personating peace officer — Every one who

(a) falsely represents himself to be a peace officer or a public officer, or

(b) not being a peace officer or public officer, uses a badge or article of uniform or equipment in a manner that is likely to cause persons to believe that he is a peace officer or a public officer, as the case may be,

is guilty of an offence punishable on summary conviction.

Misleading Justice

131. (1) Perjury — Subject to subsection (3), every one commits perjury who, with intent to mislead, makes before a person who is authorized by law to permit it to be made before him, a false statement under oath or solemn affirmation, by affidavit, solemn declaration or deposition or orally, knowing that the statement is false.

(1.1) Video links, etc. — Subject to subsection (3), every person who gives evidence under subsection 46(2) of the *Canada Evidence Act*, or gives evidence or a statement pursuant to an order made under section 22.2 of the *Mutual Legal Assistance in Criminal Matters Act,* commits perjury who, with intent to mislead, makes a false statement knowing that it is false, whether or not the false statement was made under oath or solemn affirmation in accordance with subsection (1), so long as the false statement was made in accordance with any formalities required by the law of the place outside Canada in which the person is virtually present or heard.

(2) Idem — Subsection (1) applies whether or not a statement referred to in that subsection is made in a judicial proceeding.

(3) Application — Subsections (1) and (1.1) do not apply to a statement referred to in either of those subsections that is made by a person who is not specially permitted, authorized or required by law to make that statement.

R.S. 1985, c. 27 (1st Supp.), s. 17; 1999, c. 18, s. 92

132. Punishment — Every one who commits perjury is guilty of an indictable offence and liable to imprisonment for a term not exceeding fourteen years.

R.S. 1985, c. 27 (1st Supp.), s. 17.; 1998, c. 35, s. 119,

133. Corroboration — No person shall be convicted of an offence under section 132 on the evidence of only one witness unless the evidence of that witness is corroborated in a material particular by evidence that implicates the accused.

R.S. 1985, c. 27 (1st Supp.), s. 17.

134. (1) Idem — Subject to subsection (2), every one who, not being specially permitted, authorized or required by law to make a statement under oath or solemn affirmation, makes such a statement, by affidavit, solemn declaration or deposition or orally before a person who is authorized by law to permit it to be made before him, knowing that the statement is false, is guilty of an offence punishable on summary conviction.

(2) Application — Subsection (1) does not apply to a statement referred to in that subsection that is made in the course of a criminal investigation.

R.S. 1985, c. 27 (1st Supp.), s. 17.

135. [Repealed R.S. 1985, c. 27 (1st Supp.), s. 17.]

136. (1) Witness giving contradictory evidence — Every one who, being a witness in a judicial proceeding, gives evidence with respect to any matter of fact or knowledge and who subsequently, in a judicial proceeding, gives evidence that is contrary to his previous evidence is guilty of an indictable offence and liable to imprisonment for a term not exceeding fourteen years, whether or not the prior or later evidence or either is true, but no person shall be convicted under this section unless the court, judge or provincial court judge, as the case may be, is satisfied beyond a reasonable doubt that the accused, in giving evidence in either of the judicial proceedings, intended to mislead.

(1.1) Evidence in specific cases — Evidence given under section 714.1, 714.2, 714.3 or 714.4 or under subsection 46(2) of the *Canada Evidence Act* or evidence or a statement given pursuant to an order made under section 22.2 of the *Mutual Legal Assistance in Criminal Matters Act* is deemed to be evidence given by a witness in a judicial proceeding for the purposes of subsection (1).

(2) "Evidence" — Notwithstanding the definition "evidence" in section 118, **"evidence"**, for the purposes of this section, does not include evidence that is not material.

(2.1) Proof of former trial — Where a person is charged with an offence under this section, a certificate specifying with reasonable particularity the proceeding in which that person is alleged to have given the evidence in respect of which the offence is charged, is evidence that it was given in a judicial proceeding, without proof of the signature or official character of the person by whom the certificate purports to be signed if it purports to be signed by the clerk of the court or other official having the custody of the record of that proceeding or by his lawful deputy.

(3) Consent required — No proceedings shall be instituted under this section without the consent of the Attorney General.

R.S. 1985, c. 27 (1st Supp.), ss. 18, 203; 1999, c. 18, s. 93

137. Fabricating evidence — Every one who, with intent to mislead, fabricates anything with intent that it shall be used as evidence in a judicial proceeding, existing or proposed, by any means other than perjury or incitement to perjury is guilty of an indictable offence and liable to imprisonment for a term not exceeding fourteen years.

138. Offences relating to affidavits — Every one who

(a) signs a writing that purports to be an affidavit or statutory declaration and to have been sworn or declared before him when the writing was not so sworn or declared or when he knows that he has no authority to administer the oath or declaration,

(b) uses or offers for use any writing purporting to be an affidavit or statutory declaration that he knows was not sworn or declared, as the case may be, by the affiant or declarant or before a person authorized in that behalf, or

(c) signs as affiant or declarant a writing that purports to be an affidavit or statutory declaration and to have been sworn or declared by him, as the case may be, when the writing was not so sworn or declared,

is guilty of an indictable offence and liable to imprisonment for a term not exceeding two years.

139. (1) Obstructing justice — Every one who wilfully attempts in any manner to obstruct, pervert or defeat the course of justice in a judicial proceeding,

(a) by indemnifying or agreeing to indemnify a surety, in any way and either in whole or in part, or

(b) where he is a surety, by accepting or agreeing to accept a fee or any form of indemnity whether in whole or in part from or in respect of a person who is released or is to be released from custody,

is guilty of

(c) an indictable offence and is liable to imprisonment for a term not exceeding two years, or

(d) an offence punishable on summary conviction.

(2) Idem — Every one who wilfully attempts in any manner other than a manner described in subsection (1) to obstruct, pervert or defeat the course of justice is guilty of an indictable offence and liable to imprisonment for a term not exceeding ten years.

(3) Idem — Without restricting the generality of subsection (2), every one shall be deemed wilfully to attempt to obstruct, pervert or defeat the course of justice who in a judicial proceeding, existing or proposed,

(a) dissuades or attempts to dissuade a person by threats, bribes or other corrupt means from giving evidence;

(b) influences or attempts to influence by threats, bribes or other corrupt means a person in his conduct as a juror; or

(c) accepts or obtains, agrees to accept or attempts to obtain a bribe or other corrupt consideration to abstain from giving evidence, or to do or to refrain from doing anything as a juror.

140. (1) Public mischief — Every one commits public mischief who, with intent to mislead, causes a peace officer to enter on or continue an investigation by

(a) making a false statement that accuses some other person of having committed an offence;

(b) doing anything that is intended to cause some other person to be suspected of having committed an offence that the other person has not committed, or to divert suspicion from himself;

(c) reporting that an offence has been committed when it has not been committed; or

(d) reporting or in any other way making it known or causing it to be made known that he or some other person has died when he or that other person has not died.

(2) Punishment — Every one who commits public mischief

(a) is guilty of an indictable offence and liable to imprisonment for a term not exceeding five years; or

(b) is guilty of an offence punishable on summary conviction.

R.S. 1985, c. 27 (1st Supp.), s. 19.

141. (1) Compounding indictable offence — Every one who asks for or obtains or agrees to receive or obtain any valuable consideration for himself or any other person by agreeing to compound or conceal an indictable offence is guilty of an indictable offence and liable to imprisonment for a term not exceeding two years.

(2) Exception for diversion agreements — No offence is committed under subsection (1) where valuable consideration is received or obtained or is to be received or obtained under an agreement for compensation or restitution or personal services that is

(a) entered into with the consent of the Attorney General; or

(b) made as part of a program, approved by the Attorney General, to divert persons charged with indictable offences from criminal proceedings.

R.S. 1985, c. 27 (1st Supp.), s. 19.

142. Corruptly taking reward for recovery of goods — Every one who corruptly accepts any valuable consideration, directly or indirectly, under pretence or on account of helping any person to recover anything obtained by the commission of an indictable offence is guilty of an indictable offence and liable to imprisonment for a term not exceeding five years.

143. **Advertising reward and immunity** — Every one who

(a) publicly advertises a reward for the return of anything that has been stolen or lost, and in the advertisement uses words to indicate that no questions will be asked if it is returned,

(b) uses words in a public advertisement to indicate that a reward will be given or paid for anything that has been stolen or lost, without interference with or inquiry about the person who produces it,

(c) promises or offers in a public advertisement to return to a person who has advanced money by way of loan on, or has bought, anything that has been stolen or lost, the money so advanced or paid, or any other sum of money for the return of that thing, or

(d) prints or publishes any advertisement referred to in paragraph (a), (b) or (c),

is guilty of an offence punishable on summary conviction.

Escapes and Rescues

144. **Prison breach** — Every one who

(a) by force or violence breaks a prison with intent to set at liberty himself or any other person confined therein, or

(b) with intent to escape forcibly breaks out of, or makes any breach in, a cell or other place within a prison in which he is confined,

is guilty of an indictable offence and liable to imprisonment for a term not exceeding ten years.

145. (1) **Escape and being at large without excuse** — Every one who

(a) escapes from lawful custody, or

(b) is, before the expiration of a term of imprisonment to which he was sentenced, at large in or out of Canada without lawful excuse, the proof of which lies on him,

is guilty of an indictable offence and liable to imprisonment for a term not exceeding two years or is guilty of an offence punishable on summary conviction.

(2) **Failure to attend court** — Every one who,

(a) being at large on his undertaking or recognizance given to or entered into before a justice or judge, fails, without lawful excuse, the proof of which lies on him, to attend court in accordance with the undertaking or recognizance, or

(b) having appeared before a court, justice or judge, fails, without lawful excuse, the proof of which lies on him, to attend court as thereafter required by the court, justice or judge, or to surrender himself in accordance with an order of the court, justice or judge, as the case may be, is guilty of an indictable offence and liable to imprisonment for a term not exceeding two years or is guilty of an offence punishable on summary conviction.

(3) Failure to comply with condition of undertaking or recognizance — Every person who is at large on an undertaking or recognizance given to or entered into before a justice or judge and is bound to comply with a condition of that undertaking or recognizance directed by a justice or judge, and every person who is bound to comply with a direction ordered under subsection 515(12) or 522(2.1), and who fails, without lawful excuse, the proof of which lies on that person, to comply with that condition or direction, is guilty of

    (a) an indictable offence and is liable to imprisonment for a term not exceeding two years; or

    (b) an offence punishable on summary conviction.

(4) Failure to appear or to comply with summons — Every one who is served with a summons and who fails, without lawful excuse, the proof of which lies on him, to appear at a time and place stated therein, if any, for the purposes of the *Identification of Criminals Act* or to attend court in accordance therewith, is guilty of

    (a) an indictable offence and is liable to imprisonment for a term not exceeding two years; or

    (b) an offence punishable on summary conviction.

(5) Failure to comply with appearance notice or promise to appear — Every person who is named in an appearance notice or promise to appear, or in a recognizance entered into before an officer in charge or another peace officer, that has been confirmed by a justice under section 508 and who fails, without lawful excuse, the proof of which lies on the person, to appear at the time and place stated therein, if any, for the purposes of the *Identification of Criminals Act*, or to attend court in accordance therewith, is guilty of

    (a) an indictable offence and is liable to imprisonment for a term not exceeding two years; or

    (b) an offence punishable on summary conviction.

(5.1) Failure to comply with conditions of undertaking — Every person who, without lawful excuse, the proof of which lies on the person, fails to comply with any condition of an undertaking entered into pursuant to subsection 499(2) or 503(2.1)

    (a) is guilty of an indictable offence and is liable to imprisonment for a term not exceeding two years; or

    (b) is guilty of an offence punishable on summary conviction.

(6) Idem — For the purposes of subsection (5), it is not a lawful excuse that an appearance notice, promise to appear or recognizance states defectively the substance of the alleged offence.

(7) [Repealed R.S. 1985, c. 27 (1st Supp.), s. 20(2).]

(8) Election of Crown under Contraventions Act — For the purposes of sub-sections (3) to (5), it is a lawful excuse to fail to comply with a condition of an undertaking or recognizance or to fail to appear at a time and place stated in a summons, an appearance notice, a promise to appear or a recognizance for the purposes of the *Identification of Criminals Act* if before the failure the Attorney General, within the meaning of the *Contraventions Act*, makes an election under section 50 of that Act.

(9) Proof of certain facts by certificate — In any proceedings under subsection (2), (4) or (5), a certificate of the clerk of the court or a judge of the court before which the accused is alleged to have failed to attend or of the person in charge of the place at which it is alleged the accused failed to attend for the purposes of the *Identification of Criminals Act* stating that,

> (a) in the case of proceedings under subsection (2), the accused gave or entered into an undertaking or recognizance before a justice or judge and failed to attend court in accordance therewith or, having attended court, failed to attend court thereafter as required by the court, justice or judge or to surrender in accordance with an order of the court, justice or judge, as the case may be,

> (b) in the case of proceedings under subsection (4), a summons was issued to and served on the accused and the accused failed to attend court in accordance therewith or failed to appear at the time and place stated therein for the purposes of the *Identification of Criminals Act*, as the case may be, and

> (c) in the case of proceedings under subsection (5), the accused was named in an appearance notice, a promise to appear or a recognizance entered into before an officer in charge or another peace officer, that was confirmed by a justice under section 508, and the accused failed to appear at the time and place stated therein for the purposes of the *Identification of Criminals Act*, failed to attend court in accordance therewith or, having attended court, failed to attend court thereafter as required by the court, justice or judge, as the case may be,

is evidence of the statements contained in the certificate without proof of the signature or the official character of the person appearing to have signed the certificate.

(10) Attendance and right to cross-examination — An accused against whom a certificate described in subsection (9) is produced may, with leave of the court, require the attendance of the person making the certificate for the purposes of cross-examination.

(11) Notice of intention to produce — No certificate shall be received in evidence pursuant to subsection (9) unless the party intending to produce it has, before the trial, given to the accused reasonable notice of his intention together with a copy of the certificate.

R.S. 1985, c. 27 (1st Supp.), s. 20; 1992, c. 47, s. 68; 1994, c. 44, s. 8; 1996, c. 7, s. 38; 1997, c. 18, s. 3

146. Permitting or assisting escape — Every one who

> (a) permits a person whom he has in lawful custody to escape, by failing to perform a legal duty,

(b) conveys or causes to be conveyed into a prison anything, with intent to facilitate the escape of a person imprisoned therein, or

(c) directs or procures, under colour of pretended authority, the discharge of a prisoner who is not entitled to be discharged,

is guilty of an indictable offence and liable to imprisonment for a term not exceeding two years.

147. Rescue or permitting escape — Every one who

(a) rescues any person from lawful custody or assists any person in escaping or attempting to escape from lawful custody,

(b) being a peace officer, wilfully permits a person in his lawful custody to escape, or

(c) being an officer of or an employee in a prison, wilfully permits a person to escape from lawful custody therein,

is guilty of an indictable offence and liable to imprisonment for a term not exceeding five years.

148. Assisting prisoner of war to escape — Every one who knowingly and wilfully

(a) assists a prisoner of war in Canada to escape from a place where he is detained, or

(b) assists a prisoner of war, who is permitted to be at large on parole in Canada, to escape from the place where he is at large on parole,

is guilty of an indictable offence and liable to imprisonment for a term not exceeding five years.

149. (1) Service of term for escape — Notwithstanding section 743.1, a court that convicts a person for an escape committed while undergoing imprisonment may order that the term of imprisonment be served in a penitentiary, even if the time to be served is less than two years.

(2) Definition of "escape" — In this section, "escape" means breaking prison, escaping from lawful custody or, without lawful excuse, being at large before the expiration of a term of imprisonment to which a person has been sentenced.

R.S. 1985, c. 27 (1st Supp.), s. 203; 1992, c. 20, s. 199; 1995, c. 22, s. 1.

PART V — SEXUAL OFFENCES, PUBLIC MORALS AND DISORDERLY CONDUCT

Interpretation

150. Definitions — In this Part,

"guardian" includes any person who has in law or in fact the custody or control of another person;

"public place" includes any place to which the public have access as of right or by invitation, express or implied;

"theatre" includes any place that is open to the public where entertainments are given, whether or not any charge is made for admission.

Sexual Offences

150.1 (1) Consent no defence — Where an accused is charged with an offence under section 151 or 152 or subsection 153(1), 160(3) or 173(2) or is charged with an offence under section 271, 272 or 273 in respect of a complainant under the age of fourteen years, it is not a defence that the complainant consented to the activity that forms the subject-matter of the charge.

(2) Exception — Notwithstanding subsection (1), where an accused is charged with an offence under section 151 or 152, subsection 173(2) or section 271 in respect of a complainant who is twelve years of age or more but under the age of fourteen years, it is not a defence that the complainant consented to the activity that forms the subject-matter of the charge unless the accused

(a) is twelve years of age or more but under the age of sixteen years;

(b) is less than two years older than the complainant; and

(c) is neither in a position of trust or authority towards the complainant nor is a person with whom the complainant is in a relationship of dependency.

(3) Exemption for accused aged twelve or thirteen — No person aged twelve or thirteen years shall be tried for an offence under section 151 or 152 or subsection 173(2) unless the person is in a position of trust or authority towards the complainant or is a person with whom the complainant is in a relationship of dependency.

(4) Mistake of age — It is not a defence to a charge under section 151 or 152, subsection 160(3) or 173(2), or section 271, 272 or 273 that the accused believed that the complainant was fourteen years of age or more at the time the offence is alleged to have been committed unless the accused took all reasonable steps to ascertain the age of the complainant.

(5) Idem — It is not a defence to a charge under section 153, 159, 170, 171 or 172 or subsection 212(2) or (4) that the accused believed that the complainant was eighteen years of age or more at the time the offence is alleged to have been committed unless the accused took all reasonable steps to ascertain the age of the complainant.

R.S. 1985, c. 19 (3d Supp.), s. 1

151. Sexual interference — Every person who, for a sexual purpose, touches, directly or indirectly, with a part of the body or with an object, any part of the body of a person under the age of fourteen years is guilty of an indictable offence and is liable to imprisonment for a term not exceeding ten years or is guilty of an offence punishable on summary conviction.

R.S. 1985, c. 19 (3d Supp.), s. 1.

152. Invitation to sexual touching — Every person who, for a sexual purpose, invites, counsels or incites a person under the age of fourteen years to touch, directly or indirectly, with a part of the body or with an object, the body of any person, including the body of the person who so invites, counsels or incites and the body of the person under the age of fourteen years, is guilty of an indictable offence and is liable to imprisonment for a term not exceeding ten years or is guilty of an offence punishable on summary conviction.

R.S. 1985, c. 19 (3d Supp.), s. 1.

153. (1) Sexual exploitation — Every person who is in a position of trust or authority towards a young person or is a person with whom the young person is in a relationship of dependency and who

    (a) for a sexual purpose, touches, directly or indirectly, with a part of the body or with an object, any part of the body of the young person, or

    (b) for a sexual purpose, invites, counsels or incites a young person to touch, directly or indirectly, with a part of the body or with an object, the body of any person, including the body of the person who so invites, counsels or incites and the body of the young person,

is guilty of an indictable offence and liable to imprisonment for a term not exceeding five years or is guilty of an offence punishable on summary conviction.

(2) Definition of "young person" — In this section, **"young person"** means a person fourteen years of age or more but under the age of eighteen years.

R.S. 1985, c. 19 (3d Supp.), s. 1.

153.1 (1) Sexual exploitation of person with disability — Every person who is in a position of trust or authority towards a person with a mental or physical disability or who is a person with whom a person with a mental or physical disability is in a relationship of dependency and who, for a sexual purpose, counsels or incites that person to touch, without that person's consent, his or her own body, the body of the person who so counsels or incites, or the body of any other person, directly or indirectly, with a part of the body or with an object, is guilty of

    (a) an indictable offence and liable to imprisonment for a term not exceeding five years; or

    (b) an offence punishable on summary conviction and liable to imprisonment for a term not exceeding eighteen months.

(2) Definition of "consent" — Subject to subsection (3), "consent" means, for the purposes of this section, the voluntary agreement of the complainant to engage in the sexual activity in question.

(3) When no consent obtained — No consent is obtained, for the purposes of this section, if

    (a) the agreement is expressed by the words or conduct of a person other than the complainant;

    (b) the complainant is incapable of consenting to the activity;

    (c) the accused counsels or incites the complainant to engage in the activity by abusing a position of trust, power or authority;

(d) the complainant expresses, by words or conduct, a lack of agreement to engage in the activity; or

(e) the complainant, having consented to engage in sexual activity, expresses, by words or conduct, a lack of agreement to continue to engage in the activity.

(4) Subsection (3) not limiting — Nothing in subsection (3) shall be construed as limiting the circumstances in which no consent is obtained.

(5) When belief in consent not a defence — It is not a defence to a charge under this section that the accused believed that the complainant consented to the activity that forms the subject-matter of the charge if

(a) the accused's belief arose from the accused's

(i) self-induced intoxication, or

(ii) recklessness or wilful blindness; or

(b) the accused did not take reasonable steps, in the circumstances known to the accused at the time, to ascertain that the complainant was consenting.

(6) Accused's belief as to consent — If an accused alleges that he or she believed that the complainant consented to the conduct that is the subject-matter of the charge, a judge, if satisfied that there is sufficient evidence and that, if believed by the jury, the evidence would constitute a defence, shall instruct the jury, when reviewing all the evidence relating to the determination of the honesty of the accused's belief, to consider the presence or absence of reasonable grounds for that belief.

1998, c. 9, s. 2

154. [Repealed R.S. 1985, c. 19 (3d Supp.), s. 1.]

155. (1) Incest — Every one commits **"incest"** who, knowing that another person is by blood relationship his or her parent, child, brother, sister, grandparent or grandchild, as the case may be, has sexual intercourse with that person.

(2) Punishment — Every one who commits incest is guilty of an indictable offence and liable to imprisonment for a term not exceeding fourteen years.

(3) Defence — No accused shall be determined by a court to be guilty of an offence under this section if the accused was under restraint, duress or fear of the person with whom the accused had the sexual intercourse at the time the sexual intercourse occurred.

(4) "brother", "sister" — In this section,**"brother"** and **"sister"**, respectively, include half-brother and half-sister.

R.S. 1985, c. 27 (1st Supp.), s. 21.

156. [Repealed R.S. 1985, c. 19 (3d Supp.), s. 2.]

157. [Repealed R.S. 1985, c. 19 (3d Supp.), s. 2.]

158. [Repealed R.S. 1985, c. 19 (3d Supp.), s. 2.]

159. (1) Anal intercourse — Every person who engages in an act of anal intercourse is guilty of an indictable offence and liable to imprisonment for a term not exceeding ten years or is guilty of an offence punishable on summary conviction.

(2) Exception — Subsection (1) does not apply to any act engaged in, in private, between

(a) husband and wife, or

(b) any two persons, each of whom is eighteen years of age or more,

both of whom consent to the act.

(3) Idem — For the purposes of subsection (2),

(a) an act shall be deemed not to have been engaged in in private if it is engaged in in a public place or if more than two persons take part or are present; and

(b) a person shall be deemed not to consent to an act

(i) if the consent is extorted by force, threats or fear of bodily harm or is obtained by false and fraudulent misrepresentations respecting the nature and quality of the act, or

(ii) if the court is satisfied beyond a reasonable doubt that the person could not have consented to the act by reason of mental disability.

R.S. 1985, c. 19 (3d Supp.), s. 3.

160. (1) Bestiality — Every person who commits bestiality is guilty of an indictable offence and is liable to imprisonment for a term not exceeding ten years or is guilty of an offence punishable on summary conviction.

(2) Compelling the commission of bestiality — Every person who compels another to commit bestiality is guilty of an indictable offence and is liable to imprisonment for a term not exceeding ten years or is guilty of an offence punishable on summary conviction.

(3) Bestiality in presence of or by child — Notwithstanding subsection (1), every person who, in the presence of a person under the age of fourteen years, commits bestiality or who incites a person under the age of fourteen years to commit bestiality is guilty of an indictable offence and liable to imprisonment for a term not exceeding ten years or is guilty of an offence punishable on summary conviction.

R.S. 1985, c. 19 (3d Supp.), s. 3.

161. (1) Order of prohibition — Where an offender is convicted, or is discharged on the conditions prescribed in a probation order under section 730, of an offence under section 151, 152, 155 or 159, subsection 160(2) or (3) or section 170, 171, 271, 272, 273 or 281, in respect of a person who is under the age of fourteen years, the court that sentences the offender or directs that the accused be discharged, as the case may be, in addition to any other punishment that may be imposed for that offence or any other condition prescribed in the order of discharge, shall consider making and may make, subject to the conditions or exemptions that the court directs, an order prohibiting the offender from

(a) attending a public park or public swimming area where persons under the age of fourteen years are present or can reasonably be expected to be present, or a daycare centre, schoolground, playground or community centre; or

(b) seeking, obtaining or continuing any employment, whether or not the employment is remunerated, or becoming or being a volunteer in a capacity, that involves being in a position of trust or authority towards persons under the age of fourteen years.

(2) Duration of prohibition — The prohibition may be for life or for any shorter duration that the court considers desirable and, in the case of a prohibition that is not for life, the prohibition begins on the later of

(a) the date on which the order is made; and

(b) where the offender is sentenced to a term of imprisonment, the date on which the offender is released from imprisonment for the offence, including release on parole, mandatory supervision or statutory release.

(3) Court may vary order — A court that makes an order of prohibition or, where the court is for any reason unable to act, another court of equivalent jurisdiction in the same province, may, on application of the offender or the prosecutor, require the offender to appear before it at any time and, after hearing the parties, that court may vary the conditions prescribed in the order if, in the opinion of the court, the variation is desirable because of changed circumstances after the conditions were prescribed.

(4) Offence — Every person who is bound by an order of prohibition and who does not comply with the order is guilty of

(a) an indictable offence and is liable to imprisonment for a term not exceeding two years; or

(b) an offence punishable on summary conviction.

1993, c. 45, s. 1; 1995, c. 22, s. 18 (Sch. IV); 1997, c. 18, s. 4; 1999, c. 31, s. 67.

162. [Repealed R.S. 1985, c. 19 (3d Supp.), s. 4.]

Offences Tending to Corrupt Morals

163. (1) Corrupting morals — Every one commits an offence who

(a) makes, prints, publishes, distributes, circulates, or has in his possession for the purpose of publication, distribution or circulation any obscene written matter, picture, model, phonograph record or other thing whatever; or

(b) makes, prints, publishes, distributes, sells or has in his possession for the purpose of publication, distribution or circulation a crime comic.

(2) Idem — Every one commits an offence who knowingly, without lawful justification or excuse,

(a) sells, exposes to public view or has in his possession for such a purpose any obscene written matter, picture, model, phonograph record or other thing whatever;

(b) publicly exhibits a disgusting object or an indecent show;

(c) offers to sell, advertises or publishes an advertisement of, or has for sale or disposal any means, instructions, medicine, drug or article intended or represented as a method of causing abortion or miscarriage; or

(d) advertises or publishes an advertisement of any means, instructions, medicine, drug or article intended or represented as a method for restoring sexual virility or curing venereal diseases or diseases of the generative organs.

(3) Defence of public good — No person shall be convicted of an offence under this section if the public good was served by the acts that are alleged to constitute the offence and if the acts alleged did not extend beyond what served the public good.

(4) Question of law and question of fact — For the purposes of this section, it is a question of law whether an act served the public good and whether there is evidence that the act alleged went beyond what served the public good, but it is a question of fact whether the acts did or did not extend beyond what served the public good.

(5) Motives irrelevant — For the purposes of this section, the motives of an accused are irrelevant.

(6) [Repealed 1993, c. 46, s. 1.]

(7) Definition of "crime comic" — In this section, **"crime comic"** means a magazine, periodical or book that exclusively or substantially comprises matter depicting pictorially

(a) the commission of crimes, real or fictitious; or

(b) events connected with the commission of crimes, real or fictitious, whether occurring before or after the commission of the crime.

(8) Obscene publication — For the purposes of this Act, any publication a dominant characteristic of which is the undue exploitation of sex, or of sex and any one or more of the following subjects, namely, crime, horror, cruelty and violence, shall be deemed to be obscene.

1993, c. 46, s. 1.

163.1 (1) Definition of "child pornography" — In this section, **"Child Pornography"** means

(a) a photographic, film, video or other visual representation, whether or not it was made by electronic or mechanical means,

(i) that shows a person who is or is depicted as being under the age of eighteen years and is engaged in or is depicted as engaged in explicit sexual activity, or

(ii) the dominant characteristic of which is the depiction, for a sexual purpose, of a sexual organ or the anal region of a person under the age of eighteen years; or

(b) any written material or visual representation that advocates or counsels sexual activity with a person under the age of eighteen years that would be an offence under this Act.

(2) Making child pornography — Every person who makes, prints, publishes or possesses for the purpose of publication any child pornography is guilty of

(a) an indictable offence and liable to imprisonment for a term not exceeding ten years; or

(b) an offence punishable on summary conviction.

(3) Distribution or sale of child pornography — Every person who imports, distributes, sells or possesses for the purpose of distribution or sale any child pornography is guilty of

(a) an indictable offence and liable to imprisonment for a term not exceeding ten years; or

(b) an offence punishable on summary conviction.

(4) Possession of child pornography — Every person who possesses any child pornography is guilty of

(a) an indictable offence and liable to imprisonment for a term not exceeding five years; or

(b) an offence punishable on summary conviction.

(5) Defences — It is not a defence to a charge under subsection (2) in respect of a visual representation that the accused believed that a person shown in the representation that is alleged to constitute child pornography was or was depicted as being eighteen years of age or more unless the accused took all reasonable steps to ascertain the age of that person and took all reasonable steps to ensure that, where the person was eighteen years of age or more, the representation did not depict that person as being under the age of eighteen years.

(6) Defences — Where the accused is charged with an offence under subsection (2), (3) or (4), the court shall find the accused not guilty if the representation or written material that is alleged to constitute child pornography has artistic merit or an educational, scientific or medical purpose.

(7) Other provisions to apply — Subsections 163(3) to (5) apply, with such modifications as the circumstances require, with respect to an offence under subsection (2), (3) or (4).

1993, c. 46, s. 1.

164. (1) Warrant of seizure — A judge who is satisfied by information on oath that there are reasonable grounds for believing that

    (a) any publication, copies of which are kept for sale or distribution in premises within the jurisdiction of the court, is obscene or a crime comic, within the meaning of section 163, or

    (b) any representation or written material, copies of which are kept in premises within the jurisdiction of the court, is child pornography within the meaning of section 163.1

may issue a warrant authorizing seizure of the copies.

(2) Summons to occupier — Within seven days of the issue of a warrant under subsection (1), the judge shall issue a summons to the occupier of the premises requiring him to appear before the court and show cause why the matter seized should not be forfeited to Her Majesty.

(3) Owner and maker may appear — The owner and the maker of the matter seized under subsection (1), and alleged to be obscene, a crime comic or child pornography, may appear and be represented in the proceedings in order to oppose the making of an order for the forfeiture of the matter.

(4) Order of forfeiture — If the court is satisfied that the publication, representation or written material referred to in subsection (1) is obscene, a crime comic or child pornography, it shall make an order declaring the matter forfeited to Her Majesty in right of the province in which the proceedings take place, for disposal as the Attorney General may direct.

(5) Disposal of matter — If the court is not satisfied that the publication, representation or written material referred to in subsection (1) is obscene, a crime comic or child pornography, it shall order that the matter be restored to the person from whom it was seized forthwith after the time for final appeal was expired.

(6) Appeal — An appeal lies from an order made under subsection (4) or (5) by any person who appeared in the proceedings

    (a) on any ground of appeal that involves a question of law alone,

    (b) on any ground of appeal that involves a question of fact alone, or

    (c) on any ground of appeal that involves a question of mixed law and fact,

as if it were an appeal against conviction or against a judgment or verdict of acquittal, as the case may be, on a question of law alone under Part XXI and sections 673 to 696 apply with such modifications as the circumstances require.

(7) Consent — Where an order has been made under this section by a judge in a province with respect to one or more copies of a publication, representation or written material, no proceedings shall be instituted or continued in that province under section 163 or 163.1 with respect to those or other copies of the same publication, representation or written material without the consent of the Attorney General.

(8) Definitions — In this section

"court" means

    (a) in the Province of Quebec, the Court of Quebec, the municipal court of Montreal and the municipal court of Quebec;

    (a.1) in the Province of Ontario, the Superior Court of Justice,

    (b) in the Provinces of New Brunswick, Manitoba, Saskatchewan and Alberta, the Court of Queen's Bench;

    (c) in the Provinces of Prince Edward Island and Newfoundland, the Trial Division of the Supreme Court;

    (d) in the Provinces of Nova Scotia and British Columbia, the Yukon Territory and the Northwest Territories, the Supreme Court; and

    (e) in Nunavut, the Nunavut Court of Justice;

"crime comic" has the same meaning as in section 163;

"judge" means a judge of a court.

R.S. 1985, c. 27 (2d Supp.), Sched.; c. 40 (4th Supp.), s. 2; 1990, c. 16, s. 3; 1990, c. 17, s. 9; 1992, c. 1, s. 58(1), Sched. 1, item 3; 1992, c. 51, s. 34; 1993, c. 28, s. 78 (Sched. III, item 28) [Repealed 1999, c. 3, (Sched., item 6).]; 1993, c. 46, s. 3; 1997, c. 18, s. 5; 1998, c. 30, s. 14(d); 1999, c. 3, s. 27.

165. Tied sale — Every one commits an offence who refuses to sell or supply to any other person copies of any publication for the reason only that the other person refuses to purchase or acquire from him copies of any other publication that the other person is apprehensive may be obscene or a crime comic.

166. [Repealed 1994, c. 44, s. 9.]

167. (1) Immoral theatrical performance — Every one commits an offence who, being the lessee, manager, agent or person in charge of a theatre, presents or gives or allows to be presented or given therein an immoral, indecent or obscene performance, entertainment or representation.

(2) Person taking part — Every one commits an offence who takes part or appears as an actor, a performer or an assistant in any capacity, in an immoral, indecent or obscene performance, entertainment or representation in a theatre.

168. Mailing obscene matter — **(1)** Every one commits an offence who makes use of the mails for the purpose of transmitting or delivering anything that is obscene, indecent, immoral or scurrilous.

(2) Exceptions — Subsection (1) does not apply to a person who

    (a) prints or publishes any matter for use in connection with any judicial proceedings or communicates it to persons who are concerned in the proceedings;

(b) prints or publishes a notice or report under the direction of a court; or

(c) prints or publishes any matter

(i) in a volume or part of a genuine series of law reports that does not form part of any other publication and consists solely of reports of proceedings in courts of law, or

(ii) in a publication of a technical character that is intended, in good faith, for circulation among members of the legal or medical profession.

169. Punishment — Every one who commits an offence under section 163, 165, 167 or 168 is guilty of

(a) an indictable offence and is liable to imprisonment for a term not exceeding two years; or

(b) an offence punishable on summary conviction.

170. Parent or guardian procuring sexual activity — Every parent or guardian of a person under the age of eighteen years who procures that person for the purpose of engaging in any sexual activity prohibited by this Act with a person other than the parent or guardian is guilty of an indictable offence and liable to imprisonment for a term not exceeding five years, if the person procured for that purpose is under the age of fourteen years or to imprisonment for a term not exceeding two years if the person so procured is fourteen years of age or more but under the age of eighteen years.

R.S. 1985, c. 19 (3d Supp.), s. 5.

171. Householder permitting sexual activity — Every owner, occupier or manager of premises or other person who has control of premises or assists in the management or control of premises who knowingly permits a person under the age of eighteen years to resort to or to be in or on the premises for the purpose of engaging in any sexual activity prohibited by this Act is guilty of an indictable offence and is liable to imprisonment for a term not exceeding five years if the person in question is under the age of fourteen years or to imprisonment for a term not exceeding two years if the person in question is fourteen years of age or more but under the age of eighteen years.

R.S. 1985, c. 19 (3d Supp.), s. 5.

172. (1) Corrupting children — Every one who, in the home of a child, participates in adultery or sexual immorality or indulges in habitual drunkenness or any other form of vice, and thereby endangers the morals of the child or renders the home an unfit place for the child to be in, is guilty of an indictable offence and liable to imprisonment for a term not exceeding two years.

(2) [Repealed R.S. 1985, c. 19 (3d Supp.), s. 6]

(3) Definition of "child" — For the purposes of this section, **"child"** means a person who is or appears to be under the age of eighteen years.

(4) Who may institute prosecutions — No proceedings shall be commenced under subsection (1) without the consent of the Attorney General, unless they are instituted by or at the instance of a recognized society for the protection of children or by an officer of a juvenile court.

R.S. 1985, c. 19 (3d Supp.), s. 6.

Disorderly Conduct

173. (1) Indecent acts — Every one who wilfully does an indecent act

(a) in a public place in the presence of one or more persons, or

(b) in any place, with intent thereby to insult or offend any person,

is guilty of an offence punishable on summary conviction.

(2) Exposure — Every person who, in any place, for a sexual purpose, exposes his or her genital organs to a person who is under the age of fourteen years is guilty of an offence punishable on summary conviction.

R.S. 1985, c. 19 (3d Supp.), s. 7.

174. (1) Nudity — Every one who, without lawful excuse,

(a) is nude in a public place, or

(b) is nude and exposed to public view while on private property, whether or not the property is his own,

is guilty of an offence punishable on summary conviction.

(2) Nude — For the purposes of this section, a person is nude who is so clad as to offend against public decency or order.

(3) Consent of Attorney General — No proceedings shall be commenced under this section without the consent of the Attorney General.

175. (1) Causing disturbance, indecent exhibition, loitering, etc. — Every one who

(a) not being in a dwelling-house, causes a disturbance in or near a public place,

(i) by fighting, screaming, shouting, swearing, singing or using insulting or obscene language,

(ii) by being drunk, or

(iii) by impeding or molesting other persons,

(b) openly exposes or exhibits an indecent exhibition in a public place,

(c) loiters in a public place and in any way obstructs persons who are in that place, or

(d) disturbs the peace and quiet of the occupants of a dwelling-house by discharging firearms or by other disorderly conduct in a public place or who, not being an occupant of a dwelling-house comprised in a particular building or structure, disturbs the peace and quiet of the occupants of a dwelling-house comprised in the building or structure by discharging firearms or by other disorderly conduct in any part of a building or structure to which, at the time of such conduct, the occupants of two or more dwelling-houses comprised in the building or structure have access as of right or by invitation, express or implied,

is guilty of an offence punishable on summary conviction.

(2) Evidence of peace officer — In the absence of other evidence, or by way of corroboration of other evidence, a summary conviction court may infer from the evidence of a peace officer relating to the conduct of a person or persons, whether ascertained or not, that a disturbance described in paragraph (1)(a) or (d) or an obstruction described in paragraph (1)(c) was caused or occurred.

1997, c. 18, s. 6.

176. (1) Obstructing or violence to or arrest of officiating clergyman — Every one who

(a) by threats or force, unlawfully obstructs or prevents or endeavours to obstruct or prevent a clergyman or minister from celebrating divine service or performing any other function in connection with his calling, or

(b) knowing that a clergyman or minister is about to perform, is on his way to perform or is returning from the performance of any of the duties or functions mentioned in paragraph (*a*)

    (i) assaults or offers any violence to him, or

    (ii) arrests him on a civil process, or under the pretence of executing a civil process,

is guilty of an indictable offence and liable to imprisonment for a term not exceeding two years.

(2) Disturbing religious worship or certain meetings — Every one who wilfully disturbs or interrupts an assemblage of persons met for religious worship or for a moral, social or benevolent purpose is guilty of an offence punishable on summary conviction.

(3) Idem — Every one who, at or near a meeting referred to in subsection (2), wilfully does anything that disturbs the order or solemnity of the meeting is guilty of an offence punishable on summary conviction.

177. Trespassing at night — Every one who, without lawful excuse, the proof of which lies on him, loiters or prowls at night on the property of another person near a dwelling-house situated on that property is guilty of an offence punishable on summary conviction.

178. Offensive volatile substance — Every one other than a peace officer engaged in the discharge of his duty who has in his possession in a public place or who deposits, throws or injects or causes to be deposited, thrown or injected in, into or near any place,

(a) an offensive volatile substance that is likely to alarm, inconvenience, discommode or cause discomfort to any person or to cause damage to property, or

(b) a stink or stench bomb or device from which any substance mentioned in paragraph (a) is or is capable of being liberated,

is guilty of an offence punishable on summary conviction.

179. (1) Vagrancy — Every one commits **"vagrancy"** who

(a) supports himself in whole or in part by gaming or crime and has no lawful profession or calling by which to maintain himself; or

(b) having at any time been convicted of an offence under section 151, 152 or 153, subsection 160(3) or 173(2) or section 271, 272 or 273, or of an offence under a provision referred to in paragraph (b) of the definition "serious personal injury offence" in section 687 of the *Criminal Code*, chapter C-34 of the Revised Statutes of Canada, 1970, as it read before January 4, 1983, is found loitering in or near a school ground, playground, public park or bathing area.

(2) Punishment — Every one who commits vagrancy is guilty of an offence punishable on summary conviction.

R.S. 1985, c. 27 (1st Supp.), s. 22; c. 19 (3d Supp.), s. 8.

Nuisances

180. (1) Common nuisance — Every one who commits a common nuisance and thereby

(a) endangers the lives, safety or health of the public, or

(b) causes physical injury to any person,

is guilty of an indictable offence and liable to imprisonment for a term not exceeding two years.

(2) Definition — For the purposes of this section, every one commits a common nuisance who does an unlawful act or fails to discharge a legal duty and thereby

(a) endangers the lives, safety, health, property or comfort of the public; or

(b) obstructs the public in the exercise or enjoyment of any right that is common to all the subjects of Her Majesty in Canada.

181. Spreading false news — Every one who wilfully publishes a statement, tale or news that he knows is false and that causes or is likely to cause injury or mischief to a public interest is guilty of an indictable offence and liable to imprisonment for a term not exceeding two years.

182. Dead body — Every one who

    (a) neglects, without lawful excuse, to perform any duty that is imposed on him by law or that he undertakes with reference to the burial of a dead human body or human remains, or

    (b) improperly or indecently interferes with or offers any indignity to a dead human body or human remains, whether buried or not,

is guilty of an indictable offence and liable to imprisonment for a term not exceeding five years.

PART VI — INVASION OF PRIVACY

Definitions

183. Definitions — In this Part,

"authorization" means an authorization to intercept a private communication given under section 186 or subsection 184.2(3), 184.3(6) or 188(2);

"electro-magnetic, acoustic, mechanical or other device" means any device or apparatus that is used or is capable of being used to intercept a private communication, but does not include a hearing aid used to correct subnormal hearing of the user to not better than normal hearing;

"intercept" includes listen to, record or acquire a communication or acquire the substance, meaning or purport thereof;

"offence" means an offence contrary to, any conspiracy or attempt to commit or being an accessory after the fact in relation to an offence contrary to, or any counselling in relation to an offence contrary to section 47 (high treason), 51 (intimidating Parliament or a legislature), 52 (sabotage), 57 (forgery, etc.), 61 (sedition), 76 (hijacking), 77 (endangering safety of aircraft or airport), 78 (offensive weapons, etc., on aircraft), 78.1 (offences against maritime navigation or fixed platforms), 80 (breach of duty), 81 (using explosives), 82 (possessing explosive), 96 (possession of weapon obtained by commission of offence), 99 (weapons trafficking), 100 (possession for purpose of weapons trafficking), 102 (making automatic firearm), 103 (importing or exporting knowing it is unauthorized), 104 (unauthorized importing or exporting), 119 (bribery, etc.), 120 (bribery, etc.), 121 (fraud on government), 122 (breach of trust), 123 (municipal corruption), 132 (perjury), 139 (obstructing justice), 144 (prison breach), 163.1 (child pornography), 184 (unlawful interception), 191 (possession of intercepting device), 235 (murder), 264.1 (uttering threats), 267 (assault with a weapon or causing bodily harm), 268 (aggravated assault), 269 (unlawfully causing bodily harm), 271 (sexual assault), 272 (sexual assault with a weapon, threats to a third party or causing bodily harm), 273 (aggravated sexual assault), 279 (kidnapping), 279.1 (hostage taking), 280 (abduction of person under sixteen), 281 (abduction of person under fourteen), 282 (abduction in contravention of custody order), 283 (abduction), 318 (advocating genocide), 327 (possession of device to obtain telecommunication facility or service), 334 (theft), 342 (theft, forgery, etc., or credit card), 342.1 (unauthorized use of computer), 342.2 (possession of device to obtain computer service), 344 (robbery), 346 (extortion), 347 (criminal interest rate), 348 (breaking and entering), 354 (possession of property obtained by crime), 356 (theft from mail), 367 (forgery), 368 (uttering forged document), 372 (false messages), 380 (fraud), 381 (using mail to defraud), 382 (fraudulent manipulation of stock exchange transactions), 424 (threat to commit offences against internationally protected person), 426 (secret commissions), 430 (mischief), 431 (attack on premises, residence or transport of internationally protected person), 433 (arson), 434 (arson), 434.1 (arson), 435 (arson for fraudulent purposes), 449 (making counterfeit money), 450 (possession, etc., of counterfeit money), 452 (uttering, etc., counterfeit money), 462.31 (laundering proceeds of crime), 467.1 (participation in criminal organization), subsection 145(1) (escape, etc.), 201(1) (keeping gaming or betting house), 210(1) (keeping common bawdy house), 212(1) (procuring), 212(2) (procuring), 212(2.1) (aggravated offence in relation to living on the avails of prostitution of a person under the age of eighteen years), 212(4) (offence — prostitution of person under eighteen) or 462.33(11) (acting in contravention of restraint order) or paragraph 163(1)(*a*) (obscene materials), or 202(1)(*e*) (pool-selling, etc.) of this Act, section 45 (conspiracy) of the *Competition Act* in relation to any of the matters referred to in paragraphs 45(4)(*a*) to (*d*) of that Act, section 47 (bid-rigging) or subsection 52.1 (3) (deceptive telemarketing) of that Act, or section 5 (trafficking), 6 (importing and exporting), 7 (production), 8 (possession of property obtained by designated substance offences) or 9 (laundering proceeds of designated substance offences of the *Controlled Drugs and Substances Act*, section 153 (false statements), 159 (smuggling), 163.1 (possession of property obtained by smuggling, etc.) or 163.2 (laundering proceeds of smuggling, etc.) of the *Customs Act*, sections 94.1 and 94.2 (organizing entry into Canada), 94.4 (disembarking persons at sea) and 94.5 (counselling false statements) of the *Immigration Act*, section 126.1 (possession of property obtained by excise offences), 126.2 (laundering proceeds of excise offences), 158 (unlawful distillation of spirits) or 163 (unlawful selling of spirits) or subsection 233(1) (unlawful packaging or stamping) or 240(1) (unlawful possession or sale of manufactured tobacco or cigars) of the *Excise Act*, section 198 (fraudulent bankruptcy) of the *Bankruptcy and Insolvency Act*, section 3 (bribing a foreign public official), section 4 (possession of property) or section 5 (laundering proceeds of the offence) of the *Corruption of Foreign Public Official Act*, section 3 (spying) of the *Official Secrets Act*, section 13 (export or attempt to export), 14 (import or attempt to import), 15 (diversion, etc.), 16 (no transfer or permits), 17 (false information) or 18 (aiding or abetting) of the *Export and Import Permits Act* or any other offence created by this Act for which an offender may be sentenced to imprisonment for five years or more that there are reasonable grounds to believe is part of a pattern of criminal activity planned and organized by a number of persons acting in concert, or any other offence created by this or any other Act of Parliament for which an offender may be sentenced to imprisonment for five years or more that there are reasonable grounds to believe is committed for the benefit of, at the direction of or in association with a criminal organization;

Proposed Amendment — 183 "offence"

"offence" means an offence contrary to, any conspiracy or attempt to commit or being an accessory after the fact in relation to an offence contrary to, or any counselling in relation to an offence contrary to section 47 (high treason), 51 (intimidating Parliament or a legislature), 52 (sabotage), 57 (forgery, etc.), 61 (sedition), 76 (hijacking), 77 (endangering safety of aircraft or airport), 78 (offensive weapons, etc., on aircraft), 78.1 (offences against maritime navigation or fixed platforms), 80 (breach of duty), 81 (using explosives), 82 (possessing explosive), 96 (possession of weapon obtained by commission of offence), 99 (weapons trafficking), 100 (possession for purpose of weapons trafficking), 102 (making automatic firearm), 103 (importing or exporting knowing it is unauthorized), 104 (unauthorized importing or exporting), 119 (bribery, etc.), 120 (bribery, etc.), 121 (fraud on government), 122 (breach of trust), 123 (municipal corruption), 132 (perjury), 139 (obstructing justice), 144 (prison breach), 163.1 (child pornography), 184 (unlawful interception), 191 (possession of intercepting device), 235 (murder), 264.1 (uttering threats), 267 (assault with a weapon or causing bodily harm), 268 (aggravated assault), 269 (unlawfully causing bodily harm), 271 (sexual assault), 272 (sexual assault with a weapon, threats to a third party or causing bodily harm), 273 (aggravated sexual assault), 279 (kidnapping), 279.1 (hostage taking), 280 (abduction of person under sixteen), 281 (abduction of person under fourteen), 282 (abduction in contravention of custody order), 283 (abduction), 318 (advocating genocide), 327 (possession of device to obtain telecommunication facility or service), 334 (theft), 342 (theft, forgery, etc., or credit card), 342.1 (unauthorized use of computer), 342.2 (possession of device to obtain computer service), 344 (robbery), 346 (extortion), 347 (criminal interest rate), 348 (breaking and entering), 354 (possession of property obtained by crime), 356 (theft from mail), 367 (forgery), 368 (uttering forged document), 372 (false messages), 380 (fraud), 381 (using mail to defraud), 382 (fraudulent manipulation of stock exchange transactions), 424 (threat to commit offences against internationally protected person), 426 (secret commissions), 430 (mischief), 431 (attack on premises, residence or transport of internationally protected person), 433 (arson), 434 (arson), 434.1 (arson), 435 (arson for fraudulent purposes), 449 (making counterfeit money), 450 (possession, etc., of counterfeit money), 452 (uttering, etc., counterfeit money), 462.31 (laundering proceeds of crime), 467.1 (participation in criminal organization), subsection 145(1) (escape, etc.), 201(1) (keeping gaming or betting house), 210(1) (keeping common bawdy house), 212(1) (procuring), 212(2) (procuring), 212(2.1) (aggravated offence in relation to living on the avails of prostitution of a person under the age of eighteen years), 212(4) (offence — prostitution of person under eighteen) or 462.33(11) (acting in contravention of restraint order) or paragraph 163(1)(*a*) (obscene materials), or 202(1)(*e*) (pool-selling, etc.) of this Act, section 45 (conspiracy) of the *Competition Act* in relation to any of the matters referred to in paragraphs 45(4)(*a*) to (*d*) of that Act, section 47 (bid-rigging) or subsection 52.1 (3) (deceptive telemarketing) of that Act, or section 5 (trafficking), 6 (importing and exporting), 7 (production), 8 (possession of property obtained by designated substance offences) or 9 (laundering proceeds of designated substance offences of the *Controlled Drugs and Substances Act*, section 153 (false statements), 159 (smuggling), 163.1 (possession of property obtained by smuggling, etc.) or 163.2 (laundering proceeds of smuggling, etc.) of the *Customs Act*, sections 94.1 and

94.2 (organizing entry into Canada), 94.4 (disembarking persons at sea) and 94.5 (counselling false statements) of the *Immigration Act*, section 126.1 (possession of property obtained by excise offences), 126.2 (laundering proceeds of excise offences), 158 (unlawful distillation of spirits) or 163 (unlawful selling of spirits) or subsection 233(1) (unlawful packaging or stamping) or 240(1) (unlawful possession or sale of manufactured tobacco or cigars) of the *Excise Act*, section 198 (fraudulent bankruptcy) of the *Bankruptcy and Insolvency Act*, section 3 (bribing a foreign public official), section 4 (possession of property) or section 5 (laundering proceeds of the offence) of the *Corruption of Foreign Public Official Act*, section 3 (spying) of the *Official Secrets Act*, section 13 (export or attempt to export), 14 (import or attempt to import), 15 (diversion, etc.), 16 (no transfer or permits), 17 (false information) or 18 (aiding or abetting) of the *Export and Import Permits Act*, any offence under the *Crimes Against Humanity and War Crimes Act*, or any other offence created by this Act for which an offender may be sentenced to imprisonment for five years or more that there are reasonable grounds to believe is part of a pattern of criminal activity planned and organized by a number of persons acting in concert, or any other offence created by this or any other Act of Parliament for which an offender may be sentenced to imprisonment for five years or more that there are reasonable grounds to believe is committed for the benefit of, at the direction of or in association with a criminal organization;

2000, c. 24, s. 43 [Not in force at date of publication.]

"private communication" means any oral communication, or any telecommunication, that is made by an originator who is in Canada or is intended by the originator to be received by a person who is in Canada and that is made under circumstances in which it is reasonable for the originator to expect that it will not be intercepted by any person other than the person intended by the originator to receive it, and includes any radio-based telephone communication that is treated electronically or otherwise for the purpose of preventing intelligible reception by any person other than the person intended by the originator to receive it;

"public switched telephone network" means a telecommunication facility the primary purpose of which is to provide a land line-based telephone service to the public for compensation;

"radio-based telephone communication" means any radiocommunication within the meaning of the *Radiocommunication Act* that is made over apparatus that is used primarily for connection to a public switched telephone network;

"sell" includes offer for sale, expose for sale, have in possession for sale or distribute or advertise for sale;

"solicitor" means, in the Province of Quebec, an advocate or a notary and, in any other province, a barrister or solicitor.

R.S. 1985, c. 27 (1st Supp.), ss. 7(2), 23; c. 1 (2d Supp.), s. 213(1), Schedule I, item 2; c. 1 (4th Supp.), s. 20; c. 29 (4th Supp.), s. 17; c. 42 (4th Supp.), s. 1; 1991, c. 28, s. 12; 1992, c. 27, s. 90(1); 1993, c. 7, s. 5; c. 25, s. 94; c. 40, s. 1; c. 46, s. 4; 1995, c. 39, s. 140; 1997, c. 18, s. 7; c. 23, s. 3; 1998, c. 34, s. 8; 1999, c. 2, s. 47; 1999, c. 5, s. 4.

183.1 Consent to interception — Where a private communication is originated by more than one person or is intended by the originator thereof to be received by more than one person, a consent to the interception thereof by any one of those persons is sufficient consent for the purposes of any provision of this Part.

1993, c. 40, s. 2.

Interception of Communications

184. (1) Interception — Every one who, by means of any electro-magnetic, acoustic, mechanical or other device, wilfully intercepts a private communication is guilty of an indictable offence and liable to imprisonment for a term not exceeding five years.

(2) Saving provision — Subsection (1) does not apply to

(a) a person who has the consent to intercept, express or implied, of the originator of the private communication or of the person intended by the originator thereof to receive it;

(b) a person who intercepts a private communication in accordance with an authorization or pursuant to section 184.4 or any person who in good faith aids in any way another person who the aiding person believes on reasonable grounds is acting with an authorization or pursuant to section 184.4;

(c) a person engaged in providing a telephone, telegraph or other communication service to the public who intercepts a private communication,

(i) if the interception is necessary for the purpose of providing the service,

(ii) in the course of service observing or random monitoring necessary for the purpose of mechanical or service quality control checks, or

(iii) if the interception is necessary to protect the person's rights or property directly related to providing the service; or

(d) an officer or servant of Her Majesty in right of Canada who engages in radio frequency spectrum management, in respect of a private communication intercepted by that officer or servant for the purpose of identifying, isolating or preventing an unauthorized or interfering use of a frequency or of a transmission.

(3) [Repealed 1993, c. 40, s. 3(3).]

1993, c. 40, s. 3.

184.1 (1) Interception to prevent bodily harm — An agent of the state may intercept, by means of any electro-magnetic, acoustic, mechanical or other device, a private communication if

(a) either the originator of the private communication or the person intended by the originator to receive it has consented to the interception;

(b) the agent of the state believes on reasonable grounds that there is a risk of bodily harm to the person who consented to the interception; and

(c) the purpose of the interception is to prevent the bodily harm.

(2) Admissibility of intercepted communicaiton — The contents of a private communication that is obtained from an interception pursuant to subsection (1) are inadmissible as evidence except for the purposes of proceedings in which actual, attempted or threatened bodily harm is alleged, including proceedings in respect of an application for an authorization under this Part or in respect of a search warrant or a warrant for the arrest of any person.

(3) Destruction of recording and transcripts — The agent of the state who intercepts a private communication pursuant to subsection (1) shall, as soon as is practicable in the circumstances, destroy any recording of the private communication that is obtained from an interception pursuant to subsection (1), any full or partial transcript of the recording and any notes made by that agent of the private communication if nothing in the private communication suggests that bodily harm, attempted bodily harm or threatened bodily harm has occurred or is likely to occur.

(4) Definition of "agent of the state" — For the purposes of this section, **"Agent of the state"** means

(a) a peace officer; and

(b) a person acting under the authority of, or in cooperation with, a peace officer.

1993, c. 40, s. 4.

184.2 (1) Interception with consent — A person may intercept, by means of any electro-magnetic, acoustic, mechanical or other device, a private communication where either the originator of the private communication or the person intended by the originator to receive it has consented to the interception and an authorization has been obtained pursuant to subsection (3).

(2) Application for authorization — An application for an authorization under this section shall be made by a peace officer, or a public officer who has been appointed or designated to administer or enforce any federal or provincial law and whose duties include the enforcement of this or any other Act of Parliament, ex parte and in writing to a provincial court judge, a judge of a superior court of criminal jurisdiction or a judge as defined in section 552, and shall be accompanied by an affidavit, which may be sworn on the information and belief of that peace officer or public officer or of any other peace officer or public officer, deposing to the following matters:

(a) that there are reasonable grounds to believe that an offence against this or any other Act of Parliament has been or will be committed;

(b) the particulars of the offence;

(c) the name of the person who has consented to the interception;

(d) the period for which the authorization is requested; and

(e) in the case of an application for an authorization where an authorization has previously been granted under this section or section 186, the particulars of the authorization.

(3) Judge to be satisfied — An authorization may be given under this section if the judge to whom the application is made is satisfied that

(a) there are reasonable grounds to believe that an offence against this or any other Act of Parliament has been or will be committed;

(b) either the originator of the private communication or the person intended by the originator to receive it has consented to the interception; and

(c) there are reasonable grounds to believe that information concerning the offence referred to in paragraph (a) will be obtained through the interception sought.

(4) Content and limitation of authorization — An authorization given under this section shall

(a) state the offence in respect of which private communications may be intercepted;

(b) state the type of private communication that may be intercepted;

(c) state the identity of the persons, if known, whose private communications are to be intercepted, generally describe the place at which private communications may be intercepted, if a general description of that place can be given, and generally describe the manner of interception that may be used;

(d) contain the terms and conditions that the judge considers advisable in the public interest; and

(e) be valid for the period, not exceeding sixty days, set out therein.

1993, c. 40, s. 4.

184.3 (1) Application by means of telecommunication — Notwithstanding section 184.2, an application for an authorization under subsection 184.2(2) may be made ex parte to a provincial court judge, a judge of a superior court of criminal jurisdiction or a judge as defined in section 552, by telephone or other means of telecommunication, if it would be impracticable in the circumstances for the applicant to appear personally before a judge.

(2) Application — An application for an authorization made under this section shall be on oath and shall be accompanied by a statement that includes the matters referred to in paragraphs 184.2(2)(a) to (e) and that states the circumstances that make it impracticable for the applicant to appear personally before a judge.

(3) Recording — The judge shall record, in writing or otherwise, the application for an authorization made under this section and, on determination of the application, shall cause the writing or recording to be placed in the packet referred to in subsection 187(1) and sealed in that packet, and a recording sealed in a packet shall be treated as if it were a document for the purposes of section 187.

(4) Oath — For the purposes of subsection (2), an oath may be administered by telephone or other means of telecommunication.

(5) Alternative to oath — An applicant who uses a means of telecommunication that produces a writing may, instead of swearing an oath for the purposes of subsection (2), make a statement in writing stating that all matters contained in the application are true to the knowledge or belief of the applicant and such a statement shall be deemed to be a statement made under oath.

(6) Authorization — Where the judge to whom an application is made under this section is satisfied that the circumstances referred to in paragraphs 184.2(3)(a) to (c) exist and that the circumstances referred to in subsection (2) make it impracticable for the applicant to appear personally before a judge, the judge may, on such terms and conditions, if any, as are considered advisable, give an authorization by telephone or other means of telecommunication for a period of up to thirty-six hours.

(7) Giving authorization — Where a judge gives an authorization by telephone or other means of telecommunication, other than a means of telecommunication that produces a writing,

(a) the judge shall complete and sign the authorization in writing, noting on its face the time, date and place at which it is given;

(b) the applicant shall, on the direction of the judge, complete a facsimile of the authorization in writing, noting on its face the name of the judge who gave it and the time, date and place at which it was given; and

(c) the judge shall, as soon as is practicable after the authorization has been given, cause the authorization to be placed in the packet referred to in subsection 187(1) and sealed in that packet.

(8) Giving authorization where telecommunication produces writing — Where a judge gives an authorization by a means of telecommunication that produces a writing, the judge shall

(a) complete and sign the authorization in writing, noting on its face the time, date and place at which it is given;

(b) transmit the authorization by the means of telecommunication to the applicant, and the copy received by the applicant shall be deemed to be a facsimile referred to in paragraph (7)(b); and

(c) as soon as is practicable after the authorization has been given, cause the authorization to be placed in the packet referred to in subsection 187(1) and sealed in that packet.

1993, c. 40, s. 4.

184.4 Interception in exceptional circumstances — A peace officer may intercept, by means of any electro-magnetic, acoustic, mechanical or other device, a private communication where

(a) the peace officer believes on reasonable grounds that the urgency of the situation is such that an authorization could not, with reasonable diligence, be obtained under any other provision of this Part;

(b) the peace officer believes on reasonable grounds that such an interception is immediately necessary to prevent an unlawful act that would cause serious harm to any person or to property; and

(c) either the originator of the private communication or the person intended by the orginator to receive it is the person who would perform the act that is likely to cause the harm or is the victim, or intended victim, of the harm.

1993, c. 40, s. 4.

184.5 (1) Interception of radio-based telephone communications — Every person who intercepts, by means of any electro-magnetic, acoustic, mechanical or other device, maliciously or for gain, a radio-based telephone communication, if the originator of the communication or the person intended by the originator of the communication to receive it is in Canada, is guilty of an indictable offence and liable to imprisonment for a term not exceeding five years.

(2) Other provisions to apply — Section 183.1, subsection 184(2) and sections 184.1 to 190 and 194 to 196 apply, with such modifications as the circumstances require, to interceptions of radio-based telephone communications referred to in subsection (1).

1993, c. 40, s. 4.

184.6 One application for authorization sufficient — For greater certainty, an application for an authorization under this Part may be made with respect to both private communications and radio-based telephone communications at the same time.

1993, c. 40, s. 4.

185. (1) Application for authorization — An application for an authorization to be given under section 186 shall be made ex parte and in writing to a judge of a superior court of criminal jurisdiction or a judge as defined in section 552 and shall be signed by the Attorney General of the province in which the application is made or the Solicitor General of Canada or an agent specially designated in writing for the purposes of this section by

(a) the Solicitor General of Canada personally or the Deputy Solicitor General of Canada personally, if the offence under investigation is one in respect of which proceedings, if any, may be instituted at the instance of the Government of Canada and conducted by or on behalf of the Attorney General of Canada, or

(b) the Attorney General of a province personally or the Deputy Attorney General of a province personally, in any other case,

and shall be accompanied by an affidavit, which may be sworn on the information and belief of a peace officer or public officer deposing to the following matters:

(c) the facts relied on to justify the belief that an authorization should be given together with particulars of the offence,

(d) the type of private communication proposed to be intercepted,

(e) the names, addresses and occupations, if known, of all persons, the interception of whose private communications there are reasonable grounds to believe may assist the investigation of the offence, a general description of the nature and location of the place, if known, at which private communications are proposed to be intercepted and a general description of the manner of interception proposed to be used,

(f) the number of instances, if any, on which an application has been made under this section in relation to the offence and a person named in the affidavit pursuant to paragraph (*e*) and on which the application was withdrawn or no authorization was given, the date on which each application was made and the name of the judge to whom each application was made,

(g) the period for which the authorization is requested, and

(h) whether other investigative procedures have been tried and have failed or why it appears they are unlikely to succeed or that the urgency of the matter is such that it would be impractical to carry out the investigation of the offence using only other investigative procedures.

(1.1) Exception for criminal organizations — Notwithstanding paragraph (1)(*h*), that paragraph does not apply where the application for an authorization is in relation to

(a) an offence under section 467.1; or

(b) an offence committed for the benefit of, at the direction of or in association with a criminal organization.

(2) Extension of period for notification — An application for an authorization may be accompanied by an application, personally signed by the Attorney General of the province in which the application for the authorization is made or the Solicitor General of Canada if the application for the authorization is made by him or on his behalf, to substitute for the period mentioned in subsection 196(1) such longer period not exceeding three years as is set out in the application.

(3) Where extension to be granted — Where an application for an authorization is accompanied by an application referred to in subsection (2), the judge to whom the applications are made shall first consider the application referred to in subsection (2) and where, on the basis of the affidavit in support of the application for the authorization and any other affidavit evidence submitted in support of the application referred to in subsection (2), the judge is of the opinion that the interests of justice warrant the granting of the application, he shall fix a period, not exceeding three years, in substitution for the period mentioned in subsection 196(1).

(4) Where extension not granted — Where the judge to whom an application for an authorization and an application referred to in subsection (2) are made refuses to fix a period in substitution for the period mentioned in subsection 196(1) or where the judge fixes a period in substitution therefor that is less than the period set out in the application referred to in subsection (2), the person appearing before the judge on the application for the authorization may withdraw the application for the authorization and thereupon the judge shall not proceed to consider the application for the authorization or to give the authorization and shall return to the person appearing before him on the application for the authorization both applications and all other material pertaining thereto.

1993, c. 40, s. 5; 1997, c. 18, s. 8; c. 23, s. 4.

186. (1) Judge to be satisfied — An authorization under this section may be given if the judge to whom the application is made is satisfied

(a) that it would be in the best interests of the administration of justice to do so; and

(b) that other investigative procedures have been tried and have failed, other investigative procedures are unlikely to succeed or the urgency of the matter is such that it would be impractical to carry out the investigation of the offence using only other investigative procedures.

(1.1) Exception for criminal organizations — Notwithstanding paragraph (1)(*b*), that paragraph does not apply where the judge is satisfied that the application for an authorization is in relation to

(a) an offence under section 467.1; or

(b) an offence committed for the benefit of, at the direction of or in association with a criminal organization.

(2) Where authorization not to be given — No authorization may be given to intercept a private communication at the office or residence of a solicitor, or at any other place ordinarily used by a solicitor and by other solicitors for the purpose of consultation with clients, unless the judge to whom the application is made is satisfied that there are reasonable grounds to believe that the solicitor, any other solicitor practising with him, any person employed by him or any other such solicitor or a member of the solicitor's household has been or is about to become a party to an offence.

(3) Terms and conditions — Where an authorization is given in relation to the interception of private communications at a place described in subsection (2), the judge by whom the authorization is given shall include therein such terms and conditions as he considers advisable to protect privileged communications between solicitors and clients.

(4) Content and limitation of authorization — An authorization shall

(a) state the offence in respect of which private communications may be intercepted;

(b) state the type of private communication so that may be intercepted;

(c) state the identity of the persons, if known, whose private communications are to be intercepted, generally describe the place at which private communications may be intercepted, if a general description of that place can be given, and generally describe the manner of interception that may be used;

(d) contain such terms and conditions as the judge considers advisable in the public interest; and

(e) be valid for the period, not exceeding sixty days, set out therein.

(5) Persons designated — The Solicitor General of Canada or the Attorney General, as the case may be, may designate a person or persons who may intercept private communications under authorizations.

(5.1) Installation and removal of device — For greater certainty, an authorization that permits interception by means of an electro-magnetic, acoustic, mechanical or other device includes the authority to install, maintain or remove the device covertly.

(5.2) Removal after expiry of authorization — On an *ex parte* application, in writing, supported by affidavit, the judge who gave an authorization referred to in subsection (5.1) or any other judge having jurisdiction to give such an authorization may give a further authorization for the covert removal of the electro-magnetic, acoustic, mechanical or other device after the expiry of the original authorization

(a) under any terms or conditions that the judge considers advisable in the public interest; and

(b) during any specified period of not more than sixty days.

(6) Renewal of authorization — Renewals of an authorization may be given by a judge of a superior court of criminal jurisdiction or a judge as defined in section 552 on receipt by him of an *ex parte* application in writing signed by the Attorney General of the province in which the application is made or the Solicitor General of Canada or an agent specially designated in writing for the purposes of section 185 by the Solicitor General of Canada or the Attorney General, as the case may be, accompanied by an affidavit of a peace officer or public officer deposing to the following matters:

(a) the reason and period for which the renewal is required,

(b) full particulars, together with times and dates, when interceptions, if any, were made or attempted under the authorization, and any information that has been obtained by any interception, and

(c) the number of instances, if any, on which, to the knowledge and belief of the deponent, an application has been made under this subsection in relation to the same authorization and on which the application was withdrawn or no renewal was given, the date on which each application was made and the name of the judge to whom each application was made,

and supported by such other information as the judge may require.

(7) Renewal — A renewal of an authorization may be given if the judge to whom the application is made is satisfied that any of the circumstances described in subsection (1) still obtain, but no renewal shall be for a period exceeding sixty days.

1993, c. 40, s. 6; 1997, c. 23, s. 5; 1999, c. 5, s. 5.

186.1 Time limitation in relation to criminal organizations — Notwithstanding paragraphs 184.2(4)(*e*) and 186(4)(*e*) and subsection 186(7), an authorization or any renewal of an authorization may be valid for one or more periods specified in the authorization exceeding sixty days, each not exceeding one year, where the authorization is in relation to

(a) an offence under section 467.1; or

(b) an offence committed for the benefit of, at the direction of or in association with criminal organization.

1997, c. 23, s. 6.

187. (1) Manner in which application to be kept secret — All documents relating to an application made pursuant to any provision of this Part are confidential and, subject to subsection (1.1), shall be placed in a packet and sealed by the judge to whom the application is made immediately on determination of the application, and that packet shall be kept in the custody of the court in a place to which the public has no access or in such other place as the judge may authorize and shall not be dealt with except in accordance with subsections (1.2) to (1.5).

(1.1) Exception — An authorization given under this Part need not be placed in the packet except where, pursuant to subsection 184.3(7) or (8), the original authorization is in the hands of the judge, in which case that judge must place it in the packet and the facsimile remains with the applicant.

(1.2) Opening for further applications — The sealed packet may be opened and its contents removed for the purpose of dealing with an application for a further authorization or with an application for renewal of an authorization.

(1.3) Opening on order of judge — A provincial court judge, a judge of a superior court of criminal jurisdiction or a judge as defined in section 552 may order that the sealed packet be opened and its contents removed for the purpose of copying and examining the documents contained in the packet.

(1.4) Opening on order of trial judge — A judge or provincial court judge before whom a trial is to be held and who has jurisdiction in the province in which an authorization was given may order that the sealed packet be opened and its contents removed for the purpose of copying and examining the documents contained in the packet if

(a) any matter relevant to the authorization or any evidence obtained pursuant to the authorization is in issue in the trial; and

(b) the accused applies for such an order for the purpose of consulting the documents to prepare for trial.

(1.5) Order for destruction of documents — Where a sealed packet is opened, its contents shall not be destroyed except pursuant to an order of a judge of the same court as the judge who gave the authorization.

(2) Order of judge — An order under subsection (1.2), (1.3), (1.4) or (1.5) made with respect to documents relating to an application made pursuant to section 185 or subsection 186(6) or 196(2) may only be made after the Attorney General or the Solicitor General by whom or on whose authority the application for the authorization to which the order relates was made has been given an opportunity to be heard.

(3) Idem — An order under subsection (1.2), (1.3), (1.4) or (1.5) made with respect to documents relating to an application made pursuant to subsection 184.2(2) or section 184.3 may only be made after the Attorney General has been given an opportunity to be heard.

(4) Editing of copies — Where a prosecution has been commenced and an accused applies for an order for the copying and examination of documents pursuant to subsection (1.3) or (1.4), the judge shall not, notwithstanding those subsections, provide any copy of any document to the accused until the prosecutor has deleted any part of the copy of the document that the prosecutor believes would be prejudicial to the public interest, including any part that the prosecutor believes could

(a) compromise the identity of any confidential informant;

(b) compromise the nature and extent of ongoing investigations;

(c) endanger persons engaged in particular intelligence-gathering techniques and thereby prejudice future investigations in which similar techniques would be used; or

(d) prejudice the interests of innocent persons.

(5) Accused to be provided with copies — After the prosecutor has deleted the parts of the copy of the document to be given to the accused under subsection (4), the accused shall be provided with an edited copy of the document.

(6) Original documents to be returned — After the accused has received an edited copy of a document, the prosecutor shall keep a copy of the original document, and an edited copy of the document and the original document shall be returned to the packet and the packet resealed.

(7) Deleted parts — An accused to whom an edited copy of a document has been provided pursuant to subsection (5) may request that the judge before whom the trial is to be held order that any part of the document deleted by the prosecutor be made available to the accused, and the judge shall order that a copy of any part that, in the opinion of the judge, is required in order for the accused to make full answer and defence and for which the provision of a judicial summary would not be sufficient, be made available to the accused.

R.S. 1985, c. 27 (1st Supp.), s. 24; 1993, c. 40, s. 7.

188. (1) Applications to specially appointed judges — Notwithstanding section 185, an application made under that section for an authorization may be made *ex parte* to a judge of a superior court of criminal jurisdiction, or a judge as defined in section 552, designated from time to time by the Chief Justice, by a peace officer specially designated in writing, by name or otherwise, for the purposes of this section by

(a) the Solicitor General of Canada, if the offence is one in respect of which proceedings, if any, may be instituted by the Government of Canada and conducted by or on behalf of the Attorney General of Canada, or

(b) the Attorney General of a province, in respect of any other offence in the province,

if the urgency of the situation requires interception of private communications to commence before an authorization could, with reasonable diligence, be obtained under section 186.

(2) Authorizations in emergency — Where the judge to whom an application is made pursuant to subsection (1) is satisfied that the urgency of the situation requires that interception of private communications commence before an authorization could, with reasonable diligence, be obtained under section 186, he may, on such terms and conditions, if any, as he considers advisable, give an authorization in writing for a period of up to thirty-six hours.

(3) [Repealed 1993, c 40, s. 8.]

(4) Definition of "chief justice" — In this section, **"Chief Justice"** means

(a) in the Province of Ontario, the Chief Justice of the Ontario Court;

(b) in the Province of Quebec, the Chief Justice of the Superior Court;

(c) in the Provinces of Nova Scotia and British Columbia, the Chief Justice of the Supreme Court;

(d) in the Provinces of New Brunswick, Manitoba, Saskatchewan and Alberta, the Chief Justice of the Court of Queen's Bench;

(e) in the Provinces of Prince Edward Island and Newfoundland, the Chief Justice of the Supreme Court, Trial Division; and;

(f) in the Yukon Territory, the Northwest Territories and Nunavut, the senior judge within the meaning of subsection 22(3) of the *Judges Act*.

(5) Inadmissibility of evidence — The trial judge may deem inadmissible the evidence obtained by means of an interception of a private communication pursuant to a subsequent authorization given under this section, where he finds that the application for the subsequent authorization was based on the same facts, and involved the interception of the private communications of the same person or persons, or related to the same offence, on which the application for the original authorization was based.

R.S. 1985, c. 27 (1st Supp.), s. 25; c. 27 (2d Supp.), Sched., item 6; 1990, c. 17, s. 10; 1992, c. 1, s. 58(1), Sched. I, item 4; 1992, c. 51, s. 35; 1993, c. 28, s. 78 (Sched. III, item 29) [Repealed 1999, c. 3, (Sched., item 6).]; 1993, c. 40, s. 8; 1999, c. 3, s. 28.

188.1 (1) Execution of authorizations — Subject to subsection (2), the interception of a private communication authorized pursuant to section 184.2, 184.3, 186 or 188 may be carried out anywhere in Canada.

(2) Execution in another province — Where an authorization is given under section 184.2, 184.3, 186 or 188 in one province but it may reasonably be expected that it is to be executed in another province and the execution of the authorization would require entry into or upon the property of any person in the other province or would require that an order under section 487.02 be made with respect to any person in that other province, a judge in the other province may, on application, confirm the authorization and when the authorization is so confirmed, it shall have full force and effect in that other province as though it had originally been given in that other province.

1993, c. 40, s. 9.

188.2 No civil or criminal liability — No person who acts in accordance with an authorization or under section 184.1 or 184.4 or who aids, in good faith, a person who he or she believes on reasonable grounds is acting in accordance with an authorization or under one of those sections incurs any criminal or civil liability for anything reasonably done further to the authorization or to that section.

1993, c. 40, s. 9.

189. (1)–(4) [Repealed 1993, c. 40, s. 10.]

(5) Notice of intention to produce evidence — The contents of a private communication that is obtained from an interception of the private communication pursuant to any provision of, or pursuant to an authorization given under, this Part shall not be received in evidence unless the party intending to adduce it has given to the accused reasonable notice of the intention together with

(a) a transcript of the private communication, where it will be adduced in the form of a recording, or a statement setting out full particulars of the private communication, where evidence of the private communication will be given *viva voce*; and

(b) a statement respecting the time, place and date of the private communication and the parties thereto, if known.

(6) Privileged evidence — Any information obtained by an interception that, but for the interception, would have been privileged remains privileged and inadmissible as evidence without the consent of the person enjoying the privilege.

R.S. 1985, c. 27 (1st Supp.), s. 203; 1993, c. 40, s. 10.

190. Further particulars — Where an accused has been given notice pursuant to subsection 189(5), any judge of the court in which the trial of the accused is being or is to be held may at any time order that further particulars be given of the private communication that is intended to be adduced in evidence.

191. (1) Possession, etc. — Every one who possesses, sells or purchases any electro-magnetic, acoustic, mechanical or other device or any component thereof knowing that the design thereof renders it primarily useful for surreptitious interception of private communications is guilty of an indictable offence and liable to imprisonment for a term not exceeding two years.

(2) Exemptions — Subsection (1) does not apply to

(a) a police officer or police constable in possession of a device or component described in subsection (1) in the course of his employment;

(b) a person in possession of such a device or component for the purpose of using it in an interception made or to be made in accordance with an authorization;

(b.1) a person in possession of such a device or component under the direction of a police officer or police constable in order to assist that officer or constable in the course of his duties as a police officer or police constable;

(c) an officer or a servant of Her Majesty in right of Canada or a member of the Canadian Forces in possession of such a device or component in the course of his duties as such an officer, servant or member, as the case may be; and

(d) any other person in possession of such a device or component under the authority of a licence issued by the Solicitor General of Canada.

(3) Terms and conditions of licence — A licence issued for the purpose of paragraph (2)(*d*) may contain such terms and conditions relating to the possession, sale or purchase of a device or component described in subsection (1) as the Solicitor General of Canada may prescribe.

R.S. 1985, c. 27 (1st Supp.), s. 26.

192. (1) Forfeiture — Where a person is convicted of an offence under section 184 or 191, any electro-magnetic, acoustic, mechanical or other device by means of which the offence was committed or the possession of which constituted the offence, on the conviction, in addition to any punishment that is imposed, may be ordered forfeited to Her Majesty whereupon it may be disposed of as the Attorney General directs.

(2) Limitation — No order for forfeiture shall be made under subsection (1) in respect of telephone, telegraph or other communication facilities or equipment owned by a person engaged in providing telephone, telegraph or other communication service to the public or forming part of the telephone, telegraph or other communication service or system of that person by means of which an offence under section 184 has been committed if that person was not a party to the offence.

193. (1) Disclosure of information — Where a private communication has been intercepted by means of an electro-magnetic, acoustic, mechanical or other device without the consent, express or implied, of the originator thereof or of the person intended by the originator thereof to receive it, every one who, without the express consent of the originator thereof or of the person intended by the originator thereof to receive it, wilfully

(a) uses or discloses the private communication or any part thereof or the substance, meaning or purport thereof or of any part thereof, or

(b) discloses the existence thereof,

is guilty of an indictable offence and liable to imprisonment for a term not exceeding two years.

(2) Exemptions — Subsection (1) does not apply to a person who discloses a private communication or any part thereof or the substance, meaning or purport thereof or of any part thereof or who discloses the existence of a private communication

(a) in the course of or for the purpose of giving evidence in any civil or criminal proceedings or in any other proceedings in which the person may be required to give evidence on oath;

(b) in the course of or for the purpose of any criminal investigation if the private communication was lawfully intercepted;

(c) in giving notice under section 189 or furnishing further particulars pursuant to an order under section 190;

(d) in the course of the operation of

(i) a telephone, telegraph or other communication service to the public, or

(ii) a department or an agency of the Government of Canada,

if the disclosure is necessarily incidental to an interception described in paragraph 184(2)(c) or (d); or

(e) where disclosure is made to a peace officer or prosecutor in Canada or to a person or authority with responsibility in a foreign state for the investigation or prosecution of offences and is intended to be in the interests of the administration of justice in Canada or elsewhere; or

(f) where the disclosure is made to the Director of the Canadian Security Intelligence Service or to an employee of the Service for the purpose of enabling the Service to perform its duties and functions under section 12 of the *Canadian Security Intelligence Service Act.*

(3) Publishing of prior lawful disclosure — Subsection (1) does not apply to a person who discloses a private communication or any part thereof or the substance, meaning or purport thereof or of any part thereof or who discloses the existence of a private communication where that which is disclosed by him was, prior to the disclosure, lawfully disclosed in the course of or for the purpose of giving evidence in proceedings referred to in paragraph (2)(*a*).

R.S. 1985, c. 30 (4th Supp.), s. 45; 1993, c. 40, s. 11.

193.1 (1) Disclosure of information received from interception of radio-based telephone communications — Every person who wilfully uses or discloses a radio-based telephone communication or who wilfully discloses the existence of such a communication is guilty of an indictable offence and liable to imprisonment for a term not exceeding two years, if

(a) the originator of the communication or the person intended by the originator of the communication to receive it was in Canada when the communication was made;

(b) the communication was intercepted by means of an electromagnetic, acoustic, mechanical or other device without the consent, express or implied, of the originator of the communication or of the person intended by the originator to receive the communication; and

(c) the person does not have the express or implied consent of the originator of the communication or of the person intended by the originator to receive the communication.

(2) Other provisions to apply — Subsections 193(2) and (3) apply, with such modifications as the circumstances require, to disclosures of radio-based telephone communications.

1993, c. 40, s. 12.

194. (1) Damages — Subject to subsection (2), a court that convicts an accused of an offence under section 184, 184.5, 193 or 193.1 may, on the application of a person aggrieved, at the time sentence is imposed, order the accused to pay to that person an amount not exceeding five thousand dollars as punitive damages.

(2) No damages where civil proceedings commenced — No amount shall be ordered to be paid under subsection (1) to a person who has commenced an action under Part II of the *Crown Liability Act.*

(3) Judgment may be registered — Where an amount that is ordered to be paid under subsection (1) is not paid forthwith, the applicant may, by filing the order, enter as a judgment, in the superior court of the province in which the trial was held, the amount ordered to be paid, and that judgment is enforceable against the accused in the same manner as if it were a judgment rendered against the accused in that court in civil proceedings.

(4) Moneys in possession of accused may be taken — All or any part of an amount that is ordered to be paid under subsection (1) may be taken out of moneys found in the possession of the accused at the time of his arrest, except where there is a dispute respecting ownership of or right of possession to those moneys by claimants other than the accused.

1993, c. 40, s. 13.

195. (1) Annual report — The Solicitor General of Canada shall, as soon as possible after the end of each year, prepare a report relating to

(a) authorizations for which he and agents to be named in the report who were specially designated in writing by him for the purposes of section 185 made application, and

(b) authorizations given under section 188 for which peace officers to be named in the report who were specially designated by him for the purposes of that section made application,

and interceptions made thereunder in the immediately preceding year.

(2) Information respecting authorizations — The report referred to in subsection (1) shall, in relation to authorizations and interceptions made thereunder, set out

(a) the number of applications made for authorizations;

(b) the number of applications made for renewal of authorizations;

(c) the number of applications referred to in paragraphs (a) and (b) that were granted, the number of those applications that were refused and the number of applications referred to in paragraph (a) that were granted subject to terms and conditions;

(d) the number of persons identified in an authorization against whom proceedings were commenced at the instance of the Attorney General of Canada in respect of

(i) an offence specified in the authorization,

(ii) an offence other than an offence specified in the authorization but in respect of which an authorization may be given, and

(iii) an offence in respect of which an authorization may not be given;

(e) the number of persons not identified in an authorization against whom proceedings were commenced at the instance of the Attorney General of Canada in respect of

(i) an offence specified in such an authorization,

(ii) an offence other than an offence specified in such an authorization but in respect of which an authorization may be given, and

(iii) an offence other than an offence specified in such an authorization and for which no such authorization may be given,

and whose commission or alleged commission of the offence became known to a peace officer as a result of an interception of a private communication under an authorization;

(f) the average period for which authorizations were given and for which renewals thereof were granted;

(g) the number of authorizations that, by virtue of one or more renewals thereof, were valid for more than sixty days, for more than one hundred and twenty days, for more than one hundred and eighty days and for more than two hundred and forty days;

(h) the number of notifications given pursuant to section 196;

(i) the offences in respect of which authorizations were given, specifying the number of authorizations given in respect of each of those offences;

(j) a description of all classes of places specified in authorizations and the number of authorizations in which each of those classes of places was specified;

(k) a general description of the methods of interception involved in each interception under an authorization;

(l) the number of persons arrested whose identity became known to a peace officer as a result of an interception under an authorization;

(m) the number of criminal proceedings commenced at the instance of the Attorney General of Canada in which private communications obtained by interception under an authorization were adduced in evidence and the number of those proceedings that resulted in a conviction; and

(n) the number of criminal investigations in which information obtained as a result of the interception of a private communication under an authorization was used although the private communication was not adduced in evidence in criminal proceedings commenced at the instance of the Attorney General of Canada as a result of the investigations.

(3) Other information — The report referred to in subsection (1) shall, in addition to the information referred to in subsection (2), set out

(a) the number of prosecutions commenced against officers or servants of Her Majesty in right of Canada or members of the Canadian Forces for offences under section 184 or 193; and

(b) a general assessment of the importance of interception of private communications for the investigation, detection, prevention and prosecution of offences in Canada.

(4) Report to be laid before Parliament — The Solicitor General of Canada shall cause a copy of each report prepared by him under subsection (1) to be laid before Parliament forthwith on completion thereof, or if Parliament is not then sitting, on any of the first fifteen days next thereafter that Parliament is sitting.

(5) Report by Attorneys General — The Attorney General of each province shall, as soon as possible after the end of each year, prepare and publish or otherwise make available to the public a report relating to

(a) authorizations for which he and agents specially designated in writing by him for the purposes of section 185 made application, and

(b) authorizations given under section 188 for which peace officers specially designated by him for the purposes of that section made application, and interceptions made thereunder in the immediately preceding year setting out, with such modifications as the circumstances require, the information described in subsections (2) and (3).

R.S. 1985, c. 27 (1st Supp.), s. 27.

196. (1) Written notification to be given — The Attorney General of the province in which an application under subsection 185(1) was made or the Solicitor General of Canada if the application was made by or on behalf of the Solicitor General of Canada shall, within ninety days after the period for which the authorization was given or renewed or within such other period as is fixed pursuant to subsection 185(3) or subsection (3) of this section, notify in writing the person who was the object of the interception pursuant to the authorization and shall, in a manner prescribed by regulations made by the Governor in Council, certify to the court that gave the authorization that the person has been so notified.

(2) Extension of period for notification — The running of the ninety days referred to in subsection (1), or of any other period fixed pursuant to subsection 185(3) or subsection (3) of this section, is suspended until any application made by the Attorney General or the Solicitor General to a judge of a superior court of criminal jurisdiction or a judge as defined in section 552 for an extension or a subsequent extension of the period for which the authorization was given or renewed has been heard and disposed of.

(3) Where extension to be granted — Where the judge to whom an application referred to in subsection (2) is made, on the basis of an affidavit submitted in support of the application, is satisfied that

(a) the investigation of the offence to which the authorization relates, or

(b) a subsequent investigation of an offence listed in section 183 commenced as a result of information obtained from the investigation referred to in paragraph (a),

is continuing and is of the opinion that the interests of justice warrant the granting of the application, the judge shall grant an extension, or a subsequent extension, of the period, each extension not to exceed three years.

(4) Application to be accompanied by affidavit — An application pursuant to subsection (2) shall be accompanied by an affidavit deposing to

(a) the facts known or believed by the deponent and relied on to justify the belief that an extension should be granted; and

(b) the number of instances, if any, on which an application has, to the knowledge or belief of the deponent, been made under that subsection in relation to the particular authorization and on which the application was withdrawn or the application was not granted, the date on which each application was made and the judge to whom each application was made.

(5) Exception for criminal organization — Notwithstanding subsection (3) and 185(3), where the judge to whom an application referred to in subsection (2) or 185(2) is made, on the basis of an affidavit submitted in support of the application, is satisfied that the investigation is in relation to

(a) an offence under section 467.1, or

(b) an offence committed for the benefit of, at the direction of or in association with a criminal organization,

and is of the opinion that the interests of justice warrant the granting of the application, the judge shall grant an extension, or a subsequent extension, of the period, but no extension may exceed three years.

R.S. 1985, c. 27 (1st Supp.), s. 28; 1993, c. 40, s. 14; 1997, c. 23, s. 7.

PART VII — DISORDERLY HOUSES, GAMING AND BETTING

Interpretation

197. (1) Definitions — In this Part

"bet" means a bet that is placed on any contingency or event that is to take place in or out of Canada, and without restricting the generality of the foregoing, includes a bet that is placed on any contingency relating to a horse-race, fight, match or sporting event that is to take place in or out of Canada;

"common bawdy-house" means a place that is

(a) kept or occupied, or

(b) resorted to by one or more persons

for the purpose of prostitution or the practice of acts of indecency;

"common betting house" means a place that is opened, kept or used for the purpose of

(a) enabling, encouraging or assisting persons who resort thereto to bet between themselves or with the keeper, or

(b) enabling any person to receive, record, register, transmit or pay bets or to announce the results of betting;

"common gaming house" means a place that is

(a) kept for gain to which persons resort for the purpose of playing games, or

(b) kept or used for the purpose of playing games

(i) in which a bank is kept by one or more but not all of the players,

(ii) in which all or any portion of the bets on or proceeds from a game is paid, directly or indirectly, to the keeper of the place,

(iii) in which, directly or indirectly, a fee is charged to or paid by the players for the privilege of playing or participating in a game or using gaming equipment, or

(iv) in which the chances of winning are not equally favourable to all persons who play the game, including the person, if any, who conducts the game;

"disorderly house" means a common bawdy-house, a common betting house or a common gaming house;

"game" means a game of chance or mixed chance and skill;

"gaming equipment" means anything that is or may be used for the purpose of playing games or for betting;

"keeper" includes a person who

    (a) is an owner or occupier of a place,

    (b) assists or acts on behalf of an owner or occupier of a place,

    (c) appears to be, or to assist or act on behalf of an owner or occupier of a place,

    (d) has the care or management of a place, or

    (e) uses a place permanently or temporarily, with or without the consent of the owner or occupier;

"place" includes any place, whether or not

    (a) it is covered or enclosed,

    (b) it is used permanently or temporarily, or

    (c) any person has an exclusive right of user with respect to it;

"prostitute" means a person of either sex who engages in prostitution;

"public place" includes any place to which the public have access as of right or by invitation, express or implied.

(2) Exception — A place is not a common gaming house within the meaning of paragraph (*a*) or subparagraph (*b*)(ii) or (iii) of the definition "common gaming house" in subsection (1) while it is occupied and used by an incorporated genuine social club or branch thereof, if

    (a) the whole or any portion of the bets on or proceeds from games played therein is not directly or indirectly paid to the keeper thereof; and

    (b) no fee is charged to persons for the right or privilege of participating in the games played therein other than under the authority of and in accordance with the terms of a licence issued by the Attorney General of the province in which the place is situated or by such other person or authority in the province as may be specified by the Attorney General thereof.

(3) Onus — The onus of proving that, by virtue of subsection (2), a place is not a common gaming house is on the accused.

(4) Effect when game partly played on premises — A place may be a common gaming house notwithstanding that

    (a) it is used for the purpose of playing part of a game and another part of the game is played elsewhere;

    (b) the stake that is played for is in some other place, or

    (c) it is used on only one occasion in the manner described in paragraph (*b*) of the definition "common gaming house" in subsection (1), if the keeper or any person acting on behalf of or in concert with the keeper has used another place on another occasion in the manner described in that paragraph.

R.S. 1985, c. 27 (1st Supp.), s. 29.

Presumptions

198. (1) Presumptions — In proceedings under this Part,

(a) evidence that a peace officer who was authorized to enter a place was wilfully prevented from entering or was wilfully obstructed or delayed in entering is, in the absence of any evidence to the contrary, proof that the place is a disorderly house;

(b) evidence that a place was found to be equipped with gaming equipment or any device for concealing, removing or destroying gaming equipment is, in the absence of any evidence to the contrary, proof that the place is a common gaming house or a common betting house, as the case may be;

(c) evidence that gaming equipment was found in a place entered under a warrant issued pursuant to this Part, or on or about the person of anyone found therein, is, in the absence of any evidence to the contrary, proof that the place is a common gaming house and that the persons found therein were playing games, whether or not any person acting under the warrant observed any persons playing games therein; and

(d) evidence that a person was convicted of keeping a disorderly house is, for the purpose of proceedings against any one who is alleged to have been an inmate or to have been found in that house at the time the person committed the offence of which he was convicted, in the absence of any evidence to the contrary, proof that the house was, at that time, a disorderly house.

(2) Conclusive presumption from slot machine — For the purpose of proceedings under this Part, a place that is found to be equipped with a slot machine shall be conclusively presumed to be a common gaming house.

(3) "slot machine" defined — In subsection (2), **"slot machine"** means any automatic machine or slot machine

(a) that is used or intended to be used for any purpose other than vending merchandise or services, or

(b) that is used or intended to be used for the purpose of vending merchandise or services if

(i) the result of one of any number of operations of the machine is a matter of chance or uncertainty to the operator,

(ii) as a result of a given number of successive operations by the operator the machine produces different results, or

(iii) on any operation of the machine it discharges or emits a slug or token but does not include an automatic machine or slot machine that dispenses as prizes only one or more free games on that machine.

Search

199. (1) Warrant to search — A justice who is satisfied by information on oath that there are reasonable grounds to believe that an offence under section 201, 202, 203, 206, 207 or 210 is being committed at any place within the jurisdiction of the justice may issue a warrant authorizing a peace officer to enter and search the place by day or night and seize anything found therein that may be evidence that an offence under section 201, 202, 203, 206, 207 or 210, as the case may be, is being committed at that place, and to take into custody all persons who are found in or at that place and requiring those persons and things to be brought before that justice or before another justice having jurisdiction, to be dealt with according to law.

(2) Search without warrant, seizure and arrest — A peace officer may, whether or not he is acting under a warrant issued pursuant to this section, take into custody any person whom he finds keeping a common gaming house and any person whom he finds therein, and may seize anything that may be evidence that such an offence is being committed and shall bring those persons and things before a justice having jurisdiction, to be dealt with according to law.

(3) Disposal of property seized — Except where otherwise expressly provided by law, a court, judge, justice or provincial court judge before whom anything that is seized under this section is brought may declare that the thing is forfeited, in which case it shall be disposed of or dealt with as the Attorney General may direct if no person shows sufficient cause why it should not be forfeited.

(4) When declaration or direction may be made — No declaration or direction shall be made pursuant to subsection (3) in respect of anything seized under this section until

(a) it is no longer required as evidence in any proceedings that are instituted pursuant to the seizure; or

(b) the expiration of thirty days from the time of seizure where it is not required as evidence in any proceedings.

(5) Conversion into money — The Attorney General may, for the purpose of converting anything forfeited under this section into money, deal with it in all respects as if he were the owner thereof.

(6) Telephones exempt from seizure — Nothing in this section or in section 489 authorizes the seizure, forfeiture or destruction of telephone, telegraph or other communication facilities or equipment that may be evidence of or that may have been used in the commission of an offence under section 201, 202, 203, 206, 207 or 210 and that is owned by a person engaged in providing telephone, telegraph or other communication service to the public or forming part of the telephone, telegraph or other communication service or system of that person.

(7) Exception — Subsection (6) does not apply to prohibit the seizure, for use as evidence, of any facility or equipment described in that subsection that is designed or adapted to record a communication.

R.S. 1985, c. 27 (1st Supp.), s. 203; 1994, c. 44, s. 10.

200. [Repealed R.S. 1985, c. 27 (1st Supp.), s. 30.]

Gaming and Betting

201. (1) Keeping gaming or betting house — Every one who keeps a common gaming house or common betting house is guilty of an indictable offence and liable to imprisonment for a term not exceeding two years.

(2) Person found in or owner permitting use — Every one who

(a) is found, without lawful excuse, in a common gaming house or common betting house, or

(b) as owner, landlord, lessor, tenant, occupier or agent, knowingly permits a place to be let or used for the purposes of a common gaming house or common betting house,

is guilty of an offence punishable on summary conviction.

202. (1) Betting, pool-selling, book-making, etc. — Every one commits an offence who

(a) uses or knowingly allows a place under his control to be used for the purposes of recording or registering bets or selling a pool;

(b) imports, makes, buys, sells, rents, leases, hires or keeps, exhibits, employs or knowingly allows to be kept, exhibited or employed in any place under his control any device or apparatus for the purpose of recording or registering bets or selling a pool, or any machine or device for gambling or betting;

(c) has under his control any money or other property relating to a transaction that is an offence under this section;

(d) records or registers bets or sells a pool;

(e) engages in book-making or pool-selling, or in the business or occupation of betting, or makes any agreement for the purchase or sale of betting or gaming privileges, or for the purchase or sale of information that is intended to assist in book-making, pool-selling or betting;

(f) prints, provides or offers to print or provide information intended for use in connection with book-making, pool-selling or betting on any horse-race, fight, game or sport, whether or not it takes place in or outside Canada or has or has not taken place;

(g) imports or brings into Canada any information or writing that is intended or is likely to promote or be of use in gambling, book-making, pool-selling or betting on a horse-race, fight, game or sport, and where this paragraph applies it is immaterial

    (i) whether the information is published before, during or after the race, fight, game or sport, or

    (ii) whether the race, fight, game or sport takes place in Canada or elsewhere,

but this paragraph does not apply to a newspaper, magazine or other periodical published in good faith primarily for a purpose other than the publication of such information;

(h) advertises, prints, publishes, exhibits, posts up, or otherwise gives notice of any offer, invitation or inducement to bet on, to guess or to foretell the results of a contest, or a result of or contingency relating to any contest;

(i) wilfully and knowingly sends, transmits, delivers or receives any message by radio, telegraph, telephone, mail or express that conveys any information relating to book-making, pool-selling, betting or wagering, or that is intended to assist in book-making, pool-selling, betting or wagering; or

(j) aids or assists in any manner in anything that is an offence under this section.

(2) Punishment — Every one who commits an offence under this section is guilty of an indictable offence and liable

(a) for a first offence, to imprisonment for not more than two years;

(b) for a second offence, to imprisonment for not more than two years and not less than fourteen days; and

(c) for each subsequent offence, to imprisonment for not more than two years and not less than three months.

203. Placing bets on behalf of others — Every one who

(a) places or offers or agrees to place a bet on behalf of another person for a consideration paid or to be paid by or on behalf of that other person,

(b) engages in the business or practice of placing or agreeing to place bets on behalf of other persons, whether for a consideration or otherwise, or

(c) holds himself out or allows himself to be held out as engaging in the business or practice of placing or agreeing to place bets on behalf of other persons, whether for a consideration or otherwise,

is guilty of an indictable offence and liable

(d) for a first offence, to imprisonment for not more than two years,

(e) for a second offence, to imprisonment for not more than two years and not less than fourteen days, and

(f) for each subsequent offence, to imprisonment for not more than two years and not less than three months.

204. (1) Exemption — Sections 201 and 202 do not apply to

(a) any person or association by reason of his or their becoming the custodian or depository of any money, property or valuable thing staked, to be paid to

    (i) the winner of a lawful race, sport, game or exercise,

    (ii) the owner of a horse engaged in a lawful race, or

    (iii) the winner of any bets between not more than ten individuals;

(b) a private bet between individuals not engaged in any way in the business of betting;

(c) bets made or records of bets made through the agency of a pari-mutuel system on running, trotting or pacing horse-races if

    (i) the bets or records of bets are made on the race-course of an association in respect of races conducted at that race-course or another race-course in or out of Canada, and, in the case of a race conducted on a race-course situated outside Canada, the governing body that regulates the race has been certified as acceptable by the Minister of Agriculture and Agri-Food or a person designated by that Minister pursuant to subsection (8.1) and that Minister or person has permitted pari-mutuel betting in Canada on the race pursuant to that subsection, and

    (ii) the provisions of this section and the regulations are complied with.

(1.1) Exception — For greater certainty, a person may, in accordance with the regulations, do anything described in section 201 or 202, if the person does it for the purposes of legal pari-mutuel betting.

(2) Presumption — For the purposes of paragraph (1)(c), bets made, in accordance with the regulations, in a betting theatre referred to in paragraph 8(e), or by telephone calls to the race-course of an association or to such a betting theatre, are deemed to be made on the race-course of the association.

(3) Operation of pari-mutuel system — No person or association shall use a pari-mutuel system of betting in respect of a horse-race unless the system has been approved by and its operation is carried on under the supervision of an officer appointed by the Minister of Agriculture and Agri-Food.

(4) Supervision of pari-mutuel system — Every person or association operating a pari-mutuel system of betting in accordance with this section in respect of a horse-race, whether or not the person or association is conducting the race-meeting at which the race is run, shall pay to the Receiver General in respect of each individual pool of the race and each individual feature pool one-half of one per cent, or such greater fraction not exceeding one per cent as may be fixed by the Governor in Council, of the total amount of money that is bet through the agency of the pari-mutuel system of betting.

(5) Percentage that may be deducted and retained — Where any person or association becomes a custodian or depository of any money, bet or stakes under a pari-mutuel system in respect of a horse-race, that person or association shall not deduct or retain any amount from the total amount of money, bets or stakes unless it does so pursuant to subsection (6).

(6) Idem — An association operating a pari-mutuel system of betting in accordance with this section in respect of a horse-race, or any other association or person acting on its behalf, may deduct and retain from the total amount of money that is bet through the agency of the pari-mutuel system, in respect of each individual pool of each race or each individual feature pool, a percentage not exceeding the percentage prescribed by the regulations plus any odd cents over any multiple of five cents in the amount calculated in accordance with the regulations to be payable in respect of each dollar bet.

(7) Stopping of betting — Where an officer appointed by the Minister of Agriculture and Agri-Food is not satisfied that the provisions of this section and the regulations are being carried out in good faith by any person or association in relation to a race meeting, he may, at any time, order any betting in relation to the race meeting to be stopped for any period that he considers proper.

(8) Regulations — The Minister of Agriculture and Agri-Food may make regulations

(a) prescribing the maximum number of races for each race-course on which a race meeting is conducted, in respect of which a pari-mutuel system of betting may be used for the race meeting or on any one calendar day during the race meeting, and the circumstances in which the Minister of Agriculture and Agri-Food or a person designated by him for that purpose may approve of the use of that system in respect of additional races on any race-course for a particular race meeting or on a particular day during the race meeting;

(b) prohibiting any person or association from using a pari-mutuel system of betting for any race-course on which a race meeting is conducted in respect of more than the maximum number of races prescribed pursuant to paragraph (a) and the additional races, if any, in respect of which the use of a pari-mutuel system of betting has been approved pursuant to that paragraph;

(c) prescribing the maximum percentage that may be deducted and retained pursuant to subsection (6) by or on behalf of a person or association operating a pari-mutuel system of betting in respect of a horse-race in accordance with this section and providing for the determination of the percentage that each such person or association may deduct and retain;

(d) respecting pari-mutuel betting in Canada on horse-races conducted on a race-course situated outside Canada; and

(e) authorizing pari-mutuel betting and governing the conditions for pari-mutuel betting, including the granting of licences therefor, that is conducted by an association in a betting theatre owned or leased by the association in a province in which the Lieutenant Governor in Council, or such other person or authority in the province as may be specified by the Lieutenant Governor in Council thereof, has issued a licence to that association for the betting theatre.

(8.1) Approvals — The Minister of Agriculture and Agri-Food or a person designated by that Minister may, with respect to a horse-race conducted on a race-course situated outside Canada,

(a) certify as acceptable, for the purposes of this section, the governing body that regulates the race; and

(b) permit pari-mutuel betting in Canada on the race.

(9) Regulations — The Minister of Agriculture and Agri-Food may make regulations respecting

(a) the supervision and operation of pari-mutuel systems related to race meetings, and the fixing of the dates on which and the places at which an association may conduct such meetings;

(b) the method of calculating the amount payable in respect of each dollar bet;

(c) the conduct of race-meetings in relation to the supervision and operation of pari-mutuel systems, including photo-finishes, video patrol and the testing of bodily substances taken from horses entered in a race at such meetings, including, in the case of a horse that dies while engaged in racing or immediately before or after the race, the testing of any tissue taken from its body;

(d) the prohibition, restriction or regulation of

(i) the possession of drugs or medicaments or of equipment used in the administering of drugs or medicaments at or near race-courses, or

(ii) the administering of drugs or medicaments to horses participating in races run at a race meeting during which a pari-mutuel system of betting is used; and

(e) the provision, equipment and maintenance of accommodation, services or other facilities for the proper supervision and operation of pari-mutuel systems related to race meetings, by associations conducting those meetings or by other associations.

(9.1) 900 metre zone — For the purposes of this section, the Minister of Agriculture and Agri-Food may designate, with respect to any race-course, a zone that shall be deemed to be part of the race-course, if

(a) the zone is immediately adjacent to the race-course;

(b) the farthest point of that zone is no more than 900 metres from the nearest point on the race track of the race-course; and

(c) all real property situated in that zone is owned or leased by the person or association that owns or leases the race-course.

(10) Contravention — Every person who contravenes or fails to comply with any of the provisions of this section or of any regulations made under this section is guilty of

(a) an indictable offence and is liable to imprisonment for a term not exceeding two years, or

(b) an offence punishable on summary conviction.

(11) Definition of "association" — For the purposes of this section **"association"** means an association incorporated by or pursuant to an Act of the Parliament or of the legislature of a province that owns or leases a race-course and conducts horse-races in the ordinary course of its business and, to the extent that the applicable legislation requires that the purposes of the association be expressly stated in its constating instrument, having as one of its purposes the conduct of horse-races.

R.S. 1985, c. 47 (1st Supp.), s. 1; 1989, c. 2, s. 1; 1994, c. 38, s. 25(1)(g).

205. [Repealed R.S. 1985, c. 52 (1st Supp.), s. 1.]

206. (1) Offence in relation to lotteries and games of chance — Every one is guilty of an indictable offence and liable to imprisonment for a term not exceeding two years who

(a) makes, prints, advertises or publishes, or causes or procures to be made, printed, advertised or published, any proposal, scheme or plan for advancing, lending, giving, selling or in any way disposing of any property by lots, cards, tickets or any mode of chance whatever;

(b) sells, barters, exchanges or otherwise disposes of, or causes or procures, or aids or assists in, the sale, barter, exchange or other disposal of, or offers for sale, barter or exchange, any lot, card, ticket or other means or device for advancing, lending, giving, selling or otherwise disposing of any property by lots, tickets or any mode of chance whatever;

(c) knowingly sends, transmits, mails, ships, delivers or allows to be sent, transmitted, mailed, shipped or delivered, or knowingly accepts for carriage or transport or conveys any article that is used or intended for use in carrying out any device, proposal, scheme or plan for advancing, lending, giving, selling or otherwise disposing of any property by any mode of chance whatever;

(d) conducts or manages any scheme, contrivance or operation of any kind for the purpose of determining who, or the holders of what lots, tickets, numbers or chances, are the winners of any property so proposed to be advanced, lent, given, sold or disposed of;

(e) conducts, manages or is a party to any scheme, contrivance or operation of any kind by which any person, on payment of any sum of money, or the giving of any valuable security, or by obligating himself to pay any sum of money or give any valuable security, shall become entitled under the scheme, contrivance or operation to receive from the person conducting or managing the scheme, contrivance or operation, or any other person, a larger sum of money or amount of valuable security than the sum or amount paid or given, or to be paid or given, by reason of the fact that other persons have paid or given, or obligated themselves to pay or give any sum of money or valuable security under the scheme, contrivance or operation;

(f) disposes of any goods, wares or merchandise by any game of chance or any game of mixed chance and skill in which the contestant or competitor pays money or other valuable consideration;

(g) induces any person to stake or hazard any money or other valuable property or thing on the result of any dice game, three-card monte, punch board, coin table or on the operation of a wheel of fortune;

(h) for valuable consideration carries on or plays or offers to carry on or to play, or employs any person to carry on or play in a public place or a place to which the public have access, the game of three-card monte;

(i) receives bets of any kind on the outcome of a game of three-card monte; or

(j) being the owner of a place, permits any person to play the game of three-card monte therein.

(2) "three-card monte" — In this section **"three-card monte"** means the game commonly known as three-card monte and includes any other game that is similar to it, whether or not the game is played with cards and notwithstanding the number of cards or other things that are used for the purpose of playing.

(3) Exemption for fairs — Paragraphs (1)(*f*) and (*g*), in so far as they do not relate to a dice game, three-card monte, punch board or coin table, do not apply to the board of an annual fair or exhibition, or to any operator of a concession leased by that board within its own grounds and operated during the fair or exhibition on those grounds.

(3.1) Definition of "fair or exhibition" — For the purposes of this section, **"fair or exhibition"** means an event where agricultural or fishing products are presented or where activities relating to agriculture or fishing take place.

(4) Offence — Every one who buys, takes or receives a lot, ticket or other device mentioned in subsection (1) is guilty of an offence punishable on summary conviction.

(5) Lottery sale void — Every sale, loan, gift, barter or exchange of any property, by any lottery, ticket, card or other mode of chance depending on or to be determined by chance or lot, is void, and all property sold, lent, given, bartered or exchanged is forfeited to Her Majesty.

(6) Bona fide exception — Subsection (5) does not affect any right or title to property acquired by any *bona fide* purchaser for valuable consideration without notice.

(7) Foreign lottery included — This section applies to the printing or publishing, or causing to be printed or published, of any advertisement, scheme, proposal or plan of any foreign lottery, and the sale or offer for sale of any ticket, chance or share, in any such lottery, or the advertisement for sale of such ticket, chance or share, and the conducting or managing of any such scheme, contrivance or operation for determining the winners in any such lottery.

(8) Saving — This section does not apply to

(a) the division by lot or chance of any property by joint tenants or tenants in common, or persons having joint interests in any such property; or

(b) [Repealed 1999, c. 28, s. 156.]

(c) bonds, debentures, debenture stock or other securities recallable by drawing of lots and redeemable with interest and providing for payment of premiums on redemption or otherwise.

R.S. 1985, c. 52 (1st Supp.), s. 2; 1999, c. 28, s. 156.

207. (1) Permitted lotteries — Notwithstanding any of the provisions of this Part relating to gaming and betting, it is lawful

(a) for the government of a province, either alone or in conjunction with the government of another province, to conduct and manage a lottery scheme in that province, or in that and the other province, in accordance with any law enacted by the legislature of that province;

(b) for a charitable or religious organization, pursuant to a licence issued by the Lieutenant Governor in Council of a province or by such other person or authority in the province as may be specified by the Lieutenant Governor in Council thereof, to conduct and manage a lottery scheme in that province if the proceeds from the lottery scheme are used for a charitable or religious object or purpose;

(c) for the board of a fair or of an exhibition or an operator of a concession leased by that board, to conduct and manage a lottery scheme in a province where the Lieutenant Governor in Council of the province or such other person or authority in the province as may be specified by the Lieutenant Governor in Council thereof has

(i) designated that fair or exhibition as a fair or exhibition where a lottery scheme may be conducted and managed, and

(ii) issued a licence for the conduct and management of a lottery scheme to that board or operator;

(d) for any person, pursuant to a licence issued by the Lieutenant Governor in Council of a province or by such other person or authority in the province as may be specified by the Lieutenant Governor in Council thereof, to conduct and manage a lottery scheme at a public place of amusement in that province if

(i) the amount or value of each prize awarded does not exceed five hundred dollars, and

(ii) the money or other valuable consideration paid to secure a chance to win a prize does not exceed two dollars;

(e) for the government of a province to agree with the government of another province that lots, cards or tickets in relation to a lottery scheme that is by any of paragraphs (*a*) to (*d*) authorized to be conducted and managed in that other province may be sold in the province;

(f) for any person, pursuant to a licence issued by the Lieutenant Governor in Council of a province or such other person or authority in the province as may be designated by the Lieutenant Governor in Council thereof, to conduct and manage in the province a lottery scheme that is authorized to be conducted and managed in one or more other provinces where the authority by which the lottery scheme was first authorized to be conducted and managed consents thereto;

(g) for any person, for the purpose of a lottery scheme that is lawful in a province under any of paragraphs (*a*) to (*f*), to do anything in the province, in accordance with the applicable law or licence, that is required for the conduct, management or operation of the lottery scheme or for the person to participate in the scheme; and

(h) for any person to make or print anywhere in Canada or to cause to be made or printed anywhere in Canada anything relating to gaming and betting that is to be used in a place where it is or would, if certain conditions provided by law are met, be lawful to use such a thing, or to send, transmit, mail, ship, deliver or allow to be sent, transmitted, mailed, shipped or delivered or to accept for carriage or transport or convey any such thing where the destination thereof is such a place.

(2) Terms and conditions of licence — Subject to this Act, a licence issued by or under the authority of the Lieutenant Governor in Council of a province as described in paragraph (1)(b), (c), (d), or (f) may contain such terms and conditions relating to the conduct, management and operation of or participation in the lottery scheme to which the licence relates as the Lieutenant Governor in Council of that province, the person or authority in the province designated by the Lieutenant Governor in Council thereof or any law enacted by the legislature of that province may prescribe.

(3) Offence — Every one who, for the purposes of a lottery scheme, does anything that is not authorized by or pursuant to a provision of this section

(a) in the case of the conduct, management or operation of that lottery scheme

(i) is guilty of an indictable offence and liable to imprisonment for a term not exceeding two years, or

(ii) is guilty of an offence punishable on summary conviction; or

(b) in the case of participating in that lottery scheme, is guilty of an offence punishable on summary conviction.

(4) Definition of "lottery scheme" — In this section, **"lottery scheme"** means a game or any proposal, scheme, plan, means, device, contrivance or operation described in any of paragraphs 206(1)(a) to (g), whether or not it involves betting, pool selling or a pool system of betting other than

(a) three-card monte, punch board or coin table;

(b) bookmaking, pool selling or the making or recording of bets, including bets made through the agency of a pool or pari-mutuel system, on any race or fight, or on a single sport event or athletic contest; or

(c) for the purposes of paragraphs (1)(b) to (f), a game or proposal, scheme, plan, means, device, contrivance or operation described in any of paragraphs 206(1)(a) to (g) that is operated on or through a computer, video device or slot machine, within the meaning of subsection 198(3), or a dice game.

(5) Exception re: pari-mutuel betting — For greater certainty, nothing in this section shall be construed as authorizing the making or recording of bets on horseraces through the agency of a pari-mutuel system other than in accordance with section 204.

R.S. 1985, c. 27 (1st Supp.), s. 31; c. 52 (1st Supp.), s. 3; 1999, c. 5, s. 6.

207.1 (1) Exemption — lottery scheme on an international cruise ship — Despite any of the provisions of this Part relating to gaming and betting, it is lawful for the owner or operator of an international cruise ship, or their agent, to conduct, manage or operate and for any person to participate in a lottery scheme during a voyage on an international cruise ship when all of the following conditions are satisfied:

(a) all the people participating in the lottery scheme are located on the ship;

(b) the lottery scheme is not linked, by any means of communication, with any lottery scheme, betting, pool selling or pool system of betting located off the ship;

(c) the lottery scheme is not operated within five nautical miles of a Canadian port at which the ship calls or is scheduled to call; and

(d) the ship is registered

(i) in Canada and its entire voyage is scheduled to be outside Canada, or

(ii) anywhere, including Canada, and its voyage includes some scheduled voyaging within Canada and the voyage

(A) is of at least forty-eight hours duration and includes some voyaging in international waters and at least one non-Canadian port of call including the port at which the voyage begins or ends, and

(B) is not scheduled to disembark any passengers at a Canadian port who have embarked at another Canadian port, without calling on at least one non-Canadian port between the two Canadian ports.

(2) Paragraph 207(1)(h) and subsection 207(5) apply — For greater certainty, paragraph 207(1)(h) and subsection 207(5) apply for the purposes of this section.

(3) Offence — Every one who, for the purpose of a lottery scheme, does anything that is not authorized by this section

(a) in the case of the conduct, management or operation of the lottery scheme,

(i) is guilty of an indictable offence and liable to imprisonment for a term of not more than two years, or

(ii) is guilty of an offence punishable on summary conviction; and

(b) in the case of participating in the lottery scheme, is guilty of an offence punishable on summary conviction.

(4) Definitions — The definitions in this subsection apply in this section

"international cruise ship" means a passenger ship that is suitable for continuous ocean voyages of at least forty-eight hours duration, but does not include such a ship that is used or fitted for the primary purpose of transporting cargo or vehicles.

"lottery scheme" means a game or any proposal, scheme, plan, means, device, contrivance or operation described in any of paragraphs 206(1)(a) to (g), whether or not it involves betting, pool selling or a pool system of betting. It does not include

(a) three-card monte, punch board or coin table; or

(b) bookmaking, pool selling or the making or recording of bets, including bets made through the agency of a pool or pari-mutuel system, on any race or fight, or on a single sporting event or athletic contest.

1999, c. 5, s. 7.

208. [Repealed R.S. 1985, c. 27 (1st Supp.), s. 32.]

209. Cheating at play — Every one who, with intent to defraud any person, cheats while playing a game or in holding the stakes for a game or in betting is guilty of an indictable offence and liable to imprisonment for a term not exceeding two years.

Bawdy-houses

210. (1) Keeping common bawdy-house — Every one who keeps a common bawdy-house is guilty of an indictable offence and liable to imprisonment for a term not exceeding two years.

(2) Landlord, inmate, etc. — Every one who

(a) is an inmate of a common bawdy-house,

(b) is found, without lawful excuse, in a common bawdy-house, or

(c) as owner, landord, lessor, tenant, occupier, agent or otherwise having charge or control of any place, knowingly permits the place or any part thereof to be let or used for the purposes of a common bawdy-house,

is guilty of an offence punishable on summary conviction.

(3) Notice of conviction to be served on owner — Where a person is convicted of an offence under subsection (1), the court shall cause a notice of the conviction to be served on the owner, landlord or lessor of the place in respect of which the person is convicted or his agent, and the notice shall contain a statement to the effect that it is being served pursuant to this section.

(4) Duty of landlord on notice — Where a person on whom a notice is served under subsection (3) fails forthwith to exercise any right he may have to determine the tenancy or right of occupation of the person so convicted, and thereafter any person is convicted of an offence under subsection (1) in respect of the same premises, the person on whom the notice was served shall be deemed to have committed an offence under subsection (1) unless he proves that he has taken all reasonable steps to prevent the recurrence of the offence.

211. Transporting person to bawdy-house — Every one who knowingly takes, transports, directs, or offers to take, transport, or direct any other person to a common bawdy-house is guilty of an offence punishable on summary conviction.

Procuring

212. (1) Procuring — Every one who

(a) procures, attempts to procure or solicits a person to have illicit sexual intercourse with another person, whether in or out of Canada,

(b) inveigles or entices a person who is not a prostitute to a common bawdy-house for the purpose of illicit sexual intercourse or prostitution,

(c) knowingly conceals a person in a common bawdy-house,

(d) procures or attempts to procure a person to become, whether in or out of Canada, a prostitute,

(e) procures or attempts to procure a person to leave the usual place of abode of that person in Canada, if that place is not a common bawdy-house, with intent that the person may become an inmate or frequenter of a common bawdy-house, whether in or out of Canada,

(f) on the arrival of a person in Canada, directs or causes that person to be directed or takes or causes that person to be taken, to a common bawdy-house,

(g) procures a person to enter or leave Canada, for the purpose of prostitution,

(h) for the purposes of gain, exercises control, direction or influence over the movements of a person in such manner as to show that he is aiding, abetting or compelling that person to engage in or carry on prostitution with any person or generally,

(i) applies or administers to a person or causes that person to take any drug, intoxicating liquor, matter or thing with intent to stupefy or overpower that person in order thereby to enable any person to have illicit sexual intercourse with that person, or

(j) lives wholly or in part on the avails of prostitution of another person,

is guilty of an indictable offence and liable to imprisonment for a term not exceeding ten years.

(2) Idem — Notwithstanding paragraph (1)(*j*), every person who lives wholly or in part on the avails of prostitution of another person who is under the age of eighteen years is guilty of an indictable offence and liable to imprisonment for a term not exceeding fourteen years.

(2.1) Aggravated offence in relation to living on the avails of prostitution of a person under the age of eighteen years — Notwithstanding paragraph (1)(j) and subsection (2), every person who lives wholly or in part on the avails of prostitution of another person under the age of eighteen years, and who

> (a) for the purposes of profit, aids, abets, counsels or compels the person under that age to engage in or carry on prostitution with any person or generally, and

> (b) uses, threatens to use or attempts to use violence, intimidation or coercion in relation to the person under that age,

is guilty of an indictable offence and liable to imprisonment for a term not exceeding fourteen years but not less than five years.

(3) Presumption — Evidence that a person lives with or is habitually in the company of a prostitute or lives in a common bawdy-house is, in the absence of evidence to the contrary, proof that the person lives on the avails of prostitution, for the purposes of paragraph (1)(j) and subsections (2) and (2.1).

(4) Offence — prostitution of person under eighteen — Every person who, in any place, obtains for consideration, or communicates with anyone for the purpose of obtaining for consideration, the sexual services of a person who is under the age of eighteen years is guilty of an indictable offence and liable to imprisonment for a term not exceeding five years.

(5) [Repealed 1999, c. 5, s. 8.]

R.S. 1985, c. 19 (3d Supp.), s. 9; 1997, c. 16, s. 2; 1999, c. 5, s. 8.

Offence in Relation to Prostitution

213. (1) Offence in relation to prostitution — Every person who in a public place or in any place open to public view

> (a) stops or attempts to stop any motor vehicle,

> (b) impedes the free flow of pedestrian or vehicular traffic or ingress to or egress from premises adjacent to that place, or

> (c) stops or attempts to stop any person or in any manner communicates or attempts to communicate with any person

for the purpose of engaging in prostitution or of obtaining the sexual services of a prostitute is guilty of an offence punishable on summary conviction.

(2) Definition of "public place" — In this section, **"public place"** includes any place to which the public have access as of right or by invitation, express or implied, and any motor vehicle located in a public place or in any place open to public view.

R.S. 1985, c. 51 (1st Supp.), s. 1.

PART VIII — OFFENCES AGAINST THE PERSON AND REPUTATION

Interpretation

214. Definitions — In this Part,

"abandon" or **"expose"** includes

(a) a wilful omission to take charge of a child by a person who is under a legal duty to do so, and

(b) dealing with a child in a manner that is likely to leave that child exposed to risk without protection;

"aircraft" does not include a machine designed to derive support in the atmosphere primarily from reactions against the earth's surface of air expelled from the machine;

"child" includes an adopted child and an illegitimate child;

"form of marriage" includes a ceremony of marriage that is recognized as valid

(a) by the law of the place where it was celebrated, or

(b) by the law of the place where an accused is tried, notwithstanding that it is not recognized as valid by the law of the place where it was celebrated;

"guardian" includes a person who has in law or in fact the custody or control of a child.

"operate"

(a) means, in respect of a motor vehicle, to drive the vehicle,

(b) means, in respect of railway equipment, to participate in the direct control of its motion, whether

(i) as a member of the crew of the equipment,

(ii) as a person who, by remote control, acts in lieu of such crew, or

(iii) as other than a member or person described in subparagraphs (i) and (ii), and

(c) includes, in respect of a vessel or an aircraft, to navigate the vessel or aircraft;

"vessel" includes a machine designed to derive support in the atmosphere primarily from reactions against the earth's surface of air expelled from the machine.

R.S. 1985, c. 27 (1st Supp.), s. 33; c. 32 (4th Supp.), s. 56.

Duties Tending to Preservation of Life

215. (1) Duty of persons to provide necessaries — Every one is under a legal duty

    (a) as a parent, foster parent, guardian or head of a family, to provide necessaries of life for a child under the age of sixteen years;

    (b) as a married person, to provide necessaries of life to his spouse; and

Proposed Amendment — 215(1)(b)

    (b) to provide necessaries of life to their spouse or common-law partner; and

2000, c. 12, s. 93(1) [Not in force at date of publication.]

    (c) to provide necessaries of life to a person under his charge if that person

        (i) is unable, by reason of detention, age, illness, mental disorder or other cause, to withdraw himself from that charge, and

        (ii) is unable to provide himself with necessaries of life.

(2) Offence — Every one commits an offence who, being under a legal duty within the meaning of subsection (1), fails without lawful excuse, the proof of which lies on him, to perform that duty, if

    (a) with respect to a duty imposed by paragraph (l)(a) or (b),

        (i) the person to whom the duty is owed is in destitute or necessitous circumstances, or

        (ii) the failure to perform the duty endangers the life of the person to whom the duty is owed, or causes or is likely to cause the health of that person to be endangered permanently; or

    (b) with respect to a duty imposed by paragraph (1)(c), the failure to perform the duty endangers the life of the person to whom the duty is owed or causes or is likely to cause the health of that person to be injured permanently.

(3) Punishment — Every one who commits an offence under subsection (2) is guilty of

    (a) an indictable offence and is liable to imprisonment for a term not exceeding two years; or

    (b) an offence punishable on summary conviction.

(4) Presumptions — For the purpose of proceedings under this section,

    (a) evidence that a person has cohabited with a person of the opposite sex or has in any way recognized that person as being his spouse is, in the absence of any evidence to the contrary, proof that they are lawfully married;

Proposed Repeal — 215(4)(a)

    (a) [Repealed 2000, c. 12, s. 93(2). Not in force at date of publication.]

    (b) evidence that a person has in any way recognized a child as being his child is, in the absence of any evidence to the contrary, proof that the child is his child;

(c) evidence that a person has left his spouse and has failed, for a period of any one month subsequent to the time of his so leaving, to make provision for the maintenance of his spouse or for the maintenance of any child of his under the age of sixteen years is, in the absence of any evidence to the contrary, proof that he has failed without lawful excuse to provide necessaries of life for them; and

Proposed Amendment — 215(4)(c)

(c) evidence that a person has failed for a period of one month to make provision for the maintenance of any child of theirs under the age of sixteen years is, in the absence of any evidence to the contrary, proof that the person has failed without lawful excuse to provide necessaries of life for the child; and

2000, c. 12, s. 93(3) [Not in force at date of publication.]

(d) the fact that a spouse or child is receiving or has received necessaries of life from another person who is not under a legal duty to provide them is not a defence.

Proposed Amendment — 215(4)(d)

(d) the fact that a spouse or common-law partner or child is receiving or has received necessaries of life from another person who is not under a legal duty to provide them is not a defence.

2000, c. 12, s. 95(a) [Not in force at date of publication.]

1991, c. 43, s. 9, Schedule, item 2.

216. Duty of persons undertaking acts dangerous to life — Every one who undertakes to administer surgical or medical treatment to another person or to do any other lawful act that may endanger the life of another person is, except in cases of necessity, under a legal duty to have and to use reasonable knowledge, skill and care in so doing.

217. Duty of persons undertaking acts — Every one who undertakes to do an act is under a legal duty to do it if an omission to do the act is or may be dangerous to life.

218. Abandoning child — Every one who unlawfully abandons or exposes a child who is under the age of ten years, so that its life is or is likely to be endangered or its health is or is likely to be permanently injured, is guilty of an indictable offence and liable to imprisonment for a term not exceeding two years.

Criminal Negligence

219. (1) Criminal negligence — Every one is criminally negligent who

(a) in doing anything, or

(b) in omitting to do anything that it is his duty to do,

shows wanton or reckless disregard for the lives or safety of other persons.

(2) "duty" — For the purposes of this section, **"duty"** means a duty imposed by law.

220. Causing death by criminal negligence — Every person who by criminal negligence causes death to another person is guilty of an indictable offence and liable

(a) where a firearm is used in the commission of the offence, to imprisonment for life and to a minimum punishment of imprisonment for a term of four years; and

(b) in any other case, to imprisonment for life.

1995, c. 39, s. 141.

221. Causing bodily harm by criminal negligence — Every one who by criminal negligence causes bodily harm to another person is guilty of an indictable offence and liable to imprisonment for a term not exceeding ten years.

Homicide

222. (1) Homicide — A person commits homicide when, directly or indirectly, by any means, he causes the death of a human being.

(2) Kinds of homicide — Homicide is culpable or not culpable.

(3) Non culpable homicide — Homicide that is not culpable is not an offence.

(4) Culpable homicide — Culpable homicide is murder or manslaughter or infanticide.

(5) Idem — A person commits culpable homicide when he causes the death of a human being,

(a) by means of an unlawful act,

(b) by criminal negligence,

(c) by causing that human being, by threats or fear of violence or by deception, to do anything that causes his death, or

(d) by wilfully frightening that human being, in the case of a child or sick person.

(6) Exception — Notwithstanding anything in this section, a person does not commit homicide within the meaning of this Act by reason only that he causes the death of a human being by procuring, by false evidence, the conviction and death of that human being by sentence of the law.

223. (1) When child becomes human being — A child becomes a human being within the meaning of this Act when it has completely proceeded, in a living state, from the body of its mother whether or not

(a) it has breathed,

(b) it has an independent circulation, or

(c) the navel string is severed.

(2) Killing child — A person commits homicide when he causes injury to a child before or during its birth as a result of which the child dies after becoming a human being.

224. Death which might have been prevented — Where a person, by an act or omission, does any thing that results in the death of a human being, he causes the death of that human being notwithstanding that death from that cause might have been prevented by resorting to proper means.

225. Death from treatment of injury — Where a person causes to a human being a bodily injury that is of itself of a dangerous nature and from which death results, he causes the death of that human being notwithstanding that the immediate cause of death is proper or improper treatment that is applied in good faith.

226. Acceleration of death — Where a person causes to a human being a bodily injury that results in death, he causes the death of that human being notwithstanding that the effect of the bodily injury is only to accelerate his death from a disease or disorder arising from some other cause.

227. [Repealed 1999, c. 5, s. 9(1).]

> *Section 227 was repealed by S.C. 1999, c. 5, s. 9(1), which came into force on March 11, 1999. Under the terms of S.C. 1999, c. 5, s. 9(2), the s. 9(1) repeal applies with respect to an offence referred to in s. 227 if the last event by means of which a person caused or contributed to the cause of death occurs after the coming into force of that subsection or occurred not more than one year and a day before its coming into force. Immediately before its repeal, s. 227 read as follows:*

> *227.* **Death within year and a day** — *No person commits culpable homicide or the offence of causing the death of a person by criminal negligence or by means of the commission of an offence under subsection 249(4) or 255(3) unless the death occurs within one year and one day from the time of the occurrence of the last event by means of which the person caused or contributed to the cause of death.*

228. Killing by influence on the mind — No person commits culpable homicide where he causes the death of a human being

(a) by any influence on the mind alone, or

(b) by any disorder or disease resulting from influence on the mind alone,

but this section does not apply where a person causes the death of a child or sick person by wilfully frightening him.

Murder, Manslaughter and Infanticide

229. Murder — Culpable homicide is murder

(a) where the person who causes the death of a human being

(i) means to cause his death, or

(ii) means to cause him bodily harm that he knows is likely to cause his death, and is reckless whether death ensues or not;

(b) where a person, meaning to cause death to a human being or meaning to cause him bodily harm that he knows is likely to cause his death, and being reckless whether death ensues or not, by accident or mistake causes death to another human being, notwithstanding that he does not mean to cause death or bodily harm to that human being; or

(c) where a person, for an unlawful object, does anything that he knows or ought to know is likely to cause death, and thereby causes death to a human being, notwithstanding that he desires to effect his object without causing death or bodily harm to any human being.

230. Murder in commission of offences — Culpable homicide is murder where a person causes the death of a human being while committing or attempting to commit high treason or treason or an offence mentioned in section 52 (sabotage), 75 (piratical acts), 76 (hijacking an aircraft), 144 or subsection 145(1) or sections 146 to 148 (escape or rescue from prison or lawful custody), section 270 (assaulting a peace officer), section 271 (sexual assault), 272 (sexual assault with a weapon, threats to a third party or causing bodily harm), 273 (aggravated sexual assault), 279 (kidnapping and forcible confinement), 279.1 (hostage taking), 343 (robbery), 348 (breaking and entering) or 433 or 434 (arson), whether or not the person means to cause death to any human being and whether or not he knows that death is likely to be caused to any human being, if

(a) he means to cause bodily harm for the purpose of

(i) facilitating the commission of the offence, or

(ii) facilitating his flight after committing or attempting to commit the offence,

and the death ensues from the bodily harm;

(b) he administers a stupefying or overpowering thing for a purpose mentioned in paragraph (*a*), and the death ensues therefrom; or

(c) he wilfully stops, by any means, the breath of a human being for a purpose mentioned in paragraph (*a*), and the death ensues therefrom,

and the death ensues as a consequence.

R.S. 1985, c. 27 (1st Supp.), s. 40(2); 1991, c. 4, s. 1.

231. (1) Classification of murder — Murder is first degree murder or second degree murder.

(2) Planned and deliberate murder — Murder is first degree murder when it is planned and deliberate.

(3) Contracted murder — Without limiting the generality of subsection (2), murder is planned and deliberate when it is committed pursuant to an arrangement under which money or anything of value passes or is intended to pass from one person to another, or is promised by one person to another, as consideration for that other's causing or assisting in causing the death of anyone or counselling another person to do any act causing or assisting in causing that death.

(4) Murder of peace officer, etc. — Irrespective of whether a murder is planned and deliberate on the part of any person, murder is first degree murder when the victim is

(a) a police officer, police constable, constable, sheriff, deputy sheriff, sheriff's officer or other person employed for the preservation and maintenance of the public peace, acting in the course of his duties;

(b) a warden, deputy warden, instructor, keeper, jailer, guard or other officer or a permanent employee of a prison, acting in the course of his duties; or

(c) a person working in a prison with the permission of the prison authorities and acting in the course of his work therein.

(5) Hijacking, sexual assault or kidnapping — Irrespective of whether a murder is planned and deliberate on the part of any person, murder is first degree murder in respect of a person when the death is caused by that person while committing or attempting to commit an offence under one of the following sections:

(a) section 76 (hijacking an aircraft);

(b) section 271 (sexual assault);

(c) section 272 (sexual assault with a weapon, threats to a third party or causing bodily harm);

(d) section 273 (aggravated sexual assault);

(e) section 279 (kidnapping and forcible confinement); or

(f) section 279.1 (hostage taking).

(6) Criminal harassment — Irrespective of whether a murder is planned and deliberate on the part of any person, murder is first degree murder when the death is caused by that person while committing or attempting to commit an offence under section 264 and the person committing that offence intended to cause the person murdered to fear for the safety of the person murdered or the safety of anyone known to the person murdered.

(6.1) Using explosives in association with criminal organization — Irrespective of whether a murder is planned and deliberate on the part of a person, murder is first degree murder when the death is caused while committing or attempting to commit an offence under section 81 for the benefit of, at the direction of or in association with a criminal organization.

(7) Second degree murder — All murder that is not first degree murder is second degree murder.

R.S. 1985, c. 27 (1st Supp.), ss. 7(2), 35, 40(2); 1997, c. 16, s. 3; c. 23, s. 8.

232. (1) Murder reduced to manslaughter — Culpable homicide that otherwise would be murder may be reduced to manslaughter if the person who committed it did so in the heat of passion caused by sudden provocation.

(2) What is provocation — A wrongful act or insult that is of such a nature as to be sufficient to deprive an ordinary person of the power of self-control is provocation for the purposes of this section if the accused acted on it on the sudden and before there was time for his passion to cool.

(3) Questions of fact — For the purposes of this section, the questions

(a) whether a particular wrongful act or insult amounted to provocation, and

(b) whether the accused was deprived of the power of self-control by the provocation that he alleges he received,

are questions of fact, but no one shall be deemed to have given provocation to another by doing anything that he had a legal right to do, or by doing anything that the accused incited him to do in order to provide the accused with an excuse for causing death or bodily harm to any human being.

(4) Death during illegal arrest — Culpable homicide that otherwise would be murder is not necessarily manslaughter by reason only that it was committed by a person who was being arrested illegally, but the fact that the illegality of the arrest was known to the accused may be evidence of provocation for the purpose of this section.

233. Infanticide — A female person commits infanticide when by a wilful act or omission she causes the death of her newly-born child, if at the time of the act or omission she is not fully recovered from the effects of giving birth to the child and by reason thereof or of the effect of lactation consequent on the birth of the child her mind is then disturbed.

234. Manslaughter — Culpable homicide that is not murder or infanticide is manslaughter.

235. (1) Punishment for murder — Every one who commits first degree murder or second degree murder is guilty of an indictable offence and shall be sentenced to imprisonment for life.

(2) Minimum punishment — For the purposes of Part XXIII, the sentence of imprisonment for life prescribed by this section is a minimum punishment.

236. Manslaughter — Every person who commits manslaughter is guilty of an indictable offence and liable

(a) where a firearm is used in the commission of the offence, to imprisonment for life and to a minimum punishment of imprisonment for a term of four years; and

(b) in any other case, to imprisonment for life.

1995, c. 39, s. 142.

237. Punishment for infanticide — Every female person who commits infanticide is guilty of an indictable offence and liable to imprisonment for a term not exceeding five years.

238. (1) Killing unborn child in act of birth — Every one who causes the death, in the act of birth, of any child that has not become a human being, in such a manner that, if the child were a human being, he would be guilty of murder, is guilty of an indictable offence and liable to imprisonment for life.

(2) Saving — This section does not apply to a person who, by means that, in good faith, he considers necessary to preserve the life of the mother of a child, causes the death of that child.

239. Attempt to commit murder — Every person who attempts by any means to commit murder is guilty of an indictable offence and liable

    (a) where a firearm is used in the commission of the offence, to imprisonment for life and to a minimum punishment of imprisonment for a term of four years; and

    (b) in any other case, to imprisonment for life.

1995, c. 39, s. 143.

240. Accessory after fact to murder — Every one who is an accessory after the fact to murder is guilty of an indictable offence and liable to imprisonment for life.

Suicide

241. Counselling or aiding suicide — Every one who

    (a) counsels a person to commit suicide, or

    (b) aids or abets a person to commit suicide,

whether suicide ensues or not, is guilty of an indictable offence and liable to imprisonment for a term not exceeding fourteen years.

R.S. 1985, c. 27 (1st Supp.), s. 7(3).

Neglect in Child-birth and Concealing Dead Body

242. Neglect to obtain assistance in child-birth — A female person who, being pregnant and about to be delivered, with intent that the child shall not live or with intent to conceal the birth of the child, fails to make provision for reasonable assistance in respect of her delivery is, if the child is permanently injured as a result thereof or dies immediately before, during or in a short time after birth, as a result thereof, guilty of an indictable offence and is liable to imprisonment for a term not exceeding five years.

243. Concealing body of child — Every one who in any manner disposes of the dead body of a child, with intent to conceal the fact that its mother has been delivered of it, whether the child died before, during or after birth, is guilty of an indictable offence and liable to imprisonment for a term not exceeding two years.

Bodily Harm and Acts and Omissions Causing Danger to the Person

244. Causing bodily harm with intent — firearm — Every person who, with intent

    (a) to wound, maim or disfigure any person,

(b) to endanger the life of any person, or

(c) to prevent the arrest or detention of any person,

discharges a firearm at any person, whether or not that person is the person mentioned in paragraph (*a*), (*b*) or (*c*), is guilty of an indictable offence and liable to imprisonment for a term not exceeding fourteen years and to a minimum punishment of imprisonment for a term of four years.

1995, c. 39, s. 144

244.1 Causing bodily harm with intent — air gun or pistol — Every person who, with intent

(a) to wound, maim or disfigure any person,

(b) to endanger the life of any person, or

(c) to prevent the arrest or detention of any person,

discharges an air or compressed gas gun or pistol at any person, whether or not that person is the person mentioned in paragraph (*a*), (*b*) or (*c*), is guilty of an indictable offence and liable to imprisonment for a term not exceeding fourteen years.

1995, c. 39, s. 144.

245. Administering noxious thing — Every one who administers or causes to be administered to any person or causes any person to take poison or any other destructive or noxious thing is guilty of an indictable offence and liable

(a) to imprisonment for a term not exceeding fourteen years, if he intends thereby to endanger the life of or to cause bodily harm to that person; or

(b) to imprisonment for a term not exceeding two years, if he intends thereby to aggrieve or annoy that person.

246. Overcoming resistance to commission of offence — Every one who, with intent to enable or assist himself or another person to commit an indictable offence,

(a) attempts, by any means, to choke, suffocate or strangle another person, or by any means calculated to choke, suffocate or strangle, attempts to render another person insensible, unconscious or incapable of resistance, or

(b) administers, or causes to be administered to any person, or attempts to administer to any person, or causes or attempts to cause any person to take a stupefying or overpowering drug, matter or thing,

is guilty of an indictable offence and liable to imprisonment for life.

247. (1) Traps likely to cause bodily harm — Every one who, with intent to cause death or bodily harm to persons, whether ascertained or not, sets or places or causes to be set or placed a trap, device or other thing whatever that is likely to cause death or bodily harm to persons is guilty of an indictable offence and liable to imprisonment for a term not exceeding five years.

(2) Permitting traps on premises — A person who, being in occupation or possession of a place where anything mentioned in subsection (1) has been set or

placed, knowingly and wilfully permits it to remain at that place, shall be deemed, for the purposes of that subsection, to have set or placed it with the intent mentioned therein.

248. Interfering with transportation facilities — Every one who, with intent to endanger the safety of any persons, places anything on or does anything to any property that is used for or in connection with the transportation of persons or goods by land, water or air that is likely to cause death or bodily harm to persons is guilty of an indictable offence and liable to imprisonment for life.

Motor Vehicles, Vessels and Aircraft

249. (1) Dangerous operation of motor vehicles, vessels and aircraft — Every one commits an offence who operates

(a) a motor vehicle in a manner that is dangerous to the public, having regard to all the circumstances, including the nature, condition and use of the place at which the motor vehicle is being operated and the amount of traffic that at the time is or might reasonably be expected to be at that place;

(b) a vessel or any water skis, surf-board, water sled or other towed object on or over any of the internal waters of Canada or the territorial sea of Canada, in a manner that is dangerous to the public, having regard to all the circumstances, including the nature and condition of those waters or sea and the use that at the time is or might reasonably be expected to be made of those waters or sea;

(c) an aircraft in a manner that is dangerous to the public, having regard to all the circumstances, including the nature and condition of that aircraft or the place or air space in or through which the aircraft is operated; or

(d) railway equipment in a manner that is dangerous to the public, having regard to all the circumstances, including the nature and condition of the equipment or the place in or through which the equipment is operated.

(2) Punishment — Every one who commits an offence under subsection (1)

(a) is guilty of an indictable offence and liable to imprisonment for a term not exceeding five years; or

(b) is guilty of an offence punishable on summary conviction.

(3) Dangerous operation causing bodily harm — Every one who commits an offence under subsection (1) and thereby causes bodily harm to any other person is guilty of an indictable offence and liable to imprisonment for a term not exceeding ten years.

(4) Dangerous operation causing death — Every one who commits an offence under subsection (1) and thereby causes the death of any other person is guilty of an indictable offence and liable to imprisonment for a term not exceeding fourteen years.

R.S. 1985, c. 27 (1st Supp.), s. 36; c. 32 (4th Supp.), s. 57; 1994, c. 44, s. 11.

249.1 (1) Flight — Every one commits an offence who, operating a motor vehicle while being pursued by a peace officer operating a motor vehicle, fails, without reasonable excuse and in order to evade the peace officer, to stop the vehicle as soon as is reasonable in the circumstances.

(2) Punishment — Every one who commits an offence under subsection (1)

(a) is guilty of an indictable offence and liable to imprisonment for a term not exceeding five years; or

(b) is guilty of an offence punishable on summary conviction.

(3) Flight causing bodily harm or death — Every one commits an offence who causes bodily harm to or the death of another person by operating a motor vehicle in a manner described in paragraph 249(1)(a), if the person operating the motor vehicle was being pursued by a peace officer operating a motor vehicle and failed, without reasonable excuse and in order to evade the police officer, to stop the vehicle as soon as is reasonable in the circumstances.

(4) Punishment — Every person who commits an offence under subsection (3)

(a) if bodily harm was caused, is guilty of an indictable offence and liable to imprisonment for a term not exceeding 14 years; and

(b) if death was caused, is guilty of an indictable offence and liable to imprisonment for life.

2000, c. 2, s. 1

250. (1) Failure to keep watch on person towed — Every one who operates a vessel while towing a person on any water skis, surf-board, water sled or other object, when there is not on board such vessel another responsible person keeping watch on the person being towed, is guilty of an offence punishable on summary conviction.

(2) Towing of person after dark — Every one who operates a vessel while towing a person on any water skis, surf-board, water sled or other object during the period from one hour after sunset to sunrise is guilty of an offence punishable on summary conviction.

R.S. 1985, c. 27 (1st Supp.), s. 36.

251. (1) Unseaworthy vessel and unsafe aircraft — Every one who knowingly

(a) sends or being the master takes a vessel that is registered or licensed, or for which an identification number has been issued, pursuant to any Act of Parliament and that is unseaworthy

(i) on a voyage from a place in Canada to any other place in or out of Canada, or

(ii) on a voyage from a place on the inland waters of the United States to a place in Canada,

(b) sends an aircraft on a flight or operates an aircraft that is not fit and safe for flight, or

    (c) sends for operation or operates railway equipment that is not fit and safe for operation

and thereby endangers the life of any person, is guilty of an indictable offence and liable to imprisonment for a term not exceeding five years.

(2) Defences — An accused shall not be convicted of an offence under this section where the accused establishes that,

    (a) in the case of an offence under paragraph (1)(a),

        (i) the accused used all reasonable means to ensure that the vessel was seaworthy, or

        (ii) to send or take the vessel while it was unseaworthy was, under the circumstances, reasonable and justifiable;

    (b) in the case of an offence under paragraph (1)(*b*),

        (i) the accused used all reasonable means to ensure that the aircraft was fit and safe for flight, or

        (ii) to send or operate the aircraft while it was not fit and safe for flight was, under the circumstances, reasonable and justifiable; and

    (c) in the case of an offence under paragraph (1)(c),

        (i) the accused used all reasonable means to ensure that the railway equipment was fit and safe for operation, or

        (ii) to send the railway equipment for operation or to operate it while it was not fit and safe for operation was, under the circumstances, reasonable and justifiable.

(3) Consent of Attorney General — No proceedings shall be instituted under this section in respect of a vessel or aircraft, or in respect of railway equipment sent for operation or operated on a line of railway that is within the legislative authority of Parliament, without the consent in writing of the Attorney General of Canada.

R.S. 1985, c. 27 (1st Supp.), s. 36; c. 32 (4th Supp.), s. 58.

252. (1) Failure to stop at scene of accident — Every person commits an offence who has the care, charge or control of a vehicle, vessel or aircraft that is involved in an accident with

    (a) another person,

    (b) a vehicle, vessel or aircraft, or

    (c) in the case of a vehicle, cattle in the charge of another person,

and with intent to escape civil or criminal liability fails to stop the vehicle, vessel or, if possible, the aircraft, give his or her name and address and, where any person has been injured or appears to require assistance, offer assistance.

(1.1) Punishment — Every person who commits an offence under subsection (1) in a case not referred to in subsection (1.2) or (1.3) is guilty of an indictable offence and liable to imprisonment for a term not exceeding five years or is guilty of an offence punishable on summary conviction.

(1.2) Offence involving bodily harm — Every person who commits an offence under subsection (1) knowing that bodily harm has been caused to another person involved in the accident is guilty of an indictable offence and liable to imprisonment for a term not exceeding ten years.

(1.3) Offence involving bodily harm or death — Every person who commits an offence under subsection (1) is guilty of an indictable offence and liable to imprisonment for life if

(a) the person knows that another person involved in the accident is dead; or

(b) the person knows that bodily harm has been caused to another person involved in the accident and is reckless as to whether the death of the other person results from that bodily harm, and the death of that other person so results.

(2) Evidence — In proceedings under subsection (1), evidence that an accused failed to stop his vehicle, vessel or, where possible, his aircraft, as the case may be, offer assistance where any person has been injured or appears to require assistance and give his name and address is, in the absence of evidence to the contrary, proof of an intent to escape civil or criminal liability.

R.S. 1985, c. 27 (1st Supp.), s. 36; 1994, c. 44, s. 12; 1999, c. 32, s. 1.

Section 252 formerly prescribed a single maximum penalty of five years' imprisonment for all offences thereunder, regardless of circumstances. Section 1 of S.C. 1999, c. 32 increased the maximum penalty to ten years in circumstances where the accused fails to stop knowing that bodily harm has been caused and to life imprisonment where the accused fails to stop knowing that death has been caused. Section 7 of S.C. 1999, c. 32 provides, however, that where any penalty or punishment provided by the Criminal Code *is varied by 1999, c. 32, the lesser penalty or punishment applies in respect of any offence that was committed before the coming into force of section 7 (i.e. before July 1, 1999). The five year maximum would thus continue to apply for offences involving bodily harm or death committed before that date.*

253. Operation while impaired — Every one commits an offence who operates a motor vehicle or vessel or operates or assists in the operation of an aircraft or of railway equipment or has the care or control of a motor vehicle, vessel, aircraft or railway equipment, whether it is in motion or not,

(a) while the person's ability to operate the vehicle, vessel, aircraft or railway equipment is impaired by alcohol or a drug; or

(b) having consumed alcohol in such a quantity that the concentration in the person's blood exceeds eighty milligrams of alcohol in one hundred millilitres of blood.

R.S. 1985, c. 27 (1st Supp.), s. 36; c. 32 (4th Supp.), s. 59.

254. (1) Definitions — In this section and sections 255 to 258,

"analyst" means a person designated by the Attorney General as an analyst for the purposes of section 258;

"approved container" means

    (a) in respect of breath samples, a container of a kind that is designed to receive a sample of the breath of a person for analysis and is approved as suitable for the purposes of section 258 by order of the Attorney General of Canada, and

    (b) in respect of blood samples, a container of a kind that is designed to receive a sample of the blood of a person for analysis and is approved as suitable for the purposes of section 258 by order of the Attorney General of Canada;

"approved instrument" means an instrument of a kind that is designed to receive and make an analysis of a sample of the breath of a person in order to measure the concentration of alcohol in the blood of that person and is approved as suitable for the purposes of section 258 by order of the Attorney General of Canada;

"approved screening device" means a device of a kind that is designed to ascertain the presence of alcohol in the blood of a person and that is approved for the purposes of this section by order of the Attorney General of Canada;

"qualified medical practitioner" means a person duly qualified by provincial law to practise medicine.

"qualified technician" means,

    (a) in respect of breath samples, a person designated by the Attorney General as being qualified to operate an approved instrument, and

    (b) in respect of blood samples, any person or person of a class of persons designated by the Attorney General as being qualified to take samples of blood for the purposes of this section and sections 256 and 258.

(2) Testing for presence of alcohol in the blood — Where a peace officer reasonably suspects that a person who is operating a motor vehicle or vessel or operating or assisting in the operation of an aircraft or of railway equipment or who has the care or control of a motor vehicle, vessel, aircraft or railway equipment, whether it is in motion or not, has alcohol in the person's body, the peace officer may, by demand made to that person, require the person to provide forthwith such a sample of breath as in the opinion of the peace officer is necessary to enable a proper analysis of the breath to be made by means of an approved screening device and, where necessary, to accompany the peace officer for the purpose of enabling such a sample of breath to be taken.

(3) Samples of breath or blood where reasonable belief of commission of offence — Where a peace officer believes on reasonable and probable grounds that a person is committing, or at any time within the preceding three hours has committed, as a result of the consumption of alcohol, an offence under section 253, the peace officer may, by demand made to that person forthwith or as soon as practicable, require that person to provide then or as soon thereafter as is practicable

    (a) such samples of the person's breath as in the opinion of a qualified technician, or

(b) where the peace officer has reasonable and probable grounds to believe that, by reason of any physical condition of the person,

 (i) the person may be incapable of providing a sample of his breath; or

 (ii) it would be impracticable to obtain a sample of his breath,

such samples of the person's blood, under the conditions referred to in subsection(4), as in the opinion of the qualified medical practitioner or qualified technician taking the samples

are necessary to enable proper analysis to be made in order to determine the concentration, if any, of alcohol in the person's blood, and to accompany the peace officer for the purpose of enabling such samples to be taken.

(4) Exception — Samples of blood may only be taken from a person pursuant to a demand made by a peace officer under subsection (3) if the samples are taken by or under the direction of a qualified medical practitioner and the qualified medical practitioner is satisfied that the taking of those samples would not endanger the life or health of the person.

(5) Failure or refusal to provide sample — Every one commits an offence who, without reasonable excuse, fails or refuses to comply with a demand made to him by a peace officer under this section.

(6) Only one determination of guilt for failure to comply with demand — A person who is convicted of an offence committed under subsection (5) for a failure or refusal to comply with a demand made under subsection (2) or paragraph (3)(a) or (b) in respect of any transaction may not be convicted of another offence committed under subsection (5) in respect of the same transaction.

R.S. 1985, c. 27 (1st Supp.), s. 36; c. 1 (4th Supp.), s. 14; c. 32 (4th Supp.), s. 60; 1999, c. 32, s. 2.

255. (1) Punishment — Every one who commits an offence under section 253 or 254 is guilty of an indictable offence or an offence punishable on summary conviction and is liable,

(a) whether the offence is prosecuted by indictment or punishable on summary conviction, to the following minimum punishment, namely,

 (i) for a first offence, to a fine of not less than six hundred dollars,

 (ii) for a second offence, to imprisonment for not less than fourteen days, and

 (iii) for each subsequent offence, to imprisonment for not less than ninety days;

(b) where the offence is prosecuted by indictment, to imprisonment for a term not exceeding five years; and

(c) where the offence is punishable on summary conviction, to imprisonment for a term not exceeding six months.

Note: Section 3 of S.C. 1999, c. 32, increased the maximum fine prescribed by s. 255(1)(a)(i) for a first offence under s. 253 or 254 from three hundred to six hundred dollars. Section 7 of S.C. 1999, c. 32, provides, however, that where any penalty or punishment provided by the Criminal Code *is varied by 1999, c. 32, the lesser penalty or punishment applies in respect to any offence that was committed before the coming into force of section 7 (i.e. before July 1, 1999). The three hundred dollar maximum would thus continue to apply to first offences committed before that date.*

(2) Impaired driving causing bodily harm — Every one who commits an offence under paragraph 253(*a*) and thereby causes bodily harm to any other person is guilty of an indictable offence and liable to imprisonment for a term not exceeding ten years.

(3) Impaired driving causing death — Every one who commits an offence under paragraph 253(*a*) and thereby causes the death of any other person is guilty of an indictable offence and liable to imprisonment for a term not exceeding fourteen years.

Proposed Amendment — 255(3)

(3) Impaired driving causing death — Every one who commits an offence under paragraph 253(*a*) and thereby causes the death of any other person is guilty of an indictable offence and liable to imprisonment for life.

2000, c. 25, s. 2 [Not in force at date of publication.]

(4) Previous convictions — Where a person is convicted of an offence committed under paragraph 253(a) or (b) or subsection 254(5), that person shall, for the purposes of this Act, be deemed to be convicted for a second or subsequent offence, as the case may be, if the person has previously been convicted of

　(a) an offence committed under any of those provisions;

　(b) an offence under subsection (2) or (3); or

　(c) an offence under section 250, 251, 252, 253, 259 or 260 or subsection 258(4) of this Act as this Act read immediately before the coming into force of this subsection.

(5) Conditional discharge — Notwithstanding subsection 730(1), a court may, instead of convicting a person of an offence committed under section 253, after hearing medical or other evidence, if it considers that the person is in need of curative treatment in relation to his consumption of alcohol or drugs and that it would not be contrary to the public interest, by order direct that the person be discharged under section 730 on the conditions prescribed in a probation order, including a condition respecting the person's attendance for curative treatment in relation to his consumption of alcohol or drugs.

Note: s. 255(5) has been proclaimed in force in the provinces of Alberta, Manitoba, New Brunswick, Nova Scotia, Prince Edward Island, Saskatchewan and in Yukon Territory and Northwest Territories.

R.S. 1985, c. 27 (1st Supp.), s. 36; 1995, c. 22, s. 18, Sch. IV, item 26; 1999, c. 32, s. 3

255.1 Aggravating circumstances for sentencing purposes — Without limiting the generality of section 718.2, where a court imposes a sentence for an offence committed under this Act by means of a motor vehicle, vessel or aircraft or of railway equipment, evidence that the concentration of alcohol in the blood of the offender at the time when the offence was committed exceeded one hundred and sixty milligrams of alcohol in one hundred millilitres of blood shall be deemed to be aggravating circumstances relating to the offence that the court shall consider under paragraph 718.2(a).

1999, c. 32, s. 4

256. (1) Warrants to obtain blood samples — Subject to subsection (2), where a justice is satisfied, on an information on oath in Form 1 or on an information on oath submitted to the justice pursuant to section 487.1 by telephone or other means of telecommunication, that there are reasonable grounds to believe that

(a) a person has, within the preceding four hours, committed, as a result of the consumption of alcohol, an offence under, section 253 and the person was involved in an accident resulting in the death of another person or in bodily harm to himself or herself or to any other person, and

(b) a qualified medical practitioner is of the opinion that

(i) by reason of any physical or mental condition of the person that resulted from the consumption of alcohol, the accident or any other occurrence related to or resulting from the accident, the person is unable to consent to the taking of samples of his blood, and

(ii) the taking of samples of blood from the person would not endanger the life or health of the person,

the justice may issue a warrant authorizing a peace officer to require a qualified medical practitioner to take, or to cause to be taken by a qualified technician under the direction of the qualified medical practitioner, such samples of the blood of the person as in the opinion of the person taking the samples are necessary to enable a proper analysis to be made in order to determine the concentration, if any, of alcohol in his blood.

Proposed Amendment — 256(1)

(1) Warrants to obtain blood samples — Subject to subsection (2), if a justice is satisfied, on an information on oath in Form 1 or on an information on oath submitted to the justice under section 487.1 by telephone or other means of telecommunication, that there are reasonable grounds to believe that

(a) a person has, within the preceding four hours, committed, as a result of the consumption of alcohol or a drug, an offence under section 253 and the person was involved in an accident resulting in the death of another person or in bodily harm to himself or herself or to any other person, and

(b) a qualified medical practitioner is of the opinion that

(i) by reason of any physical or mental condition of the person that resulted from the consumption of alcohol or a drug, the accident or any other occurrence related to or resulting from the accident, the person is unable to consent to the taking of samples of his or her blood, and

(ii) the taking of samples of blood from the person would not endanger the life or health of the person,

the justice may issue a warrant authorizing a peace officer to require a qualified medical practitioner to take, or to cause to be taken by a qualified technician under the direction of the qualified medical practitioner, the samples of the blood of the person that in the opinion of the person taking the samples are necessary to enable a proper analysis to be made in order to determine the concentration, if any, of alcohol or drugs in the person's blood.

2000, c. 25, s. 3 [Not in force at date of publication.]

(2) Form — A warrant issued pursuant to subsection (1) may be in Form 5 or 5.1 varied to suit the case.

(3) Information on oath — Notwithstanding paragraphs 487.1(4)(*b*) and (*c*), an information on oath submitted by telephone or other means of telecommunication for the purposes of this section shall include, instead of the statements referred to in those paragraphs, a statement setting out the offence alleged to have been committed and identifying the person from whom blood samples are to be taken.

(4) Duration of warrant — Samples of blood may be taken from a person pursuant to a warrant issued pursuant to subsection (1) only during such time as a qualified medical practitioner is satisfied that the conditions referred to in subparagraphs (1)(*b*)(i) and (ii) continue to exist in respect of that person.

(5) Facsimile to person — Where a warrant issued pursuant to subsection (1) is executed, the peace officer shall, as soon as practicable thereafter, give a copy or, in the case of a warrant issued by telephone or other means of telecommunication, a facsimile of the warrant to the person from whom the blood samples were taken.

R.S. 1985, c. 27 (1st Supp.), s. 36; 1992, c. 1, s. 58(1); 1994, c. 4, s. 13.

257. (1) No offence committed — No qualified medical practitioner or qualified technician is guilty of an offence only by reason of his refusal to take a sample of blood from a person for the purposes of section 254 or 256 and no qualified medical practitioner is guilty of an offence only by reason of his refusal to cause to be taken by a qualified technician under his direction a sample of blood from a person for such purposes.

(2) No criminal or civil liability — No qualified medical practitioner by whom or under whose direction a sample of blood is taken from a person pursuant to a demand made under subsection 254(3) or a warrant issued under section 256 and no qualified technician acting under the direction of a qualified medical practitioner incurs any criminal or civil liability for anything necessarily done with reasonable care and skill in the taking of such a sample of blood.

R.S. 1985, c. 27 (1st Supp.), s. 36.

258. (1) Proceedings under section 255 — In any proceedings under subsection 255(1) in respect of an offence committed under section 253 or in any proceedings under subsection 255(2) or (3),

> (a) where it is proved that the accused occupied the seat or position ordinarily occupied by a person who operates a motor vehicle, vessel, or aircraft or any railway equipment or who assists in the operation of an aircraft or of railway equipment, the accused shall be deemed to have had the care or control of the vehicle, vessel, aircraft or railway equipment, as the case may be, unless the accused establishes that the accused did not occupy that seat or position for the purpose of setting the vehicle, vessel, aircraft or railway equipment in

motion or assisting in the operation of the aircraft or railway equipment, as the case may be;

(b) the result of an analysis of a sample of the breath or blood of the accused (other than a sample taken pursuant to a demand made under subsection 254(3)) or of the urine or other bodily substance of the accused may be admitted in evidence notwithstanding that, before the accused gave the sample, he was not warned that he need not give the sample or that the result of the analysis of the sample might be used in evidence;

(c) where samples of the breath of the accused have been taken pursuant to a demand made under subsection 254(3), if

Proposed Addition — 258(1)(c)

(i) at the time each sample was taken, the person taking the sample offered to provide to the accused a specimen of the breath of the accused in an approved container for his own use, and, at the request of the accused made at thet time, such a specimen was thereupon provided to the accused,

R.S. 1985, c. 27 (1st Supp.), s. 36 [Not in force at date of publication.]

(ii) each sample was taken as soon as practicable after the time when the offence was alleged to have been committed and, in the case of the first sample, not later than two hours after that time, with an interval of at least fifteen minutes between the times when the samples were taken,

(iii) each sample was received from the accused directly into an approved container or into an approved instrument operated by a qualified technician, and

(iv) an analysis of each sample was made by means of an approved instrument operated by a qualified technician,

evidence of the results of the analyses so made is, in the absence of evidence to the contrary, proof that the concentration of alcohol in the blood of the accused at the time when the offence was alleged to have been committed was, where the results of the analyses are the same, the concentration determined by the analyses and, where the results of the analyses are different, the lowest of the concentrations determined by the analyses;

(d) where a sample of the blood of the accused has been taken pursuant to a demand made under subsection 254(3) or otherwise with the consent of the accused or pursuant to a warrant issued under section 256, if

(i) at the time the sample was taken, the person taking the sample took an additional sample of the blood of the accused and one of the samples was retained, to permit an analysis thereof to be made by or on behalf of the accused and, in the case where the accused makes a request within six months from the taking of the samples, one of the samples was ordered to be released pursuant to subsection (4),

(ii) both samples referred to in subparagraph (i) were taken as soon as practicable after the time when the offence was alleged to have been committed and in any event not later than two hours after that time,

(iii) both samples referred to in subparagraph (i) were taken by a qualified medical practitioner or a qualified technician under the direction of a qualified medical practitioner,

(iv) both samples referred to in subparagraph (i) were received from the accused directly into, or placed directly into, approved containers that were subsequently sealed, and

(v) an analysis was made by an analyst of at least one of the samples that was contained in a sealed approved container,

evidence of the result of the analysis is, in the absence of evidence to the contrary, proof that the concentration of alcohol in the blood of the accused at the time when the offence was alleged to have been committed was the concentration determined by the analysis or, where more than one sample was analyzed and results of the analyses are the same, the concentration determined by the analyses and, where the results of the analyses are different, the lowest of the concentrations determined by the analyses;

(d.1) where samples of the breath of the accused or a sample of the blood of the accused have been taken as described in paragraph (c) or (d) under the conditions described therein and the results of the analyses show a concentration of alcohol in blood exceeding eighty milligrams of alcohol in one hundred millilitres of blood, evidence of the result of the analyses is, in the absence of evidence tending to show that the concentration of alcohol in the blood of the accused at the time when the offence was alleged to have been committed did not exceed eighty milligrams of alcohol in one hundred millilitres of blood, proof that the concentration of alcohol in the blood of the accused at the time when the offence was alleged to have been committed exceeded eighty milligrams of alcohol in one hundred millilitres of blood;

(e) a certificate of an analyst stating that the analyst has made an analysis of a sample of the blood, urine, breath or other bodily substance of the accused and stating the result of that analysis is evidence of the facts alleged in the certificate without proof of the signature or the official character of the person appearing to have signed the certificate;

(f) a certificate of an analyst stating that the analyst has made an analysis of a sample of an alcohol standard that is identified in the certificate and intended for use with an approved instrument and that the sample of the standard analyzed by the analyst was found to be suitable for use with an approved instrument, is evidence that the alcohol standard so identified is suitable for use with an approved instrument without proof of the signature or the official character of the person appearing to have signed the certificate;

(g) where samples of the breath of the accused have been taken pursuant to a demand made under subsection 254(3), a certificate of a qualified technician stating

(i) that the analysis of each of the samples has been made by means of an approved instrument operated by the technician and ascertained by the technician to be in proper working order by means of an alcohol standard, identified in the certificate, that is suitable for use with an approved instrument,

(ii) the results of the analyses so made, and

(iii) if the samples were taken by the technician,

Proposed Addition — 258(1)(g)(iii)

(A) that at the time each sample was taken the technician offered to provide the accused with a specimen of the breath of the accused in an approved container for his own use and, at the request of the accused made at that time, the accused was thereupon provided with such a specimen,

R.S. 1985, c. 27 (1st Supp.), s. 36. [Not in force at date of publication.]

(B) the time when and place where each sample and any specimen described in clause (A) was taken, and

(C) that each sample was received from the accused directly into an approved container or into an approved instrument operated by the technician,

is evidence of the facts alleged in the certificate without proof of the signature or the official character of the person appearing to have signed the certificate;

Note: paragraphs 258(1)(f) and (g) [incorrectly noted in R.S. 1985, c. 27 (1st Supp.), s. 204 as paragraphs 255(1)(f) and (g)] of the Code, as they read immediately before the coming into force of the amendments to those paragraphs, as enacted by s. 36 of the Criminal Law Amendment Act, 1985, R.S. 1985, c. 27 (1st Supp.), continue to apply to any proceedings in respect of which a certificate referred to in those paragraphs was issued prior to the coming into force of the amendments to those paragraphs.

(h) where a sample of the blood of the accused has been taken pursuant to a demand made under subsection 254(3) or otherwise with the consent of the accused or pursuant to a warrant issued under section 256,

(i) a certificate of a qualified medical practitioner stating that

(A) the medical practitioner took the sample and that before the sample was taken he was of the opinion that the taking of blood samples from the accused would not endanger the life or health of the accused and, in the case of a demand made pursuant to a warrant issued pursuant to section 256, that by reason of any physical or mental condition of the accused that resulted from the consumption of alcohol, the accident or any other occurrence related to or resulting from the accident, the accused was unable to consent to the taking of his blood,

(B) at the time the sample was taken, an additional sample of the blood of the accused was taken to permit analysis of one of the samples to be made by or on behalf of the accused,

(C) the time when and place where both samples referred to in clause (B) were taken, and

(D) both samples referred to in clause (B) were received from the accused directly into, or placed directly into, approved containers that were subsequently sealed and that are identified in the certificate,

163

(ii) a certificate of a qualified medical practitioner stating that the medical practitioner caused the sample to be taken by a qualified technician under his direction and that before the sample was taken the qualified medical practitioner was of the opinion referred to in clause (i)(A), or

(iii) a certificate of a qualified technician stating that the technician took the sample and the facts referred to in clauses (i)(B) to (D)

is evidence of the facts alleged in the certificate without proof of the signature or official character of the person appearing to have signed the certificate; and

(i) a certificate of an analyst stating that the analyst has made an analysis of a sample of the blood of the accused that was contained in a sealed approved container identified in the certificate, the date on which and place where the sample was analyzed and the result of that analysis is evidence of the facts alleged in the certificate without proof of the signature or official character of the person appearing to have signed it.

(2) No obligation to give sample except as required under s. 254 — No person is required to give a sample of urine or other bodily substance for analysis for the purposes of this section except breath or blood as required under section 254, and evidence that a person failed or refused to give such a sample or that such a sample was not taken is not admissible nor shall such a failure or refusal or the fact that a sample was not taken be the subject of comment by any person in the proceedings.

(3) Evidence of failure to comply with demand — In any proceedings under subsection 255(1) in respect of an offence committed under paragraph 253(*a*) or in any proceedings under subsection 255(2) or (3), evidence that the accused, without reasonable excuse, failed or refused to comply with a demand made to him by a peace officer under section 254 is admissible and the court may draw an inference therefrom adverse to the accused.

(4) Release of specimen for testing — A judge of a superior court of criminal jurisdiction or a court of criminal jurisdiction shall, on the summary application of the accused made within six months from the day on which samples of the blood of the accused were taken, order the release of one of the samples for the purpose of an examination or analysis thereof, subject to such terms as appear to be necessary or desirable to ensure the safeguarding of the sample and its preservation for use in any proceedings in respect of which it was retained.

(5) Testing blood for presence of drugs — Where a sample of blood of an accused has been taken pursuant to a demand made under subsection 254(3) or otherwise with the consent of the accused or pursuant to a warrant issued under section 256, the sample may be tested for the presence of drugs in the blood of the accused.

(6) Attendance and right to cross-examine — A party against whom a certificate described in paragraph (1)(*e*), (*f*), (*g*), (*h*) or (*i*) is produced may, with leave of the court, require the attendance of the qualified medical practitioner, analyst or qualified technician, as the case may be, for the purposes of cross-examination.

(7) Notice of intention to produce certificate — No certificate shall be received in evidence pursuant to paragraph (1)(*e*), (*f*), (*g*), (*h*) or (*i*) unless the party intending to produce it has, before the trial, given to the other party reasonable notice of his intention and a copy of the certificate.

R.S. 1985, c. 27 (1st Supp.), s. 36; c. 32 (4th Supp.), s. 61; 1994, c. 44, s. 14; 1997, c. 18, s. 10

259. (1) Mandatory order of prohibition — When an offender is convicted of an offence committed under section 253 or 254 or discharged under section 730 of an offence committed under section 253 and, at the time the offence was committed or, in the case of an offence committed under section 254, within the three hours preceding that time, was operating or had the care or control of a motor vehicle, vessel or aircraft or of railway equipment or was assisting in the operation of an aircraft or of railway equipment, the court that sentences the offender shall, in addition to any other punishment that may be imposed for that offence, make an order prohibiting the offender from operating a motor vehicle on any street, road, highway or other public place, or from operating a vessel or an aircraft or railway equipment, as the case may be,

(a) for a first offence, during a period of not more than three years plus any period to which the offender is sentenced to imprisonment, and not less than one year;

(b) for a second offence, during a period of not more than five years plus any period to which the offender is sentenced to imprisonment, and not less than two years; and

(c) for each subsequent offence, during a period of not less than three years plus any period to which the offender is sentenced to imprisonment.

Note: Section 5 of S.C. 1999, c. 32 increased the mandatory minimum driving prohibition to be imposed in the circumstances prescribed by s. 259 from three months to one year for a first offence (except where an offender participates in an alcohol interlock program for a specified period), from six months to two years for a second, and from one to three years on a subsequent offence, and increased the maximum prohibitions from three to five years for a second offence, and from three years to life for a subsequent offence. That section also changed the relevant operation/care/control period for the offence under s. 254 from two to three hours. Section 7 of S.C. 1999, c. 32 provides, however, that where any penalty or punishment provided by the Criminal Code *is varied by 1999, c. 32, the lesser penalty or punishment applies in respect to any offence that was committed before the coming into force of section 7 (i.e. before July 1, 1999).*

(1.1) Exception where Alcohol Ignition Interlock Program — Notwithstanding paragraph (1)(a), where the lieutenant governor in council of the province in which the prohibition order under paragraph (1)(a) is to be made has established a program governing the use of an alcohol ignition interlock device by an offender convicted of an offence for which the order is to be made, the minimum period of not less than one year is reduced to a period of not less than three months, if the offender participates in the program during the remainder of the one year period.

(2) Discretionary order of prohibition — Where an offender is convicted or discharged under section 730 of an offence under section 220, 221, 236, 249, 249.1, 250, 251 or 252, subsection 255(2) or (3) or this section committed by means of a motor vehicle, vessel or aircraft or of railway equipment, the court that sentences the offender may, in addition to any other punishment that may be imposed for that offence, make an order prohibiting the offender from operating a motor vehicle on any street, road, highway or other public place, or from operating a vessel, an aircraft or railway equipment, as the case may be

(a) during any period that the court considers proper, if the offender is liable to imprisonment for life in respect of that offence;

(b) during any period not exceeding ten years plus any period to which the offender is sentenced to imprisonment, if the offender is liable to imprisonment for more than five years but less than life in respect of that offence; and

(c) during any period not exceeding three years plus any period to which the offender is sentenced to imprisonment, in any other case.

(3) Saving — No order made under subsection (1) or (2) shall operate to prevent any person from acting as master, mate or engineer of a vessel that is required to carry officers holding certificates as master, mate or engineer.

(4) Operation while disqualified — Every one who operates a motor vehicle, vessel, aircraft or railway equipment in Canada while disqualified from doing so

(a) is guilty of an indictable offence and liable to imprisonment for a term not exceeding five years; or

(b) is guilty of an offence punishable on summary conviction.

Note: Subsection 5(2) of S.C. 1999, c. 32 increased the maximum sentence available in indictable proceedings for the offence under s. 259(4) from two to five years. Section 7 of S.C. 1999, c. 32 provides, however, that where any penalty or punishment provided by the Criminal Code *is varied by 1999, c. 32, the lesser penalty or punishment applies in respect to any offence that was committed before the coming into force of section 7 (i.e. before July 1, 1999). The two year maximum would thus continue to apply for offences involving bodily harm or death committed before that date.*

(5) Definition of "disqualification" — For the purposes of this section, **"disqualification"** means

(a) a prohibition from operating a motor vehicle, vessel, aircraft or railway equipment ordered pursuant to subsection (1) or (2); or

(b) a disqualification or any other form of legal restriction of the right or privilege to operate a motor vehicle, vessel or aircraft imposed

(i) in the case of a motor vehicle, under the law of a province, or

(ii) in the case of a vessel or an aircraft, under an Act of Parliament,

in respect of a conviction or discharge under section 730 of any offence referred to in subsection (1) or (2).

R.S. 1985, c. 27 (1st Supp.), s. 36; c. 32 (4th Supp.), s. 62; 1995, c. 22, ss. 10, 18; 1997, c. 18, s. 11; 1999, c. 32, s. 5; 2000, c. 2, s. 2.

260. (1) Proceedings on making of prohibition order — Where a court makes a prohibition order under subsection 259(1) or (2) in relation to an offender, it shall cause

(a) the order to be read by or to the offender;

(b) a copy of the order to be given to the offender; and

(c) the offender to be informed of subsection 259(4).

(2) Endorsement by offender — After subsection (1) has been complied with in relation to an offender who is bound by an order referred to in that subsection, the offender shall endorse the order, acknowledging receipt of a copy thereof and that the order has been explained to him.

(3) Validity of order not affected — The failure of an offender to endorse an order pursuant to subsection (2) does not affect the validity of the order.

(4) Onus — In the absence of evidence to the contrary, where it is proved that a disqualification referred to in paragraph 259(5)(*b*) has been imposed on a person and that notice of the disqualification has been mailed by registered or certified mail to that person, that person shall, after five days following the mailing of the notice, be deemed to have received the notice and to have knowledge of the disqualification, of the date of its commencement and of its duration.

(5) Certificate admissible in evidence — In proceedings under section 259, a certificate setting out with reasonable particularity that a person is disqualified from

(a) driving a motor vehicle in a province, purporting to be signed by the registrar of motor vehicles for that province, or

(b) operating a vessel or aircraft, purporting to be signed by the Minister of Transport or any person authorized by the Minister of Transport for that purpose

is evidence of the facts alleged therein without proof of the signature or official character of the person by whom it purports to be signed.

(6) Notice to accused — Subsection (5) does not apply in any proceedings unless at least seven days notice in writing is given to the accused that it is intended to tender the certificate in evidence.

(7) Definition of "registrar of motor vehicles" — In subsection (5), **"registrar of motor vehicles"** includes the deputy of that registrar and any other person or body, by whatever name or title designated, that from time to time performs the duties of superintending the registration of motor vehicles in the province.

R.S. 1985, c. 27 (1st Supp.), s. 36.

261. (1) Stay of order pending appeal — Where an appeal is taken against a conviction or discharge under section 730 for an offence committed under any of sections 220, 221, 236, 249 to 255 and 259, a judge of the court being appealed to may direct that any order under subsection 259(1) or (2) arising out of the conviction or discharge shall, on such conditions as the judge or court may impose, be stayed pending the final disposition of the appeal or until otherwise ordered by that court.

(2) Effect of conditions — Where conditions are imposed pursuant to a direction made under subsection (1) that a prohibition order under subsection 259(1) or (2) be stayed, the direction shall not operate to decrease the period of prohibition provided in the order made under subsection 259(1) or (2).

R.S. 1985, c. 27 (1st Supp.), s. 36; 1994, c. 44, s. 15; 1994, c. 44. s. 103; 1997, c. 18, ss. 12, 141(a).

262. Impeding attempt to save life — Every one who

(a) prevents or impedes or attempts to prevent or impede any person who is attempting to save his own life, or

(b) without reasonable cause prevents or impedes or attempts to prevent or impede any person who is attempting to save the life of another person,

is guilty of an indictable offence and liable to imprisonment for a term not exceeding ten years.

263. (1) Duty to safeguard opening in ice — Every one who makes or causes to be made an opening in ice that is open to or frequented by the public is under a legal duty to guard it in a manner that is adequate to prevent persons from falling in by accident and is adequate to warn them that the opening exists.

(2) Excavation on land — Every one who leaves an excavation on land that he owns or of which he has charge or supervision is under a legal duty to guard it in a manner that is adequate to prevent persons from falling in by accident and is adequate to warn them that the excavation exists.

(3) Offences — Every one who fails to perform a duty imposed by subsection (1) or (2) is guilty of

(a) manslaughter, if the death of any person results therefrom;

(b) an offence under section 269, if bodily harm to any person results therefrom; or

(c) an offence punishable on summary conviction.

264. (1) Criminal harassment — No person shall, without lawful authority and knowing that another person is harassed or recklessly as to whether the other person is harassed, engage in conduct referred to in subsection (2) that causes that other person reasonably, in all the circumstances, to fear for their safety or the safety of anyone known to them.

(2) Prohibited conduct — The conduct mentioned in subsection (1) consists of

(a) repeatedly following from place to place the other person or anyone known to them;

(b) repeatedly communicating with, either directly or indirectly, the other person or anyone known to them;

(c) besetting or watching the dwelling-house, or place where the other person, or anyone known to them, resides, works, carries on business or happens to be; or

(d) engaging in threatening conduct directed at the other person or any member of their family.

(3) Punishment — Every person who contravenes this section is guilty of

(a) an indictable offence and is liable to imprisonment for a term not exceeding five years; or

(b) an offence punishable on summary conviction.

(4) Factors to be considered — Where a person is convicted of an offence under this section, the court imposing the sentence on the person shall consider as an aggravating factor that, at the time the offence was committed, the person contravened

(a) the terms or conditions of an order made pursuant to section 161 or a recognizance entered into pursuant to section 810, 810.1 or 810.2; or

(b) the terms or conditions of any other order or recognizance made or entered into under the common law or a provision of this or any other Act of Parliament or of a province that is similar in effect to an order or recognizance referred to in paragraph (a)

(5) Reasons — Where the court is satisfied of the existence of an aggravating factor referred to in subsection (4), but decides not to give effect to it for sentencing purposes, the court shall give reasons for its decision.

R.S. 1985, c. 27 (1st Supp.), s. 37; 1993, c. 45, s. 2; 1997, c. 16, s. 4; c. 17, s. 9(3).

Assaults

264.1 (1) Uttering threats — Every one commits an offence who, in any manner, knowingly utters, conveys or causes any person to receive a threat

(a) to cause death or bodily harm to any person;

(b) to burn, destroy or damage real or personal property; or

(c) to kill, poison or injure an animal or bird that is the property of any person.

(2) Punishment — Every one who commits an offence under paragraph (1)(a) is guilty of

(a) an indictable offence and liable to imprisonment for a term not exceeding five years; or

(b) an offence punishable on summary conviction and liable to imprisonment for a term not exceeding eighteen months.

(3) Idem — Every one who commits an offence under paragraph (1)(b) or (c)

(a) is guilty of an indictable offence and liable to imprisonment for a term not exceeding two years; or

(b) is guilty of an offence punishable on summary conviction.

R.S. 1985, c. 27 (1st Supp.), s. 38; 1994, c. 44, s. 16.

265. (1) Assault — A person commits an assault when

(a) without the consent of another person, he applies force intentionally to that other person, directly or indirectly;

(b) he attempts or threatens, by an act or a gesture, to apply force to another person, if he has, or causes that other person to believe on reasonable grounds that he has, present ability to effect his purpose; or

(c) while openly wearing or carrying a weapon or an imitation thereof, he accosts or impedes another person or begs.

(2) Application — This section applies to all forms of assault, including sexual assault, sexual assault with a weapon, threats to a third party or causing bodily harm and aggravated sexual assault.

(3) Consent — For the purposes of this section, no consent is obtained where the complainant submits or does not resist by reason of

(a) the application of force to the complainant or to a person other than the complainant;

(b) threats or fear of the application of force to the complainant or to a person other than the complainant;

(c) fraud; or

(d) the exercise of authority.

(4) Accused's belief as to consent — Where an accused alleges that he believed that the complainant consented to the conduct that is the subject-matter of the charge, a judge, if satisfied that there is sufficient evidence and that, if believed by the jury, the evidence would constitute a defence, shall instruct the jury, when reviewing all the evidence relating to the determination of the honesty of the accused's belief, to consider the presence or absence of reasonable grounds for that belief.

266. Assault — Every one who commits an assault is guilty of

(a) an indictable offence and is liable to imprisonment for a term not exceeding five years; or

(b) an offence punishable on summary conviction.

267. Assault with a weapon or causing bodily harm — Every one who, in committing an assault,

(a) carries, uses or threatens to use a weapon or an imitation thereof, or

(b) causes bodily harm to the complainant,

is guilty of an indictable offence and liable to imprisonment for a term not exceeding ten years or an offence punishable on summary conviction and liable to imprisonment for a term not exceeding eighteen months.

1994, c. 44 s. 17.

268. (1) Aggravated assault — Every one commits an aggravated assault who wounds, maims, disfigures or endangers the life of the complainant.

(2) Punishment — Every one who commits an aggravated assault is guilty of an indictable offence and liable to imprisonment for a term not exceeding fourteen years.

(3) Excision — For greater certainty, in this section, "wounds" or "maims" includes to excise, infibulate or mutilate, in whole or in part, the labia majora, labia minora or clitoris of a person, except where

(a) a surgical procedure is performed, by a person duly qualified by provincial law to practise medicine, for the benefit of the physical health of the person or for the purpose of that person having normal reproductive functions or normal sexual appearance or function; or

(b) the person is at least eighteen years of age and there is no resulting bodily harm.

(4) Consent — For the purposes of this section and section 265, no consent to the excision, infibulation or mutilation, in whole or in part, of the labia majora, labia minora or clitoris of a person is valid, except in the cases described in paragraphs (3)(*a*) and (*b*)

1997, c. 16, s. 5.

269. Unlawfully causing bodily harm — Every one who unlawfully causes bodily harm to any person is guilty of

(a) an indictable offence and liable to imprisonment for a term not exceeding ten years; or

(b) an offence punishable on summary conviction and liable to imprisonment for a term not exceeding eighteen months.

1994, c. 44, s. 18.

269.1 (1) Torture — Every official, or every person acting at the instigation of or with the consent or acquiescence of an official, who inflicts torture on any other person is guilty of an indictable offence and is liable to imprisonment for a term not exceeding fourteen years.

(2) Definitions — For the purposes of this section,

"official" means

(a) a peace officer,

(b) a public officer,

(c) a member of the Canadian Forces, or

(d) any person who may exercise powers, pursuant to a law in force in a foreign state, that would, in Canada be exercised by a person referred to in paragraph (*a*), (*b*), or (*c*),

whether the person exercises powers in Canada or outside Canada;

"torture" means any act or omission by which severe pain or suffering, whether physical or mental, is intentionally inflicted on a person

(a) for a purpose including

(i) obtaining from the person or from a third person information or a statement,

(ii) punishing the person for an act that the person or a third person has committed or is suspected of having committed, and

(iii) intimidating or coercing the person or a third person, or

(b) for any reason based on discrimination of any kind,

but does not include any act or omission arising only from, inherent in or incidental to lawful sanctions.

(3) No defence — It is no defence to a charge under this section that the accused was ordered by a superior or a public authority to perform the act or omission that forms the subject-matter of the charge or that the act or omission is alleged to have been justified by exceptional circumstances, including a state of war, a threat of war, internal political instability or any other public emergency.

(4) Evidence — In any proceedings over which Parliament has jurisdiction, any statement obtained as a result of the commission of an offence under this section is inadmissible in evidence except as evidence that the statement was so obtained.

R.S. 1985, c. 10 (3d Supp.), s. 2.

270. (1) Assaulting a peace officer — Every one commits an offence who

(a) assaults a public officer or peace officer engaged in the execution of his duty or a person acting in aid of such an officer;

(b) assaults a person with intent to resist or prevent the lawful arrest or detention of himself or another person; or

(c) assaults a person

(i) who is engaged in the lawful execution of a process against lands or goods or in making a lawful distress or seizure, or

(ii) with intent to rescue anything taken under lawful process, distress or seizure.

(2) Punishment — Every one who commits an offence under subsection (1) is guilty of

(a) an indictable offence and is liable to imprisonment for a term not exceeding five years; or

(b) an offence punishable on summary conviction.

271. (1) Sexual assault — Every one who commits a sexual assault is guilty of

(a) an indictable offence and is liable to imprisonment for a term not exceeding ten years; or

(b) an offence punishable on summary conviction and liable to imprisonment for a term not exceeding eighteen months.

(2) [Repealed R.S. 1985, c. 19 (3d Supp.), s. 10.]

R.S. 1985, c. 19 (3d Supp.), s. 10; 1994, c. 44, s. 19.

272. (1) Sexual assault with a weapon, threats to a third party or causing bodily harm — Every person commits an offence who, in committing a sexual assault,

(a) carries, uses or threatens to use a weapon or an imitation of a weapon;

(b) threatens to cause bodily harm to a person other than the complainant;

(c) causes bodily harm to the complainant; or

(d) is a party to the offence with any other person.

(2) Punishment — Every person who commits an offence under subsection (1) is guilty of an indictable offence and liable

(a) where a firearm is used in the commission of the offence, to imprisonment for a term not exceeding fourteen years and to a minimum punishment of imprisonment for a term of four years; and

(b) in any other case, to imprisonment for a term not exceeding fourteen years.

1995, c. 39, s. 145.

273. (1) Aggravated sexual assault — Every one commits an aggravated sexual assault who, in committing a sexual assault, wounds, maims, disfigures or endangers the life of the complainant.

(2) Aggravated sexual assault — Every person who commits an aggravated sexual assault is guilty of an indictable offence and liable

(a) where a firearm is used in the commission of the offence, to imprisonment for life and to a minimum punishment of imprisonment for a term of four years; and

(b) in any other case, to imprisonment for life.

1995, c. 39, s. 146.

273.1 (1) Meaning of "consent" — Subject to subsection (2) and subsection 265(3), **"consent"** means, for the purposes of sections 271, 272 and 273, the voluntary agreement of the complainant to engage in the sexual activity in question.

(2) Where no consent obtained — No consent is obtained, for the purposes of sections 271, 272 and 273, where

(a) the agreement is expressed by the words or conduct of a person other than the complainant;

(b) the complainant is incapable of consenting to the activity;

(c) the accused induces the complainant to engage in the activity by abusing a position of trust, power or authority;

(d) the complainant expresses, by words or conduct, a lack of agreement to engage in the activity; or

(e) the complainant, having consented to engage in sexual activity, expresses, by words or conduct, a lack of agreement to continue to engage in the activity.

(3) Subsection (2) not limiting — Nothing in subsection (2) shall be construed as limiting the circumstances in which no consent is obtained.

1992, c. 38, s. 1

273.2 Where belief in consent not a defence — It is not a defence to a charge under section 271, 272 or 273 that the accused believed that the complainant consented to the activity that forms the subject-matter of the charge, where

(a) the accused's belief arose from the accused's

(i) self-induced intoxication, or

173

(ii) recklessness or wilful blindness; or

(b) the accused did not take reasonable steps, in the circumstances known to the accused at the time, to ascertain that the complainant was consenting.

1992, c. 38, s. 1.

273.3 (1) Removal of child from Canada — No person shall do anything for the purpose of removing from Canada a person who is ordinarily resident in Canada and who is

(a) under the age of fourteen years, with the intention that an act be committed outside Canada that if it were committed in Canada would be an offence against section 151 or 152 or subsection 160(3) or 173(2) in respect of that person;

(b) fourteen years of age or more but under the age of eighteen years, with the intention that an act be committed outside Canada that if it were committed in Canada would be an offence against section 153 in respect of that person; or

(c) under the age of eighteen years, with the intention that an act be committed outside Canada that if it were committed in Canada would be an offence against section 155 or 159, subsection 160(2) or section 170, 171, 267, 268, 269, 271, 272 or 273 in respect of that person.

(2) Punishment — Every person who contravenes this section is guilty of

(a) an indictable offence and is liable to imprisonment for a term not exceeding five years; or

(b) an offence punishable on summary conviction.

1993, c. 45, s. 3; 1997, c. 18, s. 13.

274. Corroboration not required — Where an accused is charged with an offence under section 151, 152, 153, 155, 159, 160, 170, 171, 172, 173, 212, 271, 272 or 273, no corroboration is required for a conviction and the judge shall not instruct the jury that it is unsafe to find the accused guilty in the absence of corroboration.

R.S. 1985, c. 19 (3d Supp.), s. 11.

275. Rules respecting recent complaint abrogated — The rules relating to evidence of recent complaint are hereby abrogated with respect to offences under sections 151, 152, 153, 155 and 159, subsections 160(2) and (3), and sections 170, 171, 172, 173, 271, 272 and 273.

R.S. 1985, c. 19 (3d Supp.), s. 11.

276. (1) Evidence of complainant's sexual activity — In proceedings in respect of an offence under section 151, 152, 153, 155 or 159, subsections 160(2) or (3), or section 170, 171, 172, 173, 271, 272 or 273, evidence that the complainant has engaged in sexual activity, whether with the accused or with any other person, is not admissible to support an inference that, by reason of the sexual nature of that activity, the complainant

(a) is more likely to have consented to the sexual activity that forms the subject-matter of the charge; or

(b) is less worthy of belief.

(2) Idem — In proceedings in respect of an offence referred to in subsection (1), no evidence shall be adduced by or on behalf of the accused that the complainant has engage in sexual activity other than the sexual activity that forms the subject-matter of the charge, whether with the accused or with any other person, unless the judge, provincial court judge or justice determines, in accordance with the procedures set out in sections 276.1 and 276.2, that the evidence

(a) is of specific instances of sexual activity;

(b) is relevant to an issue at trial; and

(c) has significant probative value that is not substantially outweighed by the danger of prejudice to the proper administration of justice.

(3) Factors that judge must consider — In determining whether evidence is admissible under subsection (2), the judge, provincial court judge or justice shall take into account

(a) the interests of justice, including the right of the accused to make a full answer and defence;

(b) society's interest in encouraging the reporting of sexual assault offences;

(c) whether there is a reasonable prospect that the evidence will assist in arriving at a just determination in the case;

(d) the need to remove from the fact-finding process any discriminatory belief or bias;

(e) the risk that the evidence may unduly arouse sentiments of prejudice, sympathy or hostility in the jury;

(f) the potential prejudice to the complainant's personal dignity and right of privacy;

(g) the right of the complainant and of every individual to personal security and to the full protection and benefit of the law; and

(h) any other factor that the judge, provincial court judge or justice considers relevant.

R.S. 1985, c. 19 (3d Supp.), s. 12; 1992, c. 38, s. 2.

276.1 (1) Application for hearing — Application may be made to the judge, provincial court judge or justice by or on behalf of the accused for a hearing under section 276.2 to determine whether evidence is admissible under subsection 276(2).

(2) Form and content of application — An application referred to in subsection (1) must be made in writing and set out

(a) detailed particulars of the evidence that the accused seeks to adduce, and

(b) the relevance of that evidence to an issue at trial,

and a copy of the application must be given to the prosecutor and to the clerk of the court.

(3) Jury and public excluded — The judge, provincial court judge or justice shall consider the application with the jury and the public excluded.

(4) Judge may decide to hold hearing — Where the judge, provincial court judge or justice is satisfied

    (a) that the application was made in accordance with subsection (2),

    (b) that a copy of the application was given to the prosecutor and to the clerk of the court at least seven days previously, or such shorter interval as the judge, provincial court judge or justice may allow where the interests of justice so require, and

    (c) that the evidence sought to be adduced is capable of being admissible under subsection 276(2),

the judge, provincial court judge or justice shall grant the application and hold a hearing under section 276.2 to determine whether the evidence is admissible under subsection 276(2).

1992, c. 38, s. 2.

276.2 (1) Jury and public excluded — At a hearing to determine whether evidence is admissible under subsection 276(2), the jury and the public shall be excluded.

(2) Complainant not compellable — The complainant is not a compellable witness at the hearing.

(3) Judge's determination and reasons — At the conclusion of the hearing, the judge, provincial court judge or justice shall determine whether the evidence, or any part thereof, is admissible under subsection 276(2) and shall provide reasons for that determination, and

    (a) where not all of the evidence is to be admitted, the reasons must state the part of the evidence that is to be admitted;

    (b) the reasons must state the factors referred to in subsection 276(3) that affected the determination; and

    (c) where all or any part of the evidence is to be admitted, the reasons must state the manner in which that evidence is expected to be relevant to an issue at trial.

(4) Record of reasons — The reasons provided under subsection (3) shall be entered in the record of the proceedings or, where the proceedings are not recorded, shall be provided in writing.

1992, c. 38, s. 2.

276.3 (1) Publication prohibited — No person shall publish in a newspaper, as defined in section 297, or in a broadcast, any of the following:

    (a) the contents of an application made under section 276.1;

    (b) any evidence taken, the information given and the representations made at an application under section 276.1 or at a hearing under section 276.2;

    (c) the decision of a judge, provincial court judge or justice under subsection 276.1(4), unless the judge, provincial court judge or justice, after taking into account the complainant's right of privacy and the interests of justice, orders that the decision may be published; and

(d) the determination made and the reasons provided under section 276.2, unless

(i) that determination is that evidence is admissible, or

(ii) the judge, provincial court judge or justice, after taking into account the complainant's right of privacy and the interests of justice, orders that the determination and reasons may be published.

(2) Offence — Every person who contravenes subsection (1) is guilty of an offence punishable on summary conviction.

1992, c.38, s. 2.

276.4 Judge to instruct jury re use of evidence — Where evidence is admitted at trial pursuant to a determination made unde section 276.2, the judge shall instruct the jury as to the uses that the jury may and may not make of that evidence.

1992, c. 38, s. 2.

276.5 Appeal — For the purposes of sections 675 and 676, a determination made under section 276.2 shall be deemed to be a question of law.

1992, c. 38, s. 2.

277. Reputation evidence — In proceedings in respect of an offence under section 151, 152, 153, 155 or 159, subsection 160(2) or (3), or section 170, 171, 172, 173, 271, 272 or 273, evidence of sexual reputation, whether general or specific, is not admissible for the purpose of challenging or supporting the credibility of the complainant.

R.S. 1985, c. 19 (3d Supp.), s. 13.

278. Spouse may be charged — A husband or wife may be charged with an offence under section 271, 272 or 273 in respect of his or her spouse, whether or not the spouses were living together at the time the activity that forms the subject-matter of the charge occurred.

278.1 Definition of "record" — For the purposes of sections 278.2 to 278.9, **"record"** means any form of record that contains personal information for which there is a reasonable expectation of privacy and includes, without limiting the generality of the foregoing, medical, psychiatric, therapeutic, counselling, education, employment, child welfare, adoption and social services records, personal journals and diaries, and records containing personal information the production or disclosure of which is protected by any other Act of Parliament or a provincial legislature, but does not include records made by persons responsible for the investigation or prosecution of the offence.

1997, c. 30, s. 1.

278.2 Production of record to accused — **(1)** No record relating to a complainant or a witness shall be produced to an accused in any proceedings in respect of

(a) an offence under section 151, 152, 153, 153.1, 155, 159, 160, 170, 171, 172, 173, 210, 211, 212, 213, 271, 272 or 273,

(b) an offence under section 144, 145, 149, 156, 245 or 246 of the *Criminal Code*, chapter C-34 of the Revised Statutes of Canada, 1970, as it read immediately before January 4, 1983, or

(c) an offence under section 146, 151, 153, 155, 157, 166 or 167 of the *Criminal Code*, chapter C-34 of the Revised Statutes of Canada, 1970, as it read immediately before January 1, 1988,

or in any proceedings in respect of two or more offences that include an offence referred to in any of paragraphs (a) to (c), except in accordance with sections 278.3 to 278.91.

(2) Application of provisions — Section 278.1, this section and sections 278.3 to 278.91 apply where a record is in the possession or control of any person, including the prosecutor in the proceedings, unless, in the case of a record in the possession or control of the prosecutor, the complainant or witness to whom the record relates has expressly waived the application of those sections.

(3) Duty of prosecutor to give notice — In the case of a record in respect of which this section applies that is in the possession or control of the prosecutor, the prosecutor shall notify the accused that the record is in the prosecutor's possession but, in doing so, the prosecutor shall not disclose the record's contents.

1997, c. 30, s. 1, 1998, c. 9, s. 3.

278.3 (1) Application for production — An accused who seeks production of a record referred to in subsection 278.2(1) must make an application to the judge before whom the accused is to be, or is being, tried.

(2) No application in other proceedings — For greater certainty, an application under subsection (1) may not be made to a judge or justice presiding at any other proceedings, including a preliminary inquiry.

(3) Form and content of application — An application must be made in writing and set out

(a) particulars identifying the record that the accused seeks to have produced and the name of the person who has possession or control of the record; and

(b) the grounds on which the accused relies to establish that the record is likely relevant to an issue at trial or to the competence of a witness to testify.

(4) Insufficient grounds — Any one or more of the following assertions by the accused are not sufficient on their own to establish that the record is likely relevant to an issue at trial or to the competence of a witness to testify:

(a) that the record exists;

(b) that the record relates to medical or psychiatric treatment, therapy or counselling that the complainant or witness has received or is receiving;

(c) that that record relates to the incident that is the subject-matter of the proceedings;

(d) that the record may disclose a prior inconsistent statement of the complainant or witness;

(e) that the record may relate to the credibility of the complainant or witness;

(f) that the record may relate to the reliability of the testimony of the complainant or witness merely because the complainant or witness has received or is receiving psychiatric treatment, therapy or counselling;

(g) that the record may reveal allegations of sexual abuse of the complainant by a person other than the accused;

(h) that the record relates to the sexual activity of the complainant with any person, including the accused;

(i) that the record relates to the presence or absence of a recent complaint;

(j) that the record relates to the complainant's sexual reputation; or

(k) that the record was made close in time to a complaint or to the activity that forms the subject-matter of the charge against the accused.

(5) Service of application and subpoena — The accused shall serve the application on the prosecutor, on the person who has possession or control of the record, on the complainant or witness, as the case may be, and on any other person to who, to the knowledge of the accused, the record relates, at least seven days before the hearing referred to in subsection 278.4(1) or any shorter interval that the judge may allow in the interests of justice. The accused shall also serve a subpoena issued under Part XXII in Form 16.1 on the person who has possession or control of the record at the same time as the application is served.

(6) Service on other persons — The judge may at any time order that the application be served on any person to whom the judge considers the record may relate.

1997, c. 30, s. 1.

278.4 (1) Hearing *in camera* — The judge shall hold a hearing *in camera* to determine whether to order the person who has possession or control of the record to produce it to the court for review by the judge.

(2) Persons who may appear at hearing — The person who has possession or control of the record, the complainant or witness, as the case may be, and any other person to whom the record relates may appear and make submissions at the hearing, but they are not compellable as witnesses at the hearing.

(3) Costs — No order for costs may be made against a person referred to in subsection (2) in respect of their participation in the hearing.

1997, c. 30, s. 1.

278.5 (1) Judge may order production of record for review — The judge may order the person who has possession or control of the record to produce the record or part of the record to the court for review by the judge if, after the hearing referred to in subsection 278.4(1), the judge is satisfied that

(a) the application was made in accordance with subsections 278.3(2) to (6);

(b) the accused has established that the record is likely relevant to an issue at trial or to the competence of a witness to testify; and

(c) the production of the record is necessary in the interests of justice.

(2) Factors to be considered — In determining whether to order the production of the record or part of the record for review pursuant to subsection (1), the judge shall consider the salutary and deleterious effects of the determination on the accused's right to make a full answer and defence and on the right to privacy and equality of the complainant or witness, as the case may be, and any other person to whom the record relates. In particular, the judge shall take the following factors into account:

(a) the extent to which the record is necessary for the accused to make a full answer and defence;

(b) the probative value of the record;

(c) the nature and extent of the reasonable expectation of privacy with respect to the record;

(d) whether production of the record is based on a discriminatory belief or bias;

(e) the potential prejudice to the personal dignity and right to privacy of any person to whom the record relates;

(f) society's interest in encouraging the reporting of sexual offences;

(g) society's interest in encouraging the obtaining of treatment by complainants of sexual offences; and

(h) the effect of the determination on the integrity of the trial process.

1997, c. 30, s. 1.

278.6 (1) Review of record by judge — Where the judge has ordered the production of the record or part of the record for review, the judge shall review it in the absence of the parties in order to determine whether the record or part of the record should be produced to the accused.

(2) Hearing *in camera* — The judge may hold a hearing *in camera* if the judge considers that it will assist in making the determination.

(3) Provisions re hearing — Subsections 278.4(2) and (3) apply in the case of a hearing under subsection (2).

1997, c. 30, s. 1.

278.7 (1) Judge may order production of record to accused — Where the judge is satisfied that the record or part of the record is likely relevant to an issue at trial or to the competence of a witness to testify and its production is necessary in the interests of justice, the judge may order that the record or part of the record that is likely relevant be produced to the accused, subject to any conditions that may be imposed pursuant to subsection (3).

(2) Factors to be considered — In determining whether to order the production of the record or part of the record to the accused, the judge shall consider the salutary and deleterious effects of the determination on the accused's right to make a full answer and the defence and on the right to privacy and equality of the complainant or witness, as the case may be, and any other person to whom the record relates and, in particular, shall take the factors specified in paragraphs 278.5(2)(a) to (h) into account.

(3) Conditions on production — Where the judge orders the production of the record or part of the record to the accused, the judge may impose conditions on the production to protect the interest of justice and, to the greatest extent possible, the privacy and equality interests of the complainant or witness, as the case may be, and any other person to whom the record relates, including, for example, the following conditions:

(a) that the record be edited as directed by the judge;

(b) that a copy of the record, rather than the original, be produced;

(c) that the accused and counsel for the accused not disclose the contents of the record to any other person, except with the approval of the court;

(d) that the record be viewed only at the offices of the court;

(e) that no copies of the record be made or that restrictions be imposed on the number of copies of the record that may be made; and

(f) that information regarding any person named in the record, such as their address, telephone number and place of employment, be severed from the record.

(4) Copy to prosecutor — Where the judge orders the production of the record or part of the record to the accused, the judge shall direct that a copy of the record or part of the record be provided to the prosecutor, unless the judge determines that it is not in the interests of justice to do so.

(5) Record not to be used in other proceedings — The record or part of the record that is produced to the accused pursuant to an order under subsection (1) shall not be used in any other proceedings.

(6) Retention of record by court — Where the judge refuses to order the production of the record or part of the record to the accused, the record or part of the record shall, unless a court orders otherwise, be kept in a sealed package by the court until the later of the expiration of the time for any appeal and the completion of any appeal in the proceedings against the accused, whereupon the record or part of the record shall be returned to the person lawfully entitled to possession or control of it.

1997, c. 30, s. 1.

278.8 (1) Reasons for decision — The judge shall provide reasons for ordering or refusing to order the production of the record or part of the record pursuant to subsection 278.5(1) or 278.7(1).

(2) Record of reasons — The reasons referred to in subsection (1) shall be entered in the record of the proceedings or, where the proceedings are not recorded, shall be provided in writing.

1997, c. 30, s. 1.

278.9 (1) Publication prohibited — No person shall publish in a newspaper, as defined in section 297, or in a broadcast, any of the following:

(a) the contents of an application made under section 278.3;

(b) any evidence taken, information given or submissions made at a hearing under subsection 278.4(1) or 278.6(2); or

(c) the determination of the judge pursuant to subsection 278.5(1) or 278.7(1) and the reasons provided pursuant to section 278.8, unless the judge, after taking into account the interests of justice and the right to privacy of the person to whom the record relates, orders that the determination may be published.

(2) Offence — Every person who contravenes subsection (1) is guilty of an offence punishable on summary conviction.

1997, c. 30, s. 1.

278.91 Appeal — For the purposes of sections 675 and 676, a determination to make or refuse to make an order pursuant to subsection 278.5(1) or 278.7(1) is deemed to be a question of law.

1997, c. 30, s. 1.

Kidnapping, Hostage Taking and Abduction

279. (1) Kidnapping — Every person commits an offence who kidnaps a person with intent

(a) to cause the person to be confined or imprisoned against the person's will;

(b) to cause the person to be unlawfully sent or transported out of Canada against the person's will; or

(c) to hold the person for ransom or to service against the person's will.

(1.1) Punishment — Every person who commits an offence under subsection (1) is guilty of an indictable offence and liable

(a) where a firearm is used in the commission of the offence, to imprisonment for life and to a minimum punishment of imprisonment for a term of four years; and

(b) in any other case, to imprisonment for life.

(2) Forcible confinement — Every one who, without lawful authority, confines, imprisons or forcibly seizes another person is guilty of

(a) an indictable offence and liable to imprisonment for a term not exceeding ten years; or

(b) an offence punishable on summary conviction and liable to imprisonment for a term not exceeding eighteen months.

(3) Non-resistance — In proceedings under this section, the fact that the person in relation to whom the offence is alleged to have been committed did not resist is not a defence unless the accused proves that the failure to resist was not caused by threats, duress, force or exhibition or force.

R.S. 1985, c. 27 (1st Supp.), s. 39; 1995, c. 39. s. 147; 1997, c. 18, s. 14.

279.1 (1) Hostage taking — Every one takes a person hostage who

(a) confines, imprisons, forcibly seizes or detains that person, and

(b) in any manner utters, conveys or causes any person to receive a threat that the death of, or bodily harm to, the hostage will be caused or that the confinement, imprisonment or detention of the hostage will be continued

with intent to induce any person, other than the hostage, or any group of persons or any state or international or intergovernmental organization to commit or cause to be committed any act or omission as a condition, whether express or implied, of the release of the hostage.

(2) Hostage–taking — Every person who takes a person hostage is guilty of an indictable offence and liable

(a) where a firearm is used in the commission of the offence, to imprisonment for life and to a minimum punishment of imprisonment for a term of four years; and

(b) in any other case, to imprisonment for life.

(3) Non–resistance — Subsection 279(3) applies to proceedings under this section as if the offence under this section were an offence under section 279.

R.S. 1985, c. 27 (1st Supp.), s. 40(1); 1995, c. 39, s. 148.

280. (1) Abduction of person under sixteen — Every one who, without lawful authority, takes or causes to be taken an unmarried person under the age of sixteen years out of the possession of and against the will of the parent or guardian of that person or of any other person who has the lawful care or charge of that person is guilty of an indictable offence and liable to imprisonment for a term not exceeding five years.

(2) Definition of "guardian" — In this section and sections 281 to 283, **"guardian"** includes any person who has in law or in fact the custody or control of another person.

281. Abduction of person under fourteen — Every one who, not being the parent, guardian or person having the lawful care or charge of a person under the age of fourteen years, unlawfully takes, entices away, conceals, detains, receives or harbours that person with intent to deprive a parent or guardian, or any other person who has the lawful care or charge of that person, of the possession of that person is guilty of an indictable offence and liable to imprisonment for a term not exceeding ten years.

282. (1) Abduction in contravention of custody order — Every one who, being the parent, guardian or person having the lawful care or charge of a person under the age of fourteen years, takes, entices away, conceals, detains, receives or harbours that person, in contravention of the custody provisions of a custody order in relation to that person made by a court anywhere in Canada, with intent to deprive a parent or guardian or any other person who has the lawful care or charge of that person, of the possession of that person is guilty of

  (a) an indictable offence and is liable to imprisonment for a term not exceeding ten years; or

  (b) an offence punishable on summary conviction.

(2) Where no belief in validity of custody order — Where a count charges an offence under subsection (1) and the offence is not proven only because the accused did not believe that there was a valid custody order but the evidence does prove an offence under section 283, the accused may be convicted of an offence under section 283.

1993, c. 45, s. 4.

283. (1) Abduction — Every one who, being the parent, guardian or person having the lawful care or charge of a person under the age of fourteen years, takes, entices away, conceals, detains, receives or harbours that person, whether or not there is a custody order in relation to that person made by a court anywhere in Canada, with intent to deprive a parent or guardian, or any other person who has the lawful care or charge of that person, of the possession of that person, is guilty of

  (a) an indictable offence and is liable to imprisonment for a term not exceeding ten years; or

  (b) an offence punishable on summary conviction.

(2) Consent required — No proceedings may be commenced under subsection (1) without the consent of the Attorney General or counsel instructed by him for that purpose.

1993, c. 45, s. 5.

284. Defence — No one shall be found guilty of an offence under sections 281 to 283 if he establishes that the taking, enticing away, concealing, detaining, receiving or harbouring of any young person was done with the consent of the parent, guardian or other person having the lawful possession, care or charge of that young person.

285. Defence — No one shall be found guilty of an offence under sections 280 to 283 if the court is satisfied that the taking, enticing away, concealing, detaining, receiving or harbouring of any young person was necessary to protect the young person from danger of imminent harm or if the person charged with the offence was escaping from danger of imminent harm.

286. No defence — In proceedings in respect of an offence under sections 280 to 283, it is not a defence to any charge that a young person consented to or suggested any conduct of the accused.

Abortion

287. (1) Procuring miscarriage — Every one who, with intent to procure the miscarriage of a female person, whether or not she is pregnant, uses any means for the purpose of carrying out his intention is guilty of an indictable offence and liable to imprisonment for life.

(2) Woman procuring her own miscarriage — Every female person who, being pregnant, with intent to procure her own miscarriage, uses any means or permits any means to be used for the purpose of carrying out her intention is guilty of an indictable offence and liable to imprisonment for a term not exceeding two years.

(3) "means" — In this section, **"means"** includes

    (a) the administration of a drug or other noxious thing;

    (b) the use of an instrument; and

    (c) manipulation of any kind.

(4) Exceptions — Subsections (1) and (2) do not apply to

    (a) a qualified medical practitioner, other than a member of a therapeutic abortion committee for any hospital, who in good faith uses in an accredited or approved hospital any means for the purpose of carrying out his intention to procure the miscarriage of a female person, or

    (b) a female person who, being pregnant, permits a qualified medical practitioner to use in an accredited or approved hospital any means for the purpose of carrying out her intention to procure her own miscarriage,

if, before the use of those means, the therapeutic abortion committee for that accredited or approved hospital, by a majority of the members of the committee and at a meeting of the committee at which the case of the female person has been reviewed,

    (c) has by certificate in writing stated that in its opinion the continuation of the pregnancy of the female person would or would be likely to endanger her life or health, and

    (d) has caused a copy of that certificate to be given to the qualified medical practitioner.

(5) Information requirement — The Minister of Health of a province may by order

    (a) require a therapeutic abortion committee for any hospital in that province, or any member thereof, to furnish him with a copy of any certificate described in paragraph (4)(*c*) issued by that committee, together with such other information relating to the circumstances surrounding the issue of that certificate as he may require, or

(b) require a medical practitioner who, in that province, has procured the miscarriage of any female person named in a certificate described in paragraph (4)(*c*), to furnish him with a copy of that certificate, together with such other information relating to the procuring of the miscarriage as he may require.

(6) Definitions — For the purposes of subsections (4) and (5) and this subsection

"accredited hospital" means a hospital accredited by the Canadian Council on Hospital Accreditation in which diagnostic services and medical, surgical and obstetrical treatment are provided;

"approved hospital" means a hospital in a province approved for the purposes of this section by the Minister of Health of that province;

"board" means the board of governors, management or directors, or the trustees, commission or other person or group of persons having the control and management of an accredited or approved hospital;

"Minister of Health" means

(a) in the Provinces of Ontario, Quebec, New Brunswick, Prince Edward Island, Manitoba, and Newfoundland, the Minister of Health,

(b) in the Provinces of Nova Scotia and Saskatchewan, the Minister of Public Health, and

(c) in the Province of British Columbia, the Minister of Health Services and Hospital Insurance,

(d) in the Province of Alberta, the Minister of Hospitals and Medical Care,

(e) in the Yukon Territory, the Northwest Territories and Nunavut, the Minister of National Health and Welfare;

"qualified medical practitioner" means a person entitled to engage in the practice of medicine under the laws of the province in which the hospital referred to in subsection (4) is situated;

"therapeutic abortion committee" for any hospital means a committee, comprised of not less than three members each of whom is a qualified medical practitioner, appointed by the board of that hospital for the purpose of considering and determining questions relating to terminations of pregnancy within that hospital.

(7) Requirement of consent not affected — Nothing in subsection (4) shall be construed as making unnecessary the obtaining of any authorization or consent that is or may be required, otherwise than under this Act, before any means are used for the purpose of carrying out an intention to procure the miscarriage of a female person.

1993, c. 28, s. 78 (Sched. III, item 30); 1996, c. 8, s. 32(1)(d).

288. Supplying noxious things — Every one who unlawfully supplies or procures a drug or other noxious thing or an instrument or thing, knowing that it is intended to be used or employed to procure the miscarriage of a female person, whether or not she is pregnant, is guilty of an indictable offence and liable to imprisonment for a term not exceeding two years.

Venereal Diseases

289. [Repealed R.S. 1985, c. 27 (1st Supp.), s. 41.]

Offences Against Conjugal Rights

290. (1) Bigamy — Every one commits **"bigamy"** who

(a) in Canada,

(i) being married, goes through a form of marriage with another person,

(ii) knowing that another person is married, goes through a form of marriage with that person, or

(iii) on the same day or simultaneously, goes through a form of marriage with more than one person; or

(b) being a Canadian citizen resident in Canada leaves Canada with intent to do anything mentioned in subparagraphs (a)(i) to (iii) and, pursuant thereto, does outside Canada anything mentioned in those subparagraphs in circumstances mentioned therein.

(2) Matters of defence — No person commits bigamy by going through a form of marriage if

(a) that person in good faith and on reasonable grounds believes that his spouse is dead,

(b) the spouse of that person has been continuously absent from him for seven years immediately preceding the time when he goes through the form of marriage, unless he knew that his spouse was alive at any time during those seven years,

(c) that person has been divorced from the bond of the first marriage, or

(d) the former marriage has been declared void by a court of competent jurisdiction.

(3) Incompetency no defence — Where a person is alleged to have committed bigamy, it is not a defence that the parties would, if unmarried, have been incompetent to contract marriage under the law of the place where the offence is alleged to have been committed.

(4) Validity presumed — Every marriage or form of marriage shall, for the purpose of this section, be deemed to be valid unless the accused establishes that it was invalid.

(5) Act or omission by accused — No act or omission on the part of an accused who is charged with bigamy invalidates a marriage or form of marriage that is otherwise valid.

291. (1) Punishment — Every one who commits bigamy is guilty of an indictable offence and liable to imprisonment for a term not exceeding five years.

(2) Certificate of marriage — For the purposes of this section, a certificate of marriage issued under the authority of law is evidence of the marriage or form of marriage to which it relates without proof of the signature or official character of the person by whom it purports to be signed.

292. (1) Procuring feigned marriage — Every person who procures or knowingly aids in procuring a feigned marriage between himself and another person is guilty of an indictable offence and liable to imprisonment for a term not exceeding five years.

(2) Corroboration — No person shall be convicted of an offence under this section on the evidence of only one witness unless the evidence of that witness is corroborated in a material particular by evidence that implicates the accused.

293. (1) Polygamy — Every one who

(a) practises or enters into or in any manner agrees or consents to practise or enter into

(i) any form of polygamy, or

(ii) any kind of conjugal union with more than one person at the same time, whether or not it is by law recognized as a binding form of marriage; or

(b) celebrates, assists or is a party to a rite, ceremony, contract or consent that purports to sanction a relationship mentioned in subparagraph (a)(i) or (ii),

is guilty of an indictable offence and liable to imprisonment for a term not exceeding five years.

(2) Evidence in case of polygamy — Where an accused is charged with an offence under this section, no averment or proof of the method by which the alleged relationship was entered into, agreed to or consented to is necessary in the indictment or on the trial of the accused, nor is it necessary on the trial to prove that the persons who are alleged to have entered into the relationship had or intended to have sexual intercourse.

Unlawful Solemnization of Marriage

294. Pretending to solemnize marriage — Every one who

(a) solemnizes or pretends to solemnize a marriage without lawful authority, the proof of which lies upon him, or

(b) procures a person to solemnize a marriage knowing that he is not lawfully authorized to solemnize the marriage,

is guilty of an indictable offence and liable to imprisonment for a term not exceeding two years.

295. Marriage contrary to law — Every one who, being lawfully authorized to solemnize marriage, knowingly and wilfully solemnizes a marriage in contravention of the laws of the province in which the marriage is solemnized is guilty of an indictable offence and liable to imprisonment for a term not exceeding two years.

Blasphemous Libel

296. (1) Offence — Every one who publishes a blasphemous libel is guilty of an indictable offence and liable to imprisonment for a term not exceeding two years.

(2) Question of fact — It is a question of fact whether or not any matter that is published is a blasphemous libel.

(3) Saving — No person shall be convicted of an offence under this section for expressing in good faith and in decent language, or attempting to establish by argument used in good faith and conveyed in decent language, an opinion on a religious subject.

Defamatory Libel

297. "Newspaper" — In sections 303, 304 and 308, **"newspaper"** means any paper, magazine or periodical containing public news, intelligence or reports of events, or any remarks or observations thereon, printed for sale and published periodically or in parts or numbers, at intervals not exceeding thirty-one days between the publication of any two such papers, parts or numbers, and any paper, magazine or periodical printed in order to be dispersed and made public, weekly or more often, or at intervals not exceeding thirty-one days, that contains advertisements, exclusively or principally.

298. (1) Definition — A **"defamatory libel"** is matter published, without lawful justification or excuse, that is likely to injure the reputation of any person by exposing him to hatred, contempt or ridicule, or that is designed to insult the person of or concerning whom it is published.

(2) Mode of expression — A defamatory libel may be expressed directly or by insinuation or irony

    (a) in words legibly marked upon any substance, or

    (b) by any object signifying a defamatory libel otherwise than by words.

299. Publishing — A person publishes a libel when he

    (a) exhibits it in public,

    (b) causes it to be read or seen, or

(c) shows or delivers it, or causes it to be shown or delivered, with intent that it should be read or seen by the person whom it defames or by any other person.

300. Punishment of libel known to be false — Every one who publishes a defamatory libel that he knows is false is guilty of an indictable offence and liable to imprisonment for a term not exceeding five years.

301. Punishment for defamatory libel — Every one who publishes a defamatory libel is guilty of an indictable offence and liable to imprisonment for a term not exceeding two years.

302. (1) Extortion by libel — Every one commits an offence who, with intent

    (a) to extort money from any person, or

    (b) to induce a person to confer on or procure for another person an appointment or office of profit or trust,

publishes or threatens to publish or offers to abstain from publishing or to prevent the publication of a defamatory libel.

(2) Idem — Every one commits an offence who, as the result of the refusal of any person to permit money to be extorted or to confer or procure an appointment or office of profit or trust, publishes or threatens to publish a defamatory libel.

(3) Punishment — Every one who commits an offence under this section is guilty of an indictable offence and liable to imprisonment for a term not exceeding five years.

303. (1) Proprietor of newspaper presumed responsible — The proprietor of a newspaper shall be deemed to publish defamatory matter that is inserted and published therein, unless he proves that the defamatory matter was inserted in the newspaper without his knowledge and without negligence on his part.

(2) General authority to manager when negligence — Where the proprietor of a newspaper gives to a person general authority to manage or conduct the newspaper as editor or otherwise, the insertion by that person of defamatory matter in the newspaper shall, for the purposes of subsection (1), be deemed not to be negligence on the part of the proprietor unless it is proved that

    (a) he intended the general authority to include authority to insert defamatory matter in the newspaper; or

    (b) he continued to confer general authority after he knew that it had been exercised by the insertion of defamatory matter in the newspaper.

(3) Selling newspapers — No person shall be deemed to publish a defamatory libel by reason only that he sells a number or part of a newspaper that contains a defamatory libel, unless he knows that the number or part contains defamatory matter or that defamatory matter is habitually contained in the newspaper.

304. (1) Selling book containing defamatory libel — No person shall be deemed to publish a defamatory libel by reason only that he sells a book, magazine, pamphlet or other thing, other than a newspaper that contains defamatory matter if, at the time of the sale, he does not know that it contains the defamatory matter.

(2) Sale by servant — Where a servant, in the course of his employment, sells a book, magazine, pamphlet or other thing, other than a newspaper, the employer shall be deemed not to publish any defamatory matter contained therein unless it is proved that the employer authorized the sale knowing that

    (a) defamatory matter was contained therein; or

    (b) defamatory matter was habitually contained therein, in the case of a periodical.

305. Publishing proceedings of courts of justice — No person shall be deemed to publish a defamatory libel by reason only that he publishes defamatory matter

    (a) in a proceeding held before or under the authority of a court exercising judicial authority; or

    (b) in an inquiry made under the authority of an Act or by order of Her Majesty, or under the authority of a public department or a department of the government of a province.

306. Parliamentary papers — No person shall be deemed to publish a defamatory libel by reason only that he

    (a) publishes to the Senate or House of Commons or to a legislature of a province defamatory matter contained in a petition to the Senate or House of Commons or to the legislature of a province, as the case may be;

    (b) publishes by order or under the authority of the Senate or House of Commons or of the legislature of a province a paper containing defamatory matter; or

    (c) publishes, in good faith and without ill-will to the person defamed, an extract from or abstract of a petition or paper mentioned in paragraph (a) or (b).

307. (1) Fair reports of Parliamentary or judicial proceedings — No person shall be deemed to publish a defamatory libel by reason only that he publishes in good faith, for the information of the public, a fair report of the proceedings of the Senate or House of Commons or the legislature of a province, or a committee thereof, or of the public proceedings before a court exercising judicial authority, or publishes, in good faith, any fair comment on any such proceedings.

(2) Divorce proceedings an exception — This section does not apply to a person who publishes a report of evidence taken or offered in any proceeding before the Senate or House of Commons or any committee thereof, on a petition or bill relating to any matter of marriage or divorce, if the report is published without authority from or leave of the House in which the proceeding is held or is contrary to any rule, order or practice of that House.

308. Fair report of public meeting — No person shall be deemed to publish a defamatory libel by reason only that he publishes in good faith, in a newspaper, a fair report of the proceedings of any public meeting if

(a) the meeting is lawfully convened for a lawful purpose and is open to the public;

(b) the report is fair and accurate;

(c) the publication of the matter complained of is for the public benefit; and

(d) he does not refuse to publish in a conspicuous place in the newspaper a reasonable explanation or contradiction by the person defamed in respect of the defamatory matter.

309. Public benefit — No person shall be deemed to publish a defamatory libel by reason only that he publishes defamatory matter that, on reasonable grounds, he believes is true, and that is relevant to any subject of public interest, the public discussion of which is for the public benefit.

310. Fair comment on public person or work of art — No person shall be deemed to publish a defamatory libel by reason only that he publishes fair comments

(a) upon the public conduct of a person who takes part in public affairs; or

(b) upon a published book or other literary production, or on any composition or work of art or performance publicly exhibited, or on any other communication made to the public on any subject, if the comments are confined to criticism thereof.

311. When truth a defence — No person shall be deemed to publish a defamatory libel where he proves that the publication of the defamatory matter in the manner in which it was published was for the public benefit at the time when it was published and that the matter itself was true.

312. Publication invited or necessary — No person shall be deemed to publish a defamatory libel by reason only that he publishes defamatory matter

(a) on the invitation or challenge of the person in respect of whom it is published, or

(b) that it is necessary to publish in order to refute defamatory matter published in respect of him by another person, if he believes that the defamatory matter is true and it is relevant to the invitation, challenge or necessary refutation, as the case may be, and does not in any respect exceed what is reasonably sufficient in the circumstances.

313. Answer to inquiries — No person shall be deemed to publish a defamatory libel by reason only that he publishes, in answer to inquiries made to him, defamatory matter relating to a subject-matter in respect of which the person by whom or on whose behalf the inquiries are made has an interest in knowing the truth or who, on reasonable grounds, the person who publishes the defamatory matter believes has such an interest, if

(a) the matter is published, in good faith, for the purpose of giving information in answer to the inquiries;

(b) the person who publishes the defamatory matter believes that it is true;

(c) the defamatory matter is relevant to the inquiries; and

(d) the defamatory matter does not in any respect exceed what is reasonably sufficient in the circumstances.

314. Giving information to person interested — No person shall be deemed to publish a defamatory libel by reason only that he publishes to another person defamatory matter for the purpose of giving information to that person with respect to a subject-matter in which the person to whom the information is given has, or is believed on reasonable grounds by the person who gives it to have, an interest in knowing the truth with respect to that subject-matter if

(a) the conduct of the person who gives the information is reasonable in the circumstances;

(b) the defamatory matter is relevant to the subject-matter; and

(c) the defamatory matter is true, or if it is not true, is made without ill-will toward the person who is defamed and is made in the belief, on reasonable grounds, that it is true.

315. Publication in good faith for redress of wrong — No person shall be deemed to publish a defamatory libel by reason only that he publishes defamatory matter in good faith for the purpose of seeking remedy or redress for a private or public wrong or grievance from a person who has, or who on reasonable grounds he believes has, the right or is under an obligation to remedy or redress the wrong or grievance, if

(a) he believes that the defamatory matter is true;

(b) the defamatory matter is relevant to the remedy or redress that is sought; and

(c) the defamatory matter does not in any respect exceed what is reasonably sufficient in the circumstances.

316. (1) Proving publication by order of legislature — An accused who is alleged to have published a defamatory libel may, at any stage of the proceedings, adduce evidence to prove that the matter that is alleged to be defamatory was contained in a paper published by order or under the authority of the Senate or House of Commons or the legislature of a province.

(2) Directing verdict — Where at any stage in proceedings referred to in subsection (1) the court, judge, justice or provincial court judge is satisfied that the matter alleged to be defamatory was contained in a paper published by order or under the authority of the Senate or House of Commons or the legislature of a province, he shall direct a verdict of not guilty to be entered and shall discharge the accused.

(3) Certificate of order — For the purposes of this section, a certificate under the hand of the Speaker or clerk of the Senate or House of Commons or the legislature of a province to the effect that the matter that is alleged to be defamatory was contained in a paper published by order or under the authority of the Senate, House of Commons or the legislature of a province, as the case may be, is conclusive evidence thereof.

R.S. 1985, c. 27 (1st Supp.), s. 203.

Verdicts

317. Verdicts in cases of defamatory libel — Where, on the trial of an indictment for publishing a defamatory libel, a plea of not guilty is pleaded, the jury that is sworn to try the issue may give a general verdict of guilty or not guilty on the whole matter put in issue on the indictment, and shall not be required or directed by the judge to find the defendant guilty merely on proof of publication by the defendant of the alleged defamatory libel, and of the sense ascribed thereto in the indictment, but the judge may, in his discretion, give a direction or opinion to the jury on the matter in issue as in other criminal proceedings, and the jury may, on the issue, find a special verdict.

Hate Propaganda

318. (1) Advocating genocide — Every one who advocates or promotes genocide is guilty of an indictable offence and liable to imprisonment for a term not exceeding five years.

(2) Definition of "genocide" — In this section **"genocide"** means any of the following acts committed with intent to destroy in whole or in part any identifiable group, namely,

    (a) killing members of the group; or

    (b) deliberately inflicting on the group conditions of life calculated to bring about its physical destruction.

(3) Consent — No proceeding for an offence under this section shall be instituted without the consent of the Attorney General.

(4) Definition of "identifiable group" — In this section **"identifiable group"** means any section of the public distinguished by colour, race, religion or ethnic origin.

319. (1) Public incitement of hatred — Every one who, by communicating statements in any public place, incites hatred against any identifiable group where such incitement is likely to lead to a breach of the peace is guilty of

(a) an indictable offence and is liable to imprisonment for a term not exceeding two years; or

(b) an offence punishable on summary conviction.

(2) Wilful promotion of hatred — Every one who, by communicating statements, other than in private conversation, wilfully promotes hatred against any identifiable group is guilty of

(a) an indictable offence and is liable to imprisonment for a term not exceeding two years; or

(b) an offence punishable on summary conviction.

(3) Defences — No person shall be convicted of an offence under subsection (2)

(a) if he establishes that the statements communicated were true;

(b) if, in good faith, he expressed or attempted to establish by argument an opinion upon a religious subject;

(c) if the statements were relevant to any subject of public interest, the discussion of which was for the public benefit, and if on reasonable grounds he believed them to be true; or

(d) if, in good faith, he intended to point out, for the purpose of removal, matters producing or tending to produce feelings of hatred towards an identifiable group in Canada.

(4) Forfeiture — Where a person is convicted of an offence under section 318 or subsection (1) or (2) of this section, anything by means of or in relation to which the offence was committed, on such conviction, may, in addition to any other punishment imposed, be ordered by the presiding provincial court judge or judge to be forfeited to Her Majesty in right of the province in which that person is convicted, for disposal as the Attorney General may direct.

(5) Exemption from seizure of communication facilities — Subsections 199(6) and (7) apply with such modifications as the circumstances require to section 318 or subsection (1) or (2) of this section.

(6) Consent — No proceeding for an offence under subsection (2) shall be instituted without the consent of the Attorney General.

(7) Definitions — In this section,

"communicating" includes communicating by telephone, broadcasting or other audible or visible means;

"identifiable group" has the same meaning as in section 318;

"public place" includes any place to which the public have access as of right or by invitation, express or implied;

"statements" includes words spoken or written or recorded electronically or electro-magnetically or otherwise, and gestures, signs or other visible representations.

320. (1) Warrant of seizure — A judge who is satisfied by information on oath that there are reasonable grounds for believing that any publication, copies of which are kept for sale or distribution in premises within the jurisdiction of the court, is hate propaganda shall issue a warrant under his hand authorizing seizure of the copies.

(2) Summons to occupier — Within seven days of the issue of a warrant under subsection (1), the judge shall issue a summons to the occupier of the premises requiring him to appear before the court and show cause why the matter seized should not be forfeited to Her Majesty.

(3) Owner and author may appear — The owner and the author of the matter seized under subsection (1) and alleged to be hate propaganda may appear and be represented in the proceedings in order to oppose the making of an order for the forfeiture of the matter.

(4) Order of forfeiture — If the court is satisfied that the publication referred to in subsection (1) is hate propaganda, it shall make an order declaring the matter forfeited to Her Majesty in right of the province in which the proceedings take place, for disposal as the Attorney General may direct.

(5) Disposal of matter — If the court is not satisfied that the publication referred to in subsection (1) is hate propaganda, it shall order that the matter be restored to the person from whom it was seized forthwith after the time for final appeal has expired.

(6) Appeal — An appeal lies from an order made under subsection (4) or (5) by any person who appeared in the proceedings

    (a) on any ground of appeal that involves a question of law alone,

    (b) on any ground of appeal that involves a question of fact alone, or

    (c) on any ground of appeal that involves a question of mixed law and fact,

as if it were an appeal against conviction or against a judgment or verdict of acquittal, as the case may be, on a question of law alone under Part XXI, and sections 673 to 696 apply with such modifications as the circumstances require.

(7) Consent — No proceeding under this section shall be instituted without the consent of the Attorney General.

(8) Definitions — In this section

"court" means

    (a) in the Province of Quebec, the Court of Quebec;

    (a.1) in the Province of Ontario, the Superior Court of Justice;

(b) in the Provinces of New Brunswick, Manitoba, Saskatchewan and Alberta, the Court of Queen's Bench;

(c) in the Provinces of Prince Edward Island and Newfoundland, the Supreme Court, Trial Division;

(d) in the Provinces of Nova Scotia and British Columbia, the Yukon Territory and Northwest Territories, the Supreme Court; and

(e) in Nunavut, the Nunavut Court of Justice;

"genocide" has the same meaning as it has in section 318;

"hate propaganda" means any writing, sign or visible representation that advocates or promotes genocide or the communication of which by any person would constitute an offence under section 319;

"judge" means a judge of a court.
 R.S. 1985, c. 27 (2d Supp.), Sched., item 6; c. 40 (4th Supp.), s. 2; 1990, c. 16, s. 4; c. 17, s. 11; 1992, c. 1, s. 58(1) (Sched. 1, item 6); 1993, c. 28, s. 78 (Sched. III, item 31) [Repealed 1999, c. 3, (Sched., item 7).]; 1998, c. 30, s. 14(d); 1999, c. 3, s. 29.

PART IX — OFFENCES AGAINST RIGHTS OF PROPERTY

Interpretation

321. Definitions — In this Part,

"break" means

(a) to break any part, internal or external, or

(b) to open any thing that is used or intended to be used to close or to cover an internal or external opening;

"credit card" means any card, plate, coupon book or other device issued or otherwise distributed for the purpose of being used

(a) on presentation to obtain, on credit, money, goods, services or any other thing of value, or

(b) in an automated teller machine, a remote service unit or a similar automated banking device to obtain any of the services offered through the machine, unit or device;

"document" means any paper, parchment or other material on which is recorded or marked anything that is capable of being read or understood by a person, computer system or other device, and includes a credit card, but does not include trade marks on articles of commerce or inscriptions on stone or metal or other like material;

"exchequer bill" means a bank note, bond, note, debenture or security that is issued or guaranteed by Her Majesty under the authority of Parliament or the legislature of a province;

"exchequer bill paper" means paper that is used to manufacture exchequer bills;

"false document" means a document

    (a) the whole or a material part of which purports to be made by or on behalf of a person

        (i) who did not make it or authorize it to be made, or

        (ii) who did not in fact exist,

    (b) that is made by or on behalf of the person who purports to make it but is false in some material particular,

    (c) that is made in the name of an existing person, by him or under his authority, with a fraudulent intention that it should pass as being made by a person, real or fictitious, other than the person who makes it or under whose authority it is made;

"revenue paper" means paper that is used to make stamps, licences or permits or for any purpose connected with the public revenue.

R.S. 1985, c. 27 (1st Supp.), s. 42.

Theft

322. (1) Theft — Every one commits theft who fraudulently and without colour of right takes, or fraudulently and without colour of right converts to his use or to the use of another person, anything, whether animate or inanimate, with intent,

    (a) to deprive, temporarily or absolutely, the owner of it, or a person who has a special property or interest in it, of the thing or of his property or interest in it;

    (b) to pledge it or deposit it as security;

    (c) to part with it under a condition with respect to its return that the person who parts with it may be unable to perform; or

    (d) to deal with it in such a manner that it cannot be restored in the condition in which it was at the time it was taken or converted.

(2) Time when theft completed — A person commits theft when, with intent to steal anything, he moves it or causes it to move or to be moved, or begins to cause it to become movable.

(3) Secrecy — A taking or conversion of anything may be fraudulent notwithstanding that it is effected without secrecy or attempt at concealment.

(4) Purpose of taking — For the purposes of this Act, the question whether anything that is converted is taken for the purpose of conversion, or whether it is, at the time it is converted, in the lawful possession of the person who converts it is not material.

(5) Wild living creature — For the purposes of this section, a person who has a wild living creature in captivity shall be deemed to have a special property or interest in it while it is in captivity and after it has escaped from captivity.

323. Oysters — **(1)** Where oysters and oyster brood are in oyster beds, layings or fisheries that are the property of any person and are sufficiently marked out or known as the property of that person, that person shall be deemed to have a special property or interest in them.

(2) Oyster bed — An indictment is sufficient if it describes an oyster bed, laying or fishery by name or in any other way, without stating that it is situated in a particular territorial division.

324. Theft by bailee of things under seizure — Every one who is a bailee of anything that is under lawful seizure by a peace officer or public officer in the execution of the duties of his office, and who is obliged by law or agreement to produce and deliver it to that officer or to another person entitled thereto at a certain time and place, or on demand, steals it if he does not produce and deliver it in accordance with his obligation, but he does not steal it if his failure to produce and deliver it is not the result of a wilful act or omission by him.

325. Agent pledging goods, when not theft — A factor or an agent does not commit theft by pledging or giving a lien on goods or documents of title to goods that are entrusted to him for the purpose of sale or for any other purpose, if the pledge or lien is for an amount that does not exceed the sum of

    (a) the amount due to him from his principal at the time the goods or documents are pledged or the lien is given; and

    (b) the amount of any bill of exchange that he has accepted for or on account of his principal.

326. (1) Theft of telecommunication service — Every one commits theft who fraudulently, maliciously, or without colour of right,

    (a) abstracts, consumes or uses electricity or gas or causes it to be wasted or diverted; or

    (b) uses any telecommunication facility or obtains any telecommunication service.

(2) Definition of "telecommunication" — In this section and section 327, **"telecommunication"** means any transmission, emission or reception of signs, signals, writing, images or sounds or intelligence of any nature by wire, radio, visual, or other electro-magnetic system.

327. (1) Possession of device to obtain telecommunication facility or service — Every one who, without lawful excuse, the proof of which lies on him, manufactures, possesses, sells or offers for sale or distributes any instrument or device or any component thereof, the design of which renders it primarily useful for obtaining the use of any telecommunication facility or service, under circumstances that give rise to a reasonable inference that the device has been used or is or was intended to be used to obtain the use of any telecommunication facility or service without payment of a lawful charge therefor, is guilty of an indictable offence and liable to imprisonment for a term not exceeding two years.

(2) Forfeiture — Where a person is convicted of an offence under subsection (1) or paragraph 326(1)(*b*), any instrument or device in relation to which the offence was committed or the possession of which constituted the offence, upon such conviction, in addition to any punishment that is imposed, may be ordered forfeited to Her Majesty, whereupon it may be disposed of as the Attorney General directs.

(3) Limitation — No order for forfeiture shall be made under subsection (2) in respect of telephone, telegraph or other communication facilities or equipment owned by a person engaged in providing telephone, telegraph or other communication service to the public or forming part of the telephone, telegraph or other communication service or system of such a person by means of which an offence under subsection (1) has been committed if such person was not a party to the offence.

328. Theft by or from person having special property or interest — A person may be convicted of theft notwithstanding that anything that is alleged to have been stolen was stolen

(a) by the owner of it from a person who has a special property or interest in it;

(b) by a person who has a special property or interest in it from the owner of it;

(c) by a lessee of it from his reversioner;

(d) by one of several joint owners, tenants in common or partners of or in it from the other persons who have an interest in it; or

(e) by the directors, officers or members of a company, body corporate, unincorporated body or of a society associated together for a lawful purpose from the company, body corporate, unincorporated body or society, as the case may be.

329. (1) Husband or wife — Subject to subsection (2), no husband or wife, during cohabitation, commits theft of anything that is by law the property of the other.

(2) Theft by spouse while living apart — A husband or wife commits theft who, intending to desert or on deserting the other or while living apart from the other, fraudulently takes or converts anything that is by law the property of the other in a manner that, if it were done by another person, would be theft.

(3) Assisting or receiving — Every one commits theft who, during cohabitation of a husband and wife, knowingly

(a) assists either of them in dealing with anything that is by law the property of the other in a manner that would be theft if they were not married, or;

(b) receives from either of them anything that is by law the property of the other and has been obtained from the other by dealing with it in a manner that would be theft if they were not married.

Proposed Repeal — 329.

329. [Repealed 2000, c. 12, s. 94. Not in force at date of publication.]

330. (1) Theft by person required to account — Every one commits theft who, having received anything from any person on terms that require him to account for or pay it or the proceeds of it or a part of the proceeds to that person or another person, fraudulently fails to account for or pay it or the proceeds of it or the part of the proceeds of it accordingly.

(2) Effect of entry in account — Where subsection (1) otherwise applies, but one of the terms is that the thing received or the proceeds or part of the proceeds of it shall be an item in a debtor and creditor account between the person who receives the thing and the person to whom he is to account for or to pay it, and that the latter shall rely only on the liability of the other as his debtor in respect thereof, a proper entry in that account of the thing received or the proceeds or part of the proceeds of it, as the case may be, is a sufficient accounting therefor, and no fraudulent conversion of the thing or the proceeds or part of the proceeds of it thereby accounted for shall be deemed to have taken place.

331. Theft by person holding power of attorney — Every one commits theft who, being entrusted, whether solely or jointly with another person, with a power of attorney for the sale, mortgage, pledge or other disposition of real or personal property, fraudulently sells, mortgages, pledges or otherwise disposes of the property or any part of it, or fraudulently converts the proceeds of a sale, mortgage, pledge or other disposition of the property, or any part of the proceeds, to a purpose other than that for which he was entrusted by the power of attorney.

332. (1) Misappropriation of money held under direction — Every one commits theft who, having received, either solely or jointly with another person, money or valuable security or a power of attorney for the sale of real or personal property, with a direction that the money or a part of it, or the proceeds or a part of the proceeds of the security or the property shall be applied to a purpose or paid to a person specified in the direction, fraudulently and contrary to the direction applies to any other purpose or pays to any other person the money or proceeds or any part of it.

(2) Effect of entry in account — This section does not apply where a person who receives anything mentioned in subsection (1) and the person from whom he receives it deal with each other on such terms that all money paid to the former would, in the absence of any such direction, be properly treated as an item in a debtor and creditor account between them, unless the direction is in writing.

333. Taking ore for scientific purpose — No person commits theft by reason only that he takes, for the purpose of exploration or scientific investigation, a specimen of ore or mineral from land that is not enclosed and is not occupied or worked as a mine, quarry or digging.

334. Punishment for theft — Except where otherwise provided by law, every one who commits theft

(a) is guilty of an indictable offence and liable to imprisonment for a term not exceeding ten years, where the property stolen is a testamentary instrument or the value of what is stolen exceeds five thousand dollars; or

(b) is guilty

> (i) of an indictable offence and is liable to imprisonment for a term not exceeding two years, or

> (ii) of an offence punishable on summary conviction,

where the value of what is stolen does not exceed five thousand dollars.

R.S. 1985, c. 27 (1st Supp.), s. 43; 1994, c. 44, s. 20.

Offences Resembling Theft

335. (1) Taking motor vehicle or vessel or found therein without consent — Subject to subsection (1.1), every one who, without the consent of the owner, takes a motor vehicle or vessel with intent to drive, use, navigate or operate it or cause it to be driven, used, navigated or operated, or is an occupant of a motor vehicle or vessel knowing that it was taken without the consent of the owner, is guilty of an offence punishable on summary conviction.

(1.1) Exception — Subsection (1) does not apply to an occupant of a motor vehicle or vessel who, on becoming aware that it was taken without the consent of the owner, attempted to leave the motor vehicle or vessel, to the extent that it was feasible to do so, or actually left the motor vehicle or vessel.

(2) Definition of "vessel" — For the purposes of subsection (1), **"vessel"** has the meaning assigned by section 214.

R.S. 1985, c. 1 (4th Supp.), s. 22; 1997, c. 18, s. 15.

336. Criminal breach of trust — Every one who, being a trustee of anything for the use or benefit, whether in whole or in part, of another person, or for a public or charitable purpose, converts, with intent to defraud and in contravention of his trust, that thing or any part of it to a use that is not authorized by the trust is guilty of an indictable offence and liable to imprisonment for a term not exceeding fourteen years.

337. Public servant refusing to deliver property — Every one who, being or having been employed in the service of Her Majesty in right of Canada or in right of a province, or in the service of a municipality, and entrusted by virtue of that employment with the receipt, custody, management or control of anything, refuses or fails to deliver it to a person who is authorized to demand it and does demand it is guilty of an indictable offence and liable to imprisonment for a term not exceeding fourteen years.

338. (1) Fraudulently taking cattle or defacing brand — Every one who, without the consent of the owner,

> (a) fraudulently takes, holds, keeps in his possession, conceals, receives, appropriates, purchases or sells cattle that are found astray, or

> (b) fraudulently, in whole or in part,

>> (i) obliterates, alters or defaces a brand or mark on cattle, or

>> (ii) makes a false or counterfeit brand or mark on cattle,

is guilty of an indictable offence and liable to imprisonment for a term not exceeding five years.

(2) Punishment for theft of cattle — Every one who commits theft of cattle is guilty of an indictable offence and liable to imprisonment for a term not exceeding ten years.

(3) Evidence of property in cattle — In any proceedings under this Act, evidence that cattle are marked with a brand or mark that is recorded or registered in accordance with any Act is, in the absence of any evidence to the contrary, proof that the cattle are owned by the registered owner of that brand or mark.

(4) Presumption from possession — Where an accused is charged with an offence under subsection (1) or (2), the burden of proving that the cattle came lawfully into the possession of the accused or his employee or into the possession of another person on behalf of the accused is on the accused, if the accused is not the registered owner of the brand or mark with which the cattle are marked, unless it appears that possession of the cattle by an employee of the accused or by another person on behalf of the accused was without the knowledge and authority, sanction or approval of the accused.

339. (1) Taking possession, etc., of drift timber — Every one is guilty of an indictable offence and liable to imprisonment for a term not exceeding five years who, without the consent of the owner,

   (a) fraudulently takes, holds, keeps in his possession, conceals, receives, appropriates, purchases or sells,

   (b) removes, alters, obliterates or defaces a mark or number on, or

   (c) refuses to deliver up to the owner or to the person in charge thereof on behalf of the owner or to a person authorized by the owner to receive it,

any lumber or lumbering equipment that is found adrift, cast ashore or lying on or embedded in the bed or bottom, or on the bank or beach, of a river, stream or lake in Canada, or in the harbours or any of the coastal waters of Canada.

(2) Dealer in second-hand goods — Every one who, being a dealer in second-hand goods of any kind, trades or traffics in or has in his possession for sale or traffic any lumbering equipment that is marked with the mark, brand, registered timber mark, name or initials of a person, without the written consent of that person, is guilty of an offence punishable on summary conviction.

(3) Search for timber unlawfully detained — A peace officer who suspects, on reasonable grounds, that any lumber owned by any person and bearing the registered timber mark of that person is kept or detained in or on any place without the knowledge or consent of that person, may enter into or on that place to ascertain whether or not it is detained there without the knowledge or consent of that person.

(4) Evidence of property in timber — Where any lumber or lumbering equipment is marked with a timber mark or a boom chain brand registered under any Act, the mark or brand is, in proceedings under subsection (1), and, in the absence of any evidence to the contrary, proof that it is the property of the registered owner of the mark or brand.

(5) Presumption from possession — Where an accused or his servants or agents are in possession of lumber or lumbering equipment marked with the mark, brand, registered timber mark, name or initials of another person, the burden of proving that it came lawfully into his possession or into possession of his servants or agents is, in proceedings under subsection (1), on the accused.

(6) Definitions — In this section

"coastal waters of Canada" includes all of Queen Charlotte Sound, all the Strait of Georgia and the Canadian waters of the Strait of Juan de Fuca;

"lumber" means timber, mast, spar, shingle bolt, sawlog or lumber of any description;

"lumbering equipment" includes a boom chain, chain, line and shackle.

340. Destroying documents of title — Every one who, for a fraudulent purpose, destroys, cancels, conceals or obliterates

    (a) a document of title to goods or lands,

    (b) a valuable security or testamentary instrument, or

    (c) a judicial or official document,

is guilty of an indictable offence and liable to imprisonment for a term not exceeding ten years.

341. Fraudulent concealment — Every one who, for a fraudulent purpose, takes, obtains, removes or conceals anything is guilty of an indictable offence and liable to imprisonment for a term not exceeding two years.

342. (1) Theft, forgery, etc., of credit card — Every person who

    (a) steals a credit card,

    (b) forges or falsifies a credit card,

    (c) possesses, uses or traffics in a credit card or a forged or falsified credit card, knowing that it was obtained, made or altered

        (i) by the commission in Canada of an offence, or

        (ii) by an act or omission anywhere that, if it had occurred in Canada, would have constituted an offence, or

    (d) uses a credit card knowing that it has been revoked or cancelled,

is guilty of

    (e) an indictable offence and is liable to imprisonment for a term not exceeding ten years, or

    (f) an offence punishable on summary conviction.

(2) Jurisdiction — An accused who is charged with an offence under subsection (1) may be tried and punished by any court having jurisdiction to try that offence in the place where the offence is alleged to have been committed or in the place where the accused is found, is arrested or is in custody, but where the place where the accused is found, is arrested or is in custody is outside the province in which the offence is alleged to have been committed, no proceedings in respect of that offence shall be commenced in that place without the consent of the Attorney General of that province.

(3) Unauthorized use of credit card data — Every person who, fraudulently and without colour of right, possesses, uses, traffics in or permits another person to use credit card data, whether or not authentic, that would enable a person to use a credit card or to obtain the services that are provided by the issuer of a credit card to credit card holders is guilty of

> (a) an indictable offence and is liable to imprisonment for a term not exceeding ten years; or

> (b) an offence punishable on summary conviction.

(4) Definition of "traffic" — In this section, **"traffic"** means, in relation to a credit card or credit card data, to sell, export from or import into Canada, distribute or deal with in any other way.

(3) [Repealed R.S. 1985, c. 27 (1st Supp.), s. 44.]

R.S. 1985, c. 27 (1st Supp.), s. 44; 1997, c. 18, s. 16.

342.01 (1) Making having or dealing in instruments for forging or falsifying credit cards — Every person who, without lawful justification or excuse,

> (a) makes or repairs,

> (b) buys or sells,

> (c) exports from or imports into Canada, or

> (d) possesses

any instrument, device, apparatus, material or thing that the person knows has been used or knows is adapted or intended for use in forging or falsifying credit cards is guilty of an indictable offence and liable to imprisonment for a term not exceeding ten years, or is guilty of an offence punishable on summary conviction.

(2) Forfeiture — Where a person is convicted of an offence under subsection (1), any instrument, device, apparatus, material or thing in relation to which the offence was committed or the possession of which constituted the offence may, in addition to any other punishment that may be imposed, be ordered forfeited to Her Majesty, whereupon it may be disposed of as the Attorney General directs.

(3) Limitation — No order of forfeiture may be made under subsection (2) in respect of any thing that is the property of a person who was not a party to the offence under subsection (1).

1997, c. 18, s. 17.

342.1 (1) Unauthorized use of computer — Every one who, fraudulently and without color of right,

> (a) obtains, directly or indirectly, any computer service,

(b) by means of an electro-magnetic, acoustic, mechanical or other device, intercepts or causes to be intercepted, directly or indirectly, any function of a computer system,

(c) uses or causes to be used, directly or indirectly, a computer system with intent to commit an offence under paragraph (a) or (b) or an offence under section 430 in relation to data or a computer system, or

(d) uses, possesses, traffics in or permits another person to have access to a computer password that would enable a person to commit an offence under paragraph (*a*), (*b*) or (*c*)

is guilty of an indictable offence and liable to imprisonment for a term not exceeding ten years, or is guilty of an offence punishable on summary conviction.

(2) Definitions — In this section,

"computer password" means any data by which a computer service or computer system is capable of being obtained or used;

"computer program" means data representing instructions or statements that, when executed in a computer system, causes the computer system to perform a function;

"computer service" includes data processing and the storage or retrieval of data;

"computer system" means a device that, or a group of interconnected or related devices one or more of which,

(a) contains computer programs or other data, and

(b) pursuant to computer programs,

    (i) performs logic and control, and

    (ii) may perform any other function;

"data" means representations of information or of concepts that are being prepared or have been prepared in a form suitable for use in a computer system;

"electro-magnetic, acoustic, mechanical or other device" means any device or apparatus that is used or is capable of being used to intercept any function of a computer system, but does not include a hearing aid used to correct subnormal hearing of the user to not better than normal hearing;

"function" includes logic, control, arithmetic, deletion, storage and retrieval and communication or telecommunication to, from or within a computer system;

"intercept" includes listen to or record a function of a computer system, or acquire the substance, meaning or purport thereof.

"traffic" means, in respect of a computer password, to sell, export from or import into Canada, distribute or deal with in any other way.

R.S. 1985, c. 27 (1st Supp.), s. 45; 1997, c. 18, s. 18.

342.2 (1) Possession of device to obtain computer service — Every person who, without lawful justification or excuse, makes, possesses, sells, offers for sale or distributes any instrument or device or any component thereof, the design of which renders it primarily useful for committing an offence under section 342.1, under circumstances that give rise to a reasonable inference that the instrument, device or component has been used or is or was intended to be used to commit an offence contrary to that section,

(a) is guilty of an indictable offence and liable to imprisonment for a term not exceeding two years; or

(b) is guilty of an offence punishable on summary conviction.

(2) Forfeiture — Where a person is convicted of an offence under subsection (1), any instrument or device, in relation to which the offence was committed or the possession of which constituted the offence, may, in addition to any other punishment that may be imposed, be ordered forfeited to Her Majesty, whereupon it may be disposed of as the Attorney General directs.

(3) Limitation — No order of forfeiture may be made under subsection (2) in respect of any thing that is the property of a person who was not a party to the offence under subsection (1).

1997, c. 18, s. 19.

343. Robbery — Every one commits robbery who

(a) steals, and for the purpose of extorting whatever is stolen or to prevent or overcome resistance to the stealing, uses violence or threats of violence to a person or property;

(b) steals from any person and, at the time he steals or immediately before or immediately thereafter, wounds, beats, strikes or uses any personal violence to that person;

(c) assaults any person with intent to steal from him; or

(d) steals from any person while armed with an offensive weapon or imitation thereof.

344. Robbery — Every person who commits robbery is guilty of an indictable offence and liable

(a) where a firearm is used in the commission of the offence, to imprisonment for life and to a minimum punishment of imprisonment for a term of four years; and

(b) in any other case, to imprisonment for life.

1995, c. 39, s. 149.

345. Stopping mail with intent — Every one who stops a mail conveyance with intent to rob or search it is guilty of an indictable offence and liable to imprisonment for life.

346. (1) Extortion — Every one commits extortion who, without reasonable justification or excuse and with intent to obtain anything, by threats, accusations, menaces or violence induces or attempts to induce any person, whether or not he is the person threatened, accused or menaced or to whom violence is shown, to do anything or cause anything to be done.

(1.1) Extortion — Every person who commits extortion is guilty of an indictable offence and liable

> (a) where a firearm is used in the commission of the offence, to imprisonment for life and to a minimum punishment of imprisonment for a term of four years; and

> (b) in any other case, to imprisonment for life.

(2) Saving — A threat to institute civil proceedings is not a threat for the purposes of this section.

R.S. 1985, c. 27 (1st Supp.), s. 46; 1995, c. 39, s. 150.

Criminal Interest Rate

347. (1) Criminal interest rate — Notwithstanding any Act of Parliament, every one who

> (a) enters into an agreement or arrangement to receive interest at a criminal rate, or

> (b) receives a payment or partial payment of interest at a criminal rate,

is guilty of

> (c) an indictable offence and is liable to imprisonment for a term not exceeding five years, or

> (d) an offence punishable on summary conviction and is liable to a fine not exceeding twenty-five thousand dollars or to imprisonment for a term not exceeding six months or to both.

(2) Definitions — In this section,

"credit advanced" means the aggregate of the money and the monetary value of any goods, services or benefits actually advanced or to be advanced under an agreement or arrangement minus the aggregate of any required deposit balance and any fee, fine, penalty, commission and other similar charge or expense directly or indirectly incurred under the original or any collateral agreement or arrangement;

"criminal rate" means an effective annual rate of interest calculated in accordance with generally accepted actuarial practices and principles that exceeds sixty per cent on the credit advanced under an agreement or arrangement;

"insurance charge" means the cost of insuring the risk assumed by the person who advances or is to advance credit under an agreement or arrangement, where the face amount of the insurance does not exceed the credit advanced;

"interest" means the aggregate of all charges and expenses, whether in the form of a fee, fine, penalty, commission or other similar charge or expense or in any other form, paid or payable for the advancing of credit under an agreement or arrangement, by or on behalf of the person to whom the credit is or is to be advanced, irrespective of the person to whom any such charges and expenses are or are to be paid or payable, but does not include any repayment of credit advanced or any insurance charge, official fee, overdraft charge, required deposit balance or, in the case of a mortgage transaction, any amount required to be paid on account of property taxes;

"official fee" means a fee required by law to be paid to any governmental authority in connection with perfecting any security under an agreement or arrangement for the advancing of credit;

"overdraft charge" means a charge not exceeding five dollars for the creation of or increase in an overdraft, imposed by a credit union or caisse populaire the membership of which is wholly or substantially comprised of natural persons or a deposit taking institution the deposits in which are insured, in whole or in part, by the Canada Deposit Insurance Corporation or guaranteed, in whole or in part, by the Quebec Deposit Insurance Board;

"required deposit balance" means a fixed or an ascertainable amount of the money actually advanced or to be advanced under an agreement or arrangement that is required, as a condition of the agreement or arrangement, to be deposited or invested by or on behalf of the person to whom the advance is or is to be made and that may be available, in the event of his defaulting in any payment, to or for the benefit of the person who advances or is to advance the money.

(3) Presumption — Where a person receives a payment or partial payment of interest at a criminal rate, he shall, in the absence of evidence to the contrary, be deemed to have knowledge of the nature of the payment and that it was received at a criminal rate.

(4) Proof of effective annual rate — In any proceedings under this section, a certificate of a Fellow of the Canadian Institute of Actuaries stating that he has calculated the effective annual rate of interest on any credit advanced under an agreement or arrangement and setting out the calculations and the information on which they are based is, in the absence of evidence to the contrary, proof of the effective annual rate without proof of the signature or official character of the person appearing to have signed the certificate.

(5) Notice — A certificate referred to in subsection (4) shall not be received in evidence unless the party intending to produce it has given to the accused or defendant reasonable notice of that intention together with a copy of the certificate.

(6) Cross examination with leave — An accused or a defendant against whom a certificate referred to in subsection (4) is produced may, with leave of the court, require the attendance of the actuary for the purposes of cross-examination.

(7) Consent required for proceedings — No proceedings shall be commenced under this section without the consent of the Attorney General.

(8) Application — This section does not apply to any transaction to which the *Tax Rebate Discounting Act* applies.

Breaking and Entering

348. (1) Breaking and entering with intent, committing offence or breaking out — Every one who

(a) breaks and enters a place with intent to commit an indictable offence therein,

(b) breaks and enters a place and commits an indictable offence therein, or

(c) breaks out of a place after

(i) committing an indictable offence therein, or

(ii) entering the place with intent to commit an indictable offence therein,

is guilty

(d) if the offence is committed in relation to a dwelling-house, of an indictable offence and liable to imprisonment for life, and

(e) if the offence is committed in relation to a place other than a dwelling-house, of an indictable offence and liable to imprisonment for a term not exceeding ten years or of an offence punishable on summary conviction.

(2) Presumptions — For the purposes of proceedings under this section, evidence that an accused

(a) broke and entered a place or attempted to break and enter a place is, in the absence of any evidence to the contrary, proof that he broke and entered the place or attempted to do so, as the case may be, with intent to commit an indictable offence therein; or

(b) broke out of a place is, in the absence of any evidence to the contrary, proof that he broke out after

(i) committing an indictable offence therein, or

(ii) entering with intent to commit an indictable offence therein.

(3) Definition of "place" — For the purposes of this section, and section 351, **"place"** means

(a) a dwelling-house;

(b) a building or structure or any part thereof, other than a dwelling-house;

(c) a railway vehicle, a vessel, an aircraft or a trailer; or

(d) a pen or an enclosure in which fur-bearing animals are kept in captivity for breeding or commercial purposes.

R.S. 1985, c. 27 (1st Supp.), s. 47; 1997, c. 18, s. 20.

349. (1) Being unlawfully in dwelling-house — Every person who, without lawful excuse, the proof of which lies on that person, enters or is in a dwelling-house with intent to commit an indictable offence in it is guilty of an indictable offence and liable to imprisonment for a term not exceeding ten years or of an offence punishable on summary conviction.

(2) Presumption — For the purposes of proceedings under this section, evidence that an accused, without lawful excuse, entered or was in a dwelling-house is, in the absence of any evidence to the contrary, proof that he entered or was in the dwelling-house with intent to commit an indictable offence therein.

1997, c. 18, s. 21.

350. Entrance — For the purposes of sections 348 and 349,

(a) a person enters as soon as any part of his body or any part of an instrument that he uses is within any thing that is being entered; and

(b) a person shall be deemed to have broken and entered if

(i) he obtained entrance by a threat or artifice or by collusion with a person within, or

(ii) he entered without lawful justification or excuse, the proof of which lies on him, by a permanent or temporary opening.

351. (1) Possession of break-in instrument — Every one who, without lawful excuse, the proof of which lies on him, has in his possession any instrument suitable for the purpose of breaking into any place, motor vehicle, vault or safe under circumstances that give rise to a reasonable inference that the instrument has been used or is or was intended to be used for any such purpose, is guilty of an indictable offence and liable to imprisonment for a term not exceeding ten years.

(2) Disguise with intent — Every one who, with intent to commit an indictable offence, has his face masked or coloured or is otherwise disguised is guilty of an indictable offence and liable to imprisonment for a term not exceeding ten years.

R.S. 1985, c. 27 (1st Supp.), s. 48.

352. Possession of instruments for breaking into coin-operated or currency exchange devices — Every one who, without lawful excuse, the proof of which lies on him, has in his possession any instrument suitable for breaking into a coin-operated device or a currency exchange device, under circumstances that give rise to a reasonable inference that the instrument has been used or is or was intended to be used for breaking into a coin-operated device or a currency exchange device, is guilty of an indictable offence and liable to imprisonment for a term not exceeding two years.

353. (1) Selling, etc., automobile master key — Every one who

(a) sells, offers for sale or advertises in a province an automobile master key otherwise than under the authority of a licence issued by the Attorney General of that province, or

(b) purchases or has in his possession in a province an automobile master key otherwise than under the authority of a licence issued by the Attorney General of that province, is guilty of an indictable offence and liable to imprisonment for a term not exceeding two years.

(1.1) Exception — A police officer specially authorized by the chief of the police force to possess an automobile master key is not guilty of an offence under subsection (1) by reason only that the police officer possesses an automobile master key for the purposes of the execution of the police officer's duties.

(2) Terms and conditions of licence — A licence issued by the Attorney General of a province as described in paragraph (1)(*a*) or (*b*) may contain such terms and conditions relating to the sale, offering for sale, advertising, purchasing, having in possession or use of an automobile master key as the Attorney General of that province may prescribe.

(2.1) Fees — The Attorney General of a province may prescribe fees for the issue or renewal of licences as described in paragraph (1)(*a*) or (*b*).

(3) Record to be kept — Every one who sells an automobile master key

(a) shall keep a record of the transaction showing the name and address of the purchaser and particulars of the licence issued to the purchaser as described in paragraph (1)(*b*); and

(b) shall produce the record for inspection at the request of a peace officer.

(4) Failure to comply with subsection (3) — Every one who fails to comply with subsection (3) is guilty of an offence punishable on summary conviction.

(5) Definitions — The definitions in this subsection apply in this section.

"automobile master key" includes a key, pick, rocker key or other instrument designed or adapted to operate the ignition or other switches or locks of a series of motor vehicles.

"licence" includes any authorization,

1997, c. 18, s. 22.

Having in Possession

354. (1) Possession of property obtained by crime — Every one commits an offence who has in his possession any property or thing or any proceeds of any property or thing knowing that all or part of the property or thing or of the proceeds was obtained by or derived directly or indirectly from

(a) the commission in Canada of an offence punishable by indictment; or

(b) an act or omission anywhere that, if it had occurred in Canada, would have constituted an offence punishable by indictment.

(2) Obliterated vehicle identification number — In proceedings in respect of an offence under subsection (1), evidence that a person has in his possession a motor vehicle the vehicle identification number of which has been wholly or partially removed or obliterated or a part of a motor vehicle being a part bearing a vehicle identification number that has been wholly or partially removed or obliterated is, in the absence of any evidence to the contrary, proof that the motor vehicle or part, as the case may be, was obtained, and that such person had the motor vehicle or part, as the case may be, in his possession knowing that it was obtained,

(a) by the commission in Canada of an offence punishable by indictment; or

(b) by an act or omission anywhere that, if it had occurred in Canada, would have constituted an offence punishable by indictment.

(3) "vehicle identification number" defined — For the purposes of subsection (2), **"vehicle identification number "**means any number or other mark placed on a motor vehicle for the purpose of distinguishing the motor vehicle from other similar motor vehicles.

(4) Exception — A peace officer or a person acting under the direction of a peace officer is not guilty of an offence under this section by reason only that the peace officer or person possesses property or a thing or the proceeds of property or a thing mentioned in subsection (1) for the purposes of an investigation or otherwise in the execution of the peace officer's duties.

1997, c. 18, s. 23.

355. Punishment — Every one who commits an offence under section 354

(a) is guilty of an indictable offence and liable to imprisonment for a term not exceeding ten years, where the subject-matter of the offence is a testamentary instrument or the value of the subject-matter of the offence exceeds five thousand dollars; or

(b) is guilty

(i) of an indictable offence and is liable to imprisonment for a term not exceeding two years, or

(ii) of an offence punishable on summary conviction,

where the value of the subject-matter of the offence does not exceed five thousand dollars.

1985, c. 27 (1st Supp.), s. 49; 1994, c. 44, s. 21.

356. (1) Theft from mail — Every one who

(a) steals

(i) any thing sent by post, after it is deposited at a post office and before it is delivered,

(ii) a bag, sack or other container or covering in which mail is conveyed, whether or not it contains mail, or

(iii) a key suited to a lock adopted for use in the Canada Post Corporation, or

(b) has in his possession anything in respect of which he knows that an offence has been committed under paragraph (a),

is guilty of an indictable offence and liable to imprisonment for a term not exceeding ten years.

(2) Allegation of value not necessary — In proceedings for an offence under this section it is not necessary to allege in the indictment or to prove on the trial that anything in respect of which the offence was committed had any value.

357. Bringing into Canada property obtained by crime — Every one who brings into or has in Canada anything that he has obtained outside Canada by an act that, if it had been committed in Canada, would have been the offence of theft or an offence under section 342 or 354, is guilty of an indictable offence and liable to a term of imprisonment not exceeding ten years.

R.S. 1985, c. 27 (1st Supp.), s. 50.

358. Having in possession when complete — For the purposes of sections 342 and 354 and paragraph 356(1)(b), the offence of having in possession is complete when a person has, alone or jointly with another person, possession of or control over anything mentioned in those sections or when he aids in concealing or disposing of it, as the case may be.

R.S. 1985, c. 27 (1st Supp.), s. 50.

359. (1) Evidence — Where an accused is charged with an offence under section 342 or 354 or paragraph 356(1)(b), evidence is admissible at any stage of the proceedings to show that property other than the property that is the subject-matter of the proceedings

(a) was found in the possession of the accused, and

(b) was stolen within twelve months before the proceedings were commenced,

and that evidence may be considered for the purpose of proving that the accused knew that the property that forms the subject-matter of the proceedings was stolen property.

(2) Notice to accused — Subsection (1) does not apply unless

(a) at least three days notice in writing is given to the accused that in the proceedings it is intended to prove that property other than the property that is the subject-matter of the proceedings was found in his possession; and

(b) the notice sets out the nature or description of the property and describes the person from whom it is alleged to have been stolen.

R.S. 1985, c. 27 (1st Supp.), s. 51.

360. (1) Evidence of previous conviction — Where an accused is charged with an offence under section 354 or paragraph 356(1)(b) and evidence is adduced that the subject-matter of the proceedings was found in his possession, evidence that the accused was, within five years before the proceedings were commenced, convicted of an offence involving theft or an offence under section 354 is admissible at any stage of the proceedings and may be taken into consideration for the purpose of proving that the accused knew that the property that forms the subject-matter of the proceedings was unlawfully obtained.

(2) Notice to accused — Subsection (1) does not apply unless at least three days notice in writing is given to the accused that in the proceedings it is intended to prove the previous conviction.

False Pretences

361. (1) False pretence — A false pretence is a representation of a matter of fact either present or past, made by words or otherwise, that is known by the person who makes it to be false and that is made with a fraudulent intent to induce the person to whom it is made to act on it.

(2) Exaggeration — Exaggerated commendation or depreciation of the quality of anything is not a false pretence unless it is carried to such an extent that it amounts to a fraudulent misrepresentation of fact.

(3) Question of fact — For the purposes of subsection (2), it is a question of fact whether commendation or depreciation amounts to a fraudulent misrepresentation of fact.

362. (1) False pretence or false statement — Every one commits an offence who

(a) by a false pretence, whether directly or through the medium of a contract obtained by a false pretence, obtains anything in respect of which the offence of theft may be committed or causes it to be delivered to another person;

(b) obtains credit by a false pretence or by fraud;

(c) knowingly makes or causes to be made, directly or indirectly, a false statement in writing with intent that it should be relied on, with respect to the financial condition or means or ability to pay of himself or any person, firm or corporation that he is interested in or that he acts for, for the purpose of procuring, in any form whatever, whether for his benefit or the benefit of that person, firm or corporation,

(i) the delivery of personal property,

(ii) the payment of money,

(iii) the making of a loan,

(iv) the grant or extension of credit,

(v) the discount of an account receivable, or

(vi) the making, accepting, discounting or endorsing of a bill of exchange, cheque, draft or promissory note; or

(d) knowing that a false statement in writing has been made with respect to the financial condition or means or ability to pay of himself or another person, firm or corporation that he is interested in or that he acts for, procures on the faith of that statement, whether for his benefit or for the benefit of that person, firm or corporation, anything mentioned in subparagraphs (c)(i) to (vi).

(2) Punishment — Every one who commits an offence under paragraph (1)(*a*)

(a) is guilty of an indictable offence and liable to a term of imprisonment not exceeding ten years, where the property obtained is a testamentary instrument or the value of what is obtained exceeds five thousand dollars; or

(b) is guilty

(i) of an indictable offence and is liable to imprisonment for a term not exceeding two years, or

(ii) of an offence punishable on summary conviction,

where the value of what is obtained does not exceed five thousand dollars.

(3) Idem — Every one who commits an offence under paragraph (1)(*b*), (*c*) or (*d*) is guilty of an indictable offence and liable to imprisonment for a term not exceeding ten years.

(4) Presumption from cheque issued without funds — Where, in proceedings under paragraph (1)(*a*), it is shown that anything was obtained by the accused by means of a cheque that, when presented for payment within a reasonable time, was dishonoured on the ground that no funds or insufficient funds were on deposit to the credit of the accused in the bank or other institution on which the cheque was drawn, it shall be presumed to have been obtained by a false pretence, unless the court is satisfied by evidence that when the accused issued the cheque he believed on reasonable grounds that it would be honoured if presented for payment within a reasonable time after it was issued.

(5) Definition of "cheque" — In this section, **"cheque"** includes, in addition to its ordinary meaning, a bill of exchange drawn on any institution that makes it a business practice to honour bills of exchange or any particular kind thereof drawn on it by depositors.

R.S. 1985, c. 27 (1st Supp.), s. 52; 1994, c. 44, s. 22.

363. Obtaining execution of valuable security by fraud — Every one who, with intent to defraud or injure another person, by a false pretence causes or induces any person

(a) to execute, make, accept, endorse or destroy the whole or any part of a valuable security, or

(b) to write, impress or affix a name or seal on any paper or parchment in order that it may afterwards be made or converted into or used or dealt with as a valuable security,

is guilty of an indictable offence and liable to imprisonment for a term not exceeding five years.

364. (1) Fraudulently obtaining food, beverage or accommodation — Every one who fraudulently obtains food, a beverage or accommodation at any place that is in the business of providing those things is guilty of an offence punishable on summary conviction.

(2) Presumption — In proceedings under this section, evidence that the accused obtained food, a beverage or accommodation at a place that is in the business of providing those things and did not pay for it and

(a) made a false or fictitious show or pretence of having baggage,

(b) had any false or pretended baggage,

(c) surreptitiously removed or attempted to remove his baggage or any material part of it,

(d) absconded or surreptitiously left the premises,

(e) knowingly made a false statement to obtain credit or time for payment, or

(f) offered a worthless cheque, draft or security in payment for the food, beverage or accommodation,

is, in the absence of any evidence to the contrary, proof of fraud.

(3) Definition of "cheque" — In this section **"cheque"** includes, in addition to its ordinary meaning, a bill of exchange drawn on any institution that makes it a business practice to honour bills of exchange or any particular kind thereof drawn on it by depositors.

1994, c. 44, s. 23.

365. Pretending to practise witchcraft, etc. — Every one who fraudulently

(a) pretends to exercise or to use any kind of witchcraft, sorcery, enchantment or conjuration,

(b) undertakes, for a consideration, to tell fortunes, or

(c) pretends from his skill in or knowledge of an occult or crafty science to discover where or in what manner anything that is supposed to have been stolen or lost may be found,

is guilty of an offence punishable on summary conviction.

Forgery and Offences Resembling Forgery

366. (1) Forgery — Every one commits forgery who makes a false document, knowing it to be false, with intent

(a) that it should in any way be used or acted on as genuine, to the prejudice of any one whether within Canada or not, or

(b) that a person should be induced, by the belief that it is genuine, to do or to refrain from doing anything, whether within Canada or not.

(2) Making false document — Making a false document includes

(a) altering a genuine document in any material part;

(b) making a material addition to a genuine document or adding to it a false date, attestation, seal or other thing that is material; or

(c) making a material alteration in a genuine document by erasure, obliteration, removal or in any other way.

(3) When forgery complete — Forgery is complete as soon as a document is made with the knowledge and intent referred to in subsection (1), notwithstanding that the person who makes it does not intend that any particular person should use or act on it as genuine or be induced, by the belief that it is genuine, to do or refrain from doing anything.

(4) Forgery complete though document incomplete — Forgery is complete notwithstanding that the false document is incomplete or does not purport to be a document that is binding in law, if it is such as to indicate that it was intended to be acted on as genuine.

367. Punishment for forgery — Every one who commits forgery

(a) is guilty of an indictable offence and liable to imprisonment for a term not exceeding ten years; or

(b) is guilty of an offence punishable on summary conviction.

1994, c. 44, s. 24; 1997, c. 18, s. 24.

368. (1) Uttering forged document — Every one who, knowing that a document is forged,

(a) uses, deals with or acts upon it, or

(b) causes or attempts to cause any person to use, deal with or act upon it,

as if the document were genuine,

(c) is guilty of an indictable offence and liable to imprisonment for a term not exceeding ten years; or

(d) is guilty of an offence punishable on summary conviction.

(2) Wherever forged — For the purposes of proceedings under this section, the place where a document was forged is not material.

1994, c. 44, s. 24; 1997, c. 18, s. 25.

369. Exchequer bill paper, public seals, etc. — Every one who, without lawful authority or excuse, the proof of which lies on him,

(a) makes, uses or knowingly has in his possession

(i) any exchequer bill paper, revenue paper or paper that is used to make bank notes, or

(ii) any paper that is intended to resemble paper mentioned in subparagraph (i),

(b) makes, offers or disposes of or knowingly has in his possession any plate, die, machinery, instrument or other writing or material that is adapted and intended to be used to commit forgery, or

(c) makes, reproduces or uses a public seal of Canada or of a province, or the seal of a public body or authority in Canada, or of a court of law,

is guilty of an indictable offence and liable to imprisonment for a term not exceeding fourteen years.

370. Counterfeit proclamation, etc. — Every one who knowingly

(a) prints a proclamation, order, regulation or appointment, or notice thereof, and causes it falsely to purport to have been printed by the Queen's Printer for Canada, or the Queen's Printer for a province, or

(b) tenders in evidence a copy of a proclamation, order, regulation or appointment that falsely purports to have been printed by the Queen's Printer for Canada or the Queen's Printer for a province,

is guilty of an indictable offence and liable to imprisonment for a term not exceeding five years.

371. Telegram, etc., in false name — Every one who, with intent to defraud, causes or procures a telegram, cablegram or radio message to be sent or delivered as being sent by the authority of another person, knowing that it is not sent by his authority and with intent that the message should be acted on as being sent by his authority, is guilty of an indictable offence and liable to imprisonment for a term not exceeding five years.

372. (1) False messages — Every one who, with intent to injure or alarm any person, conveys or causes or procures to be conveyed by letter, telegram, telephone, cable, radio or otherwise information that he knows is false is guilty of an indictable offence and liable to imprisonment for a term not exceeding two years.

(2) Indecent telephone calls — Every one who, with intent to alarm or annoy any person, makes any indecent telephone call to that person is guilty of an offence punishable on summary conviction.

(3) Harassing telephone calls — Every one who, without lawful excuse and with intent to harass any person, makes or causes to be made repeated telephone calls to that person is guilty of an offence punishable on summary conviction.

373. [Repealed R.S. 1985, c. 27 (1st Supp.), s. 53.]

374. Drawing document without authority, etc. — Every one who

(a) with intent to defraud and without lawful authority makes, executes, draws, signs, accepts or endorses a document in the name or on the account of another person by procuration or otherwise, or

(b) makes use of or utters a document knowing that it has been made, executed, signed, accepted or endorsed with intent to defraud and without lawful authority, in the name or on the account of another person, by procuration or otherwise,

is guilty of an indictable offence and liable to imprisonment for a term not exceeding fourteen years.

375. Obtaining, etc., by instrument based on forged document — Every one who demands, receives or obtains anything, or causes or procures anything to be delivered or paid to any person under, on or by virtue of any instrument issued under the authority of law, knowing that it is based on a forged document, is guilty of an indictable offence and liable to imprisonment for a term not exceeding fourteen years.

376. (1) Counterfeiting stamp, etc. — Every one who

(a) fraudulently uses, mutilates, affixes, removes or counterfeits a stamp or part thereof,

(b) knowingly and without lawful excuse, the proof of which lies on him, has in his possession

(i) a counterfeit stamp or a stamp that has been fraudulently mutilated, or

(ii) anything bearing a stamp of which a part has been fraudulently erased, removed or concealed, or

(c) without lawful excuse, the proof of which lies on him, makes or knowingly has in his possession a die or instrument that is capable of making the impression of a stamp or part thereof,

is guilty of an indictable offence and liable to imprisonment for a term not exceeding fourteen years.

(2) Counterfeiting mark — Every one who, without lawful authority,

(a) makes a mark,

(b) sells, or exposes for sale, or has in his possession a counterfeit mark,

(c) affixes a mark to anything that is required by law to be marked, branded, sealed or wrapped other than the thing to which the mark was originally affixed or was intended to be affixed, or

(d) affixes a counterfeit mark to anything that is required by law to be marked, branded, sealed or wrapped,

is guilty of an indictable offence and liable to imprisonment for a term not exceeding fourteen years.

(3) Definitions — In this section

"mark" means a mark, brand, seal, wrapper or design used by or on behalf of

(a) the Government of Canada or a province,

(b) the government of a state other than Canada, or

(c) any department, board, commission or agent established by a government mentioned in paragraph (*a*) or (*b*) in connection with the service or business of that government;

"stamp" means an impressed or adhesive stamp used for the purpose of revenue by the Government of Canada or of a province or by the government of a state other than Canada.

377. (1) Damaging documents — Every one who unlawfully

(a) destroys, defaces or injures a register, or any part of a register of births, baptisms, marriages, deaths or burials that is required or authorized by law to be kept in Canada, or a copy or any part of a copy of such a register that is required by law to be transmitted to a registrar or other officer,

(b) inserts or causes to be inserted in a register or copy referred to in paragraph (*a*) an entry, that he knows is false, of any matter relating to a birth, baptism, marriage, death or burial, or erases any material part from that register or copy,

(c) destroys, damages or obliterates an election document or causes an election document to be destroyed, damaged or obliterated, or

(d) makes or causes to be made an erasure, alteration or interlineation in or on an election document,

is guilty of an indictable offence and liable to imprisonment for a term not exceeding five years.

(2) Definition of "election document" — In this section, **"election document"** means any document or writing issued under the authority of an Act of Parliament or the legislature of a province with respect to an election held pursuant to the authority of that Act.

378. Offences in relation to registers — Every one who

(a) being authorized or required by law to make or issue a certified copy of, extract from or certificate in respect of a register, record or document, knowingly makes or issues a false certified copy, extract or certificate,

(b) not being authorized or required by law to make or issue a certified copy of, extract from or certificate in respect of a register, record or document, fraudulently makes or issues a copy, extract or certificate that purports to be certified as authorized or required by law, or

(c) being authorized or required by law to make a certificate or declaration concerning any particular required for the purpose of making entries in a register, record or document, knowingly and falsely makes the certificate or declaration,

is guilty of an indictable offence and liable to imprisonment for a term not exceeding five years.

PART X — FRAUDULENT TRANSACTIONS RELATING TO CONTRACTS AND TRADE

Interpretation

379. Definitions — In this Part,

"goods" means anything that is the subject of trade or commerce;

"trading stamps" includes any form of cash receipt, receipt, coupon, premium ticket or other device, designed or intended to be given to the purchaser of goods by the vendor thereof or on his behalf, and to represent a discount on the price of the goods or a premium to the purchaser thereof

    (a) that may be redeemed

        (i) by any person other than the vendor, the person from whom the vendor purchased the goods or the manufacturer of the goods,

        (ii) by the vendor, the person from whom the vendor purchased the goods or the manufacturer of the goods in cash or in goods that are not his property in whole or in part, or

        (iii) by the vendor elsewhere than in the premises where the goods are purchased, or

    (b) that does not show on its face the place where it is delivered and the merchantable value thereof, or

    (c) that may not be redeemed on demand at any time,

but an offer, endorsed by the manufacturer on a wrapper or container in which goods are sold, of a premium or reward for the return of that wrapper or container to the manufacturer is not a trading stamp.

Fraud

380. (1) Fraud — Every one who, by deceit, falsehood or other fraudulent means, whether or not it is a false pretence within the meaning of this Act, defrauds the public or any person, whether ascertained or not, of any property, money or valuable security or any service.

    (a) is guilty of an indictable offence and liable to a term of imprisonment not exceeding ten years, where the subject-matter of the offence is a testamentary instrument or the value of the subject-matter of the offence exceeds five thousand dollars; or

    (b) is guilty

        (i) of an indictable offence and is liable to imprisonment for a term not exceeding two years, or

        (ii) of an offence punishable on summary conviction,

where the value of the subject-matter of the offence does not exceed five thousand dollars.

(2) Affecting public market — Every one who, by deceit, falsehood or other fraudulent means, whether or not it is a false pretence within the meaning of this Act, with intent to defraud, affects the public market price of stocks, shares, merchandise or anything that is offered for sale to the public, is guilty of an indictable offence and liable to imprisonment for a term not exceeding ten years.

R.S. 1985, c. 27 (1st Supp.), s. 54; 1994, c. 44, s. 25; 1997, c. 18, s. 26.

381. Using mails to defraud — Every one who makes use of the mails for the purpose of transmitting or delivering letters or circulars concerning schemes devised or intended to deceive or defraud the public, or for the purpose of obtaining money under false pretences, is guilty of an indictable offence and liable to imprisonment for a term not exceeding two years.

382. Fraudulent manipulation of stock exchange transactions — Every one who, through the facility of a stock exchange, curb market or other market, with intent to create a false or misleading appearance of active public trading in a security or with intent to create a false or misleading appearance with respect to the market price of a security,

(a) effects a transaction in the security that involves no change in the beneficial ownership thereof,

(b) enters an order for the purchase of the security, knowing that an order of substantially the same size at substantially the same time and at substantially the same price for the sale of the security has been or will be entered by or for the same or different persons, or

(c) enters an order for the sale of the security, knowing that an order of substantially the same size at substantially the same time and at substantially the same price for the purchase of the security has been or will be entered by or for the same or different persons,

is guilty of an indictable offence and liable to imprisonment for a term not exceeding five years.

383. (1) Gaming in stocks or merchandise — Every one is guilty of an indictable offence and liable to imprisonment for a term not exceeding five years who, with intent to make gain or profit by the rise or fall in price of the stock of an incorporated or unincorporated company or undertaking, whether in or outside Canada, or of any goods, wares or merchandise,

(a) makes or signs, or authorizes to be made or signed, any contract or agreement, oral or written, purporting to be for the purchase or sale of shares of stock or goods, wares or merchandise, without the *bona fide* intention of acquiring the shares, goods, wares or merchandise or of selling them, as the case may be, or

(b) makes or signs, or authorizes to be made or signed, any contract or agreement, oral or written, purporting to be for the sale or purchase of shares of stock or goods, wares or merchandise in respect of which no delivery of the thing sold or purchased is made or received, and without the *bona fide* intention of making or receiving delivery thereof, as the case may be,

but this section does not apply where a broker, on behalf of a purchaser, receives delivery, notwithstanding that the broker retains or pledges what is delivered as security for the advance of the purchase money or any part thereof.

(2) Onus — Where, in proceedings under this section, it is established that the accused made or signed a contract or an agreement for the sale or purchase of shares of stock or goods, wares or merchandise, or acted, aided or abetted in the making or signing thereof, the burden of proof of a *bona fide* intention to acquire or to sell the shares, goods, wares or merchandise or to deliver or to receive delivery thereof, as the case may be, lies on the accused.

384. Broker reducing stock by selling for his own account — Every one is guilty of an indictable offence and liable to imprisonment for a term not exceeding five years who, being an individual, or a member or an employee of a partnership, or a director, an officer or an employee of a corporation, where he or the partnership or corporation is employed as a broker by any customer to buy and carry on margin any shares of an incorporated or unincorporated company or undertaking, whether in or out of Canada, thereafter sells or causes to be sold shares of the company or undertaking for any account in which

    (a) he or his firm or a partner thereof, or

    (b) the corporation or a director thereof,

has a direct or indirect interest, if the effect of the sale is, otherwise than unintentionally, to reduce the amount of those shares in the hands of the broker or under his control in the ordinary course of business below the amount of those shares that the broker should be carrying for all customers.

385. (1) Fraudulent concealment of title documents — Every one who, being a vendor or mortgagor of property or of a chose in action or being a solicitor for or agent of a vendor or mortgagor of property or a chose in action, is served with a written demand for an abstract of title by or on behalf of the purchaser or mortgagee before the completion of the purchase or mortgage, and who

    (a) with intent to defraud and for the purpose of inducing the purchaser or mortgagee to accept the title offered or produced to him, conceals from him any settlement, deed, will or other instrument material to the title, or any encumbrance on the title, or

    (b) falsifies any pedigree on which the title depends,

is guilty of an indictable offence and liable to imprisonment for a term not exceeding two years.

(2) Consent required — No proceedings shall be instituted under this section without the consent of the Attorney General.

386. Fraudulent registration of title — Every one who, as principal or agent, in a proceeding to register title to real property, or in a transaction relating to real property that is or is proposed to be registered, knowingly and with intent to deceive,

> (a) makes a material false statement or representation,
>
> (b) suppresses or conceals from a judge or registrar, or any person employed by or assisting the registrar, any material document, fact, matter or information, or
>
> (c) is privy to anything mentioned in paragraph (a) or (b),

is guilty of an indictable offence and liable to imprisonment for a term not exceeding five years.

387. Fraudulent sale of real property — Every one who, knowing of an unregistered prior sale or of an existing unregistered grant, mortgage, hypothec, privilege or encumbrance of or on real property, fraudulently sells the property or any part thereof is guilty of an indictable offence and liable to imprisonment for a term not exceeding two years.

388. Misleading receipt — Every one who wilfully

> (a) with intent to mislead, injure or defraud any person, whether or not that person is known to him, gives to a person anything in writing that purports to be a receipt for or an acknowledgment of property that has been delivered to or received by him, before the property referred to in the purported receipt or acknowledgment has been delivered to or received by him, or
>
> (b) accepts, transmits or uses a purported receipt or acknowledgment to which paragraph (a) applies,

is guilty of an indictable offence and liable to imprisonment for a term not exceeding two years.

389. (1) Fraudulent disposal of goods on which money advanced — Every one who

> (a) having shipped or delivered to the keeper of a warehouse or to a factor, an agent or a carrier anything on which the consignee thereof has advanced money or has given valuable security, thereafter, with intent to deceive, defraud or injure the consignee, disposes of it in a manner that is different from and inconsistent with any agreement that has been made in that behalf between him and the consignee, or
>
> (b) knowingly and wilfully aids or assists any person to make a disposition of anything to which paragraph (a) applies for the purpose of deceiving, defrauding or injuring the consignee,

is guilty of an indictable offence and liable to imprisonment for a term not exceeding two years.

(2) Saving — No person is guilty of an offence under this section where, before disposing of anything in a manner that is different from and inconsistent with any agreement that has been made in that behalf between him and the consignee, he pays or tenders to the consignee the full amount of money or valuable security that the consignee has advanced.

390. Fraudulent receipts under Bank Act — Every one is guilty of an indictable offence and liable to imprisonment for a term not exceeding two years who

(a) wilfully makes a false statement in any receipt, certificate or acknowledgment for anything that may be used for a purpose mentioned in the *Bank Act*; or

(b) wilfully,

(i) after giving to another person,

(ii) after a person employed by him has, to his knowledge, given to another person, or

(iii) after obtaining and endorsing or assigning to another person,

any receipt, certificate or acknowledgment for anything that may be used for a purpose mentioned in the *Bank Act*, without the consent in writing of the holder or endorsee or the production and delivery of the receipt, certificate or acknowledgment, alienates or parts with, or does not deliver to the holder or owner the property mentioned in the receipt, certificate or acknowledgment.

391. Saving — Where an offence is committed under section 388, 389 or 390 by a person who acts in the name of a corporation, firm or partnership, no person other than the person who does the act by means of which the offence is committed or who is secretly privy to the doing of that act is guilty of the offence.

392. Disposal of property to defraud creditors — Every one who,

(a) with intent to defraud his creditors,

(i) makes or causes to be made any gift, conveyance, assignment, sale, transfer or delivery of his property, or

(ii) removes, conceals or disposes of any of his property, or

(b) with intent that any one should defraud his creditors, receives any property by means of or in relation to which an offence has been committed under paragraph (*a*),

is guilty of an indictable offence and liable to imprisonment for a term not exceeding two years.

393. (1) Fraud in relation to fares, etc. — Every one whose duty it is to collect a fare, toll, ticket or admission who wilfully

(a) fails to collect it,

(b) collects less than the proper amount payable in respect thereof, or

(c) accepts any valuable consideration for failing to collect it or for collecting less than the proper amount payable in respect thereof,

is guilty of an indictable offence and liable to imprisonment for a term not exceeding two years.

(2) Idem — Every one who gives or offers to a person whose duty it is to collect a fare, toll, ticket or admission fee, any valuable consideration

(a) for failing to collect it, or

(b) for collecting an amount less than the amount payable in respect thereof,

is guilty of an indictable offence and liable to imprisonment for a term not exceeding two years.

(3) Fraudulently obtaining transportation — Every one who, by any false pretence or fraud, unlawfully obtains transportation by land, water or air is guilty of an offence punishable on summary conviction.

394. (1) Fraud in relation to valuable minerals — No person who is the holder of a lease or licence issued under an Act relating to the mining of valuable minerals, or by the owner of land that is supposed to contain valuable minerals, shall

(a) by a fraudulent device or contrivance, defraud or attempt to defraud any person of

(i) any valuable minerals obtained under or reserved by the lease or licence, or

(ii) any money or valuable interest or thing payable in respect of valuable minerals obtained or rights reserved by the lease or licence; or

(b) fraudulently conceal or make a false statement with respect to the amount of valuable minerals obtained under the lease or licence.

(2) Sale of valuable minerals — No person, other than the owner or the owner's agent or someone otherwise acting under lawful authority, shall sell any valuable mineral that is unrefined, partly refined, uncut or otherwise unprocessed.

(3) Purchase of valuable minerals — No person shall buy any valuable mineral that is unrefined, partly refined, uncut or otherwise unprocessed from anyone who the person has reason to believe is not the owner or the owner's agent or someone otherwise acting under lawful authority.

(4) Presumption — In any proceeding in relation to subsection (2) or (3), in the absence of evidence raising a reasonable doubt to the contrary, it is presumed that

(a) in the case of a sale, the seller is not the owner of the valuable mineral or the owner's agent or someone otherwise acting under lawful authority; and

(b) in the case of a purchase, the purchaser, when buying the valuable mineral, had reason to believe that the seller was not the owner of the mineral or the owner's agent or someone otherwise acting under lawful authority.

(5) Offence — A person who contravenes subsection (1), (2) or (3) is guilty of an indictable offence and liable to imprisonment for a term of not more than five years.

(6) Forfeiture — If a person is convicted of an offence under this section, the court may order anything by means of or in relation to which the offence was committed, on such conviction, to be forfeited to Her Majesty.

(7) Exception — Subsection (6) does not apply to real property other than real property built or significantly modified for the purpose of facilitating the commission of an offence under this section.

R.S. 1985, c. 27 (1st Supp.), s. 186; 1999, c. 5, s. 10.

394.1 (1) Possession of stolen or fraudulently obtained valuable minerals — No person shall possess any valuable mineral that is unrefined, partly refined, uncut or otherwise unprocessed that has been stolen or dealt with contrary to section 394.

(2) Evidence — Reasonable grounds to believe that the valuable mineral has been stolen or dealt with contrary to section 394 are, in the absence of evidence raising a reasonable doubt to the contrary, proof that the valuable mineral has been stolen or dealt with contrary to section 394.

(3) Offence — A person who contravenes subsection (1) is guilty of an indictable offence and liable to imprisonment for a term of not more than five years.

(4) Forfeiture — If a person is convicted of an offence under this section, the court may, on that conviction, order that anything by means of or in relation to which the offence was committed be forfeited to Her Majesty.

(5) Exception — Subsection (4) does not apply to real property, other than real property built or significantly modified for the purpose of facilitating the commission of an offence under subsection (3).

1999, c. 5, s. 10.

395. (1) Search for valuable minerals — If an information in writing is laid under oath before a justice by a peace officer or by a public officer who has been appointed or designated to administer or enforce a federal or provincial law and whose duties include the enforcement of this Act or any other Act of Parliament and the justice is satisfied that there are reasonable grounds to believe that, contrary to this Act or any other Act of Parliament, any valuable mineral is deposited in a place or held by a person, the justice may issue a warrant authorizing a peace officer or a public officer, if the public officer is named in it, to search any of the places or persons mentioned in the information.

(2) Power to seize — Where, on search, anything mentioned in subsection (1) is found, it shall be seized and carried before the justice who shall order

(a) that it be detained for the purposes of an inquiry or a trial; or

(b) if it is not detained for the purposes of an inquiry or a trial,

(i) that it be restored to the owner, or

(ii) that it be forfeited to Her Majesty in right of the province in which the proceedings take place if the owner cannot be ascertained.

(3) Appeal — An appeal lies from an order made under paragraph (2)(*b*) in the manner in which an appeal lies in summary conviction proceedings under Part XXVII and the provisions of that Part relating to appeals apply to appeals under this subsection.

1999, c. 5, s. 11.

396. (1) Offences in relation to mines — Every one who

(a) adds anything to or removes anything from any existing or prospective mine, mining claim or oil well with a fraudulent intent to affect the result of an assay, a test or a valuation that has been made or is to be made with respect to the mine, mining claim or oil well, or

(b) adds anything to, removes anything from or tampers with a sample or material that has been taken or is being or is about to be taken from any existing or prospective mine, mining claim or oil well for the purpose of being assayed, tested or otherwise valued, with a fraudulent intent to affect the result of the assay, test or valuation,

is guilty of an indictable offence and liable to imprisonment for a term not exceeding ten years.

(2) Presumption — For the purposes of proceedings under subsection (1), evidence that

(a) something has been added to or removed from anything to which subsection (1) applies, or

(b) anything to which subsection (1) applies has been tampered with,

is, in the absence of any evidence to the contrary, proof of a fraudulent intent to affect the result of an assay, test or a valuation.

Falsification of Books and Documents

397. (1) Books and documents — Every one who, with intent to defraud,

(a) destroys, mutilates, alters, falsifies, or makes a false entry in, or

(b) omits a material particular from, or alters a material particular in, a book, paper, writing, valuable security or document is guilty of an indictable offence and liable to imprisonment for a term not exceeding five years.

(2) Privy — Every one who, with intent to defraud his creditors, is privy to the commission of an offence under subsection (1) is guilty of an indictable offence and liable to imprisonment for a term not exceeding five years.

398. Falsifying employment record — Every one who, with intent to deceive, falsifies an employment record by any means, including the punching of a time clock, is guilty of an offence punishable on summary conviction.

399. False return by public officer — Every one who, being entrusted with the receipt, custody or management of any part of the public revenues, knowingly furnishes a false statement or return of

(a) any sum of money collected by him or entrusted to his care, or

(b) any balance of money in his hands or under his control,

is guilty of an indictable offence and liable to imprisonment for a term not exceeding five years.

400. (1) False prospectus, etc. — Every one who makes, circulates or publishes a prospectus, statement or an account, whether written or oral, that he knows is false in a material particular, with intent

(a) to induce persons, whether ascertained or not, to become shareholders or partners in a company,

(b) to deceive or defraud the members, shareholders or creditors, whether ascertained or not, of a company, or

(c) to induce any person to

(i) entrust or advance anything to a company, or

(ii) enter into any security for the benefit of a company,

is guilty of an indictable offence and liable to imprisonment for a term not exceeding ten years.

(2) Definition of "company" — In this section, **"company"** means a syndicate, body corporate or company, whether existing or proposed to be created.

1994, c. 44, s. 26.

401. (1) Obtaining carriage by false billing — Every one who, by means of a false or misleading representation, knowingly obtains or attempts to obtain the carriage of anything by any person into a country, province, district or other place, whether or not within Canada, where the importation or transportation of it is, in the circumstances of the case, unlawful is guilty of an offence punishable on summary conviction.

(2) Forfeiture — Where a person is convicted of an offence under subsection (1), anything by means of or in relation to which the offence was committed, on such conviction, in addition to any punishment that is imposed, is forfeited to Her Majesty and shall be disposed of as the court may direct.

402. (1) Trader failing to keep accounts — Every one who, being a trader or in business,

(a) is indebted in an amount exceeding one thousand dollars,

(b) is unable to pay his creditors in full, and

(c) has not kept books of account that, in the ordinary course of the trade or business in which he is engaged, are necessary to exhibit or explain his transactions,

is guilty of an indictable offence and liable to imprisonment for a term not exceeding two years.

(2) Saving — No person shall be convicted of an offence under this section

(a) where, to the satisfaction of the court or judge, he

(i) accounts for his losses, and

(ii) shows that his failure to keep books was not intended to defraud his creditors; or

(b) where his failure to keep books occurred at a time more than five years prior to the day on which he was unable to pay his creditors in full.

Personation

403. Personation with intent — Every one who fraudulently personates any person, living or dead,

(a) with intent to gain advantage for himself or another person,

(b) with intent to obtain any property or an interest in any property, or

(c) with intent to cause disadvantage to the person whom he personates or another person,

is guilty of an indictable offence and liable to imprisonment for a term not exceeding ten years or an offence punishable on summary conviction.

1994, c. 44, s. 27.

404. Personation at examination — Every one who falsely, with intent to gain advantage for himself or some other person, personates a candidate at a competitive or qualifying examination held under the authority of law or in connection with a university, college or school or who knowingly avails himself of the results of such personation is guilty of an offence punishable on summary conviction.

405. Acknowledging instrument in false name — Every one who, without lawful authority or excuse, the proof of which lies on him, acknowledges, in the name of another person before a court or a judge or other person authorized to receive the acknowledgment, a recognizance of bail, a confession of judgment, a consent to judgment or a judgment, deed or other instrument is guilty of an indictable offence and liable to imprisonment for a term not exceeding five years.

Forgery of Trade-marks and Trade Descriptions

406. Forging trade-mark — For the purposes of this Part, every one forges a trade-mark who

(a) without the consent of the proprietor of the trade-mark, makes or reproduces in any manner that trade-mark or a mark so nearly resembling it as to be calculated to deceive; or

(b) falsifies, in any manner, a genuine trade-mark.

407. Offence — Every one commits an offence who, with intent to deceive or defraud the public or any person, whether ascertained or not, forges a trade-mark.

408. Passing off — Every one commits an offence who, with intent to deceive or defraud the public or any person, whether ascertained or not,

(a) passes off other wares or services as and for those ordered or required; or

(b) makes use, in association with wares or services, of any description that is false in a material respect regarding

(i) the kind, quality, quantity or composition,

(ii) the geographical origin, or

(iii) the mode of the manufacture, production or performance

of those wares or services.

409. (1) Instruments for forging trade-mark — Every one commits an offence who makes, has in his possession or disposes of a die, block, machine or other instrument designed or intended to be used in forging a trade-mark.

(2) Saving — No person shall be convicted of an offence under this section where he proves that he acted in good faith in the ordinary course of his business or employment.

410. Other offences in relation to trade-marks — Every one commits an offence who, with intent to deceive or defraud,

(a) defaces, conceals or removes a trade-mark or the name of another person from anything without the consent of that other person; or

(b) being a manufacturer, dealer, trader or bottler, fills any bottle or siphon that bears the trade-mark or name of another person, without the consent of that other person, with a beverage, milk, by-product of milk or other liquid commodity for the purpose of sale or traffic.

411. Used goods sold without disclosure — Every one commits an offence who sells, exposes or has in his possession for sale, or advertises for sale, goods that have been used, reconditioned or remade and that bear the trade-mark or the trade-name of another person, without making full disclosure that the goods have been reconditioned, rebuilt or remade for sale and that they are not then in the condition in which they were originally made or produced.

412. (1) Punishment — Every one who commits an offence under section 407, 408, 409, 410 or 411 is guilty of

(a) an indictable offence and is liable to imprisonment for a term not exceeding two years; or

(b) an offence punishable on summary conviction.

(2) Forfeiture — Anything by means of or in relation to which a person commits an offence under section 407, 408, 409, 410 or 411 is, unless the court otherwise orders, forfeited on the conviction of that person for that offence.

413. Falsely claiming royal warrant — Every one who falsely represents that goods are made by a person holding a royal warrant, or for the service of Her Majesty, member of the Royal Family or public department is guilty of an offence punishable on summary conviction.

414. Presumption from port of shipment — Where, in proceedings under this Part, the alleged offence relates to imported goods, evidence that the goods were shipped to Canada from a place outside Canada is, in the absence of any evidence to the contrary, proof that the goods were made or produced in the country from which they were shipped.

Wreck

415. Offences in relation to wreck — Every one who

(a) secretes wreck, defaces or obliterates the marks on wreck, or uses any means to disguise or conceal the fact that anything is wreck, or in any manner conceals the character of wreck, from a person who is entitled to inquire into the wreck,

(b) receives wreck, knowing that it is wreck, from a person other than the owner thereof or a receiver of wreck, and does not within forty-eight hours thereafter inform the receiver of wreck thereof,

(c) offers wreck for sale or otherwise deals with it, knowing that it is wreck, and not having a lawful authority to sell or deal with it,

(d) keeps wreck in his possession knowing that it is wreck, without lawful authority to keep it, for any time longer than the time reasonably necessary to deliver it to the receiver of wreck, or

(e) boards, against the will of the master, a vessel that is wrecked, stranded or in distress unless he is a receiver of wreck or a person acting under orders of a receiver of wreck,

is guilty of

(f) an indictable offence and is liable to imprisonment for a term not exceeding two years, or

(g) an offence punishable on summary conviction.

Public Stores

416. Distinguishing mark on public stores — The Governor in Council may, by notice to be published in the *Canada Gazette*, prescribe distinguishing marks that are appropriate for use on public stores to denote the property of Her Majesty therein, whether the stores belong to Her Majesty in right of Canada or to Her Majesty in any other right.

417. (1) Applying or removing marks without authority — Every one who,

(a) without lawful authority, the proof of which lies on him, applies a distinguishing mark to anything, or

(b) with intent to conceal the property of Her Majesty in public stores, removes, destroys or obliterates, in whole or in part, a distinguishing mark,

is guilty of an indictable offence and liable to imprisonment for a term not exceeding two years.

(2) Unlawful transactions in public stores — Every one who, without lawful authority, the proof of which lies on him, receives, possesses, keeps, sells or delivers public stores that he knows bear a distinguishing mark is guilty of

(a) an indictable offence and is liable to imprisonment for a term not exceeding two years; or

(b) an offence punishable on summary conviction.

(3) Definition of "distinguishing mark" — For the purposes of this section, **"distinguishing mark"** means a distinguishing mark that is appropriated for use on public stores pursuant to section 416.

418. (1) Selling defective stores to Her Majesty — Every one who knowingly sells or delivers defective stores to Her Majesty or commits fraud in connection with the sale, lease or delivery of stores to Her Majesty or the manufacture of stores for Her Majesty is guilty of an indictable offence and liable to imprisonment for a term not exceeding fourteen years.

(2) Offences by officers and employees of corporations — Every one who, being a director, an officer, an agent or an employee of a corporation that commits, by fraud, an offence under subsection (1),

(a) knowingly takes part in the fraud, or

(b) knows or has reason to suspect that the fraud is being committed or has been or is about to be committed and does not inform the responsible government, or a department thereof, of Her Majesty,

is guilty of an indictable offence and liable to imprisonment for a term not exceeding fourteen years.

419. Unlawful use of military uniforms or certificates — Every one who without lawful authority, the proof of which lies on him,

(a) wears a uniform of the Canadian Forces or any other naval, army or air force or a uniform that is so similar to the uniform of any of those forces that it is likely to be mistaken therefor,

(b) wears a distinctive mark relating to wounds received or service performed in war, or a military medal, ribbon, badge, chevron or any decoration or order that is awarded for war services, or any imitation thereof, or any mark or device or thing that is likely to be mistaken for any such mark, medal, ribbon, badge, chevron, decoration or order,

(c) has in his possession a certificate of discharge, certificate of release, statement of service or identity card from the Canadian Forces or any other naval, army or air force that has not been issued to and does not belong to him, or

(d) has in his possession a commission or warrant or a certificate of discharge, certificate of release, statement of service or identity card issued to an officer or a person in or who has been in the Canadian Forces or any other naval, army or air force, that contains any alteration that is not verified by the initials of the officer who issued it, or by the initials of an officer thereto lawfully authorized,

is guilty of an offence punishable on summary conviction.

420. (1) Military stores — (1) Every one who buys, receives or detains from a member of the Canadian Forces or a deserter or an absentee without leave therefrom any military stores that are owned by Her Majesty or for which the member, deserter or absentee without leave is accountable to Her Majesty is guilty of

(a) an indictable offence and is liable to imprisonment for a term not exceeding five years; or

(b) an offence punishable on summary conviction.

(2) Exception — No person shall be convicted of an offence under this section where he establishes that he did not know and had no reason to suspect that the military stores in respect of which the offence was committed were owned by Her Majesty or were military stores for which the member, deserter or absentee without leave was accountable to Her Majesty.

421. (1) Evidence of enlistment — In proceedings under sections 417 to 420, evidence that a person was at any time performing duties in the Canadian Forces is, in the absence of any evidence to the contrary, proof that his enrolment in the Canadian Forces prior to that time was regular.

(2) Presumption when accused a dealer in stores — An accused who is charged with an offence under subsection 417(2) shall be presumed to have known that the stores in respect of which the offence is alleged to have been committed bore a distinguishing mark within the meaning of that subsection at the time the offence is alleged to have been committed if he was, at that time, in the service or employment of Her Majesty or was a dealer in marine stores or in old metals.

Breach of Contract, Intimidation and Discrimination Against Trade Unionists

422. (1) Criminal breach of contract — Every one who wilfully breaks a contract, knowing or having reasonable cause to believe that the probable consequences of doing so, whether alone or in combination with others, will be

(a) to endanger human life,

(b) to cause serious bodily injury,

(c) to expose valuable property, real or personal, to destruction or serious injury,

(d) to deprive the inhabitants of a city or place, or part thereof, wholly or to a great extent, of their supply of light, power, gas or water, or

(e) to delay or prevent the running of any locomotive engine, tender, freight or passenger train or car, on a railway that is a common carrier, is guilty of

(f) an indictable offence and is liable to imprisonment for a term not exceeding five years, or

(g) an offence punishable on summary conviction.

(2) Saving — No person wilfully breaks a contract within the meaning of subsection (1) by reason only that

(a) being the employee of an employer, he stops work as a result of the failure of his employer and himself to agree on any matter relating to his employment, or,

(b) being a member of an organization of employees formed for the purpose of regulating relations between employers and employees, he stops work as a result of the failure of the employer and a bargaining agent acting on behalf of the organization to agree on any matter relating to the employment of members of the organization,

if, before the stoppage of work occurs, all steps provided by law with respect to the settlement of industrial disputes are taken and any provision for the final settlement of differences, without stoppage of work, contained in or by law deemed to be contained in a collective agreement is complied with and effect given thereto.

(3) Consent required — No proceedings shall be instituted under this section without the consent of the Attorney General.

423. (1) Intimidation — Every one who, wrongfully and without lawful authority, for the purpose of compelling another person to abstain from doing anything that he has a lawful right to do, or to do anything that he has a lawful right to abstain from doing,

(a) uses violence or threats of violence to that person or his spouse or children, or injures his property,

Proposed Amendment — 423(1)(a)

(a) uses violence or threats of violence to that person or his spouse or common-law partner or children, or injures his property,

2000, c. 12, s. 95(b) [Not in force at date of publication.]

(b) intimidates or attempts to intimidate that person or a relative of that person by threats that, in Canada or elsewhere, violence or other injury will be done to or punishment inflicted on him or a relative of his, or that the property of any of them will be damaged,

(c) persistently follows that person about from place to place,

(d) hides any tools, clothes or other property owned or used by that person, or deprives him of them or hinders him in the use of them,

(e) with one or more other persons, follows that person, in a disorderly manner, on a highway,

(f) besets or watches the dwelling-house or place where that person resides, works, carries on business or happens to be, or

(g) blocks or obstructs a highway,

is guilty of an offence punishable on summary conviction.

(2) Exception — A person who attends at or near or approaches a dwelling-house or place, for the purpose only of obtaining or communicating information, does not watch or beset within the meaning of this section.

424. Threat to commit offence against internationally protected person — Every one who threatens to commit an offence under section 235, 266, 279 or 279.1 against an internationally protected person or who threatens to commit an offence under section 431 is guilty of an indictable offence and liable to imprisonment for a term not exceeding five years.

R.S. 1985, c. 27 (1st Supp.), s. 55.

425. Offences by employers — Every one who, being an employer or the agent of an employer, wrongfully and without lawful authority

(a) refuses to employ or dismisses from his employment any person for the reason only that the person is a member of a lawful trade union or of a lawful association or combination of workmen or employees formed for the purpose of advancing, in a lawful manner, their interests and organized for their protection in the regulation of wages and conditions of work,

(b) seeks by intimidation, threat of loss of position or employment, or by causing actual loss of position or employment, or by threatening or imposing any pecuniary penalty, to compel workmen or employees to abstain from belonging to a trade union, association or combination to which they have a lawful right to belong, or

(c) conspires, combines, agrees or arranges with any other employer or his agent to do anything mentioned in paragraph (*a*) or (*b*),

is guilty of an offence punishable on summary conviction.

Secret Commissions

426. (1) Secret commissions — Every one commits an offence who

(a) corruptly

    (i) gives, offers or agrees to give or offer to an agent, or

    (ii) being an agent, demands, accepts or offers or agrees to accept from any person,

any reward, advantage or benefit of any kind as consideration for doing or forbearing to do, or for having done or forborne to do, any act relating to the affairs or business of his principal or for showing or forbearing to show favour or disfavour to any person with relation to the affairs or business of his principal; or

(b) with intent to deceive a principal, gives to an agent of that principal, or, being an agent, uses with intent to deceive his principal, a receipt, account or other writing

    (i) in which the principal has an interest,

(ii) that contains any statement that is false or erroneous or defective in any material particular, and

(iii) that is intented to mislead the principal.

(2) Privity to offence — Every one commits an offence who is knowingly privy to the commission of an offence under subsection (1).

(3) Punishment — A person who commits an offence under this section is guilty of an indictable offence and liable to imprisonment for a term not exceeding five years.

(4) Definitions of "agent" and "principal" — In this section **"agent"** includes an employee, and **"principal"** includes an employer.

R.S. 1985, c. 27 (1st Supp.), s. 56.

Trading Stamps

427. (1) Issuing trading stamps — Every one who, by himself or his employee or agent, directly or indirectly issues, gives, sells or otherwise disposes of, or offers to issue, give, sell or otherwise dispose of trading stamps to a merchant or dealer in goods for use in his business is guilty of an offence punishable on summary conviction.

(2) Giving to purchaser of goods — Every one who, being a merchant or dealer in goods, by himself or his employee or agent, directly or indirectly gives or in any way disposes of, or offers to give or in any way dispose of, trading stamps to a person who purchases goods from him is guilty of an offence punishable on summary conviction.

PART XI — WILFUL AND FORBIDDEN ACTS IN RESPECT OF CERTAIN PROPERTY

Interpretation

428. "Property" — In this Part, **"property"** means real or personal corporeal property.

429. (1) Wilfully causing event to occur — Every one who causes the occurrence of an event by doing an act or by omitting to do an act that it is his duty to do, knowing that the act or omission will probably cause the occurrence of the event and being reckless whether the event occurs or not, shall be deemed, for the purposes of this Part, wilfully to have caused the occurrence of the event.

(2) Colour of right — No person shall be convicted of an offence under sections 430 to 446 where he proves that he acted with legal justification or excuse and with colour of right.

(3) Interest — Where it is an offence to destroy or to damage anything,

(a) the fact that a person has a partial interest in what is destroyed or damaged does not prevent him from being guilty of the offence if he caused the destruction or damage; and

(b) the fact that a person has a total interest in what is destroyed or damaged does not prevent him from being guilty of the offence if he caused the destruction or damage with intent to defraud.

Mischief

430. (1) Mischief — Every one commits mischief who wilfully

(a) destroys or damages property;

(b) renders property dangerous, useless, inoperative or ineffective;

(c) obstructs, interrupts or interferes with the lawful use, enjoyment or operation of property; or

(d) obstructs, interrupts or interferes with any person in the lawful use, enjoyment or operation of property.

(1.1) Mischief in relation to data — Every one commits mischief who wilfully

(a) destroys or alters data;

(b) renders data meaningless, useless or ineffective;

(c) obstructs, interrupts or interferes with the lawful use of data; or

(d) obstructs, interrupts or interferes with any person in the lawful use of data or denies access to data to any person who is entitled to access thereto.

(2) Punishment — Every one who commits mischief that causes actual danger to life is guilty of an indictable offence and liable to imprisonment for life.

(3) Idem — Every one who commits mischief in relation to property that is a testamentary instrument or the value of which exceeds five thousand dollars

(a) is guilty of an indictable offence and liable to imprisonment for a term not exceeding ten years; or

(b) is guilty of an offence punishable on summary conviction.

(4) Idem — Every one who commits mischief in relation to property, other than property described in subsection (3),

(a) is guilty of an indictable offence and liable to imprisonment for a term not exceeding two years; or

(b) is guilty of an offence punishable on summary conviction.

(5) Idem — Everyone who commits mischief in relation to data

(a) is guilty of an indictable offence and liable to imprisonment for a term not exceeding ten years; or

(b) is guilty of an offence punishable on summary conviction.

(5.1) Offence — Every one who wilfully does an act or wilfully omits to do an act that it is his duty to do, if that act or omission is likely to constitute mischief causing actual danger to life, or to constitute mischief in relation to property or data,

(a) is guilty of an indictable offence and liable to imprisonment for a term not exceeding five years; or

(b) is guilty of an offence punishable on summary conviction.

(6) Saving — No person commits mischief within the meaning of this section by reason only that

(a) he stops work as a result of the failure of his employer and himself to agree on any matter relating to his employment;

(b) he stops work as a result of the failure of his employer and a bargaining agent acting on his behalf to agree on any matter relating to his employment; or

(c) he stops work as a result of his taking part in a combination of workmen or employees for their own reasonable protection as workmen or employees.

(7) Idem — No person commits mischief within the meaning of this section by reason only that he attends at or near or approaches a dwelling-house or place for the purpose only of obtaining or communicating information.

(8) Definition of "data" — In this section, **"data"** has the same meaning as in section 342.1.

R.S. 1985, c. 27 (1st Supp.), s. 57; 1994, c. 44, s. 28.

431. Attack on premises, residence or transport of internationally protected person — Every one who commits an attack on the official premises, private accommodation or means of transport of an internationally protected person that is likely to endanger the life or liberty of such person is guilty of an indictable offence and liable to imprisonment for a term not exceeding fourteen years.

R.S. 1985, c. 27 (1st Supp.), s. 58.

432. [Repealed R.S. 1985, c. 27 (1st Supp.), s. 58.]

Arson and Other Fires

433. Arson — disregard for human life — Every person who intentionally or recklessly causes damage by fire or explosion to property, whether or not that person owns the property, is guilty of an indictable offence and liable to imprisonment for life where

(a) the person knows that or is reckless with respect to whether the property is inhabited or occupied; or

(b) the fire or explosion causes bodily harm to another person.

1990, c. 15, s. 1.

434. Arson — damage to property — Every person who intentionally or recklessly causes damage by fire or explosion to property that is not wholly owned by that person is guilty of an indictable offence and liable to imprisonment for a term not exceeding fourteen years.

1990, c. 15, s. 1.

434.1 Arson — own property — Every person who intentionally or recklessly causes damage by fire or explosion to property that is owned, in whole or in part, by that person is guilty of an indictable offence and liable to imprisonment for a term not exceeding fourteen years, where the fire or explosion seriously threatens the health, safety or property of another person.

1990, c. 15, s. 1.

435. (1) Arson for fraudulent purpose — Every person who, with intent to defraud any other person, causes damage by fire or explosion to property, whether or not that person owns, in whole or in part, the property, is guilty of an indictable offence and liable to imprisonment for a term not exceeding ten years.

(2) Holder or beneficiary of fire insurance policy — Where a person is charged with an offence under subsection (1), the fact that the person was the holder of or was named as a beneficiary under a policy of fire insurance relating to the property in respect of which the offence is alleged to have been committed is a fact from which intent to defraud may be inferred by the court.

1990, c. 15, s. 1.

436. (1) Arson by negligence — Every person who owns, in whole or in part, or controls property is guilty of an indictable offence and liable to imprisonment for a term not exceeding five years where, as a result of a marked departure from the standard of care that a reasonably prudent person would use to prevent or control the spread of fires or to prevent explosions, that person is a cause of a fire or explosion in that property that causes bodily harm to another person or damage to property.

(2) Non-compliance with prevention laws — Where a person is charged with an offence under subsection (1), the fact that the person has failed to comply with any law respecting the prevention or control of fires or explosions in the property is a fact from which a marked departure from the standard of care referred to in that subsection may be inferred by the court.

1990, c. 15, s. 1.

436.1 Possession of incendiary material — Every person who possesses any incendiary material, incendiary device or explosive substance for the purpose of committing an offence under any of sections 433 to 436 is guilty of an indictable offence and liable to imprisonment for a term not exceeding five years.

1990, c. 15, s. 1.

Other Interference with Property

437. False alarm of fire — Every one who wilfully, without reasonable cause, by outcry, ringing bells, using a fire alarm, telephone or telegraph, or in any other manner, makes or circulates or causes to be made or circulated an alarm of fire is guilty of

(a) an indictable offence and is liable to imprisonment for a term not exceeding two years; or

(b) an offence punishable on summary conviction.

438. (1) **Interfering with saving of wrecked vessel** — Every one who wilfully prevents or impedes, or who wilfully endeavours to prevent or impede,

(a) the saving of a vessel that is wrecked, stranded, abandoned or in distress, or

(b) a person who attempts to save a vessel that is wrecked, stranded, abandoned or in distress,

is guilty of an indictable offence and liable to imprisonment for a term not exceeding five years.

(2) **Interfering with saving of wreck** — Every one who wilfully prevents or impedes or wilfully endeavours to prevent or impede the saving of wreck is guilty of an offence punishable on summary conviction.

439. (1) **Interfering with marine signal, etc.** — Every one who makes fast a vessel or boat to a signal, buoy or other sea-mark that is used for purposes of navigation is guilty of an offence punishable on summary conviction.

(2) **Idem** — Every one who wilfully alters, removes or conceals a signal, buoy or other sea-mark that is used for purposes of navigation is guilty of an indictable offence and liable to imprisonment for a term not exceeding ten years.

440. Removing natural bar without permission — Every one who wilfully and without the written permission of the Minister of Transport, the burden of proof of which lies on the accused, removes any stone, wood, earth or other material that forms a natural bar necessary to the existence of a public harbour, or that forms a natural protection to such a bar, is guilty of an indictable offence and liable to imprisonment for a term not exceeding two years.

441. Occupant injuring building — Every one who, wilfully and to the prejudice of a mortgagee or an owner, pulls down, demolishes or removes, all or any part of a dwelling-house or other building of which he is in possession or occupation, or severs from the freehold any fixture fixed therein or thereto is guilty of an indictable offence and liable to imprisonment for a term not exceeding five years.

442. Interfering with boundary lines — Every one who wilfully pulls down, defaces, alters or removes anything planted or set up as the boundary line or part of the boundary line of land is guilty of an offence punishable on summary conviction.

443. (1) Interfering with international boundary marks, etc. — Every one who wilfully pulls down, defaces, alters or removes

    (a) a boundary mark lawfully placed to mark an international, provincial, county or municipal boundary, or

    (b) a boundary mark lawfully placed by a land surveyor to mark any limit, boundary or angle of a concession, range, lot or parcel of land,

is guilty of an indictable offence and liable to imprisonment for a term not exceeding five years.

(2) Saving provision — A land surveyor does not commit an offence under subsection (1) where, in his operations as a land surveyor,

    (a) he takes up, when necessary, a boundary mark mentioned in paragraph (1)(*b*) and carefully replaces it as it was before he took it up, or

    (b) he takes up a boundary mark mentioned in paragraph (1)(*b*) in the course of surveying for a highway or other work that, when completed, will make it impossible or impracticable for that boundary mark to occupy its original position, and he establishes a permanent record of the original position sufficient to permit that position to be ascertained.

Cattle and Other Animals

444. Injuring or endangering cattle — Every one who wilfully

    (a) kills, maims, wounds, poisons or injures cattle, or

    (b) places poison in such a position that it may easily be consumed by cattle,

is guilty of an indictable offence and liable to imprisonment for a term not exceeding five years.

445. Injuring or endangering other animals — Every one who wilfully and without lawful excuse

    (a) kills, maims, wounds, poisons or injures dogs, birds or animals that are not cattle and are kept for a lawful purpose, or

    (b) places poison in such a position that it may easily be consumed by dogs, birds or animals that are not cattle and are kept for a lawful purpose, is guilty of an offence punishable on summary conviction.

Cruelty to Animals

446. **(1) Causing unnecessary suffering** — Every one commits an offence who

> (a) wilfully causes or, being the owner, wilfully permits to be caused unnecessary pain, suffering or injury to an animal or bird;

> (b) by wilful neglect causes damage or injury to animals or birds while they are being driven or conveyed;

> (c) being the owner or the person having the custody or control of a domestic animal or a bird or an animal or a bird wild by nature that is in captivity, abandons it in distress or wilfully neglects or fails to provide suitable and adequate food, water, shelter and care for it;

> (d) in any manner encourages, aids or assists at the fighting or baiting of animals or birds;

> (e) wilfully, without reasonable excuse, administers a poisonous or an injurious drug or substance to a domestic animal or bird or an animal or a bird wild by nature that is kept in captivity or, being the owner of such an animal or a bird, wilfully permits a poisonous or an injurious drug or substance to be administered to it;

> (f) promotes, arranges, conducts, assists in, receives money for or takes part in any meeting, competition, exhibition, pastime, practice, display, or event at or in the course of which captive birds are liberated by hand, trap, contrivance or any other means for the purpose of being shot when they are liberated; or

> (g) being the owner, occupier, or person in charge of any premises, permits the premises or any part thereof to be used for a purpose mentioned in paragraph (f).

(2) Punishment — Every one who commits an offence under subsection (1) is guilty of an offence punishable on summary conviction.

(3) Failure to exercise reasonable care as evidence — For the purposes of proceedings under paragraph (1)(a) or (b), evidence that a person failed to exercise reasonable care or supervision of an animal or a bird thereby causing it pain, suffering, damage or injury is, in the absence of any evidence to the contrary, proof that the pain, suffering, damage or injury was caused or was permitted to be caused wilfully or was caused by wilful neglect, as the case may be.

(4) Presence at baiting as evidence — For the purpose of proceedings under paragraph (1)(d), evidence that an accused was present at the fighting or baiting of animals or birds is, in the absence of any evidence to the contrary, proof that he encouraged, aided or assisted at the fighting or baiting.

(5) Order of prohibition — Where an accused is convicted of an offence under subsection (1), the court may, in addition to any other sentence that may be imposed for the offence, make an order prohibiting the accused from owning or having the custody or control of an animal or bird during any period not exceeding two years.

(6) Breach of order — Every one who owns or has the custody or control of an animal or a bird while he is prohibited from doing so by reason of an order made under subsection (5) is guilty of an offence punishable on summary conviction.

447. (1) Keeping cockpit — Every one who builds, makes, maintains or keeps a cockpit on premises that he owns or occupies, or allows a cockpit to be built, made, maintained or kept on such premises is guilty of an offence punishable on summary conviction.

(2) Confiscation — A peace officer who finds cocks in a cockpit or on premises where a cockpit is located shall seize them and take them before a justice who shall order them to be destroyed.

PART XII — OFFENCES RELATING TO CURRENCY

Interpretation

448. Definitions — In this Part,

"counterfeit money" includes

(a) false coin or false paper money that resembles or is apparently intended to resemble or pass for a current coin or current paper money,

(b) a forged bank note or forged blank bank note, whether complete or incomplete,

(c) a genuine coin or genuine paper money that is prepared or altered to resemble or pass for a current coin or current paper money of a higher denomination,

(d) a current coin from which the milling is removed by filing or cutting the edges and on which new milling is made to restore its appearance,

(e) a coin cased with gold, silver or nickel, as the case may be, that is intended to resemble or pass for a current gold, silver or nickel coin, and

(f) a coin or a piece of metal or mixed metals washed or coloured by any means with a wash or material capable of producing the appearance of gold, silver or nickel and that is intended to resemble or pass for a current gold, silver or nickel coin;

"counterfeit token of value" means a counterfeit excise stamp, postage stamp or other evidence of value, by whatever technical, trivial or deceptive designation it may be described, and includes genuine coin or paper money that has no value as money;

"current" means lawfully current in Canada or elsewhere by virtue of a law, proclamation or regulation in force in Canada or elsewhere as the case may be;

"utter" includes sell, pay, tender and put off.

Making

449. Making — Every one who makes or begins to make counterfeit money is guilty of an indictable offence and liable to imprisonment for a term not exceeding fourteen years.

Possession

450. Possession, etc., of counterfeit money — Every one who, without lawful justification or excuse, the proof of which lies on him,

    (a) buys, receives or offers to buy or receive,

    (b) has in his custody or possession, or

    (c) introduces into Canada,

counterfeit money is guilty of an indictable offence and liable to imprisonment for a term not exceeding fourteen years.

451. Having clippings, etc. — Every one who, without lawful justification or excuse, the proof of which lies on him, has in his custody or possession

    (a) gold or silver filings or clippings,

    (b) gold or silver bullion, or

    (c) gold or silver in dust, solution or otherwise,

produced or obtained by impairing, diminishing or lightening a current gold or silver coin, knowing that it has been so produced or obtained, is guilty of an indictable offence and liable to imprisonment for a term not exceeding five years.

Uttering

452. Uttering, etc., counterfeit money — Every one who, without lawful justification or excuse, the proof of which lies on him,

    (a) utters or offers to utter counterfeit money or uses counterfeit money as if it were genuine, or

    (b) exports, sends or takes counterfeit money out of Canada,

is guilty of an indictable offence and liable to imprisonment for a term not exceeding fourteen years.

453. Uttering coin — Every one who, with intent to defraud, knowingly utters

    (a) a coin that is not current, or

    (b) a piece of metal or mixed metals that resembles in size, figure or colour a current coin for which it is uttered,

is guilty of an indictable offence and liable to imprisonment for a term not exceeding two years.

454. Slugs and tokens — Every one who without lawful excuse, the proof of which lies on him,

(a) manufactures, produces or sells, or

(b) has in his possession

anything that is intended to be fraudulently used in substitution for a coin or token of value that any coin or token-operated device is designed to receive is guilty of an offence punishable on summary conviction.

Defacing or Impairing

455. Clipping and uttering clipped coin — Every one who

(a) impairs, diminishes or lightens a current gold or silver coin with intent that it should pass for a current gold or silver coin, or

(b) utters a coin, knowing that it has been impaired, diminished or lightened contrary to paragraph (a),

is guilty of an indictable offence and liable to imprisonment for a term not exceeding fourteen years.

456. Defacing current coins — Every one who

(a) defaces a current coin, or

(b) utters a current coin that has been defaced,

is guilty of an offence punishable on summary conviction.

457. (1) Likeness of bank-notes — No person shall make, publish, print, execute, issue, distribute or circulate, including by electronic or computer-assisted means, anything in the likeness of

(a) a current bank-note; or

(b) an obligation or a security of a government or bank.

(2) Exception — Subsection (1) does not apply to

(a) the Bank of Canada or its employees when they are carrying out their duties;

(b) the Royal Canadian Mounted Police or its members or employees when they are carrying out their duties; or

(c) any person acting under a contract or licence from the Bank of Canada or Royal Canadian Mounted Police.

(3) Offence — A person who contravenes subsection (1) is guilty of an offence punishable on summary conviction.

(4) Defence — No person shall be convicted of an offence under subsection (3) in relation to the printed likeness of a Canadian bank-note if it is established that the length or width of the likeness is less than three-fourths or greater than one-and-one-half times the length or width, as the case may be, of the bank-note and

    (a) the likeness is in black-and-white only; or

    (b) the likeness of the bank-note appears on only one side of the likeness.

Instruments or Materials

458. Making, having or dealing in instruments for counterfeiting — Every one who, without lawful justification or excuse, the proof of which lies on him,

    (a) makes or repairs,

    (b) begins or proceeds to make or repair,

    (c) buys or sells, or

    (d) has in his custody or possession,

any machine, engine, tool, instrument, material or thing that he knows has been used or that he knows is adapted and intended for use in making counterfeit money or counterfeit tokens of value is guilty of an indictable offence and liable to imprisonment for a term not exceeding fourteen years.

459. Conveying instruments for coining out of mint — Every one who, without lawful justification or excuse, the proof of which lies on him, knowingly conveys out of any of Her Majesty's mints in Canada,

    (a) any machine, engine, tool, instrument, material or thing used or employed in connection with the manufacture of coins,

    (b) a useful part of anything mentioned in paragraph (a), or

    (c) coin, bullion, metal or a mixture of metals,

is guilty of an indictable offence and liable to imprisonment for a term not exceeding fourteen years.

Advertising and Trafficking in Counterfeit Money or Counterfeit Tokens of Value

460. (1) Advertising and dealing in counterfeit money, etc. — Every one who

    (a) by an advertisement or any other writing, often to sell, procure or dispose of counterfeit money or counterfeit tokens of value or to give information with respect to the manner in which or the means by which counterfeit money or counterfeit tokens of value may be sold, procured or disposed of, or

    (b) purchases, obtains, negotiates or otherwise deals with counterfeit tokens of value, or offers to negotiate with a view to purchasing or obtaining them,

is guilty of an indictable offence and liable to imprisonment for a term not exceeding five years.

(2) Fraudulent use of money genuine but valueless — No person shall be convicted of an offence under subsection (1) in respect of genuine coin or genuine paper money that has no value as money unless, at the time when the offence is alleged to have been committed, he knew that the coin or paper money had no value as money and he had a fraudulent intent in his dealings with or with respect to the coin or paper money.

Special Provisions as to Proof

461. (1) When counterfeit complete — Every offence relating to counterfeit money or counterfeit tokens of value shall be deemed to be complete notwithstanding that the money or tokens of value in respect of which the proceedings are taken are not finished or perfected or do not copy exactly the money or tokens of value that they are apparently intended to resemble or for which they are apparently intended to pass.

(2) Certificate of examiner of counterfeit — In any proceedings under this Part, a certificate signed by a person designated as an examiner of counterfeit by the Solicitor General of Canada, stating that any coin, paper money or bank note described therein is counterfeit money or that any coin, paper money or bank note described therein is genuine and is or is not, as the case may be, current in Canada or elsewhere, is evidence of the statements contained in the certificate without proof of the signature or official character of the person appearing to have signed the certificate.

(3) Cross-examination and notice — Subsections 258(6) and (7) apply, with such modification as the circumstances require, in respect of a certificate described in subsection (2).

1992, c. 1, s. 58(1), Schedule I, item 7.

Forfeiture

462. (1) Ownership — Counterfeit money, counterfeit tokens of value and anything that is used or is intended to be used to make counterfeit money or counterfeit tokens of value belong to Her Majesty.

(2) Seizure — A peace officer may seize and detain

(a) counterfeit money,

(b) counterfeit tokens of value, and

(c) machines, engines, tools, instruments, materials or things that have been used or that have been adapted and are intended for use in making counterfeit money or counterfeit tokens of value,

and anything seized shall be sent to the Minister of Finance to be disposed of or dealt with as he may direct, but anything that is required as evidence in any proceedings shall not be sent to the Minister until it is no longer required in those proceedings.

PART XII.1 — INSTRUMENTS AND LITERATURE FOR ILLICIT DRUG USE

Interpretation

462.1 "Consume" — In this Part,

"consume", "consumption" includes smoking, inhaling, masticating and injecting into the human body;

"illicit drug" means a controlled substance or precursor the import, export, production, sale or possession of which is prohibited or restricted pursuant to the *Controlled Drugs and Substances Act*;

"illicit drug use" means the importation, exportation, production, sale or possession of a controlled substance or precursor contrary to the *Controlled Drugs and Substances Act* or a regulation made under that Act;

"instrument for illicit drug use" means anything designed primarily or intended under the circumstances for consuming or to facilitate the consumption of an illicit drug, but does not include a "device" as that term is defined in section 2 of the *Food and Drugs Act*;

"literature for illicit drug use" means any printed matter or video describing or depicting, and designed primarily or intended under the circumtances to promote, encourage or advocate the production, preparation or consumption of illicit drugs;

"sell" includes offer for sale, expose for sale, have in possession for sale and distribute, whether or not the distribution is made for consideration.

R.S. 1985, c. 50 (4th Supp.), s. 1; 1996, c. 19, s. 67.

Offence

462.2 Offence — Every one who knowingly imports into Canada, exports from Canada, manufactures, promotes or sells instruments or literature for illicit drug use is guilty of an offence and is liable on summary conviction

    (a) for a first offence, to a fine not exceeding one hundred thousand dollars or to imprisonment for a term not exceeding six months or to both; or

    (b) for a second or subsequent offence, to a fine not exceeding three hundred thousand dollars or to imprisonment for a term not exceeding one year or to both.

R.S. 1985, c. 50 (4th Supp.), s. 1.

PART XII.2 — PROCEEDS OF CRIME

Interpretation

462.3 Definitions — In this Part,

"designated drug offence" [Repealed 1996, c. 19, s. 68(1).]

"designated substance offence" means

(a) an offence under Part I of the *Controlled Drugs and Substances Act*, except subsection 4(1) of that Act, or

(b) a conspiracy or an attempt to commit, being an accessory after the fact in relation to, or any counselling in relation to, an offence referred to in paragraph (a);

"enterprise crime offence" means

(a) an offence against any of the following provisions, namely,

(i) subsection 99(1) (weapons trafficking),

(i.1) subsection 100(1) (possession for purpose of weapons trafficking),

(i.2) subsection 102(1) (making automatic firearm),

(i.3) subsection 103(1) (importing or exporting knowing it is unauthorized),

(i.4) subsection 104(1) (unauthorized importing or exporting),

(i.5) section 119 (bribery of judicial officers, etc.),

(ii) section 120 (bribery of officers),

(iii) section 121 (frauds on the government),

(iv) section 122 (breach of trust by public officer),

(iv.1) section 123 (municipal corruption),

(iv.2) section 124 (selling or purchasing office),

(iv.3) section 125 (influencing or negotiating appointments or dealing in offices),

(v) section 163 (corrupting morals),

(v.1) section 163.1 (child pornography),

(vi) subsection 201(1) (keeping gaming or betting house),

(vii) section 202 (betting, pool-selling, book-making, etc.),

(vii.1) paragraph 206(1)(*e*) (money increment schemes, etc.),

(viii) section 210 (keeping common bawdy-house),

(ix) section 212 (procuring),

(x) section 235 (punishment for murder),

(xi) section 334 (punishment for theft),

(xii) section 344 (punishment for robbery),

    (xiii) section 346 (extortion),

    (xiii.1) section 347 (criminal interest rate),

    (xiv) section 367 (punishment for forgery),

    (xv) section 368 (uttering forged document),

    (xvi) section 380 (fraud),

    (xvii) section 382 (fraudulent manipulation of stock exchange transactions),

    (xvii.1) section 394 (fraud in relation to valuable minerals),

    (xvii.2) section 394.1 (possession of stolen or fraudulently obtained valuable minerals),

    (xviii) section 426 (secret commissions),

    (xix) section 433 (arson),

    (xx) section 449 (making counterfeit money),

    (xxi) section 450 (possession, etc., of counterfeit money),

    (xxii) section 452 (uttering, etc., counterfeit money),

    (xxiii) section 462.31 (laundering proceeds of crime), or

    (xxiv) section 467.1 (participation in criminal organization),

(a.1) any indictable offence under this or any other Act of Parliament committed for the benefit of, at the direction of or in association with a criminal organization for which the maximum punishment is imprisonment for five years or more,

(b) an offence against subsection 96(1) (possession of weapon obtained by commission of offence) or section 354 (possession of property obtained by crime), committed in relation to any property, thing or proceeds obtained or derived directly or indirectly as a result of

    (i) the commission in Canada of an offence referred to in paragraph (*a*) or (*a*.1) or a designated substance offence, or

    (ii) an act or omission anywhere that, if it has occurred in Canada, would have constituted an offence referred to in paragraph (*a*) or (*a*.1) or a designated substance offence,

(b.1) an offence against section 126.1 or 126.2 or subsection 233(1) or 240(1) of the *Excise Act*, section 153, 159, 163.1 or 163.2 of the *Customs Act*, subsection 52.1(9) of the *Competition Act* or section 3, 4 or 5 of the *Corruption of Foreign Public Officials Act*, or

Editor's note: S.C. 1998, c. 34, s. 11 and S.C. 1999, c. 5, s. 52 each conditionally amended the definition of 'enterprise crime offence' in s. 462.3 by replacing paragraph (b.1). As a result of an oversight in legislative drafting, the conditions in both were fulfilled on the same day, with the result that there are now two in force versions of paragraph (b.1). The error will have to be corrected legislatively. S.C. 1999, c. 5, s. 52 proposed to add the offence under s. 52.1(9) of the Competition Act *to the list of enumerated offences. S.C. 1998, c. 34, s. 11 retained that addition and added the offences under ss. 3, 4 and 5 of the* Corruption of Foreign Public Officials Act. *The cumulative result is reflected in the text.*

(c) a conspiracy or an attempt to commit, being an accessory after the fact in relation to, or any counselling in relation to, an offence referred to in paragraph (*a*), (*a*.1), (*b*) or (*b.1*);

"judge" means a judge as defined in section 552 or a judge of a superior court of criminal jurisdiction;

"proceeds of crime" means any property, benefit or advantage, within or outside Canada, obtained or derived directly or indirectly as a result of

(a) the commission in Canada of an enterprise crime offence or a designated substance offence,

(b) an act or omission anywhere that, if it had occurred in Canada, would have constituted an enterprise crime offence or a designated substance offence.

R.S. 1985, c. 42 (4th Supp.), s. 2; 1993, c. 25, s. 95; 1993, c. 37, s. 32; 1993, c. 46, s. 5; 1994, c. 44, s. 29; 1995, c. 39, s. 151; 1996, c. 19, ss. 68, 70(a), (b); 1997, c. 18, s. 27; c. 23, s. 9; 1998, c. 34, ss. 9, 11; 1999, c. 5, ss. 13, 52.

Offence

462.31 (1) Laundering proceeds of crime — Every one commits an offence who uses, transfers the possession of, sends or delivers to any person or place, transports, transmits, alters, disposes of or otherwise deals with, in any manner and by any means, any property or any proceeds of any property with intent to conceal or convert that property or those proceeds, knowing or believing that all or a part of that property or of those proceeds was obtained or derived directly or indirectly as a result of

(a) the commission in Canada of an enterprise crime offence or a designated substance offence; or

(b) an act or omission anywhere that, if it had occurred in Canada, would have constituted an enterprise crime offence or a designated substance offence.

(2) Punishment — Every one who commits an offence under subsection (1)

(a) is guilty of an indictable offence and liable to imprisonment for a term not exceeding ten years; or

(b) is guilty of an offence punishable on summary conviction.

(3) Exception — A peace officer or a person acting under the direction of a peace officer is not guilty of an offence under subsection (1) if the peace officer or person does any of the things mentioned in that subsection for the purposes of an investigation or otherwise in the execution of the peace officer's duties.

R.S. 1985, c. 42 (4th Supp.), s. 2; 1996, c. 19, s. 70(c); 1997, c. 18, s. 28.

Search, Seizure and Detention of Proceeds of Crime

462.32 (1) Special search warrant — Subject to subsection (3), where a judge, on application of the Attorney General, is satisfied by information on oath in Form 1 that there are reasonable grounds to believe that there is in any building, receptacle or place, within the province in which the judge has jurisdiction or any other province, any property in respect of which an order of forfeiture may be made under subsection 462.37(1) or 462.38(2), in respect of an enterprise crime offence alleged to have been committed within the province in which the judge has jurisdiction, the judge may issue a warrant authorizing a person named therein or a peace officer to search the building, receptacle or place for that property and to seize that property and any other property in respect of which that person or peace officer believes, on reasonable grounds, that an order of forfeiture may be made under that subsection.

(2) Procedure — An application for a warrant under subsection (1) may be made *ex parte*, shall be made in writing and shall include a statement as to whether any previous applications have been made under subsection (1) with respect to the property that is the subject of the application.

(2.1) Execution of warrant — Subject to subsection (2.2), a warrant issued pursuant to subsection (1) may be executed anywhere in Canada.

(2.2) Execution in another province — Where a warrant is issued under subsection (1) in one province but it may be reasonably expected that it is to be executed in another province and the execution of the warrant would require entry into or on the property of any person in the other province, a judge in the other province may, on *ex parte* application, confirm the warrant, and when the warrant is so confirmed it shall have full force and effect in that other province as though it had originally been issued in that province.

(3) Execution of warrant in other territorial jurisdictions — Subsections 487(2) to (4) and section 488 apply, with such modifications as the circumstances require, to a warrant issued under this section.

(4) Detention and record of property seized — Every person who executes a warrant issued by a judge under this section shall

(a) detain or cause to be detained the property seized, taking reasonable care to ensure that the property is preserved so that it may be dealt with in accordance with the law;

(b) as soon as practicable after the execution of the warrant but within a period not exceeding seven days thereafter, prepare a report in Form 5.3, identifying the property seized and the location where the property is being detained, and cause the report to be filed with the clerk of the court; and

(c) cause a copy of the report to be provided, on request, to the person from whom the property was seized and to any other person who, in the opinion of the judge, appears to have a valid interest in the property.

(5) Notice — Before issuing a warrant under this section in relation to any property, a judge, may require notice to be given to and may hear any person who, in the opinion of the judge, appears to have a valid interest in the property unless the judge is of the opinion that giving such notice before the issuance of the warrant would result in the disappearance, dissipation or reduction in value of the property or otherwise affect the property so that all or a part thereof could not be seized pursuant to the warrant.

(6) Undertakings by Attorney General — Before issuing a warrant under this section, a judge shall require the Attorney General to give such undertakings as the judge considers appropriate with respect to the payment of damages or costs, or both, in relation to the issuance and execution of the warrant.

R.S. 1985, c. 42 (4th Supp.), s. 2; 1997, c. 18, s. 29.

462.33 (1) Application for restraint order — The Attorney General may make an application in accordance with subsection (2) for a restraint order under subsection (3) in respect of any property.

(2) Procedure — An application made under subsection (1) for a restraint order under subsection (3) in respect of any property may be made *ex parte* and shall be made in writing to a judge and be accompanied by an affidavit sworn on the information and belief of the Attorney General or any other person deposing to the following matters, namely,

(a) the offence or matter under investigation;

(b) the person who is believed to be in possession of the property;

(c) the grounds for the belief that an order of forfeiture may be made under subsection 462.37(1) or 462.38(2) in respect of the property;

(d) a description of the property; and

(e) whether any previous applications have been made under this section with respect to the property.

(3) Restraint order — Where an application for a restraint order is made to a judge under subsection (1), the judge may, if satisfied that there are reasonable grounds to believe that there exists within the province in which the judge has jurisdiction or any other province, any property in respect of which an order of forfeiture may be made under subsection 462.37(1) or 462.38(2), in respect of an enterprise crime offence alleged to have been committed within the province in which the judge has jurisdiction, make an order

(a) prohibiting any person from disposing of, or otherwise dealing with any interest in, the property specified in the order otherwise than in such manner as may be specified in the order; and

(b) at the request of the Attorney General, where the judge is of the opinion that the circumstances so require,

(i) appointing a person to take control of and to manage or otherwise deal with all or part of that property in accordance with the directions of the judge, which power to manage or otherwise deal with all or part of that property includes, in the case of perishable or rapidly depreciating property, the power to make an interlocutory sale of that property, and

(ii) requiring any person having possession of that property to give possession of the property to the person appointed under subparagraph (i).

(3.01) Execution in another province — Subsections 462.32(2.1) and (2.2) apply, with such modifications as the circumstances require, in respect of a restraint order.

(3.1) Appointment of minister of public works and government services — Where the Attorney General of Canada so requests, a judge appointing a person under subparagraph 462.33(3)(*b*)(*i*) shall appoint the Minister of Public Works and Government Services.

(4) Idem — An order made by a judge under subsection (3) may be subject to such reasonable conditions as the judge thinks fit.

(5) Notice — Before making an order under subsection (3) in relation to any property, a judge may require notice to be given to and may hear any person who, in the opinion of the judge, appears to have a valid interest in the property unless the judge is of the opinion that giving such notice before making the order would result in the disappearance, dissipation or reduction in value of the property or otherwise affect the property so that all or a part thereof could not be subject to an order of forfeiture under subsection 462.37(1) or 462.38(2).

(6) Order in writing — An order made under subsection (3) shall be made in writing.

(7) Undertakings by Attorney General — Before making an order under subsection (3), a judge shall require the Attorney General to give such undertakings as the judge considers appropriate with respect to the payment of damages or costs, or both, in relation to the making and execution of the order.

(8) Service of order — A copy of an order made by a judge under subsection (3) shall be served on the person to whom the order is addressed in such manner as the judge directs or as may be prescribed by rules of court.

(9) Registration of order — A copy of an order made under subsection (3), shall be registered against any property in accordance with the laws of the province in which the property is situated.

(10) Continues in force — An order made under subsection (3) remains in effect until

(a) it is revoked or varied under subsection 462.34(4) or revoked under paragraph 462.43(*a*);

(b) it ceases to be in force under section 462.35; or

(c) an order of forfeiture or restoration of the property is made under subsection 462.37(1), 462.38(2) or 462.41(3) or any other provision of this or any other Act of Parliament.

(11) Offence — Any person on whom an order made under subsection (3) is served in accordance with this section and who, while the order is in force, acts in contravention of or fails to comply with the order is guilty of an indictable offence or an offence punishable on summary conviction.

R.S. 1985, c. 42 (4th Supp.), s. 2; 1996, c. 16, s. 60(1)(d); 1997, c. 18, s. 30.

462.34 (1) Application for review of special warrants and restraint orders — Any person who has an interest in property that was seized under a warrant issued pursuant to section 462.32 or in respect of which a restraint order was made under subsection 462.33(3) may, at any time, apply to a judge

    (a) for an order under subsection (4); or

    (b) for permission to examine the property.

(2) Notice to Attorney General — Where an application is made under paragraph (1)(*a*),

    (a) the application shall not, without the consent of the Attorney General, be heard by a judge unless the applicant has given to the Attorney General at least two clear days notice in writing of the application; and

    (b) the judge may require notice of the application to be given to and may hear any person who, in the opinion of the judge, appears to have a valid interest in the property.

(3) Terms of examination order — A judge may, on an application made to the judge under paragraph (1)(*b*), order that the applicant be permitted to examine property subject to such terms as appear to the judge to be necessary or desirable to ensure that the property is safeguarded and for any purpose for which it may subsequently be required.

(4) Order of restoration of property or revocation or variation of order — On an application made to a judge under paragraph (1)(*a*) in respect of any property and after hearing the applicant and the Attorney General and any other person to whom notice was given pursuant to paragraph (2)(*b*), the judge may order that the property or a part thereof be returned to the applicant or, in the case of a restraint order made under subsection 462.33(3), revoke the order, vary the order to exclude the property or any interest in the property or part thereof from the application of the order or make the order subject to such reasonable conditions as the judge thinks fit,

    (a) if the applicant enters into a recognizance before the judge, with or without sureties, in such amount and with such conditions, if any, as the judge directs and, where the judge considers it appropriate, deposits with the judge such sum of money or other valuable security as the judge directs;

    (b) if the conditions referred to in subsection (6) are satisfied; or

    (c) for the purpose of

        (i) meeting the reasonable living expenses of the person who was in possession of the property at the time the warrant was executed or the order was made or any person who, in the opinion of the judge, has a valid interest in the property and of the dependants of that person,

        (ii) meeting the reasonable business and legal expenses of a person referred to in subparagraph (i), or

        (iii) permitting the use of the property in order to enter into a recognizance under Part XVI, if the judge is satisfied that the applicant has no other assets or means available for the purposes set out in this paragraph and that no other person appears to be the lawful owner of or lawfully entitled to possession of the property.

(5) Hearing — For the purpose of determining the reasonableness of legal expenses referred to in subparagraph (4)(c)(ii), a judge shall hold an *in camera* hearing, without the presence of the Attorney General, and shall take into account the legal aid tariff of the province.

(5.1) Expenses — For the purpose of determining the reasonableness of expenses referred to in paragraph (4)(c), the Attorney General may

(a) at the hearing of the application, make representations as to what would constitute the reasonableness of the expenses, other than legal expenses; and

(b) before or after the hearing of the application held *in camera* pursuant to subsection (5), make representations as to what would constitute reasonable legal expenses referred to in subparagraph (4)(c)(ii).

(5.2) Taxing legal fees — The judge who made an order under paragraph (4)(c) may, and on the application of the Attorney General shall, tax the legal fees forming part of the legal expenses referred to in subparagraph (4)(c)(ii) and, in so doing, shall take into account

(a) the value of property in respect of which an order of forfeiture may be made;

(b) the complexity of the proceedings giving rise to those legal expenses;

(c) the importance of the issues involved in those proceedings;

(d) the duration of any hearings held in respect of those proceedings;

(e) whether any stage of those proceedings was improper or vexatious;

(f) any representations made by the Attorney General; and

(g) any other relevant matter.

(6) Conditions to be satisfied — An order under paragraph (4)(b) in respect of property may be made by a judge if the judge is satisfied

(a) where the application is made by

(i) a person charged with an enterprise crime offence or a designated substance offence, or

(ii) any person who acquired title to or a right of possession of that property from a person referred to in subparagraph (i) under circumstances that give rise to a reasonable inference that the title or right was transferred from that person for the purpose of avoiding the forfeiture of the property,

that a warrant should not have been issued pursuant to section 462.32 or a restraint order under subsection 462.33(3) should not have been made in respect of that property, or

(b) in any other case, that the applicant is the lawful owner of or lawfully entitled to possession of the property and appears innocent of any complicity in an enterprise crime offence or designated substance offence or of any collusion in relation to such an offence, and that no other person appears to be the lawful owner of or lawfully entitled to possession of the property,

and that the property will no longer be required for the purpose of any investigation or as evidence in any proceeding.

(7) Saving provision — Section 354 of this Act and subsection 8(1) of the *Controlled Drugs and Substances Act* do not apply to a person who comes into possession of any property or thing that, pursuant to an order made under paragraph 4(c), was returned to any person after having been seized or was excluded from the application of a restraint order made under subsection 462.33(3).

(8) Form of recognizance — A recognizance entered into pursuant to paragraph (4)(*a*) may be in Form 32.

R.S. 1985, c. 42 (4th Supp.), s. 2; 1996, c. 19, ss. 69, 70(d), (e); 1997, c. 18, s. 31.

462.341 Application of property restitution provisions — Subsection 462.34(2), paragraph 462.34(4)(*c*) and subsections 462.34(5), (5.1) and (5.2) apply, with any modifications that the circumstances require, to a person who has an interest in money or bank-notes that are seized under this Act or the *Controlled Drugs and Substances Act* and in respect of which proceedings may be taken under subsection 462.37(1) or 462.38(2).

1997, c. 18, ss. 32, 140(a); 1999, c. 5, s. 14.

462.35 (1) Expiration of special warrants and restraint orders — Subject to this section, where property has been seized under a warrant issued pursuant to section 462.32 or a restraint order has been made under section 462.33 in relation to property, the property may be detained or the order may continue in force, as the case may be, for a period not exceeding six months from the seizure or the making of the order, as the case may be.

(2) Where proceedings instituted — The property may continue to be detained, or the order may continue in force, for a period that exceeds six months if proceedings are instituted in respect of which the thing detained may be forfeited.

(3) Where application made — The property may continue to be detained or the order may continue in force for a period or periods that exceed six months if the continuation is, on application made by the Attorney General, ordered by a judge, where the judge is satisfied that the property is required, after the expiration of the period or periods, for the purpose of section 462.37 or 462.38 or any other provision of this or any other Act of Parliament respecting forfeiture or for the purpose of any investigation or as evidence in any proceeding.

R.S. 1985, c. 42 (4th Supp.), s. 2; 1997, c. 18, s. 33.

462.36 Forwarding to clerk where accused to stand trial — Where a judge issues a warrant under section 462.32 or makes a restraint order under section 462.33 in respect of any property, the clerk of the court shall, when an accused is ordered to stand trial for an enterprise crime offence, cause to be forwarded to the clerk of the court to which the accused has been ordered to stand trial a copy of the report filed pursuant to paragraph 462.32(4)(*b*) or of the restraint order in respect of the property.

R.S. 1985, c. 42 (4th Supp.), s. 2.

Forfeiture of Proceeds of Crime

462.37 (1) Order of forfeiture of property on conviction — Subject to this section and sections 462.39 to 462.41, where an offender is convicted or discharged under section 730 of an enterprise crime offence and the court imposing sentence on the offender, on application of the Attorney General, is satisfied, on a balance of probabilities, that any property is proceeds of crime and that the enterprise crime offence was committed in relation to that property, the court shall order that the property be forfeited to Her Majesty to be disposed of as the Attorney General directs or otherwise dealt with in accordance with the law.

(2) Proceeds of crime derived from other offences — Where the evidence does not establish to the satisfaction of the court that the enterprise crime offence of which the offender is convicted, or discharged under section 730, was committed in relation to property in respect of which an order of forfeiture would otherwise be made under subsection (1) but the court is satisfied, beyond a reasonable doubt, that that property is proceeds of crime, the court may make an order of forfeiture under subsection (1) in relation to that property.

(3) Fine instead of forfeiture — Where a court is satisfied that an order of forfeiture under subsection (1) should be made in respect of any property of an offender, but that that property or any part thereof or interest therein cannot be made subject to such an order and, in particular,

(a) cannot, on the exercise of due diligence, be located,

(b) has been transferred to a third party,

(c) is located outside Canada,

(d) has been substantially diminished in value or rendered worthless, or

(e) has been commingled with other property that cannot be divided without difficulty,

the court may, instead of ordering that property or part thereof or interest therein to be forfeited pursuant to subsection (1), order the offender to pay a fine in an amount equal to the value of that property, part or interest.

(4) Imprisonment in default of payment of fine — Where a court orders an offender to pay a fine pursuant to subsection (3), the court shall

(a) impose, in default of payment of that fine, a term of imprisonment

(i) not exceeding six months, where the amount of the fine does not exceed ten thousand dollars,

(ii) of not less than six months and not exceeding twelve months, where the amount of the fine exceeds ten thousand dollars but does not exceed twenty thousand dollars,

(iii) of not less than twelve months and not exceeding eighteen months, where the amount of the fine exceeds twenty thousand dollars but does not exceed fifty thousand dollars,

(iv) of not less than eighteen months and not exceeding two years, where the amount of the fine exceeds fifty thousand dollars but does not exceed one hundred thousand dollars,

(v) of not less than two years and not exceeding three years, where the amount of the fine exceeds one hundred thousand dollars but does not exceed two hundred and fifty thousand dollars,

(vi) of not less than three years and not exceeding five years, where the amount of the fine exceeds two hundred and fifty thousand dollars but does not exceed one mllion dollars, or

(vii) of not less than five years and not exceeding ten years, where the amount of the fine exceeds one million dollars; and

(b) direct that the term of imprisonment imposed pursuant to paragraph (*a*) be served consecutively to any other term of imprisonment imposed on the offender or that the offender is then serving.

(5) Fine option not available to offender — Section 736 does not apply to an offender against whom a fine is imposed pursuant to subsection (3).

R.S. 1985, c. 42 (4th Supp.), s. 2; 1995, c. 22, s. 18.

462.371 (1) Definition of "order" — In this section, "order" means an order made under section 462.36 or 462.38.

(2) Execution — An order may be executed anywhere in Canada.

(3) Filing of order from another province — Where the Attorney General of a province in which property that is the subject of an order made in another province is situated receives a certified copy of the order and files it with the superior court of criminal jurisdiction of the province in which the property is situated, the order shall be entered as a judgment of that court.

(4) Attorney General of Canada — Where the Attorney General of Canada receives a certified copy of an order made in a province in respect of property situated in another province and files the order with the superior court of criminal jurisdiction of the province in which the property is situated, the order shall be entered as a judgment of the court.

(5) Effect of registered order — An order has, from the date it is filed in a court of a province under subsection (3) or (4), the same effect as if it had been an order originally made by that court.

(6) Notice — Where an order has been filed in a court under subsection (3) or (4), it shall not be executed before notice in accordance with subsection 462.41(2) is given to every person who, in the opinion of the court, appears to have a valid interest in the property.

(7) Application of section 462.42 — Section 462.42 applies, with such modifications as the circumstances require, in respect of a person who claims an interest in property that is the subject of an order filed under subsection (3) or (4).

(8) Application under section 462.42 to be made in one province — No person may make an application under section 462.42 in relation to property that is the subject of an order filed under subsection (3) or (4) if that person has previously made an application in respect of the same property in another province.

(9) Finding in one court binding — The finding by a court of a province in relation to property that is the subject of an order filed under subsection (3) or (4) as to whether or not an applicant referred to in subsection 462.42(4) is affected by the forfeiture referred to in that subsection or declaring the nature and extent of the interest of the applicant under that subsection is binding on the superior court of criminal jurisdiction of the province where the order is entered as a judgment.

1997, c. 18, s. 34.

462.38 (1) Application for forfeiture — Where an information has been laid in respect of an enterprise crime offence, the Attorney General may make an application to a judge for an order of forfeiture under subsection (2) in respect of any property.

(2) Order of forfeiture of property — Subject to sections 462.39 to 462.41, where an application is made to a judge under subsection (1), the judge shall, if the judge is satisfied that

(a) any property is, beyond a reasonable doubt, proceeds of crime,

(b) proceedings in respect of an enterprise crime offence committed in relation to that property were commenced, and

(c) the accused charged with the offence referred to in paragraph (b) has died or absconded,

order that the property be forfeited to Her Majesty to be disposed of as the Attorney General directs or otherwise dealt with in accordance with the law.

(3) Person deemed absconded — For the purposes of this section, a person shall be deemed to have absconded in connection with an enterprise crime offence if

(a) an information has been laid alleging the commission of the offence by the person,

(b) a warrant for the arrest of the person or a summons in respect of a corporation has been issued in relation to that information,

(c) reasonable attempts to arrest the person pursuant to the warrant or to serve the summons have been unsuccessful during the period of six months commencing on the day the warrant or summons was issued, or, in the case of a person who is not or never was in Canada, the person cannot be brought within that period to the jurisdiction in which the warrant or summons was issued, and the person shall be deemed to have so absconded on the last day of that period of six months.

R.S. 1985, c. 42 (4th Supp.), s. 2; 1997, c. 18, s. 35(2).

462.39 Inference — For the purpose of subsection 462.37(1) or 462.38(2), the court may infer that property was obtained or derived as a result of the commission of an enterprise crime offence where evidence establishes that the value, after the commission of that offence, of all the property of the person alleged to have committed the offence exceeds the value of all the property of that person before the commission of that offence and the court is satisfied that the income of that person from sources unrelated to enterprise crime offences or designated substance offences committed by that person cannot reasonably account for such an increase in value.

R.S. 1985, c. 42 (4th Supp.), s. 2; 1996, c. 19, s. 70(f).

462.4 Voidable transfers — A court may,

(a) prior to ordering property to be forfeited under subsection 462.37(1) or 462.38(2), and

(b) in the case of property in respect of which a restraint order was made under section 462.33, where the order was served in accordance with subsection 462.33(8),

set aside any conveyance or transfer of the property that occurred after the seizure of the property or the service of the order under section 462.33, unless the conveyance or transfer was for valuable consideration to a person acting in good faith.

R.S. 1985, c. 42 (4th Supp.), s. 2; 1997, c. 18, s. 36.

462.41 (1) Notice — Before making an order under subsection 462.37(1) or 462.38(2) in relation to any property, a court shall require notice in accordance with subsection (2) to be given to and may hear any person who, in the opinion of the court, appears to have a valid interest in the property.

(2) Manner of giving notice — A notice given under subsection (1) shall

(a) be given or served in such manner as the court directs or as may be prescribed by the rules of the court;

(b) be of such duration as the court considers reasonable or as may be prescribed by the rules of the court; and

(c) set out the enterprise crime offence charged and a description of the property.

(3) Order of restoration of property — Where a court is satisfied that any person, other than

(a) a person who is charged with, or was convicted of, an enterprise crime offence or a designated substance offence, or

(b) a person who acquired title to or a right of possession of that property from a person referred to in paragraph (a) under circumstances that give rise to a reasonable inference that the title or right was transferred for the purpose of avoiding the forfeiture of the property,

263

is the lawful owner or is lawfully entitled to possession of any property or any part thereof that would otherwise be forfeited pursuant to subsection 462.37(1) or 462.38(2) and that the person appears innocent of any complicity in an offence referred to in paragraph (a) or of any collusion in relation to such an offence, the court may order that the property or part thereof be returned to that person.

R.S. 1985, c. 42 (4th Supp.), s. 2; 1996, c. 19, s. 70(g); 1997, c. 18, ss. 37, 140(d)(ii).

462.42 (1) Application by person claiming interest for relief from forfeiture — Where any property is forfeited to Her Majesty under subsection 462.37(1) or 462.38(2), any person who claims an interest in the property, other than

(a) a person who is charged with, or was convicted of, an enterprise crime offence or a designated substance offence that was committed in relation to the property forfeited, or

(b) a person who acquired title to or a right of possession of that property from a person referred to in paragraph (a) under circumstances that give rise to a reasonable inference that the title or right was transferred from that person for the purpose of avoiding the forfeiture of the property,

may, within thirty days after that forfeiture, apply by notice in writing to a judge for an order under subsection (4).

(2) Fixing day for hearing — The judge to whom an application is made under subsection (1) shall fix a day not less than thirty days after the date of filing of the application for the hearing thereof.

(3) Notice — An applicant shall serve a notice of the application made under subsection (1) and of the hearing thereof on the Attorney General at least fifteen days before the day fixed for the hearing.

(4) Order declaring interest not subject to forfeiture — Where, on the hearing of an application made under subsection (1), the judge is satisfied that the applicant is not a person referred to in paragraph (1)(a) or (b) and appears innocent of any complicity in any enterprise crime offence or designated substance offence that resulted in the forfeiture or of any collusion in relation to any such offence, the judge may make an order declaring that the interest of the applicant is not affected by the forfeiture and declaring the nature and extent of the interest.

(5) Appeal from order under subsection (4) — An applicant or the Attorney General may appeal to the court of appeal from an order under subsection (4) and the provisions of Part XXI with respect to procedure on appeals apply, with such modifications as the circumstances require, to appeals under this subsection.

(6) Return of property — The Attorney General shall, on application made to the Attorney General by any person who has obtained an order under subsection (4) and where the periods with respect to the taking of appeals from that order have expired and any appeal from that order taken under subsection (5) has been determined,

(a) direct that the property or the part thereof to which the interest of the applicant relates be returned to the applicant; or

(b) direct that an amount equal to the value of the interest of the applicant, as declared in the order, be paid to the applicant.

R.S. 1985, c. 42 (4th Supp.), s. 2; 1996, c. 19, s. 70(h), (i); 1997, c. 18, s. 38(1), 140(d)(iii).

462.43 Residual disposal of property seized or dealt with pursuant to special warrants or restraint orders — Where property has been seized under a warrant issued pursuant to section 462.32, a restraint order has been made under section 462.33 in relation to any property or a recognizance has been entered into pursuant to paragraph 462.34(4)(*a*) in relation to any property and a judge, on application made to the judge by the Attorney General or any person having an interest in the property or on the judge's own motion, after notice given to the Attorney General and any other person having an interest in the property, is satisfied that the property will no longer be required for the purpose of section 462.37, 462.38 or any other provision of this or any other Act of Parliament respecting forfeiture or for the purpose of any investigation or as evidence in any proceeding, the judge

(a) in the case of a restraint order, shall revoke the order;

(b) in the case of a recognizance, shall cancel the recognizance; and

(c) in the case of property seized under a warrant issued pursuant to section 462.32 or property under the control of a person appointed pursuant to subparagraph 462.33(3)(*b*)(i),

(i) if possession of it by the person from whom it was taken is lawful, shall order that it be returned to that person,

(ii) if possession of it by the person from whom it was taken is unlawful and the lawful owner or person who is lawfully entitled to its possession is known, shall order that it be returned to the lawful owner or the person who is lawfully entitled to its possession, or

(iii) if possession of it by the person from whom it was taken is unlawful and the lawful owner or person who is lawfully entitled to its possession is not known, may order that it be forfeited to Her Majesty, to be disposed of as the Attorney General directs, or otherwise dealt with in accordance with the law.

R.S. 1985, c. 42 (4th Supp.), s. 2.

462.44 Appeals from certain orders — Any person who considers that they are aggrieved by an order made under subsection 462.38(2) or 462.41(3) or section 462.43 may appeal from the order as if the order were an appeal against conviction or against a judgment or verdict of acquittal, as the case may be, under Part XXI, and that Part applies, with such modifications as the circumstances require, to such an appeal.

R.S. 1985, c. 42 (4th Supp.), s. 2; 1997, c. 18, s. 39.

462.45 Suspension of forfeiture pending appeal — Notwithstanding anything in this Part, the operation of an order of forfeiture or restoration of property under subsection 462.34(4), 462.37(1), 462.38(2) or 462.41(3) or section 462.43 is suspended pending

(a) any application made in respect of the property under any of those provisions or any other provision of this or any other Act of Parliament that provides for the restoration or forfeiture of such property,

(b) any appeal taken from an order of forfeiture or restoration in respect of the property, or

(c) any other proceeding in which the right of seizure of the property is questioned, and property shall not be disposed of within thirty days after an order of forfeiture is made under any of those provisions.

R.S. 1985, c. 42 (4th Supp.), s. 2.

462.46 (1) Copies of documents returned or forfeited — Where any document is returned or ordered to be returned, forfeited or otherwise dealt with under subsection 462.34(3) or (4), 462.37(1), 462.38(2) or 462.41(3) or section 462.43, the Attorney General may, before returning the document or complying with the order, cause a copy of the document to be made and retained.

(2) Probative force — Every copy made under subsection (1) shall, if certified as a true copy by the Attorney General, be admissible in evidence and, in the absence of evidence to the contrary, shall have the same probative force as the original document would have had if it had been proved in the ordinary way.

R.S. 1985, c. 42 (4th Supp.), s. 2.

Disclosure Provisions

462.47 No civil or criminal liability incurred by informants — For greater certainty but subject to section 241 of the *Income Tax Act*, a person is justified in disclosing to a peace officer or the Attorney General any facts on the basis of which that person reasonably suspects that any property is proceeds of crime or that any person has committed or is about to commit an enterprise crime offence or a designated substance offence.

R.S. 1985, c. 42 (4th Supp.), s. 2; 1996, c. 19, s. 70(j).

462.48 (1) Disclosure of income tax information — The Attorney General may, for the purposes of an investigation in relation to

(a) a designated substance offence,

(b) an offence against section 354 or 462.31 where the offence is alleged to have been committed in relation to any property, thing or proceeds obtained or derived directly or indirectly as a result of

(i) the commission in Canada of a designated substance offence, or

(ii) an act or omission anywhere that, if it had occurred in Canada, would have constituted a designated substance offence, or

(c) an offence against section 467.1 or a conspiracy or an attempt to commit, being an accessory after the fact in relation to, or any counselling in relation to, such an offence,

make an application in accordance with subsection (2) for an order for disclosure of information under subsection (3).

(2) Application — An application under subsection (1) shall be made *ex parte* in writing to a judge and be accompanied by an affidavit sworn on the information and belief of the Attorney General or a person specially designated by the Attorney General for that purpose deposing to the following matters, namely,

(a) the offence or matter under investigation;

(b) the person in relation to whom the information or documents referred to in paragraph (c) are required;

(c) the type of information or book, record, writing, return or other document obtained by or on behalf of the Minister of National Revenue for the purposes of the *Income Tax Act* to which access is sought or that is proposed to be examined or communicated; and

(d) the facts relied on to justify the belief, on reasonable grounds, that the person referred to in paragraph (b) has committed or benefited from the commission of an offence referred to in paragraph (1)(a), (b) or (c) and that the information or documents referred to in paragraph (c) are likely to be of substantial value, whether alone or together with other material, to the investigation for the purposes of which the application is made.

(3) Order for disclosure of information — Where the judge to whom an application under subsection (1) is made is satisfied

(a) of the matters referred to in paragraph (2)(d), and

(b) that there are reasonable grounds for believing that it is in the public interest to allow access to the information or documents to which the application relates, having regard to the benefit likely to accrue to the investigation if the access is obtained,

the judge may, subject to any conditions that the judge considers advisable in the public interest, order the Commissioner of Customs and Revenue or any person specially designated in writing by the Commissioner for the purposes of this section

(c) to allow a police officer named in the order access to all such information and documents and to examine them, or

(d) where the judge considers it necessary in the circumstances, to produce all such information and documents to the police officer and allow the police officer to remove the information and documents,

within such period as the judge may specify after the expiration of seven clear days following the service of the order pursuant to subsection (4).

(4) Service of order — A copy of an order made by a judge under subsection (3) shall be served on the person to whom the order is addressed in such manner as the judge directs or as may be prescribed by rules of court.

(5) Extension of period for compliance with order — A judge who makes an order under subsection (3) may, on application of the Minister of National Revenue, extend the period within which the order is to be complied with.

(6) Objection to disclosure of information — The Minister of National Revenue or any person specially designated in writing by that Minister for the purposes of this section may object to the disclosure of any information or document in respect of which an order under subsection (3) has been made by certifying orally or in writing that the information or document should not be disclosed on the ground that

(a) the Minister of National Revenue is prohibited from disclosing the information or document by any bilateral or international treaty, convention or other agreement respecting taxation to which the Government of Canada is signatory;

(b) a privilege is attached by law to the information or document;

(c) the information or document has been placed in a sealed package pursuant to law or an order of a court of competent jurisdiction; or

(d) disclosure of the information or document would not, for any other reason, be in the public interest.

(7) Determination of objection — Where an objection to the disclosure of information or a document is made under subsection (6), the objection may be determined, on application, in accordance with subsection (8), by the Chief Justice of the Federal Court, or by such other judge of that court as the Chief Justice may designate to hear such applications.

(8) Judge may examine information — A judge who is to determine an objection pursuant to subsection (7) may, if the judge considers it necessary to determine the objection, examine the information or document in relation to which the objection is made and shall grant the objection and order that disclosure of the information or document be refused where the judge is satisfied of any of the grounds mentioned in subsection (6).

(9) Limitation period — An application under subsection (7) shall be made within ten days after the objection is made or within such greater or lesser period as the Chief Justice of the Federal Court, or such other judge of that court as the Chief Justice may designate to hear such applications, considers appropriate.

(10) Appeal to federal court of appeal — An appeal lies from a determination under subsection (7) to the Federal Court of Appeal.

(11) Limitation period for appeal — An appeal under subsection (10) shall be brought within ten days from the date of the determination appealed from or within such further time as the Federal Court of Appeal considers appropriate in the circumstances.

(12) Special rules for hearing — An application under subsection (7) or an appeal brought in respect of that application shall

(a) be heard in *camera*; and

(b) on the request of the person objecting to the disclosure of information, be heard and determined in the National Capital Region described in the schedule to the *National Capital Act*.

(13) Ex parte representations — During the hearing of an application under subsection (7) or an appeal brought in respect of that application, the person who made the objection in respect of which the application was made or the appeal was brought shall, on the request of that person, be given the opportunity to make representations *ex parte*.

(14) Copies — When any information or document is examined or provided under subsection (3), the person by whom it is examined or to whom it is provided or any officer of the Canada Customs and Revenue Agency may make, or cause to be made, one or more copies of it, and any copy purporting to be certified by the Minister of National Revenue or an authorized person to be a copy made under this subsection is evidence of the nature and content of the original information or document and has the same probative force as the original information or document would have had if it had been proved in the ordinary way.

(15) Further disclosure — No person to whom information or documents have been disclosed or provided pursuant to this subsection or pursuant to an order made under subsection (3) shall further disclose the information or documents except for the purposes of the investigation in relation to which the order was made.

(16) Form — An order made under subsection (3) may be in Form 47.

(17) Definition of "police officer" — In this section, **"police officer"** means any officer, constable or other person employed for the preservation and maintenance of the public peace.

R.S. 1985, c. 42 (4th Supp.), s. 2; 1994, c. 13, s. 7(1)(b); 1996, c. 19, s. 70(k); 1997, c. 23, s. 10(2); 1999, c. 17, s. 120.

Specific Rules of Forfeiture

462.49 (1) Specific forfeiture provisions unaffected by this part — This Part does not affect the operation of any other provision of this or any other Act of Parliament respecting the forfeiture of property.

(2) Priority for restitution to victims of crime — The property of an offender may be used to satisfy the operation of a provision of this or any other Act of Parliament respecting the forfeiture of property only to the extent that it is not required to satisfy the operation of any other provision of this or any other Act of Parliament respecting the restitution or compensation of persons affected by the commission of offences.

R.S. 1985, c. 42 (4th Supp.), s. 2.

Regulations

462.5 Regulations — The Attorney General may make regulations governing the manner of disposing of or otherwise dealing with, in accordance with the law, property, forfeited under this Part.

R.S. 1985, c. 42 (4th Supp.), s. 2.

PART XIII — ATTEMPTS — CONSPIRACIES — ACCESSORIES

463. Attempts, accessories — Except where otherwise expressly provided by law, the following provisions apply in respect of persons who attempt to commit or are accessories after the fact to the commission of offences:

> (a) every one who attempts to commit or is an accessory after the fact to the commission of an indictable offence for which, on conviction, an accused is liable to be sentenced to imprisonment for life is guilty of an indictable offence and liable to imprisonment for a term not exceeding fourteen years;

(b) every one who attempts to commit or is an accessory after the fact to the commission of an indictable offence for which, on conviction, an accused is liable to imprisonment for fourteen years or less is guilty of an indictable offence and liable to imprisonment for a term that is one-half of the longest term to which a person who is guilty of that offence is liable;

(c) every one who attempts to commit or is an accessory after the fact to the commission of an offence punishable on summary conviction is guilty of an offence punishable on summary conviction; and

(d) every one who attempts to commit or is an accessory after the fact to the commission of an offence for which the offender may be prosecuted by indictment or for which he is punishable on summary conviction

(i) is guilty of an indictable offence and liable to imprisonment for a term not exceeding a term that is one-half of the longest term to which a person who is guilty of that offence is liable, or

(ii) is guilty of an offence punishable on summary conviction.

R.S. 1985, c. 27 (1st Supp.), s. 59; 1998, c. 35, s. 120

464. Counselling offence that is not committed — Except where otherwise expressly provided by law, the following provisions apply in respect of persons who counsel other persons to commit offences, namely,

(a) every one who counsels another person to commit an indictable offence is, if the offence is not committed, guilty of an indictable offence and liable to the same punishment to which a person who attempts to commit that offence is liable; and

(b) every one who counsels another person to commit an offence punishable on summary conviction is, if the offence is not committed, guilty of an offence punishable on summary conviction.

R.S. 1985, c. 27 (1st Supp.), s. 60.

465. (1) Conspiracy — Except where otherwise expressly provided by law, the following provisions apply in respect of conspiracy:

(a) every one who conspires with any one to commit murder or to cause another person to be murdered, whether in Canada or not, is guilty of an indictable offence and liable to a maximum term of imprisonment for life;

(b) every one who conspires with any one to prosecute a person for an alleged offence, knowing that he did not commit that offence, is guilty of an indictable offence and liable

(i) to imprisonment for a term not exceeding ten years, if the alleged offence is one for which, on conviction, that person would be liable to be sentenced to imprisonment for life or for a term not exceeding fourteen years, or

(ii) to imprisonment for a term not exceeding five years, if the alleged offence is one for which, on conviction, that person would be liable to imprisonment for less than fourteen years; and

(c) every one who conspires with any one to commit an indictable offence not provided for in paragraph (*a*) or (*b*) is guilty of an indictable offence and liable to the same punishment as that to which an accused who is guilty of that offence would, on conviction, be liable; and

(d) every one who conspires with any one to commit an offence punishable on summary conviction is guilty of an offence punishable on summary conviction.

(2) [Repealed R.S. 1985, c. 27 (1st Supp.), s. 61(3).]

(3) **Conspiracy to commit offences** — Every one who, while in Canada, conspires with any one to do anything referred to in subsection (1) in a place outside Canada that is an offence under the laws of that place shall be deemed to have conspired to do that thing in Canada.

(4) **Idem** — Every one who, while in a place outside Canada, conspires with any one to do anything referred to in subsection (1) in Canada shall be deemed to have conspired in Canada to do that thing.

(5) **Jurisdiction** — Where a person is alleged to have conspired to do anything that is an offence by virtue of subsection (3) or (4), proceedings in respect of that offence may, whether or not that person is in Canada, be commenced in any territorial division in Canada, and the accused may be tried and punished in respect of that offence in the same manner as if the offence had been committed in that territorial division.

(6) **Appearance of accused at trial** — For greater certainty, the provisions of this Act relating to

(a) requirements that an accused appear at and be present during proceedings, and

(b) the exceptions to those requirements,

apply to proceedings commenced in any territorial division pursuant to subsection (5).

(7) **Where previously tried outside Canada** — Where a person is alleged to have conspired to do anything that is an offence by virtue of subsection (3) or (4) and that person has been tried and dealt with outside Canada in respect of the offence in such a manner that, if the person had been tried and dealt with in Canada, he would be able to plead *autrefois acquit, autrefois convict* or pardon, the person shall be deemed to have been so tried and dealt with in Canada.

R.S. 1985, c. 27 (1st Supp.), s. 61; 1998, c. 35, s. 121

466. (1) Conspiracy in restraint of trade — A conspiracy in restraint of trade is an agreement between two or more persons to do or to procure to be done any unlawful act in restraint of trade.

(2) Trade union, exception — The purposes of a trade union are not, by reason only that they are in restraint of trade, unlawful within the meaning of subsection (1).

467. (1) Saving — No person shall be convicted of the offence of conspiracy by reason only that he

(a) refuses to work with a workman or for an employer; or

(b) does any act or causes any act to be done for the purpose of a trade combination, unless such act is an offence expressly punishable by law.

(2) "trade combination" — In this section, **"trade combination"** means any combination between masters or workmen or other persons for the purpose of regulating or altering the relations between masters or workmen, or the conduct of a master or workman in or in respect of his business, employment or contract of employment or service.

467.1 (1) Participation in criminal organization — Every one who

(a) participates in or substantially contributes to the activities of a criminal organization knowing that any or all of the members of the organization engage in or have, within the preceding five years, engaged in the commission of a series of indictable offence under this or any other Act of Parliament for each of which the maximum punishment is imprisonment for five years or more, and

(b) is a party to the commission of an indictable offence for the benefit of, at the direction of or in association with the criminal organization for which the maximum punishment is imprisonment for five years or more

is guilty of an indictable offence and liable to imprisonment for a term not exceeding fourteen years.

(2) Sentences to be served consecutively — A sentence imposed on a person for an offence under subsection (1) shall be served consecutively to any other punishment imposed on the person for an offence arising out of the same event or series of events and to any other sentence to which is subject at the time the sentence is imposed on the person for an offence under subsection (1).

1997, c. 23, s. 11.

467.2 (1) Powers of the Attorney General of Canada — Notwithstanding the definition of "Attorney General" in section 2, the Attorney General of Canada may conduct proceedings in respect of a criminal organization offence where the alleged offence arises out of conduct that in whole or in part is in relation to an alleged contravention of an Act of Parliament or a regulation made under such an Act, other than this Act or a regulation made under this Act, and, for that purpose, the Attorney General of Canada may exercise all the powers and perform all the duties and functions assigned to the Attorney General by or under this Act.

(2) Powers of Attorney General of a province — Subsection (1) does not affect the authority of the Attorney General of a province to conduct proceedings in respect of an offence referred to in subsection 467.1(1) or to exercise any of the powers or perform any of the duties and functions assigned to the Attorney General by or under this Act.

1997, c. 23, s. 11.

PART XIV — JURISDICTION

General

468. Superior court of criminal jurisdiction — Every superior court of criminal jurisdiction has jurisdiction to try any indictable offence.

469. Court of criminal jurisdiction — Every court of criminal jurisdiction has jurisdiction to try an indictable offence other than

    (a) an offence under any of the following sections:

        (i) section 47 (treason),

        (ii) section 49 (alarming Her Majesty),

        (iii) section 51 (intimidating Parliament or a legislature),

        (iv) section 53 (inciting to mutiny),

        (v) section 61 (seditious offences),

        (vi) section 74 (piracy),

        (vii) section 75 (piratical acts), or

        (viii) section 235 (murder),

    (b) **Accessories** — the offence of being an accessory after the fact to high treason or treason or murder,

    (c) **Corrupting justice** — an offence under section 119 (bribery) by the holder of a judicial office,

Proposed Addition — 469(c.1)

(c.1) **Crimes against humanity** — an offence under any of sections 4 to 7 of the *Crimes Against Humanity and War Crimes Act*;

2000, c. 24, s. 44 [Not in force at date of publication.]

    (d) **Attempts** — the offence of attempting to commit any offence mentioned in subparagraphs (*a*)(i) to (vii), or

    (e) **Conspiracy** — the offence of conspiring to commit any offence mentioned in paragraph (*a*).

R.S. 1985, c. 27 (1st Supp.), s. 62.

470. Jurisdiction over person — Subject to this Act, every superior court of criminal jurisdiction and every court of criminal jurisdiction that has power to try an indictable offence is competent to try an accused for that offence

    (a) if the accused is found, is arrested or is in custody within the territorial jurisdiction of the court; or

(b) if the accused has been ordered to be tried by

    (i) that court, or

    (ii) any other court, the jurisdiction of which has by lawful authority been transferred to that court.

R.S. 1985, c. 27 (1st Supp.), s. 101(3).

471. Trial by jury compulsory — Except where otherwise expressly provided by law, every accused who is charged with an indictable offence shall be tried by a court composed of a judge and jury.

472. [Repealed R.S. 1985, c. 27 (1st Supp.), s. 63.]

473. (1) Trial without jury — Notwithstanding anything in this Act, an accused charged with an offence listed in section 469 may, with the consent of the accused and the Attorney General, be tried without a jury by a judge of a superior court of criminal jurisdiction.

(1.1) Joinder of other offences — Where the consent of the accused and the Attorney General is given in accordance with subsection (1), the judge of the superior court of criminal jurisdiction may order that any offence be tried by that judge in conjunction with the offence listed in section 469.

(2) Withdrawal of consent — Notwithstanding anything in this Act, where the consent of an accused and the Attorney General is given in accordance with subsection (1), such consent shall not be withdrawn unless both the accused and the Attorney General agree to the withdrawal.

R.S. 1985, c. 27 (1st Supp.), s. 63; 1994, c. 44, s. 30.

474. (1) Adjournment when no jury summoned — Where the competent authority has determined that a panel of jurors is not to be summoned for a term or sittings of the court for the trial of criminal cases in any territorial division, the clerk of the court may, on the day of the opening of the term or sittings, if a judge is not present to preside over the court, adjourn the court and the business of the court to a subsequent day.

(2) Adjournment on instructions of judge — A clerk of the court for the trial of criminal cases in any territorial division may, at any time, on the instructions of the presiding judge or another judge of the court, adjourn the court and the business of the court to a subsequent day.

1994, c. 44, s. 31.

475. (1) Accused absconding during trial — Notwithstanding any other provision of this Act, where an accused, whether or not he is charged jointly with another, absconds during the course of his trial,

    (a) he shall be deemed to have waived his right to be present at his trial, and

    (b) the court may

        (i) continue the trial and proceed to a judgment or verdict and, if it finds the accused guilty, impose a sentence on him in his absence, or

(ii) if a warrant in Form 7 is issued for the arrest of the accused, adjourn the trial to await his appearance,

but where the trial is adjourned pursuant to subparagraph (b)(ii), the court may, at any time, continue the trial if it is satisfied that it is no longer in the interests of justice to await the appearance of the accused.

(2) Adverse inference — Where a court continues a trial pursuant to subsection (1), it may draw an inference adverse to the accused from the fact that he has absconded.

(3) Accused not entitled to re-opening — Where an accused reappears at his trial that is continuing pursuant to subsection (1), he is not entitled to have any part of the proceedings that was conducted in his absence re-opened unless the court is satisfied that because of exceptional circumstances it is in the interests of justice to re-open the proceedings.

(4) Counsel for accused may continue to act — Where an accused has absconded during the course of his trial and the court continues the trial, counsel for the accused is not thereby deprived of any authority he may have to continue to act for the accused in the proceedings.

Special Jurisdiction

476. Special jurisdictions — For the purposes of this Act,

(a) where an offence is committed in or on any water or on a bridge between two or more territorial divisions, the offence shall be deemed to have been committed in any of the territorial divisions;

(b) where an offence is committed on the boundary of two or more territorial divisions or within five hundred metres of any such boundary, or the offence was commenced within one territorial division and completed within another, the offence shall be deemed to have been committed in any of the territorial divisions;

(c) where an offence is committed in or on a vehicle employed in a journey, or on board a vessel employed on a navigable river, canal or inland water, the offence shall be deemed to have been committed in any territorial division through which the vehicle or vessel passed in the course of the journey or voyage on which the offence was committed, and where the center or other part of the road, or navigable river, canal or inland water on which the vehicle or vessel passed in the course of the journey or voyage is the boundary of two or more territorial divisions, the offence shall be deemed to have been committed in any of the territorial divisions;

(d) where an offence is committed in an aircraft in the course of a flight of that aircraft, it shall be deemed to have been committed

(i) in the territorial division in which the flight commenced,

(ii) in any territorial division over which the aircraft passed in the course of the flight, or

(iii) in the territorial division in which the flight ended; and

(e) where an offence is committed in respect of a mail in the course of its door-to-door delivery, the offence shall be deemed to have been committed in any territorial division through which the mail was carried on that delivery.

R.S. 1985, c. 27 (lst Supp.), s. 186; 1992, c. 1, s. 58(1), Schedule I, item 8.

477. (1) Definition of "ship" — In sections 477.1 to 477.4, **"ship"** includes any description of vessel, boat or craft designed, used or capable of being used solely or partly for marine navigation, without regard to method or lack of propulsion.

(2) Saving — Nothing in sections 477.1 to 477.4 limits the operation of any other Act of Parliament or the jurisdiction that a court may exercise apart from those sections.

1990, c. 44, s. 15; 1996, c. 31, s. 67.

477.1 (1) Offences outside of Canada — Every person who commits an act or omission that, if it occurred in Canada, would be an offence under a federal law, within the meaning of section 2 of the *Oceans Act*, is deemed to have committed that act or omission in Canada if it is an act or omission

(a) in the exclusive economic zone of Canada that

(i) is committed by a person who is in the exclusive economic zone of Canada in connection with exploring or exploiting, conserving or managing the natural resources, whether living or non-living, of the exclusive economic zone of Canada, and

(ii) is committed by or in relation to a person who is a Canadian citizen or a permanent resident within the meaning of the *Immigration Act*,

(b) that is committed in a place in or above the continental shelf of Canada and that is an offence in that place by virtue of section 20 of the *Oceans Act*,

(c) that is committed outside Canada on board or by means of a ship registered or licensed, or for which an identification number has been issued, pursuant to any Act of Parliament;

(d) that is committed outside Canada in the course of hot pursuit; or

(e) that is committed outside the territory of any state by a Canadian citizen.

1990, c. 44, s. 15; 1996, c. 31, s. 68.

477.2 (1) Consent of Attorney General of Canada — No proceedings in respect of an offence committed in or on the territorial sea of Canada shall be continued unless the consent of the Attorney General of Canada is obtained not later than eight days after the proceedings are commenced, if the accused is not a Canadian citizen and the offence is alleged to have been committed on board any ship registered outside Canada.

(1.1) Exception — Subsection (1) does not apply to proceedings by way of summary conviction.

(2) Consent of Attorney General of Canada — No proceedings in respect of which courts have jurisdiction by virtue only of paragraph 477.1(a) or (b) shall be continued unless the consent of the Attorney General of Canada is obtained not later than eight days after the proceedings are commenced, if the accused is not a Canadian citizen and the offence is alleged to have been committed on board any ship registered outside Canada.

(3) Consent of Attorney General of Canada — No proceedings in respect of which courts have jurisdiction by virtue only of paragraph 477.1(*d*) or (*e*) shall be continued unless the consent of the Attorney General of Canada is obtained not later than eight days after the proceedings are commenced.

(4) Consent to be filed — The consent of the Attorney General required by subsection (1), (2) or (3) must be filed with the clerk of the court in which the proceedings have been instituted.

1990, c. 44, s. 15; 1994, c. 44, s. 32; 1996, c. 31, s. 69.

477.3 (1) Exercising powers of arrest, entry, etc. — Every power of arrest, entry, search or seizure or other power that could be exercised in Canada in respect of an act or omission referred to in section 477.1 may be exercised, in the circumstances referred to in that section,

> (a) at the place or on board the ship or marine installation or structure, within the meaning of section 2 of the *Oceans Act*, where the act or omission occurred; or
>
> (b) where hot pursuit has been commenced, at any place on the seas, other than a place that is part of the territorial sea of any other state.

(2) Arrest, search, seizure, etc. — A justice or judge in any territorial division in Canada has jurisdiction to authorize an arrest, entry, search or seizure or an investigation or other ancillary matter related to an offence

> (a) committed in or on the territorial sea of Canada or any area of the sea that forms part of the internal waters of Canada, or
>
> (b) referred to in section 477.1

in the same manner as if the offence had been committed in that territorial division.

(3) Limitation — Where an act or omission that is an offence by virtue only of section 477.1 is alleged to have been committed on board any ship registered outside Canada, the powers referred to in subsection (1) shall not be exercised outside Canada with respect to that act or omission without the consent of the Attorney General of Canada.

1990, c. 44, s. 15; 1996, c. 34, s. 70.

477.4 (1) [Repealed, 1996, c. 31, s. 71(1)]

(2) [Repealed, 1996, c. 31, s. 71(1)]

(3) Evidence — In proceedings in respect of an offence,

> (a) a certificate referred to in subsection 23(1) of the *Oceans Act*, or
>
> (b) a certificate issued by or under the authority of the Minister of Foreign Affairs containing a statement that any geographical location specified in the certificate was, at any time material to the proceedings, in an area of a fishing zone of Canada that is not within the internal waters of Canada or the territorial sea of Canada or outside the territory of any state

is conclusive proof of the truth of the statement without proof of the signature or official character of the person appearing to have issued the certificate.

(4) Certificate cannot be compelled — A certificate referred to in subsection (3) is admissible in evidence in proceedings referred to in that subsection but its production cannot be compelled.

1990, c. 44, s. 15; 1995, c. 5, s. 25(1)(g); 1996, c. 31, s. 71.

478. (1) Offence committed entirely in one province — Subject to this Act, a court in a province shall not try an offence committed entirely in another province.

(2) Exception — Every proprietor, publisher, editor or other person charged with the publication of a defamatory libel in a newspaper or with conspiracy to publish a defamatory libel in a newspaper shall be dealt with, indicted, tried and punished in the province where he resides or in which the newspaper is printed.

(3) Idem — An accused who is charged with an offence that is alleged to have been committed in Canada outside the province in which the accused is may, if the offence is not an offence mentioned in section 469 and

(a) in the case of proceedings instituted at the instance of the Government of Canada and conducted by or on behalf of that Government, if the Attorney General of Canada consents, or

(b) in any other case, if the Attorney General of the province where the offence is alleged to have been committed consents,

appear before a court or judge that would have had jurisdiction to try that offence if it had been committed in the province where the accused is, and where the accused consents to plead guilty and pleads guilty to that offence, the court or judge shall determine the accused to be guilty of the offence and impose the punishment warranted by law, but where the accused does not consent to plead guilty and does not plead guilty, the accused shall, if the accused was in custody prior to appearance, be returned to custody and shall be dealt with according to law.

(4) Where accused committed to stand trial — Notwithstanding that an accused described in subsection (3) has been ordered to stand trial or that an indictment has been preferred against the accused in respect of the offence to which he desires to plead guilty, the accused shall be deemed simply to stand charged of that offence without a preliminary inquiry having been conducted or an indictment having been preferred with respect thereto.

(5) "newspaper" — In this section **"newspaper"** has the same meaning that it has in section 297.

R.S. 1985, c. 27 (1st Supp.), ss. 64, 101(3); 1994, c. 44, s. 33.

479. Offence outstanding in same province — Where an accused is charged with an offence that is alleged to have been committed in the province in which he is, he may, if the offence is not an offence mentioned in section 469, and

(a) in the case of proceedings instituted at the instance of the Government of Canada and conducted by or on behalf of that Government, the Attorney General of Canada consents, or

(b) in any other case, the Attorney General of the province where the offence is alleged to have been committed consents,

appear before a court or judge that would have had jurisdiction to try that offence if it had been committed in the place where the accused is, and where the accused consents to plead guilty and pleads guilty to that offence, the court or judge shall determine the accused to be guilty of the offence and impose the punishment warranted by law, but where the accused does not consent to plead guilty and does not plead guilty, the accused shall, if the accused was in custody prior to appearance, be returned to custody and shall be dealt with according to law.

R.S. 1985, c. 27 (1st Supp.), s. 65; 1994, c. 44, s. 34.

480. (1) Offence in unorganized territory — Where an offence is committed in an unorganized tract of country in any province or on a lake, river or other water therein, not included in a territorial division or in a provisional judicial district, proceedings in respect thereof may be commenced and an accused may be charged, tried and punished in respect thereof within any territorial division or provisional judicial district of the province in the same manner as if the offence had been committed within that territorial division or provisional judicial district.

(2) New territorial division — Where a provisional judicial district or a new territorial division is constituted in an unorganized tract referred to in subsection (1), the jurisdiction conferred by that subsection continues until appropriate provision is made by law for the administration of criminal justice within the provisional judicial district or new territorial division.

481. Offence not in a province — Where an offence is committed in a part of Canada not in a province, proceedings in respect thereof may be commenced and the accused may be charged, tried and punished within any territorial division in any province in the same manner as if that offence had been committed in that territorial division.

481.1 Offence in Canadian waters — Where an offence is committed in or on the territorial sea of Canada or any area of the sea that forms part of the internal waters of Canada, proceedings in respect thereof may, whether or not the accused is in Canada, be commenced and an accused may be charged, tried and punished within any territorial division in Canada in the same manner as if the offence had been committed in that territorial division.

1996, c. 31, s. 72.

481.2 Offence outside Canada — Subject to this or any other Act of Parliament, where an act or omission is committed outside Canada and the act or omission, when committed in those circumstances, is an offence under this or any other Act of Parliament, proceedings in respect thereof may, whether or not the accused is in Canada, be commenced, and an accused may be charged, tried and punished within any territorial division in Canada in the same manner as if the offence had been committed in that territorial division.

1996, c. 31, s. 72.

481.3 Appearance of accused at trial — For greater certainty, the provisions of this Act relating to

(a) the requirement of the appearance of an accused at proceedings, and

(b) the exceptions to that requirement

apply to proceedings commenced in any territorial division pursuant to section 481, 481.1 or 481.2

1996, c. 31, s. 72.

Rules of Court

482. (1) Power to make rules — Every superior court of criminal jurisdiction and every court of appeal may make rules of court not inconsistent with this or any other Act of Parliament, and any rules so made apply to any prosecution, proceeding, action or appeal, as the case may be, within the jurisdiction of that court, instituted in relation to any matter of a criminal nature or arising from or incidental to any such prosecution, proceeding, action or appeal.

(2) Idem — Every court of criminal jurisdiction for a province and every appeal court within the meaning of section 812 that is not a court referred to in subsection (1) may, subject to the approval of the lieutenant governor in council of the province, make rules of court not inconsistent with this Act or any other Act of Parliament, and any rules so made apply to any prosecution, proceeding, action or appeal, as the case may be, within the jurisdiction of that court, instituted in relation to any matter of a criminal nature or arising from or incidental to any such prosecution, proceeding, action or appeal.

(3) Purpose of rules — Rules under subsection (1) or (2) may be made

(a) generally to regulate the duties of the officers of the court and any other matter considered expedient to attain the ends of justice and carry into effect the provisions of the law;

(b) to regulate the sittings of the court or any division thereof, or of any judge of the court sitting in chambers, except in so far as they are regulated by law;

(c) to regulate in criminal matters the pleading, practice and procedure in the court including pre-hearing conferences held pursuant to section 625.1 and proceedings with respect to judicial interim release and, in the case of rules under subsection (1), proceedings with respect to *mandamus, certiorari, habeas corpus*, prohibition and *procedendo* and proceedings on an appeal under section 830; and

(d) to carry out the provisions of this Act relating to appeals from conviction, acquittal or sentence and, without restricting the generality of this paragraph,

(i) for furnishing necessary forms and instructions in relation to notices of appeal or applications for leave to appeal to officials or other persons requiring or demanding them,

(ii) for ensuring the accuracy of notes taken at a trial and the verification of any copy or transcript,

(iii) for keeping writings, exhibits or other things connected with the proceedings on the trial,

(iv) for securing the safe custody of property during the period in which the operation of an order with respect to that property is suspended under subsection 689(1), and

(v) for providing that the Attorney General and counsel who acted for the Attorney General at the trial be supplied with certified copies of writings, exhibits and things connected with the proceedings that are required for the purposes of their duties.

(4) Publication — Rules of court that are made under the authority of this section shall be published in the *Canada Gazette*.

(5) Regulations to secure uniformity — Notwithstanding anything in this section, the Governor in Council may make such provision as he considers proper to secure uniformity in the rules of court in criminal matters, and all uniform rules made under the authority of this subsection prevail and have effect as if enacted by this Act.

R.S. 1985, c. 27 (1st Supp.), s. 66; 1994, c. 44, s. 35.

PART XV — SPECIAL PROCEDURE AND POWERS

General Powers of Certain Officials

483. Officials with powers of two justices — Every judge or provincial court judge authorized by the law of the province in which he is appointed to do anything that is required to be done by two or more justices may do alone anything that this Act or any other Act of the Parliament authorizes two or more justices to do.

R.S. 1985, c. 27 (1st Supp.), s. 203

484. Preserving order in court — Every judge or provincial court judge has the same power and authority to preserve order in a court over which he presides as may be exercised by the superior court of criminal jurisdiction of the province during the sittings thereof.

R.S. 1985, c. 27 (1st Supp.), s. 203

485. (1) Procedural irregularities — Jurisdiction over an offence is not lost by reason of the failure of any court, judge, provincial court judge or justice to act in the exercise of that jurisdiction at any particular time, or by reason of a failure to comply with any of the provisions of this Act respecting adjournments or remands.

(1.1) Where accused not present — Jurisdiction over an accused is not lost by reason of the failure of the accused to appear personally, so long as paragraph 537(1)(j) or subsection 650(1.1) applies and the accused is to appear by counsel.

(2) Summons or warrant — Where jurisdiction over an accused or a defendant is lost and has not been regained, a court, judge, provincial court judge or justice may, within three months after the loss of jurisdiction, issue a summons, or if it or he considers it necessary in the public interest, a warrant for the arrest of the accused or defendant.

(3) Dismissal for want of prosecution — Where no summons or warrant is issued under subsection (2) within the period provided therein, the proceedings shall be deemed to be dismissed for want of prosecution and shall not be recommenced except in accordance with section 485.1.

(4) Adjournment and order — Where, in the opinion of the court, judge, provincial court judge or justice, an accused or a defendant who appears at a proceeding has been misled or prejudiced by reason of any matter referred to in subsection (1), the court, judge, provincial court judge or justice may adjourn the proceeding and may make such order as it or he considers appropriate.

(5) Part XVI to apply — The provisions of Part XVI apply with such modifications as the circumstances require where a summons or warrant is issued under subsection (2).

R.S. 1985, c. 27 (1st Supp.), ss. 67, 203; 1997, c. 18, s. 40

485.1 Recommencement where dismissal for want of prosecution — Where an indictment in respect of a transaction is dismissed or deemed by any provision of this Act to be dismissed for want of prosecution, a new information shall not be laid and a new indictment shall not be preferred before any court in respect of the same transaction without

(a) the personal consent in writing of the Attorney General or Deputy Attorney General, in any prosecution conducted by the Attorney General or in which the Attorney General intervenes; or

(b) the written order of a judge of that court, in any prosecution conducted by a prosecutor other than the Attorney General and in which the Attorney General does not intervene.

R.S. 1985, c. 27 (1st Supp.), s. 67

486. (1) Exclusion of public in certain cases — Any proceedings against an accused shall be held in open court, but where the presiding judge, provincial court judge or justice, as the case maybe, is of the opinion that it is in the interest of public morals, the maintenance of order or the proper administration of justice to exclude all or any members of the public from the court room for all or part of the proceedings, he may so order.

(1.1) Protection of child witnesses — For the purposes of subsections (1) and (2.3) and for greater certainty, the "proper administration of justice" includes ensuring that the interests of witnesses under the age of eighteen years are safeguarded in proceedings in which the accused is charged with a sexual offence, an offence against any of sections 271, 272 and 273 or an offence in which violence against the person is alleged to have been used, threatened or attempted.

(1.2) Support person — In proceedings referred to in subsection (1.1), the presiding judge, provincial court judge or justice may, on application of the prosecutor or a witness who, at the time of the trial or preliminary hearing, is under the age of fourteen years or who has a mental or physical disability, order that a support person of the witness' choice be permitted to be present and to be close to the witness while testifying.

(1.3) Witness not to be a support person — The presiding judge, provincial court judge or justice shall not permit a witness in the proceedings referred to in subsection (1.1) to be a support person unless the presiding judge, provincial court judge or justice is of the opinion that the proper administration of justice so requires.

(1.4) No communication while testifying — The presiding judge, provincial court judge or justice may order that the support person and the witness not communicate with each other during the testimony of the witness.

(2) Reasons to be stated — Where an accused is charged with an offence mentioned in section 274 and the prosecutor or the accused makes an application for an order under subsection (1), the presiding judge, provincial court judge or justice, as the case may be, shall, if no such order is made, state, by reference to the circumstances of the case, the reason for not making an order.

(2.1) Testimony outside court room — Notwithstanding section 650, where an accused is charged with an offence under section 151, 152, 153, 155 or 159, subsection 160(2) or (3), or section 163.1, 170, 171, 172, 173, 210, 211, 212, 213, 266, 267, 268, 271, 272 or 273 and the complainant or any witness, at the time of the trial or preliminary inquiry, is under the age of eighteen years or is able to communicate evidence but may have difficulty doing so by reason of a mental or physical disability, the presiding judge or justice, as the case may be, may order that the complainant or witness testify outside the court room or behind a screen or other device that would allow the complainant or witness not to see the accused, if the judge or justice is of the opinion that the exclusion is necessary to obtain a full and candid account of the acts complained of from the complainant or witness.

(2.11) Same procedure for opinion — Where the judge or justice is of the opinion that it is necessary for the complainant or witness to testify in order to determine whether an order under subsection (2.1) should be made in respect of that complainant or witness, the judge or justice shall order that the complainant or witness testify pursuant to that subsection.

(2.2) Condition of exclusion — A complainant or witness shall not testify outside the court room pursuant to subsection (2.1) or (2.11) unless arrangements are made for the accused, the judge or justice and the jury to watch the testimony of the complainant or other witness by means of closed-circuit television or otherwise and the accused is permitted to communicate with counsel while watching the testimony.

(2.3) Accused not to cross-examine child witness — In proceedings referred to in subsection (1.1), the accused shall not personally cross-examine a witness who at the time of the proceedings is under the age of eighteen years, unless the presiding judge, provincial court judge or justice is of the opinion that the proper administration of justice requires the accused to personally conduct the cross-examination and, if the accused is not personally conducting the cross-examination, the presiding judge, provincial court judge or justice shall appoint counsel for the purpose of conducting the cross-examination.

(3) Order restricting publication — Subject to subsection (4), the presiding judge or justice may make an order directing that the identity of a complainant or a witness and any information that could disclose the identity of the complainant or witness shall not be published in any document or broadcast in any way, when an accused is charged with

(a) any of the following offences:

(i) an offence under section 151, 152, 153, 153.1, 155, 159, 160, 170, 171, 172, 173, 210, 211, 212, 213, 271, 272, 273, 346 or 347,

(ii) an offence under section 144, 145, 149, 156, 245 or 246 of the *Criminal Code*, chapter C-34 of the Revised Statutes of Canada, 1970, as it read immediately before January 4, 1983, or

(iii) an offence under section 146, 151, 153, 155, 157, 166 or 167 of the *Criminal Code*, chapter C-34 of the Revised Statutes of Canada, 1970, as it read immediately before January 1, 1988; or

(b) two or more offences being dealt with in the same proceeding, at least one of which is an offence referred to in any of subparagraphs (a)(i), (ii) and (iii).

(3.1) Limitation — An order made under subsection (3) does not apply in respect of the disclosure of information in the course of the administration of justice where it is not the purpose of the disclosure to make the information known in the community.

(4) Mandatory order on application — The presiding judge or justice shall

(a) at the first reasonable opportunity, inform any witness under the age of eighteen years and the complainant to proceedings in respect of an offence mentioned in subsection (3) of the right to make an application for an order under subsection (3); and

(b) on application made by the complainant, the prosecutor or any such witness, make an order under that subsection.

(4.1) Ban on publication — A judge or justice may, in any proceedings against an accused other than in respect of an offence set out in subsection (3), make an order directing that the identity of a victim or witness, or any information that could disclose their identity, shall not be published in any document or broadcast in any way, if the judge or justice is satisfied that the order is necessary for the proper administration of justice.

(4.2) Order restricting publication — An order made under subsection (4.1) does not apply in respect of the disclosure of information in the course of the administration of justice if it is not the purpose of the disclosure to make the information known in the community.

(4.3) Application — An order under subsection (4.1) may be made on the application of the prosecutor, a victim or a witness. The application must be made to the presiding judge or justice or, if the judge or justice has not been determined, to a judge of a superior court of criminal jurisdiction in the judicial district where the proceedings will take place.

(4.4) Contents of application — The application must be in writing and set out the grounds on which the applicant relies to establish that the order is necessary for the proper administration of justice.

(4.5) Notice of application — The applicant shall provide notice of the application to the prosecutor, the accused and any other person affected by the order that the judge or justice specifies.

(4.6) Hearing may be held — The judge or justice may hold a hearing to determine whether an order under subsection (4.1) should be made, and the hearing may be in private.

(4.7) Factors to be considered — In determining whether to make an order under subsection (4.1), the judge or justice shall consider

    (a) the right to a fair and public hearing;

    (b) whether there is a real and substantial risk that the victim or witness would suffer significant harm if their identity were disclosed;

    (c) whether the victim or witness needs the order for their security or to protect them from intimidation or retaliation;

    (d) society's interest in encouraging the reporting of offences and the participation of victims and witnesses;

    (e) whether effective alternatives are available to protect the identity of the victim or witness;

    (f) the salutary and deleterious effects of the proposed order;

    (g) the impact of the proposed order on the freedom of expression of those affected by it; and

    (h) any other factor that the judge or justice considers relevant.

(4.8) Conditions — An order made under subsection (4.1) may be subject to any conditions that the judge or justice thinks fit.

(4.9) Publication of application prohibited — Unless the presiding judge or justice refuses to make an order under subsection (4.1), no person shall publish in any document or broadcast in any way

    (a) the contents of an application referred to in subsection (4.3);

    (b) any evidence taken, information given, or submissions made at a hearing under subsection (4.6); or

    (c) any other information that could identify the person to whom the application relates as a victim or witness in the proceedings.

(5) Failure to comply with order — Every person who fails to comply with an order made under subsection (3) or (4.1) is guilty of an offence punishable on summary conviction.

(6) [Repealed R.S. 1985, c. 19 (3d Supp.), s. 14(2).]

R.S. 1985, c. 27 (1st Supp.), s. 203; c. 19 (3d Supp.), s. 14; c. 23 (4th Supp.), s. 1; 1992, c. 21, s. 9; 1993, c. 45, s. 7; 1997, c. 16, s. 6; 1999, c. 25, s. 2

487. (1) Information for search warrant — A justice who is satisfied by information on oath in Form 1 that there are reasonable grounds to believe that there is in a building, receptacle or place

(a) anything on or in respect of which any offence against this Act or any other Act of Parliament has been or is suspected to have been committed,

(b) anything that there are reasonable grounds to believe will afford evidence with respect to the commission of an offence, or will reveal the whereabouts of a person who is believed to have committed an offence, against this Act or any other Act of Parliament,

(c) anything that there are reasonable grounds to believe is intended to be used for the purpose of committing any offence against the person for which a person may be arrested without warrant, or

(c.1) any offence-related property,

may at any time issue a warrant authorizing a peace officer or a public officer who has been appointed or designated to administer or enforce a federal or provincial law and whose duties include the enforcement of this Act or any other Act of Parliament and who is named in the warrant

(d) to search the building, receptacle or place for any such thing and to seize it, and

(e) subject to any other Act of Parliament, to, as soon as practicable, bring the thing seized before, or make a report in respect thereof to, the justice or some other justice for the same territorial division in accordance with section 489.1.

(2) Endorsement of search warrant — Where the building, receptacle, or place in which anything mentioned in subsection (1) is believed to be is in any other territorial division, the justice may issue his warrant in like form modified according to the circumstances, and the warrant may be executed in the other territorial division after it has been endorsed, in Form 28, by a justice having jurisdiction in that territorial division.

(2.1) Operation of computer system and copying equipment — A person authorized under this section to search a computer system in a building or place for data may

(a) use or cause to be used any computer system at the building or place to search any data contained in or available to the computer system;

(b) reproduce or cause to be reproduced any data in the form of a print-out or other intelligible output;

(c) seize the print-out or other output for examination or copying; and

(d) use or cause to be used any copying equipment at the place to make copies of the data.

(2.2) Duty of person in possession or control — Every person who is in possession or control of any building or place in respect of which a search is carried out under this section shall, on presentation of the warrant, permit the person carrying out the search

(a) to use or cause to be used any computer system at the building or place in order to search any data contained in or available to the computer system for data that the person is authorized by this section to search for;

(b) to obtain a hard copy of the data and to seize it; and

(c) to use or cause to be used any copying equipment at the place to make copies of the data.

(3) Form — A search warrant issued under this section may be in the form set out as Form 5 in Part XXVIII, varied to suit the case.

(4) Effect of endorsement — An endorsement that is made on a warrant as provided for in subsection (2) is sufficient authority to the peace officers or public officers to whom it was originally directed, and to all peace officers within the jurisdiction of the justice by whom it is endorsed, to execute the warrant and to deal with the things seized in accordance with section 489.1 or as otherwise provided by law.

R.S. 1985, c. 27 (1st Supp.), s. 68; 1994, c. 44, s. 36; 1997, c. 18, s. 41; 1997, c. 23, s. 12; 1999, c. 5, s. 16

487.01 (1) Information for general warrant — A provincial court judge, a judge of a superior court of criminal jurisdiction or a judge as defined in section 552 may issue a warrant in writing authorizing a peace officer to, subject to this section, use any device or investigative technique or procedure or do any thing described in the warrant that would, if not authorized, constitute an unreasonable search or seizure in respect of a person or a person's property if

(a) the judge is satisfied by information on oath in writing that there are reasonable grounds to believe that an offence against this or any other Act of Parliament has been or will be committed and that information concerning the offence will be obtained through the use of the technique, procedure or device or the doing of the thing;

(b) the judge is satisfied that it is in the best interests of the administration of justice to issue the warrant; and

(c) there is no other provision in this or any other Act of Parliament that would provide for a warrant, authorization or order permitting the technique, procedure or device to be used or the thing to be done.

(2) Limitation — Nothing in subsection (1) shall be construed as to permit interference with the bodily integrity of any person.

(3) Search or seizure to be reasonable — A warrant issued under subsection (1) shall contain such terms and conditions as the judge considers advisable to ensure that any search or seizure authorized by the warrant is reasonable in the circumstances.

(4) Video surveillance — A warrant issued under subsection (1) that authorizes a peace officer to observe, by means of a television camera or other similar electronic device, any person who is engaged in activity in circumstances in which the person has a reasonable expectation of privacy shall contain such terms and conditions as the judge considers advisable to ensure that the privacy of the person or of any other person is respected as much as possible.

(5) Other provisions to apply — The definition "offence" in section 183 and sections 183.1, 184.2, 184.3 and 185 to 188.2, subsection 189(5), and sections 190, 193 and 194 to 196 apply, with such modifications as the circumstances require, to a warrant referred to in subsection (4) as though references in those provisions to interceptions of private communications were read as references to observations by peace officers by means of television cameras or similar electronic devices of activities in circumstances in which persons had reasonable expectations of privacy.

(5.1) Notice after covert entry — A warrant issued under subsection (1) that authorizes a peace officer to enter and search a place covertly shall require, as part of the terms and conditions referred to in subsection (3), that notice of the entry and search be given within any time after the execution of the warrant that the judge considers reasonable in the circumstances.

(5.2) Extension of period for giving notice — Where the judge who issues a warrant under subsection (1) or any other judge having jurisdiction to issue such a warrant is, on the basis of an affidavit submitted in support of an application to vary the period within which the notice referred to in subsection (5.1) is to be given, is satisfied that the interests of justice warrant the granting of the application, the judge may grant an extension, or a subsequent extension, of the period, but no extension may exceed three years.

(6) Provisions to apply — Subsections 487(2) and (4) apply, with such modifications as the circumstances require, to a warrant issued under subsection (1).

(7) Telewarrant provisions to apply — Where a peace officer believes that it would be impracticable to appear personally before a judge to make an application for a warrant under this section, a warrant may be issued under this section on an information submitted by telephone or other means of telecommunication and, for that purpose, section 487.1 applies, with such modifications as the circumstances require, to the warrant.

1997, c. 18, s. 42; 1997, c. 23, s. 13

487.02 Assistance order — Where an authorization is given under section 184.2, 184.3, 186 or 188, a warrant is issued under this Act or an order is made under subsection 492.2(2), the judge or justice who gives the authorization, issues the warrant or makes the order may order any person to provide assistance, where the person's assistance may reasonably be considered to be required to give effect to the authorization, warrant or order.

1993, c. 40, s. 15; 1997, c. 18, s. 43

487.03 (1) Execution in another province — Where

(a) a warrant is issued under section 487.01, 487.05 or 492.1 or subsection 492.2(1) in one province,

(b) it may reasonably be expected that the warrant is to be executed in another province, and

(c) the execution of the warrant would require entry into or on the property of any person in the other province or would require that an order be made under section 487.02 with respect to any person in that other province,

a judge or justice, as the case may be, in the other province may, on application, endorse the warrant and the warrant, after being so endorsed, has the same force in that other province as though it had originally been issued in that other province.

(2) Execution in another province — taking of bodily substances — When an order or authorization referred to in section 487.051, 487.052, 487.055 or 487.091 is made or granted, and it may reasonably be expected to be executed in another province, a provincial court judge of that province may, on application, endorse the order or authorization in Form 28.1. Once the order or authorization is endorsed, it has the same force in that province as though it had originally been issued there.

1993, c. 40, s. 15; 1995, c. 27, s. 1; 2000, c. 10, s. 13

Forensic DNA Analysis

487.04 Definitions — In this section and sections 487.05 to 487.09,

"adult" has the meaning assigned by subsection 2(1) of the *Young Offenders Act*;

"designated offence" means a primary designated offence or a secondary designated offence;

"DNA" means deoxyribonucleic acid;

"forensic DNA analysis"

(a) in relation to a bodily substance that is taken from a person in execution of a warrant under section 487.05, means forensic DNA analysis of the bodily substance and the comparison of the results of that analysis with the results of the analysis of the DNA in the bodily substance referred to in paragraph 487.05(1)(b), and includes any incidental tests associated with that analysis, and

(b) in relation to a bodily substance that is provided voluntarily in the course of an investigation of a designated offence or taken from a person in execution of an order under section 487.051 or 487.052 or under an authorization under section 487.055 or 487.091, or a bodily substance referred to in paragraph 487.05(1)(b), means forensic DNA analysis of the bodily substance;

"primary designated offence" means

(a) an offence under any of the following provisions, namely,

(i) section 151 (sexual interference),

(ii) section 152 (invitation to sexual touching),

(iii) section 153 (sexual exploitation),

(iv) section 155 (incest),

(v) subsection 212(4) (offence in relation to juvenile prostitution),

(vi) section 233 (infanticide),

(vii) section 235 (murder),

(viii) section 236 (manslaughter),

(ix) section 244 (causing bodily harm with intent),

(x) section 267 (assault with a weapon or causing bodily harm),

(xi) section 268 (aggravated assault),

(xii) section 269 (unlawfully causing bodily harm),

(xiii) section 271 (sexual assault),

(xiv) section 272 (sexual assault with a weapon, threats to a third party or causing bodily harm),

(xv) section 273 (aggravated sexual assault), and

(xvi) section 279 (kidnapping),

(b) an offence under any of the following provisions of the *Criminal Code*, chapter C-34 of the Revised Statutes of Canada, 1970, as they read from time to time before January 4, 1983, namely,

(i) section 144 (rape),

(ii) section 146 (sexual intercourse with female under fourteen and between fourteen and sixteen), and

(iii) section 148 (sexual intercourse with feeble-minded, etc.),

(c) an offence under paragraph 153(1)(a) (sexual intercourse with step-daughter, etc.) of the Criminal Code, chapter C-34 of the Revised Statutes of Canada, 1970, as it read from time to time before January 1, 1988, and

(d) an attempt to commit or, other than for the purposes of subsection 487.05(1), a conspiracy to commit an offence referred to in any of paragraphs (a) to (c);

"provincial court judge", in relation to a young person, includes a youth court judge within the meaning of subsection 2(1) of the *Young Offenders Act*.

"secondary designated offence" means

(a) an offence under any of the following provisions, namely,

(i) section 75 (piratical acts),

(ii) section 76 (hijacking),

(iii) section 77 (endangering safety of aircraft or airport),

(iv) section 78.1 (seizing control of ship or fixed platform),

(v) paragraph 81(1)(a) or (b) (using explosives),

(vi) subsection 160(3) (bestiality in the presence of or by child),

(vii) section 163.1 (child pornography),

(viii) section 170 (parent or guardian procuring sexual activity),

(ix) section 173 (indecent acts),

(x) section 220 (causing death by criminal negligence),

(xi) section 221 (causing bodily harm by criminal negligence),

    (xii) subsection 249(3) (dangerous operation causing bodily harm),

    (xiii) subsection 249(4) (dangerous operation causing death),

    (xiv) section 252 (failure to stop at scene of accident),

    (xv) subsection 255(2) (impaired driving causing bodily harm),

    (xvi) subsection 255(3) (impaired driving causing death),

    (xvii) section 266 (assault),

    (xviii) section 269.1 (torture),

    (xix) paragraph 270(1)(a) (assaulting a peace officer),

    (xx) section 279.1 (hostage taking),

    (xxi) section 344 (robbery),

    (xxii) subsection 348(1) (breaking and entering with intent, committing offence or breaking out),

    (xxiii) subsection 430(2) (mischief that causes actual danger to life),

    (xxiv) section 433 (arson — disregard for human life), and

    (xxv) section 434.1 (arson — own property),

(b) an offence under any of the following provisions of the *Criminal Code*, as they read from time to time before July 1, 1990, namely,

    (i) section 433 (arson), and

    (ii) section 434 (setting fire to other substance), and

(c) an attempt to commit or, other than for the purposes of subsection 487.05(1), a conspiracy to commit an offence referred to in paragraph (a) or (b);

"young person" has the meaning assigned by subsection 2(1) of the *Young Offenders Act*.

1995, c. 27, s. 1; 1998, c. 37, s. 15

487.05 (1) Information for warrant to take bodily substances for forensic DNA analysis — A provincial court judge who on *ex parte* application made in Form 5.01 is satisfied by information on oath that there are reasonable grounds to believe

    (a) that a designated offence has been committed,

    (b) that a bodily substance has been found or obtained

        (i) at the place where the offence was committed,

        (ii) on or within the body of the victim of the offence,

        (iii) on anything worn or carried by the victim at the time when the offence was committed, or

        (iv) on or within the body of any person or thing or at any place associated with the commission of the offence,

    (c) that a person was a party to the offence, and

(d) that forensic DNA analysis of a bodily substance from the person will provide evidence about whether the bodily substance referred to in paragraph (b) was from that person

and who is satisfied that it is in the best interests of the administration of justice to do so may issue a warrant in Form 5.02 authorizing the taking, from that person, for the purpose of forensic DNA analysis, of any number of samples of one or more bodily substances that is reasonably required for that purpose, by means of the investigative procedures described in subsection 487.06(1).

(2) Criteria — In considering whether to issue the warrant, the provincial court judge shall have regard to all relevant matters, including

(a) the nature of the designated offence and the circumstances of its commission; and

(b) whether there is

(i) a peace officer who is able, by virtue of training or experience, to take samples of bodily substances from the person, by means of the investigative procedures described in subsection 487.06(1), or

(ii) another person who is able, by virtue of training or experience, to take, under the direction of a peace officer, samples of bodily substances from the person, by means of those investigative procedures.

(3) Telewarrant — Where a peace officer believes that it would be impracticable to appear personally before a judge to make an application for a warrant under this section, a warrant may be issued under this section on an information submitted by telephone or other means of telecommunication and, for that purpose, section 487.1 applies, with such modifications as the circumstances require, to the warrant.

1995, c. 27, s. 1; 1997, c. 18, s. 44; 1998, c. 37, s. 16

487.051 Order — **(1)** Subject to section 487.053, if a person is convicted, discharged under section 730 or, in the case of a young person, found guilty under the *Young Offenders Act*, of a designated offence, the court

(a) shall, subject to subsection (2), in the case of a primary designated offence, make an order in Form 5.03 authorizing the taking, from that person, for the purpose of forensic DNA analysis, of any number of samples of one or more bodily substances that is reasonably required for that purpose, by means of the investigative procedures described in subsection 487.06(1); or

(b) may, in the case of a secondary designated offence, make an order in Form 5.04 authorizing the taking of such samples if the court is satisfied that it is in the best interests of the administration of justice to do so.

(2) Exception — The court is not required to make an order under paragraph (1)(a) if it is satisfied that the person or young person has established that, were the order made, the impact on the person's or young person's privacy and security of the person would be grossly disproportionate to the public interest in the protection of society and the proper administration of justice, to be achieved through the early detection, arrest and conviction of offenders.

(3) Criteria — In deciding whether to make an order under paragraph (1)(b), the court shall consider the criminal record of the person or young person, the nature of the offence and the circumstances surrounding its commission and the impact such an order would have on the person's or young person's privacy and security of the person and shall give reasons for its decision.

1998, c. 37, s. 17

487.052 (1) Offences committed before *DNA Identification Act* in force — Subject to section 487.053, if a person is convicted, discharged under section 730 or, in the case of a young person, found guilty under the *Young Offenders Act*, of a designated offence committed before the coming into force of subsection 5(1) of the *DNA Identification Act*, the court may, on application by the prosecutor, make an order in Form 5.04 authorizing the taking, from that person or young person, for the purpose of forensic DNA analysis, of any number of samples of one or more bodily substances that is reasonably required for that purpose, by means of the investigative procedures described in subsection 487.06(1), if the court is satisifed that it is in the best interests of the administration of justice to do so.

(2) Criteria — In deciding whether to make the order, the court shall consider the criminal record of the person or young person, the nature of the offence and the circumstances surrounding its commission and the impact such an order would have on the person's or young person's privacy and security of the person and shall give reasons for its decision.

1998, c. 37, s. 17

487.053 No order — An order shall not be made under section 487.051 or 487.052 if the prosecutor advises the court that the national DNA data bank, established under the *DNA Identification Act*, contains a DNA profile, within the meaning of section 2 of that Act, of the person or young person in question.

1998, c. 37, s. 17; 2000, c. 10, s. 14

487.054 Appeal — The offender or the prosecutor may appeal from a decision of the court made under subsection 487.051(1) or 487.052(1).

1998, c. 37, s. 17

487.055 (1) Offenders serving sentences — A provincial court judge may, on *ex parte* application made in Form 5.05, authorize, in Form 5.06, the taking, from a person who

(a) before the coming into force of this subsection, had been declared a dangerous offender under Part XXIV,

(b) before the coming into force of this subsection, had been convicted of more than one murder committed at different times, or

(c) before the coming into force of this subsection, had been convicted of more than one sexual offence within the meaning of subsection (3) and, on the date of the application, is serving a sentence of imprisonment of at least two years for one or more of those offences,

for the purpose of forensic DNA analysis, of any number of samples of one or more bodily substances that is reasonably required for that purpose, by means of the investigative procedures described in subsection 487.06(1).

293

(2) Certificate — The application shall be accompanied by a certificate referred to in paragraph 667(1)(a) that establishes that the person is a person referred to in subsection (1). The certificate may be received in evidence without giving the notice referred to in subsection 667(4).

(3) Definition of "sexual offence" — For the purposes of subsection (1), **"sexual offence"** means

    (a) an offence under any of the following provisions, namely,

        (i) section 151 (sexual interference),

        (ii) section 152 (invitation to sexual touching),

        (iii) section 153 (sexual exploitation),

        (iv) section 155 (incest),

        (v) subsection 212(4) (offence in relation to juvenile prostitution),

        (vi) section 271 (sexual assault),

        (vii) section 272 (sexual assault with a weapon, threats to a third party or causing bodily harm), and

        (viii) section 273 (aggravated sexual assault);

    (b) an offence under any of the following provisions of the *Criminal Code*, chapter C-34 of the Revised Statutes of Canada, 1970, as they read from time to time before January 4, 1983, namely,

        (i) section 144 (rape),

        (ii) section 146 (sexual intercourse with female under fourteen or between fourteen and sixteen), or

        (iii) section 148 (sexual intercourse with feeble-minded, etc.);

    (c) an offence under paragraph 153(1)(a) (sexual intercourse with step-daughter, etc.) of the *Criminal Code*, chapter C-34 of the Revised Statutes of Canada, 1970, as it read from time to time before January 1, 1988; and

    (d) an attempt to commit an offence referred to in any of paragraphs (a) to (c).

(3.1) Criteria — In deciding whether to grant an authorization under subsection (1), the court shall consider the person's criminal record, the nature of the offence and the circumstances surrounding its commission and the impact such an authorization would have on the privacy and security of the person and shall give reasons for its decision.

(4) Summons — A summons shall be directed to a person referred to in subsection (1) who is on conditional release requiring the person to report at the place, day and time set out in the summons in order to submit to the taking from the person of samples of bodily substances under an authorization granted under that subsection and setting out the matters referred to in paragraphs 487.07(1)(b) to (e).

(5) Service on individual — The summons shall be accompanied by a copy of the authorization referred to in subsection (1) and be served by a peace officer who shall either deliver it personally to the person to whom it is directed or, if that person cannot conveniently be found, leave it for the person at their latest or usual place of residence with any person found there who appears to be at least sixteen years of age.

(6) Proof of service — Service of a summons may be proved by the oral evidence, given under oath, of the peace officer who served it or by the peace officer's affidavit made before a justice of the peace or other person authorized to administer oaths or to take affidavits.

(7) Content of summons — The text of subsection (8) shall be set out in the summons.

(8) Failure to appear — If the person to whom a summons is directed does not report at the place, day and time set out in the summons, a justice of the peace may issue a warrant for the arrest of the person in order to allow the taking of samples of bodily substances from the person under the authorization.

(9) Contents of warrant to arrest — The warrant shall name or describe the person and order that the person be arrested without delay for the purpose of allowing the taking from them of samples of bodily substances under the authorization.

(10) No return day — A warrant issued under subsection (8) remains in force until it is executed and need not be made returnable at any particular time.

1998, c. 37, s. 17; 2000, c. 10, s. 15

487.056 (1) When collection to take place — Samples of bodily substances referred to in sections 487.051 and 487.052 shall be taken at the time the person is convicted, discharged under section 730 or, in the case of a young person, found guilty under the *Young Offenders Act*, or as soon as is feasible afterwards, even though an appeal may have been taken.

(2) Collection under authorization — Samples of bodily substances referred to in section 487.055 or 487.091 shall be taken as soon as is feasible after the authorization referred to in that section is granted.

(3) Who collects — The samples shall be taken by a peace officer, or another person acting under the direction of a peace officer, who is able, by virtue of training or experience, to take them.

1998, c. 37, s. 17; 2000, c. 10, s. 16

487.057 (1) Report of peace officer — A peace officer who is authorized to take, or cause to be taken under the direction of the peace officer, samples of bodily substances from a person in execution of a warrant under section 487.05 or an order under section 487.051 or 487.052 or under an authorization under section 487.055 or 487.091 shall, as soon as is feasible after the samples have been taken, make a written report in Form 5.07 and cause the report to be filed with

(a) the provincial court judge who issued the warrant or granted the authorization, or another judge of that provincial court; or

(b) the court that made the order.

(2) Contents of report — The report shall include

    (a) a statement of the time and date the samples were taken; and

    (b) a description of the bodily substances that were taken.

1998, c. 37, s. 17; 2000, c. 10, s. 17

487.058 No criminal or civil liability — No peace officer or person acting under the direction of a peace officer incurs any criminal or civil liability for anything necessarily done with reasonable care and skill in the taking of samples of bodily substances from a person in execution of a warrant under section 487.05 or an order under section 487.051 or 487.052 or under an authorization under section 487.055 or 487.091.

1998, c. 37, s. 17; 2000, c. 10, s. 18

487.06 (1) Investigative procedures — A peace officer or another person under the direction of a peace officer is authorized to take samples of bodily substances from a person by a warrant under section 487.05 or an order under section 487.051 or 487.052 or an authorization under section 487.055 or 487.091, by any of the following means:

    (a) the plucking of individual hairs from the person, including the root sheath;

    (b) the taking of buccal swabs by swabbing the lips, tongue and inside cheeks of the mouth to collect epithelial cells; or

    (c) the taking of blood by pricking the skin surface with a sterile lancet.

(2) Terms and conditions — The warrant, order or authorization shall include any terms and conditions that the provincial court judge or court, as the case may be, considers advisable to ensure that the taking of the samples authorized by the warrant, order or authorization is reasonable in the circumstances.

(3) Fingerprints — A peace officer, or any person acting under a peace officer's direction, who is authorized to take samples of bodily substances from a person by an order under section 487.051 or 487.052 or an authorization under section 487.055 or 487.091 may take fingerprints from the person for the purpose of the *DNA Identification Act*.

1995, c. 27, s. 1; 1998, c. 37, s. 18; 2000, c. 10, s. 19

487.07 (1) Duty to inform — Before taking samples of bodily substances from a person, or causing samples of bodily substances to be taken from a person under the direction of a peace officer, in execution of a warrant under section 487.05 or an order under section 487.051 or 487.052 or under an authorization under section 487.055 or 487.091, the peace officer shall inform the person from whom the samples are to be taken of

    (a) the contents of the warrant, order or authorization;

    (b) the nature of the investigative procedures by means of which the samples are to be taken;

    (c) the purpose of taking the samples;

(d) the authority of the peace officer and any other person under the direction of the peace officer to use as much force as is necessary for the purpose of taking the samples; and

(d.1) [Repealed 2000, c. 10, s. 20(2).]

(e) in the case of samples of bodily substances taken in execution of a warrant,

> (i) the possibility that the results of forensic DNA analysis may be used in evidence, and

> (ii) if the sample is taken from a young person, the rights of the young person under subsection (4).

(2) Detention of person — A person from whom samples of bodily substances are to be taken may

(a) be detained for that purpose for a period that is reasonable in the circumstances; and

(b) be required to accompany a peace officer for that purpose.

(3) Respect of privacy — A peace officer who takes samples of bodily substances from a person, or a person who takes such samples under the direction of a peace officer, shall ensure that the person's privacy is respected in a manner that is reasonable in the circumstances.

(4) Execution of warrant against young person — A young person against whom a warrant is executed has, in addition to any other rights arising from his or her detention under the warrant,

(a) the right to a reasonable opportunity to consult with, and

(b) the right to have the warrant executed in the presence of

counsel and a parent or, in the absence of a parent, an adult relative or, in the absence of a parent and an adult relative, any other appropriate adult chosen by the young person.

(5) Waiver of rights of young person — A young person may waive his or her rights under subsection (4) but any such waiver

(a) must be recorded on audio tape or video tape or otherwise; or

(b) must be made in writing and contain a statement signed by the young person that he or she has been informed of the right being waived.

1995, c. 27, ss. 1, 3; 1998, c. 37, s. 19; 2000, c. 10, s. 20

487.071 (1) Transmission of results to Commissioner — There shall be transmitted to the Commissioner of the Royal Canadian Mounted Police for entry in the convicted offenders index of the national DNA data bank established under the *DNA Identification Act* the results of forensic DNA analysis of bodily substances that are taken in execution of an order under section 487.051 or 487.052 or an authorization under section 487.055 or 487.091.

(2) Transmission of bodily substances — Any portions of samples of bodily substances referred to in subsection (1) that are not used in forensic DNA analysis shall be transmitted to the Commissioner of the Royal Canadian Mounted Police for the purposes of the *DNA Identification Act*.

1998, c. 37, s. 20 ; 2000, c. 10, s. 21

487.08 (1) Use of bodily substances — warrant — No person shall use bodily substances that are taken in execution of a warrant under section 487.05 or under section 196.12 of the *National Defence Act* except to use them for the purpose of forensic DNA analysis in the course of an investigation of a designated offence.

(1.1) Use of bodily substances — order, authorization — No person shall use bodily substances that are taken in execution of an order under section 487.051 or 487.052, under an authorization under section 487.055 or 487.091, in execution of an order under section 196.14 or 196.15 of the *National Defence Act*, or under an authorization under section 196.24 of that Act except

(a) to use them for the purpose of forensic DNA analysis; or

(b) to transmit any portions of samples of those bodily substances that are not used in forensic DNA analysis to the Commissioner of the Royal Canadian Mounted Police under subsection 487.071(2).

(2) Use of results — warrant — No person shall use the results of forensic DNA analysis of bodily substances that are taken in execution of a warrant under section 487.05 or under section 196.12 of the *National Defence Act* except

(a) in the course of an investigation of the designated offence or any other designated offence in respect of which a warrant was issued or a bodily substance was found in the circumstances described in paragraph 487.05(1)(b) or in paragraph 196.12(1)(b) of the *National Defence Act*; or

(b) in any proceeding for such an offence.

(2.1) Use of results — order, authorization — No person shall use the results of forensic DNA analysis of bodily substances that are taken in execution of an order under section 487.051 or 487.052 or under an authorization under section 487.055 or 487.091, or in execution of an order under section 196.14 or 196.15 of the *National Defence Act*, or under an authorization under section 196.24 of that Act, except to transmit them to the Commissioner of the Royal Canadian Mounted Police.

(3) Offence — Every person who contravenes subsection (1) or (2) is guilty of an offence punishable on summary conviction.

(4) Offence — Every person who contravenes subsection (1.1) or (2.1)

(a) is guilty of an indictable offence and liable to imprisonment for a term not exceeding two years; or

(b) is guilty of an offence punishable on summary conviction and liable to a fine not exceeding $2,000 or to imprisonment for a term not exceeding six months, or to both.

1995, c. 27, s. 1; 1998, c. 37, s. 21; 2000, c. 10, s. 22

487.09 (1) Destruction of bodily substances, etc. — warrant — Subject to subsection (2), bodily substances that are taken from a person in execution of a warrant under section 487.05 and the results of forensic DNA analysis shall be destroyed or, in the case of results in electronic form, access to those results shall be permanently removed, without delay after

(a) the results of that analysis establish that the bodily substance referred to in paragraph 487.05(1)(b) was not from that person;

(b) the person is finally acquitted of the designated offence and any other offence in respect of the same transaction; or

(c) the expiration of one year after

(i) the person is discharged after a preliminary inquiry into the designated offence or any other offence in respect of the same transaction,

(ii) the dismissal, for any reason other than acquittal, or the withdrawal of any information charging the person with the designated offence or any other offence in respect of the same transaction, or

(iii) any proceeding against the person for the offence or any other offence in respect of the same transaction is stayed under section 579 or under that section as applied by section 572 or 795,

unless during that year a new information is laid or an indictment is preferred charging the person with the designated offence or any other offence in respect of the same transaction or the proceeding is recommenced.

(2) Exception — A provincial court judge may order that the bodily substances that are taken from a person and the results of forensic DNA analysis not be destroyed during any period that the provincial court judge considers appropriate if the provincial court judge is satisfied that the bodily substances or results might reasonably be required in an investigation or prosecution of the person for another designated offence or of another person for the designated offence or any other offence in respect of the same transaction.

(3) Destruction of bodily substances, etc. voluntarily given — Bodily substances that are provided voluntarily by a person and the results of forensic DNA analysis shall be destroyed or, in the case of results in electronic form, access to those results shall be permanently removed, without delay after the results of that analysis establish that the bodily substance referred to in paragraph 487.05(1)(b) was not from that person.

1995, c. 27, s. 1; 1998, c. 37, s. 22

487.091 (1) Collection of additional bodily substances — If a DNA profile could not be derived from the bodily substances that were taken from a person in execution of an order under section 487.051 or 487.052 or under an authorization under section 487.055, a provincial court judge may, on *ex parte* application made in Form 5.08 within a reasonable time after it is determined that the DNA profile could not be derived, grant an authorization in Form 5.09 authorizing the taking, from that person, for the purpose of forensic DNA analysis, of any number of additional samples of bodily substances that is required for that purpose, by means of the investigative procedures described in subsection 487.06(1).

(2) Reasons — The application shall state the reasons why a DNA profile could not be derived from the bodily substances that were taken from the person under the initial order or authorization.

(3) Persons not in custody — Subsections 487.055(4) to (10) apply, with any modifications that the circumstances require and without regard to the words "referred to in subsection (1) who is on conditional release" in subsection 487.055(4), in respect of any person who is not in custody and from whom bodily substances are authorized to be taken under this section.

1998, c. 37, s. 23; 2000, c. 10, s. 23

487.092 (1) Information for impression warrant — A justice may issue a warrant in writing authorizing a peace officer to do any thing, or cause any thing to be done under the direction of the peace officer, described in the warrant in order to obtain any handprint, fingerprint, footprint, foot impression, teeth impression or other print or impression of the body or any part of the body in respect of a person if the justice is satisfied

(a) by information on oath in writing that there are reasonable grounds to believe that an offence against this or any other Act of Parliament has been committed and that information concerning the offence will be obtained by the print or impression; and

(b) that it is in the best interests of the administration of justice to issue the warrant.

(2) Search or seizure to be reasonable — A warrant issued under subsection (1) shall contain such terms and conditions as the justice considers advisable to ensure that any search or seizure authorized by the warrant is reasonable in the circumstances.

(3) Provisions to apply — Subsections 487(2) and (4) apply, with such modifications as the circumstances require, to a warrant issued under subsection (1).

(4) Telewarrant — Where a peace officer believes that it would be impracticable to appear personally before a justice to make an application for a warrant under this section, a warrant may be issued under this section on an information submitted by telephone or other means of telecommunication and, for that purpose, section 487.1 applies, with such modifications as the circumstances require, to the warrant.

1997, c. 18, s. 45; 1998, c. 37, s. 23

Editor's Note: This section was originally enacted as s. 487.091 by 1997, c. 18, s. 45 and was renumbered as s. 487.092 by 1998, c. 37, s. 23.

487.1 (1) Telewarrants — Where a peace officer believes that an indictable offence has been committed and that it would be impracticable to appear personally before a justice to make application for a warrant in accordance with section 256 or 487, the peace officer may submit an information on oath by telephone or other means of telecommunication to a justice designated for the purpose by the chief judge of the provincial court having jurisdiction in the matter.

(2) Information on oath and record — An information submitted by telephone or other means of telecommunication, other than a means of telecommunication that produces a writing, shall be on oath and shall be recorded verbatim by the justice, who shall, as soon as practicable, cause to be filed, with the clerk of the court for the territorial division in which the warrant is intended for execution, the record or a transcription of it, certified by the justice as to time, date and contents.

(2.1) Information submitted by other means of telecommunication — The justice who receives an information submitted by a means of telecommunication that produces a writing shall, as soon as practicable, cause to be filed, with the clerk of the court for the territorial division in which the warrant is intended for execution, the information certified by the justice as to time and date of receipt.

(3) Administration of oath — For the purposes of subsection (2), an oath may be administered by telephone or other means of telecommunication.

(3.1) Alternative to oath — A peace officer who uses a means of telecommunication referred to in subsection (2.1) may, instead of swearing an oath, make a statement in writing stating that all matters contained in the information are true to his or her knowledge and belief and such a statement is deemed to be a statement made under oath.

(4) Contents of information — An information submitted by telephone or other means of telecommunication shall include

(a) a statement of the circumstances that make it impracticable for the peace officer to appear personally before a justice;

(b) a statement of the indictable offence alleged, the place or premises to be searched and the items alleged to be liable to seizure;

(c) a statement of the peace officer's grounds for believing that items liable to seizure in respect of the offence alleged will be found in the place or premises to be searched; and

(d) a statement as to any prior application for a warrant under this section or any other search warrant, in respect of the same matter, of which the peace officer has knowledge.

(5) Issuing warrant — A justice referred to in subsection (1) who is satisfied that an information submitted by telephone or other means of telecommunication

(a) is in respect of an indictable offence and conforms to the requirements of subsection (4),

(b) discloses reasonable grounds for dispensing with an information presented personally and in writing, and

(c) discloses reasonable grounds, in accordance with subsection 256(1) or paragraph 487(1)(a), (b) or (c), as the case may be, for the issuance of a warrant in respect of an indictable offence,

may issue a warrant to a peace officer conferring the same authority respecting search and seizure as may be conferred by a warrant issued by a justice before whom the peace officer appears personally pursuant to subsection 256(1) or 487(1), as the case may be, and may require that the warrant be executed within such period as the justice may order.

(6) Formalities respecting warrant and facsimiles — Where a justice issues a warrant by telephone or other means of telecommunication, other than a means of telecommunication that produces a writing,

    (a) the justice shall complete and sign the warrant in Form 5.1, noting on its face the time, date and place of issuance;

    (b) the peace officer, on the direction of the justice, shall complete, in duplicate, a facsimile of the warrant in Form 5.1, noting on its face the name of the issuing justice and the time, date and place of issuance; and

    (c) the justice shall, as soon as practicable after the warrant has been issued, cause the warrant to be filed with the clerk of the court for the territorial division in which the warrant is intended for execution.

(6.1) Issuance of warrant where telecommunication produces writing — Where a justice issues a warrant by a means of telecommunication that produces a writing,

    (a) the justice shall complete and sign the warrant in Form 5.1, noting on its face the time, date and place of issuance;

    (b) the justice shall transmit the warrant by the means of telecommunication to the peace officer who submitted the information and the copy of the warrant received by the peace officer is deemed to be a facsimile within the meaning of paragraph (6)(b);

    (c) the peace officer shall procure another facsimile of the warrant; and

    (d) the justice shall, as soon as practicable after the warrant has been issued, cause the warrant to be filed with the clerk of the court for the territorial division in which the warrant is intended for execution.

(7) Providing facsimile — A peace officer who executes a warrant issued by telephone or other means of telecommunication, other than a warrant issued pursuant to subsection 256(1), shall, before entering the place or premises to be searched or as soon as practicable thereafter, give a facsimile of the warrant to any person present and ostensibly in control of the place or premises.

(8) Affixing facsimile — A peace officer who, in any unoccupied place or premises, executes a warrant issued by telephone or other means of telecommunication, other than a warrant issued pursuant to subsection 256(1), shall, on entering the place or premises or as soon as practicable thereafter, cause a facsimile of the warrant to be suitably affixed in a prominent place within the place or premises.

(9) Report of peace officer — A peace officer to whom a warrant is issued by telephone or other means of telecommunication shall file a written report with the clerk of the court for the territorial division in which the warrant was intended for execution as soon as practicable but within a period not exceeding seven days after the warrant has been executed, which report shall include

    (a) a statement of the time and date the warrant was executed or, if the warrant was not executed, a statement of the reasons why it was not executed;

    (b) a statement of the things, if any, that were seized pursuant to the warrant and the location where they are being held; and

(c) a statement of the things, if any, that were seized in addition to the things mentioned in the warrant and the location where they are being held, together with a statement of the peace officer's grounds for believing that those additional things had been obtained by, or used in, the commission of an offence.

(10) Bringing before justice — The clerk of the court shall, as soon as practicable, cause the report, together with the information and the warrant to which it pertains, to be brought before a justice to be dealt with, in respect of the things seized referred to in the report, in the same manner as if the things were seized pursuant to a warrant issued, on an information presented personally by a peace officer, by that justice or another justice for the same territorial division.

(11) Proof of authorization — In any proceeding in which it is material for a court to be satisfied that a search or seizure was authorized by a warrant issued by telephone or other means of telecommunication, the absence of the information or warrant, signed by the justice and carrying on its face a notation of the time, date and place of issuance, is, in the absence of evidence to the contrary, proof that the search or seizure was not authorized by a warrant issued by telephone or other means of telecommunication.

(12) Duplicates and facsimiles acceptable — A duplicate or a facsimile of an information or a warrant has the same probative force as the original for the purposes of subsection (11).
R.S. 1985, c. 27 (1st Supp.), s. 69; 1992, c. 1, s. 58(1) (Sched. I, items 9, 18); 1994, c. 44, s. 37

487.11 Where warrant not necessary — A peace officer, or a public officer who has been appointed or designated to administer or enforce any federal or provincial law and whose duties include the enforcement of this or any other Act of Parliament, may, in the course of his or her duties, exercise any of the powers described in subsection 487(1) or 492.1(1) without a warrant if the conditions for obtaining a warrant exist but by reason of exigent circumstances it would be impracticable to obtain a warrant.
1997, c. 18, s. 46

487.2 (1) Restriction on publicity — Where a search warrant is issued under section 487 or 487.1 or a search is made under such a warrant, every one who publishes in any newspaper or broadcasts any information with respect to

(a) the location of the place searched or to be searched, or

(b) the identity of any person who is or appears to occupy or be in possession or control of that place or who is suspected of being involved in any offence in relation to which the warrant was issued,

without the consent of every person referred to in paragraph (b) is, unless a charge has been laid in respect of any offence in relation to which the warrant was issued, guilty of an offence punishable on summary conviction.

(2) Definition of "newspaper" — In this section, **"newspaper"** has the same meaning as in section 297.
R.S. 1985, c. 27 (1st Supp.), s. 69

487.3 (1) Order denying access to information used to obtain any warrant — A judge or justice may, on application made at the time of issuing a warrant under this or any other Act of Parliament or of granting an authorization to enter a dwelling-house under section 529 or an authorization under section 529.4 or at any time thereafter, make an order prohibiting access to and the disclosure of any information relating to the warrant or authorization on the ground that

(a) the ends of justice would be subverted by the disclosure for one of the reasons referred to in subsection (2) or the information might be used for an improper purpose; and

(b) the ground referred to in paragraph (a) outweighs in importance the access to the information.

(2) Reasons — For the purposes of paragraph (1)(a), an order may be made under subsection (1) on the ground that the ends of justice would be subverted by the disclosure

(a) if disclosure of the information would

(i) compromise the identity of a confidential informant,

(ii) compromise the nature and extent of an ongoing investigation,

(iii) endanger a person engaged in particular intelligence-gathering techniques and thereby prejudice future investigations in which similar techniques would be used, or

(iv) prejudice the interests of an innocent person; and

(b) for any other sufficient reason.

(3) Procedure — Where an order is made under subsection (1), all documents relating to the application shall, subject to any terms and conditions that the justice or judge considers desirable in the circumstances, including, without limiting the generality of the foregoing, any term or condition concerning the duration of the prohibition, partial disclosure of a document, deletion of any information or the occurrence of a condition, be placed in a packet and sealed by the justice or judge immediately on determination of the application, and that packet shall be kept in the custody of the court in a place to which the public has no access or in any other place that the justice or judge may authorize and shall not be dealt with except in accordance with the terms and conditions specified in the order or as varied under subsection (4).

(4) Application for variance of order — An application to terminate the order or vary any of its terms and conditions may be made to the justice or judge who made the order or a judge of the court before which any proceedings arising out of the investigation in relation to which the warrant was obtained may be held.

1997, c. 23, s. 14; 1997, c. 39, s. 1

488. Execution of search warrant — A warrant issued under section 487 or 487.1 shall be executed by day, unless

(a) the justice is satisfied that there are reasonable grounds for it to be executed by night;

(b) the reasonable grounds are included in the information; and

(c) the warrant authorizes that it be executed by night.

R.S. 1985, c. 27 (1st Supp.), s.70; 1997, c. 18, s. 47

488.1 (1) Definitions — In this section,

"custodian" means a person in whose custody a package is placed pursuant to subsection (2);

"document" for the purposes of this section, has the same meaning as in section 321;

"judge" means a judge of a superior court of criminal jurisdiction of the province where the seizure was made;

"lawyer" means, in the Province of Quebec, an advocate, lawyer or notary and, in any other province, a barrister or solicitor;

"officer" means a peace officer or public officer.

(2) Examination or seizure of certain documents where privilege claimed — Where an officer acting under the authority of this or any other Act of Parliament is about to examine, copy or seize a document in the possession of a lawyer who claims that a named client of his has a solicitor-client privilege in respect of that document, the officer shall, without examining or making copies of the document,

(a) seize the document and place it in a package and suitably seal and identify the package; and

(b) place the package in the custody of the sheriff of the district or county in which the seizure was made or, if there is agreement in writing that a specified person act as custodian, in the custody of that person.

(3) Application to judge — Where a document has been seized and placed in custody under subsection (2), the Attorney General or the client or the lawyer on behalf of the client, may

(a) within fourteen days from the day the document was so placed in custody apply, on two days notice of motion to all other persons entitled to make application to a judge for an order

(i) appointing a place and a day, not later than twenty-one days after the date of the order, for the determination of the question whether the document should be disclosed, and

(ii) requiring the custodian to produce the document to the judge at that time and place;

(b) serve a copy of the order on all other persons entitled to make application and on the custodian within six days of the date on which it was made; and

(c) if he has proceeded as authorized by paragraph (b), apply, at the appointed time and place, for an order determining the question.

(4) Disposition of application — On an application under paragraph (3)(c), the judge

    (a) may, if the judge considers it necessary to determine the question whether the document should be disclosed, inspect the document;

    (b) where the judge is of the opinion that it would materially assist him in deciding whether or not the document is privileged, may allow the Attorney General to inspect the document;

    (c) shall allow the Attorney General and the person who objects to the disclosure of the document to make representations; and

    (d) shall determine the question summarily and,

        (i) if he is of the opinion that the document should not be disclosed, ensure that it is repackaged and resealed and order the custodian to deliver the document to the lawyer who claimed the solicitor-client privilege or to his client, or

        (ii) if he is of the opinion that the document should be disclosed, order the custodian to deliver the document to the officer who seized the document or some other person designated by the Attorney General, subject to such restrictions or conditions as the judge deems appropriate,

and shall, at the same time, deliver concise reasons for the determination in which the nature of the document is described without divulging the details thereof.

(5) Privilege continues — Where the judge determines pursuant to paragraph (4)(d) that a solicitor-client privilege exists in respect of a document, whether or not he has, pursuant to paragraph (4)(b), allowed the Attorney General to inspect the document, the document remain privileged and inadmissible as evidence unless the client consents to its admission in evidence or the privilege is otherwise lost.

(6) Order to custodian to deliver — Where a document has been seized and placed in custody under subsection (2) and a judge, on the application of the Attorney General, is satisfied that no application has been made under paragraph (3)(a) or that following such an application no further application has been made under paragraph (3)(c), the judge shall order the custodian to deliver the document to the officer who seized the document or to some other person designated by the Attorney General.

(7) Application to another judge — Where the judge to whom an application has been made under paragraph (3)(*c*) cannot act or continue to act under this section for any reason, subsequent applications under that paragraph may be made to another judge.

(8) Prohibition — No officer shall examine, make copies of or seize any document without affording a reasonable opportunity for a claim of solicitor-client privilege to be made under subsection (2).

(9) Authority to make copies — At any time while a document is in the custody of a custodian under this section, a judge may, on an *ex parte* application of a person claiming a solicitor-client privilege under this section, authorize that person to examine the document or make a copy of it in the presence of the custodian or the judge, but any such authorization shall contain provisions to ensure that the document is repackaged and that the package is resealed without alteration or damage.

(10) Hearing in private — An application under paragraph (3)(c) shall be heard in private.

(11) Exception — This section does not apply in circumstances where a claim of solicitor-client privilege may be made under the *Income Tax Act*.

> **Proposed Amendment — 488.1(11)**
>
> **(11) Exception** — This section does not apply in circumstances where a claim of solicitor-client privilege may be made under the *Income Tax Act* or under the *Proceeds of Crime (Money Laundering) Act*.
>
> 2000, c. 17, s. 89 [Not in force at date of publication.]

R.S.C. 1985, c. 27 (1st Supp.), s. 71

489. (1) Seizure of things not specified — Every person who executes a warrant may seize, in addition to the things mentioned in the warrant, any thing that the person believes on reasonable grounds

    (a) has been obtained by the commission of an offence against this or any other Act of Parliament;

    (b) has been used in the commission of an offence against this or any other Act of Parliament; or

    (c) will afford evidence in respect of an offence against this or any other Act of Parliament.

(2) Seizure without warrant — Every peace officer, and every public officer who has been appointed or designated to administer or enforce any federal or provincial law and whose duties include the enforcement of this or any other Act of Parliament, who is lawfully present in a place pursuant to a warrant or otherwise in the execution of duties may, without a warrant, seize any thing that the officer believes on reasonable grounds

    (a) has been obtained by the commission of an offence against this or any Act of Parliament;

    (b) has been used in the commission of an offence against this or any other Act of Parliament; or

    (c) will afford evidence in respect of an offence against this or any other Act of Parliament.

R.S. 1985, c. 27 (1st Supp.), s. 72; c. 42(4th Supp.), s. 3; 1993, c. 40, s. 16; 1997, c. 18, s. 48.

489.1 (1) Restitution of property or report by peace officer — Subject to this or any other Act of Parliament, where a peace officer has seized anything under a warrant issued under this Act or under section 487.11 or 489 or otherwise in the execution of duties under this or any other Act of Parliament, the peace officer shall, as soon as is practicable,

> (a) where the peace officer is satisfied,
>
>> (i) that there is no dispute as to who is lawfully entitled to possession of the thing seized, and
>>
>> (ii) that the continued detention of the thing seized is not required for the purposes of any investigation or a preliminary inquiry, trial or other proceeding,
>
> return the thing seized, on being issued a receipt therefor, to the person lawfully entitled to its possession and report to the justice who issued the warrant or some other justice for the same territorial division or, if no warrant was issued, a justice having jurisdiction in respect of the matter, that he has done so; or
>
> (b) where the peace officer is not satisfied as described in subparagraphs (a)(i) and (ii),
>
>> (i) bring the thing seized before the justice referred to in paragraph (a), or
>>
>> (ii) report to the justice that he has seized the thing and is detaining it or causing it to be detained
>
> to be dealt with by the justice in accordance with subsection 490(1).

(2) Idem — Subject to this or any other Act of Parliament, where a person, other than a peace officer, has seized anything under a warrant issued under this Act or under section 487.11 or 489 or otherwise in the execution of duties under this or any other Act of Parliament, that person shall, as soon as is practicable,

> (a) bring the thing seized before the justice who issued the warrant, or some other justice for the same territorial division or, if no warrant was issued, before a justice having jurisdiction in respect of the matter, or
>
> (b) report to the justice referred to in paragraph (a) that he has seized the thing and is detaining it or causing it to be detained,
>
> to be dealt with by the justice in accordance with subsection 490(1).

(3) Form — A report to a justice under this section shall be in the form set out as Form 5.2 in Part XXVIII, varied to suit the case and shall include, in the case of a report in respect of a warrant issued by telephone or other means of telecommunication, the statements referred to in subsection 487.1(9).

R.S. 1985, c. 27 (1st Supp.), s. 72; 1993, c. 40, s. 17; 1997, c. 18, s. 49.

490. (1) Detention of things seized — Subject to this or any other Act of Parliament, where, pursuant to paragraph 489.1(1)(b) or subsection 489.1(2), anything that has been seized is brought before a justice or a report in respect of anything seized is made to a justice, he shall,

> (a) where the lawful owner or person who is lawfully entitled to possession of the thing seized is known, order it to be returned to that owner or person, unless the prosecutor, or the peace officer or other person having custody of the thing seized, satisfies the justice that the detention of the thing seized is

required for the purposes of any investigation or a preliminary inquiry, trial or other proceeding; or

(b) where the prosecutor, or the peace officer or other person having custody of the thing seized, satisfies the justice that the thing seized should be detained for a reason set out in paragraph (a), detain the thing seized or order that it be detained, taking reasonable care to ensure that it is preserved until the conclusion of any investigation or until it is required to be produced for the purposes of a preliminary inquiry, trial or other proceeding.

(2) Further detention — Nothing shall be detained under the authority of paragraph (1)(b) for a period of more than three months after the day of the seizure, or any longer period that ends when an application made under paragraph (a) is decided, unless

(a) a justice, on the making of a summary application to him after three clear days notice thereof to the person from whom the thing detained was seized, is satisfied that, having regard to the nature of the investigation, its further detention for a specified period is warranted and he so orders; or

(b) proceedings are instituted in which the thing detained may be required.

(3) Idem — More than one order for further detention may be made under paragraph (2)(a) but the cumulative period of detention shall not exceed one year from the day of the seizure, or any longer period that ends when an application made under paragraph (a) is decided, unless

(a) a judge of a superior court of criminal jurisdiction or a judge as defined in section 552, on the making of a summary application to him after three clear days notice thereof to the person from whom the thing detained was seized, is satisfied, having regard to the complex nature of the investigation, that the further detention of the thing seized is warranted for a specified period and subject to such other conditions as the judge considers just, and he so orders; or

(b) proceedings are instituted in which the thing detained may be required.

(3.1) Detention without application where consent — A thing may be detained under paragraph (1)(b) for any period, whether or not an application for an order under subsection (2) or (3) is made, if the lawful owner or person who is lawfully entitled to possession of the thing seized consents in writing to its detention for that period.

(4) When accused ordered to stand trial — When an accused has been ordered to stand trial, the justice shall forward anything detained pursuant to subsections (1) to (3) to the clerk of the court to which the accused has been ordered to stand trial to be detained by the clerk and disposed of as the court directs.

(5) Where continued detention no longer required — Where at any time before the expiration of the periods of detention provided for or ordered under subsections (1) to (3) in respect of anything seized, the prosecutor, or the peace officer or other person having custody of the thing seized, determines that the continued detention of the thing seized is no longer required for any purpose mentioned in subsection (1) or (4), the prosecutor, peace officer or other person shall apply to

(a) a judge of a superior court of criminal jurisdiction or a judge as defined in section 552, where a judge ordered its detention under subsection (3), or

(b) a justice, in any other case,

who shall, after affording the person from whom the thing was seized or the person who claims to be the lawful owner thereof or person entitled to its possession, if known, an opportunity to establish that he is lawfully entitled to the possession thereof, make an order in respect of the property under subsection (9).

(6) Idem — Where the periods of detention provided for or ordered under subsections (1) to (3) in respect of anything seized have expired and proceedings have not been instituted in which the thing detained may be required, the prosecutor, peace officer or other person shall apply to a judge or justice referred to in paragraph (5)(a) or (b) in the circumstances set out in that paragraph, for an order in respect of the property under subsection (9) or (9.1).

(7) Application for order of return — A person from whom anything has been seized may, after the expiration of the periods of detention provided for or ordered under subsections (1) to (3) and on three clear days notice to the Attorney General, apply summarily to

(a) a judge of a superior court of criminal jurisdiction or a judge as defined in section 552, where a judge ordered the detention of the thing seized under subsection (3), or

(b) a justice, in any other case,

for an order under paragraph (9)(c) that the thing seized be returned to the applicant.

(8) Exception — A judge of a superior court of criminal jurisdiction or a judge as defined in section 552, where a judge ordered the detention of the thing seized under subsection (3), or a justice, in any other case, may allow an application to be made under subsection (7) prior to the expiration of the periods referred to therein where he is satisfied that hardship will result unless such application is so allowed.

(9) Disposal of things seized — Subject to this or any other Act of Parliament, if

(a) a judge referred to in subsection (7), where a judge ordered the detention of anything seized under subsection (3), or

(b) a justice, in any other case,

is satisfied that the periods of detention provided for or ordered under subsections (1) to (3) in respect of anything seized have expired and proceedings have not been instituted in which the thing detained may be required or, where such periods have not expired, that the continued detention of the thing seized will not be required for any purpose mentioned in subsection (1) or (4), he shall

(c) if possession of it by the person from whom it was seized is lawful, order it to be returned to that person; or

(d) if possession of it by the person from whom it was seized is unlawful and the lawful owner or person who is lawfully entitled to its possession is

known, order it to be returned to the lawful owner or to the person who is
lawfully entitled to its possession,

any may, if possession of it by the person from whom it was seized is unlawful, or
if it was seized when it was not in the possession of any person, and the lawful
owner or person who is lawfully entitled to its possession is not known, order it to
be forfeited to Her Majesty, to be disposed of as the Attorney General directs, or
otherwise dealt with in accordance with the law.

(9.1) Exception — Notwithstanding subsection (9), a judge or justice referred to
in paragraph (9)(*a*) or (*b*) may, if the periods of detention provided for or ordered
under subsections (1) to (3) in respect of a thing seized have expired but proceedings have not been instituted in which the thing may be required, order that the
thing continue to be detained for such period as the judge or justice considers necessary if the judge or justice is satisfied

    (a) that the continued detention of the thing might reasonably be required for
    a purpose mentioned in subsection (1) or (4); and

    (b) that it is in the interests of justice to do so.

(10) Application by lawful owner — Subject to this or any other Act of Parliament, a person, other than a person who may make an application under subsection
(7), who claims to be the lawful owner or person lawfully entitled to possession of
anything seized and brought before or reported to a justice under section 489.1 may,
at any time, on three clear days notice to the Attorney General and the person from
whom the thing was seized, apply summarily to

    (a) a judge referred to in subsection (7), where a judge ordered the detention
    of the thing seized under subsection (3), or

    (b) a justice, in any other case,

for an order that the thing detained be returned to the applicant.

(11) Order — Subject to this or any other Act of Parliament, on an application
under subsection (10), where a judge or justice is satisfied that

    (a) the applicant is the lawful owner or lawfully entitled to possession of the
    thing seized, and

    (b) the periods of detention provided for or ordered under subsections (1) to
    (3) in respect of the thing seized have expired and proceedings have not been
    instituted in which the thing detained may be required or, where such periods
    have not expired, that the continued detention of the thing seized will not be
    required for any purpose mentioned in subsection (1) or (4),

the judge shall order that

    (c) the thing seized be returned to the applicant; or

    (d) except as otherwise provided by law, where, pursuant to subsection (9),
    the thing seized was forfeited, sold or otherwise dealt within such a manner
    that it cannot be returned to the applicant, the applicant be paid the proceeds
    of sale or the value of the thing seized.

(12) Detention pending appeal, etc. — Notwithstanding anything in this section, nothing shall be returned, forfeited or disposed of under this section pending

any application made, or appeal taken, thereunder in respect of the thing or proceeding in which the right of seizure thereof is questioned or within thirty days after an order in respect of the thing is made under this section.

(13) Copies of documents returned — The Attorney General, the prosecutor or the peace officer or other person having custody of a document seized may, before bringing it before a justice or complying with an order that the document be returned, forfeited or otherwise dealt with under subsection (1), (9) or (11), make or cause to be made, and may retain, a copy of the document.

(14) Probative force — Every copy made under subsection (13) that is certified as a true copy by the Attorney General, the person who made the copy or the person in whose presence the copy was made is admissible in evidence and, in the absence of evidence to the contrary, has the same probative force as the original document would have if it had been proved in the ordinary way.

(15) Access to anything seized — Where anything is detained pursuant to subsections (1) to (3.1), a judge of a superior court of criminal jurisdiction, a judge as defined in section 552 or a provincial court judge may, on summary application on behalf of a person who has an interest in what is detained, after three clear days notice to the Attorney General, order that the person by or on whose behalf the application is made be permitted to examine anything so detained.

(16) Conditions — An order that is made under subsection (15) shall be made on such terms as appear to the judge to be necessary or desirable to ensure that anything in respect of which the order is made is safeguarded and preserved for any purpose for which it may subsequently be required.

(17) Appeal — A person who feels aggrieved by an order made under subsection (8),(9), (9.1) or (11) may appeal from the order to the appeal court, as defined in section 812, and for the purposes of the appeal the provisions of sections 814 to 828 apply with such modifications as the circumstances require.

(18) Waiver of notice — Any person to whom three days notice must be given under paragraph (2)(a) or (3)(a) or subsection (7), (10) or (15) may agree that the application for which the notice is given be made before the expiration of the three days.

R.S. 1985, c. 27 (1st Supp.), s. 73; 1994, c. 44, s. 38; 1997, c. 18, s. 50.

490.01 Perishable things — Where any thing seized pursuant to this Act is perishable or likely to depreciate rapidly, the person who seized the thing or any other person having custody of the thing

(a) may return it to its lawful owner or the person who is lawfully entitled to possession of it; or

(b) where, on *ex parte* application to a justice, the justice so authorizes, may

(i) dispose of it and give the proceeds of disposition to the lawful owner of the thing seized, if the lawful owner was not a party to an offence in relation to the thing or, if the identity of that lawful owner cannot be reasonably ascertained, the proceeds of disposition are forfeited to Her Majesty, or

        (ii) destroy it.

1997, c. 18, s. 51; 1999, c. 5, s. 17.

490.1 (1) Order of forfeiture of property on conviction — Subject to section 490.3 and 490.4, where a person is convicted of a criminal organization offence and, on application of the Attorney General, the court is satisfied, on a balance of probabilities, that any property is offence-related property and that the offence was committed in relation to that property, the court shall

    (a) where the prosecution of the offence was commenced at the instance of the government of a province and conducted by or on behalf of that government, order that the property be forfeited to Her Majesty in right of that province and disposed of by the Attorney General or Solicitor General of that province in accordance with the law; and

    (b) in any other case, order that the property be forfeited to Her Majesty in right of Canada and disposed of by the member of the Queen's Privy Council for Canada that may be designated for the purpose of this paragraph in accordance with the law.

(2) Property related to other offence — Where the evidence does not establish to the satisfaction of the court that the criminal organization offence of which a person has been convicted was committed in relation to property in respect of which an order of forfeiture would otherwise be made under subsection (1) but the court is satisfied, beyond a reasonable doubt, that the property is offence-related property, the court may make an order of forfeiture under subsection (1) in relation to that property.

(3) Appeal — A person who has been convicted of a criminal organization offence or the Attorney General may appeal to the court of appeal from an order or a failure to make an order under subsection (1) as if the appeal were an appeal against the sentence imposed on the person in respect of the offence.

1997, c. 23, s. 15.

490.2 (1) Application for *in rem* forfeiture — Where an information has been laid in respect of a criminal organization offence, the Attorney General may make an application to a judge for an order of forfeiture under subsection (2).

(2) Order of forfeiture of property — Subject to sections 490.3 and 490.4, where an application is made to a judge under subsection (1) and the judge is satisfied

    (a) beyond a reasonable doubt that any property is offence-related property,

    (b) that proceedings in respect of a criminal organization offence in relation to the property referred to in paragraph (*a*) were commenced, and

    (c) that the accused charged with the criminal organization offence has died or absconded,

the judge shall order that the property be forfeited and disposed of in accordance with subsection (4).

(3) Accused deemed absconded — For the purpose of subsection (2), an accused is deemed to have absconded in connection with a criminal organization offence if

(a) an information has been laid alleging the commission of the offence by the accused,

(b) a warrant for the arrest of the accused has been issued in relation to that information, and

(c) a reasonable attempts to arrest the accused under the warrant have been unsuccessful during a period of six months beginning on the day on which the warrant was issued,

and the accused is deemed to have so absconded on the last day of that six month period.

(4) Who may dispose of forfeited property — For the purpose of subsection (2), the judge shall

(a) where the prosecution of the offence was commenced at the instance of the government of a province and conducted by or on behalf of that government, order that the property be forfeited to Her Majesty in right of that province and disposed of by the Attorney General or Solicitor General of that province in accordance with the law; and

(b) in any other case, order that the property be forfeited to Her Majesty in right of Canada and disposed of by the member of the Queen's Privy Council for Canada that may be designated for the purpose of this paragraph in accordance with the law.

(5) Definition of "judge" — In this section and sections 490.5 and 490.8, "judge" means a judge as defined in section 552 or a judge of a superior court of criminal jurisdiction.

1997, c. 23, s. 15.

490.3 Voidable transfers — A court may, before ordering that offence-related property be forfeited under subsection 490.1(1) or 490.2(2), set aside any conveyance or transfer of the property that occurred after the seizure of the property, or the making of a restraint order in respect of the property, unless the conveyance or transfer was for valuable consideration to a person acting in good faith.

1997, c. 23, s. 15.

490.4 (1) Notice — Before making an order under subsection 490.1(1) or 490.2(2) in relation to any property, a court shall require notice in accordance with subsection (2) to be given to, and may hear, any person who, in the opinion of the court, appears to have a valid interest in the property.

(2) Manner of giving notice — A notice given under subsection (1) shall

(a) be given or served in the manner that the court directs or that may be specified in the rules of the court;

(b) be of any duration that the court considers reasonable or that may be specified in the rules of the court; and

314

(c) set out the criminal organization offence charged and a description of the property.

(3) Order of restoration of property — Where a court is satisfied that a person, other than

(a) a person who was charged with a criminal organization offence, or

(b) a person who acquired title to or a right of possession of the property from a person referred to in paragraph (*a*) under circumstances that give rise to a reasonable inference that the title or right was transferred for the purpose of avoiding the forfeiture of the property,

is the lawful owner or is lawfully entitled to possession of any property or a part of any property that would otherwise be forfeited pursuant to an order made under subsection 490.1(1) or 490.2(2) and that the person appears innocent of any complicity in an offence referred to in paragraph (*a*) or of any collusion in relation to such an offence, the court may order that the property or part be returned to the person.

1997, c. 23, s. 15.

490.5 (1) Application — Where any offence-related property is forfeited to Her Majesty pursuant to an order made under subsection 490.1(1) or 490.2(2), any person who claims an interest in the property, other than

(a) in the case of property forfeited pursuant to an order made under subsection 490.1(1), a person who was convicted of the criminal organization offence in relation to which the property was forfeited,

(b) in the case of property forfeited pursuant to an order made subsection 490.2(2), a person who was charged with the criminal organization offence in relation to which the property was forfeited, or

(c) a person who acquired title to or a right of possession of the property from a person referred to in paragraph (*a*) or (*b*) under circumstances that give rise to a reasonable inference that the title or right was transferred from that person for the purpose of avoiding the forfeiture of the property,

may, within thirty days after the forfeiture, apply by notice in writing to a judge for an order under subsection (4).

(2) Fixing day for hearing — The judge to whom an application is made under subsection (1) shall fix a day not less than thirty days after the date of the filing of the application for the hearing of the application.

(3) Notice — An applicant shall serve a notice of the application made under subsection (1) and of the hearing of it on the Attorney General at least fifteen days before the day fixed for the hearing.

(4) Order declaring interest not affected by forfeiture — Where, on the hearing of an application made under subsection (1), the judge is satisfied that the applicant

(a) is not a person referred to in paragraph (1)(a), (b) or(c) and appears innocent of any complicity in any criminal organization offence that resulted in the forfeiture of the property or of any collusion in relation to such an offence, and

(b) exercised all reasonable care to be satisfied that the property was not likely to have been used in connection with the commission of an unlawful act by the person who was permitted by the applicant to obtain possession of the property or from whom the applicant obtained possession or, where the applicant is a mortgagee or lienholder, by the mortgagor or lien-giver,

the judge may make an order declaring that the interest of the applicant is not affected by the forfeiture and declaring the nature and the extent or value of the interest.

(5) Appeal from order made under subsection (4) — An applicant or the Attorney General may appeal to the court of appeal from an order made under subsection (4), and the provisions of Part XXI with respect to procedure on appeals apply, with any modifications that the circumstances require, in respect of appeals under this subsection.

(6) Return of property — The Attorney General shall, on application made to the Attorney General by any person in respect of whom a judge has made an order under subsection (4), and where the periods with respect to the taking of appeals from that order under subsection (4), and where the periods with respect to the taking of appeals from that order have expired and any appeal from that order taken under subsection (5) has been determined, direct that

(a) the property, or the part of it to which the interest of the applicant relates, be returned to the applicant; or

(b) an amount equal to the value of the interest of the applicant, as declared in the order, be paid to the applicant.

1997, c. 23, s. 15.

490.6 Appeals from orders under subsection 490.2(2) — Any person who, in their opinion, is aggrieved by an order made under subsection 490.2(2) may appeal from the order as if the order were an appeal against conviction or against a judgment or verdict of acquittal, as the case may be, under Part XXI, and that Part applies, with any modifications that the circumstances require, in respect of such an appeal.

1997, c. 23, s. 15.

490.7 Suspension of order pending appeal — Notwithstanding anything in this Act, the operation of an order made in respect of property under subsection 490.1(1), 490.2(2) or 490.5(4) is suspended pending

(a) any application made in respect of the property under those provisions or any other provision of this or any other Act of Parliament that provides for restoration or forfeiture of the property, or

(b) any appeal taken from an order of forfeiture or restoration in respect of the property,

and the property shall not be disposed of or otherwise dealt with until thirty days have expired after an order is made under any of those provisions.

1997, c. 23, s. 15.

490.8 (1) Application for restraint order — The Attorney General may make an application in accordance with this section for a restraint order under this section in respect of any offence-related property.

(2) Procedure — An application made under subsection (1) for a restraint order in respect of any offence-related property may be made *ex parte* and shall be made in writing to a judge and be accompanied by an affidavit sworn on the information and belief of the Attorney General or any other person deposing to the following matters:

(a) the criminal organization offence to which the offence-related property relates;

(b) the person who is believed to be in possession of the offence-related property; and

(c) a description of the offence-related property.

(3) Restraint order — Where an application for a restraint order is made to a judge under subsection (1), the judge may, if satisfied that there are reasonable grounds to believe that the property is offence-related property, make a restraint order

(a) prohibiting any person from disposing of, or otherwise dealing with any interest in, the offence-related property specified in the order otherwise than in the manner that may be specified in the order; and

(b) at the request of the Attorney General, where the judge is of the opinion that the circumstances so require,

(i) appointing a person to take control of and to manage or otherwise deal with all or part of the property in accordance with the directions of the judge, and

(ii) requiring any person having possession of the property to give possession of it to the person appointed under subparagraph (i).

(4) Conditions — A restraint order made by a judge under this section may be subject to any reasonable conditions that the judge thinks fit.

(5) Order in writing — A restraint order made under this section shall be made in writing.

(6) Service of order — A copy of a restraint order made under this section shall be served on the person to whom the order is addressed in any manner that the judge making the order directs or in accordance with the rules of the court.

(7) Registration of order — A copy of a restraint order made under this section shall be registered against any property in accordance with the laws of the province in which the property is situated.

(8) Order continues in force — A restraint order made under this section remains in effect until

(a) an order is made under subsection 490(9) or (11) in relations to the property; or

(b) an order of forfeiture of the property is made under section 490 or subsection 490.1(1) or 490.2(2).

(9) Offence — Any person on whom a restraint order made under this section is served in accordance with this section and who, while the order is in force, acts in contravention of or fails to comply with the order is guilty of an indictable offence or offence punishable on summary conviction.

1997, c. 23, s. 15.

490.9 (1) Sections 489.1 and 490 applicable — Subject to sections 490.1 to 490.7 sections 489.1 and 490 apply, with any modifications that the circumstances require, to any offence-related property that is the subject of a restraint order made under section 490.8.

(2) Recognizance — Where, pursuant to subsection (1), an order is made under paragraph 490(9)(*c*) for the return of any offence-related property that is the subject of a restraint order under section 490.8, the judge or justice making the order may require the applicant for the order to enter into a recognizance before the judge or justice, with or without sureties, in any amount and with any conditions that the judge or justice directs and, where the judge or justice considers it appropriate, require that applicant to deposit with the judge or justice any sum of money or other valuable security that the judge or justice directs.

1997, c. 23, s. 15.

491. (1) Forfeiture of weapons and ammunition — Subject to subsection (2) where it is determined by a court that

(a) a weapon, an imitation firearm, a prohibited device, any ammunition, any prohibited ammunition or an explosive substance was used in the commission of an offence and that thing has been seized and detained, or

(b) that a person has committed an offence that involves, or the subject-matter of which is, a firearm, a cross-bow, a prohibited weapon, a restricted weapon, a prohibited device, ammunition, prohibited ammunition or an explosive substance and any such thing has been seized and detained,

the thing so seized and detained is forfeited to Her Majesty and shall be disposed of as the Attorney General directs.

(2) Return to lawful owner — If the court by which a determination referred to in subsection (1) is made is satisfied that the lawful owner of any thing that is or may be forfeited to Her Majesty under subsection (1) was not a party to the offence and had no reasonable grounds to believe that the thing would or might be used in the commission of an offence, the court shall order that the thing be returned to that lawful owner, that the proceeds of any sale of the thing be paid to that lawful owner or, if the thing was destroyed, that an amount equal to the value of the thing be paid to the owner.

(3) Application of proceeds — Where any thing in respect of which this section applies is sold, the proceeds of the sale shall be paid to the Attorney General or, where an order is made under subsection (2), to the person who was, immediately prior to the sale, the lawful owner of the thing.

1991, c. 40, s. 30; 1995, c. 39, s. 152.

491.1 (1) Order for restitution or forfeiture of property obtained by crime — Where an accused or defendant is tried for an offence and the court determines that an offence has been committed, whether or not the accused has been convicted or discharged under section 730 of the offence, and at the time of the trial any property obtained by the commission of the offence

(a) is before the court or has been detained so that it can be immediately dealt with, and

(b) will not be required as evidence in any other proceedings,

section 490 does not apply in respect of the property and the court shall make an order under subsection (2) in respect of the property.

(2) Idem — In the circumstances referred to in subsection (1), the court shall order, in respect of any property,

(a) if the lawful owner or person lawfully entitled to possession of the property is known, that it be returned to that person; and

(b) if the lawful owner or person lawfully entitled to possession of the property is not known, that it be forfeited to Her Majesty, to be disposed of as the Attorney General directs or otherwise dealt with in accordance with the law.

(3) When certain orders not to be made — An order shall not be made under subsection (2)

(a) in the case of proceedings against a trustee, banker, merchant, attorney, factor, broker or other agent entrusted with the possession of goods or documents of title to goods, for an offence under section 330, 331, 332 or 336; or

(b) in respect of

(i) property to which a person acting in good faith and without notice has acquired lawful title for valuable consideration,

(ii) a valuable security that has been paid or discharged in good faith by a person who was liable to pay or discharge it,

(iii) a negotiable instrument that has, in good faith, been taken or received by transfer or delivery for valuable consideration by a person who had no notice and no reasonable cause to suspect that an offence had been committed, or

(iv) property in respect of which there is a dispute as to ownership or right of possession by claimants other than the accused or defendant.

(4) By whom order executed — An order made under this section shall, on the direction of the court, be executed by the peace officers by whom the process of the court is ordinarily executed.

R.S.C. 1985, c. 27 (1st Supp.), s. 74; 1995, c. 22, (Sched. IV, item 26)

491.2 (1) Photographic evidence — Before any property that would otherwise be required to be produced for the purposes of a preliminary inquiry, trial or other proceeding in respect of an offence under section 334, 344, 348, 354, 362 or 380 is returned or ordered to be returned, forfeited or otherwise dealt with under section 489.1 or 490 or is otherwise returned, a peace officer or any person under the direction of a peace officer may take and retain a photograph of the property.

(2) Certified photograph admissible in evidence — Every photograph of property taken under subsection (1), accompanied by a certificate of a person containing the statements referred to in subsection (3), shall be admissible in evidence and, in the absence of evidence to the contrary, shall have the same probative force as the property would have had if it had been proved in the ordinary way.

(3) Statements made in certificate — For the purposes of subsection (2), a certificate of a person stating that

    (a) the person took the photograph under the authority of subsection (1),

    (b) the person is a peace officer or took the photograph under the direction of a peace officer, and

    (c) the photograph is a true photograph

shall be admissible in evidence and, in the absence of evidence to the contrary, is evidence of the statements contained in the certificate without proof of the signature of the person appearing to have signed the certificate.

(4) Secondary evidence of peace officer — An affidavit or solemn declaration of a peace officer or other person stating that the person has seized property and detained it or caused it to be detained from the time that person took possession of the property until a photograph of the property was taken under subsection (1) and that property was not altered in any manner before the photograph was taken shall be admissible in evidence and, in the absence of evidence to the contrary, is evidence of the statements contained in the affidavit or solemn declaration without proof of the signature or official character of the person appearing to have signed the affidavit or solemn declaration.

(5) Notice of intention to produce certified photograph — Unless the court orders otherwise, no photograph, certificate affidavit or solemn declaration shall be received in evidence at a trial or other proceeding pursuant to subsection (2), (3) or (4) unless the prosecutor has, before the trial or other proceeding, given to the accused a copy thereof and reasonable notice of intention to produce it in evidence.

(6) Attendance for examination — Notwithstanding subsection (3) or (4), the court may require the person who appears to have signed a certificate, an affidavit or a solemn declaration referred to in that subsection to appear before it for examination or cross-examination in respect of the issue of proof of any of the facts contained in the certificate, affidavit or solemn declaration.

(7) Production of property in court — A court may order any property seized and returned pursuant to section 489.1 or 490 to be produced in court or made available for examination by all parties to a proceeding at a reasonable time and place, notwithstanding that a photograph of the property has been received in evidence pursuant to subsection (2), where the court is satisfied that the interests of justice so require and that it is possible and practicable to do so in the circumstances.

(8) Definition of "photograph" — In this section, **"photograph"** includes a still photograph, a photographic film or plate, a microphotographic film, a photostatic negative, an X-ray film, a motion picture and a videotape.

R.S. 1985, c. 23 (4th Supp.), s. 2; 1992, c. 1, s. 58(1) (Sched. 1, item 10)

492. (1) Seizure of explosives — Every person who executes a warrant issued under section 487 may seize any explosive substance that he suspects is intended to be used for an unlawful purpose, and shall, as soon as possible, remove to a place of safety anything that he seizes by virtue of this section and detain it until he is ordered by a judge of a superior court to deliver it to some other person or an order is made pursuant to subsection (2).

(2) Forfeiture — Where an accused is convicted of an offence in respect of anything seized by virtue of subsection (1), it is forfeited and shall be dealt with as the court that makes the conviction may direct.

(3) Application of proceeds — Where anything to which this section applies is sold, the proceeds of the sale shall be paid to the Attorney General.

R.S. 1985, c. 27 (1st Supp.), s.70.

492.1 (1) Information for tracking warrant — A justice who is satisfied by information on oath in writing that there are reasonable grounds to suspect that an offence under this or any other Act of Parliament has been or will be committed and that information that is relevant to the commission of the offence, including the whereabouts of any person, can be obtained through the use of a tracking device, may at any time issue a warrant authorizing a peace officer or a public officer who has been appointed or designated to administer or enforce a federal or provincial law and whose duties include the enforcement of this Act or any other Act of Parliament and who is named in the warrant

(a) to install, maintain and remove a tracking device in or on any thing, including a thing carried, used or worn by any person; and

(b) to monitor, or to have monitored, a tracking device installed in or on any thing.

(2) Time limit for warrant — A warrant issued under subsection (1) is valid for the period, not exceeding sixty days, mentioned in it.

(3) Further warrants — A justice may issue further warrants under this section.

(4) Definition of "tracking device" — For the purposes of this section, **"tracking device"** means any device that, when installed in or on any thing, may be used to help ascertain, by electronic or other means, the location of any thing or person.

(5) Removal after expiry of warrant — On *ex parte* application in writing supported by affidavit, the justice who issued a warrant under subsection (1) or a further warrant under subsection (3) or any other justice having jurisdiction to issue such warrants may authorize that the tracking device be covertly removed after the expiry of the warrant

(a) under any terms or conditions that the justice considers advisable in the public interest; and

(b) during any specified period of not more than sixty days.

1993, c. 40, s. 18; 1999, c. 5, s. 18

492.2 (1) Information re number recorder — A justice who is satisfied by information on oath in writing that there are reasonable grounds to suspect that an offence under this or any other Act of Parliament has been or will be committed and that information that would assist in the investigation of the offence could be obtained through the use of a number recorder, may at any time issue a warrant authorizing a peace officer or a public officer who has been appointed or designated to administer or enforce a federal or provincial law and whose duties include the enforcement of this Act or any other Act of Parliament and who is named in the warrant

(a) to install, maintain and remove a number recorder in relation to any telephone or telephone line; and

(b) to monitor, or to have monitored, the number recorder.

(2) Order re telephone records — When the circumstances referred to in subsection (1) exist, a justice may order that any person or body that lawfully possesses records of telephone calls originated from, or received or intended to be received at, any telephone give the records, or a copy of the records, to a person named in the order.

(3) Other provisions to apply — Subsections 492.1(2) and (3) apply to warrants and orders issued under this section, with such modifications as the circumstances require.

(4) Definition of "number recorder" — For the purposes of this section, **"number recorder"** means any device that can be used to record or identify the telephone number or location of the telephone from which a telephone call originates, or at which it is received or is intended to be received.

1993, c. 40, s. 18; 1999, c. 5, s. 19

PART XVI — COMPELLING APPEARANCE OF AN ACCUSED BEFORE A JUSTICE AND INTERIM RELEASE

Interpretation

493. Definitions — In this Part

"accused" includes

(a) a person to whom a peace officer has issued an appearance notice under section 496, and

(b) a person arrested for a criminal offence;

"appearance notice" means a notice in Form 9 issued by a peace officer;

"judge" means

(a) in the Province of Ontario, a judge of the superior court of criminal jurisdiction of the Province,

(b) in the Province of Quebec, a judge of the superior court of criminal jurisdiction of the province or three judges of the Court of Quebec,

(c) [Repealed 1992, c. 51, s. 37.],

(d) in the Provinces of Nova Scotia, New Brunswick, Manitoba, British Columbia, Prince Edward Island, Saskatchewan, Alberta and Newfoundland, a judge of the superior court of criminal jurisdiction of the Province,

(e) in the Yukon Territory and the Northwest Territories, a judge of the Supreme Court of the territory, and

(f) in Nunavut, a judge of the Nunavut Court of Justice;

"officer in charge" means the officer for the time being in command of the police force responsible for the lock-up or other place to which an accused is taken after arrest or a peace officer designated by him for the purposes of this Part who is in charge of that place at the time an accused is taken to that place to be detained in custody;

"promise to appear" means a promise in Form 10

"recognizance", when used in relation to a recognizance entered into before an officer in charge, or other peace officer, means a recognizance in Form 11, and when used in relation to a recognizance entered into before a justice or judge, means a recognizance in Form 32;

"summons" means a summons in Form 6 issued by a justice or a judge;

"undertaking" means an undertaking in Form 11.1 or 12;

"warrant", when used in relation to a warrant for the arrest of a person, means a warrant in Form 7 and, when used in relation to a warrant for the committal of a person, means a warrant in Form 8.

R.S. 1985, c. 11 (1st Supp.), Sched.; c. 27 (2d Supp.) (Sched., item 6); c. 40 (4th Supp.) (Sched.); 1990, c. 16, s. 5; c. 17, s. 12; 1992, c. 51, s. 37; 1993, c. 28, s. 78 (Sched. III, item 32) [Repealed 1999, c. 3, (Sched., item 7).]; 1994, c. 44, s. 39; 1999, c. 3, s. 30

Arrest without Warrant and Release from Custody

494. (1) Arrest without warrant by any person — Any one may arrest without warrant

(a) a person whom he finds committing an indictable offence; or

(b) a person who, on reasonable grounds, he believes

(i) has committed a criminal offence, and

(ii) is escaping from and freshly pursued by persons who have lawful authority to arrest that person.

(2) Arrest by owner, etc., of property — Any one who is

(a) the owner or a person in lawful possession of property, or

(b) a person authorized by the owner or by a person in lawful possession of property may arrest without warrant a person whom he finds committing a criminal offence on or in relation to that property.

(3) Delivery to peace officer — Any one other than a peace officer who arrests a person without warrant shall forthwith deliver the person to a peace officer.

495. (1) Arrest without warrant by peace officer — A peace officer may arrest without warrant

(a) a person who has committed an indictable offence or who, on reasonable grounds, he believes has committed or is about to commit an indictable offence,

(b) a person whom he finds committing a criminal offence, or

(c) a person in respect of whom he has reasonable grounds to believe that a warrant of arrest or committal, in any form set out in Part XXVIII in relation thereto, is in force within the territorial jurisdiction in which the person is found.

(2) Limitation — A peace officer shall not arrest a person without warrant for

(a) an indictable offence mentioned in section 553,

(b) an offence for which the person may be prosecuted by indictment or for which he is punishable on summary conviction, or

(c) an offence punishable on summary conviction,

in any case where

(d) he believes on reasonable grounds that the public interest, having regard to all the circumstances including the need to

(i) establish the identity of the person,

(ii) secure or preserve evidence of or relating to the offence, or

(iii) prevent the continuation or repetition of the offence or the commission of another offence,

may be satisfied without so arresting the person, and

(e) he has no reasonable grounds to believe that, if he does not so arrest the person, the person will fail to attend court in order to be dealt with according to law.

(3) Consequences of arrest without warrant — Notwithstanding subsection (2), a peace officer acting under subsection (1) is deemed to be acting lawfully and in the execution of his duty for the purposes of

(a) any proceedings under this or any other Act of Parliament; and

(b) any other proceedings, unless in any such proceedings it is alleged and established by the person making the allegation that the peace officer did not comply with the requirements of subsection (2).

R.S. 1985, c. 27 (1st Supp.), s. 75

496. Issue of appearance notice by peace officer — Where, by virtue of subsection 495(2), a peace officer does not arrest a person, he may issue an appearance notice to the person if the offence is

(a) an indictable offence mentioned in section 553,

(b) an offence for which the person may be prosecuted by indictment or for which he is punishable on summary conviction, or

(c) an offence punishable on summary conviction.

497. (1) Release from custody by peace officer — Subject to subsection (1.1), if a peace officer arrests a person without warrant for an offence described in paragraph 496(a), (b) or (c), the peace officer shall, as soon as practicable,

(a) release the person from custody with the intention of compelling their appearance by way of summons; or

(b) issue an appearance notice to the person and then release them.

(1.1) Exception — A peace officer shall not release a person under subsection (1) if the peace officer believes, on reasonable grounds,

(a) that it is necessary in the public interest that the person be detained in custody or that the matter of their release from custody be dealt with under another provision of this Part, having regard to all the circumstances including the need to

(i) establish the identity of the person,

(ii) secure or preserve evidence of or relating to the offence,

(iii) prevent the continuation or repetition of the offence or the commission of another offence, or

(iv) ensure the safety and security of any victim of or witness to the offence; or

(b) that if the person is released from custody, the person will fail to attend court in order to be dealt with according to law.

(2) Where subsection (1) does not apply — Subsection (1) does not apply in respect of a person who has been arrested without warrant by a peace officer for an offence described in subsection 503(3).

(3) Consequences of non-release — A peace officer who has arrested a person without warrant for an offence described in subsection (1) and who does not release the person from custody as soon as practicable in the manner described in that subsection shall be deemed to be acting lawfully and in the execution of the peace officer's duty for the purposes of

(a) any proceedings under this or any other Act of Parliament; and

(b) any other proceedings, unless in any such proceedings it is alleged and established by the person making the allegation that the peace officer did not comply with the requirements of subsection (1).

1999, c. 25, s. 3

498. (1) Release from custody by officer in charge — Subject to subsection (1.1), if a person who has been arrested without warrant by a peace officer is taken into custody, or if a person who has been arrested without warrant and delivered to a peace officer under subsection 494(3) or placed in the custody of a peace officer under subsection 163.5(3) of the *Customs Act* is detained in custody under subsection 503(1) for an offence described in paragraph 496(a), (b) or (c), or any other offence that is punishable by imprisonment for five years or less, and has not been taken before a justice or released from custody under any other provision of this Part, the officer in charge or another peace officer shall, as soon as practicable,

(a) release the person with the intention of compelling their appearance by way of summons;

(b) release the person on their giving a promise to appear;

(c) release the person on the person's entering into a recognizance before the officer in charge or another peace officer without sureties in an amount not exceeding $500 that the officer directs, but without deposit of money or other valuable security; or

(d) if the person is not ordinarily resident in the province in which the person is in custody or does not ordinarily reside within 200 kilometres of the place in which the person is in custody, release the person on the person's entering into a recognizance before the officer in charge or another peace officer without sureties in an amount not exceeding $500 that the officer directs and, if the officer so directs, on depositing with the officer a sum of money or other valuable security not exceeding in amount or value $500, that the officer directs.

(1.1) Exception — The officer in charge or the peace officer shall not release a person under subsection (1) if the officer in charge or peace officer believes, on reasonable grounds,

(a) that it is necessary in the public interest that the person be detained in custody or that the matter of their release from custody be dealt with under another provision of this Part, having regard to all the circumstances including the need to

(i) establish the identity of the person,

(ii) secure or preserve evidence of or relating to the offence,

(iii) prevent the continuation or repetition of the offence or the commission of another offence, or

(iv) ensure the safety and security of any victim of or witness to the offence; or

(b) that, if the person is released from custody, the person will fail to attend court in order to be dealt with according to law.

(2) Where subsection (1) does not apply — Subsection (1) does not apply in respect of a person who has been arrested without warrant by a peace officer for an offence described in subsection 503(3).

(3) Consequences of non-release — An officer in charge or another peace officer who has the custody of a person taken into or detained in custody for an offence described in subsection (1) and who does not release the person from custody as soon as practicable in the manner described in that subsection shall be deemed to be acting lawfully and in the execution of the officer's duty for the purposes of

(a) any proceedings under this or any other Act of Parliament; or

(b) any other proceedings, unless in any such proceedings it is alleged and established by the person making the allegation that the officer in charge or other peace officer did not comply with the requirements of subsection (1).

R.S. 1985, c. 27 (lst Supp.), s. 186; 1997, c. 18, s. 52; 1998, c. 7, s. 2; 1999, c. 25, ss. 4, 30

499. (1) Release from custody by officer in charge where arrest made with warrant — Where a person who has been arrested with a warrant by a peace officer is taken into custody for an offence other than one mentioned in section 522, the officer in charge may, if the warrant has been endorsed by a justice under subsection 507(6),

(a) release the person on the person's giving a promise to appear;

(b) release the person on the person's entering into a recognizance before the officer in charge without sureties in the amount not exceeding five hundred dollars that the officer in charge directs, but without deposit of money or other valuable security; or

(c) if the person is not ordinarily resident in the province in which the person is in custody or does not ordinarily reside within two hundred kilometres of the place in which the person is in custody, release the person on the person's entering into a recognizance before the officer in charge without sureties in the amount not exceeding five hundred dollars that the officer in charge directs and, if the officer in charge so directs, on depositing with the officer in charge such sum of money or other valuable security not exceeding in amount or value five hundred dollars, as the officer in charge directs.

(2) **Additional conditions** — In addition to the conditions for release set out in paragraphs (1)(a), (b) and (c), the officer in charge may also require the person to enter into an undertaking in Form 11.1 in which the person, in order to be released, undertakes to do one or more of the following things:

(a) to remain within a territorial jurisdiction specified in the undertaking;

(b) to notify a peace officer or another person mentioned in the undertaking of any change in his or her address, employment or occupation;

(c) to abstain from communicating, directly or indirectly, with any victim, witness or other person identified in the undertaking, or from going to a place specified in the undertaking, except in accordance with the conditions specified in the undertaking;

(d) to deposit the person's passport with the peace officer or other person mentioned in the undertaking;

(e) to abstain from possessing a firearm and to surrender any firearm in the possession of the person and any authorization, licence or registration certificate or other document enabling that person to acquire or possess a firearm;

(f) to report at the times specified in the undertaking to a peace officer or other person designated in the undertaking;

(g) to abstain from

(i) the consumption of alcohol or other intoxicating substances, or

(ii) the consumption of drugs except in accordance with a medical prescription; and

(h) to comply with any other condition specified in the undertaking that the officer in charge considers necessary to ensure the safety and security of any victim of or witness to the offence.

(3) Application to justice — A person who has entered into an undertaking under subsection (2) may, at any time before or at his or her appearance pursuant to a promise to appear or recognizance, apply to a justice for an order under subsection 515(1) to replace his or her undertaking, and section 515 applies, with such modifications as the circumstances require, to such a person.

(4) Application by prosecutor — Where a person has entered into an undertaking under subsection (2), the prosecutor may

(a) at any time before the appearance of the person pursuant to a promise to appear or recognizance, after three days notice has been given to that person, or

(b) at the appearance

apply to a justice for an order under subsection 515(2) to replace the undertaking, and section 515 applies, with such modifications as the circumstances require, to such a person.

R.S. 1985, c. 27 (lst Supp.), s. 186; 1994, c. 44, s. 40; 1997, c. 18, s. 53; 1999, c. 25, s. 5

500. Money or other valuable security to be deposited with justice — If a person has, under paragraph 498(1)(d) or 499(1)(c), deposited any sum of money or other valuable security with the officer in charge, the officer in charge shall, without delay after the deposit, cause the money or valuable security to be delivered to a justice for deposit with the justice.

1999, c. 25, s. 6

501. (1) Contents of appearance notice, promise to appear and recognizance — An appearance notice issued by a peace officer or a promise to appear given to, or a recognizance entered into before, an officer in charge or another peace officer shall

(a) set out the name of the accused;

(b) set out the substance of the offence that the accused is alleged to have committed; and

(c) require the accused to attend court at a time and place to be stated therein and to attend thereafter as required by the court in order to be dealt with according to law.

(2) Idem — An appearance notice issued by a peace officer or a promise to appear given to, or a recognizance entered into before, an officer in charge or another peace officer shall set out the text of subsections 145(5) and (6) and section 502.

(3) Attendance for purposes of Identification of Criminals Act — An appearance notice issued by a peace officer or a promise to appear given to, or a recognizance entered into before, an officer in charge or another peace officer may require the accused to appear at a time and place stated in it for the purposes of the *Identification of Criminals Act*, where the accused is alleged to have committed an indictable offence and, in the case of an offence designated as a contravention under the *Contraventions Act*, the Attorney General, within the meaning of that Act has not made an election under section 50 of that Act.

(4) Signature of accused — An accused shall be requested to sign in duplicate his appearance notice, promise to appear or recognizance and, whether or not he complies with that request, one of the duplicates shall be given to the accused, but if the accused fails or refuses to sign, the lack of his signature does not invalidate the appearance notice, promise to appear or recognizance, as the case may be.

(5) Proof of issue of appearance notice — The issue of an appearance notice by any peace officer may be proved by the oral evidence, given under oath, of the officer who issued it or by the officer's affidavit made before a justice or other person authorized to administer oaths or to take affidavits.

R.S. 1985, c. 27 (1st Supp.), s. 76; 1992, c. 47, s. 69 [Amended 1996, c. 7, s. 38.]; 1994, c. 44, s. 41

502. Failure to appear — Where an accused who is required by an appearance notice or promise to appear or by a recognizance entered into before an officer in charge or another peace officer to appear at a time and place stated therein for the purposes of the *Identification of Criminals Act* does not appear at that time and place, a justice may, where the appearance notice, promise to appear or recognizance has been confirmed by a justice under section 508, issue a warrant for the arrest of the accused for the offence with which the accused is charged.

1992, c. 47, s. 70 [Amended 1996, c. 7, s. 38.]; 1997, c. 18, s. 54

Appearance of Accused before Justice

503. (1) Taking before justice — A peace officer who arrests a person with or without warrant or to whom a person is delivered under subsection 494(3) or into whose custody a person is placed under subsection 163.5(3) of the *Customs Act* shall cause the person to be detained in custody and, in accordance with the following provisions, to be taken before a justice to be dealt with according to law:

(a) where a justice is available within a period of twenty-four hours after the person has been arrested by or delivered to the peace officer, the person shall be taken before a justice without unreasonable delay and in any event within that period, and

(b) where a justice is not available within a period of twenty-four hours after the person has been arrested by or delivered to the peace officer, the person shall be taken before a justice as soon as possible,

unless, at any time before the expiration of the time prescribed in paragraph (*a*) or (*b*) for taking the person before a justice,

(c) the peace officer or officer in charge releases the person under any other provision of this Part, or

(d) the peace officer or officer in charge is satisfied that the person should be released from custody, whether unconditionally under subsection (4) or otherwise conditionally or unconditionally, and so releases him.

(2) Conditional release — If a peace officer or an officer in charge is satisfied that a person described in subsection (1) should be released from custody conditionally, the officer may, unless the person is detained in custody for an offence mentioned in section 522, release that person on the person's giving a promise to appear or entering into a recognizance in accordance with paragraphs 498(1)(b) to (d) and subsection (2.1).

(2.1) Undertaking — In addition to the conditions referred to in subsection (2), the peace officer or officer in charge may, in order to release the person, require the person to enter into an undertaking in Form 11.1 in which the person undertakes to do one or more of the following things:

(a) to remain within a territorial jurisdiction specified in the undertaking;

(b) to notify the peace officer or another person mentioned in the undertaking of any change in his or her address, employment or occupation;

(c) to abstain from communicating, directly or indirectly, with any victim, witness or other person identified in the undertaking, or from going to a place specified in the undertaking, except in accordance with the conditions specified in the undertaking;

(d) to deposit the person's passport with the peace officer or other person mentioned in the undertaking;

(e) to abstain possessing a firearm and to surrender any firearm in the possession of the person and any authorization, licence or registration certificate or other document enabling that person to acquire or possess a firearm;

(f) to report at the times specified in the undertaking to a peace officer or other person designated in the undertaking;

(g) to abstain from

(i) the consumption of alcohol or other intoxicating substances, or

(ii) the consumption of drugs except in accordance with a medical prescription; or

(h) to comply with any other condition specified in the undertaking that the peace officer or officer in charge considers necessary to ensure the safety and security of any victim of or witness to the offence.

(2.2) Application to justice — A person who has entered into an undertaking under subsection (2.1) may, at any time before or at his or her appearance pursuant to a promise to appear or recognizance, apply to a justice for an order under subsection 515(1) to replace his or her undertaking, and section 515 applies, with such modifications as the circumstances require, to such a person.

(2.3) Application by prosecutor — Where a person has entered into an undertaking under subsection (2.1), the prosecutor may

(a) at any time before the appearance of the person pursuant to a promise to appear or recognizance, after three days notice has been given to that person, or

(b) at the appearance,

apply to justice for an order under subsection 515(2) to replace the undertaking, and section 515 applies, with such modifications as the circumstances require, to such a person.

(3) Remand in custody for return to jurisdiction where offence alleged to have been committed — Where a person has been arrested without warrant for an indictable offence alleged to have been committed in Canada outside the territorial division where the arrest took place, the person shall, within the time prescribed in paragraph (1)(a) or (b), be taken before a justice within whose jurisdiction the person was arrested unless, where the offence was alleged to have been committed within the province in which the person was arrested, the person was taken before a justice within whose jurisdiction the offence was alleged to have been committed, and the justice within whose jurisdiction the person was arrested

(a) if the justice is not satisfied that there are reasonable grounds to believe that the person arrested is the person alleged to have committed the offence, shall release that person; or

(b) if the justice is satisfied that there are reasonable grounds to believe that the person arrested is the person alleged to have committed the offence, may

(i) remand the person to the custody of a peace officer to await execution of a warrant for his or her arrest in accordance with section 528, but if no warrant is so executed within a period of six days after the time he or she is remanded to such custody, the person in whose custody he or she then is shall release him or her, or

(ii) where the offence was alleged to have been committed within the province in which the person was arrested, order the person to be taken before a justice having jurisdiction with respect to the offence.

(3.1) Interim release — Notwithstanding paragraph (3)(b), a justice may, with the consent of the prosecutor, order that the person referred to in subsection (3), pending the execution of a warrant for arrest of that person, be released

(a) unconditionally, or

(b) on any of the following terms to which the prosecutor consents, namely,

(i) giving an undertaking, including an undertaking to appear at a specified time before the court that has jurisdiction with respect to the indictable offence that the person is alleged to have committed, or

(ii) entering into a recognizance described in any of paragraphs 515(2)(a) to (e)

with such conditions described in subsection 515(4) as the justice considers desirable and to which the prosecutor consents.

(4) Release of person about to commit indictable offence — A peace officer or officer in charge having the custody of a person who has been arrested without warrant as a person about to commit an indictable offence shall release that person unconditionally as soon as practicable after he is satisfied that the continued detention of that person in custody is no longer necessary in order to prevent the commission by him of an indictable offence.

(5) Consequences of non-release — Notwithstanding subsection (4), a peace officer or officer in charge having the custody of a person referred to in that subsection who does not release the person before the expiration of the time prescribed in paragraph (1)(a) or (b) for taking the person before the justice shall be deemed to be acting lawfully and in the execution of his duty for the purposes of

(a) any proceedings under this or any other Act of Parliament; or

(b) any other proceedings, unless in such proceedings it is alleged and established by the person making the allegation that the peace officer or officer in charge did not comply with the requirements of subsection (4).

R.S. 1985, c. 27 (1st Supp.), s. 77; 1994, c. 44 s. 42; 1997, c. 18, s. 55; 1998, c. 7, s. 3; 1999, c. 25, s. 7

Information, Summons and Warrant

504. In what cases justice may receive information — Any one who, on reasonable grounds, believes that a person has committed an indictable offence may lay an information in writing and under oath before a justice, and the justice shall receive the information, where it is alleged

(a) that the person has committed, anywhere, an indictable offence that may be tried in the province in which the justice resides, and that the person

(i) is or is believed to be, or

(ii) resides or is believed to reside,

within the territorial jurisdiction of the justice;

(b) that the person, wherever he may be, has committed an indictable offence within the territorial jurisdiction of the justice;

(c) that the person has, anywhere, unlawfully received property that was unlawfully obtained within the territorial jurisdiction of the justice; or

(d) that the person has in his possession stolen property within the territorial jurisdiction of the justice.

505. Time within which information to be laid in certain cases — Where

(a) an appearance notice has been issued to an accused under section 496, or

(b) an accused has been released from custody under section 497 or 498,

an information relating to the offence alleged to have been committed by the accused or relating to an included or other offence alleged to have been committed by him shall be laid before a justice as soon as practicable thereafter and in any event before the time stated in the appearance notice, promise to appear or recognizance issued to or given or entered into by the accused for his attendance in court.

506. Form — An information laid under section 504 or 505 may be in Form 2.

507. (1) Justice to hear informant and witnesses — Subject to subsection 523(1.1), a justice who receives an information, other than an information laid before the justice under section 505, shall, except where an accused has already been arrested with or without a warrant,

(a) hear and consider, *ex parte*,

(i) the allegations of the informant, and

(ii) the evidence of witnesses, where he considers it desirable or necessary to do so; and

(b) where he considers that a case for so doing is made out, issue, in accordance with this section, either a summons or a warrant for the arrest of the accused to compel the accused to attend before him or some other justice for the same territorial division to answer to a charge of an offence.

(2) Process compulsory — No justice shall refuse to issue a summons or warrant by reason only that the alleged offence is one for which a person may be arrested without warrant.

(3) Procedure when witnesses attend — A justice who hears the evidence of a witness pursuant to subsection (1) shall

(a) take the evidence on oath; and

(b) cause the evidence to be taken in accordance with section 540 in so far as that section is capable of being applied.

(4) Summons to be issued except in certain cases — Where the justice considers that a case is made out for compelling an accused to attend before him to answer to a charge of an offence, he shall issue a summons to the accused unless the allegations of the informant or the evidence of any witness or witnesses taken in accordance with subsection (3) disclose reasonable grounds to believe that it is necessary in the public interest to issue a warrant for the arrest of the accused.

(5) No process in blank — A justice shall not sign a summons or warrant in blank.

(6) Endorsement of warrant by justice — A justice who issues a warrant under this section or section 508 or 512 may, unless the offence is one mentioned in section 522, authorize the release of the accused pursuant to section 499 by making an endorsement on the warrant in Form 29.

(7) Promise to appear or recognizance deemed to have been confirmed — Where, pursuant to subsection (6), a justice authorizes the release of an accused pursuant to section 499, a promise to appear given by the accused or a recognizance entered into by the accused pursuant to that section shall be deemed, for the purposes of subsection 145(5), to have been confirmed by a justice under section 508.

(8) Issue of summons or warrant — Where, on an appeal from or review of any decision or matter of jurisdiction, a new trial or hearing or a continuance or renewal of a trial or hearing is ordered, a justice may issue either a summons or a warrant for the arrest of the accused in order to compel the accused to attend at the new or continued or renewed trial or hearing.

R.S. 1985, c. 27 (1st Supp.), s. 78; 1994, c. 44, s. 43

508. (1) Justice to hear informant and witnesses — A justice who receives an information laid before him under section 505 shall

(a) hear and consider, *ex parte*,

(i) the allegations of the informant, and

(ii) the evidence of witnesses, where he considers it desirable or necessary to do so;

(b) where he considers that a case for so doing is made out, whether the information relates to the offence alleged in the appearance notice, promise to appear or recognizance or to an included or other offence,

(i) confirm the appearance notice, promise to appear or recognizance, as the case may be, and endorse the information accordingly, or

(ii) cancel the appearance notice, promise to appear or recognizance, as the case may be, and issue, in accordance with section 507, either a summons or a warrant for the arrest of the accused to compel the accused to attend before him or some other justice for the same territorial division to answer to a charge of an offence and endorse on the summons or warrant that the appearance notice, promise to appear or recognizance, as the case may be, has been cancelled; and

(c) where he considers that a case is not made out for the purposes of paragraph (b), cancel the appearance notice, promise to appear or recognizance, as the case may be, and cause the accused to be notified forthwith of such cancellation.

(2) Procedure when witnesses attend — A justice who hears the evidence of a witness pursuant to subsection (1) shall

(a) take the evidence upon oath; and

(b) cause the evidence to be taken in accordance with section 540 in so far as that section is capable of being applied.

R.S. 1985, c. 27 (1st Supp.), s. 79.

508.1 (1) Information laid otherwise than in person — For the purposes of sections 504 to 508, a peace officer may lay an information by any means of telecommunication that produces a writing.

(2) Alternative to oath — A peace officer who uses a means of telecommunication referred to in subsection (1) shall, instead of swearing an oath, make a statement in writing stating that all matters contained in the information are true to the officer's knowledge and belief, and such a statement is deemed to be a statement made under oath.

1997, c. 18, s. 56

509. (1) Summons — A summons issued under this Part shall

(a) be directed to the accused;

(b) set out briefly the offence in respect of which the accused is charged; and

(c) require the accused to attend court at a time and place to be stated therein and to attend thereafter as required by the court in order to be dealt with according to law.

(2) Service on individual — A summons shall be served by a peace officer who shall deliver it personally to the person to whom it is directed or, if that person cannot conveniently be found, shall leave it for him at his latest or usual place of abode with an inmate thereof who appears to be at least sixteen years of age.

(3) Proof of service — Service of a summons may be proved by the oral evidence, given under oath, of the peace officer who served it or by his affidavit made before a justice or other person authorized to administer oaths or to take affidavits.

(4) Content of summons — There shall be set out in every summons the text of subsection 145(4) and section 510.

(5) Attendance for purposes of Identification of Criminals Act — A summons may require the accused to appear at a time and place stated in it for the purposes of the *Identification of Criminals Act*, where the accused is alleged to have committed an indictable offence and, in the case of an offence designated as a contravention under the *Contraventions Act*, the Attorney General, within the meaning of that Act, has not made an election under section 50 of that Act.

R.S. 1985, c. 27 (1st Supp.), s. 80; 1992, c. 47, s. 71 [Amended 1996, c. 7, s. 38.]

510. Failure to appear — Where an accused who is required by a summons to appear at a time and place stated in it for the purposes of the *Identification of Criminals Act* does not appear at that time and place and, in the case of an offence designated as a contravention under the *Contraventions Act*, the Attorney General, within the meaning of that Act, has not made an election under section 50 of that Act, a justice may issue a warrant for the arrest of the accused for the offence with which the accused is charged.

1992, c. 47, s. 72 [Amended 1996, c. 7, s. 38.]

511. (1) Contents of warrant to arrest — A warrant issued under this Part shall

(a) name or describe the accused;

(b) set out briefly the offence in respect of which the accused is charged; and

(c) order that the accused be forthwith arrested and brought before the judge or justice who issued the warrant or before some other judge or justice having jurisdiction in the same territorial division, to be dealt with according to law.

(2) No return day — A warrant issued under this Part remains in force until it is executed, and need not be made returnable at any particular time.

(3) Discretion to postpone execution — Notwithstanding paragraph (1)(*c*), a judge or justice who issues a warrant may specify in the warrant the period before which the warrant shall not be executed, to allow the accused to appear voluntarily before a judge or justice having jurisdiction in the territorial division in which the warrant was issued.

(4) Deemed execution of warrant — Where the accused appears voluntarily for the offence in respect of which the accused is charged, the warrant is deemed to be executed.

R.S. 1985, c. 27 (1st Supp.), s. 81; 1997, c. 18, s. 57.

512. (1) Certain actions not to preclude issue of warrant — A justice may, where the justice has reasonable grounds to believe that it is necessary in the public interest to issue a summons or a warrant for the arrest of the accused, issue a summons or a warrant notwithstanding that

(a) an appearance notice or a promise to appear or a recognizance entered into before an officer in charge or another peace officer has been confirmed or cancelled under subsection 508(1);

(b) a summons has previously been issued under subsection 507(4); or

(c) the accused has been released unconditionally or with the intention of compelling his appearance by way of summons.

(2) Warrant in default of appearance — Where

(a) service of a summons is proved and the accused fails to attend court in accordance with the summons,

(b) an appearance notice or a promise to appear or a recognizance entered into before an officer in charge or another peace officer has been confirmed under subsection 508(1) and the accused fails to attend court in accordance therewith in order to be dealt with according to law, or

(c) it appears that a summons cannot be served because the accused is evading service,

a justice may issue a warrant for the arrest of the accused.

R.S. 1985, c. 27 (1st Supp.), s.82; 1997, c. 18, s. 58.

513. Formalities of warrant — A warrant in accordance with this Part shall be directed to the peace officers within the territorial jurisdiction of the justice, judge or court by whom or by which it is issued.

514. (1) Execution of warrant — A warrant in accordance with this Part may be executed by arresting the accused

(a) wherever he is found within the territorial jurisdiction of the justice, judge or court by whom or by which the warrant was issued; or

(b) wherever he is found in Canada, in the case of fresh pursuit.

(2) By whom warrant may be executed — A warrant in accordance with this Part may be executed by a person who is one of the peace officers to whom it is directed, whether or not the place in which the warrant is to be executed is within the territory for which the person is a peace officer.

Judicial Interim Release

515. (1) Order of release — Subject to this section, where an accused who is charged with an offence other than an offence listed in section 469 is taken before a justice the justice shall, unless a plea of guilty by the accused is accepted, order, in respect of that offence, that the accused be released on his giving an undertaking without conditions, unless the prosecutor, having been given a reasonable opportunity to do so, shows cause, in respect of that offence, why the detention of the accused in custody is justified or why an order under any other provision of this section should be made and where the justice makes an order under any other provision of this section, the order shall refer only to the particular offence for which the accused was taken before the justice.

(2) Release on undertaking with conditions, etc. — Where the justice does not make an order under subsection (1), he shall, unless the prosecutor shows cause why the detention of the accused is justified, order that the accused be released

(a) on his giving an undertaking with such conditions as the justice directs;

(b) on his entering into a recognizance before the justice, without sureties, in such amount and with such conditions, if any, as the justice directs but without deposit of money or other valuable security;

(c) on his entering into a recognizance before the justice with sureties in such amount and with such conditions, if any, as the justice directs but without deposit of money or other valuable security;

(d) with the consent of the prosecutor, on his entering into a recognizance before the justice, without sureties, in such amount and with such conditions, if any, as the justice directs and on his depositing with the justice such sum of money or other valuable security as the justice directs, or

(e) if the accused is not ordinarily resident in the province in which the accused is in custody or does not ordinarily reside within two hundred kilometres of the place in which he is in custody, on his entering into a recognizance before the justice with or without sureties in such amount and with such conditions, if any, as the justice directs, and on his depositing with the justice such sum of money or other valuable security as the justice directs.

(2.1) Power of justice to name sureties in order — Where, pursuant to subsection (2) or any other provision of this Act, a justice, judge or court orders that an accused be released on his entering into a recognizance with sureties, the justice, judge or court may, in the order, name particular persons as sureties.

(2.2) Alternative to physical presence — Where, by this Act, the appearance of an accused is required for the purposes of judicial interim release, the appearance shall be by actual physical attendance of the accused but the justice may, subject to subsection (2.3), allow the accused to appear by means of any suitable telecommunication device, including telephone, that is satisfactory to the justice.

(2.3) Where consent required — The consent of the prosecutor and the accused is required for the purposes of an appearance if the evidence of a witness is to be taken at the appearance and the accused cannot appear by closed-circuit television or any other means that allow the court and the accused to engage in simultaneous visual and oral communication.

(3) Release on undertaking with conditions etc. — The justice shall not make an order under any of paragraphs (2)(b) to (e) unless the prosecution shows cause why an order under the immediately preceding paragraph should not be made.

(4) Conditions authorized — The justice may direct as conditions under subsection (2) that the accused shall do any one or more of the following things as specified in the order:

(a) report at times to be stated in the order to a peace officer or other person designated in the order;

(b) remain within a territorial jurisdiction specified in the order;

(c) notify the peace officer or other person designated under paragraph (a) of any change in his address or his employment or occupation;

(d) abstain from communicating, directly or indirectly, with any victim, witness or other person identified in the order, or refrain from going to any place specified in the order, except in accordance with the conditions specified in the order that the justice considers necessary;

(e) where the accused is the holder of a passport, deposit his passport as specified in the order;

(e.1) comply with any other condition specified in the order that the justice considers necessary to ensure the safety and security of any victim of or witness to the offence; and

(f) comply with such other reasonable conditions specified in the order as the justice considers desirable.

(4.1) Condition prohibiting possession of firearms, etc. — When making an order under subsection (2), in the case of an accused who is charged with

(a) an offence in the commission of which violence against a person was used, threatened or attempted,

(b) an offence under section 264 (criminal harassment),

(c) an offence relating to the contravention of subsection 5(3) or (4) or 6(3) or 7(2) of the *Controlled Drugs and Substances Act*, or

(d) an offence that involves, or the subject-matter of which is, a firearm, a cross-bow, a prohibited weapon, a restricted weapon, a prohibited device, ammunition, prohibited ammunition or an explosive substance,

the justice shall add to the order a condition prohibiting the accused from possessing a firearm, cross-bow, prohibited weapon, restricted weapon, prohibited device, ammunition, prohibited ammunition or explosive substance, or all those things, until the accused is dealt with according to law unless the justice considers that such a condition is not required in the interests of the safety of the accused or the safety and security of a victim of the offence or of any other person.

(4.11) Surrender, etc. — Where the justice adds a condition described in subsection (4.1) to an order made under subsection (2), the justice shall specify in the order the manner and method by which

(a) the things referred to in subsection (4.1) that are in the possession of the accused shall be surrendered, disposed of, detained, stored or dealt with; and

(b) the authorizations, licences and registration certificates held by the person shall be surrendered.

(4.12) Reasons — Where the justice does not add a condition described in subsection (4.1) to an order made under subsection (2), the justice shall include in the record a statement of the reasons for not adding the condition.

(4.2) Additional conditions — Before making an order under subsection (2), in the case of an accused who is charged with an offence described in section 264, or an offence in the commission of which violence against a person was used, threatened or attempted, the justice shall consider whether it is desirable, in the interests of the safety and security of any person, particularly a victim of or witness to the offence, to include as a condition of the order

(a) that the accused abstain from communicating, directly or indirectly, with any victim, witness or other person identified in the order, or refrain from going to any place specified in the order; or

(b) that the accused comply with any other condition specified in the order that the justice considers necessary to ensure the safety and security of those persons.

(5) Detention in custody — Where the prosecutor shows cause why the detention of the accused in custody is justified, the justice shall order that the accused be detained in custody until he is dealt with according to law and shall include in the record a statement of his reasons for making the order.

(6) Order of detention — Notwithstanding any provision of this section, where an accused is charged

(a) with an indictable offence, other than an offence listed in section 469,

(i) that is alleged to have been committed while at large after being released in respect of another indictable offence pursuant to the provisions of this Part or section 679 or 680, or

(ii) that is an offence under section 467.1 or an offence under this or any other Act of Parliament alleged to have been committed for the benefit of, at the direction of or in association with a criminal organization for which the maximum punishment is imprisonment for five years or more,

(b) with an indictable offence, other than an offence listed in section 469 and is not ordinarily resident in Canada,

(c) with an offence under any of subsections 145(2) to (5) that is alleged to have been committed while he was at large after being released in respect of another offence pursuant to the provisions of this Part or section 679, 680 or 816, or

(d) with having committed an offence punishable by imprisonment for life under subsection 5(3), 6(3) or 7(2) of the *Controlled Drugs and Substances Act* or the offence of conspiring to commit such an offence,

the justice shall order that the accused be detained in custody until he is dealt with according to law, unless the accused, having been given a reasonable opportunity to do so, shows cause why his detention in custody is not justified, but where the justice orders that the accused be released, he shall include in the record a statement of his reasons for making the order.

(7) Order of release — Where an accused to whom paragraph 6(a), (c) or (d) applies shows cause why the accused's detention in custody is not justified, the justice shall order that the accused be released on giving an undertaking or entering into a recognizance described in any of paragraphs (2)(a) to (e) with the conditions described in subsections (4) to (4.2) or, where the accused was at large on an undertaking or recognizance with conditions, the additional conditions described in subsections (4) to (4.2), that the justice considers desirable, unless the accused, having been given a reasonable opportunity to do so, shows cause why the conditions or additional conditions should not be imposed.

(8) Idem — Where an accused to whom paragraph (6)(b) applies shows cause why the accused's detention in custody is not justified, the justice shall order that the accused be released on giving an undertaking or entering into a recognizance described in any of paragraphs (2)(a) to (e) with the conditions, described in subsections (4) to (4.2), that the justice considers desirable.

(9) Sufficiency of record — For the purposes of subsections (5) and (6), it is sufficient if a record is made of the reasons in accordance with the provisions of Part XVIII relating to the taking of evidence at preliminary inquiries.

(10) Justification for detention in custody — For the purposes of this section, the detention of an accused in custody is justified only on one or more of the following grounds:

    (a) where the detention is necessary to ensure his or her attendance in court in order to be dealt with according to law;

    (b) where the detention is necessary for the protection or safety of the public, including any victim of or witness to the offence, having regard to all the circumstances including any substantial likelihood that the accused will, if released from custody, commit a criminal offence or interfere with the administration of justice; and

    (c) on any other just cause being shown and without limiting the generality of the foregoing, where the detention is necessary in order to maintain confidence in the administration of justice, having regard to all the circumstances, including the apparent strength of the prosecution's case, the gravity of the nature of the offence, the circumstances surrounding its commission and the potential for a lengthy term of imprisonment.

(11) Detention in custody for offence mentioned in s. 469 — Where an accused who is charged with an offence mentioned in section 469 is taken before a justice, the justice shall order that the accused be detained in custody until he is dealt with according to law and shall issue a warrant in Form 8 for the committal of the accused.

(12) Order re no communication — A justice who orders that an accused be detained in custody under this section may include in the order a direction that the accused abstain from communicating, directly or indirectly, with any victim, witness or other person identified in the order, except in accordance with such conditions specified in the order as the justice considers necessary.

R.S. 1985, c. 27 (1st Supp.), ss. 83, 186; 1991, c. 40, s. 31; 1993, c. 45, s. 8; 1994, c. 44, s. 44; 1995, c. 39, ss. 153, 188(b); 1996, c. 19, ss. 71, 93.3; 1997, c. 18, s. 59; c. 23, s. 16; 1999, c. 5, s. 21; 1999, c. 25, s. 8

515.1 Variation of undertaking or recognizance — An undertaking or recognizance pursuant to which the accused was released that has been entered into under section 499, 503 or 515 may, with the written consent of the prosecutor, be varied, and where so varied, is deemed to have been entered into pursuant to section 515.

1997, c. 18, s. 60

516. (1) Remand in custody — A justice may, before or at any time during the course of any proceedings under section 515, on application by the prosecutor or the accused, adjourn the proceedings and remand the accused to custody in prison by warrant in Form 19, but no adjournment shall be for more than three clear days except with the consent of the accused.

(2) Detention pending bail hearing — A justice who remands an accused to custody under subsection (1) or subsection 515(11) may order that the accused abstain from communicating, directly or indirectly, with any victim, witness or other person identified in the order, except in accordance with any conditions specified in the order that the justice considers necessary.

1999, c. 5, s. 22; 1999, c. 25, s. 31(3)

517. (1) Order directing matters not to be published for specified period — Where the prosecutor or the accused intends to show cause under section 515, he shall so state to the justice and the justice may, and shall on application by the accused, before or at any time during the course of the proceedings under that section, make an order directing that the evidence taken, the information given or the representations made and the reasons, if any, given or to be given by the justice shall not be published in any newspaper or broadcast before such time as

(a) if a preliminary inquiry is held, the accused in respect of whom the proceedings are held is discharged; or

(b) if the accused in respect of whom the proceedings are held is tried or committed for trial, the trial is ended.

(2) Failure to comply — Every one who fails without lawful excuse, the proof of which lies on him, to comply with an order made under subsection (1) is guilty of an offence punishable on summary conviction.

(3) "newspaper" — In this section, **"newspaper"** has the same meaning as in section 297.

R.S. 1985, c. 27 (1st Supp.), s. 101(2).

518. (1) Inquiries to be made by justice and evidence — In any proceedings under section 515,

(a) the justice may, subject to paragraph (*b*), make such inquiries, on oath or otherwise, of and concerning the accused as he considers desirable;

(b) the accused shall not be examined by the justice or any other person except counsel for the accused respecting the offence with which the accused is charged, and no inquiry shall be made of the accused respecting that offence by way of cross-examination unless the accused has testified respecting the offence;

(c) the prosecutor may, in addition to any other relevant evidence, lead evidence

(i) to prove that the accused has previously been convicted of a criminal offence,

(ii) to prove that the accused has been charged with and is awaiting trial for another criminal offence,

(iii) to prove that the accused has previously committed an offence under section 145, or

(iv) to show the circumstances of the alleged offence, particularly as they relate to the probability of conviction of the accused;

(d) the justice may take into consideration any relevant matters agreed on by the prosecutor and the accused or his counsel;

(d.1) the justice may receive evidence obtained as a result of an interception of a private communication under and within the meaning of Part VI, in writing, orally or in the form of a recording and, for the purposes of this section, subsection 189(5) does not apply to such evidence;

(d.2) the justice shall take into consideration any evidence submitted regarding the need to ensure the safety or security of any victim of or witness to an offence; and

(e) the justice may receive and base his decision on evidence considered credible or trustworthy by him in the circumstances of each case.

(2) Release pending sentence — Where, before or at any time during the course of any proceedings under section 515, the accused pleads guilty and that plea is accepted, the justice may make any order provided for in this Part for the release of the accused until the accused is sentenced.

R.S. 1985, c. 27 (1st Supp.), s. 84; 1994, c. 44, s. 45; 1999, c. 25, s. 9

519. (1) Release of accused — Where a justice makes an order under subsection 515(1), (2), (7) or (8),

(a) if the accused thereupon complies with the order, the justice shall direct that the accused be released

(i) forthwith, if the accused is not required to be detained in custody in respect of any other matter, or

(ii) as soon thereafter as the accused is no longer required to be detained in custody in respect of any other matter; and

(b) if the accused does not thereupon comply with the order, the justice who made the order or another justice having jurisdiction shall issue a warrant for the committal of the accused and may endorse thereon an authorization to the person having the custody of the accused to release the accused when the accused complies with the order

(i) forthwith after the compliance, if the accused is not required to be detained in custody in respect of any other matter, or

(ii) as soon thereafter as the accused is no longer required to be detained in custody in respect of any other matter

and if the justice so endorses the warrant, he shall attach to it a copy of the order.

(2) Discharge from custody — Where the accused complies with an order referred to in paragraph (1)(b), and is not required to be detained in custody in respect of any other matter, the justice who made the order or another justice having jurisdiction shall, unless the accused has been or will be released pursuant to an authorization referred to in that paragraph, issue an order for discharge in Form 39.

(3) Warrant for committal — Where the justice makes an order under subsection 515(5) or (6) for the detention of the accused, he shall issue a warrant for the committal of the accused.

R.S. 1985, c. 27 (1st Supp.), s. 85.

520. (1) Review of order — If a justice, or a judge of the Nunavut Court of Justice, makes an order under subsection 515(2), (5), (6), (7), (8) or (12) or makes or vacates any order under paragraph 523(2)(*b*), the accused may, at any time before the trial of the charge, apply to a judge for a review of the order.

(2) Notice to prosecutor — An application under this section shall not, unless the prosecutor otherwise consents, be heard by a judge unless the accused has given to the prosecutor at least two clear days notice in writing of the application.

(3) Accused to be present — If the judge so orders or the prosecutor or the accused or his counsel so requests, the accused shall be present at the hearing of an application under this section and, where the accused is in custody, the judge may order, in writing, the person having the custody of the accused to bring him before the court.

(4) Adjournment of proceedings — A judge may, before or at any time during the hearing of an application under this section, on application by the prosecutor or the accused, adjourn the proceedings, but if the accused is in custody no adjournment shall be for more than three clear days except with the consent of the accused.

(5) Failure of accused to attend — Where an accused, other than an accused who is in custody, has been ordered by a judge to be present at the hearing of an application under this section and does not attend the hearing, the judge may issue a warrant for the arrest of the accused.

(6) Execution — A warrant issued under subsection (5) may be executed anywhere in Canada.

(7) Evidence and powers of judge on review — On the hearing of an application under this section, the judge may consider

    (a) the transcript, if any, of the proceedings heard by the justice and by any judge who previously reviewed the order made by the justice,

    (b) the exhibits, if any, filed in the proceedings before the justice, and

    (c) such additional evidence or exhibits as may be tendered by the accused or the prosecutor,

and shall either

    (d) dismiss the application, or

    (e) if the accused shows cause, allow the application, vacate the order previously made by the justice and make any other order provided for in section 515 that he considers is warranted.

(8) Limitation of further applications — Where an application under this section or section 521 has been heard, a further or other application under this section or section 521 shall not be made with respect to that same accused, except with leave of a judge, prior to the expiration of thirty days from the date of the decision of the judge who heard the previous application.

(9) Application of ss. 517, 518 and 519 — The provisions of sections 517, 518 and 519 apply with such modifications as the circumstances require in respect of an application under this section.

R.S. 1985, c. 27 (1st Supp.), s. 86; 1994, c. 44, s. 46; 1999, c. 3, s. 31

521. (1) Review of order — If a justice, or a judge of the Nunavut Court of Justice, makes an order under subsection 515(1), (2), (7), (8) or (12) or makes or vacates any order under paragraph 523(2)(*b*), the prosecutor may, at any time before the trial of the charge, apply to a judge for a review of the order.

(2) Notice to accused — An application under this section shall not be heard by a judge unless the prosecutor has given to the accused at least two clear days notice in writing of the application.

(3) Accused to be present — If the judge so orders or the prosecutor or the accused or his counsel so requests, the accused shall be present at the hearing of an application under this section and, where the accused is in custody, the judge may order, in writing, the person having the custody of the accused to bring him before the court.

(4) Adjournment of proceedings — A judge may, before or at any time during the hearing of an application under this section, on application of the prosecutor or the accused, adjourn the proceedings, but if the accused is in custody no such adjournment shall be for more than three clear days except with the consent of the accused.

(5) Failure of accused to attend — Where an accused, other than an accused who is in custody, has been ordered by a judge to be present at the hearing of an application under this section and does not attend the hearing, the judge may issue a warrant for the arrest of the accused.

(6) Warrant for detention — Where, pursuant to paragraph (8)(*e*), the judge makes an order that the accused be detained in custody until he is dealt with according to law, he shall, if the accused is not in custody, issue a warrant for the committal of the accused.

(7) Execution — A warrant issued under subsection (5) or (6) may be executed anywhere in Canada.

(8) Evidence and powers of judge on review — On the hearing of an application under this section, the judge may consider

    (a) the transcript, if any, of the proceedings heard by the justice and by any judge who previously reviewed the order made by the justice,

    (b) the exhibits, if any, filed in the proceedings before the justice, and

(c) such additional evidence or exhibits as may be tendered by the prosecutor or the accused,

and shall either

(d) dismiss the application, or

(e) if the prosecutor shows cause, allow the application, vacate the order previously made by the justice and make any other order provided for in section 515 that he considers to be warranted.

(9) Limitation of further applications — Where an application under this section or section 520 has been heard, a further or other application under this section or section 520 shall not be made with respect to the same accused, except with leave of a judge, prior to the expiration of thirty days from the date of the decision of the judge who heard the previous application.

(10) Application of ss. 517, 518 and 519 — The provisions of sections 517, 518 and 519 apply with such modifications as the circumstances require in respect of an application under this section.

R.S. 1985, c. 27 (1st Supp.), s. 87; 1994, c. 44, s. 47; 1999, c. 3, s. 32

522. (1) Interim release by judge only — Where an accused is charged with an offence listed in section 469, no court, judge or justice, other than a judge of or a judge presiding in a superior court of criminal jurisdiction for the province in which the accused is so charged, may release the accused before or after the accused has been ordered to stand trial.

(2) Idem — Where an accused is charged with an offence listed in section 469, a judge of or a judge presiding in a superior court of criminal jurisdiction for the province in which the accused is charged shall order that the accused be detained in custody unless the accused, having been given a reasonable opportunity to do so, shows cause why his detention in custody is not justified within the meaning of subsection 515(10).

(2.1) Order re no communication — A judge referred to in subsection (2) who orders that an accused be detained in custody under this section may include in the order a direction that the accused abstain from communicating, directly or indirectly, with any victim, witness or other person identified in the order except in accordance with such conditions specified in the order as the judge considers necessary.

(3) Release of accused — If the judge does not order that the accused be detained in custody under subsection (2), the judge may order that the accused be released on giving an undertaking or entering into a recognizance described in any of paragraphs 515(2)(a) to (e) with such conditions described in subsections 515(4), (4.1) and (4.2) as the judge considers desirable.

(4) Order not reviewable except under s. 680 — An order made under this section is not subject to review, except as provided in section 680.

(5) Application of ss. 517, 518 and 519 — The provisions of sections 517, 518 except subsection (2) thereof, and 519 apply with such modifications as the circumstances require in respect of an application for an order under subsection (2).

(6) Other offences — Where an accused is charged with an offence mentioned in section 469 and with any other offence, a judge acting under this section may apply the provisions of this Part respecting judicial interim release to that other offence.

R.S. 1985, c. 27 (1st Supp.), s. 88; 1991, c. 40, s. 32; 1994, c. 44, s. 48; 1999, c. 25, s. 10

523. (1) Period for which appearance notice, etc., continues in force — Where an accused, in respect of an offence with which he is charged, has not been taken into custody or has been released from custody under or by virtue of any provision of this Part, the appearance notice, promise to appear, summons, undertaking or recognizance issued to, given or entered into by the accused continues in force, subject to its terms, and applies in respect of any new information charging the same offence or an included offence that was received after the appearance notice, promise to appear, summons, undertaking or recognizance was issued, given or entered into,

(a) where the accused was released from custody pursuant to an order of a judge made under subsection 522(3), until his trial is completed; or

(b) in any other case,

(i) until his trial is completed, and

(ii) where the accused is, at his trial, determined to be guilty of the offence, until a sentence within the meaning of section 673 is imposed on the accused unless, at the time the accused is determined to be guilty, the court, judge or justice orders that the accused be taken into custody pending such sentence.

(1.1) Where new information charging same offence — Where an accused, in respect of an offence with which he is charged, has not been taken into custody or is being detained or has been released from custody under or by virtue of any provision of this Part and after the order for interim release or detention has been made, or the appearance notice, promise to appear, summons, undertaking or recognizance has been issued, given or entered into, a new information charging the same offence or an included offence, is received, section 507 or 508, as the case may be, does not apply in respect of the new information and the order for interim release or detention of the accused and the appearance notice, promise to appear, summons, undertaking or recognizance, if any, applies in respect of the new information.

(2) Order vacating previous order for release or detention — Notwithstanding subsections (1) and (1.1),

(a) the court, judge or justice before whom an accused is being tried, at any time,

(b) the justice, on completion of the preliminary inquiry in relation to an offence for which an accused is ordered to stand trial, other than an offence listed in section 469, or

(c) with the consent of the prosecutor and the accused or, where the accused or the prosecutor applies to vacate an order that would otherwise apply pursuant to subsection (1.1), without such consent, at any time

(i) where the accused is charged with an offence other than an offence listed in section 469, the justice by whom an order was made under this Part or any other justice,

(ii) where the accused is charged with an offence listed in section 469, a judge of or a judge presiding in a superior court of criminal jurisdiction for the province, or

(iii) the court, judge or justice before which or whom an accused is to be tried,

may, on cause being shown, vacate any order previously made under this Part for the interim release or detention of the accused and make any other order provided for in this Part for the detention or release of the accused until his trial is completed that the court, judge or justice considers to be warranted.

(3) Provisions applicable to proceedings under subsection (2) — The provisions of sections 517, 518 and 519 apply, with such modifications as the circumstances require, in respect of any proceedings under subsection (2), except that subsection 518(2) does not apply in respect of an accused who is charged with an offence listed in section 469.

R.S. 1985, c. 27 (1st Supp.), s. 89.

Arrest of Accused on Interim Release

524. (1) Issue of warrant for arrest of accused — Where a justice is satisfied that there are reasonable grounds to believe that an accused

(a) has contravened or is about to contravene any summons, appearance notice, promise to appear, undertaking or recognizance that was issued or given to him or entered into by him, or

(b) has committed an indictable offence after any summons, appearance notice, promise to appear, undertaking or recognizance was issued or given to him or entered into by him,

he may issue a warrant for the arrest of the accused.

(2) Arrest of accused without warrant — Notwithstanding anything in this Act, a peace officer who believes on reasonable grounds that an accused

(a) has contravened or is about to contravene any summons, appearance notice, promise to appear, undertaking or recognizance that was issued or given to him or entered into by him, or

(b) has committed an indictable offence after any summons, appearance notice, promise to appear, undertaking or recognizance was issued or given to him or entered into by him,

may arrest the accused without warrant.

(3) Hearing — Where an accused who has been arrested with a warrant issued under subsection (1), or who has been arrested under subsection (2), is taken before a justice, the justice shall

(a) where the accused was released from custody pursuant to an order made under subsection 522(3) by a judge of the superior court of criminal jurisdiction of any province, order that the accused be taken before a judge of that court; or

(b) in any other case, hear the prosecutor and his witnesses, if any, and the accused and his witnesses, if any.

(4) Detention of accused — Where an accused described in paragraph (3)(a) is taken before a judge and the judge finds

(a) that the accused has contravened or had been about to contravene his summons, appearance notice, promise to appear, undertaking or recognizance, or

(b) that there are reasonable grounds to believe that the accused has committed an indictable offence after any summons, appearance notice, promise to appear, undertaking or recognizance was issued or given to him or entered into by him,

he shall cancel the summons, appearance notice, promise to appear, undertaking or recognizance and order that the accused be detained in custody unless the accused, having been given a reasonable opportunity to do so, shows cause why his detention in custody is not justified within the meaning of subsection 515(10).

(5) Release of accused — Where the judge does not order that the accused be detained in custody pursuant to subsection (4), he may order that the accused be released upon his giving an undertaking or entering into a recognizance described in any of paragraphs 515(2)(a) to (e) with such conditions described in subsection 515(4) or, where the accused was at large on an undertaking or a recognizance with conditions, such additional conditions, described in subsection 515(4), as the judge considers desirable.

(6) Order not reviewable — Any order made under subsection (4) or (5) is not subject to review, except as provided in section 680.

(7) Release of accused — Where the judge does not make a finding under paragraph (4)(a) or (b), he shall order that the accused be released from custody.

(8) Powers of justice after hearing — Where an accused described in subsection (3), other than an accused to whom paragraph (a) of that subsection applies, is taken before the justice and the justice finds

(a) that the accused has contravened or had been about to contravene his summons, appearance notice, promise to appear, undertaking or recognizance, or

(b) that there are reasonable grounds to believe that the accused has committed an indictable offence after any summons, appearance notice, promise to appear, undertaking or recognizance was issued or given to him or entered into by him,

he shall cancel the summons, appearance notice, promise to appear, undertaking or recognizance and order that the accused be detained in custody unless the accused, having been given a reasonable opportunity to do so, shows cause why his detention in custody is not justified within the meaning of subsection 515(10).

(9) Release of accused — Where the accused shows cause why his detention in custody is not justified within the meaning of subsection 515(10), the justice shall order that the accused be released on his giving an undertaking or entering into a recognizance described in any of paragraphs 515(2)(a) to (e) with such conditions, described in subsection 515(4), as the justice considers desirable.

(10) Reasons — Where the justice makes an order under subsection (9), he shall include in the record a statement of his reasons for making the order, and subsection 515(9) is applicable with such modification as the circumstances require in respect thereof.

(11) Where justice to order that accused be released — Where the justice does not make a finding under paragraph (8)(a) or (b), he shall order that the accused be released from custody.

(12) Provisions applicable to proceedings under this section — The provisions of sections 517, 518 and 519 apply with such modifications as the circumstances require in respect of any proceedings under this section, except that subsection 518(2) does not apply in respect of an accused who is charged with an offence mentioned in section 522.

(13) Certain provisions applicable to order under this section — Section 520 applies in respect of any order made under subsection (8) or (9) as though the order were an order made by a justice or a judge of the Nunavut Court of Justice under subsection 515(2) or (5), and section 521 applies in respect of any order made under subsection (9) as though the order were an order made by a justice or a judge of the Nunavut Court of Justice under subsection 515(2).

1999, c. 3, s. 33

Review of Detention where Trial Delayed

525. (1) Time for application to judge — Where an accused who has been charged with an offence other than an offence listed in section 469 and who is not required to be detained in custody in respect of any other matter is being detained in custody pending his trial for that offence and the trial has not commenced

    (a) in the case of an indictable offence, within ninety days from

        (i) the day on which the accused was taken before a justice under section 503, or

        (ii) where an order that the accused be detained in custody has been made under section 521 or 524, or a decision has been made with respect to a review under section 520, the later of the day on which the accused was taken into custody under that order and the day of the decision, or

(b) in the case of an offence for which the accused is being prosecuted in proceedings by way of summary conviction, within thirty days from

(i) the day on which the accused was taken before a justice under subsection 503(1), or

(ii) where an order that the accused be detained in custody has been made under section 521 or 524, or a decision has been made with respect to a review under section 520, the later of the day on which the accused was taken into custody under that order and the day of the decision,

the person having the custody of the accused shall, forthwith on the expiration of those ninety or thirty days, as the case may be, apply to a judge having jurisdiction in the place in which the accused is in custody to fix a date for a hearing to determine whether or not the accused should be released from custody.

(2) Notice of hearing — On receiving an application under subsection (1), the judge shall

(a) fix a date for the hearing described in subsection (1) to be held in the jurisdiction

(i) where the accused is in custody, or

(ii) where the trial is to take place; and

(b) direct that notice of the hearing be given to such persons, including the prosecutor and the accused, and in such manner, as the judge may specify.

(3) Matters to be considered on hearing — On the hearing described in subsection (1), the judge may, in deciding whether or not the accused should be released from custody, take into consideration whether the prosecutor or the accused has been responsible for any unreasonable delay in the trial of the charge.

(4) Order — If, following the hearing described in subsection (1), the judge is not satisfied that the continued detention of the accused in custody is justified within the meaning of subsection 515(10), the judge shall order that the accused be released from custody pending the trial of the charge on his giving an undertaking or entering into a recognizance described in any of paragraphs 515(2)(a) to (e) with such conditions described in subsection 515(4) as the judge considers desirable.

(5) Warrant of judge for arrest — Where a judge having jurisdiction in the province where an order under subsection (4) for the release of an accused has been made is satisfied that there are reasonable grounds to believe that the accused

(a) has violated or is about to violate the undertaking or recognizance on which he has been released, or

(b) has, after his release from custody on his undertaking or recognizance, committed an indictable offence,

he may issue a warrant for the arrest of the accused.

(6) Arrest without warrant by peace officer — Notwithstanding anything in this Act, a peace officer who believes on reasonable grounds that an accused who has been released from custody under subsection (4)

(a) has contravened or is about to contravene the undertaking or recognizance on which he has been released, or

(b) has, after his release from custody on his undertaking or recognizance, committed an indictable offence,

may arrest the accused without warrant and take him or cause him to be taken before a judge having jurisdiction in the province where the order for his release was made.

(7) Hearing and order — A judge before whom an accused is taken pursuant to a warrant issued under subsection (5) or pursuant to subsection (6) may, where the accused shows cause why his detention in custody is not justified within the meaning of subsection 515(10), order that the accused be released on his giving an undertaking or entering into a recognizance described in any of paragraphs 515(2)(*a*) to (*e*) with such conditions, described in subsection 515(4), as the judge considers desirable.

(8) Provisions applicable to proceedings — The provisions of sections 517, 518 and 519 apply with such modifications as the circumstances require in respect of any proceedings under this section.

(9) Directions for expediting trial — Where an accused is before a judge under any of the provisions of this section, the judge may give directions for expediting the trial of the accused.

R.S. 1985, c. 27 (1st Supp.), s. 90; 1994, c. 44, s. 49; 1997, c. 18, s. 61

526. Directions for expediting proceedings — Subject to subsection 525(9), a court, judge or justice before which or whom an accused appears pursuant to this Part may give directions for expediting any proceedings in respect of the accused.

R.S. 1985, c. 27 (1st Supp.), s. 91.

Procedure to Procure Attendance of a Prisoner

527. (1) Procuring attendance — A judge of a superior court of criminal jurisdiction may order in writing that a person who is confined in a prison be brought before the court, judge, justice or provincial court judge before whom the prisoner is required to attend, from day to day as may be necessary, if

(a) the applicant for the order sets out the facts of the case in an affidavit and produces the warrant, if any; and

(b) the judge is satisfied that the ends of justice require that an order be made.

(2) Provincial court judge's order — A provincial court judge has the same powers for the purposes of subsection (1) or (7) as a judge has under that subsection where the person whose attendance is required is within the province in which the provincial court judge has jurisdiction.

(3) Conveyance of prisoner — An order that is made under subsection (1) or (2) shall be addressed to the person who has custody of the prisoner, and on receipt thereof that person shall

(a) deliver the prisoner to any person who is named in the order to receive him; or

(b) bring the prisoner before the court, judge, justice or provincial court judge, as the case may be, upon payment of his reasonable charges in respect thereof.

(4) Detention of prisoner required as witness — Where the prisoner is required as a witness, the judge or provincial court judge shall direct, in the order, the manner in which the prisoner shall be kept in custody and returned to the prison from which he is brought.

(5) Detention in other cases — Where the appearance of the prisoner is required for the purposes of paragraph (1)(a) or (b), the judge or provincial court judge shall give appropriate directions in the order with respect to the manner in which the prisoner is

(a) to be kept in custody, if he is committed for trial; or

(b) to be returned, if he is discharged upon a preliminary inquiry or if he is acquitted of the charge against him.

(6) Application of sections respecting sentence — Sections 718.3 and 743.1 apply where a prisoner to whom this section applies is convicted and sentenced to imprisonment by the court, judge, justice or provincial court judge.

(7) Transfer of prisoner — On application by the prosecutor, a judge of a superior court of criminal jurisdiction may, if a prisoner or a person in the custody of a peace officer consents in writing, order the transfer of the prisoner or other person to the custody of a peace officer named in the order for a period specified in the order, where the judge is satisfied that the transfer is required for the purpose of assisting a peace officer acting in the execution of his or her duties.

(8) Conveyance of prisoner — An order under subsection (7) shall be addressed to the person who has custody of the prisoner and on receipt thereof that person shall deliver the prisoner to the peace officer who is named in the order to receive him.

(9) Return — When the purposes of any order made under this section have been carried out, the prisoner shall be returned to the place where he was confined at the time the order was made.

R.S. 1985, c. 27 (1st Supp.), ss. 92, 101(2), 203; 1994, c. 44, s. 50; 1995, c. 22, s. 10 (Sched. I, item 18); 1997, c. 18, s. 62.

Endorsement of Warrant

528. (1) Endorsing warrant — Where a warrant for the arrest or committal of an accused, in any form set out in Part XXVIII in relation thereto, cannot be executed in accordance with section 514 or 703, a justice within whose jurisdiction the accused is or is believed to be shall, on application and proof on oath or by affidavit of the signature of the justice who issued the warrant, authorize the arrest of the accused within his jurisdiction by making an endorsement, which may be in Form 28, on the warrant.

(1.1) Copy of affidavit or warrant — A copy of an affidavit or warrant submitted by a means of telecommunication that produces a writing has the same probative force as the original for the purposes of subsection (1).

(2) Effect of endorsement — An endorsement that is made upon a warrant pursuant to subsection (1) is sufficient authority to the peace officers to whom it was originally directed, and to all peace officers within the territorial jurisdiction of the justice by whom it is endorsed, to execute the warrant and to take the accused before the justice who issued the warrant or before any other justice for the same territorial division.

R.S.1985, c. 27 (1st Supp.), s. 93; 1994, c. 44, s. 51.

529. (1) Including authorization to enter in warrant of arrest — A warrant to arrest or apprehend a person issued by a judge or justice under this or any other Act of Parliament may authorize a peace officer, subject to subsection (2), to enter a dwelling-house described in the warrant for the purpose of arresting or apprehending the person if the judge or justice is satisfied by information on oath in writing that there are reasonable grounds to believe that the person is or will be present in the dwelling house.

(2) Execution — An authorization to enter a dwelling-house granted under subsection (1) is subject to the condition that the peace officer may not enter the dwelling-house unless the peace officer has, immediately before entering the dwelling-house, reasonable grounds to believe that the person to be arrested or apprehended is present in the dwelling-house.

1997, c. 39, s. 2.

529.1 Warrant to enter dwelling-house — A judge or justice may issue a warrant in Form 7.1 authorizing a peace officer to enter a dwelling-house described in the warrant for the purpose of arresting or apprehending a person identified or identifiable by the warrant if the judge or justice is satisfied by information on oath that there are reasonable grounds to believe that the person is or will be present in the dwelling-house and that

(a) a warrant referred to in this or any other Act of Parliament to arrest or apprehend the person is in force anywhere in Canada;

(b) grounds exist to arrest the person without warrant under paragraph 495(1)(a) or (b); or

(c) grounds exist to arrest or apprehend without warrant the person under an Act of Parliament, other than this Act.

1997, c. 39, s. 2.

529.2 Reasonable terms and conditions — Subject to section 529.4, the judge or justice shall include in a warrant referred to in section 529 or 529.1 any terms and conditions that the judge or justice considers advisable to ensure that the entry into the dwelling-house is reasonable in the circumstances.

1997, c. 39, s. 2.

529.3 (1) Authority to enter dwelling without warrant — Without limiting or restricting any power a peace officer may have to enter a dwelling-house under this or any other Act or law, the peace officer may enter the dwelling-house for the purpose of arresting or apprehending a person, without a warrant referred to in section 529 or 529.1 authorizing the entry, if the peace officer has reasonable grounds to believe that the person is present in the dwelling-house, and the conditions for obtaining a warrant under section 529.1 exist but by reason of exigent circumstances it would be impracticable to obtain a warrant.

(2) Exigent circumstances — For the purposes of subsection (1), exigent circumstances include circumstances in which the peace officer

(a) has reasonable grounds to suspect that entry into the dwelling-house is necessary to prevent imminent bodily harm or death to any person; or

(b) has reasonable grounds to believe that evidence relating to the commission of an indictable offence is present in the dwelling-house and that entry into the dwelling-house is necessary to prevent the imminent loss or imminent destruction of evidence.

1997, c. 39, s. 2.

529.4 (1) Omitting announcement before entry — A judge or justice who authorizes a peace officer to enter a dwelling-house under section 529 or 529.1, or any judge or justice, may authorize the peace officer to enter the dwelling-house without prior announcement if the judge or justice is satisfied by information on oath that there are reasonable grounds to believe that prior announcement of the entry would

(a) expose the peace officer or any other person to imminent bodily harm or death; or

(b) result in the imminent loss or imminent destruction of evidence relating to the commission of an indictable offence.

(2) Execution of authorization — An authorization under this section is subject to the condition that the peace officer may not enter the dwelling-house without prior announcement despite being authorized to do so unless the peace officer has, immediately before entering the dwelling-house,

(a) reasonable grounds to suspect that prior announcement of the entry would expose the peace officer or any other person to imminent bodily harm or death; or

(b) reasonable grounds to believe that prior announcement of the entry would result in the imminent loss or imminent destruction of evidence relating to the commission of an indictable offence.

(3) Exception — A peace officer who enters a dwelling-house without a warrant under section 529.3 may not enter the dwelling-house without prior announcement unless the peace officer has, immediately before entering the dwelling-house,

(a) reasonable grounds to suspect that prior announcement of the entry would expose the peace officer or any other person to imminent bodily harm or death; or

(b) reasonable grounds to believe that prior announcement of the entry would result in the imminent loss or imminent destruction of evidence relating to the commission of an indictable offence.

1997, c. 39, s. 2.

529.5 Telewarrant — If a peace officer believes that it would be impracticable in the circumstances to appear personally before a judge or justice to make an application for a warrant under section 529.1 or an authorization under section 529 or 529.4, the warrant or authorization may be issued on an information submitted by telephone or other means of telecommunication and, for that purpose, section 487.1 applies, with any modifications that the circumstances require, to the warrant or authorization.

1997, c. 39, s. 2.

PART XVII — LANGUAGE OF ACCUSED

530. (1) Language of accused — On application by an accused whose language is one of the official languages of Canada, made not later than

(a) the time of the appearance of the accused at which his trial date is set, if

(i) he is accused of an offence mentioned in section 553 or punishable on summary conviction, or

(ii) the accused is to be tried on an indictment preferred under section 557,

(b) the time of the accused's election, if the accused elects under section 536 to be tried by a provincial court judge or under section 536.1 to be tried by a judge without a jury and without having a preliminary inquiry, or

(c) the time when the accused is ordered to stand trial, if the accused

(i) is charged with an offence listed in section 469,

(ii) has elected to be tried by a court composed of a judge or a judge and jury, or

(iii) is deemed to have elected to be tried by a court composed of a judge and jury,

a justice of the peace, provincial court judge or judge of the Nunavut Court of Justice shall grant an order directing that the accused be tried before a justice of the peace, provincial court judge, judge or judge and jury, as the case may be, who speak the official language of Canada that is the language of the accused or, if the circumstances warrant, who speak both official languages of Canada.

(2) Idem — On application by an accused whose language is not one of the official languages of Canada, made not later than whichever of the times referred to in paragraphs (1)(a) to (c) is applicable, a justice of the peace or provincial court judge may grant an order directing that the accused be tried before a justice of the peace, provincial court judge, judge or judge and jury, as the case may be, who speak the official language of Canada in which the accused, in the opinion of the justice or provincial court judge, can best give testimony or, if the circumstances warrant, who speak both official languages of Canada.

(3) Accused to be advised of right — The justice of the peace or provincial court judge before whom an accused first appears shall, if the accused is not represented by counsel, advise the accused of his right to apply for an order under subsection (1) or (2) and of the time before which such an application must be made.

(4) Remand — Where an accused fails to apply for an order under subsection (1) or (2) and the justice of the peace, provincial court judge or judge before whom the accused is to be tried, in this Part referred to as "the court", is satisfied that it is in the best interests of justice that the accused be tried before a justice of the peace, provincial court judge, judge or judge and jury who speak the official language of Canada that is the language of the accused or, if the language of the accused is not one of the official languages of Canada, the official language of Canada in which the accused, in the opinion of the court, can best give testimony, the court may, if it does not speak that language, by order remand the accused to be tried by a justice of the peace, provincial court judge, judge or judge and jury, as the case may be, who speak that language or, if the circumstances warrant, who speak both official languages of Canada.

(5) Variation of order — An order under this section that an accused be tried before a justice of the peace, provincial court judge, judge or judge and jury who speak the official language of Canada that is the language of the accused or the official language of Canada in which the accused can best give testimony may, if the circumstances warrant, be varied by the court to require that the accused be tried before a justice of the peace, provincial court judge, judge or judge and jury who speak both official languages of Canada.

R.S. 1985, c. 27 (1st Supp.), ss. 94, 203; 1999, c. 3, s. 34.

530.1 Where order granted under section 530 — Where an order is granted under section 530 directing that an accused be tried before a justice of the peace, provincial court judge, judge or judge and jury who speak the official language that is the language of the accused or in which the accused can best give testimony,

    (a) the accused and his counsel have the right to use either official language for all purposes during the preliminary inquiry and trial of the accused;

    (b) the accused and his counsel may use either official language in written pleadings or other documents used in any proceedings relating to the preliminary inquiry or trial of the accused;

    (c) any witness may give evidence in either official language during the preliminary inquiry or trial;

    (d) the accused has a right to have a justice presiding over the preliminary inquiry who speaks the official language that is the language of the accused;

(e) except where the prosecutor is a private prosecutor, the accused has a right to have a prosecutor who speaks the official language that is the language of the accused;

(f) the court shall make interpreters available to assist the accused, his counsel or any witness during the preliminary inquiry or trial;

(g) the record of proceedings during the preliminary inquiry or trial shall include

    (i) a transcript of everything that was said during those proceedings in the official language in which it was said,

    (ii) a transcript of any interpretation into the other language of what was said, and

    (iii) any documentary evidence that was tendered during those proceedings in the official language in which it was tendered; and

(h) any trial judgment, including any reasons given therefor, issued in writing in either official language, shall be made available by the court in the official language that is the language of the accused.

R.S. 1985, c. 31 (4th Supp.), s. 94.

531. Change of venue — Notwithstanding any other provision of this Act but subject to any regulations made pursuant to section 533, the court shall order that the trial of an accused be held in a territorial division in the same province other than that in which the offence would otherwise be tried if an order has been made that the accused be tried before a justice of the peace, provincial court judge, judge or judge and jury who speak the official language of Canada that is the language of the accused or the official language of Canada in which the accused can best give testimony or both official languages of Canada and such order cannot be conveniently complied with in the territorial division in which the offence would otherwise be tried.

R.S. 1985, c. 27 (1st Supp.), s. 203.

532. Saving — Nothing in this Part or the *Official Languages Act* derogates from or otherwise adversely affects any right afforded by a law of a province in force on the coming into force of this Part in that province or thereafter coming into force relating to the language of proceedings or testimony in criminal matters that is not inconsistent with this Part or that Act.

533. Regulations — The Lieutenant Governor in Council of a province may make regulations generally for carrying into effect the purposes and provisions of this Part in the province and the Commissioner of the Yukon Territory, the Commissioner of the Northwest Territories and the Commissioner of Nunavut may make regulations generally for carrying into effect the purposes and provisions of this Part in the Yukon Territory, the Northwest Territories and Nunavut, respectively.

1993, c. 28, s. 78 (Sched. III, item 33)

534. [Repealed 1997, c. 18, s. 63.]

PART XVIII — PROCEDURE ON PRELIMINARY INQUIRY

Jurisdiction

535. Inquiry by justice — Where an accused who is charged with an indictable offence is before a justice, the justice shall, in accordance with this Part, inquire into that charge and any other indictable offence, in respect of the same transaction, founded on the facts that are disclosed by the evidence taken in accordance with this Part.

R.S. 1985, c. 27 (1st Supp.), s. 96.

536. (1) Remand by justice to provincial court judge in certain cases — Where an accused is before a justice other than a provincial court judge charged with an offence over which a provincial court judge has absolute jurisdiction under section 553, the justice shall remand the accused to appear before a provincial court judge having jurisdiction in the territorial division in which the offence is alleged to have been committed.

(2) Election before justice in certain cases — Where an accused is before a justice charged with an offence, other than an offence listed in section 469, and the offence is not one over which a provincial court judge has absolute jurisdiction under section 553, the justice shall, after the information has been read to the accused, put the accused to his election in the following words:

> You have the option to elect to be tried by a provincial court judge without a jury and without having had a preliminary inquiry; or you may elect to have a preliminary inquiry and to be tried by a judge without a jury; or you may elect to have a preliminary inquiry and to be tried by a court composed of a judge and jury. If you do not elect now, you shall be deemed to have elected to have a preliminary inquiry and to be tried by a court composed of a judge and jury. How do you elect to be tried?

(3) Procedure where accused elects trial by provincial court judge — Where an accused elects to be tried by a provincial court judge, the justice shall endorse on the information a record of the election and shall

> (a) where the justice is not a provincial court judge, remand the accused to appear and plead to the charge before a provincial court judge having jurisdiction in the territorial division in which the offence is alleged to have been committed; or

> (b) where the justice is a provincial court judge, call on the accused to plead to the charge and if the accused does not plead guilty, proceed with the trial or fix a time for the trial.

(4) Procedure where accused elects trial by judge alone or by judge and jury or deemed election — Where an accused elects to have a preliminary inquiry and to be tried by a judge without a jury or by a court composed of a judge and jury or does not elect when put to his election, the justice shall hold a preliminary inquiry into the charge and if the accused is ordered to stand trial, the justice shall endorse on the information and, where the accused is in custody, on the warrant of committal, a statement showing the nature of the election of the accused or that the accused did not elect, as the case may be.

(5) Jurisdiction — Where a justice before whom a preliminary inquiry is being or is to be held has not commenced to take evidence, any justice having jurisdiction in the province where the offence with which the accused is charged is alleged to have been committed has jurisdiction for the purposes of subsection (4).

R.S. 1985, c. 27 (1st Supp.), ss. 96, 203.

536.1 (1) Remand by justice — Nunavut — If an accused is before a justice of the peace charged with an indictable offence mentioned in section 553, the justice of the peace shall remand the accused to appear before a judge.

(2) Election before justice in certain cases — Nunavut — If an accused is before a justice of the peace or a judge charged with an indictable offence, other than an offence mentioned in section 469 or 553, the justice of the peace or judge shall, after the information has been read to the accused, put the accused to an election in the following words:

> You have the option to elect to be tried by a judge without a jury and without having had a preliminary inquiry; or you may elect to have a preliminary inquiry and to be tried by a judge without a jury; or you may elect to have a preliminary inquiry and to be tried by a court composed of a judge and jury. If you do not elect now, you shall be deemed to have elected to have a preliminary inquiry and to be tried by a court composed of a judge and jury. How do you elect to be tried?

(3) Procedure if accused elects trial by judge — Nunavut — If an accused elects to be tried by a judge without a jury and without having had a preliminary inquiry, the justice of the peace or judge shall endorse on the information a record of the election and,

(a) if the accused is before a justice of the peace, the justice of the peace shall remand the accused to appear and plead to the charge before a judge; or

(b) if the accused is before a judge, the judge shall call on the accused to plead to the charge and if the accused does not plead guilty, proceed with the trial or fix a time for the trial.

(4) Procedure if accused elects trial by judge alone or by judge and jury or deemed election — Nunavut — If an accused elects to have a preliminary inquiry and to be tried by a judge without a jury or by a court composed of a judge and jury or does not elect when put to an election, the justice of the peace or judge shall hold a preliminary inquiry into the charge and if the accused is ordered to stand trial, the justice of the peace or judge shall endorse on the information and, if the accused is in custody, on the warrant of committal, a statement showing the nature of the election of the accused or that the accused did not elect, as the case may be.

(5) Jurisdiction — Nunavut — If a justice of the peace before whom a preliminary inquiry is being or is to be held has not commenced to take evidence, any justice of the peace having jurisdiction in Nunavut has jurisdiction for the purposes of subsection (4).

(6) Application to Nunavut — This section, and not section 536, applies in respect of criminal proceedings in Nunavut.

1999, c. 3, s. 35.

Powers of Justice

537. (1) Powers of justice — A justice acting under this Part may

(a) adjourn an inquiry from time to time and change the place of hearing, where it appears to be desirable to do so by reason of the absence of a witness, the inability of a witness who is ill to attend at the place where the justice usually sits or for any other sufficient reason;

(b) remand the accused to custody for the purposes of the *Identification of Criminals Act*;

(b) [Repealed 1991, c. 43, s. 9, Schedule, item 3(1).]

(c) except where the accused is authorized pursuant to Part XVI to be at large, remand the accused to custody in a prison by warrant in Form 19;

(d) resume an inquiry before the expiration of a period for which it has been adjourned with the consent of the prosecutor and the accused or his counsel;

(e) order in writing, in Form 30, that the accused be brought before him, or any other justice for the same territorial division, at any time before the expiration of the time for which the accused has been remanded;

(f) grant or refuse permission to the prosecutor or his counsel to address him in support of the charge, by way of opening or summing up or by way of reply on any evidence that is given on behalf of the accused;

(g) receive evidence on the part of the prosecutor or the accused, as the case may be, after hearing any evidence that has been given on behalf of either of them;

(h) order that no person other than the prosecutor, the accused and their counsel shall have access to or remain in the room in which the inquiry is held, where it appears to him that the ends of justice will be best served by so doing;

(i) regulate the course of the inquiry in any way that appears to him to be desirable and that is not inconsistent with this Act;

(j) where the prosecutor and the accused so agree, permit the accused to appear by counsel or by closed-circuit television or any other means that allow the court and the accused to engage in simultaneous visual and oral communication, for any part of the inquiry other than a part in which the evidence of a witness is taken; and

(k) for any part of the inquiry other than a part in which the evidence of a witness is taken require an accused who is confined in prison to appear by closed-circuit television or any other means that allow the court and the accused to engage in simultaneous visual and oral communication, if the accused is given the opportunity to communicate privately with counsel, in a case in which the accused is represented by counsel.

(2) Change of venue — Where a justice changes the place of hearing under paragraph (1) (a) to a place in the same province, other than a place in territorial division in which the justice has jurisdiction, any justice who has jurisdiction in the place to which the hearing is changed may continue the hearing.

(2)–(4) [Repealed 1991, c. C-43, s. 9 (Sched., item 3(2)).]

1991, c. 43, s. 9, Schedule, item 3; 1994, c. 44, s. 53; 1997, c. 18, s. 64.

538. Corporation — Where an accused is a corporation, subsections 556(1) and (2) apply, with such modifications as the circumstances require.

Taking Evidence of Witnesses

539. (1) Order restricting publication of evidence taken at preliminary inquiry — Prior to the commencement of the taking of evidence at a preliminary inquiry, the justice holding the inquiry

(a) may, if application therefor is made by the prosecutor, and

(b) shall, if application therefor is made by any of the accused,

make an order directing that the evidence taken at the inquiry shall not be published in any newspaper or broadcast before such time as, in respect of each of the accused,

(c) he is discharged; or

(d) if he is ordered to stand trial, the trial is ended.

(2) Accused to be informed of right to apply for order — Where an accused is not represented by counsel at a preliminary inquiry, the justice holding the inquiry shall, prior to the commencement of the taking of evidence at the inquiry, inform the accused of his right to make application under subsection (1).

(3) Failure to comply with order — Every one who fails to comply with an order made pursuant to subsection (1) is guilty of an offence punishable on summary conviction.

(4) "Newspaper" — In this section, **"newspaper"** has the same meaning as in section 297.

R.S. 1985, c. 27 (1st Supp.), s. 97.

540. (1) Taking evidence — Where an accused is before a justice holding a preliminary inquiry, the justice shall

(a) take the evidence under oath, in the presence of the accused, of the witnesses called on the part of the prosecution and allow the accused or his counsel to cross-examine them; and

(b) cause a record of the evidence of each witness to be taken

(i) in legible writing in the form of a deposition, in Form 31, or by a stenographer appointed by him or pursuant to law, or

(ii) in a province where a sound recording apparatus is authorized by or under provincial legislation for use in civil cases, by the type of apparatus so authorized and in accordance with the requirements of the provincial legislation.

(2) Reading and signing depositions — Where a deposition is taken down in writing, the justice shall, in the presence of the accused, before asking the accused if he wishes to call witnesses,

(a) cause the deposition to be read to the witness;

(b) cause the deposition to be signed by the witness; and

(c) sign the deposition himself.

(3) Authentication by justice — Where depositions are taken down in writing, the justice may sign

(a) at the end of each deposition; or

(b) at the end of several or of all the depositions in a manner that will indicate that his signature is intended to authenticate each deposition.

(4) Stenographer to be sworn — Where the stenographer appointed to take down the evidence is not a duly sworn court stenographer, he shall make oath that he will truly and faithfully report the evidence.

(5) Authentication of transcript — Where the evidence is taken down by a stenographer appointed by the justice or pursuant to law, it need not be read to or signed by the witnesses, but, on request of the justice or of one of the parties, shall be transcribed, in whole or in part, by the stenographer and the transcript shall be accompanied by

(a) an affidavit of the stenographer that it is a true report of the evidence; or

(b) a certificate that it is a true report of the evidence if the stenographer is a duly sworn court stenographer.

(6) Transcription of record taken by sound recording apparatus — Where, in accordance with this Act, a record is taken in any proceedings under this Act by a sound recording apparatus, the record so taken shall, on request of the justice or of one of the parties, be dealt with and transcribed, in whole or in part, and the transcription certified and used in accordance with the provincial legislation, with such modifications as the circumstances require mentioned in subsection (1).

R.S. 1985, c. 27 (1st Supp.), s. 98; 1997, c. 18, s. 65.

541. (1) Hearing of witnesses — When the evidence of the witnesses called on the part of the prosecution has been taken down and, where required by this Part, has been read, the justice shall, subject to this section, hear the witnesses called by the accused.

(2) Contents of address to accused — Before hearing any witness called by an accused who is not represented by counsel, the justice shall address the accused as follows or to the like effect:

"Do you wish to say anything in answer to these charges or to any other charges which might have arisen from the evidence led by the prosecution? You are not obliged to say anything. but whatever you do say may be given in evidence against you at your trial. You should not make any confession or admission of guilt because of any promise or threat made to you but if you do make any statement it may be given in evidence against you at your trial in spite of the promise or threat."

(3) Statement of accused — Where the accused who is not represented by counsel says anything in answer to the address made by the justice pursuant to sub-section (2), the answer shall be taken down in writing and shall be signed by the justice and kept with the evidence of the witnesses and dealt with in accordance with this Part.

(4) Witnesses for accused — Where an accused is not represented by counsel, the justice shall ask the accused if he or she wishes to call any witnesses after sub-sections (2) and (3) have been complied with.

(5) Depositions of such witnesses — The justice shall hear each witness called by the accused who testifies to any matter relevant to the inquiry, and for the purposes of this subsection, section 540 applies with such modifications as the circumstances require.

R.S. 1985, c. 27 (1st Supp.) s. 99; 1994, c. 44, s. 54.

542. (1) Confession or admission of accused — Nothing in this Act prevents a prosecutor giving in evidence at a preliminary inquiry any admission, confession or statement made at any time by the accused that by law is admissible against him.

(2) Restriction of publication of reports of preliminary inquiry — Every one who publishes in any newspaper, or broadcasts, a report that any admission or confession was tendered in evidence at a preliminary inquiry or a report of the nature of such admission or confession so tendered in evidence unless

(a) the accused has been discharged, or

(b) if the accused has been committed for trial, the trial has ended, is guilty of an offence punishable on summary conviction.

(3) "Newspaper" — In this section **"newspaper"** has the same meaning as in section 297.

R.S. 1985, c. 27 (1st Supp.), s. 101(2).

Remand Where Offence Committed in Another Jurisdiction

543. (1) Order that accused appear or be taken before justice where offence committed — Where an accused is charged with an offence alleged to have been committed out of the limits of the jurisdiction in which he has been charged, the justice before whom he appears or is brought may, at any stage of the inquiry after hearing both parties,

(a) order the accused to appear, or

(b) if the accused is in custody, issue a warrant in Form 15 to convey the accused

before a justice having jurisdiction in the place where the offence is alleged to have been committed, who shall continue and complete the inquiry.

(2) Transmission of transcript and documents and effect of order or warrant — Where a justice makes an order or issues a warrant pursuant to subsection (1), he shall cause the transcript of any evidence given before him in the inquiry and all documents that were then before him and that are relevant to the inquiry to be transmitted to a justice having jurisdiction in the place where the offence is alleged to have been committed and

(a) any evidence the transcript of which is so transmitted shall be deemed to have been taken by the justice to whom it is transmitted; and

(b) any appearance notice, promise to appear, undertaking or recognizance issued to or given or entered into by the accused under Part XVI shall be deemed to have been issued, given or entered into in the jurisdiction where the offence is alleged to have been committed and to require the accused to appear before the justice to whom the transcript and documents are transmitted at the time provided in the order made in respect of the accused under paragraph (1)(*a*).

Absconding Accused

544. (1) Accused absconding during inquiry — Notwithstanding any other provision of this Act, where an accused, whether or not he is charged jointly with another, absconds during the course of a preliminary inquiry into an offence with which he is charged,

(a) he shall be deemed to have waived his right to be present at the inquiry; and

(b) the justice

(i) may continue the inquiry and, when all the evidence has been taken, shall dispose of the inquiry in accordance with section 548, or

(ii) if a warrant is issued for the arrest of the accused, may adjourn the inquiry to await his appearance,

but where the inquiry is adjourned pursuant to subparagraph (*b*)(ii), the justice may continue it at any time pursuant to subparagraph(*b*)(i) if he is satisfied that it would no longer be in the interests of justice to await the appearance of the accused.

(2) Adverse inference — Where the justice continues a preliminary inquiry pursuant to subsection (1), he may draw an inference adverse to the accused from the fact that he has absconded.

(3) Accused not entitled to re-opening — Where an accused reappears at a preliminary inquiry that is continuing pursuant to subsection (1), he is not entitled to have any part of the proceedings that was conducted in his absence re-opened unless the justice is satisfied that because of exceptional circumstances it is in the interests of justice to re-open the inquiry.

(4) Counsel for accused may continue to act — Where the accused has absconded during the course of a preliminary inquiry and the justice continues the inquiry, counsel for the accused is not thereby deprived of any authority he may have to continue to act for the accused in the proceedings.

(5) Accused calling witnesses — Where, at the conclusion of the evidence on the part of the prosecution at a preliminary inquiry that has been continued pursuant to subsection (1), the accused is absent but counsel for the accused is present, he or she shall be given an opportunity to call witnesses on behalf of the accused and subsection 541(5) applies with such modifications as the circumstances require.

1994, c. 44, s. 55.

Procedure where Witness Refuses to Testify

545. (1) Witness refusing to be examined — Where a person, being present at a preliminary inquiry and being required by the justice to give evidence,

> (a) refuses to be sworn,

> (b) having been sworn, refuses to answer the questions that are put to him,

> (c) fails to produce any writings that he is required to produce, or

> (d) refuses to sign his deposition,

without offering a reasonable excuse for his failure or refusal, the justice may adjourn the inquiry and may, by warrant in Form 20, commit the person to prison for a period not exceeding eight clear days or for the period during which the inquiry is adjourned, whichever is the lesser period.

(2) Further commitment — Where a person to whom subsection (1) applies is brought before the justice on the resumption of the adjourned inquiry and again refuses to do what is required of him, the justice may again adjourn the inquiry for a period not exceeding eight clear days and commit him to prison for the period of adjournment or any part thereof, and may adjourn the inquiry and commit the person to prison from time to time until the person consents to do what is required of him.

(3) Saving — Nothing in this section shall be deemed to prevent the justice from sending the case for trial on any other sufficient evidence taken by him.

Remedial Provisions

546. Irregularity or variance not to affect validity — The validity of any proceeding at or subsequent to a preliminary inquiry is not affected by

> (a) any irregularity or defect in the substance or form of the summons or warrant,

> (b) any variance between the charge set out in the summons or warrant and the charge set out in the information, or

(c) any variance between the charge set out in the summons, warrant or information and the evidence adduced by the prosecution at the inquiry.

547. Adjournment if accused misled — Where it appears to the justice that the accused has been deceived or misled by any irregularity, defect or variance mentioned in section 546, he may adjourn the inquiry and may remand the accused or grant him interim release in accordance with Part XVI.

547.1 Inability of justice to continue — Where a justice acting under this Part has commenced to take evidence and dies or is unable to continue for any reason, another justice may

(a) continue taking the evidence at the point at which the interruption in the taking of the evidence occurred, where the evidence was recorded pursuant to section 540 and is available; or

(b) commence taking the evidence as if no evidence had been taken, where no evidence was recorded pursuant to section 540 or where the evidence is not available.

R.S. 1985, c. 27 (1st Supp.), s. 100.

Adjudication and Recognizances

548. (1) Order to stand trial or discharge — When all the evidence has been taken by the justice, he shall,

(a) if in his opinion there is sufficient evidence to put the accused on trial for the offence charged or any other indictable offence in respect of the same transaction, order the accused to stand trial; or

(b) discharge the accused, if in his opinion on the whole of the evidence no sufficient case is made out to put the accused on trial for the offence charged or any other indictable offence in respect of the same transaction.

(2) Endorsing charge — Where the justice orders the accused to stand trial for an indictable offence, other than or in addition to the one with which the accused was charged, the justice shall endorse on the information the charges on which he orders the accused to stand trial.

(2.1) Where accused ordered to stand trial — A justice who orders that an accused is to stand trial has the power to fix the date for the trial or the date on which the accused must appear in the trial court to have that date fixed.

(3) Defect not to affect validity — The validity of an order to stand trial is not affected by any defect apparent on the face of the information in respect of which the preliminary inquiry is held or in respect of any charge on which the accused is ordered to stand trial unless, in the opinion of the court before which an objection to the information or charge is taken, the accused has been misled or prejudiced in his defence by reason of that defect.

R.S. 1985, c. 27 (1st Supp.), s. 101(1); 1994, c. 44, s. 56.

549. (1) Order to stand trial at any stage of inquiry with consent — Notwithstanding any other provision of this Act, the justice may, at any stage of the preliminary inquiry, with the consent of the accused and the prosecutor, order the accused to stand trial in the court having criminal jurisdiction, without taking or recording any evidence or further evidence.

(2) Procedure — Where an accused is ordered to stand trial under subsection (1), the justice shall endorse on the information a statement of the consent of the accused and the prosecutor, and the accused shall thereafter be dealt with in all respects as if ordered to stand trial under section 548.

R.S. 1985, c. 27 (1st Supp.), s. 101(3).

550. (1) Recognizance of witness — Where an accused is ordered to stand trial, the justice who held the preliminary inquiry may require any witness whose evidence is, in his opinion, material to enter into a recognizance to give evidence at the trial of the accused and to comply with such reasonable conditions prescribed in the recognizance as the justice considers desirable for securing the attendance of the witness to give evidence at the trial of the accused.

(2) Form — The recognizance entered into pursuant to this section may be in Form 32, and may be set out at the end of a deposition or be separate therefrom.

(3) Sureties or deposit for appearance of witness — A justice may, for any reason satisfactory to him, require any witness entering into a recognizance pursuant to this section.

    (a) to produce one or more sureties in such amount as he may direct; or

    (b) to deposit with him a sum of money sufficient in his opinion to ensure that the witness will appear and give evidence.

(4) Witness refusing to be bound — Where a witness does not comply with subsection (1) or (3) when required to do so by a justice, he may be committed by the justice, by warrant in Form 24, to a prison in the territorial division where the trial is to be held, there to be kept until he does what is required of him or until the trial is concluded.

(5) Discharge — Where a witness has been committed to prison pursuant to subsection (4), the court before which the witness appears or a justice having jurisdiction in the territorial division where the prison is situated may, by order in Form 39, discharge the witness from custody when the trial is concluded.

R.S. 1985, c. 27 (1st Supp.), s. 101(3).

Transmission of Record

551. Transmitting record — Where a justice orders an accused to stand trial, the justice shall forthwith send to the clerk or other proper officer of the court by which the accused is to be tried, the information, the evidence, the exhibits, the statement if any of the accused taken down in writing under section 541, any promise to appear, undertaking or recognizance given or entered into in accordance with Part XVI, or any evidence taken before a coroner, that is in the possession of the justice.

R.S. 1985, c. 27 (1st Supp.), s. 102.

PART XIX — INDICTABLE OFFENCES — TRIAL WITHOUT A JURY

Interpretation

552. Definitions — In this Part

"judge" means,

> (a) in the Province of Ontario, a judge of the superior court of criminal jurisdiction of the Province,
>
> (b) in the Province of Quebec, a judge of the Court of Quebec,
>
> (c) in the Province of Nova Scotia, a judge of the superior court of criminal jurisdiction of the Province,
>
> (d) in the Province of New Brunswick, a judge of the Court of Queen's Bench,
>
> (e) in the Province of British Columbia, the Chief Justice or a puisne judge of the Supreme Court,
>
> (f) in the Provinces of Prince Edward Island and Newfoundland, a judge of the Supreme Court,
>
> (g) in the Province of Manitoba, the Chief Justice, or a puisne judge of the Court of Queen's Bench,
>
> (h) in the Provinces of Saskatchewan and Alberta, a judge of the superior court of criminal jurisdiction of the province,
>
> (i) in the Yukon Territory and the Northwest Territories, a judge of the Supreme Court of the territory, and
>
> (j) in Nunavut, a judge of the Nunavut Court of Justice.

R.S. 1985, c. 11 (1st Supp.), s. 2; c. 27 (1st Supp.), s. 103(1); c. 27 (2d Supp.), Schedule, item 6; c. 40 (4th Supp.), s. 2; 1990, c. 16, s. 6; 1990, c. 17, s. 13; 1992, c. 51, s. 38; 1993, c. 28, s. 78 (Sched. III, item 33) [Repealed 1999, c. 3, (Sched., item 8).]; 1999, c. 3, s. 36.

Jurisdiction of Provincial Court Judges

Absolute Jurisdiction

553. Absolute jurisdiction — The jurisdiction of a provincial court judge, or in Nunavut, of a judge of the Nunavut Court of Justice, to try an accused is absolute and does not depend on the consent of the accused where the accused is charged in an information

> (a) with
>
> > (i) theft, other than theft of cattle,
> >
> > (ii) obtaining money or property by false pretences,
> >
> > (iii) unlawfully having in his possession any property or thing or any proceeds of any property or thing knowing that all or a part of the prop-

erty or thing or of the proceeds was obtained by or derived directly or indirectly from the commission in Canada of an offence punishable by indictment or an act or omission anywhere that, if it had occurred in Canada, would have constituted an offence punishable by indictment,

(iv) having, by deceit, falsehood or other fraudulent means, defrauded the public or any person, whether ascertained or not, of any property, money or valuable security, or

(v) mischief under subsection 430(4),

where the subject-matter of the offence is not a testamentary instrument and the alleged value of the subject-matter of the offence does not exceed five thousand dollars;

(b) with counselling or with a conspiracy or attempt to commit or with being an accessory after the fact to the commission of

(i) any offence referred to in paragraph (*a*) in respect of the subject-matter and value thereof referred to in that paragraph, or

(ii) any offence referred to in paragraph (*c*); or

(c) with an offence under

(i) section 201 (keeping gaming or betting house),

(ii) section 202 (betting, pool-selling, book-making, etc.),

(iii) section 203 (placing bets),

(iv) section 206 (lotteries and games of chance),

(v) section 209 (cheating at play),

(vi) section 210 (keeping common bawdy-house),

(vii) subsection 259(4) (driving while disqualified),

Proposed Repeal — 553(c)(vii)

(vii) [Repealed 2000, c. 25, s. 4. Not in force at date of publication.]

(viii) section 393 (fraud in relation to fares),

(viii.1) section 811 (breach of recognizance),

(ix) subsection 733.1(1) (failure to comply with probation order),

(x) paragraph 4(4)(a) of the *Controlled Drugs and Substances Act*, or

(xi) subsection 5(4) of the *Controlled Drugs and Substances Act*.

R.S. 1985, c. 27 (1st Supp.), s. 104; 1992, c. 1, s. 58(1), Schedule I, item 11; 1994, c. 44, s. 57; 1995, c. 22, s. 2; 1996, c. 19, s. 72; 1997, c. 18, s. 66; 1999, c. 3, s. 37.

Provincial Court Judge's Jurisdiction with Consent

554. (1) Trial by provincial court judge with consent — Subject to subsection (2), if an accused is charged in an information with an indictable offence other than an offence that is mentioned in section 469, and the offence is not one over which a provincial court judge has absolute jurisdiction under section 553, a provincial court judge may try the accused if the accused elects to be tried by a provincial court judge.

(2) Nunavut — With respect to criminal proceedings in Nunavut, if an accused is charged in an information with an indictable offence other than an offence that is mentioned in section 469, and the offence is not one over which a judge of the Nunavut Court of Justice has absolute jurisdiction under section 553, a judge of the Nunavut Court of Justice may try the accused if the accused elects to be tried by a judge without a jury and without having a preliminary inquiry.

(3) [Repealed R.S. 1985, c. 27 (1st Supp.), s. 105.]

(4) [Repealed R.S. 1985, c. 27 (1st Supp.), s. 105.]

R.S. 1985, c. 27 (1st Supp.), ss. 105, 203; 1999, c. 3, s. 38.

555. (1) Provincial court judge may decide to hold preliminary inquiry — Where in any proceedings under this Part an accused is before a provincial court judge and it appears to the provincial court judge that for any reason the charge should be prosecuted by indictment, he may, at any time before the accused has entered upon his defence, decide not to adjudicate and shall thereupon inform the accused of his decision and continue the proceedings as a preliminary inquiry.

(2) Where subject-matter is a testamentary instrument or exceeds $5,000 in value — Where an accused is before a provincial court judge charged with an offence mentioned in paragraph 553(*a*) or subparagraph 553(*b*)(i), and, at any time before the provincial court judge makes an adjudication, the evidence establishes that the subject-matter of the offence is a testamentary instrument or that its value exceeds five thousand dollars, the provincial court judge shall put the accused to his or her election in accordance with subsection 536(2).

(3) Continuing proceedings — Where an accused is put to his election pursuant to subsection (2), the following provisions apply, namely,

(a) if the accused elects to be tried by a judge without a jury or a court composed of a judge and jury or does not elect when put to his election, the provincial court judge shall continue the proceedings as a preliminary inquiry under Part XVIII and, if he orders the accused to stand trial, the provincial court judge shall comply with subsection 536(4); and

(b) if the accused elects to be tried by a provincial court judge, the provincial court judge shall endorse on the information a record of the election and continue with the trial.

R.S. 1985, c. 27 (1st Supp.), ss. 106, 203; 1994, c. 44, s. 58

555.1 (1) Decision to hold preliminary inquiry — Nunavut — If in any criminal proceedings under this Part an accused is before a judge of the Nunavut Court of Justice and it appears to the judge that for any reason the charge should be prosecuted by indictment, the judge may, at any time before the accused has entered a defence, decide not to adjudicate and shall then inform the accused of the decision and continue the proceedings as a preliminary inquiry.

(2) If subject-matter is a testamentary instrument or exceeds $5,000 in value — Nunavut — If an accused is before a judge of the Nunavut Court of Justice charged with an indictable offence mentioned in paragraph 553(a) or subparagraph 553(b)(i), and, at any time before the judge makes an adjudication, the evidence establishes that the subject-matter of the offence is a testamentary instrument or that its value exceeds five thousand dollars, the judge shall put the accused to an election in accordance with subsection 536.1(2).

(3) Continuation as preliminary inquiry — Nunavut — If an accused is put to an election under subsection (2) and the accused elects to have a preliminary inquiry and to be tried by a judge without a jury or a court composed of a judge and jury or does not elect when put to the election, the judge shall continue the proceedings as a preliminary inquiry under Part XVIII and, if the judge orders the accused to stand trial, the judge shall endorse on the information and, if the accused is in custody, on the warrant of committal, a statement showing the nature of the election of the acccused or that the accused did not elect, as the case may be.

(4) Continuing proceedings — Nunavut — If an accused is put to an election under subsection (2), and the accused elects to be tried by a judge without a jury and without having a preliminary inquiry, the judge shall endorse on the information a record of the election and continue with the trial.

(5) Application to Nunavut — This section, and not section 555, applies in respect of criminal proceedings in Nunavut.

1999, c. 3, s. 39.

556. (1) Corporation — An accused corporation shall appear by counsel or agent.

(2) Non-appearance — Where an accused corporation does not appear pursuant to a summons and service of the summons on the corporation is proved, the provincial court judge, or in Nunavut, the judge of the Nunavut Court of Justice

(a) may, if the charge is one over which he has absolute jurisdiction, proceed with the trial of the charge in the absence of the accused corporation; and

(b) shall, if the charge is not one over which he has absolute jurisdiction, hold a preliminary inquiry in accordance with Part XVIII in the absence of the accused corporation.

(3) Corporation not electing — If an accused corporation appears but does not elect when put to an election under subsection 536(2) or 536.1(2), the provincial court judge or judge of the Nunavut Court of Justice shall hold a preliminary inquiry in accordance with Part XVIII.

R.S. 1985, c. 27 (1st Supp.), s. 107; 1999, c. 3, s. 40.

557. Taking evidence — If an accused is tried by a provincial court judge or a judge of the Nunavut Court of Justice in accordance with this Part, the evidence of witnesses for the prosecutor and the accused shall be taken in accordance with the provisions of Part XVIII relating to preliminary inquiries.

R.S. 1985, c. 27 (1st Supp.), s. 203; 1999, c. 3, s. 41.

Jurisdiction of Judges

Judge's Jurisdiction with Consent

558. Trial by judge without a jury — If an accused who is charged with an indictable offence, other than an offence mentioned in section 469, elects under section 536 or 536.1 or re-elects under section 561 or 561.1 to be tried by a judge without a jury, the accused shall, subject to this Part, be tried by a judge without a jury.

R.S. 1985, c. 27 (1st Supp.), s. 108; 1999, c. 3, s. 41.

559. (1) Court of record — A judge who holds a trial under this Part shall, for all purposes thereof and proceedings connected therewith or relating thereto, be a court of record.

(2) Custody of records — The record of a trial that a judge holds under this Part shall be kept in the court over which the judge presides.

Election

560. (1) Duty of judge — If an accused elects, under section 536 or 536.1 to have a preliminary inquiry and to be tried by a judge without a jury, a judge having jurisdiction shall,

    (a) on receiving a written notice from the sheriff or other person having custody of the accused stating that the accused is in custody and setting out the nature of the charge against him, or

    (b) on being notified by the clerk of the court that the accused is not in custody and of the nature of the charge against him,

fix a time and place for the trial of the accused.

(2) Notice by sheriff, when given — The sheriff or other person having custody of the accused shall give the notice mentioned in paragraph (1)(*a*) within twenty-four hours after the accused is ordered to stand trial, if he is in custody pursuant to that order or if, at the time of the order, he is in custody for any other reason.

(3) Duty of sheriff when date set for trial — Where, pursuant to subsection (1), a time and place is fixed for the trial of an accused who is in custody, the accused

    (a) shall be notified forthwith by the sheriff or other person having custody of the accused of the time and place so fixed; and

    (b) shall be produced at the time and place so fixed.

(4) Duty of accused when not in custody — Where an accused is not in custody, the duty of ascertaining from the clerk of the court the time and place fixed for the trial, pursuant to subsection (1), is on the accused, and he shall attend for his trial at the time and place so fixed.

(5) [Repealed R.S. 1985, c. 27 (1st Supp.), s. 109(2).]

R.S. 1985, c. 27 (1st Supp.), ss. 101(3), 109; 1999, c. 3, s. 42.

561. (1) Right to re-elect — An accused who elects or is deemed to have elected a mode of trial other than trial by a provincial court judge may re-elect,

(a) at any time before or after the completion of the preliminary inquiry, with the written consent of the prosecutor, to be tried by a provincial court judge;

(b) at any time before the completion of the preliminary inquiry or before the fifteenth day following the completion of the preliminary inquiry, as of right, another mode of trial other than trial by a provincial court judge; and

(c) on or after the fifteenth day following the completion of the preliminary inquiry, any mode of trial with the written consent of the prosecutor.

(2) Idem — An accused who elects to be tried by a provincial court judge may, not later than fourteen days before the day first appointed for the trial, re-elect as of right another mode of trial, and may do so thereafter with the written consent of the prosecutor.

(3) Notice — Where an accused wishes to re-elect under subsection (1) before the completion of the preliminary inquiry, the accused shall give notice in writing that he wishes to re-elect, together with the written consent of the prosecutor, where that consent is required, to the justice presiding at the preliminary inquiry who shall on receipt of the notice,

(a) in the case of a re-election under paragraph (1)(*b*), put the accused to his re-election in the manner set out in subsection (7); or

(b) where the accused wishes to re-elect under paragraph (1)(*a*) and the justice is not a provincial court judge, notify a provincial court judge or clerk of the court of the accused's intention to re-elect and send to the provincial court judge or clerk the information and any promise to appear, undertaking or recognizance given or entered into in accordance with Part XVI, or any evidence taken before a coroner, that is in the possession of the justice.

(4) Idem — Where an accused wishes to re-elect under section (2), the accused shall give notice in writing that he wishes to re-elect together with the written consent of the prosecutor, where that consent is required, to the provincial court judge before whom the accused appeared and pleaded or to a clerk of the court.

(5) Notice and transmitting record — Where an accused wishes to re-elect under subsection (1) after the completion of the preliminary inquiry, the accused shall give notice in writing that he wishes to re-elect, together with the written consent of the prosecutor, where such consent is required, to a judge or clerk of the court of his original election who shall, on receipt of the notice, notify the judge or provincial court judge or clerk of the court by which the accused wishes to be tried of the accused's intention to re-elect and send to that judge or provincial court judge or clerk the information, the evidence, the exhibits and the statement, if any, of the accused taken down in writing under section 541 and any promise to appear, undertaking or recognizance given or entered into in accordance with Part XVI, or any evidence taken before a coroner, that is in the possession of the first-mentioned judge or clerk.

(6) Time and place for re-election — Where a provincial court judge or judge or clerk of the court is notified under paragraph (3)(*b*) or subsection (4) or (5) that the accused wishes to re-elect, the provincial court judge or judge shall forthwith appoint a time and place for the accused to re-elect and shall cause notice thereof to be given to the accused and the prosecutor.

(7) Proceedings on re-election — The accused shall attend or, if he is in custody, shall be produced at the time and place appointed under subsection (6) and shall, after

> (a) the charge on which he has been ordered to stand trial or the indictment, where an indictment has been preferred pursuant to section 566, 574 or 577 or is filed with the court before which the indictment is to be preferred pursuant to section 577, or

> (b) in the case of a re-election under subsection (1) before the completion of the preliminary inquiry or under subsection (2), the information

has been read to the accused, be put to his re-election in the following words or in words to the like effect: You have given notice of your wish to re-elect the mode of your trial. You now have the option to do so. How do you wish to re-elect?

R.S. 1985, c. 27 (1st Supp.), s. 110.

561.1 (1) Right to re-elect — Nunavut — An accused who has elected or is deemed to have elected a mode of trial may re-elect any other mode of trial at any time with the written consent of the prosecutor, except that an accused who has had a preliminary inquiry may not elect to be tried by a judge without a jury and without having had a preliminary inquiry.

(2) Right to re-elect — Nunavut — An accused who has elected to be tried by a judge without a jury and without a preliminary inquiry may, as of right, re-elect to be tried by any other mode of trial at any time up to 14 days before the day first appointed for the trial.

(3) Right to re-elect — Nunavut — An accused who has elected to be tried by a judge and jury or to have a preliminary inquiry and to be tried by a judge without jury may, as of right, re-elect to be tried by the other mode of trial at any time before the completion of the preliminary inquiry or before the fifteenth day following its completion.

(4) Notice of re-election under subsection (1) or (3) — Nunavut — If an accused wishes to re-elect under subsection (1) or (3), before the completion of the preliminary inquiry, the accused shall give notice in writing of the wish to re-elect, together with the written consent of the prosecutor, if that consent is required, to the justice of the peace or judge presiding at the preliminary inquiry who shall on receipt of the notice put the accused to a re-election in the manner set out in subsection (9).

(5) Notice of re-election under subsection (1) — Nunavut — If an accused wishes to re-elect under subsection (1) to be tried by a judge without a jury and without having had a preliminary inquiry and a justice of the peace is presiding at the preliminary inquiry, the justice of the peace shall notify a judge or a clerk of the Nunavut Court of Justice of the accused's intention to re-elect and send to the judge or clerk the information and any promise to appear, undertaking or recognizance given or entered into in accordance with Part XVI, or any evidence taken before a coroner, that is in the possession of the justice of the peace.

(6) Notice of re-election under subsection (1) or (3) — Nunavut — If an accused wishes to re-elect under subsection (1) or (3) after the completion of a preliminary inquiry or after having elected a trial by judge without a jury and without having had a preliminary inquiry, the accused shall give notice in writing of the wish to re-elect together with the written consent of the prosecutor, if that consent is required, to the judge before whom the accused appeared and pleaded or to a clerk of the Nunavut Court of Justice.

(7) Notice of re-election under subsection (2) — Nunavut — If an accused wishes to re-elect under subsection (2), the accused shall give notice in writing of the wish to re-elect to the judge before whom the accused appeared and pleaded or to a clerk of the Nunavut Court of Justice.

(8) Time and place for re-election — Nunavut — On receipt of a notice given under any of subsections (4) to (7) that the accused wishes to re-elect, a judge shall immediately appoint a time and place for the accused to re-elect and shall cause notice of the time and place to be given to the accused and the prosecutor.

(9) Proceedings on re-election — Nunavut — The accused shall attend or, if in custody, shall be produced at the time and place appointed under subsection (8) and shall, after

(a) the charge on which the accused has been ordered to stand trial or the indictment, if an indictment has been preferred pursuant to section 566, 574 or 577 or is filed with the court before which the indictment is to be preferred pursuant to section 577, or

(b) in the case of a re-election under subsection (1) or (3), before the completion of the preliminary inquiry or under subsection (2), the information

has been read to the accused, be put to a re-election in the following words or in words to the like effect:

You have given notice of your wish to re-elect the mode of your trial. You now have the option to do so. How do you wish to re-elect?

(10) Application to Nunavut — This section, and not section 561, applies in respect of criminal proceedings in Nunavut.

1999, c. 3, s. 43.

562. (1) Proceedings following re-election — Where the accused re-elects under paragraph 561(1)(*a*) before the completion of the preliminary inquiry or under subsection 561(1) after the completion of the preliminary inquiry, the provincial court judge or judge, as the case may be, shall proceed with the trial or appoint a time and place for the trial.

(2) Idem — Where the accused re-elects under paragraph 561(1)(*b*) before the completion of the preliminary inquiry or under subsection 561(2), the justice shall proceed with the preliminary inquiry.

R.S. 1985, c. 27 (1st Supp.), s. 110.

562.1 (1) Proceedings following re-election — Nunavut — If the accused re-elects under subsection 561.1(1) to be tried by a judge without a jury and without a preliminary inquiry, the judge shall proceed with the trial or appoint a time and place for the trial.

(2) Proceedings following re-election — Nunavut — If the accused re-elects under section 561.1 before the completion of the preliminary inquiry to be tried by judge and jury or to have a preliminary inquiry and to be tried by a judge without a jury, the justice of the peace or judge shall proceed with the preliminary inquiry.

(3) Application to Nunavut — This section, and not section 562, applies in respect of criminal proceedings in Nunavut.

1999, c. 3, s. 44.

563. Proceedings on re-election to be tried by provincial court judge without jury — Where an accused re-elects under section 561 to be tried by a provincial court judge,

    (a) the accused shall be tried on the information that was before the justice at the preliminary inquiry, subject to any amendments thereto that may be allowed by the provincial court judge by whom the accused is tried; and

    (b) the provincial court judge before whom the re-election is made shall endorse on the information a record of the re-election.

R.S. 1985, c. 27 (1st Supp.), s. 110.

563.1 (1) Proceedings on re-election to be tried by judge without jury — Nunavut — If an accused re-elects under section 561.1 to be tried by a judge without a jury and without having a preliminary inquiry,

    (a) the accused shall be tried on the information that was before the justice of the peace or judge at the preliminary inquiry, subject to any amendments that may be allowed by the judge by whom the accused is tried; and

    (b) the judge before whom the re-election is made shall endorse on the information a record of the re-election.

(2) Application to Nunavut — This section, and not section 563, applies in respect of criminal proceedings in Nunavut.

1999, c. 3, s. 45.

564. [Repealed R.S. 1985, c. 27 (1st Supp.), s. 110.]

565. (1) Election deemed to have been made — Subject to subsection (1.1), if an accused is ordered to stand trial for an offence that, under this Part, may be tried by a judge without a jury, the accused shall, for the purposes of the provisions of this Part relating to election and re-election, be deemed to have elected to be tried by a court composed of a judge and jury if

    (a) he was ordered to stand trial by a provincial court judge who, pursuant to subsection 555(1), continued the proceedings before him as a preliminary inquiry;

(b) the justice, provincial court judge or judge, as the case may be, declined pursuant to section 567 to record the election or re-election of the accused; or

(c) the accused does not elect when put to an election under section 536.

(1.1) Nunavut — With respect to criminal proceedings in Nunavut, if an accused is ordered to stand trial for an offence that, under this Part, may be tried by a judge without a jury, the accused shall, for the purposes of the provisions of this Part relating to election and re-election, be deemed to have elected to be tried by a court composed of a judge and jury if

(a) the accused was ordered to stand trial by a judge who, under subsection 555.1(1), continued the proceedings as a preliminary inquiry;

(b) the justice of the peace or judge, as the case may be, declined pursuant to subsection 567.1(1) to record the election or re-election of the accused; or

(c) the accused did not elect when put to an election under section 536.1.

(2) Where direct indictment preferred — Where an accused is to be tried after an indictment has been preferred against him pursuant to a consent or order given under section 577, the accused shall, for the purposes of the provisions of this Part relating to election and re-election, be deemed to have elected to be tried by a court composed of a judge and jury and may, with the written consent of the prosecutor, re-elect to be tried by a judge without a jury.

(3) Notice of re-election — Where an accused wishes to re-elect under subsection (2), he shall give notice in writing that he wishes to re-elect, together with the written consent of the prosecutor, to a judge or clerk of the court where the indictment has been filed or preferred who shall, on receipt of the notice, notify a judge having jurisdiction or clerk of the court by which the accused wishes to be tried of the accused's intention to re-elect and send to that judge or clerk the indictment and any promise to appear, undertaking or recognizance given or entered into in accordance with Part XVI, any summons or warrant issued under section 578, or any evidence taken before a coroner, that is in the possession of the first-mentioned judge or clerk.

(4) Application — Subsections 561(6) and (7), or subsections 561.1(8) and (9), as the case may be, apply to a re-election made under subsection (3).

R.S. 1985, c. 27 (1st Supp.), s. 111; 1999, c. 3, s. 46.

Trial

566. (1) Indictment — The trial of an accused for an indictable offence, other than a trial before a provincial court judge, shall be on an indictment in writing setting forth the offence with which he is charged.

(2) Preferring indictment — Where an accused elects under section 536 or re-elects under section 561 to be tried by a judge without a jury, an indictment in Form 4 may be preferred.

(3) What counts may be included and who may prefer indictment — Section 574 and subsection 576(1) apply, with such modifications as the circumstances require, to the preferring of an indictment pursuant to subsection (2).

R.S. 1985, c. 27 (1st Supp.), s. 111; 1997, c. 18, s. 67.

566.1 (1) Indictment — Nunavut — The trial of an accused for an indictable offence, other than an indictable offence mentioned in section 553 or an offence in respect of which the accused has elected or re-elected to be tried by a judge without a jury without having had a preliminary inquiry, shall be on an indictment in writing setting forth the offence with which the accused is charged.

(2) Preferring indictment — Nunavut — If an accused elects under section 536.1 or re-elects under section 561.1 to have a preliminary inquiry and to be tried by a judge without a jury, an indictment in Form 4 may be preferred.

(3) What counts may be included and who may prefer indictment — Nunavut — Section 574 and subsection 576(1) apply, with any modifications that the circumstances require, to the preferring of an indictment under subsection (2).

(4) Application to Nunavut — This section, and not section 566, applies in respect of criminal proceedings in Nunavut.

1999, c. 3, s. 47.

General

567. Mode of trial where two or more accused — Notwithstanding any other provision of this Part, where two or more persons are charged with the same offence, unless all of them elect or re-elect or are deemed to have elected, as the case may be, the same mode of trial, the justice, provincial court judge or judge

(a) may decline to record any election, re-election or deemed election for trial by a provincial court judge or a judge without a jury; and

(b) if he declines to do so, shall hold a preliminary inquiry unless a preliminary inquiry has been held prior to the election, re-election or deemed election.

R.S. 1985, c. 27 (1st Supp.), s. 111.

567.1 (1) Mode of trial if two or more accused — Nunavut — Despite any other provision of this Part, if two or more persons are charged with the same indictable offence, unless all of them elect or re-elect or are deemed to have elected, as the case may be, the same mode of trial, the justice of the peace or judge

(a) may decline to record any election, re-election or deemed election

(i) for trial by a judge without a jury and without having a preliminary inquiry, or

(ii) to have a preliminary inquiry and to be tried by a judge without a jury; and

(b) if the justice of the peace or judge declines to do so, shall hold a preliminary inquiry unless a preliminary inquiry has been held prior to the election, re-election or deemed election.

(2) Application to Nunavut — This section, and not section 567, applies in respect of criminal proceedings in Nunavut.

1999, c. 3, s. 48.

568. Attorney General may require trial by jury — The Attorney General may, notwithstanding that an accused elects under section 536 or re-elects under section 561 to be tried by a judge or provincial court judge, as the case may be, require the accused to be tried by a court composed of a judge and jury, unless the alleged offence is one that is punishable with imprisonment for five years or less, and where the Attorney General so requires, a judge or provincial court judge has no jurisdiction to try the accused under this Part and a preliminary inquiry shall be held before a justice unless a preliminary inquiry has been held prior to the requirement by the Attorney General that the accused be tried by a court composed of a judge and jury.

R.S. 1985, c. 27 (1st Supp.), s. 111.

569. (1) Attorney General may require trial by jury — Nunavut — The Attorney General may, despite that an accused elects under section 536.1 or re-elects under section 561.1 to be tried by a judge without a jury and without having had a preliminary inquiry or to have a preliminary inquiry and to be tried by a judge without a jury, require the accused to be tried by a court composed of a judge and jury, unless the alleged offence is one that is punishable with imprisonment for five years or less, and if the Attorney General so requires, a judge has no jurisdiction to try the accused under this Part and a preliminary inquiry shall be held before a justice of the peace or a judge unless a preliminary inquiry has been held prior to the requirement by the Attorney General that the accused be tried by a court composed of a judge and jury.

(2) Application to Nunavut — This section, and not section 568, applies in respect of criminal proceedings in Nunavut.

1999, c. 3, s. 49.

570. (1) Record of conviction or order — Where an accused who is tried under this Part is determined by a judge or provincial court judge to be guilty of an offence on acceptance of a plea of guilty or on a finding of guilt, the judge or provincial court judge, as the case may be, shall endorse the information accordingly and shall sentence the accused or otherwise deal with the accused in the manner authorized by law and, on request by the accused, the prosecutor, a peace officer, or any other person, shall cause a conviction in Form 35 and a certified copy of it, or an order in Form 36 and a certified copy of it, to be drawn up and shall deliver the certified copy to the person making the request.

(2) Acquittal and record of acquittal — Where an accused who is tried under this Part is found not guilty of an offence with which the accused is charged, the judge or provincial court judge, as the case may be, shall immediately acquit the accused in respect of that offence and shall cause an order in Form 37 to be drawn up, and on request shall make out and deliver to the accused a certified copy of the order.

(3) Transmission of record — Where an accused elects to be tried by a provincial court judge under this Part, the provincial court judge shall transmit the written charge, the memorandum of adjudication and the conviction, if any, into such custody as the Attorney General may direct.

(4) Proof of conviction order or acquittal — A copy of a conviction in Form 35 or of an order in Form 36 or 37, certified by the judge or by the clerk or other proper officer of the court, or by the provincial court judge, as the case may be, or proved to be a true copy, is, on proof of the identity of the person to whom the conviction or order relates, sufficient evidence in any legal proceedings to prove the conviction of that person or the making of the order against that person or his acquittal, as the case may be, for the offence mentioned in the copy of the conviction or order.

(5) Warrant of committal — Where an accused other than a corporation is convicted, the judge or provincial court judge, as the case may be, shall issue or cause to be issued a warrant of committal in Form 21, and section 528 applies in respect of a warrant of committal issued under this subsection.

(6) Admissibility of certified copy — Where a warrant of committal is issued by a clerk of a court, a copy of the warrant of committal, certified by the clerk, is admissible in evidence in any proceeding.

R.S. 1985, c. 27 (1st Supp.), ss. 112, 203; 1994, c. 44, s. 59.

571. Adjournment — A judge or provincial court judge acting under this Part may from time to time adjourn a trial until it is finally terminated.

R.S. 1985, c. 27 (1st Supp.), s. 203.

572. Application of Parts XVI, XVIII, XX and XXIII — The provisions of Part XVI, the provisions of Part XVIII relating to transmission of the record by a provincial court judge where he holds a preliminary inquiry, and the provisions of Parts XX and XXIII, in so far as they are not inconsistent with this Part, apply, with such modifications as the circumstances require to proceedings under this Part.

R.S. 1985, c. 27 (1st Supp.), s. 203.

PART XIX.1 — NUNAVUT COURT OF JUSTICE

573. (1) Nunavut Court of Justice — The powers to be exercised and the duties and functions to be performed under this Act by a court of criminal jurisdiction, a summary conviction court, a judge, a provincial court judge, a justice or a justice of the peace may be exercised or performed by a judge of the Nunavut Court of Justice.

(2) Status when exercising power — A power exercised or a duty or function performed by a judge of the Nunavut Court of Justice under subsection (1) is exercised or performed by that judge as a judge of a superior court.

(3) Interpretation — Subsection (2) does not authorize a judge of the Nunavut Court of Justice who is presiding at a preliminary inquiry to grant a remedy under section 24 of the *Canadian Charter of Rights and Freedoms*.

1999, c. 3, s. 50

573.1 (1) Application for review — Nunavut — An application for review may be made by the Attorney General or the accused, or by any person directly affected by the decision or order, to a judge of the Court of Appeal of Nunavut in respect of a decision or order of a judge of the Nunavut Court of Justice

(a) relating to a warrant or summons;

(b) relating to the conduct of a preliminary inquiry, including an order under subsection 548(1);

(c) relating to a subpoena;

(d) relating to the publication or broadcasting of information or access to the court room for all or part of the proceedings;

(e) to refuse to quash an information or indictment; or

(f) relating to the detention, disposal or forfeiture of any thing seized under a warrant or order.

(2) Limitation — A decision or order may not be reviewed under this section if

(a) the decision or order is of a kind that could only be made in a province or a territory other than Nunavut by a superior court of criminal jurisdiction or a judge as defined in section 552; or

(b) another statutory right of review is available.

(3) Grounds of review — The judge of the Court of Appeal of Nunavut may grant relief under subsection (4) only if the judge is satisfied that

(a) in the case of any decision or order mentioned in subsection (1),

(i) the judge of the Nunavut Court of Justice failed to observe a principle of natural justice or failed or refused to exercise the judge's jurisdiction, or

(ii) the decision or order was made as a result of an irrelevant consideration or for an improper purpose;

(b) in the case of a decision or order mentioned in paragraph (1)(a), that

(i) the judge failed to comply with a statutory requirement for the making of the deciaion or order,

(ii) the decision or order was made in the absence of any evidence that a statutory requirement for the making of the decision or order was met,

(iii) the decision or order was made as a result of reckless disregard for the truth, fraud, intentional misrepresentation of material facts or intentional omission to state material facts,

(iv) the warrant is so vague or lacking in particularity that it authorizes an unreasonable search, or

(v) the warrant lacks a material term or condition that is required by law;

(c) in the case of a decision or order mentioned in paragraph (1)(b), that the judge of the Nunavut Court of Justice

(i) failed to follow a mandatory provision of this Act relating to the conduct of a preliminary inquiry,

(ii) ordered the accused to stand trial when there was no evidence adduced on which a properly instructed jury acting reasonably could convict, or

(iii) discharged the accused when there was some evidence adduced on which a properly instructed jury acting reasonably could convict;

(d) in the case of a decision or order mentioned in paragraph (1)(c) or (d), that the judge of the Nunavut Court of Justice erred in law;

(e) in the case of a decision or order mentioned in paragraph (1)(e), that

(i) the information or indictment failed to give the accused notice of the charge,

(ii) the judge of the Nunavut Court of Justice did not have jurisdiction to try the offence, or

(iii) the provision creating the offence alleged to have been committed by the accused is unconstitutional; or

(f) in the case of a decision or order mentioned in paragraph (1)(f), that

(i) the judge failed to comply with a statutory requirement for the making of the decision or order,

(ii) the decision or order was made in the absence of any evidence that a statutory requirement for the making of the decision or order was met, or

(iii) the decision or order was made as a result of reckless disregard for the truth, fraud, intentional misrepresentation of material facts or intentional omission to state material facts.

(4) Powers of judge — On the hearing of the application for review, the judge of the Court of Appeal of Nunavut may do one or more of the following:

(a) order a judge of the Nunavut Court of Justice to do any act or thing that the judge or any other judge of that court failed or refused to do or has delayed in doing;

(b) prohibit or restrain a decision, order or proceeding of a judge of the Nunavut Court of Justice;

(c) declare invalid or unlawful, quash or set aside, in whole or in part, a decision, order or proceeding of a judge of the Nunavut Court of Justice;

(d) refer back for determination in accordance with any directions that the judge considers to be appropriate, a decision, order or proceeding of a judge of the Nunavut Court of Justice;

(e) grant any remedy under subsection 24(1) of the *Canadian Charter of Rights and Freedoms*;

(f) refuse to grant any relief if the judge is of the opinion that no substantial wrong or miscarriage of justice has occurred or that the subject-matter of the application should be determined at trial or on appeal; and

(g) dismiss the application.

(5) Interim orders — If an application for review is made, a judge of the Court of Appeal of Nunavut may make any interim order that the judge considers appropriate pending the final disposition of the application for review.

(6) Rules — A person who proposes to make an application for review shall do so in the manner and within the period that may be directed by rules of court, except that a judge of the Court of Appeal of Nunavut may at any time extend any period specified in the rules.

(7) Appeal — An appeal lies to the Court of Appeal of Nunavut against a decision or order made under subsection (4). The provisions of Part XXI apply, with any modifications that the circumstances require, to the appeal.

1999, c. 3, s. 50

573.2 (1) *Habeas corpus* — *Habeas corpus* proceedings may be brought before a judge of the Court of Appeal of Nunavut in respect of an order made or warrant issued by a judge of the Nunavut Court of Justice, except where

(a) the order or warrant is of a kind that could only be made or issued in a province or a territory other than Nunavut by a superior court of criminal jurisdiction or a judge as defined in section 552; or

(b) another statutory right of review or appeal is available.

(2) Exception — Despite subsection (1), *habeas corpus* proceedings may be brought before a judge of the Court of Appeal of Nunavut with respect to an order or warrant of a judge of the Nunavut Court of Justice if the proceedings are brought to challenge the constitutionality of a person's detention or confinement.

(3) Provisions apply — Subsections 784(2) to (6) apply in respect of any proceedings brought under subsection (1) or (2).

1999, c. 3, s. 50

PART XX — PROCEDURE IN JURY TRIALS AND GENERAL PROVISIONS

Preferring Indictment

574. (1) Prosecutor may prefer indictment — Subject to subsection (3) and section 577, the prosecutor may prefer an indictment against any person who has been ordered to stand trial in respect of

(a) any charge on which that person was ordered to stand trial, or

(b) any charge founded on the facts disclosed by the evidence taken on the preliminary inquiry, in addition to or in substitution for any charge on which that person was ordered to stand trial, whether or not the charges were included in one information.

(2) Consent to inclusion of other charges — An indictment preferred under subsection (1) may, if the accused consents, include any charge that is not referred to in paragraph (1)(a) or (b), and the offence charged may be dealt with, tried and determined and punished in all respects as if it were an offence in respect of which the accused had been ordered to stand trial, but if the offence was committed wholly in a province other than that in which the accused is before the court, subsection 478(3) applies.

(3) Private prosecutor requires consent — In any prosecution conducted by a prosecutor other than the Attorney General and in which the Attorney General does not intervene, an indictment shall not be preferred under subsection (1) before any court without the written order of a judge of that court.

R.S. 1985, c. 27 (1st Supp.), s. 113.

575. [Repealed R.S. 1985, c. 27 (1st Supp.), s. 113.]

576. (1) Indictment — Except as provided in this Act, no indictment shall be preferred.

(2) Criminal information and bill of indictment — No criminal information shall be laid or granted and no bill of indictment shall be preferred before a grand jury.

(3) Coroner's inquisition — No person shall be tried on a coroner's inquisition.

R.S. 1985, c. 27 (1st Supp.), s. 114.

577. Direct indictments — In any prosecution,

    (a) where a preliminary inquiry has not been held, an indictment shall not be preferred, or

    (b) where a preliminary inquiry has been held and the accused has been discharged, an indictment shall not be preferred or a new information shall not be laid

before any court without,

    (c) where the prosecution is conducted by the Attorney General or the Attorney General intervenes in the prosecution, the personal consent in writing of the Attorney General or Deputy Attorney General, or

    (d) where the prosecution is conducted by a prosecutor other than the Attorney General and the Attorney General does not intervene in the prosecution, the written order of a judge of that court.

R.S. 1985, c. 27 (1st Supp.) s. 115.

578. (1) Summons or warrant — Where notice of the recommencement of proceedings has been given pursuant to subsection 579(2) or an indictment has been filed with the court before which the proceedings are to commence or recommence, the court, if it considers it necessary, may issue

    (a) a summons addressed to, or

(b) a warrant for the arrest of,

the accused or defendant, as the case may be, to compel him to attend before the court to answer the charge described in the indictment.

(2) Part XVI to apply — The provisions of Part XVI apply with such modifications as the circumstances require where a summons or warrant is issued under subsection (1).

R.S. 1985, c. 27 (1st Supp.), s. 116.

579. (1) Attorney General may direct stay — The Attorney General or counsel instructed by him for that purpose may, at any time after any proceedings in relation to an accused or a defendant are commenced and before judgment, direct the clerk or other proper officer of the court to make an entry on the record that the proceedings are stayed by his direction, and such entry shall be made forthwith thereafter, whereupon the proceedings shall be stayed accordingly and any recognizance relating to the proceedings is vacated.

(2) Recommencement of proceedings — Proceedings stayed in accordance with subsection (1) may be recommenced, without laying a new information or preferring a new indictment, as the case may be, by the Attorney General or counsel instructed by him for that purpose giving notice of the recommencement to the clerk of the court in which the stay of the proceedings was entered, but where no such notice is given within one year after the entry of the stay of proceedings, or before the expiration of the time within which the proceedings could have been commenced, whichever is the earlier, the proceedings shall be deemed never to have been commenced.

R.S. 1985, c. 27 (1st Supp.), s. 117.

579.1 (1) Intervention by Attorney General of Canada — The Attorney General of Canada or counsel instructed by him or her for that purpose may intervene in proceedings in the following circumstances:

(a) the proceedings are in respect of a contravention of, a conspiracy or attempt to contravene or counselling the contravention of an Act of Parliament or a regulation made under that Act, other than this Act or a regulation made under this Act;

(b) the proceedings have not been instituted by an Attorney General;

(c) judgment has not been rendered; and

(d) the Attorney General of the province in which the proceedings are taken has not intervened.

(2) Section 579 to apply — Section 579 applies, with such modifications as the circumstances require, to proceedings in which the Attorney General of Canada intervenes pursuant to this section.

1994, c. 44, s. 60.

580. Form of indictment — An indictment is sufficient if it is on paper and is in Form 4.

R.S. 1985, c. 27 (1st Supp.), s. 117.

General Provisions respecting Counts

581. (1) Substance of offence — Each count in an indictment shall in general apply to a single transaction and shall contain in substance a statement that the accused or defendant committed an indictable offence therein specified.

(2) Form of statement — The statement referred to in subsection (1) may be

(a) in popular language without technical averments or allegations of matters that are not essential to be proved;

(b) in the words of the enactment that describes the offence or declares the matters charged to be an indictable offence; or

(c) in words that are sufficient to give to the accused notice of the offence with which he is charged.

(3) Details of circumstances — A count shall contain sufficient detail of the circumstances of the alleged offence to give to the accused reasonable information with respect to the act or omission to be proved against him and to identify the transaction referred to, but otherwise the absence or insufficiency of details does not vitiate the count.

(4) Indictment for treason — Where an accused is charged with an offence under section 47 or sections 49 to 53, every overt act that is to be relied on shall be stated in the indictment.

(5) Reference to section — A count may refer to any section, subsection, paragraph or subparagraph of the enactment that creates the offence charged, and for the purpose of determining whether a count is sufficient, consideration shall be given to any such reference.

(6) General provisions not restricted — Nothing in this Part relating to matters that do not render a count insufficient shall be deemed to restrict or limit the application of this section.

R.S. 1985, c. 27 (1st Supp.), s. 118.

582. High treason and first degree murder — No person shall be convicted for the offence of high treason or first degree murder unless in the indictment charging the offence he is specifically charged with that offence.

583. Certain omissions not grounds for objection — No count in an indictment is insufficient by reason of the absence of details where, in the opinion of the court, the count otherwise fulfils the requirements of section 581 and, without restricting the generality of the foregoing, no count in an indictment is insufficient by reason only that

(a) it does not name the person injured or intended or attempted to be injured,

(b) it does not name the person who owns or has a special property or interest in property mentioned in the count;

(c) it charges an intent to defraud without naming or describing the person whom it was intended to defraud;

(d) it does not set out any writing that is the subject of the charge;

(e) it does not set out the words used where words that are alleged to have been used are the subject of the charge;

(f) it does not specify the means by which the alleged offence was committed;

(g) it does not name or describe with precision any person, place or thing; or

(h) it does not, where the consent of a person, official or authority is required before proceedings may be instituted for an offence, state that the consent has been obtained.

Special Provisions Respecting Counts

584. (1) Sufficiency of count charging libel — No count for publishing a blasphemous, seditious or defamatory libel, or for selling or exhibiting an obscene book, pamphlet, newspaper or other written matter, is insufficient by reason only that it does not set out the words that are alleged to be libellous or the writing that is alleged to be obscene.

(2) Specifying sense — A count for publishing a libel may charge that the published matter was written in a sense that by innuendo made the publication thereof criminal, and may specify that sense without any introductory assertion to show how the matter was written in that sense.

(3) Proof — It is sufficient, on the trial of a count for publishing a libel, to prove that the matter published was libellous, with or without innuendo.

585. Sufficiency of count charging perjury, etc. — No count that charges

    (a) perjury,

    (b) the making of a false oath or a false statement,

    (c) fabricating evidence, or

    (d) procuring the commission of an offence mentioned in paragraph (*a*), (*b*) or (*c*)

is insufficient by reason only that it does not state the nature of the authority of the tribunal before which the oath or statement was taken or made, or the subject of the inquiry, or the words used or the evidence fabricated, or that it does not expressly negative the truth of the words used.

586. Sufficiency of count relating to fraud — No count that alleges false pretences, fraud or any attempt or conspiracy by fraudulent means is insufficient by reason only that it does not set out in detail the nature of the false pretence, fraud or fraudulent means.

Particulars

587. (1) What may be ordered — A court may, where it is satisfied that it is necessary for a fair trial, order the prosecutor to furnish particulars and, without restricting the generality of the foregoing, may order the prosecutor to furnish particulars

(a) of what is relied on in support of a charge of perjury, the making of a false oath or of a false statement, fabricating evidence or counselling the commission of any of those offences;

(b) of any false pretense or fraud that is alleged;

(c) of any alleged attempt or conspiracy by fraudulent means;

(d) setting out the passages in a book, pamphlet, newspaper or other printing or writing that are relied on in support of a charge of selling or exhibiting an obscene book, pamphlet, newspaper, printing or writing;

(e) further describing any writing or words that are the subject of a charge;

(f) further describing the means by which an offence is alleged to have been committed; or

(g) further describing a person, place or thing referred to in an indictment.

(2) Regard to evidence — For the purpose of determining whether or not a particular is required, the court may give consideration to any evidence that has been taken.

(3) Particular — Where a particular is delivered pursuant to this section,

(a) a copy shall be given without charge to the accused or his counsel,

(b) the particular shall be entered in the record, and

(c) the trial shall proceed in all respects as if the indictment had been amended to conform with the particular.

R.S. 1985, c. 27 (1st Supp.), s. 7(2).

Ownership of Property

588. Ownership — The real and personal property of which a person has, by law, the management, control or custody shall, for the purposes of an indictment or proceeding against any other person for an offence committed on or in respect of the property, be deemed to be the property of the person who has the management, control or custody of it.

Joinder or Severance of Counts

589. Count for murder — No count that charges an indictable offence other than murder shall be joined in an indictment to a count that charges murder unless

(a) the count that charges the offence other than murder arises out of the same transaction as a count that charges murder; or

(b) the accused signifies consent to the joinder of the counts.

1991, c. 4, s. 2.

590. (1) Offences may be charged in the alternative — A count is not objectionable by reason only that

(a) it charges in the alternative several different matters, acts or omissions that are stated in the alternative in an enactment that describes as an indictable offence the matters, acts or omissions charged in the count; or

(b) it is double or multifarious.

(2) Application to amend or divide counts — An accused may at any stage of his trial apply to the court to amend or to divide a count that

(a) charges in the alternative different matters, acts or omissions that are stated in the alternative in the enactment that describes the offence or declares that the matters, acts or omissions charged are an indictable offence, or

(b) is double or multifarious,

on the ground that, as framed, it embarrasses him in his defence.

(3) Order — The court may, where it is satisfied that the ends of justice require it, order that a count be amended or divided into two or more counts, and thereupon a formal commencement may be inserted before each of the counts into which it is divided.

591. (1) Joinder of counts — Subject to section 589, any number of counts for any number of offences may be joined in the same indictment, but the counts shall be distinguished in the manner shown in Form 4.

(2) Each count separate — Where there is more than one count in an indictment, each count may be treated as a separate indictment.

(3) Severance of accused and counts — The court may, where it is satisfied that the interests of justice so require, order

(a) that the accused or defendant be tried separately on one or more of the counts; and

(b) where there is more than one accused or defendant, that one or more of them be tried separately on one or more of the counts.

(4) Order for severance — An order under subsection (3) may be made before or during the trial but, if the order is made during the trial, the jury shall be discharged from giving a verdict on the counts

(a) on which the trial does not proceed; or

(b) in respect of the accused or defendant who has been granted a separate trial.

(5) Subsequent procedure — The counts in respect of which a jury is discharged pursuant to paragraph (4)(*a*) may subsequently be proceeded on in all respects as if they were contained in a separate indictment.

(6) Idem — Where an order is made in respect of an accused or defendant under paragraph (3)(*b*), the accused or defendant may be tried separately on the counts in relation to which the order was made as if they were contained in a separate indictment.

R.S. 1985, c. 27 (1st Supp.), s. 119.

Joinder of Accused in Certain Cases

592. Accessories after the fact — Any one who is charged with being an accessory after the fact to any offence may be indicted, whether or not the principal or any other party to the offence has been indicted or convicted or is or is not amenable to justice.

593. (1) Trial of persons jointly for having in possession — Any number of persons may be charged in the same indictment with an offence under section 354 or paragraph 356(1)(b), notwithstanding that

    (a) the property was had in possession at different times; or

    (b) the person by whom the property was obtained

        (i) is not indicted with them, or

        (ii) is not in custody or is not amenable to justice.

(2) Conviction of one or more — Where, pursuant to subsection (1), two or more persons are charged in the same indictment with an offence referred to in that subsection, any one or more of those persons who separately committed the offence in respect of the property or any part of it may be convicted.

594. [Repealed R.S. 1985, c. 27 (1st Supp.), s. 120.]

595. [Repealed R.S. 1985, c. 27 (1st Supp.), s. 120.]

596. [Repealed R.S. 1985, c. 27 (1st Supp.), s. 120.]

Proceedings when Person Indicted is at Large

597. (1) Bench warrant — Where an indictment has been preferred against a person who is at large, and that person does not appear or remain in attendance for his trial, the court before which the accused should have appeared or remained in attendance may issue a warrant in Form 7 for his arrest.

(2) Execution — A warrant issued under subsection (1) may be executed anywhere in Canada.

(3) Interim release — Where an accused is arrested under a warrant issued under subsection (1), a judge of the court that issued the warrant may order that the accused be released on his giving an undertaking that he will do any one or more of the following things as specified in the order, namely,

    (a) report at times to be stated in the order to a peace officer or other person designated in the order;

(b) remain within a territorial jurisdiction specified in the order;

(c) notify the peace officer or other person designated under paragraph (a) of any change in his address or his employment or occupation;

(d) abstain from communicating with any witness or other person expressly named in the order except in accordance with such conditions specified in the order as the judge deems necessary;

(e) where the accused is the holder of a passport, deposit his passport as specified in the order; and

(f) comply with such other reasonable conditions specified in the order as the judge considers desirable.

(4) Discretion to postpone execution — A judge who issues a warrant may specify in the warrant the period before which the warrant shall not be executed, to allow the accused to appear voluntarily before a judge having jurisdiction in the territorial division in which the warrant was issued.

(5) Deemed execution of warrant — Where the accused appears voluntarily for the offence in respect of which the accused is charged, the warrant is deemed to be executed.

R.S. 1985, c. 27 (1st Supp), s. 121; 1997, c. 18, s. 68.

598. (1) Election deemed to be waived — Notwithstanding anything in this Act, where a person to whom subsection 597(1) applies has elected or is deemed to have elected to be tried by a court composed of a judge and jury and, at the time he failed to appear or to remain in attendance for his trial, he had not re-elected to be tried by a court composed of a judge without a jury or a provincial court judge without a jury, he shall not be tried by a court composed of a judge and jury unless

(a) he establishes to the satisfaction of a judge of the court in which he is indicted that there was a legitimate excuse for his failure to appear or remain in attendance for his trial; or

(b) the Attorney General requires pursuant to section 568 or 569 that the accused be tried by a court composed of a judge and jury.

(2) Election deemed to be waived — An accused who, pursuant to subsection (1), may not be tried by a court composed of a judge and jury is deemed to have elected under section 536 or 536.1 to be tried by a judge without a jury and section 561 or 561.1, as the case may be, does not apply in respect of the accused.

R.S. 1985, c. 27 (1st Supp.), ss. 122, 203; 1999, c. 3, s. 51.

Change of Venue

599. (1) Reasons for change of venue — A court before which an accused is or may be indicted, at any term or sittings thereof, or a judge who may hold or sit in that court, may at any time before or after an indictment is found, on the application of the prosecutor or the accused, order the trial to be held in a territorial division in the same province other than that in which the offence would otherwise be tried if

(a) it appears expedient to the ends of justice; or

(b) a competent authority has directed that a jury is not to be summoned at the time appointed in a territorial division where the trial would otherwise by law be held.

(2) [Repealed 1988, c. 2, s. 23.]

(3) Conditions as to expense — The court or judge may, in an order made on an application by the prosecutor under subsection (1), prescribe conditions that he thinks proper with respect to the payment of additional expenses caused to the accused as a result of the change of venue

(4) Transmission of record — Where an order is made under subsection (1), the officer who has custody of the indictment, if any, and the writings and exhibits relating to the prosecution, shall transmit them forthwith to the clerk of the court before which the trial is ordered to be held, and all proceedings in the case shall be held or, if previously commenced, shall be continued in that court.

(5) Idem — Where the writings and exhibits referred to in subsection (4) have not been returned to the court in which the trial was to be held at the time an order is made to change the place of trial, the person who obtains the order shall serve a true copy thereof on the person in whose custody they are and that person shall thereupon transmit them to the clerk of the court before which the trial is to be held.

R.S. 1985, c. 1 (4th Supp.), s. 23.

600. Order is authority to remove prisoner — An order that is made under section 599 is sufficient warrant, justification and authority to all sheriffs, keepers of prisons and peace officers for the removal, disposal and reception of an accused in accordance with the terms of the order, and the sheriff may appoint and authorize any peace officer to convey the accused to a prison in the territorial division in which the trial is ordered to be held.

Amendment

601. (1) Amending defective indictment or count — An objection to an indictment or to a count in an indictment for a defect apparent on the face thereof shall be taken by motion to quash the indictment or count before the accused has pleaded, and thereafter only by leave of the court before which the proceedings take place, and the court before which an objection is taken under this section may, if it considers it necessary, order the indictment or count to be amended to cure the defect.

(2) Amendment where variance — Subject to this section, a court may, on the trial of an indictment, amend the indictment or a count therein or a particular that is furnished under section 587, to make the indictment, count or particular conform to the evidence, where there is a variance between the evidence and

    (a) a count in the indictment as preferred; or

    (b) a count in the indictment

        (i) as amended, or

(ii) as it would have been if it had been amended in conformity with any particular that has been furnished pursuant to section 587.

(3) Amending indictment — Subject to this section, a court shall, at any stage of the proceedings, amend the indictment or a count therein as may be necessary where it appears

(a) that the indictment has been preferred under a particular Act of Parliament instead of another Act of Parliament;

(b) that the indictment or a count thereof

(i) fails to state or states defectively anything that is requisite to constitute the offence,

(ii) does not negative an exception that should be negatived,

(iii) is in any way defective in substance,

and the matters to be alleged in the proposed amendment are disclosed by the evidence taken on the preliminary inquiry or on the trial; or

(c) that the indictment or a count thereof is in any way defective in form.

(4) Matters to be considered by the court — The court shall, in considering whether or not an amendment should be made to the indictment or a count in it, consider

(a) the matters disclosed by the evidence taken on the preliminary inquiry;

(b) the evidence taken on the trial, if any;

(c) the circumstances of the case;

(d) whether the accused has been misled or prejudiced in his defence by any variance, error or omission mentioned in subsection (2) or (3); and

(e) whether, having regard to the merits of the case, the proposed amendment can be made without injustice being done.

(4.1) Variance not material — A variance between the indictment or a count therein and the evidence taken is not material with respect to

(a) the time when the offence is alleged to have been committed, if it is proved that the indictment was preferred within the prescribed period of limitation, if any; or

(b) the place where the subject-matter of the proceedings is alleged to have arisen, if it is proved that it arose within the territorial jurisdiction of the court.

(5) Adjournment if accused prejudiced — Where, in the opinion of the court, the accused has been misled or prejudiced in his defence by a variance, error or omission in an indictment or a count therein, the court may, if it is of the opinion that the misleading or prejudice may be removed by an adjournment, adjourn the proceedings to a specified day or sittings of the court and may make such an order with respect to the payment of costs resulting from the necessity for amendment as it considers desirable.

(6) Question of law — The question whether an order to amend an indictment or a count thereof should be granted or refused is a question of law.

(7) Endorsing indictment — An order to amend an indictment or a count therein shall be endorsed on the indictment as part of the record and the proceedings shall continue as if the indictment or count had been originally preferred as amended.

(8) Mistakes not material — A mistake in the heading of an indictment shall be corrected as soon as it is discovered but, whether corrected or not, is not material.

(9) Limitation — The authority of a court to amend indictments does not authorize the court to add to the overt acts stated in an indictment for high treason or treason or for an offence against any provision in sections 49, 50, 51 and 53.

(10) Definition of "court" — In this section, **"court"** means a court, judge, justice or provincial court judge acting in summary conviction proceedings or in proceedings on indictment.

(11) Application — This section applies to all proceedings, including preliminary inquiries, with such modifications as the circumstances require.

R.S. 1985, c. 27 (1st Supp.), s. 123; 1999, c. 5, s. 23.

602. [Repealed R.S. 1985, c. 27 (1st Supp.), s. 124.]

Inspection and Copies of Documents

603. Right of accused — An accused is entitled, after he has been ordered to stand trial or at his trial,

(a) to inspect without charge the indictment, his own statement, the evidence and the exhibits, if any; and

(b) to receive, on payment of a reasonable fee determined in accordance with a tariff of fees fixed or approved by the Attorney General of the province, a copy

(i) of the evidence,

(ii) of his own statement, if any, and

(iii) of the indictment;

but the trial shall not be postponed to enable the accused to secure copies unless the court is satisfied that the failure of the accused to secure them before the trial is not attributable to lack of diligence on the part of the accused.

R.S. 1985, c. 27 (1st Supp.), s. 101(2).

604. [Repealed 1997, c. 18, s. 69.]

605. (1) Release of exhibits for testing — A judge of a superior court of criminal jurisdiction or a court of criminal jurisdiction may, on summary application on behalf of the accused or the prosecutor, after three days notice to the accused or prosecutor, as the case may be, order the release of any exhibit for the purpose of a scientific or other test or examination, subject to such terms as appear to be necessary or desirable to ensure the safeguarding of the exhibit and its preservation for use at the trial.

(2) Disobeying orders — Every one who fails to comply with the terms of an order made under subsection (1) is guilty of contempt of court and may be dealt with summarily by the judge or provincial court judge who made the order or before whom the trial of the accused takes place.

R.S. 1985, c. 27 (1st Supp.), s. 203.

Pleas

606. (1) Pleas permitted — An accused who is called on to plead may plead guilty or not guilty, or the special pleas authorized by this Part and no others.

(2) Refusal to plead — Where an accused refuses to plead or does not answer directly, the court shall order the clerk of the court to enter a plea of not guilty.

(3) Allowing time — An accused is not entitled as of right to have his trial postponed but the court may, if it considers that the accused should be allowed further time to plead, move to quash, or prepare for his defence or for any other reason, adjourn the trial to a later time in the session or sittings of the court, or to the next of any subsequent session or sittings of the court, on such terms as the court considers proper.

(4) Included or other offence — Notwithstanding any other provision of this Act, where an accused or defendant pleads not guilty of the offence charged but guilty of any other offence arising out of the same transaction, whether or not it is an included offence, the court may, with the consent of the prosecutor, accept that plea of guilty and, if the plea is accepted, the court shall find the accused or defendant not guilty of the offence charged and find him guilty of the offence in respect of which the plea of guilty was accepted and enter those findings in the record of the court.

R.S. 1985, c. 27 (1st Supp.), s. 125.

607. (1) Special pleas — An accused may plead the special pleas of

    (a) *autrefois acquit*;

    (b) *autrefois convict*; and

    (c) pardon.

(2) In case of libel — An accused who is charged with defamatory libel may plead in accordance with sections 611 and 612.

(3) Disposal — The pleas of *autrefois acquit, autrefois convict* and pardon shall be disposed of by the judge without a jury before the accused is called on to plead further.

(4) Pleading over — When the pleas referred to in subsection (3) are disposed of against the accused, he may plead guilty or not guilty.

(5) Statement sufficient — Where an accused pleads *autrefois acquit* or *autrefois convict*, it is sufficient if he

(a) states that he has been lawfully acquitted, convicted or discharged under subsection 730(1), as the case may be, of the offence charged in the count to which the plea relates; and

(b) indicates the time and place of the acquittal, conviction or discharge under subsection 730(1).

(6) Exceptions: foreign trials in absentia — A person who is alleged to have committed an act or omission outside Canada that is an offence in Canada by virtue of any of subsections 7(2) to (3.4) or subsection 7(3.7) or (3.71), and in respect of which that person has been tried and convicted outside Canada, may not plead *autrefois convict* with respect to a count that charges that offence if

(a) at the trial outside Canada the person was not present and was not represented by counsel acting under the person's instructions, and

(b) the person was not punished in accordance with the sentence imposed on conviction in respect of the act or omission,

notwithstanding that the person is deemed by virtue of subsection 7(6) to have been tried and convicted in Canada in respect of the act or omission.

Proposed Amendment — 607(6)

(6) Exception: foreign trials *in absentia* — A person who is alleged to have committed an act or omission outside Canada that is an offence in Canada by virtue of any of subsections 7(2) to (3.4) or (3.7), or an offence under the *Crimes Against Humanity and War Crimes Act*, and in respect of which the person has been tried and convicted outside Canada, may not plead *autrefois convict* with respect to a count that charges that offence if

(a) at the trial outside Canada the person was not present and was not represented by counsel acting under the person's instructions, and

(b) the person was not punished in accordance with the sentence imposed on conviction in respect of the act or omission,

notwithstanding that the person is deemed by virtue of subsection 7(6), or subsection 12(1) of the *Crimes Against Humanity and War Crimes Act*, as the case may be, to have been tried and convicted in Canada in respect of the act or omission.

2000, c. 24, s. 45 [Not in force at date of publication.]

R.S. 1985, c. 27 (1st Supp.), s. 126; c. 30 (3d Supp.), s. 2; 1995, c. 22, s. 10.

608. Evidence of identity of charges — Where an issue on a plea of *autrefois acquit* or *autrefois convict* is tried, the evidence and adjudication and the notes of the judge and official stenographer on the former trial and the record transmitted to the court pursuant to section 551 on the charge that is pending before that court are admissible in evidence to prove or to disprove the identity of the charges.

609. (1) What determines identity — Where an issue on a plea of *autrefois acquit* or *autrefois convict* to a count is tried and it appears

(a) that the matter on which the accused was given in charge on the former trial is the same in whole or in part as that on which it is proposed to give him in charge, and

(b) that on the former trial, if all proper amendments had been made that might then have been made, he might have been convicted of all the offences of which he may be convicted on the count to which the plea of *autrefois acquit* or *autrefois convict* is pleaded,

the judge shall give judgment discharging the accused in respect of that count.

(2) Allowance of special plea in part — The following provisions apply where an issue on a plea of *autrefois acquit* or *autrefois convict* is tried:

(a) where it appears that the accused might on the former trial have been convicted of an offence of which he may be convicted on the count in issue, the judge shall direct that the accused shall not be found guilty of any offence of which he might have been convicted on the former trial; and

(b) where it appears that the accused may be convicted on the count in issue of an offence of which he could not have been convicted on the former trial, the accused shall plead guilty or not guilty with respect to that offence.

610. (1) Circumstances of aggravation — Where an indictment changes substantially the same offence as that charged in an indictment on which an accused was previously convicted or acquitted, but adds a statement of intention or circumstances of aggravation tending, if proved, to increase the punishment, the previous conviction or acquittal bars the subsequent indictment.

(2) Effect of previous charge of murder or manslaughter — A conviction or an acquittal on an indictment for murder bars a subsequent indictment for the same homicide charging it as manslaughter or infanticide, and a conviction or acquittal on an indictment for manslaughter or infanticide bars a subsequent indictment for the same homicide charging it as murder.

(3) Previous charges of first degree murder — A conviction or an acquittal on an indictment for first degree murder bars a subsequent indictment for the same homicide charging it as second degree murder, and a conviction or acquittal on an indictment for second degree murder bars a subsequent indictment for the same homicide charging it as first degree murder.

(4) Effect of previous charge of infanticide or manslaughter — A conviction or an acquittal on an indictment for infanticide bars a subsequent indictment for the same homicide charging it as manslaughter, and a conviction or acquittal on an indictment for manslaughter bars a subsequent indictment for the same homicide charging it as infanticide.

611. (1) Libel, plea of justification — An accused who is charged with publishing a defamatory libel may plead that the defamatory matter published by him was true, and that it was for the public benefit that the matter should have been published in the manner in which and at the time when it was published.

(2) Where more than one sense alleged — A plea that is made under subsection (1) may justify the defamatory matter in any sense in which it is specified in the count, or in the sense that the defamatory matter bears without being specified, or separate pleas justifying the defamatory matter in each sense may be pleaded separately to each count as if two libels had been charged in separate counts.

(3) Plea in writing — A plea that is made under subsection (1) shall be in writing and shall set out the particular facts by reason of which it is alleged to have been for the public good that the matter should have been published.

(4) Reply — The prosecutor may in his reply deny generally the truth of a plea that is made under this section.

612. (1) Plea of justification necessary — The truth of the matters charged in an alleged libel shall not be inquired into in the absence of a plea of justification under section 611 unless the accused is charged with publishing the libel knowing it to be false, in which case evidence of the truth may be given to negative the allegation that the accused knew that the libel was false.

(2) Not guilty, in addition — The accused may, in addition to a plea that is made under section 611, plead not guilty and the pleas shall be inquired into together.

(3) Effect of plea on punishment — Where a plea of justification is pleaded and the accused is convicted, the court may, in pronouncing sentence, consider whether the guilt of the accused is aggravated or mitigated by the plea.

613. Plea of not guilty — Any ground of defence for which a special plea is not provided by this Act may be relied on under the plea of not guilty.

614. [Repealed 1991, c. 43, s. 3.]

615. [Repealed 1991, c. 43, s. 3.]

616. [Repealed 1991, c. 43, s. 3.]

617. [Repealed 1991, c. 43, s. 3.]

618. [Repealed 1991, c. 43, s. 3.]

619. [Repealed 1991, c. 43, s. 3.]

Corporations

620. Appearance by attorney — Every corporation against which an indictment is filed shall appear and plead by counsel or agent.

1997, c. 18, s. 70.

621. (1) Notice to corporation — The clerk of the court or the prosecutor may, where an indictment is filed against a corporation, cause a notice of the indictment to be served on the corporation.

(2) Contents of notice — A notice of an indictment referred to in subsection (1) shall set out the nature and purport of the indictment and advise that, unless the corporation appears on the date set out in the notice or the date fixed pursuant to subsection 548(2.1), and enters a plea, a plea of not guilty will be entered for the accused by the court, and that the trial of the indictment will be proceeded with as though the corporation had appeared and pleaded.

1997, c. 18, s. 71.

622. Procedure on default of appearance — Where a corporation does not appear in accordance with the notice referred to in section 621, the presiding judge may, on proof of service of the notice, order the clerk of the court to enter a plea of not guilty on behalf of the corporation, and the plea has the same force and effect as if the corporation had appeared by its counsel oar agent and pleaded that plea.

1997, c. 18, s. 72.

623. Trial of corporation — Where a corporation appears and pleads to the indictment or a plea of not guilty is entered by order of the court pursuant to section 622, the court shall proceed with the trial of the indictment and, where the corporation is convicted, section 735 applies.

Record of Proceedings

624. (1) How recorded — It is sufficient, in making up the record of a conviction or acquittal on an indictment, to copy the indictment and the plea that was pleaded, without a formal caption or heading.

(2) Record of proceedings — The court shall keep a record of every arraignment and of proceedings subsequent to arraignment.

625. Form of record in case of amendment — Where it is necessary to draw up a formal record in proceedings in which the indictment has been amended, the record shall be drawn up in the form in which the indictment remained after the amendment, without reference to the fact that the indictment was amended.

Pre-hearing Conference

625.1 (1) Pre-hearing conference — Subject to subsection (2), on application by the prosecutor or the accused or on its own motion, the court, or a judge of the court, before which, or the judge, provincial court judge or justice before whom, any proceedings are to be held may order that a conference between the prosecutor and the accused or counsel for the accused, to be presided over by the court, judge, provincial court judge or justice, be held prior to the proceedings to consider the matters that, to promote a fair and expeditious hearing, would be better decided before the start of the proceedings, and other similar matters, and to make arrangements for decisions on those matters.

(2) Mandatory pre-trial hearing for jury trials — In any case to be tried with a jury, a judge of the court before which the accused is to be tried shall, prior to the trial, order that a conference between the prosecutor and the accused or counsel for the accused, to be presided over by a judge of that court, be held in accordance with the rules of court made under section 482 to consider such matters as will promote a fair and expeditious trial.

R.S. 1985, c. 27 (1st Supp.), s. 127; 1997, c. 18, s. 73.

Juries

626. (1) Qualification of jurors — A person who is qualified as a juror according to, and summoned as a juror in accordance with, the laws of a province is qualified to serve as a juror in criminal proceedings in that province.

(2) No disqualification based on sex — Notwithstanding any law of a province referred to in subsection (1), no person may be disqualified, exempted or excused from serving as a juror in criminal proceedings on the grounds of his or her sex.

R.S. 1985, c.27 (1st Supp.), s. 128.

627. Support for juror with physical disability — The judge may permit a juror with a physical disability who is otherwise qualified to serve as a juror to have technical, personal, interpretative or other support services.

1998, c. 9, s. 4.

628. [Repealed R.S. 1985, c. 27 (1st Supp.), s. 129.]

629. (1) Challenging the jury panel — The accused or the prosecutor may challenge the jury panel only on the ground of partiality, fraud or wilful misconduct on the part of the sheriff or other officer by whom the panel was returned.

(2) In writing — A challenge under subsection (1) shall be in writing and shall state that the person who returned the panel was partial or fraudulent or that he wilfully misconducted himself, as the case may be.

(3) Form — A challenge under this section may be in Form 40.

R.S. 1985, c. 27 (1st Supp.), s. 130.

630. Trying ground of challenge — Where a challenge is made under section 629, the judge shall determine whether the alleged ground of challenge is true or not, and where he is satisfied that the alleged ground of challenge is true, he shall direct a new panel to be returned.

Empanelling Jury

631. (1) Names of jurors on cards — The name of each juror on a panel of jurors that has been returned, his number on the panel and his address shall be written on a separate card, and all the cards shall, as far as possible, be of equal size.

(2) To be placed in box — The sheriff or other officer who returns the panel shall deliver the cards referred to in subsection (1) to the clerk of the court who shall cause them to be placed together in a box to be provided for the purpose and to be thoroughly shaken together.

(3) To be drawn by clerk of court — Where

    (a) the array of jurors is not challenged, or

    (b) the array of jurors is challenged but the judge does not direct a new panel to be returned,

the clerk of the court shall, in open court, draw out the cards referred to in subsection (1), one after another, and shall call out the name and number on each card as it is drawn, until the number of persons who have answered to their names is, in the opinion of the judge, sufficient to provide a full jury after allowing for orders to excuse, challenges and directions to stand by.

(4) Juror and other persons to be sworn — The clerk of the court shall swear each member of the jury in the order in which the names of the jurors were drawn and shall swear any other person providing technical, personal, interpretative or other support services to a juror with a physical disability.

(5) Drawing additional names if necessary — Where the number of persons who answer to their names under subsection (3) is not sufficient to provide a full jury, the clerk of the court shall proceed in accordance with subsections (3) and (4) until twelve jurors are sworn.

R.S. 1985, c. 27 (1st Supp.), s. 131, 1992, c. 41, s. 1; 1998, c. 9, s. 5.

632. Excusing jurors — The judge may, at any time before the commencement of a trial, order that any juror be excused from jury service, whether or not the juror has been called pursuant to subsection 631(3) or any challenge has been made in relation to the juror, for reasons of

    (a) personal interest in the matter to be tried;

    (b) relationship with the judge, prosecutor, accused, counsel for the accused or a prospective witness; or

    (c) personal hardship or any other reasonable cause that, in the opinion of the judge, warrants that the juror be excused.

1992, c. 41, s. 2.

633. Stand by — The judge may direct a juror whose name has been called pursuant to subsection 631(3) to stand by for reasons of personal hardship or any other reasonable cause.

1992, c. 41, s. 2.

634. (1) Peremptory challenges — A juror may be challenged peremptorily whether or not the juror has been challenged for cause pursuant to section 638.

(2) Maximum number — Subject to subsections (3) and (4), the prosecutor and the accused are each entitled to

(a) twenty peremptory challenges, where the accused is charged with high treason or first degree murder;

(b) twelve peremptory challenges, where the accused is charged with an offence, other than an offence mentioned in paragraph (*a*), for which the accused may be sentenced to imprisonment for a term exceeding five years; or

(c) four peremptory challenges, where the accused is charged with an offence that is not referred to in paragraph (*a*) or (*b*).

(3) Where there are multiple counts — Where two or more counts in an indictment are to be tried together, the prosecutor and the accused are each entitled only to the number of peremptory challenges provided in respect of the count for which the greatest number of peremptory challenges is available.

(4) Where there are joint trials — Where two or more accused are to be tried together,

(a) each accused is entitled to the number of peremptory challenges to which the accused would be entitled if tried alone; and

(b) the prosecutor is entitled to the total number of peremptory challenges available to all the accused.

1992, c. 41, s. 2.

635. (1) Order of challenges — The accused shall be called on before the prosecutor is called on to declare whether the accused challenges the first juror, for cause or peremptorily, and thereafter the prosecutor and the accused shall be called on alternately, in respect of each of the remaining jurors, to first make such a declaration.

(2) Where there are joint trials — Subsection (1) applies where two or more accused are to be tried together, but all of the accused shall exercise the challenges of the defence in turn, in the order in which their names appear in the indictment or in any other order agreed on by them,

(a) in respect of the first juror, before the prosecutor; and

(b) in respect of each of the remaining jurors, either before or after the prosecutor, in accordance with subsection (1).

R.S. 1985, c. 2 (1st Supp.), ss. 1, 3; 1992, c. 41, s. 2.

636. [Repealed 1992, c. 41, s. 2.]

637. [Repealed 1992, c. 41, s. 2.]

638. (1) Challenge for cause — A prosecutor or an accused is entitled to any number of challenges on the ground that

(a) the name of a juror does not appear on the panel, but no misnomer or misdescription is a ground of challenge where it appears to the court that the description given on the panel sufficiently designates the person referred to;

(b) a juror is not indifferent between the Queen and the accused;

(c) a juror has been convicted of an offence for which he was sentenced to death or to a term of imprisonment exceeding twelve months;

(d) a juror is an alien;

(e) a juror, even with the aid of technical, personal, interpretative or other support services provided to the juror under section 627, is physically unable to perform properly the duties of a juror; or

(f) a juror does not speak the official language of Canada that is the language of the accused or the official language of Canada in which the accused can best give testimony or both official languages of Canada, where the accused is required by reason of an order under section 530 to be tried before a judge and jury who speak the official language of Canada that is the language of the accused or the official language of Canada in which the accused can best give testimony or who speak both official languages of Canada, as the case may be.

(2) No other ground — No challenge for cause shall be allowed on a ground not mentioned in subsection (1).

(3) [Repealed 1997, c. 18, s. 74]

(4) [Repealed 1997, c. 18, s. 74]

R.S. 1985, c. 27 (1st Supp.), s. 132; c. 31 (4th Supp.), s. 96; 1997, c. 18, s. 74.

S. 638(1)(f) has been proclaimed in force in the provinces of Manitoba, New Brunswick, Ontario and in Yukon Territory and Northwest Territories.

639. (1) Challenge in writing — Where a challenge is made on a ground mentioned in section 638, the court may, in its discretion, require the party that challenges to put the challenge in writing.

(2) Form — A challenge may be in Form 41.

(3) Denial — A challenge may be denied by the other party to the proceedings on the ground that it is not true.

640. (1) Objection that name not on panel — Where the ground of a challenge is that the name of a juror does not appear on the panel, the issue shall be tried by the judge on the *voir dire* by the inspection of the panel, and such other evidence that the judge thinks fit to receive.

(2) Other grounds — Where the ground of a challenge is one not mentioned in subsection (1), the two jurors who were last sworn, or if no jurors have then been sworn, two persons present whom the court may appoint for the purpose, shall be sworn to determine whether the ground of challenge is true.

(3) If challenge not sustained, or if sustained — Where the finding, pursuant to subsection (1) or (2) is that the ground of challenge is not true, the juror shall be sworn, but if the finding is that the ground of challenge is true, the juror shall not be sworn.

(4) Disagreement of triers — Where, after what the court considers to be a reasonable time, the two persons who are sworn to determine whether the ground of challenge is true are unable to agree, the court may discharge them from giving a verdict and may direct two other persons to be sworn to determine whether the ground of challenge is true.

641. (1) Calling jurors who have stood by — Where a full jury has not been sworn and no names remain to be called, the names of those who have been directed to stand by shall be called again in the order in which their names were drawn and they shall be sworn, unless excused by the judge or challenged by the accused or the prosecutor.

(2) Other jurors becoming available — Where, before a juror is sworn pursuant to subsection (1), other jurors in the panel become available, the prosecutor may require the names of those jurors to be put into and drawn from the box in accordance with section 631, and those jurors shall be challenged, directed to stand by, excused or sworn, as the case may be, before the names of the jurors who were originally directed to stand by are called again.

1992, c. 41, s. 3.

642. (1) Summoning other jurors when panel exhausted — Where a full jury cannot be provided notwithstanding that the relevant provisions of this Part have been complied with, the court may, at the request of the prosecutor, order the sheriff or other proper officer forthwith to summon as many persons, whether qualified jurors or not, as the court directs for the purpose of providing a full jury.

(2) Orally — Jurors may be summoned under subsection (1) by word of mouth, if necessary.

(3) Adding names to panel — The names of the persons who are summoned under this section shall be added to the general panel for the purposes of the trial, and the same proceedings shall be taken with respect to calling and challenging those persons, excusing them and directing them to stand by as are provided in this Part with respect to the persons named in the original panel.

1992, c. 41, s. 4.

643. (1) Who shall be jury — The twelve jurors whose names are drawn and who are sworn in accordance with this Part shall be the jury to try the issues of the indictment, and the names of the jurors so drawn and sworn shall be kept apart until the jury gives its verdict or until it is discharged, whereupon the names shall be returned to the box as often as occasion arises, as long as an issue remains to be tried before a jury.

(2) Same jury may try another issue by consent — The court may try an issue with the same jury in whole or in part that previously tried or was drawn to try another issue, without the jurors being sworn again, but if the prosecutor or the accused objects to any of the jurors or the court excuses any of the jurors, the court shall order those persons to withdraw and shall direct that the required number of names to make up a full jury be drawn and, subject to the provisions of this Part relating to challenges, orders to excuse and directions to stand by, the persons whose names are drawn shall be sworn.

(3) Sections directory — Failure to comply with the directions of this section or section 631, 635 or 641 does not affect the validity of a proceeding.

1992, c. 41, s. 5.

644. (1) Discharge of juror — Where in the course of a trial the judge is satisfied that a juror should not, by reason of illness or other reasonable cause, continue to act, the judge may discharge the juror.

(1.1) Replacement of juror — A judge may select another juror to take the place of a juror who by reason of illness or other reasonable cause cannot continue to act, if the jury has not yet begun to hear evidence, either by drawing a name from a panel of persons who were summoned to act as jurors and who are available at the court at the time of replacing the juror or by using the procedure referred to in section 642.

(2) Trial may continue — Where in the course of a trial a member of the jury dies or is discharged pursuant to subsection (1), the jury shall, unless the judge otherwise directs and if the number of jurors is not reduced below ten, be deemed to remain properly constituted for all purposes of the trial and the trial shall proceed and a verdict may be given accordingly.

1992, c. 41, s. 6; 1997, c. 18, s. 75.

Trial

645. (1) Trial continuous — The trial of an accused shall proceed continuously subject to adjournment by the court.

(2) Adjournment — The judge may adjourn the trial from time to time in the same sittings.

(3) Formal adjournment unnecessary — No formal adjournment of trial or entry thereof is required.

(4) Questions reserved for decision — A judge, in any case tried without a jury, may reserve final decision on any question raised at the trial, or any matter raised further to a pre-hearing conference, and the decision, when given, shall be deemed to have been given at the trial.

(5) Questions reserved for decision in a trial with a jury — In any case to be tried with a jury, the judge before whom an accused is or is to be tried has jurisdiction, before any juror on a panel of jurors is called pursuant to subsection 631(3) and in the absence of any such juror, to deal with any matter that would ordinarily or necessarily be dealt with in the absence of the jury after it has been sworn.

R.S. 1985, c. 27 (1st Supp.), s. 133; 1997, c. 18, s. 76.

646. Taking evidence — On the trial of an accused for an indictable offence, the evidence of the witnesses for the prosecutor and the accused and the address of the prosecutor and the accused or counsel for the accused by way of summing up shall be taken in accordance with the provisions of Part XVIII relating to the taking of evidence at preliminary inquiries.

647. (1) Separation of jurors — The judge may, at any time before the jury retires to consider its verdict, permit the members of the jury to separate.

(2) Keeping in charge — Where permission to separate under subsection (1) cannot be given or is not given, the jury shall be kept under the charge of an officer of the court as the judge directs, and that officer shall prevent the jurors from communicating with anyone other than himself or another member of the jury without leave of the judge.

(3) Non-compliance with subsection (2) — Failure to comply with subsection (2) does not affect the validity of the proceedings.

(4) Empanelling new jury in certain cases — Where the fact that there has been a failure to comply with this section or section 648 is discovered before the verdict of the jury is returned, the judge may, if he considers that the failure to comply might lead to a miscarriage of justice, discharge the jury and

(a) direct that the accused be tried with a new jury during the same session or sittings of the court; or

(b) postpone the trial on such terms as justice may require.

(5) Refreshment and accommodation — The judge shall direct the sheriff to provide the jurors who are sworn with suitable and sufficient refreshment, food and lodging while they are together until they have given their verdict.

648. (1) Restriction on publication — Where permission to separate is given to members of a jury under subsection 647(1), no information regarding any portion of the trial at which the jury is not present shall be published, after the permission is granted, in any newspaper or broadcast before the jury retires to consider its verdict.

(2) Offence — Every one who fails to comply with subsection (1) is guilty of an offence punishable on summary conviction.

(3) "Newspaper" — In this section, **"newspaper"** has the same meaning as in section 297.

649. Disclosure of jury proceedings — Every member of a jury, and every person providing technical, personal, interpretative or other support services to a juror with a physical disability, who except for the purposes of

(a) an investigation of an alleged offence under subsection 139(2) in relation to a juror, or

(b) giving evidence in criminal proceedings in relation to such an offence, discloses any information relating to the proceedings of the jury when it was absent from the courtroom that was not subsequently disclosed in open court is guilty of an offence punishable on summary conviction.

1998, c. 9, s. 7.

650. (1) Accused to be present — Subject to subsections (1.1) and (2), an accused other than a corporation shall be present in court during the whole of the accused's trial.

(1.1) Video links — Where the court so orders, and where the prosecutor and the accused so agree, the accused may appear by counsel or by closed-circuit television or any other means that allow the court and the accused to engage in simultaneous visual and oral communication, for any part of the trial other than a part in which the evidence of a witness is taken.

(1.2) Video links — Where the court so orders, an accused who is confined in prison may appear by closed-circuit in prison television or any other means that allow the court and the accused to engage in simultaneous visual and oral communication, for any part of the trial other than a part in which the evidence of a witness is taken, if the accused is given the opportunity to communicate privately with counsel, in a case in which the accused is represented by counsel.

(2) Exceptions — The court may

(a) cause the accused to be removed and to be kept out of court, where he misconducts himself by interrupting the proceedings so that to continue the proceedings in his presence would not be feasible;

(b) permit the accused to be out of court during the whole or any part of his trial on such conditions as the court considers proper; or

(c) cause the accused to be removed and to be kept out of court during the trial of an issue as to whether the accused is unfit to stand trial, where it is satisfied that failure to do so might have an adverse effect on the mental condition of the accused.

(3) To make defence — An accused is entitled, after the close of the case for the prosecution, to make full answer and defence personally or by counsel.

1997, c. 18, s. 77(2).

650.1 Pre-charge conference — A judge in a jury trial may, before the charge to the jury, confer with the accused or counsel for the accused and the prosecutor with respect to the matters that should be explained to the jury and with respect to the choice of instructions to the jury.

1997, c. 18, s. 78.

651. (1) Summing up by prosecutor — Where an accused, or any one of several accused being tried together, is defended by counsel, the counsel shall, at the end of the case for the prosecution, declare whether or not he intends to adduce evidence on behalf of the accused for whom he appears and if he does not announce his intention to adduce evidence, the prosecutor may address the jury by way of summing up.

(2) Summing up by accused — Counsel for the accused or the accused, where he is not defended by counsel, is entitled, if he thinks fit, to open the case for the defence, and after the conclusion of that opening to examine such witnesses as he thinks fit, and when all the evidence is concluded to sum up the evidence.

(3) Accused's right of reply — Where no witnesses are examined for an accused, he or his counsel is entitled to address the jury last, but otherwise counsel for the prosecution is entitled to address the jury last.

(4) Prosecutor's right of reply where more than one accused — Where two or more accused are tried jointly and witnesses are examined for any of them, all the accused or their respective counsel are required to address the jury before it is addressed by the prosecutor.

652. (1) View — The judge may, where it appears to be in the interests of justice, at any time after the jury has been sworn and before it give its verdict, direct the jury to have a view of any place, thing or person, and shall give directions respecting the manner in which, and the persons by whom, the place, thing or person shall be shown to the jury, and may for that purpose adjourn the trial.

(2) Directions to prevent communication — Where a view is ordered under subsection (1), the judge shall give any directions that he considers necessary for the purpose of preventing undue communication by any person with members of the jury, but failure to comply with any directions given under this subsection does not affect the validity of the proceedings.

(3) Who shall attend — Where a view is ordered under subsection (1) the accused and the judge shall attend.

653. (1) Disagreement of jury — Where the judge is satisfied that the jury is unable to agree on its verdict and that further detention of the jury would be useless, he may in his discretion discharge that jury and direct a new jury to be empanelled during the sittings of the court, or may adjourn the trial on such terms as justice may require.

(2) Discretion not reviewable — A discretion that is exercised under subsection (1) by a judge is not reviewable.

654. Proceeding on Sunday, etc., not invalid — The taking of the verdict of a jury and any proceeding incidental thereto is not invalid by reason only that it is done on Sunday or on a holiday.

Evidence on Trial

655. Admissions at trial — Where an accused is on trial for an indictable offence, he or his counsel may admit any fact alleged against him for the purpose of dispensing with proof thereof.

656. Presumption — valuable minerals — In any proceeding in relation to theft or possession of a valuable mineral that is unrefined, partly refined, uncut or otherwise unprocessed by any person actively engaged in or on a mine, if it is established that the person possesses the valuable mineral, the person is presumed, in the absence of evidence raising a reasonable doubt to the contrary, to have stolen or unlawfully possessed the valuable mineral.

657. Use in evidence of statement by accused — A statement made by an accused under subsection 541(3) and purporting to be signed by the justice before whom it was made may be given in evidence against the accused at his or her trial without proof of the signature of the justice, unless it is proved that the justice by whom the statement purports to be signed did not sign it.

1994, c. 44, s. 62.

657.1 (1) Proof of ownership and value of property — In any proceedings, an affidavit or a solemn declaration of a person who claims to be the lawful owner of, or the person lawfully entitled to possession of, property that was the subject-matter of the offence, or any other person who has specialized knowledge of the property or of that type of property, containing the statements referred to in subsection (2), shall be admissible in evidence and, in the absence of evidence to the contrary, is evidence of the statements contained in the affidavit or solemn declaration without proof of the signature of the person appearing to have signed the affidavit or solemn declaration.

(2) Statements to be made — For the purposes of subsection (1), a person shall state in an affidavit or a solemn declaration

(a) that the person is the lawful owner of, or is lawfully entitled to possession of, the property, or otherwise has specialized knowledge of the property or of property of the same type as that property;

(b) the value of the property;

(c) in the case of a person who is the lawful owner of or is lawfully entitled to possession of the property, that the person has been deprived of the property by fraudulent means or otherwise without the lawful consent of the person;

(c.1) in the case of proceedings in respect of an offence under section 342, that the credit card had been revoked or cancelled, is a false document within the meaning of section 321 or that no credit card that meets the exact description of that credit card was ever issued; and

(d) any facts within the personal knowledge of the person relied on to justify the statements referred to in paragraphs (a) to (c.1).

(3) Notice of intention to produce affidavit or solemn declaration — Unless the court orders otherwise, no affidavit or solemn declaration shall be received in evidence pursuant to subsection (1) unless the prosecutor has, before the trial or other proceeding, given to the accused a copy of the affidavit or solemn declaration and reasonable notice of intention to produce it in evidence.

(4) Attendance for examination — Notwithstanding subsection (1), the court may require the person who appears to have signed an affidavit or solemn declaration referred to in that subsection to appear before it for examination or cross-examination in respect of the issue of proof of any of the statements contained in the affidavit or solemn declaration.

R.S. 1985, c. 23 (4th Supp.), s. 3; 1994, c. 44, s. 63; 1997, c. 18, s. 79

657.2 (1) Theft and possession — Where an accused is charged with possession of any property obtained by the commission of an offence, evidence of the conviction or discharge of another person of theft of the property is admissible against the accused, and in the absence of evidence to the contrary is proof that the property was stolen.

(2) Accessory after the fact — Where an accused is charged with being an accessory after the fact to the commission of an offence, evidence of the conviction or discharge of another person of the offence is admissible against the accused, and in the absence of evidence to the contrary is proof that the offence was committed.

657.3 (1) Expert testimony — In any proceedings, the evidence of a person as an expert may be given by means of a report accompanied by the affidavit or solemn declaration of the person, setting out, in particular, the qualifications of the person as an expert if

(a) the court recognizes that person as an expert; and

(b) the party intending to produce the report in evidence has, before the proceeding, given to the other party a copy of the affidavit or solemn declaration and the report and reasonable notice of the intention to produce it in evidence.

(2) Attendance for examination — Notwithstanding subsection (1), the court may require the person who appears to have signed an affidavit or solemn declaration referred to in that subsection to appear before it for examination or cross-examination in respect of the issue of proof of any of the statements contained in the affidavit or solemn declaration or report.

1997, c. 18, s. 80

Children and Young Persons

658. (1) Testimony as to date of birth — In any proceedings to which this Act applies, the testimony of a person as to the date of his or her birth is admissible as evidence of that date.

(2) Testimony of parent — In any proceedings to which this Act applies, the testimony of a parent as to the age of a person of whom he or she is a parent is admissible as evidence of the age of that person.

(3) Proof of age — In any proceedings to which this act applies,

(a) a birth or baptismal certificate or a copy of such a certificate purporting to be certified under the hand of the person in whose custody the certificate is held is evidence of the age of that person; and

(b) an entry or record of an incorporated society or its officers who have had the control or care of a child or young person at or about the time the child or young person was brought to Canada is evidence of the age of the child or young person if the entry or record was made before the time when the offence is alleged to have been committed.

(4) Other evidence — In the absence of any certificate, copy, entry or record mentioned in subsection (3), or in corroboration of any such certificate, copy, entry or record, a jury, judge, justice or provincial court judge, as the case may be, may receive and act on any other information relating to age that they consider reliable.

(5) Inference from appearance — In the absence of other evidence, or by way of corroboration of other evidence, a jury, judge, justice or provincial court judge, as the case may be, may infer the age of a child or young person from his or her appearance.

1994, c. 44, s. 64.

Corroboration

659. Children's evidence — Any requirement whereby it is mandatory for a court to give the jury a warning about convicting an accused on the evidence of a child is abrogated.

1993, c. 45, s. 9.

660. Full offence charged, attempt proved — Where the complete commission of an offence charged is not proved but the evidence establishes an attempt to commit the offence, the accused may be convicted of the attempt.

661. (1) Attempt charged, full offence proved — Where an attempt to commit an offence is charged but the evidence establishes the commission of the complete offence, the accused is not entitled to be acquitted, but the jury may convict him of the attempt unless the judge presiding at the trial, in his discretion, discharges the jury from giving a verdict and directs that the accused be indicted for the complete offence.

(2) Conviction a bar — An accused who is convicted under this section is not liable to be tried again for the offence that he was charged with attempting to commit.

662. (1) Offence charged, part only proved — A count in an indictment is divisible and where the commission of the offence charged, as described in the enactment creating it or as charged in the count, includes the commission of another offence, whether punishable by indictment or on summary conviction, the accused may be convicted

(a) of an offence so included that is proved, notwithstanding that the whole offence that is charged is not proved; or

(b) of an attempt to commit an offence so included.

(2) First degree murder charged — For greater certainty and without limiting the generality of subsection (1), where a count charges first degree murder and the evidence does not prove first degree murder but proves second degree murder or an attempt to commit second degree murder, the jury may find the accused not guilty of first degree murder but guilty of second degree murder or an attempt to commit second degree murder, as the case may be.

(3) Conviction for infanticide or manslaughter on charge of murder — Subject to subsection (4), where a count charges murder and the evidence proves manslaughter or infanticide but does not prove murder, the jury may find the accused not guilty of murder but guilty of manslaughter or infanticide, but shall not on that count find the accused guilty of any other offence.

(4) Conviction for concealing body of child where murder or infanticide charged — Where a count charges the murder of a child or infanticide and the evidence proves the commission of an offence under section 243 but does not prove murder or infanticide, the jury may find the accused not guilty of murder or infanticide, as the case may be, but guilty of an offence under section 243.

(5) Conviction for dangerous driving where manslaughter charged — For greater certainty, where a court charges an offence under section 220, 221 or 236 arising out of the operation of a motor vehicle or the navigation or operation of a vessel or aircraft, and the evidence does not prove such offence but does prove an offence under section 249 or subsection 249.1(3), the accused may be convicted of an offence under section 249 or subsection 249.1(3), as the case may be.

(6) Conviction for break and enter with intent — Where a count charges an offence under paragraph 348(1)(b) and the evidence does not prove such offence but does prove an offence under paragraph 348(1)(a), the accused may be convicted of an offence under paragraph 348(1)(a).

R.S. 1985, c. 27 (1st Supp.), s. 134; 2000, c. 2, s. 3.

663. No acquittal unless act or omission not wilful — Where a female person is charged with infanticide and the evidence establishes that she caused the death of her child but does not establish that, at the time of the act or omission by which she caused the death of the child,

(a) she was not fully recovered from the effects of giving birth to the child or from the effect of lactation consequent on the birth of the child, and

(b) the balance of her mind was, at that time, disturbed by reason of the effect of giving birth to the child or of the effect of lactation consequent on the birth of the child,

she may be convicted unless the evidence establishes that the act or omission was not wilful.

Previous Convictions

664. No reference to previous conviction — No indictment in respect of an offence for which, by reason of previous convictions, a greater punishment may be imposed shall contain any reference to previous convictions.

665. [Repealed 1995, c. 22, s. 3.]

666. Evidence of character — Where, at a trial, the accused adduces evidence of his good character, the prosecutor may, in answer thereto, before a verdict is returned, adduce evidence of the previous conviction of the accused for any offences, including any previous conviction by reason of which a greater punishment may be imposed.

667. (1) Proof of previous conviction — In any proceedings,

(a) a certificate setting out with reasonable particularity the conviction, discharge under section 730 or the conviction and sentence in Canada of an offender signed by

(i) the person who made the conviction or order for the discharge,

(ii) the clerk of the court in which the conviction or order for the discharge was made, or

(iii) a fingerprint examiner,

is, on proof that the accused or defendant is the offender referred to in the certificate, evidence that the accused or defendant was so convicted, so discharged or so convicted and sentenced without proof of the signature or the official character of the person appearing to have signed the certificate;

(b) evidence that the fingerprints of the accused or defendant are the same as the fingerprints of the offender whose fingerprints are reproduced in or attached to a certificate issued under subparagraph (a)(iii) is, in the absence of evidence to the contrary, proof that the accused or defendant is the offender referred to in that certificate;

(c) a certificate of a fingerprint examiner stating that he has compared the fingerprints reproduced in or attached to that certificate with the fingerprints reproduced in or attached to a certificate issued under subparagraph (a)(iii) and that they are those of the same person is evidence of the statements contained in the certificate without proof of the signature or the official character of the person appearing to have signed the certificate; and

(d) a certificate under subparagraph (a)(iii) may be in Form 44, and a certificate under paragraph (c) may be in Form 45.

(2) Idem — In any proceedings, a copy of the summary conviction or discharge under section 730 in Canada of an offender, signed by the person who made the conviction or order for the discharge or by the clerk of the court in which the conviction or order for the discharge was made, is, on proof that the accused or defendant is the offender referred to in the copy of the summary conviction, evidence of the conviction or discharge under section 730 of the accused or defendant, without proof of the signature or the official character of the person appearing to have signed it.

(2.1) Proof of identity — In any summary conviction proceedings, where the name of a defendant is similar to the name of an offender referred to in a certificate made under subparagraph (1)(a)(i) or (ii) in respect of a summary conviction or referred to in a copy of a summary conviction mentioned in subsection (2), that similarity of name is, in the absence of evidence to the contrary, evidence that the defendant is the offender referred to in the certificate or the copy of the summary conviction.

(3) Attendance and right to cross-examine — An accused against whom a certificate issued under subparagraph (1)(a)(iii) or paragraph (1)(c) is produced may, with leave of the court, require the attendance of the person who signed the certificate for the purposes of cross-examination.

(4) Notice of intention to produce certificate — No certificate issued under subparagraph (1)(a)(iii) or paragraph (1)(c) shall be received in evidence unless the party intending to produce it has given to the accused reasonable notice of his intention together with a copy of the certificate.

(5) "fingerprint examiner" — In this section **"fingerprint examiner"** means a person designated as such for the purposes of this section by the Solicitor General of Canada.

R.S. 1985, c. 27 (1st Supp.), s. 136; 1995, c. 22, s. 10.

668. [Repealed 1995, c. 22, s. 4.]

669. [Repealed 1995, c. 22, s. 4.]

Jurisdiction

669.1 (1) Jurisdiction — Where any judge, court or provincial court judge by whom or which the plea of the accused or defendant to an offence was taken has not commenced to hear evidence, any judge, court or provincial court judge having jurisdiction to try the accused or defendant has jurisdiction for the purpose of the hearing and adjudication.

(2) Adjournment — Any court, judge or provincial court judge having jurisdiction to try an accused or a defendant, or any clerk or other proper officer of the court, or in the case of an offence punishable on summary conviction, any justice, may, at any time before or after the plea of the accused or defendant is taken, adjourn the proceedings.

R.S. 1985, c. 27 (1st Supp.), s. 137.

669.2 (1) Continuation of proceedings — Subject to this section, where an accused or a defendant is being tried by

(a) a judge or provincial court judge,

(b) a justice or other person who is, or is a member of, a summary conviction court, or

(c) a court composed of a judge and jury,

as the case may be, and the judge, provincial court judge, justice or other person dies or is for any reason unable to continue, the proceedings may be continued before another judge, provincial court judge, justice or other person, as the case may be, who has jurisdiction to try the accused or defendant.

(2) Where adjudication is made — Where a verdict was rendered by a jury or an adjudication was made by a judge, provincial court judge, justice or other person before whom the trial was commenced, the judge, provincial court judge, justice or other person before whom the proceedings are continued shall, without further election by an accused, impose the punishment or make the order that is authorized by law in the circumstances.

(3) Where no adjudication is made — Subject to subsections (4) and (5), where the trial was commenced but no adjudication was made or verdict rendered, the judge, provincial court judge, justice or other person before whom the proceedings are continued shall, without further election by an accused, commence the trial again as if no evidence had been taken.

(4) Where no adjudication is made - jury trials — Where a trial that is before a court composed of a judge and a jury was commenced but no adjudication was made or verdict rendered, the judge before whom the proceedings are continued may, without further election by an accused,

(a) continue the trial; or

(b) commence the trial again as if no evidence had been taken.

(5) Where trial continued — Where a trial is continued under paragraph (4)(a), any evidence that was adduced before a judge referred to in paragraph (1)(c) is deemed to have been adduced before the judge before whom the trial is continued but, where the prosecutor and the accused so agree, any part of that evidence may be adduced again before the judge before whom the trial is continued.

R.S. 1985, c. 27 (1st Supp.), s. 137; 1994, c. 44, s. 65.

669.3 Jurisdiction when appointment to another court — Where a court composed of a judge and a jury, a judge or a provincial court judge is conducting a trial and the judge or provincial court judge is appointed to another court, he or she continues to have jurisdiction in respect of the trial until its completion.

1994, c. 44, s. 66.

Formal Defects in Jury Process

670. Judgment not to be stayed on certain grounds — Judgment shall not be stayed or reversed after verdict on an indictment

(a) by reason of any irregularity in the summoning or empanelling of the jury; or

(b) for the reason that a person who served on the jury was not returned as a juror by a sheriff or other officer.

671. Directions respecting jury or jurors directory — No omission to observe the directions contained in any Act with respect to the qualification, selection, balloting or distribution of jurors, the preparation of the jurors' book, the selecting of jury lists or the drafting of panels from the jury lists is a ground for impeaching or quashing a verdict rendered in criminal proceedings.

672. Saving powers of court — Nothing in this Act alters, abridges or affects any power or authority that a court or judge had immediately before April 1, 1955, or any practice or form that existed immediately before April 1, 1955, with respect to trials by jury, jury process, juries or jurors, except where the power or authority, practice or form is expressly altered by or is inconsistent with this Act.

PART XX.1 — MENTAL DISORDER

Interpretation

672.1 Definitions — In this Part,

"accused" includes a defendant in summary conviction proceedings and an accused in respect of whom a verdict of not criminally responsible on account of mental disorder has been rendered;

"assessment" means an assessment by a medical practitioner of the mental condition of the accused pursuant to an assessment order made under section 672.11, and any incidental observation or examination of the accused;

"chairperson" includes any alternate that the chairperson of a Review Board may designate to act on the chairperson's behalf;

"court" includes a summary conviction court as defined in section 785, a judge, a justice and a judge of the court of appeal as defined in section 673;

"disposition" means an order made by a court or Review Board under section 672.54 or an order made by a court under section 672.58;

"dual status offender" means an offender who is subject to a sentence of imprisonment in respect of one offence and a custodial disposition under paragraph 672.54(c) in respect of another offence;

"hospital" means a place in a province that is designated by the Minister of Health for the province for the custody, treatment or assessment of an accused in respect of whom an assessment order, a disposition or a placement decision is made.

"medical practitioner" means a person who is entitled to practise medicine by the laws of a province;

"party", in relation to proceedings of a court or Review Board to make or review a disposition, means

(a) the accused,

(b) the person in charge of the hospital where the accused is detained or is to attend pursuant to an assessment order or a disposition,

(c) an Attorney General designated by the court or Review Board under subsection 672.5(3),

(d) any interested person designated by the court or Review Board under subsection 672.5(4), or

(e) where the disposition is to be made by a court, the prosecutor of the charge against the accused;

"placement decision" means a decision by a Review Board under subsection 672.68(2) as to the place of custody of a dual status offender;

"prescribed" means prescribed by regulations made by the Governor in Council under section 672.95;

"Review Board" means the Review Board established or designated for a province pursuant to subsection 672.38(1);

"verdict of not criminally responsible on account of mental disorder" means a verdict that the accused committed the act or made the omission that formed the basis of the offence with which the accused is charged but is not criminally responsible on account of mental disorder.

1991, c. 43, s. 4

Assessment Orders

672.11 Assessment order — A court having jurisdiction over an accused in respect of an offence may order an assessment of the mental condition of the accused, if it has reasonable grounds to believe that such evidence is necessary to determine

(a) whether the accused is unfit to stand trial;

(b) whether the accused was, at the time of the commission of the alleged offence, suffering from a mental disorder so as to be exempt from criminal responsibility by virtue of subsection 16(1);

(c) whether the balance of the mind of the accused was disturbed at the time of commission of the alleged offence, where the accused is a female person charged with an offence arising out of the death of her newly-born child;

(d) the appropriate disposition to be made, where a verdict of not criminally responsible on account of mental disorder or unfit to stand trial has been rendered in respect of the accused; or

(e) whether an order should be made under subsection 747.1(1) to detain the accused in a treatment facility, where the accused has been convicted of the offence.

1991, c. 43, s. 4; 1995, c. 22, s. 10

672.12 (1) Where court may order assessment — The court may make an assessment order at any stage of proceedings against the accused of its own motion, on application of the accused or, subject to subsections (2) and (3), on application of the prosecutor.

(2) Limitation on prosecutor's application for assessment of fitness — Where the prosecutor applies for an assessment in order to determine whether the accused is unfit to stand trial for an offence that is prosecuted by way of summary conviction, the court may only order the assessment if

(a) the accused raised the issue of fitness; or

(b) the prosecutor satisfies the court that there are reasonable grounds to doubt that the accused is fit to stand trial.

(3) Limitation on prosecutor's application for assessment — Where the prosecutor applies for an assessment in order to determine whether the accused was suffering from a mental disorder at the time of the offence so as to be exempt from criminal responsibility, the court may only order the assessment if

(a) the accused puts his or her mental capacity for criminal intent into issue; or

(b) the prosecutor satisfies the court that there are reasonable grounds to doubt that the accused is criminally responsible for the alleged offence, on account of mental disorder.

1991, c. 43, s. 4.

672.13 (1) Contents of assessment order — An assessment order must specify

(a) the service that or the person who is to make the assessment, or the hospital where it is to be made;

(b) whether the accused is to be detained in custody while the order is in force; and

(c) the period that the order is to be in force, including the time required for the assessment and for the accused to travel to and from the place where the assessment is to be made.

(2) Form — An assessment order may be in Form 48.

1991, c. 43, s. 4.

672.14 (1) General rule for period — An assessment order shall not be in force for more than thirty days.

(2) Exception in fitness cases — No assessment order to determine whether the accused is unfit to stand trial shall be in force for more than five days, excluding holidays and the time required for the accused to travel to and from the place where the assessment is to be made, unless the accused and the prosecutor agree to a longer period not exceeding thirty days.

(3) Exception for compelling circumstances — Notwithstanding subsections (1) and (2), a court may make an assessment order that remains in force for sixty days where the court is satisfied that compelling circumstances exist that warrant it.

1991, c. 43, s. 4.

672.15 (1) Extensions — Subject to subsection (2), a court may extend an assessment order, of its own motion or on the application of the accused or the prosecutor made during or after the period that the order is in force, for any further period that is required, in its opinion, to complete the assessment of the accused.

(2) Maximum duration of extensions — No extension of an assessment order shall exceed thirty days, and the period of the initial order together with all extensions shall not exceed sixty days.

1991, c. 43, s. 4.

672.16 (1) Presumption against custody — Subject to subsection (3), an accused shall not be detained in custody pursuant to an assessment order unless

(a) the court is satisfied that on the evidence custody is necessary to assess the accused, or that on the evidence of a medical practitioner custody is desirable to assess the accused and the accused consents to custody;

(b) custody of the accused is required in respect of any other matter or by virtue of any other provision of this Act; or

(c) the prosecutor, having been given a reasonable opportunity to do so, shows that detention of the accused in custody is justified on either of the grounds set out in subsection 515(10).

(2) Report of medical practitioner — For the purposes of paragraph (1)(*a*), where the prosecutor and the accused agree, the evidence of a medical practitioner may be received in the form of a report in writing.

(3) Presumption of custody in certain circumstances — An accused who is charged with an offence described in any of paragraphs 515(6)(a) to (d) in the circumstances described in that paragraph, or an offence described in subsection 522(2), shall be detained in custody pursuant to an assessment order, unless the accused shows that custody is not justified under the terms of that paragraph or subsection.

1991, c. 43, s. 4.

672.17 Assessment order takes precedence over bail hearing — During the period that an assessment order of an accused charged with an offence is in force, no order for the interim release or detention of the accused may be made by virtue of Part XVI or section 679 in respect of that offence or an included offence.

1991, c. 43, s. 4.

672.18 Application to vary assessment order — Where at any time while an assessment order made by a court is in force the prosecutor or an accused shows cause, the court may vary the terms of the order respecting the interim release or detention of the accused in such manner as it considers appropriate in the circumstances.

1991, c. 43, s. 4.

672.19 No treatment order on assessment — No assessment order may direct that psychiatric or any other treatment of the accused be carried out, or direct the accused to submit to such treatment.

1991, c. 43, s. 4.

672.191 When assessment completed — An accused in respect of whom an assessment order is made shall appear before the court that made the order as soon as is practicable after the assessment is completed and not later than the last day of the period that the order is to be in force.

1997, c. 18, s. 81.

Assessment Reports

672.2 (1) Assessment reports — An assessment order may require the person who makes the assessment to submit in writing an assessment report on the mental condition of the accused.

(2) Assessment report to be filed with court — An assessment report shall be filed with the court that ordered it, within the period fixed by the court.

(3) Court to send assessment report to Review Board — The court shall send to the Review Board without delay a copy of any report filed with it pursuant to subsection (2), to assist in determining the appropriate disposition to be made in respect of the accused.

(4) Copies of reports to accused and prosecutor — Subject to subsection 672.51(3), copies of any report filed with a court pursuant to subsection (2) shall be provided without delay to the prosecutor, the accused and any counsel representing the accused.

1991, c. 43, s. 4.

Protected Statements

672.21 (1) Definition of "protected statement" — In this section, "protected statement" means a statement made by the accused during the course and for the purposes of an assessment or treatment directed by a disposition, to the person specified in the assessment order or the disposition, or to anyone acting under that person's direction.

(2) Protected statements not admissible against accused — No protected statement or reference to a protected statement made by an accused is admissible in evidence, without the consent of the accused, in any proceeding before a court, tribunal, body or person with jurisdiction to compel the production of evidence.

(3) Exceptions — Notwithstanding subsection (2), evidence of a protected statement is admissible for the purpose of

(a) determining whether the accused is unfit to stand trial;

(b) making a disposition or placement decision respecting the accused;

(c) finding whether the accused is a dangerous mentally disordered accused under section 672.65;

(d) determining whether the balance of the mind of the accused was disturbed at the time of commission of the alleged offence, where the accused is a female person charged with an offence arising out of the death of her newly-born child;

(e) determining whether the accused was, at the time of the commission of an alleged offence, suffering from automatism or a mental disorder so as to be exempt from criminal responsibility by virtue of subsection 16(1), if the accused puts his or her mental capacity for criminal intent into issue, or if the prosecutor raises the issue after verdict;

(f) challenging the credibility of an accused in any proceeding where the testimony of the accused is inconsistent in a material particular with a protected statement that the accused made previously; or

(g) establishing the perjury of an accused who is charged with perjury in respect of a statement made in any proceeding.

1991, c. 43, s. 4

Fitness to Stand Trial

672.22 Presumption of fitness — An accused is presumed fit to stand trial unless the court is satisfied on the balance of probabilities that the accused is unfit to stand trial.

1991, c. 43, s. 4

672.23 (1) Court may direct issue to be tried — Where the court has reasonable grounds, at any state of the proceedings before a verdict is rendered, to believe that the accused is unfit to stand trial, the court may direct, of its own motion or on application of the accused or the prosecutor, that the issue of fitness of the accused be tried.

(2) Burden of proof — An accused or a prosecutor who makes an application under subsection (1) has the burden of proof that the accused is unfit to stand trial.

1991, c. 43, s. 4

672.24 (1) Counsel — Where the court has reasonable grounds to believe that an accused is unfit to stand trial and the accused is not represented by counsel, the court shall order that the accused be represented by counsel.

(2) Counsel fees and disbursements — Where counsel is assigned pursuant to subsection (1) and legal aid is not granted to the accused pursuant to a provincial legal aid program, the fees and disbursements of counsel shall be paid by the Attorney General to the extent that the accused is unable to pay them.

(3) Taxation of fees and disbursements — Where counsel and the Attorney General cannot agree on the fees or disbursements of counsel, the Attorney General or the counsel may apply to the registrar of the court and the registrar may tax the disputed fees and disbursements.

1991, c. 43, s. 4; 1997, c. 18, s. 82

672.25 (1) Postponing trial of issue — The court shall postpone directing the trial of the issue of fitness of an accused in proceedings for an offence for which the accused may be prosecuted by indictment or that is punishable on summary conviction, until the prosecutor has elected to proceed by way of indictment or summary conviction.

(2) Idem — The court may postpone directing the trial of the issue of fitness of an accused

(a) where the issue arises before the close of the case for the prosecution at a preliminary inquiry, until a time that is not later than the time the accused is called on to answer to the charge; or

(b) where the issue arises before the close of the case for the prosecution at trial, until a time not later than the opening of the case for the defence or, on motion of the accused, any later time that the court may direct.

1991, c. 43, s. 4

672.26 Trial of issue by judge and jury — Where an accused is tried or is to be tried before a court composed of a judge and jury,

(a) if the judge directs that the issue of fitness of the accused be tried before the accused is given in charge to a jury for trial on the indictment, a jury composed of the number of jurors required in respect of the indictment in the province where the trial is to be held shall be sworn to try that issue and, with the consent of the accused, the issues to be tried on the indictment; and

(b) if the judge directs that the issue of fitness of the accused be tried after the accused has been given in charge to a jury for trial on the indictment, the jury shall be sworn to try that issue in addition to the issues in respect of which it is already sworn.

1991, c. 43, s. 4

672.27 Trial of issue by court — The court shall try the issue of fitness of an accused and render a verdict where the issue arises

(a) in respect of an accused who is tried or is to be tried before a court other than a court composed of a judge and jury; or

(b) before a court at a preliminary inquiry or at any other stage of the proceedings.

1991, c. 43, s. 4

672.28 Proceeding continues where accused is fit — Where the verdict on trial of the issue is that an accused is fit to stand trial, the arraignment, preliminary inquiry, trial or other stage of the proceeding shall continue as if the issue of fitness of the accused had never arisen.

1991, c. 43, s. 4

672.29 Where continued detention in custody — Where an accused is detained in custody on delivery of a verdict that the accused is fit to stand trial, the court may order the accused to be detained in a hospital until the completion of the trial, if the court has reasonable grounds to believe that the accused would become unfit to stand trial if released.

1991, c. 43, s. 4

672.3 Acquittal — Where the court has postponed directing the trial of the issue of fitness of an accused pursuant to subsection 672.25(2) and the accused is discharged or acquitted before the issue is tried, it shall not be tried.

1991, c. 43, s. 4

672.31 Verdict of unfit to stand trial — Where the verdict on trial of the issue is that an accused is unfit to stand trial, any plea that has been made shall be set aside and any jury shall be discharged.

1991, c. 43, s. 4

672.32 (1) Subsequent proceedings — A verdict of unfit to stand trial shall not prevent the accused from being tried subsequently where the accused becomes fit to stand trial.

(2) Burden of proof — The burden of proof that the accused has subsequently become fit to stand trial is on the party who asserts it, and is discharged by proof on the balance of probabilities.

1991, c. 43, s. 4

672.33 (1) Prima facie case to be made every two years — The court that has jurisdiction in respect of the offence charged against an accused who is found unfit to stand trial shall hold an inquiry, not later than two years after the verdict is rendered and every two years thereafter until the accused is acquitted pursuant to subsection (6) or tried, to decide whether sufficient evidence can be adduced at that time to put the accused on trial.

(2) Court may order inquiry to be held — On application of the accused, the court may order an inquiry under this section to be held at any time if it is satisfied, on the basis of the application and any written material submitted by the accused, that there is reason to doubt that there is a *prima facie* case against the accused.

(3) Burden of proof — At an inquiry under this section, the burden of proof that sufficient evidence can be adduced to put the accused on trial is on the prosecutor.

(4) Admissible evidence at an inquiry — In an inquiry under this section, the court shall admit as evidence

(a) any affidavit containing evidence that would be admissible if given by the person making the affidavit as a witness in court; or

(b) any certified copy of the oral testimony given at a previous inquiry or hearing held before a court in respect of the offence with which the accused is charged.

(5) Conduct of inquiry — The court may determine the manner in which an inquiry under this section is conducted and may follow the practices and procedures in respect of a preliminary inquiry under Part XVIII where it concludes that the interests of justice so require.

(6) Where prima facie case not made — Where, on the completion of an inquiry under this section, the court is satisfied that sufficient evidence cannot be adduced to put the accused on trial, the court shall acquit the accused.

1991, c. 43, s. 4

Verdict of Not Criminally Responsible on Account of Mental Disorder

672.34 Verdict of not criminally responsible on account of mental disorder — Where the jury, or the judge or provincial court judge where there is no jury, finds that an accused committed the act or made the omission that formed the basis of the offence charged, but was at the time suffering from mental disorder so as to be exempt from criminal responsibility by virtue of subsection 16(1), the jury or the judge shall render a verdict that the accused committed the act or made the omission but is not criminally responsible on account of mental disorder.

1991, c. 43, s. 4

672.35 Effect of verdict of not criminally responsible on account of mental disorder — Where a verdict of not criminally responsible on account of mental disorder is rendered, the accused shall not be found guilty or convicted of the offence, but

(a) the accused may plead *autrefois acquit* in respect of any subsequent charge relating to that offence;

(b) any court may take the verdict into account in considering an application for judicial interim release or in considering what dispositions to make or sentence to impose for any other offence; and

(c) the National Parole Board or any provincial parole board may take the verdict into account in considering an application by the accused for parole or pardon in respect of any other offence.

1991, c. 43, s. 4

672.36 Verdict not a previous conviction — A verdict of not criminally responsible on account of mental disorder is not a previous conviction for the purposes of any offence under any Act of Parliament for which a greater punishment is provided by reason of previous convictions.

1991, c. 43, s. 4

672.37 (1) Definition of "application for federal employment" — In this section, **"application for federal employment"** means an application form relating to

    (a) employment in any department, as defined in section 2 of the *Financial Administration Act*;

    (b) employment by any Crown corporation as defined in subsection 83(1) of the *Financial Administration Act*;

    (c) enrolment in the Canadian Forces; or

    (d) employment in connection with the operation of any work, undertaking or business that is within the legislative authority of Parliament.

(2) Application for federal employment — No application for federal employment shall contain any question that requires the applicant to disclose any charge or finding that the applicant committed an offence that resulted in a finding or a verdict of not criminally responsible on account of mental disorder if the applicant was discharged absolutely or is no longer subject to any disposition in respect of that offence.

(3) Punishment — Any person who uses or authorizes the use of an application for federal employment that contravenes subsection (2) is guilty of an offence punishable on summary conviction.

1991, c. 43, s. 4.

Review Boards

672.38 (1) Review boards to be established — A Review Board shall be established or designated for each province to make or review dispositions concerning any accused in respect of whom a verdict of not criminally responsible by reason of mental disorder or unfit to stand trial is rendered, and shall consist of not fewer than five members appointed by the lieutenant governor in council of the province.

(2) Treated as provincial board — A Review Board shall be treated as having been established under the laws of the province.

(3) Personal liability — No member of a Review Board is liable for any act done in good faith in the exercise of the member's powers or the performance of the member's duties and functions or for any default or neglect in good faith in the exercise of those powers or the performance of those duties and functions.

1991, c. 43, s. 4; 1997, c. 18, s. 83.

672.39 Members of Review Board — A Review Board must have at least one member who is entitled under the laws of a province to practise psychiatry and, where only one member is so entitled, at least one other member must have training and experience in the field of mental health, and be entitled under the laws of a province to practise medicine or psychology.

1991, c. 43, s. 4.

672.4 (1) Chairperson of a Review Board — Subject to subsection (2), the chairperson of a Review Board shall be a judge of the Federal Court or of a superior, district or county court of a province, or a person who is qualified for appointment to, or has retired from, such a judicial office.

(2) Transitional — Where the chairperson of a Review Board that was established before the coming into force of subsection (1) is not a judge or other person referred to therein, the chairperson may continue to act until the expiration of his or her term of office if at least one other member of the Review Board is a judge or other person referred to in subsection (1) or is a member of the bar of the province.

1991, c. 43, s. 4.

672.41 (1) Quorum of Review Board — Subject to subsection (2), the quorum of a Review Board is constituted by the chairperson, a member who is entitled under the laws of a province to practise psychiatry, and any other member.

(2) Transitional — Where the chairperson of a Review Board that was established before the coming into force of this section is not a judge or other person referred to in subsection 672.4(1), the quorum of the Review Board is constituted by the chairperson, a member who is entitled under the laws of a province to practise psychiatry, and a member who is a person referred to in that subsection or a member of the bar of the province.

1991, c. 43, s. 4.

672.42 Majority vote — A decision of a majority of the members present and voting is the decision of a Review Board.

1991, c. 43, s. 4.

672.43 Powers of Review Boards — At a hearing held by a Review Board to make a disposition or review a disposition in respect of an accused, the chairperson has all the powers that are conferred by sections 4 and 5 of the *Inquiries Act* on persons appointed as commissioners under Part I of that Act.

1991, c. 43, s. 4.

672.44 (1) Rules of Review Board — A Review Board may, subject to the approval of the lieutenant governor in council of the province, make rules providing for the practice and procedure before the Review Board.

(2) Application and publication of rules — The rules made by a Review Board under subsection (1) apply to any proceeding within its jurisdiction, and shall be published in the *Canada Gazette*.

(3) Regulations — Notwithstanding anything in this section, the Governor in Council may make regulations to provide for the practice and procedure before Review Boards, in particular to make the rules of Review Boards uniform, and all regulations made under this subsection prevail over any rules made under subsection (1).

1991, c. 43, s. 4.

Disposition Hearings

672.45 (1) Hearing to be held by a court — Where a verdict of not criminally responsible on account of mental disorder or unfit to stand trial is rendered in respect of an accused, the court may of its own motion, and shall on application by the accused or the prosecutor, hold a disposition hearing.

(2) Disposition to be made — At a disposition hearing, the court shall make a disposition in respect of the accused, if it is satisfied that it can readily do so and that a disposition should be made without delay.

1991, c. 43, s. 4.

672.46 (1) Status quo pending Review Board hearing — Where the court does not make a disposition in respect of the accused at a disposition hearing, any order for the interim release or detention of the accused or any appearance notice, promise to appear, summons, undertaking or recognizance in respect of the accused that is in force at the time the verdict of not criminally responsible on account of mental disorder or unfit to stand trial is rendered continues in force, subject to its terms, until the Review Board makes a disposition.

(2) Variation of order — Notwithstanding subsection (1), a court may, on cause being shown, vacate any order, appearance notice, promise to appear, summons, undertaking or recognizance referred to in that subsection and make any other order for the interim release or detention of the accused that the court considers to be appropriate in the circumstances, including an order directing that the accused be detained in custody in a hospital pending a disposition by the Review Board in respect of the accused.

1991, c. 43, s. 4.

672.47 (1) Review board to make disposition where court does not — Where a verdict of not criminally responsible on account of mental disorder or unfit to stand trial is rendered and the court makes no disposition in respect of an accused, the Review Board shall, as soon as is practicable but not later than forty-five days after the verdict was rendered, hold a hearing and make a disposition.

(2) Extension of time for hearing — Where the court is satisfied that there are exceptional circumstances that warrant it, the court may extend the time for holding a hearing under subsection (1) to a maximum of ninety days after the verdict was rendered.

(3) Where disposition made by court — Where a court makes a disposition under section 672.54 other than an absolute discharge in respect of an accused, the Review Board shall hold a hearing on a day not later than the day on which the disposition ceases to be in force, and not later than ninety days after the disposition was made, and shall make a disposition in respect of the accused.

1991, c. 43, s. 4.

672.48 (1) Review board to determine fitness — Where a Review Board holds a hearing to make or review a disposition in respect of an accused who has been found unfit to stand trial, it shall determine whether in its opinion the accused is fit to stand trial at the time of the hearing.

(2) Review board shall send accused to court — If a Review Board determines that the accused is fit to stand trial, it shall order that the accused be sent back to court, and the court shall try the issue and render a verdict.

(3) Chairperson may send accused to court — The chairperson of a Review Board may, with the consent of the accused and the person in charge of the hospital where an accused is being detained, order that the accused be sent back to court for trial of the issue of whether the accused is unfit to stand trial, where the chairperson is of the opinion that

(a) the accused is fit to stand trial, and

(b) the Review Board will not hold a hearing to make or review a disposition in respect of the accused within a reasonable period.

1991, c. 43, s. 4.

672.49 (1) Continued detention in hospital — In a disposition made pursuant to section 672.47 the Review Board or chairperson may require the accused to continue to be detained in a hospital until the court determines whether the accused is fit to stand trial, if the Review Board or chairperson has reasonable grounds to believe that the accused would become unfit to stand trial if released.

(2) Copy of disposition to be sent to court — The Review Board or chairperson shall send a copy of a disposition made pursuant to section 672.47 without delay to the court having jurisdiction over the accused and to the Attorney General of the province where the accused is to be tried.

1991, c. 43, s. 4.

672.5 (1) Procedure at disposition hearing — A hearing held by a court or Review Board to make or review a disposition in respect of an accused shall be held in accordance with this section.

(2) Hearing to be informal — The hearing may be conducted in as informal a manner as is appropriate in the circumstances.

(3) Attorneys general may be parties — On application, the court or Review Board shall designate as a party the Attorney General of the province where the disposition is to be made and, where an accused is transferred from another province, the Attorney General of the province from which the accused is transferred.

(4) Interested person may be a party — The court or Review Board may designate as a party any person who has a substantial interest in protecting the interests of the accused, if the court or Review Board is of the opinion that it is just to do so.

(5) Notice of hearing — Notice of the hearing shall be given to the parties, the Attorney General of the province where the disposition is to be made and, where the accused is transferred to another province, the Attorney General of the province from which the accused is transferred, within the time and in the manner prescribed, or within the time and in the manner fixed by the rules of the court or Review Board.

(6) Order excluding the public — Where the court or Review Board considers it to be in the best interests of the accused and not contrary to the public interest, the court or Review Board may order the public or any members of the public to be excluded from the hearing or any part of the hearing.

(7) Right to counsel — The accused or any other party has the right to be represented by counsel.

(8) Assigning counsel — The court or Review Board shall, if an accused is not represented by counsel, assign counsel to act for any accused

(a) who has been found unfit to stand trial; or

(b) wherever the interests of justice so require.

(8.1) Counsel fees and disbursements — Where counsel is assigned pursuant to subsection (8) and legal aid is not granted to the accused pursuant to a provincial legal aid program, the fees and disbursements of counsel shall be paid by the Attorney General to the extent that the accused is unable to pay them.

(8.2) Taxation of fees and disbursements — Where counsel and the Attorney General cannot agree on the fees or disbursements of counsel, the Attorney General or the counsel may apply to the registrar of the court and the registrar may tax the disputed fees and disbursements.

(9) Right of accused to be present — Subject to subsection (10), the accused has the right to be present during the whole of the hearing.

(10) Removal or absence of accused — The court or the chairperson of the Review Board may

(a) permit the accused to be absent during the whole or any part of the hearing on such conditions as the court or chairperson considers proper; or

(b) cause the accused to be removed and barred from re-entry for the whole or any part of the hearing

(i) where the accused interrupts the hearing so that to continue in the presence of the accused would not be feasible,

(ii) on being satisfied that failure to do so would likely endanger the life or safety of another person or would seriously impair the treatment or recovery of the accused, or

(iii) in order to hear, in the absence of the accused, evidence, oral or written submissions, or the cross-examination of any witness concerning whether grounds exist for removing the accused pursuant to subparagraph (ii).

(11) Rights of parties at hearing — Any party may adduce evidence, make oral or written submissions, call witnesses and cross-examine any witness called by any other party and, on application, cross-examine any person who made an assessment report that was submitted to the court or Review Board in writing.

(12) Request to compel attendance of witnesses — A party may not compel the attendance of witnesses, but may request the court or the chairperson of the Review Board to do so.

(13) Video links — Where the accused so agrees, the court or the chairperson of the Review Board may permit the accused to appear by closed-circuit television or any other means that allow the court or Review Board and the accused to engage in simultaneous visual and oral communication, for any part of the hearing.

(14) Victim impact statement — A victim of the offence may prepare and file with the court or Review Board a written statement describing the harm done to, or loss suffered by, the victim arising from the commission of the offence.

(15) Copy of statement — The court or Review Board shall ensure that a copy of any statement filed in accordance with subsection (14) is provided to the accused or counsel for the accused, and the prosecutor, as soon as practicable after a verdict of not criminally responsible on account of mental disorder is rendered in respect of the offence.

(16) Definition of "victim" — In subsection (14), "victim" has the same meaning as in subsection 722(4).

1991, c. 43, s. 4; 1997, c. 18, s. 84; 1999, c. 25, s. 11

672.51 (1) Definition of "disposition information" — In this section, "disposition information" means all or part of an assessment report submitted to the court or Review Board and any other written information before the court or Review Board about the accused that is relevant to making a disposition.

(2) Disposition information to be made available to parties — Subject to this section, all disposition information shall be made available for inspection by, and the court or Review Board shall provide a copy of it to, each party and any counsel representing the accused.

(3) Exception where disclosure dangerous to any person — The court or Review Board shall withhold some or all of the disposition information from an accused where it is satisfied, on the basis of that information and the evidence or report of the medical practitioner responsible for the assessment or treatment of the accused, that disclosure of the information would be likely to endanger the life or safety of another person or would seriously impair the treatment or recovery of the accused.

(4) Idem — Notwithstanding subsection (3), the court or Review Board may release some or all of the disposition information to an accused where the interests of justice make disclosure essential in its opinion.

(5) Exception where disclosure unnecessary or prejudicial — The court or Review Board shall withold disposition information from a party other than the accused or an Attorney General, where disclosure to that party, in the opinion of the court or Review Board, is not necessary to the proceeding and may be prejudicial to the accused.

(6) Exclusion of certain persons from hearing — A court or Review Board that withholds disposition information from the accused or any other party pursuant to subsection (3) or (5) shall exclude the accused or the other party, as the case may be, from the hearing during

> (a) the oral presentation of that disposition information; or

> (b) the questioning by the court or Review Board or the cross-examination of any person concerning that disposition information.

(7) Prohibition of disclosure in certain cases — No disposition information shall be made available for inspection or disclosed to any person who is not a party to the proceedings

> (a) where the disposition information has been withheld from the accused or any other party pursuant to subsection (3) or (5); or

> (b) where the court or Review Board is of the opinion that disclosure of the disposition information would be seriously prejudicial to the accused and that, in the circumstances, protection of the accused takes precedence over the public interest in disclosure.

(8) Idem — No part of the record of the proceedings in respect of which the accused was excluded pursuant to subparagraph 672.5(10)(b)(ii) or (iii) shall be made available for inspection to the accused or to any person who is not a party to the proceedings.

(9) Information to be made available to specified persons — Notwithstanding subsections (7) and (8), the court or Review Board may make any disposition information, or a copy of it, available on request to any person or member of a class of persons

> (a) that has a valid interest in the information for research or statistical purposes, where the court or Review Board is satisfied that disclosure is in the public interest;

> (b) that has a valid interest in the information for the purposes of the proper administration of justice; or

> (c) that the accused requests or authorizes in writing to inspect it, where the court or Review Board is satisfied that the person will not disclose or give to the accused a copy of any disposition information withheld from the accused pursuant to subsection (3), or of any part of the record of proceedings referred to in subsection (8), or that the reasons for withholding that information from the accused no longer exist.

(10) Disclosure for research or statistical purposes — A person to whom the court or Review Board makes disposition information available under paragraph (9)(a) may disclose it for research or statistical purposes, but not in any form or manner that could reasonably be expected to identify any person to whom it relates.

(11) Prohibition on publication — No person shall publish in any newspaper within the meaning of section 297 or broadcast

> (a) any disposition information that is prohibited from being disclosed pursuant to subsection (7); or

> (b) any part of the record of the proceedings in respect of which the accused was excluded pursuant to subparagraph 672.5(10)(b)(ii) or (iii).

(12) Powers of courts not limited — Except as otherwise provided in this section, nothing in this section limits the powers that a court may exercise apart from this section.

1991, c. 43, s. 4; 1997, c. 18, s. 85.

672.52 (1) Record of proceedings — The court or Review Board shall cause a record of the proceedings of its disposition hearings to be kept, and include in the record any assessment report submitted.

(2) Transmittal of transcript to Review Board — Where a court makes a disposition, it shall send without delay a transcript of the disposition hearing, any document or information relating thereto in the possession of the court, and all exhibits filed with the court or copies of those exhibits, to the Review Board that has jurisdiction in respect of the matter.

(3) Reasons for disposition and copies to be provided — The court or Review Board shall state its reasons for making a disposition in the record of the proceedings, and shall provide every party with a copy of the disposition and those reasons.

1991, c. 43, s. 4.

672.53 Proceedings not invalid — Any procedural irregularity in relation to a disposition hearing does not affect the validity of the hearing unless it causes the accused substantial prejudice.

1992, c. 43, s. 4.

Dispositions by a Court or Review Board

Terms of Dispositions

672.54 Dispositions that may be made — Where a court or Review Board makes a disposition pursuant to subsection 672.45(2) or section 672.47, it shall, taking into consideration the need to protect the public from dangerous persons, the mental condition of the accused, the reintegration of the accused into society and the other needs of the accused, make one of the following dispositions that is the least onerous and least restrictive to the accused:

(a) where a verdict of not criminally responsible on account of mental disorder has been rendered in respect of the accused and, in the opinion of the court or Review Board, the accused is not a significant threat to the safety of the public, by order, direct that the accused be discharged absolutely;

(b) by order, direct that the accused be discharged subject to such conditions as the court or Review Board considers appropriate; or

(c) by order, direct that the accused be detained in custody in a hospital, subject to such conditions as the court or Review Board considers appropriate.

1991, c. 43, s. 4.

672.541 Victim impact statement — When a verdict of not criminally responsible on account of mental disorder has been rendered in respect of an accused, the court or Review Board shall, at a hearing held under section 672.45 or 672.47, take into consideration any statement filed in accordance with subsection 672.5(14) in determining the appropriate disposition or conditions under section 672.54, to the extent that the statement is relevant to its consideration of the criteria set out in section 672.54.

1999, c. 25, s. 12

672.55 (1) Treatment not a condition — No disposition made under section 672.54 shall direct that any psychiatric or other treatment of the accused be carried out or that the accused submit to such treatment except that the disposition may include a condition regarding psychiatric or other treatment where the accused has consented to the condition and the court or Review Board considers the condition to be reasonable and necessary in the interests of the accused.

(2) Effective period of disposition — No disposition made under paragraph 672.54(c) by a court shall continue in force for more than ninety days after the day that it is made.

1991, c. 43, s. 4; 1997, c. 18, s. 86.

672.56 (1) Delegated authority to vary restrictions on liberty of accused — A Review Board that makes a disposition in respect of an accused under paragraph 672.54(b) or (c) may delegate to the person in charge of the hospital authority to direct that the restrictions on the liberty of the accused be increased or decreased within any limits and subject to any conditions set out in that disposition, and any direction so made is deemed for the purposes of this Act to be a disposition made by the Review Board.

(2) Notice to accused and Review Board of increase in restrictions — A person who increases the restrictions on the liberty of the accused significantly pursuant to authority delegated to the person by a Review Board shall

(a) make a record of the increased restrictions on the file of the accused; and

(b) give notice of the increase as soon as is practicable to the accused and, if the increased restrictions remain in force for a period exceeding seven days, to the Review Board.

1991, c. 43, s. 4.

672.57 Warrant of committal — Where the court or Review Board makes a disposition under paragraph 672.54(c), it shall issue a warrant of committal of the accused, which may be in Form 49.

1991, c. 43, s. 4.

672.58 Treatment disposition — Where a verdict of unfit to stand trial is rendered and the court has not made a disposition under section 672.54 in respect of an accused, the court may, on application by the prosecutor, by order, direct that treatment of the accused be carried out for a specified period not exceeding sixty days, subject to such conditions as the court considers appropriate and, where the accused is not detained in custody, direct that the accused submit to that treatment by the person or at the hospital specified.

1991, c. 43, s. 4.

672.59 (1) Criteria for disposition — No disposition may be made under section 672.58 unless the court is satisfied, on the basis of the testimony of a medical practitioner, that a specific treatment should be administered to the accused for the purpose of making the accused fit to stand trial.

(2) Evidence required — The testimony required by the court for the purposes of subsection (1) shall include a statement that the medical practitioner has made an assessment of the accused and is of the opinion, based on the grounds specified, that

(a) the accused, at the time of the assessment, was unfit to stand trial;

(b) the psychiatric treatment and any other related medical treatment specified by the medical practitioner will likely make the accused fit to stand trial within a period not exceeding sixty days and that without that treatment the accused is likely to remain unfit to stand trial;

(c) the risk of harm to the accused from the psychiatric and other related medical treatment specified is not disproportionate to the benefit anticipated to be derived from it; and

(d) the psychiatric and other related medical treatment specified is the least restrictive and least intrusive treatment that could, in the circumstances, be specified for the purpose referred to in subsection (1), considering the opinions referred to in paragraphs (*b*) and (*c*).

1991, c. 43, s. 4.

672.6 (1) Notice required — The court shall not make a disposition under section 672.58 unless the prosecutor notifies the accused, in writing and as soon as practicable, of the application.

(2) Challenge by accused — On receiving the notice referred to in subsection (1), the accused may challenge the application and adduce evidence for that purpose.

1991, c. 43, s. 4; 1997, c. 18, s. 87.

672.61 (1) Exception — The court shall not direct, and no disposition made under section 672.58 shall include, the performance of psychosurgery or electro-convulsive therapy or any other prohibited treatment that is prescribed.

(2) Definitions — In this section,

"electro-convulsive therapy" means a procedure for the treatment of certain mental disorders that induces, by electrical stimulation of the brain, a series of generalized convulsions;

"psychosurgery" means any procedure that by direct or indirect access to the brain removes, destroys or interrupts the continuity of histologically normal brain tissue, or inserts indwelling electrodes for pulsed electrical stimulation for the purpose of altering behaviour or treating psychiatric illness, but does not include neurological procedures used to diagnose or treat intractable physical pain, organic brain conditions, or epilepsy, where any of those conditions is clearly demonstrable.

1991, c. 43, s. 4.

672.62 (1) Consent of hospital required for treatment — No court shall make a disposition under section 672.58 without the consent of

(a) the person in charge of the hospital where the accused is to be treated; or

(b) the person to whom responsibility for the treatment of the accused is assigned by the court.

(2) Consent of accused not required for treatment — The court may direct that treatment of an accused be carried out pursuant to a disposition made under section 672.58 without the consent of the accused or a person who, according to the laws of the province where the disposition is made, is authorized to consent for the accused.

1991, c. 43, s. 4.

672.63 Effective date of disposition — A disposition shall come into force on the day that it is made or on any later day that the court or Review Board specifies in it, and shall remain in force until the date of expiration that the disposition specifies or until the Review Board holds a hearing pursuant to section 672.47 or 672.81.

1991, c. 43, s. 4.

Proposed Addition — 672.64

Capping of Dispositions

672.64 (1) Definitions — In this section, sections 672.65, 672.79 and 672.8,

"designated offence" means an offence included in the schedule to this Part, an offence under the *National Defence Act* referred to in subsection (2), or any conspiracy or attempt to commit, being an accessory after the fact in relation to, or any counselling in relation to, such an offence;

"cap" means the maximum period during which an accused is subject to one or more dispositions in respect of an offence, beginning at the time when the verdict is rendered.

(2) Additional designated offences under the national defence act — An offence contrary to any of the following sections of the *National Defence Act* is a designated offence if it is committed in the circumstances described:

(a) section 73 (offences by commanders when in action), where the accused person acted from cowardice;

(b) section 74 (offences by any person in presence of enemy), 75 (offences related to security) or 76 (offences related to prisoners of war), where the accused person acted otherwise than traitorously;

(c) section 77 (offences related to operations), where the accused person committed the offence on active service;

(d) section 107 (wrongful acts in relation to aircraft or aircraft material) or 127 (injurious or destructive handling of dangerous substances), where the accused person acted wilfully;

(e) section 130 (service trial of civil offences), where the civil offence is included in the schedule to this Part; and

(f) section 132 (offences under law applicable outside Canada), where a court martial determines that the offence is substantially similar to an offence included in the schedule to this Part.

(3) Cap for various offences — Where a verdict of not criminally responsible on account of mental disorder or unfit to stand trial is rendered in respect of an accused, the cap is

(a) life, where the offence is

(i) high treason under subsection 47(1) or first or second degree murder under section 229,

(ii) an offence under section 73 (offences by commanders when in action), section 74 (offences by any person in presence of enemy), section 75 (offences related to security) or section 76 (offences related to prisoners of war) of the *National Defence Act*, if the accused person acted traitorously, or first or second degree murder punishable under section 130 of that Act,

(iii) any other offence under any Act of Parliament for which a minimum punishment of imprisonment for life is provided by law;

(b) ten years, or the maximum period during which the accused is liable to imprisonment in respect of the offence, whichever is shorter, where the offence is a designated offence that is prosecuted by indictment; or

(c) two years, or the maximum period during which the accused is liable to imprisonment in respect of the offence, whichever is shorter, where the offence is an offence under this Act or any other Act of Parliament, other than an offence referred to in paragraph (a) or (b).

(4) Longest cap applies where two or more offences — Subject to subsection (5), where an accused is subject to a verdict in relation to two or more offences, even if they arise from the same transaction, the offence with the longest maximum period of imprisonment as a punishment shall be used to determine the cap that applies to the accused in respect of all the offences.

(5) Offence committed while subject to previous disposition — Where a verdict of not criminally responsible on account of mental disorder or unfit to stand trial is rendered in respect of an accused who is subject to a disposition other than an absolute discharge in respect of a previous offence, the court may order that any disposition that it makes in respect of the offence be consecutive to the previous disposition, even if the duration of all the dispositions exceeds the cap for the offences determined pursuant to subsections (3) and (4).

1991, c. 43, s. 4 [Not in force at date of publication.]

Proposed Addition — 672.65

Dangerous Mentally Disordered Accused

672.65 (1) Definition of "serious personal injury offence" — In this section, **"serious personal injury offence"** means

(a) an offence or attempt to commit an offence mentioned in section 271 (sexual assault), 272 (sexual assault with a weapon, threats to a third party or causing bodily harm) or 273 (aggravated sexual assault); or

(b) any designated offence prosecuted by indictment involving

(i) the use or attempted use of violence against another person, or

(ii) conduct endangering or likely to endanger the life or safety of another person or inflicting or likely to inflict severe psychological damage on another person,

and for which the accused is liable to imprisonment for ten years or more.

(2) Application for a finding that accused is a dangerous mentally disordered accused — Where a verdict of not criminally responsible on account of mental disorder is rendered in respect of an accused, the prosecutor may, before any disposition is made, apply to the court that rendered the verdict or to a superior court of criminal jurisdiction for a finding that the accused is a dangerous mentally disordered accused.

(3) Grounds for finding — On an application made under this section, the court may find the accused to be a dangerous mentally disordered accused where it is satisfied that

(a) the offence that resulted in the verdict is a serious personal injury offence described in paragraph (1)(*b*), and the accused constitutes a threat to the life, safety, physical or mental well-being of other persons on the basis of evidence establishing

(i) a pattern of repetitive behaviour by the accused, of which the offence that resulted in the verdict is a part, that shows a failure to exercise behavioural restraint and a likelihood that the accused will cause death or injury to other persons or inflict severe psychological damage on other persons, through failure in the future to exercise restraint,

(ii) a pattern of persistent aggressive behaviour by the accused, of which the offence that resulted in the verdict is a part, or

(iii) any behaviour by the accused, associated with the offence that resulted in the verdict, that is of such a brutal nature as to compel the conclusion that the behaviour of the accused in future is unlikely to be inhibited by normal standards of behavioural restraint; or

(b) the offence that resulted in the verdict is a serious personal injury offence described in paragraph (1)(*a*), and the accused, by conduct in any sexual matter including the conduct in the commission of the offence that resulted in the verdict, has shown a failure to control sexual impulses and a likelihood that the accused will cause injury, pain or other harm to other persons through failure in the future to control such impulses.

(4) Court may increase duration of disposition — Where the court finds the accused to be a dangerous mentally disordered accused under this section, it may increase the cap in respect of the offence to a maximum of life.

1991, c. 43, s. 4 [Not in force at date of publication.]

Proposed Addition — 672.66

672.66 (1) Sections 754 to 758 apply — Sections 754 to 758 apply, with such modifications as the circumstances require, to an application under section 672.65 as if it were made under Part XXIV and the accused were an offender.

(2) Transmittal of transcript to Review Board — Where a court makes a finding that the accused is a dangerous mentally disordered accused, it shall send without delay to the Review Board that has jurisdiction in respect of the matter a transcript of the hearing of the application, any document or information relating to it in the possession of the court, and all exhibits filed with the court or copies of them.

1991, c. 43, s. 4 [Not in force at date of publication.]

Dual Status Offenders

672.67 (1) Where court imposes a sentence — Where a court imposes a sentence of imprisonment on an offender who is, or thereby becomes, a dual status offender, that sentence takes precedence over any prior custodial disposition, pending any placement decision by the Review Board.

(2) Custodial disposition by court — Where a court imposes a custodial disposition on an accused who is, or thereby becomes, a dual status offender, the disposition takes precedence over any prior sentence of imprisonment except a hospital order, as defined in section 747, pending any placement decision by the Review Board.

1991, c. 43, s. 4; 1995, c. 22, s. 10.

672.68 (1) Definition of "minister" — In this section and in sections 672.69 and 672.7, **"Minister"** means the Solicitor General of Canada or the Minister responsible for correctional services of the province to which a dual status offender may be sent pursuant to a sentence of imprisonment.

(2) Placement decision by Review Board — On application by the Minister or of its own motion, where the Review Board is of the opinion that the place of custody of a dual status offender pursuant to a sentence or custodial disposition made by the court is inappropriate to meet the mental health needs of the offender or to safeguard the well-being of other persons, the Review Board shall, after giving the offender and the Minister reasonable notice, decide whether to place the offender in custody in a hospital or in a prison.

(3) Idem — In making a placement decision, the Review Board shall take into consideration

(a) the need to protect the public from dangerous persons;

(b) the treatment needs of the offender and the availability of suitable treatment resources to address those needs;

(c) whether the offender would consent to or is a suitable candidate for treatment;

(d) any submissions made to the Review Board by the offender or any other party to the proceedings and any assessment report submitted in writing to the Review Board; and

(e) any other factors that the Review Board considers relevant.

(4) Time for making placement decision — The Review Board shall make its placement decision as soon as practicable but not later than thirty days after receiving an application from, or giving notice to, the Minister under subsection (2), unless the Review Board and the Minister agree to a longer period not exceeding sixty days.

(5) Effects of placement decision — Where the offender is detained in a prison pursuant to the placement decision of the Review Board, the Minister is responsible for the supervision and control of the offender.

1991, c. 43, s. 4.

672.69 (1) Minister and Review Board entitled to access — The Minister and the Review Board are entitled to have access to any dual status offender in respect of whom a placement decision has been made, for the purpose of conducting a review of the sentence or disposition imposed.

(2) Review of placement decisions — The Review Board shall hold a hearing as soon as is practicable to review a placement decision, on application by the Minister or the dual status offender who is the subject of the decision, where the Review Board is satisfied that a significant change in circumstances requires it.

(3) Idem — The Review Board may of its own motion hold a hearing to review a placement decision after giving the Minister and the dual status offender who is subject to it reasonable notice.

(4) Minister shall be a party — The Minister shall be a party in any proceedings relating to the placement of a dual status offender.

1991, c. 43, s. 4.

672.7 (1) Notice of discharge — Where the Minister or the Review Board intends to discharge a dual status offender from custody, each shall give written notice to the other indicating the time, place and conditions of the discharge.

(2) Warrant of committal — A Review Board that makes a placement decision shall issue a warrant of committal of the accused, which may be in Form 50.

1991, c. 43, s. 4.

672.71 (1) Detention to count as service of term — Each day of detention of a dual status offender pursuant to a placement decision or a custodial disposition shall be treated as a day of service of the term of imprisonment, and the accused shall be deemed, for all purposes, to be lawfully confined in a prison.

(2) Disposition takes precedence over probation orders — When a dual status offender is convicted or discharged on the conditions set out in a probation order made under section 730 in respect of an offence but is not sentenced to a term of imprisonment, the custodial disposition in respect of the accused comes into force and, notwithstanding subsection 732.2(1), takes precedence over any probation order made in respect of the offence.

1991, c. 43, s. 4; 1995, c. 22, s. 10.

Appeals

672.72 (1) Grounds for appeal — Any party may appeal against a disposition made by a court or a Review Board, or a placement decision made by a Review Board, to the court of appeal of the province where the disposition or placement decision was made on any ground of appeal that raises a question of law or fact alone or of mixed law and fact.

(2) Limitation period for appeal — An appellant shall give notice of an appeal against a disposition or placement decision in the manner directed by the applicable rules of the court within fifteen days after the day on which the appellant receives a copy of the placement decision or disposition and the reasons for it or within any further time that the court of appeal, or a judge of that court, may direct.

(3) Appeal to be heard expeditiously — The court of appeal shall hear an appeal against a disposition or placement decision in or out of the regular sessions of the court, as soon as practicable after the day on which the notice of appeal is given, within any period that may be fixed by the court of appeal, a judge of the court of appeal, or the rules of that court.

1991, c. 43, s. 4; 1997, c. 18, s. 88.

672.73 (1) Appeal on the transcript — An appeal against a disposition by a court or Review Board or placement decision by a Review Board shall be based on a transcript of the proceedings and any other evidence that the court of appeal finds necessary to admit in the interests of justice.

(2) Additional evidence — For the purpose of admitting additional evidence under this section, subsections 683(1) and (2) apply, with such modifications as the circumstances require.

1991, c. 43, s. 4.

672.74 (1) Notice of appeal to be given to court or Review Board — The clerk of the court of appeal, on receiving notice of an appeal against a disposition or placement decision, shall notify the court or Review Board that made the disposition.

(2) Transmission of records to court of appeal — On receipt of notification under subsection (1), the court or Review Board shall transmit to the court of appeal, before the time that the appeal is to be heard or within any time that the court of appeal or a judge of that court may direct,

(a) a copy of the disposition or placement decision;

(b) all exhibits filed with the court or Review Board or a copy of them; and

(c) all other material in its possession respecting the hearing.

(3) Record to be kept by court of appeal — The clerk of the court of appeal shall keep the material referred to in subsection (2) with the records of the court of appeal.

(4) Appellant to provide transcript of evidence — Unless it is contrary to an order of the court of appeal or any applicable rules of court, the appellant shall provide the court of appeal and the respondent with a transcript of any evidence taken before a court or Review Board by a stenographer or a sound recording apparatus, certified by the stenographer or in accordance with subsection 540(6), as the case may be.

(5) Saving — An appeal shall not be dismissed by the court of appeal by reason only that a person other than the appellant failed to comply with this section.

1991, c. 43, s. 4.

672.75 Automatic suspension of certain dispositions — The filing of a notice of appeal against a disposition made under paragraph 672.54(*a*) or section 672.58 suspends the application of the disposition pending the determination of the appeal.

1991, c. 43, s. 4.

672.76 (1) Application respecting dispositions under appeal — Any party who gives notice to each of the other parties, within the time and in the manner prescribed, may apply to a judge of the court of appeal for an order under this section respecting a disposition or placement decision that is under appeal.

(2) Discretionary powers respecting suspension of dispositions — On receipt of an application made pursuant to subsection (1) a judge of the court of appeal may, if satisfied that the mental condition of the accused justifies it,

(a) by order, direct that a disposition made under paragraph 672.54(*a*) or section 672.58 be carried out pending the determination of the appeal, notwithstanding section 672.75;

(b) by order, direct that the application of a placement decision or a disposition made under paragraph 672.54(*b*) or (*c*) be suspended pending the determination of the appeal;

(c) where the application of a disposition is suspended pursuant to section 672.75 or paragraph (*b*), make any other disposition in respect of the accused that is appropriate in the circumstances, other than a disposition under paragraph 672.54(*a*) or section 672.58, pending the determination of the appeal;

(d) where the application of a placement decision is suspended pursuant to an order made under paragraph (b), make any other placement decision that is appropriate in the circumstances, pending the determination of the appeal; and

(e) give any directions that the judge considers necessary for expediting the appeal.

(3) Copy of order to parties — A judge of the court of appeal who makes an order under this section shall send a copy of the order to each of the parties without delay.

1991, c. 43, s. 4.

672.77 Effect of suspension of disposition — Where the application of a disposition or placement decision appealed from is suspended, a disposition, or in the absence of a disposition any order for the interim release or detention of the accused, that was in effect immediately before the disposition or placement decision appealed from took effect, shall be in force pending the determination of the appeal, subject to any disposition made under paragraph 672.76(2)(c).

1991, c. 43, s. 4.

672.78 (1) Powers of court of appeal — The court of appeal may allow an appeal against a disposition or placement decision and set aside an order made by the court or Review Board, where the court of appeal is of the opinion that

(a) it is unreasonable or cannot be supported by the evidence;

(b) it is based on a wrong decision on a question of law; or

(c) there was a miscarriage of justice.

(2) Idem — The court of appeal may dismiss an appeal against a disposition or placement decision where the court is of the opinion

(a) that paragraphs (1)(a), (b) and (c) do not apply; or

(b) that paragraph (1)(b) may apply, but the court finds that no substantial wrong or miscarriage of justice has occurred.

(3) Orders that the court may make — Where the court of appeal allows an appeal against a disposition or placement decision, it may

(a) make any disposition under section 672.54 or any placement decision that the Review Board could have made;

(b) refer the matter back to the court or Review Board for rehearing, in whole or in part, in accordance with any directions that the court of appeal considers appropriate; or

(c) make any other order that justice requires.

1991, c. 43, s. 4; 1997, c. 18, s. 89.

672.79 (1) Appeal by dangerous mentally disordered accused — Where a court finds an accused to be a dangerous mentally disordered accused and increases the cap applicable to the accused pursuant to section 672.65, the accused may appeal to the court of appeal against the increase in the cap on any ground of law or fact or mixed law and fact.

(2) Disposition of appeal — On an appeal by an accused under subsection (1), the court of appeal may

(a) quash any increase in the cap and impose any other cap that might have been imposed in respect of the offence, or order a new hearing; or

(b) dismiss the appeal.

1991, c. 43, s. 4.

672.8 (1) Appeal by Attorney General — The Attorney General may appeal against the dismissal of an application for a finding that the accused is a dangerous mentally disordered accused on any ground of law.

(2) Disposition of appeal — On an appeal by the Attorney General under subsection (1), the court of appeal may

(a) allow the appeal, designate the accused as a dangerous mentally disordered accused, and increase the cap in respect of the offence to a maximum of life, or order a new hearing; or

(b) dismiss the appeal.

(3) Part XXI applies to appeal — The provisions of Part XXI with respect to procedure on appeals apply, with such modifications as the circumstances require, to appeals under this section or section 672.79.

1991, c. 43, s. 4.

Review of Dispositions

672.81 (1) Mandatory review of dispositions — A Review Board shall hold a hearing not later than twelve months after making a disposition and every twelve months thereafter for as long as the disposition remains in force, to review any disposition that it has made in respect of an accused, other than an absolute discharge under paragraph s. 672.54(*a*).

(2) Additional mandatory reviews in custody cases — The Review Board shall hold a hearing to review any disposition made under paragraph 672.54(*b*) or (*c*) as soon as is practicable after receiving notice that the person in charge of the place where the accused is detained or directed to attend

(a) has increased the restrictions on the liberty of the accused significantly for a period exceeding seven days; or

(b) requests a review of the disposition.

(3) Idem — Where an accused is detained in custody pursuant to a disposition made under paragraph 672.54(*c*) and a sentence of imprisonment is subsequently imposed on the accused in respect of another offence, the Review Board shall hold a hearing to review the disposition as soon as is practicable after receiving notice of that sentence.

1991, c. 43, s. 4.

672.82 (1) Discretionary review on request — A Review Board may hold a hearing to review any of its dispositions at any time, at the request of the accused or any other party.

(2) Review cancels appeal — Where a party requests a review of a disposition under this section, the party is deemed to abandon any appeal against the disposition taken under section 672.72.

1991, c. 43, s. 4.

672.83 (1) Disposition by Review Board — At a hearing held pursuant to section 672.81 or 672.82, the Review Board shall, except where a determination is made under subsection 672.48(1) that the accused is fit to stand trial, review the disposition made in respect of the accused and make any other disposition that the Review Board considers to be appropriate in the circumstances.

(2) Certain provisions applicable — Subsection 672.52(3), and sections 672.64 and 672.71 to 672.82 apply to a disposition made under this section, with such modifications as the circumstances require.

1991, c. 43, s. 4; 1997, c. 18, s. 90.

672.84 Procedure for review — The Review Board shall hold a hearing to review a disposition under section 672.81 or 672.82 in accordance with the procedures described in section 672.5.

1991, c. 43, s. 4.

672.85 Bringing accused before Review Board — For the purpose of bringing the accused in respect of whom a hearing under section 672.81 is to be held before the Review Board, the chairperson

(a) shall order the person having custody of the accused to bring the accused to the hearing at the time and place fixed for it; or

(b) may issue a summons or warrant to compel the accused to appear at the time and place fixed for the hearing, if the accused is not in custody.

1991, c. 43, s. 4.

Interprovincial Transfers

672.86 (1) Interprovincial transfers — An accused who is detained in custody or directed to attend at a hospital pursuant to a disposition made by a court or Review Board under paragraph 672.54(c) or a court under section 672.58 may be transferred to any other place in Canada where

(a) the Review Board of the province where the accused is detained or directed to attend recommends a transfer for the purpose of the reintegration of the accused into society or the recovery, treatment or custody of the accused; and

(b) the Attorneys General of the provinces to and from which the accused is to be transferred give their consent.

444

(2) Transfer where accused in custody — Where an accused who is detained in custody is to be transferred, an officer authorized by the Attorney General of the province where the accused is being detained shall sign a warrant specifying the place in Canada to which the accused is to be transferred.

(3) Transfer where accused not in custody — Where an accused who is not detained in custody is to be transferred, the Review Board of the province where the accused is directed to attend shall, by order,

> (a) direct that the accused be taken into custody and transferred pursuant to a warrant described in subsection (2); or

> (b) direct the accused to attend at a specified place in Canada, subject to any conditions that the Review Board considers appropriate.

1991, c. 43, s. 4.

672.87 Delivery and detention of accused — A warrant described in subsection 672.86(2) is sufficient authority

> (a) for any person who is responsible for the custody of an accused to have the accused taken into custody and conveyed to the person in charge of the place specified in the warrant; and

> (b) for the person specified in the warrant to detain the accused in accordance with any disposition made in respect of the accused under paragraph 672.54(c).

1991, c. 43, s. 4.

672.88 (1) Review board of receiving province has jurisdiction over transferee — The Review Board of the province to which an accused is transferred pursuant to section 672.86 has exclusive jurisdiction over the accused, and may exercise the powers and shall perform the duties mentioned in sections 672.5 and 672.81 to 672.83 as if that Review Board had made the disposition in respect of the accused.

(2) Agreement — Notwithstanding subsection (1), the Attorney General of the province to which an accused is transferred may enter into an agreement subject to this Act with the Attorney General of the province from which the accused is transferred, enabling the Review Board of that province to exercise the powers and perform the duties referred to in subsection (1) in respect of the accused, in the circumstances and subject to the terms and conditions set out in agreement.

1991, c. 43, s. 4.

672.89 (1) Other interprovincial transfers — Where an accused who is detained in custody pursuant to a disposition made by a Review Board is transferred to another province otherwise than pursuant to section 672.86, the Review Board of the province from which the accused is transferred has exclusive jurisdiction over the accused and may continue to exercise the powers and shall continue to perform the duties mentioned in sections 672.5 and 672.81 to 672.83.

(2) Agreement — Notwithstanding subsection (1), the Attorneys General of the provinces to and from which the accused is to be transferred as described in that subsection may, after the transfer is made, enter into an agreement subject to this

Act, enabling the Review Board of the province to which an accused is transferred to exercise the powers and perform the duties referred to in subsection (1) in respect of the accused, subject to the terms and conditions and in the circumstances set out in the agreement.

1991, c. 43, s. 4.

Enforcement of Orders and Regulations

672.9 Execution of warrant anywhere in Canada — Any warrant or process issued in relation to an assessment order or disposition made in respect of an accused may be executed or served in any place in Canada outside the province where the order or disposition was made as if it had been issued in that province.

1991, c. 43, s. 4; 1997, c. 18, s. 91.

672.91 Arrest without warrant for contravention of disposition — A peace officer may arrest an accused without a warrant at any place in Canada if the peace officer has reasonable grounds to believe that the accused has contravened or wilfully failed to comply with the disposition or any condition of it, or is about to do so.

1991, c. 43, s. 4.

672.92 (1) Accused to be brought before justice — An accused who is arrested pursuant to section 672.91 shall be taken before a justice having jurisdiction in the territorial division in which the accused is arrested, without unreasonable delay and in any event within twenty-four hours after the arrest.

(2) Idem — If a justice described in subsection (1) is not available within twenty-four hours after the arrest, the accused shall be taken before a justice as soon as is practicable.

1991, c. 43, s. 4.

672.93 (1) Where justice to release accused — A justice shall release an accused who is brought before the justice pursuant to section 672.92 unless the justice is satisfied that there are reasonable grounds to believe that the accused has contravened or failed to comply with a disposition.

(2) Order of justice pending decision of Review Board — If the justice is satisfied that there are reasonable grounds to believe that the accused has contravened or failed to comply with a disposition, the justice may make an order that is appropriate in the circumstances in relation to the accused, pending a hearing of the Review Board of the province where the disposition was made, and shall cause notice of that order to be given to that Review Board.

1991, c. 43, s. 4.

672.94 Powers of Review Board — Where a Review Board receives a notice given pursuant to subsection 672.93(2), it may exercise the powers and shall perform the duties mentioned in sections 672.5 and 672.81 to 672.83 as if the Review Board were reviewing a disposition.

1991, c. 43, s. 4.

672.95 Regulations — The Governor in Council may make regulations

(a) prescribing anything that may be prescribed under this Part; and

(b) generally to carry out the purposes and provisions of this Part.

1991, c. 43, s. 4.

Schedule to Part XX.1 Designated Offences - Criminal Code

(Subsection 672.64(1))

1. Section 49 — acts intended to alarm Her Majesty or break public peace

2. Section 50 — assisting alien enemy to leave Canada, or omitting to prevent treason

3. Section 51 — intimidating Parliament or legislature

4. Section 52 — sabotage

5. Section 53 — inciting to mutiny

6. Section 75 — piratical acts

7. Section 76 — hijacking

8. Section 77 — endangering safety of aircraft

9. Section 78 — offensive weapons and explosive substances

10. Section 80 — breach of duty (explosive substances)

11. Section 81 — using explosives

12. Section 82 — possession of explosives without lawful excuse

13. Subsection 85(1) — using firearm in commission of offence
13.1 Subsection 85(2) — using imitation firearm in commission of offence
14. Subsection 86(1) — careless use of firearm, etc.
15. Subsection 87(1) — pointing a firearm
16. Subsection 88(1) — possession of weapon for dangerous purpose

17. Section 151 — sexual interference

18. Section 152 — invitation to sexual touching

19. Section 153 — sexual exploitation

20. Section 155 — incest

21. Section 159 — anal intercourse

22. Subsection 160(2) — compelling commission of bestiality

23. Subsection 160(3) — bestiality in presence of child or inciting child to commit bestiality

24. Section 220 — causing death by criminal negligence

25. Section 221 — causing bodily harm by criminal negligence

26. Section 223 — causing injury to child before or during birth

27. Section 236 — manslaughter

28. Section 238 — killing unborn child in act of birth

29. Section 239 — attempt to commit murder

30. Section 241 — counselling or aiding suicide

31. Section 244 — causing bodily harm with intent

32. Paragraph 245(a) — administering noxious thing with intent to endanger life or cause bodily harm

33. Section 246 — overcoming resistance to commission of offence

34. Section 247 — setting traps likely to cause death or bodily harm

35. Section 248 — interfering with transportation facilities

36. Subsection 249(3) — dangerous operation of motor vehicles, vessels and aircraft causing bodily harm

37. Subsection 249(4) — dangerous operation of motor vehicles, vessels and aircraft causing death

38. Subsection 255(2) — impaired driving causing bodily harm

39. Subsection 255(3) — impaired driving causing death

40. Section 262 — impeding attempt to save life

41. Paragraph 265(1)(a) — assault

42. Section 267 — assault with a weapon or causing bodily harm

43. Section 268 — aggravated assault

44. Section 269 — unlawfully causing bodily harm

45. Subsection 269.1(1) — torture

46. Paragraph 271(1)(a) — sexual assault

47. Section 272 — sexual assault with a weapon, threats to a third party or causing bodily harm

48. Section 273 — aggravated sexual assault

49. Subsection 279(1) — kidnapping

50. Subsection 279(2) — forcible confinement

51. Section 279.1 — hostage taking

52. Section 280 — abduction of person under sixteen

53. Section 281 — abduction of person under fourteen

54. Paragraph 282(a) — abduction in contravention of custody order

55. Paragraph 283(1)(a) — abduction where no custody order

56. Section 344 — robbery

57. Section 345 — stopping mail with intent

58. Section 346 — extortion

59. Section 348 — breaking and entering with intent, committing offence or breaking out

60. Subsection 349(1) — being unlawfully in dwelling-house

61. Subsection 430(2) — mischief that causes actual danger to life

62. Section 431 — attack on premises, etc., of internationally protected person

63. Section 433 — arson (disregard for human life)

64. Section 434 — arson (damage to property)

65. Section 434.1 — arson (own property)

66. Section 435 — arson for fraudulent purpose

Atomic Energy Control Act

67. Section 20 — offence and punishment

Proposed Repeal — Conditional Amendment — Part XX.1, Schedule, item 67

67. [Repealed 1997, c. 9, s. 124(a). Not in force at date of publication.]

On the later of the day on which subsection 672.64(1) of the *Criminal Code*, as enacted by 1991, c. 43, s. 4, comes into force [Not in force at date of publication.] and the day 1997, c. 9, s. 124 comes into force [In force May 31, 2000.] item 67 of the schedule to Part XX.1 is repealed.

Emergencies Act

68A. Subparagraph 8(1)(j)(ii) — contravention of public welfare emergency regulation

69. Subparagraph 19(1)(e)(ii) — contravention of public order emergency regulation

70. Subparagraph 30(1)(l)(ii) — contravention of international emergency regulation

71. Paragraph 40(3)(b) — contravention of war emergency regulation

Canadian Environmental Protection Act

72. Section 274 — damage to environment and death or harm to persons

Controlled Drugs and Substances Act

73. Subsections 4(3) and (4) — possession

74. Subsections 5(3) and (4) — trafficking

75. Subsection 6(3) — importing and exporting

76. Subsection 7(2) — production

77. [Repealed 1996, c. 19, s. 73.]

National Defence Act

78. Section 78 — offence of being spy

79. Section 79 — mutiny with violence

80. Section 80 — mutiny without violence

81. Section 81 — offences related to mutiny

82. Section 82 — advocating governmental change by force

83. Section 83 — disobedience of lawful command

84. Section 84 — striking or offering violence to a superior officer

85. Section 88 — desertion

86. Paragraph 98(c) — maiming or injuring self or another person

87. Section 105 — offences in relation to convoys

88. Section 106 — disobedience of captain's orders — ships

89. Section 110 — disobedience of captain's orders — aircraft

90. Section 128 — conspiracy

Proposed Addition — Conditional Amendment — Part XX.1, Schedule, item 90.1

On the later of the day on which subsection 672.64(1) of the *Criminal Code*, as enacted by 1991, c. 43, s. 4, comes into force [Not in force at date of publication.] and the day 1997, c. 9, s. 124 comes into force [In force May 31, 2000.], the schedule to Part XX.1 is amended by 1997, c. 9, s. 124(b) by adding the following after item 90:

Nuclear Safety and Control Act

     90.1 Paragraphs 48(a) and (b) and section 50 — offence

Official Secrets Act

91. Section 3 — spying

92. Section 4 — wrongful communication, etc., of information

93. Section 5 — unauthorized use of uniforms, falsification of reports, etc.

1991, c. 43, s. 4; 1995, c. 39, s. 154; 1996, c. 19, s. 73; 1999, c. 33, s. 346

PART XXI — APPEALS — INDICTABLE OFFENCES

Interpretation

673. Definitions — In this Part,

"court of appeal" means the court of appeal, as defined by the definition "court of appeal" in section 2, for the province or territory in which the trial of a person by indictment is held;

"indictment" includes an information or charge in respect of which a person has been tried for an indictable offence under Part XIX;

"registrar" means the registrar or clerk of the court of appeal;

"sentence" includes

     (a) a declaration made under subsection 199(3),

     (b) an order made under subsection 109(1) or 110(1), section 161, subsection 194(1) or 259(1) or (2), section 261 or 462.37, subsection 491.1(2), 730(1) or 737(3) or (5) or section 738, 739, 742.1, 742.3, 743.6, 745.4, 745.5 or 747.1,

     (c) a disposition made under section 731 or 732 or subsection 732.2(3) or (5), 742.4(3) or 742.6(9), and

     (d) an order made under subsection 16(1) of the *Controlled Drugs and Substances Act;*

*[Editor's note: S.C. 1999, c. 25, ss. 31(5) and (8) each conditionally amended the definition of "**sentence**" in s. 673 by replacing paragraph (b). As a result of an oversight in legislative drafting, the conditions in both were fulfilled on the same day, with the result that there would now appear to be two in force versions of paragraph (b). Section 32(5) proposed to replace the references to s. 100(1) and (2) with references to ss. 109(1) and 110(1), respectively, and to replace the reference to s. 737 with a reference to 737(3) or (5) in the list of enumerated orders. Section 32(8) retained those amendments and added a reference to an order under s. 747.1 to the list. The cumulative result is reflected in the text. Note that s. 747.1 was not in force at date of publication.]*

"**trial court**" means the court by which an accused was tried and includes a judge or a provincial court judge acting under Part XIX.

R.S. 1985, c. 27 (1st Supp.), ss. 138, 203; c. 23 (4th Supp.), s. 4; c. 42 (4th Supp.), s. 4; 1992, c. 1, s. 58(1) (Sched. 1, item 12); 1993, c. 45, ss. 10, 16, 19; 1995, c. 22, s. 5(1); 1995, c. 39, ss. 155, 190(a); 1996, c. 19, s. 74(2); 1999, c. 5, s. 25; 1999, c. 25, ss. 13, 31(5), (8)

Right of Appeal

674. Procedure abolished — No proceedings other than those authorized by this Part and Part XXVI shall be taken by way of appeal in proceedings in respect of indictable offences.

675. (1) Right of appeal of person convicted — A person who is convicted by a trial court in proceedings by indictment may appeal to the court of appeal

(a) against his conviction

(i) on any ground of appeal that involves a question of law alone,

(ii) on any ground of appeal that involves a question of fact or a question of mixed law and fact, with leave of the court of appeal or a judge thereof or on the certificate of the trial judge that the case is a proper case for appeal, or

(iii) on any ground of appeal not mentioned in subparagraph (i) or (ii) that appears to the court of appeal to be a sufficient ground of appeal, with leave of the court of appeal; or

(b) against the sentence passed by the trial court, with leave of the court of appeal or a judge thereof unless that sentence is one fixed by law.

(1.1) Summary conviction appeals — A person may appeal, pursuant to subsection (1), with leave of the court of appeal or a judge of that court, to that court in respect of a summary conviction or a sentence passed with respect to a summary conviction as if the summary conviction had been a conviction in proceedings by indictment if

(a) there has not been an appeal with respect to the summary conviction;

(b) the summary conviction offence was tried with an indictable offence; and

(c) there is an appeal in respect of the indictable offence.

(2) Appeal against absolute term in excess of 10 years — A person who has been convicted of second degree murder and sentenced to imprisonment for life without eligibility for parole for a specified number of years in excess of ten may appeal to the court of appeal against the number of years in excess of ten of his imprisonment without eligibility for parole.

(2.1) Appeal against s. 741.2 order — A person against whom an order under section 741.2 has been made may appeal to the court of appeal against the order.

(2.2) Persons under eighteen — A person who was under the age of eighteen at the time of the commission of the offence for which the person was convicted of first degree murder or second degree murder and sentenced to imprisonment for life without eligibility for parole until the person has served the period specified by the judge presiding at the trial may appeal to the court of appeal against the number of years in excess of the minimum number of years of imprisonment without eligibility for parole that are required to be served in respect of that person's case.

(3) Appeals against verdicts based on mental disorder — Where a verdict of not criminally responsible on account of mental disorder or unfit to stand trial is rendered in respect of a person, that person may appeal to the court of appeal against that verdict on any ground of appeal mentioned in subparagraph (1)(*a*)(i), (ii) or (iii) and subject to the conditions described therein.

(4) Where application for leave to appeal refused by judge — Where a judge of the court of appeal refuses leave to appeal under this section otherwise than under paragraph (1)(*b*), the appellant may, by filing notice in writing with the court of appeal within seven days after refusal, have the application for leave to appeal determined by the court of appeal.

1991, c. 43, s. 9 (Sched., item 5); 1995, c. 42, s. 73; 1997, c. 18, s. 92; 1999, c. 31, s. 68.

676. (1) Right of Attorney General to appeal — The Attorney General or counsel instructed by him for the purpose may appeal to the court of appeal

(a) against a judgment or verdict of acquittal or a verdict of not criminally responsible on account of mental disorder of a trial court in proceedings by indictment on any ground of appeal that involves a question of law alone;

(b) against an order of a superior court of criminal jurisdiction that quashes an indictment or in any manner refuses or fails to exercise jurisdiction on an indictment;

(c) against an order of a trial court that stays proceedings on an indictment or quashes an indictment; or

(d) with leave of the court of appeal or a judge thereof, against the sentence passed by a trial court in proceedings by indictment, unless that sentence is one fixed by law.

(1.1) Summary conviction appeals — The Attorney General or counsel instructed by the Attorney General may appeal, pursuant to subsection (1), with leave of the court of appeal or a judge of that court, to that court in respect of a summary conviction or a sentence passed with respect to a summary conviction or a sentence passed with respect to a summary conviction as if the summary conviction had been a conviction in proceedings by indictment if

> (a) there has not been an appeal with respect to the summary conviction;

> (b) the summary conviction offence was tried with an indictable offence; and

> (c) there is an appeal in respect of the indictable offence.

(2) Acquittal — For the purposes of this section, a judgment or verdict of acquittal includes an acquittal in respect of an offence specifically charged where the accused has, on the trial thereof, been convicted or discharged under section 730 of any other offence.

(3) Appeal against verdict of unfit — The Attorney General or counsel instructed by the Attorney General for the purpose may appeal to the court of appeal against a verdict that an accused is unfit to stand trial, on any ground of appeal that involves a question of law alone.

(4) Appeal against ineligible parole period — The Attorney General or counsel instructed by him for the purpose may appeal to the court of appeal in respect of a conviction for second degree murder, against the number of years of imprisonment without eligibility for parole, being less than twenty-five, that has been imposed as a result of that conviction.

(5) Appeal against decision not to make s. 741.2 order — The Attorney General or counsel instructed by the Attorney General for the purpose may appeal to the court of appeal against the decision of the court not to make an order under section 741.2.

R.S. 1985, c. 27 (1st Supp.), s. 139; 1991, c. 43, s. 9, Schedule, item 6; 1995, c. 22, s. 10; 1995, c. 42, s. 74; 1997, c. 18, s. 93.

676.1 Appeal re costs — A party who is ordered to pay costs may, with leave of the court of appeal or a judge of a court of appeal, appeal the order or the amount of costs ordered.

1997, c. 18, s. 94.

677. Specifying grounds of dissent — Where a judge of the court of appeal expresses an opinion dissenting from the judgment of the court, the judgment of the court shall specify any grounds in law on which the dissent, in whole or in part, is based.

1994, c. 44, s. 67.

Procedure on Appeals

678. (1) Notice of appeal — An appellant who proposes to appeal to the court of appeal or to obtain the leave of that court to appeal shall give notice of appeal or notice of his application for leave to appeal in such manner and within such period as may be directed by rules of court.

(2) Extension of time — The court of appeal or a judge thereof may at any time extend the time within which notice of appeal or notice of an application for leave to appeal may be given.

678.1 Service where respondent cannot be found — Where a respondent cannot be found after reasonable efforts have been made to serve him with a notice of appeal or notice of an application for leave to appeal, service of the notice of appeal or the notice of the application for leave to appeal may be effected substitutionally in the manner and within the period directed by a judge of the court of appeal.

R.S. 1985, c. 27 (1st Supp.), s. 140.

679. (1) Release pending determination of appeal — A judge of the court of appeal may, in accordance with this section, release an appellant from custody pending the determination of his appeal if,

(a) in the case of an appeal to the court of appeal against conviction, the appellant has given notice of appeal or, where leave is required, notice of his application for leave to appeal pursuant to section 678;

(b) in the case of an appeal to the court of appeal against sentence only, the appellant has been granted leave to appeal; or

(c) in the case of an appeal or an application for leave to appeal to the Supreme Court of Canada, the appellant has filed and served his notice of appeal or, where leave is required, his application for leave to appeal.

(2) Notice of application for release — Where an appellant applies to a judge of the court of appeal to be released pending the determination of his appeal, he shall give written notice of the application to the prosecutor or to such other person as a judge of the court of appeal directs.

(3) Circumstances in which appellant may be released — In the case of an appeal referred to in paragraph (1)(a) or (c), the judge of the court of appeal may order that the appellant be released pending the determination of his appeal if the appellant establishes that

(a) the appeal or application for leave to appeal is not frivolous,

(b) he will surrender himself into custody in accordance with the terms of the order, and

(c) his detention is not necessary in the public interest.

(4) Idem — In the case of an appeal referred to in paragraph (1)(b), the judge of the court of appeal may order that the appellant be released pending the determination of his appeal or until otherwise ordered by a judge of the court of appeal if the appellant establishes that

(a) the appeal has sufficient merit that, in the circumstances, it would cause unnecessary hardship if he were detained in custody;

(b) he will surrender himself into custody in accordance with the terms of the order; and

(c) his detention is not necessary in the public interest.

(5) Conditions of order — Where the judge of the court of appeal does not refuse the application of the appellant, he shall order that the appellant be released

(a) on his giving an undertaking to the judge, without conditions or with such conditions as the judge directs, to surrender himself into custody in accordance with the order, or

(b) on his entering into a recognizance

(i) with one or more sureties,

(ii) with deposit of money or other valuable security,

(iii) with both sureties and deposit, or

(iv) with neither sureties nor deposit,

in such amount, subject to such conditions, if any, and before such justice as the judge directs,

and the person having the custody of the appellant shall, where the appellant complies with the order, forthwith release the appellant.

(5.1) Conditions — The judge may direct that the undertaking or recognizance referred to in subsection (5) include the conditions described in subsections 515(4), (4.1) and (4.2) that the judge considers desirable.

(6) Application of certain provisions of s. 525 — The provisions of subsections 525(5), (6) and (7) apply with such modification as the circumstances require in respect of a person who has been released from custody under subsection (5) of this section.

(7) Release or detention pending hearing of reference — Where, with respect to any person, the Minister of Justice gives a direction or makes a reference under section 690, this section applies to the release or detention of that person pending the hearing and determination of the reference as though that person were an appellant in an appeal described in paragraph (1)(a).

(7.1) Release or detention pending new trial or new hearing — Where, with respect to any person, the court of appeal or the Supreme Court of Canada orders a new trial, section 515 or 522, as the case may be, applies to the release or detention of that person pending the new trial or new hearing as though that person were charged with the offence for the first time, except that the powers of a justice under section 515 or of a judge under section 522 are exercised by a judge of the court of appeal.

(8) Application to appeals on summary conviction proceedings — This section applies to applications for leave to appeal and appeals to the Supreme Court of Canada in summary conviction proceedings.

(9) Form of undertaking or recognizance — An undertaking under this section may be in Form 12 and a recognizance under this section may be in Form 32.

(10) Directions for expediting appeal, new trial, etc. — A judge of the court of appeal, where on the application of an appellant he does not make an order under subsection (5) or where he cancels an order previously made under this section, or a judge of the Supreme Court of Canada on application by an appellant in the case of an appeal to that Court, may give such directions as he thinks necessary for expediting the hearing of the appellant's appeal or for expediting the new trial or new hearing or the hearing of the reference, as the case may be.

R.S. 1985, c. 27 (1st Supp.), s. 141; 1997, c. 18, s. 95; 1999, c. 25, s. 14

680. (1) Review by court of appeal — A decision made by a judge under section 522 or subsection 524(4) or (5) or a decision made by a judge of the court of appeal under section 261 or 679 may, on the direction of the chief justice or acting chief justice of the court of appeal, be reviewed by that court and that court may, if it does not confirm the decision,

(a) vary the decision; or

(b) substitute such other decision as, in its opinion, should have been made.

(2) Single judge acting — On consent of the parties, the powers of the court of appeal under subsection (1) may be exercised by a judge of that court.

(3) Enforcement of decision — A decision as varied or substituted under this section shall have effect and may be enforced in all respects as though it were the decision originally made.

R.S. 1985, c. 27 (1st Supp.), s. 142; 1994, c. 44, s. 68.

681. [Repealed 1991, c. 43, s. 9, Schedule, item 7.]

682. (1) Report by judge — Where, under this Part, an appeal is taken or an application for leave to appeal is made, the judge or provincial court judge who presided at the trial shall, at the request of the court of appeal or a judge thereof, in accordance with rules of court, furnish it or him with a report on the case or on any matter relating to the case that is specified in the request.

(2) Transcript of evidence — A copy or transcript of

(a) the evidence taken at the trial,

(b) any charge to the jury and any objections that were made to a charge to the jury,

(c) the reasons for judgment, if any, and

(d) the addresses of the prosecutor and the accused, if a ground for the appeal is based on either of the addresses,

shall be furnished to the court of appeal, except in so far as it is dispensed with by order of a judge of that court.

(3) [Repealed 1997, c. 18, s. 96(2).]

(4) Copies to interested parties — A party to an appeal is entitled to receive, on payment of any charges that are fixed by rules of court, a copy or transcript of any material that is prepared under subsections (1) and (2).

(5) Copy for minister of justice — The Minister of Justice is entitled, on request, to receive a copy or transcript of any material that is prepared under subsection (1) and (2).

R.S. 1985, c. 27 (1st Supp.), ss. 143, 203; 1997, c. 18, s. 96.

683. (1) Powers of court of appeal — For the purposes of an appeal under this Part, the court of appeal may, where it considers it in the interests of justice,

(a) order the production of any writing, exhibit, or other thing connected with the proceedings;

(b) order any witness who could have been a compellable witness at the trial, whether or not he was called at the trial,

(i) to attend and be examined before the court of appeal, or

(ii) to be examined in the manner provided by rules of court before a judge of the court of appeal, or before any officer of the court of appeal or justice of the peace or other person appointed by the court of appeal for the purposes;

(c) admit, as evidence, an examination that is taken under subparagraph (b)(ii);

(d) receive the evidence, if tendered, of any witness, including the appellant, who is a competent but not compellable witness;

(e) order that any question arising on the appeal that

(i) involves prolonged examination of writings or accounts, or scientific or local investigation,

(ii) cannot in the opinion of the court of appeal conveniently be inquired into before the court of appeal,

be referred for inquiry and report, in the manner provided by rules of court, to a special commissioner appointed by the court of appeal; and

(f) act upon the report of a commissioner who is appointed under paragraph (e) in so far as the court of appeal thinks fit to do so;

(g) amend the indictment, unless it is of the opinion that the accused has been misled or prejudiced in his defence or appeal.

(2) Parties entitled to adduce evidence and be heard — In proceedings under this section, the parties or their counsel are entitled to examine or cross-examine witnesses and, in an inquiry under paragraph (1)(e), are entitled to be present during the inquiry, and to adduce evidence and to be heard.

(3) Other powers — A court of appeal may exercise in relation to proceedings in the court, any powers not mentioned in subsection (1) that may be exercised by the court on appeals in civil matters, and may issue any process that is necessary to enforce the orders or sentences of the court, but no costs shall be allowed to the appellant or respondent on the hearing and determination of an appeal or on any proceedings preliminary or incidental thereto.

(4) Execution of process — Any process that is issued by the court of appeal under this section may be executed anywhere in Canada.

(5) Power to order suspension — Where an appeal or an application for leave to appeal has been filed in the court of appeal, that court, or a judge of that court, may, where it considers it to be in the interests of justice, order that

(a) any obligation to pay a fine,

(b) any order of forfeiture or disposition of forfeited property,

(c) any order to make restitution under section 738 or 739,

(d) any obligation to pay a victim surcharge under section 737, or

(e) the conditions prescribed in a probation order under subsections 732.1(2) and (3)

be suspended until the appeal has been determined.

(6) Revocation of suspension order — The court of appeal may revoke any order it makes under subsection (5) where it considers the revocation to be in the interests of justice.

R.S. 1985, c. 27 (1st Supp.), s. 144; c. 23 (4th Supp.), s. 5; 1995, c. 22, s. 10; 1997, c. 18, ss. 97, 141(b); 1999, c. 25, s. 15

684. (1) Legal assistance for appellant — A court of appeal or a judge of that court may, at any time, assign counsel to act on behalf of an accused who is a party to an appeal or to proceedings preliminary or incidental to an appeal where, in the opinion of the court or judge, it appears desirable in the interests of justice that the accused should have legal assistance and where it appears that the accused has not sufficient means to obtain that assistance.

(2) Counsel fees and disbursements — Where counsel is assigned pursuant to subsection (1) and legal aid is not granted to the accused pursuant to a provincial legal aid program, the fees and disbursements of counsel shall be paid by the Attorney General who is the appellant or respondent, as the case may be, in the appeal.

(3) Taxation of fees and disbursements — Where subsection (2) applies and where counsel and the Attorney General cannot agree on fees or disbursements of counsel, the Attorney General or the counsel may apply to the registrar of the court of appeal and the registrar may tax the disputed fees and disbursements.

R.S. 1985, c. 34 (3d Supp.), s. 9.

685. Summary determination of frivolous appeals — Where it appears to the registrar that a notice of appeal, which purports to be on a ground of appeal that involves a question of law alone, does not show a substantial ground of appeal, the registrar may refer the appeal to the court of appeal for summary determination, and, where an appeal is referred under this section, the court of appeal may, if it considers that the appeal is frivolous or vexatious and can be determined without being adjourned for a full hearing, dismiss the appeal summarily, without calling on any person to attend the hearing or to appear for the respondent on the hearing.

Powers of the Court of Appeal

686. (1) Powers — On the hearing of an appeal against a conviction or against a verdict that the appellant is unfit to stand trial or not criminally responsible on account of mental disorder, the court of appeal

(a) may allow the appeal where it is of the opinion that

(i) the verdict should be set aside on the ground that it is unreasonable or cannot be supported by the evidence,

(ii) the judgment of the trial court should be set aside on the ground of a wrong decision on a question of law, or

(iii) on any ground there was a miscarriage of justice;

(b) may dismiss the appeal where

(i) the court is of the opinion that the appellant, although he was not properly convicted on a count or part of the indictment, was properly convicted on another count or part of the indictment,

(ii) the appeal is not decided in favour of the appellant on any ground mentioned in paragraph (*a*),

(iii) notwithstanding that the court is of the opinion that on any ground mentioned in subparagraph (*a*)(ii) the appeal might be decided in favour of the appellant, it is of the opinion that no substantial wrong or miscarriage of justice has occurred; or

(iv) notwithstanding any procedural irregularity at trial, the trial court had jurisdiction over the class of offence of which the appellant was convicted and the court of appeal is of the opinion that the appellant suffered no prejudice thereby;

(c) may refuse to allow the appeal where it is of the opinion that the trial court arrived at a wrong conclusion respecting the effect of a special verdict, may order the conclusion to be recorded that appears to the court to be required by the verdict, and may pass a sentence that is warranted in law in substitution for the sentence passed by the trial court; or

(d) may set aside a conviction and find the appellant unfit to stand trial or not criminally responsible on account of mental disorder and may exercise any of the powers of the trial court conferred by or referred to in section 672.45 in any manner deemed appropriate to the court of appeal in the circumstances.

(2) Order to be made — Where a court of appeal allows an appeal under paragraph (1)(*a*), it shall quash the conviction and

(a) direct a judgment or verdict of acquittal to be entered; or

(b) order a new trial.

(3) Substituting verdict — Where a court of appeal dismisses an appeal under subparagraph (1)(*b*)(i), it may substitute the verdict that in its opinion should have been found and

(a) affirm the sentence passed by the trial court; or

(b) impose a sentence that is warranted in law or remit the matter to the trial court and direct the trial court to impose a sentence that is warranted in law.

(4) Appeal from acquittal — If an appeal is from an acquittal or verdict that the appellant or respondent was unfit to stand trial or not criminally responsible on account of mental disorder, the court of appeal may

(a) dismiss the appeal; or

(b) allow the appeal, set aside the verdict and

(i) order a new trial, or

(ii) except where the verdict is that of a court composed of a judge and jury, enter a verdict of guilty with respect to the offence of which, in its opinion, the accused should have been found guilty but for the error in law, and pass a sentence that is warranted in law, or remit the matter to the trial court and direct the trial court to impose a sentence that is warranted in law.

(5) New trial under Part XIX — Subject to subsection (5.01), if an appeal is taken in respect of proceedings under Part XIX and the court of appeal orders a new trial under this Part, the following provisions apply:

(a) if the accused, in his notice of appeal or notice of application for leave to appeal, requested that the new trial, if ordered, should be held before a court composed of a judge and jury, the new trial shall be held accordingly;

(b) if the accused, in his notice of appeal or notice of application for leave to appeal, did not request that the new trial, if ordered, should be held before a court composed of a judge and jury, the new trial shall, without further election by the accused, be held before a judge or provincial court judge, as the case may be, acting under Part XIX, other than a judge or provincial court judge who tried the accused in the first instance, unless the court of appeal directs that the new trial be held before the judge or provincial court judge who tried the accused in the first instance;

(c) if the court of appeal orders that the new trial shall be held before a court composed of a judge and jury the new trial shall be commenced by an indictment in writing setting forth the offence in respect of which the new trial was ordered; and

(d) notwithstanding paragraph (*a*), if the conviction against which the accused appealed was for an offence mentioned in section 553 and was made by a provincial court judge, the new trial shall be held before a provincial court judge acting under Part XIX, other than the provincial court judge who tried the accused in the first instance, unless the court of appeal directs that the new trial be held before the provincial court judge who tried the accused in the first instance.

(5.01) New trial under Part XIX — Nunavut — If an appeal is taken in respect of proceedings under Part XIX and the Court of Appeal of Nunavut orders a new trial under Part XXI, the following provisions apply:

(a) if the accused, in the notice of appeal or notice of application for leave to appeal, requested that the new trial, if ordered, should be held before a court composed of a judge and jury, the new trial shall be held accordingly;

(b) if the accused, in the notice of appeal or notice of application for leave to appeal, did not request that the new trial, if ordered, should be held before a court composed of a judge and jury, the new trial shall, without further election by the accused, and without a further preliminary inquiry, be held before a judge, acting under Part XIX, other than a judge who tried the accused in the first instance, unless the Court of Appeal of Nunavut directs that the new trial be held before the judge who tried the accused in the first instance;

(c) if the Court of Appeal of Nunavut orders that the new trial shall be held before a court composed of a judge and jury, the new trial shall be commenced by an indictment in writing setting forth the offence in respect of which the new trial was ordered; and

(d) despite paragraph (a), if the conviction against which the accused appealed was for an indictable offence mentioned in section 553, the new trial shall be held before a judge acting under Part XIX, other than the judge who tried the accused in the first instance, unless the Court of Appeal of Nunavut directs that the new trial be held before the judge who tried the accused in the first instance.

(5.1) Election if new trial a jury trial — Subject to subsection (5.2), if a new trial ordered by the court of appeal is to be held before a court composed of a judge and jury,

(a) the accused may, with the consent of the prosecutor, elect to have the trial heard before a judge without a jury or a provincial court judge;

(b) the election shall be deemed to be a re-election within the meaning of subsection 561(5); and

(c) subsection 561(5) applies, with such modifications as the circumstances require, to the election.

(5.2) Election if new trial a jury trial — Nunavut — If a new trial ordered by the Court of Appeal of Nunavut is to be held before a court composed of a judge and jury, the accused may, with the consent of the prosecutor, elect to have the trial heard before a judge without a jury. The election shall be deemed to be a re-election within the meaning of subsection 561.1(1), and subsection 561.1(6) applies, with any modifications that the circumstances require, to the election.

(6) Where appeal allowed against verdict of unfit to stand trial — Where a court of appeal allows an appeal against a verdict that the accused is unfit to stand trial, it shall, subject to subsection (7), order a new trial.

(7) Appeal court may set aside verdict of unfit to stand trial — Where the verdict that the accused is unfit to stand trial was returned after the close of the case for the prosecution, the court of appeal may, notwithstanding that the verdict is proper, if it is of the opinion that the accused should have been acquitted at the close of the case for the prosecution, allow the appeal, set aside the verdict and direct a judgment or verdict of acquittal to be entered.

(8) Additional powers — Where a court of appeal exercises any of the powers conferred by subsection (2), (4), (6) or (7), it may make any order, in addition, that justice requires.

R.S. 1985, c. 27 (1st Supp.), ss. 145, 203; 1991, c. 43, s. 9, Schedule, item 8; 1997, c. 18, s. 98; 1999, c. 3, s. 52; 1999, c. 5, s. 26

687. (1) Powers of court on appeal against sentence — Where an appeal is taken against sentence the court of appeal shall, unless the sentence is one fixed by law, consider the fitness of the sentence appealed against, and may on such evidence, if any, as it thinks fit to require or to receive,

(a) vary the sentence within the limits prescribed by law for the offence of which the accused was convicted; or

(b) dismiss the appeal.

(2) Effect of judgment — A judgment of a court of appeal that varies the sentence of an accused who was convicted has the same force and effect as if it were a sentence passed by the trial court.

688. (1) Right of appellant to attend — Subject to subsection (2), an appellant who is in custody is entitled, if he desires, to be present at the hearing of the appeal.

(2) Appellant represented by counsel — An appellant who is in custody and who is represented by counsel is not entitled to be present

(a) at the hearing of the appeal, where the appeal is on a ground involving a question of law alone,

(b) on an application for leave to appeal, or

(c) on any proceedings that are preliminary or incidental to an appeal,

unless rules of court provide that he is entitled to be present or the court of appeal or a judge thereof gives him leave to be present.

(3) Argument may be oral or in writing — An appellant may present his case on appeal and his argument in writing instead of orally, and the court of appeal shall consider any case of argument so presented.

(4) Sentence in absence of appellant — A court of appeal may exercise its power to impose sentence notwithstanding that the appellant is not present.

689. (1) Restitution or forfeiture of property — Where the trial court makes an order for compensation or for the restitution of property under section 738 or 739 or an order of forfeiture of property under subsection 462.37(1), the operation of the order is suspended

(a) until the expiration of the period prescribed by rules of court for the giving of notice of appeal or of notice of application for leave to appeal, unless the accused waives an appeal; and

(b) until the appeal or application for leave to appeal has been determined, where an appeal is taken or application for leave to appeal is made.

(2) Annulling or varying order — The court of appeal may by order annul or vary an order made by the trial court with respect to compensation or the restitution of property within the limits prescribed by the provision under which the order was made by the trial court, whether or not the conviction is quashed.

Powers of Minister of Justice

690. Powers of minister of justice — The Minister of Justice may, on an application for the mercy of the Crown by or on behalf of a person who has been convicted in proceedings by indictment or who has been sentenced to preventive detention under Part XXIV,

(a) direct, by order in writing, a new trial or, in the case of a person under sentence of preventive detention, a new hearing, before any court that he thinks proper, if after inquiry he is satisfied that in the circumstances a new trial or hearing, as the case may be, should be directed;

(b) refer the matter at any time to the court of appeal for hearing and determination by that court as if it were an appeal by the convicted person or the person under sentence of preventive detention, as the case may be; or

(c) refer to the court of appeal at any time, for its opinion, any question on which he desires the assistance of that court, and the court shall furnish its opinion accordingly.

Appeals to the Supreme Court of Canada

691. (1) Appeal from conviction — A person who is convicted of an indictable offence and whose conviction is affirmed by the court of appeal may appeal to the Supreme Court of Canada

(a) on any question of law on which a judge of the court of appeal dissents; or

(b) on any question of law, if leave to appeal is granted by the Supreme Court of Canada.

(2) Appeal where acquittal set aside — A person who is acquitted of an indictable offence other than by reason of a verdict of not criminally responsible on account of mental disorder and whose acquittal is set aside by the court of appeal may appeal to the Supreme Court of Canada

(a) on any question of law on which a judge of the court of appeal dissents;

(b) on any question of law, if the Court of Appeal enters a verdict of guilty against the person; or

(c) on any question of law, if leave to appeal is granted by the Supreme Court of Canada.

R.S. 1985, c. 34 (3d Supp.), s. 10; 1991, c. 43, s. 9, Schedule, item 9; 1997, c. 18, s. 99.

692. (1) Appeal against affirmation of special verdict of not criminally responsible on account of mental disorder — A person who has been found not criminally responsible on account of mental disorder and

(a) whose verdict is affirmed on that ground by the court of appeal, or

(b) against whom a verdict of guilty is entered by the court of appeal under subparagraph 686(4)(*b*)(ii),

may appeal to the Supreme Court of Canada.

(2) Appeal against affirmation of verdict of unfit to stand trial — A person who is found unfit to stand trial and against whom that verdict is affirmed by the court of appeal may appeal to the Supreme Court of Canada.

(3) Grounds of appeal — An appeal under subsection (1) or (2) may be

(a) on any question of law on which a judge of the court of appeal dissents; or

(b) on any question of law, if leave to appeal is granted by the Supreme Court of Canada.

R.S. 1985, c. 34 (3d Supp.), s. 11; 1991, c. 43, s. 9 (Sched., item 10).

693. (1) Appeal by Attorney General — Where a judgment of a court of appeal sets aside a conviction pursuant to an appeal taken under section 675 or dismisses an appeal taken pursuant to paragraph 676(1)(*a*), (*b*) or (*c*) or subsection 676(3), the Attorney General may appeal to the Supreme Court of Canada

    (a) on any question of law on which a judge of the court of appeal dissents, or

    (b) on any question of law, if leave to appeal is granted by the Supreme Court of Canada.

(2) Terms — Where leave to appeal is granted under paragraph (1)(*b*), the Supreme Court of Canada may impose such terms as it sees fit.

R.S. 1985, c. 27 (1st Supp.), s. 146; c. 34 (3d Supp.), s. 12.

694. Notice of appeal — No appeal lies to the Supreme Court of Canada unless notice of appeal in writing is served by the appellant on the respondent in accordance with the *Supreme Court Act*.

R.S. 1985, c. 34 (3d Supp.), s. 13.

694.1 (1) Legal assistance for accused — The Supreme Court of Canada or a judge thereof may, at any time, assign counsel to act on behalf of an accused who is a party to an appeal to the Court or to proceedings preliminary or incidental to an appeal to the Court where, in the opinion of the Court or judge, it appears desirable in the interests of justice that the accused should have legal assistance and where it appears that the accused has not sufficient means to obtain that assistance.

(2) Counsel fees and disbursements — Where counsel is assigned pursuant to subsection (1) and legal aid is not granted to the accused pursuant to a provincial legal aid program, the fees and disbursements of counsel shall be paid by the Attorney General who is the appellant or respondent, as the case may be, in the appeal.

(3) Taxation of fees and disbursements — Where subsection (2) applies and counsel and the Attorney General cannot agree on fees or disbursements of counsel, the Attorney General or the counsel may apply to the Registrar of the Supreme Court of Canada, and the Registrar may tax the disputed fees and disbursements.

R.S. 1985, c. 34 (3d Supp.), s. 13.

694.2 (1) Right of appellant to attend — Subject to subsection (2), an appellant who is in custody and who desires to be present at the hearing of the appeal before the Supreme Court of Canada is entitled to be present at it.

(2) Appellant represented by counsel — An appellant who is in custody and who is represented by counsel is not entitled to be present before the Supreme Court of Canada

    (a) on an application for leave to appeal,

    (b) on any proceedings that are preliminary or incidental to an appeal, or

    (c) at the hearing of the appeal,

unless rules of court provide that entitlement or the Supreme Court of Canada or a judge thereof gives the appellant leave to be present.

R.S. 1987, c. 34 (3d Supp.), s. 13.

695. (1) Order of Supreme Court of Canada — The Supreme Court of Canada may, on an appeal under this Part, make any order that the court of appeal might have made and may make any rule or order that is necessary to give effect to its judgment.

(2) [Repealed 1999, c. 5, s. 27.]

Appeals by Attorney General of Canada

696. Right of Attorney General of Canada to appeal — The Attorney General of Canada has the same rights of appeal in proceedings instituted at the instance of the Government of Canada and conducted by or on behalf of that Government as the Attorney General of a province has under this Part.

PART XXII — PROCURING ATTENDANCE

Application

697. Application — Except where section 527 applies, this Part applies where a person is required to attend to give evidence in a proceeding to which this Act applies.

R.S. 1985, c. 27 (1st Supp.), s. 147.

Process

698. (1) Subpoena — Where a person is likely to give material evidence in a proceeding to which this Act applies, a subpoena may be issued in accordance with this Part requiring that person to attend to give evidence.

(2) Warrant in form 17 — Where it is made to appear that a person who is likely to give material evidence

    (a) will not attend in response to a subpoena if a subpoena is issued, or

    (b) is evading service of a subpoena,

a court, justice or provincial court judge having power to issue a subpoena to require the attendance of that person to give evidence may issue a warrant in Form 17 to cause that person to be arrested and to be brought to give evidence.

(3) Subpoena issued first — Except where paragraph (2)(a) applies, a warrant in Form 17 shall not be issued unless a subpoena has first been issued.

R.S. 1985, c. 27 (1st Supp.), s. 203.

699. (1) Who may issue — If a person is required to attend to give evidence before a superior court of criminal jurisdiction, a court of appeal, an appeal court or a court of criminal jurisdiction other than a provincial court judge acting under Part XIX, a subpoena directed to that person shall be issued out of the court before which the attendance of that person is required.

(2) Order of judge — If a person is required to attend to give evidence before a provincial court judge acting under Part XIX or a summary conviction court under Part XXVII or in proceedings over which a justice has jurisdiction, a subpoena directed to the person shall be issued

(a) by a provincial court judge or a justice, where the person whose attendance is required is within the province in which the proceedings were instituted; or

(b) by a provincial court judge or out of a superior court of criminal jurisdiction of the province in which the proceedings were instituted, where the person whose attendance is required is not within the province.

(3) Order of judge — A subpoena shall not be issued out of a superior court of criminal jurisdiction pursuant to paragraph (2)(*b*), except pursuant to an order of a judge of the court made on application by a party to the proceedings.

(4) Seal — A subpoena or warrant that is issued by a court under this Part shall be under the seal of the court and shall be signed by a judge of the court or by the clerk of the court.

(5) Signature — A subpoena or warrant that is issued by a justice or provincial court judge under this Part shall be signed by the justice or provincial court judge.

(5.1) Sexual offences — Notwithstanding anything in subsection (1) to (5), in the case of an offence referred to in subsection 278.2(1), a subpoena requiring a witness to bring to the court a record, the production of which is governed by sections 278.1 to 278.91, must be issued and signed by a judge.

(6) Form of subpoena — Subject to subsection (7), a subpoena issued under this Part may be in Form 16.

(7) Form of subpoena in sexual offences — In the case of an offence referred to in subsection 278.2(1), a subpoena requiring a witness to bring anything to the court shall be in Form 16.1

R.S. 1985, c. 27 (1st Supp.), s. 203; 1994, c. 44, s. 69; 1997, c. 30, s. 2; 1999, c. 5, s. 28.

700. (1) Contents of subpoena — A subpoena shall require the person to whom it is directed to attend, at a time and place to be stated in the subpoena, to give evidence and, if required, to bring with him anything that he has in his possession or under his control relating to the subject-matter of the proceedings.

(2) Witness to appear and remain — A person who is served with a subpoena issued under this Part shall attend and shall remain in attendance throughout the proceedings unless he is excused by the presiding judge, justice or provincial court judge.

R.S. 1985, c. 27 (1st Supp.), ss. 148, 203.

700.1 (1) Video links, etc. — If a person is to give evidence under section 714.1 or 714.3 or under subsection 46(2) of the *Canada Evidence Act* — or is to give evidence or a statement pursuant to an order made under section 22.2 of the *Mutual Legal Assistance in Criminal Matters Act* — at a place within the jurisdiction of a court referred to in subsection 699(1) or (2) where the technology is available, a subpoena shall be issued out of the court to order the person to give that evidence at such a place.

(2) Sections of *Criminal Code* — Sections 699, 700 and 701 to 703.2 apply, with any modifications that the circumstances require, to a subpoena issued under this section.

1999, c. 18, s. 94

Execution or Service of Process

701. (1) Service — Subject to subsection (2), a subpoena shall be served in a province by a peace officer or any other person who is qualified in that province to serve civil process, in accordance with subsection 509(2), with such modifications as the circumstances require.

(2) Personal service — A subpoena that is issued pursuant to paragraph 699(2)(*b*) shall be served personally on the person to whom it is directed.

(3) Proof of service — Service of a subpoena may be proved by the affidavit of the person who effected service.

1994, c. 44, s. 70.

701.1 Service in accordance with provincial laws — Notwithstanding section 701, in any province service and proof of service of any subpoena, summons or other document may be made in accordance with the laws of the province relating to offences created by the laws of the province.

1997, c. 18, s. 100.

702. (1) Subpoena effective throughout Canada — A subpoena that is issued by a provincial court judge or out of a superior court of criminal jurisdiction, a court of appeal, an appeal court or a court of criminal jurisdiction has effect anywhere in Canada according to its terms.

(2) Subpoena effective throughout province — A subpoena that is issued by a justice has effect anywhere in the province in which it is issued.

R.S. 1985, c. 27 (1st Supp.), s. 203; 1994, c. 44, s. 71.

703. (1) Warrant effective throughout Canada — Notwithstanding any other provision of this Act, a warrant of arrest or committal that is issued out of a superior court of criminal jurisdiction, a court of appeal, an appeal court within the meaning of section 812 or a court of criminal jurisdiction other than a provincial court judge acting under Part XIX may be executed anywhere in Canada.

(2) Warrant effective in a province — Notwithstanding any other provision of this Act but subject to subsection 705(3), a warrant of arrest or committal that is issued by a justice or provincial court judge may be executed anywhere in the province in which it is issued.

R.S. 1985, c. 27 (1st Supp.), s. 149.

703.1 Summons effective throughout Canada — A summons may be served anywhere in Canada and, if served, is effective notwithstanding the territorial jurisdiction of the authority that issued the summons.

R.S. 1985, c. 27 (1st Supp.), s. 149.

703.2 Service of process on a corporation — Where any summons, notice or other process is required to be or may be served on a corporation, and no other method of service is provided, service may be effected by delivery

(a) in the case of a municipal corporation, to the mayor, warden, reeve or other chief officer of the corporation, or to the secretary, treasurer or clerk of the corporation; and

(b) in the case of any other corporation, to the manager, secretary or other executive officer of the corporation or of a branch thereof.

R.S. 1985, c. 27 (1st Supp.), s. 149.

Defaulting or Absconding Witness

704. (1) Warrant for absconding witness — Where a person is bound by recognizance to give evidence in any proceedings, a justice who is satisfied on information being made before him in writing and under oath that the person is about to abscond or has absconded may issue his warrant in Form 18 directing a peace officer to arrest that person and to bring him before the court, judge, justice or provincial court judge before whom he is bound to appear.

(2) Endorsement of warrant — Section 528 applies, with such modifications as the circumstances require, to a warrant issued under this section.

(3) Copy of information — A person who is arrested under this section is entitled, on request, to receive a copy of the information upon which the warrant for his arrest was issued.

R.S. 1985, c. 27 (1st Supp.), s. 203.

705. (1) Warrant when witness does not attend — Where a person who has been served with a subpoena to give evidence in a proceeding does not attend or remain in attendance, the court, judge, justice or provincial court judge before whom that person was required to attend may, if it is established

(a) that the subpoena has been served in accordance with this Part, and

(b) that the person is likely to give material evidence,

issue or cause to be issued a warrant in Form 17 for the arrest of that person.

(2) Warrant where witness bound by recognizance — Where a person who has been bound by a recognizance to attend to give evidence in any proceeding does not attend or does not remain in attendance, the court, judge, justice or provincial court judge before whom that person was bound to attend may issue or cause to be issued a warrant in Form 17 for the arrest of that person.

(3) Warrant effective throughout Canada — A warrant that is issued by a justice or provincial court judge pursuant to subsection (1) or (2) may be executed anywhere in Canada.

R.S. 1985, c. 27 (1st Supp.), s. 203.

706. Order where witness arrested under warrant — Where a person is brought before a court, judge, justice or provincial court judge under a warrant issued pursuant to subsection 698(2), or section 704 or 705, the court, judge, justice or provincial court judge may order that the person

    (a) be detained in custody, or

    (b) be released on recognizance in Form 32, with or without sureties, to appear and give evidence when required.

R.S. 1985, c. 27 (1st Supp.), s. 203.

707. (1) Maximum period for detention of witness — No person shall be detained in custody under the authority of any provision of this Act, for the purpose only of appearing and giving evidence when required as a witness, for any period exceeding thirty days unless prior to the expiration of those thirty days he has been brought before a judge of a superior court of criminal jurisdiction in the province in which he is being detained.

(2) Application by witness to judge — Where at any time prior to the expiration of the thirty days referred to in subsection (1), a witness being detained in custody as described in that subsection applies to be brought before a judge of a court described therein, the judge before whom the application is brought shall fix a time prior to the expiration of those thirty days for the hearing of the application and shall cause notice of the time so fixed to be given to the witness, the person having custody of the witness and such other persons as the judge may specify, and at the time so fixed for the hearing of the application the person having custody of the witness shall cause the witness to be brought before a judge of the court for that purpose.

(3) Review of detention — If the judge before whom a witness is brought under this section is not satisfied that the continued detention of the witness is justified, he shall order him to be discharged, or to be released on recognizance in Form 32, with or without sureties, to appear and to give evidence when required, but if the judge is satisfied that the continued detention of the witness is justified, he may order his continued detention until the witness does what is required of him pursuant to section 550 or the trial is concluded, or until the witness appears and gives evidence when required, as the case may be, except that the total period of detention of the witness from the time he was first detained in custody shall not in any case exceed ninety days.

708. (1) Contempt — A person who, being required by law to attend or remain in attendance for the purpose of giving evidence, fails, without lawful excuse, to attend or remain in attendance accordingly is guilty of contempt of court.

(2) Punishment — A court, judge, justice or provincial court judge may deal summarily with a person who is guilty of contempt of court under this section and that person is liable to a fine not exceeding one hundred dollars or to imprisonment for a term not exceeding ninety days or to both, and may be ordered to pay the costs that are incident to the service of any process under this Part and to his detention, if any.

(3) Form — A conviction under this section may be in Form 38 and a warrant of committal in respect of a conviction under this section may be in Form 25.

R.S. 1985, c. 27 (1st Supp.), s. 203.

Electronically Transmitted Copies

708.1 Electronically transmitted copies — A copy of a summons, warrant or subpoena transmitted by a means of telecommunication that produces a writing has the same probative force as the original for the purposes of this Act.

1997, c. 18, s. 101.

Evidence on Commission

709. (1) Order appointing commissioner — A party to proceedings by way of indictment or summary conviction may apply for an order appointing a commissioner to take the evidence of a witness who

(a) is, by reason of

(i) physical disability arising out of illness, or

(ii) any other good and sufficient cause,

not likely to be able to attend at the time the trial is held; or

(b) is out of Canada.

(2) Idem — A decision under subsection (1) is deemed to have been made at the trial held in relation to the proceedings mentioned in that subsection.

R.S. 1985, c. 27 (1st Supp.), s. 150; 1994, c. 44, s. 72.

710. (1) Application where witness is ill — An application under paragraph 709(1)(a) shall be made

(a) to a judge of a superior court of the province in which the proceedings are taken,

(b) to a judge of a county or district court in the territorial division in which the proceedings are taken, or

(c) to a provincial court judge, where

(i) at the time the application is made, the accused is before a provincial court judge presiding over a preliminary inquiry under Part XVIII, or

(ii) the accused or defendant is to be tried by a provincial court judge acting under Part XIX or XXVII.

(2) Evidence of medical practitioner — An application under subparagraph 709(1)(a)(i) may be granted on the evidence of a registered medical practitioner.

R.S. 1985, c. 27 (1st Supp.), s. 151; 1994, c. 44, s. 73.

711. Admitting evidence of witness who is ill — Where the evidence of a witness mentioned in paragraph 709(1)(a) is taken by a commissioner appointed under section 710, it may be admitted in evidence in the proceedings if

(a) it is proved by oral evidence or by affidavit that the witness is unable to attend by reason of death or physical disability arising out of illness or some other good and sufficient cause,

(b) the transcript of the evidence is signed by the commissioner by or before whom it purports to have been taken; and

(c) it is proved to the satisfaction of the court that reasonable notice of the time for taking the evidence was given to the other party, and that the accused or his counsel, or the prosecutor or his counsel, as the case may be, had or might have had full opportunity to cross-examine the witness.

R.S. 1985, c. 27 (1st Supp.), s. 152; 1994, c. 44, s. 74; 1997, c. 18, s. 102.

712. (1) Application for order when witness out of Canada — An application that is made under paragraph 709(1)(b)(1) shall be made

(a) to a judge of a superior court of criminal jurisdiction or of a court of criminal jurisdiction before which the accused is to be tried; or

(b) to a provincial court judge, where the accused or defendant is to be tried by a provincial court judge acting under Part XIX or XXVII.

(2) Admitting evidence of witness out of Canada — Where the evidence of a witness is taken by a commissioner appointed under this section, it may be admitted in evidence in the proceedings.

(3) [Repealed R.S. 1985, c. 27 (1st Supp.), s. 153.]

R.S. 1985, c. 27 (1st Supp.), s. 153; 1994, c. 44, s. 75; 1997, c. 18, s. 103.

713. (1) Providing for presence of accused counsel — A judge or provincial court judge who appoints a commissioner may make provision in the order to enable an accused to be present or represented by counsel when the evidence is taken, but failure of the accused to be present or to be represented by counsel in accordance with the order does not prevent the admission of the evidence in the proceedings if the evidence has otherwise been taken in accordance with the order and with this Part.

(2) Return of evidence — An order for the taking of evidence by commission shall indicate the officer of the court to whom the evidence that is taken under the order shall be returned.

R.S. 1985, c. 27 (1st Supp.), s. 203; 1997, c. 18, s. 104.

713.1 Evidence not excluded — Evidence taken by a commissioner appointed under section 712 shall not be excluded by reason only that it would have been taken differently in Canada, provided that the process used to take the evidence is consistent with the law of the country where it was taken and that the process used to take the evidence was not contrary to the principles of fundamental justice.

1994, c. 44, s. 76.

714. Rules and practice same as in civil cases — Except where otherwise provided by this Part or by rules of court, the practice and procedure in connection with the appointment of commissioners under this Part, the taking of evidence by commissioners, the certifying and return thereof and the use of the evidence in the proceedings shall, as far as possible, be the same as those that govern like matters in civil proceedings in the superior court of the province in which the proceedings are taken.

Video and Audio Evidence

714.1 Video links, etc. — witness in Canada — A court may order that a witness in Canada give evidence by means of technology that permits the witness to testify elsewhere in Canada in the virtual presence of the parties and the court, if the court is of the opinion that it would be appropriate in all the circumstances, including

(a) the location and personal circumstances of the witness;

(b) the costs that would be incurred if the witness had to be physically present; and

(c) the nature of the witness' anticipated evidence.

1999, c. 18, s. 95

714.2 (1) Video links, etc. — witness outside Canada — A court shall receive evidence given by a witness outside Canada by means of technology that permits the witness to testify in the virtual presence of the parties and the court unless one of the parties satisfies the court that the reception of such testimony would be contrary to the principles of fundamental justice.

(2) Notice — A party who wishes to call a witness to give evidence under subsection (1) shall give notice to the court before which the evidence is to be given and the other parties of their intention to do so not less than ten days before the witness is scheduled to testify.

1999, c. 18, s. 95

714.3 Audio evidence — witness in Canada — The court may order that a witness in Canada give evidence by means of technology that permits the parties and the court to hear and examine the witness elsewhere in Canada, if the court is of the opinion that it would be appropriate, considering all the circumstances including

(a) the location and personal circumstances of the witness;

(b) the costs that would be incurred if the witness had to be physically present;

(c) the nature of the witness' anticipated evidence; and

(d) any potential prejudice to either of the parties caused by the fact that the witness would not be seen by them.

1999, c. 18, s. 95

714.4 Audio evidence — witness outside Canada — The court may receive evidence given by a witness outside Canada by means of technology that permits the parties and the court in Canada to hear and examine the witness, if the court is of the opinion that it would be appropriate, considering all the circumstances including

(a) the nature of the witness' anticipated evidence; and

(b) any potential prejudice to either of the parties caused by the fact that the witness would not be seen by them.

1999, c. 18, s. 95

714.5 Oath or affirmation — The evidence given under section 714.2 or 714.4 shall be given

(a) under oath or affirmation in accordance with Canadian law;

(b) under oath or affirmation in accordance with the law in the place in which the witness is physically present; or

(c) in any other manner that demonstrates that the witness understands that they must tell the truth.

1999, c. 18, s. 95

714.6 Other laws about witnesses to apply — When a witness who is outside Canada gives evidence under section 714.2 or 714.4, the evidence is deemed to be given in Canada, and given under oath or affirmation in accordance with Canadian law, for the purposes of the laws relating to evidence, procedure, perjury and contempt of court.

1999, c. 18, s. 95

714.7 Costs of technology — A party who wishes to call a witness to give evidence by means of the technology referred to in section 714.1, 714.2, 714.3 or 714.4 shall pay any costs associated with the use of the technology.

1999, c. 18, s. 95

714.8 Consent — Nothing in sections 714.1 to 714.7 is to be construed as preventing a court from receiving evidence by means of the technology referred to in sections 714.1 to 714.4 if the parties so consent.

1999, c. 18, s. 95

Evidence Previously Taken

715. (1) Evidence at preliminary inquiry may be read at trial in certain cases — Where, at the trial of an accused, a person whose evidence was given at a previous trial on the same charge, or whose evidence was taken in the investigation of the charge against the accused or on the preliminary inquiry into the charge, refuses to be sworn or to give evidence, or if facts are proved on oath from which it can be inferred reasonably that the person

(a) is dead,

(b) has since become and is insane,

(c) is so ill that he is unable to travel or testify, or

(d) is absent from Canada,

and where it is proved that the evidence was taken in the presence of the accused, it may be admitted as evidence in the proceedings without further proof, unless the accused proves that the accused did not have full opportunity to cross-examine the witness.

(2) Admission of evidence — Evidence that has been taken on the preliminary inquiry or other investigation of a charge against an accused may be admitted as evidence in the prosecution of the accused for any other offence on the same proof and in the same manner in all respects, as it might, according to law, be admitted as evidence in the prosecution of the offence with which the accused was charged when the evidence was taken.

(3) Absconding accused deemed present — For the purposes of this section, where evidence was taken at a previous trial or preliminary hearing or other proceeding in respect of an accused in the absence of the accused, who was absent by reason of having absconded, the accused is deemed to have been present during the taking of the evidence and to have had full opportunity to cross-examine the witness.

1994, c. 44, s. 77; 1997, c. 18, s. 105.

Videotaped Evidence

715.1 Evidence of complainant or witness — In any proceeding relating to an offence under section 151, 152, 153, 155 or 159, subsection 160(2) or (3), or section 163.1, 170, 171, 172, 173, 210, 211, 212, 213, 266, 267, 268, 271, 272 or 273, in which the complainant or other witness was under the age of eighteen years at the time the offence is alleged to have been committed, a videotape made within a reasonable time after the alleged offence, in which the complainant or witness describes the acts complained of, is admissible in evidence if the complainant or witness, while testifying, adopts the contents of the videotape.

R.S. 1985, c. 19 (3d Supp.), s. 16; 1997, c. 16, s. 7.

715.2 (1) Evidence of complainant — In any proceedings relating to an offence under section 151, 152, 153, 153.1, 155 or 159, subsection 160(2) or (3) or section 163.1, 170, 171, 172, 173, 210, 211, 212, 213, 266, 267, 268, 271, 272 or 273 in which the complainant or other witness is able to communicate evidence but may have difficulty doing so by reason of a mental or physical disability, a videotape, made within a reasonable time after the alleged offence, in which the complainant or witness describes the acts complained of is admissible in evidence if the complainant or witness adopts the contents of the videotape while testifying.

(2) Order prohibiting use — The presiding judge may prohibit any other use of a videotape referred to in subsection (1).

1998, c. 9, s. 8.

PART XXIII — SENTENCING

Interpretation

716. Definitions — In this Part,

"accused" includes a defendant;

"alternative measures" means measures other than judicial proceedings under this Act used to deal with a person who is eighteen years of age or over and alleged to have committed an offence;

"court" means

(a) a superior court of criminal jurisdiction,

(b) a court of criminal jurisdiction,

(c) a justice or provincial court judge acting as a summary conviction court under Part XXVII, or

(d) a court that hears an appeal;

"fine" includes a pecuniary penalty or other sum of money, but does not include restitution.

1995, c. 22, s. 6; 1999, c. 5, s. 29.

Alternative Measures

717. (1) When alternative measures may be used — Alternative measures may be used to deal with a person alleged to have committed an offence only if it is not inconsistent with the protection of society and the following conditions are met:

(a) the measures are part of a program of alternative measures authorized by the Attorney General or the Attorney General's delegate or authorized by a person, or a person within a class of persons, designated by the Lieutenant Governor in Council of a province;

(b) the person who is considering whether to use the measures is satisfied that they would be appropriate, having regard to the needs of the person alleged to have committed the offence and the interests of society and of the victim;

(c) the person, having been informed of the alternative measures, fully and freely consents to participate therein;

(d) the person has, before consenting to participate in the alternative measures, been advised of the right to be represented by counsel;

(e) the person accepts responsibility for the act or omission that forms the basis of the offence that the person is alleged to have committed;

(f) there is, in the opinion of the Attorney General or the Attorney General's agent, sufficient evidence to proceed with the prosecution of the offence; and

(g) the prosecution of the offence is not in any way barred at law.

(2) Restriction on use — Alternative measures shall not be used to deal with a person alleged to have committed an offence if the person

(a) denies participation or involvement in the commission of the offence; or

(b) expresses the wish to have any charge against the person dealt with by the court.

(3) Admissions not admissible in evidence — No admission, confession or statement accepting responsibility for a given act or omission made by a person alleged to have committed an offence as a condition of the person being dealt with by alternative measures is admissible in evidence against that person in any civil or criminal proceedings.

(4) No bar to proceedings — The use of alternative measures in respect of a person alleged to have committed an offence is not a bar to proceedings against the person under this Act, but, if a charge is laid against that person in respect of that offence,

(a) where the court is satisfied on a balance of probabilities that the person has totally complied with the terms and conditions of the alternative measures, the court shall dismiss the charge; and

(b) where the court is satisfied on a balance of probabilities that the person has partially complied with the terms and conditions of the alternative measures, the court may dismiss the charge if, in the opinion of the court, the prosecution of the charge would be unfair, having regard to the circumstances and that person's performance with respect to the alternative measures.

(5) Laying of information, etc. — Subject to subsection (4), nothing in this section shall be construed as preventing any person from laying an information, obtaining the issue or confirmation of any process, or proceeding with the prosecution of any offence, in accordance with law.

1995, c. 22, s. 6.

Note: 1997, c. 18, s. 106 was not in force at the date of publication. This section purported to amend s. 717 of the Criminal Code as it existed prior to the 1995, c. 22 amendments. The reference to s. 717 of the Code has been replaced by s. 718.3 in accordance with 1995, c. 22, s. 18 (Sch. IV).

717.1 Records of persons dealt with — Sections 717.2 to 717.4 apply only in respect of persons who have been dealt with by alternative measures, regardless of the degree of their compliance with the terms and conditions of the alternative measures.

1995, c. 22, s. 6.

717.2 (1) Police records — A record relating to any offence alleged to have been committed by a person, including the original or a copy of any fingerprints or photographs of the person, may be kept by any police force responsible for, or participating in, the investigation of the offence.

(2) Disclosure by peace officer — A peace officer may disclose to any person any information in a record kept pursuant to this section that it is necessary to disclose in the conduct of the investigation of an offence.

(3) Idem — A peace officer may disclose to an insurance company any information in a record kept pursuant to this section for the purpose of investigating any claim arising out of an offence committed or alleged to have been committed by the person to whom the record relates.

1995, c. 22, s. 6.

717.3 (1) Government records — A department or agency of any government in Canada may keep records containing information obtained by the department or agency

    (a) for the purposes of an investigation of an offence alleged to have been committed by a person;

    (b) for use in proceedings against a person under this Act; or

    (c) as a result of the use of alternative measures to deal with a person.

(2) Private records — A person or organization may keep records containing information obtained by the person or organization as a result of the use of alternative measures to deal with a person alleged to have committed an offence.

1995, c. 22, s. 6.

717.4 (1) Disclosure of records — Any record that is kept pursuant to section 717.2 or 717.3 may be made available to

    (a) any judge or court for any purpose relating to proceedings relating to offences committed or alleged to have been committed by the person to whom the record relates;

    (b) any peace officer

        (i) for the purpose of investigating any offence that the person is suspected on reasonable grounds of having committed, or in respect of which the person has been arrested or charged, or

        (ii) for any purpose related to administration of the case to which the record relates;

    (c) any member of a department or agency of a government in Canada, or any agent thereof, that is

        (i) engaged in the administration of alternative measures in respect of the person, or

        (ii) preparing a report in respect of the person pursuant to this Act; or

    (d) any other person who is deemed, or any person within a class of persons that is deemed, by a judge of a court to have a valid interest in the record, to the extent directed by the judge, if the judge is satisfied that the disclosure is

        (i) desirable in the public interest for research or statistical purposes, or

        (ii) desirable in the interest of the proper administration of justice.

(2) Subsequent disclosure — Where a record is made available for inspection to any person under subparagraph (1)(d)(i), that person may subsequently disclose information contained in the record, but may not disclose the information in any form that would reasonably be expected to identify the person to whom it relates.

(3) Information, copies — Any person to whom a record is authorized to be made available under this section may be given any information contained in the record and may be given a copy of any part of the record.

(4) Evidence — Nothing in this section authorizes the introduction into evidence of any part of a record that would not otherwise be admissible in evidence.

(5) Idem — A record kept pursuant to section 717.2 or 717.3 may not be introduced into evidence, except for the purposes set out in paragraph 721(3)(c), more than two years after the end of the period for which the person agreed to participate in the alternative measures.

1995, c. 22, s. 6.

Purpose and Principles of Sentencing

718. Purpose — The fundamental purpose of sentencing is to contribute, along with crime prevention initiatives, to respect for the law and the maintenance of a just, peaceful and safe society by imposing just sanctions that have one or more of the following objectives:

(a) to denounce unlawful conduct;

(b) to deter the offender and other persons from committing offences;

(c) to separate offenders from society, where necessary;

(d) to assist in rehabilitating offenders;

(e) to provide reparations for harm done to victims or to the community; and

(f) to promote a sense of responsibility in offenders, and acknowledgment of the harm done to victims and to the community.

1995, c. 22, s. 6.

718.1 Fundamental principle — A sentence must be proportionate to the gravity of the offence and the degree of responsibility of the offender.

1995, c. 22, s. 6.

718.2 Other sentencing principles — A court that imposes a sentence shall also take into consideration the following principles:

(a) a sentence should be increased or reduced to account for any relevant aggravating or mitigating circumstances relating to the offence or the offender, and, without limiting the generality of the foregoing,

(i) evidence that the offence was motivated by bias, prejudice or hate based on race, national or ethnic origin, language, colour, religion, sex, age, mental or physical disability, sexual orientation, or any other similar factor, or

(ii) evidence that the offender, in committing the offence, abused the offender's spouse or child,

Proposed Amendment — 718.2(a)(ii)

(ii) evidence that the offender, in committing the offence, abused the offender's spouse or common-law partner or child,

2000, c. 12, s. 95(c) [Not in force at date of publication.]

(iii) evidence that the offender, in committing the offence, abused a position of trust or authority in relation to the victim, or

(iv) evidence that the offence was committed for the benefit of, at the direction of or in association with a criminal organization

shall be deemed to be aggravating circumstances;

(b) a sentence should be similar to sentences imposed on similar offenders for similar offences committed in similar circumstances;

(c) where consecutive sentences are imposed, the combined sentence should not be unduly long or harsh;

(d) an offender should not be deprived of liberty, if less restrictive sanctions may be appropriate in the circumstances; and

(e) all available sanctions other than imprisonment that are reasonable in the circumstances should be considered for all offenders, with particular attention to the circumstances of aboriginal offenders.

1995, c. 22, s. 6; 1997, c. 23, s. 17.

Punishment Generally

718.3 (1) Degrees of punishment — Where an enactment prescribes different degrees or kinds of punishment in respect of an offence, the punishment to be imposed is, subject to the limitations prescribed in the enactment, in the discretion of the court that convicts a person who commits the offence.

(2) Discretion respecting punishment — Where an enactment prescribes a punishment in respect of an offence, the punishment to be imposed is, subject to the limitations prescribed in the enactment, in the discretion of the court that convicts a person who commits the offence, but no punishment is a minimum punishment unless it is declared to be a minimum punishment.

(3) Imprisonment in default where term not specified — Where an accused is convicted of an offence punishable with both fine and imprisonment and a term of imprisonment in default of payment of the fine is not specified in the enactment that prescribes the punishment to be imposed, the imprisonment that may be imposed in default of payment shall not exceed the term of imprisonment that is prescribed in respect of the offence.

(4) Cumulative punishments — Where an accused

(a) is sentenced while under sentence for an offence, and a term of imprisonment, whether in default of payment of a fine or otherwise, is imposed,

(b) is convicted of an offence punishable with both a fine and imprisonment and both are imposed, or

(c) is convicted of more offences than one, and

    (i) more than one fine is imposed,

    (ii) terms of imprisonment for the respective offences are imposed, or

    (iii) a term of imprisonment is imposed in respect of one offence and a fine is imposed in respect of another offence,

the court that sentences the accused may direct that the terms of imprisonment that are imposed by the court or result from the operation of subsection 734(4) shall be served consecutively.

Proposed Amendment — 718.3

the court that sentences the accused may direct that the terms of imprisonment shall be served one after the other.

1997, c. 18, s. 106(3) [Not in force at date of publication.]

1995, c. 22, s. 6; 1997, c. 18, ss. 106, 141(c); 1999, c. 5, s. 30.

The following subsection was enacted by S.C. 1995, c. 22, s. 6:

(5) *Idem* — *Where an offender who is under a conditional sentence imposed under section 742.1 is convicted of a second offence that was committed while the offender was under the conditional sentence,*

    (a) *a sentence of imprisonment imposed for the second offence shall be served consecutively to the conditional sentence; and*

    (b) *the offender shall be imprisoned until the expiration of the sentence imposed for the second offence, or for any longer period resulting from the operation of subparagraph 742.6(9)(c)(i) or paragraph 742.6(9)(d).*

This subsection was never proclaimed in force and was later repealed by S.C. 1999, c. 5, s. 30.

719. (1) Commencement of sentence — A sentence commences when it is imposed, except where a relevant enactment otherwise provides.

(2) Time at large excluded from term of imprisonment — Any time during which a convicted person is unlawfully at large or is lawfully at large on interim release granted pursuant to any provision of this Act does not count as part of any term of imprisonment imposed on the person.

(3) Determination of sentence — In determining the sentence to be imposed on a person convicted of an offence, a court may take into account any time spent in custody by the person as a result of the offence.

(4) When time begins to run — Notwithstanding subsection (1), a term of imprisonment, whether imposed by a trial court or the court appealed to, commences or shall be deemed to be resumed, as the case may be, on the day on which the convicted person is arrested and taken into custody under the sentence.

(5) When fine imposed — Notwithstanding subsection (1), where the sentence that is imposed is a fine with a term of imprisonment in default of payment, no time prior to the day of execution of the warrant of committal counts as part of the term of imprisonment.

(6) Application for leave to appeal — An application for leave to appeal is an appeal for the purposes of this section.

1995, c. 22, s. 6.

Procedure and Evidence

720. Sentencing proceedings — A court shall, as soon as practicable after an offender has been found guilty, conduct proceedings to determine the appropriate sentence to be imposed.

1995, c. 22, s. 6.

721. (1) Report by probation officer — Subject to regulations made under subsection (2), where an accused, other than a corporation, pleads guilty to or is found guilty of an offence, a probation officer shall, if required to do so by a court, prepare and file with the court a report in writing relating to the accused for the purpose of assisting the court in imposing a sentence or in determining whether the accused should be discharged pursuant to section 730.

(2) Provincial regulations — The Lieutenant Governor in Council of a province may make regulations respecting the types of offences for which a court may require a report, and respecting the content and form of the report.

(3) Content of report — Unless otherwise specified by the court, the report must, wherever possible, contain information on the following matters:

(a) the offender's age, maturity, character, behaviour, attitude and willingness to make amends;

(b) the history of previous dispositions under the Young Offenders Act and of previous findings of guilt under this Act and any other Act of Parliament;

(c) the history of any alternative measures used to deal with the offender, and the offender's response to those measures; and

(d) any matter required, by any regulation made under subsection (2), to be included in the report.

(4) Idem — The report must also contain information on any other matter required by the court, after hearing argument from the prosecutor and the offender, to be included in the report, subject to any contrary regulation made under subsection (2).

(5) Copy of report — The clerk of the court shall provide a copy of the report, as soon as practicable after filing, to the offender or counsel for the offender, as directed by the court, and to the prosecutor.

1995, c. 22, s. 6; 1999, c. 25, s. 16

722. (1) Victim impact statement — For the purpose of determining the sentence to be imposed on an offender or whether the offender should be discharged pursuant to section 730 in respect of any offence, the court shall consider any statement that may have been prepared in accordance with subsection (2) of a victim of

481

the offence describing the harm done to, or loss suffered by, the victim arising from the commission of the offence.

(2) Procedure for victim impact statement — A statement referred to in subsection (1) must be

(a) prepared in writing in the form and in accordance with the procedures established by a program designated for that purpose by the Lieutenant Governor in Council of the province in which the court is exercising its jurisdiction; and

(b) filed with the court.

(2.1) Presentation of statement — The court shall, on the request of a victim, permit the victim to read a statement prepared and filed in accordance with subsection (2), or to present the statement in any other manner that the court considers appropriate.

(3) Evidence concerning victim admissible — Whether or not a statement has been prepared and filed in accordance with subsection (2), the court may consider any other evidence concerning any victim of the offence for the purpose of determining the sentence to be imposed on the offender or whether the offender should be discharged under section 730.

(4) Definition of "victim" — For the purposes of this section and section 722.2, "victim", in relation to an offence,

(a) means a person to whom harm was done or who suffered physical or emotional loss as a result of the commission of the offence; and

(b) where the person described in paragraph (a) is dead, ill or otherwise incapable of making a statement referred to in subsection (1), includes the spouse or any relative of that person, anyone who is in law or fact the custody of that person or is responsible for the care or support of that person or any dependant of that person.

Proposed Amendment — 722(4)(b)

(b) where the person described in paragraph (a) is dead, ill or otherwise incapable of making a statement referred to in subsection (1), includes the spouse or common-law partner or any relative of that person, anyone who is in law or fact the custody of that person or is responsible for the care or support of that person or any dependant of that person.

2000, c. 12, s. 95(d) [Not in force at date of publication.]

1995, c. 22, s. 6; 1999, c. 25, s. 17

722.1 Copy of statement — The clerk of the court shall provide a copy of a statement referred to in subsection 722(1), as soon as practicable after a finding of guilt, to the offender or counsel for the offender, and to the prosecutor.

1995, c. 22, s. 6; 1999, c. 25, s. 18

722.2 (1) Inquiry by court — As soon as practicable after a finding of guilt and in any event before imposing sentence, the court shall inquire of the prosecutor or a victim of the offence, or any person representing a victim of the offence, whether the victim or victims have been advised of the opportunity to prepare a statement referred to in subsection 722(1).

(2) Adjournment — On application of the prosecutor or a victim or on its own motion, the court may adjourn the proceedings to permit the victim to prepare a statement referred to in subsection 722(1) or to present evidence in accordance with subsection 722(3), if the court is satisfied that the adjournment would not interfere with the proper administration of justice.

1999, c. 25, s. 18

723. (1) Submissions on facts — Before determining the sentence, a court shall give the prosecutor and the offender an opportunity to make submissions with respect to any facts relevant to the sentence to be imposed.

(2) Submission of evidence — The court shall hear any relevant evidence presented by the prosecutor or the offender.

(3) Production of evidence — The court may, on its own motion, after hearing argument from the prosecutor and the offender, require the production of evidence that would assist it in determining the appropriate sentence.

(4) Compel appearance — Where it is necessary in the interests of justice, the court may, after consulting the parties, compel the appearance of any person who is a compellable witness to assist the court in determining the appropriate sentence.

(5) Hearsay evidence — Hearsay evidence is admissible at sentencing proceedings, but the court may, if the court considers it to be in the interests of justice, compel a person to testify where the person

(a) has personal knowledge of the matter;

(b) is reasonably available; and

(c) is a compellable witness.

1995, c. 22, s. 6.

724. (1) Information accepted — In determining a sentence, a court may accept as proved any information disclosed at the trial or at the sentencing proceedings and any facts agreed on by the prosecutor and the offender.

(2) Jury — Where the court is composed of a judge and jury, the court

(a) shall accept as proven all facts, express or implied, that are essential to the jury's verdict of guilty; and

(b) may find any other relevant fact that was disclosed by evidence at the trial to be proven, or hear evidence presented by either party with respect to that fact.

(3) Disputed facts — Where there is a dispute with respect to any fact that is relevant to the determination of a sentence,

(a) the court shall request that evidence be adduced as to the existence of the fact unless the court is satisfied that sufficient evidence was adduced at the trial;

(b) the party wishing to rely on a relevant fact, including a fact contained in a presentence report, has the burden of proving it;

(c) either party may cross-examine any witness called by the other party;

(d) subject to paragraph (e), the court must be satisfied on a balance of probabilities of the existence of the disputed fact before relying on it in determining the sentence; and

(e) the prosecutor must establish, by proof beyond a reasonable doubt, the existence of any aggravating fact or any previous conviction by the offender.
1995, c. 22, s. 6.

725. (1) Other offences — In determining the sentence, a court

(a) shall consider, if it is possible and appropriate to do so, any other offences of which the offender was found guilty by the same court, and shall determine the sentence to be imposed for each of those offences;

(b) shall consider, if the Attorney General and the offender consent, any outstanding charges against the offender to which the offender consents to plead guilty and pleads guilty, if the court has jurisdiction to try those charges, and shall determine the sentence to be imposed for each charge unless the court is of the opinion that a separate prosecution for the other offence is necessary in the public interest;

(b.1) shall consider any outstanding charges against the offender, unless the court is of the opinion that a separate prosecution for one or more of the other offences is necessary in the public interest, subject to the following conditions:

(i) the Attorney General and the offender consent,

(ii) the court has jurisdiction to try each charge,

(iii) each charge has been described in open court,

(iv) the offender has agreed with the facts asserted in the description of each charge, and

(v) the offender has acknowledged having committed the offence described in each charge; and

(c) may consider any facts forming part of the circumstances of the offence that could constitute the basis for a separate charge.

(1.1) Attorney General's consent — For the purpose of paragraphs (1)(b) and (b.1), the Attorney General shall take the public interest into account before consenting.

(2) No further proceedings — The court shall, on the information or indictment, note

(a) any outstanding charges considered in determining the sentence under paragraph (1)(b.1), and

(b) any facts considered in determining the sentence under paragraph (1)(c), and no further proceedings may be taken with respect to any offence described in those charges or disclosed by those facts unless the conviction for the offence of which the offender has been found guilty is set aside or quashed on appeal.

1995, c. 22, s. 6; 1999, c. 5, s. 31.

726. Offender may speak to sentence — Before determining the sentence to be imposed, the court shall ask whether the offender, if present, has anything to say.

1995, c. 22, s. 6.

726.1 Relevant information — In determining the sentence, a court shall consider any relevant information placed before it, including any representations or submissions made by or on behalf of the prosecutor or the offender.

1995, c. 22, s. 6.

726.2 Reasons for sentence — When imposing a sentence, a court shall state the terms of the sentence imposed, and the reasons for it, and enter those terms and reasons into the record of the proceedings.

1995, c. 22, s. 6.

727. (1) Previous conviction — Subject to subsections (3) and (4), where an offender is convicted of an offence for which a greater punishment may be imposed by reason of previous convictions, no greater punishment shall be imposed on the offender by reason thereof unless the prosecutor satisfies the court that the offender, before making a plea, was notified that a greater punishment would be sought by reason thereof.

(2) Procedure — Where an offender is convicted of an offence for which a greater punishment may be imposed by reason of previous convictions, the court shall, on application by the prosecutor and on being satisfied that the offender was notified in accordance with subsection (1), ask whether the offender was previously convicted and, if the offender does not admit to any previous convictions, evidence of previous convictions may be adduced.

(3) Where hearing ex parte — Where a summary conviction court holds a trial pursuant to subsection 803(2) and convicts the offender, the court may, whether or not the offender was notified that a greater punishment would be sought by reason of a previous conviction, make inquiries and hear evidence with respect to previous convictions of the offender and, if any such conviction is proved, may impose a greater punishment by reason thereof.

(4) Corporations — Where, pursuant to section 623, the court proceeds with the trial of a corporation that has not appeared and pleaded and convicts the corporation, the court may, whether or not the corporation was notified that a greater punishment would be sought be reason of a previous conviction, make inquiries and hear evidence with respect to previous convictions of the corporation and, if any such conviction is proved, may impose a greater punishment by reason thereof.

(5) Section does not apply — This section does not apply to a person referred to in paragraph 745(b).

1995, c. 22, s. 6.

728. Sentence justified by any count — Where one sentence is passed on a verdict of guilty on two or more counts of an indictment, the sentence is good if any of the counts would have justified the sentence.

1995, c. 22, s. 6.

729. (1) Proof of certificate of analyst — In

    (a) a prosecution for failure to comply with a condition in a probation order that the accused not have in possession or use drugs,

or

    (b) a hearing to determine whether the offender breached a condition of a conditional sentence that the offender not have in possession or use drugs,

a certificate purporting to be signed by an analyst stating that the analyst has analyzed or examined a substance and stating the result of the analysis or examination is admissible in evidence and, in the absence of evidence to the contrary, is proof of the statements contained in the certificate without proof of the signature or official character of the person appearing to have signed the certificate.

(2) Definition of "analyst" — In this section, "analyst" means a person designated as an analyst under the *Controlled Drugs and Substances Act*.

(3) Notice of intention to produce certificate — No certificate shall be admitted in evidence unless the party intending to produce it has, before the trial or hearing, as the case may be, given reasonable notice and a copy of the certificate to the party against whom it is to be produced.

(4) Proof of service — Service of any certificate referred to in subsection (1) may be proved by oral evidence given under oath by, or by the affidavit or solemn declaration of, the person claiming to have served it.

(5) Attendance for examination — Notwithstanding subsection (4), the court may require the person who appears to have signed an affidavit or solemn declaration referred to in that subsection to appear before it for examination or cross-examination in respect of the issue of proof of service.

(6) Requiring attendance of analyst — The party against whom a certificate of an analyst is produced may, with leave of the court, require the attendance of the analyst for cross-examination.

1995, c. 22, s. 6; 1999, c. 31, s. 69.

Absolute and Conditional Discharges

730. (1) Conditional and absolute discharge — Where an accused, other than a corporation, pleads guilty to or is found guilty of an offence other than an offence for which a minimum, punishment is prescribed by law or an offence punishable by imprisonment for fourteen years or for life, the court before which the accused appears may, if it considers it to be in the best interests of the accused and not contrary to the public interest, instead of convicting the accused, by order direct that the accused be discharged absolutely or on the conditions prescribed in a probation order made under subsection 731(2).

(2) Period for which appearance notice, etc., continues in force — Subject to Part XVI, where an accused who has not been taken into custody or who has been released from custody under or by virtue of any provision of Part XVI pleads guilty of or is found guilty of an offence but is not convicted, the appearance notice, promise to appear, summons, undertaking or recognizance issued to or given or entered into by the accused continues in force, subject to its terms, until a disposition in respect of the accused is made under subsection (1) unless, at the time the accused pleads guilty or is found guilty, the court, judge or justice orders that the accused be taken into custody pending such a disposition.

(3) Effect of discharge — Where a court directs under subsection (1) that an offender be discharged of an offence, the offender shall be deemed not to have been convicted of the offence except that

(a) the offender may appeal from the determination of guilt as if it were a conviction in respect of the offence;

(b) the Attorney General and, in the case of summary conviction proceedings, the informant or the informant's agent may appeal from the decision of the court not to convict the offender of the offence as if that decision were a judgment or verdict of acquittal of the offence or a dismissal of the information against the offender; and

(c) the offender may plead autrefois convict in respect of any subsequent charge relating to the offence.

(4) Where person bound by probation order convicted of offence — Where an offender who is bound by the conditions of a probation order made at a time when the offender was directed to be discharged under this section is convicted of an offence, including an offence under section 733.1, the court that made the probation order may, in addition to or in lieu of exercising its authority under subsection 732.2(5), at any time when it may take action under that subsection, revoke the discharge, convict the offender of the offence to which the discharge relates and impose any sentence that could have been imposed if the offender had been convicted at the time of discharge, and no appeal lies from a conviction under this subsection where an appeal was taken from the order directing that the offender be discharged.

1995, c. 22, s. 6; 1997, c. 18, ss. 107, 141(d).

Note: 1997, c. 18, s. 107 was not in force at the date of publication. This section purported to amend s. 736 of the Criminal Code as it existed prior to the 1995, c. 22 amendments. The reference to s. 736 of the Code has been replaced by s. 730 in accordance with 1995, c. 22, s. 18 (Sch. IV). If proclaimed in force, 1997, c. 18, s. 107 will amend s. 730(1) by deleting the words "made under s. 731(2)" from the last line.

Probation

731. (1) Making of probation order — Where a person is convicted of an offence, a court may, having regard to the age and character of the offender, the nature of the offence and the circumstances surrounding its commission,

(a) if no minimum punishment is prescribed by law, suspend the passing of sentence and direct that the offender be released on the conditions prescribed in a probation order; or

(b) in addition to fining or sentencing the offender to imprisonment for a term not exceeding two years, direct that the offender comply with the conditions prescribed in a probation order.

(2) Idem — A court may also make a probation order where it discharges an accused under subsection 730(1).

1995, c. 22, s. 6.

731.1 (1) Firearm, etc., prohibitions — Before making a probation order, the court shall consider whether section 100 is applicable.

(2) Idem — For greater certainty, a condition of a probation order referred to in paragraph 732.1(3)(d) does not affect the operation of section 100.

1995, c. 22, s. 6.

732. (1) Intermittent sentence — Where the court imposes a sentence of imprisonment of ninety days or less on an offender convicted of an offence, whether in default of payment of a fine or otherwise, the court may, having regard to the age and character of the offender, the nature of the offence and the circumstances surrounding its commission, and the availability of appropriate accommodation to ensure compliance with the sentence, order

(a) that the sentence be served intermittently at such times as are specified in the order; and

(b) that the offender comply with the conditions prescribed in a probation order when not in confinement during the period that the sentence is being served and, if the court so orders, on release from prison after completing the intermittent sentence.

(2) Application to vary intermittent sentence — An offender who is ordered to serve a sentence of imprisonment intermittently may, on giving notice to the prosecutor, apply to the court that imposed the sentence to allow it to be served on consecutive days.

(3) Court may vary intermittent sentence if subsequent offence — Where a court imposes a sentence of imprisonment on a person who is subject to an intermittent sentence in respect of another offence, the unexpired portion of the intermittent sentence shall be served on consecutive days unless the court otherwise orders.

1995, c. 22, s. 6.

732.1 (1) Definitions — In this section and section 732.2,

"change", in relation to optional conditions, includes deletions and additions;

"optional conditions" means the conditions referred to in subsection (3).

(2) Compulsory conditions of probation order — The court shall prescribe, as conditions of a probation order, that the offender do all of the following:

(a) keep the peace and be of good behaviour;

(b) appear before the court when required to do so by the court; and

(c) notify the court or the probation officer in advance of any change of name or address, and promptly notify the court or the probation officer of any change of employment or occupation.

(3) Optional conditions of probation order — The court may prescribe, as additional conditions of a probation order, that the offender do one or more of the following:

(a) report to a probation officer

(i) within two working days, or such longer period as the court directs, after the making of the probation order, and

(ii) thereafter, when required by the probation officer and in the manner directed by the probation officer;

(b) remain within the jurisdiction of the court unless written permission to go outside that jurisdiction is obtained from the court or the probation officer;

(c) abstain from

(i) the consumption of alcohol or other intoxicating substances, or

(ii) the consumption of drugs except in accordance with a medical prescription;

(d) abstain from owning, possessing or carrying a weapon;

(e) provide for the support or care of dependants;

(f) perform up to 240 hours of community service over a period not exceeding eighteen months;

(g) if the offender agrees, and the subject to the program director's acceptance of the offender, participate actively in a treatment program approved by the province;

(g.1) where the lieutenant governor in council of the province in which the probation order is made has established a program for curative treatment in relation to the consumption of alcohol or drugs, attend at a treatment facility, designated by the lieutenant governor in council of the province, for assessment and curative treatment in relation to the consumption by the offender of alcohol or drugs that is recommended pursuant to the program;

(g.2) where the lieutenant governor in council of the province in which the probation order is made has established a program governing the use of an alcohol ignition interlock device by an offender and if the offender agrees to participate in the program, comply with the program; and

(h) comply with such other reasonable conditions as the court considers desirable, subject to any regulations made under subsection 738(2), for protecting society and for facilitating the offender's successful reintegration into the community.

(4) Form and period of order — A probation order may be in Form 46, and the court that makes the probation order shall specify therein the period for which it is to remain in force.

(5) Proceedings on making order — A court that makes a probation order shall

(a) cause to be given to the offender

(i) a copy of the order,

(ii) an explanation of the substance of subsections 732.2(3) and (5) and section 733.1, and

(iii) an explanation of the procedure for applying under subsection 732.2(3) for a change to the optional conditions; and

(b) take reasonable measures to ensure that the offender understands the order and the explanations given to the offender under paragraph (a).

1995, c. 22, s. 6; 1999, c. 32, s. 6.

732.2 (1) Coming into force of order — A probation order comes into force

(a) on the date on which the order is made;

(b) where the offender is sentenced to imprisonment under paragraph 731(1)(b) or was previously sentenced to imprisonment for another offence, as soon as the offender is released from prison or, if released from prison on conditional release, at the expiration of the sentence of imprisonment; or

(c) where the offender is under a conditional sentence, at the expiration of the conditional sentence.

(2) Duration of order and limit on term of order — Subject to subsection (5),

(a) where an offender who is bound by a probation order is convicted of an offence, including an offence under section 733.1, or is imprisoned under paragraph 731(1)(b) in default of payment of a fine, the order continues in force except in so far as the sentence renders it impossible for the offender for the time being to comply with the order; and

(b) no probation order shall continue in force for which more than three years after the date on which the order came into force.

(3) Changes to probation order — A court that makes a probation order may at any time, on application by the offender, the probation officer or the prosecutor, require the offender to appear before it and, after hearing the offender and one or both of the probation officer and the prosecutor,

(a) make any changes to the optional conditions that in the opinion of the court are rendered desirable by a change in the circumstances since those conditions were prescribed,

(b) relieve the offender, either absolutely or on such terms or for such period as the court deems desirable, of compliance with any optional condition, or

(c) decrease the period for which the probation order is to remain in force, and the court shall thereupon endorse the probation order accordingly and, if it changes the optional conditions, inform the offender of its action and give the offender a copy of the order so endorsed.

(4) Judge may act in chambers — All the functions of the court under subsection (3) may be exercised in chambers.

(5) Where person convicted of offence — Where an offender who is bound by a probation order is convicted of an offence, including an offence under section 733.1, and

(a) the time within which an appeal may be taken against that conviction has expired and the offender has not taken an appeal,

(b) the offender has taken an appeal against that conviction and the appeal has been dismissed, or

(c) the offender has given written notice to the court that convicted the offender that the offender elects not to appeal the conviction or has abandoned the appeal, as the case may be,

in addition to any punishment that may be imposed for that offence, the court that made the probation order may, on application by the prosecutor, require the offender to appear before it and, after hearing the prosecutor and the offender,

(d) where the probation order was made under paragraph 731(1)(a), revoke the order and impose any sentence that could have been imposed if the passing of sentence had not been suspended, or

(e) make such changes to the optional conditions as the court deems desirable, or extend the period for which the order is to remain in force for such period, not exceeding one year, as the court deems desirable,

and the court shall thereupon endorse the probation order accordingly and, if it changes the optional conditions or extends the period for which the order is to remain in force, inform the offender of its action and give the offender a copy of the order so endorsed.

(6) Compelling appearance of person bound — The provisions of Parts XVI and XVIII with respect to compelling the appearance of an accused before a justice apply, with such modifications as the circumstances require, to proceedings under subsections (3) and (5).

1995, c. 22, s. 6.

733. (1) Transfer of order — Where an offender who is bound by a probation order becomes a resident of, or is convicted or discharged under section 730 of an offence including an offence under section 733.1 in, a territorial division other than the territorial division where the order was made, on the application of a probation officer, the court that made the order may, subject to subsection (1.1), transfer the order to a court in that other territorial division that would, having regard to the mode of trial of the offender, have had jurisdiciton to make the order in that other territorial division if the offender had been tried and convicted there of the offence in respect of which the order was made, and the order may thereafter be dealt with and enforced by the court to which it is so transferred in all respects as if that court had made the order.

(1.1) Attorney General's consent — The transfer may be granted only with

(a) the consent of the Attorney General of the province in which the probation order was made, if the two territorial divisions are not in the same province; or

(b) the consent of the Attorney General of Canada, if the proceedings that led to the issuance of the probation order were instituted by or on behalf of the Attorney General of Canada.

(2) Where court unable to act — Where a court that has made a probation order or to which a probation order has been transferred pursuant to subsection (1) is for any reason unable to act, the powers of that court in relation to the probation order may be exercised by any other court that has equivalent jurisdiction in the same province.

1995, c. 22, s. 6; 1999, c. 5, s. 32.

733.1 (1) Failure to comply with probation order — An offender who is bound by a probation order and who, without reasonable excuse, fails or refuses to comply with that order is guilty of

(a) an indictable offence and is liable to imprisonment for a term not exceeding two years; or

(b) an offence punishable on summary conviction and is liable to imprisonment for a term not exceeding eighteen months, or to a fine not exceeding two thousand dollars, or both.

(2) Where accused may be tried and punished — An accused who is charged with an offence under subsection (1) may be tried and punished by any court having jurisdiction to try that offence in the place where the offence is alleged to have been committed or in the place where the accused is found, is arrested or is in custody, but where the place where the accused is found, is arrested or is in custody is outside the province in which the offence is alleged to have been committed, no proceedings in respect of that offence shall be instituted in that place without the consent of the Attorney General of that province.

1995, c. 22, s. 6.

Fines and Forfeiture

734. (1) Power of court to impose fine — Subject to subsection (2), a court that convicts a person, other than a corporation, of an offence may fine the offender by making an order under section 734.1

(a) if the punishment for the offence does not include a minimum term of imprisonment, in addition to or in lieu of any other sanction that the court is authorized to impose; or

(b) if the punishment for the offence includes a minimum term of imprisonment, in addition to any other sanction that the court is required or authorized to impose.

(2) Offender's ability to pay — Except when the punishment for an offence includes a minimum fine or a fine is imposed in lieu of a forfeiture order, a court may fine an offender under this section only if the court is satisfied that the offender is able to pay the fine or discharge it under section 736.

(3) Meaning of default of payment — For the purposes of this section and sections 734.1 to 737, a person is in default of payment of a fine if the fine has not been paid in full by the time set out in the order made under section 734.1.

(4) Imprisonment in default of payment — Where an offender is fined under this section, a term of imprisonment, determined in accordance with subsection (5), shall be deemed to be imposed in default of payment of the fine.

(5) Determination of term — The length, in days, of the term of imprisonment referred to in subsection (4) is the lesser of

(a) a fraction, rounded down to the nearest whole number, of which

(i) the numerator is the unpaid amount of the fine plus the costs and charges of committing and conveying the defaulter to prison, calculated in accordance with regulations made under subsection (7), and

(ii) the denominator is equal to eight times the provincial minimum hourly wage, at the time of default, in the province in which the fine was imposed, and

(b) the maximum term of imprisonment, expressed in days, that the court could itself impose on conviction.

(6) Moneys found on offender — All or any part of a fine imposed under this section may be taken out of moneys found in the possession of the offender at the time of the arrest of the offender if the court making the order, on being satisfied that ownership of or right to possession of those moneys is not disputed by claimants other than the offender, so directs.

(7) Provincial regulations — The lieutenant governor in council of a province may make regulations repecting the calculation of the costs and charges referred to in subparagraph (5)(a)(i) and in paragraph 734.8(1)(b).

(8) Application to other law — This section and sections 734.1 to 734.8 and 736 apply to a fine imposed under any Act of Parliament, except that subsections (4) and (5) do not apply if the term of imprisonment in default of payment of the fine provided for in that Act or regulation is

(a) calculated by a different method; or

(b) specified, either as a minimum or a maximum.

1995, c. 22, s. 6; 1999, c. 5, s. 33.

734.1 Terms of order imposing fine — A court that fines an offender under section 734 shall do so by making an order that clearly sets out

(a) the amount of the fine;

(b) the manner in which the fine is to be paid;

(c) the time or times by which the fine, or any portion thereof, must be paid; and

(d) such other terms respecting the payment of the fine as the court deems appropriate.

1995, c. 22, s. 6.

734.2 Proceedings on making order — A court that makes an order under section 734.1 shall

(a) cause to be given to the offender

(i) a copy of the order,

(ii) an explanation of the substance of sections 734 to 734.8 and 736,

(iii) an explanation of available programs referred to in section 736 and of the procedure for applying for admission to such programs, and

(iv) an explanation of the procedure for applying under section 734.3 for a change in the terms of the order; and

(b) take reasonable measures to ensure that the offender understands the order and the explanations given to the offender under paragraph (a).

1995, c. 22, s. 6.

734.3 Change in terms of order — A court that makes an order under section 734.1, or a person designated, either by name or by title of office, by that court, may, on application by or on behalf of the offender, subject to any rules made by the court under section 482, change any term of the order except the amount of the fine, and any reference in this section and sections 734, 734.1, 734.2 and 734.6 to an order shall be read as including a reference to the order as changed pursuant to this section.

1995, c. 22, s. 6.

734.4 (1) Proceeds to go to provincial treasurer — Where a fine or forfeiture is imposed or a recognizance is forfeited and no provision, other than this section, is made by law for the application of the proceeds thereof, the proceeds belong to Her Majesty in right of the province in which the fine or forfeiture was imposed or the recognizance was forfeited, and shall be paid by the person who receives them to the treasurer of that province.

(2) Proceeds to go to receiver general for Canada — Where

(a) a fine or forfeiture is imposed

(i) in respect of a contravention of a revenue law of Canada,

(ii) in respect of a breach of duty or malfeasance in office by an officer or employee of the Government of Canada, or

(iii) in respect of any proceedings instituted at the instance of the Government of Canada in which that government bears the costs of prosecution, or

(b) a recognizance in connection with proceedings mentioned in paragraph (a) is forfeited,

the proceeds of the fine, forfeiture or recognizance belong to Her Majesty in right of Canada and shall be paid by the person who receives them to the Receiver General.

(3) Direction for payment to municipality — Where a provincial, municipal or local authority bears, in whole or in part, the expense of administering the law under which a fine or forfeiture is imposed or under which proceedings are taken in which a recognizance is forfeited,

> (a) the Lieutenant Governor in Council of a province may direct that the proceeds of a fine, forfeiture or recognizance that belongs to Her Majesty in right of the province shall be paid to that authority; and

> (b) the Governor in Council may direct that the proceeds of a fine, forfeiture or recognizance that belongs to Her Majesty in right of Canada shall be paid to that authority.

734.5 Licences, permits, etc. — If an offender is in default of payment of a fine,

> (a) where the proceeds of the fine belong to Her Majesty in right of a province by virtue of subsection 734.4(1), the person reponsible, by or under an Act of the legislature of the province, for issuing, renewing or suspending a licence, permit or other similar instrument in relation to the offender may refuse to issue or renew or may suspend the licence, permit or other instrument until the fine is paid in full, proof of which lies on the offender; or

> (b) where the proceeds of the fine belong to Her Majesty in right of Canada by virtue of subsection 734.4(2), the person responsible, by or under an Act of Parliament, for issuing or renewing a licence, permit or other similar instrument in relation to the offender may refuse to issue or renew or may suspend the licence, permit or other instrument until the fine is paid in full, proof of which lies on the offender.

1995, c. 22, s. 6; 1999, c. 5, s. 34

734.6 (1) Civil enforcement of fines, forfeiture — Where

> (a) an offender is in default of payment of a fine, or

> (b) a forfeiture imposed by law is not paid as required by the order imposing it,

then, in addition to any other method provided by law for recovering the fine or forfeiture,

> (c) the Attorney General of the province to whom the proceeds of the fine or forfeiture belong, or

> (d) the Attorney General of Canada, where the proceeds of the fine or forfeiture belong to Her Majesty in right of Canada,

may, by filing the order, enter as a judgment the amount of the fine or forfeiture, and costs, if any, in any civil court in Canada that has jurisdiction to enter a judgment for that amount.

(2) Effect of filing order — An order that is entered as a judgment under this section is enforceable in the same manner as if it were a judgment obtained by the Attorney General of the province or the Attorney General of Canada, as the case may be, in civil proceedings.

1995, c. 22, s. 6

734.7 (1) Warrant of committal — Where time has been allowed for payment of a fine, the court shall not issue a warrant of committal in default of payment of the fine

    (a) until the expiration of the time allowed for payment of the fine in full; and

    (b) unless the court is satisfied

        (i) that the mechanisms provided by sections 734.5 and 734.6 are not appropriate in the circumstances, or

        (ii) that the offender has, without reasonable excuse, refused to pay the fine or discharge it under section 736.

(2) Reasons for committal — Where no time has been allowed for payment of a fine and a warrant committing the offender to prison for default of payment of the fine is issued, the court shall state in the warrant the reason for immediate committal.

(2.1) Period of imprisonment — The period of imprisonment in default of payment of the fine shall be specified in a warrant of committal referred to in subsection (1) or (2).

(3) Compelling appearance of person bound — The provisions of Parts XVI and XVIII with respect to compelling the appearance of an accused before a justice apply, with such modifications as the circumstances require, to proceedings under paragraph (1)(b).

(4) Effect of imprisonment — The imprisonment of an offender for default of payment of a fine terminates the operation of sections 734.5 and 734.6 in relation to that fine.

1995, c. 22, s. 6; 1999, c. 5, s. 35.

734.8 (1) Definition of "penalty" — In this section, "penalty" means the aggregate of

    (a) the fine, and

    (b) the costs and charges of committing and conveying the defaulter to prison, calculated in accordance with regulations made under subsection 734(7).

(2) Reduction of imprisonment on part payment — The term of imprisonment in default of payment of a fine shall, on payment of a part of the penalty, whether the payment was made before or after the execution of a warrant of committal, be reduced by the number of days that bears the same proportion to the number of days in the term as the part paid bears to the total penalty.

(3) Minimum that can be accepted — No amount offered in part payment of a penalty shall be accepted after the execution of a warrant of committal unless it is sufficient to secure a reduction of sentence of one day, or a whole number multiple of one day, and no part payment shall be accepted until any fee that is payable in respect of the warrant or its execution has been paid.

(4) To whom payment made — Payment may be made under this section to the person that the Attorney General directs or, if the offender is imprisoned, to the person who has lawful custody of the prisoner or to any other person that the Attorney General directs.

(5) Application of money paid — A payment under this section shall be applied firstly to the payment in full of costs and charges, secondly to the payment in full of any victim surcharge imposed under section 737, and then to payment of any part of the fine that remains unpaid.

1995, c. 22, s. 6; 1999, c. 5, s. 36; 1999, c. 25, s. 19

735. (1) Fines on corporations — A corporation that is convicted of an offence is liable, in lieu of any imprisonment that is prescribed as punishment for that offence, to be fined in an amount, except where otherwise provided by law,

(a) that is in the discretion of the court, where the offence is an indictable offence; or

(b) not exceeding twenty-five thousand dollars, where the offence is a summary conviction offence.

(1.1) Application of certain provisions — fines — A court that imposes a fine under subsection (1) or under any other Act of Parliament shall make an order that clearly sets out

(a) the amount of the fine;

(b) the manner in which the fine is to be paid;

(c) the time or times by which the fine, or any portion of it, must be paid; and

(d) any other terms respecting the payment of the fine that the court deems appropriate.

(2) Effect of filing order — Section 734.6 applies, with any modifications that are required, when a corporate offender fails to pay the fine in accordance with the terms of the order.

1995, c. 22, s. 6; 1999, c. 5, s. 37.

736. (1) Fine option program — An offender who is fined under section 734 may, whether or not the offender is serving a term of imprisonment imposed in default of payment of the fine, discharge the fine in whole or in part by earning credits for work performed during a period not greater than two years in a program established for that purpose by the Lieutenant Governor in Council

(a) of the province in which the fine was imposed, or

(b) of the province in which the offender resides, where an appropriate agreement is in effect between the government of that province and the government of the province in which the fine was imposed,

if the offender is admissible to such a program.

(2) Credits and other matters — A program referred to in subsection (1) shall determine the rate at which credits are earned and may provide for the manner of crediting any amounts earned against the fine and any other matters necessary for or incidental to carrying out the program.

(3) Deemed payment — Credits earned for work performed as provided by subsection (1) shall, for the purposes of this Act, be deemed to be payment in respect of a fine.

(4) Federal-provincial agreement — Where, by virtue of subsection 734.4(2), the proceeds of a fine belong to Her Majesty in right of Canada, an offender may discharge the fine in whole or in part in a fine option program of a province pursuant to subsection (1), where an appropriate agreement is in effect between the government of the province and the Government of Canada.

1995, c. 22, s. 6.

Note: 1997, c. 18, s. 107 was not in force at the date of publication. This section purported to amend s. 736 of the Criminal Code as it existed prior to the 1995, c. 22 amendments. The reference to s. 736 of the Code has been replaced by s. 730 in accordance with 1995, c. 22, s. 18 (Sch. IV).

737. (1) Victim surcharge — Subject to subsection (5), an offender who is convicted or discharged under section 730 of an offence under this Act or the *Controlled Drugs and Substances Act* shall pay a victim surcharge, in addition to any other punishment imposed on the offender.

(2) Amount of surcharge — Subject to subsection (3), the amount of the victim surcharge in respect of an offence is

    (a) 15 per cent of any fine that is imposed on the offender for the offence; or

    (b) if no fine is imposed on the offender for the offence,

        (i) $50 in the case of an offence punishable by summary conviction, and

        (ii) $100 in the case of an offence punishable by indictment.

(3) Increase in surcharge — The court may order an offender to pay a victim surcharge in an amount exceeding that set out in subsection (2) if the court considers it appropriate in the circumstances and is satisfied that the offender is able to pay the higher amount.

(4) Time for payment — The victim surcharge imposed in respect of an offence is payable at the time at which the fine imposed for the offence is payable and, when no fine is imposed, within the time established by the lieutenant governor in council of the province in which the surcharge is imposed for payment of any such surcharge.

(5) Exception — When the offender establishes to the satisfaction of the court that undue hardship to the offender or the dependants of the offender would result from payment of the victim surcharge, the court may, on application of the offender, make an order exempting the offender from the application of subsection (1).

(6) Reasons — When the court makes an order under subsection (5), the court shall state its reasons in the record of the proceedings.

(7) Amounts applied to aid victims — A victim surcharge imposed under subsection (1) shall be applied for the purposes of providing such assistance to victims of offences as the lieutenant governor in council of the province in which the surcharge is imposed may direct from time to time.

(8) Notice — The court shall cause to be given to the offender a written notice setting out

(a) the amount of the victim surcharge;

(b) the manner in which the victim surcharge is to be paid;

(c) the time by which the victim surcharge must be paid; and

(d) the procedure for applying for a change in any terms referred to in paragraphs (b) and (c) in accordance with section 734.3.

(9) Enforcement — Subsections 734(3) to (7) and sections 734.3, 734.5, 734.7 and 734.8 apply, with any modifications that the circumstances require, in respect of a victim surcharge imposed under subsection (1) and, in particular,

(a) a reference in any of those provisions to "fine", other than in subsection 734.8(5), must be read as if it were a reference to "victim surcharge"; and

(b) the notice provided under subsection (8) is deemed to be an order made under section 734.1.

(10) Section 736 does not apply — For greater certainty, the program referred to in section 736 for the discharge of a fine may not be used in respect of a victim surcharge.

1995, c. 22, s. 6; 1996, c. 19, s. 75 [Amended 1995, c. 22, s. 18 (Sched. IV, item 15).]; 1999, c. 5, s. 38; 1999, c. 25, s. 20

Restitution

738. (1) Restitution to victims of offences — Where an offender is convicted or discharged under section 730 of an offence, the court imposing sentence on or discharging the offender may, on application of the Attorney General or on its own motion, in addition to any other measure imposed on the offender, order that that offender make restitution to another person as follows:

(a) in the case of damage to, or the loss or destruction of, the property of any person as a result of the commission of the offence or the arrest or attempted arrest of the offender, by paying to the person an amount not exceeding the replacement value of the property as of the date the order is imposed, less the value of any part of the property that is returned to that person as of the date it is returned, where the amount is readily ascertainable;

(b) in the case of bodily harm to any person as a result of the commission of the offence or the arrest or attempted arrest of the offender, by paying to the person an amount not exceeding all pecuniary damages, including loss of income or support, incurred as a result of the bodily harm, where the amount is readily ascertainable; and

(c) in the case of bodily harm or threat of bodily harm to the offender's spouse or child, or any other person, as a result of the commission of the offence or the arrest or attempted arrest of the offender, where the spouse, child or other person was a member of the offender's household at the relevant time, by paying to the person in question, independently of any amount ordered to be paid under paragraphs (a) and (b), an amount not exceeding actual and reasonable expenses incurred by that person, as a result of moving out of the offender's household, for temporary housing, food, child care and transportation, where the amount is readily ascertainable.

Proposed Amendment — 738(1)(c)

(c) in the case of bodily harm or threat of bodily harm to the offender's spouse or common-law partner or child, or any other person, as a result of the commission of the offence or the arrest or attempted arrest of the offender, where the spouse or common-law partner, child or other person was a member of the offender's household at the relevant time, by paying to the person in question, independently of any amount ordered to be paid under paragraphs (a) and (b), an amount not exceeding actual and reasonable expenses incurred by that person, as a result of moving out of the offender's household, for temporary housing, food, child care and transportation, where the amount is readily ascertainable.

2000, c. 12, s. 95(e) [Not in force at date of publication.]

(2) Regulations — The Lieutenant Governor in Council of a province may make regulations precluding the inclusion of provisions on enforcement of restitution orders as an optional condition of a probation order or of a conditional sentence order.

1995, c. 22, s. 6.

739. Restitution to persons acting in good faith — Where an offender is convicted or discharged under section 730 of an offence and

(a) any property obtained as a result of the commission of the offence has been conveyed or transferred for valuable consideration to a person acting in good faith and without notice, or

(b) the offender has borrowed money on the security of that property from a person acting in good faith and without notice,

the court may, where that property has been returned to the lawful owner or the person who had lawful possession of that property at the time the offence was committed, order the offender to pay as restitution to the person referred to in paragraph (a) or (b) an amount not exceeding the amount of consideration for that property or the total amount outstanding in respect of the loan, as the case may be.

1995, c. 22, s. 6.

740. Priority to restitution — Where the court finds it applicable and appropriate in the circumstances of a case to make, in relation to an offender, an order of restitution under section 738 or 739, and

(a) an order of forfeiture under this or any other Act of Parliament may be made in respect of property that is the same as property in respect of which the order of restitution may be made, or

(b) the court is considering ordering the offender to pay a fine and it appears to the court that the offender would not have the means or ability to comply with both the order of restitution and the order to pay the fine, the court shall first make the order of restitution and shall then consider whether and to what extent an order of forfeiture or an order to pay a fine is appropriate in the circumstances.

1995, c. 22, s. 6.

741. (1) Enforcing restitution order — Where an amount that is ordered to be paid under section 738 or 739 is not paid forthwith, the person to whom the amount was ordered to be paid may, by filing the order, enter as a judgment the amount ordered to be paid in any civil court in Canada that has jurisdiction to enter a judgment for that amount, and that judgment is enforceable against the offender in the same manner as if it were a judgment rendered against the offender in that court in civil proceedings.

(2) Moneys found on offender — All or any part of an amount that is ordered to be paid under section 738 or 739 may be taken out of moneys found in the possession of the offender at the time of the arrest of the offender if the court making the order, on being satisfied that ownership of or right to possession of those moneys is not disputed by claimants other than the offender, so directs.

1995, c. 22, s. 6.

741.1 Notice of orders of restitution — Where a court makes an order of restitution under section 738 or 739, it shall cause notice of the content of the order, or a copy of the order, to be given to the person to whom the restitution is ordered to be paid.

1995, c. 22, s. 6.

741.2 Civil remedy not affected — A civil remedy for an act or omission is not affected by reason only that an order for restitution under section 738 or 739 has been made in respect of that act or omission.

1995, c. 22, s. 6.

Conditional Sentence of Imprisonment

742. Definitions — In sections 742.1 to 742.7,

"change", in relation to optional conditions, includes deletions and additions;

"optional conditions" means the conditions referred to in subsection 742.3(2);

"supervisor" means a person designated by the Attorney General, either by name or by title of office, as a supervisor for the purposes of sections 742.1 to 742.7.

1995, c. 22, s. 6.

742.1 Imposing of conditional sentence — Where a person is convicted of an offence, except an offence that is punishable by a minimum term of imprisonment, and the court

    (a) imposes a sentence of imprisonment of less than two years, and

(b) is satisfied that serving the sentence in the community would not endanger the safety of the community and would be consistent with the fundamental purpose and principles of sentencing set out in sections 718 to 718.2,

the court may, for the purposes of supervising the offender's behaviour in the community, order that the offender serve the sentence in the community, subject to the offender's complying with the conditions of a conditional sentence order made under section 742.3.

1995, c. 22, s. 6; 1997, c. 18, s. 107.1.

742.2 (1) Firearm, etc., prohibitions — Before imposing a conditional sentence under section 742.1, the court shall consider whether section 100 is applicable.

(2) Idem — For greater certainty, a condition of a conditional sentence referred to in paragraph 742.3(2)(b) does not affect the operation of section 100.

1995, c. 22, s. 6.

742.3 (1) Compulsory conditions of conditional sentence order — The court shall prescribe, as conditions of a conditional sentence order, that the offender do all of the following:

(a) keep the peace and be of good behaviour;

(b) appear before the court when required to do so by the court;

(c) report to a supervisor

(i) within two working days, or such longer period as the court directs, after the making of the conditional sentence order, and

(ii) thereafter, when required by the supervisor and in the manner directed by the supervisor;

(d) remain within the jurisdiction of the court unless written permission to go outside that jurisdiction is obtained from the court or the supervisor; and

(e) notify the court or the supervisor in advance of any change of name or address, and promptly notify the court or the supervisor of any change of employment or occupation.

(2) Optional conditions of conditional sentence order — The court may prescribe, as additional conditions of a conditional sentence order, that the offender do one or more of the following:

(a) abstain from

(i) the consumption of alcohol or other intoxicating substances, or

(ii) the consumption of drugs except in accordance with a medical prescription;

(b) abstain from owning, possessing or carrying a weapon;

(c) provide for the support or care of dependants;

(d) perform up to 240 hours of community service over a period not exceeding eighteen months;

(e) attend a treatment program approved by the province; and

(f) comply with such other reasonable conditions as the court considers desirable, subject to any regulations made under subsection 738(2), for securing the good conduct of the offender and for preventing a repetition by the offender of the same offence or the commission of other offences.

(3) Proceedings on making order — A court that makes an order under this section shall

(a) cause to be given to the offender

(i) a copy of the order,

(ii) an explanation of the substance of sections 742.4 and 742.6, and

(iii) an explanation of the procedure for applying under section 742.4 for a change to the optional conditions; and

(b) take reasonable measures to ensure that the offender understands the order and the explanations given to the offender under paragraph (a).

1995, c. 22, s. 6.

742.4 (1) Supervisor may propose changes to optional conditions — Where an offender's supervisor is of the opinion that a change in circumstances makes a change to the optional conditions desirable, the supervisor shall give written notification of the proposed change, and the reasons for it, to the offender, to the prosecutor and to the court.

(2) Hearing — Within seven days after receiving a notification referred to in subsection (1),

(a) the offender or the prosecutor may request the court to hold a hearing to consider the proposed change, or

(b) the court may, of its own initiative, order that a hearing be held to consider the proposed change,

and a hearing so requested or ordered shall be held within thirty days after the receipt by the court of the notification referred to in subsection (1).

(3) Decision at hearing — At a hearing held pursuant to subsection (2), the court

(a) shall approve or refuse to approve the proposed change; and

(b) may make any other change to the optional conditions that the court deems appropriate.

(4) Where no hearing requested or ordered — Where no request or order for a hearing is made within the time period stipulated in subsection (2), the proposed change takes effect fourteen days after the receipt by the court of the notification referred to in subsection (1), and the supervisor shall so notify the offender and file proof of that notification with the court.

(5) Changes proposed by offender or prosecutor — Subsections (1) and (3) apply, with such modifications as the circumstances require, in respect of a change proposed by the offender or the prosecutor to the optional conditions, and in all such cases a hearing must be held, and must be held within thirty days after the receipt by the court of the notification referred to in subsection (1).

(6) Judge may act in chambers — All the functions of the court under this section may be exercised in chambers.

1995, c. 22, s. 6; 1999, c. 5, s. 39.

742.5 (1) Transfer of order — Where an offender who is bound by a conditional sentence order becomes a resident of a territorial division, other than the territorial division where the order was made, on the application of a supervisor, the court that made the order may, subject to subsection (1.1), transfer the order to a court in that other territorial division that would, having regard to the mode of trial of the offender, have had jurisdiction to make the order in that other territorial division if the offender had been tried and convicted there of the offence in respect of which the order was made, and the order may thereafter be dealt with and enforced by the court to which it is so transferred in all respects as if that court had made the order.

(1.1) Attorney General's consent — The transfer may be granted only with

(a) the consent of the Attorney General of the province in which the conditional sentence order was made, if the two territorial divisions are not in the same province; or

(b) the consent of the Attorney General of Canada, if the proceedings that led to the issuance of the conditional sentence order were instituted by or on behalf of the Attorney General of Canada.

(2) Where court unable to act — Where a court that has made a conditional sentence order or to which a conditional sentence order has been transferred pursuant to subsection (1) is for any reason unable to act, the powers of that court in relation to the conditional sentence order may be exercised by any other court that has equivalent jurisdiction in the same province.

1995, c. 22, s. 6; 1999, c. 5, s. 40.

742.6 (1) Procedure on breach of condition — For the purpose of proceedings under this section,

(a) the provisions of Parts XVI and XVIII with respect to compelling the appearance of an accused before a justice apply, with any modifications that the circumstances require, and any reference in those Parts to committing an offence shall be read as a reference to breaching a condition of a conditional sentence order;

(b) the powers of arrest for breach of a condition are those that apply to an indictable offence, with any modifications that the circumstances require, and subsection 495(2) does not apply;

(c) despite paragraph (a), if an allegation of breach of condition is made, the proceeding is commenced by

(i) the issuance of a warrant for the arrest of the offender for the alleged breach,

(ii) the arrest without warrant of the offender for the alleged breach, or

(iii) the compelling of the offender's appearance in accordance with paragraph (d);

(d) if the offender is already detained or before a court, the offender's appearance may be compelled under the provisions referred to in paragraph (a);

(e) if an offender is arrested for the alleged breach, the peace officer who makes the arrest, the officer in charge or a judge or justice may release the offender and the offender's appearance may be compelled under the provisions referred to in paragraph (a); and

(f) any judge of a superior court of criminal jurisdiction or of a court of criminal jurisdiction or any justice of the peace may issue a warrant to arrest no matter which court, judge or justice sentenced the offender, and the provisions that apply to the issuance of telewarrants apply, with any modifications that the circumstances require, as if a breach of condition were an indictable offence.

(2) Interim release — For the purpose of the application of section 515, the release from custody of an offender who is detained on the basis of an alleged breach of a condition of a conditional sentence order shall be governed by subsection 515(6).

(3) Hearing — The hearing of an allegation of a breach of condition shall be commenced within thirty days, or as soon thereafter as is practicable, after

(a) the offender's arrest; or

(b) the compelling of the offender's appearance in accordance with paragraph (1)(d).

(3.1) Place — The allegation may be heard by any court having jurisdiction to hear that allegation in the place where the breach is alleged to have been committed or the offender is found, arrested or in custody.

(3.2) Attorney General's consent — If the place where the offender is found, arrested or in custody is outside the province in which the breach is alleged to have been committed, no proceedings in respect of that breach shall be instituted in that place without

(a) the consent of the Attorney General of the province in which the breach is alleged to have been committed; or

(b) the consent of the Attorney General of Canada, if the proceedings that led to the issuance of the conditional sentence order were instituted by or on behalf of the Attorney General of Canada.

(3.3) Adjournment — A judge may, at any time during a hearing of an allegation of breach of condition, adjourn the hearing for a reasonable period.

(4) Report of supervisor — An allegation of a breach of condition must be supported by a written report of the supervisor, which report must include, where appropriate, signed statements of witnesses.

(5) Admission of report on notice of intent — The report is admissible in evidence if the party intending to produce it has, before the hearing, given the offender reasonable notice and a copy of the report.

(6) Proof of service — Service of any report referred to in subsection (4) may be proved by oral evidence given under oath by, or by the affidavit or solemn declaration of, the person claiming to have served it.

(7) Attendance for examination — Notwithstanding subsection (6), the court may require the person who appears to have signed an affidavit or solemn declaration referred to in that subsection to appear before it for examination or cross-examination in respect of the issue of proof of service.

(8) Requiring attendance of supervisor or witness — The offender may, with leave of the court, require the attendance, for cross-examination, of the supervisor or of any witness whose signed statement is included in the report.

(9) Powers of court — Where the court is satisfied, on a balance of probabilities, that the offender has without reasonable excuse, the proof of which lies on the offender, breached a condition of the conditional sentence order, the court may

    (a) take no action;

    (b) change the optional conditions;

    (c) suspend the conditional sentence order and direct

        (i) that the offender serve in custody a portion of the unexpired sentence, and

        (ii) that the conditional sentence order resume on the offender's release from custody, either with or without changes to the optional conditions; or

    (d) terminate the conditional sentence order and direct that the offender be committed to custody until the expiration of the sentence.

(10) Warrant or arrest — suspension of running of conditional sentence — The running of a conditional sentence imposed on an offender is suspended during the period that ends with the determination of whether a breach of condition had occurred and begins with the earliest of

    (a) the issuance of a warrant for the arrest of the offender for the alleged breach,

    (b) the arrest without warrant of the offender for the alleged breach, and

    (c) the compelling of the offender's appearance in accordance with paragraph (1)(d).

(11) Conditions continue — If the offender is not detained in custody during any period referred to in subsection (10), the conditions of the order continue to apply, with any changes made to them under section 742.4, and any subsequent breach of those conditions may be dealt with in accordance with this section.

(12) Detention under s. 515(6) — A conditional sentence referred to in subsection (10) starts running again on the making of an order to detain the offender in custody under subsection 515(6) and, unless section 742.7 applies, continues running while the offender is detained under the order.

(13) Earned remission does not apply — Section 6 of the *Prisons and Reformatories Act* does not apply to the period of detention in custody under subsection 515(6).

(14) Unreasonable delay in execution — Despite subsection (10), if there was unreasonable delay in the execution of a warrant, the court may, at any time, order that any period between the issuance and execution of the warrant that it considers appropriate in the interest of justice is deemed to be time served under the conditional sentence unless the period has been so deemed under subsection (15).

(15) Allegation dismissed or reasonable excuse — If the allegation is withdrawn or dismissed or the offender is found to have had a reasonable excuse for the breach, the sum of the following periods is deemed to be time served under the conditional sentence:

(a) any period for which the running of the conditional sentence was suspended; and

(b) if subsection (12) applies, a period equal to one half of the period that the conditional sentence runs while the offender is detained under an order referred to in that subsection.

(16) Powers of court — If a court is satisfied, on a balance of probabilities, that the offender has without reasonable excuse, the proof of which lies on the offender, breached a condition of the conditional sentence order, the court may, in exceptional cases and in the interests of justice, order that some or all of the period of suspension referred to in subsection (10) is deemed to be time served under the conditional sentence.

(17) Considerations — In exercising its discretion under subsection (16), a court shall consider

(a) the circumstances and seriousness of the breach;

(b) whether not making the order would cause the offender undue hardship based on the offender's individual circumstances; and

(c) the period for which the offender was subject to conditions while the running of the conditional sentence was suspended and whether the offender complied with those conditions during that period.

1995, c. 22, s. 6; 1999, c. 5, s. 41.

742.7 (1) If person imprisoned for new offence — If an offender who is subject to a conditional sentence is imprisoned as a result of a sentence imposed for another offence, whenever committed, the running of the conditional sentence is suspended during the period of imprisonment for that other offence.

(2) Breach of condition — If an order is made under paragraph 742.6(9)(c) or (d) to commit an offender to custody, the custodial period ordered shall, unless the court considers that it would not be in the interests of justice, be served consecutively to any other period of imprisonment that the offender is serving when that order is made.

(3) Multiple sentences — If an offender is serving both a custodial period referred to in subsection (2) and any other period of imprisonment, the periods shall, for the purpose of section 743.1 and section 139 of the *Corrections and Conditional Release Act*, be deemed to constitute one sentence of imprisonment.

(4) Conditional sentence resumes — The running of any period of the conditional sentence that is to be served in the community resumes upon the release of the offender from prison on parole, on statutory release, on earned remission, or at the expiration of the sentence.

1995, c. 22, s. 6; 1999, c. 5, s. 42.

Imprisonment

743. Imprisonment when no other provision — Every one who is convicted of an indictable offence for which no punishment is specially provided is liable to imprisonment for a term not exceeding five years.

1995, c. 22, s. 6.

743.1 (1) Imprisonment for life or more than two years — Except where otherwise provided, a person who is sentenced to imprisonment for

    (a) life,

    (b) a term of two years or more, or

    (c) two or more terms of less than two years each that are to be served one after the other and that, in the aggregate, amount to two years or more,

shall be sentenced to imprisonment in a penitentiary.

(2) Subsequent term less than two years — Where a person who is sentenced to imprisonment in a penitentiary is, before the expiration of that sentence, sentenced to imprisonment for a term of less than two years, the person shall serve that term in a penitentiary, but if the previous sentence of imprisonment in a penitentiary is set aside, that person shall serve that term in accordance with subsection (3).

(3) Imprisonment for term less than two years — A person who is sentenced to imprisonment and who is not required to be sentenced as provided in subsection (1) or (2) shall, unless a special prison is prescribed by law, be sentenced to imprisonment in a prison or other place of confinement, other than a penitentiary, within the province in which the person is convicted, in which the sentence of imprisonment may be lawfully executed.

(3.1) Long-term supervision — Notwithstanding subsection (3), an offender who is required to be supervised by an order made under paragraph 753.1(3)(b) and who is sentenced for another offence during the period of the supervision shall be sentenced to imprisonment in a penitentiary.

(4) Sentence to penitentiary of person serving sentence elsewhere — Where a person is sentenced to imprisonment in a penitentiary while the person is lawfully imprisoned in a place other than a penitentiary, that person shall, except where otherwise provided, be sent immediately to the penitentiary, and shall serve in the penitentiary the unexpired portion of the term of imprisonment that the person was serving when sentenced to the penitentiary as well as the term of imprisonment for which that person was sentenced to the penitentiary.

(5) Transfer to penitentiary — Where, at any time, a person who is imprisoned in a prison or place of confinement other than a penitentiary is subject to two or more terms of imprisonment, each of which is for less than two years, that are to be served one after the other, and the aggregate of the unexpired portions of those terms at that time amounts to two years or more, the person shall be transferred to a penitentiary to serve those terms, but if any one or more of such terms is set aside or reduced and the unexpired portions of the remaining term or terms on the day on which that person was transferred under this section amounted to less than two years, that person shall serve that term or terms in accordance with subsection (3).

(6) Newfoundland — For the purposes of subsection (3), "penitentiary" does not, until a day to be fixed by order of the Governor in Council, include the facility mentioned in subsection 15(2) of the *Corrections and Conditional Release Act*.

1995, c. 22, s. 6; 1997, c. 17, s. 1.

743.2 Report by court to correctional service — A court that sentences or commits a person to penitentiary shall forward to the Correctional Service of Canada its reasons and recommendation relating to the sentence or committal, any relevant reports that were submitted to the court, and any other information relevant to administering the sentence or committal.

1995, c. 22, s. 6.

743.3 Sentence served according to regulations — A sentence of imprisonment shall be served in accordance with the enactments and rules that govern the institution to which the prisoner is sentenced.

1995, c. 22, s. 6.

743.4 (1) Transfer of young person to place of custody — Where a young person is sentenced to imprisonment under this or any other Act of Parliament, the young person may, with the consent of the provincial director, be transferred to a place of custody for any portion of the young person's term of imprisonment, but in no case shall that young person be kept in a place of custody under this section after that young person attains the age of twenty years.

(2) Removal of young person from place of custody — Where the provincial director certifies that a young person transferred to a place of custody under subsection (1) can no longer be held therein without significant danger of escape or of detrimentally affecting the rehabilitation or reformation of other young persons held therein, the young person may be imprisoned during the remainder of his term of imprisonment in any place where that young person might, but for subsection (1), have been imprisoned.

(3) Words and expressions — For the purposes of this section, the expressions "provincial director" and "young person" have the meanings assigned by subsection 2(1) of the *Young Offenders Act*, and the expression "place of custody" means "open custody" or "secure custody" within the meaning assigned by subsection 24.1(1) of that Act.

1995, c. 22, s. 6.

743.5 (1) Transfer of jurisdiction — Where a person is or has been sentenced for an offence while subject to a disposition made under paragraph 20(1)(j), (k) or (k.1) of the *Young Offenders Act*, on the application of the Attorney General or the Attorney General's agent, a court of criminal jurisdiction may, unless to so order would bring the administration of justice into disrepute, order that the remaining portion of the disposition made under that Act be dealt with, for all purposes under this Act or any other Act of Parliament, as if it had been a sentence imposed under this Act.

(2) Whether sentence to be served concurrently or consecutively — Where an order is made under subsection (1), in respect of a disposition made under paragraph 20(1)(k) or (k.1) of the *Young Offenders Act*, the remaining portion of the disposition to be served pursuant to the order shall be served concurrently with the sentence referred to in subsection (1), where it is a term of imprisonment, unless the court making the order orders that it be served consecutively.

(3) Remaining portion deemed to constitute one sentence — For greater certainty, the remaining portion of the disposition referred to in subsection (2) shall, for the purposes of section 139 of the *Corrections and Conditional Release Act* and section 743.1 of this Act, be deemed to constitute one sentence of imprisonment.

1995, c. 22, s. 6, s. 19(b), s. 20(b).

Eligibility for Parole

743.6 (1) Power of court to delay parole — Notwithstanding subsection 120(1) of the *Corrections and Conditional Release Act*, where an offender is sentenced, after the coming into force of this section, to a term of imprisonment of two years or more, including a sentence of imprisonment for life imposed otherwise than as a minimum punishment, on conviction for an offence set out in Schedule I or II to that Act that were prosecuted by way of indictment, the court may, if satisfied, having regard to the circumstances of the commission of the offence and the character and circumstances of the offender, that the expression of society's denunciation of the offences or the objective of specific or general deterrence so requires, order that the portion of the sentence that must be served before the offender may be released on full parole is one half of the sentence or ten years, whichever is less.

(1.1) Power of court to delay parole — Notwithstanding subsection 120(1) of the *Corrections and Conditional Release Act*, where an offender receives a sentence of imprisonment of two years or more, including a sentence of imprisonment for life imposed otherwise than as a minimum punishment, on conviction for a criminal organization offence, the court may order that the portion of the sentence that must be served before the offender may be released on full parole is one half of the sentence or ten years, whichever is less.

(2) Principles that are to guide the court — For greater certainty, the paramount principles that are to guide the court under this section are denunciation and specific or general deterrence, with rehabilitation of the offender, in all cases, being subordinate to those paramount principles.

1995, c. 22, s. 6; c. 42, s. 86(b); 1997, c. 23, s. 18.

Delivery of Offender to Keeper of Prison

744. Execution of warrant of committal — A peace officer or other person to whom a warrant of committal authorized by this or any other Act of Parliament is directed shall arrest the person named or described therein, if it is necessary to do so in order to take that person into custody, convey that person to the prison mentioned in the warrant and deliver that person, together with the warrant, to the keeper of the prison who shall thereupon give to the peace officer or other person who delivers the prisoner a receipt in Form 43 setting out the state and condition of the prisoner when delivered into custody.

1995, c. 22, s. 6.

Imprisonment for Life

745. Sentence of life imprisonment — Subject to section 745.1, the sentence to be pronounced against a person who is to be sentenced to imprisonment for life shall be

(a) in respect of a person who has been convicted of high treason or first degree murder, that the person be sentenced to imprisonment for life without eligibility for parole until the person has served twenty-five years of the sentence;

(b) in respect of a person who has been convicted of second degree murder where that person has previously been convicted of culpable homicide that is murder, however described in this Act, that the person be sentenced to imprisonment for life without eligibility for parole until the person has served twenty-five years of the sentence;

Proposed Addition — 745(b.1)

(b.1) in respect of a person who has been convicted of second degree murder where that person has previously been convicted of an offence under section 4 or 6 of the *Crimes Against Humanity and War Crimes Act* that had as its basis an intentional killing, whether or not it was planned and deliberate, that that person be sentenced to imprisonment for life without eligibility for parole until the person has served twenty-five years of the sentence;

2000, c. 24, s. 46 [Not in force at date of publication.]

(c) in respect of a person who has been convicted of second degree murder, that the person be sentenced to imprisonment for life without eligibility for parole until the person has served at least ten years of the sentence or such greater number of years, not being more than twenty-five years, as has been substituted therefor pursuant to section 745.4; and

(d) in respect of a person who has been convicted of any other offence, that the person be sentenced to imprisonment for life with normal eligibility for parole.

1995, c. 22, s. 6

745.01 Information in respect of parole — Except where subsection 745.6(2) applies, at the time of sentencing under paragraph 745(a), (b) or (c), the judge who presided at the trial of the offender shall state the following, for the record:

> The offender has been found guilty of (*state offence*) and sentenced to imprisonment for life. The offender is not eligible for parole until (*state date*). However, after serving at least 15 years of the sentence, the offender may apply under section 745.6 of the *Criminal Code* for a reduction in the number of years of imprisonment without eligibility for parole. If the jury hearing the application reduces the period of parole ineligibility, the offender may then make an application for parole under the *Corrections and Conditional Release Act* at the end of that reduced period.

1999, c. 25, s. 21

745.1 Persons under eighteen — The sentence to be pronounced against a person who was under the age of eighteen at the time of the commission of the offence for which the person was convicted of first degree murder or second degree murder and who is to be sentenced to imprisonment for life shall be that the person be sentenced to imprisonment for life without eligibility for parole until the person has served

(a) such period between five and seven years of the sentence as is specified by the judge presiding at the trial, or if no period is specified by the judge presiding at the trial, five years, in the case of a person who was under the age of sixteen at the time of the commission of the offence;

(b) ten years, in the case of a person convicted of first degree murder who was sixteen or seventeen years of age at the time of the commission of the offence; and

(c) seven years, in the case of a person convicted of second degree murder who was sixteen or seventeen years of age at the time of the commission of the offence.

1995, c. 22, s. 6, s. 21(b).

745.2 Recommendation by jury — Subject to section 745.3, where a jury finds an accused guilty of second degree murder, the judge presiding at the trial shall, before discharging the jury, put to them the following question:

You have found the accused guilty of second degree murder and the law requires that I now pronounce a sentence of imprisonment for life against the accused. Do you wish to make any recommendation with respect to the number of years that the accused must serve before the accused is eligible for release on parole? You are not required to make any recommendation but if you do, your recommendation will be considered by me when I am determining whether I should substitute for the ten year period, which the law would otherwise require the accused to serve before the accused is eligible to be considered for release on parole, a number of years that is more than ten but not more than twenty-five.

1995, c. 22, s. 6.

745.3 Persons under sixteen — Where a jury finds an accused guilty of first degree murder or second degree murder and the accused was under the age of sixteen at the time of the commission of the offence, the judge presiding at the trial shall, before discharging the jury, put to them the following question:

You have found the accused guilty of first degree murder (or second degree murder) and the law requires that I now pronounce a sentence of imprisonment for life against the accused. Do you wish to make any recommendation with respect to the period of imprisonment that the accused must serve before the accused is eligible for release on parole? You are not required to make any recommendation but if you do, your recommendation will be considered by me when I am determining the period of imprisonment that is between five years and seven years that the law would require the accused to serve before the accused is eligible to be considered for release on parole.

1995, c. 22, s. 6, s. 22(b).

745.4 Ineligibility for parole — Subject to section 745.5, at the time of the sentencing under section 745 of an offender who is convicted of second degree murder, the judge who presided at the trial of the offender or, if that judge is unable to do so, any judge of the same court may, having regard to the character of the offender, the nature of the offence and the circumstances surrounding its commission, and to the recommendation, if any, made pursuant to section 745.2, by order, substitute for ten years a number of years of imprisonment (being more than ten but nor more than twenty-five) without eligibility for parole, as the judge deems fit in the circumstances.

1995, c. 22, s. 6.

745.5 Idem — At the time of the sentencing under section 745.1 of an offender who is convicted of first degree murder or second degree murder and who was under the age of sixteen at the time of the commission of the offence, the judge who presided at the trial of the offender or, if that judge is unable to do so, any judge of the same court, may, having regard to the age and character of the offender, the nature of the offence and the circumstances surrounding its commission, and to the recommendation, if any, made pursuant to section 745.3, by order, decide the period of imprisonment the offender is to serve that is between five years and seven years without eligibility for parole, as the judge deems fit in the circumstances.

1995, c. 22, s. 6, 23(b).

745.6 (1) Application for judicial review — Subject to subsection (2), a person may apply, in writing, to the appropriate Chief Justice in the province in which their conviction took place for a reduction in the number of years of imprisonment without eligibility for parole if the person

(a) has been convicted of murder or high treason;

(b) has been sentenced to imprisonment for life without eligibility for parole until more than fifteen years of their sentence has been served; and

(c) has served at least fifteen years of their sentence.

(2) Exception — multiple murderers — A person who has been convicted of more than one murder may not make an application under subsection (1), whether or not proceedings were commenced in respect of any of the murders before another murder was committed.

(3) Definition of "appropriate chief justice" — For the purposes of this section and sections 745.61 to 745.64, the **"appropriate Chief Justice"** is

(a) in relation to the Province of Ontario, the Chief Justice of the Ontario Court;

(b) in relation to the Province of Quebec, the Chief Justice of the Superior Court;

(c) in relation to the Provinces of Prince Edward Island and Newfoundland, the Chief Justice of the Supreme Court, Trial Division;

(d) in relation to the Provinces of New Brunswick, Manitoba, Saskatchewan and Alberta, the Chief Justice of the Court of Queen's Bench;

(e) in relation to the Provinces of Nova Scotia and British Columbia, the Chief Justice of the Supreme Court; and

(f) in relation to the Yukon Territory, the Northwest Territories and Nunavut, the Chief Justice of the Court of Appeal thereof.

1995, c. 22, s. 6; 1996, c. 34, s. 2(2); 1998, c. 15, s. 20.

745.61 (1) Judicial screening — On receipt of an application under subsection 745.6(1), the appropriate Chief Justice shall determine, or shall designate a judge of the superior court of criminal jurisdiction to determine, on the basis of the following written material, whether the applicant has shown, on a balance of probabilities, that there is a reasonable prospect that the application will succeed:

(a) the application;

(b) any report provided by the Correctional Service of Canada or other correctional authorities; and

(c) any other written evidence presented to the Chief Justice or judge by the applicant or the Attorney General.

(2) Criteria — In determining whether the applicant has shown that there is a reasonable prospect that the application will succeed, the Chief Justice or judge shall consider the criteria set out in paragraphs 746.63(1)(a) to (e), with such modifications as the circumstances require.

(3) Decision re new application — If the Chief Justice or judge determines that the applicant has not shown that there is a reasonable prospect that the application will succeed, the Chief Justice or judge may

(a) set a time, not earlier than two years after the date of the determination, at or after which another application may be made by the applicant under subsection 745.6(1); or

(b) decide that the applicant may not make another application under that subsection.

(4) Where no decision re new application — If the Chief Justice or judge determines that the applicant has not shown that there is a reasonable prospect that the application will succeed but does not set a time for another application or decide that such an application may not be made, the applicant may make another application no earlier than two years after the date of the determination.

(5) Designation of judge to empanel jury — If the Chief Justice or judge determines that the applicant has shown that there is a reasonable prospect that the application will succeed, the Chief Justice shall designate a judge of the superior court of criminal jurisdiction to empanel a jury to hear the application.

1996, c. 34, s. 2(2).

Editor's Note: Section 745.61 of the Criminal Code applies in respect of applications for judicial review made after January 9, 1997 in respect of crimes committed before or after that date, unless the applicant has, before that date, made an application under s. 745.6(1) of the Code as it read immediately before that date and the application had not yet been disposed of before that date: see 1996, c. 34, s. 7.

745.62 (1) Appeal — The applicant or the Attorney General may appeal to the Court of Appeal from a determination or a decision made under section 745.61 on any question of law or fact or mixed law and fact.

(2) Documents to be considered — The appeal shall be determined on the basis of the documents presented to the Chief Justice or judge who made the determination or decision, any reasons for the determination or decision and any other documents that the Court of Appeal requires.

(3) Sections to apply — Sections 673 to 696 apply, with such modifications as the circumstances require.

1996, c. 34, s. 2(2).

Editor's Note: Section 745.62 of the Criminal Code applies in respect of applications for judicial review made after January 9, 1997, in respect of crimes committed before or after that date, unless the applicant has, before that date, made an application under s. 745.61(1) of the Code as it read immediately before that date and the application had not yet been disposed of before that date: see 1996, c. 34, s. 7.

745.63 (1) Hearing of application — The jury empaneled under subsection 745.61(5) to hear the application shall consider the following criteria and determine whether the applicant's number of years of imprisonment without eligibility for parole ought to be reduced:

    (a) the character of the applicant;

    (b) the applicant's conduct while serving the sentence;

    (c) the nature of the offence for which the applicant was convicted;

    (d) any information provided by a victim at the time of the imposition of the sentence or at the time of the hearing under this section; and

    (e) any other matters that the judge considers relevant in the circumstances.

(1.1) Information provided by victim — Information provided by a victim referred to in paragraph (1)(d) may be provided either orally or in writing, at the discretion of the victim, or in any other manner that the judge considers appropriate.

(2) Definition of "victim" — In paragraph (1)(d), **"victim"** has the same meaning as in subsection 722(4).

(3) Reduction — The jury hearing an application under subsection (1) may determine that the applicant's number of years of imprisonment without eligibility for parole ought to be reduced. The determination to reduce the number of years must be by unanimous vote.

(4) No reduction — The applicant's number of years of imprisonment without eligibility for parole is not reduced if

(a) the jury hearing an application under subsection (1) determines that the number of years ought not to be reduced;

(b) the jury hearing an application under subsection (1) concludes that it cannot unanimously determine that the number of years ought to be reduced; or

(c) the presiding judge, after the jury has deliberated for a reasonable period, concludes that the jury is unable to unanimously determine that the number of years ought to be reduced.

(5) Where determination to reduce number of years — If the jury determines that the number of years of imprisonment without eligibility for parole ought to be reduced, the jury may, by a vote of not less than two thirds of the members of the jury,

(a) substitute a lesser number of years of imprisonment without eligibility for parole than that then applicable; or

(b) terminate the ineligibility for parole.

(6) Decision re new application — If the applicant's number of years of imprisonment without eligibility for parole is not reduced, the jury may

(a) set a time, not earlier than two years after the date of the determination or conclusion under subsection (4), at or after which another application may be made by the applicant under subsection 745.6(1); or

(b) decide that the applicant may not make another application under that subsection.

(7) Two-thirds decision — The decision of the jury under paragraph (6)(a) or (b) must be made by not less than two thirds of its members.

(8) If no decision re new application — If the jury does not set a date at or after which another application may be made or decide that such an application may not be made, the applicant may make another application no earlier than two years after the date of the determination or conclusion under subsection (4).

1996, c. 34, s. 2(2); 1999, c. 25, s. 22

Editor's Note: Section 745.63 of the Criminal Code, other than paragraph 745.63(1)(d), applies in respect of applications for judicial review made after January 9, 1997, in respect of crimes committed before or after that date, unless the applicant has, before that date, made an application under s. 745.6(1) of the Code as it read immediately before that date and the application had not yet been disposed of before that date. Paragraph 745.63(1)(d) applies in respect of hearings held after January 9, 1997, with respect to applications for judicial review in respect of crimes committed before or after that date: see 1996, c. 34, ss. 7, 8 (as amended by 1997, c. 18, s. 139.1).

745.64 (1) Rules — The appropriate Chief Justice in each province or territory may make such rules as are required for the purposes of sections 745.6 to 745.63.

(2) Territories — When the appropriate Chief Justice is designating a judge of the superior court of criminal jurisdiction, for the purpose of a judicial screening under subsection 745.61(1) or to empanel a jury to hear an application under subsection 745.61(5), in respect of a conviction that took place in the Yukon Territory, the Northwest Territories or Nunavut, the appropriate Chief Justice may designate the judge from the Court of Appeal of the Yukon Territory, the Northwest Territories or Nunavut, or the Supreme Court of the Yukon Territory or the Northwest Territories or the Nunavut Court of Justice, as the case may be.

1996, c. 34, s. 2(2); 1998, c. 15, s. 20 [Repealed 1999, c. 3, s. 12 (Sched., item 9).]; 1999, c. 3, s. 53.

746. Time spent in custody — In calculating the period of imprisonment served for the purposes of section 745, 745.1, 745.4 745.5 or 745.6, there shall be included any time spent in custody between,

(a) in the case of a sentence of imprisonment for life imposed after July 25, 1976, the day on which the person was arrested and taken into custody in respect of the offence for which that person was sentenced to imprisonment for life and the day the sentence was imposed; or

(b) in the case of a sentence of death that has been or is deemed to have been commuted to a sentence of imprisonment for life, the day on which the person was arrested and taken into custody in respect of the offence for which that person was sentenced to death and the day the sentence was commuted or deemed to have been commuted to a sentence of imprisonment for life.

1995, c. 22, s. 6, s. 24(b).

746.1 (1) Parole prohibited — Unless Parliament otherwise provides by an enactment making express reference to this section, a person who has been sentenced to imprisonment for life without eligibility for parole for a specified number of years pursuant to this Act shall not be considered for parole or released pursuant to a grant of parole under the *Corrections and Conditional Release Act* or any other Act of Parliament until the expiration or termination of the specified number of years of imprisonment.

(2) Absences with or without escort and day parole — Subject to subsection (3), in respect of a person sentenced to imprisonment for life without eligibility for parole for a specified number of years pursuant to this Act, until the expiration of all but three years of the specified number of years of imprisonment,

(a) no day parole may be granted under the *Corrections and Conditional Release Act*;

(b) no absence without escort may be authorized under that Act or the *Prisons and Reformatories Act*; and

(c) except with the approval of the National Parole Board, no absence with escort otherwise than for medical reasons or in order to attend judicial proceedings or a coroner's inquest may be authorized under either of those Acts.

(3) Young offenders — In the case of any person convicted of first degree murder or second degree murder who was under the age of eighteen at the time of the commission of the offence and who is sentenced to imprisonment for life without eligibility for parole for a specified number of years pursuant to this Act, until the expiration of all but one fifth of the period of imprisonment the person is to serve without eligibility for parole,

> (a) no day parole may be granted under the *Corrections and Conditional Release Act*;
>
> (b) no absence without escort may be authorized under that Act or the *Prisons and Reformatories Act*; and
>
> (c) except with the approval of the National Parole Board, no absence with escort otherwise than for medical reasons or in order to attend judicial proceedings or a coroner's inquest may be authorized under either of those Acts.

1995, c. 22, s. 6; 1995, c. 42, s. 87(b); 1997, c. 17, s. 2

Proposed Addition — 747 to 747.8

Hospital Orders

747. Definitions — In this section and sections 747.1 to 747.8,

"assessment report" means a written report made pursuant to an assessment order made under section 672.11 by a psychiatrist who is entitled under the laws of a province to practise psychiatry or, where a psychiatrist is not practicably available, by a medical practitioner;

"hospital order" means an order by a court under section 747.1 that an offender be detained in a treatment facility;

"medical practitioner" means a person who is entitled to practise medicine by the laws of a province;

"treatment facility" means any hospital or place for treatment of the mental disorder of an offender, or a place within a class of such places, designated by the Governor in Council, the Lieutenant Governor in Council of the province in which the offender is sentenced or a person to whom authority has been delegated in writing for that purpose by the Governor in Council or that Lieutenant Governor in Council.

1995, c. 22, s. 6 [Not in force at date of publication.]

747.1 (1) Court may make a hospital order — A court may order that an offender be detained in a treatment facility as the initial part of a sentence of imprisonment where it finds, at the time of sentencing, that the offender is suffering from a mental disorder in an acute phase and the court is satisfied, on the basis of an assessment report and any other evidence, that immediate treatment of the mental disorder is urgently required to prevent further significant deterioration of the mental or physical health of the offender, or to prevent the offender from causing serious bodily harm to any person.

(2) Limitation on hospital order — A hospital order shall be for a single period of treatment not exceeding sixty days, subject to any terms and conditions that the court considers appropriate.

(3) Form — A hospital order may be in Form 51.

(4) Warrant of committal — A court that makes a hospital order shall issue a warrant for committal of the offender, which may be in Form 8.

1995, c. 22, s. 6 [Not in force at date of publication.]

747.2 (1) Recommended treatment facility — In a hospital order, the court shall specify that the offender be detained in a particular treatment facility recommended by the central administration of any penitentiary, prison or other institution to which the offender has been sentenced to imprisonment, unless the court is satisfied, on the evidence of a medical practitioner, that serious harm to the mental or physical health of the offender would result from travelling to that treatment facility or from that delay occasioned in travelling there.

(2) Court chooses treatment facility — Where the court does not follow a recommendation referred to in subsection (1), it shall order that the offender be detained in a treatment facility that is reasonably accessible to the place where the accused is detained when the hospital order is made or to the place where the court is located.

1995, c. 22, s. 6 [Not in force at date of publication.]

747.3 Condition — No hospital order may be made unless the offender and the person in charge of the treatment facility where the offender is to be detained consent to the order and its terms and conditions, but nothing in this section shall be construed as making unnecessary the obtaining of any authorization or consent to treatment from any other person that is or may be required otherwise than under this Act.

1995, c. 22, s. 6 [Not in force at date of publication.]

747.4 Exception — No hospital order may be made in respect of an offender

(a) who is convicted of or is serving a sentence imposed in respect of a conviction for an offence for which a minimum punishment of imprisonment for life is prescribed by law;

(b) who has been found to be a dangerous offender pursuant to section 753;

(c) where the term of imprisonment to be served by the offender does not exceed sixty days;

(d) where the term of imprisonment is imposed on the offender in default of payment of a fine or of a victim fine surcharge imposed under subsection 737(1); or

Proposed Amendment — Conditional Amendment-747.4(d)

On the later of the coming into force of 1999, c. 25 [In force December 1, 1999.] and the coming into force of paragraph 747.4(d) of the *Criminal Code*, as enacted by 1995, c. 22, s. 6 [Not in force at date of publication.], paragraph (d) is replaced by the following:

(d) where the term of imprisonment is imposed on the offender in default of payment of a fine or of a victim surcharge imposed under section 737; or

1999, c. 25, s. 29(1)

(e) where the sentence of imprisonment imposed on the offender is ordered under paragraph 732(1)(a) to be served intermittently.

1995, c. 22, s. 6 [Not in force at date of publication.]

747.5 (1) Offender to serve remainder of sentence — An offender shall be sent or returned to a prison to serve the portion of the offender's sentence that remains unexpired where

(a) the hospital order expires before the expiration of the sentence; or

(b) the consent to the detention of the offender in the treatment facility pursuant to the hospital order is withdrawn either by the offender or by the person in charge of the treatment facility.

(2) Transfer from one treatment facility to another — Before the expiration of a hospital order in respect of an offender, the offender may be transferred from the treatment facility specified in the hospital order to another treatment facility where treatment of the offender's mental disorder is available, if the court authorizes the transfer in writing and the person in charge of the treatment facility consents.

1995, c. 22, s. 6 [Not in force at date of publication.]

747.6 Detention to count as service of term — Each day that an offender is detained under a hospital order shall be treated as a day of service of the term of imprisonment of the offender, and the offender shall be deemed, for all purposes, to be lawfully confined in a prison during that detention.

1995, c. 22, s. 6 [Not in force at date of publication.]

747.7 Application of section 12 of *Corrections and Conditional Release Act* — Notwithstanding section 12 of the *Corrections and Conditional Release Act*, an offender in respect of whom a hospital order is made and who is sentenced or committed to a penitentiary may, during the period for which that order is in force, be received in a penitentiary before the expiration of the time limited by law for an appeal and shall be detained in the treatment facility specified in the order during that period.

1995, c. 22, s. 6 [Not in force at date of publication.]

747.8 Copy of warrant and order given to prison and hospital — Where a court makes a hospital order in respect of an offender, the court shall cause a copy of the order and of the warrant of committal issued pursuant to subsection 747.1 to be sent to the central administration of the penitentiary, prison or other institution where the term of imprisonment imposed on the offender is to be served and to the treatment facility where the offender is to be detained for treatment.

1995, c. 22, s. 6 [Not in force at date of publication.]

Pardons and Remissions

748. (1) To whom pardon may be granted — Her Majesty may extend the royal mercy to a person who is sentenced to imprisonment under the authority of an Act of Parliament, even if the person is imprisoned for failure to pay money to another person.

(2) Free or conditional pardon — The Governor in Council may grant a free pardon or a conditional pardon to any person who has been convicted of an offence.

(3) Effect of free pardon — Where the Governor in Council grants a free pardon to a person, that person shall be deemed thereafter never to have committed the offence in respect of which the pardon is granted.

(4) Punishment for subsequent offence not affected — No free pardon or conditional pardon prevents or mitigates the punishment to which the person might otherwise be lawfully sentenced on a subsequent conviction for an offence other than that for which the pardon was granted.

1995, c. 22, s. 6.

748.1 (1) Remission by Governor in Council — The Governor in Council may order the remission, in whole or in part, of a fine or forfeiture imposed under an Act of Parliament, whoever the person may be to whom it is payable or however it may be recoverable.

(2) Terms of remission — An order for remission under subsection (1) may include the remission of costs incurred in the proceedings, but no costs to which a private prosecutor is entitled shall be remitted.

1995, c. 22, s. 6.

749. Royal prerogative — Nothing in this Act in any manner limits or affects Her Majesty's royal prerogative of mercy.

Disabilities

750. (1) Public office vacated for conviction — Where a person is convicted of an indictable offence for which the person is sentenced to imprisonment for two years or more and holds, at the time that person is convicted, an office under the Crown or other public employment, the office or employment forthwith becomes vacant.

(2) When disability ceases — A person to whom subsection (1) applies is, until undergoing the punishment imposed on the person or the punishment substituted therefor by competent authority or receives a free pardon from Her Majesty, incapable of holding any office under the Crown or other public employment, or of being elected or sitting or voting as a member of Parliament or of a legislature or of exercising any right of suffrage.

(3) Disability to contract — No person who is convicted of an offence under section 121, 124 or 418 has, after that conviction, capacity to contract with Her Majesty or to receive any benefit under a contract between Her Majesty and any other person or to hold office under Her Majesty.

(4) Application for restoration of privileges — A person to whom subsection (3) applies may, at any time before a pardon is granted to the person under section 4.1 of the *Criminal Records Act*, apply to the Governor in Council for the restoration of one or more of the capacities lost by the person by virtue of that subsection.

Proposed Amendment — 750(4)

(4) Application for restoration of privileges — A person to whom subsection (3) applies may, at any time before a pardon is granted or issued to the person under section 4.1 of the *Criminal Records Act*, apply to the Governor in Council for the restoration of one or more of the capacities lost by the person by virtue of that subsection.

2000, c. 1, s. 9 [Not in force at date of publication.]

(5) Order of restoration — Where an application is made under subsection (4), the Governor in council may order that the capacities lost by the applicant by virtue of subsection (3) be restored to that applicant in whole or in part and subject to such conditions as the Governor in Council considers desirable in the public interest.

(6) Removal of disability — Where a conviction is set aside by competent authority, any disability imposed by this section is removed.

1995, c. 22, s. 6.

Miscellaneous Provisions

751. Costs to successful party in case of libel — The person in whose favour judgment is given in proceedings by indictment for defamatory libel is entitled to recover from the opposite party costs in a reasonable amount to be fixed by order of the court.

1995, c. 22, s. 6.

751.1 How recovered — Where costs that are fixed under section 751 are not paid forthwith, the party in whose favour judgment is given may enter judgment for the amount of the costs by filing the order in any civil court of the province in which the trial was held that has jurisdiction to enter a judgment for that amount, and that judgment is enforceable against the opposite party in the same manner as if it were a judgment rendered against that opposite party in that court in civil proceedings.

1995, c. 22, s. 6.

PART XXIV — DANGEROUS OFFENDERS AND LONG-TERM OFFENDERS

Interpretation

752. Definitions — In this Part,

"court" means the court by which an offender in relation to whom an application under this Part is made was convicted, or a superior court of criminal jurisdiction;

"serious personal injury offence" means

(a) an indictable offence, other than high treason, treason, first degree murder or second degree murder, involving

(i) the use or attempted use of violence against another person, or

(ii) conduct endangering or likely to endanger the life or safety of another person or inflicting or likely to inflict severe psychological damage upon another person,

and for which the offender may be sentenced to imprisonment for ten years or more, or

(b) an offence or attempt to commit an offence mentioned in section 271 (sexual assault), 272 (sexual assault with a weapon, threats to a third party or causing bodily harm) or 273 (aggravated sexual assault).

Dangerous Offenders and Long-Term Offenders

752.1 (1) Application for remand for assessment — Where an offender is convicted of a serious personal injury offence or an offence referred to in paragraph 753.1(2)(a) and, before sentence is imposed on the offender, on application by the prosecution, the court is of the opinion that there are reasonable grounds to believe that the offender might be found to be a dangerous offender under section 753 or a long-term offender under section 753.1, the court may, by order in writing remand the offender, for a period not exceeding sixty days, to the custody of the person that the court directs and who can perform an assessment, or can have an assessment performed by experts. The assessment is to be used as evidence in an application under section 753 or 753.1.

(2) Report — The person to whom the offender is remanded shall file a report of the assessment with the court not later than fifteen days after the end of the assessment period and make copies of it available to the prosecutor and counsel for the offender.

1997, c. 17, s. 4

753. (1) Application for finding that an offender is a dangerous offender — The court may, on application made under this Part following the filing

523

of an assessment report under subsection 752.1(2), find the offender to be a dangerous offender if it is satisfied

(a) that the offence for which the offender has been convicted is a serious personal injury offence described in paragraph (a) of the definition of that expression in section 752 and the offender constitutes a threat to the life, safety or physical or mental well-being of other persons on the basis of evidence establishing

(i) a pattern of repetitive behaviour by the offender, of which the offence for which he or she has been convicted forms a part, showing a failure to restrain his or her behaviour and a likelihood of causing death or injury to other persons, or inflicting severe psychological damage on other persons, through failure in the future to restrain his or her behaviour,

(ii) a pattern of persistent aggressive behaviour by the offender, of which the offence for which he or she has been convicted forms a part, showing a substantial degree of indifference on the part of the offender respecting the reasonably foreseeable consequences to other persons of his or her behaviour, or

(iii) any behaviour by the offender, associated with the offence for which he or she has been convicted, that is of such a brutal nature as to compel the conclusion that the offender's behaviour in the future is unlikely to be inhibited by normal standards of behavioural restraint; or

(b) that the offence for which the offender has been convicted is a serious personal injury offence described in paragraph (b) of the definition of that expression in section 752 and the offender, by his or her conduct in any sexual matter including that involved in the commission of the offence for which he or she has been convicted, has shown a failure to control his or her sexual impulses and a likelihood of causing injury, pain or other evil to other persons through failure in the future to control his or her sexual impulses.

(2) Time for making application — An application under subsection (1) must be made before sentence is imposed on the offender unless

(a) before the imposition of sentence, the prosecution gives notice to the offender of a possible intention to make an application under section 752.1 and an application under subsection (1) not later than six months after that imposition; and

(b) at the time of the application under subsection (1) that is not later than six months after imposition of sentence, it is shown that relevant evidence that was not reasonably available to the prosecution at the time of the imposition of sentence became available in the interim.

(3) Application for remand for assessment after imposition of sentence — Notwithstanding subsection 752.1(1), an application under that subsection may be made after the imposition of sentence or after an offender begins to serve the sentence in a case to which paragraphs (2)(a) and (b) apply.

(4) If offender found to be dangerous offender — If the court finds an offender to be a dangerous offender, it shall impose a sentence of detention in a penitentiary for an indeterminate period.

(4.1) If application made after sentencing — If the application was made after the offender begins to serve the sentence in a case to which paragraphs (2)(*a*) and (*b*) apply, the sentence of detention in a penitentiary for an indeterminate period referred to in subsection (4) replaces the sentence that was imposed for the offence for which the offender was convicted.

(5) If offender not found to be dangerous offender — If the court does not find an offender to be a dangerous offender,

(a) the court may treat the application as an application to find the offender to be a long-term offender, section 753.1 applies to the application and the court may either find that the offender is a long-term offender or hold another hearing for that purpose; or

(b) the court may impose sentence for the offence for which the offender has been convicted.

(6) Victim evidence — Any evidence given during the hearing of an application made under subsection (1) by victim of an offence for which the offender was convicted is deemed also to have been given during any hearing under paragraph (5)(*a*) held with respect to the offender.

1997, c. 17, s. 4

753.1 (1) Application for finding that an offender is a long-term offender — The court may, on application made under this Part following the filing of an assessment report under subsection 752.1(2), find an offender to be a long-term offender if it is satisfied that

(a) it would be appropriate to impose a sentence of imprisonment of two years or more for the offence for which the offender has been convicted;

(b) there is a substantial risk that the offender will reoffend; and

(c) there is a reasonable possibility of eventual control of the risk in the community.

(2) Substantial risk — The court shall be satisfied that there is a substantial risk that the offender will reoffend if

(a) the offender has been convicted of an offence under section 151 (sexual interference), 152 (invitation to sexual touching) or 153 (sexual exploitation), subsection 173(2) (exposure) or section 271 (sexual assault), 272 (sexual assault with a weapon) or 273 (aggravated sexual assault), or has engaged in serious conduct of a sexual nature in the commission of another offence of which the offender has been convicted; and

(b) the offender

(i) has shown a pattern of repetitive behaviour, of which the offence for which he or she has been convicted forms a part, that shows a likelihood of the offender's causing death or injury to other persons or inflicting severe psychological damage on other persons, or

(ii) by conduct in any sexual matter including that involved in the commission of the offence for which the offender has been convicted, has shown a likelihood of causing injury, pain or other evil to other persons in the future through similar offence.

(3) If offender found to be long-term offender — Subject to subsection (3.1), (4) and (5), if the court finds an offender to be a long-term offender, it shall

(a) impose a sentence for the offence for which the offender has been convicted, which sentence must be a minimum punishment of imprisonment for a term of two years; and

(b) order the offender to be supervised in the community, for a period not exceeding ten years, in accordance with section 753.2 and the *Corrections and Conditional Release Act*.

(3.1) Exception – if application made after sentencing — The court may not impose a sentence under paragraph (3)(*a*) and the sentence that was imposed for the offence for which the offender was convicted stands despite the offender's being found to be a long-term offender, if the application was one that

(a) was made after the offender begins to serve the sentence in a case to which paragraphs 753(2)(*a*) and (*b*) apply; and

(b) was treated as an application under this section further to the court deciding to do so under paragraph 753(5)(*a*).

(4) Exception-life sentence — The court shall not make an order under paragraph (3)(*b*) if the offender has been sentenced to life imprisonment.

(5) Exception to length of supervision where new declaration — If the offender commits another offence while required to be supervised by an order made under paragraph (3)(*b*), and is thereby found to be a long-term offender, the periods of supervision to which the offender is subject at any particular time must not total more than ten years.

(6) If offender not found to be long-term offender — If the court does not find an offender to be a long-term offender, the court shall impose sentence for the offence for which the offender has been convicted.

1997, c. 17, s. 4

753.2 (1) Long-term supervision — Subject to subsection (2), an offender who is required to be supervised by an order made under paragraph 753.1(3)(*b*) shall be supervised in accordance with the *Corrections and Conditional Release Act* when the offender has finished serving

(a) the sentence for the offence for which the offender has been convicted; and

(b) all other sentences for offences for which the offender is convicted and for which sentence of a term of imprisonment is imposed on the offender, either before or after the conviction for the offence referred to in paragraph (*a*).

(2) Non-carceral sentences — A sentence imposed on an offender referred to in subsection (1), other than a sentence that requires imprisonment of the offender, is to be served concurrently with the long-term supervision ordered under paragraph 753.1(3)(*b*).

(3) Application for reduction in period of long- term supervision — An offender who is required to be supervised, a member of the National Parole Board, or, on approval of that Board, the parole supervisor, as that expression is defined in subsection 134.2(2) of the *Corrections and Conditional Release Act*, of the offender, may apply to a superior court of criminal jurisdiction for an order reducing the period of long-term supervision or terminating it on the ground that the offender no longer presents a substantial risk of reoffending and thereby being a danger to the community. The onus of proving that ground is on the applicant.

(4) Notice to Attorney General — The applicant must give notice of an application under subsection (3) to the Attorney General at the time the application is made.

1997, c. 17, s. 4

753.3 (1) Breach of order of long-term supervision — An offender who is required to be supervised by an order made under paragraph 753.1(3)(*b*) and who, without reasonable excuse, fails or refuses to comply with that order is guilty of an indictable offence and liable to imprisonment for a term not exceeding ten years.

(2) Where accused may be tried and punished — An accused who is charged with an offence under subsection (1) may be tried and punished by any court having jurisdiction to try that offence in the place where the offence is alleged to have been committed or in the place where the accused is found, is arrested or is in custody, but if the place where the accused is found, is arrested or is in custody is outside the province in which the offence is alleged to have been committed, no proceedings in respect of that offence shall be instituted in that place without the consent of the Attorney General of that province.

1997, c. 17, s. 4

753.4 (1) Where new offence — Where an offender who is required to be supervised by an order made under paragraph 753.1(3)(*b*) commits one or more offences under this or any other Act and a court imposes a sentence of imprisonment for the offence or offence, the long-term supervision is interrupted until the offender has finished serving all the sentences, unless the court orders its termination.

(2) Reduction in term of long-term supervision — A court that imposes a sentence of imprisonment under subsection (1) may order a reduction in the length of the period of the offender's long-term supervision.

1997, c. 17, s. 4

754. (1) Hearing of application — Where an application under this Part has been made, the court shall hear and determine the application except that no such application shall be heard unless

(a) the Attorney General of the province in which the offender was tried has, either before or after the making of the application, consented to the application;

(b) at least seven days notice has been given to the offender by the prosecutor, following the making of the application, outlining the basis on which it is intended to found the application; and

(c) a copy of the notice has been filed with the clerk of the court or the provincial court judge, as the case may be.

(2) By court alone — An application under this Part shall be heard and determined by the court without a jury.

(3) When proof unnecessary — For the purposes of an application under this Part, where an offender admits any allegations contained in the notice referred to in paragraph (1)(*b*), no proof of those allegations is required.

(4) Proof of consent — The production of a document purporting to contain any nomination or consent that may be made or given by the Attorney General under this Part and purporting to be signed by the Attorney General is, in the absence of any evidence to the contrary, proof of that nomination or consent without proof of the signature or the official character of the person appearing to have signed the document.

R.S. 1985, c. 27 (1st Supp.), s. 203.

755. [Repealed 1997, c. 17, s. 5.]

756. [Repealed 1997, c. 17, s. 5.]

757. Evidence of character — Without prejudice to the right of the offender to tender evidence as to his or her character and repute, evidence of character and repute may, if the court thinks fit, be admitted on the question of whether the offender is or is not a dangerous offender or a long-term offender.

1997, c. 17, s. 5

758. (1) Presence of accused at hearing of application — The offender shall be present at the hearing of the application under this Part and if at the time the application is to be heard

(a) he is confined in a prison, the court may order, in writing, the person having the custody of the accused to bring him before the court; or

(b) he is not confined in a prison, the court shall issue a summons or a warrant to compel the accused to attend before the court and the provisions of Part XVI relating to summons and warrant are applicable with such modifications as the circumstances require.

(2) Exception — Notwithstanding subsection (1), the court may

(a) cause the offender to be removed and to be kept out of court, where he misconducts himself by interrupting the proceedings so that to continue the proceedings in his presence would not be feasible; or

(b) permit the offender to be out of court during the whole or any part of the hearing on such conditions as the court considers proper.

759. (1) Appeal – dangerous offender — An offender who is found to be a dangerous offender under this Part may appeal to the court of appeal against that finding on any ground of law or fact or mixed law and fact.

(1.1) Appeal – long-term offender — An offender who is found to be a long-term offender under this Part may appeal to the court of appeal against that finding or against the length of the period of long-term supervision ordered, on any ground of law or fact or mixed law and fact.

(2) Appeal by Attorney General — The Attorney General may appeal to the court of appeal against the dismissal of an application for an order under this Part, or against the length of the period of long-term supervision of a long-term offender, on any ground of law.

(3) Disposition of appeal – dangerous offender — On an appeal against a finding that an offender is a dangerous offender, the court of appeal may

(a) allow the appeal and

(i) find that the offender is not a dangerous offender, find that the offender is a long-term offender, impose a minimum sentence of imprisonment for two years, for the offence for which the offender has been convicted, and order the offender to be supervised in the community, for a period that does not, subject to subsection 753.1(5), exceed ten years, in accordance with section 753.2 and the *Corrections and Conditional Release Act*,

(ii) find that the offender is not a dangerous offender and impose sentence for the offence for which the offender has been convicted, or

(iii) order a new hearing; or

(b) dismiss the appeal.

(3.1) Disposition of appeal – long-term offender — On an appeal against a finding that an offender is a long-term offender, the court of appeal may

(a) allow the appeal and

(i) find that the offender is not a long-term offender and quash the order for long-term supervision, or

(ii) order a new hearing; or

(b) dismiss the appeal,

(3.2) Disposition of appeal – long-term offender — On an appeal by a long-term offender against the length of a period of long-term supervision of the long-term offender, the court of appeal may

(a) allow the appeal and change the length of the period; or

(b) dismiss the appeal.

(4) Disposition of appeal by Attorney General — On an appeal against the dismissal of an application for an order that an offender is a dangerous offender under this Part, the court of appeal may

(a) allow the appeal and

(i) find that the offender is a dangerous offender,

(ii) find that the offender is not a dangerous offender, find that the offender is a long-term offender, impose a minimum sentence of imprisonment for two years, for the offence for which the offender has been convicted, and order the offender to be supervised in the community, for a period that does not, subject to subsection 753.1(5), exceed ten years, in accordance with section 753.2 and the *Corrections and Conditional Release Act*, or

(iii) order a new hearing; or

(b) dismiss the appeal.

(4.1) Disposition of appeal by Attorney General — On an appeal by the Attorney General against the length of a period of long-term supervision of a long-term offender, the court of appeal may

(a) allow the appeal and change the length of the period; or

(b) dismiss the appeal.

(4.2) Disposition of appeal by Attorney General — On an appeal against the dismissal of an application for a finding that an offender is a long-term offender under this Part, the court of appeal may

(a) allow the appeal and

(i) find that the offender is a long-term offender, impose a minimum sentence of imprisonment for two years, for the offence for which the offender has been convicted, and order the offender to be supervised in the community, for a period that does not, subject to subsection 753.1(5), exceed ten years, in accordance with section 753.2 and the *Corrections and Conditional Release Act*, or

(ii) order a new hearing; or

(b) dismiss the appeal.

(5) Effect of judgment — A judgment of the court of appeal finding that an offender is or is not a dangerous offender or a long-term offender, or changing the length of the period of long-term supervision ordered, has the same force and effect as if it were a finding by or judgment of the trial court.

(6) Commencement of sentence — Notwithstanding subsection 719(1), a sentence imposed on an offender by the court of appeal pursuant to this section shall be deemed to have commenced when the offender was sentenced by the court by which he was convicted.

(7) Part XXI applies re appeals — The provisions of Part XXI with respect to procedure on appeals apply, with such modifications as the circumstances require, to appeals under this section.

1995, c. 22, s. 10; 1997, c. 17, s. 6

760. Disclosure to Correctional Service of Canada — Where a court finds an offender to be a dangerous offender or a long-term offender, the court shall order that a copy of all reports and testimony given by psychiatrists, psychologists, criminologists and other experts and any observations of the court with respect to the reasons for the finding, together with a transcript of the trial of the offender, be forwarded to the Correctional Service of Canada for information.

1997, c. 17, s. 7

761. (1) Review for parole — Subject to subsection (2), where a person is in custody under a sentence of detention in a penitentiary for an indeterminate period, the National Parole Board shall, as soon as possible after the expiration of seven years from the day on which that person was taken into custody and not later than every two years after the previous review, review the condition, history and circumstances of that person for the purposes of determining whether he or she should be granted parole under Part II of the *Corrections and Conditional Release Act* and, if so, on what conditions.

(2) Idem — Where a person is in custody under a sentence of detention in a penitentiary for an indeterminate period that was imposed before October 15, 1977, the National Parole Board shall, at least once in every year, review the condition, history and circumstances of that person for the purpose of determining whether he should be granted parole under Part II of the *Corrections and Conditional Release Act* and, if so, on what conditions.

1992, c. 20, s. 215(1)(a); 1997, c. 17, s. 8.

PART XXV — EFFECT AND ENFORCEMENT OF RECOGNIZANCES

762. (1) Applications for forfeiture of recognizances — Applications for the forfeiture of recognizances shall be made to the courts, designated in column II of the schedule, of the respective provinces designated in column I of the schedule.

(2) Definitions — In this Part

"clerk of the court" means the officer designated in column III of the schedule in respect of the court designated in column II of the schedule;

"schedule" means the schedule to this Part.

763. Recognizance binding — Where a person is bound by recognizance to appear before a court, justice or provincial court judge for any purpose and the session or sittings of that court or the proceedings are adjourned or an order is made changing the place of trial, that person and his sureties continue to be bound by the recognizance in like manner as if it had been entered into with relation to the resumed proceedings or the trial at the time and place at which the proceedings are ordered to be resumed or the trial is ordered to be held.

R.S. 1985, c. 27 (1st Supp.), s. 203.

764. (1) Responsibility of sureties — Where an accused is bound by recognizance to appear for trial, his arraignment or conviction does not discharge the recognizance, but it continues to bind him and his sureties, if any, for his appearance until he is discharged or sentenced, as the case may be.

(2) Committal or new sureties — Notwithstanding subsection (1), the court, justice or provincial court judge may commit an accused to prison or may require him to furnish new or additional sureties for his appearance until he is discharged or sentenced, as the case may be.

(3) Effect of committal — The sureties of the accused who is bound by recognizance to appear for trial are discharged if he is committed to prison pursuant to subsection (2).

(4) Endorsement on recognizance — The provisions of section 763 and subsections (1) to (3) of this section shall be endorsed on any recognizance entered into pursuant to this Act.

R.S. 1985, c. 27 (1st Supp.), s. 203.

765. Effect of subsequent arrest — Where an accused is bound by recognizance to appear for trial, his arrest on another charge does not vacate the recognizance, but it continues to bind him and his sureties, if any, for his appearance until he is discharged or sentenced, as the case may be, in respect of the offence to which the recognizance relates.

766. (1) Render of accused by sureties — A surety for a person who is bound by recognizance to appear may, by an application in writing to a court, justice or provincial court judge, apply to be relieved of his obligation under the recognizance, and the court, justice or provincial court judge shall thereupon issue an order in writing for committal of that person to the prison nearest to the place where he was, under the recognizance, bound to appear.

(2) Arrest — An order under subsection (1) shall be given to the surety and upon receipt thereof he or any peace officer may arrest the person named in the order and deliver that person with the order to the keeper of the prison named herein, and the keeper shall receive and imprison that person until he is discharged according to law.

(3) Certificate and entry of render — Where a court, justice or provincial court judge issues an order under subsection (1) and receives from the sheriff a certificate that the person named in the order has been committed to prison pursuant to subsection (2), the court, justice or provincial court judge shall order an entry of the committal to be endorsed on the recognizance.

(4) Discharge of sureties — An endorsement under subsection (3) vacates the recognizance and discharges the sureties.

R.S. 1985, c. 27 (1st Supp.), s. 203.

767. Render of accused in court by sureties — A surety for a person who is bound by recognizance to appear may bring that person into the court at which he is required to appear at any time during the sittings thereof and before his trial and the surety may discharge his obligation under the recognizance by giving that person into the custody of the court, and the court shall thereupon commit that person to prison until he is discharged according to law.

767.1 (1) Substitution of surety — Notwithstanding subsection 766(1) and section 767, where a surety for a person who is bound by a recognizance has rendered the person into the custody of a court pursuant to section 767 or applies to be relieved of his obligation under the recognizance pursuant to subsection 766(1), the court, justice or provincial court judge, as the case may be, may, instead of committing or issuing an order for the committal of the person to prison, substitute any other suitable person for the surety under the recognizance.

(2) Signing of recognizance by new sureties — Where a person substituted for a surety under a recognizance pursuant to subsection (1) signs the recognizance, the original surety is discharged, but the recognizance and the order for judicial interim release pursuant to which the recognizance was entered into are not otherwise affected.

R.S. 1985, c. 27 (1st Supp.), s. 167.

768. Rights of surety preserved — Nothing in this Part limits or restricts any right that a surety has of taking and giving into custody any person for whom, under a recognizance, he is a surety.

769. Application of judicial interim release provisions — Where a surety for a person has rendered him into custody and that person has been committed to prison, the provisions of Parts XVI, XXI and XXVII relating to judicial interim release apply, with such modifications as the circumstances require, in respect of him and he shall forthwith be taken before a justice or judge as an accused charged with an offence or as an appellant, as the case may be, for the purposes of those provisions.

770. (1) Default to be endorsed — Where, in proceedings to which this Act applies, a person who is bound by recognizance does not comply with a condition of the recognizance, a court, justice or provincial court judge having knowledge of the facts shall endorse or cause to be endorsed on the recognizance a certificate in Form 33 setting out

(a) the nature of the default,

(b) the reason for the default, if it is known,

(c) whether the ends of justice have been defeated or delayed by reason of the default, and

(d) the names and addresses of the principal and sureties.

(2) Transmission to clerk of court — A recognizance that has been endorsed pursuant to subsection (1) shall be sent to the clerk of the court and shall be kept by him with the records of the court.

(3) Certificate is evidence — A certificate that has been endorsed on a recognizance pursuant to subsection (1) is evidence of the default to which it relates.

(4) Transmission of deposit — Where, in proceedings to which this section applies, the principal or surety has deposited money as security for the performance of a condition of a recognizance, that money shall be sent to the clerk of the court with the defaulted recognizance, to be dealt with in accordance with this Part.

R.S. 1985, c. 27 (1st Supp.), s. 203; 1997, c. 18, s. 108.

771. (1) Proceedings in case of default — Where a recognizance has been endorsed with a certificate pursuant to section 770 and has been received by the clerk of the court pursuant to that section,

(a) a judge of the court shall, on the request of the clerk of the court or the Attorney General or counsel acting on his behalf, fix a time and place for the hearing of an application for the forfeiture of the recognizance; and

(b) the clerk of the court shall, not less than ten days before the time fixed under paragraph (*a*) for the hearing, send by registered mail, or have served in the manner directed by the court or prescribed by the rules of court, to each principal and surety named in the recognizance, directed to the principal or surety at the address set out in the certificate, a notice requiring the person to appear at the time and place fixed by the judge to show cause why the recognizance should not be forfeited.

(2) Order of judge — Where subsection (1) has been complied with, the judge may, after giving the parties an opportunity to be heard, in his discretion grant or refuse the application and make any order with respect to the forfeiture of the recognizance that he considers proper.

(3) Judgment debtors of the crown — Where, pursuant to subsection (2), a judge orders forfeiture of a recognizance, the principal and his sureties become judgment debtors of the Crown, each in the amount that the judge orders him to pay.

(3.1) Order may be filed — An order made under subsection (2) may be filed with the clerk of the superior court and if an order is filed, the clerk shall issue a writ of *fieri facias* in Form 34 and deliver it to the sheriff of each of the territorial divisions in which the principal or any surety resides, carries on business or has property.

(4) Transfer of deposit — Where a deposit has been made by a person against whom an order for forfeiture of a recognizance has been made, no writ of *fieri facias* shall issue, but the amount of the deposit shall be transferred by the person who has custody of it to the person who is entitled by law to receive it.

R.S. 1985, c. 27 (1st Supp.), s. 168; 1994, c. 44, s. 78; 1999, c. 5, s. 43.

772. (1) Levy under writ — Where a writ of *fieri facias* is issued pursuant to section 771, the sheriff to whom it is delivered shall execute the writ and deal with the proceeds thereof in the same manner in which he is authorized to execute and deal with the proceeds of writs of *fieri facias* issued out of superior courts in the province in civil proceedings.

(2) Costs — Where this section applies, the Crown is entitled to the costs of execution and of proceedings incidental thereto that are fixed, in the Province of Quebec, by any tariff applicable in the Superior Court in civil proceedings, and in any other province, by any tariff applicable in the superior court of the province in civil proceedings, as the judge may direct.

773. (1) Committal when writ not satisfied — Where a writ of *fieri facias* has been issued under this Part and it appears from a certificate in a return made by the sheriff that sufficient goods and chattels, lands and tenements cannot be found to satisfy the writ, or that the proceeds of the execution of the writ are not sufficient to satisfy it, a judge of the court may, upon the application of the Attorney General or counsel acting on his behalf, fix a time and place for the sureties to show cause why a warrant of committal should not be issued in respect of them.

(2) Notice — Seven clear days notice of the time and place fixed for the hearing pursuant to subsection (1) shall be given to the sureties.

(3) Hearing — The judge shall, at the hearing held pursuant to subsection (1), inquire into the circumstances of the case and may in his discretion

(a) order the discharge of the amount for which the surety is liable; or

(b) make any order with respect to the surety and to his imprisonment that he considers proper in the circumstances and issue a warrant of committal in Form 27.

(4) Warrant to committal — A warrant of committal issued pursuant to this section authorizes the sheriff to take into custody the person in respect of whom the warrant was issued and to confine him in a prison in the territorial division in which the writ was issued or in the prison nearest to the court, until satisfaction is made or until the period of imprisonment fixed by the judge has expired.

(5) Definition of "Attorney General" — In this section and in section 771, **"Attorney General"** means, where subsection 734.4(2) applies, the Attorney General of Canada.

1995, c.22, s. 10.

Schedule Part XXV
(Section 762)

Column I.	Column II.	Column III.
Ontario	A judge of the Court of Appeal in respect of a recognizance for the appearance of a person before the Court.	The Registrar of the Court of Appeal.

	The Superior Court of Justice in respect of all other recognizances.	A Registrar of the Superior Court of Justice.
Quebec	The Court of Quebec, Criminal and Penal Division.	The Clerk of the Court.
Nova Scotia	The Supreme Court.	A Prothonotary of the Supreme Court.
New Brunswick	The Court of Queen's Bench.	The Registrar of the Court of Queen's Bench.
British Columbia	The Supreme Court in respect of a recognizance for the appearance of a person before that court or the Court of Appeal.	The District Registrar of the Supreme Court.
Prince Edward Island	The Supreme Court, Trial Division.	The Prothonotary.
Manitoba	The Court of Queen's Bench.	The Registrar or a Deputy Registrar of the Court of Queen's Bench.
Saskatchewan	The Court of Queen's Bench.	The Local Registrar of the of Queen's Bench.
Alberta	The Court of Queen's Bench.	The Clerk of the Court of Queen's Bench.
Newfoundland	The Supreme Court.	The Registrar of the Supreme Court.
Yukon Territory	The Supreme Court.	The Clerk of the Supreme Court.
Northwest Territories	The Supreme Court.	The Clerk of the Supreme Court.
Nunavut	The Nunavut Court of Justice	The Clerk of the Nunavut Court of Justice

R.S. 1985, c. 11 (1st Supp.), s. 2; c. 27 (2d Supp.), (Sched., item 6); 1992, c. 1, s. 58(1), (Sched. I, item 15); 1992, c. 51, ss. 40–42; 1993, c. 28, s. 78 (Sched. III, item 35) [Amended 1998, c. 15, s. 20; Repealed 1999, c. 3, (Sched., item 9).]; 1998, c. 30, s. 14(d); 1999, c. 3. s. 54; 1999, c. 5, s. 44

PART XXVI — EXTRAORDINARY REMEDIES

774. Application of Part — This Part applies to proceedings in criminal matters by way of *certiorari, habeas corpus, mandamus, procedendo* and prohibition.

R.S. 1985, c. 27 (1st Supp.), s. 169.

775. Detention on inquiry to determine legality of imprisonment — Where proceedings to which this Part applies have been instituted before a judge or court having jurisdiction, by or in respect of a person who is in custody by reason that he is charged with or has been convicted of an offence, to have the legality of his imprisonment determined, the judge or court may, without determining the question, make an order for the further detention of that person and direct the judge, justice or provincial court judge under whose warrant he is in custody, or any other judge, justice or provincial court judge to take any proceedings, hear such evidence or do any other thing that, in the opinion of the judge or court, will best further the ends of justice.

R.S. 1985, c. 27 (1st Supp.), s. 203.

776. Where conviction of order not reviewable — No conviction or order shall be removed by *certiorari*

(a) where an appeal was taken, whether or not the appeal has been carried to a conclusion; or

(b) where the defendant appeared and pleaded and the merits were tried, and an appeal might have been taken, but the defendant did not appeal.

777. (1) Conviction or order remediable, when — No conviction, order or warrant for enforcing a conviction or order shall, on being removed by *certiorari*, be held to be invalid by reason of any irregularity, informality or insufficiency therein, where the court before which or the judge before whom the question is raised, on perusal of the evidence, is satisfied

(a) that an offence of the nature described in the conviction, order or warrant, as the case may be, was committed,

(b) that there was jurisdiction to make the conviction or order or issue the warrant, as the case may be, and

(c) that the punishment imposed, if any, was not in excess of the punishment that might lawfully have been imposed,

but the court or judge has the same powers to deal with the proceedings in the manner that the court or judge considers proper that are conferred on a court to which an appeal might have been taken.

(2) Correcting punishment — Where, in proceedings to which subsection (1) applies, the court or judge is satisfied that a person was properly convicted of an offence but the punishment that was imposed is greater than the punishment that might lawfully have been imposed, the court or judge

(a) shall correct the sentence,

(i) where the punishment is a fine, by imposing a fine that does not exceed the maximum fine that might lawfully have been imposed,

(ii) where the punishment is imprisonment, and the person has not served a term of imprisonment under the sentence that is equal to or greater than the term of imprisonment that might lawfully have been imposed, by imposing a term of imprisonment that does not exceed the maximum term of imprisonment that might lawfully have been imposed, or

(iii) where the punishment is a fine and imprisonment, by imposing a punishment in accordance with subparagraph (i) or (ii), as the case requires; or

(b) shall remit the matter to the convicting judge, justice or provincial court judge and direct him to impose a punishment that is not greater than the punishment that may be lawfully imposed.

(3) Amendment — Where an adjudication is varied pursuant to subsection (1) or (2), the conviction and warrant of committal, if any, shall be amended to conform with the adjudication as varied.

(4) Sufficiency of statement — Any statement that appears in a conviction and is sufficient for the purpose of the conviction is sufficient for the purposes of an information, summons, order or warrant in which it appears in the proceedings.

R.S. 1985, c. 27 (1st Supp.), s. 203.

778. Irregularities within section 777 — Without restricting the generality of section 777, that section shall be deemed to apply where

(a) the statement of the adjudication or of any other matter or thing is in the past tense instead of in the present tense;

(b) the punishment imposed is less than the punishment that might by law have been imposed for the offence that appears by the evidence to have been committed; or

(c) there has been an omission to negative circumstances, the existence of which would make the act complained of lawful, whether those circumstances are stated by way of exception or otherwise in the provision under which the offence is charged or are stated in another provision.

779. (1) General order for security by recognizance — A court that has authority to quash a conviction, order or other proceeding on *certiorari* may prescribe by general order that no motion to quash any such conviction, order or other proceeding removed to the court by *certiorari*, shall be heard unless the defendant has entered into a recognizance with one or more sufficient sureties, before one or more justices of the territorial division in which the conviction or order was made or before a judge or other officer, or has made a deposit to be prescribed with a condition that the defendant will prosecute the writ of *certiorari* at his own expense, without wilful delay, and, if ordered, will pay to the person in whose favour the conviction, order or other proceeding is affirmed his full costs and charges to be taxed according to the practice of the court where the conviction, order or proceeding is affirmed.

(2) Provisions of Part XXV — The provisions of Part XXV relating to forfeiture of recognizances apply to a recognizance entered into under this section.

780. Effect of order dismissing application to quash — Where a motion to quash a conviction, order or other proceeding is refused, the order of the court refusing the application is sufficient authority for the clerk of the court forthwith to return the conviction, order or proceeding to the court from which or the person from whom it was removed, and for proceedings to be taken with respect thereto for the enforcement thereof.

781. (1) Want of proof of order in council — No order, conviction or other proceeding shall be quashed or set aside, and no defendant shall be discharged, by reason only that evidence has not been given

(a) of a proclamation or order of the Governor in Council or the lieutenant governor in council;

(b) of rules, regulations or by-laws made by the Governor in Council under an Act of Parliament or by the lieutenant governor in council under an Act of the legislature of the province; or

(c) of the publication of a proclamation, order, rule, regulation or by-law in the *Canada Gazette* or in the official gazette for the province.

(2) Judicial notice — Proclamations, orders, rules, regulations and by-laws mentioned in subsection (1) and the publication thereof shall be judicially noticed.

782. Defect in form — No warrant of committal shall, on *certiorari* or *habeas corpus*, be held to be void by reason only of any defect therein, where

(a) it is alleged in the warrant that the defendant was convicted; and

(b) there is a valid conviction to sustain the warrant.

783. No action against official when conviction, etc., quashed — Where an application is made to quash a conviction, order or other proceeding made or held by a provincial court judge acting under Part XIX or a justice on the ground that he exceeded his jurisdiction, the court to which or the judge to whom the application is made may, in quashing the conviction, order or other proceeding, order that no civil proceedings shall be taken against the justice or provincial court judge or against any officer who acted under the conviction, order or other proceeding or under any warrant issued to enforce it.

784. (1) Appeal in mandamus etc. — An appeal lies to the court of appeal from a decision granting or refusing the relief sought in proceedings by way of *mandamus, certiorari* or prohibition.

(2) Application of Part XXI — Except as provided in this section, Part XXI applies, with such modifications as the circumstances require, to appeals under this section.

(3) Refusal of application, and appeal — Where an application for a writ of *habeas corpus ad subjiciendum* is refused by a judge of a court having jurisdiction therein, no application may again be made on the same grounds, whether to the same or to another court or judge, unless fresh evidence is adduced, but an appeal from that refusal shall lie to the court of appeal, and where on the appeal the application is refused a further appeal shall lie to the Supreme Court of Canada, with leave of that Court.

(4) Where writ granted — Where a writ of *habeas corpus ad subjiciendum* is granted by any judge, no appeal therefrom shall lie at the instance of any party including the Attorney General of the province concerned or the Attorney General of Canada.

(5) Appeal from judgment on return of writ — Where a judgment is issued on the return of a writ of *habeas corpus ad subjiciendum*, an appeal therefrom lies to the court of appeal, and from a judgment of the court of appeal to the Supreme Court of Canada, with the leave of that court, at the instance of the applicant or the Attorney General of the province concerned or the Attorney General of Canada, but not at the instance of any other party.

(6) Hearing of appeal — An appeal in *habeas corpus* matters shall be heard by the court to which the appeal is directed at an early date, whether in or out of the prescribed sessions of the court.

1997, c. 18, s. 109.

PART XXVII — SUMMARY CONVICTIONS

Interpretation

785. (1) Definitions — In this Part

"clerk of the appeal court" includes a local clerk of the appeal court;

"informant" means a person who lays an information;

"information" includes

(a) a count in an information, and

(b) a complaint in respect of which a justice is authorized by an Act of Parliament or an enactment made thereunder to make an order;

"order" means any order, including an order for the payment of money;

"proceedings" means

(a) proceedings in respect of offences that are declared by an Act of Parliament or an enactment made thereunder to be punishable on summary conviction, and

(b) proceedings where a justice is authorized by an Act of Parliament or an enactment made thereunder to make an order;

"prosecutor" means the Attorney General or where the Attorney General does not intervene, the informant, and includes counsel or an agent acting on behalf of either of them;

"sentence" includes

(a) a declaration made under subsection 199(3),

(b) an order made under subsection 110(1) or 259(1) or (2), section 261, subsection 730(1) or 737(3) or (5) or section 738, 739 or 742.3, and

Proposed Amendment — 785 "sentence"(b)

On the coming into force of section 747.1 of the *Criminal Code*, as enacted by section 6 of 1995, c. 22, paragraph (b) of the definition "sentence" in section 785 of the *Criminal Code* is replaced by the following:

(b) an order made under subsection 100(2) or 259(1) or (2), section 261, subsection 730(1), section 737, 738, 739 or 742.3 or subsection 747.1(1) and

1995, c. 22, s. 7(2) [Not in force at date of publication.]

Proposed Amendment — Conditional Amendment 785 "sentence"(b)

On the later of the coming into force of 1999, c. 25 [In force December 1, 1999.] and the coming into force of paragraph (b) of the definition "sentence" in section 785 of the *Criminal Code*, as enacted by 1995, c. 22, s. 7(2) [Not in force at date of publication.], paragraph (b) is replaced by the following:

(b) an order made under subsection 110(1) or 259(1) or (2), section 261, subsection 730(1) or 737(3) or (5), section 738, 739 or 742.3 or subsection 747.1(1), and

1999, c. 25, s. 29(2)

(c) a disposition made under section 731 or 732 or subsection 732.2(3) or (5), 742.4(3) or 742.6(9);

(d) an order made under subsection 16(1) of the *Controlled Drugs and Substances Act*;

"summary conviction court" means a person who has jurisdiction in the territorial division where the subject-matter of the proceedings is alleged to have arisen and who

(a) is given jurisdiction over the proceedings by the enactment under which the proceedings are taken,

(b) is a justice or provincial court judge, where the enactment under which the proceedings are taken does not expressly give jurisdiction to any person or class of persons, or

(c) is a provincial court judge, where the enactment under which the proceedings are taken gives jurisdiction in respect thereof to two or more justices;

"trial" includes the hearing of a complaint.

R.S. 1985, c. 27 (1st Supp.), ss. 170, 203; 1992, c. 1, s. 58(1) (Sched. 1, item 16); 1995, c. 22, s. 7; 1995, c. 39, s. 156; 1996, c. 19, s. 76; 1999, c. 25, s. 23

786. (1) Application of Part — Except where otherwise provided by law, this Part applies to proceedings as defined in this Part.

(2) Limitation — No proceedings shall be instituted more than six months after the time when the subject-matter of the proceedings arose, unless the prosecutor and the defendant so agree.

1997, c. 18, s. 110

Punishment

787. (1) General penalty — Except where otherwise provided by law, every one who is convicted of an offence punishable on summary conviction is liable to a fine of not more than two thousand dollars or to imprisonment for six months or to both.

(2) Imprisonment in default where not otherwise specified — Where the imposition of a fine or the making of an order for the payment of money is authorized by law, but the law does not provide that imprisonment may be imposed in default of payment of the fine or compliance with the order, the court may order that in default of payment of the fine or compliance with the order, as the case may be, the defendant shall be imprisoned for a term not exceeding six months.

(3) to (11) [Repealed R.S. 1985, c. 27 (1st Supp.), s. 171.]

R.S. 1985, c. 27 (1st Supp.), s. 171.

Information

788. (1) Commencement of proceedings — Proceedings under this Part shall be commenced by laying an information in Form 2.

(2) One justice may act before the trial — Notwithstanding any other law that requires an information to be laid before or to be tried by two or more justices, one justice may

(a) receive the information;

(b) issue a summons or warrant with respect to the information; and

(c) do all other things preliminary to the trial.

789. (1) Formalities of information — In proceedings to which this Part applies, an information

(a) shall be in writing and under oath; and

(b) may charge more than one offence or relate to more than one matter of complaint, but where more than one offence is charged or the information relates to more than one matter of complaint, each offence or matter of complaint, as the case may be, shall be set out in a separate count.

(2) No reference to previous convictions — No information in respect of an offence for which, by reason of previous convictions, a greater punishment may be imposed shall contain any reference to previous convictions.

790. (1) Any justice may act before and after trial — Nothing in this Act or any other law shall be deemed to require a justice before whom proceedings are commenced or who issues process before or after the trial to be the justice or one of the justices before whom the trial is held.

(2) Two or more justices — Where two or more justices have jurisdiction with respect to proceedings, they shall be present and act together at the trial, but one justice may thereafter do anything that is required or is authorized to be done in connection with the proceedings.

(3) and (4) [Repealed R.S. 1985, c. 27 (1st Supp.), s. 172.]

R.S. 1985, c. 27 (1st Supp.), s. 172.

791. [Repealed R.S. 1985, c. 27 (1st Supp.), s. 173.]

792. [Repealed R.S. 1985, c. 27 (1st Supp.), s. 174.]

793. [Repealed R.S. 1985, c. 27 (1st Supp.), s. 175.]

794. (1) No need to negative exception, etc. — No exception, exemption, proviso, excuse or qualification prescribed by law is required to be set out or negatived, as the case may be, in an information.

(2) Burden of proving exception, etc. — The burden of proving that an exception, exemption, proviso, excuse or qualification prescribed by law operates in favour of the defendant is on the defendant, and the prosecutor is not required, except by way of rebuttal, to prove that the exception, exemption, proviso, excuse or qualification does not operate in favour of the defendant, whether or not it is set out in the information.

Application

795. Application of Parts XVI, XVIII, and XX.1 — The provisions of Parts XVI and XVIII with respect to compelling the appearance of an accused before a justice, and the provisions of Parts XX and XX.1, in so far as they are not inconsistent with this Part, apply, with such modifications as the circumstances require, to proceedings under this Part.

R.S. 1985, c. 27 (1st Supp.), s. 176; 1991, c. 43, s. 7.

796. [Repealed R.S. 1985, c. 27 (1st Supp.), s. 176.]

797.]Repealed R.S. 1985, c. 27 (1st Supp.), s. 176.]

798. Jurisdiction — Every summary conviction court has jurisdiction to try, determine and adjudge proceedings to which this Part applies in the territorial division over which the person who constitutes that court has jurisdiction.

799. Non-appearance of prosecutor — Where, in proceedings to which this Part applies, the defendant appears for the trial and the prosecutor, having had due notice, does not appear, the summary conviction court may dismiss the information or may adjourn the trial to some other time on such terms as it considers proper.

800. (1) When both parties appear — Where the prosecutor and defendant appear for the trial, the summary conviction court shall proceed to hold the trial.

(2) Counsel or agent — A defendant may appear personally or by counsel or agent, but the summary conviction court may require the defendant to appear personally and may, if it thinks fit, issue a warrant in Form 7 for the arrest of the defendant and adjourn the trial to await his appearance pursuant thereto.

(2.1) Video links — Where the court so orders and the defendant agrees, the defendant who is confined in prison may appear by closed-circuit television or any other means that allow the court and the defendant to engage in simultaneous visual and oral communication, if the defendant is given the opportunity to communicate privately with counsel, in a case in which the defendant is represented by counsel.

(3) Appearance by corporation — Where the defendant is a corporation, it shall appear by counsel or agent, and if it does not appear, the summary conviction court may, on proof of service of the summons, proceed *ex parte* to hold the trial.
1997, c. 18, s. 111.

801. (1) Arraignment — Where the defendant appears for the trial, the substance of the information laid against him shall be stated to him, and he shall be asked,

> (a) whether he pleads guilty or not guilty to the information, where the proceedings are in respect of an offence that is punishable on summary conviction; or

> (b) whether he has cause to show why an order should not be made against him, in proceedings where a justice is authorized by law to make an order.

(2) Finding of guilt, conviction or order if charge admitted — Where the defendant pleads guilty or does not show sufficient cause why an order should not be made against him, as the case may be, the summary conviction court shall convict the defendant, discharge the defendant under section 730 or make an order against the defendant accordingly.

(3) Procedure if charge not admitted — Where the defendant pleads not guilty or states that he has cause to show why an order should not be made against him, as the case may be, the summary conviction court shall proceed with the trial, and shall take the evidence of witnesses for the prosecutor and the defendant in accordance with the provisions of Part XVIII relating to preliminary inquiries.

(4) and (5) [Repealed R.S. 1985, c. 27 (1st Supp.), s. 177(2).]
R.S. 1985, c. 27 (1st Supp.), s. 177; 1995, c. 22, s. 10.

802. (1) Right to make full answer and defence — The prosecutor is entitled personally to conduct his case and the defendant is entitled to make his full answer and defence.

(2) Examination of witnesses — The prosecutor or defendant, as the case may be, may examine and cross-examine witnesses personally or by counsel or agent.

(3) On oath — Every witness at a trial in proceedings to which this Part applies shall be examined under oath.

803. (1) Adjournment — The summary conviction court may, in its discretion, before or during the trial, adjourn the trial to a time and place to be appointed and stated in the presence of the parties or their counsel or agents.

(2) Non-appearance of defendant — Where a defendant does not appear at the time and place appointed for the trial after having been notified of that time and place, or where a defendant does not appear for the resumption of a trial that has been adjourned in accordance with subsection (1), the summary conviction court

(a) may proceed *ex parte* to hear and determine the proceedings in the absence of the defendant as fully and effectually as if the defendant had appeared; or

(b) may, if it thinks fit, issue a warrant in Form 7 for the arrest of the defendant and adjourn the trial to await his appearance pursuant thereto.

(3) Consent of Attorney General required — Where, at the trial of a defendant, the summary conviction court proceeds in the manner described in paragraph (2)(*a*), no proceedings under section 145 arising out of the failure of the defendant to appear at the time and place appointed for the trial or for the resumption of the trial shall be instituted or if instituted shall be proceeded with, except with the consent of the Attorney General.

(4) Non-appearance of prosecutor — Where the prosecutor does not appear at the time and place appointed for the resumption of an adjourned trial, the summary conviction court may dismiss the information with or without costs.

(5)–(8) [Repealed 1991, c. 43, s. 9, Schedule, item 11.]

1991, c. 43, s. 9, Schedule, item 11; 1994, c. 44, s. 79; 1997, c. 18, s. 112.

Adjudication

804. Finding of guilt, conviction, order or dismissal — When the summary conviction court has heard the prosecutor, defendant and witnesses, it shall, after considering the matter, convict the defendant, discharge the defendant under section 730, make an order against the defendant or dismiss the information, as the case may be.

R.S. 1985, c. 27 (1st Supp.), s. 178; 1995, c. 22, s. 10.

805. [Repealed R.S. 1985, c. 27 (1st Supp.), s. 179.]

806. (1) Memo of conviction or order — Where a defendant is convicted or an order is made in relation to the defendant, a minute or memorandum of the conviction or order shall be made by the summary conviction court indicating that the matter was dealt with under this Part and, on request by the defendant, the prosecutor or any other person, the court shall cause a conviction or order in Form 35 or 36, as the case may be, and a certified copy of the conviction or order to be drawn up and shall deliver the certified copy to the person making the request.

(2) Warrant of committal — Where a defendant is convicted or an order is made against him, the summary conviction court shall issue a warrant of committal in Form 21 or 22, and section 528 applies in respect of a warrant of committal issued under this subsection.

(3) Admissibility of certified copy — Where a warrant of committal in Form 21 is issued by a clerk of a court, a copy of the warrant of committal, certified by the clerk, is admissible in evidence in any proceeding.

1994, c. 44, s. 80.

807. Disposal of penalties when joint offenders — Where several persons join in committing the same offence and upon conviction each is adjudged to pay an amount to a person aggrieved, no more shall be paid to that person than an amount equal to the value of the property destroyed or injured or the amount of the injury done, together with costs, if any, and the residue of the amount adjudged to be paid shall be applied in the manner in which other penalties imposed by law are directed to be applied.

808. (1) Order of dismissal — Where the summary conviction court dismisses an information, it may, if requested by the defendant, draw up an order of dismissal, and shall give to the defendant a certified copy of the order of dismissal.

(2) Effect of certificate — A copy of an order of dismissal, certified in accordance with subsection (1) is, without further proof, a bar to any subsequent proceedings against the defendant in respect of the same cause.

809. (1) Costs — The summary conviction court may in its discretion award and order such costs as it considers reasonable and not inconsistent with such of the fees established by section 840 as may be taken or allowed in proceedings before that summary conviction court, to be paid

(a) to the informant by the defendant, where the summary conviction court convicts or makes an order against the defendant; or

(b) to the defendant by the informant, where the summary conviction court dismisses an information.

(2) Order set out — An order under subsection (1) shall be set out in the conviction, order or order of dismissal, as the case may be.

(3) Costs are part of fine — Where a fine or sum of money or both are adjudged to be paid by a defendant and a term of imprisonment in default of payment is imposed, the defendant is, in default of payment, liable to serve the term of imprisonment imposed, and for the purposes of this subsection, any costs that are awarded against the defendant shall be deemed to be part of the fine or sum of money adjudged to be paid.

(4) Where no fine imposed — Where no fine or sum of money is adjudged to be paid by a defendant, but costs are awarded against the defendant or informant, the person who is liable to pay them is, in default of payment, liable to imprisonment for one month.

(5) Definition of "costs" — In this section, **"costs"** includes the costs and charges, after they have been ascertained, of committing and conveying to prison the person against whom costs have been awarded.

Sureties to Keep the Peace

810. (1) Where injury or damage feared — An information may be laid before a justice by or on behalf of any person who fears on reasonable grounds that another person will cause personal injury to him or her or to his or her spouse or child or will damage his or her property.

Proposed Amendment — 810(1)

(1) Where injury or damage feared — An information may be laid before a justice by or on behalf of any person who fears on reasonable grounds that another person will cause personal injury to him or her or to his or her spouse or common-law partner or child or will damage his or her property.

2000, c. 12, s. 95(f) [Not in force at date of publication.]

(2) Duty of justice — A justice who receives an information under subsection (1) shall cause the parties to appear before him or before a summary conviction court having jurisdiction in the same territorial division.

(3) Adjudication — The justice or the summary conviction court before which the parties appear may, if satisfied by the evidence adduced that the person on whose behalf the information was laid has reasonable grounds for his or her fears,

(a) order that the defendant enter into a recognizance, with or without sureties, to keep the peace and be of good behaviour for any period that does not exceed twelve months, and comply with such other reasonable conditions prescribed in the recognizance, including the conditions set out in subsections (3.1) and (3.2), as the court considers desirable for securing the good conduct of the defendant; or

(b) commit the defendant to prison for a term not exceeding twelve months if he or she fails or refuses to enter into the recognizance.

(3.1) Conditions — Before making an order under subsection (3), the justice or the summary conviction court shall consider whether it is desirable, in the interests of the safety of the defendant or any other person, to include as a condition of the recognizance that the defendant be prohibited from possessing any firearm, crossbow, prohibited weapon, restricted weapon, prohibited device, ammunition, prohibited ammunition or explosive substance, or all such things, for any period specified in the recognizance and, where the justice or summary conviction court decides that it is so desirable, the justice or summary conviction court shall add such a condition to the recognizance.

(3.11) Where the justice or summary conviction court adds a condition described in subsection (3.1) to a recognizance order, the justice or summary conviction court shall specify in the order the manner and method by which

(a) the things referred to in that subsection that are in the possession of the accused shall be surrendered, disposed of, detained, stored or dealt with; and

(b) the authorizations, licences and registration certificates held by the person shall be surrendered.

(3.12) Where the justice or summary conviction court does not add a condition described in subsection (3.1) to a recognizance order, the justice or summary conviction court shall include in the record a statement of the reasons for not adding the condition.

(3.2) Idem — Before making an order under subsection (3), the justice or the summary conviction court shall consider whether it is desirable, in the interests of the safety of the informant, of the person on whose behalf the information was laid or of that person's spouse or child, as the case may be, to add either or both of the following conditions to the recognizance, namely, a condition

(a) prohibiting the defendant from being at, or within a distance specified in the recognizance from, a place specified in the recognizance where the person on whose behalf the information was laid or that person's spouse or child, as the case may be, is regularly found; and

(b) prohibiting the defendant from communicating, in whole or in part, directly or indirectly, with the person on whose behalf the information was laid or that person's spouse or child, as the case may be.

Proposed Amendment — 810(3.2)

(3.2) Idem — Before making an order under subsection (3), the justice or the summary conviction court shall consider whether it is desirable, in the interests of the safety of the informant, of the person on whose behalf the information was laid or of that person's spouse or common-law partner or child, as the case may be, to add either or both of the following conditions to the recognizance, namely, a condition

(a) prohibiting the defendant from being at, or within a distance specified in the recognizance from, a place specified in the recognizance where the person on whose behalf the information was laid or that person's spouse or common-law partner or child, as the case may be, is regularly found; and

(b) prohibiting the defendant from communicating, in whole or in part, directly or indirectly, with the person on whose behalf the information was laid or that person's spouse or common-law partner or child, as the case may be.

2000, c. 12, s. 95(g) [Not in force at date of publication.]

(4) Forms — A recognizance and committal to prison in default of recognizance under subsection (3) may be in Forms 32 and 23, respectively.

(4.1) Modification of recognizance — The justice or the summary conviction court may, on application of the informant or the defendant, vary the conditions fixed in the recognizance.

(5) Procedure — The provisions of this Part apply, with such modifications as the circumstances require, to proceedings under this section.

1991, c. 40, s. 33; 1994, c. 44, s. 81; 1995, c. 22, s. 8; 1995, c. 39, s. 157

810.01 (1) When fear of criminal organization offence — A person who fears on reasonable grounds that another person will commit a criminal organization offence may, with the consent of the Attorney General, lay an information before a provincial court judge.

(2) Appearances — A provincial court judge who receives an information under subsection (1) may cause the parties to appear before the provincial court judge.

(3) Adjudication — The provincial court judge before whom the parties appear may, if satisfied by the evidence adduced that the informant has reasonable grounds for the fear, order that the defendant enter into a recognizance to keep the peace and be of good behaviour for any period that does not exceed twelve months and to comply with any other reasonable conditions prescribed in the recognizance, including the conditions set out in subsection (5), that the provincial court judge considers desirable for preventing the commission of a criminal organization offence.

(4) Refusal to enter into recognizance — The provincial court judge may commit the defendant to prison for a term not exceeding twelve months if the defendant fails or refuses to enter into the recognizance.

(5) Conditions-firearms — Before making an order under subsection (3), the provincial court judge shall consider whether it is desirable, in the interests of the safety of the defendant or of any other person, to include as a condition of the recognizance that the defendant be prohibited from possessing any firearm, crossbow, prohibited weapon, restricted weapon, prohibited device, ammunition, prohibited ammunition or explosive substance, or all of those things, for any period specified in the recognizance, and where the provincial court judge decides that it is so desirable, the provincial court judge shall add such a condition to the recognizance.

(5.1) Surrender, etc. — Where the provincial court judge adds a condition described in subsection (5) to a recognizance, the provincial court judge shall specify in the recognizance the manner and method by which

(a) the things referred to in that subsection that are in the possession of the defendant shall be surrendered, disposed of, detained, stored or dealt with; and

(b) the authorizations, licences and registration certificates held by the defendant shall be surrendered.

(5.2) Reasons — Where the provincial court judge does not add a condition described in subsection (5) to a recognizance, the provincial court judge shall include in the record a statement of the reasons for not adding the condition.

(6) Variance of conditions — The provincial court judge may, on application of the informant, the Attorney General or the defendant, vary the conditions fixed in the recognizance.

(7) Other provisions to apply — Subsections 810(4) and (5) apply, with any modifications that the circumstances require, to recognizance made under this section.

1997, c. 23, s. 19, 26.

810.1 (1) Where fear of sexual offence — Any person who fears on reasonable grounds that another person will commit an offence under section 151, 152, 155 or 159, subsection 160(2) or (3), section 170 or 171, subsection 173(2) or section 271, 272 or 273, in respect of one or more persons who are under the age of fourteen years, may lay an information before a provincial court judge, whether or not the person or persons in respect of whom it is feared that the offence will be committed are named.

(2) Duty of provincial court judge — A provincial court judge who receives an information under subsection (1) shall cause the parties to appear before the provincial court judge.

(3) Adjudication — The provincial court judge before whom the parties appear may, if satisfied by the evidence adduced that the informant has reasonable grounds for the fear, order the defendant to enter into a recognizance and comply with the conditions fixed by the provincial court judge, including a condition prohibiting the defendant from engaging in any activity that involves contact with persons under the age of fourteen years and prohibiting the defendant from attending a public park or public swimming area where persons under the age of fourteen years are present or can reasonably be expected to be present, or a daycare centre, schoolground, playground or community centre, for any period fixed by the provincial court judge that does not exceed twelve months.

(3.1) Refusal to enter into recognizance — The provincial court judge may commit the defendant to prison for a term not exceeding twelve months if the defendant fails or refuses to enter into the recognizance.

(4) Judge may vary recognizance — The provincial court judge may, on application of the informant or the defendant, vary the conditions fixed in the recognizance.

(5) Other provisions to apply — Subsections 810(4) and (5) apply, with such modifications as the circumstances require, to recognizances made under this section.

1993, c. 45, s. 11; 1997, c. 18, s. 113(2).

810.2 (1) Where fear of serious personal injury offence — Any person who fears on reasonable grounds that another person will commit a serious personal injury offence, as that expression is defined in section 752, may, with the consent of the Attorney General, lay an information before a provincial court judge, whether or not the person or persons in respect of whom it is feared that the offence will be committed are named.

(2) Duty of provincial court judge — A provincial court judge who receives an information under subsection (1) may cause the parties to appear before the provincial court judge.

(3) Adjudication — The provincial court judge before whom the parties appear may, if satisfied by the evidence adduced that the informant has reasonable grounds for the fear, order that the defendant enter into a recognizance to keep the peace and be of good behaviour for any period that does not exceed twelve months and to comply with any other reasonable conditions prescribed in the recognizance, including the conditions set out in subsection (5) and (6), that the provincial court judge considers desirable for securing the good conduct of the defendant.

(4) Refusal to enter into recognizance — The provincial court judge may commit the defendant to prison for a term not exceeding twelve months if the defendant fails or refuses to enter into the recognizance.

(5) Conditions — firearms — Before making an order under subsection (3), the provincial court judge shall consider whether it is desirable, in the interests of the safety of the defendant or of any other person, to include as a condition of the recognizance that the defendant be prohibited from possessing any firearm, crossbow, prohibited weapon, restricted weapon, prohibited device, ammunition, prohibited ammunition or explosive substance, or all such things, for any period specified in the recognizance, and where the provincial court judge decides that it is so desirable, the provincial court judge shall add such a condition to the recognizance.

(5.1) Surrender, etc. — Where the provincial court judge adds a condition described in subsection (5) to a recognizance order, the provincial court judge shall specify in the order the manner and method by which

(a) the things referred to in that subsection that are in the possession of the defendant shall be surrendered, disposed of, detained, stored or dealt with; and

(b) the authorization, licences and registration certificates held by the defendant shall be surrendered.

(5.2) Reasons — Where the provincial court judge does not add a condition described in subsection (5) to a recognizance order, the provincial court judge shall include in the record a statement of the reasons for not adding the condition.

(6) Conditions — reporting and monitoring — Before making an order under subsection (3), the provincial court judge shall consider whether it is desirable to include as a condition of the recognizance that the defendant report to the correctional authority of a province or to an appropriate police authority, and where the provincial court judge decides that it is desirable for the defendant to so report, the provincial court judge may add the appropriate condition to the recognizance.

(7) Variance of conditions — The provincial court judge may, on application of the informant, of the Attorney General or of the defendant, vary the conditions fixed in the recognizance.

(8) Other provisions to apply — Subsections 810(4) and (5) apply, with such modifications as the circumstances require, to recognizance made under this section.

1997, c. 17, s. 9

811. Breach of recognizance — A person bound by a recognizance under section 810, 810.01, 810.1 or 810.2 who commits a breach of the recognizance is guilty of

(a) an indictable offence and liable to imprisonment for a term not exceeding two years; or

(b) an offence punishable on summary conviction.

1993, c. 45, s. 11; 1994, c. 44, s. 82; 1997, c. 17, s. 10; c. 23, ss. 20, 27.

Appeal

812. (1) Definition of "appeal court" — For the purposes of sections 813 to 828 "appeal court" means

(a) in the Province of Ontario, the Superior Court of Justice sitting in the region, district or county or group of counties where the adjudication was made;

(b) in the Province of Quebec, the Superior Court;

(c) in the Provinces of Nova Scotia and British Columbia, the Supreme Court;

(d) in the Provinces of New Brunswick, Manitoba, Saskatchewan and Alberta, the Court of Queen's Bench;

(e) [Repealed 1992, c. 51, s. 43(2).];

(f) in the Province of Prince Edward Island, the Trial Division of the Supreme Court;

(g) in the Province of Newfoundland, the Trial Division of the Supreme Court; and

(h) in the Yukon Territory and Northwest Territories, a judge of the Supreme Court of the territory; and

(i) in Nunavut, a judge of the Nunavut Court of Justice.

(2) When appeal court is Court of Appeal of Nunavut — A judge of the Court of Appeal of Nunavut is the appeal court for the purposes of sections 813 to 828 if the appeal is from a conviction, order, sentence or verdict of a summary conviction court consisting of a judge of the Nunavut Court of Justice.

R.S. 1985, c. 11 (1st Supp.), s. 2; c. 27 (2d Supp.) (Sched., item 6); 1990, c. 16, s. 7; 1990, c. 17, s. 15; 1992, c. 51, s. 43; 1993, c. 28, s. 78 (Sched. III, item 36) [Repealed 1999, c. 3, (Sched., item 9).]; 1998, c. 30, s. 14(d); 1999, c. 3, s. 55.

813. Appeal by defendant, informant or Attorney General — Except where otherwise provided by law,

    (a) the defendant in proceedings under this Part may appeal to the appeal court

        (i) from a conviction or order made against him;

        (ii) against a sentence passed on him; or

        (iii) against a verdict of unfit to stand trial or not criminally responsible on account of mental disorder; and

    (b) the informant, the Attorney General or his agent in proceedings under this Part may appeal to the appeal court

        (i) from an order that stays proceedings on an information or dismisses an information,

        (ii) against a sentence passed upon a defendant; or

        (iii) against a verdict of not criminally responsible on account of mental disorder or unfit to stand trial,

and the Attorney General of Canada or his agent has the same rights of appeal in proceedings instituted at the instance of the Government of Canada and conducted by or on behalf of that government as the Attorney General of a province or his agent has under this paragraph.

R.S. 1985, c. 27 (1st Supp.), s. 180; 1991, c. 43, s. 9, Schedule, item 12.

814. (1) Manitoba and Alberta — In the Provinces of Manitoba and Alberta, an appeal under section 813 shall be heard at the sittings of the appeal court that is held nearest to the place where the cause of the proceedings arose, but the judge of the appeal court may, on the application of one of the parties, appoint another place for the hearing of the appeal.

(2) Saskatchewan — In the Province of Saskatchewan, an appeal under section 813 shall be heard at the sittings of the appeal court at the judicial centre nearest to the place where the adjudication was made, but the judge of the appeal court may, on the application of one of the parties, appoint another place for the hearing of the appeal.

(3) British Columbia — In the Province of British Columbia, an appeal under section 813 shall be heard at the sittings of the appeal court that is held nearest to the place where the adjudication was made, but the judge of the appeal court may, on the application of one of the parties, appoint another place for the hearing of the appeal.

(4) Territories — In the Yukon Territory, the Northwest Territories and Nunavut, an appeal under section 813 shall be heard at the place where the cause of the proceedings arose or at the place nearest thereto where a court is appointed to be held.

1993, c. 28, s. 78 (Sched. III, item 37).

815. (1) Notice of appeal — An appellant who proposes to appeal to the appeal court shall give notice of appeal in such manner and within such period as may be directed by rules of court.

(2) Extension of time — The appeal court or a judge thereof may extend the time within which notice of appeal may be given.

Interim Release of Appellant

816. (1) Undertaking or recognizance of appellant — A person who was the defendant in proceedings before a summary conviction court and by whom an appeal is taken under section 813 shall, if he is in custody, remain in custody unless the appeal court at which the appeal is to be heard orders that the appellant be released

(a) on his giving an undertaking to the appeal court, without conditions or with such conditions as the appeal court directs, to surrender himself into custody in accordance with the order,

(b) on his entering into a recognizance without sureties in such amount, with such conditions, if any, as the appeal court directs, but without deposit of money or other valuable security, or

(c) on his entering into a recognizance with or without sureties in such amount, with such conditions, if any, as the appeal court directs, and on his depositing with that appeal court such sum of money or other valuable security as the appeal court directs,

and the person having the custody of the appellant shall, where the appellant complies with the order, forthwith release the appellant.

(2) Application of certain provisions of section 525 — The provisions of subsections 525(5), (6) and (7) apply with such modifications as the circumstances require in respect of a person who has been released from custody under subsection (1).

R.S. 1985, c. 27 (1st Supp.), s. 181.

817. (1) Undertaking or recognizance of prosecutor — The prosecutor in proceedings before a summary conviction court by whom an appeal is taken under section 813 shall, forthwith after filing the notice of appeal and proof of service thereof in accordance with section 815, appear before a justice, and the justice shall, after giving the prosecutor and the respondent a reasonable opportunity to be heard, order that the prosecutor

(a) give an undertaking as prescribed in this section; or

(b) enter into a recognizance in such amount, with or without sureties and with or without deposit of money or other valuable security, as the justice directs.

(2) Condition — The condition of an undertaking or recognizance given or entered into under this section is that the prosecutor will appear personally or by counsel at the sittings of the appeal court at which the appeal is to be heard.

(3) Appeals by Attorney General — This section does not apply in respect of an appeal taken by the Attorney General or by counsel acting on behalf of the Attorney General.

(4) Form of undertaking or recognizance — An undertaking under this section may be in Form 14 and a recognizance under this section may be in Form 32.

818. (1) Application to appeal court for review — Where a justice makes an order under section 817, either the appellant or the respondent may, before or at any time during the hearing of the appeal, apply to the appeal court for a review of the order made by the justice.

(2) Disposition of application by appeal court — On the hearing of an application under this section, the appeal court, after giving the appellant and the respondent a reasonable opportunity to be heard, shall

    (a) dismiss the application; or

    (b) if the person applying for the review shows cause, allow the application, vacate the order made by the justice and make the order that in the opinion of the appeal court should have been made.

(3) Effect of order — An order made under this section shall have the same force and effect as if it had been made by the justice.

819. (1) Application to fix date for hearing of appeal — Where, in the case of an appellant who has been convicted by a summary conviction court and who is in custody pending the hearing of his appeal, the hearing of his appeal has not commenced within thirty days from the day on which notice of his appeal was given in accordance with the rules referred to in section 815, the person having the custody of the appellant shall, forthwith on the expiration of those thirty days, apply to the appeal court to fix a date for the hearing of the appeal.

(2) Order fixing date — On receiving an application under subsection (1), the appeal court shall, after giving the prosecutor a reasonable opportunity to be heard, fix a date for the hearing of the appeal and give such directions as it thinks necessary for expediting the hearing of the appeal.

820. (1) Payment of fine not a waiver of appeal — A person does not waive his right of appeal under section 813 by reason only that he pays the fine imposed on conviction, without in any way indicating an intention to appeal or reserving the right to appeal.

(2) Presumption — A conviction, order or sentence shall be deemed not to have been appealed against until the contrary is shown.

Procedure on Appeal

821. (1) Notification and transmission of conviction, etc. — Where a notice of appeal has been given in accordance with the rules referred to in section 815, the clerk of the appeal court shall notify the summary conviction court that made the conviction or order appealed from or imposed the sentence appealed against of the appeal and on receipt of the notification that summary conviction court shall transmit the conviction, order or order of dismissal and all other material in its possession in connection with the proceedings to the appeal court before the time when the appeal is to be heard, or within such further time as the appeal court may direct, and the material shall be kept by the clerk of the appeal court with the records of the appeal court.

(2) Saving — An appeal shall not be dismissed by the appeal court by reason only that a person other than the appellant failed to comply with the provisions of this Part relating to appeals.

(3) Appellant to furnish transcript of evidence — Where the evidence on a trial before a summary conviction court has been taken by a stenographer duly sworn or by a sound recording apparatus, the appellant shall, unless the appeal court otherwise orders or the rules referred to in section 815 otherwise provide, cause a transcript thereof, certified by the stenographer or in accordance with subsection 540(6), as the case may be, to be furnished to the appeal court and the respondent for use on the appeal.

822. (1) Certain sections applicable to appeals — Where an appeal is taken under section 813 in respect of any conviction, acquittal, sentence, verdict or order, sections 683 to 689, with the exception of subsections 683(3) and 686(5), apply, with such modifications as the circumstances require.

(2) New trial — Where an appeal court orders a new trial, it shall be held before a summary conviction court other than the court that tried the defendant in the first instance, unless the appeal court directs that the new trial be held before the summary conviction court that tried the defendant in the first instance.

(3) Order of detention or release — Where an appeal court orders a new trial, it may make such order for the release or detention of the appellant pending the trial as may be made by a justice pursuant to section 515 and the order may be enforced in the same manner as if it had been made by a justice under that section, and the provisions of Part XVI apply with such modifications as the circumstances require to the order.

(4) Trial de novo — Notwithstanding subsections (1) to (3), where an appeal is taken under section 813 and where, because of the condition of the record of the trial in the summary conviction court or for any other reason, the appeal court, upon application of the defendant, the informant, the Attorney General or his agent, is of the opinion that the interests of justice would be better served by hearing and determining the appeal by holding a trial *de novo*, the appeal court may order that the appeal shall be heard by way of trial *de novo* in accordance with such rules as may be made under section 482 and for this purpose the provisions of sections 793 to 809 apply with such modifications as the circumstances require.

(5) Former evidence — The appeal court may, for the purpose of hearing and determining an appeal under subsection (4), permit the evidence of any witness taken before the summary conviction court to be read if that evidence has been authenticated in accordance with section 540 and if

(a) the appellant and respondent consent,

(b) the appeal court is satisfied that the attendance of the witness cannot reasonably be obtained, or

(c) by reason of the formal nature of the evidence or otherwise the court is satisfied that the opposite party will not be prejudiced, and any evidence that is read under the authority of this subsection has the same force and effect as if the witness had given the evidence before the appeal court.

(6) Appeal against sentence — Where an appeal is taken under subsection (4) against sentence, the appeal court shall, unless the sentence is one fixed by law, consider the fitness of the sentence appealed against and may, on such evidence, if any, as it thinks fit to require or receive, by order,

(a) dismiss the appeal, or

(b) vary the sentence within the limits prescribed by law for the offence of which the defendant was convicted;

and in making any order under paragraph (b) the appeal court may take into account any time spent in custody by the defendant as a result of the offence.

(7) General provisions re appeals — The following provisions apply in respect of appeals under subsection (4):

(a) where an appeal is based on an objection to an information or any process, judgment shall not be given in favour of the appellant

(i) for any alleged defect therein in substance or in form, or

(ii) for any variance between the information or process and the evidence adduced at the trial,

unless it is shown

(iii) that the objection was taken at the trial, and

(iv) that an adjournment of the trial was refused notwithstanding that the variance referred to in subparagraph (ii) had deceived or misled the appellant; and

(b) where an appeal is based on a defect in a conviction or an order, judgment shall not be given in favour of the appellant, but the court shall make an order curing the defect.

1991, c. 43, s. 9, Schedule, item 13.

823. [Repealed 1991, c. 43, s. 9, Schedule, item 14.]

824. Adjournment — The appeal court may adjourn the hearing of an appeal from time to time as may be necessary.

825. Dismissal for failure to appear or want of prosecution — The appeal court may, on proof that notice of an appeal has been given and that

(a) the appellant has failed to comply with any order made under section 816 or 817 or with the conditions of any undertaking or recognizance given or entered into as prescribed in either of those sections, or

(b) the appeal has not been proceeded with or has been abandoned, order that the appeal be dismissed.

826. Costs — Where an appeal is heard and determined or is abandoned or is dismissed for want of prosecution, the appeal court may make any order with respect to costs that it considers just and reasonable.

827. (1) To whom costs payable, and when — Where the appeal court orders the appellant or respondent to pay costs, the order shall direct that the costs be paid to the clerk of the court, to be paid by him to the person entitled to them, and shall fix the period within which the costs shall be paid.

(2) Certificate of non-payment of costs — Where costs are not paid in full within the period fixed for payment and the person who has been ordered to pay them has not been bound by a recognizance to pay them, the clerk of the court shall, on application by the person entitled to the costs, or by any person on his behalf, and on payment of any fee to which the clerk of the court is entitled, issue a certificate in Form 42 certifying that the costs or a part thereof, as the case may be, have not been paid.

(3) Committal — A justice having jurisdiction in the territorial division in which a certificate has been issued under subsection (2) may, upon production of the certificate, by warrant in Form 26, commit the defaulter to imprisonment for a term not exceeding one month, unless the amount of the costs and, where the justice thinks fit so to order, the costs of the committal and of conveying the defaulter to prison are sooner paid.

828. (1) Enforcement of conviction or order by court of appeal — A conviction or order made by the appeal court may be enforced

(a) in the same manner as if it had been made by the summary conviction court; or

(b) by process of the appeal court.

(2) Enforcement by justice — Where an appeal taken against a conviction or order adjudging payment of a sum of money is dismissed, the summary conviction court that made the conviction or order or a justice for the same territorial division may issue a warrant of committal as if no appeal had been taken.

(3) Duty of clerk of court — Where a conviction or order that has been made by an appeal court is to be enforced by a justice, the clerk of the appeal court shall send to the justice the conviction or order and all writings relating thereto, except the notice of intention to appeal and any recognizance.

Summary Appeal on Transcript or Agreed Statement of Facts

829. (1) Definition of "appeal court" — Subject to subsection (2), for the purposes of sections 830 to 838, **"appeal court"** means, in any province, the superior court of criminal jurisdiction for the province.

(2) Nunavut — If the appeal is from a conviction, judgment, verdict or other final order or determination of a summary conviction court consisting of a judge of the Nunavut Court of Justice, **"appeal court"** means a judge of the Court of Appeal of Nunavut.

R.S. 1985, c. 27 (1st Supp.), s. 182; 1999, c. 3, s. 56.

830. (1) Appeals — A party to proceedings to which this Part applies or the Attorney General may appeal against a conviction, judgment, verdict of acquittal or verdict of not criminally responsible on account of mental disorder or of unfit to stand trial or other final order or determination of a summary conviction court on the ground that

(a) it is erroneous in point of law;

(b) it is in excess of jurisdiction; or

(c) it constitutes a refusal or failure to exercise jurisdiction.

(2) Form of appeal — An appeal under this section shall be based on a transcript of the proceedings appealed from unless the appellant files with the appeal court, within fifteen days of the filing of the notice of appeal, a statement of facts agreed to in writing by the respondent.

(3) Rules for appeals — An appeal under this section shall be made within the period and in the manner directed by any applicable rules of court and where there are no such rules otherwise providing, a notice of appeal in writing shall be served on the respondent and a copy thereof, together with proof of service, shall be filed with the appeal court within thirty days after the date of the conviction, judgment or verdict of acquittal or other final order or determination that is the subject of the appeal.

(4) Rights of Attorney General of Canada — The Attorney General of Canada has the same rights of appeal in proceedings instituted at the instance of the Government of Canada and conducted by or on behalf of that Government as the Attorney General of a province has under this section.

R.S. 1985, c. 27 (1st Supp.), s. 182; 1991, c. 43, s. 9, Schedule, item 15.

831. Application — The provisions of sections 816, 817, 819 and 825 apply, with such modifications as the circumstances require, in respect of an appeal under section 830, except that on receiving an application by the person having the custody of an appellant described in section 819 to appoint a date for the hearing of the appeal, the appeal court shall, after giving the prosecutor a reasonable opportunity to be heard, give such directions as it thinks necessary for expediting the hearing of the appeal.

R.S. 1985, c. 27 (1st Supp.), s. 182.

832. (1) Undertaking or recognizance — When a notice of appeal is filed pursuant to section 830, the appeal court may order that the appellant appear before a justice and give an undertaking or enter into a recognizance as provided in section 816 where the defendant is the appellant, or as provided in section 817, in any other case.

(2) Attorney General — Subsection (1) does not apply where the appellant is the Attorney General or counsel acting on behalf of the Attorney General.

R.S. 1985, c. 27 (1st Supp.), s. 182.

833. No writ required — No writ of *certiorari* or other writ is required to remove any conviction, judgment, verdict or other final order or determination of a summary conviction court for the purpose of obtaining the judgment, determination or opinion of the appeal court.

R.S. 1985, c. 27 (1st Supp.), s. 182; 1991, c. 43, s. 9, Schedule, item 16.

834. (1) Powers of appeal court — When a notice of appeal is filed pursuant to section 830, the appeal court shall hear and determine the grounds of appeal and may

    (a) affirm, reverse or modify the conviction, judgment or verdict or other final order or determination, or

    (b) remit the matter to the summary conviction court with the opinion of the appeal court,

and may make any other order in relation to the matter or with respect to costs that it considers proper.

(2) Authority of judge — Where the authority and jurisdiction of the appeal court may be exercised by a judge of that court, the authority and jurisdiction may, subject to any applicable rules of court, be exercised by a judge of the court sitting in chambers as well in vacation as in term time.

R.S. 1985, c. 27 (1st Supp.), s. 182; 1991, c. 43, s. 9, Schedule, item 17.

835. (1) Enforcement — Where the appeal court renders its decision on an appeal, the summary conviction court from which the appeal was taken or a justice exercising the same jurisdiction has the same authority to enforce a conviction, order or determination that has been affirmed, modified or made by the appeal court as the summary conviction court would have had if no appeal had been taken.

(2) Idem — An order of the appeal court may be enforced by its own process.

R.S. 1985, c. 27 (1st Supp.), s. 182.

836. Appeal under section 830 — Every person who appeals under section 830 from any conviction, judgment, verdict or other final order or determination in respect of which that person is entitled to an appeal under section 813 shall be taken to have abandoned all the person's rights of appeal under section 813.

1985, c. 27 (1st Supp.), s. 182; 1991, c. 43, s. 9, Schedule, item 18.

837. Appeal barred — Where it is provided by law that no appeal lies from a conviction or order, no appeal under section 830 lies from such a conviction or order.

R.S. 1985, c. 27 (1st Supp.), s. 182.

838. Extension of time — The appeal court or a judge thereof may at any time extend any time period referred to in section 830, 831 or 832.

R.S. 1985, c. 27 (1st Supp.), s. 182.

Appeals to Court of Appeal

839. (1) Appeal on question of law — Subject to subsection (1.1), an appeal to the court of appeal, as defined in section 673 may, with leave of that court or a judge thereof, be taken on any ground that involves a question of law alone, against

(a) a decision of a court in respect of an appeal under section 822; or

(b) a decision of an appeal court under section 834, except where that court is the court of appeal.

(1.1) Nunavut — An appeal to the Court of Appeal of Nunavut may, with leave of that court or a judge of that court, be taken on any ground that involves a question of law alone, against a decision of a judge of the Court of Appeal of Nunavut acting as an appeal court under subsection 812(2) or 829(2).

(2) Sections applicable — Sections 673 to 689 apply with such modifications as the circumstances require to an appeal under this section.

(3) Costs — Notwithstanding subsection (2), the court of appeal may make any order with respect to costs that it considers proper in relation to an appeal under this section.

(4) Enforcement of decision — The decision of the court of appeal may be enforced in the same manner as if it had been made by the summary conviction court before which the proceedings were originally heard and determined.

(5) Right of Attorney General of Canada to appeal — The Attorney General of Canada has the same rights of appeal in proceedings instituted at the instance of the Government of Canada and conducted by or on behalf of that Government as the Attorney General of a province has under this Part.

R.S. 1985, c. 27 (1st Supp.), s. 183.

Fees and Allowances

840. (1) Fees and allowances — Subject to subsection (2), the fees and allowances mentioned in the schedule to this Part are the fees and allowances that may be taken or allowed in proceedings before summary conviction courts and justices under this Part.

(2) Order of lieutenant governor in council — The lieutenant governor in council of a province may order that all or any of the fees and allowances mentioned in the schedule to this Part shall not be taken or allowed in proceedings before summary conviction courts and justices under this Part in that province and, when the lieutenant governor in council so orders, he or she may fix any other fees and allowances for any items similar to those mentioned in the schedule, or any other items, to be taken or allowed instead.

1994, c. 44, s. 83; 1997, c. 18, s. 114.

Schedule

(Section 840)

FEES AND ALLOWANCES THAT MAY BE CHARGED BY SUMMARY CONVICTION COURTS AND JUSTICES

1.	Information	$1.00
2.	Summons or warrant	0.50
3.	Warrant where summons issued in first instance	0.30
4.	Each necessary copy of summons or warrant	0.30
5.	Each subpoena or warrant to or for witnesses	0.30
	(A subpoena may contain any number of names. Only one subpoena may be issued on behalf of a party in any proceeding, unless the summary conviction court or the justice considers it necessary or desirable that more than one subpoena be issued.)	
6.	Information for warrant for witness and warrant for witness	1.00
7.	Each necessary copy of subpoena to or warrant for witness	$0.20
8.	Each recognizance	1.00
9.	Hearing and determining proceeding	1.00
10.	Where hearing lasts more than two hours	2.00
11.	Where two or more justices hear and determine a proceeding, each is entitled to the fee authorized by item 9.	
12.	Each warrant of committal	0.50
13.	Making up record of conviction or order on request of a party to the proceedings	1.00
14.	Copy of a writing other than a conviction or order, on request of a party to the proceedings; for each folio of one hundred words	0.10
15.	Bill of costs, when made out in detail on request of a party to the proceedings	0.20
	(Items 14 and 15 may be charged only where there has been an adjudication.)	
16.	Attending to remand prisoner	1.00
17.	Attending to take recognizance of bail	1.00
18.	Arresting a person on a warrant or without a warrant	1.50
19.	Serving summons or subpoena	0.50
20.	Mileage to serve summons or subpoena or to make an arrest, both ways, for each mile	0.10
	(Where a public conveyance is not used, reasonable costs of transportation may be allowed.)	
21.	Mileage where service cannot be effected on proof of a diligent ,attempt to effect service, each way, for each mile	0.10

22.	Returning with prisoner after arrest to take him before a summary conviction court or justice at a place different from the place where the peace officer received the warrant to arrest, if the journey is of necessity over a route different from that taken by the peace officer to make the arrest, each way, for each mile	0.10
23.	Taking a prisoner to prison on remand or committal, each way, for each mile . . . . (Where a public conveyance is not used, reasonable costs of may be allowed. No charge may be made under this item in respect of a service for which a charge is made under item 22.)	0.10
24.	Attending summary conviction court or justice on summary conviction proceedings, for each day necessarily employed (No more than $2.00 may be charged under this item in respect of any day notwithstanding the number of proceedings that the peace officer attended on that day before that summary conviction court or justice.)	2.00
	FEES AND ALLOWANCES THAT MAY BE ALLOWED TO WITNESSES	
25.	Each day attending trial	$4.00
26.	Mileage travelled to attend trial, each way, for each mile . . .	0.10
	FEES AND ALLOWANCES THAT MAY BE ALLOWED TO INTERPRETERS	
27.	Each half day attending trial	$2.50
28.	Actual living expenses when away from ordinary place of residence, not to exceed per day	10.00
29.	Mileage travelled to attend trial, each way, for each mile . . .	0.10

PART XXVIII — FORMS

841. (1) Forms — The forms set out in this Part varied to suit the case or forms to the like effect shall be deemed to be good, valid and sufficient in the circumstances for which, respectively, they are provided.

(2) Seal not required — No justice is required to attach or affix a seal to any writing or process that he is authorized to issue and in respect of which a form is provided by this Part.

(3) Official languages — Any pre-printed portions of a form set out in this Part varied to suit the case or of a form to the like effect shall be printed in both official languages.

Form 1 — Information To Obtain A Search Warrant
(Section 487)

Canada,

           Province of ....,

           (*territorial division*).

This is the information of A.B., of ...., in the said (*territorial division*), (*occupation*), hereinafter called the informant, taken before me.

The informant says that (*describe things to be searched for and offence in respect of which search is to be made*), and that he believes on reasonable grounds that the said things, or some part of them, are in the (*dwelling-house, etc.*) of C.D., of ...., in the said (*territorial division*). (*Here add the grounds of belief, whatever they may be*).

Wherefore the informant prays that a search warrant may be granted to search the said (*dwelling-house, etc.*) for the said things.

Sworn before me

this .... day of

.........., A.D. ...., ...

at ....   (*Signature of Informant*)

....

A Justice of the Peace in and for

Form 2 — Information
(Section 506 and 788)

Canada,

           Province of ....,

           (*territorial division*).

This is the information of C.D., of ...., (*occupation*), hereinafter called the informant.

The informant says that (*if the informant has no personal knowledge state that he believes on reasonable grounds and state the offence*).

Sworn before me

this .... day of

.........., A.D. ...., ...

at ....   (*Signature of Informant*)

....

A Justice of the Peace in and for

Note: The date of birth of the accused may be mentioned on the information or indictment.

Form 3

Repealed R.S., c. 27 (1st Supp.), s. 184(2).

Form 4 — Heading of Indictment
(Sections 566, 566.1, 580 and 591)

Canada,
            Province of ....,
            (*territorial division*).

In the (*set out name of the court*) —

Her Majesty the Queen —

against —

(*name of accused*)

(*Name of accused*) stands charged

    1. That he (*state offence*).

    2. That he (*state offence*).

Dated this .... day of .... A.D. ...., at ....

. . . .
            *(Signature of signing officer, Agent
            of Attorney General, etc., as the
            case may be)*

1999, c. 3, s. 58.

Note: The date of birth of the accused may be mentioned on the information or indictment.

Form 5 — Warrant to Search
(Section 487)

Canada,
            Province of ....,
            (*territorial division*).

To the peace officers in the said (*territorial division*) or to the (*named public officers*):

Whereas it appears on the oath of A.B., of .... that there are reasonable grounds for believing that (*describe things to be searched for and offence in respect of which search is to be made*) are in .... at.......... , hereinafter called the premises;

This is, therefore, to authorize and require you between the hours of (*as the justice may direct*) to enter into the said premises and to search for the said things and to bring them before me or some other justice.

Dated this .... day of .... A.D. ...., at ....

. . . .
A Justice of the Peace in and for

. . . .
1999, c. 5, s. 45

Form 5.01 — Information to Obtain a Warrant to take Bodily Substances for Forensic DNA Analysis
(Subsection 487.05(1))

Canada,

Province of ....,

(*territorial division*)

This is the information of (*name of peace officer*), (*occupation*), of .... in the said (*territorial division*), hereinafter called the informant, taken before me.

The informant says that he or she has reasonable grounds to believe

(a) that (*offence*), a designated offence within the meaning of section 487.04 of the *Criminal Code*, has been committed;

(b) that a bodily substance has been found

(i) at the place where the offence was committed,

(ii) on or within the body of the victim of the offence,

(iii) on anything worn or carried by the victim at the time when the offence was committed, or

(iv) on or within the body of any person or thing or at any place associated with the commission of the offence;

(c) that (*name of person*) was a party to the offence; and

(d) that forensic DNA analysis of a bodily substance from (*name of person*) will provide evidence about whether the bodily substance referred to in paragraph (b) was from that person.

The reasonable grounds are:

The informant therefore requests that a warrant be issued authorizing the taking from (*name of person*) of the number of samples of bodily substances that are reasonably required for forensic DNA analysis, provided that the person taking the samples is able by virtue of training or experience to take them by means of the investigative procedures described in subsection 487.06(1) of the *Criminal Code* and provided that, if the person taking the samples is not a peace officer, he or she take the samples under the direction of a peace officer.

Sworn to before me

this ....day of.........,

A.D. ...., at ....

....

(*Signature of informant*)

....

(*Signature of provincial court judge*)

1998, c. 37, s. 24

Form 5.02 — Warrant Authorizing the Taking of Bodily Substances for Forensic DNA Analysis

(Subsection 487.05(1))

Canada,

Province of ....,

(*territorial division*)

To the peace officers in (*territorial division*):

Whereas it appears on the oath of (*name of peace officer*) of .... in the said (*territorial division*), that there are reasonable grounds to believe

(a) that (*offence*), a designated offence within the meaning of section 487.04 of the *Criminal Code*, has been committed,

(b) that a bodily substance has been found

(i) at the place where the offence was committed,

(ii) on or within the body of the victim of the offence,

(iii) on anything worn or carried by the victim at the time when the offence was committed, or

(iv) on or within the body of any person or thing or at any place associated with the commission of the offence,

(c) that (*name of person*) was a party to the offence, and

(d) that forensic DNA analysis of a bodily substance from (*name of person*) will provide evidence about whether the bodily substance referred to in paragraph (b) was from that person;

And whereas I am satisfied that it is in the best interests of the administration of justice to issue this warrant;

This is therefore to authorize and require you to take from (*name of person*) or cause to be taken by a person acting under your direction, the number of samples of bodily substances that are reasonably required for forensic DNA analysis, provided that the person taking the samples is able by virtue of training or experience to take them by means of the investigative procedures described in subsection 487.06(1) of the *Criminal Code* and provided that, if the person taking the samples is not a peace officer, he or she take the samples under the direction of a peace officer. This warrant is subject to the following terms and conditions that I consider advisable to ensure that the taking of the samples is reasonable in the circumstances:

Dated this ...... day of ....

A.D. ...., at ....

....

(*Signature of provincial court judge*)

1998, c. 37, s. 24

Form 5.03 — Order Authorizing the Taking of Bodily Substances for Forensic DNA Analysis

(Paragraph 487.05(1)(a))

Canada,

Province of ....,

(*territorial division*)

To the peace officers in (*territorial division*):

Whereas (*name of offender*) has been convicted, discharged under section 730 of the *Criminal Code* or, in the case of a young person, found guilty under the *Young Offenders Act* of (*offence*), an offence that is a primary designated offence within the meaning of section 487.04 of the *Criminal Code*.

Therefore, you are authorized to take from (*name of offender*) or cause to be taken by a person acting under your direction, the number of samples of bodily substances that are reasonably required for forensic DNA analysis, provided that the person taking the samples is able by virtue of training or experience to take them by means of the investigative procedures described in subsection 487.06(1) of the *Criminal Code* and provided that, if the person taking the samples is not a peace officer, he or she take the samples under the direction of a peace officer.

This order is subject to the following terms and conditions that I consider advisable to ensure that the taking of the samples is reasonable in the circumstances:

Dated this ...... day of ....

A.D. ...., at ....

....

(*Signature of judge of the court*)

1998, c. 37, s. 24

Form 5.04 — Order Authorizing the Taking of Bodily Substances for Forensic DNA Analysis

(Paragraph 487.05(1)(b) and subsection 487.052(1))

Canada,

Province of ....,

(*territorial division*)

To the peace officers in (*territorial division*):

Whereas (*name of offender*), in this order called the "offender", has been convicted, discharged under section 730 of the *Criminal Code* or, in the case of a young person, found guilty under the *Young Offenders Act* of (*offence*), an offence that is

    (a) a secondary designated offence within the meaning of section 487.04 of the *Criminal Code*, or

(b) a designated offence within the meaning of section 487.04 of the *Criminal Code* committed before subsection 5(1) of the *DNA Identification Act* came into force;

Whereas I have considered the offender's criminal record, the nature of the offence and the circumstances surrounding its commission and the impact that this order would have on the offender's privacy and security of the person;

And whereas I am satisfied that it is in the best interests of the administration of justice to make this order;

Therefore, you are authorized to take from (*name of offender*) or cause to be taken by a person acting under your direction, the number of samples of bodily substances that are reasonably required for forensic DNA analysis, provided that the person taking the samples is able by virtue of training or experience to take them by means of the investigative procedures described in subsection 487.06(1) of the *Criminal Code* and provided that, if the person taking the samples is not a peace officer, he or she take the samples under the direction of a peace officer.

This order is subject to the following terms and conditions that I consider advisable to ensure that the taking of the samples is reasonable in the circumstances:

Dated this ...... day of ....

A.D. ...., at ....

....

(*Signature of judge of the court*)

1998, c. 37, s. 24

Form 5.05 — Application for an Authorization to take Bodily Substances for Forensic DNA Analysis

(Subsection 487.055(1))

Canada,

Province of ....,

(*territorial division*)

I, (*name of peace officer*), (*occupation*), of .... in the said (*territorial division*), apply for an authorization to take bodily substances for forensic DNA analysis. A certificate referred to in paragraph 667(1)(a) of the *Criminal Code* is filed with this application.

Whereas (*name of offender*)

(a) before subsection 487.055(1) of the *Criminal Code* came into force, had been declared a dangerous offender under Part XXIV of that Act,

(b) before subsection 487.055(1) of the *Criminal Code* came into force, had been convicted of more than one murder committed at different times, or

(c) before subsection 487.055(1) of the *Criminal Code* came into force, had been convicted of more than one sexual offence within the meaning of subsection 487.055(3) of the *Criminal Code* and is currently serving a sentence of at least two years imprisonment for one or more of those offences;

And whereas I have considered the offender's criminal record, the nature of the offence and the circumstances surrounding its commission and the impact that this authorization would have on the offender's privacy and security of the person;

Therefore, I request that an authorization be granted under subsection 487.055(1) of the *Criminal Code* to take from (*name of offender*) the number of samples of bodily substances that is reasonably required for forensic DNA analysis, provided that the person taking the samples is able by virtue of training or experience to take them by means of the investigative procedures described in subsection 487.06(1) of the *Criminal Code* and provided that, if the person taking the samples is not a peace officer, he or she take the samples under the direction of a peace officer.

Dated this ...... day of ....

A.D. ...., at ....

....

(*Signature of applicant*)

1998, c. 37, s. 24

Form 5.06 — Authorization for the Taking of Bodily Substances for Forensic DNA Analysis
(Subsection 487.055(1))

Canada,

Province of ....,

(*territorial division*)

To the

peace officers in (*territorial division*):

Whereas (*name of offender*)

> (a) before subsection 487.055(1) of the *Criminal Code* came into force, had been declared a dangerous offender under Part XXIV of that Act,

> (b) before subsection 487.055(1) of the *Criminal Code* came into force, had been convicted of more than one murder committed at different times, or

> (c) before subsection 487.055(1) of the *Criminal Code* came into force, had been convicted of more than one sexual offence within the meaning of subsection 487.055(3) of the *Criminal Code* and is currently serving a sentence of at least two years imprisonment for one or more of those offences;

Whereas (*name of peace officer*), a peace officer of the said territorial division, has applied for an authorization for the taking of the number of samples of bodily substances from (*name of offender*) that is reasonably required for forensic DNA analysis by means of the investigative procedures described in subsection 487.06(1) of that Act;

And whereas I have considered the offender's criminal record, the nature of the offence and the circumstances surrounding its commission and the impact that this authorization would have on the offender's privacy and security of the person;

Therefore, the peace officers of the said territorial division, are authorized to take from (*name of offender*) or cause to be taken by a person acting under their direction those samples, provided that the person taking the samples is able by virtue of training or experience to take them by means of the investigative procedures described in subsection 487.06(1) of the *Criminal Code* and provided that, if the person taking the samples is not a peace officer, he or she take the samples under the direction of a peace officer.

This authorization is subject to the following terms and conditions that I consider advisable to ensure that the taking of the samples is reasonable in the circumstances:

Dated this ...... day of ....

A.D. ...., at ....

....

(*Signature of provincial court judge*)

1998, c. 37, s. 24

Form 5.07 — Report to a Provincial Court Judge or the Court

(Subsection 487.057(1))

Canada,

Province of ....,

(*territorial division*)

❏ To (*name of judge*), a judge of the provincial court who issued a warrant under section 487.05 or granted an authorization under section 487.055 or 487.091 of the *Criminal Code* or to another judge of that court:

❏ To the court from which an order under section 487.051 or 487.052 of the *Criminal Code* was made:

I, (*name of peace officer*), have (*state here whether you have acted in execution of a warrant under section 487.05 or an order under section 487.051 or 487.052, or under an authorization under section 487.055 or 487.091*) of the *Criminal Code*.

I have (*state here whether you have taken the samples yourself or caused them to be taken under your direction*) from (*name of offender*) the number of samples of bodily substances that I believe are reasonably required for forensic DNA analysis, in accordance with (*state whether the taking of the samples was under the warrant issued or an authorization granted by the judge or another judge of the court or an order made by the court.*)

The samples were taken at .... a.m./p.m. on the .... day of .... A.D. ......

I (*or state the name of the person who took the samples*) was able by virtue of training or experience to take the following samples from (*name of offender*) in accordance with subsection 487.06(1) of the *Criminal Code* and did so take them:

❏ individual hairs, including the root sheath

❏ epithelial cells taken by swabbing the lips, tongue or inside cheeks of the mouth

❏ blood taken by pricking the skin surface with a sterile lancet

Any terms or conditions in the (*warrant, order or authorization*) have been complied with.

Dated this ...... day of ....

A.D. ...., at ....

....

(*Signature of peace officer*)

1998, c. 37, s. 24

Form 5.08 — Application for an Authorization for Taking Additional Samples of Bodily Substances for Forensic DNA Analysis

(Subsection 487.091(1))

Canada,

Province of ....,

(*territorial division*)

I, (*name of peace officer*), (*occupation*), of .... in the said (*territorial division*), apply for an authorization to take additional samples of bodily substances for forensic DNA analysis.

Whereas samples of bodily substances were taken from (*name of offender*) for the purpose of forensic DNA analysis, in execution of an order made under section 487.051 or 487.052 of the *Criminal Code* or an authorization granted under section 487.055 of the *Criminal Code* (*attach a copy of the order or authorization*);

And whereas on (*day/month/year*) it was determined that a DNA profile could not be derived from the samples for the following reasons:

Therefore, I request that an authorization be granted under subsection 487.091(1) of the *Criminal Code* to take from (*name of offender*) the number of additional samples of bodily substances that is reasonably required for forensic DNA analysis, provided that the person taking the samples is able by virtue of training or experience to take them by means of the investigative procedures described in subsection 487.06(1) of the *Criminal Code* and provided that, if the person taking the samples is not a peace officer, he or she take the samples under the direction of a peace officer.

Dated this ...... day of ....

A.D. ...., at ....

....

(*Signature of applicant*)

1998, c. 37, s. 24

Form 5.09 — Authorization for the Taking of Additional Samples of Bodily Substances for Forensic DNA Analysis

(Subsection 487.091(1))

Canada,

Province of ....,

(*territorial division*)

To the peace officers in (*territorial division*):

Whereas samples of bodily substances were taken from (*name of offender*) for the purpose of forensic DNA analysis, in execution of an order made under section 487.051 or 487.052 of the *Criminal Code* or an authorization granted under section 487.055 of the *Criminal Code*;

Whereas on (*day/month/year*) it was determined that a DNA profile could not be derived from the samples for the following reasons:

And whereas (*name of peace officer*), a peace officer of the said territorial division, has applied for an authorization for the taking of the number of additional samples of bodily substances from (*name of offender*) that is reasonably required for forensic DNA analysis by means of the investigative procedures described in subsection 487.06(1) of that Act;

Therefore, the peace officers of the said territorial division, are authorized to take from (*name of offender*) or cause to be taken by a person acting under their direction those additional samples, provided that the person taking the samples is able by virtue of training or experience to take them by means of the investigative procedures described in subsection 487.06(1) of the *Criminal Code* and provided that, if the person taking the samples is not a peace officer, he or she take the samples under the direction of a peace officer.

This authorization is subject to the following terms and conditions that I consider advisable to ensure that the taking of the samples is reasonable in the circumstances:

Dated this ...... day of ....

A.D. ...., at ....

....

(*Signature of provincial court judge*)

1998, c. 37, s. 24

Form 5.1 — Warrant To Search

(Section 487.1)

Canada,

Province of ....,

(*territorial division*).

To A.B. and other peace officers in the (*territorial division in which the warrant is intended for execution*):

Whereas it appears on the oath of A.B., a peace officer in the (*territorial division in which the warrant is intended for execution*), that there are reasonable grounds for dispensing with an information presented personally and in writing; and that there are reasonable grounds for believing that the following things

    (*describe things to be searched for*)

relevant to the investigation of the following indictable offence

    (*describe offence in respect of which search is to be made*)

are to be found in the following place or premises

    (*describe place or premises to be searched*):

This is, therefore, to authorize you to enter the said place or premises between the hours of (*as the justice may direct*) and to search for and seize the said things and to report thereon as soon as practicable but within a period not exceeding seven days after the execution of the warrant to the clerk of the court for the (*territorial division in which the warrant is intended for execution*).

Issued at (*time*) on the (*day*) of (*month*) A.D. (*year*), at (*place*).

....

A Judge of the Provincial Court in and for the Province of (*specify province*).

To the Occupant: This search warrant was issued by telephone or other means of telecommunication. If you wish to know the basis on which this warrant was issued, you may apply to the clerk of the court for the territorial division in which the warrant was executed, at *address*, to obtain a copy of the information on oath.

You may obtain from the clerk of the court a copy of the report filed by the peace officer who executed this warrant. That report will indicate the things, if any, that were seized and the location where they are being held.

Form 5.2 — Report To A Justice
Section 489.1

Canada

    Province of ....,

    (*territorial division*)

.

To the justice who issued a warrant to the undersigned pursuant to section 256, 487 or 487.1 of the *Criminal Code* (*or another justice for the same territorial division or, if no warrant was issued, any justice having jurisdiction in respect of the matter*).

I, (*name of the peace officer or other person*) have (*state here whether you have acted under a warrant issued pursuant to section 256, 487 or 487.1 of the Criminal Code or under section 489 of the Code or otherwise in the execution of duties under the Criminal Code or another Act of Parliament to be specified*)

1. searched the premises situated at ....; and

2. seized the following things and dealt with them as follows:

Property Seized *(describe (each thing (seized)*	Disposition *(state, in respect of each thing (seized, whether*
	(a) it was returned to the person lawfully entitled to its possession, in which case the receipt therefor shall be attached hereto, or
	(b) it is being detained to be dealt with according to law, and the location and manne in which, or where applicable, the person by whom it is being detained).

1. . . . .
2. . . . .
3. . . . .
4. . . . .

In the case of a warrant issued by telephone or other means of telecommunication, the statements referred to in subsection 487.1(9) of the *Criminal Code* shall be specified in the report.

Dated this . . . . day of . . . . A.D. . . . ., at . . . .

. . . .
Signature of peace
officer or other
person
R.S. 1985, c.27(1st Supp.), s.184(3).

Form 5.3 — Report To A Judge of Property Seized

(Section 462.32)

Canada
        Province of . . . .,
        (territorial division)

To a judge of the court from which the warrant was issued *(specify court)*:

I, *(name of the peace officer or other person)* have acted under a warrant issued under section 462.32 of the *Criminal Code* and have

        1. searched the premises situated at . . . .; and

        2. seized the following property:

Property Seized	Location

(*describe*	(*state, in respect of each*
each item	*item of property seized,*
of proper-	*the location where it is*
ty	
seized)	*being detained*).

1. . . . .
2. . . . .
3. . . . .
4. . . . .

Dated this .... day of .... A.D. . . . . at
....

. . . .
Signature of peace
officer or other
person
R.S. 1985, c. 42 (4th Supp.), s. 6.

Form 6 — Summons to a Person Charged With an Offence

(Sections 493, 508 and 512)

Canada,

Province of ....,
(*territorial division*).

To A.B., of ...., (*occupation*):

Whereas you have this day been charged before me that (*set out briefly the offence in respect of which the accused is charged*);

This is therefore to command you, in Her Majesty's name:

(a) to attend court on ...., the .... day of .... A.D. ...., at ....
o'clock in the .... noon, at .... or before any justice for the said (*territorial division*) who is there, and to attend thereafter as required by the court, in order to be dealt with according to law; and

(b) to appear on ...., the .... day of .... A.D........... , at ....
o'clock in the .... noon, at ...., for the purposes of the *Identification of Criminals Act*. (*Ignore, if not filled in*).

You are warned that failure without lawful excuse to attend court in accordance with this summons is an offence under subsection 145(4) of the *Criminal Code*.

Section 145(4) of the *Criminal Code* states as follows:

> (4) Every one who is served with a summons and who fails, without lawful excuse, the proof of which lies on him, to appear at a time and place stated therein, if any, for the purposes of the *Identification of Criminals Act* or to attend court in accordance therewith, is guilty of
>
>> (a) an indictable offence and is liable to imprisonment for a term not exceeding two years; or
>>
>> (b) an offence punishable on summary conviction.

Section 510 of the *Criminal Code* states as follows:

> 510. Where an accused who is required by a summons to appear at a time and place stated therein for the purposes of the *Identification of Criminals Act* does not appear at that time and place, a justice may issue a warrant for the arrest of the accused for the offence with which he is charged.

Dated this .... day of .... A.D. ...., at ....

. . . .
A Justice of the Peace in
and for .... *or* Judge
R.S. 1985, c. 27 (1st Supp.), s. 184(4).

Form 7 — Warrant for Arrest

(Sections 475, 493, 597, 800 and 803)

Canada,

Province of ....,
(*territorial division*).

To the peace officers in the said (*territorial division*):

This warrant is issued for the arrest of A.B., of ...., (*occupation*), hereinafter called the accused.

Whereas the accused has been charged that (*set out briefly the offence in respect of which the accused is charged*);

And whereas:*

(a) there are reasonable grounds to believe that it is necessary in the public interest to issue this warrant for the arrest of the accused [507(4), 512(1)];

(b) the accused failed to attend court in accordance with the summons served on him [512(2)];

(c) (an appearance notice *or* a promise to appear *or* a recognizance entered into before an officer in charge) was confirmed and the accused failed to attend court in accordance therewith [512(2)];

(d) it appears that a summons cannot be served because the accused is evading service [512(2)];

(e) the accused was ordered to be present at the hearing of an application for a review of an order made by a justice and did not attend the hearing [520(5), 521(5)];

(f) there are reasonable grounds to believe that the accused has contravened or is about to contravene the (promise to appear *or* undertaking *or* recognizance) on which he was released [524(1), 525(5), 679(6)];

(g) there are reasonable grounds to believe that the accused has since his release from custody on (a promise to appear *or* an undertaking *or* a recognizance) committed an indictable offence [524(1), 525(5), 679(6)];

(h) the accused was required by (an appearance notice *or* a promise to appear *or* a recognizance entered into before an officer in charge *or* a summons) to attend at a time and place stated therein for the purposes of the *Identification of Criminals Act* and did not appear at that time and place [502, 510];

(i) an indictment has been found against the accused and the accused has not appeared or remained in attendance before the court for his trial [597];

(j)**

This is, therefore, to command you, in Her Majesty's name, forthwith to arrest the said accused and to bring him before (*state court, judge or justice*), to be dealt with according to law.

(*Add where applicable*) Whereas there are reasonable grounds to believe that the accused is or will be present in (*here describe dwelling-house*);

This warrant is also issued to authorize you to enter the dwelling-house for the purpose of arresting or apprehending the accused, subject to the condition that you may not enter the dwelling-house unless you have, immediately before entering the dwelling-house, reasonable grounds to believe that the person to be arrested or apprehended is present in the dwelling-house.

Dated this .... day of .... A.D. ...., at ....

. . . .

Judge, Clerk of the Court,
Provincial Court Judge *or* Justice

_____

*Initial applicable recital.

**For any case not covered by recitals (a) to (i), insert recital in the words of the statute authorizing the warrant.

1999, c. 5, s. 46

Form 7.1 — Warrant to Enter Dwelling-House

(Section 529.1)

Canada,

Province of ....,
(*territorial division*).

To the peace officers in the said (*territorial division*):

This warrant is issued in respect of the arrest of A.B., or a person with the following description ( ), of ...., (*occupation*).

Whereas there are reasonable grounds to believe:[*]

    (a) a warrant referred to in this or any other Act of Parliament to arrest or apprehend the person is in force anywhere in Canada;

    (b) grounds exist to arrest the person without warrant under paragraph 495(1)(a) or (b) of the *Criminal Code*; or

    (c) grounds exist to arrest or apprehend without warrant the person under an Act of Parliament, other than this Act;

And whereas there are reasonable grounds to believe that the person is or will be present in (*here describe dwelling-house*);

This warrant is issued to authorize you to enter the dwelling-house for the purpose of arresting or apprehending the person.

Dated this .... day of .... A.D. ...., at ....

                 . . . .

                 Judge, Clerk of the Court,
                 Provincial Court Judge or Justice

---

[*]*Initial applicable recital.*

1997, c. 39, s. 3.

Form 8 — **Warrant for Committal**

(Sections 493 and 515)

Canada,

           Province of ....,
           (*territorial division*).

To the peace officers in the said (*territorial division*) and to the keeper of the (*prison*) at ....:

This warrant is issued for the committal of A.B., of ...., (*occupation*), hereinafter called the accused.

Whereas the accused has been charged that (*set out briefly the offence in respect of which the accused is charged*);

And whereas:[*]

    (a) the prosecutor has shown cause why the detention of the accused in custody is justified [515(5)];

    (b) an order has been made that the accused be released on (giving an undertaking *or* entering into a recognizance) but the accused has not yet complied with the order [519(1), 520(9), 524(12), 525(8)];[**]

    (c) the application by the prosecutor for a review of the order of a justice in respect of the interim release of the accused has been allowed and that order has been vacated, and the prosecutor has shown cause why the detention of the accused in custody is justified [521];

(d) the accused has contravened or was about to contravene his (promise to appear *or* undertaking *or* recognizance) and the same was cancelled, and the detention of the accused in custody is justified or seems proper in the circumstances [524(4), 524(8)];

(e) there are reasonable and probable grounds to believe that the accused has after his release from custody on (a promise to appear *or* an undertaking *or* a recognizance) committed an indictable offence and the detention of the accused in custody is justified or seems proper in the circumstances [524(4), 524(8)];

(f) the accused has contravened or was about to contravene the (undertaking *or* recognizance) on which he was released and the detention of the accused in custody seems proper in the circumstances [525(7), 679(6)];

(g) there are reasonable grounds to believe that the accused has after his release from custody on (an undertaking *or* a recognizance) committed an indictable offence and the detention of the accused in custody seems proper in the circumstances [525(7), 679(6)];

(h)***

This is, therefore, to command you, in Her Majesty's name, to arrest, if necessary, and take the accused and convey him safely to the (*prison*) at ...., and there deliver him to the keeper thereof, with the following precept:

I do hereby command you the said keeper to receive the accused in your custody in the said prison and keep him safely there until he is delivered by due course of law.

Dated this .... day of .... A.D. ...., at ....

....
Judge, Clerk of the Court,
Provincial Court Judge *or* Justice

---

*Initial applicable recital.

**If the person having custody of the accused is authorized under paragraph 519(1)(b) to release him upon his complying with an order, endorse the authorization on this warrant and attach a copy of the order.

***For any case not covered by recitals (a) to (g), insert recital in the words of the statute authorizing the warrant.

Form 9 — Appearance Notice Issued By a Peace Officer to a Person Not Yet Charged With an Offence

(Section 493)

Canada,

       Province of ....,
       (*territorial division*).

To A.B., of ...., (*occupation*):

You are alleged to have committed (*set out substance of offence*).

1. You are required to attend court on .... day, the .... day of .... A.D. ...., at .... o'clock in the .... noon, in courtroom No. ...., at .... court, in the municipality of.........., and to attend thereafter as required by the court, in order to be dealt with according to law.

2. You are also required to appear on .... day, the .... day of.......... A.D. ...., at .... o'clock in the .... noon, at (*police station*), (*address*), for the purposes of the *Identification of Criminals Act*. (*Ignore, if not filled in*).

You are warned that failure to attend court in accordance with this appearance notice is an offence under subsection 145(5) of the *Criminal Code*.

Section 145(5) and (6) of the *Criminal Code* state as follows:

"

(5) Every person who is named in an appearance notice or promise to appear, or in a recognizance entered into before an officer in charge, that has been confirmed by a justice under section 508 and who fails, without lawful excuse, the proof of which lies on the person, to appear at a time and place stated therein, if any, for the purposes of the *Identification of Criminals Act* or to attend court in accordance therewith, is guilty of

    (a) an indictable offence and is liable to imprisonment for a term not exceeding two years; or

    (b) an offence punishable on summary conviction.

(6) For the purposes of subsection (5), it is not a lawful excuse that an appearance notice, promise to appear or recognizance states defectively the substance of the alleged offence."

Section 502 of the *Criminal Code* states as follows:

"

502. Where an accused who is required by an appearance notice or promise to appear or by a recognizance entered into before an officer in charge or another peace officer to appear at a time and place stated therein for the purposes of the *Identification of Criminals Act* does not appear at that time and place, a justice may, where the appearance notice, promise to appear or recognizance has been confirmed by a justice under section 508, issue a warrant for the arrest of the accused for the offence with which the accused is charged."

Issued at .... a.m./p.m. this .... day of .... A.D............ , at ....

         . . . .
         (*Signature of peace officer*)

         . . . .
         (*Signature of accused*)

                          1997, c. 18, s. 115.

Form 10 — Promise to Appear

(Section 493)

Canada,

        Province of ....,
        (*territorial division*).

I, A.B., of ...., (*occupation*), understand that it is alleged that I have committed (*set out substance of offence*).

In order that I may be released from custody,

1. I promise to attend court on .... day, the .... day of.......... A.D. ...., at .... o'clock in the .... noon, in courtroom No. ...., at court, in the municipality of ...., and to attend thereafter as required by the court, in order to be dealt with according to law.

2. I also promise to appear on .... day, the .... day of.......... A.D. ...., at .... o'clock in the .... noon, at (*police station*), (*address*), for the purposes of the *Identification of Criminals Act*. (*Ignore if not filled in*).

I understand that failure without lawful excuse to attend court in accordance with this promise to appear is an offence under subsection 145(5) of the *Criminal Code*.

Subsections 145(5) and (6) of the *Criminal Code* state as follows:

"

(5) Every one who is named in an appearance notice or promise to appear, or in a recognizance entered into before an officer in charge, or another peace officer, that has been confirmed by a justice under section 508 and who fails, without lawful excuse, the proof of which lies on the person, to appear at a time and place stated therein, if any, for the purposes of the *Identification of Criminals Act* or to attend court in accordance therewith, is guilty of

(a) an indictable offence and is liable to imprisonment for a term not exceeding two years; or

(b) an offence punishable on summary conviction.

(6) For the purposes of subsection (5), it is not a lawful excuse that an appearance notice, promise to appear or recognizance states defectively the substance of the alleged offence."

Section 502 of the *Criminal Code* states as follows:

"

502. Where an accused who is required by an appearance notice or promise to appear or by a recognizance entered into before an officer in charge or another peace officer to appear at a time and place stated therein for the purposes of the *Identification of Criminals Act* does not appear at that time and place, a justice may, where the appearance notice, promise to appear or recognizance has been confirmed by a justice under section 508, issue a warrant for the arrest of the accused for the offence with which the accused is charged."

Dated this .... day of .... A.D. ...., at ....

. . . .
(Signature of accused)

1997, c. 18, s. 115.

Form 11 — Recognizance Entered Into Before an Officer in Charge or Other Peace Officer

(Section 493)

Canada,

Province of ....,
(*territorial division*).

I, A.B., of ...., (*occupation*), understand that it is alleged that I have committed (*set out substance of offence*).

In order that I may be released from custody, I hereby acknowledge that I owe $ (*not exceeding $500*) to Her Majesty the Queen to be levied on my real and personal property if I fail to attend court as hereinafter required. (*or, for a person not ordinarily resident in the province in which the person is in custody or within two hundred kilometers of the place in which the person is in custody*)

In order that I may be released from custody, I hereby acknowledge that I owe $ (*not exceeding $500*) to Her Majesty the Queen and deposit herewith (*money or other valuable security not exceeding in amount or value $500*) to be forfeited if I fail to attend court as hereinafter required.

1. I acknowledge that I am required to attend court on .... day, the.......... day of .... A.D. ...., at .... o'clock in the.......... noon, in courtroom No. ...., at .... court, in the municipality of ...., and to attend thereafter as required by the court, in order to be dealt with according to law.

2. I acknowledge that I am also required to appear on .... day, the.......... day of .... A.D. ...., at .... o'clock in the.......... noon, at (*police station*), (*address*), for the purposes of the *Identification of Criminals Act*. (*Ignore if not filled in*).

I understand that failure without lawful excuse to attend court in accordance with this recognizance to appear is an offence under subsection 145(5) of the *Criminal Code*.

Section 145(5) and (6) of the *Criminal Code* state as follows:

"

(5) Every person who is named in an appearance notice or promise to appear, or in a recognizance entered into before an officer in charge or another peace officer, that has been confirmed by a justice under section 508 and who fails, without lawful excuse, the proof of which lies on the person, to appear at a time and place stated therein, if any, for the purposes of the *Identification of Criminals Act* or to attend court in accordance therewith, is guilty of

(a) an indictable offence and is liable to imprisonment for a term not exceeding two years; or

(b) an offence punishable on summary conviction.

(6) For the purposes of subsection (5), it is not a lawful excuse that an appearance notice, promise to appear or recognizance states defectively the substance of the alleged offence."

Section 502 of the *Criminal Code* states as follows:

"

502. Where an accused who is required by an appearance notice or promise to appear or by a recognizance entered into before an officer in charge or another peace officer to appear at a time and place stated therein for the purposes of the *Identification of Criminals Act* does not appear at that time and place, a justice may, where the appearance notice, promise to appear or recognizance has been confirmed by a justice under section 508, issue a warrant for the arrest of the accused for the offence with which he is charged."

Dated this .... day of .... A.D. ...., at ....

. . . .
(Signature of accused)

1997, c. 18, s. 115.

Form 11.1 — Undertaking Given to a Peace Officer or an Officer in Charge

(Sections 493, 499 and 503)

Canada,

Province of ....,

(territorial division).

I, A.B., of ...., *(occupation)*, understand that it is alleged that I have committed *(set out substance of the offence)*.

In order that I may be released from custody by way of (a promise to appear *or* a recognizance entered into before an officer in charge), I undertake to *(insert any conditions that are directed)*:

(a) remain within *(designated territorial jurisdiction)*;

(b) notify *(name of peace officer or other person designated)* of any change in my address, employment or occupation;

(c) abstain from communicating, directly or indirectly, with *(identification of victim, witness or other person)* or from going to *(name or description of place)* except in accordance with the following conditions: *(as the peace officer or other person designated specifies)*;

(d) deposit my passport with *(name of peace officer or other person designated)*;

(e) to abstain from possession a firearm and to surrender to *(name of peace officer or other person designated)* any firearm in my possession and any authorization, license or registration certificate or other document enabling the acquisition or possession of a firearm;

(f) report at *(state times)* to *(name of peace officer or other person designated)*;

(g) to abstain from

(i) the consumption of alcohol or other intoxicating substances, or

(ii) the consumption of drugs except in accordance with a medical prescription; and

(h) comply with any other conditions that the peace officer or officer in charge considers necessary to ensure the safety and security of any victim of or witness to the offence.

I understand that I am not required to give an undertaking to abide by the conditions specified above, but that if I do not, I may be kept in custody and brought before a justice so that the prosecutor may be given a reasonable opportunity to show cause why I should not be released on giving an undertaking without conditions.

I understand that if I give an undertaking to abide by the conditions specified above, then I may apply, at any time before I appear, or when I appear, before a justice pursuant to (a promise to appear *or* a recognizance entered into before an officer in charge or another peace officer), to have this undertaking vacated or varied and that my application will be considered as if I were before a justice pursuant to section 515 of the *Criminal Code*.

I also understand that this undertaking remains in effect until it is vacated or varied.

I also understand that failure without lawful excuse to abide by any of the conditions specified above is an offence under subsection 145(5.1) of the *Criminal Code*.

"

> (5.1) Every person who, without lawful excuse, the proof of which lies on the person, fails to comply with any condition of an undertaking entered into pursuant to subsection 499(2) or 503(2.1)
>
> > (a) is guilty of an indictable offence and is liable to imprisonment for a term not exceeding two years; or
> >
> > (b) is guilty of an offence punishable on summary conviction."

Dated this .... day of .... A.D. ...., at ....

. . . .
(Signature of accused)
1997, c. 18, s. 115; 1999, c. 25, s. 24

Form 12 — Undertaking Given to a Justice or a Judge

(Sections 493 and 679)

Canada,

Province of ....,

(territorial division).

I, A.B., of ...., *(occupation)*, understand that I have been charged that (*set out briefly the offence in respect of which accused is charged*).

In order that I may be released from custody, I undertake to attend court on .... day, the .... day of .... A.D. ...., and to attend thereafter as required by the court in order to be dealt with according to law (*or, where date and place of appearance before court are not known at the time undertaking is given*, to attend at the time and place fixed by the court and thereafter as required by the court in order to be dealt with according to law). (*and where applicable*)

I also undertake to (*insert any conditions that are directed*)

(a) report at (*state times*) to (*name of peace officer or other person designated*);

(b) remain within (*designated territorial jurisdiction*);

(c) notify (*name of peace officer or other person designated*) of any change in my address, employment or occupation;

(d) abstain from communicating, directly or indirectly, with (*identification of victim, witness or other person*) except in accordance with the following conditions: (*as the justice or judge specifies*);

(e) deposit my passport (*as the justice or judge directs*); and

(f) (*any other reasonable conditions*).

I understand that failure without lawful excuse to attend court in accordance with this undertaking is an offence under subsection 145(2) of the *Criminal Code*.

Subsection 145(2) and (3) of the *Criminal Code* state as follows:

> (2) Every one who,
>
>> (a) being at large on his undertaking or recognizance given to or entered into before a justice or judge, fails, without lawful excuse, the proof of which lies on him, to attend court in accordance with the undertaking or recognizance, or
>>
>> (b) having appeared before a court, justice or judge, fails, without lawful excuse, the proof of which lies on him, to attend court as thereafter required by the court, justice or judge,
>
> or to surrender himself in accordance with an order of the court, justice or judge, as the case may be, is guilty of an indictable offence and liable to imprisonment for a term not exceeding two years or is guilty of an offence punishable on summary conviction.
>
> (3) Every person who is at large on an undertaking or recognizance given to or entered into before a justice or judge and is bound to comply with a condition of that undertaking or recognizance directed by a justice or judge, and every person who is bound to comply with a direction ordered under subsection 515(12) or 522(2.1), and who fails, without lawful excuse, the proof of which lies on that person, to comply with that condition or direction, is guilty of
>
>> (a) an indictable offence and is liable to imprisonment for a term not exceeding two years; or
>>
>> (b) an offence punishable on summary conviction.

Dated this .... day of .... A.D. ...., at ....)

. . . .
(Signature of appellant)

1999, c. 25, s. 25

Form 13 — Undertaking By Appellant (Defendant)

(Sections 816, 832 and 834)

Canada,

Province of ....,
(*territorial division*).

I, A.B., of ...., (*occupation*), being the appellant against conviction (*or against sentence or against an order or by way of stated case*) in respect of the following matter (*set out the offence, subject-matter of order or question of law*) undertake to appear personally at the sittings of the appeal court at which the appeal is to be heard. (*and where applicable*)

I also undertake to (*insert any conditions that are directed*)

(a) report at (*state times*) to (*name of peace officer or other person designated*);

(b) remain within (*designated territorial jurisdiction*);

(c) notify (*name of peace officer or other person designated*) of any change in my address, employment or occupation;

(d) abstain from communicating, directly or indirectly, with (*identification of victim, witness or other person*) except in accordance with the following conditions: (*as the justice or judge specifies*);

(e) deposit my passport (*as the justice or judge directs*); and

(f) (*any other reasonable conditions*).

Dated this .... day of .... A.D ...., at ....

. . . .
(Signature of appellant)

1999, c. 25, s. 26

Form 14 — Undertaking by Appellant (Prosecutor)
(Section 817)

Canada,

                    Province of ....,
                    (*territorial division*).

I, A.B., of ...., (*occupation*), being the appellant against an order of dismissal (*or against sentence*) in respect of the following charge (*set out the name of the defendant and the offence, subject-matter of order or question of law*) undertake to appear personally or by counsel at the sittings of the appeal court at which the appeal is to be heard.

Dated this .... day of .... A.D ...., at ....

....
(Signature of appellant)

Form 15 — Warrant to Convey Accused Before Justice Of Another Territorial Division
(Section 543)

Canada,

                    Province of ....,
                    (*territorial division*).

To the peace officers in the said (*territorial division*):

Whereas A.B., of .... hereinafter called the accused, has been charged that (*state place of offence and charge*);

And Whereas I have taken the deposition of X.Y. in respect of the said charge;

And Whereas the charge is for an offence committted in the (*territorial division*);

This is to command you, in Her Majesty's name, to convey the said A.B., before a justice of the (*last mentioned territorial division*).

Dated this .... day of .... A.D. ...., at ....

. . . .
A Justice of the Peace in and for

. . . .

Form 16 — Subpoena to a Witness
(Section 699)

Canada,

Province of ....,
(*territorial division*).

To E.F., of ...., (*occupation*);

Whereas A.B. has been charged that (*state offence as in the information*), and it has been made to appear that you are likely to give material evidence for (the prosecution *or* the defence);

This is therefore to command you to attend before (*set out court or justice*), on .... the .... day of .... A.D. ...., at.......... o'clock in the .... noon at .... to give evidence concerning the said charge.*

**Where a witness is required to produce anything, add the following:*

and to bring with you anything in your possession or under your control that relates to the said charge, and more particularly the following: (*specify any documents, objects or other things required*).

Dated this .... day of .... A.D. ...., at ....

....
A Judge, Justice *or* Clerk of the court

(*Seal if required*) ....

1999, c. 5, s. 47

Form 16.1 — Subpoena to a witness in the case of proceedings in respect of an offence referred to in s. 278.2(1) of the Criminal Code
(Subsections 278.3(5) and 699(7))

Canada,

Province of ....,
(*territorial division*).

To E.F., of ...., (*occupation*);

Whereas A.B. has been charged that (*state offence as in the information*), and it has been made to appear that you are likely to give material evidence for (the prosecution *or* the defence);

This is therefore to command you to attend before (*set out court or justice*), on .... the .... day of .... A.D. ...., at.......... o'clock in the .... noon at .... to give evidence concerning the said charge, and to bring with you anything in your possession or under your control that relates to the said charge, and more particularly the following: (*specify any documents, objects or other things required*).

Dated this .... day of .... A.D. ...., at ....

Take Note

You are only required to bring the things specified above to the court on the date and at the time indicated, and you are not required to provide the things specified to any person or to discuss their contents with any person unless and until ordered by the court to do so.

If anything specified above is a "record" as defined in section 278.1 of the *Criminal Code*, it may be subject to a determination by the court in accordance with sections 278.1 to 278.91 of the *Criminal Code* as to whether and to what extent it should be produced.

If anything specified above is a "record" as defined in section 278.1 of the *Criminal Code*, the production of which is governed by sections 278.1 to 278.91 of the *Criminal Code*, this subpoena must be accompanied by a copy of an application for the production of the record made pursuant to section 278.3 of the *Criminal Code*, and you will have an opportunity to make submissions to the court concerning the production of the record.

If anything specified above is a "record" as defined in section 278.1 of the *Criminal Code*, the production of which is governed by sections 278.1 to 278.91 of the *Criminal Code*, you are not required to bring it with you until a determination is made in accordance with those sections as to whether and to what extent it should be produced.

As defined in section 278.1 of the *Criminal Code*, "record" means any form of record that contains personal information for which there is a reasonable expectation of privacy and includes, without limiting the generality of the foregoing, medical, psychiatric, therapeutic, counselling, education, employment, child welfare, adoption and social services records, personal journals and diaries, and records containing personal information the production or disclosure of which is protected by any other Act of Parliament or a provincial legislature, but does not include records made by persons responsible for the investigation or prosecution of the offence.

. . . .
Judge, Clerk of the Court
Provincial Court Judge *or*Justice

(Seal if required)   . . . .

3.1 (1) **Review after three years** — On the expiration of three years after the coming into force of this Act, the provisions contained herein shall be referred to such committee of the House of Commons, of the Senate or of both Houses of Parliament as may be designated or established by Parliament for that purpose.

(2) **Report** — The committee designated or established by Parliament for the purpose of subsection (1) shall, as soon as practicable, undertake a comprehensive review of the provisions and operation of this Act and shall, within one year after the review is undertaken or within such further time as the House of Commons may authorize, submit a report to Parliament thereon including such recommendations pertaining to the continuation of those sections and changes required therein as the committee may wish to make.

1997, c. 30, s. 3.

Form 17 — Warrant for Witness
(Sections 698 and 705)

Canada,

Province of ....,
(*territorial division*).

To the peace officers in the (*territorial division*):

Whereas A.B. of ...., has been charged that (*state offence as in the information*);

And Whereas it has been made to appear that E.F. of .... hereinafter called the witness, is likely to give material evidence for (the prosecution *or* the defence) and that*

Insert whichever of the following is appropriate:

  (a) the said E.F. will not attend unless compelled to do so;

  (b) the said E.F. is evading service of a subpoena;

  (c) the said E.F. was duly served with a subpoena and has neglected (to attend at the time and place appointed therein *or* to remain in attendance);

  (d) the said E.F. was bound by a recognizance to attend and give evidence and has neglected (to attend *or* to remain in attendance).

This is therefore to command you, in Her Majesty's name, to arrest and bring the witness forthwith before (*set out court or justice*) to be dealt with in accordance with section 706 of the *Criminal Code*.

Dated this .... day of .... A.D. ...., at ....

....
A Justice*or* Clerk of the Court

Form 18 — Warrant to Arrest an Absconding Witness

(Section 704)

Canada,

                    Province of ....,
                    (*territorial division*).

To the peace officers in the (*territorial division*):

Whereas A.B., of .... has been charged that (*state offence as in the information*);

And Whereas I am satisfied by information in writing and under oath that C.D., of ...., hereinafter called the witness, is bound by recognizance to give evidence on the trial of the accused on the said charge, and that the witness (has absconded *or* is about to abscond):

This is therefore to command you, in Her Majesty's name, to arrest the witness and bring him forthwith before (*the court, judge, justice or provincial court judge before whom the witness is bound to appear*) to be dealt with in accordance with section 706 of the *Criminal Code*.

Dated this .... day of .... A.D. ...., at ....

....
A Justice of the Peace in and for

....
A Justice of the Peace in and for

....

R.S. 1985, c. 27(1st Supp.), s.
184(9).

Form 19 — Warrant Remanding a Prisoner

(Sections 516 and 537)

Canada,

Province of ....,

(*territorial division*).

To the peace officers in the (*territorial division*):

You are hereby commanded forthwith to arrest, if necessary, and convey to the (*prison*) at .... the persons named in the following schedule each of whom has been remanded to the time mentioned in the schedule:

Person charged   Offence   Remanded to

And I hereby command you, the keeper of the said prison, to receive each of the said persons into your custody in the prison and keep him safely until the day when his remand expires and then to have him before me or any other justice at .... at .... o'clock in the .... noon of the said day, there to answer to the charge and to be dealt with according to law, unless you are otherwise ordered before that time.

Dated this .... day of .... A.D. ...., at ....

. . . .

A Justice of the Peace in and for

. . . .

R.S. 1985, c. 27(1st Supp.), s.
184(9).

Form 20 — Warrant of Committal of Witness for Refusing to be Sworn or to Give Evidence

(Section 545)

Canada,

Province of ....,

(*territorial division*).

To the peace officers in the (*territorial division*):

Whereas A.B. of .... , hereinafter called the accused, has been charged that (*set out offence as in the information*);

And Whereas E.F. .... , hereinafter called the witness, attending before me to give evidence for (the prosecution *or* the defence) concerning the charge against the accused (refused to be sworn *or* being duly sworn as a witness refused to answer certain questions concerning the charge that were put to him *or* refused or neglected to produce the following writings, namely .... *or* refused to sign his deposition)

591

having been ordered to do so, without offering any just excuse for such refusal or neglect;

This is therefore to command you, in Her Majesty's name, to arrest, if necessary, and take the witness and convey him safely to the prison at.......... , and there deliver him to the keeper thereof, together with the following precept:

I do hereby command you, the said keeper, to receive the said witness into your custody in the said prison and safely keep him there for the term of .... days, unless he sooner consents to do what was required of him, and for so doing this is a sufficient warrant.

Dated this .... day of .... A.D. ...., at ....

....
A Justice of the Peace in and for

....
R.S. 1985, c. 27(1st Supp.), s. 184(19).

Form 21 — Warrant of Committal on Conviction
(Sections 570 and 806)

Canada

Province of ....,

(*territorial division*).

To the peace officers in the territorial division of (*name*) and to the keeper of a federal penitentiary (or provincial correctional institution for the province of ...., as the case may be)

Whereas (*name*), hereinafter called the offender was on the.......... day of .... 19.........., convicted by (name of judge and court) of having committed the following offence(s) and it was adjudged that the offender be sentenced as follows:

Offence	*Sentence*	*Remarks*
(*state offence of which offender was convicted*)	(*state term of imprisonment for the offence and, in case of imprisonment for default of payment of fine, so indicate together with the amount thereof and costs applicable and whether payable forthwith or within a timed fixed*)	(*state whether the sentence is consecutive or concurrent, and specify consecutive or concurrent to/with what other sentence*)
1.		
2.		
3.		
4.		

You are hereby commanded, in Her Majesty's name, to arrest the offender if it is necessary to do so in order to take the offender into custody, and to take and convey him safely to a federal penitentiary (or provincial correctional institution for the province of ...., as the case may be) and deliver him to the keeper thereof, who is hereby commanded to receive the accused into custody and to imprison him there for the term(s) of his sentence, unless, where a term of imprisonment was imposed only in default of payment of a fine or costs, the said amounts and the costs and charges of the committal and of conveying the offender to the said prison are sooner paid, and this is a sufficient warrant for so doing.

Dated this .... day of .... A.D. ...., at ....

. . . .
Clerk of the Court,
Justice, Judge or
Provincial Court Judge
R.S. 1985, c. 27(1st Supp.), s. 184(10);
1995, c. 22, s. 9.

Form 22 — Warrant of Committal on an Order For the Payment of Money

(Section 806)

Canada,

    Province of ....,
    (*territorial division*).

To the peace officers in the (*territorial division*) and to the keeper of the (*prison*) at ....:

Whereas A.B., hereinafter called the defendant, was tried on an information alleging that (*set out matter of complaint*), and it was ordered that (*set out the order made*), and in default that the defendant be imprisoned in the (*prison*) at .... for a term of.......... ;

I hereby command you, in Her Majesty's name, to arrest, if necessary, and take the defendant and convey him safely to the (*prison*) at ...., and deliver him to the keeper thereof, together with the following precept:

I hereby command you, the keeper of the said prison, to receive the defendant into your custody in the said prison and imprison him there for the term of ...., unless the said amounts and the costs and charges of the committal and of conveying the defendant to the said prison are sooner paid, and for so doing this is a sufficient warrant.

Dated this .... day of .... A.D. ...., at ....

. . . .
A Justice of the Peace in and for

. . . .
R.S. 1985, c. 27(1st Supp.), s. 184(19).

Form 23 — Warrant of Committal for Failure to Furnish Recognizance to Keep the Peace

(Sections 810 and 810.1)

Canada,

         Province of ....,
         (*territorial division*).

To the peace officers in the (*territorial division*) and to the keeper of the (*prison*) at ....:

Whereas A.B., hereinafter called the accused, has been ordered to enter into a recognizance to keep the peace and be of good behaviour, and has (refused *or* failed) to enter into a recognizance accordingly;

You are hereby commanded, in Her Majesty's name, to arrest, if necessary, and take the accused and convey him safely to the (*prison*) at.......... and deliver him to the keeper thereof, together with the following precept:

You, the said keeper, are hereby commanded to receive the accused into your custody in the said prison and imprison him there until he enters into a recognizance as aforesaid or until he is discharged in due course of law.

Dated this .... day of .... A.D. ...., at ....

     . . . .
         Clerk of the Court, Justice
         or Provincial Court Judge
         R.S. 1985, c. 27 (1st Supp.), ss. 184(19), 206; 1993; c. 45, s. 12.

(Seal, if required)

Form 24 — Warrant of Committal of Witness for Failure to Enter into Recognizance

(Section 550)

Canada,

         Province of ....,
         (*territorial division*).

To the peace officers in the (*territorial division*) and to the keeper of the (*prison*) at ....:

Whereas A.B., hereinafter called the accused, was committed for trial on a charge that (*state offence as in the information*);

And Whereas E.F., hereinafter called the witness, having appeared as a witness on the preliminary inquiry into the said charge, and being required to enter into a recognizance to appear as a witness on the trial of the accused on the said charge, has (failed *or* refused) to do so;

This is therefore to command you, in Her Majesty's name, to arrest, if necessary, and take and safely convey the said witness to the (*prison*) at .... and there deliver him to the keeper thereof, together with the following precept:

I do hereby command you, the said keeper, to receive the witness into your custody in the said prison and keep him there safely until the trial of the accused on the said charge, unless before that time the witness enters into the said recognizance.

Dated this .... day of .... A.D. ...., at ....

. . . .
A Justice of the Peace in and for

. . . .
R.S. 1985, c. 27 (1st Supp.), s. 184(19).

Form 25 — Warrant of Committal for Contempt
(Section 708)

Canada,

Province of ....,
(*territorial division*).

To the peace officers in the said (*territorial division*) and to the keeper of the (*prison*) at ....:

Whereas E.F. of ...., hereinafter called the defaulter, was on the.......... day of .... A.D. ...., at ...., convicted before.......... for contempt in that he did not attend before .... to give evidence on the trial of a charge that (*state offence as in the information*) against A.B. of ...., although (duly subpoenaed *or* bound by recognizance to appear and give evidence in that behalf, *as the case may be*) and did not show any sufficient excuse for his default;

And Whereas in and by the said conviction it was adjudged that the defaulter (*set out punishment adjudged*);

And Whereas the defaulter has not paid the amounts adjudged to be paid; (*delete if not applicable*)

This is therefore to command you, in Her Majesty's name, to arrest, if necessary, and take the defaulter and convey him safely to the prison at.......... and there deliver him to the keeper thereof, together with the following precept:

I do hereby command you, the said keeper, to receive the defaulter into your custody in the said prison and imprison him there* and for so doing this is a sufficient warrant.

*Insert whichever of the following is applicable:

  (a) for the term of ....;

  (b) for the term of .... unless the said sums and the costs and charges of the committal and of conveying the defaulter to the said prison are sooner paid; *or*

(c) for the term of .... and for the term of (*if consecutive so state*) unless the said sums and costs and charges of the committal and of conveying the defaulter to the said prison are sooner paid.

Dated this .... day of .... A.D. ...., at ....

....

A Justice *or* Clerk of

the Court

(Seal, if required)

Form 26 — Warrant of Committal in Default of Payment of Costs of an Appeal

(Section 827)

Canada,

Province of ....,

(*territorial division*).

To the peace officers of (*territorial division*) and to the keeper of the (*prison*) at ....:

Whereas it appears that on the hearing of an appeal before the (*set out court*), it was adjudged that A.B., of ...., hereinafter called the defaulter, should pay to the Clerk of the Court the sum of .... dollars in respect of costs;

And Whereas the Clerk of the Court has certified that the defaulter has not paid the sum within the time limited therefor;

I do hereby command you, the said peace officers, in Her Majesty's name, to take the defaulter and safely convey him to the (*prison*) at.......... and deliver him to the keeper thereof, together with the following precept:

I do hereby command you, the said keeper, to receive the defaulter into your custody in the said prison and imprison him for the term of ...., unless the said sum and the costs and charges of the committal and of conveying the defaulter to the said prison are sooner paid, and for so doing this is a sufficient warrant.

Dated this .... day of .... A.D. ...., at ....

....

A Justice of the Peace in and for

....

Form 27 — Warrant of Committal on Forfeiture of a Recognizance

(Section 773)

Canada,

Province of ....,

(*territorial division*).

To the sheriff of (*territorial division*) and to the keeper of the (*prison*) at ....:

You are hereby commanded to arrest, if necessary, and take (A.B. and C.D. *as the case may be*) hereinafter called the defaulters, and to convey them safely to the (*prison*) at .... and deliver them to the keeper thereof, together with the following precept:

You, the said keeper, are hereby commanded to receive the defaulters into your custody in the said prison and imprison them for a period of .... or until satisfaction is made of a judgment debt of .... dollars due to Her Majesty the Queen in respect of the forfeiture of a recognizance entered into by .... on the .... day of .... A.D. ....

Dated this .... day of .... A.D. ...., at ....

. . . .
A Justice of the Peace in and for

. . . .

. . . .
A Justice of the Peace in and for

. . . .

Form 28 — Endorsement of Warrant
(Sections 487 and 528)

Canada,

Province of ....,
(*territorial division*).

Pursuant to application this day made to me, I hereby authorize the arrest of the accused (*or* defendant) (*or* execution of this warrant, in the case of a warrant issued pursuant to section 487), within the said (*territorial division*).

Dated this .... day of .... A.D. ...., at ....
....

. . . .
A Justice of the Peace in and for

. . . .
R.S. 1985, c. 27 (1st Supp.), s.
184(12).

Form 28.1 — Endorsement (Order or Authorization)
(Subsection 487.03(2))

Canada,
Province of ....,
(*territorial division*).

Pursuant to application this day made to me, I hereby authorize the execution of this order, *in the case of an order issued under section 487.051 or 487.052* (or execution of this authorization *in the case of an authorization issued under section 487.055 or 487.091*), within the said (*territorial division*).

Dated this ...... day of ....

A.D. ...., at ....

....

Judge of the Provincial Court

2000, c. 10, s. 24

Form 29 — Endorsement of Warrant
(Section 507)

Canada,

Province of ....,

(*territorial division*).

Whereas this warrant is issued under section 507, 508 or 512 of the *Criminal Code* in respect of an offence other than an offence mentioned in section 522 of the *Criminal Code*, I hereby authorize the release of the accused pursuant to section 499 of that Act.

Dated this .... day of .... A.D. ...., at ....

              . . . .

              A Justice of the Peace in and for

              . . . .

Form 30 — Order for Accused to be Brought Before Justice Prior to Expiration of Period of Remand
(Section 537)

Canada,

Province of ....,

(*territorial division*).

To the keeper of the (*prison*) at ....:

Whereas by warrant dated the .... day of .... A.D. ...., I committed A.B., hereinafter called the accused, to your custody and required you safely to keep [him] until the .... day of .... A.D. ...., and then to have him before me or any other justice at .... at .... o'clock in the .... noon to answer to the charge against him and to be dealt with according to law unless you should be ordered otherwise before that time;

Now, therefore, I order and direct you to have the accused before.......... at .... at .... o'clock in the .... noon to answer to the charge against him and to be dealt with according to law.

Dated this .... day of .... A.D. ...., at ....

. . . .
A Justice of the Peace in and for

. . . .

Form 31 — Deposition of a Witness
(Section 540)

Canada,

Province of ....,
(*territorial division*).

These are the depositions of X.Y., of ...., and M.N., of ...., taken before me, this .... day of .... A.D., ... at.......... , in the presence and hearing of A.B., hereinafter called the accused, who stands charged (*state offence as in the information*).

X.Y., having been duly sworn, deposes as follows: (*insert deposition as nearly as possible in words of witness*).

M.N., having been duly sworn, deposes as follows:

I certify that the depositions of X.Y., and M.N., written on the several sheets of paper hereto annexed to which my signature is affixed, were taken in the presence and hearing of the accused (and signed by them respectively, in is presence, *where they are required to be signed by witness*). In witness whereof I have hereto signed my name.

. . . .
A Justice of the Peace in and for

. . . .

Form 32 — Recognizance
(Sections 493, 550, 679, 706, 707, 810, 810.1 and 817)

Canada,

Province of ....,
(*territorial division*).

Be it remembered that on this day the persons named in the following schedule personally came before me and severally acknowledged themselves to owe to Her Majesty the Queen the several amounts set opposite their respective names, namely,

Name	Address	Occupation	Amount
A.B.			
C.D.			
E.F.			

to be made and levied of their several goods and chattels, lands and tenements, respectively, to the use of Her Majesty the Queen, if the said A.B. fails in any of the conditions hereunder written.

Taken and acknowledged before me on the .... day of .... A.D............ , at ....

. . . .
Judge, Clerk of the Court,
Provincial Court Judge *or* Justice

1. Whereas the said ...., hereinafter called the accused, has been charged that (*set out the offence in respect of which the accused has been charged*);

Now, therefore, the condition of this recognizance is that if the accused attends court on .... day, the .... day of .... A.D............ , at .... o'clock in the .... noon and attends thereafter as required by the court in order to be dealt with according to law (*or, where date and place of appearance before court are not known at the time recognizance is entered into* if the accused attends at the time and place fixed by the court and attends thereafter as required by the court in order to be dealt with according to law) [515, 520, 521, 522, 523, 524, 525, 680];

And further, if the accused (*insert in Schedule of Conditions any additional conditions that are directed*), the said recognizance is void, otherwise it stands in full force and effect.

2. Whereas the said ...., hereinafter called the appellant, is an appellant against his conviction (*or against his sentence*) in respect of the following charge (*set out the offence for which the appellant was convicted*) [679, 680];

Now, therefore, the condition of this recognizance is that if the appellant attends as required by the court in order to be dealt with according to law;

And further, if the appellant (*insert in Schedule of Conditions any additional conditions that are directed*), the said recognizance is void, otherwise it stands in full force and effect.

3. Whereas the said ...., hereinafter called the appellant, is an appellant against his conviction (*or against his sentence or against an order or by way of stated case*) in respect of the following matter (*set out offence, subject-matter of order or question of law*) [816, 831, 832, 834];

Now, therefore, the condition of this recognizance is that if the appellant appears personally at the sittings of the appeal court at which the appeal is to be heard;

And further, if the appellant (*insert in Schedule of Conditions any additional conditions that are directed*), the said recognizance is void, otherwise it stands in full force and effect.

4. Whereas the said ...., hereinafter called the appellant, is an appellant against an order of dismissal (*or against sentence*) in respect of the following charge (*set out the name of the accused and the offence, subject-matter of order or question of law*) [817, 831, 832, 834];

Now, therefore, the condition of this recognizance is that if the appellant appears personally or by counsel at the sittings of the appeal court at which the appeal is to be heard the said recognizance is void, otherwise it stands in full force and effect.

5. Whereas the said ...., hereinafter called the accused, was ordered to stand trial on a charge that (*set out the offence in respect of which the accused has been charged*);

And whereas A.B. appeared as a witness on the preliminary inquiry into the said charge [550, 706, 707];

Now, therefore, the condition of this recognizance is that if the said A.B. appears at the time and place fixed for the trial of the accused to give evidence on the indictment that is found against the accused, the said recognizance is void, otherwise it stands in full force and effect.

6. The condition of the above written recognizance is that if A.B. keeps the peace and is of good behaviour for the term of .... commencing on.........., the said recognizance is void, otherwise it stands in full force and effect [810 and 810.1].

7. Whereas a warrant was issued under section 462.32 or a restraint order was made under subsection 462.33(3) of the *Criminal Code* in relation to any property (*set out a description of the property and its location*);

Now, therefore, the condition of this recognizance is that A.B. shall not do or cause anything to be done that would result, directly or indirectly, in the disappearance, dissipaton or reduction in value of the property or otherwise affect the property so that all or a part thereof could not be subject to an order of forfeiture under section 462.37 or 462.38 of the *Criminal Code* or any other provision of the *Criminal Code* or any other Act of Parliament [462.34].

Schedule of Conditions

     (a) reports at (*state times*) to (*name of peace officer or other person designated*),

     (b) remains within (*designated territorial jurisdiction*),

     (c) notifies (*name of peace officer or other person designated*) of any change in his address, employment or occupation,

     (d) abstains from communicating, directly or indirectly, with (*identification of victim, witness or other person*) except in accordance with the following conditions: (*as the justice or judge specifies*);

     (e) deposits his passport (*as the justice or judge directs*), and

     (f) (*any other reasonable conditions*).

Note: Section 763 and subsections 764(1) to (3) of the Criminal Code state as follows:

763. Where a person is bound by recognizance to appear before a court, justice or provincial court judge for any purpose and the session or sittings of that court or the proceedings are adjourned or an order is made changing the place of trial, that person and his sureties continue to be bound by the recognizance in like manner as if it had been entered into with relation to the resumed proceedings or the trial at the time and place at which the proceedings are ordered to be resumed or the trial is ordered to be held.

764. (1) Where an accused is bound by recognizance to appear for trial, his arraignment or conviction does not discharge the recognizance, but it continues to bind him and his sureties, if any, for his appearance until he is discharged or sentenced, as the case may be.

(2) Notwithstanding subsection (1), the court, justice or provincial court judge may commit an accused to prison or may require him to furnish new or additional sureties for his appearance until he is discharged or sentenced, as the case may be.

(3) The sureties of an accused who is bound by recognizance to appear for trial are discharged if he is committed to prison pursuant to subsection (2).

1999, c. 25, s. 27

Form 33 — Certificate of Default to be Endorsed on Recognizance

(Section 770)

I hereby certify that A.B. (has not appeared as required by this recognizance *or* has not complied with a condition of this recognizance) and that by reason thereof the ends of justice have been (defeated *or* delayed, *as the case may be*).

The nature of the default is .... and the reason for the default is.......... (*state reason if known*).

The names and addresses of the principal and sureties are as follows:

Dated this .... day of .... A.D. ...., at ....

. . . .
Clerk of the Court, Judge,
Justice *or* Provincial Court Judge

(Seal, if required)

Form 34 — Writ of Fieri Facias

(Section 771)

Elizabeth II by the Grace of God, etc.

To the sheriff of (*territorial division*), *Greeting*.

You are hereby commanded to levy of the goods and chattels, lands and tenements of each of the following persons the amount set opposite the name of each:

Name	Address	Occupation	Amount

And you are further commanded to make a return of what you have done in execution of this writ.

Dated this .... day of .... A.D. ...., at ....

. . . .
Clerk of the . . . .

(Seal)

Form 35 — Conviction
(Sections 570 and 806)

Canada,

Province of ....,
(*territorial division*).

Be it remembered that on the .... day of .... at ...., A.B., (*date of birth*)
hereinafter called the accused, was tried under Part (XIX *or* XXVII) of the *Criminal
Code* on the charge that (*state fully the offence of which accused was convicted*),
was convicted of the said offence and the following punishment was imposed on
him, namely,*

Use whichever of the following forms of sentence is applicable:

(a) That the said accused be imprisoned in the (*prison*) at .... for the term of ....;

(b) That the said accused forfeit and pay the sum of .... dollars to be applied according to law
and also pay to .... the sum of.......... dollars in respect of costs and in default of payment of the
said sums (forthwith *or within a time fixed, if any*) to be imprisoned in the (*prison*) at .... for the
term of .... unless the said sums and costs and charges of the committal and of conveying the
accused to the said prison are sooner paid;

(c) That the said accused be imprisoned in the (*prison*) at.......... for the term of .... and in addition forfeit and pay the sum of .... dollars to be applied according to law and also pay to ....
the sum of .... dollars in respect of costs and in default of payment of the said sums (forthwith
or within a time fixed, if any), to be imprisoned in the (*prison*) at .... for the term of .... (*if
sentence to be consecutive, state accordingly*) unless the said sums and costs and charges of the
committal and of conveying the accused to the said prison are sooner paid.

Dated this .... day of .... A.D. ...., at ....

. . . .
Clerk of the Court, Justice
or Provincial Court Judge

(*Seal, if required*)

Form 36 — Order Against an Offender
(Sections 570 and 806)

Canada,

Province of ....,
(*territorial division*).

Be it remembered that on the .... day of .... A.D. ...., at ...., A.B.,
(*date of birth*) of ...., was tried on an information (*indictment*) alleging that (*set
out matter of complaint or alleged offence*), and it was ordered and adjudged that
(*set out the order made*).

Dated this .... day of .... A.D. ...., at ....

. . . .
Justice *or* Clerk

of the Court
R.S. 1985, c. 27 (1st Supp.), s. 184(15).

Form 37 — Order Acquitting Accused
(Section 570)

Canada,

Province of ....,
(*territorial division*).

Be it remembered that on the .... day of .... A.D. ...., at ...., A.B., of
.........., (*occupation*), (*date of birth*) was tried on the charge that (*state fully the
offence of which the accused was acquitted*) and was found not guilty of the said
offence.

Dated this .... day of .... A.D. ...., at ....

. . . .
Provincial Court Judge *or* Clerk of the Court
(*Seal, if required*)

R.S. 1985, c. 27(1st Supp.), ss.184(16), 203,
206.

Form 38 — Conviction for Contempt
(Section 708)

Canada,

Province of ....,
(*territorial division*).

Be it remembered that on the .... day of .... A.D. ...., at .... in the
(*territorial division*), E.F. of ...., hereinafter called the defaulter, is convicted by
me for contempt in that he did not attend before (*set out court or justice*) *to give
evidence on the trial of a charge that* (*state fully offence with which accused was
charged*), although (duly subpoenaed *or* bound by recognizance to attend to give
evidence, *as the case may be*) and has not shown before me any sufficient excuse
for his default;

Wherefore I adjudge the defaulter for his said default, (*set out punishment as authorized and determined in accordance with section 708 of the Criminal Code*).

Dated this .... day of .... A.D. ...., at ....

. . . .
A Justice *or* Clerk of the
Court

(*Seal, if required*)

Form 39 — Order for Discharge of a Person in Custody
(Sections 519 and 550)

Canada,

Province of ....,
(*territorial division*).

To the keeper of the (*prison*) at ....:

I hereby direct you to release E.F., detained by you under a (warrant of committal *or* order) dated the .... day of .... A.D............ , if the said E.F. is detained by you for no other cause.

. . . .

A Judge, Justice *or* Clerk
of the Court

(Seal, if required)

Form 40 — Challenge to Array
(Section 629)

Canada,

Province of . . . .
(*territorial division*).

The Queen —

v. —

C.D.

The (prosecutor *or* accused) challenges the array of the panel on the ground that X.Y., (sheriff *or* deputy sheriff), who returned the panel, was guilty of (partiality *or* fraud *or* wilful misconduct) on returning it.

Dated this .... day of .... A.D. ...., at ....

. . . .

Counsel for (prosecutor
*or*accused)

Form 41 — Challenge for Cause
(Section 639)

Canada,

Province of . . . .

(territorial division).

. . . .
Counsel for (prosecutor
or accused)

The Queen —

v. —

C.D.

The (prosecutor *or* accused) challenges G.H. on the ground that (*set out ground of challenge in accordance with s. 638(1) of the Criminal Code*).

. . . .
Counsel for (prosecutor *or* accused)

Form 42 — Certificate of Non-Payment of Costs of Appeal

(Section 827)

In the Court of ....

(Style of Cause)

I hereby certify that A.B. (the appellant *or* respondent, *as the case may be*) in this appeal, having been ordered to pay costs in the sum of .... dollars, has failed to pay the said costs within the time limited for the payment thereof.

Dated this .... day of .... A.D. ...., at ....

. . . .

. . . .
Clerk of the Court of
. . . .

(Seal)

Form 43 — Jailer's Receipt to Peace Officer for Prisoner

(Section 734)

I hereby certify that I have received from X.Y., a peace officer for (*territorial division*), one A.B., together with a (warrant *or* order) issued by (*set out court or justice, as the case may be*).*

Add a statement of the condition of the prisoner

Dated this .... day of .... A.D. ...., at ....

. . . .
Keeper of *(prison)*

Form 44 — Fingerprint Examiner's Certificate
(Section 667)

I, *(name)*, a fingerprint examiner designated as such for the purposes of section 667 of the *Criminal Code* by the Solicitor General of Canada, do hereby certify that *(name)* also known as *(aliases if any)*, FPS Number ...., whose fingerprints are shown reproduced below *(reproduction of fingerprints)* or attached hereto, has been convicted, discharged under section 736 of the *Criminal Code* or convicted and sentenced in Canada as follows:

(record)

Dated this .... day of .... A.D. ...., at ....

. . . .
Fingerprint Examiner
R.S. 1985, c. 27(1st Supp.), s. 184(17).

Form 45 — Fingerprint Examiner's Certificate
(Section 667)

I, *(name)*, a fingerprint examiner designated as such for the purposes of section 667 of the *Criminal Code* by the Solicitor General of Canada, do hereby certify that I have compared the fingerprints reproduced in or attached to exhibit A with the fingerprints reproduced in or attached to the certificate in Form 44 attached marked exhibit B and that they are those of the same person.

Dated this .... day of .... A.D. ...., at ....

. . . .
Fingerprint Examiner
R.S. 1985, c. 27(1st Supp.), s. 184(18).

Form 46 — Probation Order
(Section 732.1)

Canada,

Province of . . . .
(territorial division).

Whereas on the .... day of .... at ...., A.B., hereinafter called the accused, (pleaded guilty to *or* was tried under *(here insert Part XIX, XX or XXVII, as the case may be)* of the *Criminal Code* and was *(here insert convicted or found guilty, as the case may be)* on the charge that *(here state the offence to which the accused pleaded guilty or for which the accused was convicted or found guilty, as the case may be))*;

And whereas on the .... day of .... the court adjudged*

Use whichever of the following forms of disposition is applicable:

    (a) that the accused be discharged on the conditions hereinafter prescribed:

    (b) that the passing of sentence on the accused be suspended and that the said the accused be released on the conditions hereinafter prescribed:

    (c) that the accused forfeit and pay the sum of .... dollars to be applied according to law and in default of payment of the said sum forthwith (*or within a time fixed, if any*), be imprisoned in the (*prison*) at .... for the term of .... unless the said sum and charges of the committal and of conveying the said accused to the said prison are sooner paid, and in addition thereto, that the said accused comply with the conditions hereinafter prescribed:

    (d) that the accused be imprisoned in the (*prison*) at .... for the term of .... and, in addition thereto, that the said accused comply with the conditions hereinafter prescribed:

Now therefore the said accused shall, for the period of .... from the date of this order (*or, where paragraph (d) is applicable* the date of expiration of his sentence of imprisonment) comply with the following conditions, namely, that the said accused shall keep the peace and be of good behaviour and appear before the court when required to do so by the court, and, in addition,

(*here state any additional conditions prescribed pursuant to subsection 732.1(3) of the Criminal Code*).

Dated this .... day of .... A.D. ...., at ....

                    . . . .

                    Clerk of the Court, Justice

                    or Provincial Court Judge

                    R.S. 1985, c. 27(1st Supp.), s. 206; 1995, c. 22, s. 10 (Sch. I, item 35).

Form 47 — Order To Disclose Income Tax Information

(Section 462.48)

Canada,

                Province of

                  . . . . ,

                    (*territorial division*).

To A.B., of ...., (*office or occupation*):

Whereas, it appears on the oath of C.D., of ...., that there are reasonable grounds for believing that E.F., of ...., has committed or benefited from the commission of the offence of .... and that the information or documents (*describe information or documents*) are likely to be of substantial value to an investigation of that offence or a related matter; and

Whereas there are reasonable grounds for believing that it is in the public interest to allow access to the information or documents, having regard to the benefit likely to accrue to the investigation if the access is obtained;

This is, therefore, to authorize and require you between the hours of (*as the judge may direct*), during the period commencing on .... and ending on ...., to produce all the above-mentioned information and documents to one of the following police officers, namely, (*here name police officers*) and allow the police officer to remove the information or documents, *or* to allow the police officer access to the above-mentioned information and documents and to examine them, *as the judge directs*, subject to the following conditions (*state conditions*): ....

Dated this .... day of .... A.D. ...., at ....

. . . .

Signature of
Judge
R.S. 1985, c. 42(4th Supp.), s. 8.

Form 48 — Assessment Order

(Section 672.13)

Canada,
Province of
(*territorial division*)

Whereas, I have reasonable grounds to believe that evidence of the mental condition of (*name of accused*, who has been charged with .... may be necessary to determine*

❏ whether the accused is unfit to stand trial

❏ whether the accused suffered from a mental disorder so as to exempt the accused from criminal responsibility by virtue of subsection 16(1) of the *Criminal Code* at the time of the act or omission charged against the accused

❏ whether the accused is a dangerous mentally disordered accused under section 672.65 of the *Criminal Code*

❏ whether the balance of the mind of the accused was disturbed at the time of commission of the alleged offence, where the accused is a female person charged with an offence arising out of the death of her newly-born child

❏ where a verdict of unfit to stand trial or a verdict of not criminally responsible on account of mental disorder has been rendered in respect of the accused, the appropriate disposition to be made in respect of the accused pursuant to section 672.54 or 672.58 of the *Criminal Code*

❏ where the accused has been convicted of the offence, whether an order under subsection 747.1(1) of the *Criminal Code* should be made in respect of the accused

I hereby order an assessment of the mental condition of (*name of accused*) to be conducted by/at (*name of person or service by whom or place where assessment is to be made*) for a period of ....days

This order is to be in force for a total of .... days, including travelling time, during which time the accused is to remain*

❏   in custody at (*place where accused is to be detained*)

❏   out of custody, on the following conditions:
     set out conditions, where applicable)

*Check applicable option.

Dated this .... day of .... A.D. ...., at ....

....
(Signature of justice or judge or clerk of the court, as the case may be)

1995, c. 22, s. 10 (Sch. I, item 36).

Form 49 — Warrant of Committal Disposition of Detention
(Section 672.57)

Canada,

Province of

(*territorial division*)

To the peace officers, in the said (*territorial division*) and to the keeper (*administrator, warden*) of the (*prison, hospital or other appropriate place where the accused is detained*).

This warrant is issued for the committal of A.B., of .... (*occupation*), hereinafter called the accused.

Whereas the accused has been charged that (*set out briefly the offence in respect of which the accused was charged*);

And whereas the accused was found*

❏   unfit to stand trial

❏   not criminally responsible on account of mental disorder

This is, therefore, to command you, in Her Majesty's name, to take the accused in custody and convey the accused safely to the (*prison, hospital or other appropriate place*) at .... and there deliver the accused to the keeper (*administrator, warden*) with the following precept:

I do therefore command you the said keeper (*administrator, warden*) to receive the accused in your custody in the said (*prison, hospital or other appropriate place*) and to keep the accused safely there until the accused is delivered by due course of law.

The following are the conditions to which the accused shall be subject while in your (*prison, hospital or other appropriate place*):

The following are the powers regarding the restrictions (*and the limits and conditions on these restrictions*) on the liberty of the accused that are hereby delegated to you the said keeper (*administrator, warden*) of the said (*prison, hospital or other appropriate place*):

*Check applicable option.

Dated this .... day of .... A.D. ...., at ....

....
(Signature of judge, clerk of the court, provinical court
judge or chairperson of the Review Board)

Form 50 — **Warrant of Committal Placement Decision**
(Section 672.7(2))

Canada,
Province of
(*territorial division*)

To the peace officers, in the said (*territorial division*) and to the keeper (*administrator, warden*) of the (*prison, hospital or other appropriate place where the accused is detained*).

This warrant is issues for the committal of A.B., of .... (*occupation*), hereinafter called the accused.

Whereas the accused has been charged that (*set out briefly the offence in respect of which the accused was charged*);

And whereas the accused was found*

❏   unfit to stand trial

❏   not criminally responsible on account of mental disorder

And whereas the Review Board has held a hearing and decided that the accused shall be detained in custody;

And whereas the accused is required to be detained in custody pursuant to a warrant of committal issued by (*set out the name of the Judge, Clerk of the Court, Provincial Court Judge or Justice as well as the name of the court and territorial division*), dated the .... day of .... in respect of the offence that (*set out briefly the offence in respect of which the accused was charged or convicted*);

This is, therefore to command you, in Her Majesty's name, to*

❏   execute the warrant of committal issued by the court, according to its terms

❏   execute the warrant of committal issued herewith by the Review Board

*Check the applicable option.

Dated this .... day of .... A.D. ...., at ....

....
(Signature of chairperson of the Review Board)

Form 51

Form 51 — Hospital Order

(Section 747.1(3))

Canada,

Province of

(territorial division)

Whereas (*name of offender*), who has been convicted of (*offence*) and sentenced to a term of imprisonment of (*length of term of imprisonment*), is suffering from a mental disorder in an acute phase and immediate treatment of the mental disorder is urgently required to prevent significant deterioration of the mental or physical health of the offender or to prevent the offender from causing serious bodily harm to any person;

And whereas (*name of offender*) and (*name of treatment facility*) have consented to this order and its terms and conditions;

I hereby order that (*name of offender*) be detained for treatment at (*name of treatment facility*) for a period not to exceed (*length of period not to exceed sixty days*) subject to the following terms and conditions:

(*set out terms and conditions, where applicable*)

Dated this .... day of .... A.D. ...., at ....

....
(Signature of justice or judge or clerk of the court, as
the case may be)
1995, c. 22, s. 10 (Sch. I, item 37).

CANADA EVIDENCE ACT

TABLE OF CONCORDANCE

R.S.C. 1970, c. E-10	R.S.C. 1985, c. C-5	R.S.C. 1970, c. E-10	R.S.C. 1985, c. C-5
1	1	28	28
2	2	29	29
3	3	30	30
4	4	31	31
5	5	32	32
6	6	33	33
7	7	34	34
8	8	35	35
9	79	36	36
10	10	36.1	37
11	11	36.2	38
12	12	36.2	39
13	13	37	40
14	14	38	41
15	15	39	42
16	16	40	43
17	17	41	44
18	18	42	45
19	19	43	46
20	20	44	47
21	21	45	48
22	22	46	49
23	23	47	50
24	24	48	51
25	25	49	52
26	26	50	53
27	27	51	54

CANADA EVIDENCE ACT

An Act respecting Witnesses and Evidence

R.S.C. 1985, c. C-5, as am. R.S.C. 1985, c. 19 (3rd Supp.), ss. 17, 18;
S.C. 1992, c. 1, s. 142 (Sched. V, item 9); 1992, c. 47, s. 66; 1993, c. 28,
s. 78 (Sched. III, item 8); 1993, c. 34, s. 15; 1994, c. 44, ss. 85–93; 1995,
c. 28, s. 47; 1997, c. 18, ss. 116–118; 1998, c. 9, s. 1; 1999, c. 18, ss.
89–91; 1999, c. 28, ss. 149, 150; 2000, c. 5, ss. 52–57.

Short Title

1. Short title — This Act may be cited as the *Canada Evidence Act*.

PART I — APPLICATION

2. Application — This Part applies to all criminal proceedings and to all civil proceedings and other matters whatever respecting which Parliament has jurisdiction.

Witnesses

3. Interest or crime — A person is not incompetent to give evidence by reason of interest or crime.

4. (1) Accused and spouse — Every person charged with an offence, and, except as otherwise provided in this section, the wife or husband, as the case may be, of the person so charged, is a competent witness for the defence whether the person so charged is charged solely or jointly with any other person.

(2) Idem — The wife or husband of a person charged with an offence against subsection 50(1) of the *Young Offenders Act* or with an offence against any of sections 151, 152, 153, 155 or 159, subsection 160(2) or (3), or sections 170 to 173, 179, 212, 215, 218, 271 to 273, 280 to 283, 291 to 294 or 329 of the *Criminal Code*, or an attempt to commit any such offence, is a competent and compellable witness for the prosecution without the consent of the person charged.

(3) Communications during marriage — No husband is compellable to disclose any communication made to him by his wife during their marriage, and no wife is compellable to disclose any communication made to her by her husband during their marriage.

(4) Offences against young persons — The wife or husband of a person charged with an offence against any of ections 220, 221, 235, 236, 237, 239, 240,

266, 267, 268 or 269 of the *Criminal Code* where the complainant or victim is under the age of fourteen years is a competent and compellable witness for the prosecution without the consent of the person charged.

(5) Saving — Nothing in this section affects a case where the wife or husband of a person charged with an offence may at common law be called as a witness without the consent of that person.

(6) Failure to testify — The failure of the person charged, or of the wife or husband of such person, to testify shall not be made the subject of comment by the judge or by counsel for the prosecution.

R.S. 1985, c. 19 (3d Supp.), s. 17

5. (1) Incriminating questions — No witness shall be excused from answering any question on the ground that the answer to the question may tend to criminate him, or may tend to establish his liability to a civil proceeding at the instance of the Crown or of any person.

(2) Answer not admissible against witness — Where with respect to any question a witness objects to answer on the ground that his answer may tend to criminate him, or may tend to establish his liability to a civil proceeding at the instance of the Crown or of any person, and if but for this Act, or the Act of any provincial legislature, the witness would therefore have been excused from answering the question, then although the witness is by reason of this Act or the provincial Act compelled to answer, the answer so given shall not be used or admissible in evidence against him in any criminal trial or other criminal proceeding against him thereafter taking place, other than a prosecution for perjury in the giving of that evidence or for the giving of contradictory evidence.

1997, c. 18, s. 116

6. (1) Evidence of person with physical disability — If a witness has difficulty communicating by reason of a physical disability, the court may order that the witness be permitted to give evidence by any means that enables the evidence to intelligible.

(2) Evidence of person with mental disability — If a witness with a mental disability is determined under section 16 to have the capacity to give evidence and difficulty communicating by reason of disability, the court may order that the witness be permitted to give evidence by any means that enables the evidence to be intelligible.

(3) Inquiry — The court may conduct an inquiry to determine if the means by which a witness may be permitted to give evidence under subsection (1) or (2) is necessary and reliable.

1998, c. 9, s. 1

6.1 Identification of accused — For greater certainty, a witness may give evidence as to the identity of an accused whom the witness is able to identify visually or in any other sensory manner.

1998, c. 9, s. 1

7. Expert witnesses — Where, in any trial or other proceeding, criminal or civil, it is intended by the prosecution or the defence, or by any party, to examine as witnesses professional or other experts entitled according to the law or practice to give opinion evidence, not more than five of such witnesses may be called on either side without the leave of the court or judge or person presiding.

8. Handwriting comparison — Comparison of a disputed writing with any writing proved to the satisfaction of the court to be genuine shall be permitted to be made by witnesses, and such writings, and the evidence of witnesses respecting those writings, may be submitted to the court and jury as proof of the genuineness or otherwise of the writing in dispute.

9. (1) Adverse witnesses — A party producing a witness shall not be allowed to impeach his credit by general evidence of bad character, but if the witness, in the opinion of the court, proves adverse, the party may contradict him by other evidence, or, by leave of the court, may prove that the witness made at other times a statement inconsistent with his present testimony, but before the last mentioned proof can be given the circumstances of the supposed statement, sufficient to designate the particular occasion, shall be mentioned to the witness, and he shall be asked whether or not he did make the statement.

(2) Previous statements in writing by witness not proved adverse — Where the party producing a witness alleges that the witness made at other times a statement in writing, reduced to writing, or recorded on audio tape or video tape or otherwise, inconsistent with the witness' present testimony, the court may, without proof that the witness is adverse, grant leave to that party to cross-examine the witness as to the statement and the court may consider the cross-examination in determining whether in the opinion of the court the witness is adverse.

1994, c. 44, s. 85

10. (1) Cross-examination as to previous statements — On any trial a witness may be cross-examined as to previous statements that the witness made in writing, or that have been reduced to writing, or recorded on audio tape or video tape or otherwise, relative to the subject-matter of the case, without the writing being shown to the witness or the witness being given the opportunity to listen to the audio tape or view the video tape or otherwise take cognizance of the statements, but, if it is intended to contradict the witness, the witness' attention must, before the contradictory proof can be given, be called to those parts of the statement that are to be used for the purpose of so contradicting the witness, and the judge, at any time during the trial, may require the production of the writing or tape or other medium for inspection, and thereupon make such use of it for the purposes of the trial as the judge thinks fit.

(2) Deposition of witness in criminal investigation — A deposition of a witness, purporting to have been taken before a justice on the investigation of a criminal charge and to be signed by the witness and the justice, returned to and produced from the custody of the proper officer shall be presumed, in the absence of evidence to the contrary, to have been signed by the witness.

1994, c. 44, s. 86

11. Cross-examination as to previous oral statements — Where a witness, on cross-examination as to a former statement made by him relative to the subject-matter of the case and inconsistent with his present testimony, does not distinctly admit that he did make the statement, proof may be given that he did in fact make it, but before the proof can be given the circumstances of the supposed statement, sufficient to designate the particular occasion, shall be mentioned to the witness, and he shall be asked whether or not he did make the statement.

12. (1) Examination as to previous convictions — A witness may be questioned as to whether the witness has been convicted of any offence, excluding any offence designated as a contravention under the Contraventions Act, but including such an offence where the conviction was entered after a trial on an indictment.

(1.1) Proof of previous convictions — If the witness either denies the fact or refuses to answer, the opposite party may prove the conviction.

(2) How conviction proved — A conviction may be proved by producing

(a) a certificate containing the substance and effect only, omitting the formal part, of the indictment and conviction, if it is for an indictable offence, or a copy of the summary conviction, if it is for an offence punishable on summary conviction, purporting to be signed by the clerk of the court or other officer having the custody of the records of the court in which the conviction, if on indictment, was had, or to which the conviction, if summary, was returned; and

(b) proof of identity.

1992, c. 47, s. 66

Oaths and Solemn Affirmations

13. Who may administer oaths — Every court and judge, and every person having, by law or consent of parties, authority to hear and receive evidence, has power to administer an oath to every witness who is legally called to give evidence before that court, judge or person.

14. (1) Solemn affirmation by witness instead of oath — A person may, instead of taking an oath, make the following solemn affirmation:

I solemnly affirm that the evidence to be given by me shall be the truth, the whole truth and nothing but the truth.

(2) Effect — Where a person makes a solemn affirmation in accordance with subsection (1), his evidence shall be taken and have the same effect as if taken under oath.

1994, c. 44, s. 87

15. (1) Solemn affirmation by deponent — Where a person who is required or who desires to make an affidavit or deposition in a proceeding or on an occasion on which or concerning a matter respecting which an oath is required or is lawful, whether on the taking of office or otherwise, does not wish to take an oath, the court or judge, or other officer or person qualified to take affidavits or depositions, shall permit the person to make a solemn affirmation in the words following, namely, "I, ..., do solemnly affirm, etc.", and that solemn affirmation has the same force and effect as if that person had taken an oath.

(2) Effect — Any witness whose evidence is admitted or who makes a solemn affirmation under this section or section 14 is liable to indictment and punishment for perjury in all respects as if he had been sworn.

1994, c. 44, s. 88

16. (1) Witness whose capacity is in question — Where a proposed witness is a person under fourteen years of age or a person whose mental capacity is challenged, the court shall, before permitting the person to give evidence, conduct an inquiry to determine

(a) whether the person understands the nature of an oath or a solemn affirmation; and

(b) whether the person is able to communicate the evidence.

(2) Testimony under oath or solemn affirmation — A person referred to in subsection (1) who understands the nature of an oath or a solemn affirmation and is able to communicate the evidence shall testify under oath or solemn affirmation.

(3) Testimony on promise to tell truth — A person referred to in subsection (1) who does not understand the nature of an oath or a solemn affirmation but is able to communicate the evidence may, notwithstanding any provision of any Act requiring an oath or a solemn affirmation, testify on promising to tell the truth.

(4) Inability to testify — A person referred to in subsection (1) who neither understands the nature of an oath or a solemn affirmation nor is able to communicate the evidence shall not testify.

(5) Burden as to capacity of witness — A party who challenges the mental capacity of a proposed witness of fourteen years of age or more has the burden of satisfying the court that there is an issue as to the capacity of the proposed witness to testify under an oath or a solemn affirmation.

R.S. 1985, c. 19 (3d Supp.), s. 18; 1994, c. 44, s. 89

Judicial Notice

17. Imperial Acts, etc — Judicial notice shall be taken of all Acts of the Imperial Parliament, of all ordinances made by the Governor in Council, or the lieutenant governor in council of any province or colony that, or some portion of which, now forms or hereafter may form part of Canada, and of all the Acts of the legislature of any such province or colony, whether enacted before or after the passing of the *Constitution Act, 1867.*

18. Acts of Canada — Judicial notice shall be taken of all Acts of Parliament, public or private, without being specially pleaded.

Documentary Evidence

19. Copies by Queen's Printer — Every copy of any Act of Parliament, public or private, published by the Queen's Printer, is evidence of that Act and of its contents, and every copy purporting to be published by the Queen's Printer shall be deemed to be so published, unless the contrary is shown.

2000, c. 5, s. 52

20. Imperial proclamations, etc — Imperial proclamations, orders in council, treaties, orders, warrants, licences, certificates, rules, regulations, or other Imperial official records, Acts or documents may be proved

    (a) in the same manner as they may from time to time be provable in any court in England;

    (b) by the production of a copy of the *Canada Gazette*, or a volume of the Acts of Parliament purporting to contain a copy of the same or a notice thereof; or

    (c) by the production of a copy of them purporting to be published by the Queen's Printer.

2000, c. 5, s. 53

21. Proclamations, etc., of Governor General — Evidence of any proclamation, order, regulation or appointment, made or issued by the Governor General or by the Governor in Council, or by or under the authority of any minister or head of any department of the Government of Canada and evidence of a treaty to which Canada is a party, may be given in all or any of the following ways:

    (a) by the production of a copy of the *Canada Gazette*, or a volume of the Acts of Parliament purporting to contain a copy of the treaty, proclamation, order, regulation or appointment or a notice thereof;

    (b) by the production of a copy of the proclamation, order, regulation or appointment, purporting to be published by the Queen's Printer;

    (c) by the production of a copy of the treaty purporting to be published by the Queen's Printer;

    (d) by the production, in the case of any proclamation, order, regulation or appointment made or issued by the Governor General or by the Governor in Council, of a copy or extract purporting to be certified to be true by the clerk or assistant or acting clerk of the Queen's Privy Council for Canada; and

    (e) by the production, in the case of any order, regulation or appointment made or issued by or under the authority of any minister or head of a department of the Government of Canada, of a copy or extract purporting to be certified to be true by the minister, by his deputy or acting deputy, or by the secretary or acting secretary of the department over which he presides.

2000, c. 5, s. 54

22. (1) Proclamations, etc., of Lieutenant Governor — Evidence of any proclamation, order, regulation or appointment made or issued by a lieutenant governor or lieutenant governor in council of any province, or by or under the authority of any member of the executive council, being the head of any department of the government of the province, may be given in all or any of the following ways:

(a) by the production of a copy of the official gazette for the province, purporting to contain a copy of the proclamation, order, regulation or appointment, or a notice thereof;

(b) by the production of a copy of the proclamation, order, regulation or appointment purporting to be published by the government or Queen's Printer for the province; and

(c) by the production of a copy or extract of the proclamation, order, regulation or appointment purporting to be certified to be true by the clerk or assistant or acting clerk of the executive council, by the head of any department of the government of a province, or by his deputy or acting deputy, as the case may be.

(2) In the case of the territories — Evidence of any proclamation, order, regulation or appointment made by the Lieutenant Governor or Lieutenant Governor in Council of the Northwest Territories, as constituted prior to September 1, 1905, or by the Commissioner in Council of the Yukon Territory, the Commissioner in Council of the Northwest Territories or the Legislature for Nunavut, may be given by the production of a copy of the *Canada Gazette* purporting to contain a copy of the proclamation, order, regulation or appointment, or a notice thereof.

2000, c. 5, s. 55

23. (1) Evidence of judicial proceedings, etc. — Evidence of any proceeding or record whatever of, in or before any court in Great Britain, the Supreme Court, Federal Court or Tax Court of Canada, any court in any province, any court in any British colony or possession or any court of record of the United States, of any state of the United States or of any other foreign country, or before any justice of the peace or coroner in any province, may be given in any action or proceeding by an exemplification or certified copy of the proceeding or record, purporting to be under the seal of the court or under the hand or seal of the justice or coroner or court stenographer, as the case may be, without any proof of the authenticity of the seal or of the signature of the justice or coroner or court stenographer or other proof whatever.

(2) Certificate where court has no seal — Where any court, justice or coroner or court stenographer referred to in subsection (1) has no seal, or so certifies, the evidence may be given by a copy purporting to be certified under the signature of a judge or presiding provincial court judge or of the justice or coroner or court stenographer, without any proof of the authenticity of the signature or other proof whatever.

1993, c. 34, s. 15; 1997, c. 18, s. 117

24. Certified copies — In every case in which the original record could be admitted in evidence,

>(a) a copy of any official or public document of Canada or of any province, purporting to be certified under the hand of the proper officer or person in whose custody the official or public document is placed, or

>(b) a copy of a document, by-law, rule, regulation or proceeding, or a copy of any entry in any register or other book of any municipal or other corporation, created by charter or Act of Parliament or the legislature of any province, purporting to be certified under the seal of the corporation, and the hand of the presiding officer, clerk or secretary thereof,

is admissible in evidence without proof of the seal of the corporation, or of the signature or official character of the person or persons appearing to have signed it, and without further proof thereof.

25. Books and documents — Where a book or other document is of so public a nature as to be admissible in evidence on its mere production from the proper custody, and no other Act exists that renders its contents provable by means of a copy, a copy thereof or extract therefrom is admissible in evidence in any court of justice or before a person having, by law or by consent of parties, authority to hear, receive and examine evidence, if it is proved that it is a copy or extract purporting to be certified to be true by the officer to whose custody the original has been entrusted.

26. (1) Books kept in offices under government of Canada — A copy of any entry in any book kept in any office or department of the Government of Canada, or in any commission, board or other branch of the public service of Canada, shall be admitted as evidence of that entry, and of the matters, transactions and accounts therein recorded, if it is proved by the oath or affidavit of an officer of the office or department, commission, board or other branch of the public service of Canada that the book was, at the time of the making of the entry, one of the ordinary books kept in the office, department, commission, board or other branch of the public service of Canada, that the entry was made in the usual and ordinary course of business of the office, department, commission, board or other branch of the public service of Canada and that the copy is a true copy thereof.

(2) Proof of non-issue of licence or document — Where by any Act of Parliament or regulation made thereunder provision is made for the issue by a department, commission, board or other branch of the public service of Canada of a licence requisite to the doing or having of any act or thing or for the issue of any other document, an affidavit of an officer of the department, commission, board or other branch of the public service, sworn before any commissioner or other person authorized to take affidavits, setting out that he has charge of the appropriate records and that after careful examination and search of those records he has been unable to find in any given case that any such licence or other document has been issued, shall be admitted in evidence as proof, in the absence of evidence to the contrary, that in that case no licence or other document has been issued.

(3) Proof of mailing departmental matter — Where by any Act of Parliament or regulation made thereunder provision is made for sending by mail any request for information, notice or demand by a department or other branch of the public service of Canada, an affidavit of an officer of the department or other branch of the public service, sworn before any commissioner or other person authorized to take affidavits, setting out that he has charge of the appropriate records, that he has a knowledge of the facts in the particular case, that the request, notice or demand was sent by registered letter on a named date to the person or firm to whom it was addressed (including that address) and that he identifies as exhibits attached to the affidavit the post office certificate of registration of the letter and a true copy of the request, notice or demand, shall, on production and proof of the post office receipt for the delivery of the registered letter to the addressee, be admitted in evidence as proof, in the absence of evidence to the contrary, of the sending and of the request, notice or demand.

(4) Proof of official character — Where proof is offered by affidavit pursuant to this section it is not necessary to prove the official character of the person making the affidavit if that information is set out in the body of the affidavit.

27. Notarial acts in Quebec — Any document purporting to be a copy of a notarial act or instrument made, filed or registered in the Province of Quebec, and to be certified by a notary or prothonotary to be a true copy of the original in his possession as such notary or prothonotary, shall be admitted in evidence in the place and stead of the original and has the same force and effect as the original would have if produced and proved, but it may be proved in rebuttal that there is no original, that the copy is not a true copy of the original in some material particular or that the original is not an instrument of such nature as may, by the law of the Province of Quebec, be taken before a notary or be filed, enrolled or registered by a notary in that Province.

28. (1) Notice of production of book or document — No copy of any book or other document shall be admitted in evidence, under the authority of section 23, 24, 25, 26 or 27, on any trial, unless the party intending to produce the copy has before the trial given to the party against whom it is intended to be produced reasonable notice of that intention.

(2) Not less than 7 days — The reasonableness of the notice referred to in subsection (1) shall be determined by the court, judge or other person presiding, but the notice shall not in any case be less than seven days.

29. (1) Copies of entries — Subject to this section, a copy of any entry in any book or record kept in any financial institution shall in all legal proceedings be admitted in evidence as proof, in the absence of evidence to the contrary, of the entry and of the matters, transactions and accounts therein recorded.

(2) Admission in evidence — A copy of an entry in the book or record described in subsection (1) shall not be admitted in evidence under this section unless it is first proved that the book or record was, at the time of the making of the entry, one of the ordinary books or records of the financial institution, that the entry was made in the usual and ordinary course of business, that the book or record is in the custody or control of the financial institution and that the copy is a true copy of it, and such proof may be given by any person employed by the financial institution who has knowledge of the book or record or the manager or accountant of the financial institution, and may be given orally or by affidavit sworn before any commissioner or other person authorized to take affidavits.

(3) Cheques, proof of "no account" — Where a cheque has been drawn on any financial institution or branch thereof by any person, an affidavit of the manager or accountant of the financial institution or branch, sworn before any commissioner or other person authorized to take affidavits, setting out that he is the manager or accountant, that he has made a careful examination and search of the books and records for the purpose of ascertaining whether or not that person has an account with the financial institution or branch and that he has been unable to find such an account, shall be admitted in evidence as proof, in the absence of evidence to the contrary, that that person has no account in the financial institution or branch.

(4) Proof of official character — Where evidence is offered by affidavit pursuant to this section, it is not necessary to prove the signature or official character of the person making the affidavit if the official character of that person is set out in the body of the affidavit.

(5) Compulsion of production or appearance — A financial institution or officer of a financial institution is not in any legal proceedings to which the financial institution is not a party compellable to produce any book or record, the contents of which can be proved under this section, or to appear as a witness to prove the matters, transactions and accounts therein recorded unless by order of the court made for special cause.

(6) Order to inspect and copy — On the application of any party to a legal proceeding, the court may order that that party be at liberty to inspect and take copies of any entries in the books or records of a financial institution for the purposes of the legal proceeding, and the person whose account is to be inspected shall be notified of the application at least two clear days before the hearing thereof, and if it is shown to the satisfaction of the court that he cannot be notified personally, the notice may be given by addressing it to the financial institution.

(7) Warrants to search — Nothing in this section shall be construed as prohibiting any search of the premises of a financial institution under the authority of a warrant to search issued under any other Act of Parliament, but unless the warrant is expressly endorsed by the person under whose hand it is issued as not being limited by this section, the authority conferred by any such warrant to search the premises of a financial institution and to seize and take away anything in it shall, with respect to the books or records of the institution, be construed as limited to the searching of those premises for the purpose of inspecting and taking copies of entries in those books or records, and section 490 of the *Criminal Code* does not apply in respect of the copies of those books or records obtained under a warrant referred to in this section.

(8) Computation of time — Holidays shall be excluded from the computation of time under this section.

(9) Definitions — In this section,

"court" means the court, judge, arbitrator or person before whom a legal proceeding is held or taken;

"financial institution" means the Bank of Canada, the Business Development Bank of Canada and any institution that accepts in Canada deposits of money from its members or the public, and includes a branch, agency or office of any of those Banks or institutions;

"legal proceeding" means any civil or criminal proceeding or inquiry in which evidence is or may be given, and includes an arbitration.

1994, c. 44, s. 90; 1995, c. 28, s. 47(a); 1999, c. 28, s. 149

30. (1) Business records to be admitted in evidence — Where oral evidence in respect of a matter would be admissible in a legal proceeding, a record made in the usual and ordinary course of business that contains information in respect of that matter is admissible in evidence under this section in the legal proceeding on production of the record.

(2) Inference where information not in business record — Where a record made in the usual and ordinary course of business does not contain information in respect of a matter the occurrence or existence of which might reasonably be expected to be recorded in that record, the court may on production of the record admit the record for the purpose of establishing that fact and may draw the inference that the matter did not occur or exist.

(3) Copy of records — Where it is not possible or reasonably practicable to produce any record described in subsection (1) or (2), a copy of the record accompanied by two documents, one that is made by a person who states why it is not possible or reasonably practicable to produce the record and one that sets out the source from which the copy was made, that attests to the copy's authenticity and that is made by the person who made the copy, is admissible in evidence under this section in the same manner as if it were the original of the record if each document is

    (a) an affidavit of each of those persons sworn before a commissioner or other person authorized to take affidavits; or

    (b) a certificate or other statement pertaining to the record in which the person attests that the certificate or statement is made in conformity with the laws of a foreign state, whether or not the certificate or statement is in the form of an affidavit attested to before an official of the foreign state.

(4) Where record kept in form requiring explanation — Where production of any record or of a copy of any record described in subsection (1) or (2) would not convey to the court the information contained in the record by reason of its having been kept in a form that requires explanation, a transcript of the explanation of the record or copy prepared by a person qualified to make the explanation is admissible in evidence under this section in the same manner as if it were the original of the record if it is accompanied by a document that sets out the person's qualifications to make the explanation, attests to the accuracy of the explanation, and is

    (a) an affidavit of that person sworn before a commissioner or other person authorized to take affidavits; or

    (b) a certificate or other statement pertaining to the record in which the person attests that the certificate or statement is made in conformity with the laws of a foreign state, whether or not the certificate or statement is in the form of an affidavit attested to before an official of the foreign state.

(5) Court may order other part of record to be produced — Where part only of a record is produced under this section by any party, the court may examine any other part of the record and direct that, together with the part of the record previously so produced, the whole or any part of the other part thereof be produced by that party as the record produced by him.

(6) Court may examine record and hear evidence — For the purpose of determining whether any provision of this section applies, or for the purpose of determining the probative value, if any, to be given to information contained in any record admitted in evidence under this section, the court may, on production of any record, examine the record, admit any evidence in respect thereof given orally or by affidavit including evidence as to the circumstances in which the information contained in the record was written, recorded, stored or reproduced, and draw any reasonable inference from the form or content of the record.

(7) Notice of intention to produce record or affidavit — Unless the court orders otherwise, no record or affidavit shall be admitted in evidence under this section unless the party producing the record or affidavit has, at least seven days before its production, given notice of his intention to produce it to each other party to the legal proceeding and has, within five days after receiving any notice in that behalf given by any such party, produced it for inspection by that party.

(8) Not necessary to prove signature and official character — Where evidence is offered by affidavit under this section, it is not necessary to prove the signature or official character of the person making the affidavit if the official character of that person is set out in the body of the affidavit.

(9) Examination on record with leave of court — Subject to section 4, any person who has or may reasonably be expected to have knowledge of the making or contents of any record produced or received in evidence under this section may, with leave of the court, be examined or cross-examined thereon by any party to the legal proceeding.

(10) Evidence inadmissible under this section — Nothing in this section renders admissible in evidence in any legal proceeding

    (a) such part of any record as is proved to be

        (i) a record made in the course of an investigation or inquiry,

        (ii) a record made in the course of obtaining or giving legal advice or in contemplation of a legal proceeding.

        (iii) a record in respect of the production of which any privilege exists and is claimed, or

        (iv) a record of or alluding to a statement made by a person who is not, or if he were living and of sound mind would not be, competent and compellable to disclose in the legal proceeding a matter disclosed in the record;

    (b) any record the production of which would be contrary to public policy; or

(c) any transcript or recording of evidence taken in the course of another legal proceeding.

(11) Construction of this section — The provisions of this section shall be deemed to be in addition to and not in derogation of

(a) any other provision of this or any other Act of Parliament respecting the admissibility in evidence of any record or the proof of any matter; or

(b) any existing rule of law under which any record is admissible in evidence or any matter may be proved.

(12) Definitions — In this section,

"business" means any business, profession, trade, calling, manufacture or undertaking of any kind carried on in Canada or elsewhere whether for profit or otherwise, including any activity or operation carried on or performed in Canada or elsewhere by any government, by any department, branch, board, commission or agency of any government, by any court or other tribunal or by any other body or authority performing a function of government;

"copy" in relation to any record, includes a print, whether enlarged or not, from a photographic film of the record, and **"photographic film"** includes a photographic plate, microphotographic film or photostatic negative;

"court" means the court, judge, arbitrator or person before whom a legal proceeding is held or taken;

"legal proceeding" means any civil or criminal proceeding or inquiry in which evidence is or may be given, and includes an arbitration;

"record" includes the whole or any part of any book, document, paper, card, tape or other thing on or in which information is written, recorded, stored or reproduced, and, except for the purposes of subsections (3) and (4), any copy or transcript admitted in evidence under this section pursuant to subsection (3) or (4).

1994, c. 44, s. 91

31. (1) Definitions — In this section,

"corporation" means any bank, including the Bank of Canada and the Business Development Bank of Canada, any authorized foreign bank within the meaning of section 2 of the *Bank Act* and each of the following carrying on business in Canada, namely, every railway, express, telegraph and telephone company (except a street railway and tramway company), insurance company or society, trust company and loan company;

"government" means the government of Canada or of any province and includes any department, commission, board or branch of any such government; and

"photographic film" includes any photographic plate, microphotographic film and photostatic negative.

(2) When print admissible in evidence — A print, whether enlarged or not, from any photographic film of

(a) an entry in any book or record kept by any government or corporation and destroyed, lost or delivered to a customer after the film was taken,

(b) any bill of exchange, promissory note, cheque, receipt, instrument or document held by any government or corporation and destroyed, lost or delivered to a customer after the film was taken, or

(c) any record, document, plan, book or paper belonging to or deposited with any government or corporation,

is admissible in evidence in all cases in which and for all purposes for which the object photographed would have been admitted on proof that

(d) while the book, record, bill of exchange, promissory note, cheque, receipt, instrument or document, plan, book or paper was in the custody or control of the government or corporation, the photographic film was taken thereof in order to keep a permanent record thereof, and

(e) the object photographed was subsequently destroyed by or in the presence of one or more of the employees of the government or corporation, or was lost or was delivered to a customer.

(3) Evidence of compliance with conditions — Evidence of compliance with the conditions prescribed by this section may be given by any one or more of the employees of the government or corporation, having knowledge of the taking of the photographic film, of the destruction, loss or delivery to a customer, or of the making of the print, as the case may be, either orally or by affidavit sworn in any part of Canada before any notary public or commissioner for oaths.

(4) Proof by notarial copy — Unless the court otherwise orders, a notarial copy of an affidavit under subsection (3) is admissible in evidence in lieu of the original affidavit.

1992, c. 1, s. 142 (Sch. V, item 9); 1999, c. 28, s. 150

31.1 Authentication of electronic documents — Any person seeking to admit an electronic document as evidence has the burden of proving its authenticity by evidence capable of supporting a finding that the electronic document is that which it is purported to be.

2000, c. 5, s. 56

31.2 (1) Application of best evidence rule — electronic documents — The best evidence rule in respect of an electronic document is satisfied

(a) on proof of the integrity of the electronic documents system by or in which the electronic document was recorded or stored; or

(b) if an evidentiary presumption established under section 31.4 applies.

(2) Printouts — Despite subsection (1), in the absence of evidence to the contrary, an electronic document in the form of a printout satisfies the best evidence rule if the printout has been manifestly or consistently acted on, relied on or used as a record of the information recorded or stored in the printout.

2000, c. 5, s. 56

31.3 Presumption of integrity — For the purposes of subsection 31.2(1), in the absence of evidence to the contrary, the integrity of an electronic documents system by or in which an electronic document is recorded or stored is proven

(a) by evidence capable of supporting a finding that at all material times the computer system or other similar device used by the electronic documents system was operating properly or, if it was not, the fact of its not operating properly did not affect the integrity of the electronic document and there are no other reasonable grounds to doubt the integrity of the electronic documents system;

(b) if it is established that the electronic document was recorded or stored by a party who is adverse in interest to the party seeking to introduce it; or

(c) if it is established that the electronic document was recorded or stored in the usual and ordinary course of business by a person who is not a party and who did not record or store it under the control of the party seeking to introduce it.

2000, c. 5, s. 56

31.4 Presumptions regarding secure electronic signatures — The Governor in Council may make regulations establishing evidentiary presumptions in relation to electronic documents signed with secure electronic signatures, including regulations respecting

(a) the association of secure electronic signatures with persons; and

(b) the integrity of information contained in electronic documents signed with secure electronic signatures.

2000, c. 5, s. 56

31.5 Standards may be considered — For the purpose of determining under any rule of law whether an electronic document is admissible, evidence may be presented in respect of any standard, procedure, usage or practice concerning the manner in which electronic documents are to be recorded or stored, having regard to the type of business, enterprise or endeavour that used, recorded or stored the electronic document and the nature and purpose of the electronic document.

2000, c. 5, s. 56

31.6 (1) Proof by affidavit — The matters referred to in subsection 31.2(2) and sections 31.3 and 31.5 and in regulations made under section 31.4 may be established by affidavit.

(2) Cross-examination — A party may cross-examine a deponent of an affidavit referred to in subsection (1) that has been introduced in evidence

(a) as of right, if the deponent is an adverse party or is under the control of an adverse party; and

(b) with leave of the court, in the case of any other deponent.

2000, c. 5, s. 56

31.7 Application — Sections 31.1 to 31.4 do not affect any rule of law relating to the admissibility of evidence, except the rules relating to authentication and best evidence.

2000, c. 5, s. 56

31.8 Definitions — The definitions in this section apply in sections 31.1 to 31.6.

"computer system" means a device that, or a group of interconnected or related devices one or more of which,

    (a) contains computer programs or other data; and

    (b) pursuant to computer programs, performs logic and control, and may perform any other function.

"data" means representations of information or of concepts, in any form.

"electronic document" means data that is recorded or stored on any medium in or by a computer system or other similar device and that can be read or perceived by a person or a computer system or other similar device. It includes a display, printout or other output of that data.

"electronic documents system" includes a computer system or other similar device by or in which data is recorded or stored and any procedures related to the recording or storage of electronic documents.

"secure electronic signature" means a secure electronic signature as defined in subsection 31(1) of the *Personal Information Protection and Electronic Documents Act*.

2000, c. 5, s. 56

32. (1) Order signed by Secretary of State — An order signed by the Secretary of State of Canada and purporting to be written by command of the Governor General shall be admitted in evidence as the order of the Governor General.

(2) Copies published in *Canada Gazette* — All copies of official and other notices, advertisements and documents published in the *Canada Gazette* are admissible in evidence as proof, in the absence of evidence to the contrary, of the originals and of their contents.

2000, c. 5, s. 57

33. (1) Proof of handwriting of person certifying — No proof shall be required of the handwriting or official position of any person certifying, in pursuance of this Act, to the truth of any copy of or extract from any proclamation, order, regulation, appointment, book or other document.

(2) Printed or written — Any copy or extract referred to in subsection (1) may be in print or in writing, or partly in print and partly in writing.

34. (1) Attesting witness — It is not necessary to prove by the attesting witness any instrument to the validity of which attestation is not requisite.

(2) Instrument, how proved — Any instrument referred to in subsection (1) may be proved by admission or otherwise as if there had been no attesting witness thereto.

35. Impounding of forged instrument — Where any instrument that has been forged or fraudulently altered is admitted in evidence, the court or the judge or person who admits the instrument may, at the request of any person against whom it is admitted in evidence, direct that the instrument shall be impounded and be kept in the custody of an officer of the court or other proper person for such period and subject to such conditions as to the court, judge or person admitting the instrument seem meet.

36. Construction — This Part shall be deemed to be in addition to and not in derogation of any powers of proving documents given by any existing Act or existing at law.

Disclosure of Government Information

37. (1) Objection to disclosure of information — A minister of the Crown in right of Canada or other person interested may object to the disclosure of information before a court, person or body with jurisdiction to compel the production of information by certifying orally or in writing to the court, person or body that the information should not be disclosed on the grounds of a specified public interest.

(2) Where objection made to superior court — Subject to sections 38 and 39, where an objection to the disclosure of information is made under subsection (1) before a superior court, that court may examine or hear the information and order its disclosure, subject to such restrictions or conditions as it deems appropriate, if it concludes that, in the circumstances of the case, the public interest in disclosure outweighs in importance the specified public interest.

(3) Where objection not made to superior court — Subject to sections 38 and 39, where an objection to the disclosure of information is made under subsection (1) before a court, person or body other than a superior court, the objection may be determined, on application, in accordance with subsection (2) by

    (a) the Federal Court-Trial Division, in the case of a person or body vested with power to compel production by or pursuant to an Act of Parliament if the person or body is not a court established under a law of a province; or

    (b) the trial division or trial court of the superior court of the province within which the court, person or body exercises its jurisdiction, in any other case.

(4) Limitation period — An application pursuant to subsection (3) shall be made within ten days after the objection is made or within such further or lesser time as the court having jurisdiction to hear the application considers appropriate in the circumstances.

(5) Appeal to Court of Appeal — An appeal lies from a determination under subsection (2) or (3)

> (a) to the Federal Court of Appeal from a determination of the Federal Court-Trial Division; or

> (b) to the court of appeal of a province from a determination of a trial division or trial court of a superior court of a province.

(6) Limitation period for appeal under subsection (5) — An appeal under subsection (5) shall be brought within ten days from the date of the determination appealed from or within such further time as the court having jurisdiction to hear the appeal considers appropriate in the circumstances.

(7) Limitation periods for appeals to Supreme Court of Canada — Notwithstanding any other Act of Parliament,

> (a) an application for leave to appeal to the Supreme Court of Canada from a judgment made pursuant to subsection (5) shall be made within ten days from the date of the judgment appealed from or within such further time as the court having jurisdiction to grant leave to appeal considers appropriate in the circumstances; and

> (b) where leave to appeal is granted, the appeal shall be brought in the manner set out in subsection 60(1) of the *Supreme Court Act* but within such time as the court that grants leave specifies.

38. (1) Objection relating to international relations or national defence or security — Where an objection to the disclosure of information is made under subsection 37(1) on grounds that the disclosure would be injurious to international relations or national defence or security, the objection may be determined, on application, in accordance with subsection 37(2) only by the Chief Justice of the Federal Court, or such other judge of that court as the Chief Justice may designate to hear such applications.

(2) Limitation period — An application under subsection (1) shall be made within ten days after the objection is made or within such further or lesser time as the Chief Justice of the Federal Court, or such other judge of that court as the Chief Justice may designate to hear such applications, considers appropriate.

(3) Appeal to Federal Court of Appeal — An appeal lies from a determination under subsection (1) to the Federal Court of Appeal.

(4) Subsections 37(6) and (7) apply — Subsection 37(6) applies in respect of appeals under subsection (3), and subsection 37(7) applies in respect of appeals from judgments made pursuant to subsection (3), with such modifications as the circumstances require.

(5) Special rules for hearings — An application under subsection (1) or an appeal brought in respect of the application shall

> (a) be heard *in camera*; and

(b) on the request of the person objecting to the disclosure of information, be heard and determined in the National Capital Region described in the schedule to the *National Capital Act*.

(6) Ex parte representations — During the hearing of an application under subsection (1) or an appeal brought in respect of the application, the person who made the objection in respect of which the application was made or the appeal was brought shall, on the request of that person, be given the opportunity to make representations *ex parte*.

39. (1) Objection relating to a confidence of the Queen's Privy Council — Where a minister of the Crown or the Clerk of the Privy Council objects to the disclosure of information before a court, person or body with jurisdiction to compel the production of information by certifying in writing that the information constitutes a confidence of the Queen's Privy Council for Canada, disclosure of the information shall be refused without examination or hearing of the information by the court, person or body.

(2) Definition — For the purpose of subsection (1), "a confidence of the Queen's Privy Council for Canada" includes, without restricting the generality thereof, information contained in

(a) a memorandum the purpose of which is to present proposals or recommendations to Council;

(b) a discussion paper the purpose of which is to present background explanations, analyses of problems or policy options to Council for consideration by Council in making decisions;

(c) an agendum of Council or a record recording deliberations or decisions of Council;

(d) a record used for or reflecting communications or discussions between ministers of the Crown on matters relating to the making of government decisions or the formulation of government policy;

(e) a record the purpose of which is to brief ministers of the Crown in relation to matters that are brought before, or are proposed to be brought before, Council or that are the subject of communications or discussions referred to in paragraph (d); and

(f) draft legislation.

(3) Definition of "council" — For the purposes of subsection (2), "Council" means the Queen's Privy Council for Canada, committees of the Queen's Privy Council for Canada, Cabinet and committees of Cabinet.

(4) Exception — Subsection (1) does not apply in respect of

(a) a confidence of the Queen's Privy Council for Canada that has been in existence for more than twenty years; or

(b) a discussion paper described in paragraph (2)(b)

(i) if the decisions to which the discussion paper relates have been made public, or

(ii) where the decisions have not been made public, if four years have passed since the decisions were made.

Provincial Laws of Evidence

40. How applicable — In all proceedings over which Parliament has legislative authority, the laws of evidence in force in the province in which those proceedings are taken, including the laws of proof of service of any warrant, summons, subpoena or other document, subject to this Act and other Acts of Parliament, apply to those proceedings.

Statutory Declarations

41. Solemn declaration — Any judge, notary public, justice of the peace, police or provincial court judge, recorder, mayor or commissioner authorized to take affidavits to be used either in the provincial or federal courts, or any other functionary authorized by law to administer an oath in any matter, may receive the solemn declaration of any person voluntarily making the declaration before him, in the following form, in attestation of the execution of any writing, deed or instrument, or of the truth of any fact, or of any account rendered in writing:

I, ..., solemnly declare that (*state the fact or facts declared to*), and I make this solemn declaration conscientiously believing it to be true, and knowing that it is of the same force and effect as if made under oath.

Declared before me ..... at ..... this ..... day of ..... 19 ...

Insurance Proofs

42. Affidavits, etc — Any affidavit, solemn affirmation or declaration required by any insurance company authorized by law to do business in Canada, in regard to any loss of or injury to person, property or life insured or assured therein, may be taken before any commissioner or other person authorized to take affidavits, before any justice of the peace or before any notary public for any province, and the commissioner, person, justice of the peace or notary public is required to take the affidavit, solemn affirmation or declaration.

PART II

Application

43. Foreign courts — This Part applies to the taking of evidence relating to proceedings in courts out of Canada.

Interpretation

44. Definitions — In this Part,

"cause" includes a proceeding against a criminal;

"court" means any superior court in any province;

"judge" means any judge of any superior court in any province;

"oath" includes a solemn affirmation in cases in which, by the law of Canada, or of a province, as the case may be, a solemn affirmation is allowed instead of an oath.

45. Construction — This Part shall not be so construed as to interfere with the right of legislation of the legislature of any province requisite or desirable for the carrying out of the objects hereof.

Procedure

46. (1) Order for examination of witness in Canada — If, on an application for that purpose, it is made to appear to any court or judge that any court or tribunal outside Canada, before which any civil, commercial or criminal matter is pending, is desirous of obtaining the testimony in relation to that matter of a party or witness within the jurisdiction of the first mentioned court, of the court to which the judge belongs or of the judge, the court or judge may, in its or their discretion, order the examination on oath on interrogatories, or otherwise, before any person or persons named in the order, of that party or witness accordingly, and by the same or any subsequent order may command the attendance of that party or witness for the purpose of being examined, and for the production of any writings or other documents mentioned in the order and of any other writings or documents relating to the matter in question that are in the possession or power of that party or witness.

(2) Video links, etc. — For greater certainty, testimony for the purposes of subsection (1) may be given by means of technology that permits the virtual presence of the party or witness before the court or tribunal outside Canada or that permits that court or tribunal, and the parties, to hear and examine the party or witness.

1999, c. 18, s. 89

47. Enforcement of the order — On the service on the party or witness of an order referred to in section 46, and of an appointment of a time and place for the examination of the party or witness signed by the person named in the order for taking the examination, or, if more than one person is named, by one of the persons named, and on payment or tender of the like conduct money as is properly payable on attendance at a trial, the order may be enforced in like manner as an order made by the court or judge in a cause pending in that court or before that judge.

48. Expenses and conduct money — Every person whose attendance is required in manner described in section 47 is entitled to the like conduct money and payment for expenses and loss of time as on attendance at a trial.

49. Administering oath — On any examination of parties or witnesses, under the authority of any order made in pursuance of this Part, the oath shall be administered by the person authorized to take the examination, or, if more than one person is authorized, by one of those persons.

50. (1) Right of refusal to answer or produce document — Any person examined under any order made under this Part has the like right to refuse to answer questions tending to criminate himself, or other questions, as a party or witness, as the case may be, would have in any cause pending in the court by which, or by a judge whereof, the order is made.

(1.1) Laws about witnesses to apply — video links etc. — Despite subsection (1), when a party or witness gives evidence under subsection 46(2), the evidence shall be given as though they were physically before the court or tribunal outside Canada, for the purposes of the laws relating to evidence and procedure but only to the extent that giving the evidence would not disclose information otherwise protected by the Canadian law of non-disclosure of information or privilege.

(1.2) Contempt of court in Canada — When a party or witness gives evidence under subsection 46(2), the Canadian law relating to contempt of court applies with respect to a refusal by the party or witness to answer a question or to produce a writing or document referred to in subsection 46(1), as ordered under that subsection by the court or judge.

(2) Nature of right — No person shall be compelled to produce, under any order referred to in subsection (1), any writing or other document that he could not be compelled to produce at a trial of such a cause.

1999, c. 18, s. 90

51. (1) Rules of court — The court may frame rules and orders in relation to procedure and to the evidence to be produced in support of the application for an order for examination of parties and witnesses under this Part, and generally for carrying this Part into effect.

(2) Letters rogatory — In the absence of any order in relation to the evidence to be produced in support of the application referred to in subsection (1), letters rogatory from a court or tribunal outside Canada in which the civil, commercial or criminal matter is pending, are deemed and taken to be sufficient evidence in support of the application.

1999, c. 18, s. 91

PART III

Application

52. Application of this Part — This Part extends to the following classes of persons:

    (a) officers of any of Her Majesty's diplomatic or consular services while performing their functions in any foreign country, including ambassadors, envoys, ministers, charges d'affaires, counsellors, secretaries, attaches, consuls general, consuls, vice-consuls, pro-consuls, consular agents, acting consuls general, acting consuls, acting vice-consuls and acting consular agents;

(b) officers of the Canadian diplomatic, consular and representative services while performing their functions in any foreign country or in any part of the Commonwealth and Dependent Territories other than Canada, including, in addition to the diplomatic and consular officers mentioned in paragraph (a), high commissioners, permanent delegates, acting high commissioners, acting permanent delegates, counsellors and secretaries;

(c) Canadian Government Trade Commissioners and Assistant Canadian Government Trade Commissioners while performing their functions in any foreign country or in any part of the Commonwealth and Dependent Territories other than Canada;

(d) honorary consular officers of Canada while performing their functions in any foreign country or in any part of the Commonwealth and Dependent Territories other than Canada;

(e) judicial officials in a foreign country in respect of oaths, affidavits, solemn affirmations, declarations or similar documents that the official is authorized to administer, take or receive; and

(f) persons locally engaged and designated by the Deputy Minister of Foreign Affairs or any other persons authorized by that Deputy Minister while performing their functions in any foreign country or in any part of the Commonwealth and Dependent Territories other than Canada.

1994, c. 44, s. 92; 1997, c. 18, s. 118

Oaths and Solemn Affirmations

53. Oaths taken abroad — Oaths, affidavits, solemn affirmations or declarations administered, taken or received outside Canada by any person mentioned in section 52, are as valid and effectual and are of the like force and effect to all intents and purposes as if they had been administered, taken or received in Canada by a person authorized to administer, take or receive oaths, affidavits, solemn affirmations or declarations therein that are valid and effectual under this Act.

Documentary Evidence

54. (1) Documents to be admitted in evidence — Any document that purports to have affixed, impressed or subscribed on it or to it the signature of any person authorized by any of paragraphs 52 (a) to (d) to administer, take or receive oaths, affidavits, solemn affirmations or declarations, together with their seal or with the seal or stamp of their office, or the office to which the person is attached, in testimony of any oath, affidavit, solemn affirmation or declaration being administered, taken or received by the person, shall be admitted in evidence, without proof of the seal or stamp or of the person's signature or official character.

(2) Status of statements — An affidavit, solemn affirmation, declaration or other similar statement taken or received in a foreign country by an official referred to in paragraph 52(e) shall be admitted in evidence without proof of the signature or official character of the official appearing to have signed the affidavit, solemn affirmation, declaration or other statement.

1994, c. 44, s. 93

CANADIAN BILL OF RIGHTS

R.S.C. 1985, Appendix III

Preamble — The Parliament of Canada, affirming that the Canadian Nation is founded upon principles that acknowledge the supremacy of God, the dignity and worth of the human person and the position of the family in a society of free men and free institutions;

Affirming also that men and institutions remain free only when freedom is founded upon respect for moral and spiritual values and the rule of law;

And being desirous of enshrining these principles and the human rights and fundamental freedoms derived from them, in a Bill of Rights which shall reflect the respect of Parliament for its constitutional authority and which shall ensure the protection of these rights and freedoms in Canada:

Therefore, Her Majesty, by and with the advice and consent of the Senate and House of Commons of Canada, enacts as follows:

PART I — BILL OF RIGHTS

1. Recognition and declaration of rights and freedoms — It is hereby recognized and declared that in Canada there have existed and shall continue to exist without discrimination by reason of race, national origin, colour, religion or sex, the following human rights and fundamental freedoms, namely,

> (a) the right of the individual to life, liberty, security of the person and enjoyment of property, and the right not to be deprived thereof except by due process of law;

> (b) the right of the individual to equality before the law and the protection of the law;

> (c) freedom of religion;

> (d) freedom of speech;

> (e) freedom of assembly and association; and

> (f) freedom of the press.

2. Construction of law — Every law of Canada shall, unless it is expressly declared by an Act of the Parliament of Canada that it shall operate notwithstanding the *Canadian Bill of Rights*, be so construed and applied as not to abrogate, abridge or infringe or to authorize the abrogation, abridgment or infringement of any of the rights or freedoms herein recognized and declared, and in particular, no law of Canada shall be construed or applied so as to

(a) authorize or effect the arbitrary detention, imprisonment or exile of any person;

(b) impose or authorize the imposition of cruel and unusual treatment or punishment;

(c) deprive a person who has been arrested or detained

(i) of the right to be informed promptly of the reason for his arrest or detention,

(ii) of the right to retain and instruct counsel without delay, or

(iii) of the remedy by way of *habeas corpus* for the determination of the validity of his detention and for his release if the detention is not lawful;

(d) authorize a court, tribunal, commission, board or other authority to compel a person to give evidence if he is denied counsel, protection against self crimination or other constitutional safeguards;

(e) deprive a person of the right to a fair hearing in accordance with the principles of fundamental justice for the determination of his rights and obligations;

(f) deprive a person charged with a criminal offence of the right to be presumed innocent until proved guilty according to law in a fair and public hearing by an independent and impartial tribunal, or of the right to reasonable bail without just cause; or

(g) deprive a person of the right to the assistance of an interpreter in any proceedings in which he is involved or in which he is a party or a witness, before a court, commission, board or other tribunal, if he does not understand or speak the language in which such proceedings are conducted.

3. (1) Duties of Minister of Justice — Subject to subjection (2), the Minister of Justice shall, in accordance with such regulations as may be prescribed by the Governor in Council, examine every regulation transmitted to the Clerk of the Privy Council for registration pursuant to the *Statutory Instruments Act* and every Bill introduced in or presented to the House of Commons by a Minister of the Crown in order to ascertain whether any of the provisions thereof are inconsistent with the purposes and provisions of this Part and he shall report any such inconsistency to the House of Commons at the first convenient opportunity.

(2) Exception — A regulation need not be examined in accordance with subsection (1) if prior to being made it was examined as a proposed regulation in accordance with section 3 of the Statutory Instruments Act to ensure that it was not inconsistent with the purposes and provisions of this Part.

4. Short title — The provisions of this Part shall be known as the *Canadian Bill of Rights*.

PART II

5. (1) Savings — Nothing in Part I shall be construed to abrogate or abridge any human right or fundamental freedom not enumerated therein that may have existed in Canada at the commencement of this Act.

(2) "Law of Canada" defined — The expression **"law of Canada"** in Part I means an Act of the Parliament of Canada enacted before or after the coming into force of this Act, any order, rule or regulation thereunder, and any law in force in Canada or in any part of Canada at the commencement of this Act that is subject to be repealed, abolished or altered by the Parliament of Canada.

(2) Jurisdiction of Parliament — The provisions of Part I shall be construed as extending only to matters coming within the legislative authority of the Parliament of Canada.

CONSTITUTION ACT, 1982

R.S.C. 1985, Appendix II, No. 44
En. Canada Act 1982 (U.K.), c. 11 Am. Constitution Amendment Proclamation, 1983, SI/84-102, Schedule.

. . . . .

PART VII — GENERAL

52. (1) Primacy of Constitution of Canada — The Constitution of Canada is
the supreme law of Canada, and any law that is inconsistent with the provisions of
the Constitution is, to the extent of the inconsistency, of no force or effect.

(2) Constitution of Canada — The Constitution of Canada includes

  (a) the *Canada Act 1982*, including this Act;

  (b) the Acts and orders referred to in the schedule; and

  (c) any amendment to any Act or order referred to in paragraph (a) or (b).

(3) Amendments to the Constitution of Canada — Amendments to the Constitution of Canada shall be made only in accordance with the authority contained in
the Constitution of Canada.

PART I — CANADIAN CHARTER OF RIGHTS AND FREEDOMS

Whereas Canada is founded upon principles that recognize the supremacy of God
and the rule of law:

Guarantee of Rights and Freedoms

1. Rights and freedoms in Canada — The *Canadian Charter of Rights and
Freedoms* guarantees the rights and freedoms set out in it subject only to such reasonable limits prescribed by law as can be demonstrably justified in a free and democratic society.

Fundamental Freedoms

2. Fundamental freedoms — Everyone has the following fundamental
freedoms:

  (a) freedom of conscience and religion;

(b) freedom of thought, belief, opinion and expression, including freedom of the press and other media of communication;

(c) freedom of peaceful assembly; and

(d) freedom of association.

Democratic Rights

3. Democratic rights of citizens — Every citizen of Canada has the right to vote in an election of members of the House of Commons or of a legislative assembly and to be qualified for membership therein.

4. (1) Maximum duration of legislative bodies — No House of Commons and no legislative assembly shall continue for longer than five years from the date fixed for the return of the writs at a general election of its members.

(2) Continuation in special circumstances — In time of real or apprehended war, invasion or insurrection, a House of Commons may be continued by Parliament and a legislative assembly may be continued by the legislature beyond five years if such continuation is not opposed by the votes of more than one-third of the members of the House of Commons or the legislative assembly, as the case may be.

5. Annual sitting of legislative bodies — There shall be a sitting of Parliament and of each legislature at least once every twelve months.

Mobility Rights

6. (1) Mobility of citizens — Every citizen of Canada has the right to enter, remain in and leave Canada.

(2) Rights to move and gain livelihood — Every citizen of Canada and every person who has the status of a permanent resident of Canada has the right

(a) to move to and take up residence in any province; and

(b) to pursue the gaining of a livelihood in any province.

(3) Limitation — The rights specified in subsection (2) are subject to

(a) any laws or practices of general application in force in a province other than those that discriminate among persons primarily on the basis of province of present or previous residence; and

(b) any laws providing for reasonable residency requirements as a qualification for the receipt of publicly provided social services.

(4) Affirmative action programs — Subsections (2) and (3) do not preclude any law, program or activity that has as its object the amelioration in a province of conditions of individuals in that province who are socially or economically disadvantaged if the rate of employment in that province is below the rate of employment in Canada.

Legal Rights

7. Life, liberty and security of person — Everyone has the right to life, liberty and security of the person and the right not to be deprived thereof except in accordance with the principles of fundamental justice.

8. Search or seizure — Everyone has the right to be secure against unreasonable search or seizure.

9. Detention or imprisonment — Everyone has the right not to be arbitrarily detained or imprisoned.

10. Arrest or detention — Everyone has the right on arrest or detention

   (a) to be informed promptly of the reasons therefor;

   (b) to retain and instruct counsel without delay and to be informed of that right; and

   (c) to have the validity of the detention determined by way of *habeas corpus* and to be released if the detention is not lawful.

11. Proceedings in criminal and penal matters — Any person charged with an offence has the right

   (a) to be informed without unreasonable delay of the specific offence;

   (b) to be tried within a reasonable time;

   (c) not to be compelled to be a witness in proceedings against that person in respect of the offence;

   (d) to be presumed innocent until proven guilty according to law in a fair and public hearing by an independent and impartial tribunal;

   (e) not to be denied reasonable bail without just cause;

   (f) except in the case of an offence under military law tried before a military tribunal, to the benefit of trial by jury where the maximum punishment for the offence is imprisonment for five years or a more severe punishment;

   (g) not to be found guilty on account of any act or omission unless, at the time of the act or omission, it constituted an offence under Canadian or international law or was criminal according to the general principles of law recognized by the community of nations;

   (h) if finally acquitted of the offence, not to be tried for it again and, if finally found guilty and punished for the offence, not to be tried or punished for it again; and

   (i) if found guilty of the offence and if the punishment for the offence has been varied between the time of commission and the time of sentencing, to the benefit of the lesser punishment.

12. Treatment or punishment — Everyone has the right not to be subjected to any cruel and unusual treatment or punishment.

13. Self-crimination — A witness who testifies in any proceedings has the right not to have any incriminating evidence so given used to incriminate that witness in any other proceedings, except in a prosecution for perjury or for the giving of contradictory evidence.

14. Interpreter — A party or witness in any proceedings who does not understand or speak the language in which the proceedings are conducted or who is deaf has the right to the assistance of an interpreter.

Equality Rights

15. (1) Equality before and under law and equal protection and benefit of law — Every individual is equal before and under the law and has the right to the equal protection and equal benefit of the law without discrimination and, in particular, without discrimination based on race, national or ethnic origin, colour, religion, sex, age or mental or physical disability.

(2) Affirmative action programs — Subsection (1) does not preclude any law, program or activity that has as its object the amelioration of conditions of disadvantaged individuals or groups including those that are disadvantaged because of race, national or ethnic origin, colour, religion, sex, age or mental or physical disability.

Official Languages of Canada

16. (1) Official languages of Canada — English and French are the official languages of Canada and have equality of status and equal rights and privileges as to their use in all institutions of the Parliament and government of Canada.

(2) Official languages of New Brunswick — English and French are the official languages of New Brunswick and have equality of status and equal rights and privileges as to their use in all institutions of the legislature and government of New Brunswick.

(3) Advancement of status and use — Nothing in this Charter limits the authority of Parliament or a legislature to advance the equality of status or use of English and French.

17. (1) Proceedings of Parliament — Everyone has the right to use English or French in any debates and other proceedings of Parliament.

(2) Proceedings of New Brunswick legislature — Everyone has the right to use English or French in any debates and other proceedings of the legislature of New Brunswick.

18. (1) Parliamentary statutes and records — The statutes, records and journals of Parliament shall be printed and published in English and French and both language versions are equally authoritative.

(2) New brunswick statutes and records — The statutes, records and journals of the legislature of New Brunswick shall be printed and published in English and French and both language versions are equally authoritative.

19. (1) Proceedings in courts established by Parliament — Either English or French may be used by any person in, or in any pleading in or process issuing from, any court established by Parliament.

(2) Proceedings in New Brunswick courts — Either English or French may be used by any person in, or in any pleading in or process issuing from, any court of New Brunswick.

20. (1) Communications by public with federal institutions — Any member of the public in Canada has the right to communicate with, and to receive available services from, any head or central office of an institution of the Parliament or government of Canada in English or French, and has the same right with respect to any other office of any such institution where

(a) there is a significant demand for communications with and services from that office in such language; or

(b) due to the nature of the office, it is reasonable that communications with and services from that office be available in both English and French.

(2) Communications by public with New Brunswick institutions — Any member of the public in New Brunswick has the right to communicate with, and to receive available services from, any office of an institution of the legislature or government of New Brunswick in English or French.

21. Continuation of existing Constitutional provisions — Nothing in sections 16 to 20 abrogates or derogates from any right, privilege or obligation with respect to the English and French languages, or either of them, that exists or is continued by virtue of any other provision of the Constitution of Canada.

22. Rights and privileges preserved — Nothing in sections 16 to 20 abrogates or derogates from any legal or customary right or privilege acquired or enjoyed either before or after the coming into force of this Charter with respect to any language that is not English or French.

Minority Language Educational Rights

23. (1) Language of instruction — Citizens of Canada

(a) whose first language learned and still understood is that of the English or French linguistic minority population of the province in which they reside, or

(b) who have received their primary school instruction in Canada in English or French and reside in a province where the language in which they received that instruction is the language of the English or French linguistic minority population of the province, have the right to have their children receive primary and secondary school instruction in that language in that province.

(2) Continuity of language instruction — Citizens of Canada of whom any child has received or is receiving primary or secondary school instruction in English or French in Canada, have the right to have all their children receive primary and secondary school instruction in the same language.

(3) Application where numbers warrant — The right of citizens of Canada under subsections (1) and (2) to have their children receive primary and secondary school instruction in the language of the English or French linguistic minority population of a province

> (a) applies wherever in the province the number of children of citizens who have such a right is sufficient to warrant the provision to them out of public funds of minority language instruction; and

> (b) includes, where the number of those children so warrants, the right to have them receive that instruction in minority language educational facilities provided out of public funds.

Enforcement

24. (1) Enforcement of guaranteed rights and freedoms — Anyone whose rights or freedoms, as guaranteed by this Charter, have been infringed or denied may apply to a court of competent jurisdiction to obtain such remedy as the court considers appropriate and just in the circumstances.

(2) Exclusion of evidence bringing administration of justice into disrepute — Where, in proceedings under subsection (1), a court concludes that evidence was obtained in a manner that infringed or denied any rights or freedoms guaranteed by this Charter, the evidence shall be excluded if it is established that, having regard to all the circumstances, the admission of it in the proceedings would bring the administration of justice into disrepute.

25. Aboriginal rights and freedoms not affected by Charter — The guarantee in this Charter of certain rights and freedoms shall not be construed so as to abrogate or derogate from any aboriginal treaty or other rights or freedoms that pertain to the aboriginal peoples of Canada including

> (a) any rights or freedoms that have been recognized by the Royal Proclamation of October 7, 1763; and

> (b) any rights or freedoms that now exist by way of land claims agreements or may be so acquired.

26. Other rights and freedoms not affected by Charter — The guarantee in this Charter of certain rights and freedoms shall not be construed as denying the existence of any other rights or freedoms that exist in Canada.

27. Multicultural heritage — This Charter shall be interpreted in a manner consistent with the preservation and enhancement of the multicultural heritage of Canadians.

28. Rights guaranteed equally to both sexes — Notwithstanding anything in this Charter, the rights and freedoms referred to in it are guaranteed equally to male and female persons.

29. Rights respecting certain schools preserved — Nothing in this Charter abrogates or derogates from any rights or privileges guaranteed by or under the Constitution of Canada in respect of denominational, separate or dissentient schools.

30. Application to Territories and territorial authorities — A reference in this Charter to a province or to the legislative assembly or legislature of a province shall be deemed to include a reference to the Yukon Territory and the Northwest Territories, or to the appropriate legislative authority thereof, as the case may be.

31. Legislative powers not extended — Nothing in this Charter extends the legislative powers of any body or authority.

Application of Charter

32. (1) Application of Charter — This Charter applies

    (a) to the Parliament and government of Canada in respect of all matters within the authority of Parliament including all matters relating to the Yukon Territory and Northwest Territories; and

    (b) to the legislature and government of each province in respect of all matters within the authority of the legislature of each province.

(2) Exception — Notwithstanding subsection (1), section 15 shall not have effect until three years after this section comes into force.

33. (1) Exception where express declaration — Parliament or the legislature of a province may expressly declare in an Act of Parliament or of the legislature, as the case may be, that the Act or a provision thereof shall operate notwithstanding a provision included in section 2 or sections 7 to 15 of this Charter.

(2) Operation of exception — An Act or a provision of an Act in respect of which a declaration made under this section is in effect shall have such operation as it would have but for the provision of this Charter referred to in the declaration.

(3) Five year limitation — A declaration made under subsection (1) shall cease to have effect five years after it comes into force or on such earlier date as may be specified in the declaration.

(4) Re-enactment — Parliament or a legislature of a province may re-enact a declaration made under subsection (1).

(5) Five year limitation — Subsection (3) applies in respect of a re-enactment made under subsection (4).

Citation

34. Citation — This Part may be cited as the *Canadian Charter of Rights and Freedoms.*

CONTROLLED DRUGS AND SUBSTANCES ACT

TABLE OF CONCORDANCE

[Note: The Controlled Drugs and Substances Act repeals and replaces the Narcotic Control Act and Parts III and IV of the Food and Drugs Act. Note that the Controlled Drugs and Substances Act replaced Parts III and IV of the Food and Drugs Act, however, some of the Controlled Drugs and Substances Act sections pertain to interpretation, administration and enforcement which, while dealt with somewhat in Parts III and IV of the Food and Drugs Act, are also covered in Parts I and II; as such, there are some sections in the Controlled Drugs and Substances Act which equate to section in Parts I and II of the FDA.]

CDA, S.C. 1996, c. 19	NCA, R.S.C. c. N-1	FDA, R.S.C. 1985, c. F-27
1	1	1
2(1)	2	2; 38; 46
2(2)	—	—
2(3)	—	—
3	—	—
4(1)	3(1)	47(1)
4(2)	3.1(1)	38.1(1)
4(3)(a)	3(2)(b)	—
4(3)(b)	3(2)(a)	—
4(4)(a)	3(2)(b)	—
4(4)(b)	3(2)(a)	—
4(5)	—	—
4(6)	—	47(2)
4(7)	3.1(2)	38.1(2)
4(8)	—	—
5(1)	4(1)	39(1); 48(1)
5(2)	4(2)	39(2); 48(2)
5(3)(a)	4(3)	—
5(3)(b)	—	48(3)
5(3)(c)	—	39(3)
5(4)	—	—
5(5)	—	—
5(6)	—	—
6(1)	5(1)	39(1); 48(1)

CDA, S.C. 1996, c. 19	NCA, R.S.C. c. N-1	FDA, R.S.C. 1985, c. F-27
6(2)	—	39(2); 48(2)
6(3)(a)	5(2)	—
6(3)(b)	—	48(3)
6(3)(c)	—	39(3)
7(1)	4(1), (2); 6(1)	39(1); 48(1)
7(2)(a)	4(3); 6(2)	—
7(2)(b)	6(2)	—
7(2)(c)	—	48(3)
7(2)(d)	—	39(3)
8(1)(a), (b)	19.1(1)	44.2(1)(a); 50.1; 50.2(1)
8(1)(c)	—	44.1; 50.1
8(2)	19.1(2)	44.2(2); 50.2(2)
9(1)(a), (b)	—	44.1; 44.3(1); 50.1; 50.3(1)
9(1)(c)	—	44.1
9(2)	19.2(2)	44.3(2); 44.3(1); 50.1; 50.3(1)
10	—	—
11(1)	12	42(3); 51
11(2)-(4)	—	—
11(5), (6)	11	42(2); 51
11(7)	10	42(1); 51
11(8)	11	42(2); 51
12	14	42(5); 51
13	15	43; 51
14-15	—	—
16(1)	16	27; 44; 51
16(2), (3)	—	—
17	—	—
18	—	—
19	—	—
20(1)-(5)	17	—
20(6)	19	—
21	—	—
22	—	—
23	19.3	44.4; 51
24(1)-(4)	15	43; 51
24(5)	—	—
25	15(4)	43(4); 51
26	—	—

CDA, S.C. 1996, c. 19	NCA, R.S.C. c. N-1	FDA, R.S.C. 1985, c. F-27
27	—	—
28	—	27(1)
29	6(3)	—
30	—	22
31(1)	—	23(1)
31(2)	—	23(1.1)
31(3)	—	23(1.2)
31(4)	—	23(1.3)
31(5)	—	23(5)
31(6)	—	25
31(7)	—	—
31(8)	—	26
31(9)	—	—
32	—	24
33-43	—	—
44	21	28
45	—	29
46	—	—
47(1)	3.1(3)	38.1(3)
47(2)	—	33
48	7	41; 50
49, 50	—	—
51	9(1)-(3)	35(1)-(3)
52	9(4), (5)	35(4), (5)
53, 54	—	—
55	20	30; 45(1); 51
56-59	—	—
60	22	45(2); 51

CONTROLLED DRUGS AND SUBSTANCES ACT

S.C. 1996, c. 19, as am. S.C. 1996, c. 8, s. 35(a); 1997, c. 18, s. 140;
SOR/97-230; SOR/98-157; SOR/98-173; 1999, c. 5, ss. 48, 49; SOR/99-
371; SOR/99-421; SOR/2000-220 [To come into force September 1,
2000.].

An Act respecting the control of certain drugs, their precursors and other substances
and to amend certain other Acts and repeal the Narcotic Control Act in consequence
thereof.

*[Note: The Narcotic Control Act, R.S.C. 1985, c. N-1, is no longer in force. It was
repealed by the Controlled Drugs and Substances Act, S.C. 1996, c. 19 on May 14,
1997. We have, however, retained the Narcotic Control Act, because the Act remains of relevance to offences occurring before its repeal. It will therefore continue
to be of great practical importance for some time to come. The Narcotic Control
Act appears immediately following the Controlled Drugs and Substances Act. The
Narcotic Control Act is replaced by the following:]*

Short Title

1. Short title — This Act may be cited as the *Controlled Drugs and Substances
Act*.

Interpretation

2. (1) Definitions — In this Act,

"adjudicator" means a person appointed or employed under the *Public Service
Employment Act* who performs the duties and functions of an adjudicator under this
Act and the regulations;

"analogue" means a substance that, in relation to a controlled substance, has a substantially similar chemical structure;

"analyst" means a person who is designated as an analyst under section 44;

"Attorney General" means

    (a) the Attorney General of Canada, and includes their lawful deputy, or

    (b) with respect to proceedings commenced at the instance of the government
of a province and conducted by or on behalf of that government, the Attorney
General of that province, and includes their lawful deputy;

"controlled substance" means a substance included in Schedule I, II, III, IV or V;

"designated substance offence" means

> (a) an offence under Part I, except subsection 4(1), or

> (b) a conspiracy or an attempt to commit, being an accessory after the fact in relation to, or any counselling in relation to, an offence referred to in paragraph (a);

"inspector" means a person who is designated as an inspector under section 30;

"judge" means a judge as defined in section 552 of the *Criminal Code* or a judge of a superior court of criminal jurisdiction;

"justice" has the same meaning as in section 2 of the *Criminal Code*;

"Minister" means the Minister of Health;

"offence-related property" means any property, within or outside Canada,

> (a) by means of or in respect of which a designated substance offence is committed,

> (b) that is used in any manner in connection with the commission of a designated substance offence, or

> (c) that is intended for use for the purpose of committing a designated substance offence,

but does not include a controlled substance or real property, other than real property built or significantly modified for the purpose of facilitating the commission of a designated substance offence;

"possession" means possession within the meaning of subsection 4(3) of the *Criminal Code*;

"practitioner" means a person who is registered and entitled under the laws of a province to practise in that province the profession of medicine, dentistry or veterinary medicine, and includes any other person or class or persons prescribed as a practitioner;

"precursor" means a substance included in Schedule VI;

"prescribed" means prescribed by the regulations;

"produce" means, in respect of a substance included in any of Schedules I to IV, to obtain the substance by any method or process including

> (a) manufacturing, synthesizing or using any means of altering the chemical or physical properties of the substance, or

> (b) cultivating, propagating or harvesting the substance or any living thing from which the substance may be extracted or otherwise obtained,

and includes offer to produce;

"provide" means to give, transfer or otherwise make available in any manner, whether directly or indirectly and whether or not for consideration;

"sell" includes offer for sale, expose for sale, have in possession for sale and distribute, whether or not the distribution is made for consideration;

"traffic" means, in respect of a substance included in any of Schedules I to IV,

(a) to sell, administer, give, transfer, transport, send or deliver the substance,

(b) to sell an authorization to obtain the substance, or

(c) to offer to do anything mentioned in paragraph (a) or (b),

otherwise than under the authority of the regulations.

(2) Interpretation — For the purposes of this Act,

(a) a reference to a controlled substance includes a reference to any substance that contains a controlled substance; and

(b) a reference to a controlled substance includes a reference to

(i) all synthetic and natural forms of the substance, and

(ii) any thing that contains or has on it a controlled substance and that is used or intended or designed for use

(A) in producing the substance, or

(B) in introducing the substance into a human body.

(3) Idem — For the purposes of this Act, where a substance is expressly named in any of Schedules I to VI, it shall be deemed not to be included in any other of those Schedules.

1996, c. 8, s. 35(a)

3. (1) Interpretaton — Every power or duty imposed under this Act that may be exercised or performed in respect of an offence under this Act may be exercised or performed in respect of a conspiracy, or an attempt to commit, being an accessory after the fact in relation to, or any counselling in relation to, an offence under this Act.

(2) Idem — For the purposes of sections 16 and 20, a reference to a person who is or was convicted of a designated substance offence includes a reference to an offender who is discharged under section 730 of the *Criminal Code*.

1995, c. 22, s. 18 (Sched. IV, item 26)

PART I — OFFENCES AND PUNISHMENT

Particular Offences

4. (1) Possession of substance — Except as authorized under the regulations, no person shall possess a substance included in Schedule I, II or III.

(2) Obtaining substance — No person shall seek or obtain

(a) a substance included in Schedule I, II, III or IV, or

(b) an authorization to obtain a substance included in Schedule I, II, III or IV

from a practitioner, unless the person discloses to the practitioner particulars relating to the acquisition by the person of every substance in those Schedules, and of every authorization to obtain such substances, from any other practitioner within the preceding thirty days.

(3) Punishment — Every person who contravenes subsection (1) where the subject-matter of the offence is a substance included in Schedule I

> (a) is guilty of an indictable offence and liable to imprisonment for a term not exceeding seven years; or
>
> (b) is guilty of an offence punishable on summary conviction and liable
>
>> (i) for a first offence, to a fine not exceeding one thousand dollars or to imprisonment for a term not exceeding six months, or to both, and
>>
>> (ii) for a subsequent offence, to a fine not exceeding two thousand dollars or to imprisonment for a term not exceeding one year, or to both.

(4) Punishment — Subject to subsection (5), every person who contravenes subsection (1) where the subject-matter of the offence is a substance included in Schedule II

> (a) is guilty of an indictable offence and liable to imprisonment for a term not exceeding five years less a day; or
>
> (b) is guilty of an offence punishable on summary conviction and liable
>
>> (i) for a first offence, to a fine not exceeding one thousand dollars or to imprisonment for a term not exceeding six months, or to both, and
>>
>> (ii) for a subsequent offence, to a fine not exceeding two thousand dollars or to imprisonment for a term not exceeding one year, or to both.

(5) Punishment — Every person who contravenes subsection (1) where the subject-matter of the offence is a substance included in Schedule II in an amount that does not exceed the amount set out for that substance in Schedule VIII is guilty of an offence punishable on summary conviction and liable to a fine not exceeding one thousand dollars or to imprisonment for a term not exceeding six months, or to both.

(6) Punishment — Every person who contravenes subsection (1) where the subject-matter of the offence is a substance included in Schedule III

> (a) is guilty of an indictable offence and liable to imprisonment for a term not exceeding three years; or
>
> (b) is guilty of an offence punishable on summary conviction and liable
>
>> (i) for a first offence, to a fine not exceeding one thousand dollars or to imprisonment for a term not exceeding six months, or to both, and
>>
>> (ii) for a subsequent offence, to a fine not exceeding two thousand dollars or to imprisonment for a term not exceeding one year, or to both.

(7) Punishment — Every person who contravenes subsection (2)

> (a) is guilty of an indictable offence and liable
>
>> (i) to imprisonment for a term not exceeding seven years, where the subject-matter of the offence is a substance included in Schedule I,

(ii) to imprisonment for a term not exceeding five years less a day, where the subject-matter of the offence is a substance included in Schedule II,

(iii) to imprisonment for a term not exceeding three years, where the subject-matter of the offence is a substance included in Schedule III, or

(iv) to imprisonment for a term not exceeding eighteen months, where the subject-matter of the offence is a substance included in Schedule IV; or

(b) is guilty of an offence punishable on summary conviction and liable

(i) for a first offence, to a fine not exceeding one thousand dollars or to imprisonment for a term not exceeding six months, or to both, and

(ii) for a subsequent offence, to a fine not exceeding two thousand dollars or to imprisonment for a term not exceeding one year, or to both.

(8) Determination of amount — For the purposes of subsection (5) and Schedule VIII, the amount of the substance means the entire amount of any mixture or substance, or the whole of any plant, that contains a detectable amount of the substance.

5. (1) Trafficking in substance — No person shall traffic in a substance included in Schedule I, II, III or IV or in any substance represented or held out by that person to be such a substance.

(2) Possession for purpose of trafficking — No person shall, for the purposes of trafficking, possess a substance included in Schedule I, II, III or IV.

(3) Punishment — Every person who contravenes subsection (1) or (2)

(a) subject to subsection (4), where the subject-matter of the offence is a substance included in Schedule I or II, is guilty of an indictable offence and liable to imprisonment for life;

(b) where the subject-matter of the offence is a substance included in Schedule III,

(i) is guilty of an indictable offence and liable to imprisonment for a term not exceeding ten years, or

(ii) is guilty of an offence punishable on summary conviction and liable to imprisonment for a term not exceeding eighteen months; and

(c) where the subject-matter of the offence is a substance included in Schedule IV,

(i) is guilty of an indictable offence and liable to imprisonment for a term not exceeding three years, or

(ii) is guilty of an offence punishable an summary conviction and liable to imprisonment for a term not exceeding one year.

(4) Punishment in repect of specified substance — Every person who contravenes subsection (1) or (2), where the subject-matter of the offence is a substance included in Schedule II in an amount that does not exceed the amount set out for that substance in Schedule VII, is guilty of an indictable offence and liable to imprisonment for a term not exceeding five years less a day.

(5) Interpretation — For the purposes of applying subsection (3) or (4) in respect or an offence under subsection (1), a reference to a substance included in Schedule I, II, III or IV include a reference to any substance represented or held out to be a substance included in that Schedule.

(6) Interpretation — For the purposes of subsection (4) and Schedule VII, the amount of the substance means the entire amount of any mixture or substance, or the whole of any plant, that contains a detectable amount of the substance

6. (1) Importing and exporting — Except as authorized under the regulations, no person shall import into Canada or export from Canada a substance included in Schedule I, II, III, IV, V or VI.

(2) Possession for the purpose of exporting — Except as authorized under the regulations, no person shall possess a substance included in Schedule I, II, III, IV, V or VI for the purpose of exporting it from Canada.

(3) Punishment — Every person who contravenes subsection (1) or (2)

  (a) where the subject-matter of the offence is a substance included in Schedule I or II, is guilty of an indictable offence and liable to imprisonment for life;

  (b) where the subject-matter of the offence is a substance included in Schedule III or VI,

   (i) is guilty of an indictable offence and liable to imprisonment for a term not exceeding ten years, or

   (ii) is guilty of an offence punishable on summary conviction and liable to imprisonment for a term not exceeding eighteen months; and

  (c) where the subject-matter of the offence is a substance included in Schedule IV or V,

   (i) is guilty of an indictable offence and liable to imprisonment for a term not exceeding three years, or

   (ii) is guilty of an offence punishable on summary conviction and liable to imprisonment for a term not exceeding one year.

7. (1) Production of substance — Except as authorized under the regulations, no person shall produce a substance included in Schedule I, II, III or IV.

(2) Punishment — Every person who contravenes subsection (1)

  (a) where the subject-matter of the offence is a substance included in Schedule I or II, other than cannabis (marihuana), is guilty of an indictable offence and liable to imprisonment for life.

  (b) where the subject-matter of the offence is cannabis (marihuana), is guilty of an indictable offence and liable to imprisonment for a term not exceeding seven years;

(c) where the subject-matter of the offence is a substance included in Schedule III,

> (i) is guilty of an indictable offence and liable to imprisonment for a term not exceeding ten years, or

> (ii) is guilty of an offence punishable on summary conviction and liable to imprisonment for a term not exceeding eighteen months; and

(d) where the subject-matter of the offence is a substance included in Schedule IV,

> (i) is guilty of an indictable offence and liable to imprisonment for a term not exceeding three years, or

> (ii) is guilty of an offence punishable on summary conviction and liable to imprisonment for a term not exceeding one year.

8. (1) Possession of property obtained by certain offences — No person shall possess any property or any proceeds of any property knowing that all or part of the property or proceeds was obtained or derived directly or indirectly as a result of

(a) the commission in Canada of an offence under this Part except subsection 4(1) and this subsection;

(b) an act or omission anywhere that, if it had occurred in Canada, would have constituted an offence referred to in paragraph (a); or

(c) a conspiracy or an attempt to commit, being an accessory after the fact in relation to, or any counselling in relation to, an offence referred to in paragraph (a) or an act or omission referred to in paragraph (b).

(2) Punishment — Every person who contravenes subsection (1)

(a) is guilty of an indictable offence and liable to imprisonment for a term not exceeding ten years, where the value of the property or the proceeds exceeds one thousand dollars; or

(b) is guilty

> (i) of an indictable offence and liable to imprisonment for a term not exceeding two years, or

> (ii) of an offence punishable on summary conviction and liable to a fine not exceeding two thousand dollars or to imprisonment for a term not exceeding six months, or to both,

where the value of the property or the proceeds does not exceed one thousand dollars.

(3) Exception — A peace officer or a person acting under the direction of a peace officer is not guilty of an offence under this section by reason only that the peace officer or person possesses property or the proceeds of property mentioned in subsection (1) for the purposes of an investigation or otherwise in the execution of the peace officer's duties.

1997, c. 18, s. 140(b)

9. (1) Laundering proceeds of certain offences — No person shall use, transfer the possession of, send or deliver to any person or place, transport, transmit, alter, dispose of or otherwise deal with, in any manner or by any means, any property or any proceeds of any property with intent to conceal or convert that property or those proceeds and knowing or believing that all or a part of that property or of those proceeds was obtained or derived directly or indirectly as a result of

    (a) the commission in Canada of an offence under this Part except subsection 4(1);

    (b) an act or omission anywhere that, if it had occured in Canada, would have constituted an offence referred to in paragraph (a); or

    (c) a conspiracy or an attempt to commit, being an accessory after the fact in relation to, or any counselling in relation to, an offence referred to in paragraph (a) or an act or ommission referred to in paragraph (b).

(2) Punishment — Every person who contravenes subsection (1)

    (a) is guilty of an indictable offence and liable to imprisonment for a term not exceeding ten years; or

    (b) is guilty of an offence punishable on summary conviction and liable to a fine not exceeding two thousand dollars or to imprisonment for a term not exceeding six months, or to both.

(3) Exception — A peace officer or a person acting under the direction of a peace officer is not guilty of an offence under subsection (2) if the peace officer or person does anything mentioned in subsection (1) for the purposes of an investigation or otherwise in the execution of their duties.

1997, c. 18, s. 140(c)(i), (ii); 1999, c. 5, s. 48

Sentencing

10. (1) Purpose of sentencing — Without restricting the generality of the *Criminal Code*, the fundamental purpose of any sentence for an offence under this Part is to contribute to the respect for the law and the maintenance of a just, peaceful and safe society while encouraging rehabilitation, and treatment in appropriate circumstances, of offenders and acknowledging the harm done to victims and to the community.

(2) Circumstances to take into consideration — If a person is convicted of a designated substance offence, the court imposing sentence on the person shall consider any relevant aggravating factors including that the person

    (a) in relation to the commission of the offence,

        (i) carried, used or threatened to use a weapon,

        (ii) used or threatened to use violence,

        (iii) trafficked in a substance included in Schedule I, II, III or IV or possessed such a substance for the purpose of trafficking, in or near a school, on or near school grounds or in or near any other public place usually frequented by persons under the age of eighteen years, or

(iv) trafficked in a substance included in Schedule I, II, III or IV, or possessed such a substance for the purpose of trafficking, to a person under the age of eighteen years;

(b) was previously convicted of a designated substance offence; or

(c) used the services of a person under the age of eighteen years to commit, or involved such a person in the commission of, a designated substance offence.

(3) Reasons — If, under subsection (1), the court is satisfied of the existence of one or more of the aggravating factors enumerated in paragraphs (2)(a) to (c), but decides not to sentence the person to imprisonment, the court shall give reasons for that decision.

1999, c. 5, s. 49

PART II — ENFORCEMENT

Search, Seizure and Detention

11. (1) Information for search warrant — A justice who, on *ex parte* application, is satisfied by information on oath that there are reasonable grounds to believe that

(a) a controlled substance or precursor in respect of which this Act has been contravened,

(b) any thing in which a controlled substance or precursor referred to in paragraph (a) is contained or concealed,

(c) offence-related property, or

(d) any thing that will afford evidence in respect of an offence under this Act

is in a place may, at any time, issue a warrant authorizing a peace officer, at any time, to search the place for any such controlled substance, precursor, property or thing and to seize it.

(2) Application of s. 487.1 of the Criminal Code — For the purposes of subsection (1), an information may be submitted by telephone or other means of telecommunication in accordance with section 487.1 of the *Criminal Code*, with such modifications as the circumstances require.

(3) Execution in another province — A justice may, where a place referred to in subsection (1) is in a province other than that in which the justice has jurisdiction, issue the warrant referred to in that subsection and the warrant may be executed in the other province after it has been endorsed by a justice having jurisdiction in that other province.

(4) Effect of endorsement — An endorsement that is made on a warrant as provided for in subsection (3) is sufficient authority to any peace officer to whom it was originally directed and to all peace officers within the jurisdiction of the justice by whom it is endorsed to execute the warrant and to deal with the things seized in accordance with the law.

(5) Search of person and seizure — Where a peace officer who executes a warrant issued under subsection (1) has reasonable grounds to believe that any person found in the place set out in the warrant has on their person any controlled substance, precursor, property or thing set out in the warrant, the peace officer may search the person for the controlled substance, precursor, property or thing and seize it.

(6) Seizure of things not specified — A peace officer who executes a warrant issued under subsection (1) may seize, in addition to the things mentioned in the warrant,

(a) any controlled substance or precursor in respect of which the peace officer believes on reasonable grounds that this Act has been contravened;

(b) any thing that the peace officer believes on reasonable grounds to contain or conceal a controlled substance or precursor referred to in paragraph (a);

(c) any thing that the peace officer believes on reasonable grounds is offence-related property; or

(d) any thing that the peace officer believes on reasonable grounds will afford evidence in respect of an offence under this Act.

(7) Where warrant not necessary — A peace officer may exercise any of the powers described in subsection (1), (5) or (6) without a warrant if the conditions for obtaining a warrant exist but by reason of exigent circumstances it would be impracticable to obtain one.

(8) Seizure of additional things — A peace officer who executes a warrant issued under subsection (1) or exercises powers under subsection (5) or (7) may seize, in addition to the things mentioned in the warrant and in subsection (6), any thing that the peace officer believes on reasonble grounds has been obtained by or used in the commission of an offence or that will afford evidence in respect of an offence.

12. Assistance and use of force — For the purpose of exercising any of the powers described in section 11, a peace officer may

(a) enlist such assistance as the officer deems necessary; and

(b) use as much force as is necessary in the circumstances.

13. (1) Sections 489.1 and 490 of the Criminal Code applicable — Subject to subsections (2) and (3), sections 489.1 and 490 of the *Criminal Code* apply to any thing seized under this Act.

(2) Sections 489.1 and 490 of the Criminal Code applicable — Where a thing seized under this Act is offence-related property, sections 489.1 and 490 of the *Criminal Code* apply subject to sections 16 to 22 of this Act.

(3) Provisions of this Act applicable — Where a controlled substance is seized under this Act or any other Act of Parliament or pursuant to a power of seizure at common law, this Act and the regulations apply in respect of that substance.

(4) Report to justice — Subject to the regulations, every peace officer who, pursuant to section 11, seizes a controlled substance shall, as soon as is reasonable in the circumstances after the seizure,

(a) prepare a report identifying the place searched, the controlled substance and the location where it is being detained;

(b) cause the report to be filed with the justice who issued the warrant or another justice for the same territorial division or, where by reason of exigent circumstances a warrant was not issued, a justice who would have had jurisdiction to issue a warrant; and

(c) cause a copy of the report to be sent to the Minister.

(5) Report to justice — A report in Form 5.2 of the *Criminal Code* may be filed as a report for the purposes of subsection (4).

(6) Recognizance — Where, pursuant to this section, an order is made under paragraph 490(9)(c) of the *Criminal Code* for the return of any offence-related property seized under this Act, the judge or justice making the order may require the applicant for the order to enter into a recognizance before the judge or justice, with or without sureties, in such amount and with such conditions, if any, as the judge of justice directs and, where the judge or justice considers it appropriate, require the applicant to deposit with the judge or justice such sum of money or other valuable security as the judge or justice directs.

Restraint Orders

14. (1) Application for restraint order — The Attorney General may make an application in accordance with this section for a restraint order under this section in respect of any offence-related property.

(2) Procedure — An application made under subsection (1) for a restraint order in respect of any offence-related property may be made *ex parte* and shall be made in writing to a judge and be accompanied by an affidavit sworn on the information and belief of the Attorney General or any other person deposing to the following matters:

(a) the offence against this Act to which the offence-related property relates;

(b) the person who is believed to be in possession of the offence-related property; and

(c) a description of the offence-related property.

(3) Restraint order — Where an application for a restraint order is made to a judge under subsection (1), the judge may, if satisfied that there are reasonable grounds to believe that the property is offence-related property, make a restraint order

(a) prohibiting any person from disposing of, or otherwise dealing with any interest in, the offence-related property specified in the order otherwise than in such manner as may be specified in the order; and

(b) at the request of the Attorney General, where the judge is of the opinion that the circumstances so require,

(i) appointing a person to take control of and to manage or otherwise deal with all or part of that property in accordance with the directions of the judge, and

(ii) requiring any person having possession of that property to give possession of the property to the person appointed under subparagraph (i).

(4) Minister of Supply and Services — Where the Attorney General so requests, a judge appointing a person under subparagraph (3)(b)(i) shall appoint the Minister of Supply and Services.

(5) Conditions — A restraint order made by a judge under this section may be subject to such reasonable conditions as the judge thinks fit.

(6) Order in writing — A restraint order made under this section shall be made in writing.

(7) Service of order — A copy of a restraint order made under this section shall be served on the person to whom the order is addressed in such manner as the judge making the order directs or in accordance with the rules of the court.

(8) Registration of order — A copy of a restraint order made under this section shall be registered against any property in accordance with the laws of the province in which the property is situated.

(9) Order continues in force — A restraint order made under this section remains in effect until

(a) an order is made under subsection 490(9) or (11) of the *Criminal Code* in relation to the property; or

(b) an order of forfeiture of the property is made under subsection 16(1) or 17(2) of this Act or section 490 of the *Criminal Code*.

(10) Offence — Any person on whom a restraint order made under this section is served in accordance with this section and who, while the order is in force, acts in contravention of or fails to comply with the order is guilty of an indictable offence or an offence punishable on summary conviction.

15. (1) Sections 489.1 and 490 of the Criminal Code applicable — Subject to sections 16 to 22, sections 489.1 and 490 of the *Criminal Code* apply, with such modifications as the circumstances require, to any offence-related property that is the subject-matter of a restraint order made under section 14.

(2) Recognizance — Where, pursuant to subsection (1), an order is made under paragraph 490(9)(c) of the *Criminal Code* for the return of any offence-related property that is the subject of a restraint order under section 14, the judge or justice making the order may require the applicant for the order to enter into a recognizance before the judge or justice, with or without sureties, in such amount and with such conditions, if any, as the judge or justice directs and, where the judge or justice considers it appropriate, require the applicant to deposit with the judge or justice such sum of money or other valuable security as the judge or justice directs.

Forfeiture of Offence-related Property

16. (1) Order of forfeiture of property on conviction — Subject to sections 18 and 19, where a person is convicted of a designated substance offence and, on application of the Attorney General, the court is satisfied, on a balance of probabilities, that any property is offence-related property and that the offence was committed in relation to that property, the court shall

(a) in the case of a substance included in Schedule VI, order that the substance be forfeited to Her Majesty in right of Canada and disposed of by the Minister as the Minister thinks fit; and

(b) in the case of any other offence-related property,

(i) where the prosecution of the offence was commenced at the instance of the government of a province and conducted by or on behalf of that government, order that the property be forfeited to Her Majesty in right of that province and disposed of by the Attorney General or Solicitor General of that province in accordance with the law, and

(ii) in any other case, order that the property be forfeited to Her Majesty in right of Canada and disposed of by such member of the Queen's Privy Council for Canada as may be designated for the purposes of this subparagraph in accordance with the law.

(2) Property related to other offences — Where the evidence does not establish to the satisfaction of the court that the designated substance offence of which a person has been convicted was committed in relation to property in respect of which an order of forfeiture would otherwise be made under subsection (1) but the court is satisfied, beyond a reasonable doubt, that that property is offence-related property, the court may make an order of forfeiture under subsection (1) in relation to that property.

(3) Appeal — A person who has been convicted of a designated substance offence or the Attorney General may appeal to the court of appeal from an order or a failure to make an order under subsection (1) as if the appeal were an appeal against the sentence imposed on the person in respect of the offence.

17. (1) Application for *in rem* forfeiture — Where an information has been laid in respect of a designated substance offence, the Attorney General may make an application to a judge for an order of forfeiture under subsection (2).

(2) Order of forfeiture of property — Subject to sections 18 and 19, where an application is made to a judge under subsection (1) and the judge is satisfied

(a) beyond a reasonable doubt that any property is offence-related property.

(b) that proceedings in respect of a designated substance offence in relation to the property referred to in paragraph (a) were commenced, and

(c) that the accused charged with the designated substance offence has died or absconded,

the judge shall order that the property be forfeited and disposed of in accordance with subsection (4).

(3) Accused deemed absconded — For the purposes of subsection (2), an accused shall be deemed to have absconded in connection with a designated substance offence if

(a) an information has been laid alleging the commission of the offence by the accused,

(b) a warrant for the arrest of the accused has been issued in relation to that information, and

(c) reasonable attempts to arrest the accused pursuant to the warrant have been unsuccessful during a period of six months beginning on the day on which the warrant was issued,

and the accused shall be deemed to have so absconded on the last day of that six month period.

(4) Who may dispose of forfeited property — For the purposes of subsection (2),

(a) in the case of a substance included in Schedule VI, the judge shall order that the substance be forfeited to Her Majesty in right of Canada and disposed of by the Minister as the Minister thinks fit; and

(b) in the case of any other offence-related property,

(i) where the proceedings referred to in paragraph (2)(b) were commenced at the instance of the government of a province, the judge shall order that the property be forfeited to Her Majesty in right of that province and disposed of by the Attorney General or Solicitor General of that province in accordance with the law, and

(ii) in any other case, the judge shall order that the property be forfeited to Her Majesty in right of Canada and disposed of by such member of the Queen's Privy Council for Canada as may be designated for the purposes of this subparagraph in accordance with the law.

18. Voidable transfers — A court may, before ordering that offence-related property be forfeited under subsection 16(1) or 17(2), set aside any conveyance or transfer of the property that occurred after the seizure of the property, or the making of a restraint order in respect of the property, unless the conveyance or transfer was for valuable consideration to a person acting in good faith.

19. (1) Notice — Before making an order under subsection 16(1) or 17(2) in relation to any property, a court shall require notice in accordance with subsection (2) to be given to, and may hear, any person who, in the opinion of the court, appears to have a valid interest in the property.

(2) Manner of giving notice — A notice given under subsection (1) shall

(a) be given or served in such manner as the court directs or as may be specified in the rules of the court;

(b) be of such duration as the court considers reasonable or as may be specified in the rules of the court; and

(c) set out the designated substance offence charged and a description of the property.

(3) Order of restoration of property — Where a court is satisfied that any person, other than

(a) a person who was charged with a designated substance offence, or

(b) a person who acquired title to or a right of possession of the property from a person referred to in paragraph (a) under circumstances that give rise to a reasonable inference that the title or right was transferred for the purpose of voiding the forfeiture of the property,

is the lawful owner or is lawfully entitled to possession of any property or any part of any property that would otherwise be forfeited pursuant to an order made under subsection 16(1) or 17(2) and that the person appears innocent of any complicity in an offence referred to in paragraph (a) or of any collusion in relation to such an offence, the court may order that the property or part be returned to that person.

20. (1) Application — Where any offence-related property is forfeited to Her Majesty pursuant to an order made under subsection 16(1) or 17(2), any person who claims an interest in the property, other than

(a) in the case of property forfeited pursuant to an order made under subsection 16(1), a person who was convicted of the designated substance offence in relation to which the property was forfeited,

(b) in the case of property forfeited pursuant to an order made under subsection 17(2), a person who was charged with the designated substance offence in relation to which the property was forfeited, or

(c) a person who acquired title to or a right of possession of the property from a person referred to in paragraph (a) or (b) under circumstances that give rise to a reasonable inference that the title or right was transferred from that person for the purpose of avoiding the forfeiture of the property,

may, within thirty days after the forfeiture, apply by notice in writing to a judge for an order under subsection (4).

(2) Fixing day for hearing — The judge to whom an application is made under subsection (1) shall fix a day not less than thirty days after the date of the filing of the application for the hearing of the application.

(3) Notice — An applicant shall serve a notice of the application made under subsection (1) and of the hearing of it on the Attorney General at least fifteen days before the day fixed for the hearing.

(4) Order declaring interest not affected by forfeiture — Where, on the hearing of an application made under subsection (1), the judge is satisfied that the applicant

(a) is not a person referred to in paragraph (1)(a), (b) or (c) and appears innocent of any complicity in any designated substance offence that resulted in the forfeiture of the property or of any collusion in relation to such an offence, and

(b) exercised all reasonable care to be satisfied that the property was not likely to have been used in connection with the commission of an unlawful act by the person who was permitted by the applicant to obtain possession of the property or from whom the applicant obtained possession or, where the applicant is a mortgagee or lienholder, by the mortgagor or lien-giver,

the judge may make an order declaring that the interest of the applicant is not affected by the forfeiture and declaring the nature and the extent or value of the interest.

(5) Appeal from order made under subsection (4) — An applicant or the Attorney General may appeal to the court of appeal from an order made under subsection (4), and the provisions of Part XXI of the *Criminal Code* with respect to procedure on appeals apply, with such modifications as the circumstances require, in respect of appeals under this subsection.

(6) Return of property — The Minister shall, on application made to the Minister by any person in respect of whom a judge has made an order under subsection (4), and where the periods with respect to the taking of appeals from that order have expired and any appeal from that order taken under subsection (5) has been determined, direct that

(a) the property, or the part of it to which the interest of the applicant relates, be returned to the applicant; or

(b) an amount equal to the value of the interest of the applicant, as declared in the order, be paid to the applicant.

21. Appeals from orders under subsection 17(2) — Any person who, in their opinion, is aggrieved by an order made under subsection 17(2) may appeal from the order as if the order were an appeal against conviction or against a judgment or verdict of acquittal, as the case may be, under Part XXI of the *Criminal Code*, and that Part applies, with such modifications as the circumstances require, in respect of such an appeal.

22. Suspension of order pending appeal — Notwithstanding anything in this Act, operation of an order made in respect of property under subsection 16(1), 17(2) or 20(4) is suspended pending

(a) any application made in respect of the property under any of those provisions or any other provision of this or any other Act of Parliament that provides for restoration or forfeiture of the property, or

(b) any appeal taken from an order of forfeiture or restoration in respect of the property,

and the property shall not be disposed of or otherwise dealt with until thirty days have expired after an order is made under any of those provisions.

Forfeiture of Proceeds of Crime

23. (1) Application of sections 462.3 and 462.32 to 462.5 of the Criminal Code respecting proceeds — Sections 462.3 and 462.32 to 462.5 of the *Crimi-*

nal Code apply, with such modifications as the circumstances require, in respect of proceedings for a designated substance offence.

(2) Application of sections 462.3 and 462.32 to 462.5 of the Criminal Code respecting proceeds — For the purposes of subsection (1),

    (a) a reference in section 462.37 or 462.38 or subsection 462.41(2) of the *Criminal Code* to an enterprise crime offence shall be deemed to be a reference to a designated substance offence;

    (b) a reference in subsection 462.37(1) or 462.42(6), paragraph 462.43(c) or section 462.5 of the *Criminal Code* to the Attorney General in relation to the manner in which forfeited property is to be disposed of or otherwise dealt with shall be deemed to be a reference to

        (i) where the prosecution of the offence in respect of which the property was forfeited was commenced at the instance of the government of a province and conducted by or on behalf of that government, the Attorney General or Solicitor General of that province, and

        (ii) in any other case, such member of the Queen's Privy Council for Canada as may be designated for the purposes of this subparagraph; and

    (c) a reference in subsection 462.38(2) of the *Criminal Code* to the Attorney General in relation to the manner in which forfeited property is to be disposed of or otherwise dealt with shall be deemed to be a reference to

        (i) where the prosecution of the offence in respect of which the property was forfeited was commenced at the instance of the government of a province, the Attorney General or Solicitor General of that province, and

        (ii) in any other case, such member of the Queen's Privy Council for Canada as may be designated for the purposes of this subparagraph.

PART III — DISPOSAL OF CONTROLLED SUBSTANCES

24. (1) Application for return of substance — Where a controlled substance has been seized, found or otherwise acquired by a peace officer or an inspector, any person may, within sixty days after the date of the seizure, finding or acquisition, on prior notification being given to the Attorney General in the prescribed manner, apply, by notice in writing to a justice in the jurisdiction in which the substance is being detained, for an order to return that substance to the person.

(2) Order to return substance forthwith — Where, on the hearing of an application made under subsection (1), a justice is satisfied that an applicant is the lawful owner or is lawfully entitled to possession of the controlled substance and the Attorney General does not indicate that the substance or a portion of it may be required for the purposes of a preliminary inquiry, trial or other proceeding under this or any other Act of Parliament, the justice shall, subject to subsection (5), order that the substance or the portion not required for the purposes of the proceeding be returned forthwith to the applicant.

(3) Order to return substance at specified time — Where, on the hearing of an application made under subsection (1), a justice is satisfied that an applicant is the lawful owner or is lawfully entitled to possession of the controlled substance but the Attorney General indicates that the substance or a portion of it may be required for the purposes of a preliminary inquiry, trial or other proceeding under this or any other Act of Parliament, the justice shall, subject to subsection (5), order that the substance or the portion required for the purposes of the proceeding be returned to the applicant.

    (a) on the expiration of one hundred and eighty days after the application was made, if no proceeding in relation to the substance has been commenced before that time; or

    (b) on the final conclusion of the proceeding or any other proceeding in relation to the substance, where the applicant is not found guilty in those proceedings of an offence committed in relation to the substance.

(4) Order to return substance refused — Where, on the hearing of an application made under subsection (1), a justice is not satisfied that an applicant is the lawful owner or is lawfully entitled to possession of the controlled substance, the justice shall order that the substance or the portion not required for the purposes of a preliminary inquiry, trial or other proceeding under this or any other Act of Parliament be forfeited to Her Majesty to be disposed of or otherwise dealt with in accordance with the regulations or, if there are no applicable regulations, in such manner as the Minister directs.

(5) Payment of compensation in lieu — Where, on the hearing of an application made under subsection (1), a justice is satisfied that an applicant is the lawful owner or is lawfully entitled to possession of a controlled substance, but an order has been made under subsection 26(2) in respect of the substance, the justice shall make an order that an amount equal to the value of the substance be paid to the applicant.

25. Disposal by Minister where no application — Where no application for the return of a controlled substance has been made under subsection 24(1) within sixty days after the date of the seizure, finding or acquisition by a peace officer or inspector and the substance or a portion of it is not required for the purposes of any preliminary inquiry, trial or other proceeding under this Act or any other Act of Parliament, the substance or the portion not required for the purposes of the proceeding shall be delivered to the Minister to be disposed of or otherwise dealt with in accordance with the regulations or, if there are no applicable regulations, in such manner as the Minister directs.

26. (1) Security, health or safety hazard — Where the Minister has reasonable grounds to believe that a controlled substance that has been seized, found or otherwise acquired by a peace officer or inspector constitutes a potential security, public health or safety hazard, the Minister may, on prior notification being given to the Attorney General in the prescribed manner, at any time, make an application, *ex parte*, to a justice for an order that the substance or a portion of it be forfeited to Her Majesty to be disposed of or otherwise dealt with in accordance with the regulations or, if there are no applicable regulations, in such manner as the Minister directs.

(2) Security, health or safety hazard — Where, on the hearing of an application made under subsection (1), a justice is satisfied that there are reasonable grounds to believe that the controlled substance constitutes a potential security, public health or safety hazard, the justice shall order that the substance or any portion not required for the purposes of a preliminary inquiry, trial or other proceeding under this or any other Act of Parliament be forfeited to Her Majesty to be disposed of or otherwise dealt with in accordance with the regulations or, if there are no applicable regulations, in such manner as the Minister directs.

27. Disposal following proceedings — Subject to section 24, where, pursuant to a preliminary inquiry, trial or other proceeding under this or any other Act of Parliament, the court before which the proceedings have been brought is satisfied that any controlled substance that is the subject of proceedings before the court is no longer required by that court or any other court, the court

(a) shall

(i) where it is satisfied that the person from whom the substance was seized came into possession of the substance in accordance with the regulations and continued to deal with it in accordance with the regulations, order that the substance be returned to the person, or

(ii) where it is satisfied that possession of the substance by the person from whom it was seized is unlawful and the person who is lawfully entitled to its possession is known, order that the substance be returned to the person who is the lawful owner or is lawfully entitled to its possession; and

(b) may, where it is not satisfied that the substance should be returned pursuant to subparagraph (i) or (ii) or where possession of the substance by the person from whom it was seized is unlawful and the person who is the lawful owner or is lawfully entitled to its possession is not known, order that the substance be forfeited to Her Majesty to be disposed of or otherwise dealt with in accordance with the regulations or, if there are no applicable regulations, in such manner as the Minister directs.

28. Disposal with consent — Where a controlled substance has been seized, found or otherwise acquired by a peace officer or inspector under this Act or the regulations and the substance or a portion of it is not required for the purposes of a preliminary inquiry, trial or other proceeding under this or any other Act of Parliament, the person who is the lawful owner or is lawfully entitled to its possession may consent to its disposal, and on such consent being given the substance or portion is thereupon forfeited to Her Majesty and may be disposed of or otherwise otherwise dealt with in accordance with the regulations or, if there are no applicable regulations, in such manner as the Minister directs.

29. Destruction of plant — The Minister may, on prior notification being given to the Attorney General, cause to be destroyed any plant from which a substance included in Schedule I, II III or IV may be extracted that is being produced otherwise than under the authority of and in accordance with a licence issued under the regulations.

PART IV — ADMINISTRATION AND COMPLIANCE

Inspectors

30. (1) Designation of inspectors — The Minister may designate, in accordance with the regulations made pursuant to paragraph 55(1)(n), any person as an inspector for the purposes of this Act and the regulations.

(2) Certificate of designation — An inspector shall be furnished with a prescribed certificate of designation, and on entering any place pursuant to subsection 31(1) shall, on request, produce the certificate to the person in charge of the place.

31. (1) Powers of inspector — Subject to subsection (2), an inspector may, to ensure compliance with the regulations, at any reasonable time enter any place the inspector believes on reasonable grounds is used for the purpose of conducting the business or professional practice of any person licensed or otherwise authorized under the regulations to deal in a controlled substance or a precursor and may for that purpose

(a) open and examine any receptacle or package found in that place in which a controlled substance or a precursor may be found;

(b) examine any thing found in that place that is used or may be capable of being used for the production, preservation, packaging or storage of a controlled substance or a precursor;

(c) examine any labels or advertising material or records, books, electronic data or other documents found in that place with respect to any controlled substance or precursor, other than the records of the medical condition of persons, and make copies thereof or take extracts therefrom;

(d) use or cause to be used any computer system at that place to examine any electronic data referred to in paragraph (c);

(e) reproduce any document from any electronic data referred to in paragraph (c) or cause it to be reproduced, in the form of a printout or other output;

(f) take the labels or advertising material or records, books or other documents referred to in paragraph (c) or the printout or other output referred to in paragraph (e) for examination or copying;

(g) use or cause to be used any copying equipment at that place to make copies of any document;

(h) examine any substance found in that place and take, for the purpose of analysis, such samples thereof as are reasonably required; and

(i) seize and detain in accordance with this Part, any controlled substance or precursor the seizure and detention of which the inspector believes on reasonable grounds is necessary.

(2) Warrant required to enter dwelling-place — Where a place referred to in subsection (1) is a dwelling-place, an inspector may not enter the dwelling-place without the consent of an occupant thereof except under the authority of a warrant issued under subsection (3).

(3) Authority to issue warrant — Where, on *ex parte* application, a justice is satisfied by information on oath that

(a) a place referred to in subsection (1) is a dwelling-place but otherwise meets the conditions for entry described in that subsection,

(b) entry to the dwelling-place is necessary for the purpose of ensuring compliance with the regulations, and

(c) entry to the dwelling-place has been refused or there are reasonable grounds to believe that entry will be refused,

the justice may issue a warrant authorizing the inspector named in it to enter that dwelling-place and exercise any of the powers mentioned in paragraphs (1)(a) to (i), subject to such conditions as may be specified in the warrant.

(4) Use of force — In executing a warrant issued under subsection (3), an inspector shall not use force unless the inspector is accompanied by a peace officer and the use of force is specifically authorized in the warrant.

(5) Assistance to inspector — The owner or other person in charge of a place entered by an inspector under subsection (1) and every person found there shall give the inspector all reasonable assistance in the power of that person and furnish the inspector with such information as the inspector may reasonably require.

(6) Storage of substances seized — Where an inspector seizes and detains a controlled substance or a precursor, the substance or precursor may, at the discretion of the inspector, be kept or stored at the place where it was seized or, at the direction of the inspector, be removed to any other proper place.

(7) Notice — An inspector who seizes a controlled substance or a precursor shall take such measures as are reasonable in the circumstances to give to the owner or other person in charge of the place where the seizure occurred notice of the seizure and of the location where the controlled substance or precursor is being kept or stored.

(8) Return by inspector — Where an inspector determines that to ensure compliance with the regulations it is no longer necessary to detain a controlled substance or a precursor seized by the inspector under paragraph (1)(i), the inspector shall notify in writing the owner or other person in charge of the place where the seizure occurred of that determination and, on being issued a receipt for it, shall return the controlled substance or precursor to that person.

(9) Return or disposal by Minister — Notwithstanding sections 24, 25 and 27, where a period of one hundred and twenty days has elapsed after the date of a seizure under paragraph (1)(i) and the controlled substance or precursor has not been returned in accordance with subsection (8), the controlled substance or precursor shall be returned, disposed of or otherwise dealt with in such manner as the Minister directs, in accordance with any applicable regulations.

32. (1) Obstructing inspector — No person shall, by act or omission, obstruct an inspector who is engaged in the performance of duties under this Act or the regulations.

(2) False statements — No person shall knowingly make any false or misleading statement verbally or in writing to an inspector who is engaged in the performance of duties under this Act or the regulations.

(3) Interference — No person shall, without the authority of an inspector, remove, alter or interfere in any way with anything seized, detained or taken under section 31.

PART V — ADMINISTRATIVE ORDERS FOR CONTRAVENTIONS OF DESIGNATED REGULATIONS

33. Designation of regulations — The Governor in Council may, by regulation, designate any regulation made under this Act (in this Part referred to as a **"designated regulation"**) as a regulation the contravention of which shall be dealt with under this Part.

34. Contravention of designated regulation — Where the Minister has reasonable grounds to believe that a person has contravened a designated regulation, the Minister shall

(a) in the prescribed manner, serve a notice to appear on the person; and

(b) send a copy of the notice to appear to an adjudicator and direct the adjudicator to conduct a hearing to determine whether the contravention has occurred and to notify the Minister of the adjudicator's determination.

35. (1) Interim order — Where the Minister has reasonable grounds to believe that a person has contravened a designated regulation and the Minister is of the opinion that, as a result of that contravention, there is a substantial risk of immediate danger to the health or safety of any person, the Minister may, without giving prior notice to the person believed to have contravened the designated regulation, make an interim order in respect of the person

(a) prohibiting the person from doing anything that the person would otherwise be permitted to do under their licence, permit or authorization, or

(b) subjecting the doing of anything under the designated regulation by the person to the terms and conditions specified in the interim order,

and may, for that purpose, suspend, cancel or amend the licence, permit or authorization issued or granted to the person or take any other measures set out in the regulations.

(2) Idem — Where the Minister makes an interim order under subsection (1), the Minister shall forthwith

(a) in the prescribed manner, serve the interim order on the person;

(b) in the prescribed manner, serve a notice to appear on the person; and

(c) send a copy of the interim order and the notice to appear to an adjudicator and direct the adjudicator to conduct a hearing to determine whether the contravention has occurred and to notify the Minister of the adjudicator's determination.

36. (1) Hearing by adjudicator — Where an adjudicator receives from the Minister a copy of a notice to appear under paragraph 34(b) or 35(2)(c), the adjudicator shall conduct a hearing on a date to be fixed by the adjudicator at the request of the person on whom the notice was served, on two days notice being given to the adjudicator, which hearing date may not

(a) in the case of a notice served under paragraph 34(a), be less than thirty days, or more than forty-five days, after the day of service of the notice; or

(b) in the case of a notice served under paragraph 35(2)(b), be less than three days, or more than forty-five days, after the day of service of the notice.

(2) Change of hearing date — Where the adjudicator is unable to conduct a hearing on the date referred to in subsection (1), the adjudicator shall forthwith notify the person and fix, for the purpose of holding the hearing, the earliest possible date to which the adjudicator and the person agree.

(3) Proceedings on default — Where an adjudicator has received a copy of a notice to appear referred to in subsection (1) and where the person on whom the notice is served has not requested a date for a hearing within forty-five days after the notice was served on that person, or where the person, having requested a hearing, fails to appear for the hearing, the adjudicator shall proceed to make a determination in the absence of the person.

(4) Time and place — An adjudicator may, subject to the regulations, determine the time and place of any hearing or other proceeding under this Part.

37. Notice to appear — A notice to appear served on a person under paragraph 34(a) or 35(2)(b) shall

(a) specify the designated regulation that the Minister believes the person has contravened;

(b) state the grounds on which the Minister believes the contravention has occurred;

(c) state that the matter has been referred to an adjudicator for a hearing to be conducted on a date within the applicable period described in paragraph 36(1)(a) or (b); and

(d) set out such other information as is prescribed.

38. Proof of service — Proof of service of any notice, order or interim order under this Part shall be given in the prescribed manner.

39. Powers of adjudicator — For the purposes of this Act, an adjudicator has and may exercise the powers of a person appointed as a commissioner under Part I of the *Inquiries Act.*

40. Hearing procedure — An adjudicator shall deal with all matters as informally and expeditiously as the circumstances and considerations of fairness and natural justice permit.

41. (1) Determination by adjudicator — An adjudicator shall, after the conclusion of a hearing referred to in subsection 36(1) or a proceeding referred to in subsection 36(3), within the prescribed time, make a determination that the person who is the subject of the hearing or proceeding contravened or did not contravene the designated regulation.

(2) Notice of determination — Where an adjudicator has made a determination under subsection (1), the adjudicator shall

(a) forthwith notify the person and the Minister of the adjudicator's determination and the reasons; and

(b) where the adjudicator has determined that the person has contravened the designated regulation, notify the person of the opportunity to make representations to the Minister in writing in accordance with the regulations and within the prescribed time.

(3) Ministerial orders — Where an adjudicator has made a determination referred to in paragraph (2)(b) and the Minister has considered the determination and any representations referred to in that paragraph, the Minister shall forthwith make an order

(a) prohibiting the person from doing anything that they would, if they were in compliance with the designated regulation, be permitted to do, or

(b) subjecting the doing of anything under the designated regulation by the person to the terms and conditions specified in the order,

and may, for that purpose, suspend, cancel or amend any licence, permit or authorization issued or granted to the person under the regulations or take any other measures set out in the regulations.

(4) Ministerial orders — An order made under subsection (3) shall be served on the person to whom it is directed in the prescribed manner.

42. (1) Effect of order — An interim order made under subsection 35(1) and an order made under subsection 41(3) have effect from the time that they are served on the person to whom they are directed.

(2) Cessation of effect — An interim order that was made in respect of a person believed to have contravened a designated regulation ceases to have effect

(a) where the Minister makes an order under subsection 41(3), at the time the order is served on the person; and

(b) where an adjudicator has determined that the person did not contravene the designated regulation, at the time the adjudicator makes the determination.

(3) Application to revoke order — A person in respect of whom an order was made under subsection 41(3) may make an application in writing to the Minister in accordance with the regulations to revoke the order.

(4) Revocation of order — The Minister may, in the prescribed circumstances, revoke, in whole or in part, any order made under subsection 41(3).

43. Offence for contravention of order — Every person commits an offence who contravenes an order or an interim order made under this Part.

PART VI — GENERAL

Analysis

44. Designation of Analysts — The Minister may designate, in accordance with the regulations made pursuant to paragraph 55(1)(o), any person as an analyst for the purposes of this Act and the regulations.

45. (1) Analysis — An inspector or peace officer may submit to an analyst for analysis or examination any substance or sample thereof taken by the inspector or peace officer.

(2) Report — An analyst who has made an analysis or examination under subsection (1) may prepare a certificate or report stating that the analyst has analysed or examined a substance or a sample thereof and setting out the results of the analysis or examination.

Offence and Punishment

46. Penalty — Every person who contravenes a provision of this Act for which punishment is not otherwise provided or a regulation, other than a designated regulation within the meaning of Part V,

(a) is guilty of an indictable offence and liable to a fine not exceeding five thousand dollars or to imprisonment for a term not exceeding three years, or to both; or

(b) is guilty of an offence punishable on summary conviction and liable to a fine not exceeding one thousand dollars or to imprisonment for a term not exceeding six months, or to both.

Evidence and Procedure

47. (1) Limitation — No summary conviction proceedings in respect of an offence under subsection 4(2) or 32(2), section 43 or the regulations shall be commenced after the expiration of one year after the time when the subject-matter of the proceedings arose.

(2) Venue — Proceedings in respect of a contravention of any provision of this Act or the regulations may be held in the place where the offence was committed or where the subject-matter of the proceedings arose or in any place where the accused is apprehended or happens to be located.

48. (1) Burden of proving exception, etc. — No exception, exemption, excuse or qualification prescribed by law is required to be set out or negatived, as the case may be, in an information or indictment for an offence under this Act or the regulations or under section 463, 464 or 465 of the *Criminal Code* in respect of such an offence.

(2) Burden of proving exception, etc. — In any prosecution under this Act, the prosecutor is not required, except by way of rebuttal, to prove that a certificate, licence, permit or other qualification does not operate in favour of the accused, whether or not the qualification is set out in the information or indictment.

49. (1) Copies of documents — A copy of any document filed with a department, ministry, agency, municipality or other body established by or pursuant to a law of a province, or of any statement containing information from the records kept by any such department, ministry, agency, municipality or body, purporting to be certified by any official having custody of that document or those records, is admissible in evidence in any prosecution for an offence referred to in subsection 48(1) and, in the absence of evidence to the contrary, is proof of the facts contained in that document or statement, without proof of the signature or official character of the person purporting to have certified it.

(2) Authentication — For the purposes of subsection (1), an engraved, lithographed, photocopied, photographed, printed or otherwise electronically or mechanically reproduced facsimile signature of an official referred to in that subsection is sufficient authentication of any copy referred to in that subsection.

(3) Evidence inadmissible under this section — Nothing in subsection (1) renders admissible in evidence in any legal proceeding such part of any record as is proved to be a record made in the course of an investigation or inquiry.

50. (1) Certificate issued pursuant to regulations — Subject to subsection (2), any certificate or other document issued pursuant to regulations made under paragraph 55(2)(c) is admissible in evidence in a preliminary inquiry, trial or other proceeding under this or any other Act of Parliament and, in the absence of evidence to the contrary, is proof that the certificate or other document was validly issued and of the facts contained in it, without proof of the signature or official character of the person purporting to have certified it.

(2) Certificate issued pursuant to regulations — The defence may, with leave of the court, require that the person who issued the certificate or other document

    (a) produce an affidavit or solemn declaration attesting to any of the matters deemed to be proved under subsection (1); or

    (b) appear before the court for examination or cross-examination in respect of the issuance of the certificate or other document.

51. (1) Certificate of analyst — Subject to this section, a certificate or report prepared by an analyst under subsection 45(2) is admissible in evidence in any prosecution for an offence under this Act or the regulations or any other Act of Parliament and, in the absence of evidence to the contrary, is proof of the statements set out in the certificate or report, without proof of the signature or official character of the person appearing to have signed it.

(2) Attendance of analyst — The party against whom a certificate or report of an analyst is produced under subsection (1) may, with leave of the court, require the attendance of the analyst for the purpose of cross-examination.

(3) Notice — Unless the court otherwise orders, no certificate or report shall be received in evidence under subsection (1) unless the party intending to produce it has, before its production at trial, given to the party against whom it is intended to be produced reasonable notice of that intention, together with a copy of the certificate or report.

52. (1) Proof of notice — For the purposes of this Act and the regulations, the giving of any notice, whether orally or in writing, or the service of any document may be proved by the oral evidence of, or by the affidavit or solemn declaration of, the person claiming to have given that notice or served that document.

(2) Proof of notice — Notwithstanding subsection (1), the court may require the affiant or declarant to appear before it for examination or cross-examination in respect of the giving of notice or proof of service.

53. (1) Continuity of possession — In any proceeding under this Act or the regulations, continuity of possession of any exhibit tendered as evidence in that proceeding may be proved by the testimony of, or the affidavit or solemn declaration of, the person claiming to have had it in their possession.

(2) Alternative method of proof — Where an affidavit or solemn declaration is offered in proof of continuity of possession under subsection (1), the court may require the affiant or declarant to appear before it for examination or cross-examination in respect of the issue of continuity of possession.

54. Copies of records, books or documents — Where any record, book, electronic data or other document is examined or seized under this Act or the regulations, the Minister, or the officer by whom the record, book, electronic data or other document is examined or seized, may make or cause to be made one or more copies thereof, and a copy of any such record, book, electronic data or other document purporting to be certified by the Minister or a person authorized by the Minister is admissible in evidence and, in the absence of evidence to the contrary, has the same probative force as the original record, book, electronic data or other document would have had if it had been proved in the ordinary way.

Regulations, Exemptions and Disqualifications

55. (1) Regulations — The Governor in Council may make regulations for carrying out the purposes and provisions of this Act, including the regulation of the medical, scientific and industrial uses and distribution of controlled substances and precursors and the enforcement of this Act and, without restricting the generality of the foregoing, may make regulations

(a) governing, controlling, limiting, authorizing the importation into Canada, exportation from Canada, production, packaging, sending, transportation, delivery, sale, provision, administration, possession or obtaining of or other dealing in any controlled substances or precursor or any class thereof;

(b) respecting the circumstances in which, the conditions subject to which and the persons or classes of persons by whom any controlled substances or precursor or any class thereof may be imported into Canada, exported from Canada, produced, packaged, sent, transported, delivered, sold, provided, administered, possessed, obtained or otherwise dealt in, as well as the means by which and the persons or classes of persons by whom such activities may be authorized;

(c) respecting the issuance, suspension, cancellation, duration and terms and conditions of any class of licence for the importation into Canada, exportation from Canada, production, packaging, sale, provision or administration of any substance included in Schedule I, II, III, IV, V or VI or any class thereof;

(d) respecting the issuance, suspension, cancellation, duration and terms and conditions of any permit for the importation into Canada, exportation from Canada or production of a specified quantity of a substance included in Schedule I, II, III, IV, V or VI or any class thereof;

(e) prescribing the fees payable on application for any of the licences or permits provided for in paragraphs (c) and (d);

(f) respecting the method of production, preservation, testing, packaging or storage of any controlled substance or precursor or any class thereof;

(g) respecting the premises, processes or conditions for the production or sale of any controlled substance or any class thereof, and deeming such premises, processes or conditions to be or not to be suitable for the purposes of the regulations;

(h) respecting the qualifications of persons who are engaged in the production, preservation, testing, packaging, storage, selling, providing or otherwise dealing in any controlled substance or precursor or any class thereof and who do so under the supervision of a person licensed under the regulations to do any such thing;

(i) prescribing standards of composition, strength, concentration, potency, purity or quality or any other property of any controlled substance or precursor;

(j) respecting the labelling, packaging, size, dimensions, fill and other specifications of packages used for the importation into Canada, exportation from Canada, sending, transportation, delivery, sale or provision of or other dealing in any substance included in Schedule I, II, III, IV, V or VI or any class thereof;

(k) respecting the distribution of samples of any substance included in Schedule I, II, III, IV, V or VI or any class thereof;

(l) controlling and limiting the advertising for sale of any controlled substance or precursor or any class thereof;

(m) respecting the records, books, electronic data or other documents in respect of controlled substances and precursors that are required to be kept and provided by any person or class of persons who imports into Canada, exports from Canada, produces, packages, sends, transports, delivers, sells, provides, administers, possesses, obtains or otherwise deals in any controlled substance or precursor or any class thereof;

(n) respecting the qualifications for inspectors and their powers and duties in relation to the enforcement of, and compliance with, the regulations;

(o) respecting the qualifications for analysts and their powers and duties;

(p) respecting the detention and disposal of or otherwise dealing with any controlled substance;

(q) respecting the disposal of or otherwise dealing with any precursor;

(r) respecting the taking of samples of substances under paragraph 31(1)(h);

(s) respecting the communication of any information obtained under this Act or the regulations from or relating to any person or class of persons who is or may be authorized to import into Canada, export from Canada, produce, package, send, transport, deliver, sell, provide, administer, possess, obtain or otherwise deal in any controlled substance or precursor or any class thereof

    (i) to any provincial professional licensing authority, or

    (ii) to any person or class of persons where, in the opinion of the Governor in Council, it is necessary to communicate that information for the proper administration or enforcement of this Act or the regulations;

(t) respecting the making, serving, filing and manner of proving service of any notice, order, report or other document required or authorized under this Act or the regulations;

(u) prescribing the circumstances in which an order made under subsection 41(3) may be revoked by the Minister pursuant to subsection 42(4);

(v) prescribing forms for the purposes of this Act or the regulations;

(w) establishing classes or groups of controlled substances or precursors;

(x) conferring powers or imposing duties and functions on adjudicators in relation to hearings conducted and determinations made by them under Part V;

(y) governing the practice and procedure of hearings conducted and determinations made by adjudicators under Part V;

(z) exempting, on such terms and conditions as may be specified in the regulations, any person or class of persons or any controlled substance or precursor or any class thereof from the application of this Act or regulations; and

(z.1) prescribing anything that, by this Act, is to be or may be prescribed.

(2) Regulations pertaining to law enforcement — The Governor in Council, on the recommendation of the Solicitor General of Canada, may make regulations that pertain to investigations and other law enforcement activities conducted under this Act by a member of a police force and other persons acting under the direction and control of a member and, without restricting the generality of the foregoing, may make regulations

(a) authorizing the Solicitor General of Canada, or the provincial minister responsible for policing in a province, to designate a police force within the Solicitor General's jurisdiction or the minister's jurisdiction, as the case may be, for the purposes of this subsection;

(b) exempting, on such terms and conditions as may be specified in the regulations, a member of a police force that has been designated pursuant to paragraph (a) and other persons acting under the direction and control of the member from the application of any provision of Part I or the regulations;

(c) respecting the issuance, suspension, cancellation, duration and terms and conditions of a certificate, other document or, in exigent circumstances, an approval to obtain a certificate or other document, that is issued to a member of a police force that has been designated pursuant to paragraph (a) for the purpose of exempting the member from the application of this Act or the regulations;

(d) respecting the detention, storage, disposal or otherwise dealing with any controlled substance or precursor;

(e) respecting records, reports, electronic data or other documents in respect of a controlled substance or precursor that are required to be kept and provided by any person or class of persons; and

(f) prescribing forms for the purposes of the regulations.

(3) Incorporation by reference — Any regulations made under this Act incorporating by reference a classification, standard, procedure or other specification may incorporate the classification, standard, procedure or specification as amended from time to time, and, in such a case, the reference shall be read accordingly.

56. Exemption by Minister — The Minister may, on such terms and conditions as the Minister deems necessary, exempt any person or class of persons or any controlled substance or precursor or any class thereof from the application of all or any of the provisions of this Act or the regulations if, in the opinion of the Minister, the exemption is necessary for a medical or scientific purpose or is otherwise in the public interest.

57. Powers, duties and functions of Minister or Solicitor General of Canada — Any power, duty or function of

(a) the Minister under this Act or the regulations, or

(b) the Solicitor General of Canada under the regulations

may be exercised or performed by any person designated, or any person occupying a position designated, by the Minister or the Solicitor General, as the case may be, for that purpose.

58. Paramountcy of this Act and the regulations — In the case of any inconsistency or conflict between this Act or the regulations made under it, and the *Food* *and Drugs Act* or the regulations made under that Act, this Act and the regulations made under it prevail to the extent of the inconsistency or conflict.

59. Offence of making false or deceptive statements — No person shall knowingly make, or participate in, assent to or acquiesce in the making of, a false or misleading statement in any book, record, return or other document however recorded, required to be maintained, made or furnished pursuant to this Act or the regulations.

Amendments to Schedules

60. Schedules — The Governor in Council may, by order, amend any of Schedules I to VIII by adding to them or deleting from them any item or portion of an item, where the Governor in Council deems the amendment to be necessary in the public interest.

PART VII — TRANSITIONAL PROVISIONS, CONSEQUENTIAL AMENDMENTS, REPEAL AND COMING INTO FORCE

Transitional Provisions

61. References to prior enactments — Any reference in a designation by the Solicitor General of Canada under Part VI of the *Criminal Code* to an offence contrary to the *Narcotic Control Act* or Part III or IV of the *Food and Drugs Act* or any conspiracy or attempt to commit or being an accessory after the fact or any counselling in relation to such an offence shall be deemed to be a reference to an offence contrary to section 5 (trafficking), 6 (importing and exporting), 7 (production), 8 (possession of property obtained by certain offences) or 9 (laundering proceeds of certain offences) of this Act, as the case may be, or a conspiracy or attempt to commit or being an accessory after the fact or any counselling in relation to such an offence.

62. (1) Sentences for prior offences — Subject to subsection (2), where, before the coming into force of this Act, a person has committed an offence under the *Narcotic Control Act* or Part III or IV of the *Food and Drugs Act* but a sentence has not been imposed on the person for that offence, a sentence shall be imposed on the person in accordance with this Act.

(2) Application of increased punishment — Where any penalty, forfeiture or punishment provided by the *Narcotic Control Act* or section 31 or Part III or IV of the *Food and Drugs Act*, as those Acts read immediately before the coming into force of sections 4 to 9 of this Act, is varied by this Act, the lesser penalty, forfeiture or punishment applies in respect of any offence that was committed before the coming into force of those sections.

63. Validation — Every authorization issued by the Minister under subsection G.06.001(1) or J.01.033(1) of the *Food and Drug Regulations* or subsection 68(1) of the *Narcotic Control Regulations* before the coming into force of sections 78 and 90 of this Act is hereby declared to have been validly issued and every such authorization that is in force on the coming into force of sections 78 and 90 of this Act shall continue in force under this Act until it is revoked, as if it were an exemption made under section 56 of this Act.

. . . . .

Repeal

Narcotic Control Act

94. Repeal of R.S., c. N-1 — The *Narcotic Control Act* is repealed.

Coming into Force

95. Coming into force — This Act or any of its provisions comes into force on a day or days to be fixed by order of the Governor in Council.

Schedule I

(Sections 2 to 7, 29, 55 and 60)

1. Opium Poppy (Papaver somniferum), its preparations, derivatives, alkaloids and salts, including:

(1) Opium

(2) Codeine (methylmorphine)

(3) Morphine (7,8-didehydro-4,5-epoxy-17-methylmorphinan-3,6-diol)

(4) Thebaine (paramorphine),

and the salts, derivatives and salts of derivatives of substances set out in subitems (1) to (4), including:

(5) Acetorphine (acetyletorphine)

(6) Acetyldihydrocodeine (4,5-epoxy-3-methoxy-17-methylmorphinan-6 -ol acetate)

(7) Benzylmorphine (7,8-didehydro-4,5-epoxy-17-methyl-3 -(phenylmethoxy) morphinan-6-ol)

(8) codoxime (dihydrocodeinone O-(carboxymethyl) oxime)

(9) Desomorphine (dihydrodeoxymorphine)

(10) Diacetylmorphine (heroin)

(11) Dihydrocodeine (4,5-epoxy-3-methoxy-17-methylmorphinan-6-ol)

(12) Dihydromorphine (4,5-epoxy-17-methylmorphinan-3,6-diol)

(13) Ethylmorphine (7,8-didehydro-4,5-epoxy-3-ethoxy-17-methylmorphinan-6-ol)

(14) Etorphine (tetrahydro-7α-(1-hydroxy-1-methylbutyl) -6,14-endo-ethenooripavine)

(15) Hydrocodone (dihydrocodeinone)

(16) Hydromorphinol (dihydro-14-hydroxymorphine)

(17) Hydromorphone (dihydromorphinone)

(18) Methyldesorphine (δ6-deoxy-6-methylmorphine)

(19) Methyldihydromorphine (dihydro-6-methylmorphine)

(20) Metopon (dihydromethylmorphinone)

(21) Morphine-N-oxide (morphine oxide)

(22) Myrophine (benzylmorphine myristate)

(23) Nalorphine (N-allylnormorphine)

(24) Nicocodine (6-nicotinylcodeine)

(25) Nicomorphine (dinicotinylmorphine)

(26) Norcodeine (N-desmethylcodeine)

(27) Normorphine (N-desmethylmorphine)

(28) Oxycodone (dihydrohydroxycodeinone)

(29) Oxymorphone (dihydrohydroxymorphinone)

(30) Pholcodine (3-[2-(4-morphonlinyl)ethylmorphine)

(31) Thebacon (acetyldihydrocodeinone)
but not including:

(32) Apomorphine (5,6,6a,7-tetrahydro-6-methyl-4H-dibenzo[de,g] quinoline-10,11-diol)

(33) Cyprenorphine (N-(cyclopropylmethyl)-6,7,8,14-tetrahydro-7α -(1-hydroxy-1-methylethyl)-6,14-endo -ethenonororipavine)

(34) Nalmefene (17-(cyclopropylmethyl)-4,5α-epoxy-6-methylenemorphinan-3,14-diol)

(34.1) Naloxone (4,5α-epoxy-3,14-dihydroxy-17-(2-propenyl)morphinan-6-one)

(34.2) Naltrexone (17-(cyclopropylmethyl)-4,5α-epoxy-3,14-dihydroxymorphinan-6-one)

(35) Narcotine (6,7-dimethoxy-3-(5,6,7,8-tetrahydro-4-me thoxy-6-methyl-1,3-di-oxolos [4,5-g]isoquinolin-5-yl)-1(3H)-isobenzofuranone)

(36) Papaverine (1-[(3,4-dimethoxyphenyl)methyl]-6,7-dimethoxyisoquinoline)

(37) Poppy seed

SOR/97-230; SOR/99-371, s. 1

2. Coca (Erythroxylon), its preparations, derivatives, alkaloids and salts, including:

(1) Coca leaves

(2) Cocaine (benzoylmethylecgonine)

(3) Ecgonine (3-hydroxy-2-tropane carboxylic acid)

3. Phenylpiperidines, their intermediates, salts, derivatives and analogues and salts of intermediates, derivatives and analogues, including:

(1) Allylprodine (3-allyl-1-methyl-4-phenyl-4-piperidinol propionate)

(2) Alphameprodine (α-3-ethyl-1-methyl-4-phenyl- 4-piperidinol propionate)

(3) Alphaprodine (α-1,3-dimethyl-4-phenyl-4-piperidi nolpropionate)

(4) Anileridine (ethyl 1-[2-(p-aminophenyl)ethyl]-4-phenylpiperidine -4-carboxylate)

(5) Betameprodine (β-3-ethyl-1-methyl-4-phenyl-4-piperidinol propionate)

(6) Betaprodine (β-1,3-dimethyl-4-phenyl-4-piperidinol propionate)

(7) Benzethidine (ethyl 1-(2-benzyloxyethyl)-4-phenyl-piperidine- 4-carboxylate)

(8) Diphenoxylate (ethyl 1-(3-cyano-3,3-diphenyl-propyl)-4-p henylpiperidine-4-carboxylate)

(9) Difenoxin (1-(3-cyno-3,3-diphenylpropyl)-4-phenylpiperidine-4-carboxylate)

(10) Etoxeridine (ethyl 1-[2-(2-hydroxyethoxy) ethyl]-4-phenylpiperidine-4-carboxylate)

(11) Farethidine (ethyl 1-(2-tetrahydrofurfury loxyethyl)-4-phenylpiperidine-4-carboxylate)

(12) Hydroxypethidine (ethyl 4-(m-hydroxyphenyl)-1-methylpiperidine-4-carboxylate)

(13) Ketobemidone (1-[4-(m-hydroxyphenyl)-1-methyl-4- piperidyl]-1-propanone)

(14) Methylphenylisonipecotonitrile (4-cyano-1-methyl-4-phenylpiperidine)

(15) Morpheridine (ethyl 1-(2-morpholinoethyl)-4-phenylpiperidine-4 -carboxylate)

(16) Norpethidine (ethyl 4-phenylpiperidine-4-carboxylate)

(17) Pethidine (ethyl 1-methyl-4-phenylpiperidine-4-carboxylate)

(18) Phenoperidine (ethyl 1-(3-hydroxy-3-phenylpropyl)-4-phenylpiperidine-4-carboxylate)

(19) Piminodine (ethyl 1-[3-(phenylamino)propyl]-4-phenylpiperidine-4-carboxylate)

(20) Properidine (isopropyl 1-methyl-4-phenylpiperidine-4-carboxylate)

(21) Trimeperidine (1,2,5-trimethyl-4-phenyl-4-piperidinol propionate)

(22) Pethidine Intermediate C (1-methyl-4-phenylpiperidine-4-carboxylate)
but not including

(23) Carbomethidine (ethyl 1-(2-carbamylethyl)-4-phenylpiperidine-4-carboxylate)

(24) Oxpheneridine (ethyl 1-(2-hydroxy-2-phenylethyl)-4-phenylpiperidine-4-carboxylate)

SOR/97-230

4. Phenazepines, their salts, derivatives and salts of derivatives including:

(1) Proheptazine (hexahydro-1,3-dimethyl-4-phenyl-1H-azepin-4-ol propionate)
but not including

(2) Ethoheptazine (ethyl hexahydro-1-methyl-4-phenyl-azepine-4-carboxylate)

(3) Metethoheptazine (ethyl hexahydro-1,3-dimethyl-4-phenylazepine-4-carboxylate)

(4) Metheptazine (ethyl hexahydro-1,2-dimethyl-4-phenylazepine-4-carboxylate)
SOR/97-230

5. Amidones, their intermediates, salts, derivatives and salts of intermediates and derivatives including:

(1) Dimethylaminodiphenylbutanonitrile (4-cyano-2-dimethylamino-4,4-4-diphenylbutane)

(2) Dipipanone (4,4-diphenyl-6-piperidino-3-heptanone)

(3) Isomethadone (6-dimethylamino-5-methyl-4,4-diphenyl-3-hexanone)

(4) Methadone (6-dimethylamino-4,4-diphenyl-3-heptanone)

(5) Normethadone (6-dimethylamino-4,4-diphenyl-3-hexanone)

(6) Norpipanone (4,4-diphenyl-6-piperidino-3-hexanone)

(7) Phenadoxone (6-morpholino-4,4-diphenyl-3-heptanone)

6. Methadols, their salts, derivatives and salts of derivatives including:

(1) Acetylmethadol (6-dimethylamino-4,4-diphenyl-3-heptanyl acetate)

(2) Alphacetylmethadol (α-6-dimethylamino-4,4-diphenyl-3-heptanol acetate)

(3) Alphamethadol (α-6-dimethylamino-4,4-diphenyl-3-h eptanol)

(4) Betacetylmethadol (β-6-dimethylamino-4,4-diphenyl-3-he ptanol acetate)

(5) Betamethadol (β-6-dimethylamino-4,4-diphenyl-3-he ptanol)

(6) Dimepheptanol (6-dimethylamino-4,4-diphenyl-3-heptanol)

(7) Noracymethadol (α-6-methylamino-4,4-diphenyl-3-hep tanol acetate)

SOR/97-230

7. Phenalkoxams, their salts, derivatives and salts of derivatives including:

(1) Dimenoxadol (dimethylaminoethyl 1-ethoxy-1,1-diphenylacetate)

(2) Dioxaphetyl butyrate (ethyl 2,2-diphenyl-4-morpholinobutyrate)

(3) Dextropropoxyphene ([S-(R*,S*)]-α-[2-(di-methylamino)- 1-methylethyl]-α-phenylbenzeneethanol, propanoate ester)

SOR/97-230

8. Thiambutenes, their salts, derivatives and salts of derivatives including:

(1) Diethylthiambutene (N,N-diethyl-1-methyl-3,3-di-2-thienylallylamine)

(2) Dimethylthiambutene (N,N,1-trimethyl-3,3-di-2-thienylallylamine)

(3) Ethylmethylthiambutene (N-ethyl-N,1-dimethyl-3,3-di-2-thie nylallylamine)

9. Moramides, their intermediates, salts, derivatives and salts of intermediates and derivatives including:

(1) Dextromoramide (d-1-(3-methyl-4-morpholino-2,2-diphenylbutyryl)pyrrolidine)

(2) Diphenylmorpholinoisovaleric acid (2-methyl-3-morpholino-1,1-diphenylpro-pionic acid)

(3) Levomoramide (1-1-(3-methyl-4-morpholino-2,2-diphenylbutyryl)pyrrolidine)

(4) Racemoramide (d,1-1-(3-methyl-4-morpholino-2,2-diphenylbutyryl) pyrrolidine)

10. Morphinans, their salts, derivatives and salts of derivatives including:

(1) Buprenorphine (17-(cyclopropylmethyl)-α-(1,1-dimethylethyl) -4,5-epoxy-18,19-dihydro-3-hydroxy- 6-methoxy-α-methyl-6,14-ethenomorphinan -7-methanol)

(2) Drotebanol (6β,14-dihydroxy-3,4-dimethoxy-17-methylmo rphinan)

(3) Levomethorphan (1-3-methoxy-17-methylmorphinan)

(4) Levorphanol (1-3-hydroxy-17-methylmorphinan)

(5) Levophenacylmorphan (1-3-hydroxy-17-phenacylmorphinan

(6) Norlevorphanol (1-3-hydroxymorphinan)

(7) Phenomorphan (3-hydroxy-17-(2-phenylethyl) morphinan)

(8) Racemethorphan (d,1-3-methoxy-17-methylmorphinan)

(9) Racemorphan (*d,l*-3-hydroxy-N-methylmorphinan)

(10) Dextromethorphan (d-1,2,3,9,10,10a-hexahydro-6-methoxy-11- methyl-4H-10,4a-iminoethano-phenanthren)

(11) Dextrorphan (d-1,2,3,9,10,10a-hexahydro-11-methyl-4H- 10,4a-iminoethanophenanthren-6-ol)

(12) Levallorphan (1-11-allyl-1,2,3,9,10,10a-hexahydro-4H-10,4a-iminoethanophenanthren-6-ol)

(13) Levargorphan (*l*-11-propargyl-1,2,3,9,10,10a-hexahydro-4H -10,4a-iminoethanophenanthren-6-ol)

(14) Butorphanol (17-(cyclobutylmethyl)morphinan-3,14-diol)

(15) Nalbuphine (17-(cyclobutylmethyl)-4,5α-epoxy-morphinan -3,6α, 14-triol)
SOR/97-230; SOR/99-421, s. 1

11. Benzazocines, their salts, derivatives and salts of derivatives including:

(1) Phenazocine (1,2,3,4,5,6-hexahydro-6,11-dimethyl-3-phenethyl-2,6-methano-3-benzazocin-8-ol)

(2) Metazocine (1,2,3,4,5,6-hexahydro-3,6,11-trimethyl-2,6-methano-3-benzazocin-8-ol)

(3) Pentazocine (1,2,3,4,5,6-hexahydro-6,11-dimethyl-3-(3 -methyl-2-butenyl)-2,6-methano-3-be nzazocin-8-ol)
but not including

(4) Cyclazocine (1,2,3,4,5,6-hexahydro-6,11-dimethyl-3-(cyclopropylmethyl)-2, 6-methano-3-benzazocin-8-ol)

12. Ampromides, their salts, derivatives and salts of derivatives including:

(1) Diampromide (N-[2-(methylphenethylamino) propyl] propionanilide)

(2) Phenampromide (N-(1-methyl-2-piperidino) ethyl) propionanilide)

(3) Propiram (N-(1-methyl-2-piperidinoethyl)-N-2 -pyridylpropionamide)

13. Benzimidazoles, their salts, derivatives and salts of derivatives including:

(1) Clonitazene (2-(p-chlorobenzyl)-1-diethylaminoethyl-5 -nitrobenzimidazole)

(2) Etonitazene (2-(p-ethoxybenzyl)-1-diethylaminoethyl-5 -nitrobenzimidazole)

(3) Bezitramide (1-(3-cyano-3,3-diphenylpropyl)-4-(2´-oxo-3-propionyl-1-benzimidazolinyl)-pipe ridine)

14. Phencyclidine (1-(1-phenylcyclohexyl)piperidine), its salts, derivatives and analogues and salts of derivatives and analogues

15. Piritramide (1-(3-cyano-3,3-diphenylpropyl)-4-(1´-piperidino)piperidine-4-carboxylic acid amide), its salts, derivatives and salts of derivatives

16. Fentanyls, their salts, derivatives, and analogues and salts of derivatives and analogues, including:

(1) Acetyl-α-methylfentanyl (N-[1-(α-methylphenethyl)-4-piperidyl] acetanilide)

(2) Alfentanil (N-[1-[2-(4-ethyl-4,5-dihydro-5´-oxo-1H-tetrazol-1-yl)ethyl]-4-(methoxymethyl)-4-piperidyl]propionanilide)

(3) Carfentanil (methyl 4-[(1-oxopropyl)phenylamino]-1-(2-phenethyl)-4-piperidinecarboxylate)

(4) p-Fluorofentanyl (4'fluoro-N-(1-phenethyl-4-piperidyl) propionanilide)

(5) Fentanyl (N-(1-phenethyl-4-piperidyl) propionanilide)

(6) β-Hydroxyfentanyl (N-[1-(β-hydroxyphenethyl)-4-piperidyl] propionanilide)

(7) β-Hydroxy-3-methylfentanyl (N-[1-(β-hydroxyphenethyl)-3-methyl-4-piperidyl] propionanilide)

(8) α-Methylfentanyl (N-[1-(α-methylphenethyl)-4-piperidyl] propionanilide)

(9) α-Methylthiofentanyl (N-[1-[1-methyl-2-(2-thienyl) ethyl]-4-piperidyl] propionanilide)

(10) 3-Methylfentanyl (N-(3-methyl-1-phenethyl-4-piperidyl) propionanilide)

(11) 3-Methylthiofentanyl (N-[3-methyl-1-[2-(2-thienyl) ethyl]-4-piperidyl] propionanilide)

(11.1) Remifentanil (dimethyl 4-carboxy-4-(N-phenylpropionamido)-1-piperidinepropionate)

(12) Sufentanil (N-[4-(methoxymethyl)-1-[2-(2-thienyl)ethyl]-4-piperidyl] propionanilide)

(13) Thiofentanyl (N-[1-[2-(2-thienyl)ethyl]-4-piperidyl]propionilide)

SOR/99-371, s. 2

17. Tilidine (ethyl2-(dimethylamino)-1-phenyl-3-cyclohexene-1-carboxylate), its salts, derivatives and salts of derivatives

Schedule II

(Sections 2, 3, 4 to 7, 10, 29, 55 and 60)

1. Cannabis, its preparations, derivatives and similar synthetic preparations, including:

(1) Cannabis resin

(2) Cannabis (marihuana)

(3) Cannabidiol (2-[3-methyl-6-(1-methylethenyl)-2-cyclohexen-1-yl]-5-pentyl-1,3-benzenediol)

(4) Cannabinol(3-n-amyl-6,6,9-trimethyl-6-dibenzopyran-1-ol)

(5) Nabilone ((±)-trans-3-(1,1-dimethylheptyl)-6,6a,7,8,10,10a-hexahydro-1-hydroxy-6,6-dimethyl-9H-dibenzo[b,d]pyran-9-one)

(6) Pyrahexyl(3-n-hexyl-6,6,9-trimethyl-7,8,9,10-tetrahydro-6-dibenzopyran-1-ol)

(7) Tetrahydrocannabinol(tetrahydro-6,6,9-trimethyl-3-pentyl-6H-dibenzo[b,d]pyran-1-ol)

but not including

(8) Non-viable Cannabis seed, with the exception of its derivatives

SOR/98-157, s. 1

Schedule III

(Sections 2 to 7, 29, 55 and 60)

1. Amphetamines, their salts, derivatives, isomers and analogues and salts of derivatives, isomers and analogues including:

(1) amphetamine (α-methylbenzeneethanamine)

(2) methamphetamine (N,α-dimethylbenzeneethanamine)

(3) N-ethylamphetamine (N-ethyl-α-methylbenzeneethanamine)

(4) 4-methyl-2,5-dimethoxyamphetamine (STP) (2,5-dimenthoxy-4,α-dimethylbenzeneethanamine)

(5) 3,4-methylenedioxyamphetamine (MDA) (α-methyl-1,3-benzodioxide-5-ethanamine)

(6) 2,5-dimethoxyamphetamine (2,5-dimethoxy-α-methylbenzeneethanamine)

(7) 4-methoxyamphetamine (4-methoxy-α-methylbenzeneethanamine)

(8) 2,4,5-trimethoxyamphetamine (2,4,5-trimethoxy-α-methylbenzeneethanamine)

(9) N-methyl-3,4-methylenedioxyamphetamine (N,α-dimethyl-1,3-benzodioxole-5-ethanamine)

(10)   4-ethoxy-2,5-dimethoxyamphetamine(4-ethoxy-2,5-dimethoxy-α-methylbenzeneethanamine)

(11)   5-methoxy-3,4-methylenedioxyamphetamine   (7-methoxy-α-methyl-1,3-benzodioxole-5-ethanamine)

(12)   N,N-dimethyl-3,4-methylenedioxyamphetamine   (N,N,α-trimethyl-1,3-benzodioxole-5-ethanamine)

(13) N-ethyl-3,4-methylenedioxyamphetamine (N-ethyl-α-methyl-1,3-benzodioxole-5-ethanamine)

(14)   4-ethyl-2,5-dimethoxyamphetamine   (DOET)(4-ethyl-2,5-dimethoxy-α-methylbenzeneethanamine)

(15)   4-bromo-2,5-dimethoxyamphetamine   (4-bromo-2,5-dimethoxy-α-methylbenzeneethanamine)

(16)   4-chloro-2,5-dimethoxyamphetamine   (4-chloro-2,5-dimethoxy-α-methylbenzeneethanamine)

(17) 4-ethoxyamphetamine (4-ethoxy-α-methyl-benzeneethanamine)

(18) Benzphetamine (N-benzyl-N,α-dimethylbenzeneethanamine)

(19) N-Propyl-3,4-methylenedioxyamphetamine (α-methyl-N-propyl-1,3-benzodioxole-5-ethanamine

(20) N-(2-Hydroxyethyl)-α-methylbenzeneethanamine

SOR/97-230

2. Methylphenidate (α-phenyl-2-piperidineacetic acid methyl ester) and any salt thereof

SOR/97-230

3. Methaqualone (2-methyl-3-(2-methylphenyl)-4(3H)-quinazolinone) and any salt thereof

4. Mecloqualone (2-methyl-3-(2-chlorophenyl)-4(3H)-quinazolinone) and any salt thereof

5. Lysergic acid diethylamide (LSD) (N,N-diethyllysergamide) and any salt thereof

6. N,N-Diethyltryptamine (DET) (3-[(2-diethylamino) ethyl]indole) and any salt thereof

7. N,N-Dimethyltryptamine (DMT) (3-[(2-dimethylamino)ethyl]indole) and any salt thereof

8. N-Methyl-3-piperidyl benzilate (LBJ) (3-[(hydroxydiphenylacetyl)oxy]-1-methylpiperidine) and any salt thereof

9. Harmaline (4,9-dihydro-7-methoxy-1-methyl-3H- pyrido(3,4-b)indole) and any salt thereof

10. Harmalol (4,9-dihydro-1-methyl-3H-pyrido (3,4-b)indol-7-ol) and any salt thereof

11. Psilocin (3-[2-(dimethylamino)ethyl]-4-hydroxyindole) and any salt thereof

12. Psilocybin (3-[2-(dimethylamino)ethyl]-4-phosphoryloxyindole) and any salt thereof

13. N-(1-phenylcyclohexyl)ethylamine (PCE) and any salt thereof

14. 1-[1-(2-Thienyl) cyclohexyl]piperidine (TCP) and any salt thereof

15. 1-Phenyl-N-propylcyclohexanamine and any salt thereof

16. 1-(1-Phenylcyclohexyl)pyrrolidine and any salt thereof

17. Mescaline (3,4,5-trimethoxybenzeneethanamine) and any salt thereof, but not peyote (lophophora)

18. 4-Methylaminorex (4,5-dihydro-4-methyl-5-phenyl-2-oxazolamine) and any salt thereof

19. Cathinone ((-)-α-aminopropiophenome) and any salt thereof

20. Fenetylline (d,1-3,7-dihydro-1,3-dimethyl-7-(2- [(1-methyl-2-phenethyl)amino]ethyl)-1H-purine -2, 6-dione) and any salt thereof

21. 2-Methylamino-1-phenyl-1-propanone and any salt thereof

22. 1-[1-(Phenylmethyl)cyclohexyl]piperidine and any salt thereof

23. 1-[1-(4-Methylphenyl)cyclohexyl]piperidine and any salt thereof

24. 4-bromo-2,5-dimethoxybenezeneethanamine and any salt, isomer or salt of iso-mer therof

SOR/97-230

25. Flunitrazepam (5-(o-fluorophenyl)-1,3-dihydro-1-methyl-7-nitro-2H-1,4-benzodiazepin-2-one)

Proposed Amendment — Schedule III, item 25

25. Flunitrazepam   (5-(o-fluorophenyl)-1,3-dihydro-1-methyl-7-nitro-2H-1,4-benzodiazepin-2-one) and any salts or derivatives thereof

SOR/2000-220, s. 1 [To come into force September 1, 2000.]

SOR/98-173

26. 4-hydroxybutanoic acid (GHB) and any salf thereof

SOR/98-173

Schedule IV

(Sections 2 to 4, 5 to 7, 29, 55 and 60)

1. Barbiturates, their salts and derivatives including

(1) Allobarbital (5,5-diallylbarbituric acid)

(2) Alphenal (5-allyl-5-phenylbarbituric acid)

(3) Amobarital (5-ethyl-5-(3-methylbutyl) barbituric acid)

(4) Aprobarbital (5-allyl-5-isopropylbarbituric acid)

(5) Barbital (5,5-diethylbarbituric acid)

(6) Barbituric Acid (2,4,6(1H,3H,5H)-pyrimidinetrione)

(7) Butabarbital (5-sec-butyl-5-ethylbarbituric acid)

(8) Butalbital (5-allyl-5-isobutylbarbituric acid)

(9) Butallylonal (5-(2-bromoallyl)-5-sec-butylbarbituric acid)

(10) Butethal (5-butyl-5-ethylbarbituric acid)

(11) Cyclobarbital (5-(1-cyclohexen-1-yl)-5-ethylbarbituric acid)

(12) Cyclopal (5-allyl-5-(2-cyclopenten-1-yl)barbituric acid

(13) Heptabarbital (5-(1-cyclohepten-1-yl)-5-ethylbarbituric acid)

(14) Hexethal (5-ethyl-5-hexylbarbituric acid)

(15) Hexobarbital (5-(1-cyclohexen-1-yl)-1,5-dimethylbarbituric acid)

(16) Mephobarbital (5-ethyl-1-methyl-5-phenylbarbituric acid)

(17) Methabarbital (5,5-diethyl-1-methylbarbituric acid)

(18) Methylphenobarbital (5-ethyl-1-methyl-5-phenylbarbituric acid)

(19) Propallylonal(5-(2-bromoally)-5-isopropylbarbituric acid)

(20) Pentobarbital (5-ethyl-5-(1-methylbutyl)barbituric acid)

(21) Phenobarbital (5-ethyl-5-phenylbarbituric acid)

(22) Probarbital (5-ethyl-5-isopropylbarbituric acid)

(23) Phenylmethylbarbituric Acid (5-methyl-5-phenylbarbituric acid)

(24) Secobarbital (5-allyl-5-(1-methylbutyl)barbituric acid)

(25) Sigmodal (5-(2-bromoallyl)-5-(1-methylbutyl)barbituric acid)

(26) Talbutal (5-allyl-5-sec-butylbarbituric acid)

(27) Vinbarbital (5-ethyl-5-(1-methy-1-butenyl)barbituric acid)

(28) Vinylbital (5-(1-methylbutyl)-5-vinylbarbituric acid)

2. Thiobarbiturates, their salts and derivatives including:

(1) Thialbarbital (5-allyl-5-(2-cyclohexen-1-yl)-2-thiobarbituric acid)

(2) Thiamylal (5-allyl-5-(1-methylbutyl)-2-thiobarbituric acid)

(3) Thiobarbituric Acid (2-thiobarbituric acid)

(4) Thiopental (5-ethyl-5-(1-methylbutyl)-2-thiobarbituric acid)

3. Chlorphentermine (1-(p-chlorophenyl)-2-methyl-2-aminopropane) and any salt thereof

4. Diethylpropion (2-(diethylamino)propiophenone) and any salt thereof

5. Phendimetrazine (d-3,4-dimethyl-2-phenylmorpholine) and any salt thereof

6. Phenmetrazine (3-methyl-2-phenylmorpholine) and any salt thereof

7. Pipradol (α,α-diphenyl-2-piperidinemethanol) and any salt thereof

8. Phentermine (α,α-dimethylbenzeneethanamine) and any salt thereof

9. Butorphanol (1-N-cyclobutylmethyl-3,14-dihydroxymorphinan) and any salt thereof

10. Nalbuphine (N-cyclobutylmethyl-4,5-epoxy-morphinan-3,6,14-triol) and any salt thereof

11. Glutethiamide (2-ethyl-2-phenylglutarimide)

12. Clotiazepam (5-(o-chlorophenyl)-7-ethyl-1,3-dihydro-1-methyl-2H-thieno[2,3-e]-1,4-diazepin-2-one) and any salt thereof

SOR/97-230; SOR/99-421, s. 2

13. Ethchlorvynol (ethyl-2-chlorovinyl ethynyl carbinol)

14. Ethinamate (1-ethynylcyclohexanol carbamate)

15. Mazindol (5-(p-chlorophenyl)-2,5-dihydro-3H-imidazo[2,1-a]isoindol-5-ol)

16. Meprobamate (2-methyl-2-propyl-1,3-propanediol dicarbonate)

17. Methyprylon (3,3-diethyl-5-methyl-2,4-piperidinedione)

18. Benzodiazepines, their salts and derivatives, including:

(1)   Alprazolam   (8-chloro-1-methyl-6-phenyl-4H-s-triazolo[4,3-a][1,4] benzodiazepine)

(2) Bromazepam (7-bromo-1,3-dihydro-5-(2-pyridyl)- 2H-1, 4-benzodiazepin-2-one)

Proposed Addition — Schedule IV, item 18(2.1)

(2.1)   Brotizolam   (2-bromo-4-(o-chlorophenyl)-9-methyl-6H-thieno[3,2-f]-s-triazolo[4,3-a][1,4]diazepine)

SOR/2000-220, s. 2(1) [To come into force September 1, 2000.]

(3) Camazepam (7-chloro-1,3-dihydro-3-(N,N-dime=thylcarbamoyl)-1-methyl-5-phenyl-2H-1,4-ben=zodiazepin-2-one)

(4) Chlodiazepoxide(7-chloro-2-(methylamino)-5-phenyl-3H-1,4-benzodiazepine-4-oxide)

(5)   Clobazam(7-chloro-1-methyl-5-phenyl-1H-1,5-benzodiazepine-2,4(3H,5H)-dione)

(6)   Clonazepam(5-(o-chlorophenyl)-1,3-dihydro-7-nitro-2H-1,4-benzodiazepin-2-one)

(7)   Clorazepate(7-chloro-2,3-dihydro-2,2-dihydroxy-5   -phenyl-1H-1,4-benzodiazepine-3-carboxylic acid)

(8) Cloxazolam(10-chloro-11b-(o-chlorophenyl)-2,3,7,11b-tetrahydrooxazolo[3,2-d][1,4]benzodiazepin=6-(5H)-one)

(9) Delorazepam (7-chloro-5-(o-chlorophenyl)-1,3-dihydro-2H-1,4=benzodiazepin-2-one)

(10) Diazepam (7-chloro-1,3-dihydro-1-methyl-5-phenyl-2H-1,4-benzodiazepin-2-one)

(11) Estazolam (8-chloro-6-phenyl-4H-s-triazolo[4,3-a][1,4]benzodiazepine)

(12) Ethyl Loflazepate (ethyl7-chloro-5-(o-flourophenyl)-2,3-dihydro-2-oxo-1H-1,4-benzodiazepine-3-carboxylate)

(13)   Fludiazepam(7-chloro-5-(o-flourophenyl)-1,3-dihydro-1-methyl-2H-1,4-benzodiazepin-2-one)

(14) [Repealed SOR/98-173]

(15)   Flurazepam(7-chloro-1-[2-(diethylamino)ethyl]-5-(o-flourophenyl)-1,3-dihydro-2H-1,4-benzodiazepin-2-one)

(16) Halazepam(7-chloro-1,3-dihydro-5=phenyl-1-(2,2,2-triflouroethyl)-2H-1,4-benzodiazepin-2-one)

(17)   Haloxazolam(10-bromo-11b-(o-flourophenyl)-2,3,7,11b-tetrahydrooxazolo[3,2-d][1,4] benzodiazepin-6(5H)-one)

(18) Ketazolam (11-chloro-8,12b-dihydro-2,8-dimethyl-12b -phenyl-4H-[1,3]-oxazino-[3,2-d][1,4] benzo=diazepine-4,7(6H)-dione)

(19) Loprazolam (6-(o-chlorophenyl)-2,4-dihydro-2-[(4 -methyl-1-piperazinyl)methylene]-8-nitro- 1H-imidazo[1,2-a][1,4]benzodiazepin-1-one)

(20) Lorazepam (7-chloro-5-(o-chlorophenyl)-1,3-dihydro -3-hydroxy-2H-1,4-benzodiazepin-2-o ne)

(21) Lormetazepam (7-chloro-5(o-chlorophenyl)-1,3-dihydro-3 -hydroxy-1-methyl-2H-1,4-benzodiazepin -2-one)

(22)   Medazepam   (7-chloro-2,3-dihydro-1-methyl-5-ph   enyl-1H-1,4-benzodiazepine)

Proposed Addition — Schedule IV, item 18(22.1)

(22.1)   Midazolam   (8-chloro-6-(o-fluorophenyl)-1-methyl-4H-imidazo[1,5-a][1,4]benzodiazepine)

SOR/2000-220, s. 2(2) [To come into force September 1, 2000.]

(23) Nimetazepam (1,3-dihydro-1-methyl-7-nitro-5-phe nyl-2H-1,4-benzodiazepin-2-one)

(24) Nitrazepam (1,3-dihydro-7-nitro-5-phenyl-2H-1, 4-benzodiazepin-2-one)

(25) Nordazepam (7-chloro-1,3-dihydro-5-phenyl-(2H-1,4-benzodiazepin-2-one)

(26) Oxazepam (7-chloro-1,3-dihydro-3-hydroxy-5-p henyl-2H-1,4-benzodiazepin-2-one)

(27) Oxazolam (10-chloro-2,3,7,11b-tetrahydro-2-methyl- 11b-phenyloxazolo[3,2-d] [1,4]benzodiazepin-6(5H)-one)

(28) Pinazepam   (7-chloro-1,3-dihydro-5-phenyl-1-(2 -propynyl)-2H-1,   4-benzodiazepin-2-one)

(29) Prazepam (7-chloro-1-(cyclopropylmethyl)-1,3-dihydro -5-phenyl-2H-1,4-benzodiazepin-2-one)

Proposed Addition — Schedule IV, item 18(29.1)

(29.1)   Quazepam   (7-chloro-5-(o-fluorophenyl)-1,3-dihydro-1-(2,2,2-trifluoroethyl)-2H-1,4-benzodiazepine-2-thione)
SOR/2000-220, s. 2(3) [To come into force September 1, 2000.]

(30)   Temazepam   (7-chloro-1,3-dihydro-3-hydroxy-1-methyl-5-phenyl-2H-1,4-benzodiazepin-2=one)

(31)   Tetrazepam   (7-chloro-5-(cyclohexen-1-yl)-1,3-dihdyro-1-methyl-2H-1,4-benzodiazepin-2-one)

(32)   Triazolam   (8-chloro-6-(o-chlorophenyl)-1-methyl   -4H-s-triazolo[4,3-a][1,4]benzodiazepine)

Proposed Addition — Schedule IV, item 18(32.1)

(32.1)   Clozapine   (8-chloro-11-(4-methyl-1-piperazinyl)-5H-dibenzo[b,e][1,4]diazepine) and any salt thereof
SOR/2000-220, s. 2(4) [To come into force September 1, 2000.]

(33)   Flunitrazepam   (5-(o-flurophenyl)-1,3-dihydro-1-methyl-7-nitro-2H-1,4-benzodiazepin-2-one)

Proposed Amendment — Schedule IV, item 18(33)

(33)   Flunitrazepam   (5-(o-fluorophenyl)-1,3-dihydro-1-methyl-7-nitro-2H-1,4-benzodiazepin-2-one) and any salts or derivatives thereof
SOR/2000-220, s. 2(4) [To come into force September 1, 2000.]

(34)   Olanzapine   (2-methyl-4-(4-methyl-1-piperazinyl)-10H-thieno[2,3-b][1,5]benzodiazepine) and its salts

SOR/97-230; SOR/98-173; SOR/99-371, s. 3

19. Catha edulis Forsk., its preparations, derivatives, alkaloids and salts, including:

(1) Cathine (d-threo-2-amino-1-hydroxy-1-phenylpropane)

20. Fencamfamin (d,1-N-ethyl-3-phenylbicyclo[2,2,1] heptan-2-amine) and any salt thereof

21. Fenproporex (d,1-3-[(α-methylphenethyl)amino] propionitrile) and my salt thereof

22. Mefenorex (d,1-N-(3-chloropropyl)-α-methylbenzeneethanamine) and any salt thereof

23. Anabolic steroids and their derivatives including:

(1) Androisoxazole (17β-hydroxy-17α-methylandrostano [3,2-c]isoxazole)

(2) Androstanolone (17β-hydroxy-5α-androstan-3-one)

(3) Androstenediol (androst-5-ene-3β,17β-diol)

(4) Bolandiol (estr-4-ene-3β,17β-diol)

(5) Bolasterone (17β-hydroxy-7α,17-dimethylandrost-4 -en-3-one)

(6) Bolazine (17β-hydroxy-2α-methyl-5α-androstan-3-one azine)

(7) Boldenone (17β-hydroxyandrosta-1,4-dien-3-one)

(8) Bolenol (19-nor-17α-pregn-5-en-17-ol)

(9) Calusterone (17β-hydroxy-7β,17-dimethylandrost-4- en-3-one)

(10) Clostebol (4-chloro-17β-hydroxyandrost-4-en-3 -one)

(11) Drostanolone (17β-hydroxy-2α-methyl-5α-androstan-3-one)

(12) Enestebol (4,17β-dihydroxy-17-methylandrosta-1,4-dien-3-one)

(13) Epitiostanol (2α, 3α-epithio-5α-androstan-17β-ol)

(14) Ethylestrenol (19-nor-17α-pregn-4-en-17-ol)

(15) 4-Hydroxy-19-nor testosterone

(16) Fluoxymesterone (9-fluoro-11β,17β-dihydroxy-17-methylandrost-4-en-3-one)

(17) Formebolone (11α,17β-dihydroxy-17-methyl-3-oxoandrosta-1,4 dien-2-carboxaldehyde)

(18) Furazabol (17-methyl-5α-androstano[2,3-c] furazan-17β-ol)

(19) Mebolazine (17β-hydroxy-2α,17-dimethyl-5α -androstan-3-one azine)

(20) Mesabolone (17β1/n[(1-methoxycyclohexyl)oxy]-5α-androst- 1-en-3-one)

(21) Mesterolone (17β-hydroxy-1α-methyl-5α-androstan-3-one)

(22) Metandienone (17β-hydroxy-17-methylandrosta-1,4-dien -3-one)

(23) Metenolone (17β-hydroxy-1-methyl-5α-androst -1-en-3-one)

(24) Methandriol (17α-methylandrost-5-ene-3β,17β -diol)

(25) Methyltestosterone (17β-hydroxy-17-methylandrost-4-en-3 -one)

(26) Metribolone (17β-hydroxy-17-methylestra-4,9,11-trien -3-one)

(27) Mibolerone (17β-hydroxy-7α,17-dimethylestr-4-en -3-one)

(28) Nandrolone (17β-hydroxyestr-4-en-3-one)

(29) Norboletone (13-ethyl-17β-hydroxy-18,19-dinorpregn -4-en-3-one)

(30) Norclostebol (4-chloro-17β-hydroxyestr-4-en-3 -one)

(31) Norethandrolone (17α-ethyl-17β-hydroxyestr-4-en -3-one)

(32) Oxabolone (4,17β-dihydroxyestr-4-en-3-one)

(33) Oxandrolone (17β-hydroxy-17-methyl-2-oxa-5 α-androstan-3-one)

(34) Oxymesterone (4,17β-dihydroxy-17-methylandrost-4-en -3-one)

(35) Oxymetholone (17β-hydroxy-2-(hydroxymethylene)-17-methyl-5α-androstan-3-one)

(36) Prasterone (3β-hydroxyandrost-5-en-17-one)

(37) Quinbolone (17β-(1-cyclopenten-1-yloxy) androsta-1,4-dien-3-one)

(38) Stanozolol (17β-hydroxy-17-methyl-5α-androstano [3,2-c]pyrazole)

(39) Stenbolone (17β-hydroxy-2-methyl-5α-androst -1-en-3-one)

(40) Testosterone (17β-hydroxyandrost-4-en-3-one)

(41) Tibolone ((7α, 17α)-17-hydroxy-7-methyl-19-norpregn-5 (10)en-20-yn-3-one)

(42) Tiomesterone (1α,7α-bis(acetylthio)-17β-hydroxy-17-methylandrost-4-en-3-one)

(43) Trenbolone (17β-hydroxyestra-4,9,11-trien-3-one)

SOR/97-230

24. Zeranol (3,4,5,6,7,8,9,10,11,12-decahydro-7,14,16- trihydroxy-3-methyl-1H-2-benzoxacyclotetradecin -1- one)

Schedule V
(Sections 2, 4, 6, 55 and 60)

1. Phenylpropanolamine (2-amino-1-phenyl-1-propanol) and any salt thereof

2. Propylhexedrine (1-cyclohexyl-2-methylaminopropane) and any salt thereof

3. Pyrovalerone (1-(1-pyrrolidinyl)butyl p-tolyl ketone and any salt thereof

Schedule VI
(Section 2, 6, 55, and 60)

1. Benzyl methyl ketone (P2P) (1-phenyl-2-propanone)

2. Ephedrine (1-erythro-2-(methylamino)-1-phenylpropan-1-ol)

3. Ergometrine (9,10-didehydro-N-(2-hydroxy-1-methylethy l)-6-methylergoline-8-carboxamide)

4. Ergotamine (12'-hydroxy-2'-methyl-5'-(phenylmethyl) ergotaman-3',6', 18-trione)

5. Lysergic acid (9,10-didehydro-6-methylergoline-8-carboxylic acid)

6. Pseudoephedrine (d-threo-2-(methylamino)-1-phenylpropan-1 -ol)

Schedule VII

(Sections 5 and 60)

1. *Substance*: cannabis resin
Amount: 3kg

2. *Substance*: cannabis (marihuana)
Amount: 3kg

Schedule VIII

(Sections 4 and 60)

1. *Substance*: cannabis resin
Amount: 1g

2. *Substance*: cannabis (marihuana)
Amount: 30g

NARCOTIC CONTROL ACT

TABLE OF CONCORDANCE

NCA

NARCOTIC CONTROL ACT

An Act to provide for the control of narcotic drugs

R.S.C. 1985, c. N-1, Am. R.S. 1985, c. 27 (1st Supp.), ss. 196–200, 203, 208; c. 27 (2d Supp.), s. 10; c. 42 (4th Supp.), s. 12; 1990, c. 16, s. 18; 1990, c. 17, s. 36; 1992, c. 1, s. 98; 1992, c. 20, ss. 215, 216; 1992, c. 51, s. 59; 1993, c. 28, s. 78 (Sch. III, item 113); 1993, c. 37, ss. 25–29; 1996, c. 8, ss. 32, 35; 1996, c. 16, ss. 60, 62, Repealed 1996, c. 19, s. 94.

[Note: The Narcotic Control Act is no longer in force. It was repealed by the Controlled Drugs and Substances Act, S.C. 1996, c. 19, on May 14, 1997. We have, however, retained the Narcotic Control Act because the Act remains of relevance to offences occurring before its repeal (see sections 61 and 62 of the Controlled Drugs and Substances Act. It will therefore continue to be of great practical importance for some time to come.]

Short Title

1. Short title — This Act may be cited as the *Narcotic Control Act*.

repealed 1996, c. 19, s. 94.

Interpretation

2. Definitions — In this Act,

"analyst" means a person designated as an analyst under the *Food and Drugs Act* or this Act;

"conveyance" includes any aircraft, vessel, motor vehicle or other conveyance of any description whatever;

"marihuana" means *Cannabis sativa* L.;

"minister" means

(a) with respect to Part I, the Minister of Health, and

(b) with respect to Part II, the Minister of Justice;

"narcotic" means any substance included in the schedule or anything that contains any substance included in the schedule;

"narcotic addict" means a person who through the use of narcotics,

(a) has developed a desire or need to continue to take a narcotic, or

(b) has developed a psychological or physical dependence upon the effect of a narcotic;

"opium poppy" means *Papaver somniferum* L.;

"possession" means possession as defined in the *Criminal Code*;

"practitioner" means a person who is registered and entitled under the laws of a province to practise in that province the profession of medicine, dentistry or veterinary medicine;

"prescription" means, in respect of a narcotic, an authorization given by a practitioner that a stated amount of the narcotic be dispensed for the person named therein;

"traffic" means

    (a) to manufacture, sell, give, administer, transport, send, deliver or distribute, or

    (b) to offer to do anything referred to in paragraph (*a*)

otherwise than under the authority of this Act or the regulations.

        R.S. 1985, c. 27 (1st Supp.), s. 196; 1996, c. 8, s. 32(1)(j); repealed 1996, c. 19, s. 94.

PART I — OFFENCES AND ENFORCEMENT

Particular Offences

3. (1) Possession of narcotic — Except as authorized by this Act or the regulations, no person shall have a narcotic in his possession.

(2) Offence and punishment — Every person who contravenes subsection (1) is guilty of an offence and liable

    (a) on summary conviction for a first offence, to a fine not exceeding one thousand dollars or to imprisonment for a term not exceeding six months or to both and, for a subsequent offence, to a fine not exceeding two thousand dollars or to imprisonment for a term not exceeding one year or to both; or

    (b) on conviction on indictment, to imprisonment for a term not exceeding seven years.

        repealed 1996, c. 19, s. 94.

3.1 (1) Failure to disclose previous prescriptions — No person shall, at any time, seek or obtain a narcotic or a prescription for a narcotic from a practitioner unless that person discloses to the practitioner particulars of every narcotic or prescription for a narcotic issued to that person by a different practitioner within the preceding thirty days.

(2) Offence and punishment — Every person who contravenes subsection (1)

    (a) is guilty of an indictable offence and liable to imprisonment for a term not exceeding seven years; or

    (b) is guilty of an offence punishable on summary conviction and liable

        (i) for a first offence, to a fine not exceeding one thousand dollars or to imprisonment for a term not exceeding six months, and

(ii) for a subsequent offence, to a fine not exceeding two thousand dollars or to imprisonment for a term not exceeding one year.

(3) Limitation period — Summary conviction proceedings in respect of an offence under this section may be instituted at any time within but not later than one year from the time when the subject-matter of the proceedings arose.

R.S. 1985, c. 27 (1st Supp.), s. 197; repealed 1996, c. 19, s. 94.

4. (1) Trafficking — No person shall traffic in a narcotic or any substance represented or held out by the person to be a narcotic.

(2) Possession for purpose of trafficking — No person shall have in his possession any narcotic for the purpose of trafficking.

(3) Offence and punishment — Every person who contravenes subsection (1) or (2) is guilty of an indictable offence and liable to imprisonment for life.

repealed 1996, c. 19, s. 94.

5. (1) Importing and exporting — Except as authorized by this Act or the regulations, no person shall import into Canada or export from Canada any narcotic.

(2) Offence and punishment — Every person who contravenes subsection (1) is guilty of an indictable offence and liable to imprisonment for life but not less than seven years.

repealed 1996, c. 19, s. 94.

6. (1) Cultivation of opium poppy or marihuana — No person shall cultivate opium poppy or marihuana except under the authority of, and in accordance with, a licence issued to the person under the regulations.

(2) Offence and punishment — Every person who contravenes subsection (1) is guilty of an indictable offence and liable to imprisonment for a term not exceeding seven years.

(3) Destruction of plant — The Minister may cause to be destroyed any growing plant of opium poppy or marihuana cultivated otherwise than under authority of and in accordance with a licence issued under the regulations.

repealed 1996, c. 19, s. 94.

Prosecutions

7. (1) Setting out or negativing exception, etc. not required — No exception, exemption, excuse or qualification prescribed by law is required to be set out or negatived, as the case may be, in an information or indictment for an offence under this Act or under section 463, 464 or 465 of the *Criminal Code* in respect of an offence under this Act.

(2) Burden of proving exception, etc — In any prosecution under this Act the burden of proving that an exception, exemption, excuse or qualification prescribed by law operates in favour of the accused is on the accused, and the prosecutor is not required, except by way of rebuttal, to prove that the exception, exemption, excuse or qualification does not operate in favour of the accused, whether or not it is set out in the information or indictment.

repealed 1996, c. 19, s. 94.

8. (1) Procedure in prosecution for trafficking — In any prosecution for a contravention of subsection 4(2), if the accused does not plead guilty, the trial shall proceed as if it were a prosecution for an offence under section 3.

(2) Idem — After the close of the case for the prosecution pursuant to subsection (1) and after the accused has had an opportunity to make full answer and defence, the court shall make a finding as to whether or not the accused contravened subsection 3(1) and, if the court finds that the accused did not contravene subsection 3(1), the accused shall be acquitted but, if the court finds that the accused contravened subsection 3(1), the accused shall be given an opportunity of establishing that he was not in possession of the narcotic for the purpose of trafficking and, thereafter, the prosecutor shall be given an opportunity of adducing evidence to establish the contrary.

(3) Conviction of possession or conviction of trafficking — After compliance with subsection (2), in the case of finding a contravention by the accused of subsection 3(1),

> (a) if the accused establishes that he was not in possession of the narcotic for the purpose of trafficking, the accused shall be acquitted of the offence as charged but shall be convicted of an offence under section 3 and sentenced accordingly; or

> (b) if the accused fails to establish that he was not in possession of the narcotic for the purpose of trafficking, the accused shall be convicted of the offence as charged and sentenced accordingly.

repealed 1996, c. 19, s. 94

9. (1) Certificate of analyst — Subject to this section, a certificate purporting to be signed by an analyst stating that the analyst has analyzed or examined a substance and stating the result of the analysis or examination is admissible in evidence in any prosecution for an offence referred to in subsection 7(1), and, in the absence of evidence to the contrary, is proof of the statements contained in the certificate without proof of the signature or official character of the person appearing to have signed the certificate.

(2) Requiring attendance of analyst — The party against whom a certificate of an analyst is produced pursuant to subsection (1) may, with leave of the court, require the attendance of the analyst for the purposes of cross-examination.

(3) Notice of intention to produce certificate — No certificate shall be admitted in evidence pursuant to subsection (1) unless the party intending to produce it has, before the trial, given to the party against whom it is intended to be produced reasonable notice of that intention together with a copy of the certificate.

(4) Proof of service — For the purposes of this Act, service of any certificate referred to in subsection (1) may be proved by oral evidence given under oath by, or by the affidavit or solemn declaration of, the person claiming to have served it.

(5) Attendance for examination — Notwithstanding subsection (4), the court may require the person who appears to have signed an affidavit or solemn declaration referred to in that subsection to appear before it for examination or cross-examination in respect of the issue of proof of service.

R.S. 1985, c. 27 (1st Supp.), s. 198; repealed 1996, c. 19, s. 94.

Search, Seizure and Forfeiture

10. Entry and search — A peace officer may, at any time, without a warrant enter and search any place other than a dwelling-house, and under the authority of a warrant issued under section 12, enter and search any dwelling-house in which the peace officer believes on reasonable grounds there is a narcotic by means of or in respect of which an offence under this Act has been committed.

R.S. 1985, c. 27 (1st Supp.), s. 199; repealed 1996, c. 19, s. 94.

11. Search of person and seizure — A peace officer may search any person found in a place entered pursuant to section 10 and may seize and, from a place so entered, take away any narcotic found therein, anything therein in which the peace officer reasonably suspects a narcotic is contained or concealed, or any other thing by means of or in respect of which that officer believes on reasonable grounds an offence under this Act has been committed or that may be evidence of the commission of such an offence.

repealed 1996, c. 19, s. 94.

12. Warrant to search dwelling-house — A justice who is satisfied by information on oath that there are reasonable grounds for believing that there is a narcotic, by means of or in respect of which an offence under this Act has been committed, in any dwelling-house may issue a warrant, under the hand of the justice, authorizing a peace officer named therein at any time to enter the dwelling-house and search for narcotics.

repealed 1996, c. 19, s. 94.

13. [Repealed R.S. 1985, c. 27 (1st Supp.), s. 200.]

R.S. 1985, c. 27 (1st Supp.), s. 208 states:

> Nothing in sections 190, 195, 199 and 200 of this Act [Criminal Law Amendment Act, 1985] shall be construed as rendering invalid or inadmissible in any proceedings any evidence obtained by the exercise of a writ of assistance prior to the coming into force of those sections.

14. Powers of peace officer — For the purpose of exercising authority pursuant to any of sections 10 to 13, a peace officer may, with such assistance as that officer deems necessary, break open any door, window, lock, fastener, floor, wall, ceiling, compartment, plumbing fixture, box, container or any other thing.

repealed 1996, c. 19, s. 94.

15. (1) Application for restoration — Where a narcotic or other thing has been seized under section 11, any person may, within two months after the date of the seizure, on prior notification being given to the Crown in the manner prescribed by the regulations, apply to a provincial court judge within whose territorial jurisdiction the seizure was made for an order of restoration under this section.

(2) Order of immediate restoration — Subject to section 16, where on the hearing of an application made under subsection (1) the provincial court judge is satisfied that the applicant is entitled to possession of the narcotic or other thing seized and that the thing seized is not or will not be required as evidence in any proceedings in respect of an offence under this Act, the provincial court judge shall order that the thing seized be restored forthwith to the applicant.

(3) Order of restoration at specified time — Where on the hearing of an application made under subsection (1) the provincial court judge is satisfied that the applicant is entitled to possession of the thing seized but is not satisfied that the thing is not or will not be required as evidence in any proceedings in respect of an offence under this Act, the provincial court judge shall order that the thing seized be restored to the applicant.

> (a) on the expiration of four months after the date of the seizure, if no proceedings in respect of an offence under this Act have been commenced before that time; or

> (b) on the final conclusion of any such proceedings, in any other case.

(4) Where application not made or order refused — Where no application has been made for the return of any narcotic or other thing seized under section 11 within two months after the date of the seizure, or an application therefor has been made but, on the hearing of the application, no order of restoration is made, the thing seized shall be delivered

> (a) in the case of a narcotic, to the Minister, who may make such disposition thereof as the Minister thinks fit; and

> (b) in the case of any other thing,

>> (i) where the proseuction of the offence in respect of which the thing was seized was commenced at the instance of the government of a province and conducted by or on behalf of that government, to the Attorney General or Solicitor General of that province, and

>> (ii) in any other case, to the Minister of Public Works and Government Services,

who may dispose of the thing in accordance with the law.

R.S. 1985, c. 27 (1st Supp.), s. 203; 1993, c. 37, s. 25; 1996, c. 16, s. 60(1)(n); repealed 1996, c. 19, s. 94.

16. (1) Forfeiture on conviction — Where a person has been convicted of an offence under section 3, 4 or 5, any narcotic seized under section 11 by means of or in respect of which the offence was committed and any hypodermic needle, syringe, capping machine or other apparatus so seized that was used in any manner in connection with the offence, is forfeited to Her Majesty and shall be disposed of as the Minister directs.

(1.1) Idem — Where a person has been convicted of an offence under section 3, 4 or 5, any money seized under section 11 that was used for the purchase of the narcotic by means of or in respect of which the offence was committed is,

(a) where the prosecution of the offence was commenced at the instance of the government of a province and conducted by or on behalf of that government, forfeited to Her Majesty in right of that province and shall be disposed of by the Attorney General or the Solicitor General of the province in accordance with the law; and

(b) in any other case, forfeited to Her Majesty in right of Canada and shall be disposed of by the Minister of Public Works and Government Services in accordance with the law.

(2) Forfeiture of conveyance on application — Where a person has been convicted of an offence under section 4 or 5, the court may, on application by counsel for the Crown, order that any conveyance seized under section 11 that has been proved to have been used in any manner in connection with the offence be forfeited

(a) where the prosecution of the offence was commenced at the instance of the government of a province and conducted by or on behalf of that government, to Her Majesty in right of that province, and

(b) in any other case, to Her Majesty in right of Canada,

and, on the making of that order, the conveyance, except as provided in sections 17 to 19, shall, on the expiration of thirty days after the date of the forfeiture, be disposed of by the Attorney General or the Solicitor General of the province, or by the Minister of Public Works and Government Services, as the case may be, in accordance with the law.

R.S. 1985, c. 27 (1st Supp.), s. 203; 1993, c. 37, s. 26; 1996, c. 16, s. 60(1)(n); repealed 1996, c. 19, s. 94.

17. (1) Application by person claiming interest in forfeited conveyance — Where any conveyance is forfeited to Her Majesty under subsection 16(2), any person (other than a person convicted of the offence that resulted in the forfeiture or a person in whose possession the conveyance was when seized) who claims an interest therein as owner, mortgagee, lienholder or holder of any like interest may, within thirty days after the forfeiture, apply by notice in writing to a judge for an order under subsection (4).

(2) Date of hearing — The judge to whom an application is made under subsection (1) shall fix a day not less than thirty days after the date of filing of the application for the hearing thereof.

(3) Notice to Minister or Attorney General of a province — The applicant for an order under subsection (4) shall, at least fifteen days before the day fixed for the hearing, serve a notice of the application and of the hearing on

(a) where the prosecution of the offence was commenced at the instance of the government of a province and conducted by or on behalf of that government, the Attorney General or the Solicitor General of the province, as the case may be; and

(b) in any other case, the Minister of Public Works and Government Services.

(4) Order by judge — Where, on the hearing of an application made under subsection (1), it is made to appear to the satisfaction of the judge

(a) that the applicant is innocent of any complicity in the offence that resulted in the forfeiture and of any collusion in relation to that offence with the person who was convicted thereof, and

(b) that the applicant exercised, with respect to the person permitted to obtain possession of the conveyance, all reasonable care that the conveyance was not likely to be used in connection with the commission of an unlawful act or, in the case of a mortgagee or lienholder, that the applicant exercised, with respect to the mortgagor or lien-giver, all reasonable care in order to be so satisfied,

the applicant is entitled to an order declaring that the interest of the applicant is not affected by the forfeiture and declaring the nature and extent of the interest.

(5) Appeal — The applicant, the Attorney General or the Solicitor General of the province or the Minister of Public Works and Government Services, as the case may be, may appeal to the court of appeal from an order made under subsection (4) and the appeal shall be asserted, heard and decided according to the ordinary procedure governing appeals to the court of appeal from orders or judgments of a judge.

1993, c. 37, s. 27; 1996, c. 16, s. 60(1)(n); repealed 1996, c. 19, s. 94.

18. Definitions — In section 17,

"court of appeal" means, in the province in which an order under section 17 is made, the court of appeal for that province as defined in the definition "court of appeal" in section 2 of the *Criminal Code*;

"judge" means

(a) in the Province of Ontario, a judge of the Ontario Court (General Division),

(b) in the Province of Quebec, a judge of the Superior Court for the district in which the conveyance, in respect of which an application for an order under section 17 is made, was seized,

(c) [Repealed 1992, c. 51, s. 59(1).]

(d) in the Provinces of New Brunswick, Manitoba, Saskatchewan and Alberta, a judge of the Court of Queen's Bench,

(e) in the Provinces of Nova Scotia and British Columbia, the Yukon Territory and the Northwest Territories, a judge of the Supreme Court, and

(f) in the Provinces of Prince Edward Island and Newfoundland, a judge of the Trial Division of the Supreme Court.

R.S. 1985, c. 27 (2d Supp.), s. 10; 1990, c. 16, s. 18; 1990, c. 17, s. 36; 1992, c, 1, s. 98; 1992, c. 51, s. 59; repealed 1996, c. 19, s. 94.

19. Direction for restoration or payment — The Minister of Public Works and Government Services or the Attorney General or the Solicitor General of the province, as the case may be, shall, on application made to that Minister or to the Attorney General or the Solicitor General of the province by any person who has obtained a final order under section 17, direct that the conveyance to which the

interest of the applicant relates be returned to the applicant or that an amount equal to the value of that interest, as declared in the order, be paid to the applicant.

1993, c. 37, s. 28; 1996, c. 16, s. 60(1)(n); repealed 1996, c. 19, s. 94.

Proceeds of Crime

19.1 (1) Possession of property obtained by certain offences — No person shall possess any property or any proceeds of any property knowing that all or part of the property or of those proceeds was obtained or derived directly or indirectly as a result of

(a) the commission in Canada of an offence under section 4, 5 or 6; or

(b) an act or omission anywhere that, if it had occurred in Canada, would have constituted an offence under section 4, 5 or 6.

(2) Punishment — Every person who contravenes subsection (1)

(a) is guilty of an indictable offence and is liable to imprisonment for a term not exceeding ten years, where the value of the subject-matter of the offence exceeds one thousand dollars; or

(b) is guilty

(i) of an indictable offence and is liable to imprisonment for a term not exceeding two years, or

(ii) of an offence punishable on summary conviction,

where the value of the subject-matter of the offence does not exceed one thousand dollars.

R.S. 1985, c. 42 (4th Supp.), s. 12; repealed 1996, c. 19, s. 94.

19.2 (1) Laundering proceeds of certain offences — No person shall use, transfer the possession of, send or deliver to any person or place, transport, transmit, alter, dispose of or otherwise deal with, in any manner and by any means, any property or any proceeds of any property with intent to conceal or convert that property or those proceeds and knowing that all or a part of that property or of those proceeds was obtained by or derived directly or indirectly as a result of

(a) the commission in Canada of an offence under section 4, 5 or 6; or

(b) an act or omission anywhere that, if it had occurred in Canada, would have constituted an offence under section 4, 5 or 6.

(2) Punishment — Every person who contravenes subsection (1)

(a) is guilty of an indictable offence and is liable to imprisonment for a term not exceeding ten years; or

(b) is guilty of an offence punishable on summary conviction.

R.S. 1985, c. 42 (4th Supp.), s. 12; repealed 1996, c. 19, s. 94.

19.3 (1) Part XII.2 of the Criminal Code applicable — Sections 462.3 and 462.32 to 462.5 of the *Criminal Code* apply, with such modifications as the circumstances require, in respect of proceedings for

(a) an offence under section 4, 5, 6, 19.1 or 19.2; or

(b) a conspiracy or an attempt to commit, being an accessory after the fact in relation to, or any counselling in relation to an offence referred to in paragraph (*a*).

(2) Idem — For the purposes of subsection (1),

(a) a reference in section 462.37 or 462.38 or subsection 462.41(2) of the *Criminal Code* to an enterprise crime offence shall be deemed to be a reference to an offence mentioned in paragraph (1)(*a*) or (*b*); and

(b) a reference, in relation to the manner in which forfeited property is to be disposed of, in subsection 462.37(1) or 462.38(2), paragraph 462.43(*c*) or section 462.5 of the *Criminal Code*, to the Attorney General shall be deemed to be a reference to

(i) where the prosecution of the offence in respect of which the thing was forfeited was commenced at the instance of the government of a province and conducted by or on behalf of that government, the Attorney General or Solicitor General of that province, and

(ii) in any other case, the Minister of Public Works and Government Services.

R.S. 1985, c. 42 (4th Supp.), s. 12; 1993, c. 37, s. 29; 1996, c. 16, s. 60(1)(n); repealed 1996, c. 19, s. 94.

General

20. Regulations — The Governor in Council may make regulations

(a) providing for the issue of licences for the importation, export, sale, manufacture, production or distribution of narcotics and for the cultivation of opium poppy or marihuana;

(b) prescribing the form, duration and terms and conditions of any licence described in paragraph (*a*) and the fees payable therefor, and providing for the cancellation and suspension of licences described in that paragraph;

(c) authorizing the sale or possession of or other dealing in narcotics and prescribing the circumstances and conditions under which, and the persons by whom, narcotics may be sold, had in possession or otherwise dealt in;

(d) requiring physicians, dentists, veterinarians, pharmacists and other persons who deal in narcotics as authorized by this Act or the regulations to keep records and make returns;

(e) authorizing the communication of any information obtained under this Act or the regulations to provincial professional licensing authorities;

(f) prescribing the punishment by a fine not exceeding five hundred dollars or imprisonment for a term not exceeding six months, or both, to be imposed upon summary conviction for breach of any regulation; and

(g) generally, for carrying out the purposes and provisions of this Act.

repealed 1996, c. 19, s. 94

21. Designation of analyst — The Minister may designate any person as an analyst for the purpose of this Act.

repealed 1996, c. 19, s. 94.

22. Amendment of schedule — The Governor in Council may amend the schedule by adding thereto or deleting therefrom any substance, the inclusion or exclusion of which, as the case may be, is deemed necessary by the Governor in Council in the public interest.

repealed 1996, c. 19, s. 94.

[Note: Part II as enacted by 1992, c. 20 was never proclaimed into force and as such has been omitted from the text of the Narcotic Control Act.]

Coming into Force

28. Coming into force — Part II or any provision thereof shall come into force on a day or days to be fixed by proclamation of the Governor in Council.

Repealed 1996, c. 19, s. 94.

Schedule

(Sections 2 and 22)

1. Opium Poppy (*Papaver somniferum*) its preparations, derivatives, alkaloids and salts, including:

(1) Opium,

(2) Codeine (Methylmorphine),

(3) Morphine,

(4) Thebaine,

and their preparations, derivatives and salts, including:

(5) Acetorphine,

(6) Acetyldihydrocodeine,

(7) Benzylmorphine,

(7.1) Buprenorphine,

(8) Codoxime,

(9) Desomorphine (dihydrodeoxymorphine),

(10) Diacetylmorphine (heroin),

(11) Dihydrocodeine

(12) Dihydromorphine,

(13) Ethylmorphine,

(14) Etorphine,

(15) Hydrocodone (dihydrocodeinone),

717

(16) Hydromorphone (dihydromorphinone),

(17) Hydromorphinol (dihydro-14-hydroxymorphine),

(18) Methyldesorphine (δ^6-deoxy-6-methylmorphine),

(19) Methyldihydromorphine (dihydro-6-methylmorphine),

(20) Metopon (dihydromethylmorphinone),

(21) Morphine-N-oxide (morphine-N-oxide),

(22) Myrophine (benzylmorphine myristate),

(23) Nalorphine (N-allylnormorphine),

(24) Nicocodine (6-nicotinylcodeine),

(25) Nicomorphine (dinicotinylmorphine),

(26) Norcodeine,

(27) Normorphine,

(28) Oxycodone (dihydrohydroxycodeinone),

(29) Oxymorphone (dihydrohydroxymorphinone),

(30) Pholcodine (β-4-morpholinoethylmorphine), and

(31) Thebacon (acetyldihydrocodeinone),
but not including:

(32) Apomorphine,

(33) Cyprenorphine,

(34) Naloxone,

(34.1) Naltrexone,

(35) Narcotine,

(36) Papaverine, and

(37) Poppy seed.

2. Coca (*Erythroxylon*), its preparations, derivatives, alkaloids and salts, including:

(1) Coca leaves,

(2) Cocaine, and

(3) Ecgonine (3-hydroxy-2-tropane carboxylic acid).

3. *Cannabis sativa*, its preparation, derivatives and similar synthetic preparations, including:

(1) Cannabis resin,

(2) Cannabis (marihuana),

(3) Cannabidiol,

(4) Cannabinol (3-n-amyl-6,6,9-trimethyl-6-dibenzopyran-1-ol),

(4.1) Nabilone ((±)-trans-3 (1,1-dimethylheptyl)-6, 6a, 7, 8, 10, 10a-hexahydro-1-hydroxy-6,6- dimethyl-9H-dibenzo[b,d] phyran-9-one),

(5) Pyrahexyl (3-n-hexyl-6,6,9-trimethyl-7,8,9,10-tetrahydro-6-dibenzopyran-1-ol), and

(6) Tetrahydrocannabinol,

but not including:

(7) non-viable Cannabis seed.

4. Phenylpiperidines, their preparations, intermediates, derivatives and salts, including:

(1) Allyprodine (3-allyl-1-methyl-4-phenyl-4-phenyl-4-piperidyl propionate),

(2) Alphameprodine (α-3-ethyl-1-methyl-4-phenyl-4-piperidyl propionate),

(3) Alphaprodine (α-1-,3-dimethyl-4-phenyl-4-piperidyl propionate),

(4) Anileridine (ethyl 1-[2-p-aminophenyl) ethyl]-4-phenylpiperidine-4-carboxylate),

(5) Betameprodine (β-3-ethyl-1-methyl-4-phenyl-4-piperidyl propionate),

(6) Betaprodine (β-1,3-dimethyl-4-phenyl-4-piperidyl propionate),

(7) Benzethidine (ethyl 1-(2-benzyloxyethyl)-4-phenylpiperidine-4-carboxylate),

(8) Diphenoxylate (ethyl 1-(3-cyano-3,3-diphenylpropyl)-4-phenylpiperidine-4-carboxylate),

(9) Etoxeridine (ethyl 1-[2-(2-hydroxyethoxy) ethyl]-4-phenylpiperidine-4-carboxylate),

(10) Furethidine (ethyl 1-(2-tetrahydrofurfuryloxyethyl)-4-phenylpiperidine-4-carboxylate),

(11) Hydroxypethidine (ethyl 4-(m-hydroxyphenyl)-1-methyl-4-phenylpiperidine-4-carboxylate),

(12) Ketobemidone (1-[4-(m-hydroxyphenyl)-1-methyl-4-piperidyl]-1-propanone),

(13) Methylphenylisonipecotonitrile (4-cyano-1-methyl-4-phenylpiperidine),

(14) Morpheridine (ethyl 1-(2-morpholinoethyl)-4-phenylpiperidine-4-carboxylate),

(15) Norpethidine (ethyl 4-phenylpiperidine-4-carboxylate),

(16) Pethidine (ethyl 1-methyl-4-phenylpiperidine-4-carboxylate),

(17) Phenoperidine (ethyl 1-(3-hydroxy-3-phenylpropyl)-4-phenylpiperidine-4-carboxylate),

(18) Piminodine (ethyl 1-[3-(phenylamino) propyl]-4-phenylpiperidine-4-carboxylate),

(19) Properidine (isopropyl 1-methyl-4-phenyl-piperidine-4-carboxylate), and

(20) Trimeperidine (1,2,5-trimethyl-4-phenyl-4-piperidyl propionate),

and not including:

(21) Carbamethidine (ethyl 1-(2-carbamylethyl)-4-phenylpiperidine-4-carboxylate), and

(22) Oxpheneridine (ethyl 1-(2-hydroxy-2-phenylethyl)-4-phenylpiperidine-4-carboxylate).

5. Phenazepines, their preparations, derivatives and salts, inlcuding:

(1) Proheptazine (hexahydro-1,3-dimethyl-4-phenyl-4-azepinyl propionate),

but not including:

(2) Ethoheptazine (ethyl hexahydro-1-methyl-4-phenylazepine-4-carboxylate),

(3) Metethoheptazine (ethyl hexahydro-1,3-dimethyl-4-phenylazepine-4-carboxylate), and

(4) Metheptazine (ethyl hexahydro-1,2-dimethyl-4-phenylazepine-4-carboxylate).

6. Amidones, their preparations, intermediates, derivatives and salts, including:

(1) Dimethylaminodiphenylbutanonitrile (4-cyano-2-dimethylamino-4,4-diphenyl butane),

(2) Dipipanone (4,4-diphenyl-6-piperidino-3-heptanone),

(3) Isomethadone (6-dimethylamino-5-methyl-4,4-diphenyl-3-hexanone),

(4) Methadone (6-dimethylamino-4,4-diphenyl-3-heptanone),

(5) Normethadone (6-dimethylamino-4,4-diphenyl-3-hexanone), and

(6) Phenadoxone (6-morpholino-4,4-diphenyl-3-heptanone).

7. Methadols, their preparations, derivatives and salts, including:

(1) Acetylmethadol (6-dimethylamino-4,4-diphenyl-3-heptanyl acetate),

(2) Alphacetylmethadol (α-6-dimethylamino-4,4-diphenyl-3-heptanyl acetate),

(3) Alphamethadol (α-6-dimethylamino-4,4-diphenyl-3-heptanol),

(4) Betacetylmethadol (β-6-dimethylamino-4,4-diphenyl-3-heptanyl acetate),

(5) Betamethadol (β-6-dimethylamino-4,4-diphenyl-3-heptanol),

(6) Dimepheptanol (6-dimethylamino-4,4-diphenyl-3-heptanol), and

(7) Noracymethadol (α-6-methylamino-4,4-diphenyl-3-heptanyl acetate).

8. Phenalkoxams, their preparations, derivatives and salts, including:

(1) Dimenoxadol (dimethylaminoethyl 1-ethoxy-1,1-diphenylacetate),

(2) Dioxaphetylbutyrate (ethyl 2,2-diphenyl-4-morpholino butyrate), and

(3) Dextropropoxyphene ([S-(R*,S*)]-α-[2-(dimethylamino)-1-methylethyl]- α-phenyl-benzeneethanol, propanoate ester)

9. Thiambutenes, their preparations, derivatives and salts, including:

(1) Diethylthiambutene (N,N-diethyl-1-methyl-3,3-di-2-thienylallylamine),

(2) Dimethylthiambutene (N,N,1-trimethyl-3,3-di-2-thienylallylamine), and

(3) Ethylmethylthiambutene (N-ethyl-N,1-dimethyl-3,3-di-2-thienylallylamine).

10. Moramides, their preparations, intermediates, derivatives and salts, including:

(1) Dextromoramide (*d*-1-(3-methyl-4-morpholino-2,2-di-phenylbutyryl) pyrrolidine),

(2) Diphenylmorpholinoisovaleric acid (2-methyl-3-morpholino-1,1-diphenylpropionic acid),

(3) Levomoramide (*l*-1-(3-methyl-4-morpholino-2,2-diphenylbutyryl) pyrrolidine), and

(4) Racemoramide (*d,l*-1-(3-methyl-4-morpholino-2,2-diphenylbutyryl) pyrrolidine).

11. Morphinans, their preparations, derivatives and salts, including:

(1) Levomethorphan (*l*-1,2,3,9,10,10a-hexahydro-6-methoxy-11-methyl-4H-10, 4a-iminoethanophenanthrene),

(2) Levorphanol (*l*-1,2,3,9,10,10a-hexahydro-11-methyl-4H-10, 4a-iminoethanophenanthren-6-ol),

(3) Levophenacylmorphan (*l*-1,2,3,9,10,10a-hexahydro-11-phenacyl-4H-10, 4a-iminoethanophenanthren-6-ol),

(4) Norlevorphanol (*l*-1,2,3,9,10,10a-hexahydro-4H-10, 4a-iminoethanophenanthren-6-ol),

(5) Phenomorphan (*d,l*-1,2,3,9,10,10a-hexahydro-11-phenethyl-4H-10, 4a-iminoethanophenanthren-6-ol),

(6) Racemethorphan (d,l-1,2,3,9,10,10a-hexahydro-6-methoxy-11-methyl-4H-10,4a-iminoethano phenanthrene), and

(7) Racemorphan (d,l-1,2,3,9,10,10a-hexahydro-11-methyl-4H-10, 4a-iminoethanophenanthren-6-ol),

but not including:

(8) Dextromethorphan (d,-1,2,3,9,10,10a-hexahydro-6-methoxy-11-methyl-4H-10, 4a-iminoethanophenanthrene),

(9) Dextrorphan (d,1,2,3,9,10,10-hexahydro-11-methyl-4H-10, 4a-iminoethanophenanthren-6-ol),

(10) Levallorphan (l-11-allyl-1,2,3,9,10,10a-hexahydro-4H-10, 4a-iminoethanophenanthren-6-ol),

(11) Levargorphan (l-11-propargyl-1,2,3,9,10,10a-hexahydro-4H-10, 4a-iminoethanophenanthren-6-ol),

(12) Butorphanol and its salts, and

(13) Nalbuphine (17-(cyclobutylmethyl)-4,5α-epoxymorphinan-3,6α,14-triol).

12. Benzazocines, their preparations, derivatives and salts, including:

(1) Phenazocine (1,2,3,4,5,6-hexahydro-6,11-dimethyl-3-phenethyl-2,6-methano-3-benzazocin-8-o l),

(2) Metazocine (1,2,3,4,5,6-hexahydro-3,6,11-trimethyl-2,6-methano-3-benzazocin-8-ol), and

(3) Pentazocine (1,2,3,4,5,6-hexahydro-6,11-dimethyl-3-(3-methyl-2-butenyl)-2,6-methano-3-ben zazocin-8-ol),

but not including:

(4) Cyclazocine (1,2,3,4,5,6-hexahydro-6-11-dimethyl-3-(cyclopropylmethyl)-2,6-methano-3-benz azocin-8-ol).

13. Ampromides, their preparations, derivatives and salts, including:

(1) Diampromide (N-[2-(methylphenethylamino)-propyl]-propionanilide),

(2) Phenampromide (N-[2-(1-methyl-2-piperidyl)-ethyl]-propionanilide), and

(3) Propiram (N- (1-methyl-2-piperidinoethyl)-N-2-pyridylpropionamide).

14. Benzimidazoles, their preparations, derivatives and salts, including:

(1) Clonitazene (2-(p-chlorobenzyl)-1-diethylaminoethyl-5-nitrobenzimidazole), and

(2) Etonitazene (2-(p-ethoxybenzyl)-1-diethylaminoethyl-5-nitrobenzimidazole).

15. Phencyclidine, its salts and derivatives.

16. Fentanyl (1-phenylethyl-4-(phenylpropionylamino)-piperidine), its salts and derivatives.

17. Sufentanil (N-[4-(methoxymethyl)-1-[2-(2-thienyl) ethyl]-4-piperidinyl]-N-phenylpropanamide), its salts and derivatives.

18. Tilidine (3-cyclohexene-1-carboxylic acid, 2-(dimethylamino)-1-phenylethyl ester, trans (±)), its preparations, derivatives and salts.

19. Carfentanil (methyl 4-[1-oxoprophyl)phenylamino]-1-(2-phenylethyl)-4-piperi-dine-carboxylate), its salts and derivatives.

20. Alfentanil (N-[1-[2-(4-ethyl-4,5-dihydro-5-oxo-1H-tetrazol-1-yl)ethyl]-4-(methoxymethyl) -4-piperidinyl]-N-phenylpropanamide), its salts and derivatives.

repealed 1996, c. 19, s. 94.

FOOD AND DRUGS ACT

TABLE OF CONCORDANCE

FDA

FOOD AND DRUGS ACT

An Act respecting food, drugs, cosmetics and therapeutic devices

R.S.C. 1985, c. F-27,

as am. R.S.C. 1985, c. 27 (1st Supp.), ss. 191–195; R.S.C. 1985, c. 31 (1st
Supp.), s. 11; R.S.C. 1985, c. 27 (3rd Supp.), s. 1; R.S.C. 1985, c. 42 (4th
Supp.), ss. 9–11; S.C. 1992, c. 1; 1993, c. 34, ss. 71, 73; 1993, c. 37, ss.
22–24; 1993, c. 44, s. 158; 1994, c. 38, ss. 18, 19; 1995, c.1, ss. 62, 63;
1996, c. 8, ss. 23.1, 23.2, 32; 1996, c. 16, ss. 60, 62; 1996, c. 19, ss. 77-
82; 1997, c. 6, s. 62-66, 91; 1997, c. 18, ss. 123–126; 1999, c. 33, s. 347.

Short Title

1. Short title — This Act may be cited as the *Food and Drugs Act*.

Interpretation

2. Definitions — In this Act,

"advertisement" includes any representation by any means whatever for the purpose of promoting directly or indirectly the sale or disposal of any food, drug, cosmetic or device;

"analyst" means a person designated as an analyst for the purpose of the enforcement of this Act under section 28 or under section 13 of the *Canadian Food Inspection Agency Act*;

"contraceptive device" means any instrument, apparatus, contrivance or any substance other than a drug, that is manufactured, sold or represented for use in the
prevention of conception;

"cosmetic" includes any substance or mixture of substances manufactured, sold or
represented for use in cleansing, improving or altering the complexion, skin, hair or
teeth, and includes deodorants and perfumes;

"Department" means the Department of National Health and Welfare;

"device" means any article, instrument, apparatus or contrivance, including any
component, part or accessory thereof, manufactured, sold or represented for use in

(a) the diagnosis, treatment, mitigation or prevention of a disease, disorder or
abnormal physical state, or its symptoms, in human beings or animals,

(b) restoring, correcting or modifying a body function or the body structure of human beings or animals,

(c) the diagnosis of pregnancy in human beings or animals, or

(d) the care of human beings or animals during pregnancy and at and after birth of the offspring, including care of the offspring,

and includes a contraceptive device but does not include a drug;

"drug" includes any substance or mixture of substances manufactured, sold or represented for use in

(a) the diagnosis, treatment, mitigation or prevention of a disease, disorder or abnormal physical state, or its symptoms, in human beings or animals,

(b) restoring, correcting or modifying organic functions in human beings or animals, or

(c) disinfection in premises in which food is manufactured, prepared or kept;

"food" includes any article manufactured, sold or represented for use as food or drink for human beings, chewing gum, and any ingredient that may be mixed with food for any purpose whatever;

"inspector" means any person designated as an inspector for the purpose of the enforcement of this Act under subsection 22(1) or under section 13 of the *Canadian Food Inspection Agency Act*;

"label" includes any legend, word or mark attached to, included in, belonging to or accompanying any food, drug, cosmetic, device or package;

"Minister" means the Minister of Health;

"package" includes any thing in which any food, drug, cosmetic or device is wholly or partly contained, placed or packed;

"prescribed" means prescribed by the regulations;

"sell" includes offer for sale, expose for sale, have in possession for sale and distribute, whether or not the distribution is made for consideration;

"unsanitary conditions" means such conditions or circumstances as might contaminate a food, drug or cosmetic with dirt or filth, or render injurious to health a food, drug or cosmetic.

R.S. 1985, c. 27 (1st Supp.), s. 191; 1993, c. 34, s. 71; 1994, c. 38, s. 18; 1995, c. 1, s. 63; 1996, c. 8, ss. 23.1, 32(1)(g); 1997, c. 6, s. 62.

PART I — FOODS, DRUGS, COSMETICS AND DEVICES

General

3. (1) Prohibited advertising — No person shall advertise any food, drug, cosmetic or device to the general public as a treatment, preventative or cure for any of the diseases, disorders or abnormal physical states referred to in Schedule A.

(2) Prohibited label or advertisement where sale made — No person shall sell any food, drug, cosmetic or device

(a) that is represented by label, or

(b) that the person advertises to the general public

as a treatment, preventative or cure for any of the diseases, disorders or abnormal physical states referred to in Schedule A.

(3) Unauthorized advertising of contraceptive device prohibited — Except as authorized by regulation, no person shall advertise to the general public any contraceptive device or any drug manufactured, sold or represented for use in the prevention of conception.

Food

4. Prohibited sales of food — No person shall sell an article of food that

(a) has in or on it any poisonous or harmful substance;

(b) is unfit for human consumption;

(c) consists in whole or in part of any filthy, putrid, disgusting, rotten, decomposed or diseased animal or vegetable substance;

(d) is adulterated; or

(e) was manufactured, prepared, preserved, packaged or stored under unsanitary conditions.

5. (1) Deception, etc., regarding food — No person shall label, package, treat, process, sell or advertise any food in a manner that is false, misleading or deceptive or is likely to create an erroneous impression regarding its character, value, quantity, composition, merit or safety.

(2) Food labelled or packaged in contravention of regulations — An article of food that is not labelled or packaged as required by, or is labelled or packaged contrary to, the regulations shall be deemed to be labelled or packaged contrary to subsection (1).

6. (1) Importation and interprovincial movement of food — Where a standard for a food has been prescribed, no person shall

    (a) import into Canada,

    (b) send, convey or receive for conveyance from one province to another, or

    (c) have in possession for the purpose of sending or conveying from one province to another

any article that is intended for sale and that is likely to be mistaken for such food unless the article complies with the prescribed standard.

(2) Not applicable to carriers — Paragraphs (1)(*b*) and (*c*) do not apply to an operator of a conveyance that is used to carry an article or to a carrier of an article whose sole concern, in respect of the article, is the conveyance of the article unless the operator or carrier could, with reasonable diligence, have ascertained that the conveying or receiving for conveyance of the article or the possession of the article for the purpose of conveyance would be in violation of subsection (1).

(3) Labelling, etc., of food that is imported or moved interprovincially — Where a standard for a food has been prescribed, no person shall label, package, sell or advertise any article that

    (a) has been imported into Canada,

    (b) has been sent or conveyed from one province to another, or

    (c) is intended to be sent or conveyed from one province to another

in such a manner that it is likely to be mistaken for such food unless the article complies with the prescribed standard.

R.S. 1985, c. 27 (3d Supp.), s. 1.

6.1 (1) Governor in Council may identify standard or portion thereof — The Governor in Council may, by regulation, identify a standard or any portion of a standard prescribed for a food as being necessary to prevent injury to the health of the consumer or purchaser of the food.

(2) Where standard or portion thereof is identified — Where a standard or any portion of a standard prescribed for a food is identified by the Governor in Council pursuant to subsection (1), no person shall label, package, sell or advertise any article in such a manner that it is likely to be mistaken for such food unless the article complies with the standard or portion of a standard so identified.

R.S. 1985, c. 27 (3d Supp.), s. 1.

7. Unsanitary manufacture, etc., of food — No person shall manufacture, prepare, preserve, package or store for sale any food under unsanitary conditions.

Drugs

8. Prohibited sales of drugs — No person shall sell any drug that

    (a) was manufactured, prepared, preserved, packaged or stored under unsanitary conditions; or

    (b) is adulterated.

9. (1) Deception, etc., regarding drugs — No person shall label, package, treat, process, sell or advertise any drug in a manner that is false, misleading or deceptive or is likely to create an erroneous impression regarding its character, value, quantity, composition, merit or safety.

(2) Drugs labelled or packaged in contravention of regulations — A drug that is not labelled or packaged as required by, or is labelled or packaged contrary to, the regulations shall be deemed to be labelled or packaged contrary to subsection (1).

10. (1) Where standard prescribed for drug — Where a standard has been prescribed for a drug, no person shall label, package, sell or advertise any substance in such a manner that it is likely to be mistaken for that drug, unless the substance complies with the prescribed standard.

(2) Trade standards — Where a standard has not been prescribed for a drug, but a standard for the drug is contained in any publication referred to in Schedule B, no person shall label, package, sell or advertise any substance in such a manner that it is likely to be mistaken for that drug, unless the substance complies with the standard.

(3) Where no prescribed or trade standard — Where a standard for a drug has not been prescribed and no standard for the drug is contained in any publication referred to in Schedule B, no person shall sell the drug unless

    (a) it is in accordance with the professed standard under which it is sold; and

    (b) it does not resemble, in a manner likely to deceive, any drug for which a standard has been prescribed or is contained in any publication referred to in Schedule B.

11. Unsanitary manufacture, etc., of drug — No person shall manufacture, prepare, preserve, package or store for sale any drug under unsanitary conditions.

12. Drugs not to be sold unless safe manufacture indicated — No person shall sell any drug described in Schedule C or D unless the Minister has, in prescribed form and manner, indicated that the premises in which the drug was manufactured and the process and conditions of manufacture therein are suitable to ensure that the drug will not be unsafe for use.

13. Drugs not to be sold unless safe batch indicated — No person shall sell any drug described in Schedule E unless the Minister has, in prescribed form and manner, indicated that the batch from which the drug was taken is not unsafe for use.

14. (1) Samples — No person shall distribute or cause to be distributed any drug as a sample.

(2) Exception — Subsection (1) does not apply to the distribution, under prescribed conditions, of samples of drugs to physicians, dentists, veterinary surgeons or pharmacists.

15. Schedule f drugs not to be sold — No person shall sell any drug described in Schedule F.

Cosmetics

16. Prohibited sales of cosmetics — No person shall sell any cosmetic that

(a) has in or on it any substance that may cause injury to the health of the user when the cosmetic is used,

(i) according to the directions on the label or accompanying the cosmetic, or

(ii) for such purposes and by such methods of use as are customary or usual therefor;

(b) consists in whole or in part of any filthy or decomposed substance or of any foreign matter; or

(c) was manufactured, prepared, preserved, packaged or stored under unsanitary conditions.

17. Where standard prescribed for cosmetic — Where a standard has been prescribed for a cosmetic, no person shall label, package, sell or advertise any article in such a manner that it is likely to be mistaken for that cosmetic. unless the article complies with the prescribed standard.

18. Unsanitary conditions — No person shall manufacture, prepare, preserve, package or store for sale any cosmetic under unsanitary conditions.

Devices

19. Prohibited sales of devices — No person shall sell any device that, when used according to directions or under such conditions as are customary or usual, may cause injury to the health of the purchaser or user thereof.

20. (1) Deception, etc., regarding devices — No person shall label, package, treat, process, sell or advertise any device in a manner that is false, misleading or deceptive or is likely to create an erroneous impression regarding its design, construction, performance, intended use, quantity, character, value, composition, merit or safety.

(2) Devices labelled or packaged in contravention of regulations — A device that is not labelled or packaged as required by, or is labelled or packaged contrary to, the regulations shall be deemed to be labelled or packaged contrary to subsection (1).

21. Where standard prescribed for device — Where a standard has been prescribed for a device, no person shall label, package, sell or advertise any article in such a manner that is likely to be mistaken for such device, unless the article complies with the prescribed standard.

PART II

Administration and Enforcement

Inspection, Seizure and Forfeiture

22. (1) Inspectors — The Minister may designate any person as an inspector for the purpose of the enforcement of this Act.

(2) Certificate to be produced — An inspector shall be given a certificate in a form established by the Minister or the President of the Canadian Food Inspection Agency attesting to the inspector's designation and, on entering any place pursuant to subsection 23(1), an inspector shall, if so required, produce the certificate to the person in charge of that place.

23. (1) Powers of inspectors — Subject to subsection (1.1), an inspector may at any reasonable time enter any place where the inspector believes on reasonable grounds any article to which this Act or the regulations apply is manufactured, prepared, preserved, packaged or stored, and may

(a) examine any such article and take samples thereof, and examine anything that the inspector believes on reasonable grounds is used or capable of being used for that manufacture, preparation, preservation, packaging or storing;

(a.1) enter any conveyance that the inspector believes on reasonable grounds is used to carry any article to which section 6 or 6.1 applies and examine any such article found therein and take samples thereof;

(b) open and examine any receptacle or package that the inspector believes on reasonable grounds contains any article to which this Act or the regulations apply;

(c) examine and make copies of, or extracts from, any books, documents or other records found in any place referred to in this subsection that the inspector believes on reasonable grounds contain any information relevant to the enforcement of this Act with respect to any article to which this Act or the regulations apply and

(d) seize and detain for such time as may be necessary any article by means of or in relation to which the inspector believes on reasonable grounds any provision of this Act or the regulations has been contravened.

(1.1) Warrant required to enter dwelling-house — Where any place mentioned in subsection (1) is a dwelling-house, an inspector may not enter that dwelling-house without the consent of the occupant except under the authority of a warrant issued under subsection (1.2).

(1.2) Authority to issue warrant — Where on *ex parte* application a justice of the peace is satisfied by information on oath

(a) that the conditions for entry described in subsection (1) exist in relation to a dwelling-house,

(b) that entry to the dwelling-house is necessary for any purpose relating to the administration or enforcement of this Act, and

(c) that entry to the dwelling-house has been refused or that there are reasonable grounds for believing that entry thereto will be refused,

the justice of the peace may issue a warrant under his hand authorizing the inspector named therein to enter that dwelling-house subject to such conditions as may be specified in the warrant.

(1.3) Use of force — In executing a warrant issued under subsection (1.2), the inspector named therein shall not use force unless the inspector is accompanied by a peace officer and the use of force has been specifically authorized in the warrant.

(2) Definition of "article to which this Act or the regulations apply" — In subsection (1), "article to which this Act or the regulations apply" includes

(a) any food, drug, cosmetic or device;

(b) anything used for the manufacture, preparation, preservation, packaging or storing thereof; and

(c) any labelling or advertising material.

(3) Assistance and information to be given inspector — The owner or person in charge of a place entered by an inspector pursuant to subsection (1) and every person found therein shall give the inspector all reasonable assistance and furnish the inspector with any information he may reasonably require.

R.S. 1985, c. 31 (1st Supp.), s. 11; c. 27 (3d Supp.), s. 2.

24. (1) Obstruction and false statements — No person shall obstruct or hinder, or knowingly make any false or misleading statement either orally or in writing to, an inspector while the inspector is engaged in carrying out his duties or functions under this Act or the regulations.

(2) Interference — Except with the authority of an inspector, no person shall remove, alter or interfere in any way with anything seized under this Part.

25. Storage and removal — Any article seized under this Act may, at the option of an inspector, be kept or stored in the building or place where it was seized or, at the direction of an inspector, the article may be removed to any other proper place.

26. Release of seized articles — An inspector who has seized any article under this Part shall release it when he is satisfied that all the provisions of this Act and the regulations with respect thereto have been complied with.

27. (1) Destruction with consent — Where an inspector has seized an article under this Part and its owner or the person in whose possession the article was at the time of seizure consents to its destruction, the article is thereupon forfeited to Her Majesty and may be destroyed or otherwise disposed of as the Minister or the Minister of Agriculture and Agri-Food may direct.

(2) Forfeiture — Where a person has been convicted of a contravention of this Act or the regulations, the court or judge may order that any article by means of or in relation to which the offence was committed, and any thing of a similar nature belonging to or in relation to which the offence was committed, and any thing of a similar nature belonging to or in the possession of the person or found with the article, be forfeited. On the making of the order, the article and thing are forfeited to Her Majesty and may be disposed of as the Minister or the Minister of Agriculture and Agri-Food may direct.

(3) Order for forfeiture on application of inspector — Without prejudice to subsection (2), a judge of a superior court of the province in which any article is seized under this Part may, on the application of an inspector and on such notice to such persons as the judge directs, order that the article and any thing of a similar nature found with it be forfeited to Her Majesty, if the judge finds, after making such inquiry as the judge considers necessary, that the article is one by means of or in relation to which any of the provisions of this Act or the regulations have been contravened. On the making of the order, the article or thing may be disposed of as the Minister or the Minister of Agriculture and Agri-Food may direct.

1994, c. 38, s. 19;1995, c. 1, s. 62; 1994, c. 38, s. 19; 1995, c. 1, s. 62; 1996, c. 8, s. 23.2; 1997, c. 6, s. 64.

Analysis

28. Analysts — The Minister may designate any person as an analyst for the purpose of the enforcement of this Act.

29. (1) Analysis and examination — An inspector may submit to an analyst for analysis or examination, any article seized by the inspector, any sample therefrom or any sample taken by the inspector.

(2) Certificate or report — An analyst who has made an analysis or examination may issue a certificate or report setting out the results of the examination or analysis.

Regulations

30. (1) Regulations — The Governor in Council may make regulations for carrying the purposes and provisions of this Act into effect, and, in particular, but without restricting the generality of the foregoing, may make regulations

(a) declaring that any food or drug or class of food or drugs is adulterated if any prescribed substance or class of substances is present therein or has been added thereto or extracted or omitted therefrom;

(b) respecting

(i) the labelling and packaging and the offering, exposing and advertising for sale of food, drugs, cosmetics and devices,

(ii) the size, dimensions, fill and other specifications of packages of food, drugs, cosmetics and devices,

(iii) the sale or the conditions of sale of any food, drug, cosmetic or device, and

(iv) the use of any substance as an ingredient in any food, drug, cosmetic or device,

to prevent the purchaser or consumer thereof from being deceived or misled in respect of the design, construction, performance, intended use, quantity, character, value, composition, merit or safety thereof, or to prevent injury to the health of the purchaser or consumer;

(c) prescribing standards of composition, strength, potency, purity, quality or other property of any article of food, drug, cosmetic or device;

(d) respecting the importation of foods, drugs, cosmetics and devices in order to ensure compliance with this Act and the regulations;

(e) respecting the method of manufacture, preparation, preserving, packing, storing and testing of any food, drug, cosmetic or device in the interest of, or for the prevention of injury to, the health of the purchaser or consumer;

(f) requiring persons who sell food, drugs, cosmetics or devices to maintain such books and records as the Governor in Council considers necessary for the proper enforcement and administration of this Act and the regulations;

(g) respecting the form and manner of the Minister's indication under section 12, including the fees payable therefor, and prescribing what premises or what processes or conditions of manufacture, including qualifications of technical staff, shall or shall not be deemed to be suitable for the purposes of that section;

(h) requiring manufacturers of any drugs described in Schedule E to submit test portions of any batch of those drugs and respecting the form and manner of the Minister's indication under section 13, including the fees payable therefor;

(i) respecting the powers and duties of inspectors and analysts and the taking of samples and the seizure, detention, forfeiture and disposition of articles;

(j) exempting any food, drug, cosmetic or device from all or any of the provisions of this Act and prescribing the conditions of the exemption;

(k) prescribing forms for the purposes of this Act and the regulations;

(l) providing for the analysis of food, drugs or cosmetics other than for the purposes of this Act and prescribing a tariff of fees to be paid for that analysis;

(l.1) respecting the assessment of the effect on the environment or on human life and health of the release into the environment of any food, drug, cosmetic or device, and the measures to take before importing or selling any such food, drug, cosmetic or device;

(m) adding anything to any of the schedules, in the interest of, or for the prevention of injury to, the health of the purchaser or consumer, or deleting anything therefrom;

(n) respecting the distribution or the conditions of distribution of samples of any drug;

(o) respecting

   (i) the method of manufacture, preparation, preserving, packing, labelling, storing and testing of any new drug, and

   (ii) the sale or the conditions of sale of any new drug,

and defining for the purposes of this Act the expression "new drug"; and

(p) authorizing the advertising to the general public of contraceptive devices and drugs manufactured, sold or represented for use in the prevention of conception and prescribing the circumstances and conditions under which, and the persons by whom, those devices and drugs may be so advertised.

(2) Regulations respecting drugs manufactured outside Canada — Without limiting or restricting the authority conferred by any other provisions of this Act or any Part thereof for carrying into effect the purposes and provisions of this Act or any Part thereof, the Governor in Council may make such regulations governing, regulating or prohibiting

   (a) the importation into Canada of any drug or class of drugs manufactured outside Canada, or

(b) the distribution or sale in Canada, or the offering, exposing or having in possession for sale in Canada, of any drug or class of drugs manufactured outside Canada,

as the Governor in Council deems necessary for the protection of the public in relation to the safety and quality of any such drug or class of drugs.

(3) Regulations re the North American Free Trade Agreement — Without limiting or restricting the authority conferred by any other provisions of this Act or any Part thereof for carrying into effect the purposes and provisions of this Act or any Part thereof, the Governor in Council may, for the purpose of implementing Article 1711 of the North American Free Trade Agreement, make regulations respecting the extent to which, if any, a person may, in seeking to establish the safety or effectiveness of a new drug for the purposes of any regulations made under subsection (1) or (2), rely on test or other data submitted by any other person to the Minister in accordance with such regulations.

(4) Definition — In subsection (3), "North American Free Trade Agreement" has the meaning given to the word "Agreement" by subsection 2(1) of the *North American Free Trade Agreement Implementation Act*.

1993, c. 44, s. 158; 1999, c. 33, s. 347

Offences and Punishment

31. Contravention of Act and regulations — Subject to section 31.1, every person who contravenes any of the provisions of this Act or of the regulations made under this Part is guilty of an offence and liable

(a) on summary conviction for a first offence to a fine not exceeding five hundred dollars or to imprisonment for a term not exceeding three months or to both and, for a subsequent offence to a fine not exceeding one thousand dollars or to imprisonment for a term not exceeding six months or to both; and

(b) on conviction on indictment to a fine not exceeding five thousand dollars or to imprisonment for a term not exceeding three years or to both.

31.1 Offences relating to food — Every person who contravenes any provision of this Act or the regulations, as it relates to food, is guilty of an offence and liable

(a) on summary conviction, to a fine not exceeding $50,000 or to imprisonment for a term not exceeding six months or to both; or

(b) on conviction by indictment, to a fine not exceeding $250,000 or to imprisonment for a term not exceeding three years or to both.

1997, c. 6, s. 66(1).

32. (1) Limitation period — A prosecution for a summary conviction offence under this Act may be instituted at any time within two years after the time the subject-matter of the prosecution becomes known to the Minister or, in the case of a contravention of a provision of the Act that relates to food, to the Minister of Agriculture and Agri-Food.

(2) Minister's certificate — A document purporting to have been issued by the Minister referred to in subsection (1), certifying the day on which the subject-matter of any prosecution became known to the Minister, is admissible in evidence without proof of the signature or official character of the person appearing to have signed the document and is evidence of the matters asserted in it.

1997, c. 6, s. 66(2) states: for greater certainty, the two year limitation period provided for in subsection 32(1) of the Food and Drugs Act, as amended by 1997, c. 6, s. 66(1), only applies in respect of offences committed after the coming into force of that subsection.

33. Venue — A prosecution for a contravention of this Act or the regulations may be instituted, heard, tried or determined in the place in which the offence was committed or the subject-matter of the prosecution arose or in any place in which the accused is apprehended or happens to be.

34. (1) Want of knowledge — Subject to subsection (2), in a prosecution for the sale of any article in contravention of this Act, except Parts III and IV, or of the regulations made under this Part, if the accused proves to the satisfaction of the court or judge that

(a) the accused purchased the article from another person in packaged form and sold it in the same package and in the same condition the article was in at the time it was so purchased, and

(b) that the accused could not with reasonable diligence have ascertained that the sale of the article would be in contravention of this Act or the regulations,

the accused shall be acquitted.

(2) Notice of reliance on want of knowledge — Subsection (1) does not apply in any prosecution unless the accused, at least ten days before the day fixed for the trial, has given to the prosecutor notice in writing that the accused intends to avail himself of the provisions of subsection (1) and has disclosed to the prosecutor the name and address of the person from whom the accused purchased the article and the date of purchase.

35. (1) Certificate of analyst — Subject to this section, in any prosecution for an offence under section 31, a certificate purporting to be signed by an analyst and stating that an article, sample or substance has been submitted to, and analysed or examined by, the analyst and stating the results of the analysis or examination is admissible in evidence and, in the absence of evidence to the contrary, is proof of the statements contained in the certificate without proof of the signature or official character of the person appearing to have signed it.

(2) Requiring attendance of analyst — The party against whom a certificate of an analyst is produced pursuant to subsection (1) may, with leave of the court, require the attendance of the analyst for the purposes of cross-examination.

(3) Notice of intention to produce certificate — No certificate shall be admitted in evidence pursuant to subsection (1) unless, before the trial, the party intending to produce the certificate has given reasonable notice of that intention, together with a copy of the certificate, to the party against whom it is intended to be produced.

(4) Proof of service — For the purposes of this Act, service of any certificate referred to in subsection (1) may be proved by oral evidence given under oath by, or by the affidavit or solemn declaration of, the person claiming to have served it.

(5) Attendance for examination — Notwithstanding subsection (4), the court may require the person who appears to have signed an affidavit or solemn declaration referred to in that subsection to appear before it for examination or cross-examination in respect of the issue of proof of service.

R.S. 1985, c. 27 (1st Supp.), s. 192; 1996, c. 19, s. 78.

36. (1) Proof as to manufacturer or packager — In a prosecution for a contravention of this Act or of the regulations made under this Part, proof that a package containing any article to which this Act or the regulations apply bore a name or address purporting to be the name or address of the person by whom it was manufactured or packaged is, in the absence of evidence to the contrary, proof that the article was manufactured or packaged, as the case may be, by the person whose name or address appeared on the package.

(2) Offence by employee or agent — In a prosecution for a contravention described in subsection (1), it is sufficient proof of the offence to establish that it was committed by an employee or agent of the accused whether or not the employee or agent is identified or has been prosecuted for the offence.

(3) Certified copies and extracts — In a prosecution for a contravention described in subsection (1), a copy of a record or an extract therefrom certified to be a true copy by the inspector who made it pursuant to paragraph 23(1)(c) is admissible in evidence and is, in the absence of evidence to the contrary, proof of its contents.

(4) Where accused had adulterating substances — Where a person is prosecuted under this Part for having manufactured an adulterated food or drug for sale, and it is established that the person had in his possession or on his premises any substance the addition of which to that food or drug has been declared by regulation to cause the adulteration of the food or drug, the onus of proving that the food or drug was not adulterated by the addition of that substance lies on the accused.

Exports

37. (1) Conditions under which exports exempt — This Act does not apply to any packaged food, drug, cosmetic or device, not manufactured for consumption in Canada and not sold for consumption in Canada, if the package is marked in distinct overprinting with the word "Export" or "Exportation" and a certificate that the package and its contents do not contravene any known requirement of the law of the country to which it is or is about to be consigned has been issued in respect of the package and its contents in prescribed form and manner.

(2) [Repealed 1996, c. 19, s. 80.]

1993, c. 34, s. 73; 1996, c. 19, s. 80.

PART III — CONTROLLED DRUGS

[Note: Part III of the Food and Drugs Act *repealed 1996, c. 19, s. 81. Please note Part III of the Act was repealed by the* Controlled Drugs and Substances Act *on May 14, 1997. We have, however, retained the text of Part III as it remains of relevance to offences occurring before its repeal and will therefore continue to be of great practical importance for some time to come.]*

Controlled Drugs

38. Definitions — In this Part,

"controlled drug" means any drug or other substance included in Schedule G;

"possession" means possession within the meaning of subsection 4(3) of the *Criminal Code*;

"practitioner" means a person who is registered and entitled under the laws of a province to practise in that province the profession of medicine, dentistry or veterinary medicine;

"prescription" means, in respect of a controlled drug, an authorization given by a practitioner that a stated amount of the controlled drug be dispensed for the person named therein;

"traffic" means to manufacture, sell, export from or import into Canada, transport or deliver, otherwise than under the authority of this Part or the regulations.

R.S. 1985, c. 27 (1st Supp.), s. 193; repealed 1996, c. 19, s. 81.

38.1 (1) Failure to disclose previous prescriptions — No person shall, at any time, seek or obtain a controlled drug or a prescription for a controlled drug from a practitioner unless that person discloses to the practitioner particulars of every controlled drug or prescription for a controlled drug issued to that person by a different practitioner within the preceding thirty days.

(2) Offence and punishment — Every person who contravenes subsection (1)

    (a) is guilty of an indictable offence and is liable to a fine not exceeding five thousand dollars or to imprisonment for a term not exceeding three years; or

    (b) is guilty of an offence punishable on summary conviction and is liable

        (i) for a first offence, to a fine not exceeding one thousand dollars or to imprisonment for a term not exceeding six months, and

        (ii) for a subsequent offence, to a fine not exceeding two thousand dollars or to imprisonment for a term not exceeding one year.

(3) Limitation period — Summary conviction proceedings in respect of an offence under this section may be instituted at any time within but not later than one year from the time when the subject-matter of the proceedings arose.

R.S. 1985, c. 27 (1st Supp), s. 194; repealed 1996, c. 19, s. 81.

39. (1) Trafficking in controlled drug — No person shall traffic in a controlled drug or any substance represented or held out by the person to be a controlled drug.

(2) Possession for trafficking — No person shall have in possession any controlled drug for the purpose of trafficking.

(3) Offence and punishment — Every person who contravenes subsection (1) or (2) is guilty of an offence and liable

    (a) on summary conviction, to imprisonment for a term not exceeding eighteen months; or

    (b) on conviction on indictment, to imprisonment for a term not exceeding ten years.

repealed 1996, c. 19, s. 81.

40. (1) Procedure in prosecution for possession for trafficking — In any prosecution for a contravention of subsection 39(2), if the accused does not plead guilty, the trial shall proceed as if the issue to be tried is whether the accused was in possession of a controlled drug.

(2) Procedure on finding in respect of possession — If, pursuant to subsection (1), the court finds that the accused was not in possession of a controlled drug, the accused shall be acquitted but, if the court finds that the accused was in possession of a controlled drug, the accused shall be given an opportunity of establishing that he was not in possession of the controlled drug for the purpose of trafficking and, thereafter, the prosecutor shall be given an opportunity of adducing evidence to the contrary.

(3) Acquittal on conviction — If the accused establishes, pursuant to subsection (2), that he was not in possession of the controlled drug for the purpose of trafficking, the accused shall be acquitted of the offence as charged and, if the accused fails to so establish, the accused shall be convicted of the offence as charged and sentenced accordingly.

repealed 1996, c. 19, s. 81.

41. (1) Setting out or negativing exception, etc., not required — No exception, exemption, excuse or qualification prescribed by law is required to be set out or negatived, as the case may be, in an information or indictment for an offence under section 39 or under section 463, 464 or 465 of the *Criminal Code* in respect of an offence under section 39.

(2) Burden of proving exception, etc — In any prosecution under this Part, the burden of proving that an exception, exemption, excuse or qualification prescribed by law operates in favour of the accused is on the accused, and the prosecutor is not required, except by way of rebuttal, to prove that the exception, exemption, excuse or qualification does not operate in favour of the accused, whether or not it is set out in the information or indictment.

repealed 1996, c. 19, s. 81

42. (1) Entry and search — A peace officer may, at any time, without a warrant enter and search any place other than a dwelling-house, and under the authority of a warrant issued under subsection (3), enter and search any dwelling-house in which the peace officer believes on reasonable grounds there is a controlled drug by means of or in respect of which an offence under this Part has been committed.

(2) Search of person and seizure — A peace officer may search any person found in a place entered pursuant to subsection (1) and may seize and take away any controlled drug found in that place and any other thing that may be evidence that an offence under this Part has been committed.

(3) Warrant to search dwelling-house — A justice who is satisfied by information on oath that there are reasonable grounds for believing that there is a controlled drug, by means of or in respect of which an offence under this Part has been committed, in any dwelling-house may issue a warrant under his hand authorizing a peace officer named therein at any time to enter the dwelling-house and search for controlled drugs.

(4) [Repealed R.S. 1985, c. 27 (1st Supp.), s. 195(2).]

(5) Powers of peace officer — For the purpose of exercising authority under this section, a peace officer may, with such assistance as that officer deems necessary, break open any door, window, lock, fastener, floor, wall, ceiling, compartment, plumbing fixture, box, container or any other thing.

R.S. 1985, c. 27 (1st Supp.), s. 195; repealed 1996, c. 19, s. 81.

43. (1) Application for restoration — Where a controlled drug or other thing has been seized under this section, any person may, within two months after the date of the seizure, where prior notification has been given to the Crown in the manner prescribed by the regulations, apply to a provincial court judge within whose territorial jurisdiction the seizure was made for an order of restoration under subsection (2).

(2) Order of immediate restoration — Subject to section 44, where, on the hearing of an application made under subsection (1), the provincial court judge is satisfied that the applicant is entitled to possession of the controlled drug or other thing seized, and that the thing seized is not or will not be required as evidence in any proceedings in respect of an offence under this Part, he shall order that the thing seized be restored forthwith to the applicant.

(3) Order of restoration at later time — Where on the hearing of an application made under subsection (1) the provincial court judge is satisfied that the applicant is entitled to possession of the thing seized but is not satisfied that the thing is not or will not be required as evidence in any proceedings in respect of an offence under this Part, he shall order that the thing seized be restored to the applicant

(a) on the expiration of four months after the date of seizure, if no proceedings in respect of an offence under this Part have been commenced before that time; or

(b) on the final conclusion of any such proceedings, in any other case.

(4) Where application not made or order refused — Where no application has been made for the return of any controlled drug or other thing seized pursuant to subsection 42(2) within two months after the date of the seizure, or an application therefor has been made but, on the hearing of the application, no order of restoration is made, the thing seized shall be delivered

(a) in the case of a controlled drug, to the Minister, who may make such disposition thereof as the Minister thinks fit; and

(b) in the case of any other thing,

(i) where the prosecution of the offence in respect of which the thing was seized was commenced at the instance of the government of a province and conducted by or on behalf of that government, to the Attorney General or Solicitor General of that province, and

(ii) in any other case, to the Minister of Public Works and Government Services,

who may dispose of the thing in accordance with the law.

R.S. 1985, c. 27 (1st Supp.), s. 203; 1993, c. 37, s. 22; 1996, c. 16, s. 60(1)(i); repealed 1996, c. 19, s. 81.

44. Forfeiture on conviction — Where a person has been convicted of an offence under this Part,

(a) any controlled drug seized pursuant to subsection 42(2) by means of or in respect of which the offence was committed is forfeited to Her Majesty in right of Canada and shall be disposed of by the Minister as the Minister thinks fit, and

(b) any money so seized that was used for the purchase of that controlled drug is,

(i) where the prosecution of the offence in respect of which the money was seized was commenced at the instance of the government of a province and conducted by or on behalf of that government, forfeited to Her Majesty in right of that province and shall be disposed of by the Attorney General or Solicitor General of that province in accordance with the law, and

(ii) in any other case, forfeited to Her Majesty in right of Canada and shall be disposed of by the Minister of Public Works and Government Services in accordance with the law.

1993, c. 37, s. 23; 1996, c. 16, s. 60(1)(i); repealed 1996, c. 19, s. 81.

44.1 Interpretation — For the purposes of sections 44.2 to 44.4, a reference therein to an offence under section 39, 44.2 or 44.3 shall be deemed to include a reference to a conspiracy or an attempt to commit, being an accessory after the fact in relation to, or any counselling in relation to, such an offence.

R.S. 1985, c. 42 (4th Supp.), s. 9; repealed 1996, c. 19, s. 81.

44.2 (1) Possession of property obtained by trafficking in controlled drugs — No person shall possess any property or any proceeds of any property knowing that all or part of the property or of those proceeds was obtained or derived directly or indirectly as a result of

(a) the commission in Canada of an offence under section 39; or

(b) an act or omission anywhere that, if it had occurred in Canada, would have constituted an offence under section 39.

(2) Punishment — Every person who contravenes subsection (1)

(a) is guilty of an indictable offence and liable to imprisonment for a term not exceeding ten years, where the value of the subject-matter of the offence exceeds one thousand dollars; or

(b) is guilty

(i) of an indictable offence and liable to imprisonment for a term not exceeding two years, or

(ii) of an offence punishable on summary conviction, where the value of the subject-matter of the offence does not exceed one thousand dollars.

(3) Exception — A peace officer or a person acting under the direction of a peace officer is not guilty of an offence under this section by reason only that the peace officer or person possesses property or the proceeds of property mentioned in subsection (1) for the purposes of an investigation or otherwise in the execution of the peace officer's duties.

R.S. 1985, c. 42 (4th Supp.), s. 9; 1997, c. 18, s. 123; repealed 1996, c. 19, s. 81

44.3 (1) Laundering proceeds of trafficking in controlled drugs — No person shall use, transfer the possession of, send or deliver to any person or place, transport, transmit, alter, dispose of or otherwise deal with, in any manner or by any means, any property or any proceeds of any property with intent to conceal or convert that property or those proceeds and knowing or believing that all or a part of that property or of those proceeds was obtained or derived directly or indirectly as a result of

(a) the commission in Canada of an offence under section 39; or

(b) an act or omission anywhere that, if it had occurred in Canada, would have constituted an offence under section 39.

(2) Punishment — Every person who contravenes subsection (1)

(a) is guilty of an indictable offence and liable to imprisonment for a term not exceeding ten years; or

(b) is guilty of an offence punishable on summary conviction.

(3) Exception — A peace officer or a person acting under the direction of a peace officer is not guilty of an offence under this section by reason only that the peace officer or person does any of the things mentioned in subsection (1) for the purposes of an investigation or otherwise in the execution of the peace officer's duties.

R.S. 1985, c. 42 (4th Supp.), s. 9; 1997, c. 18, s. 124; repealed 1996, c. 19, s. 81.

44.4 (1) Part XII.2 of the Criminal Code applicable — Sections 462.3 and 462.32 to 462.5 of the *Criminal Code* apply, with such modifications as the circumstances require, in respect of proceedings for an offence under section 39, 44.2 or 44.3.

(2) Idem — For the purposes of subsection (1),

(a) a reference in section 462.37 or 462.38 or subsection 462.41(2) of the *Criminal Code* to an enterprise crime offence shall be deemed to be a reference to an offence under section 39, 44.2 or 44.3; and

(b) a reference, in relation to the manner in which forfeited property is to be disposed of, in subsection 462.37(1) or 462.38(2), paragraph 462.43(c) or section 462.5 of the *Criminal Code*, to the Attorney General shall be deemed to be a reference to

(i) where the prosecution of the offence in respect of which the thing was forfeited was commenced at the instance of the government of a province and conducted by or on behalf of that government, the Attorney General or Solicitor General of that province, and

(ii) in any other case, the Minister of Public Works and Government Services.

R.S. 1985, c. 42 (4th Supp.), s. 9; 1993, c. 37, s. 24; 1996, c. 16, s. 60(1)(i); repealed 1996, c. 19, s. 81

45. (1) Regulations respecting controlled drugs — The Governor in Council may make regulations for carrying out the purposes and provisions of this Part, and, in particular, but without restricting the generality of the foregoing, may make regulations

(a) authorizing the manufacture, sale, importation, transportation, delivery or other dealing in controlled drugs and prescribing the circumstances and conditions under which, and the persons by whom, controlled drugs may be manufactured, sold, imported, transported, delivered, or otherwise dealt in;

(b) providing for the issue of licences for the importation, manufacture or sale of controlled drugs;

(c) prescribing the form, duration and terms and conditions of any licence described in paragraph (b) and the fees payable therefor, and providing for the cancellation and suspension of those licences;

(d) requiring persons who import, manufacture, sell, administer or deal in controlled drugs to maintain such books and records as the Governor in Council considers necessary for the proper administration and enforcement of this Part and the regulations made under this Part and to make such returns and furnish such information relating to the said controlled drugs as the Governor in Council may require;

(e) authorizing the communication of any information obtained under this Part or the regulations to provincial professional licensing authorities; and

(f) prescribing a fine not exceeding five hundred dollars or a term of imprisonment not exceeding six months, or both, to be imposed on summary conviction, as punishment for the contravention of any regulation.

(2) Amendment of schedule g — The Governor in Council may amend Schedule G by adding thereto or deleting therefrom any substance, the inclusion or exclusion of which, as the case may be, is deemed necessary by the Governor in Council in the public interest.

repealed 1996, c. 19, s. 81

PART IV — RESTRICTED DRUGS

[Note: Part IV of the Food and Drugs Act *repealed 1996, c. 19, s. 81. Please note Part IV of the Act was repealed by the* Controlled Drugs and Substances Act *on May 14, 1997. We have, however, retained the text of Part IV as it remains of relevance to offences occurring before its repeal and will therefore continue to be of great practical importance for some time to come.]*

Restricted Drugs

46. Definitions — In this Part,

"possession" means possession within the meaning of subsection 4(3) of the *Criminal Code;*

"regulations" means regulations made as provided for by or under section 51;

"restricted drug" means any drug or other substance included in Schedule H;

"traffic" means to manufacture, sell, export from or import into Canada, transport or deliver, otherwise than under the authority of this Part or the regulations.

repealed 1996, c. 19, s. 81

47. (1) Possession of restricted drug — Except as authorized by this Part or the regulations, no person shall have a restricted drug in his possession.

(2) Offence — Every person who contravenes subsection (1) is guilty of an offence and liable

(a) on summary conviction for a first offence, to a fine not exceeding one thousand dollars or to imprisonment for a term not exceeding six months, or to both and, for a subsequent offence, to a fine not exceeding two thousand dollars or to imprisonment for a term not exceeding one year or to both; or

(b) on conviction on indictment, to a fine not exceeding five thousand dollars or to imprisonment for a term not exceeding three years or to both.

repealed 1996, c. 19, s. 81.

48. (1) Trafficking in restricted drug — No person shall traffic in a restricted drug or any substance represented or held out by the person to be a restricted drug.

(2) Possession for trafficking — No person shall have in possession any restricted drug for the purpose of trafficking.

(3) Offence — Every person who contravenes subsection (1) or (2) is guilty of an offence and liable

(a) on summary conviction, to imprisonment for a term not exceeding eighteen months; or

(b) on conviction on indictment, to imprisonment for a term not exceeding ten years.

repealed 1996, c. 19, s. 81.

49. (1) Procedure in prosecution for possession for trafficking — In any prosecution for a contravention of subsection 48(2), if the accused does not plead guilty, the trial shall proceed as if the issue to be tried is whether the accused was in possession of a restricted drug contrary to subsection 47(1).

(2) Procedure on finding in respect of possession — If, pursuant to subsection (1), the court finds that the accused was not in possession of a restricted drug contrary to subsection 47(1), the accused shall be acquitted but, if the court finds that the accused was in possession of a restricted drug contrary to subsection 47(1), the accused shall be given an opportunity of establishing that he was not in possession of the restricted drug for the purpose of trafficking, and thereafter, the prosecutor shall be given an opportunity of adducing evidence to the contrary.

(3) Acquittal and conviction — If the accused establishes, pursuant to subsection (2), that he was not in possession of the restricted drug for the purpose of trafficking, the accused shall be acquitted of the offence as charged but shall be convicted of an offence under subsection 47(1) and sentenced accordingly, and if the accused fails to so establish, the accused shall be convicted of the offence as charged and sentenced accordingly.

repealed 1996, c. 19, s. 81.

50. (1) Setting out or negativing exception, etc., not required — No exception, exemption, excuse or qualification prescribed by law is required to be set out or negatived, as the case may be, in an information or indictment for an offence under this Part or under section 463, 464 or 465 of the *Criminal Code* in respect of an offence under this Part.

(2) Burden of proving exception, etc — In any prosecution under this Part, the burden of proving that an exception, exemption, excuse or qualification prescribed by law operates in favour of the accused is on the accused, and the prosecutor is not required, except by way of rebuttal, to prove that the exception, exemption, excuse or qualification does not operate in favour of the accused, whether or not it is set out in the information or indictment.

repealed 1996, c. 19, s. 81.

50.1 Interpretation — For the purposes of section 44.4, as that section is applicable in respect of this Part by virtue of section 51, and sections 50.2 to 51, a reference therein to an offence under section 48, 50.2 or 50.3 shall be deemed to include a reference to a conspiracy or an attempt to commit, being an accessory after the fact in relation to, or any counselling in relation to, such an offence.

R.S. 1985, c. 42 (4th Supp.), s. 10; repealed 1996, c. 19, s. 81.

50.2 (1) Possession of property obtained by trafficking in restricted drugs — No person shall possess any property or any proceeds of any property knowing that all or part of the property or of those proceeds was obtained or derived directly or indirectly as a result of

    (a) the commission in Canada of an offence under section 48; or

    (b) an act or omission anywhere that, if it had occurred in Canada, would have constituted an offence under section 48.

(2) Punishment — Every person who contravenes subsection (1)

(a) is guilty of an indictable offence and is liable to imprisonment for a term not exceeding ten years, where the value of the subject-matter of the offence exceeds one thousand dollars; or

(b) is guilty

(i) of an indictable offence and is liable to imprisonment for a term not exceeding two years, or

(ii) of an offence punishable on summary conviction,

where the value of the subject-matter of the offence does not exceed one thousand dollars.

(3) Exception — A peace officer or a person acting under the direction of a peace officer is not guilty of an offence under this section by reason only that the peace officer or person possesses property or the proceeds of property mentioned in subsection (1) for the purposes of an investigation or otherwise in the execution of the peace officer's duties.

R.S. 1985, c. 42 (4th Supp.), s. 10; 1997, c. 18, s. 125; repealed 1996, c. 19, s. 81

50.3 (1) Laundering proceeds of trafficking in restricted drugs — No person shall use, transfer the possession of, send or deliver to any person or place, transport, transmit, alter, dispose of or otherwise deal with, in any manner or by any means, any property or any proceeds of any property with intent to conceal or convert that property or those proceeds and knowing or believing that all or a part of that property or of those proceeds was obtained or derived directly or indirectly as a result of

(a) the commission in Canada of an offence under section 48; or

(b) an act or omission anywhere that, if it had occurred in Canada, would have constituted an offence under section 48.

(2) Punishment — Every person who contravenes subsection (1)

(a) is guilty of an indictable offence and is liable to imprisonment for a term not exceeding ten years; or

(b) is guilty of an offence punishable on summary conviction.

(3) Exception — A peace officer or a person acting under the direction of a peace officer is not guilty of an offence under this section by reason only that the peace officer or person does any of the things mentioned in subsection (1) for the purposes of an investigation or otherwise in the execution of the peace officer's duties.

R.S. 1985, c. 42 (4th Supp.), s. 10; 1997, c. 18, s. 126; repealed 1996, c. 19, s. 81

51. (1) Application of certain provisions of Part III — Sections 42 to 45 apply in respect of this Part.

(2) Modification for purpose of application — For the purposes of subsection (1),

(a) there shall be substituted for the expression "controlled drug", wherever it appears in any of the sections referred to in that subsection, the expression "restricted drug";

(b) a reference in any of those sections

(i) to "Schedule G" shall be deemed to be a reference to Schedule H, and

(ii) to "this Part" shall be deemed to be a reference to Part IV; and

(c) a reference in section 44.4 or in a provision of the *Criminal Code* mentioned therein

(i) to "an offence under section 39, 44.2 or 44.3" shall be deemed to be a reference under section 48, 50.2 or 50.3, and

(ii) to "this Part" shall be deemed to be a reference to Part IV.

(3) Additional regulations — In addition to the regulations provided for by subsection (1), the Governor in Council may make regulations authorizing the possession or export of restricted drugs and prescribing the circumstances and conditions under which, and the persons by whom restricted drugs may be had in possession or exported.

R.S., c. F-27, s. 45; R.S. 1985, c. 42 (4th Supp.), s. 11; repealed 1996, c. 19, s. 81.

[Editor's Note: Schedules A–F have been omitted.]

SCHEDULE G

[Note: Schedule G of the Food and Drugs Act *repealed 1996, c. 19, s. 82. Please note Schedule G of the Act was repealed by the* Controlled Drugs and Substances Act *on May 14, 1997. We have, however, retained the text of Schedule G as it remains of relevance to offences occurring before its repeal and will therefore continue to be of great practical importance for some time to come.]*

(Sections 30, 38, 45 and 51)

Amphetamine and its salts

Androisoxazole

Androstanolone

Androstenediol and its derivatives

Barbituric acid and its salts and derivatives

Benzphetamine and its salts

Bolandiol and its derivatives

Bolasterone

Bolazine

Boldenone and its derivatives

Bolenol

Butorphanol and its salts
Chlorphentermine and its salts
Calusterone
Clostebol and its derivatives
Diethylpropion and its salts
Drostanolone and its derivatives
Enestebol
Epitiostanol
Ethylestrenol
Fluoxymesterone
Formebolone
Furazabol
4-Hydroxy-19-nortestosterone and its derivatives
Mebolazine
Mesabolone
Mesterolone
Metandienone
Metenolone and its derivatives
Methamphetamine and its salts
Methandriol
Methaqualone and its salts
Methylphenidate and its salts
Methyltestosterone and its derivatives
Metribolone
Mibolerone
Nalbuphine and its salts
Nandrolone and its derivatives
Norboletone
Norclostebol and its derivatives
Norethandrolone
Oxabolone and its derivatives
Oxandrolone
Oxymesterone
Oxymetholone
Phendimetrazine and its salts
Phenmetrazine and its salts
Phentermine and its salts
Prasterone

Quinbolone

Stanozolol

Stenbolone and its derivatives

Testosterone and its derivatives

Thiobarbituric acid and its salts and derivatives

Tibolone

Tiomesterone

Trembolone and its derivatives

Zeranol

repealed 1996, c. 19, s. 82.

SCHEDULE H

[Note: Schedule H of the Food and Drugs Act *repealed 1996, c. 19, s. 82. Please note Schedule H of the Act was repealed by the* Controlled Drugs and Substances Act *on May 14, 1997. We have, however, retained the text of Schedule H as it remains of relevance to offences occurring before its repeal and will therefore continue to be of great practical importance for some time to come.]*

(Sections 30, 46 and 51)

Lysergic acid diethylamide (LSD) or any salt thereof

N,N-Diethyltryptamine (DET) or any salt thereof

N,N-Dimethyltryptamine (DMT) or any salt thereof

4-Methyl-2,5-dimethoxyamphetamine (STP(DOM)) or any salt thereof

3,4-methylenedioxyamphetamine (MDA) or any salt thereof

N-methyl-3-piperidyl benzilate (LBJ) or any salt thereof

2,3-dimethoxyamphetamine or any salt thereof

2,4-dimethoxyamphetamine or any salt thereof

2,5-dimethoxyamphetamine or any salt thereof

2,6-dimethoxyamphetamine or any salt thereof

3,4-dimethoxyamphetamine or any salt thereof

3,5-dimethoxyamphetamine or any salt thereof

4,9-dihydro-7-methoxy-1-methyl-3H-pyrido (3,4-b) indole (Harmaline) and any salt thereof

4,9-dihydro-1-methyl-3H-pyrido (3,4-b) indol-7-ol (Harmalol) and any salt thereof

4-methoxyamphetamine or any salt thereof

3-[2-(Dimethylamino) ethyl]-4-hydroxyindole (Psilocin) or any salt thereof

3-[2-(Dimethylamino) ethyl]-4-phosphoryloxyindole (Psilocybin) or any salt thereof

2,4,5-Trimethoxyamphetamine or any salt, isomer, or salt of isomer, thereof

3,4-methylenedioxy-N-methylamphetamine or any salt thereof

N-(1-phenycyclohexyl) ethylamine or any salt thereof

4-bromo-2, 5-dimethoxyamphetamine or any salt thereof

1-[1-(2-thienyl) cyclohexyl] piperidine and its salts

1-phenyl-N-propylcyclohexanamine or any salt thereof

3,4,5-trimethoxybenzeneethanamine (Mescaline) or any salt thereof but not including peyote (lophophora)

4-ethoxy-2, 5-dimethoxy-α-methylbenzeneethanamine or any salt, isomer, or salt of isomer, thereof

7-methoxy-α-methyl-1,3-benzodioxole-ethanamine (MMDA) or any salt, isomer or salt of isomer thereof

N,N,-α-trimethyl-1,3-benzodioxole-5-ethanamine or any salt, isomer or salt of isomer thereof

N-ethyl-α-methyl-1,3-benzodioxole-5-ethanamine or any salt, isomer or salt of isomer thereof

4-ethyl-2,5-dimethoxy-α-methylbenzeneethanamime (DOET) or any salt, isomer or salt of isomer thereof

4-ethoxy-α-methylbenzeneethanamine or any salt, isomer or salt of isomer thereof

4-chloro-2,5-dimethoxy-α-methylbenzeneethanamime or any salt, isomer or salt of isomer thereof

4,5-dihydro-4-methyl-5-phenyl-2-oxazolamine (4-methylaminorex) or any salt thereof

N-ethyl-α-methylbenzeneethanamine or any salt thereof

α-methyl-N-propyl-1, 3-benzodioxole-5-ethanamime or any salt, isomer or salt or isomer thereof

1-[1-(phenylmethyl)cyclohexyl]piperidine or any salt, isomer or salt or isomer thereof

1-[1-(4-methylphenyl)cyclohexyl]piperidine or any salt, isomer or salt of isomer thereof

2-methylamino-1-phenyl-1-propanone or any salt thereof

4-bromo-2,5-dimethoxybenzeneethanamine or any salt, isomer or salt of isomer thereof

N-(2-hydroxyethyl)-β-methylbenzeneethanamine or any salt, isomer or salt of isomer thereof

4-bromo-2,5-dimethoxybenzeneethanamine or any salt, isomer or salt of isomer thereof

N-(2-hydroxyethyl)-α-methylbenzeneethanamine or any salt, isomer or salt of isomer thereof

repealed 1996, c. 19, s. 82

CRIMINAL RECORDS ACT

CRA

CRIMINAL RECORDS ACT

An Act to provide for the relief of persons who have been convicted of offences and have subsequently re-habilitated themselves

R.S.C. 1985, c. C-47, as am. S.C. 1992, c. 22, ss. 1–10; 1995, c. 22, s. 17; 1995, c. 39, 191; 1995, c. 42, ss. 77, 78; 1997, c. 17, s. 38; 1998, c. 37, s. 25; 2000, c. 1, ss. 1–8.1 [Not in force at date of publication.].

Short Title

1. Short title — This Act may be cited as the *Criminal Records Act*.

Interpretation

2. (1) Definitions — In this Act,

"Board" means the National Parole Board;

"Commissioner" means the Commissioner of the Royal Canadian Mounted Police;

"Minister" means the Solicitor General of Canada;

"pardon" means a pardon granted or issued by the Board under section 4.1;

"period of probation" means a period during which a person convicted of an offence was directed by the court that convicted him

(a) to be released on his own recognizance to keep the peace and be of good behaviour, or

(b) to be released on or comply with the conditions prescribed in a probation order.

"sentence" has the same meaning as in the *Criminal Code*, but does not include an order made under section 109, 110, 161 or 259 of that Act or subsection 147.1(1) of the *National Defence Act*.

(2) Termination of period of probation — For the purposes of this Act, the period of probation shall be deemed to have terminated at the time the recognizance or the probation order that relates to the period of probation ceased to be in force.

1992, c. 22, s. 1

2.1 Jurisdiction of the Board — The Board has exclusive jurisdiction to grant or issue or refuse to grant or issue or to revoke a pardon.

1992, c. 22, s. 2

2.2 (1) Quorum — Applications for pardons referred to in subsection 4.1(1) shall be determined, and decisions whether to revoke pardons under section 7 shall be made, by a panel that consists of one member of the Board.

(2) Idem — The Chairperson of the Board may direct that the number of members of the Board required to constitute a panel for the determination of an application for a pardon referred to in subsection 4.1(1) or to decide whether to revoke a pardon under section 7 or for the determination of any class of those applications or for the making of any class of those decisions shall be greater than one.

1992, c. 22, s. 2

Application for Pardon

3. (1) Application for pardon — A person who has been convicted of an offence under an Act of Parliament or a regulation made under an Act of Parliament may apply to the Board for a pardon in respect of that offence and a Canadian offender within the meaning of the *Transfer of Offenders Act* who has been transferred to Canada under that Act may apply to the Board for a pardon in respect of the offence of which the offender has been found guilty.

(2) Transfer of offenders — For the purposes of this Act, the offence of which a Canadian offender within the meaning of the *Transfer of Offenders Act* who has been transferred to Canada under that Act has been found guilty is deemed to be an offence that was prosecuted by indictment.

1992, c. 22, s. 3

Procedure

4. Conviction-free period — Before an application for a pardon may be considered, the following period must have elapsed after the expiration according to law of any sentence, including a sentence of imprisonment, a period of probation and the payment of any fine, imposed for an offence, namely,

    (a) five years, in the case of

        (i) an offence prosecuted by indictment, or

        (ii) a service offence within the meaning of the *National Defence Act* for which, the offender was punished by a fine of more than two thousand dollars, detention for more than six months, dismissal from Her Majesty's service, imprisonment for more than six months or a punishment that is greater than imprisonment for less than two years in the scale of punishments set out in subsection 139(1) of that Act; or

    (b) three years, in the case of

        (i) an offence punishable on summary conviction, or

        (ii) a service offence within the meaning of the *National Defence Act*, other than a service offence referred to in subparagraph (a)(ii).

1992, c. 22, s. 4

4.01 Exception where long-term supervision — The period during which a person is being supervised pursuant to an order for long-term supervision, within the meaning of subsection 2(1) of the *Corrections and Conditional Release Act* is not included in the calculation of the period referred to in section 4 that must have elapsed after the expiration of sentence before an application for a pardon is considered.

1997, c. 17, s. 38

4.1 (1) Grant of pardon-indictable offences — The Board may grant a pardon for an offence prosecuted by indictment or a service offence referred to in subparagraph 4(a)(ii) if the Board is satisfied that the applicant, during the period of five years referred to in paragraph 4(a),

    (a) has been of good conduct; and

    (b) has not been convicted of an offence under an Act of Parliament or a regulation made under an Act of Parliament.

(2) Summary conviction offences — A pardon for an offence punishable on summary conviction or a service offence referred to in subparagraph 4(b)(ii) shall be issued if the offender has not been convicted of an offence under an Act of Parliament or a regulation made under an Act of Parliament during the period of three years referred to in paragraph 4(b).

1992, c. 22, s. 4

4.2 (1) Inquiries — On receipt of an application for a pardon for an offence referred to in paragraph 4(a), the Board shall cause inquiries to be made to ascertain the conduct of the applicant since the date of the conviction.

(2) Opportunity to make representations — If the Board proposes to refuse to grant a pardon, it shall notify the applicant of its proposal and advise the applicant that he or she is entitled to make any representations to the Board that he or she believes relevant.

Proposed Amendment — 4.2(2)

(2) Opportunity to make representations — If the Board proposes to refuse to grant a pardon, it shall notify the applicant of its proposal in writing and advise the applicant that he or she is entitled to make, or have made on his or her behalf, any representations to the Board that he or she believes relevant either in writing or, if the Board so authorizes, orally at a hearing held for that purpose.

2000, c. 1, s. 2 [Not in force at date of publication.]

(3) Board to consider representations — The Board shall, before deciding whether to refuse to grant a pardon, consider any oral or written representations made to it by or on behalf of the applicant within a reasonable time after the notification is given to the applicant pursuant to subsection (2).

Proposed Amendment — 4.2(3)

(3) Board to consider representations — The Board shall, before making its decision, consider any representations made to it within a reasonable time after the notification is given to the applicant pursuant to subsection (2).

2000, c. 1, s. 2 [Not in force at date of publication.]

Proposed Addition — 4.2(4)

(4) Waiting period — An applicant whose application is refused may not apply for a pardon until the expiration of one year after the date of the refusal.

2000, c. 1, s. 2 [Not in force at date of publication.]

1992, c. 22, s. 4

4.3 Expiration of sentence — For the purposes of section 4, a reference to the expiration according to law of a sentence of imprisonment imposed for an offence shall be read as a reference to the day on which the sentence expires, without taking into account

(a) any period during which the offender could be entitled to statutory release or any period following a statutory release date; or

(b) any remission that stands to the credit of the offender in respect of the offence.

1992, c. 22, ss. 4, 99

Proposed Amendment — Heading

Effect of Pardon

2000, c. 1, s. 3 [Not in force at date of publication.]

Effect of Grant of Pardon

5. Effect of pardon — The pardon

(a) is evidence of the fact

(i) that, in the case of a pardon for an offence referred to in paragraph 4(a), the Board, after making inquiries, was satisfied that the applicant for the pardon was of good conduct, and

(ii) that, in the case of any pardon, the conviction in respect of which the pardon is granted or issued should no longer reflect adversely on the applicant's character; and

(b) unless the pardon is subsequently revoked or ceases to have effect, vacates the conviction in respect of which it is granted and, without restricting the generality of the foregoing, removes any disqualification to which the person so convicted is, by reason of the conviction, subject by virtue of the provisions of any Act of Parliament, other than section 109, 110, 161 or 259 of the *Criminal Code* or subsection 147.1(1) of the *National Defence Act*, or of a regulation made under an Act of Parliament.

Proposed Amendment — 5(b)

(b) unless the pardon is subsequently revoked or ceases to have effect, requires the judicial record of the conviction to be kept separate and apart from other criminal records and removes any disqualification to which the person so convicted is, by reason of the conviction, subject by virtue of the provisions of any Act of Parliament, other than section 109, 110, 161 or 259 of the *Criminal Code* or subsection 147.1(1) of the *National Defence Act*, or of a regulation made under an Act of Parliament.

2000, c. 1, s. 4 [Not in force at date of publication.]

1992, c. 22, s. 5; 1995, c. 39, s. 191; 1995, c. 42, s. 78

Custody of Records

6. (1) Order respecting custody of records — The Minister may, by order in writing addressed to any person having the custody or control of any judicial record of a conviction in respect of which a pardon has been granted, require that person to deliver that record into the custody of the Commissioner.

Proposed Amendment — 6(1)

(1) Order respecting custody of records — The Minister may, by order in writing addressed to any person having the custody or control of any judicial record of a conviction in respect of which a pardon has been granted or issued, require that person to deliver that record into the custody of the Commissioner.

2000, c. 1, s. 5 [Not in force at date of publication.]

(2) Records to be kept separate and not to be disclosed — Any record of a conviction in respect of which a pardon has been granted that is in the custody of the Commissioner or of any department or agency of the Government of Canada shall be kept separate and apart from other criminal records, and no such record shall be disclosed to any person, nor shall the existence of the record or the fact of the conviction be disclosed to any person, without the prior approval of the Minister.

Proposed Amendment — 6(2)

(2) Records to be kept separate and not to be disclosed — Any record of a conviction in respect of which a pardon has been granted or issued that is in the custody of the Commissioner or of any department or agency of the Government of Canada shall be kept separate and apart from other criminal records, and no such record shall be disclosed to any person, nor shall the existence of the record or the fact of the conviction be disclosed to any person, without the prior approval of the Minister.

2000, c. 1, s. 5 [Not in force at date of publication.]

(3) Approval for disclosure — The Minister shall, before granting the approval for disclosure referred to in subsection (2), satisfy himself that the disclosure is desirable in the interests of the administration of justice or for any purpose related to the safety or security of Canada or any state allied or associated with Canada.

(4) Information in national DNA data bank — For greater certainty, a judicial record of a conviction includes any information in relation to the conviction that is contained in the convicted offenders index of the national DNA data bank established under the *DNA Identification Act*.

1998, c. 37, s. 25

6.1 (1) Discharges — No record of a discharge under section 730 of the *Criminal Code* that is in the custody of the Commissioner or of any department or agency of the Government of Canada shall be disclosed to any person, nor shall the existence of the record or the fact of the discharge be disclosed to any person, without the prior approval of the Minister, if

(a) more than one year has elapsed since the offender was discharged absolutely; or

(b) more than three years have elapsed since the offender was discharged on the conditions prescribed in a probation order.

(2) Purging C.P.I.C — The Commissioner shall remove all references to a discharge under section 730 of the *Criminal Code* from the automated criminal conviction records retrieval system maintained by the Royal Canadian Mounted Police on the expiration of the relevant period referred to in subsection (1).

1992, c. 22, s. 6; 1995, c. 22, s. 17

6.2 Disclosure to police forces — Notwithstanding section 6 and 6.1, the name, date of birth and last known address of a person who has received a pardon or a discharge referred to in section 6.1 may be disclosed to a police force if a fingerprint, identified as that of the person, is found

(a) at the scene of a crime during an investigation of the crime; or

(b) during an attempt to identify a deceased person or a person suffering from amnesia.

1992, c. 22, s. 6

Proposed Addition — 6.3, 6.4

6.3 (1) Definitions — The definitions in this subsection apply in this section.

"children" means persons who are less than 18 years of age.

"vulnerable persons" means persons who, because of their age, a disability or other circumstances, whether temporary or permanent,

(a) are in a position of dependence on others; or

(b) are otherwise at a greater risk than the general population of being harmed by persons in a position of authority or trust relative to them.

(2) Notation of records — The Commissioner shall make, in the automated criminal conviction records retrieval system maintained by the Royal Canadian Mounted Police, a notation enabling a member of a police force or other authorized body to determine whether there is a record of an individual's conviction for a sexual offence listed in the schedule in respect of which a pardon has been granted or issued.

(3) Verification — At the request of any person or organization responsible for the well-being of one or more children or vulnerable persons and to whom or to which an application is made for a paid or volunteer position, a member of a police force or other authorized body shall verify whether the applicant is the subject of a notation made in accordance with subsection (2) if

(a) the position is one of authority or trust relative to those children or vulnerable persons; and

(b) the applicant has consented in writing to the verification.

(4) Unauthorized use — Except as authorized by subsection (3), no person shall verify whether a person is the subject of a notation made in accordance with subsection (2).

(5) Request to forward record to Minister — A police force or other authorized body that identifies an applicant for a position referred to in paragraph (3)(a) as being a person who is the subject of a notation made in accordance with subsection (2) shall request the Commissioner to provide the Minister with any record of a conviction of that applicant, and the Commissioner shall transmit any such record to the Minister.

(6) Disclosure by Minister — The Minister may disclose to the police force or other authorized body all or part of the information contained in a record transmitted by the Commissioner pursuant to subsection (5).

(7) Disclosure to person or organization — A police force or other authorized body shall disclose the information referred to in subsection (6) to the person or organization that requested a verification if the applicant for a position has consented in writing to the disclosure.

(8) Use of information — A person or organization that acquires information under this section in relation to an application for a position shall not use it or communicate it except in relation to the assessment of the application.

(9) Amendment of Schedule — The Governor in Council may, by order, amend the schedule by adding or deleting a reference to a sexual offence.

2000, c. 1, s. 6 [Not in force at date of publication.]

6.4 Operation of section 6.3 — Section 6.3 applies in respect of a record of a conviction for any offence in respect of which a pardon has been granted or issued regardless of the date of the conviction or the date of the pardon.

2000, c. 1, s. 6 [Not in force at date of publication.]

Revocation

7. Revocation of pardon — A pardon may be revoked by the Board

(a) if the person to whom it is granted or issued is subsequently convicted of an offence punishable on summary conviction under an Act of Parliament or a regulation made under an Act of Parliament;

(b) on evidence establishing to the satisfaction of the Board that the person to whom it was granted or issued is no longer of good conduct; or

(c) on evidence establishing to the satisfaction of the Board that the person to whom it was granted or issued knowingly made a false or deceptive statement in relation to the application for the pardon, or knowingly concealed some material particular in relation to that application.

1992, c. 22, s. 7

7.1 (1) Opportunity to make representations — If the Board proposes to revoke a pardon, it shall notify the person to whom the pardon was granted or issued of its proposal and advise that person that he or she is entitled to make any representations to the Board that he or she believes relevant.

(2) Board to consider representation — The Board shall, before deciding whether to revoke a pardon, consider any oral or written representations made to it by or on behalf of the person to whom the pardon was granted or issued within a reasonable time after the notification is given to that person pursuant to subsection (1).

1992, c. 22, s. 7

Proposed Amendment — 7.1

7.1 (1) Opportunity to make representations — If the Board proposes to revoke a pardon, it shall notify the person to whom the pardon was granted or issued of its proposal in writing and advise that person that he or she is entitled to make, or have made on his or her behalf, any representations to the Board that he or she believes relevant either in writing or, if the Board so authorizes, orally at a hearing held for that purpose.

(2) Board to consider representations — The Board shall, before making its decision, consider any representations made to it within a reasonable time after the notification is given to a person pursuant to subsection (1).

2000, c. 1, s. 7 [Not in force at date of publication.]

7.2 Cessation of pardon's effect — A pardon ceases to have effect if the person to whom it is granted or issued is subsequently convicted of an offence prosecuted by indictment under an Act of Parliament or a regulation made under an Act of Parliament.

1992, c. 22, s. 7

Proposed Amendment — 7.2

7.2 Cessation of effect of pardon — A pardon granted or issued to a person ceases to have effect if

(a) the person is subsequently convicted of

(i) an indictable offence under an Act of Parliament or a regulation made under an Act of Parliament,

(ii) an offence under the *Criminal Code*, except subsection 255(1), or under the *Controlled Drugs and Substances Act*, the *Firearms*

Act, Part III or IV of the *Food and Drugs Act* or the *Narcotic Control Act*, chapter N-1 of the Revised Statutes of Canada, 1985, that is punishable either on conviction on indictment or on summary conviction, or

    (iii) a service offence referred to in subparagraph 4(a)(ii); or

(b) the Board is convinced by new information that the person was not eligible for a pardon at the time it was granted or issued.

2000, c. 1, s. 7 [Not in force at date of publication.]

General

8. Applications for employment — No person shall use or authorize the use of an application form for or relating to any of the following matters that contains a question that by its terms requires the applicant to disclose a conviction in respect of which a pardon that has not been revoked or ceased to have effect has been granted or issued to the applicant:

(a) employment in any department as defined in section 2 of the *Financial Administration Act*,

(b) employment by any Crown corporation as defined in section 83 of the *Financial Administration Act*,

(c) enrolment in the Canadian Forces, or

(d) employment on or in connection with the operation of any work, undertaking or business that is within the legislative authority of Parliament.

1992, c. 22, s. 8

9. Saving of other pardons — Nothing in this Act in any manner limits or affects Her Majesty's royal prerogative of mercy or the provisions of the *Criminal Code* relating to pardons, except that section 6 and 8 apply in respect of any pardon granted pursuant to the royal prerogative of mercy or those provisions.

1992, c. 22, s. 9

9.1 Regulations — The Governor in Council may make regulations for carrying out the purposes and provisions of this Act.

1992, c. 22, s. 9

Proposed Amendment — 9.1

9.1 Regulations — The Governor in Council may make regulations

(a) respecting the making of notations in respect of records of conviction, and the verification of such records, for the purposes of section 6.3;

(b) prescribing the factors that the Minister must have regard to in considering whether to authorize a disclosure under this Act of a record of a conviction;

(c) respecting the consent given by applicants to the verification of records and the disclosure of information contained in them, including the information to be given to applicants prior to obtaining their consent and the manner in which consent is to be given, for the purposes of subsections 6.3(3) and (7); and

(d) generally for carrying out the purposes and provisions of this Act.

2000, c. 1, s. 8 [Not in force at date of publication.]

Offences

10. Offence and punishment — Any person who contravenes any provision of this Act is guilty of an offence punishable on summary conviction.

SCHEDULE [1]

Number in brackets editorially added by Carswell.

[Repealed 1992, c. 22, s. 10.]

Proposed Addition — Schedule

SCHEDULE (SECTION 8.1)

Schedule (Subsections 6.3(2) and (9))

1. Offences under the following provisions of the *Criminal Code*:

(a) subsection 7(4.1) (sexual offence against a child by an act or omission outside Canada);

(b) section 151 (sexual interference with a person under 14);

(c) section 152 (invitation to a person under 14 to sexual touching);

(d) section 153 (sexual exploitation of a person 14 or more but under 18);

(e) section 153.1 (sexual exploitation of a person with a disability);

(f) section 155 (incest);

(g) section 159 (anal intercourse);

(h) subsection 160(3) (bestiality in the presence of a person under 14 or inciting a person under 14 to commit bestiality);

(i) paragraph 163(1)(a) (obscene materials);

(j) paragraph 163(2)(a) (obscene materials);

(k) section 163.1 (child pornography);

(l) section 168 (mailing obscene matter);

(m) section 170 (parent or guardian procuring sexual activity);

(n) section 171 (householder permitting sexual activity);

(o) section 172 (corrupting children);

(p) section 173 (indecent acts);

(q) subsection 212(2) (living on avails of prostitution of a person under 18);

(r) subsection 212(2.1) (living on avails of prostitution of a person under 18);

(s) subsection 212(4) (obtain, or attempt to obtain, sexual services of a person under 18);

(t) section 271 (sexual assault);

(u) subsection 272(1) and paragraph 272(2)(a) (sexual assault with firearm);

(v) subsection 272(1) and paragraph 272(2)(b) (sexual assault other than with firearm);

(w) section 273 (aggravated sexual assault);

(x) paragraph 273.3(1)(a) (removal of child under 14 from Canada for purposes of listed offences);

(y) paragraph 273.3(1)(b) (removal of child 14 or more but under 18 from Canada for purpose of listed offence);

(z) paragraph 273.3(1)(c) (removal of child under 18 from Canada for purposes of listed offences);

(z.1) section 280 (abduction of a person under 16);

(z.2) section 281 (abduction of a person under 14);

(z.3) paragraph 348(1)(a) with respect to breaking and entering a place with intent to commit in that place an indictable offence listed in this schedule;

(z.4) paragraph 348(1)(b) with respect to breaking and entering a place and committing in that place an indictable offence listed in this schedule;

(z.5) subsection 372(2) (indecent phone calls); and

(z.6) section 463 with respect to an attempt to commit an offence listed in this section or with respect to being an accessory after the fact to the commission of an offence listed in this schedule.

2000, c. 1, s. 8.1 [Not in force at date of publication.]

2. Offences under the following provisions of the *Criminal Code*, R.S.C. 1970, c. C-34, as that Act read before January 1988:

(a) subsection 146(1) (sexual intercourse with a female under 14);

(b) subsection 146(2) (sexual intercourse with a female 14 or more but under 16);

(c) section 151 (seduction of a female 16 or more but under 18);

(d) section 153 (sexual intercourse with stepdaughter, etc., or female employee);

(e) section 155 (buggery or bestiality);

(f) section 157 (gross indecency);

(g) section 166 (parent or guardian procuring defilement); and

(h) section 167 (householder permitting defilement).

2000, c. 1, s. 8.1 [Not in force at date of publication.]

3. Offences under the following provisions of the *Criminal Code*, R.S.C. 1970, c. C-34, as that Act read before January 1983:

    (a) section 144 (rape);

    (b) section 145 (attempt to commit rape);

    (c) section 149 (indecent assault on female);

    (d) section 156 (indecent assault on male);

    (e) section 245 (common assault); and

    (f) subsection 246(1) (assault with intent to commit an indictable offence).

2000, c. 1, s. 8.1 [Not in force at date of publication.]

EXTRADITION ACT, S.C. 1999, C. 18

TABLE OF CONCORDANCE

[Note: The Extradition Act, R.S.C. 1985, c. E-23, was repealed and replaced by S.C. 1999, c. 18, An Act respecting Extradition, to amend the Canada Evidence Act, Criminal Code, the Immigration Act, and the Mutual Legal Assistance in Criminal Matters Act and to amend and repeal other acts in consequence (in force June 17, 1999). The table below traces, to the extent possible, the substantive correspondences between the provisions of both of the former acts, as amended, and those of the new act.]

R.S.C. 1970, c. E-21	R.S.C. 1985, c. E-23	Extradition Act, S.C. 1999, c. 18
1	1	1
2	2	2
3	3	10(1), (2)
4	4	—
5	5	—
6	6	—
7	7	8(1), (2)
8	8	8(3)
9(1)	9(1)	2 "court", "judge"; 24
9(2)	9(2)	—
—	9(3)	25
10(1)	10(1)	3
10(2)	—	—
11	11	16(4)
12	12	6
13	13	17; 18(1); 19
14	14	32(1) "evidence otherwise admissible under Canadian law"; 32(2)
15	15	—
16	16	32(1) "evidence otherwise admissible under Canadian law"
17	17	33(4); 35
18(1)	18(1)	29(1)
18(2)	18(2)	29(3)
19	19	38

R.S.C. 1970, c. E-21	R.S.C. 1985, c. E-23	Extradition Act, S.C. 1999, c. 18
—	19.1(1)	43
—	19.1(2)	—
—	19.2	49
—	19.3	50
—	19.4	51
—	19.5	52
—	19.6	53
—	19.7	54
—	19.8	55
—	19.9	56
20	20	2 "extradition partner"
21	21	—
22(1)	22(1)	46; 47
22(2)	22(2)	48(1)
23	23	62(1)
24	24	—
25	25(1)	40(1)
—	25(2)	40(5)
—	25(3)	40(6)
—	25(4)	64(1)
—	25(5)	67
—	25.1	41
—	25.2	57
26	26	60, 61
27	27	39
28	28	69
29	29	—
30	30	78
31	31	79(1)
32	32	81(1)
33	33	80
34–40	34–40	—
Sch. I–III	Sch. I–III	—

EXTRADITION ACT

An Act respecting extradition, to amend the Canada
Evidence Act, the Criminal Code, the Immigration Act
and the Mutual Legal Assistance in Criminal Matters
Act and to amend and repeal other Acts in
consequence

S.C. 1999, c. 18, as am. S.C. 2000, c. 24, ss. 47–53 [Not in force at date
of publication.].

Her Majesty, by and with the advice and consent of the Senate and House of Commons of Canada, enacts as follows:

SHORT TITLE

1. Short title — This Act may be cited as the *Extradition Act*.

PART 1 — INTERPRETATION

2. Definitions — The definitions in this section apply in this Act.

"Attorney General" means the Attorney General of Canada.

"court" means

(a) in Ontario, the Ontario Court (General Division);

(b) in Quebec, the Superior Court;

(c) in New Brunswick, Manitoba, Alberta and Saskatchewan, the Court of Queen's Bench;

(d) in Nova Scotia, British Columbia, the Northwest Territories, the Yukon Territory and Nunavut, the Supreme Court; and

(e) in Prince Edward Island and Newfoundland, the Trial Division of the Supreme Court.

"court of appeal" means

(a) in the Province of Prince Edward Island, the Appeal Division of the Supreme Court; and

(b) in all other provinces, the Court of Appeal.

"extradition agreement" means an agreement that is in force, to which Canada is a party and that contains a provision respecting the extradition of persons, other than a specific agreement.

"extradition partner" means a State or entity with which Canada is party to an extradition agreement, with which Canada has entered into a specific agreement or whose name appears in the schedule.

Proposed Addition — 2 "International Criminal Court"

"International Criminal Court" means the International Criminal Court as defined in subsection 2(1) of the *Crimes Against Humanity and War Crimes Act*.

2000, c. 24, s. 47 [Not in force at date of publication.]

"judge" means a judge of the court.

"justice" has the same meaning as in section 2 of the *Criminal Code*.

"Minister" means the Minister of Justice.

"specific agreement" means an agreement referred to in section 10 that is in force;

"State or entity" means

 (a) a State other than Canada;

 (b) a province, state or other political subdivision of a State other than Canada;

 (c) a colony, dependency, possession, protectorate, condominium, trust territory or any territory falling under the jurisdiction of a State other than Canada;

 (d) an international criminal court or tribunal; or

 (e) a territory.

PART 2 — EXTRADITION FROM CANADA

Extraditable Conduct

3. (1) General principle — A person may be extradited from Canada in accordance with this Act and a relevant extradition agreement on the request of an extradition partner for the purpose of prosecuting the person or imposing a sentence on — or enforcing a sentence imposed on — the person if

 (a) subject to a relevant extradition agreement, the offence in respect of which the extradition is requested is punishable by the extradition partner, by imprisoning or otherwise depriving the person of their liberty for a maximum term of two years or more, or by a more severe punishment; and

(b) the conduct of the person, had it occurred in Canada, would have constituted an offence that is punishable in Canada,

> (i) in the case of a request based on a specific agreement, by imprisonment for a maximum term of five years or more, or by a more severe punishment, and

> (ii) in any other case, by imprisonment for a maximum term of two years or more, or by a more severe punishment, subject to a relevant extradition agreement.

(2) Conduct determinative — For greater certainty, it is not relevant whether the conduct referred to in subsection (1) is named, defined or characterized by the extradition partner in the same way as it is in Canada.

(3) Extradition of a person who has been sentenced — Subject to a relevant extradition agreement, the extradition of a person who has been sentenced to imprisonment or another deprivation of liberty may only be granted if the portion of the term remaining is at least six months long or a more severe punishment remains to be carried out.

4. Further proceedings — For greater certainty, the discharge of a person under this Act or an Act repealed by section 129 or 130 does not preclude further proceedings, whether or not they are based on the same conduct, with a view to extraditing the person under this Act unless the judge is of the opinion that those further proceedings would be an abuse of process.

5. Jurisdiction — A person may be extradited

(a) whether or not the conduct on which the extradition partner bases its request occurred in the territory over which it has jurisdiction; and

(b) whether or not Canada could exercise jurisdiction in similar circumstances.

6. Retrospectivity — Subject to a relevant extradition agreement, extradition may be granted under this Act whether the conduct or conviction in respect of which the extradition is requested occurred before or after this Act or the relevant extradition agreement or specific agreement came into force.

Proposed Addition — 6.1

6.1 No immunity — Despite any other Act or law, no person who is the subject of a request for surrender by the International Criminal Court or by any international criminal tribunal that is established by resolution of the Security Council of the United Nations and whose name appears in the schedule, may claim immunity under common law or by statute from arrest or extradition under this Act.

2000, c. 24, s. 48 [Not in force at date of publication.]

Functions of the Minister

7. Functions of the Minister — The Minister is responsible for the implementation of extradition agreements, the administration of this Act and dealing with requests for extradition made under them.

Publication of Extradition Agreements

8. (1) Publication in Canada Gazette — Unless the extradition agreement has been published under subsection (2), an extradition agreement — or the provisions respecting extradition contained in a multilateral extradition agreement — must be published in the *Canada Gazette* no later than 60 days after it comes into force.

(2) Publication in Canada Treaty Series — An extradition agreement — or the provisions respecting extradition contained in a multilateral extradition agreement — may be published in the *Canada Treaty Series* and, if so published, the publication must be no later than 60 days after it comes into force.

(3) Judicial notice — Agreements and provisions published in the *Canada Gazette* or the *Canada Treaty Series* are to be judicially noticed.

Designated States and Entities

9. (1) Designated extradition partners — The names of members of the Commonwealth or other States or entities that appear in the schedule are designated as extradition partners.

(2) Amendment to the schedule — The Minister of Foreign Affairs, with the agreement of the Minister, may, by order, add to or delete from the schedule the names of members of the Commonwealth or other States or entities.

Specific Agreements

10. (1) Specific agreements — The Minister of Foreign Affairs may, with the agreement of the Minister, enter into a specific agreement with a State or entity for the purpose of giving effect to a request for extradition in a particular case.

(2) Inconsistency — For greater certainty, if there is an inconsistency between this Act and a specific agreement, this Act prevails to the extent of the inconsistency.

(3) Evidence — A certificate issued by or under the authority of the Minister of Foreign Affairs to which is attached a copy of a specific agreement entered into by Canada and a State or entity is conclusive evidence of the agreement and its contents without proof of the signature or official character of the person appearing to have signed the certificate or agreement.

Minister's Power to Receive Requests

11. (1) Request to go to Minister — A request by an extradition partner for the provisional arrest or extradition of a person shall be made to the Minister.

(2) Provisional arrest request to go to Minister — A request by an extradition partner for the provisional arrest of a person may also be made to the Minister through Interpol.

Warrant for Provisional Arrest

12. Minister's approval of request for provisional arrest — The Minister may, after receiving a request by an extradition partner for the provisional arrest of a person, authorize the Attorney General to apply for a provisional arrest warrant, if the Minister is satisfied that

(a) the offence in respect of which the provisional arrest is requested is punishable in accordance with paragraph 3(1)(a); and

(b) the extradition partner will make a request for the extradition of the person.

13. (1) Provisional arrest warrant — A judge may, on *ex parte* application of the Attorney General, issue a warrant for the provisional arrest of a person, if satisfied that there are reasonable grounds to believe that

(a) it is necessary in the public interest to arrest the person, including to prevent the person from escaping or committing an offence;

(b) the person is ordinarily resident in Canada, is in Canada or is on the way to Canada; and

(c) a warrant for the person's arrest or an order of a similar nature has been issued or the person has been convicted.

(2) Contents of the warrant — A provisional arrest warrant must

(a) name or describe the person to be arrested;

(b) set out briefly the offence in respect of which the provisional arrest was requested; and

(c) order that the person be arrested without delay and brought before the judge who issued the warrant or before another judge in Canada.

(3) Execution throughout Canada — A provisional arrest warrant may be executed anywhere in Canada without being endorsed.

14. (1) Discharge if no proceedings — A person who has been provisionally arrested, whether detained or released on judicial interim release, must be discharged

(a) when the Minister notifies the court that an authority to proceed will not be issued under section 15;

(b) if the provisional arrest was made pursuant to a request made under an extradition agreement that contains a period within which a request for extradition must be made and the supporting documents provided,

    (i) when the period has expired and the extradition partner has not made the request or provided the documents, or

    (ii) when the request for extradition has been made and the documents provided within the period but the Minister has not issued an authority to proceed before the expiry of 30 days after the expiry of that period; or

(c) if the provisional arrest was not made pursuant to a request made under an extradition agreement or was made pursuant to an extradition agreement that does not contain a period within which a request for extradition must be made and the supporting documents provided,

    (i) when 60 days have expired after the provisional arrest and the extradition partner has not made the request or provided the documents, or

    (ii) when the request for extradition has been made and the documents provided within 60 days but the Minister has not issued an authority to proceed before the expiry of 30 additional days.

(2) Extension — A judge may, on application of the Attorney General, extend a period referred to in subsection (1).

Proposed Amendment — 14(2)

(2) Extension — On application of the Attorney General, a judge

    (a) may extend a period referred to in subsection (1); or

    (b) shall, in the case of a person arrested on the request of the International Criminal Court, extend a period referred to in subsection (1) for the period specified by the Attorney General, not to exceed 30 days.

2000, c. 24, s. 49 [Not in force at date of publication.]

(3) Release of person — In extending a period under subsection (2), the judge may also grant the person judicial interim release or vary the conditions of their judicial interim release.

Authority to Proceed

15. (1) Minister's power to issue — The Minister may, after receiving a request for extradition and being satisfied that the conditions set out in paragraph 3(1)(a) and subsection 3(3) are met in respect of one or more offences mentioned in the request, issue an authority to proceed that authorizes the Attorney General to seek, on behalf of the extradition partner, an order of a court for the committal of the person under section 29.

(2) Competing requests — If requests from two or more extradition partners are received by the Minister for the extradition of a person, the Minister shall determine the order in which the requests will be authorized to proceed.

(3) Contents of authority to proceed — The authority to proceed must contain

    (a) the name or description of the person whose extradition is sought;

    (b) the name of the extradition partner; and

    (c) the name of the offence or offences under Canadian law that correspond to the alleged conduct of the person or the conduct in respect of which the person was convicted, as long as one of the offences would be punishable in accordance with paragraph 3(1)(b).

(4) Copy of authority to proceed — A copy of an authority to proceed produced by a means of telecommunication that produces a writing has the same probative force as the original for the purposes of this Part.

Arrest or Summons Following Authority to Proceed

16. (1) Warrant of arrest or summons — The Attorney General may, after the Minister issues an authority to proceed, apply *ex parte* to a judge in the province in which the Attorney General believes the person is or to which the person is on their way, or was last known to be, for the issuance of a summons to the person or a warrant for the arrest of the person.

(2) When provisionally arrested — If the person has been arrested pursuant to a provisional arrest warrant issued under section 13, the Attorney General need not apply for a summons or warrant under subsection (1).

(3) Issuance of summons or warrant of arrest — The judge to whom an application is made shall issue a summons to the person, or a warrant for the arrest of the person, in accordance with subsection 507(4) of the *Criminal Code*, with any modifications that the circumstances require.

(4) Execution throughout Canada — A warrant that is issued under this section may be executed, and a summons issued under this section may be served, anywhere in Canada without being endorsed.

(5) Date of hearing — summons — A summons that is issued under this section must

    (a) set a date for the appearance of the person before a judge that is not later than 15 days after its issuance; and

    (b) require the person to appear at a time and place stated in it for the purposes of the *Identification of Criminals Act*.

(6) Effect of appearance — A person appearing as required by subsection (5) is considered, for the purposes only of the *Identification of Criminals Act*, to be in lawful custody charged with an indictable offence.

Appearance

17. (1) Appearance — A person who is arrested under section 13 or 16 is to be brought before a judge or a justice within twenty-four hours after the person is arrested, but if no judge or no justice is available during this time, the person shall be brought before a judge or a justice as soon as possible.

(2) Appearance before justice — The justice before whom a person is brought under subsection (1) shall order that the person be detained in custody and brought before a judge.

18. (1) Judicial interim release — The judge before whom a person is brought following arrest under section 13 or 16 shall order the release, with or without conditions, or detention in custody of the person.

Proposed Amendment — 18(1)

(1) Decision of judge — The judge before whom a person is brought following arrest under section 13 or 16 shall

    (a) if the person has been arrested on the request of the International Criminal Court, order the detention in custody of the person unless

        (i) the person shows cause, in accordance with subsection 522(2) of the *Criminal Code*, that their detention in custody is not justified, and

        (ii) the judge is satisfied that, given the gravity of the alleged offence, there are urgent and exceptional circumstances that justify release — with or without conditions — and that the person will appear as required; or

    (b) in any other case, order the release, with or without conditions, or detention in custody of the person.

2000, c. 24, s. 50 [Not in force at date of publication.]

Proposed Addition — 18(1.1), (1.2)

(1.1) Mandatory adjournment — An application for judicial interim release in respect of a person referred to in paragraph (1)(a) shall, at the request of the Attorney General, be adjourned to await receipt of the recommendations of the Pre-Trial Chamber of the International Criminal Court. If the recommendations are not received within six days, the judge may proceed to hear the application.

(1.2) Recommendations of Pre-Trial Chamber — If the Pre-Trial Chamber of the International Criminal Court submits recommendations, the judge shall consider them before rendering a decision.

2000, c. 24, s. 50 [Not in force at date of publication.]

(2) Review by court of appeal — A decision respecting judicial interim release may be reviewed by a judge of the court of appeal and that judge may

    (a) confirm the decision;

    (b) vary the decision; or

    (c) substitute any other decision that, in the judge's opinion, should have been made.

19. Criminal Code — Part XVI of the *Criminal Code* applies, with any modifications that the circumstances require, in respect of a person arrested under section 13 or 16 or to whom a summons has been issued under section 16.

20. Section 679 of the Criminal Code — Section 679 of the *Criminal Code* applies, with any modifications that the circumstances require, to the judicial interim release of a person pending

(a) a determination of an appeal from an order of committal made under section 29;

(b) the Minister's decision under section 40 respecting the surrender of the person; or

(c) a determination of a judicial review of the Minister's decision under section 40 to order the surrender of the person.

21. (1) Date of hearing — provisional arrest — If a person has been provisionally arrested, the judge before whom the person is brought shall

(a) order the person to appear before the court from time to time during the period referred to in paragraph 14(1)(b) or (c); and

(b) set a date for the extradition hearing if the Minister has issued an authority to proceed.

(2) Date of hearing after authority to proceed issued — If a person has been arrested or is a person to whom a summons has been issued under section 16, the judge before whom the person is brought shall set a date for the extradition hearing.

(3) Hearing — The judge shall set an early date for the extradition hearing, whether that date is in or out of the prescribed sessions of the court.

22. (1) Application for transfer — On application of the Attorney General or the person arrested or to whom a summons has been issued under section 16, the judge shall, if satisfied that the interests of justice so require, order that the proceedings be transferred to another place in Canada and that the person appear before a judge in that place, and

(a) if the person is detained, that the person be conveyed by a peace officer to the place; and

(b) if the person is not detained or has been released on judicial interim release, that the person be summoned to appear at the place.

(2) Execution throughout Canada — A summons issued under paragraph (1)(b) may be served anywhere in Canada without being endorsed.

(3) Order respecting expenses — If the order under subsection (1) was made on the application of the Attorney General, the judge may order that the Attorney General pay the person's reasonable travel expenses incurred further to the order.

Substitution and Amendment of Authority to Proceed

23. (1) Substitution of authority to proceed — The Minister may substitute another authority to proceed at any time before the extradition hearing begins. All documents issued and orders made by the court apply in respect of the new authority to proceed, unless the court, on application of the person or the Attorney General, orders otherwise.

(1.1) New date for hearing — Where the Minister substitutes another authority to proceed under subsection (1) and the person applies for another date to be set for the beginning of the extradition hearing in order to give the person an opportunity to examine the new authority, the judge may set another date for the hearing.

(2) Amendment of authority to proceed — The judge may, on application of the Attorney General, amend the authority to proceed after the hearing has begun in accordance with the evidence that is produced during the hearing.

(3) Withdrawal of the authority to proceed — The Minister may at any time withdraw the authority to proceed and, if the Minister does so, the court shall discharge the person and set aside any order made respecting their judicial interim release or detention.

Extradition Hearing

24. (1) Extradition hearing — The judge shall, on receipt of an authority to proceed from the Attorney General, hold an extradition hearing.

(2) Application of Part XVIII of the Criminal Code — For the purposes of the hearing, the judge has, subject to this Act, the powers of a justice under Part XVIII of the *Criminal Code*, with any modifications that the circumstances require.

25. Competence — For the purposes of the *Constitution Act, 1982*, a judge has, with respect to the functions that the judge is required to perform in applying this Act, the same competence that that judge possesses by virtue of being a superior court judge.

26. Order restricting publication of evidence — Before beginning a hearing in respect of a judicial interim release or an extradition hearing, a judge may, on application by the person or the Attorney General and on being satisfied that the publication or broadcasting of the evidence would constitute a risk to the holding of a fair trial by the extradition partner, make an order directing that the evidence taken not be published or broadcast before the time that the person is discharged or, if surrendered, the trial by the extradition partner has concluded.

27. Exclusion of person from hearing — The presiding judge may make an order excluding any person from the court for all or part of an extradition hearing or hearing in respect of a judicial interim release if the judge is of the opinion that it is in the interest of public morals, the maintenance of order or the proper administration of justice to exclude the person.

28. Power to compel witnesses — A judge who presides over an extradition hearing or a hearing in respect of a judicial interim release may compel a witness to attend the hearing and sections 698 to 708 of the *Criminal Code* apply, with any modifications that the circumstances require.

29. (1) Order of committal — A judge shall order the committal of the person into custody to await surrender if

(a) in the case of a person sought for prosecution, there is evidence admissible under this Act of conduct that, had it occurred in Canada, would justify committal for trial in Canada on the offence set out in the authority to proceed and the judge is satisfied that the person is the person sought by the extradition partner; and

(b) in the case of a person sought for the imposition or enforcement of a sentence, the judge is satisfied that the conviction was in respect of conduct that corresponds to the offence set out in the authority to proceed and that the person is the person who was convicted.

(2) Order of committal — The order of committal must contain

(a) the name of the person;

(b) the offence set out in the authority to proceed for which the committal is ordered;

(c) the place at which the person is to be held in custody; and

(d) the name of the extradition partner.

(3) Discharge of person — A judge shall order the person discharged if the judge does not order their committal under subsection (1).

(4) Relevant date — The date of the authority to proceed is the relevant date for the purposes of subsection (1).

(5) Extradition when person not present at conviction — Subject to a relevant extradition agreement, if a person has been tried and convicted without the person being present, the judge shall apply paragraph (1)(a).

30. (1) Authority to keep person in custody — The order of committal constitutes the authority to keep the person in custody, subject to an order of judicial interim release.

(2) Duration of order — The order of committal remains in force until the person is surrendered or discharged or until a new hearing is ordered under paragraph 54(a).

Rules of Evidence

31. Definition of "document" — For the purposes of sections 32 to 38, **"document"** means data recorded in any form, and includes photographs and copies of documents.

32. (1) Evidence — Subject to subsection (2), evidence that would otherwise be admissible under Canadian law shall be admitted as evidence at an extradition hearing. The following shall also be admitted as evidence, even if it would not otherwise be admissible under Canadian law:

> (a) the contents of the documents contained in the record of the case certified under subsection 33(3);

> (b) the contents of the documents that are submitted in conformity with the terms of an extradition agreement; and

> (c) evidence adduced by the person sought for extradition that is relevant to the tests set out in subsection 29(1) if the judge considers it reliable.

(2) Exception — Canadian evidence — Evidence gathered in Canada must satisfy the rules of evidence under Canadian law in order to be admitted.

33. (1) Record of the case — The record of the case must include

> (a) in the case of a person sought for the purpose of prosecution, a document summarizing the evidence available to the extradition partner for use in the prosecution; and

> (b) in the case of a person sought for the imposition or enforcement of a sentence,

>> (i) a copy of the document that records the conviction of the person, and

>> (ii) a document describing the conduct for which the person was convicted.

(2) Other documents — record of the case — A record of the case may include other relevant documents, including documents respecting the identification of the person sought for extradition.

(3) Certification of record of the case — A record of the case may not be admitted unless

> (a) in the case of a person sought for the purpose of prosecution, a judicial or prosecuting authority of the extradition partner certifies that the evidence summarized or contained in the record of the case is available for trial and

>> (i) is sufficient under the law of the extradition partner to justify prosecution, or

>> (ii) was gathered according to the law of the extradition partner; or

> (b) in the case of a person sought for the imposition or enforcement of a sentence, a judicial, prosecuting or correctional authority of the extradition partner certifies that the documents in the record of the case are accurate.

(4) Authentication not required — No authentication of documents is required unless a relevant extradition agreement provides otherwise.

(5) Record of the case and supplements — For the purposes of this section, a record of the case includes any supplement added to it.

34. Oath or solemn affirmation — A document is admissible whether or not it is solemnly affirmed or under oath.

35. No proof of signature — A document purporting to have been signed by a judicial, prosecuting or correctional authority, or a public officer, of the extradition partner shall be admitted without proof of the signature or official character of the person appearing to have signed it.

36. Translated documents — A translation of a document into one of Canada's official languages shall be admitted without any further formality.

37. Evidence of identity — The following are evidence that the person before the court is the person referred to in the order of arrest, the document that records the conviction or any other document that is presented to support the request:

(a) the fact that the name of the person before the court is similar to the name that is in the documents submitted by the extradition partner; and

(b) the fact that the physical characteristics of the person before the court are similar to those evidenced in a photograph, finger-print or other description of the person.

Judge's Report

38. (1) Report of the judge — A judge who issues an order of committal of a person to await surrender shall transmit to the Minister the following documents:

(a) a copy of the order;

(b) a copy of the evidence adduced at the hearing that has not already been transmitted to the Minister; and

(c) any report that the judge thinks fit.

(2) Right to appeal — When the judge orders the committal of a person, the judge shall inform the person that they will not be surrendered until after the expiry of 30 days and that the person has a right to appeal the order and to apply for judicial interim release.

Property

39. (1) Property seized — Subject to a relevant extradition agreement, a judge who makes an order of committal may order that any thing that was seized when the person was arrested and that may be used in the prosecution of the person for the offence for which the extradition was requested be transferred to the extradition partner at the time the person is surrendered.

(2) Conditions of order — The judge may include in the order any conditions that the judge considers desirable, including conditions

(a) respecting the preservation and return to Canada of a thing; and

(b) respecting the protection of the interests of third parties.

Powers of Minister

40. (1) Surrender — The Minister may, within a period of 90 days after the date of a person's committal to await surrender, personally order that the person be surrendered to the extradition partner.

(2) When refugee claim — Before making an order under subsection (1) with respect to a person who has claimed Convention refugee status under section 44 of the *Immigration Act*, the Minister shall consult with the minister responsible for that Act.

(3) Powers of the Minister — The Minister may seek any assurances that the Minister considers appropriate from the extradition partner, or may subject the surrender to any conditions that the Minister considers appropriate, including a condition that the person not be prosecuted, nor that a sentence be imposed on or enforced against the person, in respect of any offence or conduct other than that referred to in the order of surrender.

(4) No surrender — If the Minister subjects surrender of a person to assurances or conditions, the order of surrender shall not be executed until the Minister is satisfied that the assurances are given or the conditions agreed to by the extradition partner.

(5) Extension of time — If the person has made submissions to the Minister under section 43 and the Minister is of the opinion that further time is needed to act on those submissions, the Minister may extend the period referred to in subsection (1) for one additional period that does not exceed 60 days.

Proposed Amendment — 40(5)

(5) Extension of time — If the person has made submissions to the Minister under section 43 and the Minister is of the opinion that further time is needed to act on those submissions, the Minister may extend the period referred to in subsection (1) as follows:

(a) if the person is the subject of a request for surrender by the International Criminal Court, and an issue has been raised as to the admissibility of the case or the jurisdiction of that Court, for a period ending not more than 45 days after the Court's ruling on the issue; or

(b) in any other case, for one additional period that does not exceed 60 days.

2000, c. 24, s. 51 [Not in force at date of publication.]

(6) Notice of extension of time — If an appeal has been filed under section 50 and the Minister has extended the period referred to in subsection (1), the Minister shall file with the court of appeal a notice of extension of time before the expiry of that period.

41. (1) When appeal pending — The Minister may postpone the making of the order of surrender if

(a) an appeal has been filed under section 50;

(b) the Minister files a notice of postponement with the court of appeal before the expiry of the period referred to in subsection 40(1); and

(c) the order is made not later than 45 days after the date of the decision of the court of appeal.

(2) No further deferral of appeal — When the Minister has filed a notice of postponement with the court of appeal under paragraph (1)(b), that court may not defer the hearing of the appeal under subsection 51(2).

42. Amendments — The Minister may amend a surrender order at any time before its execution.

Submissions

43. (1) Submissions — The person may, at any time before the expiry of 30 days after the date of the committal, make submissions to the Minister in respect of any ground that would be relevant to the Minister in making a decision in respect of the surrender of the person.

(2) Late acceptance of submissions — The Minister may accept submissions even after the expiry of those 30 days in circumstances that the Minister considers appropriate.

Reasons for Refusal

44. (1) When order not to be made — The Minister shall refuse to make a surrender order if the Minister is satisfied that

(a) the surrender would be unjust or oppressive having regard to all the relevant circumstances; or

(b) the request for extradition is made for the purpose of prosecuting or punishing the person by reason of their race, religion, nationality, ethnic origin, language, colour, political opinion, sex, sexual orientation, age, mental or physical disability or status or that the person's position may be prejudiced for any of those reasons.

(2) When Minister may refuse to make order — The Minister may refuse to make a surrender order if the Minister is satisfied that the conduct in respect of which the request for extradition is made is punishable by death under the laws that apply to the extradition partner.

45. (1) Refusal in extradition agreement — The reasons for the refusal of surrender contained in a relevant extradition agreement, other than a multilateral extradition agreement, or the absence of reasons for refusal in such an agreement, prevail over sections 46 and 47.

(2) Exception — multilateral extradition agreement — The reasons for the refusal of surrender contained in a relevant multilateral extradition agreement prevail over sections 46 and 47 only to the extent of any inconsistency between either of those sections and those provisions.

46. (1) When order not to be made — The Minister shall refuse to make a surrender order if the Minister is satisfied that

(a) the prosecution of a person is barred by prescription or limitation under the law that applies to the extradition partner;

(b) the conduct in respect of which extradition is sought is a military offence that is not also an offence under criminal law; or

(c) the conduct in respect of which extradition is sought is a political offence or an offence of a political character.

(2) Restriction — For the purpose of subparagraph (1)(c), conduct that constitutes an offence mentioned in a multilateral extradition agreement for which Canada, as a party, is obliged to extradite the person or submit the matter to its appropriate authority for prosecution does not constitute a political offence or an offence of a political character. The following conduct also does not constitute a political offence or an offence of a political character:

(a) murder or manslaughter;

(b) inflicting serious bodily harm;

(c) sexual assault;

(d) kidnapping, abduction, hostage-taking or extortion;

(e) using explosives, incendiaries, devices or substances in circumstances in which human life is likely to be endangered or serious bodily harm or substantial property damage is likely to be caused; and

(f) an attempt or conspiracy to engage in, counselling, aiding or abetting another person to engage in, or being an accessory after the fact in relation to, the conduct referred to in any of paragraphs (a) to (e).

47. When Minister may refuse to make order — The Minister may refuse to make a surrender order if the Minister is satisfied that

(a) the person would be entitled, if that person were tried in Canada, to be discharged under the laws of Canada because of a previous acquittal or conviction;

(b) the person was convicted in their absence and could not, on surrender, have the case reviewed;

(c) the person was under the age of 18 years at the time of the offence and the law that applies to them in the territory over which the extradition partner has jurisdiction is not consistent with the fundamental principles governing the *Young Offenders Act*;

(d) the conduct in respect of which the request for extradition is made is the subject of criminal proceedings in Canada against the person; or

(e) none of the conduct on which the extradition partner bases its request occurred in the territory over which the extradition partner has jurisdiction.

Proposed Addition — 47.1

47.1 When grounds for refusal do not apply — The grounds for refusal set out in sections 44, 46 and 47 do not apply in the case of a person who is the subject of a request for surrender by the International Criminal Court.

2000, c. 24, s. 52 [Not in force at date of publication.]

48. (1) Discharge — If the Minister decides not to make a surrender order, the Minister shall order the discharge of the person.

(2) When refugee claim — When the Minister orders the discharge of a person and the person has claimed Convention refugee status under section 44 of the *Immigration Act*, the Minister shall send copies of all relevant documents to the minister responsible for that Act.

Appeal

49. Appeal — A person may appeal against an order of committal — or the Attorney General, on behalf of the extradition partner, may appeal the discharge of the person or a stay of proceedings — to the court of appeal of the province in which the order of committal, the order discharging the person or the order staying the proceedings was made,

(a) on a ground of appeal that involves a question of law alone;

(b) on a ground of appeal that involves a question of fact or a question of mixed law and fact, with leave of the court of appeal or a judge of the court of appeal; or

(c) on a ground of appeal not set out in paragraph (a) or (b) that appears to the court of appeal to be a sufficient ground of appeal, with leave of the court of appeal.

50. (1) Notice of appeal — An appellant who proposes to appeal to a court of appeal or to obtain the leave of that court to appeal must give notice of appeal or notice of the application for leave to appeal not later than 30 days after the decision of the judge with respect to the committal or discharge of the person, or the stay of proceedings, as the case may be, in any manner that may be directed by the rules of court.

(2) Extension of time — The court of appeal or a judge of the court of appeal may, either before or after the expiry of the 30 days referred to in subsection (1), extend the time within which notice of appeal or notice of an application for leave to appeal may be given.

51. (1) Hearing of appeal — An appeal under this Act shall be scheduled for hearing by the court of appeal at an early date whether that date is in or out of the prescribed sessions of that court.

(2) Deferral of appeal — The hearing of an appeal against an order of committal may be deferred by the court of appeal until the Minister makes a decision in respect of the surrender of the person under section 40.

52. (1) Provisions of the Criminal Code to apply — Sections 677, 678.1, 682 to 685 and 688 of the *Criminal Code* apply, with any modifications that the circumstances require, to appeals under this Act.

(2) Rules — Unless inconsistent with the provisions of this Act, rules made by the court of appeal under section 482 of the *Criminal Code* in relation to appeals to that court under that Act apply, with any modifications that the circumstances require, to appeals under this Act.

53. Powers of the court of appeal — On the hearing of an appeal against an order of committal of a person, the court of appeal may

(a) allow the appeal, in respect of any offence in respect of which the person has been committed, if it is of the opinion

(i) that the order of committal should be set aside on the ground that it is unreasonable or cannot be supported by the evidence,

(ii) that the order of committal should be set aside on the ground of a wrong decision on a question of law, or

(iii) that, on any ground, there was a miscarriage of justice; or

(b) dismiss the appeal

(i) if it does not allow the appeal on any ground referred to in paragraph (a), or

(ii) even though the court of appeal is of the opinion that on the ground referred to in subparagraph (a)(ii) the appeal may be decided in favour of the appellant, if it is of the opinion that no substantial wrong or miscarriage of justice has occurred and the order of committal should be upheld.

54. Effect of allowing appeal — If the court of appeal allows an appeal under paragraph 53(a), it shall

(a) set aside the order of committal and

(i) discharge the person, or

(ii) order a new extradition hearing; or

(b) amend the order of committal to exclude an offence in respect of which the court is of the opinion that the person has not been properly committed on a ground referred to in subparagraph 53(a)(i), (ii) or (iii).

55. (1) Powers — On the hearing of an appeal against the discharge of a person or against a stay of proceedings, the court of appeal may

(a) allow the appeal and set aside the order of discharge or stay, if it is of the opinion

(i) that the order of discharge should be set aside on the ground that it is unreasonable or cannot be supported by the evidence,

(ii) that the order of discharge or the stay of proceedings should be set aside on the ground of a wrong decision on a question of law, or

(iii) that, on any ground, there was a miscarriage of justice; or

(b) dismiss the appeal.

(2) Order for new extradition hearing or committal — The court of appeal may, if it sets aside a stay of proceedings, order a new extradition hearing. The court of appeal may, if it sets aside an order of discharge, order a new extradition hearing or order the committal of the person.

56. (1) Deferral of Supreme Court appeal — The Supreme Court may defer, until the Minister makes a decision with respect to the surrender of the person under section 40, the hearing of an application for leave to appeal, or the hearing of an appeal, from a decision of the court of appeal on an appeal taken under section 49, or on any other appeal in respect of a matter arising under this Act.

(2) Deferral of Supreme Court appeal — The Supreme Court may also, if an application for judicial review is made under section 57 or otherwise, defer the hearing until the court of appeal makes its determination on the application.

Judicial Review of Minister's Order

57. (1) Review of order — Despite the *Federal Court Act*, the court of appeal of the province in which the committal of the person was ordered has exclusive original jurisdiction to hear and determine applications for judicial review under this Act, made in respect of the decision of the Minister under section 40.

(2) Application — An application for judicial review may be made by the person.

(3) Time limitation — An application for judicial review shall be made, in accordance with the rules of court of the court of appeal, within 30 days after the time the decision referred to in subsection (1) was first communicated by the Minister to the person, or within any further time that the court of appeal, either before or after the expiry of those 30 days, may fix or allow.

(4) Section 679 of the Criminal Code — Section 679 of the *Criminal Code* applies, with any modifications that the circumstances require, to an application for judicial review.

(5) Hearing of application — An application for judicial review shall be scheduled for hearing by the court of appeal at an early date whether that date is in or out of the prescribed sessions of that court.

(6) Powers of court of appeal — On an application for judicial review, the court of appeal may

(a) order the Minister to do any act or thing that the Minister has unlawfully failed or refused to do or has unreasonably delayed in doing; or

(b) declare invalid or unlawful, quash, set aside, set aside and refer back for determination in accordance with any directions that it considers appropriate, prohibit or restrain the decision of the Minister referred to in subsection (1).

(7) Grounds of review — The court of appeal may grant relief under this section on any of the grounds on which the Trial Division of the Federal Court of Canada may grant relief under subsection 18.1(4) of the *Federal Court Act*.

(8) Defect in form or technical irregularity — If the sole ground for relief established in an application for judicial review is a defect in form or a technical irregularity, the court of appeal may

(a) refuse the relief if it finds that no substantial wrong or miscarriage of justice has occurred; or

(b) in the case of a defect in form or a technical irregularity in the decision, make an order validating the order, to have effect from the time and on the terms that it considers appropriate.

(9) One hearing by court of appeal — If an appeal under section 49 or any other appeal in respect of a matter arising under this Act is pending, the court of appeal may join the hearing of that appeal with the hearing of an application for judicial review.

(10) Provincial rules of judicial review apply — Unless inconsistent with the provisions of this Act, all laws, including rules, respecting judicial review in force in the province of the court of appeal apply, with any modifications that the circumstances require, to applications under this section.

Order of Surrender

58. Contents of the surrender order — An order of surrender must

(a) contain the name of the person who is to be surrendered;

(b) describe the offence in respect of which the extradition is requested, the offence for which the committal was ordered or the conduct for which the person is to be surrendered;

(c) state the extradition partner to which the person is to be conveyed;

(d) direct the person who has custody of the person to be surrendered to deliver them into the custody of the person or a member of the class of persons referred to in paragraph (e);

(e) designate the person or class of persons authorized for the purposes of section 60;

(f) set out any assurances or conditions to which the surrender is subject;

(g) fix, in the case of postponement of surrender under section 64, the period of time at or before the expiry of which the person is to be surrendered; and

(h) fix, in the case of a temporary surrender under section 66,

    (i) the period of time at or before the expiry of which the person to be surrendered must be returned to Canada, and

    (ii) the period of time at or before the expiry of which final surrender shall take place.

59. Surrender for other offences — Subject to a relevant extradition agreement, the Minister may, if the request for extradition is based on more than one offence, order the surrender of a person for all the offences even if not all of them fulfil the requirements set out in section 3, if

(a) the person is being surrendered for at least one offence that fulfils the requirements set out in section 3; and

(b) all the offences relate to conduct that, had it occurred in Canada, would have constituted offences that are punishable under the laws of Canada.

60. Power to convey — On the execution of a surrender order, the person or persons designated under paragraph 58(e) shall have the authority to receive, hold in custody and convey the person into the territory over which the extradition partner has jurisdiction.

61. (1) Escape — If the person escapes while in custody, the law that applies with respect to a person who is accused or convicted of a crime against the laws of Canada and who escapes applies with respect to the person.

(2) Arrest — If the person escapes while in custody, the person or member of the class of persons having custody of the person has the power to arrest them in fresh pursuit.

62. (1) Delay before surrender — No person may be surrendered

(a) until a period of 30 days has expired after the date of the committal for surrender; or

(b) if an appeal or a judicial review in respect of a matter arising under this Act, or any appeal from an appeal or judicial review, is pending, until after the date of the final decision of the court on the appeal or judicial review.

(2) Waiver of period of time — The person may waive the period referred to in paragraph (1)(a) if they do so in writing.

63. Place of surrender — A surrender may take place at any place within or outside Canada that is agreed to by Canada and the extradition partner.

64. (1) Postponement of surrender — Unless the Minister orders otherwise, a surrender order made in respect of a person accused of an offence within Canadian jurisdiction or who is serving a sentence in Canada after a conviction for an offence, other than an offence with respect to the conduct to which the order relates does not take effect until the person has been discharged, whether by acquittal, by expiry of the sentence or otherwise.

(2) Offence before or after surrender — For greater certainty, the person need not have been accused of the offence within Canadian jurisdiction before the surrender order was made.

65. Return to Canada — If a person returns to Canada after surrender before the expiry of a sentence that they were serving in Canada at the time of surrender, the remaining part of the sentence must be served.

Temporary Surrender

66. (1) Temporary surrender — The Minister may order the temporary surrender to an extradition partner of a person who is ordered committed under section 29 while serving a term of imprisonment in Canada so that the extradition partner may prosecute the person or to ensure the person's presence in respect of appeal proceedings that affect the person, on condition that the extradition partner give the assurances referred to in subsections (3) and (4).

(2) Time limits — An order of temporary surrender is subject to the time limits set out in subsection 40(1) and (5) and paragraph 41(1)(c).

(3) Assurances — The Minister may not order temporary surrender under subsection (1) unless the extradition partner gives an assurance that the person will remain in custody while temporarily surrendered to the extradition partner and

    (a) in the case of temporary surrender for a trial, that the person will be returned within 30 days after the completion of the trial, unless a relevant extradition agreement provides for another time limit; and

    (b) in the case of temporary surrender for an appeal, that the person will be returned within 30 days after the completion of the proceedings for which the presence of the person was required, unless a relevant extradition agreement provides for another time limit.

(4) Time limit — The Minister may require the extradition partner to give an assurance that the person will be returned no later than a specified date or that the person will be returned on request of the Minister.

(5) Assurances in extradition agreements — Any assurance referred to in subsections (3) and (4) that is included in a relevant extradition agreement need not be repeated as a specific assurance.

(6) Final surrender after temporary surrender — A person shall, subject to subsection (7), be surrendered to the extradition partner without a further request for extradition after the person

    (a) has been temporarily surrendered;

    (b) has been convicted by the extradition partner and had a term of imprisonment imposed on them;

    (c) has been returned to Canada under subsection (4); and

(d) has finished serving the portion of the sentence that they were serving in custody in Canada at the time of the temporary surrender, unless the Minister orders that they be surrendered earlier.

(7) No final surrender if circumstances warrant — The Minister may, in circumstances that the Minister considers appropriate, revoke the surrender order and order the discharge of the person.

(8) Notice — The authority who has custody of the person to be surrendered under subsection (6) shall give the Minister reasonable notice of the time when the portion of the person's sentence to be served in custody is to expire.

(9) Final surrender when Canadian sentence expires — When the sentence that the person is serving in Canada expires during the period during which the person is temporarily surrendered to an extradition partner, the surrender is considered to be a final surrender.

(10) Waiver of return — The Minister may, after consultation with the Solicitor General of Canada or the appropriate provincial minister responsible for corrections, waive the return of the person by the extradition partner.

(11) Final surrender despite subsection 3(3) — A person may be surrendered under subsection (6) even if the term of imprisonment imposed by the extradition partner, or the portion of the term remaining to be served, is less than that required by subsection 3(3).

67. Order for surrender — An order of surrender prevails over a prior warrant or other order under which the person to whom it applies is otherwise detained in Canada or at liberty under terms and conditions.

68. Calculation of sentence — For the purposes of calculating a sentence that a person to whom an order of temporary surrender applies is serving in Canada at the time of the temporary surrender, the person

(a) is credited with any time that is served in custody outside Canada under a temporary surrender order; and

(b) remains eligible for remission in accordance with the laws of the correctional system under which the person was serving the sentence in Canada.

Remedy

69. Remedy in case of delay — A judge of the superior court of the province in which the person is detained who has the power to grant a writ of *habeas corpus*, may, on application made by or on behalf of the person, and on proof that reasonable notice of the intention to make the application has been given to the Minister, order the person to be discharged out of custody unless sufficient cause is shown against the discharge if

(a) the Minister has not made an order of surrender under section 40

(i) before the expiry of the period referred to in subsection 40(1) and any additional period referred to in subsection 40(5), or

(ii) if a notice of postponement has been filed under paragraph 41(1)(b), before the expiry of 45 days after the date of the decision of the court of appeal referred to in paragraph 41(1)(c); or

(b) the person is not surrendered and conveyed to the extradition partner

(i) within 45 days after the order of surrender is made by the Minister under section 40, or

(ii) if an appeal or judicial review in respect of any matter arising under this Act, or an appeal from such an appeal or judicial review, is pending, within 45 days after the final decision of the court is made,

over and above, in any case referred to in subparagraph (i) or (ii), the time required to convey the person to the extradition partner.

Consent

70. (1) Consent to committal — A person may, at any time after the issuance of an authority to proceed, consent, in writing and before a judge, to committal.

(2) Judge to order committal — A judge before whom a person consents under subsection (1) shall

(a) order the committal of the person into custody to await surrender to the extradition partner; and

(b) transmit a copy of the consent to the Minister.

71. (1) Consent to surrender — A person may, at any time after arrest or appearance, consent, in writing and before a judge, to being surrendered.

(2) Judge to order surrender — A judge before whom a person consents to being surrendered shall

(a) order the committal of the person into custody to await surrender to the extradition partner; and

(b) transmit a copy of the consent to the Minister.

(3) When Minister receives consent — The Minister may, as soon as is feasible after receiving a consent to surrender, personally order that the person be surrendered to the extradition partner.

(4) Sections not applicable — When a person consents to being surrendered to the extradition partner, the following sections do not apply:

(a) section 43 (submissions to the Minister);

(b) section 44 (reasons for refusal);

(c) section 48 (discharge of person);

(d) section 57 (judicial review of Minister's decision); and

(e) paragraph 62(1)(a) (delay before surrender).

Waiver of Extradition

72. (1) Waiving extradition — A person may, at any time after arrest or appearance, waive extradition in writing and before a judge.

(2) Judge to inform person — A judge before whom a person gives a waiver under subsection (1) must inform the person

    (a) of the consequences of the waiver including the consequences of waiving the protection of specialty; and

    (b) that they will be conveyed without delay to the extradition partner.

(3) Judge to order conveyance — The judge shall

    (a) order the conveyance in custody of the person to the extradition partner; and

    (b) transmit a copy of the waiver and the order to the Minister.

(4) Conveyance order — The conveyance order must

    (a) contain the name of the person who is to be conveyed; and

    (b) state the extradition partner to which the person is to be conveyed.

73. (1) Escape — If the person escapes while in custody for conveyance, the law that applies with respect to a person who is accused or convicted of a crime against the laws of Canada and who escapes applies with respect to the person.

(2) Arrest — If the person escapes while in custody for conveyance, the person in whose custody the person is has the power to arrest them in fresh pursuit.

Transit

74. (1) Transit — The Minister may consent to the transit in Canada of a person surrendered by one State or entity to another, subject to any terms and conditions that the Minister considers appropriate.

(2) Consent to transit — A consent to transit constitutes authority to the officer of the surrendering State or entity or the receiving State or entity to keep the person in custody while in Canada.

(3) Sections to apply — Sections 58 (contents of surrender order), 60 (power to convey), 61 (escape) and 69 (remedy in case of delay) apply, with any modifications that the circumstances require, in respect of the consent to transit.

75. (1) Special authorization — The Minister may, in order to give effect to a request for consent to transit, authorize a person in a State or entity who is a member of an inadmissible class of persons described in section 19 of the *Immigration Act* to come into Canada at a place designated by the Minister and to go to and remain in a place in Canada so designated for the period specified by the Minister. The Minister may make the authorization subject to any conditions that the Minister considers desirable.

(2) Variation of authorization — The Minister may vary the terms of an authorization granted under subsection (1) and, in particular, may extend the period of time during which the person is authorized to remain in a place in Canada.

(3) Non-compliance with conditions of authorization — A person in respect of whom an authorization is granted under subsection (1) and who is found in a place in Canada other than the place designated in the authorization or in any place in Canada after the expiry of the period of time specified in the authorization or who fails to comply with some other condition of the authorization is, for the purposes of the *Immigration Act*, deemed to be a person who entered Canada as a visitor and remains in Canada after they have ceased to be a visitor.

76. Unscheduled landing — If a person being extradited from one State or entity to another arrives in Canada without prior consent to transit, a peace officer may, at the request of a public officer who has custody of the person being extradited while the person is being conveyed, hold the person in custody for a maximum period of 24 hours pending receipt by the Minister of a request for a consent to transit from the requesting State or entity.

Proposed Amendment — 76.

76. Unscheduled landing — If a person being extradited or surrendered from one State or entity to another arrives in Canada without prior consent to transit, a peace officer may, at the request of a public officer who has custody of the person while the person is being conveyed,

(a) if the person is being surrendered to the International Criminal Court, hold the person in custody for a maximum period of 96 hours pending receipt by the Minister of a request for a consent to transit from that Court; or

(b) in any other case, hold the person in custody for a maximum period of 24 hours pending receipt by the Minister of a request for a consent to transit from the requesting State or entity.

2000, c. 24, s. 53 [Not in force at date of publication.]

PART 3 — EXTRADITION TO CANADA

77. Definition of "competent authority" — In this Part, **"competent authority"** means

(a) in respect of a prosecution or imposition of a sentence — or of a disposition under the *Young Offenders Act* — the Attorney General, or the Attorney General of a province who is responsible for the prosecution of the case; and

(b) in respect of the enforcement of a sentence or a disposition under the *Young Offenders Act*,

(i) the Solicitor General of Canada, if the person would serve the sentence in a penitentiary, or

(ii) the appropriate provincial minister responsible for corrections, in any other case.

78. (1) Request by Canada for extradition — The Minister, at the request of a competent authority, may make a request to a State or entity for the extradition of a person for the purpose of prosecuting the person for — or imposing or enforcing a sentence, or making or enforcing a disposition under the *Young Offenders Act*, in respect of — an offence over which Canada has jurisdiction.

(2) Request for provisional arrest — The Minister, at the request of a competent authority, may make a request to a State or entity for the provisional arrest of the person.

79. (1) Order in respect of evidence — A judge may, for the purposes of acquiring evidence for a request for extradition, on the *ex parte* application of a competent authority, make any order that is necessary to

(a) secure the attendance of a witness at any place designated by the judge;

(b) secure the production as evidence of data that is recorded in any form;

(c) receive and record the evidence; and

(d) certify or authenticate the evidence in a manner and form that is required by the requested State or entity.

(2) Part XXII of the Criminal Code to apply — Part XXII of the *Criminal Code* applies, with any modifications that the circumstances require, to orders under subsection (1).

80. Specialty if person is in Canada — Subject to a relevant extradition agreement, a person who has been extradited to Canada by a requested State or entity shall not, unless the person has voluntarily left Canada after surrender or has had a reasonable opportunity of leaving Canada,

(a) be detained or prosecuted, or have a sentence imposed or executed, or a disposition made or executed under the *Young Offenders Act*, in Canada in respect of an offence that is alleged to have been committed, or was committed, before surrender other than

(i) the offence in respect of which the person was surrendered or an included offence,

(ii) another offence in respect of which the requested State or entity consents to the person being detained or prosecuted, or

(iii) another offence in respect of which the person consents to being detained or prosecuted; or

(b) be detained in Canada for the purpose of being surrendered to another State or entity for prosecution or for imposition or execution of a sentence in respect of an offence that is alleged to have been committed, or was committed, before surrender to Canada, unless the requested State or entity consents.

81. (1) Conveyance of surrendered person — A person who is surrendered to Canada by a requested State or entity may be brought into Canada by an agent of the requested State or entity if the Minister so authorizes and be delivered to an appropriate authority to be dealt with according to law.

(2) Power to convey — On the execution of a surrender order, the authorized agent of the requested State or entity shall have the authority to hold the person in custody in Canada until delivery under subsection (1).

(3) Escape — If the person escapes while in custody, the law that applies with respect to a person who is accused or convicted of a crime against the laws of Canada and who escapes applies with respect to the person.

(4) Arrest — If the person escapes, the authorized agent of the requested State or entity has the power to arrest them in fresh pursuit.

82. (1) Order of detention for temporary surrender — Subject to subsection (2), a judge shall, on application of the competent authority made at any time before the temporary surrender, order the detention in custody of a person who is serving a term of imprisonment or has otherwise lawfully been deprived of their liberty in a requested State or entity and whose temporary surrender Canada has requested for the purpose of prosecution or appeal.

(2) Time limit — The order must contain a provision that the person will not be detained in custody after

    (a) a date specified in the order;

    (b) in the case of surrender for a trial, days after the completion of the trial; or

    (c) in the case of surrender for an appeal, 30 days after the completion of the proceedings for which the presence of the person was required.

(3) Order of detention to prevail — An order made under subsection (1) prevails over an order made by a Canadian court, a judge of a Canadian court, a Canadian justice of the peace or any other person who has power in Canada to compel the appearance of a person, in respect of anything that occurred before the person is transferred to Canada.

(4) Variation of detention order — The judge who made the detention order or another judge may vary its terms and conditions and, in particular, may extend the duration of the detention.

(5) Return — Subject to subsection (6), the person shall be returned to the requested State or entity on completion of the proceedings in Canada for which the person was temporarily surrendered or on the expiry of the period set out in the order, whichever is sooner.

(6) Return if right of appeal — The person shall not be returned to the requested State or entity

    (a) if the person has been convicted in Canada, before 30 days after the conviction, unless the person or the competent authority declares that there will be no appeal; and

    (b) if the person has been acquitted, before 30 days after the acquittal, unless the competent authority declares that there will be no appeal.

(7) Return for appeal — The court of appeal may, on application, recommend that the Minister request another temporary surrender of a person who has been returned to the requested State or entity after trial, if the court of appeal is satisfied that the interests of justice require their presence for the appeal.

83. (1) Commencement of sentence or disposition — Subject to subsection (3), the sentence or disposition of a person who has been temporarily surrendered and who has been convicted and sentenced in Canada, or in respect of whom a disposition has been made under the *Young Offenders Act*, does not commence until their final extradition to Canada.

(2) Warrant of commital — The warrant of committal issued under the *Criminal Code* in respect of the person must state that the person is to be committed to custody to serve the sentence or disposition immediately on their final extradition to Canada.

(3) If concurrent sentences ordered — The sentencing judge may order that the person's sentence, or the disposition under the *Young Offenders Act*, be executed concurrently with the sentence they are serving in the requested State or entity, in which case the warrant of committal or order of disposition shall state that the person is to be committed to custody under subsection (2) only for any portion of the sentence remaining at the time of their final extradition to Canada or that the young person's disposition is to begin only on their final extradition to Canada.

PART 4 — TRANSITIONAL PROVISIONS, CONSEQUENTIAL AND RELATED AMENDMENTS AND REPEALS

Transitional Provisions

84. Cases pending — former Extradition Act — The *Extradition Act* repealed by section 129 of this Act applies to a matter respecting the extradition of a person as though it had not been repealed, if the hearing in respect of the extradition had already begun on the day on which this Act comes into force.

85. Cases pending — Fugitive Offenders Act — The *Fugitive Offenders Act* repealed by section 130 of this Act applies to a matter respecting the return under that Act of a person as though it had not been repealed, if the hearing before the provincial court judge in respect of the return had already begun on the day on which this Act comes into force.

Consequential Amendments

Corrections and Conditional Release Act, 1992, c. 20

86. Paragraph 121(1)(d) of the *Corrections and Conditional Release Act* is replaced by the following:

> (d) who is the subject of an order of surrender under the *Extradition Act* and who is to be detained until surrendered.

87. 1995, c. 42, s. 42 and par. 69(i)(E) — Subsection 128(3) of the Act is replaced by the following:

> (3) **Deeming** — Despite subsection (1), for the purposes of subsection 50(2) of the *Immigration Act* and section 40 of the *Extradition Act*, the sentence of an offender who has been released on full parole or statutory release is deemed to be completed unless the full parole or statutory release has been suspended, terminated or revoked or the offender has returned to Canada before the expiration of the sentence according to law.

Identification of Criminals Act, R.S., c.I-1

88. 1992, c. 47, s. 74(1) — Paragraph 2(1)(b) of the *Identification of Criminals Act* is replaced by the following:

> (b) any person who has been apprehended under the *Extradition Act*; or

Related Amendments

Canada Evidence Act, R.S., c. C-5

89. Section 46 of the *Canada Evidence Act* is replaced by the following:

> 46. (1) **Order for examination of witness in Canada** — If, on an application for that purpose, it is made to appear to any court or judge that any court or tribunal outside Canada, before which any civil, commercial or criminal matter is pending, is desirous of obtaining the testimony in relation to that matter of a party or witness within the jurisdiction of the first mentioned court, of the court to which the judge belongs or of the judge, the court or judge may, in its or their discretion, order the examination on oath on interrogatories, or otherwise, before any person or persons named in the order, of that party or witness accordingly, and by the same or any subsequent order may command the attendance of that party or witness for the purpose of being examined, and for the production of any writings or other documents mentioned in the order and of any other writings or documents relating to the matter in question that are in the possession or power of that party or witness.

> (2) **Video links, etc.** — For greater certainty, testimony for the purposes of subsection (1) may be given by means of technology that permits the

virtual presence of the party or witness before the court or tribunal outside Canada or that permits that court or tribunal, and the parties, to hear and examine the party or witness.

90. Section 50 of the Act is amended by adding the following after subsection (1):

(1.1) **Laws about witnesses to apply — video links etc.** — Despite subsection (1), when a party or witness gives evidence under subsection 46(2), the evidence shall be given as though they were physically before the court or tribunal outside Canada, for the purposes of the laws relating to evidence and procedure but only to the extent that giving the evidence would not disclose information otherwise protected by the Canadian law of non-disclosure of information or privilege.

(1.2) **Contempt of court in Canada** — When a party or witness gives evidence under subsection 46(2), the Canadian law relating to contempt of court applies with respect to a refusal by the party or witness to answer a question or to produce a writing or document referred to in subsection 46(1), as ordered under that subsection by the court or judge.

91. Subsection 51(2) of the Act is replaced by the following:

(2) **Letters rogatory** — In the absence of any order in relation to the evidence to be produced in support of the application referred to in subsection (1), letters rogatory from a court or tribunal outside Canada in which the civil, commercial or criminal matter is pending, are deemed and taken to be sufficient evidence in support of the application.

Criminal Code, R.S., c. C-46

92. (1) Section 131 of the *Criminal Code* is amended by adding the following after subsection (1):

(1.1) **Video links, etc.** — Subject to subsection (3), every person who gives evidence under subsection 46(2) of the *Canada Evidence Act*, or gives evidence or a statement pursuant to an order made under section 22.2 of the *Mutual Legal Assistance in Criminal Matters Act,* commits perjury who, with intent to mislead, makes a false statement knowing that it is false, whether or not the false statement was made under oath or solemn affirmation in accordance with subsection (1), so long as the false statement was made in accordance with any formalities required by the law of the place outside Canada in which the person is virtually present or heard.

(2) R.S., c. 27 (1st Supp.), s. 17 — Subsection 131(3) of the Act is replaced by the following:

(3) **Application** — Subsections (1) and (1.1) do not apply to a statement referred to in either of those subsections that is made by a person who is not specially permitted, authorized or required by law to make that statement.

93. Section 136 of the Act is amended by adding the following after subsection (1):

(1.1) **Evidence in specific cases** — Evidence given under section 714.1, 714.2, 714.3 or 714.4 or under subsection 46(2) of the *Canada Evidence Act* or evidence or a statement given pursuant to an order made under section 22.2 of the *Mutual Legal Assistance in Criminal Matters Act* is deemed to be evidence given by a witness in a judicial proceeding for the purposes of subsection (1).

94. The Act is amended by adding the following after section 700:

700.1 (1) **Video links, etc.** — If a person is to give evidence under section 714.1 or 714.3 or under subsection 46(2) of the *Canada Evidence Act* — or is to give evidence or a statement pursuant to an order made under section 22.2 of the *Mutual Legal Assistance in Criminal Matters Act* — at a place within the jurisdiction of a court referred to in subsection 699(1) or (2) where the technology is available, a subpoena shall be issued out of the court to order the person to give that evidence at such a place.

(2) **Sections of Criminal Code** — Sections 699, 700 and 701 to 703.2 apply, with any modifications that the circumstances require, to a subpoena issued under this section.

95. The Act is amended by adding the following after section 714:

Video and Audio Evidence

714.1 **Video links, etc.** — **witness in Canada** — A court may order that a witness in Canada give evidence by means of technology that permits the witness to testify elsewhere in Canada in the virtual presence of the parties and the court, if the court is of the opinion that it would be appropriate in all the circumstances, including

(a) the location and personal circumstances of the witness;

(b) the costs that would be incurred if the witness had to be physically present; and

(c) the nature of the witness' anticipated evidence.

714.2 (1) **Video links, etc.** — **witness outside Canada** — A court shall receive evidence given by a witness outside Canada by means of technology that permits the witness to testify in the virtual presence of the parties and the court unless one of the parties satisfies the court that the reception of such testimony would be contrary to the principles of fundamental justice.

(2) **Notice** — A party who wishes to call a witness to give evidence under subsection (1) shall give notice to the court before which the evidence is to be given and the other parties of their intention to do so not less than ten days before the witness is scheduled to testify.

714.3 **Audio evidence** — **witness in Canada** — The court may order that a witness in Canada give evidence by means of technology that permits the parties and the court to hear and examine the witness elsewhere in Canada, if the court is of the opinion that it would be appropriate, considering all the circumstances including

(a) the location and personal circumstances of the witness;

(b) the costs that would be incurred if the witness had to be physically present;

(c) the nature of the witness' anticipated evidence; and

(d) any potential prejudice to either of the parties caused by the fact that the witness would not be seen by them.

714.4 Audio evidence — witness outside Canada — The court may receive evidence given by a witness outside Canada by means of technology that permits the parties and the court in Canada to hear and examine the witness, if the court is of the opinion that it would be appropriate, considering all the circumstances including

(a) the nature of the witness' anticipated evidence; and

(b) any potential prejudice to either of the parties caused by the fact that the witness would not be seen by them.

714.5 Oath or affirmation — The evidence given under section 714.2 or 714.4 shall be given

(a) under oath or affirmation in accordance with Canadian law;

(b) under oath or affirmation in accordance with the law in the place in which the witness is physically present; or

(c) in any other manner that demonstrates that the witness understands that they must tell the truth.

714.6 Other laws about witnesses to apply — When a witness who is outside Canada gives evidence under section 714.2 or 714.4, the evidence is deemed to be given in Canada, and given under oath or affirmation in accordance with Canadian law, for the purposes of the laws relating to evidence, procedure, perjury and contempt of court.

714.7 Costs of technology — A party who wishes to call a witness to give evidence by means of the technology referred to in section 714.1, 714.2, 714.3 or 714.4 shall pay any costs associated with the use of the technology.

714.8 Consent — Nothing in sections 714.1 to 714.7 is to be construed as preventing a court from receiving evidence by means of the technology referred to in sections 714.1 to 714.4 if the parties so consent.

Immigration Act, R.S., c. I-2

96. Section 69.1 of the *Immigration Act* is amended by adding the following after subsection (11):

> (12) **If authority to proceed under Extradition Act** — If an authority to proceed has been issued under section 15 of the *Extradition Act* with respect to a person for an offence under Canadian law that is punishable under an Act of Parliament by a maximum term of imprisonment of 10 years or more, a hearing under subsection (1) or (2) shall not be commenced with respect to the person, or if commenced, shall be adjourned, until the final decision under that Act with respect to the discharge or surrender of the person has been made.

> (13) **When person discharged under Extradition Act** — If the person is finally discharged under the *Extradition Act*, the hearing may be commenced or continued, or the Refugee Division may proceed, as though there had not been any proceedings under the *Extradition Act*.

> (14) **When person ordered surrendered under Extradition Act** — If the person is ordered surrendered by the Minister of Justice under the *Extradition Act* and the offence for which the person was committed by the judge under section 29 of that Act is punishable under an Act of Parliament by a maximum term of imprisonment of 10 years or more, the order of surrender is deemed to be a decision by the Refugee Division that the person is not a Convention refugee because of paragraph (b) of Section F of its Article 1, except that no appeal or judicial review of the decision shall be permitted except to the extent that a judicial review of the order of surrender is provided for under the *Extradition Act*.

> (15) **If no claim made before Extradition Act order** — For greater certainty, if the person has not made a claim under section 44 before the order of surrender referred to in subsection (14), the person may not do so before the surrender.

Mutual Legal Assistance in Criminal Matters Act, R.S., c. 30 (4th Supp.)

97. (1) The definitions "foreign state" and "treaty" in subsection 2(1) of the *Mutual Legal Assistance in Criminal Matters Act* are repealed.

(2) The definitions "offence" and "request" in subsection 2(1) of the Act are replaced by the following:

> "offence" means an offence within the meaning of the relevant agreement;

> "request" means a request for assistance presented pursuant to an agreement;

(3) Subsection 2(1) of the Act is amended by adding the following in alphabetical order:

> "agreement" means a treaty, convention or other international agreement that is in force, to which Canada is a party and that contains a provision respecting mutual legal assistance in criminal matters;

> "state or entity" means

>> (a) a state, a province, state or political subdivision of the state, or a colony, dependency, possession, protectorate, condominium, trust territory or any territory falling under the jurisdiction of the state, that is a party to an agreement with Canada, or

>> (b) an international criminal court or tribunal, the name of which appears in the schedule;

(4) Subsection 2(2) of the Act is repealed.

98. Subsection 3(2) of the Act is replaced by the following:

> (2) **Preservation of informal arrangements** — Nothing in this Act or an agreement shall be construed so as to abrogate or derogate from an arrangement or practice respecting cooperation between a Canadian competent authority and a foreign or international authority or organization.

99. Sections 4 and 5 of the Act are replaced by the following:

> 4. (1) **Designation** — The names of international criminal courts and tribunals that appear in the schedule are designated as states or entities for the purpose of this Act.

> (2) **Amendments to schedule** — The Minister of Foreign Affairs may, with the agreement of the Minister, by order, add to or delete from the schedule the names of international criminal courts and tribunals.

PUBLICATION OF AGREEMENTS

> 5. (1) **Publication in Canada Gazette** — Unless the agreement has been published under subsection (2), an agreement — or the provisions respecting mutual legal assistance in criminal matters contained in a convention or other international agreement — must be published in the *Canada Gazette* no later than 60 days after it comes into force.

> (2) **Publication in Canada Treaty Series** — An agreement — or the provisions respecting mutual legal assistance in criminal matters contained in a convention or other international agreement — may be published in the *Canada Treaty Series* and, if so published, the publication must be no later than 60 days after it comes into force.

> (3) **Judicial notice** — Agreements and provisions published in the *Canada Gazette* or the *Canada Treaty Series* are to be judicially noticed.

100. 1995, c. 5, par. 25(1)(v) — Subsections 6(1) to (3) of the Act are replaced by the following:

6. (1) **Administrative arrangements** — If there is no agreement between Canada and a state or entity, or the state's or entity's name does not appear in the schedule, the Minister of Foreign Affairs may, with the agreement of the Minister, enter into an administrative arrangement with the state or entity providing for legal assistance with respect to an investigation specified in the arrangement relating to an act that, if committed in Canada, would be an indictable offence.

(2) **Administrative arrangements** — If an agreement expressly states that legal assistance may be provided with respect to acts that do not constitute an offence within the meaning of the agreement, the Minister of Foreign Affairs may, in exceptional circumstances and with the agreement of the Minister, enter into an administrative arrangement with the state or entity concerned, providing for legal assistance with respect to an investigation specified in the arrangement relating to an act that, if committed in Canada, would be a contravention of an Act of Parliament or of the legislature of a province.

(3) **Nature of administrative arrangement** — An administrative arrangement entered into under subsection (1) or (2) may be implemented by the Minister, pursuant to this Act, in the same manner as an agreement.

101. Sections 7 and 8 of the Act are replaced by the following:

7. (1) **Functions of Minister** — The Minister is responsible for the implementation of every agreement and the administration of this Act.

(2) **Agreement and Act to apply** — When a request is presented to the Minister by a state or entity or a Canadian competent authority, the Minister shall deal with the request in accordance with the relevant agreement and this Act.

PART I — FOREIGN INVESTIGATIONS OR OTHER PROCEEDINGS IN RESPECT OF OFFENCES

Implementation

8. (1) **Limitation — requests under agreements** — If a request for mutual legal assistance is made under an agreement, the Minister may not give effect to the request by means of the provisions of this Part unless the agreement provides for mutual legal assistance with respect to the subject-matter of the request.

(2) **Request by state or entity in schedule** — If a request for mutual legal assistance is made by a state or entity whose name appears in the schedule, the Minister may give effect by means of the provisions of this Part to a request with respect to any subject-matter.

102. (1) Subsection 9(1) of the Act is replaced by the following:

9. (1) **Standing and jurisdiction** — When the Minister approves a request of a state or entity to enforce the payment of a fine imposed in respect of an offence by a court of criminal jurisdiction of the state or entity, a court in Canada has jurisdiction to enforce the payment of the fine, and the fine is recoverable in civil proceedings instituted by the state or entity, as if the fine had been imposed by a court in Canada.

(2) Subsection 9(3) of the Act is replaced by the following:

(3) **Definition of "fine"** — For the purposes of this section, "fine" includes any pecuniary penalty determined by a court of criminal jurisdiction of a state or entity to represent the value of any property, benefit or advantage, irrespective of its location, obtained or derived directly or indirectly as a result of the commission of an offence.

103. Subsection 11(1) of the Act is replaced by the following:

11. **Approval of request to search or seize** — (1) When the Minister approves a request of a state or entity to have a search or a seizure carried out in Canada regarding an offence with respect to which the state or entity has jurisdiction, the Minister shall provide a competent authority with any documents or information necessary to apply for a search warrant.

104. (1) Paragraph 12(1)(a) of the Act is replaced by the following:

(a) an offence has been committed with respect to which the state or entity has jurisdiction;

(2) Paragraph 12(4)(b) of the Act is replaced by the following:

(b) state that, at that hearing, an order will be sought for the sending to the state or entity of the records or things seized in execution of the warrant; and

105. The portion of paragraph 15(1)(b) of the Act before subparagraph (i) is replaced by the following:

(b) in any other case, order that a record or thing seized in execution of the warrant be sent to the state or entity mentioned in subsection 11(1) and include in the order any terms and conditions that the judge considers desirable, including terms and conditions

106. Section 16 of the Act is replaced by the following:

16. **Terms and conditions** — No record or thing seized that has been ordered under section 15 to be sent to the state or entity mentioned in subsection 11(1) shall be so sent until the Minister is satisfied that the state or entity has agreed to comply with any terms or conditions imposed in respect of the sending abroad of the record or thing.

107. Subsection 17(1) of the Act is replaced by the following:

17. (1) **Approval of request to obtain evidence** — When the Minister approves a request of a state or entity to obtain, by means of an order of a judge, evidence regarding an offence with respect to which the state or entity has jurisdiction, the Minister shall provide a competent authority with any documents or information necessary to apply for the order.

108. (1) Paragraph 18(1)(a) of the Act is replaced by the following:

(a) an offence has been committed with respect to which the state or entity has jurisdiction; and

(2) Paragraph 18(2)(b) of the French version of the Act is replaced by the following:

b) l'ordre à une personne visée de faire une copie d'un document ou d'en établir un à partir de données et de remettre la copie ou le document à une personne désignée ou celui de remettre à une telle personne tout objet ou document en sa possession ou sous son contrôle, ainsi que des indications concernant l'affidavit ou le certificat qui, s'il y a lieu, doit accompagner la copie, l'objet ou le document, à la demande de l'État ou entité;

(3) Paragraphs 18(7)(b) and (c) of the Act are replaced by the following:

(b) to require the person to answer the questions or to produce the records or things would constitute a breach of a privilege recognized by a law in force in the state or entity that presented the request mentioned in subsection 17(1); or

(c) to answer the questions or to produce the records or things would constitute the commission by the person of an offence against a law in force in the state or entity that presented the request mentioned in subsection 17(1).

109. Subsection 19(4) of the Act is replaced by the following:

(4) **Refusals based on foreign law** — A copy of every statement given under subsection 18(9) that contains reasons that purport to be based on a law that applies to the state or entity shall be appended to any order that the judge makes under section 20.

110. (1) Subsection 20(1) of the Act is replaced by the following:

20. (1) **Sending abroad** — A judge to whom a report is made under subsection 19(1) may order that there be sent to the state or entity the report and any record or thing produced, as well as a copy of the order accompanied by a copy of any statement given under subsection 18(9) that contains reasons that purport to be based on a law that applies to the state or entity, as well as any determination of the judge made under subsection 19(3) that the reasons contained in a statement given under subsection 18(9) are well-founded.

(2) Subsection 20(3) of the Act is replaced by the following:

(3) **Further execution** — The execution of an order made under subsection 18(1) that was not completely executed because of a refusal, by reason of a law that applies to the state or entity, to answer one or more questions or to produce certain records or things to the person designated under paragraph 18(2)(c) may be continued if a court of the state or entity or a person designated by the state or entity determines that the reasons are not well-founded and the state or entity so advises the Minister.

111. Section 21 of the Act is replaced by the following:

21. **Terms and conditions** — No record or thing that has been ordered under section 20 to be sent to the state or entity mentioned in subsection 17(1) shall be so sent until the Minister is satisfied that the state or entity has agreed to comply with any terms or conditions imposed in respect of the sending abroad of the record or thing.

112. Subparagraph 22(b)(ii) of the Act is replaced by the following:

(ii) a court of the state or entity or by a person designated by the state or entity, if the reasons were based on a law that applies to the state or entity.

113. The Act is amended by adding the following after section 22:

22.1 (1) **Approval of request to obtain evidence by video link, etc.** — If the Minister approves a request of a state or entity to compel a person to provide evidence or a statement, by means of technology that permits the virtual presence of the person in the territory over which the state or entity has jurisdiction, or that permits the parties and the court to hear and examine the witness, regarding an offence with respect to which the state or entity has jurisdiction, the Minister shall provide a competent authority with any documents or information necessary to apply for the order.

(2) **Application for order** — The competent authority who is provided with the documents or information shall apply *ex parte* to a judge of the province in which the person may be found for an order for the taking of the evidence or statement from the person under subsection (1).

22.2 (1) **Order for video link, etc.** — The judge may make the order if satisfied that there are reasonable grounds to believe that

(a) an offence has been committed with respect to which the state or entity has jurisdiction; and

(b) the state or entity believes that the person's evidence or statement would be relevant to the investigation or prosecution of the offence.

(2) **Provisions of order** — An order made under subsection (1) shall order the person

(a) to attend at the place fixed by the judge for the taking of the evidence or statement by means of the technology and to remain in attendance until the person is excused by the authorities of the state or entity;

(b) to answer any questions put to the person by the authorities of the state or entity or by any person authorized by those authorities, in accordance with the law that applies to the state or entity;

(c) to make a copy of a record or to make a record from data and to bring the copy or record, when appropriate; and

(d) to bring any record or thing in his or her possession or control, when appropriate, in order to show it to the authorities by means of the technology.

(3) **Order effective throughout Canada** — An order made under subsection (1) may be executed anywhere in Canada.

(4) **Terms and conditions of order** — An order made under subsection (1) may include any terms or conditions that the judge considers desirable, including those relating to the protection of the interests of the person named in it and of third parties.

(5) **Variation** — The judge who made the order under subsection (1) or another judge of the same court may vary its terms and conditions.

(6) **Expenses** — A person named in an order made under subsection (1) is entitled to be paid the travel and living expenses to which the person would be entitled if the person were required to attend as a witness before the judge who made the order.

22.3 Other laws about witnesses to apply — For greater certainty, when a witness gives evidence or a statement pursuant to an order made under section 22.2, the evidence or statement shall be given as though the witness were physically before the court or tribunal outside Canada, for the purposes of the laws relating to evidence and procedure but only to the extent that giving the evidence would not disclose information otherwise protected by the Canadian law of non-disclosure of information or privilege.

22.4 Contempt of court in Canada — When a witness gives evidence under section 22.2, the Canadian law relating to contempt of court applies with respect to a refusal by the person to answer a question or to produce a record or thing as ordered by the judge under that section.

114. (1) Subsection 23(1) of the Act is replaced by the following:

23. Arrest warrant — (1) The judge who made the order under subsection 18(1) or section 22.2 or another judge of the same court may issue a warrant for the arrest of the person named in the order where the judge is satisfied, on an information in writing and under oath, that

(a) the person did not attend or remain in attendance as required by the order or is about to abscond;

(b) the order was personally served on the person; and

(c) in the case of an order made under subsection 18(1), the person is likely to give material evidence and, in the case of an order under section 22.2, the state or entity believes that the testimony of the person would be relevant to the prosecution of the offence.

(2) Subsection 23(3) of the Act is replaced by the following:

(3) **Order** — A peace officer who arrests a person in execution of a warrant issued under subsection (1) shall, without delay, bring the person or cause the person to be brought before the judge who issued the warrant or another judge of the same court who may, to ensure compliance with the order made under subsection 18(1) or section 22.2, order that the person be detained in custody or released on recognizance, with or without sureties.

115. Subsection 24(1) of the Act is replaced by the following:

24. (1) **Approval of transfer request** — When the Minister approves a request of a state or entity to have a detained person who is serving a term of imprisonment in Canada transferred to the state or entity, the Minister shall provide a competent authority with any documents or information necessary to apply for a transfer order.

116. (1) Subsection 25(1) of the Act is replaced by the following:

25. (1) **Making of transfer order** — If the judge to whom an application is made under subsection 24(2) is satisfied, having considered, among other things, any documents filed or information given in support of the application, that the detained person consents to the transfer and that the state or entity has requested the transfer for a fixed period, the judge may make a transfer order.

(2) Paragraph 25(3)(c) of the Act is replaced by the following:

(c) order the person receiving the detained person into custody under paragraph (b) to take him or her to the state or entity and, on the return of the detained person to Canada, to return that person to the place of confinement where he or she was when the order was made;

117. (1) Subsection 30(1) of the Act is replaced by the following:

30. (1) **Approval of loan request** — When the Minister approves the request of a state or entity to have an exhibit that was admitted in evidence in a proceeding in respect of an offence in a court in Canada lent to the state or entity, the Minister shall provide a competent authority with any documents or information necessary to apply for a loan order.

(2) Subsection 30(2) of the English version of the Act is replaced by the following:

(2) **Application for loan order** — After having given reasonable notice to the attorney general of the province where the exhibit sought to be lent to the state or entity mentioned in subsection (1) is located and to the parties to the proceeding, the competent authority who is provided with the docu-

ments or information shall apply for a loan order to the court that has possession of the exhibit.

118. Subsection 31(1) of the Act is replaced by the following:

31. (1) **Making of loan order** — If the court to which an application is made under subsection 30(2) is satisfied that the state or entity has requested the loan for a fixed period and has agreed to comply with the terms and conditions that the court proposes to include in any loan order, the court may, after having considered any representations of the persons to whom notice of the application was given in accordance with subsection 30(2), make a loan order.

119. Section 34 of the Act is replaced by the following:

34. **Presumption of continuity** — The burden of proving that an exhibit lent to a state or entity pursuant to a loan order made under subsection 31(1) and returned to Canada is not in the same condition as it was when the loan order was made or that it was tampered with after the loan order was made is on the party who makes that allegation and, in the absence of that proof, the exhibit is deemed to have been continuously in the possession of the court that made the loan order.

120. 1994, c. 44, ss. 96, 97 — The headings before section 36 and sections 36 and 37 of the Act are replaced by the following:

PART II — ADMISSIBILITY IN CANADA OF EVIDENCE OBTAINED ABROAD PURSUANT TO AN AGREEMENT

36. (1) **Foreign records** — In a proceeding with respect to which Parliament has jurisdiction, a record or a copy of the record and any affidavit, certificate or other statement pertaining to the record made by a person who has custody or knowledge of the record, sent to the Minister by a state or entity in accordance with a Canadian request, is not inadmissible in evidence by reason only that a statement contained in the record, copy, affidavit, certificate or other statement is hearsay or a statement of opinion.

(2) **Probative value** — For the purpose of determining the probative value of a record or a copy of a record admitted in evidence under this Act, the trier of fact may examine the record or copy, receive evidence orally or by affidavit, or by a certificate or other statement pertaining to the record in which a person attests that the certificate or statement is made in conformity with the laws that apply to a state or entity, whether or not the certificate or statement is in the form of an affidavit attested to before an official of the state or entity, including evidence as to the circumstances in which the information contained in the record or copy was written, stored or reproduced, and draw any reasonable inference from the form or content of the record or copy.

37. **Foreign things** — In a proceeding with respect to which Parliament has jurisdiction, a thing and any affidavit, certificate or other statement pertaining to the thing made by a person in a state or entity as to the identity and possession of the thing from the time it was obtained until its sending to a competent authority in Canada by the state or entity in accordance with a Canadian request, are not inadmissible in evidence by reason only that the affidavit, certificate or other statement contains hearsay or a statement of opinion.

121. Section 39 of the Act is replaced by the following:

39. **Service abroad** — The service of a document in the territory over which the state or entity has jurisdiction may be proved by affidavit of the person who served it.

122. The headings before section 40 of the Act are replaced by the following:

PART III — IMPLEMENTATION OF AGREEMENTS IN CANADA

Special Authorization to Come Into Canada

123. Subsection 40(1) of the Act is replaced by the following:

40. (1) **Special authorization** — The Minister may, in order to give effect to a request of a Canadian competent authority, authorize a person in a state or entity who is a member of an inadmissible class of persons described in section 19 of the *Immigration Act* to come into Canada at a place designated by the Minister and to go to and remain in a place in Canada so designated for the period of time specified by the Minister, and the Minister may make the authorization subject to any conditions that the Minister considers desirable.

124. Paragraphs 41(1)(a) and (b) of the Act are replaced by the following:

(a) may not be detained, prosecuted or punished in Canada for any act or omission that occurred before the person's departure from the state or entity pursuant to the request;

(b) is not subject to civil process in respect of any act or omission that occurred before the person's departure from the state or entity pursuant to the request; and

125. Subsection 42(1) of the Act is replaced by the following:

42. **Detention of transferred person** — (1) When the Minister, in order to give effect to a request of a Canadian competent authority, authorizes a person who is detained in a state or entity to be transferred to Canada for a period of time specified by the Minister, a judge of the province to which the person is to be transferred may make an order for the detention of the

person anywhere in Canada and for the return of the person to the state or entity.

126. Section 43 of the Act is replaced by the following:

43. **Powers of judge** — When a Canadian request is presented to a state or entity and a person in the state or entity refuses to answer one or more questions or to give up certain records or things by reason of a law in force in Canada, a judge may determine the validity of the refusal on application made, on reasonable notice to the person, by a Canadian competent authority.

127. Subsection 44(1) of the Act is replaced by the following:

44. (1) **Privilege** — Subject to subsection 38(2), a record sent to the Minister by a state or entity in accordance with a Canadian request is privileged and no person shall disclose to anyone the record or its purport or the contents of the record or any part of it before the record, in compliance with the conditions on which it was so sent, is made public or disclosed in the course or for the purpose of giving evidence.

128. SOR/90-704; SOR/93-446 — The schedule to the Act is replaced by the following:

SCHEDULE [1] — DESIGNATED STATES OR ENTITIES

Number in brackets editorially added by Carswell.

(Sections 2, 4, 6 and 8)

The International Criminal Tribunal for the Prosecution of Persons Responsible for Genocide and other Serious Violations of International Humanitarian Law Committed in the Territory of Rwanda and Rwandan citizens responsible for genocide and other such violations committed in the territory of neighbouring States, between 1 January 1994 and 31 December 1994, established by Resolution 955 (1994) of the Security Council of the United Nations

The International Tribunal for the Prosecution of Persons Responsible for Serious Violations of International Law Committed in the Territory of the Former Yugoslavia since 1991, established by Resolution 827 (1993) of the Security Council of the United Nations

Repeals

129. Repeal of R.S. c. E-23 — The *Extradition Act* is repealed.

130. Repeal of R.S. c. F-32 — The *Fugitive Offenders Act* is repealed.

SCHEDULE [1] — STATES OR ENTITIES DESIGNATED AS EXTRADITION PARTNERS

Number in brackets editorially added by Carswell.

(Sections 2 and 9)

Antigua and Barbuda

Australia

The Bahamas

Barbados

Botswana

Costa Rica

Ghana

Grenada

Guyana

The International Criminal Tribunal for the Prosecution of Persons Responsible for Genocide and other Serious Violations of International Humanitarian Law Committed in the Territory of Rwanda and Rwandan citizens responsible for genocide and other such violations committed in the territory of neighbouring States, between 1 January 1994 and 31 December 1994, established by Resolution 955 (1994) of the Security Council of the United Nations

The International Tribunal for the Prosecution of Persons Responsible for Serious Violations of International Law Committed in the Territory of the Former Yugoslavia since 1991, established by Resolution 827 (1993) of the Security Council of the United Nations

Jamaica

Japan

Lesotho

Maldives

Malta

Mauritius

Namibia

Nauru

New Zealand

Papua New Guinea

Singapore

Solomon Islands

South Africa

St. Kitts & Nevis

St. Lucia

St. Vincent & The Grenadines
Swaziland
Trinidad and Tobago
Tuvalu
United Kingdom of Great Britain and Northern Ireland
Vanuatu
Zimbabwe

EXTRADITION ACT, R.S.C. 1985, C. E-23

TABLE OF CONCORDANCE

[Note: The Extradition Act, R.S.C. 1985, c. E-23, was repealed and replaced by S.C. 1999, c. 18, An Act respecting Extradition, to amend the Canada Evidence Act, Criminal Code, the Immigration Act, and the Mutual Legal Assistance in Criminal Matter Act and to amend and repeal other acts in consequence (in force June 17, 1999). For a table of concordance tracing the substantive correspondences between the provisions of the repealed act, as amended, and those of the new act, please refer to the pages immediately preceding the text of the new act.]

EA

EXTRADITION ACT

An Act respecting the extradition of fugitive criminals

R.S.C. 1985, c. E-23,
as am. R.S.C. 1985, c. 27 (1st Supp.), ss. 187, 203, Sched. V; 1992, c. 13;
1993, c. 28, s. 78 (Sched. III, item 56); repealed by 1999, c. 18, s. 129.

[Editor's Note: Section 129 of S.C. 1999, c. 18, An Act respecting extradition, to amend the Canada Evidence Act, the Criminal Code, the Immigration Act and the Mutual Legal Assistance in Criminal Matters Act and to amend and repeal other Acts in consequence, repeals and replaces the Extradition Act, R.S.C. 1985, c. E-23. Section 84 of S.C. 1999, c. 18 provides, however, that the repealed Act will continue to apply to a matter respecting the extradition of a person as though it had not been repealed, if the hearing in respect of the extradition has already begun on the day on which the new Act comes into force.]

Short Title

1. Short title — This Act may be cited as the *Extradition Act*.

repealed 1999, c. 18, s. 129

Interpretation

2. Definitions — In this Act,

"conviction" or **"convicted"** does not include the case of a condemnation under foreign law by reason of contumacy; but **"accused person"** includes a person so condemned;

"court of appeal" means

    (a) in the Province of Ontario, the Court of Appeal,

    (b) in the Province of Quebec, the Court of Appeal,

    (c) in the Province of Nova Scotia, the Appeal Division of the Supreme Court,

    (d) in the Province of New Brunswick, the Court of Appeal,

    (e) in the Province of Manitoba, the Court of Appeal,

    (f) in the Province of British Columbia, the Court of Appeal,

    (g) in the Province of Prince Edward Island, the Appeal Division of the Supreme Court,

    (h) in the Province of Saskatchewan, the Court of Appeal,

    (i) in the Province of Alberta, the Court of Appeal,

(j) in the Province of Newfoundland, the Court of Appeal,

(k) in the Yukon Territory, the Court of Appeal, and

(l) in the Northwest Territories, the Court of Appeal;

(m) in Nunavut, the Court of Appeal;

"extradition arrangement" or **"arrangement"** means a treaty, convention or arrangement that extends to Canada made by Her Majesty with a foreign state for the surrender of fugitive criminals;

"extradition crime" means

(a) any crime that, if committed in Canada, or within Canadian jurisdiction, would be one of the crimes described in Schedule I, and

(b) in the application of this Act to the case of an extradition arrangement, any crime described in the arrangement, whether or not it is included in that Schedule;

"foreign state" includes every colony, dependency and constituent part of the foreign state, and every vessel of a foreign state is deemed to be within the jurisdiction of and to be part of the state;

"fugitive" or **"fugitive criminal"** means a person being or suspected of being in Canada, who is accused or convicted of an extradition crime committed within the jurisdiction of a foreign state;

"judge" includes any person authorized to act judicially in extradition matters;

"warrant", in the case of a foreign state, includes any judicial document that authorizes the arrest of a person accused or convicted of crime.

1992, c. 13, s. 1; 1993, c. 28, s. 78 (Sched. III, item 56); repealed 1999, c. 18, s. 129

PART I — EXTRADITION UNDER TREATY

Application of this Part

3. Existing arrangements — In the case of any foreign state with which there is an extradition arrangement this Part applies during the continuance of the arrangement; but no provision of this Part that is inconsistent with any of the terms of the arrangement has effect to contravene the arrangement, and this Part shall be so read and construed as to provide for the execution of the arrangement.

repealed 1999, c. 18, s. 129

4. Orders in council limiting application of U.K. Act and this Part — Where, with respect to a foreign state, an order of Her Majesty in Council makes the application to the United Kingdom of the Act of the Parliament of the United Kingdom entitled *The Extradition Act, 1870*, 33-34 Victoria, chapter 52 and any Act amending that Act subject to any limitation, condition, qualification or exception, the Governor in Council shall, by order, make the application of this Part subject to that limitation, condition, qualification or exception.

repealed 1999, c. 18, s. 129

5. Revocation, etc., of orders — The Governor in Council may, by order, revoke or alter, subject to the restrictions of this Part, any order made by the Governor in Council under section 4, and all the provisions of this Part with respect to the original order, in so far as applicable, apply with such modifications as the circumstances require to the new order.

repealed 1999, c. 18, s. 129

6. Date when Part applies or is affected — This Part, in so far as its application in the case of any foreign state depends on or is affected by any order in council made under section 4 or 5 or referred to in this Part, shall apply, or its application shall be affected after the time specified in the order or, if no time is specified, after the date of the publication of the order in the *Canada Gazette*.

repealed 1999, c. 18, s. 129

7. Mandatory publication in Canada Gazette — An order of Her Majesty in Council, referred to in section 4, and any order of the Governor in Council made under section 4 or 5 and any extradition arrangement shall, as soon as possible, be published in the *Canada Gazette* and laid before both Houses of Parliament.

repealed 1999, c. 18, s. 129

8. Effect of publication — The publication in the *Canada Gazette* of an extradition arrangement or an order in council is evidence of the arrangement or order, of the terms thereof and of the application of this Part pursuant and subject thereto, any court or judge shall without proof take judicial notice of the arrangement or order, and the validity of the order and the application of this Part, pursuant and subject thereto, shall not be questioned.

repealed 1999, c. 18, s. 129

Judges and Commissioners

9. (1) Judges who may act — All judges of the superior courts and of the county courts of a province, and all commissioners who are appointed for the purpose in a province by the Governor in Council, under the Great Seal, by virtue of this Part, are authorized to act judicially in extradition matters under this Part within the province, and each of those persons has for the purposes of this Part all the powers and jurisdiction of any judge or provincial court judge of the province.

(2) Habeas corpus — Nothing in this section shall be construed so as to confer on any judge any jurisdiction in habeas corpus matters.

(3) Competence — For the purposes of the *Constitution Act, 1982*, a judge who is a superior court judge or a county judge has, with respect to the functions that that judge is required to perform in applying this Act, the same competence that the judge possesses by virtue of being a superior court judge or a county court judge.

R.S., c. 27 (1st Supp.), s. 203; 1992, c. 13, s. 2; repealed 1999, c. 18, s. 129

Extradition from Canada

10. (1) Grounds for warrant — Whenever this Part applies, a judge may issue a warrant for the apprehension of a fugitive on a foreign warrant of arrest, or an information or a complaint laid before the judge, and on such evidence or after such proceedings as in the opinion of the judge would, subject to this Part, justify the issue of the warrant if the crime of which the fugitive is accused or is alleged to have been convicted had been committed in Canada.

(2) Report to Minister of Justice — The judge shall forthwith send a report of the fact of the issue of the warrant referred to in subsection (1), together with certified copies of the evidence and foreign warrant, information or complaint, to the Minister of Justice.

repealed 1999, c. 18, s. 129

11. Execution of warrant — A warrant issued under this Part may be executed in any part of Canada in the same manner as if it had been originally issued. or subsequently endorsed, by a justice of the peace having jurisdiction in the place where it was executed.

repealed 1999, c. 18, s. 129

12. Surrender not to depend on time when offence was committed, etc — Every fugitive criminal of a foreign state, to which this Part applies, is liable to be apprehended, committed and surrendered in the manner provided in this Part, wether the crime or conviction, in respect of which the surrender is sought was committed or took place before or after the time when this Part is made to apply to that state, and wether there is or is not any criminal jurisdiction in any court of Her Majesty's Realms and territories over the fugitive in respect of the crime.

repealed 1999, c. 18, s. 129

13. Fugitive to be brought before judge — The fugitive referred to in section 12 shall be brought before a judge, who shall, subject to this Part, hear the case, in the same manner, as nearly as may be, as if the fugitive was brought before a justice of the peace, charged with an indictable offence committed in Canada.

repealed 1999, c. 18, s. 129

14. Evidence of charge — The judge shall receive an oath, or solemn affirmation, if affirmation is allowed by law, the evidence of any witness tendered to show the truth of the charge or fact of conviction.

repealed 1999, c. 18, s. 129

15. Evidence that crime is not an extradition crime — The judge shall receive, in the manner set out in section 14, any evidence tendered to show that the crime of which the fugitive is accused or alleged to have been convicted is an offence of a political character, or is, for any other reason, not an extradition crime, that the proceedings are being taken with a view to prosecute or punish the fugitive for an offence of political character.

repealed 1999, c. 18, s. 129

16. Depositions or statements taken outside Canada — Depositions or statements taken in a foreign state on oath, or on solemn affirmation, where affirmation is allowed by the law of that state, and copies of the deposition or statements and foreign certificates of, or judicial documents stating the fact of, conviction may, if duly authenticated, be received in evidence in proceedings under this Part.

repealed 1999, c. 18, s. 129

17. When to be deemed authenticated — The documents referred to in section 16 shall be deemed duly authenticated if authenticated in the manner provided by law, or if

(a) the warrant purports to be signed by, the certificate purports to certified by, or the depositions or statements, or the copies thereof, purport to be certified to be the originals or true copies, by a judge, provincial court judge or officer of the foreign state; and

(b) the documents are authenticated by the oath or affirmation of a witness, or by being sealed with the official seal of the Minister of Justice or any other minister of the foreign state, or of an colony, dependency or constituent part of the foreign state, of which seal the judge shall take judicial notice without proof.

R.S., c. 27 (1st Supp.), s. 203; repealed 1999, c. 18, s. 129

18. (1) Evidence sufficient to justify committal — The judge shall issue a warrant for the committal of the fugitive to the nearest convenient prison, there to remain until surrendered to the foreign state, or discharged according to law,

(a) in the case of a fugitive alleged to have been convicted of an extradition crime, if such evidence is produced as would, according to the law of Canada, subject to this Part, justify the committal of the fugitive for trial, if the crime had been committed in Canada.

(2) Discharge — If the evidence referred to in subsection (1) is not produced, the judge shall order the fugitive to be discharged.

repealed 1999, c. 18, s. 129

19. Information to be given to fugitives — The judge who commits a fugitive to prison shall, on the committal,

(a) inform the fugitive that the fugitive will not be surrendered until after the expiration of thirty days and has a right to appeal the committal; and

(b) transmit to the Minister of Justice a certificate of the committal, with a copy of all the evidence taken before the judge not already so transmitted, and such report on the case as the judge thinks fit.

1992, c. 13, s. 3; repealed 1999, c. 18, s. 129

19.1 (1) Fugitive's submissions — A fugitive in respect of whom a requisition for surrender has been made by a foreign state may, at any time before the expiration of thirty days after the date of the committal, make submissions to the Minister of Justice with respect to any ground that would be relevant to the Minister in making a decision with respect to the possible surrender of the fugitive to the foreign state but the Minister may, in circumstances that the Minister considers appropriate, receive those submissions after the expiration of those thirty days.

(2) Right to be informed — On the commencement of any proceedings held pursuant to section 13, the judge shall inform the fugitive of the fugitive's right under subsection (1) to make submissions to the Minister of Justice.

1992, c. 13, s. 3; repealed 1999, c. 18, s. 129

19.2 Appeal — A fugitive may appeal a committal, or foreign state that has made a requisition for surrender may appeal a discharge of a fugitive or stay of any proceedings held pursuant to section 13, to the court of appeal of the province in which, as the case may be, the order of committal, the order discharging the fugitive or the order staying the proceedings was made,

    (a) on any ground of appeal that involves a question of law alone;

    (b) on any ground of appeal that involves a question of fact or a question of mixed law and fact, with leave of the court of appeal or a judge of the court of appeal; or

    (c) on any ground of appeal not mentioned in paragraph (a) or (b) that appears to the court of appeal to be a sufficient ground of appeal, with leave of the court of appeal.

1992, c. 13, s. 3; repealed 1999, c. 18, s. 129

19.3 (1) Notice of appeal — An appellant who proposes to appeal to a court of appeal or to obtain the leave of that court to appeal shall give notice of appeal or notice of the application for leave to appeal not later than thirty days after the decision of the judge with respect to the committal or discharge of the fugitive, or the stay of the proceedings, as the case may be, in such manner as may be directed by the rules of the court.

(2) Extension of time — The court of appeal or a judge of the court of appeal may, either before or after the expiration of the thirty days referred to in subsection (1), extend the time within which notice of appeal or notice of an application for leave may the appeal be given.

1992, c. 13, s. 3; repealed 1999, c. 18, s. 129

19.4 (1) Hearing of appeal — An appeal under this Act shall be scheduled for hearing by the court of appeal at an early date, whether that date is in or out of the prescribed sessions of that court.

(2) Deferral of appeal — The hearing of an appeal from a decision with respect to the committal of a fugitive or any other appeal in a matter arising under this Act may be deferred by the court of appeal until the Minister of Justice makes a decision with respect to the surrender of the fugitives under section 25.

1992, c. 13, s. 3; repealed 1999, c. 18, s. 129

19.5 (1) Provisions of Criminal Code to apply — Sections 677, 678.1, 679 to 685 and 688 of the *Criminal Code* apply, with such modifications as the circumstances require, to appeals under this Act.

(2) Rules — Unless inconsistent with the provisions of this Act, rules made by the court of appeal pursuant to section 482 of the *Criminal Code* in relation to appeals to that court under that Act apply, with such modifications as the circumstances require, to appeals under this Act.

1992, c. 13, s. 3; repealed 1999, c. 18, s. 129

19.6 Powers where committal appealed — On the hearing of an appeal against the committal of a fugitive, the court of appeal

(a) may allow the appeal, with respect to an extradition crime in respect of which the fugitive has been committed, where it is of the opinion

(i) that the order of committal should be set aside on the ground that it is unreasonable or cannot be supported by the evidence.

(ii) that the order of committal should be set aside on the ground of a wrong decision on a question of law, or

(iii) that on any ground there was a miscarriage of justice; or

(b) may dismiss the appeal

(i) where it does not allow the appeal on any ground mentioned in paragraph (a), or

(ii) not withstanding that the court of appeal is of the opinion that on any ground mentioned in subparagraph (a)(ii) the appeal might be decided in favour of the appellant, where it is of the opinion that no substantial wrong or miscarriage of justice has occurred and the order of committal should be upheld.

1992, c. 13, s. 3; repealed 1999, c. 18, s. 129

19.7 Effect of allowing appeal — Where the court of appeal allows an appeal under paragraph 19.6(a), it shall

(a) set aside the order of committal and

(i) discharge the fugitive, or

(ii) order a new hearing; or

(b) amend the order of committal to exclude any extradition crime in respect of which the court is of the opinion that the fugitive has not been properly committed on a ground referred to in subparagraph 19.6(a),(ii) or (iii).

1992, c. 13, s. 3; repealed 1999, c. 18, s. 129

19.8 Powers where discharge appealed — On the hearing of an appeal against the discharge of a fugitive with respect to any extradition crime, or against a stay of any proceedings held pursuant to section 13, the court of appeal may

(a) allow the appeal and set aside the order of discharge, or set aside the stay, where the court is of the opinion

(i) that the order of discharge should be set aside on the ground that it is unreasonable having regard to the sufficiency of the evidence,

(ii) that the order of the discharge, or the stay of proceedings, should be set aside on the ground of a wrong decision on a question of law, or

(iii) that on any ground there was a miscarriage of justice,

and, where it sets aside a stay, order a new hearing or order the committal of the fugitive with respect to the extradition crime for which the fugitive was discharged; or

(b) dismiss the appeal.

1992, c. 13, s. 3; repealed 1999, c. 18, s. 129

19.9 Deferral of Supreme Court appeal — The hearing of an application for leave to appeal, or the hearing of an appeal, from a decision of the court of appeal on an appeal taken under section 19.2, or on any other appeal in respect of a matter arising under this Act, may be deferred by the Supreme Court of Canada until the Minister of Justice makes a decision with respect to the surrender of the fugitive under section 25, or, if an application for judicial review is made under section 25.2 or otherwise, until the court of appeal makes its determination on the application.

1992, c. 13, s. 3; repealed 1999, c. 18, s. 129

20. (1) By whom requisition for surrender may be made — A requisition for the surrender of a fugitive criminal of a foreign state who is, or is suspected to be, in Canada, may be made to the Minister of Justice

(a) by any person recognized by the Minister of Justice as a consular officer of that state resident at Ottawa; or

(b) by any minister of that state communicating with the Minister of Justice through the diplomatic representative of Her Majesty in that state.

(2) By arrangement — If neither of the modes referred to in subsection (1) is convenient, the requisition shall be made in such other mode as is settled by arrangement.

repealed 1999, c. 18, s. 129

21. Fugitive not liable to surrender — No fugitive is liable to surrender under this Part if it appears that

(a) the offence in respect of which proceedings are taken under this Part is one of a political character; or

(b) the proceedings are being taken with a view to prosecute or punish the fugitive for an offence of a political character.

repealed 1999, c. 18, s. 129

22. (1) When Minister may refuse to make order — The Minister of Justice may at any time refuse to make an order for surrender referred to in section 25 where he determines that

(a) the offence in respect of which proceedings are being taken under this Part is one of a political character;

(b) the proceedings are, in fact, being taken with a view to try or punish the fugitive for an offence of a political character; or

(c) the foreign state does not intend to make a requisition for surrender.

(2) **Discharge of fugitive** — Where the Minister of justice refuses to make an order for surrender, he may, by order under his hand and seal, cancel any order made by him or any warrant issued by a judge under this Part and order the fugitive to be discharged out of custody on any committal made under this Part, and the fugitive shall be discharged accordingly.

repealed 1999, c. 18, s. 129

23. Delay before surrender — A fugitive shall not be surrendered

(a) until after the expiration of thirty days after the date of the committal for surrender; or

(b) where an appeal or judicial review in respect of any matter arising under this Act, or any appeal therefore, is pending, until after the date of the final decision of the court.

1992, c. 13, s. 4; repealed 1999, c. 18, s. 129

24. [Repealed 1992, c. 13, s. 4.]

25. (1) Surrender of fugitive to officer of a foreign state — Subject to this part, the Minister of Justice, on the requisition of a foreign state, may, within a period of ninety days after the date of a fugitive's committal for surrender, under the hand and seal of the minister, order the fugitive to be surrendered to the person or persons who are, in the Ministers opinion, duly authorized to receive the fugitive in the name and on the behalf of the foreign state, and the fugitive shall be so surrendered accordingly.

(2) **Extension where warranted** — Where a fugitive has made submissions to the Minister under the section 19.1 and the Minister is of the opinion that further time is needed to act on those submissions, the Minister may extend the period of ninety days referred to in section (1) for one additional period that does not exceed sixty days.

(3) **Notice of extension of time** — Where an appeal has been filed pursuant to section 19.2 and the Minister has extended the period of ninety days referred to in is made under subsection (1), the Minister shall file with the court of appeal a notice of extension of time before the expiration of that period.

(4) **If fugitive is an offender under Canadian law** — When an order is made under subsection (1) in respect of a fugitive who has been accused of an offence within Canadian jurisdiction, or who is undergoing a sentence in Canada under a conviction for any offence, other than the offence to which the order relates, the order shall not have effect until the fugitive has been discharged, whether by acquittal, by expiration of the sentence or otherwise, unless the Minister orders otherwise.

(5) **Order prevails** — An order made under subsection (4) may provide for the surrender of a fugitive at any time prior to the discharge of the fugitive and prevails over any prior warrant or other order under which the fugitive is detained or at liberty under terms and conditions.

1992, c. 13, s. 5; repealed 1999, c. 18, s. 129

25.1 (1) Where appeal pending — The Minister may, notwithstanding section 25, postpone the making of the order referred to in subsection 25(1), on condition that

(a) an appeal has been filed pursuant to section 19.2;

(b) the Minister files a notice of postponement with the court of appeal before the expiration of the period of ninety days referred to in subsection 25(1); and

(c) the order is made not later than forty-five days after the date of the decision of the court of appeal.

(2) No further deferral or appeal — Where the Minister has filed a notice of postponement with the court of appeal under paragraph (1)(b), that court shall not defer the hearing of the appeal under subsection 19.4(2).

1993, c. 13, s. 5; repealed 1999, c. 18, s. 129

25.2 (1) Judicial review — Notwithstanding the *Federal Court Act*, the court of appeal of the province in which the committal of a fugitive was ordered has exclusive original jurisdiction to hear and determine applications for judicial review under this Act, in accordance with subsections (2) to (10), made in respect of the decision of the Minister of Justice under section 25.

(2) Application — An application for judicial review under this section shall be made by the fugitive.

(3) Time limitation — An application for judicial review under this section shall be made, in accordance with the rules of court of the court of appeal, within thirty days after the time the decision referred to in subsection (1) was first communicated by the Minister to the fugitive, or within such further time as the court of appeal, either before or after the expiration of those thirty days, may fix or allow.

(4) Section 679 to apply — Section 679 of the *Criminal Code* applies, with such modifications as the circumstances require, to an application for judicial review under this section.

(5) Hearing of application — A hearing of an application for judicial review under this section shall be scheduled for hearing by the court of appeal at an early date, whether that date is in or out of the prescribed session of that court.

(6) Powers of court of appeal — On an application for judicial review under this section, the court of appeal may

(a) order the Minister to do any act or thing that the Minister has unlawfully failed or refused to do or has unreasonably delayed in doing; or

(b) declare invalid or unlawful, or quash, set aside, or set aside and refer back for determination in accordance with such directions as it considers appropriate, prohibit or restrain, the decision of the Minister referred to in section (1).

(7) Grounds of review — The court of appeal may grant relief under this section on any of the grounds on which the Trial Division of the Federal Court of Canada my grant relief pursuant to subsection 18.1(4) of the *Federal Court Act*.

(8) Defect in form or technical irregularity — Where the sole ground for relief established in an application for judicial review is a defect in form or a technical irregularity, the court of appeal may

(a) refuse the relief if it finds that no substantial wrong or miscarriage of justice has occurred; or

(b) in case of a defect in form or a technical irregularity in the decision, make an order validating the order, to have effect from such time and on such terms as it considers appropriate.

(9) One hearing by court of appeal — Where an appeal under section 19.2 or any other appeal in respect of a matter arising under this Act, is pending the court of appeal may join the hearing of that appeal with the hearing of an application for judicial review made under this section or otherwise.

(10) Provincial rules of judicial review apply — Unless inconsistent with the provisions of this Act, all laws, including rules, respecting judicial review in force in the province of the court of appeal apply, with such modifications as the circumstances require, to applications under this section.

1992, c. 13, s. 5; repealed 1999, c. 18, s. 129

26. Powers of such officers — Any person to whom an order of the Minister of Justice made under section 25 is directed may deliver, and the person thereto authorized by that order may receive, hold in custody and convey, the fugitive within the jurisdiction of the foreign state, and if the fugitive escapes out of any custody to which the fugitive is delivered, or in pursuance of that order, the fugitive may be retaken in the same manner as any person accused or convicted of any crime against the laws of Canada may be retaken on an escape.

repealed 1999, c. 18, s. 129

27. Property found on a fugitive — Everything found in the procession of the fugitive at the time of his arrest that may be material as evidence in making proof of the crime may be delivered up with the fugitive on his surrender, subject to all rights of third persons with regard thereto.

repealed 1999, c. 18, s. 129

28. Remedy in case of delay — Where

(a) the Minister has not made an order of surrender under section 25

(i) before the expiration of the period referred to in subsection 25(1) and any additional period referred to in subsection 25(2), or

(ii) where a notice of postponement has been filed under paragraph 25.1(1)(b), before the expiration of forty-five days after the date of the decision of the court appeal referred to in paragraph 25.1(1)(c), or

(b) a fugitive is not surrendered and conveyed out of Canada

(i) within forty-five days after the order of surrender is made by the Minister under section 25, or

(ii) where an appeal or judicial review in respect of any matter arising under this Act, or any appeal therefrom, is pending, within forty-five days after the final decision of the court is made,

over and above, in any case referred to in a subparagraph (i) or (ii), the time required to convey the fugitive from the prison to which the fugitive has been committed, by the most efficient way out of Canada,

any one or more of the judges of the superior court of the province in which the fugitive is confined, having power to grant a writ of habeas corpus, may, on application made by or on behalf of the fugitive, and on proof that reasonable notice of the intention to make the application has been given to the Minister, order the fugitive to be discharged out of custody unless sufficient cause is shown against the discharge.

1992, c. 13, s. 6; repealed 1999, c. 18, s. 129

29. Forms — The forms set out in Schedule II, or forms as near thereto as circumstances permit, may be used in the matters to which those forms refer and, when used, shall be deemed valid.

repealed 1999, c. 18, s. 129

Extradition from a Foreign State

30. (1) Requisition for a fugitive out of Canada — A requisition for the surrender of a fugitive criminal from Canada, who is or is suspected to be in any foreign state with which there is an extradition arrangement, may be made by the Minister of Justice

(a) to a consular officer of that state resident at Ottawa, or

(b) to the Minister of Justice or any other minister of that state, through the diplomatic representative of Her Majesty in that state.

(2) By arrangement — If neither of the modes referred to in subsection (1) is convenient the requisition shall be made in such other mode as is settled by arrangement.

repealed 1999, c. 18, s. 129

31. (1) Depositions for use in a foreign state — Whenever, for the purposes of this Act, it becomes necessary or expedient to secure evidence by depositions taken in Canada to be used in a foreign state, any justice of the peace or any person having authority to issue a warrant for the apprehension of persons accused of an extradition crime in like manner as he might take the depositions if the accused person were present and charged before him with the extradition crime.

(2) Summoning of witnesses — The justice of the peace or person having authority referred to in subsection (1) may, by subpoena or order, command the attendance at the time and place therein mentioned of any person or witness for the purpose of being examined respecting any extradition crime charged under this Act, and may require the production of any writings or other documents relating to the charge that are in the procession or power of that person or witness.

(3) Enforcement of subpoenas — After service of a subpoena or order referred to in subsection (2), and on payment or tender of the like conduct money as properly payable on attendance at the trial of an indictable offence in a superior court, the subpoena or order may be enforced in like manner as a subpoena or order issued by that superior court.

repealed 1999, c. 18, s. 129

32. Conveyance of fugitive surrendered — Any person accused or convicted of an extradition crime who is surrendered by a foreign state may, under the warrant for that person's surrender issued in that state, be brought into Canada and delivered to the proper authorities, to be dealt with according to law.

repealed 1999, c. 18, s. 129

33. Fugitives surrendered by a foreign state not punishable contrary to arrangement — A person accused or convicted of an extradition crime who is surrendered by a foreign state in pursuance of an extradition arrangement is not, until after having been restored or having had an opportunity of returning to the foreign state within the meaning of the arrangement, subject, in contravention of any of the terms of the arrangement, to a prosecution or punishment in Canada for any other offence committed prior to his surrender, for which that person should not, under the arrangement, be prosecuted.

repealed 1999, c. 18, s. 129

Schedule I

34. How list of crimes in Schedule I to be construed — The list of crimes set out in Schedule I shall be construed according to the law existing in Canada at the date of the commission of the alleged crime, whether by common law or by statue, and as including only such crimes, of the description comprised in the list, as are indictable offences under that law.

repealed 1999, c. 18, s. 129

PART II — EXTRADITION IRRESPECTIVE OF TREATY

35. (1) Commencement of Part — This Part does not come into force, with respect to fugitive offenders from any foreign state, until it has been declared by proclamation of the Governor General to be in force and effect with respect to that foreign state after a day to be named in the proclamation.

(2) Proclamation may be revoked — Where by proclamation the Governor General declares this Part to be no longer in operation with respect to any foreign state, its provisions shall cease to have any force or effect with respect to the fugitive offenders from that state after a day to be named in the proclamation.

repealed 1999, c. 18, s. 129

36. Application of Part — This Part applies to any crime mentioned in Schedule III that is committed after the coming into force of this Part with respect to any foreign state to which this Part has, by proclamation pursuant to subsection 35(1), been declared to apply.

repealed 1999, c. 18, s. 129

37. (1) Extradition where no arrangement, or where crime not included — Where no extradition arrangement exists between Her Majesty and a foreign state, or where an extradition arrangement extending to Canada exists between Her Majesty and a foreign state but does not include the crimes set out in Schedule III, it is nevertheless lawful for the Minister of Justice to issue his warrant for the surrender to that foreign state of any fugitive offender from that state charged with or convicted of any of the crimes set out in Schedule III.

(2) Procedure under Part I — The arrest, committal, detention, surrender and conveyance out of Canada of a fugitive offender referred to in subsection (1) is governed by Part I, and all the provisions of that Part apply to all in steps and proceedings in relation to the arrest, committal, detention, surrender and conveyance out of Canada in the same manner and to the same extent as they would apply if the crimes set out in Schedule III were included and specified in an extradition arrangement between Her Majesty and the foreign state extending to Canada.

repealed 1999, c. 18, s. 129

38. Payments of expenses — All expenses connected with the arrest, committal, detention, surrender and conveyance out of Canada of any fugitive offender under this Part shall be borne by the foreign state that applies for the surrender of the fugitive offender.

repealed 1999, c. 18, s. 129

39. Interpretation of Schedule III — The list of crimes set out in Schedule III shall be construed according to the law existing in Canada at the date of the commission of the alleged crime, whether by common law or by statue, and as including only such crimes, of the description comprised in the list, as are indictable offences under that law.

repealed 1999, c. 18, s. 129

40. When warrant may not be issued — No warrant shall issue under this Part for the extradition of any person to a state or country in which by the law in force in that state or country that person may be tried after the extradition for any other offence than that for which he has been extradited, unless an assurance has first been given by the executive authority of the state or country that the person whose extradition has been claimed will not be tried for any other offence than that in respect of which the extradition has been claimed.

repealed 1999, c. 18, s. 129

SCHEDULE I — LIST OF CRIMES

(Sections 2 and 34)

1. Murder, or attempt or conspiracy to murder
2. Manslaughter

3. Counterfeiting or altering money, and uttering counterfeit or altered money

4. Forgery, counterfeiting or altering, or uttering what is forged, counterfeiting or altered

5. Larceny or theft

6. Embezzlement

7. Obtaining money or goods, or valuable securities, by false pretences

8. Crimes against bankruptcy or insolvency law

9. Fraud committed by a bailee, banker, agent, factor, trustee, or by a director or member or officer of any company, which fraud is made criminal by any Act for the time being in force

10. Sexual assault, sexual assault with a weapon, threats to a third party or causing bodily harm or aggravated sexual assault

11. Abduction

12. Child stealing

13. Kidnapping

14. False imprisonment

15. Burglary, housebreaking or shop–breaking

16. Arson

17. Robbery

18. Threats, by letter or otherwise, with intent to extort

19. Perjury or subornation of perjury

20. Piracy by municipal law or law of nations committed on board of or against a vessel of a foreign state

21. Criminal scuttling or destruction of a vessel of a foreign state at sea, whether on the high seas or on the Great Lakes of North America, or attempting or conspiring to do so

22. Assault on board a vessel of a foreign state at sea, whether on the high seas or on the Great Lakes of North America, with intent to destroy life or to do grievous bodily harm

23. Revolt, or conspiracy to revolt, by two or more persons on board a vessel of a foreign state at sea, whether on the high seas or on the Great Lakes of North America, against the authority of the master

24. Any offence under

    (a) sections 52, 57, 58, 79 to 81, 153, 154, 178, 280 to 283, 385 to 391, 393 to 396, subsection 397(1), sections 398, 400, 401, 405 and paragraph 465(1)(a) of the *Criminal Code*,

    (b) Part VIII of the *Criminal Code*, except sections 249, 250, 252, 253, 255 and 259 in relation to a vessel and sections 264.1 and 290 to 317,

    (c) Part IX of the *Criminal Code*, except subsection 339(2),

    (d) Part XI of the *Criminal Code*, except sections 438, 440, 441, 446 and 447,

(e) Part XII of the *Criminal Code*, except section 454, that is not included in any foregoing portion of this Schedule

25. Any offence that is, in the case of the principal offender, included in any foregoing portion of this Schedule, and for which the fugitive criminal, though not the principal, is liable to be tried or punished as if he were the principle.

R.S., c. 27 (1st Supp.), s. 187, Schedule V, item 4; repealed 1999, c. 18, s. 129

SCHEDULE II

(Section 29)

Form 1 — Form of Warrant of Apprehension

..........;

To wit:

To all and each of the constables of ....

Whereas it has been shown to the undersigned, a judge under the *Extradition Act*, that .... late of .... is accused (*or* convicted) of the crime of .... within the jurisdiction of ....

This is therefore to command you, in Her Majesty's name, forthwith to apprehend the said .... and to bring that person before me, or any other judge under the said Act, to be further dealt with according to law, for which this shall be your warrant.

Given under my hand and seal at .... this .... day of ...., 19 ....

repealed 1999, c. 18, s. 129

Form 2 — Form of Warrant of Committal

..........;

To wit:

To .... one of the constables of .... and to keeper of the .... at ....

Be it remembered that on this .... day of ...., 19 .... at .... is brought before me .... a judge under the *Extradition Act*, ... who has been apprehended under the Act, to be dealt with according to law, and as I have determined that that person should be surrendered in pursuance of that Act, to be dealt with according to law, on the ground of his being accused (or convicted) of the crime of .... within the jurisdiction of ....

This is therefore to command you the said constable, in Her Majesty's name, forthwith to convey and deliver the said .... into the custody of the keeper of the .... at .... and you, the said keeper to receive the said .... into your custody, and safely to keep that person there until thence delivered pursuant to the provisions of the said Act, for which this shall be your warrant.

Given under my hand and seal at .... this .... day of ...., 19 ....

repealed 1999, c. 18, s. 129

Form 3 — Form Order of Minister of Justice for Surrender

To the keeper of the .... at .... and to ....

Whereas .... late of .... accused (or convicted) of the crime of .... within the jurisdiction of .... was delivered into the custody of you, the keeper of the .... at .... by warrant dated .... pursuant to the *Extradition Act*.

Now I do hereby, in pursuance of the said Act, order you the said keeper, to deliver the said .... into the custody of the said ...., and I command you, the said .... to receive the said .... into your custody, and to convey him within the jurisdiction of the said .... and there place him in the custody of any person or persons (or of ....) appointed by the said .... to receive him, for which this shall be your warrant.

Given under the hand and seal of the undersigned Minister of Justice of Canada, this .... day of ...., 19 ....

repealed 1999, c. 18, s. 129

SCHEDULE III

(Sections 36, 37 and 39)

1. Murder, or attempt or conspiracy to murder

2. Manslaughter

3. Counterfeiting or altering money, and uttering counterfeit or altered money

4. Forgery, counterfeiting or altering, or uttering what is forged, counterfeited or altered

5. Larceny or theft

6. Embezzlement

7. Obtaining money or goods or valuable securities, by false pretences

8. Sexual assault, sexual assault with a weapon, threats to a third party or causing bodily harm or aggravated sexual assault

9. Abduction

10. Child stealing

11. Kidnapping

12. Burglary, housebreaking or shop-breaking

13. Arson

14. Robbery

15. Fraud committed by a bailee, banker, agent, factor, trustee or by a member or public officer of any company or municipal corporation, which fraud is made criminal by any law for the time being in force

16. Any malicious act done with intent to endanger persons in a railway train

17. Piracy by municipal law or law of nations committed on board of or against a vessel of a foreign state

18. Criminal scuttling or destruction of a vessel of a foreign state at sea, whether on the high seas or on the Great Lakes of North America, or attempting or conspiring to do so

19. Assault on board a vessel of a foreign state at sea, whether on the high seas or on the Great Lakes of North America, with intent to destroy life or to do grievous bodily harm

20. Revolt, or conspiracy to revolt, by two or more persons, on board a vessel of a foreign state at sea, whether on the high seas or on the Great Lakes of North America, against the authority of the master

21. Administering drugs or using instruments with intent to produce the miscarriage of a woman

22. Any offence that is, in the case of the principle offender, included in any forego-ing portion of this Schedule, and for which the fugitive criminal, though not the principal, is liable to be tried or punished as if he were the principle.

repealed 1999, c. 18, s. 129

FIREARMS ACT — CRIMINAL CODE PART III (PRIOR TO ENACTMENT OF S.C. 1995, C. 39)

TABLE OF CONCORDANCE

[Note: The Firearms Act, S.C. 1995, c. 39 introduced a new legislative regime to govern the licensing, registration, transport, export, import, storage, display, transfer and use of firearms in Canada. In doing so, it repealed and replaced the existing firearms scheme under Part III of the Criminal Code. Certain of the matters addressed by the provisions of the former Part III are now addressed under the Firearms Act proper. What follows is a table which identifies those provisions of the new Firearms Act which correspond, directly or by analogy, to those of the former Part III. For a table delineating the substantive correspondences between the provisions of the new and former Part III of the Criminal Code, please refer to the Criminal Code Concordance.]

FA

Firearms Act, S.C. 1995, c. 39	Criminal Code, R.S.C., c. C-46, Part III (prior to enactment of S.C. 1995, c. 39)
16	—
17	109(8); 110(3.1), (3.2), (3.3)
18	—
19	109(2); 110(2), (2.1), (3), (3.1), (4)
20	110(2)(a), (2)(b)
21	—
22	94
23	95(1), (4); 97(1); 99; 109(6)
24	95(1), (3)
25-26	—
27	109(6), (7)
28	109(3)(c), (3)(d)
29	109(3)(c); 110(2)(c)
30	84(1) "geniune gun collector"
31	109(7)
32	97(1)
33	93(2); 96(2); 97(2), (4)
34	98(1)
35	96(3); 97(3); 97(4); 110(2.1)
36-39	—
40	95(1); 96(3); 97(3)
41-42	—
43	95(1), (2), (3), (5); 96(3); 97(3), (4); 105
44-53	—
54	106(8), (11); 109(1); 110(1), (2.1), (3), (3.1), (4), (9)
55	106(9), 106(9.1)
56	105(4.1), (5); 106(1); 110(5)
57	110(2.1), (3), (3.1), (4)
58	110(6), (7), (11)
59	110(1)
60	109(7)
61	106(11); 109(7); 110(11)
62	—
63	106(13); 110(10)
64	106(11); 110(5), 110(8)
65	110(1)

Firearms Act, S.C. 1995, c. 39	Criminal Code, R.S.C., c. C-46, Part III (prior to enactment of S.C. 1995, c. 39)
66	—
67	106(1.2)
68	106(5); 112(4)
69	112(3)
70	106(11); 112(2), (2.1)
71	109(4.2); 112(1)
72	106(5); 106(14), 112(5), (6), (7)
73	—
74	90.1; 106(5), (6), (7), (15); 112(8), (9)
75	106(16), (17); 112(12)
76	106(18); 112(11)
76.1	—
77	106(19), (20); 112(13), (14)
78-80	—
81	106(19); 112(13)
82	—
83	114(1)
84-86	—
87	114(1), (3)
88	—
89	114(3)
90	114(3)
91-92	—
93	117
94	114(2)
95	108; 111
96	—
97	90(3.1); 95(4); 105(1.3)
98	84(1) "chief firearms officer"
99	—
100	84(1) "local registrar of firearms"; 84(3)
101	105(1.1)(c)
102	105(1.1)(c)
103	105(1.1)(c)
104-105	—
106	113(1)

Firearms Act, S.C. 1995, c. 39	Criminal Code, R.S.C., c. C-46, Part III (prior to enactment of S.C. 1995, c. 39)
107	113(2)
108	—
109	105(6), (7), (8); 113
110	113(3)
111	113(3)
112-113	—
114	113(4)
115	113(4)
116	—
117	116; 109.1
118	116(2)
119-137	—

FIREARMS ACT

An Act respecting firearms and other weapons

S.C. 1995, c. 39, as am. S.C. 1995, c. 39, s. 137; 1996, c. 19, s. 76.1; 1999, c. 3, s. 64; 1999, c. 25, s. 31(4)(b); 2000, c. 12, ss. 116–118 [Not in force at date of publication.].

Short Title

1. Short title — This Act may be cited as the *Firearms Act*.

Interpretation

2. (1) Definitions — In this Act,

"authorization to carry" means an authorization described in section 20;

"authorization to export" means an authorization referred to in section 44;

"authorization to import" means an authorization referred to in section 46;

"authorization to transport" means an authorization described in section 18 or 19;

"business" means a person who carries on a business that includes

(a) the manufacture, assembly, possession, purchase, sale, importation, exportation, display, repair, restoration, maintenance, storage, alteration, taking in pawn, transportation, shipping, distribution or delivery of firearms, prohibited weapons, restricted weapons, prohibited devices or prohibited ammunition,

(b) the possession, purchase or sale of ammunition, or

(c) the purchase of cross-bows

and includes a museum;

"carrier" means a person who carries on a transportation business that includes the transportation of firearms, prohibited weapons, restricted weapons, prohibited devices, ammunition or prohibited ammunition;

"chief firearms officer" means

(a) in respect of a province, the individual who is designated in writing as the chief firearms officer for the province by the provincial minister of that province,

(b) in respect of a territory, the individual who is designated in writing as the chief firearms officer for the territory by the federal Minister, or

(c) in respect of any matter for which there is no chief firearms officer under paragraph (a) or (b), the individual who is designated in writing as the chief firearms officer for the matter by the federal Minister,

"commencement day", in respect of a provision of this Act or the expression "former Act" in a provision of this Act, means the day on which the provision comes into force;

Proposed Addition — 2(1) "common-law partner"

"common-law partner", in relation to an individual, means a person who is cohabiting with the individual in a conjugal relationship, having so cohabited for a period of at least one year;

2000, c. 12, s. 116 [Not in force at date of publication.]

"customs office" has the meaning assigned by subsection 2(1) of the *Customs Act*;

"customs officer" has the meaning assigned to the word "officer" by subsection 2(1) of the *Customs Act*;

"federal Minister" means the Minister of Justice;

"firearms officer" means

(a) in respect of a province, an individual who is designated in writing as a firearms officer for the province by the provincial minister of that province,

(b) in respect of a territory, an individual who is designated in writing as a firearms officer for the territory by the federal Minister, or

(c) in respect of any matter for which there is no firearms officer under paragraph (a) or (b), an individual who is designated in writing as a firearms officer for the matter by the federal Minister;

"former Act" means Part III of the *Criminal Code*, as it read from time to time before the commencement day;

"museum" means a person who operates a museum

(a) in which firearms, prohibited weapons, restricted weapons, prohibited devices or prohibited ammunition are possessed, bought, displayed, repaired, restored, maintained, stored or altered, or

(b) in which ammunition is possessed or bought;

"non-resident" means an individual who ordinarily resides outside Canada;

"prescribed" means

(a) in the case of a form or the information to be included on a form, prescribed by the federal Minister, and

(b) in any other case, prescribed by the regulations;

"provincial minister" means

(a) in respect of a province, the member of the executive council of the province who is designated by the lieutenant governor in council of the province as the provincial minister,

(b) in respect of a territory, the federal Minister, or

(c) in respect of any matter for which there is no provincial minister under paragraph (a) or (b), the federal Minister;

"regulations" means regulations made by the Governor in Council under section 117.

(2) To be interpreted with Criminal Code — For greater certainty, unless otherwise provided, words and expressions used in this Act have the meanings assigned to them by section 2 or 84 of the *Criminal Code*.

(3) Aboriginal and treaty rights — For greater certainty, nothing in this Act shall be construed so as to abrogate or derogate from any existing aboriginal or treaty rights of the aboriginal peoples of Canada under section 35 of the *Constitution Act, 1982*.

Her Majesty

3. (1) Binding on Her Majesty — This Act is binding on Her Majesty in right of Canada or a province.

(2) Canadian Forces — Notwithstanding subsection (1), this Act does not apply in respect of the Canadian Forces.

Purpose

4. Purpose — The purpose of this Act is

(a) to provide, notably by sections 5 to 16 and 54 to 73, for the issuance of

(i) licences, registration certificates and authorizations under which persons may possess firearms in circumstances that would otherwise constitute an offence under subsection 91(1), 92(1), 93(1) or 95(1) of the *Criminal Code*,

(ii) licences and authorizations under which persons may possess prohibited weapons, restricted weapons, prohibited devices and prohibited ammunition in circumstances that would otherwise constitute an offence under subsection 91(2), 92(2) or 93(1) of the *Criminal Code*, and

(iii) licences under which persons may sell, barter or give cross-bows in circumstances that would otherwise constitute an offence under subsection 97(1) of the *Criminal Code*;

(b) to authorize,

(i) notably by sections 5 to 12 and 54 to 73, the manufacture of or offer to manufacture, and

(ii) notably by sections 21 to 34 and 54 to 73, the transfer of or offer to transfer,

firearms, prohibited weapons, restricted weapons, prohibited devices, ammunition and prohibited ammunition in circumstances that would otherwise constitute an offence under subsection 99(1), 100(1) or 101(1) of the *Criminal Code*; and

(c) to authorize, notably by sections 35 to 73, the importation or exportation of firearms, prohibited weapons, restricted weapons, prohibited devices, ammunition, prohibited ammunition and components and parts designed exclusively for use in the manufacture of or assembly into automatic firearms in circumstances that would otherwise constitute an offence under subsection 103(1) or 104(1) of the *Criminal Code*.

Authorized Possession

Eligibility to Hold Licences

General Rules

5. (1) Public safety — A person is not eligible to hold a licence if it is desirable, in the interests of the safety of that or any other person, that the person not possess a firearm, a cross-bow, a prohibited weapon, a restricted weapon, a prohibited device, ammunition or prohibited ammunition.

(2) Criteria — In determining whether a person is eligible to hold a licence under subsection (1), a chief firearms officer or, on a reference under section 74, a provincial court judge shall have regard to whether the person, within the previous five years,

(a) has been convicted or discharged under section 730 of the *Criminal Code* of

(i) an offence in the commission of which violence against another person was used, threatened or attempted,

(ii) an offence under this Act or Part III of the *Criminal Code*,

(iii) an offence under section 264 of the *Criminal Code* (criminal harassment), or

(iv) an offence relating to the contravention of subsection 5(3) or (4), 6(3) or 7(2) of the *Controlled Drugs and Substances Act*;

(b) has been treated for a mental illness, whether in a hospital, mental institute, psychiatric clinic or otherwise and whether or not the person was confined to such a hospital, institute or clinic, that was associated with violence or threatened or attempted violence on the part of the person against any person; or

(c) has a history of behaviour that includes violence or threatened or attempted violence on the part of the person against any person.

Unproclaimed subsection — 5(3)

(3) Exception — Notwithstanding subsection (2), in determining whether a non-resident who is eighteen years old or older and by or on behalf of whom an application is made for a sixty-day licence authorizing the non-resident to possess firearms that are neither prohibited firearms nor restricted firearms is eligible to hold a licence under subsection (1), a chief firearms officer or, on a reference under section 74, a provincial court judge may but need not have regard to the criteria described in subsection (2).

1995, c. 39, s. 137; 1996, c. 19, s. 76.1

6. (1) Court orders — A person is eligible to hold a licence only if the person is not prohibited by a prohibition order from possessing any firearm, cross-bow, prohibited weapon, restricted weapon, prohibited device or prohibited ammunition.

(2) Exception — Subsection (1) is subject to any order made under section 113 of the *Criminal Code* (lifting of prohibition order for sustenance or employment).

7. (1) Successful completion of safety course — An individual is eligible to hold a licence only if the individual

(a) successfully completes the Canadian Firearms Safety Course, as given by an instructor who is designated by a chief firearms officer, and passes the tests, as administered by an instructor who is designated by a chief firearms officer, that form part of that Course;

(b) except in the case of an individual who is less than eighteen years old, passes the tests, as administered by an instructor who is designated by a chief firearms officer, that form part of that Course;

(c) successfully completed, before January 1, 1995, a course that the attorney general of the province in which the course was given had, during the period beginning on January 1, 1993 and ending on December 31, 1994, approved for the purposes of section 106 of the former Act; or

(d) passed, before January 1, 1995, a test that the attorney general of the province in which the test was administered had, during the period beginning on January 1, 1993 and ending on December 31, 1994, approved for the purposes of section 106 of the former Act.

(2) Restricted firearms safety course — An individual is eligible to hold a licence authorizing the individual to possess restricted firearms only if the individual

(a) successfully completes a restricted firearms safety course that is approved by the federal Minister, as given by an instructor who is designated by a chief firearms officer, and passes any tests, as administered by an instructor who is designated by a chief firearms officer, that form part of that course; or

(b) passes a restricted firearms safety test, as administered by an instructor who is designated by a chief firearms officer, that is approved by the federal Minister.

(3) After expiration of prohibition order — An individual against whom a prohibition order was made

(a) is eligible to hold a licence only if the individual has, after the expiration of the prohibition order,

(i) successfully completed the Canadian Firearms Safety Course, as given by an instructor who is designated by a chief firearms officer, and

(ii) passed the tests, as administered by an instructor who is designated by a chief firearms officer, that form part of that Course; and

(b) is eligible to hold a licence authorizing the individual to possess restricted firearms only if the individual has, after the expiration of the prohibition order,

(i) successfully completed a restricted firearms safety course that is approved by the federal Minister, as given by an instructor who is designated by a chief firearms officer, and

(ii) passed any tests, as administered by an instructor who is designated by a chief firearms officer, that form part of that course.

(4) Exceptions — Subsections (1) and (2) do not apply to an individual who

(a) in the prescribed circumstances, has been certified by a chief firearms officer as meeting the prescribed criteria relating to the safe handling and use of firearms and the laws relating to firearms;

(b) is less than eighteen years old and requires a firearm to hunt or trap in order to sustain himself of herself or his or her family;

(c) on the commencement day, possessed one or more firearms and does not require a licence to acquire other firearms;

(d) requires a licence merely to acquire cross-bows; or

Unproclaimed paragraph — 7(4)(e)

(e) is a non-resident who is eighteen years old or older and by or on behalf of whom an application is made for a sixty-day licence authorizing the non-resident to possess firearms that are neither prohibited firearms nor restricted firearms.

(5) Further exception — Subsection (3) does not apply to an individual in respect of whom an order is made under section 113 of the *Criminal Code* (lifting of prohibition order for sustenance or employment) and who is exempted by a chief firearms officer from the application of that subsection.

Special Cases — Persons

8. (1) Minors — An individual who is less than eighteen years old and who is otherwise eligible to hold a licence is not eligible to hold a licence except as provided in this section.

(2) Minors hunting as a way of life — An individual who is less than eighteen years old and who hunts or traps as a way of life is eligible to hold a licence if the individual needs to hunt or trap in order to sustain himself or herself or his or her family.

(3) Hunting, etc. — An individual who is twelve years old or older but less than eighteen years old is eligible to hold a licence authorizing the individual to possess, in accordance with the conditions attached to the licence, a firearm for the purpose of target practice, hunting or instruction in the use of firearms or for the purpose of taking part in an organized competition.

(4) No prohibited or restricted firearms — An individual who is less than eighteen years old is not eligible to hold a licence authorizing the individual to possess prohibited firearms or restricted firearms or to acquire firearms or crossbows.

(5) Consent of parent or guardian — An individual who is less than eighteen years old is eligible to hold a licence only if a parent or person who has custody of the individual has consented, in writing or in any other manner that is satisfactory to the chief firearms officer, to the issuance of the licence.

9. (1) Businesses — A business is eligible to hold a licence authorizing a particular activity only if every person who stands in a prescribed relationship to the business is eligible under sections 5 and 6 to hold a licence authorizing that activity or the acquisition of restricted firearms.

(2) Safety courses — A business other than a carrier is eligible to hold a licence only if

(a) a chief firearms officer determines that no individual who stands in a prescribed relationship to the business need be eligible to hold a licence under section 7; or

(b) the individuals who stand in a prescribed relationship to the business and who are determined by a chief firearms officer to be the appropriate individuals to satisfy the requirements of section 7 are eligible to hold a licence under that section.

(3) Employees — A business other than a carrier is eligible to hold a licence only if every employee of the business who, in the course of duties of employment, handles or would handle firearms, prohibited weapons, restricted weapons, prohibited devices or prohibited ammunition is the holder of a licence authorizing the holder to acquire restricted firearms.

(4) Exception — In subsection (3), "firearm" does not include a partially manufactured barrelled weapon that, in its unfinished state, is not a barrelled weapon

(a) from which any shot, bullet or other projectile can be discharged; and

(b) that is capable of causing serious bodily injury or death to a person.

(5) Exception — Subsection (1) does not apply in respect of a person who stands in a prescribed relationship to a business where a chief firearms officer determines that, in all the circumstances, the business should not be ineligible to hold a licence merely because of that person's ineligibility.

(6) Exception for museums — Subsection (3) does not apply in respect of an employee of a museum

(a) who, in the course of duties of employment, handles or would handle only firearms that are designed or intended to exactly resemble, or to resemble with near precision, antique firearms, and who has been trained to handle or use such a firearm; or

(b) who is designated, by name, by a provincial minister.

10. International and interprovincial carriers — Sections 5, 6 and 9 apply in respect of a carrier whose business includes the transportation of firearms, prohibited weapons, restricted weapons, prohibited devices or prohibited ammunition from one province to any other province, or beyond the limits of a province, as if each reference in those sections to a chief firearms officer were a reference to the Registrar.

Special Cases — Prohibited Firearms, Weapons, Devices and Ammunition

11. (1) Prohibited firearms, weapons, devices and ammunition — businesses — A business that is otherwise eligible to hold a licence is not eligible to hold a licence authorizing the business to possess prohibited firearms, prohibited weapons, prohibited devices or prohibited ammunition except as provided in this section.

(2) Prescribed purposes — A business other than a carrier is eligible to hold a licence authorizing the business to possess prohibited firearms, prohibited weapons, prohibited devices or prohibited ammunition if the business needs to possess them for a prescribed purpose.

(3) Carriers — A carrier is eligible to hold a licence authorizing the carrier to possess prohibited firearms, prohibited weapons, prohibited devices or prohibited ammunition.

12. (1) Prohibited firearms — individuals — An individual who is otherwise eligible to hold a licence is not eligible to hold a licence authorizing the individual to possess prohibited firearms except as provided in this section.

(2) Grandfathered individuals — pre-January 1, 1978 automatic firearms — An individual is eligible to hold a licence authorizing the individual to possess automatic firearms that, on the commencement day, were registered as restricted weapons under the former Act if the individual

(a) on January 1, 1978 possessed one or more automatic firearms;

(b) on the commencement day held a registration certificate under the former Act for one or more automatic firearms; and

(c) beginning on the commencement day was continuously the holder of a registration certificate for one or more automatic firearms.

(3) Grandfathered individuals — pre-August 1, 1992 converted automatic firearms — An individual is eligible to hold a licence authorizing the individual to possess automatic firearms that have been altered to discharge only one projectile during one pressure of the trigger and that, on the commencement day, were registered as restricted weapons under the former Act if the individual

(a) on August 1, 1992 possessed one or more automatic firearms

(i) that had been so altered, and

(ii) for which on October 1, 1992 a registration certificate under the former Act had been issued or applied for;

(b) on the commencement day held a registration certificate under the former Act for one or more automatic firearms that had been so altered; and

(c) beginning on the commencement day was continuously the holder of a registration certificate for one or more automatic firearms that have been so altered.

(4) Grandfathered individuals — Prohibited Weapons Order, No. 12 — An individual is eligible to hold a licence authorizing the individual to possess firearms that were declared to be prohibited weapons under the former Act by the *Prohibited Weapons Order, No. 12*, made by Order in Council P.C. 1992-1690 of July 23, 1992 and registered as SOR/92-471 and that, on October 1, 1992, either were registered as restricted weapons under the former Act or were the subject of an application for a registration certificate under the former Act if the individual

(a) before July 27, 1992 possessed one or more firearms that were so declared;

(b) on the commencement day held a registration certificate under the former Act for one or more firearms that were so declared; and

(c) beginning on the commencement day was continuously the holder of a registration certificate for one or more firearms that were so declared.

(5) Grandfathered individuals — Prohibited Weapons Order, No. 13 — An individual is eligible to hold a licence authorizing the individual to possess firearms that were declared to be prohibited weapons under the former Act by the *Prohibited Weapons Order, No. 13*, made by Order in Council P.C. 1994-1974 of November 29, 1994 and registered as SOR/94-741 and that, on January 1, 1995, either were registered as restricted weapons under the former Act or were the subject of an application for a registration certificate under the former Act if the individual

(a) before January 1, 1995 possessed one or more firearms that were so declared;

(b) on the commencement day held a registration certificate under the former Act for one or more firearms that were so declared; and

(c) beginning on the commencement day was continuously the holder of a registration certificate for one or more firearms that were so declared.

(6) Grandfathered individuals — pre-February 14, 1995 handguns — A particular individual is eligible to hold a licence authorizing the particular individual to possess handguns that have a barrel equal to or less than 105 mm in length or that are designed or adapted to discharge a 25 or 32 calibre cartridge and for which on February 14, 1995 a registration certificate under the former Act had been issued to or applied for by that or another individual if the particular individual

(a) on February 14, 1995

(i) held a registration certificate under the former Act for one or more of those handguns, or

(ii) had applied for a registration certificate that was subsequently issued under the former Act for one or more of those handguns;

(b) on the commencement day held a registration certificate under the former Act for one or more of those handguns; and

(c) beginning on the commencement day was continuously the holder of a registration certificate for one or more of those handguns.

(7) Next of kin of grandfathered individuals — pre-February 14, 1995 handguns — A particular individual is eligible to hold a licence authorizing the particular individual to possess a particular handgun referred to in subsection (6) that was manufactured before 1946 if the particular individual is the spouse or a brother, sister, child or grandchild of an individual who was eligible under this or that subsection to hold a licence authorizing the individual to possess the particular handgun.

> **Proposed Amendment — 12(7)**
>
> **(7) Next of kin of grandfathered individuals — pre-February 14, 1995 handguns** — A particular individual is eligible to hold a licence authorizing the particular individual to possess a particular handgun referred to in subsection (6) that was manufactured before 1946 if the particular individual is the spouse or common-law partner or a brother, sister, child or grandchild of an individual who was eligible under this or that subsection to hold a licence authorizing the individual to possess the particular handgun.
>
> 2000, c. 12, s. 117 [Not in force at date of publication.]

(8) Grandfathered individuals — regulations re prohibited firearms — An individual is, in the prescribed circumstances, eligible to hold a licence authorizing the individual to possess firearms prescribed by a provision of regulations made by the Governor in Council under section 117.15 of the *Criminal Code* to be prohibited firearms if the individual

(a) on the day on which the provision comes into force possesses one or more of those firearms; and

(b) beginning on

(i) the day on which that provision comes into force, or

(ii) in the case of an individual who on that day did not hold but had applied for a registration certificate for one or more of those firearms, the day on which the registration certificate was issued was continuously the holder of a registration certificate for one or more of those firearms.

Registration Certificates

13. Registration certificate — A person is not eligible to hold a registration certificate for a firearm unless the person holds a licence authorizing the person to possess that kind of firearm.

14. Serial number — A registration certificate may be issued only for a firearm

(a) that bears a serial number sufficient to distinguish it from other firearms; or

(b) that is described in the prescribed manner.

15. Exempted firearms — A registration certificate may not be issued for a firearm that is owned by Her Majesty in right of Canada or a province or by a police force.

16. (1) Only one person per registration certificate — A registration certificate for a firearm may be issued to only one person.

(2) Exception — Subsection (1) does not apply in the case of a firearm for which a registration certificate referred to in section 127 was issued to more than one person.

Authorized Transportation of Firearms

17. Places where prohibited and restricted firearms may be possessed — Subject to sections 18 to 20, a prohibited firearm or restricted firearm the holder of the registration certificate for which is an individual may be possessed only at the dwelling-house of the individual, as indicated on the registration certificate, or at a place authorized by a chief firearms officer.

18. Transporting and using prohibited firearms — An individual who holds a licence authorizing the individual to possess prohibited firearms may be authorized to transport a particular prohibited firearm between two or more specified places

(a) in the case of a handgun referred to in subsection 12(6) (pre-February 14, 1995 handguns), for use in target practice, or a target shooting competition, under specified conditions or under the auspices of a shooting club or shooting range that is approved under section 29; or

(b) if the individual

(i) changes residence,

(ii) wishes to transport the firearm to a peace officer, firearms officer or chief firearms officer for registration or disposal in accordance with this Act or Part III of the *Criminal Code*,

(iii) wishes to transport the firearm for repair, storage, sale, exportation or appraisal, or

(iv) wishes to transport the firearm to a gun show.

19. (1) Transporting and using restricted firearms — An individual who holds a licence authorizing the individual to possess restricted firearms may be authorized to transport a particular restricted firearm between two or more specified places for any good and sufficient reason, including, without restricting the generality of the foregoing,

(a) for use in target practice, or a target shooting competition, under specified conditions or under the auspices of a shooting club or shooting range that is approved under section 29; or

(b) if the individual

(i) changes residence,

(ii) wishes to transport the firearm to a peace officer, firearms officer or chief firearms officer for registration or disposal in accordance with this Act or Part III of the *Criminal Code*,

(iii) wishes to transport the firearm for repair, storage, sale, exportation or appraisal, or

(iv) wishes to transport the firearm to a gun show.

(2) Non-residents — A non-resident may be authorized to transport a particular restricted firearm between specified places in accordance with section 35.

20. Carrying restricted firearms and pre-February 14, 1995 handguns — An individual who holds a licence authorizing the individual to possess restricted firearms or handguns referred to in subsection 12(6) (pre-February 14, 1995 handguns) may be authorized to possess a particular restricted firearm or handgun at a place other than the place at which it is authorized to be possessed if the individual needs the particular restricted firearm or handgun

(a) to protect the life of that individual or of other individuals; or

(b) for use in connection with his or her lawful profession or occupation.

Authorized Transfers and Lending

General Provisions

21. Definition of "transfer" — For the purposes of sections 22 to 32, **"transfer"** means sell, barter or give.

22. Mental disorder, etc. — A person may transfer or lend a firearm to an individual only if the person has no reason to believe that the individual

(a) has a mental illness that makes it desirable, in the interests of the safety of that individual or any other person, that the individual not possess a firearm; or

(b) is impaired by alcohol or a drug.

Authorized Transfers

23. Authorization to transfer firearms — A person may transfer a firearm if, at the time of the transfer,

(a) the transferee produces to the person a document that purports to be a licence authorizing the transferee to acquire and possess that kind of firearm;

(b) the person

(i) has no reason to believe that the transferee is not authorized by the document to acquire and possess that kind of firearm, and

(ii) informs a chief firearms officer of the transfer and obtains the authorization of the chief firearms officer for the transfer;

(c) the transferee holds a licence authorizing the transferee to acquire and possess that kind of firearm;

(d) a new registration certificate for the firearm is issued in accordance with this Act; and

(e) the prescribed conditions are complied with.

24. (1) Authorization to transfer prohibited weapons, devices and ammunition — Subject to section 26, a person may transfer a prohibited weapon, prohibited device or prohibited ammunition only to a business.

(2) Conditions — A person may transfer a prohibited weapon, prohibited device, ammunition or prohibited ammunition to a business only if

(a) the business holds a licence authorizing the business to acquire and possess prohibited weapons, prohibited devices, ammunition or prohibited ammunition, as the case may be;

(b) the business produces to the person a document that purports to be a licence authorizing the business to acquire and possess prohibited weapons, prohibited devices, ammunition or prohibited ammunition, as the case may be;

Unproclaimed paragraphs — 24(2)(c), (d)

(c) the person

(i) has no reason to believe that the business is not authorized by the document to acquire and possess prohibited weapons, prohibited devices, ammunition or prohibited ammunition, as the case may be, and

(ii) informs a chief firearms officer of the transfer and obtains the authorization of the chief firearms officer for the transfer; and

(d) the prescribed conditions are complied with.

25. Authorization to transfer ammunition to individuals — A person may transfer ammunition that is not prohibited ammunition to an individual only if the individual

(a) until January 1, 2001, holds a licence authorizing him or her to possess firearms or a prescribed document; or

(b) after January 1, 2001, holds a licence authorizing him or her to possess firearms.

26. (1) Authorization to transfer firearms to the Crown and to the police — A person may transfer a firearm to Her Majesty in right of Canada or a province or to a police force if the person informs the Registrar of the transfer and complies with the prescribed conditions.

(2) Authorization to transfer prohibited weapons, etc., to the Crown and to the police — A person may transfer a prohibited weapon, restricted weapon, prohibited device, ammunition or prohibited ammunition to Her Majesty in right of Canada or a province or to a police force if the person informs a chief firearms officer of the transfer and complies with the prescribed conditions.

27. Chief firearms officer — On being informed of a proposed transfer of a firearm under section 23, of a proposed transfer of a firearm, prohibited weapon, prohibited device, ammunition or prohibited ammunition to a business under section 24 or of a proposed importation of a firearm that is not a prohibited firearm by an individual under paragraph 40(1)(c), a chief firearms officer shall

(a) verify

(i) whether the transferee or individual holds a licence,

(ii) whether the transferee or individual is still eligible to hold that licence, and

(iii) whether the licence authorizes the transferee or individual to acquire that kind of firearm or to acquire prohibited weapons, prohibited devices, ammunition or prohibited ammunition, as the case may be;

(b) in the case of

(i) a proposed transfer of a restricted firearm or a handgun referred to in subsection 12(6) (pre-February 14, 1995 handguns), or

(ii) a proposed importation of a restricted firearm,

verify the purpose for which the transferee or individual wishes to acquire the restricted firearm or handgun and determine whether the particular restricted firearm or handgun is appropriate for that purpose;

(c) decide whether to approve the transfer or importation and inform the Registrar of that decision; and

(d) take the prescribed measures.

28. Permitted purposes — A chief firearms officer may approve the transfer to an individual of a restricted firearm or a handgun referred to in subsection 12(6) (pre-February 14, 1995 handguns) or the importation by an individual of a restricted firearm under paragraph 40(1)(c) only if the chief firearms officer is satisfied

(a) that the individual needs the restricted firearm or handgun

(i) to protect the life of that individual or of other individuals, or

(ii) for use in connection with his or her lawful profession or occupation; or

(b) that the purpose for which the individual wishes to acquire the restricted firearm or handgun is

(i) for use in target practice, or a target shooting competition, under conditions specified in an authorization to transport or under the auspices of a shooting club or shooting range that is approved under section 29, or

(ii) to form part of a gun collection of the individual, in the case of an individual who satisfies the criteria described in section 30.

29.

Unproclaimed subsection — 29(1)

(1) Shooting clubs and shooting ranges — No person shall operate a shooting club or shooting range except under an approval of the provincial minister for the province in which the premises of the shooting club or shooting range are located.

(2) Approval — A provincial minister may approve a shooting club or shooting range for the purposes of this Act if

(a) the shooting club or shooting range complies with the regulations made under paragraph 117(e); and

(b) the premises of the shooting club or shooting range are located in that province.

(3) Revocation — A provincial minister who approves a shooting club or shooting range for the purposes of this Act may revoke the approval for any good and sufficient reason including, without limiting the generality of the foregoing, where the shooting club or shooting range contravenes a regulation made under paragraph 117(e).

(4) Delegation — A chief firearms officer who is authorized in writing by a provincial minister may perform such duties and functions of the provincial minister under this section as are specified in the authorization.

(5) Notice of refusal to approve or revocation — Where a provincial minister decides to refuse to approve or to revoke an approval of a shooting club or shooting range for the purposes of this Act, the provincial minister shall give notice of the decision to the shooting club or shooting range.

(6) Material to accompany notice — A notice given under subsection (5) must include reasons for the decision disclosing the nature of the information relied on for the decision and must be accompanied by a copy of sections 74 to 81.

(7) Non-disclosure of information — A provincial minister need not disclose any information the disclosure of which could, in the opinion of the provincial minister, endanger the safety of any person.

30. Gun collectors — The criteria referred to in subparagraph 28(b)(ii) are that the individual

(a) has knowledge of the historical, technological or scientific characteristics that relate or distinguish the restricted firearms or handguns that he or she possesses;

(b) has consented to the periodic inspection, conducted in a reasonable manner, of the premises in which the restricted firearms or handguns are to be kept; and

(c) has complied with such other requirements as are prescribed respecting knowledge, secure storage and the keeping of records in respect of restricted firearms or handguns.

31. (1) Registrar — On being informed of a proposed transfer of a firearm, the Registrar may

(a) issue a new registration certificate for the firearm in accordance with this Act; and

(b) revoke any registration certificate for the firearm held by the transferor.

(2) Transfers of firearms to the Crown and to the police — On being informed of a transfer of a firearm to Her Majesty in right of Canada or a province or to a police force, the Registrar shall revoke any registration certificate for the firearm.

32. Mail-order transfers of firearms — A person may transfer a firearm by mail only if

(a) the verifications, notifications, issuances and authorizations referred to in sections 21 to 28, 30, 31, 40 to 43 and 46 to 52 take place within a reasonable period before the transfer in the prescribed manner;

Unproclaimed paragraph — 32(b)

(b) the firearm is delivered by a person designated by a chief firearms officer and the person ensures that the transferee holds a licence authorizing the transferee to acquire that kind of firearm; and

(c) the prescribed conditions are complied with.

Authorized Lending

33. Authorization to lend — Subject to section 34, a person may lend a firearm only if

    (a) the person

        (i) has reasonable grounds to believe that the borrower holds a licence authorizing the borrower to possess that kind of firearm, and

        (ii) lends the borrower the registration certificate for the firearm, except in the case of a borrower who uses the firearm to hunt or trap in order to sustain himself or herself or his or her family; or

    (b) the borrower uses the firearm under the direct and immediate supervision of the person in the same manner in which the person may lawfully use it.

34. Authorization to lend firearms, etc., to the Crown and to the police — A person may lend a firearm, prohibited weapon, restricted weapon, prohibited device, ammunition or prohibited ammunition to Her Majesty in right of Canada or a province or to a police force if

    (a) in the case of a firearm, the transferor lends the borrower the registration certificate for the firearm; and

    (b) the prescribed conditions are complied with.

Authorized Exportation and Importation

Individuals

35. (1) Authorization for non-residents who do not hold a licence to import firearms that are not prohibited firearms — A non-resident who does not hold a licence may import a firearm that is not prohibited firearm if, at the time of the importation,

    (a) the non-resident

        (i) is eighteen years old or older,

Unproclaimed subparagraph — 35(1)(a)(ii)

        (ii) declares the firearm to a customs officer in the prescribed manner and, in the case of a declaration in writing, completes the prescribed form containing the prescribed information, and

        (iii) in the case of a restricted firearm, produces an authorization to transport the restricted firearm; and

Unproclaimed paragraph — 35(1)(b)

    (b) a customs officer confirms in the prescribed manner the declaration referred to in subparagraph (a)(ii) and the authorization to transport referred to in subparagraph (a)(iii).

Unproclaimed subsections — 35(2)-(4)

(2) **Non-compliances** — Where a firearm is declared at a customs office to a customs officer but the requirements of subparagraphs (1)(a)(ii) and (iii) are not complied with, the customs officer may authorize the firearm to be exported from that customs office or may detain the firearm and give the non-resident a reasonable time to comply with those requirements.

(3) **Disposal of firearm** — Where those requirements are not complied with within a reasonable time and the firearm is not exported, the firearm shall be disposed of in the prescribed manner.

(4) **Non-compliance** — Where a firearm that is neither a prohibited firearm nor a restricted firearm is declared at a customs office to a customs officer and

(a) the non-resident has not truthfully completed the prescribed form, or

(b) the customs officer has reasonable grounds to believe that it is desirable, in the interests of the safety of the non-resident or any other person, that the declaration not be confirmed,

the customs officer may refuse to confirm the declaration and may authorize the firearm to be exported from that customs office.

Unproclaimed section — 36

36. (1) Temporary licence and registration certificate — A declaration that is confirmed under paragraph 35(1)(b) has the same effect after the importation of the firearm as a licence authorizing the non-resident to possess only that firearm and as a registration certificate for the firearm until the expiration of sixty days after the importation or, in the case of a restricted firearm, until the earlier of

(a) the expiration of those sixty days, and

(b) the expiration of the authorization to transport.

(2) **Renewal** — A chief firearms officer may renew the confirmation of a declaration for one or more periods of sixty days.

(3) **Electronic or other means** — For greater certainty, an application for a renewal of the confirmation of a declaration may be made by telephone or other electronic means or by mail and a chief firearms officer may renew that confirmation by electronic means or by mail.

Unproclaimed section — 37

37. (1) Authorization for non-residents who do not hold a licence to export firearms that are not prohibited firearms — A non-resident who does not hold a licence may export a firearm that is not a prohibited firearm and that was imported by the non-resident in accordance with section 35 if, at the time of the exportation,

> (a) the non-resident
>
>> (i) declares the firearm to a customs officer, and
>>
>> (ii) produces to a customs officer in the prescribed manner the declaration and, where applicable, the authorization to transport that were confirmed in accordance with that section; and
>
> (b) a customs officer confirms the declaration referred to in subparagraph (a)(i) in the prescribed manner.

(2) Non-compliance — Where a firearm is declared to a customs officer but the requirements of subparagraph (1)(a)(ii) are not complied with, the customs officer may detain the firearm and, with the approval of a chief firearms officer, give the non-resident a reasonable time to comply with those requirements.

(3) Disposal of firearm — Where those requirements are not complied with within a reasonable time, the firearm shall be disposed of in the prescribed manner.

Unproclaimed section — 38

38. (1) Authorization for individuals who hold a licence to export firearms — An individual who holds a licence may export a firearm if, at the time of the exportation,

> (a) the individual
>
>> (i) declares the firearm to a customs officer in the prescribed manner and, in the case of a declaration in writing, completes the prescribed form containing the prescribed information, and
>>
>> (ii) produces his or her licence and the registration certificate for the firearm and, in the case of a prohibited firearm or restricted firearm, an authorization to transport the firearm; and
>
> (b) a customs officer confirms the documents referred to in subparagraphs (a)(i) and (ii) in the prescribed manner.

(2) Non-compliance — Where a firearm is declared to a customs officer but the requirements of subparagraph (1)(a)(ii) are not complied with, the customs officer may detain the firearm.

(3) Disposal of firearm — A firearm that is detained under subsection (2) may be disposed of in the prescribed manner.

Unproclaimed section — 39

39. Authorization for individuals to export replica firearms — An individual may export a replica firearm if he or she declares the replica firearm to a customs officer in the prescribed manner.

Unproclaimed section — 40

40. (1) Authorization for individuals who hold a licence to import firearms — An individual who holds a licence may import a firearm if, at the time of the importation,

  (a) the individual declares the firearm to a customs officer in the prescribed manner;

  (b) in the case of a firearm that was exported in accordance with section 38, the individual produces the declaration confirmed in accordance with that section and, in the case of a prohibited firearm or restricted firearm, an authorization to transport the prohibited firearm or restricted firearm;

  (c) in the case of a firearm that is not a prohibited firearm and for which a registration certificate has not been issued,

>   (i) the individual completes the prescribed form containing the prescribed information, if the declaration referred to in paragraph (a) is in writing,

>   (ii) the individual holds a licence authorizing him or her to acquire and possess that kind of firearm,

>   (iii) a customs officer informs a chief firearms officer of the importation and the chief firearms officer approves the importation in accordance with section 27, and

>   (iv) in the case of a restricted firearm, the individual produces an authorization to transport the restricted firearm; and

  (d) a customs officer confirms the documents referred to in paragraph (b) or (c) in the prescribed manner.

(2) Non-compliance — Where a firearm is declared at a customs office to a customs officer but the requirements of paragraph (1)(b) or (c) are not complied with, the customs officer may authorize the firearm to be exported from that customs office or may detain the firearm and give the individual a reasonable time to comply with those requirements.

(3) Disposal of firearm — Where those requirements are not complied with within a reasonable time and the firearm is not exported, the firearm shall be disposed of in the prescribed manner.

(4) Importation of prohibited firearms — An individual who holds a licence may import a prohibited firearm only if he or she previously exported the prohibited firearm in accordance with section 38.

(5) Prohibited firearm — Where a prohibited firearm is declared at a customs office to a customs officer and the prohibited firearm was not previously exported in accordance with section 38, the customs officer may authorize the prohibited firearm to be exported from that customs office.

(6) Disposal — Prohibited firearms that are not immediately exported under subsection (5) are forfeited to Her Majesty in right of Canada and shall be disposed of in the prescribed manner.

Unproclaimed section — 41

41. Temporary registration certificate — A declaration that is confirmed in accordance with paragraph 40(1)(d) has the same effect as a registration certificate for the firearm for the period for which the confirmation is expressed to be effective.

Unproclaimed section — 42

42. Notification of Registrar — A customs officer shall inform the Registrar without delay of the exportation or importation of a firearm by an individual.

Unproclaimed sections — 43-53

Businesses

43. Authorization for businesses to import or export — A business may export or import a firearm, prohibited weapon, restricted weapon, prohibited device, component or part designed exclusively for use in the manufacture of or assembly into an automatic firearm or prohibited ammunition only if the business holds an authorization to export or an authorization to import.

44. Authorization to export — An authorization to export goods described in section 43 may be issued to a business only if the business that applies for such an authorization

    (a) in the case of a firearm, holds the registration certificate for the firearm;

    (b) in the case of a prohibited firearm, prohibited weapon, prohibited device, component or part designed exclusively for use in the manufacture of or assembly into an automatic firearm or prohibited ammunition, identifies it in the prescribed manner and specifies the prescribed purpose for the exportation;

    (c) holds a licence authorizing it to possess those goods, except where those goods are to be shipped in transit through Canada by a business that does not carry on business in Canada;

    (d) indicates the destination of those goods;

    (e) provides the Registrar with the prescribed information and any other information reasonably required by the Registrar.

45. (1) Authorization to be produced — A business that holds an authorization to export goods described in section 43 must produce the authorization to a customs officer at the time of the exportation.

(2) Customs officer — A customs officer may confirm an authorization to export.

(3) Non-compliance — Where an authorization to export is not confirmed, a customs officer may detain goods described in section 43.

(4) Disposal — A good that is detained under subsection (3) my be disposed of in the prescribed manner.

46. Authorization to import — An authorization to import goods described in section 43 may be issued to a business only if the business that applies for such an authorization

    (a) holds a licence authorizing it to acquire and possess those goods, except where those goods are to be shipped in transit through Canada by a business that does not carry on business in Canada;

    (b) identifies those goods in the prescribed manner;

    (c) in the case of either a firearm that is not a prohibited firearm or a restricted weapon, specifies the purpose for the importation;

    (d) in the case of a prohibited firearm, prohibited weapon, prohibited device, component or part designed exclusively for use in the manufacture of or assembly into an automatic firearm or prohibited ammunition, specifies the prescribed purpose for the importation;

    (e) indicates the destination in Canada of those goods; and

    (f) provides the Registrar with the prescribed information and any other information reasonably required by the Registrar.

47. (1) Authorization to be produced — A business that holds an authorization to import goods described in section 43 must produce the authorization at a customs office to a customs officer at the time of the importation.

(2) Customs officer — A customs officer may confirm an authorization to import.

(3) Non-compliance — Where an authorization to import is not confirmed, a customs officer may authorize goods described in section 43 to be exported from that customs office, in which case the goods may be exported without any other authorization.

(4) Disposal — Goods that are not exported under subsection (3) within ten days are forfeited to Her Majesty in right of Canada and shall be disposed of in the prescribed manner.

48. Temporary registration certificate — An authorization to import a firearm that is confirmed in accordance with subsection 47(2) has the same effect as a registration certificate for the firearm for the period for which the confirmation is expressed to be effective.

49. Separate authorization — Each exportation or importation of goods described in section 43 requires a separate authorization to export or authorization to import.

50. Notification of Registrar — A customs officer shall inform the Registrar without delay of the exportation or importation of goods described in section 43 by a business.

51. Notification of Minister responsible for the Export and Import Permits Act — The Registrar shall inform the member of the Queen's Privy Council for Canada who is designated by the Governor in Council as the Minister for the purposes of the *Export and Import Permits Act* of every application by a business for an authorization to export or authorization to import.

52. Only at designated customs offices — No business shall export or import goods described in section 43 except at a customs office designated for that purpose by the Minister of National Revenue.

53. No in-transit shipments of prohibited firearms, weapons, devices and ammunition — No business shall import a prohibited firearm, prohibited weapon prohibited device or prohibited ammunition that is to be shipped in transit through Canada and exported.

Licences, Registration Certificates and Authorizations

Applications

54. (1) Applications — A licence, registration certificate or authorization may be issued only on application made in the prescribed form containing the prescribed information and accompanied by payment of the prescribed fees.

(2) To whom made — An application for a licence, registration certificate or authorization must be made to

    (a) a chief firearms officer, in the case of a licence, an authorization to carry or an authorization to transport; or

    (b) the Registrar, in the case of a registration certificate, an authorization to export or an authorization to import.

(3) Pre-commencement restricted firearms and handguns — An individual who, on the commencement day, possesses one or more restricted firearms or one or more handguns referred to in subsection 12(6) (pre-February 14, 1995 handguns) must specify, in any application for a licence authorizing the individual to possess restricted firearms or handguns that are so referred to,

    (a) except in the case of a firearm described in paragraph (b), for which purpose described in section 28 the individual wishes to continue to possess restricted firearms or handguns that are so referred to; and

    (b) for which of those firearms was a registration certificate under the former Act issued because they were relics, were of value as a curiosity or rarity or were valued as a memento, remembrance or souvenir.

55. (1) Further information — A chief firearms officer or the Registrar may require an applicant for a licence or authorization to submit such information, in addition to that included in the application, as may reasonably be regarded as relevant for the purpose of determining whether the applicant is eligible to hold the licence or authorization.

(2) Investigation — Without restricting the scope of the inquiries that may be made with respect to an application for a licence, a chief firearms officer may conduct an investigation of the applicant, which may consist of interviews with neighbours, community workers, social workers, individuals who work or live with the applicant, spouse, former spouse, dependants or whomever in the opinion of the chief firearms officer may provide information pertaining to whether the applicant is eligible under section 5 to hold a licence.

Proposed Amendment — 55(2)

(2) Investigation — Without restricting the scope of the inquiries that may be made with respect to an application for a licence, a chief firearms officer may conduct an investigation of the applicant, which may consist of interviews with neighbours, community workers, social workers, individuals who work or live with the applicant, spouse or common-law partner, former spouse or former common-law partner, dependants or whomever in the opinion of the chief firearms officer may provide information pertaining to whether the applicant is eligible under section 5 to hold a licence.

2000, c. 12, s. 118 [Not in force at date of publication.]

Issuance

56. (1) Licences — A chief firearms officer is responsible for issuing licences.

(2) Only one licence per individual — Only one licence may be issued to any one individual.

(3) Separate licence for each location — A business other than a carrier requires a separate licence for each place where the business is carried on.

57. Authorizations to carry or transport — A chief firearms officer is responsible for issuing authorizations to carry and authorizations to transport.

58. (1) Conditions — A chief firearms officer who issues a licence, an authorization to carry or an authorization to transport may attach any reasonable condition to it that the chief firearms officer considers desirable in the particular circumstances and in the interests of the safety of the holder or any other person.

(2) Minors — Before attaching a condition to a licence that is to be issued to an individual who is less than eighteen years old and who is not eligible to hold a licence under subsection 8(2) (minors hunting as a way of life), a chief firearms officer must consult with a parent or person who has custody of the individual.

(3) Minors — Before issuing a licence to an individual who is less than eighteen years old and who is not eligible to hold a licence under subsection 8(2) (minors hunting as a way of life), a chief firearms officer shall have a parent or person who has custody of the individual sign the licence, including any conditions attached to it.

59. Different registered owner — An individual who holds an authorization to carry or authorization to transport need not be the person to whom the registration certificate for the particular prohibited firearm or restricted firearm was issued.

60. Registration certificates and authorizations to export or import — The Registrar is responsible for issuing registration certificates for firearms and assigning firearms identification numbers to them and for issuing authorizations to export and authorizations to import.

61. (1) Form — A licence or registration certificate must be in the prescribed form and include the prescribed information and any conditions attached to it.

(2) Form of authorizations — An authorization to carry, authorization to transport, authorization to export or authorization to import may be in the prescribed form and include the prescribed information, including any conditions attached to it.

(3) Condition attached to licence — An authorization to carry or authorization to transport may take the form of a condition attached to a licence.

(4) Businesses — A licence that is issued to a business must specify each particular activity that the licence authorizes in relation to prohibited firearms, restricted firearms, firearms that are neither prohibited firearms nor restricted firearms, crossbows, prohibited weapons, restricted weapons, prohibited devices, ammunition or prohibited ammunition.

62. Not transferable — Licences, registration certificates, authorizations to carry, authorizations to transport, authorizations to export and authorizations to import are not transferable.

63. (1) Geographical extent — Subject to subsection (2), licences, registration certificates, authorizations to transport, authorizations to export and authorizations to import are valid throughout Canada.

(2) Intraprovincial carriers — A licence that is issued to carrier, other than a carrier described in section 73, is not valid outside the province in which it is issued.

(3) Authorizations to carry — Authorizations to carry are not valid outside the province in which they are issued.

Term

64. (1) Term of licences — A licence that is issued to an individual who is eighteen years old or older expires on the earlier of

(a) five years after the birthday of the holder next following the day on which it is issued, and

(b) the expiration of the period for which it is expressed to be issued.

(2) Minors — A licence that is issued to an individual who is less than eighteen years old expires on the earlier of

(a) the day on which the holder attains the age of eighteen years, and

(b) the expiration of the period for which it is expressed to be issued.

(3) Businesses other than museums — A licence that is issued to a business other than a museum expires on the earlier of

(a) one year after the day on which it is issued, and

(b) the expiration of the period for which it is expressed to be issued.

(4) Museums — A licence that is issued to a museum expires on the earlier of

(a) three years after the day on which it is issued, and

(b) the expiration of the period for which it is expressed to be issued.

65. (1) Term of authorizations — Subject to subsections (2) to (4), an authorization expires on the expiration of the period for which it is expressed to be issued.

(2) Authorizations to transport — Subject to subsection (3), an authorization to transport that takes the form of a condition attached to a licence expires on the earlier of

(a) the expiration of the period for which the condition is expressed to be attached, and

(b) the expiration of the licence.

(3) Authorizations to transport — An authorization to transport a restricted firearm or a handgun referred to in subsection 12(6) (pre-February 14, 1995 handguns) for use in target practice, or a target shooting competition, under specified conditions or under the auspices of a shooting club or shooting range that is approved under section 29 expires

(a) in the case of an authorization to transport that takes the form of a condition attached to a licence, on the earlier of

(i) the expiration of the period for which the condition is expressed to be attached, which period may not be less than one year or more than three years, and

(ii) the expiration of the licence; and

(b) in the case of an authorization to transport that does not take the form of a condition attached to a licence, on the expiration of the period for which the authorization is expressed to be issued, which period may not be less than one year or more than three years.

(4) Authorizations to carry — An authorization to carry expires

(a) in the case of an authorization to carry that takes the form of a condition attached to a licence, on the earlier of

(i) the expiration of the period for which the condition is expressed to be attached, which period may not be more than two years, and

(ii) the expiration of the licence; and

(b) in the case of an authorization to carry that does not take the form of a condition attached to a licence, on the expiration of the period for which the authorization is expressed to be issued, which period may not be more than two years.

66. Term of registration certificates — A registration certificate for a firearm expires where

(a) the holder of the registration certificate ceases to be the owner of the firearm; or

(b) the firearm ceases to be a firearm.

67. (1) Renewal — A chief firearms officer may renew a licence, authorization to carry or authorization to transport in the same manner and in the same circumstances in which a licence, authorization to carry or authorization to transport may be issued.

(2) Restricted firearms and pre-February 14, 1995 handguns — On renewing a licence authorizing an individual to possess restricted firearms or handguns referred to in subsection 12(6) (pre-February 14, 1995 handguns), a chief firearms officer shall decide whether any of those firearms or handguns that the individual possesses are being used for

(a) the purpose described in section 28 for which the individual acquired the restricted firearms or handguns; or

(b) in the case of any of those firearms or handguns that were possessed by the individual on the commencement day, the purpose described in that section that was specified by the individual in the licence application.

(3) Registrar — A chief firearms officer who decides that any restricted firearms or any handguns referred to in subsection 12(6) (pre-February 14, 1995 handguns) that are possessed by an individual are not being used for that purpose shall

(a) give notice of that decision in the prescribed form to the individual; and

(b) inform the Registrar of that decision.

(4) Relics — Subsections (2) and (3) do not apply to a firearm

(a) that is a relic, is of value as a curiosity or rarity or is valued as a memento, remembrance or souvenir,

(b) that was specified in the licence application as being a firearm for which a registration certificate under the former Act was issued because the firearm was a relic, was of value as a curiosity or rarity or was valued as a memento, remembrance or souvenir;

(c) for which a registration certificate under the former Act was issued because the firearm was a relic, was of value as a curiosity or rarity or was valued as a memento, remembrance or souvenir; and

(d) in respect of which an individual, on the commencement day, held a registration certificate under the former Act.

(5) Material to accompany notice — A notice given under paragraph (3)(a) must include the reasons for the decision and be accompanied by a copy of sections 74 to 81.

Refusal to Issue and Revocation

68. Licences and authorizations — A chief firearms officer shall refuse to issue a licence if the applicant is not eligible to hold one and may refuse to issue an authorization to carry or authorization to transport for any good and sufficient reason.

69. Registration certificates — The Registrar may refuse to issue a registration certificate, authorization to export or authorization to import for any good and sufficient reason including, in the case of an application for a registration certificate, where the applicant is not eligible to hold a registration certificate.

70. (1) Revocation of licence or authorization — A chief firearms officer who issues a licence, authorization to carry or authorization to transport may revoke it for any good and sufficient reason including, without limiting the generality of the foregoing,

(a) where the holder of the licence or authorization

(i) is no longer or never was eligible to hold the licence or authorization,

(ii) contravenes any condition attached to the licence or authorization, or

(iii) has been convicted or discharged under section 730 of the *Criminal Code* of an offence referred to in paragraph 5(2)(a); or

(b) where, in the case of a business, a person who stands in a prescribed relationship to the business has been convicted or discharged under section 730 of the *Criminal Code* of any such offence.

(2) Registrar — The Registrar may revoke an authorization to export or authorization to import for any good and sufficient reason.

1995, c. 39, s. 137

71. (1) Revocation of registration certificate — The Registrar

(a) may revoke a registration certificate for any good and sufficient reason; and

(b) shall revoke a registration certificate for a firearm held by an individual where the Registrar is informed by a chief firearms officer under section 67 that the firearm is not being used for

(i) the purpose for which the individual acquired it, or

(ii) in the case of a firearm possessed by the individual on the commencement day, the purpose specified by the individual in the licence application.

(2) Automatic revocation of registration certificate — A registration certificate for a prohibited firearm referred to in subsection 12(3) (pre-August 1, 1992 converted automatic firearms) is automatically revoked on the change of any alteration in the prohibited firearm that was described in the application for the registration certificate.

72. (1) Notice of refusal to issue or revocation — Where a chief firearms officer decides to refuse to issue or to revoke a licence or authorization to transport or the Registrar decides to refuse to issue or to revoke a registration certificate, authorization to export or authorization to import, the chief firearms officer or Registrar shall give notice of the decision in the prescribed form to the applicant for or holder of the licence, registration certificate or authorization.

(2) Material to accompany notice — A notice given under subsection (1) must include reasons for the decision disclosing the nature of the information relied on for the decision and must be accompanied by a copy of sections 74 to 81.

(3) Non-disclosure of information — A chief firearms officer or the Registrar need not disclose any information the disclosure of which could, in the opinion of the chief firearms officer or the Registrar, endanger the safety of any person.

(4) Disposal of firearms — A notice given under subsection (1) in respect of a licence must specify a reasonable period during which the applicant for or holder of the licence may deliver to a peace officer or a firearms officer or a chief firearms officer or otherwise lawfully dispose of any firearm, prohibited weapon, restricted weapon, prohibited device or prohibited ammunition that the applicant for or holder of the licence possesses and during which sections 91, 92 and 94 of the *Criminal Code* do not apply to the applicant or holder.

(5) Idem — A notice given under subsection (1) in respect of a registration certificate must specify a reasonable period during which the applicant for or holder of the registration certificate may deliver to a peace officer or a firearms officer or a chief firearms officer or otherwise lawfully dispose of the firearm to which the registration certificate relates and during which sections 91, 92 and 94 of the *Criminal Code* and section 112 of this Act do not apply to the applicant or holder.

(6) Reference — If the applicant for or holder of the licence or registration certificate refers the refusal to issue it or revocation of it to a provincial court judge under section 74, the reasonable period of time does not begin until after the reference is finally disposed of.

International and Interprovincial Carriers

73. Application — Sections 54 to 72 apply in respect of a carrier whose business includes the transportation of firearms, prohibited weapons, restricted weapons, prohibited devices or prohibited ammunition from one province to any other province, or beyond the limits of a province, as if each reference in those sections to a chief firearms officer were a reference to the Registrar.

References to Provincial Court Judge

74. (1) Reference to judge of refusal to issue or revocation, etc. — Subject to subsection (2), where

(a) a chief firearms officer or the Registrar refuses to issue or revokes a licence, registration certificate, authorization to transport, authorization to export or authorization to import,

(b) a chief firearms officer decides under section 67 that a firearm possessed by an individual who holds a licence is not being used for

(i) the purpose for which the individual acquired the firearm, or

(ii) in the case of a firearm possessed by an individual on the commencement day, the purpose specified by the individual in the licence application, or

(c) a provincial minister refuses to approve or revokes the approval of a shooting club or shooting range for the purposes of this Act,

the applicant for or holder of the licence, registration certificate, authorization or approval may refer the matter to a provincial court judge in the territorial division in which the applicant or holder resides.

(2) Limitation period — An applicant or holder may only refer a matter to a provincial court judge under subsection (1) within thirty days after receiving notice of the decision of the chief firearms officer, Registrar or provincial minister under section 29, 67 or 72 or within such further time as is allowed by a provincial court judge, whether before or after the expiration of those thirty days.

75. (1) Hearing of reference — On receipt of a reference under section 74, the provincial court judge shall fix a date for the hearing of the reference and direct that notice of the hearing be given to the chief firearms officer, Registrar or provincial minister and to the applicant for or holder of the licence, registration certificate, authorization or approval, in such manner as the provincial court judge may specify.

(2) Evidence — At the hearing of the reference, the provincial court judge shall hear all relevant evidence presented by or on behalf of the chief firearms officer, Registrar or provincial minister and the applicant or holder.

(3) Burden of proof — At the hearing of the reference, the burden of proof is on the applicant or holder to satisfy the provincial court judge that the refusal to issue or revocation of the licence, registration certificate or authorization, the decision or the refusal to approve or revocation of the approval was not justified.

(4) Where hearing may proceed ex parte — A provincial court judge may proceed *ex parte* to hear and determine a reference in the absence of the applicant or holder in the same circumstances as those in which a summary conviction court may, under Part XXVII of the *Criminal Code*, proceed with a trial in the absence of the defendant.

76. Decision by provincial court judge — On the hearing of a reference, the provincial court judge may, by order,

(a) confirm the decision of the chief firearms officer, Registrar or provincial minister,

(b) direct the chief firearms officer or Registrar to issue a licence, registration certificate or authorization or direct the provincial minister to approve a club or shooting range; or

(c) cancel the revocation of the licence, registration certificate, authorization or approval or the decision of the chief firearms officer under section 67.

Appeals to Superior Court and Court of Appeal

76.1 Nunavut — With respect to Nunavut, the following definitions apply for the purposes of sections 77 to 81.

"provincial court judge" means a judge of the Nunavut Court of Justice.

"superior court" means a judge of the Court of Appeal of Nunavut.

1999, c. 3, s. 64

77. (1) Appeal to superior court — Subject to section 78, where a provincial court judge makes an order under paragraph 76(a), the applicant for or holder of the licence, registration certificate, authorization or approval, as the case may be, may appeal to the superior court against the order.

(2) Appeal by Attorney General — Subject to section 78, where a provincial court judge makes an order under paragraph 76(b) or (c),

(a) the Attorney General of Canada may appeal to the superior court against the order, if the order is directed to a chief firearms officer who was designated by the federal Minister, to the Registrar or to the federal Minister; or

(b) the attorney general of the province may appeal to the superior court against the order, in the case of any other order made under paragraph 76(b) or (c).

78. (1) Notice of appeal — An appellant who proposes to appeal an order made under section 76 to the superior court must give notice of appeal not later than thirty days after the order is made.

(2) Extension of time — The superior court may, either before or after the expiration of those thirty days, extend the time within which notice of appeal may be given.

(3) Contents of notice — A notice of appeal must set out the grounds of appeal, together with such further material as the superior court may require.

(4) Service of notice — A copy of any notice of appeal filed with the superior court under subsection (1) and of any further material required to be filed with it shall be served within fourteen days after the filing of the notice, unless before or after the expiration of those fourteen days further time is allowed by the superior court, on

(a) the Attorney General of Canada, in the case of an appeal of an order made under paragraph 76(a) confirming a decision of a chief firearms officer who was designated by the federal Minister, of the Registrar or of the federal Minister;

(b) the attorney general of the province, in the case of an appeal against any other order made under paragraph 76(a);

(c) the applicant for or holder of the licence, registration certificate, authorization or approval, in the case of an appeal against an order made under paragraph 76(b) or (c); and

(d) any other person specified by the superior court.   .

79. (1) Disposition of appeal — On the hearing of an appeal, the superior court may

(a) dismiss the appeal; or

(b) allow the appeal and, in the case of an appeal against an order made under paragraph 76(a),

(i) direct the chief firearms officer or Registrar to issue a licence, registration certificate or authorization or direct the provincial minister to approve a shooting club or shooting range, or

(ii) cancel the revocation of the licence, registration certificate, authorization or approval or the decision of the chief firearms officer under section 67.

(2) Burden on applicant — A superior court shall dispose of an appeal against an order made under paragraph 76(a) by dismissing it, unless the appellant establishes to the satisfaction of the court that a disposition referred to in paragraph (1)(b) is justified.

80. Appeal to court of appeal — An appeal to the court of appeal may, with leave of that court or of a judge of that court, be taken against a decision of a superior court under section 79 on any ground that involves a question of law alone.

81. Application of Part XXVII of the Criminal Code — Part XXVII of the *Criminal Code*, except sections 785 to 812, 816 to 819 and 829 to 838, applies in respect of an appeal under this Act, with such modifications as the circumstances require and as if each reference in that Part to the appeal court were a reference to the superior court.

Canadian Firearms Registration System

Registrar of Firearms

82. Appointment of Registrar of Firearms — The Commissioner of the Royal Canadian Mounted Police shall, after consulting with the federal Minister and the Solicitor General of Canada, appoint an individual as the Registrar of Firearms.

Records of the Registrar

83. (1) Canadian Firearms Registry — The Registrar shall establish and maintain a registry, to be known as the Canadian Firearms Registry, in which shall be kept a record of

(a) every licence, registration certificate and authorization that is issued or revoked by the Registrar;

(b) every application for a licence, registration certificate or authorization that is refused by the Registrar;

(c) every transfer of a firearm of which the Registrar is informed under section 26 or 27;

(d) every exportation from or importation into Canada of a firearm of which the Registrar is informed under section 42 or 50;

(e) every loss, finding, theft or destruction of a firearm of which the Registrar is informed under section 88; and

(f) such other matters as may be prescribed.

(2) Operation — The Registrar is responsible for the day-to-day operation of the Canadian Firearms Registry.

84. Destruction of records — The Registrar may destroy records kept in the Canadian Firearms Registry at such times and in such circumstances as may be prescribed.

85. (1) Other records of Registrar — The Registrar shall establish and maintain a record of

(a) firearms acquired or possessed by the following persons and used by them in the course of their duties or for the purposes of their employment, namely,

(i) peace officers,

(ii) persons training to become police officers or peace officers under the control and supervision of

(A) a police force, or

(B) a police academy or similar institution designated by the federal Minister or the lieutenant governor in council of a province,

(iii) persons or members of a class of persons employed in the public service of Canada or by the government of a province or municipality who are prescribed by the regulations made by the Governor in Council under Part III of the *Criminal Code* to be public officers, and

(iv) chief firearms officers and firearms officers; and

(b) firearms acquired or possessed by individuals on behalf of, and under the authority of, a police force or a department of the Government of Canada or of a province.

(2) Reporting of acquisitions and transfers — A person referred to in subsection (1) who acquires or transfers a firearm shall have the Registrar informed of the acquisition or transfer.

(3) Destruction of records — The Registrar may destroy any record referred to in subsection (1) at such times and in such circumstances as may be prescribed.

86. Records to be transferred — The records kept in the registry maintained pursuant to section 114 of the former Act that relate to registration certificates shall be transferred to the Registrar.

Records of Chief Firearms Officers

87. (1) Records of chief firearms officers — A chief firearms officer shall keep a record of

(a) every licence and authorization that is issued or revoked by the chief firearms officer;

(b) every application for a licence or authorization that is refused by the chief firearms officer;

(c) every prohibition order of which the chief firearms officer is informed under section 89; and

(d) such other matters as may be prescribed.

(2) Destruction of records — A chief firearms officer may destroy any record referred to in subsection (1) at such times and in such circumstances as may be prescribed.

88. Reporting of loss, finding, theft and destruction of firearms — A chief firearms officer to whom the loss, finding, theft or destruction of a firearm is reported shall have the Registrar informed without delay of the loss, finding, theft or destruction.

Reporting of Prohibition Orders

89. Reporting of prohibition orders — Every court, judge or justice that makes, varies or revokes a prohibition order shall have a chief firearms officer informed without delay of the prohibition order or its variation or revocation.

Access to Records

90. Right of access — The Registrar has a right of access to records kept by a chief firearms officer under section 87 and a chief firearms officer has a right of access to records kept by the Registrar under section 83 or 85 and to records kept by other chief firearms officers under section 87.

Electronic Filing

91. (1) Electronic filing — Subject to the regulations, notices and documents that are sent to or issued by the Registrar pursuant to this or any other Act of Parliament may be sent or issued in electronic or other form in any manner specified by the Registrar.

(2) Time of receipt — For the purposes of this Act and Part III of the *Criminal Code*, a notice or document that is sent or issued in accordance with subsection (1) is deemed to have been received at the time and date provided by the regulations.

92. (1) Records of Registrar — Records required by section 83 or 85 to be kept by the Registrar may

(a) be in bound or loose-leaf form or in photographic film form; or

(b) be entered or recorded by any system of mechanical or electronic data processing or by any other information storage device that is capable of reproducing any required information in intelligible written or printed form within a reasonable time.

(2) Storage of documents or information in electronic or other form — Subject to the regulations, a document or information received by the Registrar under this Act in electronic or other form may be entered or recorded by any information storage device, including any system of mechanical or electronic data processing, that is capable of reproducing stored documents or information in intelligible written or printed form within a reasonable time.

(3) Probative value — Where the Registrar maintains a record of a document otherwise than in written or printed form, an extract from that record that is certified by the Registrar has the same probative value as the document would have had if it had been proved in the ordinary way.

Reports

93. (1) Report to Solicitor General — The Registrar shall, as soon as possible after the end of each calendar year and at such other times as the Solicitor General of Canada may, in writing, request, submit to the Solicitor General a report, in such form and including such information as the Solicitor General may direct, with regard to the administration of this Act.

(2) Laid before Parliament — The Solicitor General of Canada shall have each report laid before each House of Parliament on any of the first fifteen days on which that House is sitting after the Solicitor General receives it.

94. Information to be submitted to Registrar — A chief firearms officer shall submit the prescribed information with regard to the administration of this Act at the prescribed time and in the prescribed form for the purpose of enabling the Registrar to compile the reports referred to in section 93.

General

Agreements with Provinces

95. Agreements with provinces — The federal Minister may, with the approval of the Governor in Council, enter into agreements with the governments of the provinces

> (a) providing for payment of compensation by Canada to the provinces in respect of administrative costs actually incurred by the provinces in relation to processing licences, registration certificates and authorizations and applications for licences, registration certificates and authorizations and the operation of the Canadian Firearms Registration System; and

> (b) notwithstanding subsections 17(1) and (4) of the *Financial Administration Act*, authorizing the governments of the provinces to withhold those costs, in accordance with the terms and conditions of the agreement, from fees under paragraph 117(p) collected or received by the governments of the provinces.

Other Matters

96. Other obligations not affected — The issuance of a licence, registration certificate or authorization under this Act does not affect the obligation of any person to comply with any other Act of Parliament or any regulation made under an Act of Parliament respecting firearms or other weapons.

97. (1) Exemptions — Subject to subsection (2), a provincial minister may exempt from the application in that province of any provision of this Act or the regulations or Part III of the *Criminal Code*, for any period not exceeding one year, the employees, in respect of any thing done by them in the course of or for the purpose of their duties or employment, of any business that holds a licence authorizing the business to acquire prohibited firearms, prohibited weapons, prohibited devices or prohibited ammunition.

(2) Public safety — Subsection (1) does not apply where it is not desirable, in the interests of the safety of any person, that the employees of the business be so exempted.

(3) Conditions — A provincial minister may attach to an exemption any reasonable condition that the provincial minister considers desirable in the particular circumstances and in the interests of the safety of any person.

Delegation

98. Authorized chief firearms officer may perform functions of provincial minister — A chief firearms officer of a province who is authorized in writing by a provincial minister may perform the function of the provincial minister of designating firearms officers for the province.

99. (1) Designated officers may perform functions of chief firearms officers — Subject to subsections (2) and (3), a firearms officer who is designated in writing by a chief firearms officer may perform such duties and functions of the chief firearms officer under this Act or Part III of the *Criminal Code* as are specified in the designation.

(2) Exception — A licence that is issued to a business authorizing the business to acquire prohibited firearms, prohibited weapons, prohibited devices or prohibited ammunition must be issued by a chief firearms officer personally.

(3) Exception — An authorization to carry must be issued by a chief firearms officer personally.

100. Designated officers may perform functions of Registrar — A person who is designated in writing by the Registrar for the purpose of this section may perform such duties and functions of the Registrar under this Act or Part III of the *Criminal Code* as are specified in the designation.

Inspection

101. Definition of "inspector" — In sections 102 to 105, **"inspector"** means a firearms officer and includes, in respect of a province, a member of a class of individuals designated by the provincial minister.

102. (1) Inspection — Subject to section 104, for the purpose of ensuring compliance with this Act and the regulations, an inspector may at any reasonable time enter and inspect any place where the inspector believes on reasonable grounds a business is being carried on or there is a record of a business, any place in which the inspector believes on reasonable grounds there is a gun collection or a record in relation to a gun collection or any place in which the inspector believes on reasonable grounds there is a prohibited firearm or there are more than 10 firearms and may

(a) open any container that the inspector believes on reasonable grounds contains a firearm or other thing in respect of which this Act or the regulations apply;

(b) examine any firearm and examine any other thing that the inspector finds and take samples of it;

(c) conduct any tests or analyses or take any measurements; and

(d) require any person to produce for examination or copying any records, books of account or other documents that the inspector believes on reasonable grounds contain information that is relevant to the enforcement of this Act or the regulations.

(2) Operation of data processing systems and copying equipment — In carrying out an inspection of a place under subsection (1), an inspector may

(a) use or cause to be used any data processing system at the place to examine any data contained in or available to the system;

(b) reproduce any record or cause it to be reproduced from the data in the form of a print-out or other intelligible output and remove the print-out or other output for examination or copying; and

(c) use or cause to be used any copying equipment at the place to make copies of any record, book of account or other document.

(3) Use of force — In carrying out an inspection of a place under subsection (1), an inspector may not use force.

(4) Receipt for things taken — An inspector who takes any thing while carrying out an inspection of a place under subsection (1) must give to the owner or occupant of the place at the time that the thing is taken a receipt for the thing that describes the thing with reasonable precision, including, in the case of a firearm, the serial number if available of the firearm.

(5) Definition of "business" — For greater certainty, in this section, "business" has the meaning assigned by subsection 2(1).

103. Duty to assist inspectors — The owner or person in charge of a place that is inspected by an inspector under section 102 and every person found in the place shall

(a) give the inspector all reasonable assistance to enable him or her to carry out the inspection and exercise any power conferred by section 102; and

(b) provide the inspector with any information relevant to the enforcement of this Act or the regulations that he or she may reasonably require.

104. (1) Inspection of dwelling-house — An inspector may not enter a dwelling-house under section 102 except

(a) on reasonable notice to the owner or occupant, except where a business is being carried on in the dwelling-house; and

(b) with the consent of the occupant or under a warrant.

(2) Authority to issue warrant — A justice who on *ex parte* application is satisfied by information on oath

(a) that the conditions for entry described in section 102 exist in relation to a dwelling-house,

(b) that entry to the dwelling-house is necessary for any purpose relating to the enforcement of this Act or the regulations, and

(c) that entry to the dwelling-house has been refused or that there are reasonable grounds for believing that entry will be refused

may issue a warrant authorizing the inspector named in it to enter that dwelling-house subject to any conditions that may be specified in the warrant.

(3) Areas that may be inspected — For greater certainty, an inspector who is carrying out an inspection of a dwelling-house may enter and inspect only

(a) that part of a room of the dwelling-house in which the inspector believes on reasonable grounds there is a firearm, prohibited weapon, restricted weapon, prohibited device, prohibited ammunition, a record in relation to a gun collection or all or part of a device or other thing required by a regulation made under paragraph 117(h) respecting the storage of firearms and restricted weapons; and

(b) in addition, in the case of a dwelling-house where the inspector believes on reasonable grounds a business is being carried on, that part of a room in which the inspector believes on reasonable grounds there is ammunition or a record of the business.

105. Demand to produce firearm — An inspector who believes on reasonable grounds that a person possesses a firearm may, by demand made to that person, require that person, within a reasonable time after the demand is made, to produce the firearm in the manner specified by the inspector for the purpose of verifying the serial number or other identifying features of the firearm and of ensuring that the person is the holder of the registration certificate for the firearm.

Offences

106. (1) False statements to procure licences, etc. — Every person commits an offence who, for the purpose of procuring a licence, registration certificate or authorization for that person or any other person, knowingly makes a statement orally or in writing that is false or misleading or knowingly fails to disclose any information that is relevant to the application for the licence, registration certificate or authorization.

(2) False statements to procure customs confirmations — Every person commits an offence who, for the purpose of procuring the confirmation by a customs officer of a document under this Act for that person or any other person, knowingly makes a statement orally or in writing that is false or misleading or knowingly fails to disclose any information that is relevant to the document.

(3) Definition of "statement" — In this section, **"statement"** means an assertion of fact, opinion, belief or knowledge, whether material or not and whether admissible or not.

107. Tampering with licences, etc. — Every person commits an offence who, without lawful excuse the proof of which lies on the person, alters, defaces or falsifies

(a) a licence, registration certificate or authorization; or

(b) a confirmation by a customs officer of a document under this Act.

108. Unauthorized possession of ammunition — Every business commits an offence that possesses ammunition, unless the business holds a licence under which it may possess ammunition.

109. Punishment — Every person who commits an offence under section 106, 107 or 108, who contravenes subsection 29(1) or who contravenes a regulation made under paragraph 117(d), (e), (f), (g), (i), (j), (l), (m) or (n) the contravention of which has been made an offence under paragraph 117(o)

(a) is guilty of an indictable offence and liable to imprisonment for a term not exceeding five years; or

(b) is guilty of an offence punishable on summary conviction.

110. Contravention of conditions of licences, etc. — Every person commits an offence who, without lawful excuse, contravenes a condition of a licence, registration certificate or authorization held by the person.

111. Punishment — Every person who commits an offence under section 110 or who does not comply with section 103

(a) is guilty of an indictable offence and liable to imprisonment for a term not exceeding two years; or

(b) is guilty of an offence punishable on summary conviction.

112. (1) Failure to register certain firearms — Subject to subsections (2) and (3), every person commits an offence who, not having previously committed an offence under this subsection or subsection 91(1) or 92(1) of the *Criminal Code*, possesses a firearm that is neither a prohibited firearm nor a restricted firearm without being the holder of a registration certificate for the firearm.

(2) Exceptions — Subsection (1) does not apply to

(a) a person who possesses a firearm while the person is under the direct and immediate supervision of a person who may lawfully possess it, for the purpose of using it in a manner in which the supervising person may lawfully use it;

(b) a person who comes into possession of a firearm by operation of law and who, within a reasonable period after acquiring possession of it, lawfully disposes of it or obtains a registration certificate for it; or

(c) a person who possesses a firearm and who is not the holder of a registration certificate for the firearm if the person

(i) has borrowed the firearm,

(ii) is the holder of a licence under which the person may possess it, and

(iii) is in possession of the firearm to hunt or trap in order to sustain himself or herself or his or her family.

(3) Transitional — Every person who, at any particular time between the commencement day and the later of January 1, 1998 and such other date as is prescribed, possesses a firearm that, as of that particular time, is neither a prohibited firearm nor a restricted firearm is deemed for the purposes of subsection (1) to be, until January 1, 2003 or such other earlier date as is prescribed, the holder of a registration certificate for the firearm.

(4) Onus on the defendant — Where, in any proceedings for an offence under this section, any question arises as to whether a person is the holder of a registration certificate, the onus is on the defendant to prove that the person is the holder of the registration certificate.

113. Non-compliance with demand to produce firearm — Every person commits an offence who, without reasonable excuse, does not comply with a demand made to the person by an inspector under section 105.

114. Failure to deliver up revoked licence, etc. — Every person commits an offence who, being the holder of a licence, registration certificate or authorization that is revoked, does not deliver it up to a peace officer or firearms officer without delay after the revocation.

115. Punishment — Every person who commits an offence under section 112, 113 or 114 is guilty of an offence punishable on summary conviction.

116. Attorney General of Canada may act — Any proceedings in respect of an offence under this Act may be commenced at the instance of the Government of Canada and conducted by or on behalf of that government.

Regulations

117. Regulations — The Governor in Council may make regulations

(a) regulating the issuance of licences, registration certificates and authorizations, including regulations respecting the purposes for which they may be issued under any provision of this Act and prescribing the circumstances in which persons are or are not eligible to hold licences;

(b) regulating the revocation of licences, registration certificates and authorizations;

(c) prescribing the circumstances in which an individual does or does not need firearms

    (i) to protect the life of that individual or of other individuals, or

    (ii) for use in connection with his or her lawful profession or occupation;

(d) regulating the use of firearms in target practice or target shooting competitions;

(e) regulating

    (i) the establishment and operation of shooting clubs and shooting ranges,

    (ii) the activities that may be carried on at shooting clubs and shooting ranges,

    (iii) the possession and use of firearms at shooting clubs and shooting ranges, and

    (iv) the keeping and destruction of records in relation to shooting clubs and shooting ranges and members of those clubs and ranges;

(f) regulating the establishment and maintenance of gun collections and the acquisition and disposal or disposition of firearms that form part or are to form part of a gun collection;

(g) regulating the operation of gun shows, the activities that may be carried on at gun shows and the possession and use of firearms at gun shows;

(h) regulating the storage, handling, transportation, shipping, display, advertising and mail-order sale of firearms and restricted weapons and defining the expression "mail-order sale" for the purposes of this Act;

(i) regulating the storage, handling, transportation shipping, possession for a prescribed purpose, transfer, exportation or importation of

    (i) prohibited firearms, prohibited weapons, restricted weapons, prohibited devices and prohibited ammunition, or

    (ii) components or parts of prohibited firearms, prohibited weapons, restricted weapons, prohibited devices and prohibited ammunition;

(j) regulating the possession and use of restricted weapons;

(k) for authorizing

    (i) the possession at any place,

    (ii) the manufacture or transfer, whether or not for consideration, or offer to manufacture or transfer, whether or not for consideration, or

    (iii) the importation or exportation

of firearms, prohibited weapons, restricted weapons, prohibited devices, ammunition, prohibited ammunition and components and parts designed exclusively for use in the manufacture of or assembly into automatic firearms;

(l) regulating the storage, handling, transportation, shipping, acquisition, possession, transfer, exportation, importation, use and disposal or disposition of firearms, prohibited weapons, restricted weapons, prohibited devices, prohibited ammunition and explosive substances

(i) by the following persons in the course of their duties or for the purposes of their employment, namely,

(A) peace officers,

(B) persons training to become police officers or peace officers under the control and supervision of a police force or a police academy or similar institution designated by the federal Minister or the lieutenant governor in council of a province,

(C) persons or members of a class of persons employed in the public service of Canada or by the government of a province or municipality who are prescribed by the regulations made by the Governor in Council under Part III of the *Criminal Code* to be public officers, and

(D) chief firearms officers and firearms officers, and

(ii) by individuals on behalf of, and under the authority of, a police force or a department of the Government of Canada or of a province;

(m) regulating the keeping and destruction of records in relation to firearms, prohibited weapons, restricted weapons, prohibited devices and prohibited ammunition;

(n) regulating the keeping and destruction of records by businesses in relation to ammunition;

(o) creating offences consisting of contraventions of the regulations made under paragraph (d), (e), (f), (g), (i), (j), (l), (m) or (n);

(p) prescribing the fees that are to be paid to Her Majesty in right of Canada for licences, registration certificates, authorizations, approvals of transfers and importations of firearms and confirmations by customs officers of documents under this Act;

(q) waiving or reducing the fees payable under paragraph (p) in such circumstances as may be specified in the regulations;

(r) prescribing the charges that are to be paid to Her Majesty in right of Canada in respect of costs incurred by Her Majesty in right of Canada in storing goods that are detained by customs officers or in disposing of goods;

(s) respecting the operation of the Canadian Firearms Registry;

(t) regulating the sending or issuance of notices and documents in electronic or other form, including

(i) the notices and documents that may be sent or issued in electronic or other form,

(ii) the persons or classes of persons by whom they may be sent or issued,

(iii) their signature in electronic or other form or their execution, adoption or authorization in a manner that pursuant to the regulations is to have the same effect for the purposes of this Act as their signature, and

(iv) the time and date when they are deemed to be received;

(u) respecting the manner in which any provision of this Act or the regulations applies to any of the aboriginal peoples of Canada, and adapting any such provision for the purposes of that application;

(v) repealing

(i) section 4 of the *Cartridge Magazine Control Regulations*, made by Order in Council P.C. 1992-1660 of July 16, 1992 and registered as SOR/92-460, and the heading before it,

(ii) the *Designated Areas Firearms Order*, C.R.C., chapter 430,

(iii) section 4 of the *Firearms Acquisition Certificate Regulations*, made by Order in Council P.C. 1992-1663 of July 16, 1992 and registered as SOR/92-461, and the heading before it,

(iv) section 7 of the *Genuine Gun Collector Regulations*, made by Order in Council P.C. 1992-1661 of July 16, 1992 and registered as SOR/92-435, and the heading before it,

(v) sections 8 and 13 of the *Prohibited Weapons Control Regulations*, made by Order in Council P.C. 1991-1925 of October 3, 1991 and registered as SOR/91-572, and the headings before them,

(vi) the *Restricted Weapon Registration Certificate for Classes of Persons other than Individuals Regulations*, made by Order in Council P.C. 1993-766 of April 20, 1993 and registered as SOR/93-200, and

(vii) sections 7, 15 and 17 of the *Restricted Weapons and Firearms Control Regulations*, made by Order in Council P.C. 1978-2572 of August 16, 1978 and registered as SOR/78-670, and the headings before them; and

(w) prescribing anything that by any provision of this Act is to be prescribed by regulation.

118. (1) Laying of proposed regulations — Subject to subsection (2), the federal Minister shall have each proposed regulation laid before each House of Parliament.

(2) Idem — Where a proposed regulation is laid pursuant to subsection (1), it shall be laid before each House of Parliament on the same day.

(3) Report by committee — Each proposed regulation that is laid before a House of Parliament shall, on the day it is laid, be referred by that House to an appropriate committee of that House, as determined by the rules of that House, and the committee may conduct inquiries or public hearings with respect to the proposed regulation and report its findings to that House.

(4) Making of regulations — A proposed regulation that has been laid pursuant to subsection (1) may be made

(a) on the expiration of thirty sitting days after it was laid; or

(b) where, with respect to each House of Parliament,

(i) the committee reports to the House, or

(ii) the committee decides not to conduct inquiries or public hearings.

(5) Definition of "sitting day" — For the purpose of this section, **"sitting day"** means a day on which either House of Parliament sits.

119. (1) Exception — No proposed regulation that has been laid pursuant to section 118 need again be laid under that section, whether or not it has been altered.

(2) Exception — minor changes — A regulation made under section 117 may be made without being laid before either House of Parliament if the federal Minister is of the opinion that the changes made by the regulation to an existing regulation are so immaterial or insubstantial that section 118 should not be applicable in the circumstances.

(3) Exception — urgency — A regulation made under paragraph 117(i), (l), (m), (n), (o), (q), (s) or (t) may be made without being laid before either House of Parliament if the federal Minister is of the opinion that the making of the regulation is so urgent that section 118 should not be applicable in the circumstances.

(4) Notice of opinion — Where the federal Minister forms the opinion described in subsection (2) or (3), he or she shall have a statement of the reasons why he or she formed that opinion laid before each House of Parliament.

(5) Exception — prescribed dates — A regulation may be made under paragraph 117(w) prescribing a date for the purposes of the application of any provision of this Act without being laid before either House of Parliament.

(6) Part III of the Criminal Code — For greater certainty, a regulation may be made under Part III of the *Criminal Code* without being laid before either House of Parliament.

Transitional Provisions

Licences

120. (1) Firearms acquisition certificates — A firearms acquisition certificate is deemed to be a licence if it

   (a) was issued under section 110 or 111 of the former Act;

   (b) had not been revoked before the commencement day; and

   (c) was valid pursuant to subsection 106(11) of the former Act, or pursuant to that subsection as applied by subsection 107(1) of the former Act, on the commencement day.

(2) Authorizations — A firearms acquisition certificate that is deemed to be a licence authorizes the holder

   (a) to acquire and possess any firearms other than prohibited firearms that are acquired by the holder on or after the commencement day and before the expiration or revocation of the firearms acquisition certificate;

   (b) in the case of an individual referred to in subsection 12(2), (3), (4), (5), (6) or (8), to acquire and possess any prohibited firearms referred to in that subsection that are acquired by the holder on or after the commencement day; and

(c) in the case of a particular individual who is eligible under subsection 12(7) to hold a licence authorizing the particular individual to possess a handgun referred to in subsection 12(6) (pre-February 14, 1995 handguns) in the circumstances described in subsection 12(7), to acquire and possess such a handgun in those circumstances, if the particular handgun is acquired by the particular individual on or after the commencement day.

(3) Expiration — A firearms acquisition certificate that is deemed to be a licence expires on the earlier of

(a) five years after the day on which it was issued, and

(b) the issuance of a licence to the holder of the firearms acquisition certificate.

(4) Lost, stolen and destroyed firearms acquisition certificates — Where a firearms acquisition certificate that is deemed to be a licence is lost, stolen or destroyed before its expiration under subsection (3), a person who has authority under this Act to issue a licence may issue a replacement firearms acquisition certificate that has the same effect as the one that was lost, stolen or destroyed.

121. (1) Minors' permits — A permit is deemed to be a licence if it

(a) was issued under subsection 110(6) or (7) of the former Act to a person who was under the age of eighteen years;

(b) had not been revoked before the commencement day; and

(c) remained in force pursuant to subsection 110(8) of the former Act on the commencement day.

(2) Authorizations — A permit that is deemed to be a licence authorizes the holder to possess firearms that are neither prohibited firearms nor restricted firearms.

(3) Geographical extent — A permit that is deemed to be a licence is valid only in the province in which it was issued, unless the permit was endorsed pursuant to subsection 110(10) of the former Act as being valid within the provinces indicated in the permit, in which case it remains valid within those provinces.

(4) Expiration — A permit that is deemed to be a licence expires on the earliest of

(a) the expiration of the period for which it was expressed to be issued,

(b) the day on which the person to whom it was issued attains the age of eighteen years, and

(c) five years after the birthday of the person next following the day on which it was issued, if that fifth anniversary occurs on or after the commencement day.

122. (1) Museum approvals — An approval of a museum, other than a museum established by the Chief of the Defence Staff, is deemed to be a licence if the approval

(a) was granted under subsection 105(1) of the former Act; and

(b) had not been revoked before the commencement day.

(2) Expiration — An approval of a museum that is deemed to be a licence expires on the earlier of

(a) the expiration of the period for which the approval was expressed to be granted, and

(b) three years after the commencement day.

123. (1) Permits to carry on business — A permit to carry on a business described in paragraph 105(1)(a) or (b) or subparagraph 105(2)(b)(i) of the former Act is deemed to be a licence if it

(a) was

(i) issued under subsection 110(5) of the former Act, or

(ii) continued under subsection 6(2) of the *Criminal Law Amendment Act, 1968–69*, chapter 38 of the Statutes of Canada, 1968–69, or subsection 48(1) of the *Criminal Law Amendment Act, 1977*, chapter 53 of the Statutes of Canada, 1976–77;

(b) had not been revoked before the commencement day;

(c) had not ceased to be in force or have any effect on October 30, 1992 under section 34 of *An Act to amend the Criminal Code and the Customs Tariff in consequence thereof*, chapter 40 of the Statutes of Canada, 1991; and

(d) remained in force pursuant to subsection 110(5) of the former Act on the commencement day.

(2) Expiration — A permit that is deemed to be a licence expires on the earlier of

(a) the expiration of the period for which the permit was expressed to be issued, and

(b) one year after the commencement day.

124. Geographical extent — A permit or an approval of a museum that is deemed to be a licence under section 122 or 123 is valid only for the location of the business or museum for which it was issued.

125. (1) Industrial purpose designations — A designation of a person is deemed to be a licence if it

(a) was made under subsection 90(3.1) or paragraph 95(3)(b) of the former Act; and

(b) had not been revoked before the commencement day.

(2) Geographical extent — A designation of a person that is deemed to be a licence is valid only in the province in which it was made.

(3) Expiration — A designation of a person that is deemed to be a licence expires on the earliest of

(a) the expiration of the period for which it was expressed to be made,

(b) one year after the commencement day, and

(c) in the case of a designation of a person who holds a permit that is deemed to be a licence under section 123, the expiration of the permit.

126. Pending applications — Every application that was pending on the commencement day for a document that would be a document referred to in any of sections 120 to 125 had it been issued before the commencement day shall be dealt with and disposed of under and in accordance with the former Act, except that

(a) a licence shall be issued instead of issuing a firearms acquisition certificate or a permit or making an approval or designation; and

(b) only a person who has authority under this Act to issue a licence may finally dispose of the application.

Registration Certificates

127. (1) Registration certificates — A registration certificate is deemed to be a registration certificate issued under section 60 if it

(a) was

(i) issued under subsection 109(7) of the former Act, or

(ii) continued under subsection 6(2) of the *Criminal Law Amendment Act, 1968–69*, chapter 38 of the Statutes of Canada, 1968–69, or subsection 48(2) of the *Criminal Law Amendment Act, 1977*, chapter 53 of the Statutes of Canada, 1976–77; and

(b) had not been revoked before the commencement day.

(2) Expiration — A registration certificate that is deemed to be a registration certificate issued under section 60 expires on the earlier of

(a) its expiration under section 66, and

(b) December 31, 2002, or such other date as is prescribed.

128. Pending applications — Every application for a registration certificate that was pending on the commencement day shall be dealt with and disposed of under and in accordance with the former Act, except that only a person who has authority under this Act to issue a registration certificate may finally dispose of the application.

Authorized Transportation of Firearms

129. (1) Permit to carry — A permit authorizing a person to possess a particular prohibited firearm or restricted firearm is deemed to be an authorization to carry or authorization to transport if it

(a) was

    (i) issued under subsection 110(1) of the former Act, or

    (ii) continued under subsection 6(2) of the *Criminal Law Amendment Act, 1968–69*, chapter 38 of the Statutes of Canada, 1968–69, or subsection 48(1) of the *Criminal Law Amendment Act, 1977*, chapter 53 of the Statutes of Canada, 1976–77;

(b) had not been revoked before the commencement day; and

(c) remained in force pursuant to subsection 110(1) of the former Act on the commencement day.

(2) Geographical extent — A permit that is deemed to be an authorization to carry or authorization to transport is valid only in the province in which the permit was issued, unless it was endorsed pursuant to subsection 110(10) of the former Act as being valid within the provinces indicated in the permit, in which case it remains valid within those provinces.

(3) Expiration — A permit that is deemed to be an authorization to carry or authorization to transport expires on the earlier of

(a) the expiration of the period for which it was expressed to be issued, and

(b) two years after the commencement day.

130. Temporary permit to carry — A permit authorizing a person who does not reside in Canada to possess and carry a particular prohibited firearm or restricted firearm is deemed to be an authorization to transport if it

(a) was issued under subsection 110(2.1) of the former Act;

(b) had not been revoked before the commencement day; and

(c) remained in force pursuant to that subsection on the commencement day.

131. Permit to transport or convey — A permit authorizing a person to transport or to convey to a local registrar of firearms a particular prohibited firearm or restricted firearm is deemed to be an authorization to transport if it

(a) was

    (i) issued under subsection 110(3) or (4) of the former Act, or

    (ii) continued under subsection 6(2) of the *Criminal Law Amendment Act, 1968–69*, chapter 38 of the Statutes of Canada, 1968–69, or subsection 48(1) of the *Criminal Law Amendment Act, 1977*, chapter 53 of the Statutes of Canada, 1976–77;

(b) had not been revoked before the commencement day; and

(c) remained in force pursuant to subsection 110(3) or (4) of the former Act on the commencement day.

132. Expiration — A permit that is deemed to be an authorization to transport under section 130 or 131 expires on the expiration of the period for which the permit was expressed to be issued.

133. Pending applications — Every application that was pending on the commencement day for a document that would be a document referred to in any of sections 129 to 131 had it been issued before the commencement day shall be dealt with and disposed of under and in accordance with the former Act, except that

(a) an authorization to carry or authorization to transport shall be issued or a condition shall be attached to a licence instead of issuing a permit; and

(b) only a person who has authority under this Act to issue an authorization to carry or authorization to transport may finally dispose of the application.

134. (1) Shooting club approvals — An approval of a shooting club is deemed to be an approval granted under this Act if the approval

(a) was granted under subparagraph 109(3)(c)(iii) or paragraph 110(2)(c) of the former Act; and

(b) had not been revoked before the commencement day.

(2) Expiration — An approval of a shooting club that is deemed to be an approval granted under this Act expires on the earlier of

(a) the expiration of the period for which it was expressed to be granted, and

(b) one year after the commencement day.

135. Temporary storage permit — Every permit authorizing a person to temporarily store a particular prohibited firearm or restricted firearm

(a) that was issued under subsection 110(3.1) of the former Act,

(b) that had not been revoked before the commencement day, and

(c) that remained in force pursuant to subsection 110(3.3) of the former Act on the commencement day

continues in force until the expiration of the period for which it was expressd to be issued, unless the permit is revoked by a chief firearms officer for any good and sufficient reason.

Conditional Amendments to this Act

136. Conditional amendment re Bill C-7 — If Bill C-7, introduced during the first session of the thirty-fifth Parliament and entitled *An Act respecting the control of certain drugs, their precursors and other substances and to amend certain other Acts and repeal the Narcotic Control Act in consequence thereof,* is assented to, then, on the later of the day on which sections 6 and 7 of that Act come into force and the day on which this Act is assented to, subparagraph 5(2)(a)(iv) of this Act is replaced by the following:

> (iv) an offence relating to a contravention of subsection 6(1) or (2) or 7(1) or (2) of the *Controlled Drugs and Substances Act*;

137. Conditional amendments re Bill C-41 — If Bill C-41, introduced in the first session of the thirty-fifth Parliament and entitled *An Act to amend the Criminal Code (sentencing) and other Acts is consequence thereof*, is assented to, then, on the later of the day on which section 730 of the *Criminal Code*, as enacted by section 6 of that Act, comes into force and the day on which this Act is assented to, the following provisions of this Act are amended by replacing the expression "section 736 of the *Criminal Code*" with the expression "section 730 of the *Criminal Code*":

> (a) paragraph 5(2)(a); and
>
> (b) paragraphs 70(1)(a) and (b).

Editor's Note

[NOTE: ss. 138-192 deal with consequential amendments to other related acts. Amendments are included in the affected acts.]

193. Coming into force — Subject to subsection (2), this Act or any of its provisions or any provision of any other Act enacted or amended by this Act, other than sections 136, 137 and 174, shall come into force on a day or days to be fixed by order of the Governor in Council.

194. Coming into force if no order made — If no order bringing this Act or any of its provisions or any provision of any other Act enacted or amended by this Act is made before January 1, 2003, this Act, other than sections 136, 137 and 174, comes into force on that date.

IDENTIFICATION OF CRIMINALS ACT

ICA

IDENTIFICATION OF CRIMINALS ACT

An act respecting the Identification of criminals

R.S.C. 1985, c. I-1, as am. S.C. 1992, c. 47, ss. 73-76 [Amended 1996, c. 7, ss. 39, 40.]; 1999, c. 18, s. 88.

Short Title

1. Short title — This act may be cited as the *Identification of Criminals Act*.

Her Majesty

1.1 Binding on Her Majesty — This Act is binding on Her Majesty in right of Canada or a province.

1992, c. 47, s. 73

Identification of Criminals

2. (1) Fingerprints and photographs — The following persons may be fingerprinted or photographed or subjected to such other measurements, processes and operations having the object of identifying persons as are approved by order of the Governor in Council:

(a) any person who is in lawful custody charged with or convicted of

(i) an indictable offence, other than an offence that is designated as a contravention under the *Contraventions Act* in respect of which the Attorney General, within the meaning of that Act, has made an election under section 50 of that Act, or

(ii) an offence under the *Official Secrets Act*;

(b) any person who has been apprehended under the *Extradition Act*; or

(c) any person alleged to have committed an indictable offence, other than an offence that is designated as a contravention under the *Contraventions Act* in respect of which the Attorney General, within the meaning of that Act, has made an election under section 50 of that Act, who is required pursuant to subsection 501(3) or 509(5) of the *Criminal Code* to appear for the purposes of this Act by an appearance notice, promise to appear, recognizance or summons.

(2) Use of force — Such force may be used as is necessary to the effectual carrying out and application of the measurements, processes and operations described under subsection (1).

(3) Publication — The results of the measurements, processes and operations to which a person has been subjected pursuant to subsection (1) may be published for the purpose of affording information to officers and others engaged in the execution or administration of the law.

1992, c. 47, s. 74 [Amended 1996, c. 7, s. 39.]; 1999, c. 18, s. 88

3. No liability for acting under Act — No liability, civil or criminal, for anything lawfully done under this Act shall be incurred by any person

    (a) having custody of a person described in subsection 2(1);

    (b) acting in the aid or under the direction of a person having such custody; or

    (c) concerned in the publication of results under subsection 2(3).

1992, c. 47, s. 75

Destruction of Fingerprints and Photographs

4. Destruction of fingerprints and photographs — Where a person charged with an offence that is designated as a contravention under the *Contraventions Act* is fingerprinted or photographed and the Attorney General, within the meaning of that Act, makes an election under section 50 of that Act, the fingerprints or photographs shall be destroyed.

1992, c. 47, s. 76 [Amended 1996, c. 7, s. 40.]

INTERPRETATION ACT

TABLE OF CONCORDANCE

R.S.C. 1970, c. I-23	R.S.C. 1985, c. I-21	R.S.C. 1970, c. I-23	R.S.C. 1985, c. I-21
1	1	24	25
2	2	25	26
3	3	25	27
4	4	25	28
5	5	25	29
6	6	25	30
7	7	26	31
8	8	26	32
9	9	26	33
10	10	27	34
11	12	28	11, 25, 35, part. 37
12	13	28.1	39
13	14	29	36
14	15	30	38
15	16	31	part. 37
16	17	32	40
17	18	33	41
18	19	34	42
19	20	35	43
20	21	36	44
21	22	37	45
22	23	38	46
23	24	Sch/Ann	Sch/Ann

INTERPRETATION ACT

An Act respecting the interpretation of statutes and regulations

R.S.C. 1985, c. I-21, as am. R.S.C. 1985, c. 11 (1st Supp.), s. 2; R.S.C. 1985, c. 27 (1st Supp.), s. 203; R.S.C. 1985, c. 27 (2nd Supp.), s. 10; S.C. 1990, c. 17, s. 26; 1992, c. 1, ss. 87–91; 1992, c. 47, s. 79; 1992, c. 51, s. 56; 1993, c. 28, s. 78 (Sched. III, item 82) [Amended 1998, c. 15, s. 28; 1999, c. 3, (Sched., item 18).]; 1993, c. 34, s. 88; 1993, c. 38, s. 87; 1995, c. 39, s. 174; 1996, c. 31, ss. 86–87; 1997, c. 39, s. 4; 1998, c. 30, s. 15(i); 1999, c. 3, s. 71; 1999, c. 28, s. 168; 1999, c. 31, ss. 146, 147 (Fr.).

Short Title

1. Short title — This Act may be cited as the *Interpretation Act*.

Interpretation

2. (1) Definitions — In this Act,

"Act" means an Act of Parliament;

"enact" includes to issue, make or establish;

"enactment" means an Act or regulation or any portion of an Act or regulation;

"public officer" includes any person in the public service of Canada who is authorized by or under an enactment to do or enforce the doing of an act or thing or to exercise a power, or on whom a duty is imposed by or under an enactment;

"regulation" includes an order, regulation, rule, rule of court, form, tariff of costs or fees, letters patent, commission, warrant, proclamation, by-law, resolution or other instrument issued, made or established

    (a) in the execution of a power conferred by or under the authority of an Act, or

    (b) by or under the authority of the Governor in Council;

"repeal" includes revoke or cancel.

(2) Expired and replaced enactments — For the purposes of this Act, an enactment that has been replaced is repealed and an enactment that has expired, lapsed or otherwise ceased to have effect is deemed to have been repealed.

1993, c. 34, s. 88; 1999, c. 31, s. 146.

Application

3. (1) Application — Every provision of this Act applies, unless a contrary intention appears, to every enactment, whether enacted before or after the commencement of this Act.

(2) Application to this Act — The provisions of this Act apply to the interpretation of this Act.

(3) Rules of construction not excluded — Nothing in this Act excludes the application to an enactment of a rule of construction applicable to that enactment and not inconsistent with this Act.

Enacting Clause of Acts

4. (1) Enacting clause — The enacting clause of an Act may be in the following form:

"Her Majesty, by and with the advice and consent of the Senate and House of Commons of Canada, enacts as follows:".

(2) Order of clauses — The enacting clause of an Act shall follow the preamble, if any, and the various provisions within the purview or body of the Act shall follow in a concise and enunciative form.

Operation

Royal Assent

5. (1) Royal Assent — The Clerk of the Parliaments shall endorse on every Act, immediately after its title, the day, month and year when the Act was assented to in Her Majesty's name and the endorsement shall be a part of the Act.

(2) Date of commencement — If no date of commencement is provided for in an Act, the date of commencement of that Act is the date of assent to the Act.

(3) Commencement provision — Where an Act contains a provision that the Act or any portion thereof is to come into force on a day later than the date of assent to the Act, that provision is deemed to have come into force on the date of assent to the Act.

(4) Commencement when no date fixed — Where an Act provides that certain provisions thereof are to come or are deemed to have come into force on a day other than the date of assent to the Act, the remaining provisions of the Act are deemed to have come into force on the date of assent to the Act.

Day Fixed for Commencement or Repeal

6. (1) Operation when date fixed for commencement or repeal — Where an enactment is expressed to come into force on a particular day, it shall be construed as coming into force on the expiration of the previous day, and where an enactment is expressed to expire, lapse or otherwise cease to have effect on a particular day, it shall be construed as ceasing to have effect upon the commencement of the following day.

(2) When no date fixed — Every enactment that is not expressed to come into force on a particular day shall be construed as coming into force

(a) in the case of an Act, on the expiration of the day immediately before the day the Act was assented to in Her Majesty's name; and

(b) in the case of a regulation, on the expiration of the day immediately before the day the regulation was registered pursuant to section 6 of the *Statutory Instruments Act* or, if the regulation is of a class that is exempted from the application of subsection 5(1) of that Act, on the expiration of the day immediately before the day the regulation was made.

(3) Judicial notice — Judicial notice shall be taken of a day for the coming into force of an enactment that is fixed by a regulation that has been published in the *Canada Gazette*.

1992, c. 1, s. 87.

Regulation Prior to Commencement

7. Preliminary proceedings — Where an enactment is not in force and it contains provisions conferring power to make regulations or do any other thing, that power may, for the purpose of making the enactment effective on its commencement, be exercised at any time before its commencement, but a regulation so made or a thing so done has no effect until the commencement of the enactment except in so far as may be necessary to make the enactment effective on its commencement.

Territorial Operation

8. (1) Territorial operation — Every enactment applies to the whole of Canada, unless a contrary intention is expressed in the enactment.

(2) Amending enactment — Where an enactment that does not apply to the whole of Canada is amended, no provision in the amending enactment applies to any part of Canada to which the amended enactment does not apply, unless it is provided in the amending enactment that it applies to that part of Canada or to the whole of Canada.

(2.1) Exclusive economic zone of Canada — Every enactment that applies in respect of exploring or exploiting, conserving or managing natural resources, whether living or non-living, applies, in addition to its application to Canada, to the exclusive economic zone of Canada, unless a contrary intention is expressed in the enactment.

(2.2) Continental shelf of Canada — Every enactment that applies in respect of exploring or exploiting natural resources that are

(a) mineral or other non-living resources of the seabed or subsoil, or

(b) living organisms belonging to sedentary species, that is to say, organisms that, at the harvestable stage, either are immobile on or under the seabed or are unable to move except in constant physical contact with the seabed or subsoil

applies, in addition to its application to Canada, to the continental shelf of Canada, unless a contrary intention is expressed in the enactment.

(3) Extra-territorial operation — Every Act now in force enacted prior to December 11, 1931 that expressly or by necessary or reasonable implication was intended, as to the whole or any part thereof, to have extra-territorial operation shall be construed as if, at the date of its enactment the Parliament of Canada had full power to make laws having extra-territorial operation as provided by the *Statute of Westminster, 1931.*

1996, c. 31, s. 86

Rules of Construction

Private Acts

9. Provisions in private Acts — No provision in a private Act affects the rights of any person, except only as therein mentioned or referred to.

Law Always Speaking

10. Law always speaking — The law shall be considered as always speaking, and where a matter or thing is expressed in the present tense, it shall be applied to the circumstances as they arise, so that effect may be given to the enactment according to its true spirit, intent and meaning.

Imperative and Permissive Construction

11. "Shall" and "may" — The expression **"shall"** is to be construed as imperative and the expression **"may"** as permissive.

Enactments Remedial

12. Enactments deemed remedial — Every enactment shall be deemed remedial, and shall be given such fair, large and liberal construction and interpretation as best ensures the attainment of its objects.

Preambles and Marginal Notes

13. Preamble — The preamble of an enactment shall be read as a part of the enactment intended to assist in explaining its purport and object.

14. Marginal notes and historical references — Marginal notes and references to former enactments that appear after the end of a section or other division in an enactment form no part of the enactment, but are inserted for convenience of reference only.

Application of Interpretation Provisions

15. (1) Application of definitions and interpretation rules — Definitions or rules of interpretation in an enactment apply to all of the provisions of the enactment, including the provisions that contain those definitions or rules of interpretation.

(2) Interpretation sections subject to exceptions — Where an enactment contains an interpretation section or provision, it shall be read and construed

(a) as being applicable only if a contrary intention does not appear, and

(b) as being applicable to all other enactments relating to the same subject-matter unless a contrary intention appears.

16. Words in regulations — Where an enactment confers power to make regulations, expressions used in the regulations have the same respective meanings as in the enactment conferring the power.

Her Majesty

17. Her Majesty not bound or affected unless stated — No enactment is binding on Her Majesty or affects Her Majesty or Her Majesty's rights or prerogatives in any manner, except only as therein mentioned or referred to in the enactment.

Proclamations

18. (1) Proclamation — Where an enactment authorizes the issue of a proclamation, the proclamation shall be understood to be a proclamation of the Governor in Council.

(2) Proclamation to be issued on advice — Where the Governor General is authorized to issue a proclamation, the proclamation shall be understood to be a proclamation issued under an order of the Governor in Council, but it is not necessary to mention in the proclamation that it is issued under such an order.

(3) Effective day of proclamations — A proclamation that is issued under an order of the Governor in Council may purport to have been issued on the day of the order or on any subsequent day and, if so, takes effect on that day.

1992, c. 1, s. 88.

Oaths

19. (1) Administration of oaths — Where by an enactment or by a rule of the Senate or House of Commons, evidence under oath is authorized or required to be taken, or an oath is authorized or directed to be made, taken or administered, the oath may be administered, and a certificate of its having been made, taken or administered may be given by

    (a) any person authorized by the enactment or rule to take the evidence; or

    (b) a judge of any court, a notary public, a justice of the peace, or a commissioner for taking affidavits, having authority or jurisdiction within the place where the oath is administered.

(2) Where justice of peace empowered — Where power is conferred upon a justice of the peace to administer an oath or solemn affirmation or to take an affidavit or declaration, the power may be exercised by a notary public or a commissioner for taking oaths.

Reports to Parliament

20. Reports to Parliament — Where an Act requires a report or other document to be laid before Parliament and, in compliance with the Act, a particular report or document has been laid before Parliament at a session thereof, nothing in the Act shall be construed as requiring the same report or document to be laid before Parliament at any subsequent session.

Corporations

21. (1) Powers vested in corporations — Words establishing a corporation shall be construed

    (a) as vesting in the corporation power to sue and be sued, to contract and be contracted with by its corporate name, to have a common seal and to alter or change it at pleasure, to have perpetual succession, to acquire and hold personal property for the purposes for which the corporation is established and to alienate that property at pleasure;

    (b) in the case of a corporation having a name consisting of an English and a French form or a combined English and French form, as vesting in the corporation power to use either the English or the French form of its name or both forms and to show on its seal both the English and French forms of its name or have two seals, one showing the English and the other showing the French form of its name;

    (c) as vesting in a majority of the members of the corporation the power to bind the others by their acts; and

    (d) as exempting from personal liability for its debts, obligations or acts such individual members of the corporation who do not contravene the provisions of the enactment establishing the corporation.

(2) Corporate name — Where an enactment establishes a corporation and in each of the English and French versions of the enactment the name of the corporation is in the form only of the language of that version, the name of the corporation shall consist of the form of its name in each of the versions of the enactment.

(3) Banking business — No corporation is deemed to be authorized to carry on the business of banking unless that power is expressly conferred on it by the enactment establishing the corporation.

Majority and Quorum

22. (1) Majorities — Where an enactment requires or authorizes more than two persons to do an act or thing, a majority of them may do it.

(2) Quorum of board, court, commission, etc — Where an enactment establishes a board, court, commission or other body consisting of three or more members, in this section called an "association",

(a) at a meeting of the association, a number of members of the association equal to,

(i) if the number of members provided for by the enactment is a fixed number, at least one-half of the number of members, and

(ii) if the number of members provided for by the enactment is not a fixed number but is within a range having a maximum or minimum, at least one-half of the number of members in office if that number is within the range,

constitutes a quorum;

(b) an act or thing done by a majority of the members of the association present at a meeting, if the members present constitute a quorum, is deemed to have been done by the association; and

(c) a vacancy in the membership of the association does not invalidate the constitution of the association or impair the right of the members in office to act, if the number of members in office is not less than a quorum.

Appointment, Retirement and Powers of Officers

23. (1) Public officers hold office during pleasure — Every public officer appointed by or under the authority of an enactment or otherwise is deemed to have been appointed to hold office during pleasure only, unless it is otherwise expressed in the enactment, commission or instrument of appointment.

(2) Effective day of appointments — Where an appointment is made by instrument under the Great Seal, the instrument may purport to have been issued on or after the day its issue was authorized, and the day on which it so purports to have been issued is deemed to be the day on which the appointment takes effect.

(3) Appointment or engagement otherwise than under Great Seal — Where there is authority in an enactment to appoint a person to a position or to engage the services of a person, otherwise than by instrument under the Great Seal, the instrument of appointment or engagement may be expressed to be effective on or after the day on which that person commenced the performance of the duties of the position or commenced the performance of the services, and the day on which it is so expressed to be effective, unless that day is more than sixty days before the day on which the instrument is issued, is deemed to be the day on which the appointment or engagement takes effect.

(4) Remuneration — Where a person is appointed to an office, the appointing authority may fix, vary or terminate that person's remuneration.

(5) Commencement of appointments or retirements — Where a person is appointed to an office effective on a specified day, or where the appointment of a person is terminated effective on a specified day, the appointment or termination is deemed to have been effected immediately on the expiration of the previous day.

24. (1) Implied powers respecting public officers — Words authorizing the appointment of a public officer to hold office during pleasure include, in the discretion of the authority in whom the power of appointment is vested, the power to

    (a) terminate the appointment or remove or suspend the public officer;

    (b) re-appoint or reinstate the public officer; and

    (c) appoint another person in the stead of, or to act in the stead of, the public officer.

(2) Powers of acting Minister, successor or deputy — Words directing or empowering a minister of the Crown to do an act or thing, regardless of whether the act or thing is administrative, legislative or judicial, or otherwise applying to that minister as the holder of the office, include

    (a) a minister acting for that minister or, if the office is vacant, a minister designated to act in the office by or under the authority of an order in council;

    (b) the successors of that minister in the office;

    (c) his or their deputy;

    (d) notwithstanding paragraph (c), a person appointed to serve, in the department or ministry of state over which the minister presides, in a capacity appropriate to the doing of the act or thing, or to the words so applying.

(3) Restriction as to public servants — Nothing in paragraph (2)(c) or (d) shall be construed as authorizing the exercise of any authority conferred on a minister to make a regulation as defined in the *Statutory Instruments Act*.

(4) Successors to and deputy of public officer — Words directing or empowering any other public officer, other than a minister of the Crown, to do any act or thing, or otherwise applying to the public officer by his name of office, include his successors in the office and his or their deputy.

(5) Powers of holder of public office — Where a power is conferred or a duty imposed on the holder of an office, the power may be exercised and the duty shall be performed by the person for the time being charged with the execution of the powers and duties of the office.

1992, c. 1, ss. 89(1), (3), (4).

Evidence

25. (1) Documentary evidence — Where an enactment provides that a document is evidence of a fact without anything in the context to indicate that the document is conclusive evidence, then, in any judicial proceedings, the document is admissible in evidence and the fact is deemed to be established in the absence of any evidence to the contrary.

(2) Queen's Printer — Every copy of an enactment having printed thereon what purports to be the name or title of the Queen's Printer and Controller of Stationery or the Queen's Printer is deemed to be a copy purporting to be printed by the Queen's Printer for Canada.

Computation of Time

26. (1) Time limits and holidays — Where the time limited for the doing of a thing expires or falls on a holiday, the thing may be done on the day next following that is not a holiday.

27. (1) Clear days — Where there is a reference to a number of clear days or "at least" a number of days between two events, in calculating that number of days the days on which the events happen are excluded.

(2) Not clear days — Where there is a reference to a number of days, not expressed to be clear days, between two events, in calculating that number of days the day on which the first event happens is excluded and the day on which the second event happens is included.

(3) Beginning and ending of prescribed periods — Where a time is expressed to begin or end at, on or with a specified day, or to continue to or until a specified day, the time includes that day.

(4) After specified day — Where a time is expressed to begin after or to be from a specified day, the time does not include that day.

(5) Within a time — Where anything is to be done within a time after, from, of or before a specified day, the time does not include that day.

28. Calculation of a period of months after or before a specified day — Where there is a reference to a period of time consisting of a number of months after or before a specified day, the period is calculated by

(a) counting forward or backward from the specified day the number of months, without including the month in which that day falls;

(b) excluding the specified day; and

(c) including in the last month counted under paragraph (*a*) the day that has the same calendar number as the specified day or, if that month has no day with that number, the last day of that month.

29. Time of the day — Where there is a reference to time expressed as a specified time of the day, the time is taken to mean standard time.

30. Time when specified age attained — A person is deemed not to have attained a specified number of years of age until the commencement of the anniversary, of the same number, of the day of that person's birth.

Miscellaneous Rules

31. (1) Reference to provincial court judge, etc — Where anything is required or authorized to be done by or before a judge, provincial court judge, justice of the peace or any functionary or officer, it shall be done by or before one whose jurisdiction or powers extend to the place where the thing is to be done.

(2) Ancillary powers — Where power is given to a person, officer or functionary to do or enforce the doing of any act or thing, all such powers as are necessary to enable the person, officer or functionary to do or enforce the doing of the act or thing are deemed to be also given.

(3) Powers to be exercised as required — Where a power is conferred or a duty imposed, the power may be exercised and the duty shall be performed from time to time as occasion requires.

(4) Power to repeal — Where a power is conferred to make regulations, the power shall be construed as including a power, exercisable in the same manner, and subject to the same consent and conditions, if any, to repeal, amend or vary the regulations and make others.

32. Forms — Where a form is prescribed, deviations from that form, not affecting the substance or calculated to mislead, do not invalidate the form used.

33. (1) Gender — Words importing female persons include male persons and corporations and words importing male persons include female persons and corporations.

(2) Number — Words in the singular include the plural, and words in the plural include the singular.

(3) Parts of speech and grammatical forms — Where a word is defined, other parts of speech and grammatical forms of the same word have corresponding meanings.

1992, c. 1, s. 90.

Offences

34. (1) Indictable and summary conviction offences — Where an enactment creates an offence,

(a) the offence is deemed to be an indictable offence if the enactment provides that the offender may be prosecuted for the offence by indictment;

(b) the offence is deemed to be one for which the offender is punishable on summary conviction if there is nothing in the context to indicate that the offence is an indictable offence; and

(c) if the offence is one for which the offender may be prosecuted by indictment or for which he is punishable on summary conviction, no person shall be considered to have been convicted of an indictable offence by reason only of having been convicted of the offence on summary conviction.

(2) Criminal Code to apply — All the provisions of the *Criminal Code* relating to indictable offences apply to indictable offences created by an enactment, and all the provisions of that Code relating to summary conviction offences apply to all other offences created by an enactment, except to the extent that the enactment otherwise provides.

(3) Documents similarly construed — In a commission, proclamation, warrant or other document relating to criminal law or procedure in criminal matters,

(a) a reference to an offence for which the offender may be prosecuted by indictment shall be construed as a reference to an indictable offence; and

(b) a reference to any other offence shall be construed as a reference to an offence for which the offender is punishable on summary conviction.

Powers to Enter Dwelling-houses to Carry out Arrests

34.1 Authorization to enter dwelling-house — Any person who may issue a warrant to arrest or apprehend a person under any Act of Parliament, other than the *Criminal Code*, has the same powers, subject to the same terms and conditions, as a judge or justice has under the *Criminal Code*

(a) to authorize the entry into a dwelling-house described in the warrant for the purpose of arresting or apprehending the person, if the person issuing the warrant is satisfied by information on oath that there are reasonable grounds to believe that the person is or will be present in the dwelling-house; and

(b) to authorize the entry into the dwelling-house without prior announcement if the requirement of subsection 529.4(1) is met.

1997, c. 39, s. 4.

Definitions

35. (1) General definitions — In every enactment,

"Act", as meaning an Act of a legislature, includes an ordinance of the Yukon Territory or of the Northwest Territories and a law of the Legislature for Nunavut;

"bank" means a bank listed in Schedule I or II to the *Bank Act*;

"British Commonwealth" or **"British Commonwealth of Nations"** has the same meaning as "Commonwealth";

"Canada", for greater certainty, includes the internal waters of Canada and the territorial sea of Canada;

"Canadian waters" includes the territorial sea of Canada and the internal waters of Canada;

"broadcasting" means any radiocommunication in which the transmissions are intended for direct reception by the general public;

"Clerk of the Privy Council" or **"Clerk of the Queen's Privy Council"** means the Clerk of the Privy Council and Secretary to the Cabinet;

"commencement", when used with reference to an enactment, means the time at which the enactment comes into force;

"Commonwealth" or **"Commonwealth of Nations"** means the association of countries named in the schedule;

"Commonwealth and dependent Territories" means the several Commonwealth countries and their colonies, possessions, dependencies, protectorates, protected states, condominiums and trust territories;

"contiguous zone",

> (a) in relation to Canada, means the contiguous zone of Canada as determined under the *Oceans Act*, and

> (b) in relation to any other state, means the contiguous zone of the other state as determined in accordance with international law and the domestic laws of that other state;

"continental shelf",

> (a) in relation to Canada, means the continental shelf of Canada as determined under the *Oceans Act*, and

> (b) in relation to any other state, means the continental shelf of the other state as determined in accordance with international law and the domestic laws of that other state;

"contravene" includes fail to comply with;

"corporation" does not include a partnership that is considered to be a separate legal entity under provincial law;

"county" includes two or more counties united for purposes to which the enactment relates;

"diplomatic or consular officer" includes an ambassador, envoy, minister, chargé d'affaires, counsellor, secretary, attaché, consul-general, consul, vice-consul, pro-consul, consular agent, acting consul-general, acting consul, acting vice-consul, acting consular agent, high commissioner, permanent delegate, adviser, acting high commissioner, and acting permanent delegate;

"exclusive economic zone",

(a) in relation to Canada, means the exclusive economic zone of Canada as determined under the *Oceans Act* and includes the seabed and subsoil below that zone, and

(b) in relation to any other state, means the exclusive economic zone of the other state as determined in accordance with international law and the domestic laws of that other state;

"Federal Court" means the Federal Court of Canada;

"Federal Court — Appeal Division" or **"Federal Court of Appeal"** means that division of the Federal Court of Canada called the Federal Court — Appeal Division or referred to as the Court of Appeal or Federal Court of Appeal by the *Federal Court Act*;

"Federal Court — Trial Division" means that division of the Federal Court of Canada so named by the *Federal Court Act*;

"Governor", **"Governor General"**, or **"Governor of Canada"** means the Governor General of Canada, or other chief executive officer or administrator carrying on the Government of Canada on behalf and in the name of the Sovereign, by whatever title that officer is designated;

"Governor General in Council", or **"Governor in Council"** means the Governor General of Canada acting by and with the advice of, or by and with the advice and consent of, or in conjunction with the Queen's Privy Council for Canada;

"Great Seal" means the Great Seal of Canada;

"Her Majesty", **"His Majesty"**, **"The Queen"**, **"The King"**, or **"The Crown"** means the Sovereign of the United Kingdom, Canada and Her other Realms and Territories, and Head of the Commonwealth;

"Her Majesty's Realm and Territories" means all realms and territories under the sovereignty of Her Majesty;

"herein" used in any section shall be understood to relate to the whole enactment, and not to that section only;

"holiday" means any of the following days, namely, Sunday; New Year's Day; Good Friday; Easter Monday; Christmas Day; the birthday or the day fixed by proclamation for the celebration of the birthday of the reigning Sovereign; Victoria Day; Canada Day; the first Monday in September, designated Labour Day; Remembrance Day; any day appointed by proclamation to be observed as a day of general prayer or mourning or day of public rejoicing or thanksgiving; and any of the following additional days, namely:

(a) in any province, any day appointed by proclamation of the lieutenant governor of the province to be observed as a public holiday or as a day of general prayer or mourning or day of public rejoicing or thanksgiving within the province, and any day that is a non-juridical day by virtue of an Act of the legislature of the province, and

(b) in any city, town, municipality or other organized district, any day appointed to be observed as a civic holiday by resolution of the council or other authority charged with the administration of the civic or municipal affairs of the city, town, municipality or district;

"internal waters",

(a) in relation to Canada, means the internal waters of Canada as determined under the *Oceans Act* and includes the airspace above and the bed and subsoil below those waters, and

(b) in relation to any other state, means the waters on the landward aside of the baselines of the territorial sea of the other state;

"legislative assembly", **"legislative council"** or **"legislature"**, includes the Lieutenant Governor in Council and the Legislative Assembly of the Northwest Territories, as constituted before September 1, 1905, the Commissioner in Council of the Yukon Territory, the Commissioner in Council of the Northwest Territories, and the Legislature for Nunavut;

"lieutenant governor" means the lieutenant governor or other chief executive officer or administrator carrying on the government of the province indicated by the enactment, by whatever title that officer is designated, and, in relation to the Yukon Territory or the Northwest Territories or Nunavut, means the Commissioner thereof;

"lieutenant governor in council" means the lieutenant governor acting by and with the advice of, or by and with the advice and consent of, or in conjunction with the executive council of the province indicated by the enactment and, in relation to the Yukon Territory, the Northwest Territories or Nunavut, means the Commissioner thereof;

"local time", in relation to any place, means the time observed in that place for the regulation of business hours;

"military" shall be construed as relating to all or any part of the Canadian Forces;

"month" means a calendar month;

"oath" includes a solemn affirmation or declaration when the context applies to any person by whom and to any case in which a solemn affirmation or declaration may be made instead of an oath, and in the same cases the expression **"sworn"** includes the expression "affirmed" or "declared";

"Parliament" means the Parliament of Canada;

"person" or any word or expression descriptive of a person, includes a corporation;

"proclamation" means a proclamation under the Great Seal;

"province" means a province of Canada, and includes the Yukon Territory, the Northwest Territories and Nunavut;

"radio" or **"radiocommunication"** means any transmission, emission or reception of signs, signals, writing, images, sounds or intelligence of any nature by means of electromagnetic waves of frequencies lower than 3,000 GHz propagated in space without artificial guide;

"regular force" means the component of the Canadian Forces that is referred to in the *National Defence Act* as the regular force;

"reserve force" means the component of the Canadian Forces that is referred to in the *National Defence Act* as the reserve force;

"security" means sufficient security, and **"sureties"** means sufficient sureties, and when those words are used one person is sufficient therefor, unless otherwise expressly required;

"standard time", except as otherwise provided by any proclamation of the Governor in Council that may be issued for the purposes of this definition in relation to any province or territory or any part thereof, means

> (a) in relation to the Province of Newfoundland, Newfoundland standard time, being three hours and thirty minutes behind Greenwich time,

> (b) in relation to the Provinces of Nova Scotia, New Brunswick and Prince Edward Island, that part of the Province of Quebec lying east of the sixty-third meridian of west longitude, and that part of Nunavut lying east of the sixty-eighth meridian of west longitude, Atlantic standard time, being four hours behind Greenwich time,

> (c) in relation to that part of the Province of Quebec lying west of the sixty-third meridian of west longitude, that part of the Province of Ontario lying between the sixty-eighth and the ninetieth meridians of west longitude, Southampton Island and the islands adjacent to Southampton Island, and that part of Nunavut lying between the sixty-eighth and the eighty-fifth meridians of west longitude, eastern standard time, being five hours behind Greenwich time,

> (d) in relation to that part of the Province of Ontario lying west of the ninetieth meridian of west longitude, the Province of Manitoba, and that part of Nunavut, except Southampton Island and the islands adjacent to Southampton Island, lying between the eighty-fifth and the one hundred and second meridians of west longitude, central standard time, being six hours behind Greenwich time,

> (e) in relation to the Provinces of Saskatchewan and Alberta, the Northwest Territories and that part of Nunavut lying west of the one hundred and second meridian of west longitude, mountain standard time, being seven hours behind Greenwich time,

> (f) in relation to the Province of British Columbia, Pacific standard time, being eight hours behind Greenwich time, and

> (g) in relation to the Yukon Territory, Yukon standard time, being nine hours behind Greenwich time;

"statutory declaration" means a solemn declaration made pursuant to section 41 of the *Canada Evidence Act*;

"superior court" means

> (a) in the Province of Prince Edward Island or Newfoundland, the Supreme Court,

> (a.1) in the Province of Ontario, the Court of Appeal for Ontario and the Superior Court of Justice

> (b) in the Province of Quebec, the Court of Appeal, and the Superior Court in and for the Province,

> (c) in the Province of New Brunswick, Manitoba, Saskatchewan or Alberta, the Court of Appeal for the Province and the Court of Queen's Bench for the Province,

> (d) in the Provinces of Nova Scotia and British Columbia, the Court of Appeal and the Supreme Court of the Province, and

> (e) in the Yukon Territory or the Northwest Territories, the Supreme Court of the territory, and in Nunavut, the Nunavut Court of Justice;

"telecommunication" means the emission, transmission or reception of signs, signals, writing, images, sounds or intelligence of any nature by any wire, cable, radio, optical or other electromagnetic system, or by any similar technical system;

"territorial sea",

> (a) in relation to Canada, means the territorial sea of Canada as determined under the *Oceans Act* and includes the airspace above and the seabed and subsoil below that sea, and

> (b) in relation to any other state, means the territorial sea of the other state as determined in accordance with international law and the domestic laws of that other state;

"territory" means the Yukon Territory, the Northwest Territories and, after section 3 of the *Nunavut Act* comes into force, Nunavut.

"two justices" means two or more justices of the peace, assembled or acting together;

"United Kingdom" means the United Kingdom of Great Britain and Northern Ireland;

"United States" means the United States of America;

"writing", or any term of like import, includes words printed, typewritten, painted, engraved, lithographed, photographed, or represented or reproduced by any mode of representing or reproducing words in visible form.

(2) Governor in Council may amend schedule — The Governor in Council may, by order, amend the schedule by adding thereto the name of any country recognized by the order to be a member of the Commonwealth or deleting therefrom the name of any country recognized by the order to be no longer a member of the Commonwealth.

1990, c. 17, s. 26; 1992, c. 1, s. 91; 1992, c. 47, s. 79; 1992, c. 51, s. 56; 1993, c. 28, s. 78 (Sched. III, item 82) [Amended by 1998, c. 15, s. 28; 1999, c. 3, (Sched., item 18).]; 1993, c. 38, s. 87; 1995, c. 39, s. 174; 1996, c. 31, s. 87; 1998, c. 30, s. 15(i); 1999, c. 3, s. 71; 1999, c. 28, s. 168.

36. Construction of "telegraph" — The expression "telegraph" and its derivatives, in an enactment or in an Act of the legislature of any province enacted before that province became part of Canada on any subject that is within the legislative powers of Parliament, are deemed not to include the word "telephone" or its derivatives.

37. (1) Construction of "year" — The expression **"year"** means any period of twelve consecutive months, except that a reference

(a) to a "calendar year" means a period of twelve consecutive months commencing on January 1;

(b) to a "financial year" or "fiscal year" means, in relation to money provided by Parliament, or the Consolidated Revenue Fund, or the accounts, taxes or finances of Canada, the period beginning on April 1 in one calendar year and ending on March 31 in the next calendar year; and

(c) by number to a Dominical year means the period of twelve consecutive months commencing on January 1 of that Dominical year.

(2) Governor in Council may define year — Where in an enactment relating to the affairs of Parliament or the Government of Canada there is a reference to a period of a year without anything in the context to indicate beyond doubt whether a financial or fiscal year, any period of twelve consecutive months or a period of twelve consecutive months commencing on January 1 is intended, the Governor in Council may prescribe which of those periods of twelve consecutive months shall constitute a year for the purposes of the enactment.

38. Common names — The name commonly applied to any country, place, body, corporation, society, officer, functionary, person, party or thing means the country, place, body, corporation, society, officer, functionary, person, party or thing to which the name is commonly applied, although the name is not the formal or extended designation thereof.

39. (1) Affirmative and negative resolutions — In every Act,

(a) the expression "subject to affirmative resolution of Parliament", when used in relation to any regulation, means that the regulation shall be laid before Parliament within fifteen days after it is made or, if Parliament is not then sitting, on any of the first fifteen days next thereafter that Parliament is sitting and shall not come into force unless and until it is affirmed by a resolution of both Houses of Parliament introduced and passed in accordance with the rules of those Houses;

(b) the expression "subject to affirmative resolution of the House of Commons", when used in relation to any regulation, means that the regulation shall be laid before the House of Commons within fifteen days after it is made or, if the House is not then sitting, on any of the first fifteen days next thereafter that the House is sitting and shall not come into force unless and until it is affirmed by a resolution of the House of Commons introduced and passed in accordance with the rules of that House;

(c) the expression "subject to negative resolution of Parliament", when used in relation to any regulation, means that the regulation shall be laid before Parliament within fifteen days after it is made or, if Parliament is not then sitting, on any of the first fifteen days next thereafter that Parliament is sitting and may be annulled by a resolution of both Houses of Parliament introduced and passed in accordance with the rules of those Houses; and

(d) the expression "subject to negative resolution of the House of Commons", when used in relation to any regulation, means that the regulation shall be laid before the House of Commons within fifteen days after it is made or, if the House is not then sitting, on any of the first fifteen days next thereafter that the House is sitting and may be annulled by a resolution of the House of Commons introduced and passed in accordance with the rules of that House.

(2) Effect of negative resolution — Where a regulation is annulled by a resolution of Parliament or of the House of Commons, it is deemed to have been revoked on the day the resolution is passed and any law that was revoked or amended by the making of that regulation is deemed to be revived on the day the resolution is passed but the validity of any action taken or not taken in compliance with a regulation so deemed to have been revoked shall not be affected by the resolution.

References and Citations

40. (1) Citation of enactment — In an enactment or document,

(a) an Act may be cited by reference to its chapter number in the Revised Statutes, by reference to its chapter number in the volume of Acts for the year or regnal year in which it was enacted or by reference to its long title or short title, with or without reference to its chapter number; and

(b) a regulation may be cited by reference to its long title or short title, by reference to the Act under which it was made or by reference to the number or designation under which it was registered by the Clerk of the Privy Council.

(2) Citation includes amendment — A citation of or reference to an enactment is deemed to be a citation of or reference to the enactment as amended.

41. (1) Reference to two or more parts, etc — A reference in an enactment by number or letter to two or more parts, divisions, sections, subsections, paragraphs, subparagraphs, clauses, subclauses, schedules, appendices or forms shall be read as including the number or letter first mentioned and the number or letter last mentioned.

(2) Reference in enactments to parts, etc — A reference in an enactment to a part, division, section, schedule, appendix or form shall be read as a reference to a part, division, section, schedule, appendix or form of the enactment in which the reference occurs.

(3) Reference in enactment to subsections, etc — A reference in an enactment to a subsection, paragraph, subparagraph, clause or subclause shall be read as a reference to a subsection, paragraph, subparagraph, clause or subclause of the section, subsection, paragraph, subparagraph or clause, as the case may be, in which the reference occurs.

(4) Reference to regulations — A reference in an enactment to regulations shall be read as a reference to regulations made under the enactment in which the reference occurs.

(5) Reference to another enactment — A reference in an enactment by number or letter to any section, subsection, paragraph, subparagraph, clause, subclause or other division or line of another enactment shall be read as a reference to the section, subsection, paragraph, subparagraph, clause, subclause or other division or line of such other enactment as printed by authority of law.

Repeal and Amendment

42. (1) Power of repeal or amendment reserved — Every Act shall be construed as to reserve to Parliament the power of repealing or amending it, and of revoking, restricting or modifying any power, privilege or advantage thereby vested in or granted to any person.

(2) Amendment or repeal at same session — An Act may be amended or repealed by an Act passed in the same session of Parliament.

(3) Amendment part of enactment — An amending enactment, as far as consistent with the tenor thereof, shall be construed as part of the enactment that it amends.

43. Effect of repeal — Where an enactment is repealed in whole or in part, the repeal does not

(a) revive any enactment or anything not in force or existing at the time when the repeal takes effect,

(b) affect the previous operation of the enactment so repealed or anything duly done or suffered thereunder,

(c) affect any right, privilege, obligation or liability acquired, accrued, accruing or incurred under the enactment so repealed,

(d) affect any offence committed against or contravention of the provisions of the enactment so repealed, or any punishment, penalty or forfeiture incurred under the enactment so repealed, or

(e) affect any investigation, legal proceeding or remedy in respect of any right, privilege, obligation, or liability, referred to in paragraph (c) or in respect of any punishment, penalty or forfeiture or referred to in paragraph (d), and an investigation, legal proceeding or remedy as described in paragraph (*e*) may be instituted, continued or enforced, and the punishment, penalty or forefeiture may be imposed as if the enactment had not been so repealed.

44. Repeal and substitution — Where an enactment, in this section called the "former enactment", is repealed and another enactment, in this section called the "new enactment", is substituted therefor,

> (a) every person acting under the former enactment shall continue to act, as if appointed under the new enactment, until another person is appointed in the stead of that person;

> (b) every bond and security given by a person appointed under the former enactment remains in force, and all books, papers, forms and things made or used under the former enactment shall continue to be used as before the repeal in so far as they are consistent with the new enactment;

> (c) every proceeding taken under the former enactment shall be taken up and continued under and in conformity with the new enactment in so far as it may be done consistently with the new enactment;

> (d) the procedure established by the new enactment shall be followed as far as it can be adapted thereto

>> (i) in the recovery or enforcement of fines, penalties and forfeitures imposed under the former enactment,

>> (ii) in the enforcement of rights, existing or accruing under the former enactment, and

>> (iii) in a proceeding in relation to matters that have happened before the repeal;

> (e) when any punishment, penalty or forfeiture is reduced or mitigated by the new enactment, the punishment, penalty or forfeiture if imposed or adjudged after the repeal shall be reduced or mitigated accordingly;

> (f) except to the extent that the provisions of the new enactment are not in substance the same as those of the former enactment, the new enactment shall not be held to operate as new law, but shall be construed and have effect as a consolidation and as declaratory of the law as contained in the former enactment;

> (g) all regulations made under the repealed enactment remain in force and are deemed to have been made under the new enactment, in so far as they are not inconsistent with the new enactment, until they are repealed or others made in their stead; and

> (h) any reference in an unrepealed enactment to the former enactment shall, with respect to a subsequent transaction, matter or thing, be read and construed as a reference to the provisions of the new enactment relating to the same subject-matter as the former enactment, but where there are no provisions in the new enactment relating to the same subject-matter, the former

enactment shall be read as unrepealed in so far as is necessary to maintain or give effect to the unrepealed enactment.

45. (1) Repeal does not imply enactment was in force — The repeal of an enactment in whole or in part shall not be deemed to be or to involve a declaration that the enactment was previously in force or was considered by Parliament or other body or person by whom the enactment was enacted to have been previously in force.

(2) Amendment does not imply change in law — The amendment of an enactment shall not be deemed to be or to involve a declaration that the law under that enactment was or was considered by Parliament or other body or person by whom the enactment was enacted to have been different from the law as it is under the enactment as amended.

(3) Repeal does not declare previous law — The repeal or amendment of an enactment in whole or in part shall not be deemed to be or to involve any declaration as to the previous state of the law.

(4) Judicial construction not adopted — A re-enactment, revision, consolidation or amendment of an enactment shall not be deemed to be or to involve an adoption of the construction that has by judicial decision or otherwise been placed on the language used in the enactment or on similar language.

Demise of Crown

46. (1) Effect of demise — Where there is a demise of the Crown,

(a) the demise does not affect the holding of any office under the Crown in right of Canada; and

(b) it is not necessary by reason of the demise that the holder of any such office again be appointed thereto or, having taken an oath of office or allegiance before the demise, again take that oath.

(2) Continuation of proceedings — No writ, action or other process or proceeding, civil or criminal, in or issuing out of any court established by an Act of the Parliament of Canada is, by reason of a demise of the Crown, determined, abated, discontinued or affected, but every such writ, action, process or proceeding remains in full force and may be enforced, carried on or otherwise proceeded with or completed as though there had been no such demise.

The text in square brackets has been editorially added by Carswell and does not form part of the text of the legislation.

SCHEDULE [1]

Number in brackets editorially added by Carswell.

(Section 35)

Antigua and Barbuda

Australia
The Bahamas
Bangladesh
Barbados
Belize
Botswana
Brunei Darussalem
Canada
Cyprus
Dominica
Fiji
Gambia
Ghana
Grenada
Guyana
India
Jamaica
Kenya
Kiribati
Lesotho
Malawi
Malaysia
Maldives
Malta
Mauritius
Nauru
New Zealand
Nigeria
Pakistan
Papua New Guinea
St. Christopher and Nevis
St. Lucia
St. Vincent and the Grenadines
Seychelles
Sierra Leone
Singapore
Solomon Islands
Sri Lanka

Swaziland
Tanzania
Tonga
Trinidad and Tobago
Tuvalu
Uganda
United Kingdom
Vanuatu
Western Samoa
Zambia
Zimbabwe

MOTOR VEHICLE TRANSPORT ACT

TABLE OF CONCORDANCE

R.S.C. 1970, c. M-14	R.S.C. 1985, c. M-12	R.S.C. 1985, c. 29 (3d Supp.)
1	1	
2	2	
—		3
3	3	4
—		5
4	4	6
—	—	7
—	—	8
—	—	9
—	—	10
—	—	11
—	—	12
—	—	13
—	—	14
—	—	15
5	6	16
6	5	18
—	—	19
—	—	20
—	—	21
—	—	22
—	—	23
—	—	24
—	—	25
—	—	26
—	—	27
—	—	28
—	—	29
—	—	30
—	—	31
—	—	32
—	—	33

MOTOR VEHICLE TRANSPORT ACT, 1987

An Act respecting motor vehicle transport by extra-provincial undertakings

R.S.C. 1985, c. 29 (3rd Supp.), as am. S.C. 1992, c. 1, s. 143 (Sched. VI, item 18); 1995, c. 5, s. 25(1)(o); 1996, c. 17, s. 19.

Short Title

1. Short title — This Act may be cited as the *Motor Vehicle Transport Act, 1987*.

Interpretation

2. (1) Definitions — In this Act,

"extra-provincial bus transport" means the transport of passengers or passengers and goods by means of an extra-provincial bus undertaking;

"extra-provincial bus undertaking" means a work or undertaking for the transport of passengers or passengers and goods by a bus, connecting a province with any other or others of the provinces, or extending beyond the limits of a province.

"extra-provincial truck transport" means the transport of goods by means of an extra-provincial truck undertaking;

"extra-provincial truck undertaking" means a work or undertaking for the transport of goods by a motor vehicle other than a bus, connecting a province with any other or others of the province, or extending beyond the limits of a province;

"law of a province" means a law of a province or municipality that provides for the control or regulation of the operation in the province or municipality of local bus undertakings or local truck undertakings;

"local bus transport" means the transport of passengers or passengers and goods by means of a local bus undertaking;

"local bus undertaking" means a work or undertaking for the transport of passengers or passengers and goods by a bus, not being an extra-provincial bus undertaking;

"local truck transport" means the transport of goods by means of a local truck undertaking;

"**local truck undertaking**" means a work or undertaking for the transport of goods by a motor vehicle other than a bus, not being an extra-provincial truck undertaking;

"**Minister**" means the Minister of Transport;

"**prescribed**" means prescribed by regulation under this Act;

"**provincial transport board**" means a board, commission or other body or person having under the law of a province authority to control or regulate the operation of local bus undertakings or local truck undertakings;

(2) **Interpretation** — For the purposes of this Act, an extra-provincial bus undertaking or extra-provincial truck undertaking is operated in a province if it is operated into, in, across or out of the province.

Safety

3. (1) Regulations — The Governor in Council may, on the recommendation of the Minister made after consultation by the Minister with the government of each province affected thereby, make regulations respecting the safe operation of extra-provincial bus undertakings or extra-provincial truck undertakings including, without limiting the generality of the foregoing, regulations respecting audit, inspection, entry on premises and the provision of information.

(2) **Incorporation by reference** — A regulation under subsection (1) may incorporate by reference the law of a province as amended from time to time.

(3) **Prohibition** — No person shall operate an extra-provincial bus undertaking or extra-provincial truck undertaking in contravention of any regulation made under subsection (1).

PART I — BUS TRANSPORT

Operating Licence

4. Operation without licence prohibited — Where in any province a licence is by the law of the province required for the operation of a local bus undertaking, no person shall operate an extra-provincial bus undertaking in that province except under and in accordance with a licence issued under the authority of this Part.

5. Issue of licence — The provincial transport board in each province may in its discretion issue a licence to a person to operate an extra-provincial bus undertaking in the province on the like terms and conditions and in the like manner as if the extra-provincial bus undertaking were a local bus undertaking.

Tariffs and Tolls

6. Tariffs and tolls — Where in any province tariffs and tolls for local bus transport are determined or regulated by the provincial transport board, the provincial transport board amy in its discretion determine or regulate the tariffs and tolls for extra-provincial bus transport on the like terms and conditions and in the like manner as if the extra-provincial bus transport were local bus transport.

PART II — TRUCKING

Operating Licence

7. Operation without licence prohibited — Where in any province a licence is by the law of the province required for the operation of a local truck undertaking, no person shall operate an extra-provincial truck undertaking in that province except under and in accordance with a licence issued under the authority of this Part.

8. (1) Issue of licence — Subject to this section and to any regulations made pursuant to section 9, the provincial transport board in each province may issue a licence to a person to operate an extra-provincial truck undertaking in the province on the like terms and conditions and in the like manner as if the extra-provincial truck undertaking were a local truck undertaking.

(2) Idem — The provincial transport board in a province shall, in exercising its powers under subsection (1), issue a licence to operate an extra-provincial truck undertaking in that province to an applicant therefor who submits to the board prescribed evidence that the applicant meets the prescribed criteria relating to the fitness of the applicant to hold such a licence.

(3) Public hearings — Notwithstanding subsection (2), where under the law of a province the provincial transport board is authorized to hold a public hearing with respect to an application for a licence to operate a local truck undertaking, the board shall not hold a public hearing with respect to an application for a licence referred to in subsection (2) unless an interested person who objects to the issue of the licence provides the board with evidence that satisfies the board that, in the absence of evidence to the contrary, the operation of the extra-provincial truck undertaking in respect of which the licence is sought would likely be detrimental to the public interest.

(4) Objection by interested person — Notwithstanding subsection (2), where under the law of a province an interested person may object to the issue by the provincial transport board of a licence to operate a local truck undertaking, the provincial transport board is not required to issue a licence referred to in subsection (2) if an interested person objects to the issue of the licence and establishes to the satisfaction of the board that the operation of the extra-provincial truck undertaking in respect of which the licence is sought would likely be detrimental to the public interest.

(5) Implementation — In applying subsection (3) and (4), a provincial transport board shall

(a) give primary emphasis to the interests of users of transportation services, whether those services are provided by the undertaking or not; and

(b) have regard to any relevant written expressions of public transportation policy issued by the Government of Canada after consultation with the government of each province affected thereby.

(6) Limitation — Subject to subsection 10(3) but notwithstanding any other provision of this Part, after the day on which subsections (3) to (5) and paragraphs 9(1)(a) to (d) cease to have effect,

(a) a provincial transport board may not attach any restrictions or conditions to a licence issued under the authority of this Part; and

(b) the restrictions and conditions to which any licence issued under the authority of this Part is subject, except the condition referred to in subsection 10(3), shall cease to have effect.

9. (1) Regulation — The Governor in Council may, on the recommendation of the Minister made after consultation by the Minister with the government of each province affected thereby, make regulations

(a) prescribing restrictions or conditions to which licences issued under the authority of this Part shall be subject;

(b) requiring an applicant for a licence under this Part to furnish to the provincial transport board information respecting the applicant's identity and service proposal;

(c) exempting corridor operations from the application of subsections 8(3) to (5);

(d) exempting from the application of subsections 8(3) to (5) the extra-provincial truck transport of such commodities as may be specified in the regulations;

(e) prescribing as the criteria relating to the fitness of an applicant to hold a licence issued under the authority of this Part

(i) the criteria set out in any agreement between the Government of Canada and the governments of all of the provinces, as amended from time to time, or

(ii) in the absence of any agreement referred to in subparagraph (i) or on the failure to renew such an agreement, such criteria as the Governor in Council may consider necessary;

(f) authorizing any person or body to determine and certify whether an applicant for a licence under this Part meets, or the holder of a licence issued under the authority of this Part continues to meet, the requirements related to safety that are included in the criteria prescribed pursuant to paragraph (e) and to determine and certify the level at which the applicant or holder of the licence meets those requirements;

(g) prescribing the type, amount and conditions of insurance and bonding coverage required to be held by an extra-provincial truck undertaking;

(h) prescribing any other matter or thing that by this Part to be prescribed; and

(i) generally as may be necessary for the purposes and provisions of this Part.

(2) Fitness criteria — The criteria relating to the fitness of an applicant referred to in paragraph (1)(e) shall include requirements related to safety and insurance, and may include requirements relating to bonding coverage, and any other requirement relating to the fitness of an applicant to hold a licence.

10. (1) Compliance with fitness criteria — The holder of a licence issued under the authority of this Part shall not operate the undertaking in respect of which the licence was issued during any period during which the holder does not meet the criteria prescribed pursuant to paragraph 9(1)(e).

(2) Licence not transferable — A licence issued under the authority of this Part is not transferable.

(3) Condition — It is a condition of every licence issued under the authority of this Part that the holder thereof will comply with subsections (1) and (2) and any regulations made under subsection 3(1).

PART III — INTRA-PROVINCIAL TRUCKING

11. [Repealed 1996, c. 17, s. 19.]

12. [Repealed 1996, c. 17, s. 19.]

13. [Repealed 1996, c. 17, s. 19.]

14. [Repealed 1996, c. 17, s. 19.]

15. [Repealed 1996, c. 17, s. 19.]

PART IV — EXEMPTIONS AND ENFORCEMENT

Exemption

16. Exemption — The Governor in Council may, by regulation, on the recommendation of the Minister made after consultation by the Minister with the government of each province affected thereby, exempt from the application of this Act or of any provision of this Act, either generally or for a limited period or in respect of a limited area, any person, the whole or any part of any extra-provincial bus undertaking or extra-provincial truck undertaking, every extra-provincial bus undertaking or extra-provincial truck undertaking, any group or class of such undertakings or any extra-provincial bus transport or extra-provincial truck transport.

Foreign Carriers

17. (1) Unfair practices — Where the Minister is of the opinion that a government in a foreign country has engaged in unfair, discriminatory or restrictive practices with regard to Canadian carriers that transport goods by motor vehicle in that country or between that country and Canada, the Minister shall, with the concurrence of the Minister of Foreign Affairs, seek elimination of such practices through consultations.

(2) Order in Council — Where the consultations referred to in subsection (1) fail to result in the elimination of the practices referred to in that subsection, the Governor in Council may, on the recommendation of the Minister and the Minister of Foreign Affairs made after consultation by the Minister with the government of each province affected thereby, notwithstanding this Act or any other Act of Parliament, by order,

(a) prohibit or restrict the issuance of any licence under the authority of this Act to any foreign carrier, all foreign carriers or any class of foreign carrier,

(b) direct any provincial transport board to amend or suspend any licence issued under the authority of this Act to any foreign carrier, all foreign carriers or any class of foreign carrier, and

(c) direct any provincial transport board to reinstate any licence suspended in accordance with a direction issued under paragraph (b),

subject to such terms and conditions as may be specified in the order, and a provincial transport board to which the order applies shall comply with the order.

1995, c. 5, s. 25(1)(o)

Offence and Punishment

18. (1) Offence — Every person who contravenes or fails to comply with any provision of this Act or any regulation or order made under this Act is guilty of an offence punishable on summary conviction.

(2) Limitation — Any proceedings in respect of an offence under this Act may be commenced at any time within, but not later than, twelve months after the time when the subject-matter of the proceedings arose.

19. (1) Punishment re individuals — An individual who is convicted of an offence under this Act is liable to a fine not exceeding five thousand dollars.

(2) Punishment re corporations — A corporation that is convicted of an offence under this Act is liable to a fine not exceeding twenty-five thousand dollars.

20. Officers, etc., of corporations — Where a corporation commits an offence under this Act, every person who at the time of the commission of the offence was director or officer of the corporation is guilty of the like offence unless the act or omission constituting the offence took place without the person's knowledge or consent or the person exercised all due diligence to prevent the commission of the offence.

21. Disposition of fines — A fine imposed under section 19 shall be paid over by the provincial court judge or officer receiving it to the treasurer of the province in which it was imposed.

22. Proof of documents — In any proceedings for an offence under this Act, any document purporting to be certified by the Secretary of a provincial transport board to be a true copy of any order or direction made by the board is, without proof of the signature or of the official character of the person appearing to have signed the document, evidence of the original document of which it purports to be a copy.

PART V — CONSEQUENTIAL AMENDMENTS AND COMING INTO FORCE

23. Repeal — The *Motor Vehicle Transport Act*, is repealed.

24. *Energy Supplies Emergency Act* — Section 38 of the *Energy Supplies Emergency Act* is amended by substituting for the references to "extra-provincial undertakings" and "*Motor Vehicle Transport Act*" references to "extra-provincial truck undertaking" and "*Motor Vehicle Transport Act, 1987*", respectively.

25. *Canada Grain Act* — The definition **"public carrier"** in section 2 of the *Canada Grain Act* is repealed and the following substituted therefor:

"public carrier" means any railway company, any operator of an extra-provincial truck undertaking within the meaning of the *Motor Vehicle Transport Act, 1987* and any owner or operator of a ship;

26. *National Transportation Act, 1987* — If, during the second session of the thirty-third Parliament, Bill C-18 entitled *An Act respecting national transportation* is assented to,

(a) subsection 184(1) of that Act is repealed and the following substituted therefor:

184. (1) *Motor Vehicle Transport Act, 1987* — While the *Motor Vehicle Transport Act, 1987* is in force and notwithstanding anything in this Act, the Division applies only in respect of such extra-provincial bus undertakings or such part thereof as is exempted from the application of the *Motor Vehicle Transport Act, 1987* pursuant to section 16 of that Act.

(b) subsection 199(1) of that Act is repealed and the following substituted therefor:

> 199. (1) *Motor Vehicle Transport Act, 1987* — While the *Motor Vehicle Transport Act, 1987* is in force and notwithstanding anything in this Act, this Division applies only in respect of such extra-provincial truck undertaking or such part thereof as is exempted from the application of the *Motor Vehicle Transport Act, 1987* pursuant to section 16 of that Act.

(c) subsection 266(1) of that Act is repealed and the following substituted therefor:

> 266. (1) **Comprehensive review** — The Governor in Council shall, in January, 1992, appoint one or more persons to carry out a comprehensive review of the operation of this Act, the provisions of the *Railway Act* amended by this Act, the *Shipping Conferences Exemption Act*, the *Motor Vehicle Transport Act, 1987* and any other Act of Parliament for which the Minister is responsible that pertains to the economic regulation of a mode of transportation; and

(d) subsection 267(1) of that Act is repealed and the following substituted therefor:

> 267. (1) **For certain years** — After the expiration of each of the years 1988, 1989, 1990 and 1991, the Agency shall make a review in respect of that year of the operation of this Act, the provisions of the *Railway Act* amended by this Act, the *Shipping Conferences Exemption Act*, the *Motor Vehicle Transport Act, 1987* and any other Act of Parliament for which the Minister is responsible that pertains to the economic regulation of a mode of transportation.

Transitional

27. Continuation of licences respecting bus undertakings — Every licence authorizing the operation of an extra-provincial bus undertaking that has been issued under the authority of the *Motor Vehicle Transport Act* and that is in effect on the day immediately before the day on which this Act, except section 26, comes into force shall be deemed to have been issued under the authority of Part I of this Act.

28. Intra-provincial bus transport — For greater certainty, every licence authorizing the operation of an extra-provincial bus undertaking between any two points in a province that purports to have been issued under a law of the province prior to the coming into force of this Act, except section 26, and that purports to be in effect on the day immediately before this Act, except section 26, comes into force shall be deemed to have been issued under the authority of Part I of this Act if that licence was issued to a person who at the time of issuance was the holder of a licence issued under the authority of the *Motor Vehicle Transport Act* in respect of the same extra-provincial bus undertaking.

29. (1) Continuation of licences respecting truck undertakings — Subject to subsection (2), every licence authorizing the operation of an extra-provincial truck undertaking that has been issued under the authority of the *Motor Vehicle Transport Act* and that is in effect on the day immediately before the day on which this Act, except section 26, comes into force shall be deemed to have been issued under the authority of Part II of this Act.

(2) Exception — Where a licence referred to in subsection (1) authorizes the holder thereof to engage in the intra-provincial truck transport of goods, within the meaning of Part III of this Act, that licence shall be deemed to have been issued under the authority of Parts II and III of this Act.

30. Intra-provincial trucking — For greater certainty, every licence authorizing the operation of an extra-provincial truck undertaking between any two points in a province that purports to have been issued under a law of the province prior to the coming into force of this Act, except section 26, and that purports to be in effect on the day immediately before this Act, except section 26, comes into force shall be deemed to have been issued under the authority of Part III of this Act if that licence was issued to a person who at the time of issuance was the holder of a licence issued under the authority of the *Motor Vehicle Transport Act* in respect of the same extra-provincial truck undertaking.

31. Pending applications — Every application for a licence made under the *Motor Vehicle Transport Act* and pending on the day immediately before the day on which this Act, except section 26, comes into force shall be deemed to have been made pursuant to section 5, 8 or 13 or this Act, whichever is applicable, and shall be dealt with in accordance with this Act.

32. Pending of exemptions — Every exemption granted under section 6 of the *Motor Vehicle Transport Act* and in force on the day immediately before the day on which this Act, except section 26, comes into force shall be deemed to have been granted under section 16 of this Act.

Coming Into Force

33. (1) Coming into force — This Act, except section 26, shall come into force on January 1, 1988 or on such earlier day as may be fixed by proclamation.

(2) Idem — Section 26 shall come into force on the later of the day on which section 16 comes into force and the day on which sections 184, 199, 266, and 267 of the Bill, mentioned in section 26, come into force.

Repeal

34. (1) Repeal — Subsection 8(3) to (5) and paragraphs 9(1)(a) to (d) shall, subject to subsections (2) to (4), cease to have effect five years after the day on which this Act, except section 26, comes into force.

(2) Review — The Minister shall, after the expiration of three years after the coming into force of subsections 8(3) to (5) and before the expiration of four years after the coming into force of those subsections, undertake and complete a comprehensive review of the operation and effect of those subsections.

(2.1) Tabling of report — After the completion of the review referred to in subsection (2), the Minister shall cause a copy of a report of the review to be laid before each House of Parliament on any of the first fifteen days on which this House is sitting after the report has been prepared.

(3) Continuation in force — The Governor in Council may, by proclamation, on the recommendation of the Minister made after consultation by the Minister with the government of each province, after the completion of the review referred to in subsection (2) and before subsections 8(3) to (5) and paragraphs 9(1)(a) to (d) cease to have effect pursuant to subsection (1), continue subsections 8(3) to (5) and paragraphs 9(1)(a) to (d) in force for such further period as is specified in proclamation.

(4) Idem — The Governor in Council may, by proclamation, on the recommendation of the Minister made after consultation by the Minister with the government of each province, at any time while subsection 8(3) to (5) and paragraphs 9(1)(a) to (d) are in force pursuant to subsection (3) or this subsection, continue subsections 8(3) to (5) and paragraphs 9(1)(a) to (d) in force for such further period as is specified in the proclamation.

Annual Report

35. (1) Annual Report — After the expiration of each of the years 1988 to 1993, the Minister shall prepare the report referred to in subsection (2) and shall cause a copy of the report to be laid before each House of Parliament on any of the first fifteen days on which that House is sitting after the Minister completes it.

(2) Contents of report — The report of the Minister shall contain the following in respect of each year referred to in subsection (1):

(a) the available statistical information respecting trends of highway accidents in Canada involving motor vehicles operated by extra-provincial bus undertakings and extra-provincial truck undertakings; and

(b) a progress report on the implementation of rules and standards respecting the safe operation of extra-provincial bus undertakings and of extra-provincial truck undertakings.

YOUNG OFFENDERS ACT

TABLE OF CONCORDANCE

YOUNG OFFENDERS ACT

An Act respecting young offenders

R.S.C. 1985, c. Y-1, as am. R.S.C. 1985, c. 27 (1st Supp.), ss. 187, 203;
R.S.C. 1985, c. 24 (2d Supp.), ss. 1–44; R.S.C. 1985, c. 1 (3d Supp.), s.
12; R.S.C. 1985, c. 1 (4th supp.), ss. 38–45; S.C. 1991, c. 43, ss. 31–35;
1992, c. 1, s. 143; 1992, c. 11, ss. 1–13; 1992, c. 47, ss. 81–83 [Not in
force at date of publication.]; 1993, c. 28, s. 78 [Sched. III, item 144)
[Amended 1998, c. 15, s. 41.]; 1993, c. 45, s. 15; 1994, c. 26, s. 76; 1995,
c. 19, ss. 1–36; 1995, c. 22, ss. 16, 17 (Sched. III, item 10), 25; 1995, c.
27, s. 2; 1995, c. 39, s. 177–187, 189; 1996, c. 19, s. 93.1; 1999, c. 3, ss.
86–89.

SHORT TITLE

1. Short title — This Act may be cited as the *Young Offenders Act*.

INTERPRETATION

2. (1) Definitions — In this Act,

"adult" means a person who is neither a young person nor a child;

"alternative measures" means measures other than judicial proceedings under this
Act used to deal with a young person alleged to have committed an offence;

"child" means a person who is or, in the absence of evidence to the contrary, appears to be under the age of twelve years;

"disposition" means a disposition made under any of sections 20, 20.1 and 28 to
32, and includes a confirmation or a variation of a disposition;

"offence" means an offence created by an Act of Parliament or by any regulation,
rule, order, by-law or ordinance made thereunder, other than an ordinance of the
Yukon Territory or the Northwest Territories or a law of the Legislature for
Nunavut;

"ordinary court" means the court that would, but for this Act, have jurisdiction in
respect of an offence alleged to have been committed;

"parent" includes, in respect of another person, any person who is under a legal
duty to provide for that other person or any person who has, in law or in fact, the
custody or control of that other person, but does not include a person who has the

custody or control of that other person by reason only of proceedings under this Act;

"predisposition report" means a report on the personal and family history and present environment of a young person made in accordance with section 14;

"progress report" means a report made in accordance with section 28 on the performance of a young person against whom a disposition has been made;

"provincial director" means a person, a group or class of persons or a body appointed or designated by or pursuant to an Act of the legislature of a province or by the Lieutenant Governor in Council of a province or his delegate to perform in that province, either generally or in a specific case, any of the duties or functions of a provincial director under this Act;

"review board" means a review board established or designated by a province for the purposes of section 30;

"young person" means a person who is or, in the absence of evidence to the contrary, appears to be twelve years of age or more, but under eighteen years of age and, where the context requires, includes any person who is charged under this Act with having committed an offence while he was a young person or is found guilty of an offence under this Act;

"youth court" means a court established or designated by or under an Act of the legislature of a province, or designated by the Governor in Council or the Lieutenant Governor in Council of a province, as a youth court for the purposes of this Act;

"youth court judge" means a person appointed to be a judge of a youth court;

"youth worker" means a person appointed or designated, whether by title of youth worker or probation officer or by any other title, by or pursuant to an Act of the legislature of a province or by the Lieutenant Governor in Council of a province or his delegate, to perform, either generally or in a specific case, in that province any of the duties or functions of a youth worker under this Act.

(2) words and expressions — Unless otherwise provided, words and expressions used in this Act have the same meaning as in the *Criminal Code*.

R.S. 1985, c. 24 (2nd Supp.), s. 1; 1993, c. 28, s. 78 (Sched. III, item 144) [Amended 1998, c. 15, s. 41.]; 1995, c. 39, s. 177

2.1 Powers, duties and functions of provincial directors — Any power, duty or function of a provincial director under this Act may be exercised or performed by any person authorized by the provincial director to do so and, if so exercised or performed, shall be deemed to have been exercised or performed by the provincial director.

R.S. 1985, c. 24 (2nd Supp.), s. 2

DECLARATION OF PRINCIPLE

3. (1) Policy for Canada with respect to young offenders — It is hereby recognized and declared that

(a) crime prevention is essential to the long-term protection of society and requires addressing the underlying causes of crime by young persons and developing multi-disciplinary approaches to identifying and effectively responding to children and young persons at risk of committing offending behaviour in the future;

(a.1) while young persons should not in all instances be held accountable in the same manner or suffer the same consequences for their behaviour as adults, young persons who commit offences should nonetheless bear responsibility for their contraventions;

(b) society must, although it has the responsibility to take reasonable measures to prevent criminal conduct by young persons, be afforded the necessary protection from illegal behaviour;

(c) young persons who commit offences require supervision, discipline and control, but, because of their state of dependency and level of development and maturity, they also have special needs and require guidance and assistance;

(c.1) the protection of society, which is a primary objective of the criminal law applicable to youth, is best served by rehabilitation, wherever possible, of young persons who commit offences, and rehabilitation is best achieved by addressing the needs and circumstances of a young person that are relevant to the young person's offending behaviour;

(d) where it is not inconsistent with the protection of society, taking no measures or taking measures other than judicial proceedings under this Act should be considered for dealing with young persons who have committed offences;

(e) young persons have rights and freedoms in their own right, including those stated in the *Canadian Charter of Rights and Freedoms* or in the *Canadian Bill of Rights*, and in particular a right to be heard in the course of, and to participate in, the processes that lead to decisions that affect them, and young persons should have special guarantees of their rights and freedoms;

(f) in the application of this Act, the rights and freedoms of young persons include a right to the least possible interference with freedom that is consistent with the protection of society, having regard to the needs of young persons and the interests of their families;

(g) young persons have the right, in every instance where they have rights or freedoms that may be affected by this Act, to be informed as to what those rights and freedoms are; and

(h) parents have responsibility for the care and supervision of their children, and, for that reason, young persons should be removed from parental supervision either partly or entirely only when measures that provide for continuing parental supervision are inappropriate.

(2) Act to be liberally construed — This Act shall be liberally construed to the end that young persons will be dealt with in accordance with the principles set out in subsection (1).

1995, c. 19, s. 1

ALTERNATIVE MEASURES

4. (1) Alternative measures — Alternative measures may be used to deal with a young person alleged to have committed an offence instead of judicial proceedings under this Act only if

(a) the measures are part of a program of alternative measures authorized by the Attorney General or his delegate or authorized by a person, or a person within a class of persons, designated by the Lieutenant Governor in Council of a province;

(b) the person who is considering whether to use such measures is satisfied that they would be appropriate, having regard to the needs of the young person and the interests of society;

(c) the young person, having been informed of the alternative measures, fully and freely consents to participate therein;

(d) the young person has, before consenting to participate in the alternative measures, been advised of his right to be represented by counsel and been given a reasonable opportunity to consult with counsel;

(e) the young person accepts responsibility for the act or omission that forms the basis of the offence that he is alleged to have committed;

(f) there is, in the opinion of the Attorney General or his agent, sufficient evidence to proceed with the prosecution of the offence; and

(g) the prosecution of the offence is not in any way barred at law.

(2) Restriction on use — Alternative measures shall not be used to deal with a young person alleged to have committed an offence if the young person

(a) denies his participation or involvement in the commission of the offence; or

(b) expresses his wish to have any charge against him dealt with by the youth court.

(3) Admissions not admissible in evidence — No admission, confession or statement accepting responsibility for a given act or omission made by a young person alleged to have committed an offence as a condition of his being dealt with by alternative measures shall be admissible in evidence against him in any civil or criminal proceedings.

(4) No bar to proceedings — The use of alternative measures in respect of a young person alleged to have committed an offence is not a bar to proceedings against him under this Act, but

(a) where the youth court is satisfied on a balance of probabilities that the young person has totally complied with the terms and conditions of the alternative measures, the youth court shall dismiss any charge against him; and

(b) where the youth court is satisfied on a balance of probabilities that the young person has partially complied with the terms and conditions of the alternative measures, the youth court may dismiss any charge against him if, in the opinion of the court, the prosecution of the charge would, having regard to the circumstances, be unfair, and the youth court may consider the young person's performance with respect to the alternative measures before making a disposition under this Act.

(5) Laying of information, etc — Subject to subsection (4), nothing in this section shall be construed to prevent any person from laying an information, obtaining the issue or confirmation of any process or proceeding with the prosecution of any offence in accordance with law.

JURISDICTION

5. (1) Exclusive jurisdiction of youth court — Notwithstanding any other Act of Parliament but subject to the *National Defence Act* and section 16, a youth court has exclusive jurisdiction in respect of any offence alleged to have been committed by a person while he was a young person and any such person shall be dealt with as provided in this Act.

Proposed Amendment — 5(1)

(1) Exclusive jurisdiction of youth Court — Notwithstanding any other Act of Parliament but subject to the *Contraventions Act* and the *National Defence Act* and section 16, a youth court has exclusive jurisdiction in respect of any offence alleged to have been committed by a person while a young person and any such person shall be dealt with as provided in this Act.

1992, c. 47, s. 81 [Not in force at date of publication.]

(2) Period of limitation — No proceedings in respect of an offence shall be commenced under this Act after the expiration of the time limit set out in any other Act of Parliament or any regulation made thereunder for the institution of proceedings in respect of that offence.

(3) Proceedings continued when adult — Proceedings commenced under this Act against a young person may be continued, after he becomes an adult, in all respects as if he remained a young person.

(4) Powers of youth court judge — A youth court judge, for the purpose of carrying out the provisions of this Act, is a justice and a provincial court judge and has the jurisdiction and powers of a summary conviction court under the *Criminal Code*.

(5) Court of record — A youth court is a court of record.

R.S. 1985, c. 27 (1st Supp.), s. 203; c. 24 (2nd Supp.), s. 3

6. Certain proceedings may be taken before justices — Any proceeding that may be carried out before a justice under the *Criminal Code*, other than a plea, a trial or an adjudication, may be carried out before a justice in respect of an offence alleged to have been committed by a young person, and any process that may be issued by a justice under the *Criminal Code* may be issued by a justice in respect of an offence alleged to have been committed by a young person.

R.S. 1985, c. 24 (2nd Supp.), s. 4

DETENTION PRIOR TO DISPOSITION

7. (1) Designated place of temporary detention — A young person who is

(a) arrested and detained prior to the making of a disposition in respect of the young person under section 20, or

(b) detained pursuant to a warrant issued under subsection 32(6)

shall, subject to subsection (4), be detained in a place of temporary detention designated as such by the Lieutenant Governor in Council of the appropriate province or his delegate or in a place within a class of such places so designated.

(1.1) Exception — A young person who is detained in a place of temporary detention pursuant to subsection (1) may, in the course of being transferred from that place to the court or from the court to that place, be held under the supervision and control of a peace officer.

(2) Detention separate from adults — A young person referred to in subsection (1) shall be held separate and apart from any adult who is detained or held in custody unless a youth court judge or a justice is satisfied that

(a) the young person cannot, having regard to his own safety or the safety of others, be detained in a place of detention for young persons; or

(b) no place of detention for young persons is available within a reasonable distance.

(3) Transfer by provincial director — A young person who is detained in custody in accordance with subsection (1) may, during the period of detention, be transferred by the provincial director from one place of temporary detention to another.

(4) Exception relating to temporary detention — Subsections (1) and (2) do not apply in respect of any temporary restraint of a young person under the supervision and control of a peace officer after arrest, but a young person who is so restrained shall be transferred to a place of temporary detention referred to in subsection (1) as soon as is reasonably practicable, and in no case later than the first reasonable opportunity after the appearance of the young person before a youth court judge or a justice pursuant to section 503 of the *Criminal Code*.

(5) Authorization of provincial authority for detention — In any province for which the Lieutenant Governor in Council has designated a person or a group of persons whose authorization is required, either in all circumstances or in circumstances specified by the Lieutenant Governor in Council, before a young person who has been arrested may be detained in accordance with this section, no young person shall be so detained unless the authorization is obtained.

(6) Determination by provincial authority of place of detention — In any province for which the Lieutenant Governor in Council has designated a person or a group of persons who may determine the place where a young person who has been arrested may be detained in accordance with this section, no young person may be so detained in a place other than the one so determined.

R.S. 1985, c. 24 (2nd Supp.), s. 5

7.1 (1) Placement of young person in care of responsible person — Where a youth court judge or a justice is satisfied that

    (a) a young person who has been arrested would, but for this subsection, be detained in custody,

    (b) a responsible person is willing and able to take care of and exercise control over the young person, and

    (c) the young person is willing to be placed in the care of that person,

the young person may be placed in the care of that person instead of being detained in custody.

(2) Condition of placement — A young person shall not be placed in the care of a person under subsection (1) unless

    (a) that person undertakes in writing to take care of and to be responsible for the attendance of the young person in court when required and to comply with such other conditions as the youth court judge or justice may specify; and

    (b) the young person undertakes in writing to comply with the arrangement and to comply with such other conditions as the youth court judge or justice may specify.

(3) Removing young person from care — Where a young person has been placed in the care of a person under subsection (1) and

    (a) that person is no longer willing or able to take care of or exercise control over the young person, or

    (b) it is, for any other reason, no longer appropriate that the young person be placed in the care of that person,

the young person, the person in whose care the young person has been placed or any other person may, by application in writing to a youth court judge or a justice, apply for an order under subsection (4).

(4) Order — Where a youth court judge or a justice is satisfied that a young person should not remain in the custody of the person in whose care he was placed under subsection (1), the youth court judge or justice shall

    (a) make an order relieving the person and the young person of the obligations undertaken pursuant to subsection (2); and

    (b) issue a warrant for the arrest of the young person.

(5) Effect of arrest — Where a young person is arrested pursuant to a warrant issued under paragraph (4)(b), the young person shall be taken before a youth court judge or justice forthwith and dealt with under section 515 of the *Criminal Code*.

R.S. 1985, c. 24 (2nd Supp.), s. 5

7.2 Offence and punishment — Any person who wilfully fails to comply with section 7, or with an undertaking entered into pursuant to subsection 7.1(2), is guilty of an offence punishable on summary conviction.

R.S. 1985, c. 24 (n2d Supp.), s. 5

8. (1) [Repealed R.S. 1985, c. 24 (2nd Supp.), s. 6.]

(2) Application to youth court — Where an order is made under section 515 of the *Criminal Code* in respect of a young person by a justice who is not a youth court judge, an application may, at any time after the order is made, be made to a youth court for the release from or detention in custody of the young person, as the case may be, and the youth court shall hear the matter as an original application.

(3) Notice to prosecutor — An application under subsection (2) for release from custody shall not be heard unless the young person has given the prosecutor at least two clear days notice in writing of the application.

(4) Notice to young person — An application under subsection (2) for detention in custody shall not be heard unless the prosecutor has given the young person at least two clear days notice in writing of the application.

(5) Waiver of notice — The requirement for a notice under subsection (3) or (4) may be waived by the prosecutor or by the young person or his counsel, as the case may be.

(6) Application for review under section 520 or 521 of Criminal Code — An application under section 520 or 521 of the *Criminal Code* for a review of an order made in respect of a young person by a youth court judge who is a judge of a superior, county or district court shall be made to a judge of the court of appeal.

(6.1) Nunavut — Despite subsection (6), an application under section 520 or 521 of the *Criminal Code* for a review of an order made in respect of a young person by a youth court judge who is a judge of the Nunavut Court of Justice shall be made to a judge of that court.

(7) Idem — No application may be made under section 520 or 521 of the *Criminal Code* for a review of an order made in respect of a young person by a justice who is not a youth court judge.

(8) Interim release by youth court judge only — Where a young person against whom proceedings have been taken under this Act is charged with an offence referred to in section 522 of the *Criminal Code*, a youth court judge, but no other court, judge or justice, may release the young person from custody under that section.

(9) Review by court of appeal — A decision made by a youth court judge under subsection (8) may be reviewed in accordance with section 680 of the *Criminal Code* and that section applies, with such modifications as the circumstances require, to any decision so made.

R.S. 1985, c. 24 (2nd Supp.), s. 6; 1999, c. 3, s. 86

NOTICES TO PARENTS

9. (1) Notice to parent in case of arrest — Subject to subsections (3) and (4), where a young person is arrested and detained in custody pending his appearance in court, the officer in charge at the time the young person is detained shall, as soon as possible, give or cause to be given, orally or in writing, to a parent of the young person notice of the arrest stating the place of detention and the reason for the arrest.

(2) Notice to parent in case of summons or appearance notice — Subject to subsections (3) and (4), where a summons or an appearance notice is issued in respect of a young person, the person who issued the summons or appearance notice, or, where a young person is released on giving his promise to appear or entering into a recognizance, the officer in charge, shall, as soon as possible, give or cause to be given, in writing, to a parent of the young person notice of the summons, appearance notice, promise to appear or recognizance.

Proposed Addition — 9(2.1)

(2.1) Notice to parent in case of ticket — Subject to subsections (3) and (4), a person who serves a ticket under the *Contraventions Act* on a young person, other than a ticket served for a contravention relating to parking a vehicle, shall, as soon as possible, give or cause to be given notice in writing of the ticket to a parent of the young person.

1992, c. 47, s. 82(1) [Not in force at date of publication.]

(3) Notice to relative or other adult — Where the whereabouts of the parents of a young person

    (a) who is arrested and detained in custody,

    (b) in respect of whom a summons or an appearance notice is issued, or

    (c) who is released on giving his promise to appear or entering into a recognizance

Proposed Addition — 9(3)(d)

    (d) on whom a ticket is served under the *Contraventions Act* other than a ticket served for a contravention relating to parking a vehicle,

1992, c. 47, s. 82(2) [Not in force at date of publication.]

are not known or it appears that no parent is available, a notice under this section may be given to an adult relative of the young person who is known to the young person and is likely to assist him or, if no such adult relative is available, to such other adult who is known to the young person and is likely to assist him as the person giving the notice considers appropriate.

(4) Notice to spouse — Where a young person described in paragraph (3)(a), (b) or (c) is married, a notice under this section may be given to the spouse of the young person instead of a parent.

Proposed Amendment — 9(4)

(4) Notice to spouse — A notice under this section may be given to the spouse of a young person described in paragraph (3)(a), (b), (c) or (d) instead of to a parent.

1992, c. 47, s. 82(3) [Not in force at date of publication.]

(5) Notice on direction of youth court judge or justice — Where doubt exists as to the person to whom a notice under this section should be given, a youth court judge or, where a youth court judge is, having regard to the circumstances, not reasonably available, a justice may give directions as to the person to whom the notice should be given, and a notice given in accordance with those directions is sufficient notice for the purposes of this section.

(6) Contents of notice — Any notice under this section shall, in addition to any other requirements under this section, include

    (a) the name of the young person in respect of whom it is given;

    (b) the charge against the young person and the time and place of appearance; and

Proposed Amendment — 9(6)(b)

(b) the charge against the young person and, except in the case of a notice of a ticket served under the *Contraventions Act,* the time and place of appearance; and

1992, c. 47, s. 82(4) [Not in force at date of publication.]

    (c) a statement that the young person has the right to be represented by counsel.

Proposed Addition — 9(6.1)

(6.1) Notice of ticket under Contraventions Act — A notice under subsection (2.1) shall include a copy of the ticket.

1992, c. 47, s. 82(5) [Not in force at date of publication.]

(7) Service of notice — Subject to subsections (9) and (10), a notice under this section given in writing may be served personally or may be sent by mail.

(8) Proceedings not invalid — Subject to subsections (9) and (10), failure to give notice in accordance with this section does not affect the validity of proceedings under this Act.

(9) Exception — Failure to give notice under subsection (2) in accordance with this section in any case renders invalid any subsequent proceedings under this Act relating to the case unless

    (a) a parent of the young person against whom proceedings are held attends court with the young person; or

    (b) a youth court judge or a justice before whom proceedings are held against the young person

        (i) adjourns the proceedings and orders that the notice be given in such manner and to such persons as the judge or justice directs, or

(ii) dispenses with the notice where the judge or justice is of the opinion that, having regard to the circumstances, the notice may be dispensed with.

(10) Where a notice not served — Where there has been a failure to give a notice under subsection (1) in accordance with this section and none of the persons to whom such notice may be given attends court with a young person, a youth court judge or a justice before whom proceedings are held against the young person may

Proposed Amendment — 9(10)

(10) Where notice is not served — Where there has been a failure to give a notice under subsection (1) or (2.1) in accordance with this section and none of the persons to whom the notice may be given attends court with the young person, a youth court judge or a justice before whom proceedings are held against the young person may

1992, c. 47, s. 82(6) [Not in force at date of publication.]

(a) adjourn the proceedings and order that the notice be given in such manner and to such person as he directs; or

(b) dispense with the notice where, in his opinion, having regard to the circumstances, notice may be dispensed with.

(11) [Repealed R.S. 1985, c. 24 (2nd Supp.), s. 7(2).]

R.S. 1985, c. 24 (2nd Supp.), s. 7(1); 1991, c. 43, ss. 31(1), (2)

10. (1) Order requiring attendance of parent — Where a parent does not attend proceedings before a youth court in respect of a young person, the court may, if in its opinion the presence of the parent is necessary or in the best interest of the young person, by order in writing require the parent to attend at any stage of the proceedings.

Proposed Addition — 10(1.1)

(1.1) No order in ticket proceedings — Subsection (1) does not apply in proceedings commenced by filing a ticket under the *Contraventions Act*.

1992, c. 47, s. 83 [Not in force at date of publication.]

(2) Service of order — A copy of any order made under subsection (1) shall be served by a peace officer or by a person designated by a youth court by delivering it personally to the parent to whom it is directed, unless the youth court authorizes service by registered mail.

(3) Failure to attend — A parent who is ordered to attend a youth court pursuant to subsection (1) and who fails without reasonable excuse, the proof of which lies on that parent, to comply with the order

(a) is guilty of contempt of court;

(b) may be dealt with summarily by the court; and

(c) is liable to the punishment provided for in the *Criminal Code* for a summary conviction offence.

(4) Appeal — Section 10 of the *Criminal Code* applies where a person is convicted of contempt of court under subsection (3).

(5) Warrant to arrest parent — If a parent who is ordered to attend a youth court pursuant to subsection (1) does not attend at the time and place named in the order or fails to remain in attendance as required and it is proved that a copy of the order was served on the parent, a youth court may issue a warrant to compel the attendance of the parent.

(6) [Repealed R.S. 1985, c. 24 (2nd Supp.), s. 8(2).]

R.S. 1985, c. 24 (2nd Supp.), s. 8(1)

RIGHT TO COUNSEL

11. (1) Right to retain counsel — A young person has the right to retain and instruct counsel without delay, and to exercise that right personally, at any stage of proceedings against the young person and prior to and during any consideration of whether, instead of commencing or continuing judicial proceedings against the young person under this Act, to use alternative measures to deal with the young person.

(2) Arresting officer to advise young person of right to counsel — Every young person who is arrested or detained shall, forthwith on his arrest or detention, be advised by the arresting officer or the officer in charge, as the case may be, of his right to be represented by counsel and shall be given an opportunity to obtain counsel.

(3) Justice, youth court or review board to advise young person of right to counsel — Where a young person is not represented by counsel

    (a) at a hearing at which it will be determined whether to release the young person or detain him in custody prior to disposition of his case,

    (b) at a hearing held pursuant to section 16,

    (c) at his trial,

    (c.1) at any proceedings held pursuant to subsection 26.1(1), 26.2(1) or 26.6(1),

    (d) at a review of a disposition held before a youth court or a review board under this Act, or

    (e) at a review of the level of custody pursuant to subsection 28.1(1),

the justice before whom, or the youth court or review board before which, the hearing, trial or review is held shall advise the young person of his right to be represented by counsel and shall give the young person a reasonable opportunity to obtain counsel.

(4) Trial, hearing or review before youth court or review board — Where a young person at his trial or at a hearing or review referred to in subsection (3) wishes to obtain counsel but is unable to do so, the youth court before which the hearing, trial or review is held or the review board before which the review is held

(a) shall, where there is a legal aid or assistance program available in the province where the hearing, trial or review is held, refer the young person to that program for the appointment of counsel; or

(b) where no legal aid or assistance program is available or the young person is unable to obtain counsel through such a program, may, and on the request of the young person shall, direct that the young person be represented by counsel.

(5) Appointment of counsel — Where a direction is made under paragraph (4)(b) in respect of a young person, the Attorney General of the province in which the direction is made shall appoint counsel, or cause counsel to be appointed, to represent the young person.

(6) Release hearing before justice — Where a young person at a hearing before a justice who is not a youth court judge at which it will be determined whether to release the young person or detain him in custody prior to disposition of his case wishes to obtain counsel but is unable to do so, the justice shall

(a) where there is a legal aid or assistance program available in the province where the hearing is held,

(i) refer the young person to that program for the appointment of counsel, or

(ii) refer the matter to a youth court to be dealt with in accordance with paragraph 4(a), or (b); or

(b) where no legal aid or assistance program is available or the young person is unable to obtain counsel through such a program, refer the matter to a youth court to be dealt with in accordance with paragraph (4)(b).

(7) Young person may be assisted by adult — Where a young person is not represented by counsel at his trial or at a hearing or review referred to in subsection (3), the justice before whom or the youth court or review board before which the proceedings are held may, on the request of the young person, allow the young person to be assisted by an adult whom the justice, court or review board considers to be suitable.

(8) Counsel independent of parents — In any case where it appears to a youth court judge or a justice that the interests of a young person and his parents are in conflict or that it would be in the best interest of the young person to be represented by his own counsel, the judge or justice shall ensure that the young person is represented by counsel independent of his parents.

(9) Statement of right to counsel — A statement that a young person has the right to be represented by counsel shall be included in

(a) any appearance notice or summons issued to the young person;

(b) any warrant to arrest the young person;

(c) any promise to appear given by the young person;

(d) any recognizance entered into before an officer in charge by the young person;

(e) any notice given to the young person in relation to any proceedings held pursuant to subsection 26.1(1), 26.2(1) or 26.6(1); or

(f) any notice of a review of a disposition given to the young person.

R.S. 1985, c. 24 (2nd Supp.), s. 9; 1992, c. 11, s. 1; 1995, c. 19, s. 2

APPEARANCE

12. (1) Where young person appears — A young person against whom an information is laid must first appear before a youth court judge or a justice, and the judge or justice shall

(a) cause the information to be read to the young person;

(b) where the young person is not represented by counsel, inform the young person of the right to be so represented; and

(c) where the young person is a young person referred to in subsection 16(1.01), inform the young person that the young person will be proceeded against in ordinary court in accordance with the law ordinarily applicable to an adult charged with the offence unless an application is made to the youth court by the young person, the young person's counsel or the Attorney General or an agent of the Attorney General to have the young person proceeded against in the youth court and an order is made to that effect.

(2) Waiver — A young person may waive the requirement under paragraph (1)(a) where the young person is represented by counsel.

(3) Where young person not represented by counsel — Where a young person is not represented in youth court by counsel, the youth court shall, before accepting a plea,

(a) satisfy itself that the young person understands the charge against him; and

(b) explain to the young person that he may plead guilty or not guilty to the charge.

(3.1) Idem — Where a young person is a young person referred to in subsection 16(1.01) and is not represented in youth court by counsel, the youth court shall satisfy itself that the young person understands

(a) the charge against the young person;

(b) the consequences of being proceeded against in ordinary court; and

(c) the young person's right to apply to be proceeded against in youth court.

(4) Where youth court not satisfied — Where the youth court is not satisfied that a young person understands the charge against the young person, as required under paragraph (3)(a), the court shall enter a plea of not guilty on behalf of the young person and shall proceed with the trial in accordance with subsection 19(2) or, with respect to proceedings in Nunavut, subsection 19.1(2).

(5) Idem — Where the youth court is not satisfied that a young person understands the matters referred to in subsection (3.1), the court shall direct that the young person be represented by counsel.

1995, c. 19, s. 3; 1999, c. 3, s. 87

MEDICAL AND PSYCHOLOGICAL REPORTS

13. (1) Medical or psychological examination — A youth court may, at any stage of proceedings against a young person

(a) with the consent of the young person and the prosecutor, or

(b) on its own motion or on application of the young person or the prosecutor, where

(i) the court has reasonable grounds to believe that the young person may be suffering from a physical or mental illness or disorder, a psychological disorder, an emotional disturbance, a learning disability or a mental disability,

(ii) the young person's history indicates a pattern of repeated findings of guilt under this Act, or

(iii) the young person is alleged to have committed an offence involving serious personal injury,

and the court believes a medical, psychological or psychiatric report in respect of the young person is necessary for a purpose mentioned in paragraphs (2)(a) to (f),

by order require that the young person be assessed by a qualified person and require the person who conducts the examination to report the results thereof in writing to the court.

(2) Purpose of assessment — A youth court may make an order under subsection (1) in respect of a young person for the purpose of

(a) considering an application under section 16;

(b) making or reviewing a disposition under this Act, other than a disposition made under section 672.54 or 672.58 of the *Criminal Code*;

(c) considering an application under subsection 26.1(1);

(d) setting conditions under subsection 26.2(1);

(e) making an order subsection 26.6(2); or

(f) authorizing disclosure under subsection 38(1.5).

(3) Presumption against custodial remand — Subject to subsections (3.1) and (3.3), for the purpose of an assessment under this section, a youth court may remand a young person to such custody as it directs for a period not exceeding thirty days.

(3.1) Report of qualified person in writing — A young person shall not be remanded in custody pursuant to an order made by a youth court under subsection (1) unless

(a) the youth court is satisfied that on the evidence custody is necessary to conduct an assessment of the young person, or that on the evidence of a qualified person detention of the young person in custody is desirable to conduct the assessment of the young person and the young person consents to custody; or

(b) the young person is required to be detained in custody in respect of any other matter or by virtue of any provision of the *Criminal Code*.

(3.2) Application to vary assessment order where circumstances change — For the purposes of paragraph (3.1)(a), when the prosecutor and the young person agree, evidence of a qualified person may be received in the form of a report in writing.

(3.3) Custody for assessment — A youth court may, at any time while an order in respect of a young person made by the court under subsection (1) is in force, on cause being shown, vary the terms and conditions specified in that order in such manner as the court considers appropriate in the circumstances.

(4) Disclosure of report — Where a youth court receives a report made in respect of a young person pursuant to subsection (1),

(a) the court shall, subject to subsection (6), cause a copy of the report to be given to

(i) the young person,

(ii) a parent of the young person, if the parent is in attendance at the proceedings against the young person,

(iii) counsel, if any, representing the young person, and

(iv) the prosecutor; and

(b) the court may cause a copy of the report to be given to a parent of the young person not in attendance at the proceedings against the young person if the parent is, in the opinion of the court, taking an active interest in the proceedings.

(5) Cross-examination — Where a report is made in respect of a young person pursuant to subsection (1), the young person, his counsel or the adult assisting him pursuant to subsection 11(7) and the prosecutor shall, subject to subsection (6), on application to the youth court, be given an opportunity to cross-examine the person who made the report.

(6) Report to be withheld where disclosure unnecessary or prejudicial — A youth court shall withhold all or part of a report made in respect of a young person pursuant to subsection (1) from a private prosecutor, where disclosure of the report or part, in the opinion of the court, is not necessary for the prosecution of the case and might be prejudicial to the young person.

(7) Report to be withheld where disclosure dangerous to any person — A youth court shall withhold all or part of a report made in respect of a young person pursuant to subsection (1) from the young person's parents or a private prosecutor where the court is satisfied, on the basis of the report or evidence given in the absence of the young person, parents or private prosecutor by the person who made the report, that disclosure of all or part of the report would seriously impair the treatment or recovery of the young person, or would be likely to endanger the life or safety of, or result in serious psychological harm to, another person.

(8) Idem — Notwithstanding subsection (7), the youth court may release all or part of the report referred to in that subsection to the young person, the young person's parents or the private prosecutor where the interests of justice make disclosure essential in the court's opinion.

(9) Report to be part of record — A report made pursuant to subsection (1) shall form part of the record of the case in respect of which it was requested.

(10) Disclosure by qualified person — Notwithstanding any other provision of this Act, a qualified person who is of the opinion that a young person held in detention or committed to custody is likely to endanger his own life or safety or to endanger the life of, or cause bodily harm to, another person may immediately so advise any person who has the care and custody of the young person whether or not the same information is contained in a report made pursuant to subsection (1).

(11) Definition of "qualified person" — In this section, **"qualified person"** means a person duly qualified by provincial law to practice medicine or psychiatry or to carry out psychological examinations or assessments, as the circumstances require, or, where no such law exists, a person who is, in the opinion of the youth court, so qualified, and includes a person or a person within a class of persons designated by the Lieutenant Governor in Council of a province or his delegate.

(12) [Repealed R.S. 1985, c. 24 (2nd Supp.), s. 10.]

1991, c. 43, ss. 32, 35(a); 1995, c. 19, s. 4

13.1 (1) Statements not admissible against young person — Subject to subsection (2), where a young person is assessed pursuant to an order made under subsection 13(1), no statement or reference to a statement made by the young person during the course and for the purposes of the assessment to the person who conducts the assessment or to anyone acting under that person's direction is admissible in evidence, without the consent of the young person, in any proceeding before a court, tribunal, body or person with jurisdiction to compel the production of evidence.

(2) Exceptions — A statement referred to in subsection (1) is admissible in evidence for the purposes of

(a) considering an application under section 16 in respect of the young person;

(b) determining whether the young person is unfit to stand trial;

(c) determining whether the balance of the mind of the young person was disturbed at the time of commission of the alleged offence, where the young person is a female person charged with an offence arising out of the death of her newly-born child;

(d) making or reviewing a disposition in respect of the young person;

(e) determining whether the young person was, at the time of the commission of an alleged offence, suffering from automatism or a mental disorder so as to be exempt from criminal responsibility by virtue of subsection 16(1) of the *Criminal Code*, if the accused puts his or her mental capacity for criminal intent into issue, or if the prosecutor raises the issue after verdict;

(f) challenging the credibility of a young person in any proceeding where the testimony of the young person is inconsistent in a material particular with a statement referred to in subsection (1) that the young person made previously;

(g) establishing the perjury of a young person who is charged with perjury in respect of a statement made in any proceeding;

(h) deciding an application for an order under subsection 26.1(1);

(i) setting the conditions under subsection 26.2(1);

(j) conducting a review under subsection 26.6(1); or

(k) deciding an application for a disclosure order under subsection 38(1.5).

1991, c. 43, ss. 33, 35(b); 1994, c. 26, s. 76; 1995, c. 19, s. 5

APPLICATION OF PART XX.1 OF THE CRIMINAL CODE (MENTAL DISORDER)

13.2 (1) Sections of Criminal Code applicable — Except to the extent that they are inconsistent with or excluded by this Act, section 16 and Part XX.1 of the *Criminal Code*, except sections 672.65 and 672.66, apply, with such modifications as the circumstances require, in respect of proceedings under this Act in relation to offences alleged to have been committed by young persons.

(2) Notice and copies to counsel and parents — For the purposes of subsection (1), wherever in Part XX.1 of the *Criminal Code* a reference is made to

(a) a copy to be sent or otherwise given to an accused or a party to the proceedings, the reference shall be read as including a reference to a copy to be sent or otherwise given to

(i) counsel, if any, representing the young person,

(ii) any parent of the young person who is in attendance at the proceedings against the young person, and

(iii) any parent of the young person who is, in the opinion of the youth court or Review Board, taking an active interest in the proceedings; and

(b) notice to be given to an accused or a party to proceedings, the reference shall be read as including a reference to notice to be given to counsel, if any, representing the young person and the parents of the young person.

(3) Proceedings not invalid — Subject to subsection (4), failure to give a notice referred to in paragraph (2)(b) to a parent of a young person does not affect the validity of proceedings under this Act.

(4) Exception — Failure to give a notice referred to in paragraph (2)(b) to a parent of a young person in any case renders invalid any subsequent proceedings under this Act relating to the case unless

(a) a parent of the young person attends at the court or Review Board with the young person; or

(b) a youth court judge or Review Board before whom proceedings are held against the young person

(i) adjourns the proceedings and orders that the notice be given in such manner and to such persons as the judge or Review Board directs, or

(ii) dispenses with the notice where the youth court or Review Board is of the opinion that, having regard to the circumstances, the notice may be dispensed with.

(5) No hospital order assessments — A youth court may not make an order under subsection 672.11 of the *Criminal Code* in respect of a young person for the purpose of assisting in the determination of an issue mentioned in paragraph 672.11(e) of that Act.

(6) Considerations of court or Review Board making a disposition — Before making or reviewing a disposition in respect of a young person under Part XX.1 of the *Criminal Code*, a youth court or Review Board shall consider the age and special needs of the young person and any representations or submissions made by the young person's parents.

(7) Cap applicable to young persons — Subject to subsection (9), for the purpose of applying subsection 672.64(3) of the *Criminal Code* to proceedings under this Act in relation to an offence alleged to have been committed by a young person, the applicable cap shall be the maximum period during which the young person would be subject to a disposition by the youth court if found guilty of the offence.

(8) Application to increase cap of unfit young person subject to transfer — Where an application is made under section 16 to proceed against a young person in ordinary court and the young person is found unfit to stand trial, the Attorney General or the agent of the Attorney General may, before the youth court makes or refuses to make an order under that section, apply to the court to increase the cap that shall apply to the young person.

(9) Consideration of youth court for increase in cap — The youth court, after giving the Attorney General and the counsel and parents of the young person in respect of whom an application is made under subsection (8) an opportunity to be heard, shall take into consideration

(a) the seriousness of the alleged offence and the circumstances in which it was allegedly committed,

(b) the age, maturity, character and background of the young person and any previous findings of guilty against the young person under any Act of Parliament,

(c) the likelihood that the young person will cause significant harm to any person if released on expiration of the cap that applies to the young person pursuant to subsection (7), and

(d) the respective caps that would apply to the young person under this Act and under the *Criminal Code*,

and the youth court shall, where satisfied that the application under section 16 would likely succeed if the young person were fit to stand trial, apply to the young person the cap that would apply to an adult for the same offence.

(10) Prima facie case to be made every year — For the purpose of applying subsection 672.33(1) of the *Criminal Code* to proceedings under this Act in relation to an offence alleged to have been committed by a young person, wherever in that subsection a reference is made to two years, there shall be substituted a reference to one year.

(11) Designation of hospitals for young persons — A reference in Part XX.1 of the *Criminal Code* to a hospital in a province shall be construed as a reference to a hospital designated by the Minister of Health of the province for the custody, treatment or assessment of young persons.

1991, c. 43, s. 33

PRE-DISPOSITION REPORT

14. (1) Pre-disposition report — Where a youth court deems it advisable before making a disposition under section 20 in respect of a young person who is found guilty of an offence it may, and where a youth court is required under this Act to consider a pre-disposition report before making an order or a disposition in respect of a young person it shall, require the provincial director to cause to be prepared a pre-disposition report in respect of the young person and to submit the report to the court.

(2) Contents of report — A pre-disposition report made in respect of a young person shall, subject to subsection (3), be in writing and shall include,

(a) the results of an interview with

(i) the young person,

(ii) where reasonably possible, the parents of the young person and,

(iii) where appropriate and reasonably possible, members of the young person's extended family;

(b) the results of an interview with the victim in the case, where applicable and where reasonably possible;

(c) such information as is applicable to the case including, where applicable,

(i) the age, maturity, character, behaviour and attitude of the young person and his willingness to make amends,

(ii) any plans put forward by the young person to change his conduct or to participate in activities or undertake measures to improve himself,

(iii) the history of previous findings of delinquency under the *Juvenile Delinquents Act*, chapter J-3 of the Revised Statutes of Canada, 1970, or previous findings of guilt under this or any other Act of Parliament or any regulation made thereunder or under an Act of the legislature of a province or any regulation made thereunder or a by-law or ordinance of a municipality, the history of community or other services rendered to the young person with respect to those findings and the response of the young person to previous sentences or dispositions and to services rendered to him,

(iv) the history of alternative measures used to deal with the young person and the response of the young person thereto,

(v) the availability and appropriateness of community services and facilities for young persons and the willingness of the young person to avail himself or herself of those services or facilities,

(vi) the relationship between the young person and the young person's parents and the degree of control and influence of the parents over the young person and, where appropriate and reasonably possible, the relationship between the young person and the young person's extended family and the degree of control and influence of the young person's extended family over the young person,

(vii) the school attendance and performance record and the employment record of the young person; and

(d) such information as the provincial director considers relevant, including any recommendation that the provincial director considers appropriate.

(3) Oral report with leave — Where a pre-disposition report cannot reasonably be committed to writing, it may, with leave of the youth court, be submitted orally in court.

(4) Report to form part of record — A pre-disposition report shall form part of the record of the case in respect of which it was requested.

(5) Copies of pre-disposition report — Where a pre-disposition report made in respect of a young person is submitted to a youth court in writing, the court

(a) shall, subject to subsection (7), cause a copy of the report to be given to

(i) the young person,

(ii) a parent of the young person, if the parent is in attendance at the proceedings against the young person,

(iii) counsel, if any, representing the young person, and

(iv) the prosecutor; and

(b) may cause a copy of the report to be given to a parent of the young person not in attendance at the proceedings against the young person if the parent is, in the opinion of the court, taking an active interest in the proceedings.

(6) Cross-examination — Where a pre-disposition report made in respect of a young person is submitted to a youth court, the young person, his counsel or the adult assisting him pursuant to subsection 11(7) and the prosecutor shall, subject to subsection (7), on application to the youth court, be given the opportunity to cross-examine the person who made the report.

(7) Report may be withheld from private prosecutor — Where a pre-disposition report made in respect of a young person is submitted to a youth court, the court may, where the prosecutor is a private prosecutor and disclosure of the report or any part thereof to the prosecutor might, in the opinion of the court, be prejudicial to the young person and is not, in the opinion of the court, necessary for the prosecution of the case against the young person,

(a) withhold the report or part thereof from the prosecutor, if the report is submitted in writing; or

(b) exclude the prosecutor from the court during the submission of the report or part thereof, if the report is submitted orally in court.

(8) Report disclosed to other persons — Where a pre-disposition report made in respect of a young person is submitted to a youth court, the court

(a) shall, on request, cause a copy or a transcript of the report to be supplied to

(i) any court that is dealing with matters relating to the young person, and

(ii) any youth worker to whom the young person's case has been assigned; and

(b) may, on request, cause a copy or a transcript of the report, or a part thereof, to be supplied to any person not otherwise authorized under this section to receive a copy or transcript of the report if, in the opinion of the court, the person has a valid interest in the proceedings.

(9) Disclosure by the provincial director — A provincial director who submits a pre-disposition report made in respect of a young person to a youth court may make the report, or any part thereof, available to any person in whose custody or under whose supervision the young person is placed or to any other person who is directly assisting in the care or treatment of the young person.

(10) Inadmissibility of statements — No statement made by a young person in the course of the preparation of a pre-disposition report in respect of the young person is admissible in evidence against him in any civil or criminal proceedings except in proceedings under section 16 or 20 or sections 28 to 32.

R.S. 1985, c. 24 (2nd Supp.), s. 11; 1995, c. 19, s. 6

DISQUALIFICATION OF JUDGE

15. (1) Disqualification of judge — Subject to subsection (2), a youth court judge who, prior to an adjudication in respect of a young person charged with an offence, examines a pre-disposition report made in respect of the young person, or hears an application under section 16 in respect of the young person, in connection with that offence shall not in any capacity conduct or continue the trial of the young person for the offence and shall transfer the case to another judge to be dealt with according to law.

(2) Exception — A youth court judge may, in the circumstances referred to in subsection (1), with the consent of the young person and the prosecutor, conduct or continue the trial of the young person if the judge is satisfied that he has not been predisposed by information contained in the pre-disposition report or by representations made in respect of the application under section 16.

TRANSFER

16. (1) Transfer to ordinary court — Subject to subsection (1.01), at any time after an information is laid against a young person alleged to have, after attaining the age of fourteen years, committed an indictable offence other than an offence referred to in section 553 of the *Criminal Code* but prior to adjudication, a youth court shall, on application of the young person or the young person's counsel or the Attorney General or an agent of the Attorney General, determine, in accordance with subsection (1.1), whether the young person should be proceeded against in ordinary court.

(1.01) Trial in ordinary court for certain offences — Every young person against whom an information is laid who is alleged to have committed

(a) first degree murder or second degree murder within the meaning of section 231 of the *Criminal Code*,

(b) an offence under section 239 of the *Criminal Code* (attempt to commit murder),

(c) an offence under section 232 or 234 of the *Criminal Code* (manslaughter), or

(d) an offence under section 273 of the *Criminal Code* (aggravated sexual assault),

and who was sixteen or seventeen years of age at the time of the alleged commission of the offence shall be proceeded against in ordinary court in accordance with the law ordinarily applicable to an adult charged with the offence unless the youth court, on application by the young person, the young person's counsel or the Attorney General or an agent of the Attorney General, makes an order under subsection (1.04) or (1.05) or subparagraph (1.1)(a)(ii) that the young person should be proceeded against in youth court.

(1.02) Making of application — An application to the youth court under subsection (1.01) must be made orally, in the presence of the other party to the proceedings, or in writing, with a notice served on the other party to the proceedings.

(1.03) Where application is opposed — Where the other party to the proceedings referred to in subsection (1.02) files a notice of opposition to the application with the youth court within twenty-one days after the making of the oral application, or the service of the notice referred to in that subsection, as the case may be, the youth court shall, in accordance with subsection (1.1), determine whether the young person should be proceeded against in youth court.

(1.04) Where application is unopposed — Where the other party to the proceedings referred to in subsection (1.02) files a notice of non-opposition to the application with the youth court within the time referred to in subsection (1.03), the youth court shall order that the young person be proceeded against in youth court.

(1.05) Deeming — Where the other party to the proceedings referred to in subsection (1.02) does not file a notice referred to in subsection (1.03) or (1.04) within the time referred to in subsection (1.03), the youth court shall order that the young person be proceeded against in youth court.

(1.06) Time may be extended — The time referred to in subsections (1.03) to (1.05) may be extended by mutual agreement of the parties to the proceedings by filing a notice to that effect with the youth court.

(1.1) Order — In making the determination referred to in subsection (1) or (1.03), the youth court, after affording both parties and the parents of the young person an opportunity to be heard, shall consider the interest of society, which includes the objectives of affording protection to the public and rehabilitation of the young person, and determine whether those objectives can be reconciled by the youth being under the jurisdiction of the youth court, and

> (a) if the court is of the opinion that those objectives can be so reconciled, the court shall
>
> > (i) in the case of an application under subsection (1), refuse to make an order that the young person be proceeded against in ordinary court, and
> >
> > (ii) in the case of an application under subsection (1.01), order that the young person be proceeded against in youth court; or
>
> (b) if the court is of the opinion that those objectives cannot be so reconciled, protection of the public shall be paramount and the court shall
>
> > (i) in the case of an application under subsection (1), order that the young person be proceeded against in ordinary court in accordance with the law ordinarily applicable to an adult charged with the offence, and
> >
> > (ii) in the case of an application under subsection (1.01), refuse to make an order that the young person be proceeded against in youth court.

(1.11) Onus — Where an application is made under subsection (1) or (1.01), the onus of satisfying the youth court of the matters referred to in subsection (1.1) rests with the applicant.

(2) Considerations by youth court — In making the determination referred to in subsection (1) or (1.03) in respect of a young person, a youth court shall take into account

> (a) the seriousness of the alleged offence and the circumstances in which it was allegedly committed;
>
> (b) the age, maturity, character and background of the young person and any record or summary of previous findings of delinquency under the *Juvenile Delinquents Act*, chapter J-3 of the Revised Statutes of Canada, 1970, or previous findings of guilt under this Act or any other Act of Parliament or any regulation made thereunder;
>
> (c) the adequacy of this Act, and the adequacy of the *Criminal Code* or any other Act of Parliament that would apply in respect of the young person if an order were made under this section to meet the circumstances of the case;
>
> (d) the availability of treatment or correctional resources;

(e) any representations made to the court by or on behalf of the young person or by the Attorney General or his agent; and

(f) any other factors that the court considers relevant.

(3) Pre-disposition reports — In making the determination referred to in subsection (1) or (1.03) in respect of a young person, a youth court shall consider a pre-disposition report.

(4) Where young person on transfer status — Notwithstanding subsections (1) and (3), where an application is made under subsection (1) by the Attorney General or the Attorney General's agent in respect of an offence alleged to have been committed by a young person while the young person was being proceeded against in ordinary court pursuant to an order previously made under this section or serving a sentence as a result of proceedings in ordinary court, the youth court may make a further order under this section without a hearing and without considering a pre-disposition report.

(5) Court to state reasons — Where a youth court makes an order or refuses to make an order under this section, it shall state the reasons for its decision and the reasons shall form part of the record of the proceedings in the youth court.

(6) No further applications for transfer — Where a youth court refuses to make an order under this section in respect of an alleged offence, no further application may be made under this section in respect of that offence.

(7) Effect of order — Where an order is made under this section pursuant to an application under subsection (1), proceedings under this Act shall be discontinued and the young person against whom the proceedings are taken shall be taken before the ordinary court.

(7.1) Idem — Where an order is made under this section pursuant to an application under subsection (1.01), the proceedings against the young person shall be in the youth court.

(8) Jurisdiction of ordinary court limited — Where a young person is proceeded against in ordinary court in respect of an offence by reason of

(a) subsection (1.01), where no application is made under that subsection,

(b) an order made under subparagraph (1.1)(b)(i), or

(c) the refusal under subparagraph (1.1)(b)(ii) to make an order,

that the court has jurisdiction only in respect of that offence; or an offence included therein.

(9) Review of youth court decision — An order made in respect of a young person under this section or a refusal to make such an order shall, on application of the young person or the young person's counsel or the Attorney General or the Attorney General's agent made within thirty days after the decision of the youth court, be reviewed by the court of appeal, and that court may, in its discretion, confirm or reverse the decision of the youth court.

(10) Extension of time to make application — The court of appeal may, at any time, extend the time within which an application under subsection (9) may be made.

(11) Notice of application — A person who proposes to apply for a review under subsection (9) shall give notice of the application in such manner and within such period of time as may be directed by rules of court.

(12) Inadmissibility of statement — No statement made by a young person in the course of a hearing held under this section is admissible in evidence against the young person in any civil or criminal proceeding held subsequent to that hearing.

(13) [Repealed 1992, c. 11, s. 16(3).]

(14) [Repealed R.S. 1985, c. 24 (2nd Supp.), s. 12.]

1992, c. 11, s. 2; 1995, c. 19, s. 8

16.1 (1) Detention pending trial — young person under eighteen — Notwithstanding anything in this or any other Act of Parliament, where a young person who is under the age of eighteen is to be proceeded against in ordinary court by reason of

    (a) subsection 16(1.01), where no application is made under that subsection,

    (b) an order under subparagraph 16(1.1)(b)(i), or

    (c) the refusal under subparagraph 16(1.1)(b)(ii) to make an order,

and the young person is to be in custody pending the proceedings in that court, the young person shall be held separate and apart from any adult who is detained or held in custody unless the youth court is satisfied, on application, that the young person, having regard to the best interests of the young person and the safety of others, cannot be detained in a place of detention for young persons.

(2) Detention pending trial — young person over eighteen — Notwithstanding anything in this or any other Act of Parliament, where a young person who is over the age of eighteen is to be proceeded against in ordinary court by reason of

    (a) subsection 16(1.01), where no application is made under that subsection,

    (b) an order under subparagraph 16(1.1)(b)(i), or

    (c) the refusal under subparagraph 16(1.1)(b)(ii) to make an order,

and the young person is to be in custody pending the proceedings in that court, the young person shall be held in a place of detention for adults unless the youth court is satisfied, on application, that the young person, having regard to the best interests of the young person and the safety of others, should be detained in a place of custody for young persons.

(3) Review — On application, the youth court shall review the placement of a young person in detention pursuant to this section and, if satisfied, having regard to the best interests of the young person and the safety of others, and after having afforded the young person, the provincial director and a representative of a provincial department responsible for adult correctional facilities an opportunity to be heard, that the young person should remain in detention where the young person is or be transferred to youth or adult detention, as the case may be, the court may so order.

(4) Who may make application — An application referred to in this section may be made by the young person, the young person's parents, the provincial director, the Attorney General or the Attorney General's agent.

(5) Notice — Where an application referred to in this section is made, the applicant shall cause a notice of the application to be given

(a) where the applicant is the young person or one of the young person's parents, to the provincial director and the Attorney General;

(b) where the applicant is the Attorney General or the Attorney General's agent, to the young person, the young person's parents and the provincial director; and

(c) where the applicant is the provincial director, to the young person, the parents of the young person and the Attorney General.

(6) Statement of rights — A notice given under subsection (5) by the Attorney General or the provincial director shall include a statement that the young person has the opportunity to be heard and the right to be represented by counsel.

(7) Limit — age 20 — Notwithstanding anything in this section, no young person shall remain in custody in a place of detention for young persons under this section after the young person attains the age of twenty years.

1992, c. 11, s. 2(3); 1995, c. 19, s. 9

16.2 (1) Placement on conviction by ordinary court — Notwithstanding anything in this or any other Act of Parliament, where a young person who is proceeded against in ordinary court by reason of subsection 16(1.01), where no application is made under that subsection, or by reason of an order under subparagraph 16(1.1)(b)(i) or the refusal under subparagraph 16(1.1)(b)(ii) to make an order, is convicted and sentenced to imprisonment, the court shall, after affording the young person, the parents of the young person, the Attorney General, the provincial director and representatives of the provincial and federal correctional systems an opportunity to be heard, order that the young person serve any portion of the imprisonment in

(a) a place of custody for young persons separate and apart from any adult who is detained or held in custody;

(b) a provincial correctional facility for adults; or

(c) where the sentence is for two years or more, a penitentiary.

(2) Factors to be taken into account — In making an order under subsection (1), the court shall take into account

(a) the safety of the young person;

(b) the safety of the public;

(c) the young person's accessibility to family;

(d) the safety of other young persons if the young person were to be held in custody in a place of custody for young persons;

(e) whether the young person would have a detrimental influence on other young persons if the young person were to be held in custody in a place of custody for young persons;

(f) the young person's level of maturity;

(g) the availability and suitability of treatment, educational and other resources that would be provided to the young person in a place of custody for young persons and in a place of custody for adults;

(h) the young person's prior experiences and behaviour while in detention or custody;

(i) the recommendations of the provincial director and representatives of the provincial and federal correctional facilities; and

(j) any other factor the court considers relevant.

(3) Report necessary — Prior to making an order under subsection (1), the court shall require that a report be prepared for the purpose of assisting the court.

(4) Review — On application, the court shall review the placement of a young person in detention pursuant to this section and, if satisfied that the circumstances that resulted in the initial order have changed materially, and after having afforded the young person, the provincial director and the representatives of the provincial and federal correctional systems an opportunity to be heard, the court may order that the young person be placed in

(a) a place of custody for young persons separate and apart from any adult who is detained or held in custody;

(b) a provincial correctional facility for adults, or

(c) where the sentence is for two years or more, a penitentiary.

(5) Who may make application — An application referred to in this section may be made by the young person, the young person's parents, the provincial director, a representative of the provincial and federal correctional systems and the Attorney General.

(6) Notice — Where an application referred to in this section is made, the applicant shall cause a notice of the application to be given

(a) where the applicant is the young person or one of the young person's parents, to the provincial director, to representatives of the provincial and federal correction systems and to the Attorney General;

(b) where the applicant is the Attorney General or the Attorney General's agent, to the young person, the young person's parents and the provincial director and representatives of the provincial and federal correction systems; and

(c) where an applicant is the provincial director, to the young person, the parents of the young person, the Attorney General and representatives of the provincial and federal correction systems.

1992, c. 11, s. 2(3); 1995, c. 19, s. 10

Note: Transitional Provision, S.C. 1992, c. 11, s. 18 provides:

> *18. Where a young person is alleged to have committed first degree murder or second degree murder within the meaning of section 231 of the Criminal Code before the coming into force of this Act and*
>
>> *(a) an application was made in respect of the young person under subsection 16(1) of the Young Offenders Act, as that subsection read immediately before the coming into force of this Act, but no decision under that subsection had been issued before the coming into force of this Act, or*
>>
>> *(b) an application is made in respect of the young person under subsection 16(1) of the Young Offenders Act after the coming into force of this Act,*
>
> *the provisions of the Young Offenders Act enacted by this Act shall apply to the young person as if the offence had occurred after the coming into force of this Act.*

17. (1) Order restricting publication of information presented at transfer hearing — Where a youth court hears an application for a transfer under section 16, it shall

(a) where the young person is not represented by counsel, or

(b) on application made by or on behalf of the young person or the prosecutor, where the young person is represented by counsel,

make an order directing that any information respecting the offence presented at the hearing shall not be published in any newspaper or broadcast before such time as

(c) an order for a transfer is refused or set aside on review and the time for all reviews against the decision has expired or all proceedings in respect of any such review have been completed; or

(d) the trial is ended, if the case is transferred to ordinary court.

(2) Offence — Every one who fails to comply with an order made pursuant to subsection (1) is guilty of an offence punishable on summary conviction.

(3) Definition of "newspaper" — In this section, "newspaper" has the meaning set out in section 297 of the *Criminal Code*.

1995, c. 19, s. 11

TRANSFER OF JURISDICTION

18. Transfer of jurisdiction — Notwithstanding subsections 478(1) and (3) of the *Criminal Code*, where a young person is charged with an offence that is alleged to have been committed in one province, he may, if the Attorney General of the province where the offence is alleged to have been committed consents, appear before a youth court of any other province and,

(a) where the young person signifies his consent to plead guilty and pleads guilty to that offence, the court shall, if it is satisfied that the facts support the charge, find the young person guilty of the offence alleged in the information; and

(b) where the young person does not signify his consent to plead guilty and does not plead guilty, or where the court is not satisfied that the facts support the charge, the young person shall, if he was detained in custody prior to his appearance, be returned to custody and dealt with according to law.

ADJUDICATION

19. (1) Where young person pleads guilty — Where a young person pleads guilty to an offence charged against him and the youth court is satisfied that the facts support the charge, the court shall find the young person guilty of the offence.

(2) Where young person pleads not guilty — Where a young person charged with an offence pleads not guilty to the offence or pleads guilty but the youth court is not satisfied that the facts support the charge, the court shall, subject to subsection (4), proceed with the trial and shall, after considering the matter, find the young person guilty or not guilty or make an order dismissing the charge, as the case may be.

(3) Application for transfer to ordinary court — The court shall not make a finding under this section in respect of a young person in respect of whom an application may be made under section 16 for an order that the young person be proceeded against in ordinary court unless it has inquired as to whether any of the parties to the proceedings wishes to make such an application, and, if any party so wishes, has given that party an opportunity to do so.

(4) Election — offence of murder — Notwithstanding section 5, where a young person is charged with having committed first degree murder or second degree murder within the meaning of section 231 of the *Criminal Code*, the youth court, before proceeding with the trial, shall ask the young person to elect to be tried by a youth court judge alone or by a judge of a superior court of criminal jurisdiction with a jury, and where a young person elects to be tried by a judge of a superior court of criminal jurisdiction with a jury, the young person shall be dealt with as provided in this Act.

(5) Where no election made — Notwithstanding section 5, where an election is not made under subsection (4), the young person shall be deemed to have elected to be tried by a judge of a superior court of criminal jurisdiction with a jury and dealt with as provided for in this Act.

(5.1) Preliminary inquiry — Where a young person elects or is deemed to have elected to be tried by a judge of a superior court of criminal jurisdiction with a jury, the youth court shall conduct a preliminary inquiry and if, on its conclusion, the young person is ordered to stand trial, the proceedings shall be before a judge of the superior court of criminal jurisdiction with a jury.

(5.2) Preliminary inquiry provisions of Criminal Code — A preliminary inquiry referred to in subsection (5.1) shall be conducted in accordance with the provisions of Part XVIII of the *Criminal Code*, except to the extent that they are inconsistent with this Act.

(6) Parts XIX and XX of the Criminal Code — Proceedings under this Act before a judge of a superior court of criminal jurisdiction with a jury shall be conducted, with such modifications as the circumstances require, in accordance with the provisions of Parts XIX and XX of the *Criminal Code*, except that

(a) the provisions of this Act respecting the protection of privacy and young persons prevail over the provisions of the *Criminal Code*; and

(b) the young person is entitled to be represented in court by counsel if the young person is removed from court pursuant to subsection 650(2) of the *Criminal Code*.

R.S. 1985, c. 24 (2nd Supp.), s. 13; 1995, c. 19, s. 12

19.1 (1) If young person pleads guilty — Nunavut — If a young person pleads guilty to an offence charged against the young person and the youth court is satisfied that the facts support the charge, the court shall find the young person guilty of the offence.

(2) If young person pleads not guilty — Nunavut — If a young person charged with an offence pleads not guilty to the offence or pleads guilty but the youth court is not satisfied that the facts support the charge, the court shall, subject to subsection (4), proceed with the trial and shall, after considering the matter, find the young person guilty or not guilty or make an order dismissing the charge, as the case may be.

(3) Application for transfer to ordinary court — Nunavut — The court shall not make a finding under this section in respect of a young person in respect of whom an application may be made under section 16 for an order that the young person be proceeded against in ordinary court unless it has inquired as to whether any of the parties to the proceedings wishes to make such an application, and, if any party so wishes, has given that party an opportunity to do so.

(4) Election re offence of murder — Nunavut — If a young person is charged with having committed first degree murder or second degree murder within the meaning of section 231 of the *Criminal Code*, the youth court, before proceeding with the trial, shall ask the young person to elect

(a) to be tried by a judge of the Nunavut Court of Justice alone, acting as a youth court, or

(b) to have a preliminary inquiry and to be tried by a judge of the Nunavut Court of Justice, acting as a youth court, with a jury,

and if a young person elects under paragraph (a) or (b), the young person shall be dealt with as provided in this Act.

(5) If no election made — Nunavut — Despite section 5, if an election is not made under subsection (4), the young person shall be deemed to have elected under paragraph (4)(b).

(6) Preliminary inquiry — Nunavut — If a young person elects or is deemed to have elected under paragraph (4)(b), a preliminary inquiry shall be held in the youth court and if, on its conclusion, the young person is ordered to stand trial, the proceedings shall be before a judge of the Nunavut Court of Justice, acting as a youth court, with a jury.

(7) Preliminary inquiry provisions of *Criminal Code* — Nunavut — A preliminary inquiry referred to in subsection (6) shall be conducted in accordance with the provisions of Part XVIII of the *Criminal Code*, except to the extent that they are inconsistent with this Act.

(8) Parts XIX and XX of the *Criminal Code* — Nunavut — Proceedings under this Act before a judge of the Nunavut Court of Justice, acting as a youth court, with a jury shall be conducted, with any modifications that the circumstances require, in accordance with the provisions of Parts XIX and XX of the *Criminal Code*, except that

(a) the provisions of this Act respecting the protection of privacy of young persons prevail over the provisions of the *Criminal Code*; and

(b) the young person is entitled to be represented in court by counsel if the young person is removed from court pursuant to subsection 650(2) of the *Criminal Code*.

(9) Application to Nunavut — This section, and not section 19, applies in respect of proceedings under this Act in Nunavut.

1999, c. 3, s. 88

DISPOSITIONS

20. (1) Dispositions that may be made — Where a youth court finds a young person guilty of an offence, it shall consider any pre-disposition report required by the court, any representations made by the parties to the proceedings or their counsel or agents and by the parents of the young person and any other relevant information before the court, and the court shall then make any one of the following dispositions, other than the disposition referred to in paragraph (k.1), or any number thereof that are not inconsistent with each other, and where the offence is first degree murder or second degree murder within the meaning of section 231 of the *Criminal Code*, the court shall make the disposition referred to in paragraph (k.1) and may make such other disposition as the court considers appropriate:

(a) by order direct that the young person be discharged absolutely, if the court considers it to be in the best interests of the young person and not contrary to the public interest;

(a.1) by order direct that the young person be discharged on such conditions as the court considers appropriate;

(b) impose on the young person a fine not exceeding one thousand dollars to be paid at such time and on such terms as the court may fix;

(c) order the young person to pay to any other person at such time and on such terms as the court may fix an amount by way of compensation for loss of or damage to property, for loss of income or support or for special damages for personal injury arising from the commission of the offence where the value thereof is readily ascertainable, but no order shall be made for general damages;

(d) order the young person to make restitution to any other person of any property obtained by the young person as a result of the commission of the offence within such time as the court may fix, if the property is owned by that other person or was, at the time of the offence, in his lawful possession;

(e) if any property obtained as a result of the commission of the offence has been sold to an innocent purchaser, where restitution of the property to its owner or any other person has been made or ordered, order the young person to pay the purchaser, at such time and on such terms as the court may fix, an amount not exceeding the amount paid by the purchaser for the property;

(f) subject to section 21, order the young person to compensate any person in kind or by way of personal services at such time and on such terms as the court may fix for any loss, damage or injury suffered by that person in respect of which an order may be made under paragraph (c) or (e);

(g) subject to section 21, order the young person to perform a community service at such time and on such terms as the court may fix;

(h) subject to section 20.1, make any order of prohibition, seizure or forfeiture that may be imposed under any Act of Parliament or any regulation made thereunder where an accused is found guilty or convicted of that offence;

(i) [Repealed 1995, c. 19, s. 13(2)].

(j) place the young person on probation in accordance with section 23 for a specified period not exceeding two years;

(k) subject to sections 24 to 24.5, commit the young person to custody, to be served continuously or intermittently, for a specified period not exceeding

    (i) two years from the date of committal, or

    (ii) where the young person is found guilty of an offence for which the punishment provided by the *Criminal Code* or any other Act of Parliament is imprisonment for life, three years from the date of committal;

(k.1) order the young person to serve a disposition not to exceed

    (i) in the case of first degree murder, ten years comprised of

        (A) a committal to custody, to be served continuously, for a period that shall not, subject to subsection 26.1(1), exceed six years from the date of committal, and

        (B) a placement under conditional supervision to be served in the community in accordance with section 26.2, and

    (ii) in the case of second degree murder, seven years comprised of

        (A) a committal to custody, to be served continuously, for a period that shall not, subject to subsection 26.1(1), exceed four years from the date of committal, and

        (B) a placement under conditional supervision to be served in the community in accordance with section 26.2; and

(l) impose on the young person such other reasonable and ancillary conditions as it deems advisable and in the best interest of the young person and the public.

(2) Coming into force of disposition — A disposition made under this section shall come into force on the date on which it is made or on such later date as the youth court specifies therein.

(3) Duration of disposition — No disposition made under this section, other than an order made under paragraph (1)(h), (k) or (k.1), shall continue in force for more than two years and, where the youth court makes more than one disposition at the same time in respect of the same offence, the combined duration of the dispositions, except in respect of an order made under paragraph (1)(h), (k) or (k.1), shall not exceed two years.

(4) Combined duration of dispositions — Subject to subsection (4.1), where more than one disposition is made under this section in respect of a young person with respect to different offences, the continuous combined duration of those dispositions shall not exceed three years, except where one of those offences is first degree murder or second degree murder within the meaning of section 231 of the *Criminal Code*, in which case the continuous combined duration of those dispositions shall not exceed ten years in the case of first degree murder, or seven years in the case of second degree murder.

(4.1) Duration of dispositions made at different times — Where a disposition is made under this section in respect of an offence committed by a young person after the commencement of, but before the completion of, any dispositions made in respect of previous offences committed by the young person,

> (a) the duration of the disposition made in respect of the subsequent offence shall be determined in accordance with subsections (3) and (4);

> (b) the disposition may be served consecutively to the dispositions made in respect of the previous offences; and

> (c) the combined duration of all the dispositions may exceed three years, except where the offence is, or one of the previous offences was,

>> (i) first degree murder within the meaning of section 231 of the *Criminal Code*, in which case the continuous combined duration of the dispositions may exceed ten years, or

>> (ii) second degree murder within the meaning of section 231 of the *Criminal Code*, in which case the continuous combined duration of the dispositions may exceed seven years.

(4.2) Custody first — Subject to subsection (4.3), where a young person who is serving a disposition made under paragraph (1)(k.1) is ordered to custody in respect of an offence committed after the commencement of, but before the completion of, that disposition, the custody in respect of that subsequent offence shall be served before the young person is placed under conditional supervision.

(4.3) Conditional supervision suspended — Where a young person referred to in subsection (4.2) is under conditional supervision at the time the young person is ordered to custody in respect of a subsequent offence, the conditional supervision shall be suspended until the young person is released from custody.

(5) Disposition continues when adult — Subject to section 743.5 of the *Criminal Code*, a disposition made under this section shall continue in effect in accordance with the terms thereof, after the young person against whom it is made becomes an adult.

(6) Reasons for the disposition — Where a youth court makes a disposition under this section, it shall state its reasons therefor in the record of the case and shall

(a) provide or cause to be provided a copy of the disposition, and

(b) on request, provide or cause to be provided a transcript or copy of the reasons for the disposition

to the young person in respect of whom the disposition was made, the young person's counsel and parents, the provincial director, where the provincial director has an interest in the disposition, the prosecutor and, in the case of a custodial disposition made under paragraph (1)(k) or (k.1), the review board, if a review board has been established or designated.

(7) Limitation on punishment — No disposition shall be made in respect of a young person under this section that results in a punishment that is greater than the maximum punishment that would be applicable to an adult who has committed the same offence.

(8) Application of Part XXIII of *Criminal Code* — Part XXIII of the *Criminal Code* does not apply in respect of proceedings under this Act except for section 722, subsection 730(2) and sections 748, 748.1 and 749, which provisions apply with such modifications as the circumstances require.

(9) Section 787 of *Criminal Code* does not apply — Section 787 of the *Criminal Code* does not apply in respect of proceedings under this Act.

(10) Contents of probation order — The youth court shall specify in any probation order made under paragraph (1)(j) the period for which it is to remain in force.

(11) No order under section 161 of *Criminal Code* — Notwithstanding paragraph (1)(h), a youth court shall not make an order of prohibition under section 161 of the *Criminal Code* against a young person.

R.S. 1985, c. 27 (1st Supp.), s. 187 (Sched.); R.S. 1985, c. 24 (2nd Supp.), s. 14; R.S. 1985, c. 1 (4th Supp.), s. 38; 1992, c. 11, s. 3; 1993, c. 45, s. 15; 1995, c. 19, s. 13; 1995, c. 22, ss. 16, 17, 25; 1995, c. 39, s. 178

20.1 (1) Mandatory prohibition order — Notwithstanding subsection 20(1), where a young person is found guilty of an offence referred to in any of paragraphs 109(1)(a) to (d) of the *Criminal Code*, the youth court shall, in addition to making any disposition referred to in subsection 20(1), make an order prohibiting the young person from possessing any firearm, cross-bow, prohibited weapon, restricted weapon, prohibited device, ammunition, prohibited ammunition and explosive substance during the period specified in the order as determined in accordance with subsection (2).

(2) Duration of prohibition order — An order made under subsection (1) begins on the day on which the order is made and ends not earlier than two years after the young person's release from custody after being found guilty of the offence or, if the young person is not then in custody or subject to custody, after the time the young person is found guilty of or discharged from the offence.

(3) Discretionary prohibition order — Notwithstanding subsection 20(1), where a young person is found guilty of an offence referred to in paragraph 110(1)(a) or (b) of the *Criminal Code*, the youth court shall, in addition to making any disposition referred to in subsection 20(1), consider whether it is desirable, in the interests of the safety of the person or of any other person, to make an order prohibiting the person from possessing any firearm, cross-bow, prohibited weapon, restricted weapon, prohibited device, ammunition, prohibited ammunition or explosive substance, or all such things, and where the court decides that it is so desirable, the court shall so order.

(4) Duration of prohibition order — An order made under subsection (3) against a young person begins on the day on which the order is made and ends not later than two years after the young person's release from custody or, if the young person is not then in custody or subject to custody, after the time the young person is found guilty of or discharged from the offence.

(5) Definition of "release from imprisonment" — In paragraph (2)(a) and subsection (4), **"release from custody"** means a release from custody in accordance with this Act, other than a release from custody under subsection 35(1), and includes the commencement of conditional supervision or probation.

(6) Reasons for the prohibition order — Where a youth court makes an order under this section, it shall state its reasons for making the order in the record of the case and shall

(a) provide or cause to be provided a copy of the order, and

(b) on request, provide or cause to be provided a transcript or copy of the reasons for making the order

to the young person against whom the order was made, the young person's counsel and parents and the provincial director.

(7) Reasons — Where the youth court does not make an order under subsection (3), or where the youth court does make such an order but does not prohibit the possession of everything referred to in that subsection, the youth court shall include in the record a statement of the youth court's reasons.

(8) Application of Criminal Code — Sections 113 to 117 of the *Criminal Code* apply in respect of any order made under this section.

(9) Report — Before making any order referred to in section 113 of the *Criminal Code* in respect of a young person, the youth court may require the provincial director to cause to be prepared, and to submit to the youth court, a report on the young person.

1995, c. 39, s. 179

21. (1) Where a fine or other payment is ordered — The youth court shall, in imposing a fine on a young person under paragraph 20(1)(b) or in making an order against a young person under paragraph 20(1)(c) or (e), have regard to the present and future means of the young person to pay.

(2) Fine option program — A young person against whom a fine is imposed under paragraph 20(1)(b) may discharge the fine in whole or in part by earning credits for work performed in a program established for that purpose

(a) by the Lieutenant Governor in Council of the province in which the fine was imposed; or

(b) by the Lieutenant Governor in Council of the province in which the young person resides, where an appropriate agreement is in effect between the government of that province and the government of the province in which the fine was imposed.

(3) Rates, crediting and other matters — A program referred to in subsection (2) shall determine the rate at which credits are earned and may provide for the manner of crediting any amounts earned against the fine and any other matters necessary for or incidental to carrying out the program.

(4) Representations respecting orders under paras. 20(1)(c) to (f) — In considering whether to make an order under paragraphs (20)(1)(c) to (f), the youth court may consider any representations made by the person who would be compensated or to whom restitution or payment would be made.

(5) Notice of orders under paras. 20(1)(c) to (f) — Where the youth court makes an order under paragraphs 20(1)(c) to (f), it shall cause notice of the terms of the order to be given to the person who is to be compensated or to whom restitution or payment is to be made.

(6) Consent of person to be compensated — No order can be made under paragraph 20(1)(f) unless the youth court has secured the consent of the person to be compensated.

(7) Order for compensation or community service — No order may be made under paragraph 20(1)(f) or (g) unless the youth court

(a) is satisfied that the young person against whom the order is made is a suitable candidate for such an order; and

(b) is satisfied that the order does not interfere with the normal hours of work or education of the young person.

(8) Duration of order for service — No order may be made under paragraph 20(1)(f) or (g) to perform personal or community services unless those services can be completed in two hundred and forty hours or less and within twelve months of the date of the order.

(9) Community service order — No order may be made under paragraph 20(1)(g) unless

(a) the community service to be performed is part of a program that is approved by the provincial director; or

(b) the youth court is satisfied that the person or organization for whom the community service is to be performed has agreed to its performance.

(10) Application for further time to complete disposition — A youth court may, on application by or on behalf of the young person in respect of whom a disposition has been made under paragraphs 20(1)(b) to (g), allow further time for the completion of the disposition subject to any regulations made pursuant to paragraph 67(b) and to any rules made by the youth court pursuant to subsection 68(1).

R.S. 1985, c. 24 (2nd Supp.), s. 15

22. [Repealed 1995, c. 19, s. 14].

23. (1) Conditions that must appear in probation orders — The following conditions shall be included in a probation order made under paragraph 20(1)(j):

(a) that the young person bound by the probation order shall keep the peace and be of good behaviour; and

(b) that the young person appear before the youth court when required by the court to do so.

(c) [Repealed R.S. 1985, c. 24 (2nd Supp.), s. 16(1).]

(2) Conditions that may appear in probation orders — A probation order made under paragraph 20(1)(j) may include such of the following conditions as the youth court considers appropriate in the circumstances of the case:

(a) that the young person bound by the probation order report to and be under the supervision of the provincial director or a person designated by the youth court;

(a.1) that the young person notify the clerk of the youth court, the provincial director or the youth worker assigned to his case of any change of address or any change in his place of employment, education or training;

(b) that the young person remain within the territorial jurisdiction of one or more courts named in the order;

(c) that the young person make reasonable efforts to obtain and maintain suitable employment;

(d) that the young person attend school or such other place of learning, training or recreation as is appropriate, if the court is satisfied that a suitable program is available for the young person at that place;

(e) that the young person reside with a parent, or such other adult as the court considers appropriate, who is willing to provide for the care and maintenance of the young person;

(f) that the young person reside in such place as the provincial director may specify; and

(g) that the young person comply with such other reasonable conditions set out in the order as the court considers desirable, including conditions for securing the good conduct of the young person and for preventing the commission by the young person of other offences.

(3) Communication of probation order to young person and parent — Where the youth court makes a probation order under paragraph 20(1)(j), it shall

(a) cause the order to be read by or to the young person bound by the probation order;

(b) explain or cause to be explained to the young person the purpose and effect of the order and ascertain that the young person understands it; and

(c) cause a copy of the order to be given to the young person and to a parent of the young person, if the parent is in attendance at the proceedings against the young person.

(4) Copy of probation order to parent — Where the youth court makes a probation order under paragraph 20(1)(j), it may cause a copy of the report to be given to a parent of the young person not in attendance at the proceedings against the young person if the parent is, in the opinion of the court, taking an active interest in the proceedings.

(5) Endorsement of order by young person — After a probation order has been read by or to a young person and explained to him pursuant to subsection (3), the young person shall endorse the order acknowledging that he has received a copy of the order and acknowledging the fact that it has been explained to him.

(6) Validity of probate order — The failure of a young person to endorse a probation order pursuant to subsection (5) does not affect the validity of the order.

(7) Commencement of probation order — A probation order made under paragraph 20(1)(j) comes into force

(a) on the date on which the order is made; or

(b) where the young person in respect of whom the order is made is committed to continuous custody, on the expiration of the period of custody.

(8) Notice to appear — A young person may be given notice to appear before the youth court pursuant to paragraph (1)(b) orally or in writing.

(9) Warrant to arrest young person — If a young person to whom a notice is given in writing to appear before the youth court pursuant to paragraph (1)(b) does not appear at the time and place named in the notice and it is proved that a copy of the notice was served on him, a youth court may issue a warrant to compel the appearance of the young person.

R.S. 1985, c. 24 (2nd Supp.), s. 16; R.S. 1985, c. 1 (4th Supp.), s. 39

24. (1) Conditions for custody — The youth court shall not commit a young person to custody under paragraph 20(1)(k) unless the court considers a committal to custody to be necessary for the protection of society having regard to the seriousness of the offence and the circumstances in which it was committed and having regard to the needs and circumstances of the young person.

(1.1) Factors — In making a determination under subsection (1), the youth court shall take the following into account:

(a) that an order of custody shall not be used as a substitute for appropriate child protection, health and other social measures;

(b) that a young person who commits an offence that does not involve serious personal injury should be held accountable to the victim and to society through non-custodial dispositions whenever appropriate; and

(c) that custody shall only be imposed when all available alternatives to custody that are reasonable in the circumstances have been considered.

(2) Pre-disposition report — Subject to subsection (3), before making an order of committal to custody, the youth court shall consider a pre-disposition report.

(3) Report dispensed with — The youth court may, with the consent of the prosecutor and the young person or his counsel, dispense with the pre-disposition report required under subsection (2) if the youth court is satisfied, having regard to the circumstances, that the report is unnecessary or that it would not be in the best interests of the young person to require one.

(4) Reasons — Where the youth court makes a disposition in respect of a young person under paragraph 20(1)(k), the youth court shall state the reasons why any other disposition or dispositions under subsection 20(1), without the disposition under paragraph 20(1)(k), would not have been adequate.

1995, c. 19, s. 15

24.1 (1) Definitions — In this section and sections 24.2, 24.3, 28 and 29,

"open custody" means custody in

(a) a community residential centre, group home, child care institution, or forest or wilderness camp, or

(b) any other like place or facility

designated by the Lieutenant Governor in Council of a province or his delegate as a place of open custody for the purposes of this Act, and includes a place or facility within a class of such places or facilities so designated;

"secure custody" means custody in a place or facility designated by the Lieutenant Governor in Council of a province for the secure containment or restraint of young persons, and includes a place or facility within a class of such places or facilities so designated.

(2) Youth court to specify type of custody — Subject to subsection (3), where the youth court commits a young person to custody under paragraph 20(1)(k) or (k.1) or makes an order under subsection 26.1(1) or paragraph 26.6(2)(b), it shall specify in the order whether the custody is to be open custody or secure custody.

(3) Provincial director to specify level of custody — In a province in which the Lieutenant Governor in Council has designated the provincial director to determine the level of custody, the provincial director shall, where a young person is committed to custody under paragraph 20(1)(k) or (k.1) or an order is made under subsection 26.1(1) or paragraph 26.6(2)(b), specify whether the young person shall be placed in open custody or secure custody.

(4) Factors — In deciding whether a young person shall be placed in open custody or secure custody, the youth court or the provincial director shall take into account the following factors:

(a) that a young person should be placed in a level of custody involving the least degree of containment and restraint, having regard to

(i) the seriousness of the offence in respect of which the young person was committed to custody and the circumstances in which that offence was committed,

(ii) the needs and circumstances of the young person, including proximity to family, school, employment and support services,

(iii) the safety of other young persons in custody, and

(iv) the interests of society;

(b) that the level of custody should allow for the best possible match of programs to the young person's needs and behaviour, having regard to the findings of any assessment in respect of the young person;

(c) the likelihood of escape if the young person is placed in open custody; and

(d) the recommendations, if any, of the youth court or the provincial director, as the case may be.

R.S. 1985, c. 24 (2nd Supp.), s. 17; 1992, c. 11, s. 4; 1995, c. 19, s. 16

24.2 (1) Place of custody — Subject to this section and sections 24.3 and 24.5, a young person who is committed to custody shall be placed in open custody or secure custody, as specified pursuant to subsection 24.1(2) or (3), at such place or facility as the provincial director may specify.

(2) Warrant of committal — Where a young person is committed to custody, the youth court shall issue or cause to be issued a warrant of committal.

(3) Exception — A young person who is committed to custody may, in the course of being transferred from custody to the court or from the court to custody, be held under the supervision and control of a peace officer or in such place of temporary detention referred to in subsection 7(1) as the provincial director may specify.

(4) Young person to be held separate from adults — Subject to this section and section 24.5, a young person who is committed to custody shall be held separate and apart from any adult who is detained or held in custody.

(5) Subsection 7(2) applies — Subsection 7(2) applies, with such modifications as the circumstances require, in respect of a person held in a place of temporary detention pursuant to subsection (3).

(6) Transfer — A young person who is committed to custody may, during the period of custody, be transferred by the provincial director from one place or facility of open custody to another or from one place or facility of secure custody to another.

(7) Transfer to open custody — youth court — No young person who is committed to secure custody pursuant to subsection 24.1(2) may be transferred to a place or facility of open custody except in accordance with sections 28 to 31.

(8) No transfer to secure custody — youth court — Subject to subsection (9), no young person who is committed to open custody pursuant to subsection 24.1(2) may be transferred to a place or facility of secure custody.

(9) Exception — transfer to secure custody — youth court — Where a young person is placed in open custody pursuant to subsection 24.1(2), the provincial director may transfer the young person from a place or facility of open custody to a place or facility of secure custody for a period not exceeding fifteen days if

(a) the young person escapes or attempts to escape lawful custody; or

(b) the transfer is, in the opinion of the provincial director, necessary for the safety of the young person or the safety of others in the place or facility of open custody.

(10) Transfer to open custody — provincial director — The provincial director may transfer a young person from a place or facility of secure custody to a place or facility of open custody when the provincial director is satisfied that the needs of the young person and the interests of society would be better served thereby.

(11) Transfer to secure custody — provincial director — The provincial director may transfer a young person from a place or facility of open custody to a place or facility of secure custody when the provincial director is satisfied that the needs of the young person and the interests of society would be better served thereby

(a) having considered the factors set out in subsection 24.1(4); and

(b) having determined that there has been a material change in circumstances since the young person was placed in open custody.

(12) Notice — The provincial director shall cause a notice in writing of the decision to transfer a young person under subsection (11) to be given to the young person and the young person's parents and set out in that notice the reasons for the transfer.

(13) Where application for review is made — Where an application for review under section 28.1 of a transfer under subsection (11) is made to a youth court,

(a) the provincial director shall cause such notice as may be directed by rules of court applicable to the youth court or, in the absence of such direction, at least five clear days notice of the review to be given in writing to the young person and the young person's parents; and

(b) the youth court shall forthwith, after the notice required under paragraph (a) is given, review the transfer.

(14) Interim custody — Where an application for review under section 28.1 of a transfer under subsection (11) is made to a youth court, the young person shall remain in a place or facility of secure custody until the review is heard by the youth court unless the provincial director directs otherwise.

R.S. 1985, c. 24 (2nd Supp.), s. 17; 1995, c. 19, s. 17

24.3 (1) Consecutive dispositions of custody — Where a young person is committed to open custody and secure custody pursuant to subsection 24.1(2), any portions of which dispositions are to be served consecutively, the disposition of secure custody shall be served first without regard to the order in which the dispositions were imposed.

(2) Concurrent dispositions of custody — Where a young person is committed to open custody and secure custody pursuant to subsection 24.1(2), any portions of which dispositions are to be served concurrently, the concurrent portions of the dispositions shall be served in secure custody.

R.S. 1985, c. 24 (2nd Supp.), s. 17; 1995, c. 19, s. 18

24.4 (1) Committal to custody deemed continuous — A young person who is committed to custody under paragraph 20(1)(k) shall be deemed to be committed to continuous custody unless the youth court specifies otherwise.

(2) Availability of place of intermittent custody — Before making an order of committal to intermittent custody under paragraph 20(1)(k), the youth court shall require the prosecutor to make available to the court for its consideration a report of the provincial director as to the availability of a place of custody in which an order of intermittent custody can be enforced and, where the report discloses that no such place of custody is available, the court shall not make the order.

R.S. 1985, c. 24 (2nd Supp.), s. 17

24.5 (1) Transfer to adult facility — Where a young person is committed to custody under paragraph 20(1)(k) or (k.1) the youth court may, on application of the provincial director made at any time after the young person attains the age of eighteen years, after affording the young person an opportunity to be heard, authorize the provincial director to direct that the young person serve the disposition or the remaining portion thereof in a provincial correctional facility for adults, if the court considers it to be in the best interests of the young person or in the public interest, but in that event, the provisions of this Act shall continue to apply in respect of that person.

(2) Where disposition and sentence concurrent — Where a young person is committed to custody under paragraph 20(1)(k) or (k.1) and is concurrently under sentence of imprisonment imposed in ordinary court, the young person may, in the discretion of the provincial director, serve the disposition and sentence, or any portion thereof, in a place of custody for young persons, in a provincial correctional facility for adults or, where the unexpired portion of the sentence is two years or more, in a penitentiary.

R.S. 1985, c. 24 (2nd Supp.), s. 17; 1992, c. 11, s. 5

25. (1) Transfer of disposition — Where a disposition has been made under paragraphs 20(1)(b) to (g) or paragraph 20(1)(j) or (l) in respect of a young person and the young person or a parent with whom the young person resides is or becomes a resident of a territorial division outside the jurisdiction of the youth court that made the disposition, whether in the same or in another province, a youth court judge in the territorial division in which the disposition was made may, on the application of the Attorney General or an agent of the Attorney General or on the application of the young person or the young person's parent with the consent of the Attorney General or an agent of the Attorney General, transfer the disposition and such portion of the record of the case as is appropriate to a youth court in the other territorial division, and all subsequent proceedings relating to the case shall thereafter be carried out and enforced by that court.

(2) No transfer outside province before appeal completed — No disposition may be transferred from one province to another under this section until the time for an appeal against the disposition or the finding on which the disposition was based has expired or until all proceedings in respect of any such appeal have been completed.

(3) Transfer to a province where person is adult — Where an application is made under subsection (1) to transfer the disposition of a young person to a province in which the young person is an adult, a youth court judge may, with the consent of the Attorney General, transfer the disposition and the record of the case to the youth court in the province to which the transfer is sought, and the youth court to which the case is transferred shall have full jurisdiction in respect of the disposition as if that court had made the disposition, and the person shall be further dealt with in accordance with this Act.

R.S. 1985, c. 24 (2nd Supp.), s. 18; 1995, c. 19, s. 19

25.1 (1) Interprovincial arrangements for probation or custody — Where a disposition has been made under paragraphs 20(1)(j) to (k.1) in respect of a young person, the disposition in one province may be dealt with in any other province pursuant to any agreement that may have been made between those provinces.

(2) Youth court retains jurisdiction — Subject to subsection (3), where a disposition made in respect of a young person is dealt with pursuant to this section in a province other than that in which the disposition was made, the youth court of the province in which the disposition was made shall, for all purposes of this Act, retain exclusive jurisdiction over the young person as if the disposition were dealt with within that province, and any warrant or process issued in respect of the young person may be executed or served in any place in Canada outside the province where the disposition was made as if it were executed or served in that province.

(3) Waiver of jurisdiction — Where a disposition made in respect of a young person is dealt with pursuant to this section in a province other than that in which the disposition was made, the youth court of the province in which the disposition was made may, with the consent in writing of the Attorney General of that province or his delegate and the young person, waive its jurisdiction, for the purpose of any proceeding under this Act, to the youth court of the province in which the disposition is dealt with, in which case the youth court in the province in which the disposition is so dealt with shall have full jurisdiction in respect of the disposition as if that court had made the disposition.

R.S. 1985, c. 24 (2nd Supp.), s. 19; 1992, c. 11, s. 6; 1995, c. 19, s. 20

26. Failure to comply with disposition — A person who is subject to a disposition made under paragraphs 20(1)(b) to (g) or paragraph 20(1)(j) or (l) and who wilfully fails or refuses to comply with that order is guilty of an offence punishable on summary conviction.

R.S. 1985, c. 24 (2nd Supp.), s. 19

26.1 (1) Continuation of custody — Where a young person is held in custody pursuant to a disposition made under paragraph 20(1)(k.1) and an application is made to the youth court by the Attorney General, or the Attorney General's agent, within a reasonable time prior to the expiration of the period of custody, the provincial director of the province in which the young person is held in custody shall cause the young person to be brought before the youth court and the youth court may, after affording both parties and the parents of the young person an opportunity to be heard and if it is satisfied that there are reasonable grounds to believe that the young person is likely to commit an offence causing the death of or serious harm to another person prior to the expiration of the disposition the young person is then serving, order that the young person remain in custody for a period not exceeding the remainder of the disposition.

(1.1) Idem — Where the hearing for an application under subsection (1) cannot be completed before the expiration of the period of custody, the court may order that the young person remain in custody pending the determination of the application if the court is satisfied that the application was made in a reasonable time, having regard to all the circumstances, and that there are compelling reasons for keeping the young person in custody.

(2) Factors — For the purpose of determining an application under subsection (1), the youth court shall take into consideration any factor that is relevant to the case of the young person including, without limiting the generality of the foregoing,

(a) evidence of a pattern of persistent violent behaviour and, in particular,

(i) the number of offences committed by the young person that caused physical or psychological harm to any other person,

(ii) the young person's difficulties in controlling violent impulses to the point of endangering the safety of any other person,

(iii) the use of weapons in the commission of any offence,

(iv) explicit threats of violence,

(v) behaviour of a brutal nature associated with the commission of any offence, and

(vi) a substantial degree of indifference on the part of the young person as to the reasonably foreseeable consequences, to other persons, of the young person's behaviour;

(b) psychiatric or psychological evidence that a physical or mental illness or disorder of the young person is of such a nature that the young person is likely to commit, prior to the expiration of the disposition the young person is then serving, an offence causing the death of or serious harm to another person;

(c) reliable information that satisfies the youth court that the young person is planning to commit, prior to the expiration of the disposition the young person is then serving, an offence causing the death of or serious harm to another person; and

(d) the availability of supervision programs in the community that would offer adequate protection to the public from the risk that the young person might otherwise present until the expiration of the disposition the young person is then serving.

(3) Youth court to order appearance of young person — Where a provincial director fails to cause a young person to be brought before the youth court under subsection (1), the youth court shall order the provincial director to cause the young person to be brought before the youth court forthwith.

(4) Report — For the purpose of determining an application under subsection (1), the youth court shall require the provincial director to cause to be prepared, and to submit to the youth court, a report setting out any information of which the provincial director is aware with respect to the factors referred to in subsection (2) that may be of assistance to the court.

(5) Written or oral report — A report referred to in subsection (4) shall be in writing unless it cannot reasonably be committed to writing, in which case it may, with leave of the youth court, be submitted orally in court.

(6) Provisions apply — Subsections 14(4) to (10) apply, with such modifications as the circumstances require, in respect of a report referred to in subsection (4).

(7) Notice of hearing — Where an application is made under subsection (1) in respect of a young person, the Attorney General or the Attorney General's agent shall cause such notice as may be directed by rules of court applicable to the youth court or, in the absence of such direction, at least five clear days notice of the hearing to be given in writing to the young person and the young person's parents and the provincial director.

(8) Statement of right to counsel — Any notice given to a parent under subsection (7) shall include a statement that the young person has the right to be represented by counsel.

(9) Service of notice — A notice under subsection (7) may be served personally or may be sent by registered mail.

(10) Where notice not given — Where notice under subsection (7) is not given in accordance with this section, the youth court may

(a) adjourn the hearing and order that the notice be given in such manner and to such person as it directs; or

(b) dispense with the giving of the notice where, in the opinion of the youth court, having regard to the circumstances, the giving of the notice may be dispensed with.

(11) Reasons — Where a youth court makes an order under subsection (1), it shall state its reasons for the order in the record of the case and shall

(a) provide or cause to be provided a copy of the order, and

(b) on request, provide or cause to be provided a transcript or copy of the reasons for the order

to the young person in respect of whom the order was made, the counsel and parents of the young person, the Attorney General or the Attorney General's agent, the provincial director and the review board, if any has been established or designated.

(12) Review provisions apply — Subsections 16(9) to (11) apply, with such modifications as the circumstances require, in respect of an order made, or the refusal to make an order, under subsection (1).

(13) Where application denied — Where an application under subsection (1) is denied, the court may, with the consent of the young person, the Attorney General and the provincial director, proceed as though the young person had been brought before the court as required under subsection 26.2(1).

1992, c. 11, s. 7

26.2 (1) Conditional supervision — The provincial director of the province in which a young person is held in custody pursuant to a disposition made under paragraph 20(1)(k.1) or, where applicable, an order made under subsection 26.1(1), shall cause the young person to be brought before the youth court at least one month prior to the expiration of the period of custody and the court shall, after affording the young person an opportunity to be heard, by order, set the conditions of the young person's conditional supervision.

(2) Conditions to be included in order — In setting conditions for the purposes of subsection (1), the youth court shall include in the order the following conditions, namely, that the young person

(a) keep the peace and be of good behaviour;

(b) appear before the youth court when required by the court to do so;

(c) report to the provincial director immediately on release, and thereafter be under the supervision of the provincial director or a person designated by the youth court;

(d) inform the provincial director immediately on being arrested or questioned by the police;

(e) report to the police, or any named individual, as instructed by the provincial director;

(f) advise the provincial director of the young person's address of residence on release and after release report immediately to the clerk of the youth court or the provincial director any change

(i) in that address,

(ii) in the young person's normal occupation, including employment, vocational or educational training and volunteer work,

(iii) in the young person's family or financial situation, and

(iv) that may reasonably be expected to affect the young person's ability to comply with the conditions of the order;

(g) not own, possess or have the control of any weapon, ammunition, prohibited ammunition, prohibited device or explosive substance, except as authorized by the order; and

(h) comply with such reasonable instructions as the provincial director considers necessary in respect of any condition of the conditional supervision in order to prevent a breach of that condition or to protect society.

(3) Order conditions — In setting conditions for the purposes of subsection (1), the youth court may include in the order the following conditions, namely, that the young person

(a) on release, travel directly to the young person's place of residence, or to such other place as is noted in the order.

(b) make reasonable efforts to obtain and maintain suitable employment;

(c) attend school or such other place of learning, training or recreation as is appropriate, if the court is satisfied that a suitable program is available for the young person at such a place;

(d) reside with a parent, or such other adult as the court considers appropriate, who is willing to provide for the care and maintenance of the young person;

(e) reside in such place as the provincial director may specify;

(f) remain within the territorial jurisdiction of one or more courts named in the order; and

(g) comply with such other reasonable conditions set out in the order as the court considers desirable, including conditions for securing the good conduct of the young person and for preventing the commission by the young person of other offences.

(4) Temporary conditions — Where a provincial director is required under subsection (1) to cause a young person to be brought before the youth court but cannot do so for reasons beyond the young person's control, the provincial director shall so advise the youth court and the court shall, by order, set such temporary conditions for the young person's conditional supervision as are appropriate in the circumstances.

(5) Conditions to be set at first opportunity — Where an order is made under subsection (4), the provincial director shall bring the young person before the youth court as soon thereafter as the circumstances permit and the court shall then set the conditions of the young person's conditional supervision.

(6) Report — For the purpose of setting conditions under this section, the youth court shall require the provincial director to cause to be prepared, and to submit to the youth court, a report setting out any information that may be of assistance to the court.

(7) Provisions apply — Subsections 26.1(3) and (5) to (10) apply, with such modifications as the circumstances require, in respect of any proceedings held pursuant to subsection (1).

(8) Idem — Subsections 16(9) to (11) and 23(3) to (9) apply, with such modifications as the circumstances require, in respect of an order made under subsection (1).

1992, c. 11, s. 7; 1995, c. 39, s. 180

26.3 Suspension of Conditional Supervision — Where the provincial director has reasonable grounds to believe that a young person has breached or is about to breach a condition of an order made under subsection 26.2(1), the provincial director may, in writing,

(a) suspend the conditional supervision; and

(b) order that the young person be remanded to such place of custody as the provincial director considers appropriate until a review is conducted under section 26.5 and, if applicable, section 26.6.

1992, c. 11, s. 7

26.4 (1) Apprehension — Where the conditional supervision of a young person is suspended under section 26.3, the provincial director may issue a warrant in writing, authorizing the apprehension of the young person and, until the young person is apprehended, the young person is deemed not to be continuing to serve the disposition the young person is then serving.

(2) Warrants — A warrant issued under subsection (1) shall be executed by any peace officer to whom it is given at any place in Canada and has the same force and effect in all parts of Canada as if it had been originally issued or subsequently endorsed by a provincial court judge or other lawful authority having jurisdiction in the place where it is executed.

(3) Peace officer may arrest — Where a peace officer believes on reasonable grounds that a warrant issued under subsection (1) is in force in respect of a young person, the peace officer may arrest the young person without the warrant at any place in Canada.

(4) Requirement to bring before provincial director — Where a young person is arrested pursuant to subsection (3) and detained, the peace officer making the arrest shall cause the young person to be brought before the provincial director or a person designated by the provincial director

(a) where the provincial director or the designated person is available within a period of twenty-four hours after the young person is arrested, without unreasonable delay and in any event within that period; and

(b) where the provincial director or the designated person is not available within the period referred to in paragraph (a), as soon as possible.

(5) Release on remand in custody — Where a young person is brought, pursuant to subsection (4), before the provincial director or a person designated by the provincial director, the provincial director or the designated person,

(a) if not satisfied that there are reasonable grounds to believe that the young person is the young person in respect of whom the warrant referred to in subsection (1) was issued, shall release the young person; or

(b) if satisfied that there are reasonable grounds to believe that the young person is the young person in respect of whom the warrant referred to in subsection (1) was issued, may remand the young person in custody to await execution of the warrant, but if no warrant for the young person's arrest is executed within a period of six days after the time the young person is remanded in such custody, the person in whose custody the young person then is shall release the young person.

1992, c. 11, s. 7

26.5 Review by provincial director — Forthwith after the remand to custody of a young person whose conditional supervision has been suspended under section

26.3, or forthwith after being informed of the arrest of such a young person, the provincial director shall review the case and, within forty-eight hours, cancel the suspension of the conditional supervision or refer the case to the youth court for a review under section 26.6.

1992, c. 11, s. 7

26.6 (1) Review by youth court — Where the case of a young person is referred to the youth court under section 26.5, the provincial director shall, as soon as is practicable, cause the young person to be brought before the youth court, and the youth court shall, after affording the young person an opportunity to be heard,

> (a) if the court is not satisfied on reasonable grounds that the young person has breached or was about to breach a condition of the conditional supervision, cancel the suspension of the conditional supervision; or

> (b) if the court is satisfied on reasonable grounds that the young person has breached or was about to breach a condition of the conditional supervision, review the decision of the provincial director to suspend the conditional supervision and make an order under subsection (2).

(2) Order — On completion of a review under subsection (1), the youth court shall order

> (a) the cancellation of the suspension of the conditional supervision, and where the court does so, the court may vary the conditions of the conditional supervision or impose new conditions; or

> (b) the continuation of the suspension of the conditional supervision for such period of time, not to exceed the remainder of the disposition the young person is then serving, as the court considers appropriate, and where the court does so, the court shall order that the young person remain in custody.

(3) Reasons — Where a youth court makes an order under subsection (2), it shall state its reasons for the order in the record of the case and shall

> (a) provide or cause to be provided a copy of the order, and

> (b) on request, provide or cause to be provided a transcript or copy of the reasons for the order

to the young person in respect of whom the order was made, the counsel and parents of the young person, the Attorney General or the Attorney General's agent, the provincial director and the review board, if any has been established or designated.

(4) Provisions apply — Subsections 26.1(3) and (5) to (10) and 26.2(6) apply, with such modifications as the circumstances require, in respect of a review under this section.

(5) Idem — Subsections 16(9) to (11) apply, with such modifications as the circumstances require, in respect of an order made under subsection (2).

1992, c. 11, s. 7

APPEALS

27. (1) Appeals for indictable offences — An appeal lies under this Act in respect of an indictable offence or an offence that the Attorney General or his agent elects to proceed with as an indictable offence in accordance with Part XXI of the *Criminal Code*, which Part applies with such modifications as the circumstances require.

(1.1) Appeals for summary conviction offences — An appeal lies under this Act in respect of an offence punishable on summary conviction or an offence that the Attorney General or his agent elects to proceed with as an offence punishable on summary conviction in accordance with Part XXVII of the *Criminal Code*, which Part applies with such modifications as the circumstances require.

(1.2) Appeals where offences are tried jointly — An appeal involving one or more indictable offences and one or more summary conviction offences that are tried jointly or in respect of which dispositions are jointly made lies under this Act in accordance with Part XXI of the *Criminal Code*, which applies with such modifications as the circumstances require.

(2) Deemed election — For the purpose of appeals under this Act, where no election is made in respect of an offence that may be prosecuted by indictment or proceeded with by way of summary conviction, the Attorney General or his agent shall be deemed to have elected to proceed with the offence as an offence punishable on summary conviction.

(3) Where the youth court is a superior court — In any province where the youth court is a superior court, an appeal under subsection (1.1) shall be made to the court of appeal of the province.

(3.1) Nunavut — Despite subsection (3), if the Nunavut Court of Justice is acting as a youth court, an appeal under subsection (1.1) shall be made to a judge of the Court of Appeal of Nunavut, and an appeal of that judge's decision shall be made to the Court of Appeal of Nunavut in accordance with section 839 of the *Criminal Code*.

(4) Where the youth court is a county or district court — In any province where the youth court is a county or district court, an appeal under subsection (1.1) shall be made to the superior court of the province.

(5) Appeal to the Supreme Court of Canada — No appeal lies pursuant to subsection (1) from a judgment of the court of appeal in respect of a finding of guilt or an order dismissing an information to the Supreme Court of Canada unless leave to appeal is granted by the Supreme Court of Canada within twenty-one days after the judgment of the court of appeal is pronounced or within such extended time as the Supreme Court of Canada or a judge thereof may, for special reasons, allow.

(6) No appeal from disposition on review — No appeal lies from a disposition under sections 28 to 32.

R.S. 1985, c. 24 (2nd Supp.), s. 20; 1995, c. 19, s. 21; 1999, c. 3, s. 89

REVIEW OF DISPOSITIONS

28. (1) Automatic review of disposition involving custody — Where a young person is committed to custody pursuant to a disposition made in respect of an offence for a period exceeding one year, the provincial director of the province in which the young person is held in custody shall cause the young person to be brought before the youth court forthwith at the end of one year from the date of the most recent disposition made in respect of the offence, and the youth court shall review the disposition.

(2) Idem — Where a young person is committed to custody pursuant to dispositions made in respect of more than one offence for a total period exceeding one year, the provincial director of the province in which the young person is held in custody shall cause the young person to be brought before the youth court forthwith at the end of one year from the date of the earliest disposition made, and the youth court shall review the dispositions.

(3) Optional review of disposition involving custody — Where a young person is committed to custody pursuant to a disposition made under subsection 20(1) in respect of an offence, the provincial director may, on the provincial director's own initiative, and shall, on the request of the young person, the young person's parent or the Attorney General or an agent of the Attorney General, on any of the grounds set out in subsection (4), cause the young person to be brought before a youth court

    (a) where the committal to custody is for a period not exceeding one year, once at any time after the expiration of the greater of

        (i) thirty days after the date of the disposition made under subsection 20(1) in respect of the offence, and

        (ii) one third of the period of the disposition made under subsection 20(1) in respect of the offence, and

    (b) where the committal to custody is for a period exceeding one year, at any time after six months after the date of the most recent disposition made in respect of the offence,

or, with leave of a youth court judge, at any other time, and where a youth court is satisfied that there are grounds for the review under subsection (4), the court shall review the disposition.

(4) Grounds for review under subsection (3) — A disposition made in respect of a young person may be reviewed under subsection (3)

    (a) on the ground that the young person has made sufficient progress to justify a change in disposition;

    (b) on the ground that the circumstances that led to the committal to custody have changed materially;

    (c) on the ground that new services or programs are available that were not available at the time of the disposition;

    (c.1) on the ground that the opportunities for rehabilitation are now greater in the community; or

(d) on such other grounds as the youth court considers appropriate.

(5) No review where appeal pending — No review of a disposition in respect of which an appeal has been taken shall be made under this section until all proceedings in respect of any such appeal have been completed.

(6) Youth court may order appearance of young person for review — Where a provincial director is required under subsections (1) to (3) to cause a young person to be brought before the youth court and fails to do so, the youth court may, on application made by the young person, his parent or the Attorney General or his agent, or on its own motion, order the provincial director to cause the young person to be brought before the youth court.

(7) Progress report — The youth court shall, before reviewing under this section a disposition made in respect of a young person, require the provincial director to cause to be prepared, and to submit to the youth court, a progress report on the performance of the young person since the disposition took effect.

(8) Additional information in progress report — A person preparing a progress report in respect of a young person may include in the report such information relating to the personal and family history and present environment of the young person as he considers advisable.

(9) Written or oral report — A progress report shall be in writing unless it cannot reasonably be committed to writing, in which case it may, with leave of the youth court, be submitted orally in court.

(10) Provisions of subsections 14(4) to (10) to apply — The provisions of subsections 14(4) to (10) apply, with such modifications as the circumstances require, in respect of progress reports.

(11) Notice of review from provincial director — Where a disposition made in respect of a young person is to be reviewed under subsection (1) or (2), the provincial director shall cause such notice as may be directed by rules of court applicable to the youth court or, in the absence of such direction, at least five clear days notice of the review to be given in writing to the young person, his parents and the Attorney General or his agent.

(12) Notice of review from person requesting it — Where a review of a disposition made in respect of a young person is requested under subsection (3), the person requesting the review shall cause such notice as may be directed by rules of court applicable to the youth court or, in the absence of such direction, at least five clear days notice of the review to be given in writing to the young person, his parents and the Attorney General or his agent.

(13) Statement of right to counsel — Any notice given to a parent under subsection (11) or (12) shall include a statement that the young person whose disposition is to be reviewed has the right to be represented by counsel.

(14) Service of notice — A notice under subsection (11) or (12) may be served personally or may be sent by registered mail.

(15) Notice may be waived — Any of the persons entitled to notice under subsection (11) or (12) may waive the right to that notice.

(16) Where notice not given — Where notice under subsection (11) or (12) is not given in accordance with this section, the youth court may

(a) adjourn the proceedings and order that the notice be given in such manner and to such person as it directs; or

(b) dispense with the notice where, in the opinion of the court, having regard to the circumstances, notice may be dispensed with.

(17) Decision of the youth court after review — Where a youth court reviews under this section a disposition made in respect of a young person, it may, after affording the young person, his parent, the Attorney General or his agent and the provincial director an opportunity to be heard, having regard to the needs of the young person and the interests of society,

(a) confirm the disposition;

(b) where the young person is in secure custody pursuant to subsection 24.1(2), by order direct that the young person be placed in open custody; or

(c) release the young person from custody and place the young person

(i) on probation in accordance with section 23 for a period not exceeding the remainder of the period for which the young person was committed to custody, or

(ii) under conditional supervision in accordance with the procedure set out in section 26.2, with such modifications as the circumstances require, for a period not exceeding the remainder of the disposition the young person is then serving.

(18) [Repealed R.S. 1985, c. 24 (2nd Supp.), s. 21.]

R.S. 1985, c. 24 (2nd Supp.), s. 21; 1992, c. 11, s. 8; 1995, c. 19, s. 22

28.1 (1) Application to court for review of level of custody — Where a young person is placed in secure custody pursuant to subsection 24.1(3) or transferred to secure custody pursuant to subsection 24.2(11), the youth court shall review the level of custody if an application therefor is made by the young person or the young person's parent.

(2) Report — The youth court shall, before conducting a review under this section, require the provincial director to cause to be prepared and to submit to the youth court, a report setting out the reasons for the placement or transfer.

(3) Provisions apply — The provisions of subsections 14(4) to (10) apply, with such modifications as the circumstances require, in respect of the report referred to in subsection (2), and the provisions of subsections 28(11) to (16) apply, with such modifications as the circumstances require, to every review under this section.

(4) Decision of the youth court — Where the youth court conducts a review under this section, it may, after affording the young person, the young person's parents and the provincial director an opportunity to be heard, confirm or alter the level of custody, having regard to the needs of the young person and the interests of society.

(5) Decision is final — A decision of the youth court on a review under this section in respect of any particular placement or transfer is, subject to any subsequent order made pursuant to a review under section 28 or 29, final.

1995, c. 19, s. 23

29. (1) Recommendation of provincial director for transfer to open custody or for probation — Where a young person is held in custody pursuant to a disposition, the provincial director may, if he is satisfied that the needs of the young person and the interests of society would be better served thereby, cause notice in writing to be given to the young person, his parent and the Attorney General or his agent that he recommends that the young person

(a) be transferred from a place or facility of secure custody to a place or facility of open custody, where the young person is held in a place or facility of secure custody pursuant to subsection 24.1(2), or

(b) be released from custody and placed on probation or, where the young person is in custody pursuant to a disposition made under paragraph 20(1)(k.1), placed under conditional supervision.

and give a copy of the notice to the youth court.

(1.1) Contents of notice — The provincial director shall include in any notice given under subsection (1) the reasons for the recommendation and

(a) in the case of a recommendation that the young person be placed on probation, the conditions that the provincial director would recommend be attached to a probation order; and

(b) in the case of a recommendation that the young person be placed under conditional supervision, the conditions that the provincial director would recommend be set pursuant to section 26.2.

(2) Application to court for review of recommendation — Where notice of a recommendation is made under subsection (1) with respect to a disposition made in respect of a young person, the youth court shall, if an application for review is made by the young person, his parent or the Attorney General or his agent within ten days after service of the notice, forthwith review the disposition.

(3) Subsections 28(5), (7) to (10) and (12) to (17) apply — Subject to subsection (4), subsections 28(5), (7) to (10) and (12) to (17) apply, with such modifications as the circumstances require, in respect of reviews made under this section and any notice required under subsection 28(12) shall be given to the provincial director.

(4) Where no application for review made under subsection (2) — A youth court that receives a notice under subsection (1) shall, if no application for a review is made under subsection (2),

(a) in the case of a recommendation that a young person be transferred from a place or facility of secure custody to a place or facility of open custody, order that the young person be so transferred;

(b) in the case of a recommendation that a young person be released from custody and placed on probation, release the young person and place him on probation in accordance with section 23;

(b.1) in the case of a recommendation that a young person be released from custody and placed under conditional supervision, release the young person and place the young person under conditional supervision in accordance with section 26.2, having regard to the recommendations of the provincial director; or

(c) where the court deems it advisable, make no direction under this subsection;

and for greater certainty, an order or direction under this subsection may be made without a hearing.

(4.1) Conditions in probation order — Where the youth court places a young person on probation pursuant to paragraph (4)(b), the court shall include in the probation order such conditions referred to in section 23 as it considers advisable, having regard to the recommendations of the provincial director.

(4.2) Notice where no direction made — Where a youth court, pursuant to paragraph (4)(c), makes no direction under subsection (4), it shall forthwith cause a notice of its decision to be given to the provincial director.

(4.3) Provincial director may request review — Where the provincial director is given a notice under subsection (4.2), he may request a review under this section.

(5) Where the provincial director requests a review — Where the provincial director requests a review pursuant to subsection (4.3),

(a) the provincial director shall cause such notice as may be directed by rules of court applicable to the youth court or, in the absence of such direction, at least five clear days notice of the review to be given in writing to the young person, his parents and the Attorney General or his agent; and

(b) the youth court shall forthwith, after the notice required under paragraph (a) is given, review the disposition.

(6) [Repealed R.S. 1985, c. 24 (2nd Supp.), s. 22.]
R.S. 1985, c. 24 (2nd Supp.), s. 22; R.S. 1985, c. 1 (4th Supp.), s. 40; 1992, c. 11, s. 9; 1995, c. 19, s. 24

30. (1) Review board — Where a review board is established or designated by a province for the purposes of this section, that board shall, subject to this section, carry out in that province the duties and functions of a youth court under sections 28 and 29, other than releasing a young person from custody and placing the young person on probation or under conditional supervision.

(2) Other duties of review board — Subject to this Act, a review board may carry out any duties or functions that are assigned to it by the province that established or designated it.

(3) Notice under section 29 — Where a review board is established or designated by a province for the purposes of this section, the provincial director shall at the same time as any notice is given under subsection 29(1) cause a copy of the notice to be given to the review board.

(4) Notice of decision of review board — A review board shall cause notice of any decision made by it in respect of a young person pursuant to section 28 or 29 to be given forthwith in writing to the young person, his parents, the Attorney General or his agent and the provincial director, and a copy of the notice to be given to the youth court.

(5) Decision of review board to take effect where no review — Subject to subsection (6), any decision of a review board under this section shall take effect ten days after the decision is made unless an application for review is made under section 31.

(6) Decision respecting release from custody and probation — Where a review board decides that a young person should be released from custody and placed on probation, it shall so recommend to the youth court and, if no application for a review of the decision is made under section 31, the youth court shall forthwith on the expiration of the ten day period referred to in subsection (5) release the young person from custody and place him on probation in accordance with section 23, and shall include in the probation order such conditions referred to in that section as the court considers advisable having regard to the recommendations of the review board.

(7) Idem — Where a review board decides that a young person should be released from custody and placed under conditional supervision, it shall so recommend to the youth court and, if no application for a review of the decision is made under section 31, the youth court shall forthwith, on the expiration of the ten day period referred to in subsection (5), release the young person from custody and place the young person under conditional supervision in accordance with section 26.2, and shall include in the order under that section such conditions as the court considers advisable, having regard to the recommendations of the review board.

R.S. 1985, c. 24 (2nd Supp.), s. 23; 1992, c. 11, s. 10

31. (1) Review by youth court — Where the review board reviews a disposition under section 30, the youth court shall, on the application of the young person in respect of whom the review was made, his parents, the Attorney General or his agent or the provincial director, made within ten days after the decision of the review board is made, forthwith review the decision.

(2) Subsections 28(5), (7) to (10) and (12) to (17) apply — Subsections 28(5), (7) to (10) and (12) to (17) apply, with such modifications as the circumstances require, in respect of reviews made under this section and any notice required under subsection 28(12) shall be given to the provincial director.

R.S. 1985, c. 1 (4th Supp.), s. 41

32. (1) Review of other dispositions — Where a youth court has made a disposition in respect of a young person, other than a disposition under paragraph 20(1)(k) or (k.1) or section 20.1, the youth court shall, on the application of the young person, the young person's parents, the Attorney General or the Attorney General's agent or the provincial director, made at any time after six months from the date of the disposition or, with leave of a youth court judge, at any earlier time, review the disposition if the court is satisfied that there are grounds for a review under subsection (2).

(2) Grounds for review — A review of a disposition may be made under this section

(a) on the ground that the circumstances that led to the disposition have changed materially;

(b) on the ground that the young person in respect of whom the review is to be made is unable to comply with or is experiencing serious difficulty in complying with the terms of the disposition;

(c) on the ground that the terms of the disposition are adversely affecting the opportunities available to the young person to obtain services, education or employment; or

(d) on such other grounds as the youth court considers appropriate.

(3) Progress report — The youth court may, before reviewing under this section a disposition made in respect of a young person, require the provincial director to cause to be prepared, and to submit to the youth court, a progress report on the performance of the young person since the disposition took effect.

(4) Subsections 28(8) to (10) apply — Subsections 28(8) to (10) apply, with such modifications as the circumstances require, in respect of any progress report required under subsection (3).

(5) Subsections 28(5) and (12) to (16) apply — Subsections 28(5) and (12) to (16) apply, with such modifications as the circumstances require, in respect of reviews made under this section and any notice required under subsection 28(12) shall be given to the provincial director.

(6) Compelling appearance of young person — The youth court may, by summons or warrant, compel a young person in respect of whom a review is to be made under this section to appear before the youth court for the purposes of the review.

(7) Decision of the youth court after review — Where a youth court reviews under this section a disposition made in respect of a young person, it may, after affording the young person, his parent, the Attorney General or his agent and the provincial director an opportunity to be heard,

(a) confirm the disposition;

(b) terminate the disposition and discharge the young person from any further obligation of the disposition; or

(c) vary the disposition or make such new disposition listed in section 20, other than a committal to custody, for such period of time, not exceeding the remainder of the period of the earlier disposition, as the court deems appropriate in the circumstances of the case.

(8) New disposition not to be more onerous — Subject to subsection (9), where a disposition made in respect of a young person is reviewed under this section, no disposition made under subsection (7) shall, without the consent of the young person, be more onerous than the remaining portion of the disposition reviewed.

(9) Exception — A youth court may under this section extend the time within which a disposition made under paragraphs 20(1)(b) to (g) is to be complied with by a young person where the court is satisfied that the young person requires more time to comply with the disposition, but in no case shall the extension be for a period of time that expires more than twelve months after the date the disposition would otherwise have expired.

(10), (11) [Repealed R.S. 1985, c. 24 (2nd Supp.), s. 24.]

R.S. 1985, c. 24 (2nd Supp.), s. 24; 1992, c. 11, s. 11; 1995, c. 39, s. 181

33. (1) Review of order made under s. 20.1 — A youth court or other court may, on application, review an order made under section 20.1 at any time after the circumstances set out in subsection 45(1) are realized in respect of any record in relation to the offence that resulted in the order being made.

(2) Grounds — In conducting a review under this section, the youth court or other court shall take into account

(a) the nature and circumstances of the offence in respect of which the order was made; and

(b) the safety of the young person and of other persons.

(3) Decision of review — Where a youth court or other court conducts a review under this section, it may, after affording the young person, one of the young person's parents, the Attorney General or an agent of the Attorney General and the provincial director an opportunity to be heard,

(a) confirm the order;

(b) revoke the order; or

(c) vary the order as it considers appropriate in the circumstances of the case.

(4) New order not to be more onerous — No variation of an order made under paragraph 3(c) may be more onerous than the order being reviewed.

(5) Application of provisions — Subsections 32(3) to (5) apply, with such modifications as the circumstances require, in respect of a review under this section.

1995, c. 39, s. 182

34. (1) Sections 20 to 26 apply to dispositions on review — Subject to sections 28 to 32, subsections 20(2) to (8) and sections 21 to 25.1 apply, with such modifications as the circumstances require, in respect of dispositions made under sections 28 to 32.

(2) Orders are dispositions — Orders under subsections 26.1(1) and 26.2(1) and paragraph 26.6(2)(b) are deemed to be dispositions for the purposes of section 28.

R.S. 1985, c. 24 (2nd Supp.), s. 25; 1992, c. 11, s. 12

TEMPORARY RELEASE FROM CUSTODY

35. (1) Temporary absence or day release — The provincial director of a province may, subject to any terms or conditions that he considers desirable, authorize a young person committed to custody in the province pursuant to a disposition made under this Act

    (a) to be temporarily released for a period not exceeding fifteen days where, in his opinion, it is necessary or desirable that the young person be absent, with or without escort, for medical, compassionate or humanitarian reasons or for the purpose of rehabilitating the young person or re-integrating him into the community; or

    (b) to be released from custody on such days and during such hours as he specifies in order that the young person may

        (i) attend school or any other educational or training institution,

        (ii) obtain or continue employment or perform domestic or other duties required by the young person's family,

        (iii) participate in a program specified by him that, in his opinion, will enable the young person to better carry out his employment or improve his education or training, or

        (iv) attend an out-patient treatment program or other program that provides services that are suitable to addressing the young person's needs.

(2) Limitation — A young person who is released from custody pursuant to subsection (1) shall be released only for such periods of time as are necessary to attain the purpose for which the young person is released.

(3) Revocation of authorization for release — The provincial director of a province may, at any time, revoke an authorization made under subsection (1).

(4) Arrest and return to custody — Where the provincial director revokes an authorization for a young person to be released from custody under subsection (3) or where a young person fails to comply with any term or condition of release from custody under this section, the young person may be arrested without warrant and returned to custody.

(5) Prohibition — A young person who has been committed to custody under this Act shall not be released from custody before the expiration of the period of his custody except in accordance with subsection (1) unless the release is ordered under sections 28 to 31 or otherwise according to law by a court of competent jurisdiction.

R.S. 1985, c. 24 (2nd Supp.), s. 26; R.S. 1985, c. 1 (4th Supp.), s. 42; 1995, c. 19, s. 25

EFFECT OF TERMINATION OF DISPOSITION

36. (1) Effect of absolute discharge or termination of dispositions — Subject to section 12 of the *Canada Evidence Act*, where a young person is found guilty of an offence, and

    (a) a youth court directs under paragraph 20(1)(a) that the young person be discharged absolutely, or

(b) all the dispositions made under subsection 20(1) in respect of the offence, and all terms of those dispositions, have ceased to have effect.

the young person shall be deemed not to have been found guilty or convicted of the offence except that,

(c) the young person may plead *autrefois convict* in respect of any subsequent charge relating to the offence;

(d) a youth court may consider the finding of guilt in considering an application for a transfer to ordinary court under section 16;

(e) any court or justice may consider the finding of guilt in considering an application for judicial interim release or in considering what dispositions to make or sentence to impose for any offence; and

(f) the National Parole Board or any provincial parole board may consider the finding of guilt in considering an application for parole or pardon.

(2) Disqualifications removed — For greater certainty and without restricting the generality of subsection (1), an absolute discharge under paragraph 20(1)(a) or the termination of all dispositions in respect of an offence for which a young person is found guilty removes any disqualification in respect of the offence to which the young person is subject pursuant to any Act of Parliament by reason of a conviction.

(3) Applications for employment — No application form for or relating to

(a) employment in any department, as defined in section 2 of the *Financial Administration Act*,

(b) employment by any Crown corporation as defined in section 83 of the *Financial Administration Act*,

(c) enrolment in the Canadian Forces, or

(d) employment on or in connection with the operation of any work, under-taking or business that is within the legislative authority of Parliament,

shall contain any question that by its terms requires the applicant to disclose that the applicant has been charged with or found guilty of an offence in respect of which the applicant has, under this Act, been discharged absolutely or has completed all the dispositions made under subsection 20(1).

(4) Punishment — Any person who uses or authorizes the use of an application form in contravention of subsection (3) is guilty of an offence punishable on summary conviction.

(5) Finding of guilt not a previous conviction — A finding of guilt under this Act is not a previous conviction for the purposes of any offence under any Act of Parliament for which a greater punishment is prescribed by reason of previous convictions.

R.S. 1985, c. 24 (2nd Supp.), s. 27; 1995, c. 19, s. 26; 1995, c. 39, ss. 183, 189

YOUTH WORKERS

37. Duties of youth worker — The duties and functions of a youth worker in respect of a young person whose case has been assigned to him by the provincial director include

(a) where the young person is bound by a probation order that requires him to be under supervision, supervising the young person in complying with the conditions of the probation order or in carrying out any other disposition made together with it;

(a.1) where the young person is placed under conditional supervision pursuant to an order made under section 26.2, supervising the young person in complying with the conditions of the order;

(b) where the young person is found guilty of any offence, giving such assistance to him as he considers appropriate up to the time the young person is discharged or the disposition of his case terminates;

(c) attending court when he considers it advisable or when required by the youth court to be present;

(d) preparing, at the request of the provincial director, a pre-disposition report or a progress report; and

(e) performing such other duties and functions as the provincial director requires.

R.S. 1985, c. 24 (2nd Supp.), s. 28; 1992, c. 11, s. 13

PROTECTION OF PRIVACY OF YOUNG PERSONS

38. (1) Identity not to be published — Subject to this section, no person shall publish by any means any report

(a) of an offence committed or alleged to have been committed by a young person, unless an order has been made under section 16 with respect thereto, or

(b) of any hearing, adjudication, disposition or appeal concerning a young person who committed or is alleged to have committed an offence

in which the name of the young person, a child or a young person who is a victim of the offence or a child or a young person who appeared as a witness in connection with the offence, or in which any information serving to identify the young person or child, is disclosed.

(1.1) Limitation — Subsection (1) does not apply in respect of the disclosure of information in the course of administration of justice including, for greater certainty, the disclosure of information for the purposes of the *Firearms Act* and Part III of the *Criminal Code*, where it is not the purpose of the disclosure to make the information known in the community.

(1.11) Preparation of reports — Subsection (1) does not apply in respect of the disclosure of information by the provincial director or a youth worker where the disclosure is necessary for procuring information that relates to the preparation of any report required by this Act.

(1.12) No subsequent disclosure — No person to whom information is disclosed pursuant to subsection (1.11) shall disclose that information to any other person unless the disclosure is necessary for the purpose of preparing the report for which the information was disclosed.

(1.13) Schools and others — Subsection (1) does not apply in respect of the disclosure of information to any professional or other person engaged in the supervision or care of a young person, including the representative of any school board or school or any other educational or training institution, by the provincial director, a youth worker, a peace officer or any other person engaged in the provision of services to young persons where the disclosure is necessary

> (a) to ensure compliance by the young person with an authorization pursuant to section 35 or an order of any court concerning bail, probation or conditional supervision; or

> (b) to ensure the safety of staff, students or other persons, as the case may be.

(1.14) No subsequent disclosure — No person to whom information is disclosed pursuant to subsection (1.13) shall disclose that information to any other person unless the disclosure is necessary for a purpose referred to in that subsection.

(1.15) Information to be kept separate — Any person to whom information is disclosed pursuant to subsections (1.13) and (1.14) shall

> (a) keep the information separate from any other record of the young person to whom the information relates;

> (b) subject to subsection (1.14), ensure that no other person has access to the information; and

> (c) destroy the information when the information is no longer required for the purpose for which it was disclosed.

(1.2) Ex parte application for leave to publish — A youth court judge shall, on the *ex parte* application of a peace officer, make an order permitting any person to publish a report described in subsection (1) that contains the name of a young person, or information serving to identify a young person, who has committed or is alleged to have committed an indictable offence, if the judge is satisfied that

> (a) there is reason to believe that the young person is dangerous to others; and

> (b) publication of the report is necessary to assist in apprehending the young person.

(1.3) Order ceases to have effect — An order made under subsection (1.2) shall cease to have effect two days after it is made.

(1.4) Application for leave to publish — The youth court may, on the application of any person referred to in subsection (1), make an order permitting any person to publish a report in which the name of that person, or information serving to identify that person, would be disclosed, if the court is satisfied that the publication of the report would not be contrary to the best interests of that person.

(1.5) Disclosure with court order — The youth court may, on the application of the provincial director, the Attorney General or an agent of the Attorney General or a peace officer, make an order permitting the applicant to disclose to such person or persons as are specified by the court such information about a young person as is specified if the court is satisfied that the disclosure is necessary, having regard to the following:

(a) the young person has been found guilty of an offence involving serious personal injury;

(b) the young person poses a risk of serious harm to persons; and

(c) the disclosure of the information is relevant to the avoidance of that risk.

(1.6) Opportunity to be heard — Subject to subsection (1.7), before making an order under subsection (1.5), the youth court shall afford the young person, the young person's parents, the Attorney General or an agent of the Attorney General an opportunity to be heard.

(1.7) Ex parte application — An application under subsection (1.5) may be made *ex parte* by the Attorney General or an agent of the Attorney General where the youth court is satisfied that reasonable efforts have been made to locate the young person and that those efforts have not been successful.

(1.8) Time limit — No information may be disclosed pursuant to subsection (1.5) after the record to which the information relates ceases to be available for inspection under subsection 45(1).

(2) Contravention — Every one who contravenes subsection (1), (1.12), (1.14) or (1.15)

(a) is guilty of an indictable offence and liable to imprisonment for a term not exceeding two years; or

(b) is guilty of an offence punishable on summary conviction.

(3) Provincial court judge has absolute jurisdiction on indictment — Where an accused is charged with an offence under paragraph (2)(a), a provincial court judge has absolute jurisdiction to try the case and his jurisdiction does not depend on the consent of the accused.

R.S. 1985, c. 27 (1st Supp.), s. 203; R.S. 1985, c. 24 (2nd Supp.), s. 29; 1995, c. 19, s. 27; 1995, c. 39, s. 184

39. (1) Exclusion from hearing — Subject to subsection (2), where a court or justice before whom proceedings are carried out under this Act is of the opinion

(a) that any evidence or information presented to the court or justice would be seriously injurious or seriously prejudicial to

(i) the young person who is being dealt with in the proceedings,

(ii) a child or young person who is a witness in the proceedings,

(iii) a child or young person who is aggrieved by or the victim of the offence charged in the proceedings, or

(b) that it would be in the interest of public morals, the maintenance of order or the proper administration of justice to exclude any or all members of the public from the court room,

the court or justice may exclude any person from all or part of the proceedings if the court or justice deems that person's presence to be unnecessary to the conduct of the proceedings.

(2) Exception — Subject to section 650 of the *Criminal Code* and except where it is necessary for the purposes of subsection 13(6) of this Act, a court or justice may not, pursuant to subsection (1), exclude from proceedings under this Act

(a) the prosecutor;

(b) the young person who is being dealt with in the proceedings, his parent, his counsel or any adult assisting him pursuant to subsection 11(7);

(c) the provincial director or his agent;or

(d) the youth worker to whom the young person's case has been assigned.

(3) Exclusion after adjudication or during review — The youth court, after it has found a young person guilty of an offence, or the youth court or the review board, during a review of a disposition under sections 28 to 32, may, in its discretion, exclude from the court or from a hearing of the review board, as the case may be, any person other than

(a) the young person or his counsel,

(b) the provincial director or his agent,

(c) the youth worker to whom the young person's case has been assigned, and

(d) the Attorney General or his agent,

when any information is being presented to the court or the review board the knowledge of which might, in the opinion of the court or review board, be seriously injurious or seriously prejudicial to the young person.

(4) Exception — The exception set out in paragraph (3)(a) is subject to subsection 13(6) of this Act and section 650 of the *Criminal Code*.

R.S. 1985, c. 24 (2nd Supp.), s. 30

MAINTENANCE AND USE OF RECORDS

Records that may be Kept

40. (1) Youth court, review board and other courts — A youth court, review board or any court dealing with matters arising out of proceedings under this Act may keep a record of any case arising under this Act that comes before it.

(2) Exception — For greater certainty, this section does not apply in respect of proceedings held in ordinary court pursuant to an order under section 16.

(3) Records of offences that result in order under s. 20.1 — Notwithstanding anything in this Act, where a young person is found guilty of an offence that results in an order under section 20.1 being made against the young person, the youth court may keep a record of the conviction and the order until the expiration of the order.

(4) Disclosure — Any record that is kept under subsection (3) may be disclosed only to establish the existence of the order in any offence involving a breach of the order.

R.S. 1985, c. 24 (2nd Supp.), s. 31; 1995, c. 39, s. 185

41. (1) Records in central repository — A record of any offence that a young person has been charged with having committed may, where the offence is an offence in respect of which an adult may be subjected to any measurement, process or operation referred to in the *Identification of Criminals Act*, be kept in such central repository as the Commissioner of the Royal Canadian Mounted Police may, from time to time, designate for the purpose of keeping criminal history files or records on offenders or keeping records for the identification of offenders.

(2) Police force may provide record — Where a young person is charged with having committed an offence referred to in subsection (1), the police force responsible for the investigation of the offence may provide a record of the offence, including the original or a copy of any fingerprints, palmprints or photographs and any other measurement, process or operation referred to in the *Identification of Criminals Act* taken of, or applied in respect of, the young person by or on behalf of the police force, for inclusion in any central repository designated pursuant to subsection (1).

(3) Police force shall provide record — Where a young person is found guilty of an offence referred to in subsection (1), the police force responsible for the investigation of the offence shall provide a record of the offence, including the original or a copy of any fingerprints, palmprints or photographs and any other measurement, process or operation referred to in the *Identification of Criminals Act* taken of, or applied in respect of, the young person by or on behalf of the police force, for inclusion in any central repository designated pursuant to subsection (1).

R.S. 1985, c. 24 (2nd Supp.), s. 31; 1995, c. 19, s. 28

42. Police records — A record relating to any offence alleged to have been committed by a young person, including the original or a copy of any fingerprints or photographs of the young person, may be kept by any police force responsible for, or participating in, the investigation of the offence.

(2)–(5) [Repealed R.S. 1985, c. 24 (2nd Supp.), s. 31.]

R.S. 1985, c. 24 (2nd Supp.), s. 31

43. (1) Government records — A department or agency of any government in Canada may keep records containing information obtained by the department or agency

    (a) for the purposes of an investigation of an offence alleged to have been committed by a young person;

    (b) for use in proceedings against a young person under this Act;

    (c) for the purpose of administering a disposition;

(d) for the purpose of considering whether, instead of commencing or continuing judicial proceedings under this Act against a young person, to use alternative measures to deal with the young person; or

(e) as a result of the use of alternative measures to deal with a young person.

(2) Private records — Any person or organization may keep records containing information obtained by the person or organization

(a) as a result of the use of alternative measures to deal with a young person alleged to have committed an offence; or

(b) for the purpose of administering or participating in the administration of a disposition.

(3), (4) [Repealed R.S. 1985, c. 24 (2nd Supp.), s. 32.]

Fingerprints and Photographs

44. (1) *Identification of Criminals Act* applies — Subject to this section, the *Identification of Criminals Act* applies in respect of young persons.

(2) Limitation — No fingerprints, palmprints or photograph or any other measurement, process or operation referred to in the *Identification of Criminals Act* shall be taken of, or applied in respect of, a young person who is charged with having committed an offence except in the circumstances in which an adult may, under that Act, be subjected to the measurements, processes and operations referred to in that Act.

(3)–(5) [Repealed R.S. 1985, c. 24 (2nd Supp.), s. 33.]

R.S. 1985, c. 24 (2nd Supp.), s. 3; 1995, c. 19, s. 29

Disclosure of Records

44.1 (1) Records made available — Subject to subsections (2), (2.1), any record that is kept pursuant to section 40 shall, and any record that is kept pursuant to sections 41 to 43 may, on request, be made available for inspection to

(a) the young person to whom the record relates;

(b) counsel acting on behalf of the young person, or any representative of that counsel;

(c) the Attorney General or his agent;

(d) a parent of the young person or any adult assisting the young person pursuant to subsection 11(7), during the course of any proceedings relating to the offence or alleged offence to which the record relates or during the term of any disposition made in respect of the offence;

(e) any judge, court or review board, for any purpose relating to proceedings relating to the young person under this Act or to proceedings in ordinary court in respect of offences committed or alleged to have been committed by the young person, whether as a young person or an adult;

(f) any peace officer,

> (i) for the purpose of investigating any offence that the young person is suspected on reasonable grounds of having committed, or in respect of which the young person has been arrested or charged, whether as a young person or an adult,

> (ii) for any purpose related to the administration of the case to which the record relates during the course of proceedings against the young person or the term of any disposition, or

> (iii) for the purpose of investigating any offence that another person is suspected on reasonable grounds of having committed against the young person while the young person is, or was, serving a disposition, or

> (iv) for any other law enforcement purpose;

(g) any member of a department or agency of a government in Canada, or any agent thereof, that is

> (i) engaged in the administration of alternative measures in respect of the young person,

> (ii) preparing a report in respect of the young person pursuant to this Act or for the purpose of assisting a court in sentencing the young person after he becomes an adult or is transferred to ordinary court pursuant to section 16,

> (iii) engaged in the supervision or care of the young person, whether as a young person or an adult, or in the administration of a disposition or a sentence in respect of the young person, whether as a young person or an adult, or

> (iv) considering an application for parole or pardon made by the young person after he becomes an adult;

(h) any person, or person within a class of persons, designated by the Governor in Council, or the Lieutenant Governor in Council of a province, for a purpose and to the extent specified by the Governor in Council or the Lieutenant Governor in Council, as the case may be;

(i) any person, for the purpose of determining whether to grant security clearances required by the Government of Canada or the government of a province or a municipality for purposes of employment or the performance of services;

(i.1) to any person for the purposes of the *Firearms Act*;

(j) any employee or agent of the Government of Canada, for statistical purposes pursuant to the *Statistics Act*; and

(k) any other person who is deemed, or any person within a class of persons that is deemed, by a youth court judge to have a valid interest in the record, to the extent directed by the judge, if the judge is satisfied that the disclosure is

> (i) desirable in the public interest for research or statistical purposes, or

> (ii) desirable in the interest of the proper administration of justice.

(2) Exception — Where a youth court has withheld the whole or a part of a report from any person pursuant to subsection 13(6) or 14(7), the report or part thereof shall not be made available to that person for inspection under subsection (1).

(2.1) Records of forensic DNA analysis of bodily substances — Notwithstanding subsections (1) and (5), any record that is kept pursuant to any of sections 40 to 43 and that is a record of the results of forensic DNA analysis of a bodily substance taken from a young person in execution of a warrant issued under section 487.05 of the *Criminal Code* may be made available for inspection under this section only under paragraphs (1)(a), (b), (c), (d), (e), (f), (h) or subparagraph (1)(k)(ii).

(3) Introduction into evidence — Nothing in paragraph (1)(e) authorizes the introduction into evidence of any part of a record that would not otherwise be admissible in evidence.

(4) Disclosures for research or statistical purposes — Where a record is made available for inspection to any person under paragraph (1)(j) or subparagraph (1)(k)(i), that person may subsequently disclose information contained in the record, but may not disclose the information in any form that would reasonably be expected to identify the young person to whom it relates.

(5) Record made available to victim — Any record that is kept pursuant to sections 40 to 43 may, on request, be made available for inspection to the victim of the offence to which the record relates.

(6) Disclosure of information and copies of records — Any person to whom a record is required or authorized to be made available for inspection under this section may be given any information contained in the record and may be given a copy of any part of the record.

R.S. 1985, c. 24 (2nd Supp.), s. 34; 1992, c. 43, s. 34; 1995, c. 19, s. 30; 1995, c. 27, s. 2; 1995, c. 39, s. 186

44.2 (1) Disclosure by peace officer during investigation — A peace officer may disclose to any person any information in a record kept pursuant to section 42 that it is necessary to disclose in the conduct of the investigation of an offence.

(2) Disclosure to insurance company — A peace officer may disclose to an insurance company information in any record that is kept pursuant to section 42 for the purpose of investigating any claim arising out of an offence committed or alleged to have been committed by the young person to whom the record relates.

R.S. 1985, c. 24 (2nd Supp.), s. 34

NON-DISCLOSURE AND DESTRUCTION OF RECORDS

45. (1) Non-disclosure — Subject to sections 45.01, 45.1 and 45.2, records kept pursuant to sections 40 to 43 may not be made available for inspection under section 44.1 or 44.2 in the following circumstances:

(a) where the young person to whom the record relates is charged with the offence to which the record relates and is acquitted otherwise than by reason of a verdict of not criminally responsible on account of mental disorder, on the expiration of two months after the expiration of the time allowed for the taking of an appeal or, where an appeal is taken on the expiration of three months after all proceedings in respect of the appeal have been completed;

(b) where the charge against the young person is dismissed for any reason other than acquittal or withdrawn, on the expiration of one year after the dismissal or withdrawal;

(c) where the charge against the young person is stayed, with no proceedings being taken against the young person for a period of one year, on the expiration of the one year;

(d) where alternative measures are used to deal with the young person, on the expiration of two years after the young person consents to participate in the alternative measures in accordance with paragraph 4(1)(c);

(d.1) where the young person is found guilty of the offence and the disposition is an absolute discharge, on the expiration of one year after the young person is found guilty;

(d.2) where the young person is found guilty of the offence and the disposition is a conditional discharge, on the expiration of three years after the young person is found guilty;

(e) subject to paragraph (g), where the young person is found guilty of the offence and it is a summary conviction offence, on the expiration of three years after all dispositions made in respect of that offence;

(f) subject to paragraph (g), where the young person is found guilty of the offence and it is an indictable offence, on the expiration of five years after all dispositions made in respect of that offence; and

(g) where, before the expiration of the period referred to in paragraph (e) or (f), the young person is, as a young person, found guilty of

(i) a subsequent summary conviction offence, on the expiration of three years after all dispositions made in respect of that offence have been completed, and

(ii) a subsequent indictable offence, five years after all dispositions made in respect of that offence have been completed.

[Note: 1995, c. 19, s. 31(4) states: Paragraphs 45(1)(d.1) to (e) of the Act, as enacted by subsection (2), apply in respect of a record relating to a finding of guilt made before the coming into force of that subsection only if the person to whom the record relates applies, after the coming into force of that subsection, to the Royal Canadian Mounted Police to have those paragraphs apply. 1995, c. 19, s. 31(2) came into force on December 1, 1995.]

(2) Destruction of record — Subject to subsections (2.1) and (2.2), when the circumstances set out in subsection (1) are realized in respect of any record kept pursuant to section 41, the record shall be destroyed forthwith.

(2.1) Transfer of records relating to serious offences — Where a special records repository has been established pursuant to subsection 45.02(1), all records in the central repository referred to in subsection 41(1) that relate to

(a) a conviction for first degree murder or second degree murder within the meaning of section 231 of the *Criminal Code*,

(b) an offence referred to in the schedule, or

(c) an order made under section 20.1,

shall, when the circumstances set out in subsection (1) are realized in respect of the records, be transferred to that special records repository.

(2.2) Transfer of fingerprints — Where a special fingerprints repository has been established pursuant to subsection 45.03(1), all fingerprints and any information necessary to identify the person to whom the fingerprints belong that are in the central repository referred to in subsection 41(1) shall, when the circumstances set out in subsection (1) are realized in respect of the records, be transferred to that special fingerprints repository.

(2.3) Meaning of "destroy" — For the purposes of subsection (2), "destroy", in respect of a record, means

(a) to shred, burn or otherwise physically destroy the record, in the case of a record other than a record in electronic form; and

(b) to delete, write over or otherwise render the record inaccessible, in the case of a record in electronic form.

(3) Other records may be destroyed — Any record kept pursuant to sections 40 to 43 may, in the discretion of the person or body keeping the record, be destroyed at any time before or after the circumstances set out in subsection (1) are realized in respect of that record.

(4) Young person deemed not to have committed offence — A young person shall be deemed not to have committed any offence to which a record kept pursuant to sections 40 to 43 relates when the circumstances set out in paragraph (1)(d), (e) or (f) are realized in respect of that record.

(5) Deemed election — For the purposes of paragraphs (1)(e) and (f), where no election is made in respect of an offence that may be prosecuted by indictment or proceeded with by way of summary conviction, the Attorney General or his agent shall be deemed to have elected to proceed with the offence as an offence punishable on summary conviction.

(5.1) Orders made under s. 20.1 not included — For the purposes of this Act, orders made under section 20.1 shall not be taken into account in determining any time period referred to in subsection (1).

(6) Application to delinquency — This section applies, with such modifications as the circumstances require, in respect of records relating to the offence of delinquency under the *Juvenile Delinquents Act*, chapter J-3 of the Revised Statutes of Canada, 1970, as it read immediately prior to April 2, 1984.

R.S. 1985, c. 24 (2nd Supp.), s. 35; 1992, c. 43, s. 34; 1995, c. 19, s. 31; 1995, c. 39, ss. 187, 189

RETENTION OF RECORDS

45.01 Retention of records — Where, before the expiration of the period referred to in paragraph 45(1)(e) or (f) or subparagraph 45(1)(g)(i) or (ii), the young person is found guilty of a subsequent offence as an adult, records kept pursuant to sections 40 to 43 shall be available for inspection under section 44.1 or 44.2 and the provisions applicable to criminal records of adults shall apply.

1995, c. 19, s. 32

SPECIAL RECORDS REPOSITORY

45.02 (1) Special records repository — The Commissioner of the Royal Canadian Mounted Police may establish a special records repository for records transferred pursuant to subsection 45(2.1).

(2) Records relating to murder — A record that relates to a conviction for the offence of first degree murder or second degree murder within the meaning of section 231 of the *Criminal Code* or an offence referred to in any of paragraphs 16(1.01)(b) to (d) may be kept indefinitely in the special records repository.

(3) Records relating to other serious offences — A record that relates to a conviction for an offence referred to in the schedule shall be kept in the special records repository for a period of five years and shall be destroyed forthwith at the expiration of that five year period, unless the young person to whom the record relates is subsequently found guilty of any offence referred to in the schedule, in which case the record shall be dealt with as the record of an adult.

(4) Disclosure — A record kept in the special records repository shall be made available for inspection to the following persons at the following times or in the following circumstances:

(a) at any time, to the person to whom the record relates and to counsel acting on behalf of the young person, or any representative of that counsel;

(b) where the young person has subsequently been charged with the commission of first degree murder or second degree murder within the meaning of section 231 of the *Criminal Code* or an offence referred to in the schedule, to any peace officer for the purpose of investigating any offence that the young person is suspected of having committed, or in respect of which the young person has been arrested or charged, whether as a young person or as an adult;

(c) where the young person has subsequently been convicted of an offence referred to in the schedule,

(i) to the Attorney General or an agent of the Attorney General,

(ii) to a parent of the young person or any adult assisting the young person,

(iii) to any judge, court or review board, for any purpose relating to proceedings relating to the young person under this Act or to proceedings in ordinary court in respect of offences committed or alleged to have been committed by the young person, whether as a young person or as an adult, or

(iv) to any member of a department or agency of a government in Canada, or any agent thereof, that is

(A) engaged in the administration of alternative measures in respect of the young person,

(B) preparing a report in respect of the young person pursuant to this Act or for the purpose of assisting a court in sentencing the young person after the young person becomes an adult or is transferred to ordinary court pursuant to section 16,

(C) engaged in the supervision or care of the young person, whether as a young person or as an adult, or in the administration of a disposition or a sentence in respect of the young person, whether as a young person or as an adult, or

(D) considering an application for parole or pardon made by the young person after the young person becomes an adult;

(c.1) to establish the existence of the order in any offence involving a breach of the order;

(c.2) for the purposes of the *Firearms Act*;

(d) at any time, to any employee or agent of the Government of Canada, for statistical purposes pursuant to the *Statistics Act*; or

(e) at any time, to any other person who is deemed, or any person within a class of persons that is deemed, by a youth court judge to have a valid interest in the record, to the extent directed by the judge, if the judge is satisfied that the disclosure is desirable in the public interest for research or statistical purposes.

1995, c. 19, s. 32; 1995, c. 39, s. 189(d)

SPECIAL FINGERPRINTS REPOSITORY

45.03 (1) Special fingerprints repository — The Commissioner of the Royal Canadian Mounted Police may establish a special fingerprints repository for fingerprints and any related information transferred pursuant to subsection 45(2.2).

(2) Disclosure for identification purposes — Fingerprints and any related information may be kept in the special fingerprints repository for a period of five years following the date of their receipt and, during that time, the name, date of birth and last known address of the young person to whom the fingerprints belong may be disclosed for identification purposes if a fingerprint identified as that of the young person is found during the investigation of a crime or during an attempt to identify a deceased person or a person suffering from amnesia.

(3) Destruction — Fingerprints and any related information in the special fingerprints repository shall be destroyed five years after the date of their receipt in the repository.

(3.1) Records of orders made under s. 20.1 — A record that relates to an order made under section 20.1 shall be kept in the special records repository until the expiration of the order and shall be destroyed forthwith at that time.

1995, c. 19, s. 32; 1995, c. 39, s. 189(c)

DISCLOSURE IN SPECIAL CIRCUMSTANCES

45.1 (1) Where records may be made available — Subject to subsection (1.1), a youth court judge may, on application by any person, order that any record to which subsection 45(1) applies, or any part thereof, be made available for inspection to that person or a copy of the record or part thereof be given to that person, if a youth court judge is satisfied that

(a) that person has a valid and substantial interest in the record or part thereof;

(b) it is necessary for the record, part thereof or copy thereof to be made available in the interest of the proper administration of justice; and

(c) disclosure of the record or part thereof or information is not prohibited under any other Act of Parliament or the legislature of a province.

(1.1) Records — Subsection (1) applies in respect of any record relating to a particular young person or to any record relating to a class of young persons where the identity of young persons in the class at the time of the making of the application referred to in that subsection cannot reasonably be ascertained and the disclosure of the record is necessary for the purpose of investigating any offence that a person is suspected on reasonable grounds of having committed against a young person while the young person is, or was, serving a disposition.

(2) Notice — Subject to subsection (2.1), an application under subsection (1) in respect of a record shall not be heard unless the person who makes the application has given the young person to whom the record relates and the person or body that has possession of the record at least five days notice in writing of the application and the young person and the person or body that has possession has had a reasonable opportunity to be heard.

(2.1) Where notice not required — A youth court judge may waive the requirement in subsection (2) to give notice to a young person where the youth court is of the opinion that

(a) to insist on the giving of the notice would frustrate the application; or

(b) reasonable efforts have not been successful in finding the young person.

(3) Use of record — In any order under subsection (1), the youth court judge shall set out the purposes for which the record may be used.

R.S. 1985, c. 24 (2nd Supp.), s. 35; 1995, c. 19, s. 34

45.2 Records in the custody, etc., of archivists — Where records originally kept pursuant to section 40, 42 or 43 are under the custody or control of the National Archivist of Canada or the archivist for any province, that person may disclose any information contained in the records to any other person if

(a) the Attorney General or his agent is satisfied that the disclosure is desirable in the public interest for research or statistical purposes; and

(b) the person to whom the information is disclosed undertakes not to disclose the information in any form that could reasonably be expected to identify the young person to whom it relates.

R.S. 1985, c. 24 (2nd Supp.), s. 35; R.S. 1985, c. 1 (3rd Supp.), s. 12

46. (1) Prohibition against disclosure — Except as authorized or required by this Act, no record kept pursuant to sections 40 to 43 may be made available for inspection, and no copy, print or negative thereof or information contained therein may be given, to any person where to do so would serve to identify the young person to whom it relates as a young person dealt with under this Act.

(2) Exception for employees — No person who is employed in keeping or maintaining records referred to in subsection (1) is restricted from doing anything prohibited under subsection (1) with respect to any other person so employed.

(3) Prohibition against use — Subject to section 45.1, no record kept pursuant to sections 40 to 43, and no copy, print or negative thereof, may be used for any purpose that would serve to identify the young person to whom the record relates as a young person dealt with under this Act after the circumstances set out in subsection 45(1) are realized in respect of that record.

(4) Offence — Any person who fails to comply with this section or subsection 45(2)

(a) is guilty of an indictable offence and liable to imprisonment for a term not exceeding two years; or

(b) is guilty of an offence punishable on summary conviction.

(5) Absolute jurisdiction of provincial court judge — The jurisdiction of a provincial court judge to try an accused is absolute and does not depend on the consent of the accused where the accused is charged with an offence under paragraph (4)(a).

R.S. 1985, c. 27 (1st Supp.), s. 203; R.S. 1985, c. 24 (2nd Supp.), s. 36

CONTEMPT OF COURT

47. (1) Contempt against youth court — Every youth court has the same power, jurisdiction and authority to deal with and impose punishment for contempt against the court as may be exercised by the superior court of criminal jurisdiction of the province in which the court is situated.

(2) Exclusive jurisdiction of youth court — The youth court has exclusive jurisdiction in respect of every contempt of court committed by a young person against the youth court whether or not committed in the face of the court and every contempt of court committed by a young person against any other court otherwise than in the face of that court.

(3) Concurrent jurisdiction of youth court — The youth court has jurisdiction in respect of every contempt of court committed by a young person against any other court in the face of that court and every contempt of court committed by an adult against the youth court in the face of the youth court, but nothing in this subsection affects the power, jurisdiction or authority of any other court to deal with or impose punishment for contempt of court.

(4) Dispositions — Where a youth court or any other court finds a young person guilty of contempt of court, it may make any one of the dispositions set out in section 20, or any number thereof that are not inconsistent with each other, but no other disposition or sentence.

(5) Section 708 of *Criminal Code* applies in respect of adults — Section 708 of the *Criminal Code* applies in respect of proceedings under this section in youth court against adults, with such modifications as the circumstances require.

(6) Appeals — A finding of guilt under this section for contempt of court or a disposition or sentence made in respect thereof may be appealed as if the finding were a conviction or the disposition or sentence were a sentence in a prosecution by indictment in ordinary court.

FORFEITURE OF RECOGNIZANCES

48. Applications for forfeiture of recognizances — Applications for the forfeiture of recognizances of young persons shall be made to the youth court.

49. (1) Proceedings in case of default — Where a recognizance binding a young person has been endorsed with a certificate pursuant to subsection 770(1) of the *Criminal Code*, a youth court judge shall,

(a) on the request of the Attorney General or his agent, fix a time and place for the hearing of an application for the forfeiture of the recognizance; and

(b) after fixing a time and place for the hearing, cause to be sent by registered mail, not less than ten days before the time so fixed, to each principal and surety named in the recognizance, directed to him at his latest known address, a notice requiring him to appear at the time and place fixed by the judge to show cause why the recognizance should not be forfeited.

(2) Order for forfeiture of recognizance — Where subsection (1) is complied with, the youth court judge may, after giving the parties an opportunity to be heard, in his discretion grant or refuse the application and make any order with respect to the forfeiture of the recognizance that he considers proper.

(3) Judgment debtors of the Crown — Where, pursuant to subsection (2), a youth court judge orders forfeiture of a recognizance, the principal and his sureties become judgment debtors of the Crown, each in the amount that the judge orders him to pay.

(4) Order may be filed — An order made under subsection (2) may be filed with the clerk of the superior court or, in the province of Quebec, the prothonotary and, where an order is filed, the clerk or the prothonotary shall issue a writ of *fieri facias* in Form 34 set out in the *Criminal Code* and deliver it to the sheriff of each of the territorial divisions in which any of the principal and his sureties resides, carries on business or has property.

(5) Where a deposit has been made — Where a deposit has been made by a person against whom an order for forfeiture of a recognizance has been made, no writ of *fieri facias* shall issue, but the amount of the deposit shall be transferred by the person who has custody of it to the person who is entitled by law to receive it.

(6) Subsections 770(2) and (4) of *Criminal Code* do not apply — Subsections 770(2) and (4) of the *Criminal Code* do not apply in respect of proceedings under this Act.

(7) Sections 772 and 773 of *Criminal Code* apply — Sections 772 and 773 of the *Criminal Code* apply in respect of writs of *fieri facias* issued pursuant to this section as if they were issued pursuant to section 771 of the *Criminal Code*.

INTERFERENCE WITH DISPOSITIONS

50. (1) Inducing a young person, etc — Every one who

(a) induces or assists a young person to leave unlawfully a place of custody or other place in which the young person has been placed pursuant to a disposition,

(b) unlawfully removes a young person from a place referred to in paragraph (a),

(c) knowingly harbours or conceals a young person who has unlawfully left a place referred to in paragraph (a),

(d) wilfully induces or assists a young person to breach or disobey a term or condition of a disposition, or

(e) wilfully prevents or interferes with the performance by a young person of a term or condition of a disposition

is guilty of an indictable offence and liable to imprisonment for a term not exceeding two years or is guilty of an offence punishable on summary conviction.

(2) Absolute jurisdiction of provincial court judge — The jurisdiction of a provincial court judge to try an adult accused of an indictable offence under this section is absolute and does not depend on the consent of the accused.

R.S. 1985, c. 27 (1st Supp.), s. 203; R.S. 1985, c. 24 (2d Supp.), s. 37

APPLICATION OF THE CRIMINAL CODE

51. Application of *Criminal Code* — Except to the extent that they are inconsistent with or excluded by this Act, all the provisions of the *Criminal Code* apply, with such modifications as the circumstances require, in respect of offences alleged to have been committed by young persons.

PROCEDURE

52. (1) Part XXVII and summary conviction trial provisions of *Criminal Code* to apply — Subject to this section and except to the extent that they are inconsistent with this Act,

>   (a) the provisions of Part XXVII of the *Criminal Code*, and

>   (b) any other provisions of the *Criminal Code* that apply in respect of summary conviction offences and relate to trial proceedings

apply to proceedings under this Act

>   (c) in respect of a summary conviction offence, and

>   (d) in respect of an indictable offence as if it were defined in the enactment creating it as a summary conviction offence.

(2) Indictable offences — For greater certainty and notwithstanding subsection (1) or any other provision of this Act, an indictable offence committed by a young person is, for the purposes of this or any other Act, an indictable offence.

(3) Attendance of young person — Section 650 of the *Criminal Code* applies in respect of proceedings under this Act, whether the proceedings relate to an indictable offence or an offence punishable on summary conviction.

(4) Limitation period — In proceedings under this Act, subsection 786(2) of the *Criminal Code* does not apply in respect of an indictable offence.

(5) Costs — Section 809 of the *Criminal Code* does not apply in respect of proceedings under this Act.

53. Counts Charged in Information — Indictable offences and offences punishable on summary conviction may under this Act be charged in the same information and tried jointly.

54. (1) Issue of subpoena — Where a person is required to attend to give evidence before a youth court, the subpoena directed to that person may be issued by a youth court judge, whether or not the person whose attendance is required is within the same province as the youth court.

(2) Service of subpoena — A subpoena issued by a youth court and directed to a person who is not within the same province as the youth court shall be served personally on the person to whom it is directed.

55. Warrant — A warrant that is issued out of a youth court may be executed anywhere in Canada.

EVIDENCE

56. (1) General law on admissibility of statements to apply — Subject to this section, the law relating to the admissibility of statements made by persons accused of committing offences applies in respect of young persons.

(2) When statements are admissible — No oral or written statement given by a young person to a peace officer or to any other person who is, in law, a person in authority on the arrest or detention of the young person or in circumstances where the peace officer or other person has reasonable grounds for believing that the young person has committed an offence is admissible against the young person unless

    (a) the statement was voluntary;

    (b) the person to whom the statement was given has, before the statement was made, clearly explained to the young person, in language appropriate to his age and understanding, that

        (i) the young person is under no obligation to give a statement,

        (ii) any statement given by him may be used as evidence in proceedings against him,

        (iii) the young person has the right to consult counsel and a parent or other person in accordance with paragraph (c), and

        (iv) any statement made by the young person is required to be made in the presence of counsel and any other person consulted in accordance with paragraph (c), if any, unless the young person desires otherwise;

    (c) the young person has, before the statement was made, been given a reasonable opportunity to consult

        (i) with counsel, and

        (ii) a parent, or in the absence of a parent, an adult relative, or in the absence of a parent and an adult relative, any other appropriate adult chosen by the young person; and

    (d) where the young person consults any person pursuant to paragraph (c), the young person has been given a reasonable opportunity to make the statement in the presence of that person.

(3) Exception in certain cases for oral statements — The requirements set out in paragraphs (2)(b), (c) and (d) do not apply in respect of oral statements where they are made spontaneously by the young person to a peace officer or other person in authority before that person has had a reasonable opportunity to comply with those requirements.

(4) Waiver of right to consult — A young person may waive the rights under paragraph (2)(c) or (d) but any such waiver shall be videotaped or be in writing, and where it is in writing it shall contain a statement signed by the young person that the young person has been apprised of the right being waived.

(5) Statements given under duress are inadmissible — A youth court judge may rule inadmissible in any proceedings under this Act a statement given by the young person in respect of whom the proceedings are taken if the young person satisfies the judge that the statement was given under duress imposed by any person who is not, in law, a person in authority.

(5.1) Misrepresentation of age — A youth court judge may in any proceedings under this Act rule admissible any statement or waiver by a young person where, at the time of the making of the statement or waiver,

> (a) the young person held himself or herself to be eighteen years of age or older;

> (b) the person to whom the statement or waiver was made conducted reasonable inquiries as to the age of the young person and had reasonable grounds for believing that the young person was eighteen years of age or older; and

> (c) in all other circumstances the statement or waiver would otherwise be admissible.

(6) Parent, etc., not a person in authority — For the purpose of this section, an adult consulted pursuant to paragraph 56(2)(c) shall, in the absence of evidence to the contrary, be deemed not to be a person in authority.

R.S. 1985, c. 24 (2nd Supp.), s. 38; 1995, c. 19, s. 35.

57. (1) Testimony of a parent — In any proceedings under this Act, the testimony of a parent as to the age of a person of whom he is a parent is admissible as evidence of the age of that person.

(2) Evidence of age by certificate or record — In any proceedings under this Act,

> (a) a birth or baptismal certificate or a copy thereof purporting to be certified under the hand of the person in whose custody those records are held is evidence of the age of the person named in the certificate or copy; and

> (b) an entry or record of an incorporated society that has had the control or care of the person alleged to have committed the offence in respect of which the proceedings are taken at or about the time the person came to Canada is evidence of the age of that person, if the entry or record was made before the time when the offence is alleged to have been committed.

(3) Other evidence — In the absence, before the youth court, of any certificate, copy, entry or record mentioned in subsection (2), or in corroboration of any such certificate, copy, entry or record, the youth court may receive and act on any other information relating to age that it considers reliable.

(4) When age may be inferred — In any proceedings under this Act, the youth court may draw inferences as to the age of a person from the person's appearance or from statements made by the person in direct examination or cross-examination.

58. (1) Admissions — A party to any proceedings under this Act may admit any relevant fact or matter for the purpose of dispensing with proof thereof, including any fact or matter the admissibility of which depends on a ruling of law or of mixed law and fact.

(2) Other party may adduce evidence — Nothing in this section precludes a party to a proceeding from adducing evidence to prove a fact or matter admitted by another party.

59. Material evidence — Any evidence material to proceedings under this Act that would not but for this section be admissible in evidence may, with the consent of the parties to the proceedings and where the young person is represented by counsel, be given in such proceedings.

60. Evidence of a child or young person — In any proceedings under this Act where the evidence of a child or a young person is taken, it shall be taken only after the youth court judge or the justice, as the case may be, has

(a) in all cases, if the witness is a child, and

(b) where he deems it necessary, if the witness is a young person,

instructed the child or young person as to the duty of the witness to speak the truth and the consequences of failing to do so.

(2), (3) [Repealed R.S. 1985, c. 24 (2d Supp.), s. 39.]

R.S. 1985, c. 24 (2d Supp.), s. 39.

61. [Repealed R.S. 1985, c. 24 (2d Supp.), s. 40.]

62. (1) Proof of service — For the purposes of this Act, service of any document may be proved by oral evidence given under oath by, or by the affidavit or statutory declaration of, the person claiming to have personally served it or sent it by mail.

(2) Proof of signature and official character unnecessary — Where proof of service of any document is offered by affidavit or statutory declaration, it is not necessary to prove the signature or official character of the person making or taking the affidavit or declaration, if the official character of that person appears on the face thereof.

63. Seal not required — It is not necessary to the validity of any information, summons, warrant, minute, disposition, conviction, order or other process or document laid, issued, filed or entered in any proceedings under this Act that any seal be attached or affixed thereto.

SUBSTITUTION OF JUDGES

64. (1) Powers of substitute youth court judge — A youth court judge who acts in the place of another youth court judge pursuant to subsection 669.2(1) of the *Criminal Code* shall,

(a) if an adjudication has been made, proceed with the disposition of the case or make the order that, in the circumstances, is authorized by law; or

(b) if no adjudication has been made, recommence the trial as if no evidence had been taken.

(2) Transcript of evidence already given — Where a youth court judge recommences a trial under paragraph (1)(b), he may, if the parties consent, admit into evidence a transcript of any evidence already given in the case.

R.S. 1985, c. 27 (1st Supp.), s. 187 (Sched. V)

FUNCTIONS OF CLERKS OF COURTS

65. Powers of clerks — In addition to any powers conferred on a clerk of a court by the *Criminal Code*, a clerk of the youth court may exercise such powers as are ordinarily exercised by a clerk of a court, and, in particular, may

(a) administer oaths or solemn affirmations in all matters relating to the business of the youth court; and

(b) in the absence of a youth court judge, exercise all the powers of a youth court judge relating to adjournment.

FORMS, REGULATIONS AND RULES OF COURT

66. (1) Forms — The forms prescribed under section 67, varied to suit the case, or forms to the like effect, are valid and sufficient in the circumstances for which they are provided.

(2) Where forms not prescribed — In any case for which forms are not prescribed under section 67, the forms set out in Part XXVIII of the *Criminal Code*, with such modifications as the circumstances require, or other appropriate forms, may be used.

R.S. 1985, c. 1 (4th Supp.), s. 43.

67. Regulations — The Governor in Council may make regulations

(a) prescribing forms that may be used for the purposes of this Act;

(b) establishing uniform rules of court for youth courts across Canada, including rules regulating the practice and procedure to be followed by youth courts; and

(c) generally for carrying out the purposes and provisions of this Act.

R.S. 1985, c. 24 (2d Supp.), s. 41.

68. (1) Youth court may make rules — Every youth court for a province may, at any time with the concurrence of a majority of the judges thereof present at a meeting held for the purpose and subject to the approval of the Lieutenant Governor in Council, establish rules of court not inconsistent with this Act or any other Act of Parliament or with any regulations made pursuant to section 67 regulating proceedings within the jurisdiction of the youth court.

(2) Rules of court — Rules under subsection (1) may be made

(a) generally to regulate the duties of the officers of the youth court and any other matter considered expedient to attain the ends of justice and carry into effect the provisions of this Act;

(b) subject to any regulations made under paragraph 67(b), to regulate the practice and procedure in the youth court; and

(c) to prescribe forms to be used in the youth court where not otherwise provided for by or pursuant to this Act.

(3) Publication of rules — Rules of court that are made under the authority of this section shall be published in the appropriate provincial gazette.

YOUTH JUSTICE COMMITTEES

69. Youth justice committees — The Attorney General of a province or such other Minister as the Lieutenant Governor in Council of the province may designate, or a delegate thereof, may establish one or more committees of citizens, to be known as youth justice committees, to assist without remuneration in any aspect of the administration of this Act or in any programs or services for young offenders and may specify the method of appointment of committee members and the functions of the committees.

AGREEMENTS WITH PROVINCES

70. Agreements with provinces — Any Minister of the Crown may, with the approval of the Governor in Council, enter into an agreement with the government of any province providing for payments by Canada to the province in respect of costs incurred by the province or a municipality for care of and services provided to young persons dealt with under this Act.

R.S. 1985, c. 24 (2d Supp.), s. 42

SCHEDULE (SS. 45(2.1), 45.02(3) AND (4))

1. An offence under any of the following provisions of the *Criminal Code*:

(a) paragraph 81(2)(a) (causing injury with intent);

(b) subsection 85(1) (using firearm in commission of offences);

(c) (section 151 (sexual interference);

(d) section 152 (invitation to sexual touching);

(e) section 153 (sexual exploitation);

(f) section 155 (incest);

(g) section 159 (anal intercourse);

(h) section 170 (parent or guardian procuring sexual activity by child);

(i) subsection 212(2) (living off the avails of prostitution by a child);

(j) subsection 212(4) (obtaining sexual services of a child);

(k) section 236 (manslaughter);

(l) section 239 (attempt to commit murder);

(m) section 267 (assault with a weapon or causing bodily harm);

(n) section 268 (aggravated assault);

(o) section 269 (unlawfully causing bodily harm);

(p) section 271 (sexual assault);

(q) section 272 (sexual assault with a weapon, threats to a third party or causing bodily harm);

(r) section 273 (aggravated sexual assault);

(s) section 279 (kidnapping);

(t) section 344 (robbery);

(u) section 433 (arson — disregard for human life);

(v) section 434.1 (arson — own property);

(w) section 436 (arson by negligence); and

(x) paragraph 465(1)(a) (conspiracy to commit murder).

2. An offence under any of the following provisions of the *Criminal Code*, as they read immediately before July 1, 1990:

(a) section 433 (arson);

(b) section 434 (setting fire to other substance); and

(c) section 436 (setting fire by negligence).

3. An offence under any of the following provisions of the *Criminal Code*, chapter C-34 of the Revised Statutes of Canada, 1970, as they read immediately before January 4, 1983:

(a) section 144 (rape);

(b) section 145 (attempt to commit rape);

(c) section 149 (indecent assault on female);

(d) section 156 (indecent assault on male); and

(e) section 246 (assault with intent).

FORMS OF CHARGES

From *The Police Officers Manual* by Gary P. Rodrigues, B.A., LL.B., of the Ontario Bar

Criminal Code

Part II — Offences Against Public Order

Section 47(1) High treason

A.B., on the..........(day) of (month) ...., (year).........., at (specify time) in (specify place), in Canada, did kill Her Majesty [OR did attempt to kill Her Majesty OR did Her Majesty bodily harm tending to death (OR destruction), OR did maim (OR wound) Her Majesty (OR did imprison (OR restrain) Her Majesty] and did thereby commit high treason, contrary to s. 47(1) of the Criminal Code of Canada.

Section 47(2) Treason

A.B., on the..........(day) of (month) ...., (year).........., at (specify time) in (specify place), in Canada, did use force or violence for the purpose of overthrowing the government of Canada [OR the government of the province of ....], to wit: (specify the particulars of the offence), contrary to s. 47(2) of the Criminal Code of Canada.

Section 49(a) Alarming the Queen

A.B., on the..........(day) of (month) ...., (year).........., at (specify time) in (specify place), willfully, in the presence of Her Majesty the Queen, did an act with intent to alarm Her Majesty [OR did an act with intent to break the public peace], to wit: (specify the particulars of the offence), contrary to s. 49(a) of the Criminal Code of Canada.

Section 49(b) Causing bodily harm to the Queen

A.B., on the..........(day) of (month) ...., (year).........., at (specify time) in (specify place), willfully, in the presence of Her Majesty the Queen, did an act with intent to cause bodily harm to Her Majesty [OR did an act likely to cause bodily harm to Her Majesty], to wit: (specify the particulars of the offence), contrary to s. 49(b) of the Criminal Code of Canada.

Section 50(1)(a) Assisting alien enemy to leave Canada

A.B., on the..........(day) of (month) ...., (year).........., at (specify time) in (specify place)

..........did incite [OR wilfully assist] C.D., a subject of (specify the country), a state that was at war with Canada, to leave Canada without the consent of the Crown and without establishing that assistance to the state that was at war with Canada was not intended thereby, to wit: (specify the particulars of the offence), contrary to s. 50(1)(a)(i) of the Criminal Code of Canada.

..........did incite [OR wilfully assist] C.D., a subject of (specify the country), a state against whose forces Canadian Forces were engaged in hostilities, whether or not a state of war existed between Canada and (specify the country), to leave Canada without the consent of the Crown and without establishing that assistance to the forces of (specify the country) was not intended thereby, to wit: (specify the particulars of the offence), contrary to s. 50(1)(a)(ii) of the Criminal Code of Canada.

Section 50(1)(b) Omitting to prevent treason

A.B., on the..........(day) of (month) ...., (year).........., at (specify time) in (specify place), knowing that C.D. was about to commit high treason [OR treason], did not, with all reasonable dispatch, inform a justice of the peace [OR peace officer] [OR did not make other reasonable efforts to prevent C.D. from committing high treason (OR treason)], to wit: (specify the particulars of the offence), contrary to s. 50(1)(b) of the Criminal Code of Canada.

Section 51 Intimidation of Parliament or legislature

A.B., on the..........(day) of (month) ...., (year).........., at (specify time) in (specify place), did an act of violence in order to intimidate Parliament [OR in order to intimidate the legislature of the Province of ....], to wit: (specify the particulars of the offence), contrary to s. 51 of the Criminal Code of Canada.

Section 52 Sabotage

A.B., on the..........(day) of (month) ...., (year).........., at (specify time) in (specify place), did a prohibited act for a purpose prejudicial to the safety [OR security OR defence] of Canada [OR the safety (OR security) of the naval (OR army OR air)] forces of (specify the country other than Canada), that were lawfully present in Canada], to wit: (specify the particulars of the offence), contrary to s. 52 of the Criminal Code of Canada.

Section 53 Inciting to mutiny

A.B., on the..........(day) of (month) ...., (year).........., at (specify time) in (specify place),

..........did attempt to seduce for a traitorous [OR mutinous] purpose C.D., a member of the Canadian Forces from his [OR her] duty and allegiance to Her Majesty, to wit: (specify the particulars of the offence), contrary to s. 53(a) of the Criminal Code of Canada.

..........did attempt to incite [OR to induce] C.D., a member of the Canadian Forces, to commit a traitorous [OR mutinous] act, to wit: (specify the particulars of the offence), contrary to s. 53(b) of the Criminal Code of Canada.

Section 54 Aiding Canadian Forces deserter

A.B., on the..........(day) of (month) ...., (year).........., at (specify time) in (specify place), did aid [OR assist OR harbour OR conceal] C.D., knowing the said C.D. to be a deserter [OR absent without leave] from the Canadian Forces, to wit: (specify the particulars of the offence), contrary to s. 54 of the Criminal Code of Canada.

Section 56 Assisting R.C.M.P. deserter

A.B., on the..........(day) of (month) ...., (year).........., at (specify time) in (specify place), wilfully

..........did persuade [OR counsel] C.D., a member of the Royal Canadian Mounted Police to desert [OR absent himself (OR herself) without leave] to wit: (specify the particulars of the offence), contrary to s. 56(a) of the Criminal Code of Canada.

..........did aid [OR assist OR harbour OR conceal] C.D., a member of the Royal Canadian Mounted Police who A.B. knew was a deserter [OR absentee without leave], to wit: (specify the particulars of the offence), contrary to s. 56(b) of the Criminal Code of Canada.

..........did aid [OR assist] C.D., a member of the Royal Canadian Mounted Police to desert [OR absent himself (OR herself) without leave], knowing that C.D. was about to desert [OR absent himself (OR herself) without leave], to wit: (specify the particulars of the offence), contrary to s. 56(c) of the Criminal Code of Canada.

Section 57(1)(a) Forgery of passport

A.B., on the..........(day) of (month) ...., (year).........., at (specify time) in (specify place), did forge a passport, to wit: (specify the particulars of the offence), contrary to s. 57(1)(a) of the Criminal Code of Canada.

Section 57(1)(b) Uttering forged passport

A.B., on the..........(day) of (month) ...., (year).........., at (specify time) in (specify place), knowing that a passport was forged,

..........did use [OR deal with OR act on] it as if the passport were genuine, to wit: (specify the particulars of the offence), contrary to s. 57(1)(b)(i) of the Criminal Code of Canada.

..........did cause [OR attempt to cause] C.D. to use [OR deal with OR act on] it as if the passport were genuine, to wit: (specify the particulars of the offence), contrary to s. 5(1)(b)(ii) of the Criminal Code of Canada.

Section 57(2) False statement to procure passport

A.B., on the..........(day) of (month) ...., (year).........., at (specify time) in (specify place),

..........did make a written [OR oral] statement that A.B. knew was false [OR misleading], for the purpose of procuring a passport for A.B. [OR C.D.], to wit: (specify the particulars of the offence), contrary to s. 57(2) of the Criminal Code of Canada.

..........did make a written [OR oral] statement that A.B. knew was false [OR misleading] for the purpose of procuring a material alteration [OR addition] to a passport for A.B. [OR C.D.], to wit: (specify the particulars of the offence), contrary to s. 57(2) of the Criminal Code of Canada.

Section 57(3) Possession of forged passport or passport obtained by false statement

A.B., on the..........(day) of (month) ...., (year).........., at (specify time) in (specify place), without lawful excuse,

.... did have in his [OR her] possession a forged passport, to wit: (specify the particulars of the offence) contrary to 57(3) of the Criminal Code of Canada.

..........did have in his [OR her] possession a passport procured by making a false or misleading statement [OR containing a material alteration or addition obtained by making a false or misleading statement], to wit: (specify the particulars of the offence), contrary to s. 57(3) of the Criminal Code.

Section 58(1) Fraudulent use of certificate of citizenship or certificate of naturalization

A.B., on the..........(day) of (month) ...., (year).........., at (specify time) in (specify place),

..........did use a certificate of citizenship [OR a certificate of naturalization] for a fraudulent purpose, to wit: (specify the particulars of the offence), contrary to s. 58(1)(a) of the Criminal Code of Canada.

..........being a person to whom a certificate of a citizenship [OR a certificate of naturalization] had been granted under the provisions of the Canadian Citizenship Act, did knowingly part with possession of that certificate with intent that it be used for a fraudulent purpose, to wit: (specify the particulars of the offence), contrary to s. 58(1)(b) of the Criminal Code of Canada.

Section 61 Seditious offences

A.B., on the..........(day) of (month) ...., (year).........., at (specify time) in (specify place), did speak seditious words [OR did publish a seditious libel OR was a party to a seditious conspiracy], to wit: [specify the particulars of the offence], contrary to s. 61(a) [OR (b) OR (c)] of the Criminal Code of Canada.

Section 62(1) Offences in relation to members of military forces

A.B., on the..........(day) of (month) ...., (year).........., at (specify time) in (specify place), wilfully

.... did interfere with [OR impair OR influence] the loyalty [OR discipline] of C.D., a member of the Canadian forces [OR a member of the naval (OR army OR air) forces of (specify a state other than Canada) lawfully present in Canada], to wit: specify the particulars of the offence), contrary to s. 62(1)(a) of the Criminal Code of Canada.

.... did publish [OR edit OR issue OR circulate OR distribute] a writing that advises [OR counsels OR urges] insubordination [OR disloyalty OR mutiny OR refusal of duty] by C.D., a member of the Canadian forces [OR a member of the naval (OR army OR air) forces of (specify a state other than Canada) lawfully present in Canada] to wit: (specify the particulars of the offence), contrary to s. 62(1)(b) of the Criminal Code of Canada.

.... did advise [OR counsel OR urge OR cause] insubordination [OR disloyalty OR mutiny OR refusal of duty] by C.D., a member of the Canadian forces [OR a member of the naval (OR army OR air) forces of (specify a state other than Canada) lawfully present in Canada], to wit: (specify the particulars of the offence), contrary to s. 62(1)(c) of the Criminal Code of Canada.

Section 65 Rioting

A.B., on the..........(day) of (month) ...., (year).........., at (specify time) in (specify place),

..........was a member of a lawful assembly that had begun to disturb the peace tumultuously, and did thereby take part in a riot, to wit: (specify the particulars of the offence), contrary to s. 65 of the Criminal Code of Canada.

..........did take part in a riot, to wit: (specify the particulars of the offence), contrary to s. 65 of the Criminal Code of Canada.

Section 66 Unlawful assembly

A.B., on the..........(day) of (month) ...., (year).........., at (specify time) in (specify place),

..........was a member of an unlawful assembly, to wit: (specify the particulars of the offence), contrary to s. 66 of the Criminal Code of Canada.

..........with C.D. and E.F., with intent to carry out the common purpose of (specify what the common purpose was), did assemble themselves in such a manner [OR so conduct themselves when assembled] as to cause persons in the neighbourhood to fear on reasonable grounds that A.B. with the other persons there assembled, would disturb the peace tumultuously [OR would by such assembly needlessly and without any reasonable cause provoke other persons to disturb the peace tumultuously], to wit: (specify the particulars of the offence), contrary to s. 66 of the Criminal Code of Canada.

Section 68 Offences relating to proclamation to disperse

A.B., on the..........(day) of (month) ...., (year).........., at (specify time) in (specify place),

..........did oppose [OR hinder OR assault] wilfully and with force C.D., a person who began to make [OR was about to begin to make OR was making] a proclamation to disperse pursuant to s. 67, so that it was not made, to wit: (specify the particulars of the offence), contrary to s. 68(a) of the Criminal Code of Canada.

..........did not peaceably disperse and depart from a place where a proclamation to disperse pursuant to s. 67 was made within 30 minutes after it was made, to wit: (specify the particulars of the offence), contrary to s. 68(b) of the Criminal Code of Canada.

..........did not depart from a place within 30 minutes when A.B. had reasonable grounds to believe that the proclamation to disperse pursuant to s. 67 would have been made in that place if A.B. [OR C.D.] had not opposed [OR hindered OR assaulted], wilfully and with force, E.F., the person who would have made it, to wit: (specify the particulars of the offence), contrary to s. 68(c) of the Criminal Code of Canada.

Section 69 Peace officer failing to suppress riot

A.B., on the..........(day) of (month) ...., (year).........., at (specify time) in (specify place), being a peace officer who had received notice that there was a riot within his [OR her] jurisdiction, without reasonable excuse, did fail to take all reasonable steps to suppress the riot, to wit: (specify the particulars of the offence), contrary to s. 69 of the Criminal of Code of Canada.

Section 70(3) Contravention of orders prohibiting unlawful drilling

A.B., on the..........(day) of (month) ...., (year).........., at (specify time) in (specify place), did contravene an order made under s. 70(1) prohibiting assemblies, without lawful authority, for the purpose of training or drilling [OR of being trained or drilled to the use of arms OR of practising military exercises], to wit: (specify the particulars of the offence), contrary to s. 70(3) of the Criminal Code of Canada.

Section 71 Duelling Offences

A.B., on the..........(day) of (month) ...., (year).........., at (specify time) in (specify place),

..........did challenge [OR attempt by any means to provoke] C.D. to fight a duel, to wit: (specify the particulars of the offence), contrary to s. 71 of the Criminal Code of Canada.

..........did attempt to provoke E.F. to challenge C.D. to fight a duel, to wit: (specify the particulars of the offence), contrary to s. 71 of the Criminal Code of Canada.

..........did accept a challenge to fight a duel with C.D., to wit: (specify the particulars of the offence), contrary to s. 71 of the Criminal Code of Canada.

Section 73 Forcible entry and detainer

A.B., on the..........(day) of (month) ...., (year).........., at (specify time) in (specify place),

..........did commit forcible entry, to wit: (specify the particulars of the offence), contrary to s. 73 of the Criminal Code of Canada.

..........did enter (specify address), real property in the actual and peaceable possession of C.D., in a manner that was likely to cause a breach of the peace [OR reasonable apprehension of a breach of the peace], to wit: (specify the particulars of the offence), contrary to s. 73 of the Criminal Code of Canada.

..........did commit forcible detainer, to wit: (specify the particulars of the offence), contrary to s. 73 of the Criminal Code of Canada.

..........being in actual possession of (specify real property), without colour of right, did detain it in a manner that was likely to cause a breach of the peace [OR reasonable apprehension of a breach of the peace], against C.D., a person who was entitled by law to possess it, to wit: (specify the particulars of the offence), contrary to s. 73 of the Criminal Code of Canada.

Section 74 Piracy

A.B., on the..........(day) of (month) ...., (year).........., at (specify time) in (specify place), did commit piracy, to wit: (specify the particulars of the offence), contrary to s. 74 of the Criminal Code of Canada.

Section 75 Offences in connection with Canadian ships

A.B., on the..........(day) of (month) ...., (year).........., at (specify time) in (specify place),

..........did steal [OR did counsel C.D. to steal] a Canadian ship [OR part of the cargo (OR part of the supplies OR part of the fittings) in a Canadian ship], to wit: (specify the particulars of the offence), contrary to s. 75 of the Criminal Code of Canada.

..........without lawful authority, did throw overboard [OR damage OR destroy] part of the cargo [OR part of the supplies OR part of the fittings] in a Canadian ship, to wit: (specify the particulars of the offence), contrary to s. 75 of the Criminal Code of Canada.

..........without lawful authority did counsel C.D. to throw overboard [OR damage OR destroy] part of the cargo [OR part of the supplies OR part of the fittings] in a Canadian ship, to wit: (specify the particulars of the offence), contrary to s. 75 of the Criminal Code of Canada.

..........did [OR attempted to do OR counselled C.D. to do] a mutinous act on a Canadian ship, to wit: (specify the particulars of the offence), contrary to s. 75 of the Criminal Code of Canada.

Section 76 Aircraft Hijacking

A.B., on the..........(day) of (month) ...., (year).........., at (specify time) in (specify place), unlawfully, by force [OR threat of force OR (specify other form of intimidation)]

..........did seize [OR exercise control of] an aircraft with intent to cause C.D., a person on board the aircraft, to be confined [OR imprisoned] against his [OR her] will, to wit: (specify the particulars of the offence), contrary to s. 76(a) of the Criminal Code of Canada.

..........did seize [OR exercise control of] an aircraft with intent to cause C.D., a person on board the aircraft to be transported against his [OR her] will to (specify), a place other than the next scheduled landing place of the aircraft, to wit: (specify the particulars of the offence), contrary to s. 76(b) of the Criminal Code of Canada.

..........did seize [OR exercise control of] an aircraft with intent to hold C.D., a person on board the aircraft, for ransom [OR to service against his [OR her] will], to wit: (specify the particulars of the offence), contrary to s. 76(c) of the Criminal Code of Canada.

..........did seize [OR exercise control of] an aircraft with intent to cause the aircraft to deviate in a material respect from its flight plan, to wit: (specify the particulars of the offence), contrary to s. 76(d) of the Criminal Code of Canada.

Section 77 Endangering safety of airport or aircraft

A.B., on the..........(day) of (month) ...., (year).........., at (specify time) in (specify place),

..........did commit an act of violence against C.D., a person on board an aircraft in flight, that was likely to endanger the safety of the aircraft, to wit: (specify the particulars of the offence), contrary to s. 77(a) of the Criminal Code of Canada.

..........using a weapon, did commit an act of violence against C.D., a person at an airport serving international civil aviation, that caused [OR was likely to cause] serious injury [OR death] that endangered [OR was likely to endanger] safety at the airport, to wit: (specify the particulars of the offence), contrary to s. 77(b) of the Criminal Code of Canada.

..........did cause damage to an aircraft in service that rendered the aircraft incapable of flight [OR was likely to endanger the safety of the aircraft in flight], to wit: (specify the particulars of the offence), contrary to s. 77(c) of the Criminal Code of Canada.

..........did place [OR cause to be placed] on board an aircraft in service a (specify the thing placed on board) which was likely to cause damage to an aircraft that would render it incapable of flight [OR was likely to endanger the safety of an aircraft in flight], to wit: (specify the particulars of the offence), contrary to s. 77(d) of the Criminal Code of Canada.

..........did damage to [OR interfere with the operation of] an air navigation facility, which damage [OR interference] was likely to endanger the safety of an aircraft in flight, to wit: (specify the particulars of the offence), contrary to s. 77(e) of the Criminal Code of Canada.

..........using a weapon [OR substance OR device] did destroy [OR cause serious damage to] the facilities of an airport serving international civil aviation [OR to an aircraft not in service located there OR did cause disruption of services of the airport] that endangered [OR was likely to endanger] safety at the airport, to wit: (specify the particulars of the offence), contrary to s. 77(f) of the Criminal Code of Canada.

..........did endanger the safety of an aircraft in flight by communicating information to C.D. that A.B. knew to be false, to wit: (specify the particulars of the offence), contrary to s. 77(g) of the Criminal Code of Canada.

Section 78 Offensive weapons and explosive substances on board an aircraft

A.B., on the..........(day) of (month) ...., (year).........., at (specify time) in (specify place),

..........did take on board a civil aircraft an offensive weapon [OR an explosive substance] without the consent of C.D., the owner [OR the operator OR a person duly authorized by E.F., the owner (OR the operator) to consent thereto] to wit: (specify the particulars of the offence), contrary to s. 78(1)(a) of the Criminal Code of Canada.

..........did take on board a civil aircraft an offensive weapon [OR an explosive substance] without the consent of C.D., the owner [OR the operator OR a person duly authorized by E.F., the owner (OR the operator) to consent thereto] but without complying with the terms and conditions on which consent was given, to wit: (specify the particulars of the offence), contrary to s. 78(1)(b) of the Criminal Code of Canada.

Section 78.1(1) Seizing control of ship or fixed platform

A.B., on the..........(day) of (month) ...., (year).........., at (specify time) in (specify place), did seize [OR exercise control over] a ship [OR fixed platform] by force [OR threat of force OR specify another form of intimidation], to wit: (specify the particulars of the offence), contrary to s. 78(1) of the Criminal Code of Canada.

Section 78.1(2) Endangering safety of ship or fixed platform

A.B., on the..........(day) of (month) ...., (year).........., at (specify time) in (specify place), did commit an act of violence against C.D., a person on board a ship [OR fixed platform], where that act was likely to endanger the safe navigation of the ship [OR the safety of the fixed platform], to wit: (specify the particulars of the offence), contrary to s. 78.1(2)(a) of the Criminal Code of Canada.

Section 78.1(2)(b) Destroying or causing damage to ship or platform

A.B., on the..........(day) of (month) ...., (year).........., at (specify time) in (specify place), did destroy [OR cause damage] to a ship [OR the cargo of a ship OR to a fixed platform], where that act was likely to endanger the safe navigation of the ship [OR the safety of the fixed platform], to wit: (specify the particulars of the offence), contrary to s. 78.1(2)(b) of the Criminal Code of Canada.

Section 78.1(2)(c) Destroying or causing damage to maritime navigational facility

A.B., on the..........(day) of (month) ...., (year).........., at (specify time) in (specify place), did destroy [OR cause damage to OR interfere with the operation of] (specify), a maritime navigational facility, where that act was likely to endanger the safe navigation of the ship [OR the safety of the fixed platform], to wit: (specify the particulars of the offence), contrary to s. 78.1(2)(c) of the Criminal Code of Canada.

Section 78.1(2)(d) Placing on board a ship or fixed platform anything likely to cause damage

A.B., on the..........(day) of (month) ...., (year).........., at (specify time) in (specify place), did place [OR cause to be placed] on board a ship [OR fixed platform] anything that was likely to cause damage to the ship [OR to the cargo of a ship OR to the fixed platform], where that act was likely to endanger the safe navigation of the ship [OR the safety of the fixed platform], to wit: (specify the particulars of the offence), contrary to s. 78.1(2)(d) of the Criminal Code of Canada.

Section 78.1(3) False communication endangering safe navigation

A.B., on the..........(day) of (month) ...., (year).........., at (specify time) in (specify place), did communicate information that endangered the safe navigation of a ship, knowing the information to be false, to wit: (specify the particulars of the offence), contrary to s. 78.1(3) of the Criminal Code of Canada.

Section 78.1(4) Threats causing damage or injury on ship or fixed platform

A.B., on the..........(day) of (month) ...., (year).........., at (specify time) in (specify place), did threaten to commit an offence under s. 78.1(2)(a) [OR (b) OR (c)] of the Criminal Code in order to compel a person to do [OR refrain from doing] any act, where the threat is likely to endanger the safe navigation of a ship [OR the safety of a fixed platform], to wit: (specify the particulars of the offence), contrary to s. 78.1(4) of the Criminal Code of Canada.

Section 80 Breach of duty of care with explosive substances

A.B., on the..........(day) of (month) ...., (year).........., at (specify time) in (specify place), being a person who had an explosive substance in his [OR her] possession [OR under his care and control], did fail without lawful excuse to perform his [OR her] legal duty to use reasonable care to prevent bodily harm to C.D. [OR death to C.D. OR damage to property] by that explosive substance, to wit: (specify the particulars of the offence), contrary to s. 80 of the Criminal Code of Canada.

Section 81(1) Explosive substances offences

A.B., on the..........(day) of (month) ...., (year).........., at (specify time) in (specify place),

..........with intent to cause an explosion of (specify the type of explosive substance), an explosive substance that was likely to cause serious bodily harm to C.D. [OR death to C.D. OR damage to (specify the property) did (specify the act), to wit: (specify the particulars of the offence), contrary to s. 81(1)(a) of the Criminal Code of Canada.

..........with intent to do bodily harm to C.D., did cause (specify the type of explosive substance), an explosive substance to explode, to wit: (specify the particulars of the offence), contrary to s. 81(1)(b)(i) of the Criminal Code of Canada.

..........with intent to do bodily harm to C.D., did send [OR deliver] to C.D. [OR cause C.D. to take (OR receive)](specify the type of explosive substance or other dangerous substance or thing), an explosive substance [OR a dangerous substance (OR thing)], to wit: (specify the particulars of the offence), contrary to s. 8(1)(b)(ii) of the Criminal Code of Canada.

..........with intent to do bodily harm to C.D., did place on C.D. [OR throw at C.D. or throw on C.D. OR throw (specify where thrown)](specify the type of substance or thing thrown), a corrosive fluid [OR an explosive substance OR a dangerous substance OR a dangerous thing], to wit: (specify the particulars of the offence), contrary to s. 81(1)(b)(iii) of the Criminal Code of Canada.

..........with intent to destroy [OR damage] property without lawful excuse, did place [OR throw] (specify the type of explosive substance), an explosive substance (specify where), to wit: (specify the particulars of the offence), contrary to s. 81(1)(c) of the Criminal Code of Canada.

..........did make [OR have in his [OR her] possession OR have under his [OR her] care OR have under his [OR her] control] (specify the type of explosive substance), an explosive substance, with intent thereby to endanger the life of C.D. [OR to cause serious damage to property OR to enable E.F. to endanger the life of C.D. OR to enable E.F. to cause serious damage to property], to wit: (specify the particulars of the offence), contrary to s. 81(1)(d) of the Criminal Code of Canada.

Section 82(1) Possession of explosive substance without lawful excuse

A.B., on the..........(day) of (month) ...., (year).........., at (specify time) in (specify place), without lawful excuse did make [OR have in his (OR her) possession OR have under his (OR her) care or control] an explosive substance, to wit: (specify the particulars of the offence), contrary to s. 82(1) of the Criminal Code of Canada.

Section 82(2) Criminal organizations and explosive substances

A.B., on the..........(day) of (month) ...., (year).........., at (specify time) in (specify place), without lawful excuse, did make [OR have in his (OR her) possession OR have under his (OR her) care or control] an explosive substance for the benefit of [OR at the direction of OR in association with] a criminal organization, to wit: (specify the particulars of the offence), contrary to s. 82(2) of the Criminal Code of Canada.

Section 83(1) Prize fights

A.B., on the..........(day) of (month) ...., (year).........., at (specify time) in (specify place),

..........did engage as a principal in a prize fight, to wit: (specify the particulars of the offence), contrary to s. 83(1)(a) of the Criminal Code of Canada.

..........did advise [OR encourage OR promote] a prize fight, to wit: (specify the particulars of the offence), contrary to s. 83(1)(b) of the Criminal Code of Canada.

..........was present at a prize fight as an aid [OR as a second OR as a surgeon OR as an umpire OR as a backer OR as a reporter] to wit: (specify the particulars of the offence), contrary to s. 83(1)(c) of the Criminal Code of Canada.

Part III — Firearms and Other Offensive Weapons

Section 86(1) Careless use of firearm, prohibited weapon, restricted weapon, prohibited device, ammunition or prohibited ammunition

A.B., on the..........(day) of (month) ...., (year).........., at (specify time) in (specify place), without lawful excuse, did use [OR carry OR handle OR ship OR transport OR store] a firearm [OR a prohibited weapon OR a restricted weapon OR a prohibited device OR ammunition OR prohibited ammunition] in a careless manner [OR without reasonable precautions for the safety of C.D.], to wit: (specify the particulars of the offence), contrary to s. 86(1) of the Criminal Code of Canada.

Section 86(2) Contravention of storage regulations made under the Firearms Act respecting firearms and restricted weapons

A.B., on the..........(day) of (month) ...., (year).........., at (specify time) in (specify place), did contravene (specify the regulation made under s. 117(h) of the Firearms Act) respecting the storage [OR handling OR transportation OR shipping OR display OR advertising OR mail order sale] of firearms [OR restricted weapons], to wit: (specify the particulars of the offence), contrary to s. 86(2) of the Criminal Code of Canada.

Section 87(1) Pointing a firearm

A.B., on the..........(day) of (month) ...., (year).........., at (specify time) in (specify place), without lawful excuse, did point a firearm at C.D., to wit: (specify the particulars of the offence), contrary to s. 87(1) of the Criminal Code of Canada.

Section 88(1) Possession of weapon, imitation of weapon, prohibited device, ammunition or prohibited ammunition for a dangerous purpose

A.B., on the..........(day) of (month) ...., (year).........., at (specify time) in (specify place), did carry [OR possess] a weapon [OR an imitation of a weapon OR a prohibited device OR ammunition OR prohibited ammunition] for a purpose dangerous to the public peace [OR for the purpose of committing an offence], to wit: (specify the particulars of the offence), contrary to s. 88(1) of the Criminal Code of Canada.

Section 89(1) Carrying a weapon, prohibited device, ammunition or prohibited ammunition while attending public meeting

A.B., on the..........(day) of (month) ...., (year).........., at (specify time) in (specify place), without lawful excuse, did carry a weapon [OR a prohibited device OR ammunition OR prohibited ammunition] while attending [OR while on the way to attend] a public meeting, to wit: (specify the particulars of the offence), contrary to s. 89(1) of the Criminal Code of Canada.

Section 90(1) Carrying concealed weapon, prohibited device or prohibited ammunition without authorization

A.B., on the..........(day) of (month) ...., (year).........., at (specify time) in (specify place), did carry a concealed weapon [OR a prohibited device OR prohibited ammunition] without being authorized under the Firearms Act, to wit: (specify the particulars of the offence), contrary to s. 90(1) of the Criminal Code of Canada.

Section 91(1) Unauthorized possession of firearm

A.B., on the..........(day) of (month) ...., (year).........., at (specify time) in (specify place), not being the holder of a licence or a registration certificate, did possess a firearm, to wit: (specify the particulars of the offence), contrary to s. 91(1) of the Criminal Code of Canada.

Section 91(2) Unauthorized possession of prohibited weapon, restricted weapon, prohibited device or prohibited ammunition

A.B., on the..........(day) of (month) ...., (year).........., at (specify time) in (specify place), not being the holder of a licence, did possess a prohibited weapon [OR a restricted weapon OR a prohibited device OR prohibited ammunition], to wit: (specify the particulars of the offence), contrary to s. 91(2) of the Criminal Code of Canada.

Section 92(1) Possession of firearm knowing its possession is unauthorized

A.B., on the..........(day) of (month) ...., (year).........., at (specify time) in (specify place), did possess a firearm knowing that A.B. was not the holder of a licence or a registration certificate for the firearm, to wit: (specify the particulars of the offence), contrary to s. 92(1) of the Criminal Code of Canada.

Section 92(2) Unauthorized possession of prohibited weapon, restricted weapon, prohibited device or prohibited ammunition

A.B., on the..........(day) of (month) ...., (year).........., at (specify time) in (specify place), did possess a prohibited weapon [OR a restricted weapon OR a prohibited device OR prohibited ammunition] knowing that A.B. was not the holder of a licence to possess it, to wit: (specify the particulars of the offence), contrary to s. 92(2) of the Criminal Code of Canada.

Section 93(1) Possession of firearm, prohibited weapon, restricted weapon, prohibited device or prohibited ammunition at unauthorized place

A.B., on the..........(day) of (month) ...., (year).........., at (specify time) in (specify place), being the holder of an authorization [OR a licence] under which A.B. may possess a firearm [OR a prohibited weapon OR a restricted weapon OR a prohibited device OR prohibited ammunition], did possess the firearm [OR prohibited weapon OR restricted weapon OR prohibited device OR prohibited ammunition] at an unauthorized place, to wit: (specify the particulars of the offence), contrary to s. 93(1) of the Criminal Code of Canada.

Section 94(1) Unauthorized presence of firearm, prohibited weapon, restricted weapon, prohibited device or prohibited ammunition in a motor vehicle

A.B., on the..........(day) of (month) ...., (year).........., at (specify time) in (specify place), was the occupant of a motor vehicle in which A.B. knew there was an unauthorized firearm [OR a prohibited weapon OR a restricted weapon OR a prohibited device OR prohibited ammunition], to wit: (specify the particulars of the offence), contrary to s. 94(1) of the Criminal Code of Canada.

Section 95(1) Possession of prohibited or restricted firearm with ammunition

A.B., on the ....(day) of (month) ...., (year).........., at (specify time) in (specify place),

..........did possess a loaded prohibited firearm [OR restricted firearm] without an authorization, a licence or a registration certificate to possess the firearm, to wit: (specify the particulars of the offence), contrary to s. 95(1) of the Criminal Code of Canada.

..........did possess an unloaded prohibited firearm [OR restricted firearm] together with readily accessible ammunition that is capable of being discharged in the firearm, without an authorization, a licence or a registration certificate to possess the firearm, to wit: (specify the particulars of the offence), contrary to s. 95(1) of the Criminal Code of Canada.

Section 96(1) Possession of firearm, prohibited weapon, restricted weapon, prohibited device or prohibited ammunition obtained by commission of offence

A.B., on the..........(day) of (month) ...., (year).........., at (specify time) in (specify place), did possess a firearm [OR a prohibited weapon OR a restricted weapon OR a prohibited device OR prohibited ammunition] that A.B. knew was obtained by the commission of an offence [OR was obtained by an act or omission that would have been an offence if it had occurred in Canada], to wit: (specify the particulars of the offence), contrary to s. 96(1) of the Criminal Code of Canada.

Section 97(1) Sales of cross-bow to person without licence

A.B., on the..........(day) of (month) ...., (year).........., at (specify time) in (specify place), did sell [OR barter OR give a cross-bow] to C.D., without inspecting a licence produced by C.D. to possess the cross-bow [OR having inspected the licence produced by C.D., had reasonable grounds to believe that it was either invalid (OR not issued to C.D.)], to wit: (specify the particulars of the offence), contrary to s. 97(1) of the Criminal Code of Canada.

Section 99(1) Trafficking in firearms, prohibited weapons, restricted weapons, prohibited device, ammunition or prohibited ammunition

A.B., on the..........(day) of (month) ...., (year).........., at (specify time) in (specify place), did manufacture [OR transfer OR offer to manufacture OR offer to transfer] a firearm [OR a prohibited weapon OR a restricted weapon OR a prohibited device OR ammunition OR prohibited ammunition] for [OR to] C.D., without authorization, to wit: (specify the particulars of the offence), contrary to s. 99(1) of the Criminal Code of Canada.

Section 100 Possession of firearm, prohibited weapon, restricted weapon, prohibited device, ammunition or prohibited ammunition for purpose of trafficking

A.B., on the..........(day) of (month) ...., (year).........., at (specify time) in (specify place), did possess a firearm [OR a prohibited weapon OR a restricted weapon OR a prohibited device OR ammunition OR prohibited ammunition] for the purpose of transferring it [OR offering to transfer it] to C.D., without authorization, to wit: (specify the particulars of the offence), contrary to s. 100 of the Criminal Code of Canada.

Section 101 Transfer of firearm, prohibited weapon, ammunition or prohibited ammunition without authority

A.B., on the..........(day) of (month) ...., (year).........., at (specify time) in (specify place), did transfer a firearm [OR a prohibited weapon OR a restricted weapon OR a prohibited device OR ammunition OR prohibited ammunition] to C.D. without being authorized by law to do so, to wit: (specify the particulars of the offence), contrary to s. 101 of the Criminal Code of Canada.

Section 102(1) Making automatic firearm

A.B., on the..........(day) of (month) ...., (year).........., at (specify time) in (specify place), without lawful excuse,

..........did alter a firearm so that it is capable of discharging projectiles in rapid succession during one pressure of the trigger, to wit: (specify the particulars of the offence), contrary to s. 102(1) of the Criminal Code of Canada.

..........did manufacture [OR assemble] a firearm that is capable of discharging projectiles in rapid succession during one pressure of the trigger, to wit: (specify the particulars of the offence), contrary to s. 102(1) of the Criminal Code of Canada.

Section 103(1) Importing or exporting of firearm, prohibited weapon, restricted weapon, prohibited device or prohibited ammunition knowing that it is not authorized

A.B., on the..........(day) of (month) ...., (year).........., at (specify time) in (specify place), did import [OR export] a firearm [OR a prohibited weapon OR a restricted weapon OR a prohibited device OR prohibited ammunition], knowing that A.B. is not authorized by law, to wit: (specify the particulars of the offence), contrary to s. 103(1) of the Criminal Code of Canada.

Section 103(1) Unauthorized importing or exporting component or part for automatic firearm knowing it is not authorized

A.B., on the..........(day) of (month) ...., (year).........., at (specify time) in (specify place), did import [OR export], a component [OR part] designed exclusively for use in the manufacture of [OR the assembly into] an automatic firearm, knowing that A.B. is not authorized by law, to wit: (specify the particulars of the offence), contrary to s. 103(1) of the Criminal Code of Canada.

Section 104(1)(a) Unauthorized importing or exporting of firearm, prohibited weapon, restricted weapon, prohibited device or prohibited ammunition

A.B., on the..........(day) of (month) ...., (year).........., at (specify time) in (specify place), did import [OR export], a firearm [OR a prohibited weapon OR a restricted weapon OR a prohibited device OR prohibited ammunition], without authorization by law, to wit: (specify the particulars of the offence), contrary to s. 104(1) of the Criminal Code of Canada.

Section 104(1)(b) Unauthorized importing or exporting component or part for automatic firearm

A.B., on the..........(day) of (month) ...., (year).........., at (specify time) in (specify place), did import [OR export], a component [OR a part] designed exclusively for use in the manufacture of [OR the assembly into] an automatic firearm, to wit: (specify the particulars of the offence), contrary to s. 104(1) of the Criminal Code of Canada.

Section 105(1)(a) Reporting the loss of a firearm, prohibited weapon, restricted weapon, prohibited device, prohibited ammunition, authorization, licence, or registration certificate

A.B., on the..........(day) of (month) ...., (year).........., at (specify time) in (specify place), did not with reasonable dispatch, report the loss of a firearm [OR a prohibited weapon OR a restricted weapon OR a prohibited device OR prohibited ammunition OR an authorization OR a licence OR a registration certificate] to a peace officer or firearms officer or chief firearms officer, to wit: (specify the particulars of the offence), contrary to s. 105(1) of the Criminal Code of Canada.

Section 105(1)(a) Reporting that firearm, prohibited weapon, restricted weapon, prohibited device, prohibited ammunition, authorization, licence, or registration certificate had been stolen

A.B., on the..........(day) of (month) ...., (year).........., at (specify time) in (specify place), did not with reasonable dispatch report that a firearm [OR a prohibited weapon OR a restricted weapon OR a prohibited device OR prohibited ammunition OR an authorization OR a licence OR a registration certificate] had been stolen to a peace officer or firearms officer or chief firearms officer, to wit: (specify the particulars of the offence), contrary to s. 105(1) of the Criminal Code of Canada.

Section 105(1)(b) Failure to deliver or report the finding of a firearm, prohibited weapon, restricted weapon, prohibited device or prohibited ammunition

A.B., on the..........(day) of (month) ...., (year).........., at (specify time) in (specify place), did not with reasonable dispatch deliver [OR report finding] a firearm [OR prohibited weapon OR restricted weapon OR prohibited device OR prohibited ammunition] that A.B. has reasonable grounds to believe has been lost or abandoned, to wit: (specify the particulars of the offence), contrary to s. 105(1) of the Criminal Code of Canada.

Section 106(1) Failure to report on destruction of firearm, prohibited weapon, restricted weapon, prohibited device or prohibited ammunition

A.B., on the..........(day) of (month) ...., (year).........., at (specify time) in (specify place), did not with reasonable dispatch report the destruction of a firearm [OR prohibited weapon OR restricted weapon OR prohibited device OR prohibited ammunition] after destroying it [OR having possession of it and become aware of its destruction], to wit: (specify the particulars of the offence), contrary to s. 106(1) of the Criminal Code of Canada.

Section 107(1) False statements regarding loss, theft or destruction of firearm, prohibited weapon, restricted weapon, prohibited device, prohibited ammunition, authorization, licence or registration certificate

A.B., on the..........(day) of (month) ...., (year).........., at (specify time) in (specify place), knowingly, did make a false report [OR statement] concerning the loss [OR theft OR destruction] of a firearm [OR a prohibited weapon OR a restricted weapon OR a prohibited device OR prohibited ammunition OR authorization OR a licence OR a registration certificate] before C.D. [a peace officer OR firearms officer OR chief firearms officer], to wit: (specify the particulars of the offence), contrary to s. 107(1) of the Criminal Code of Canada.

Section 108(1) Tampering with a serial number

A.B., on the..........(day) of (month) ...., (year).........., at (specify time) in (specify place), without lawful excuse,

.... did alter [OR deface OR remove] a serial number on a firearm, to wit: (specify the particulars of the offence), contrary to s. 108(1)(a) of the Criminal Code.

.... did possess a firearm knowing that the serial number on it had been altered [OR defaced OR removed], to wit: (specify the particulars of the offence), contrary to s. 108(1)(b) of the Criminal Code.

Part IV — Offences Against the Administration of Law and Justice

Section 119(1)(a) Corruption of judges, members of Parliament and members of provincial legislatures — accepting bribes

A.B., on the..........(day) of (month) ...., (year).........., at (specify time) in (specify place), being the holder of a judicial office [OR being a member of Parliament (OR of the legislature of a province)] corruptly did accept [OR obtain OR agree to accept OR attempt to obtain] money [OR valuable consideration OR office OR place OR employment] for himself [OR herself OR C.D.] in respect of (specify anything done OR omitted OR to be done OR to be omitted) by C.D. in his [OR her] official capacity, to wit: (specify the particulars of the offence), contrary to s. 119(1)(a) of the Criminal Code of Canada.

Section 119(1)(b) Corruption of judges, members of Parliament and members of provincial legislature — offering bribes

A.B., on the..........(day) of (month) ...., (year).........., at (specify time) in (specify place), did give [OR offer] corruptly to C.D., a person who holds a judicial office [OR is a member of Parliament (OR of the legislature of a province)] money [OR valuable consideration OR office OR place OR employment] in respect of (specify anything done OR omitted OR to be done OR to be omitted) by C.D. in his [OR her] official capacity for A.B. [OR C.D.], to wit: (specify the particulars of the offence), contrary to s. 119(1)(b) of the Criminal Code of Canada.

Section 120(a) Corruption of person employed in the administration of criminal law — accepting bribes

A.B., on the..........(day) of (month) ...., (year).........., at (specify time) in (specify place), being a justice [OR a police commissioner OR a peace officer OR a public officer OR an officer of a juvenile court OR a person who employed in the administration of criminal law] corruptly did accept [OR did obtain OR did agree to accept OR did attempt to obtain] for himself [OR herself OR C.D.] money [OR valuable consideration OR an office OR a place OR employment] with intent to interfere with the administration of justice [OR with intent to procure or facilitate the commission of an offence OR with intent to protect from detection (OR punishment) E.F., a person who has committed [OR who intends to commit] an indictable offence, to wit: (specify the particulars of the offence), contrary to s. 120(a) of the Criminal Code of Canada.

Section 120(b) Corruption of persons employed in the administration of criminal law — offering bribes

A.B., on the..........(day) of (month) ...., (year).........., at (specify time) in (specify place), did give [OR offer] corruptly to C.D., a justice [OR police commissioner OR peace officer OR public officer OR officer of a juvenile court OR a person who was employed in the administration of criminal law] money [OR valuable consideration OR office OR place OR employment] with intent that C.D. should interfere with the administration of justice [OR procure (OR facilitate) the commission of an offence OR protect from detection (OR punishment) E.F., a person who has committed (OR who intends to commit) an offence], to wit: (specify the particulars of the offence), contrary to s. 120(b) of the Criminal Code of Canada.

Section 121(1)(a) – (e) Frauds on the government

A.B., on the..........(day) of (month) ...., (year).........., at (specify time) in (specify place),

..........directly [OR indirectly] did give [OR offer OR agree to give (OR offer)] to C.D., an official [OR a member of the family of E.F., an official, OR for the benefit of E.F., an official], a loan [OR a reward OR an advantage OR a benefit] as consideration for cooperation [OR assistance OR the exercise of influence OR an act OR an omission] in connection with the transaction of business with the government [OR matter of business relating to the government OR a claim against Her Majesty OR any benefit that Her Majesty is entitled to bestow], to wit: (specify the particulars of the offence), contrary to s. 121(1)(a) of the Criminal Code of Canada.

..........having dealings of any kind with the government, did pay a commission [OR reward] to [OR confer an advantage (OR benefit of any kind) on] C.D., an employee [OR official] of the government with which A.B. dealt [OR to any member of the family of C.D. OR to E.F. for the benefit of the employee (OR official)] with respect to those dealings without the consent in writing of the head of the branch of government with which A.B. dealt, to wit: (specify the particulars of the offence), contrary to s. 121(1)(b) of the Criminal Code of Canada.

..........being an official [OR employee] of the government, did demand [OR accept OR offer (OR agree) to accept] from C.D., a person who had dealings with the government, a commission [OR reward OR advantage OR benefit of any kind] directly [OR indirectly] by himself [OR by herself OR through any one for his (OR her) benefit] without the consent in writing of the head of the branch of government that employed A.B. [OR of which A.B. was an official], to wit: (specify the particulars of the offence), contrary to s. 121(1)(c) of the Criminal Code of Canada.

..........having [OR pretending to have] influence with the government [OR with a minister of the government OR an official] did demand [OR accept OR offer OR agree to accept] for himself [OR for herself OR for C.D.] a reward [OR advantage OR benefit of any kind] as consideration for cooperation [OR assistance OR exercise of influence OR an act (OR omission)] in connection with the transaction of business with [OR any matter of business relating to] the government [OR a claim against Her Majesty OR any benefit that Her Majesty is authorized (OR is entitled) to bestow OR the appointment of A.B. (OR E.F.) to an office], to wit: (specify the particulars of the offence), contrary to s. 121(1)(d) of the Criminal Code of Canada.

..........did give [OR offer OR agree to give (OR offer)] to C.D., a minister of the government [OR an official] a reward [OR advantage OR benefit of any kind] as consideration for cooperation [OR assistance OR exercise of influence OR an act (OR omission)] in connection with the transaction of business with [OR any matter of business relating to] the government [OR a claim against Her Majesty OR any benefit that Her Majesty is authorized (OR is entitled) to bestow OR the appointment of A.B. (OR E.F.) to an office], to wit: (specify the particulars of the offence), contrary to s. 121(1)(e) of the Criminal Code of Canada.

Section 121(f) Frauds on the government — In connection with tenders

A.B., on the..........(day) of (month) ...., (year).........., at (specify time) in (specify place),

..........having made a tender to obtain a contract with the government, did give [OR offer OR agree to give (OR offer)] to C.D., a person who had made a tender [OR to a member of his (OR her) family OR to E.F. for the benefit of C.D.] a reward [OR advantage OR benefit of any kind] as consideration for the withdrawal of the tender of that person, to wit: (specify the particulars of the offence), contrary to s. 121(1)(f) of the Criminal Code of Canada.

..........having made a tender to obtain a contract with the government, did demand [OR accept OR offer (OR agree) to accept] from C.D., a person who had made a tender, a reward [OR advantage OR benefit of any kind] as consideration for the withdrawal of his (OR her) tender, to wit: (specify the particulars of the offence), contrary to s. 121(1)(f) of the Criminal Code of Canada.

Section 121(2) Frauds on the government — In connection with elections

A.B., on the..........(day) of (month) ...., (year).........., at (specify time) in (specify place), in order to obtain [OR retain] a contract with the government [OR as a term of any such contract, whether express or implied] directly [OR indirectly] did subscribe [OR give OR agree to subscribe (OR give)] to C.D., valuable consideration for the purpose of promoting the election of a candidate [OR class (OR party) of candidates] to Parliament [OR the legislature of a province] [OR with intent to influence (OR affect) in any way the result of an election conducted for the purpose of electing persons to serve in Parliament (OR the legislature of a province)], to wit: (specify the particulars of the offence), contrary to s. 121(2) of the Criminal Code of Canada.

Section 122 Fraud or breach of trust by public officer

A.B., on the..........(day) of (month) ...., (year).........., at (specify time) in (specify place), did commit fraud [OR a breach of trust] in connection with the duties of his [OR her] office, to wit: (specify the particulars of the offence), contrary to s. 122 of the Criminal Code of Canada.

Section 123(1)(a) Corrupting a municipal official

A.B., on the..........(day) of (month) ...., (year).........., at (specify time) in (specify place), did give [OR offer OR agree to give (OR offer)] to C.D., a municipal official, a loan [OR reward OR advantage OR benefit of any kind] as consideration for C.D. to abstain from voting at a meeting [OR a committee] of the municipal council [OR to vote in favour of (OR against) a measure (OR motion OR resolution) OR to aid in procuring (OR preventing) the adoption of a measure (OR motion OR resolution) OR to perform (OR fail to perform) an official act], to wit: contrary to s. 123(1)(a) of the Criminal Code of Canada.

Section 123(1)(b) Being a corrupt municipal official

A.B., on the..........(day) of (month) ...., (year).........., at (specify time) in (specify place), being a municipal official, did demand [OR accept OR offer (OR agree) to accept] from C.D. a loan [OR reward OR advantage OR benefit of any kind] as consideration for A.B. to abstain from voting at a meeting [OR a committee] of the municipal council [OR to vote in favour of (OR against) a measure (OR motion OR resolution) OR to perform (OR fail to perform) an official act], to wit: (specify the particulars of the offence), contrary to s. 123(1)(b) of the Criminal Code of Canada.

Section 123(2) Influencing municipal official

A.B., on the..........(day) of (month) ...., (year).........., at (specify time) in (specify place),

..........being a person who was under a duty to disclose the truth, did influence [OR attempt to influence] C.D., a municipal official, by suppression of the truth, to abstain from voting at a meeting [OR at a committee] of the municipal council [OR to vote in favour of (OR against) a measure (OR motion OR resolution)] [OR to aid in procuring (OR preventing) the adoption of a measure (OR motion OR resolution)] [OR to perform (OR fail to perform) an official act], to wit: (specify the particulars of the offence), contrary to s. 123(2) of the Criminal Code of Canada.

..........did influence [OR attempt to influence] C.D., a municipal official, by threats [OR by deceit OR by (specify other unlawful means)], to abstain from voting at a meeting [OR at a committee] of the municipal council [OR to vote in favour of (OR against) a measure (OR motion OR resolution)] [OR to aid in procuring (OR preventing) the adoption of a measure (OR motion OR resolution)] [OR to perform

(OR fail to perform) an official act], to wit: (specify the particulars of the offence), contrary to s. 123(2) of the Criminal Code of Canada.

Section 124(a) Selling office

A.B., on the..........(day) of (month) ...., (year).........., at (specify time) in (specify place),

..........did purport to sell [OR agree to sell] the appointment of C.D. to [OR the resignation of C.D. from OR the consent to the appointment of C.D. to OR the consent to the resignation of C.D. from] (specify the office), to wit: (specify the particulars of the offence), contrary to s. 124(a) of the Criminal Code of Canada.

..........did receive [OR agree to receive] a reward [OR profit] from the purported sale of the appointment of C.D. to [OR the resignation of C.D. from OR the consent to the appointment of C.D. to OR the consent to the resignation of C.D. from] (specify the office), to wit: (specify the particulars of the offence), contrary to s. 124(a) of the Criminal Code of Canada.

Section 124(b) Purchasing office

A.B., on the..........(day) of (month) ...., (year).........., at (specify time) in (specify place), did purport to [OR agree to OR promise to] purchase [OR give a reward (OR profit) for] the appointment of C.D. to [OR the resignation of C.D. from OR the consent to the appointment of C.D. to OR the consent to the resignation of C.D. from] (specify the office), to wit: (specify the particulars of the offence), contrary to s. 124(b) of the Criminal Code of Canada.

Section 125(a) Influencing appointments

A.B., on the..........(day) of (month) ...., (year).........., at (specify time) in (specify place), did receive [OR agree to receive] [OR give OR procure to be given] directly [OR indirectly] a reward [OR advantage OR benefit of any kind] as consideration for cooperation [OR assistance OR exercise of influence] to secure the appointment of C.D. to (specify the office), to wit: (specify the particulars of the offence), contrary to s. 125(a) of the Criminal Code of Canada.

Section 125(b) Negotiating appointments

A.B., on the..........(day) of (month) ...., (year).........., at (specify time) in (specify place), did solicit [OR recommend OR negotiate] with respect to the appointment of C.D. to [OR resignation of C.D. from] (specify the office) in expectation of a direct [OR indirect] reward [OR advantage OR benefit], to wit: (specify the particulars of the offence), contrary to s. 125(b) of the Criminal Code of Canada.

Section 125(c) Keeping a place for dealing in offices

A.B., on the..........(day) of (month) ...., (year).........., at (specify time) in (specify place), without lawful authority did keep a place for transacting [OR negotiating] business relating to the filling of vacancies in offices [OR the sale (OR purchase) of offices OR appointments to (OR resignations from) offices], to wit: (specify the particulars of the offence), contrary to s. 125(c) of the Criminal Code of Canada.

Section 126 Disobeying a statute

A.B., on the..........(day) of (month) ...., (year).........., at (specify time) in (specify place), without a lawful excuse, did contravene (specify an Act of Parliament) by wilfully doing (specify a thing it forbids) [OR by wilfully omitting to do (specify a thing it requires to be done)], to wit: (specify the particulars of the offence), contrary to s. 126 of the Criminal Code of Canada.

Section 127 Disobeying an order of court

A.B., on the..........(day) of (month) ...., (year).........., at (specify time) in (specify place), without lawful excuse, did disobey a lawful order made by (specify a court of justice) [OR by C.D., a person (OR body of persons) authorized by (specify an Act of Parliament) to make (OR give) the order], to wit: (specify the particulars of the offence), contrary to s. 127 of the Criminal Code of Canada.

Section 128 Misconduct in the execution of process

A.B., on the..........(day) of (month) ...., (year).........., at (specify time) in (specify place), being a peace officer [OR coroner], being entrusted with the execution of a process, wilfully, did misconduct himself [OR herself] in the execution of the process [OR did make a false return to the process], to wit: (specify the particulars of the offence), contrary to s. 128 of the Criminal Code of Canada.

Section 129(a) Resisting or obstructing peace officer

A.B., on the..........(day) of (month) ...., (year).........., at (specify time) in (specify place), did resist (OR wilfully obstruct) C.D., a peace officer [OR a public officer] in the execution of his [OR her] duty, to wit: (specify the particulars of the offence), contrary to s. 129(a) of the Criminal Code of Canada.

Section 129(b) Omitting to assist public officer or peace officer

A.B., on the..........(day) of (month) ...., (year).........., at (specify time) in (specify place), without reasonable excuse, did omit to assist C.D., a public [OR peace] officer, in the execution of his [OR her] duty in arresting E.F. [OR in preserving the peace] after having reasonable notice that A.B. was required to do so, to wit: (specify the particulars of the offence), contrary to s. 129(b) of the Criminal Code of Canada.

Section 129(c) Execution of process

A.B., on the..........(day) of (month) ...., (year).........., at (specify time) in (specify place),

..........did resist [OR wilfully obstruct] C.D. in the lawful execution of a process against land [OR goods], to wit: (specify the particulars of the offence), contrary to s. 129(c) of the Criminal Code of Canada.

..........did resist [OR wilfully obstruct] C.D. in making a lawful distress [OR seizure], to wit: (specify the particulars of the offence), contrary to s. 129(c) of the Criminal Code of Canada.

Section 130 Personating a peace officer or a public officer

A.B., on the..........(day) of (month) ...., (year).........., at (specify time) in (specify place),

..........did falsely represent himself [OR herself] to be a peace officer [OR public officer], to wit: (specify the particulars of the offence), contrary to s. 130(a) of the Criminal Code of Canada.

..........not being a peace officer [OR public officer], did use a badge [OR article of uniform OR equipment] in a manner that was likely to cause C.D. to believe that A.B. was a peace officer [OR public officer], to wit: (specify the particulars of the offence), contrary to s. 130(b) of the Criminal Code of Canada.

Section 132 Perjury

A.B., on the..........(day) of (month) ...., (year).........., at (specify time) in (specify place),

..........did commit perjury, to wit: (specify the particulars of the offence), contrary to s. 132 of the Criminal Code of Canada.

..........being specially permitted, authorized or required by law to make a statement under oath or solemn affirmation, did make a false statement by affidavit [OR solemn declaration OR deposition OR orally] before C.D., a person authorized by law to permit it to be made before him [OR her], knowing that the statement was false, to wit: (specify the particulars of the offence), contrary to s. 132 of the Criminal Code of Canada.

Section 134(1) False statements

A.B., on the..........(day) of (month) ...., (year).........., at (specify time) in (specify place), not being specially permitted, authorized or required by law to make a statement under oath or solemn affirmation, did make a statement by affidavit [OR solemn declaration OR deposition OR orally] before C.D., a person authorized by law to permit it to be made before him, knowing that the statement was false, to wit: (specify the particulars of the offence), contrary to s. 134(1) of the Criminal Code of Canada.

Section 136(1) Witness giving contradictory evidence

A.B., on the..........(day) of (month) ...., (year).........., at (specify time) in (specify place), being a witness in a judicial proceeding, gave evidence with respect to a matter of fact [OR knowledge] and subsequently, in a judicial proceeding, gave evidence that was contrary to his [OR her] previous evidence, to wit: (specify the particulars of the offence), contrary to s. 136(1) of the Criminal Code of Canada.

Section 137 Fabricating evidence

A.B., on the..........(day) of (month) ...., (year).........., at (specify time) in (specify place), with intent to mislead, did fabricate (specify the thing fabricated) with intent that it should be used as evidence in a judicial proceeding, by a means other than perjury or incitement to perjury, to wit: (specify the particulars of the offence), contrary to s. 137 of the Criminal Code of Canada.

Section 138(a) Offences relating to affidavits

A.B., on the..........(day) of (month) ...., (year).........., at (specify time) in (specify place), did sign a writing that purported to be an affidavit [OR statutory declaration] and to have been sworn [OR declared] before him [OR her] when the writing was not so sworn [OR when the writing was not so declared OR when he (OR she) knew that he (OR she) had no authority to administer the oath (OR declaration)], to wit: (specify the particulars of the offence), contrary to s. 138(a) of the Criminal Code of Canada.

..........did use [OR offered for use] writing purporting to be an affidavit [OR statutory declaration] that he (OR she) knew was not sworn [OR declared (as the case may be)] by the affiant [OR declarant OR before a person authorized in that behalf], to wit: (specify the particulars of the offence), contrary to s. 138(b) of the Criminal Code of Canada.

..........did sign as affiant [OR declarant] a writing that purported to be an affidavit [OR statutory declaration] and to have been sworn [OR declared] by A.B. when the writing was not so sworn [OR declared], to wit: (specify the particulars of the offence), contrary to s. 138(c) of the Criminal Code of Canada.

Section 139(1) Obstructing justice

A.B., on the..........(day) of (month) ...., (year).........., at (specify time) in (specify place),

..........did wilfully attempt to obstruct [OR pervert OR defeat] the course of justice in a judicial proceeding, by indemnifying [OR by agreeing to indemnify] C.D., a surety, to wit: (specify the particulars of the offence), contrary to s. 139(1)(a) of the Criminal Code of Canada.

..........being a surety, did wilfully attempt to obstruct [OR pervert OR defeat] the course of justice in a judicial proceeding, by accepting [OR by agreeing to accept] a fee [OR an indemnity] from [OR in respect of] C.D., a person who was released [OR who was to be released] from custody, to wit: (specify the particulars of the offence), contrary to s. 139(1)(b) of the Criminal Code of Canada.

Section 140(1)(a) Public mischief

A.B., on the..........(day) of (month) ...., (year).........., at (specify time) in (specify place),

..........with intent to mislead, did cause C.D., a peace officer, to enter on [OR continue] an investigation by making a false statement that accused E.F. of having committed an offence, to wit: (specify the particulars of the offence), contrary to s. 140(1)(a) of the Criminal Code of Canada.

..........with intent to mislead, did cause C.D., a peace officer, to enter on [OR continue] an investigation by (specify anything), with the intention of causing E.F. to be suspected of having committed an offence which E.F. had not committed [OR with the intention of diverting suspicion from himself (OR herself)], to wit: (specify the particulars of the offence), contrary to s. 140(1)(b) of the Criminal Code of Canada.

..........with intent to mislead, did cause C.D., a peace officer, to enter on [OR continue] an investigation by reporting that the offence of (specify an offence) had been committed when it had not been committed, to wit: (specify the particulars of the offence), contrary to s. 140(1)(c) of the Criminal Code of Canada.

..........with intent to mislead, did cause C.D., a peace officer, to enter on [OR continue] an investigation by reporting [OR by making it known OR by causing it to be made known that A.B. [OR E.F.] had died, when A.B. [OR E.F.] had not died, to wit: (specify the particulars of the offence), contrary to s. 140(1)(d) of the Criminal Code of Canada.

Section 141(1) Compounding indictable offence

A.B., on the..........(day) of (month) ...., (year).........., at (specify time) in (specify place), did ask for [OR obtain OR agree to receive OR agree to obtain] valuable consideration for himself [OR for herself OR for C.D.] by agreeing to compound [OR conceal] an indictable offence of (specify the indictable offence), to wit: (specify the particulars of the offence), contrary to s. 141(1) of the Criminal Code of Canada.

Section 142 Corruptly taking reward for recovery of goods

A.B., on the..........(day) of (month) ...., (year).........., at (specify time) in (specify place), corruptly did accept valuable consideration under pretence [OR upon account] of helping C.D. to recover (specify the thing recovered) obtained by the commission of an indictable offence of (specify the indictable offence), to wit: (specify the particulars of the offence), contrary to s. 142 of the Criminal Code of Canada.

Section 143 Advertising reward and immunity

A.B., on the..........(day) of (month) ...., (year).........., at (specify time) in (specify place),

..........publicly did advertise a reward for the return of (specify thing) that had been stolen [OR lost] and in the advertisement did use words to indicate that no questions would be asked if it was returned, to wit: (specify the particulars of the offence), contrary to s. 143(a) of the Criminal Code of Canada.

..........in a public advertisement did use words to indicate that a reward would be given [OR paid] for (specify thing) that had been stolen [OR lost] without interference with [OR inquiry about] the person who produced it, to wit: (specify the particulars of the offence), contrary to s. 143(b) of the Criminal Code of Canada.

..........in a public advertisement did promise [OR offer] to return to a person who had advanced money by way of loan on [OR had bought] (specify thing) that had been stolen [OR lost] the money so advanced [OR paid OR any other sum of money] for the return of that thing, to wit: (specify the particulars of the offence), contrary to s. 143(c) of the Criminal Code of Canada.

..........did print [OR publish] an advertisement (specify as provided in s. 143(a) [OR s. 143(b) OR s. 143(c)), to wit: (specify the particulars of the offence), contrary to s. 143(d) of the Criminal Code of Canada.

Section 144 Prison breach

A.B., on the..........(day) of (month) ...., (year).........., at (specify time) in (specify place),

..........by force [OR violence] did break a prison, with intent to set at liberty himself [OR herself OR C.D., a person confined therein], to wit: (specify the particulars of the offence), contrary to s. 144(a) of the Criminal Code of Canada.

..........with intent to escape did forcibly break out of [OR make a breach in] the cell [OR (specify what other place) within the prison in which A.B. was confined], to wit: (specify the particulars of the offence), contrary to s. 144(b) of the Criminal Code of Canada.

Section 145(1)(a) Escaping lawful custody

A.B., on the..........(day) of (month) ...., (year).........., at (specify time) in (specify place), did escape from lawful custody, to wit: (specify the particulars of the offence), contrary to s. 145(1)(a) of the Criminal Code of Canada.

Section 145(1)(b) Being at large without lawful excuse

A.B., on the..........(day) of (month) ...., (year).........., at (specify time) in (specify place), was at large within [OR outside] Canada without lawful excuse before the expiration of a term of imprisonment to which A.B. was sentenced, to wit: (specify the particulars of the offence), contrary to s. 145(1)(b) of the Criminal Code of Canada.

Section 145(2)(a) Failure to attend at court when at large on undertaking or recognizance

A.B., on the..........(day) of (month) ...., (year).........., at (specify time) in (specify place), being at large on an undertaking [OR recognizance] given to [OR entered into before] C.D., a justice [OR judge], did fail without lawful excuse to attend at court in accordance therewith [OR to surrender himself (OR herself) in accordance with the order of C.D.], to wit: (specify the particulars of the offence), contrary to s. 145(2)(a) of the Criminal Code of Canada.

Section 145(2)(b) Failure to attend at court after appearing before court, justice or judge

A.B., on the..........(day) of (month) ...., (year).........., at (specify time) in (specify place), having appeared before a court [OR C.D., a justice OR C.D., a judge], did fail without lawful excuse to attend court as thereafter required by the court [OR C.D.] [OR to surrender himself in accordance with the order of the court (OR C.D.)], to wit: (specify the particulars of the offence), contrary to s. 145(1)(b) of the Criminal Code of Canada.

Section 145(3) Failure to comply with condition of undertaking or recognizance

A.B., on the..........(day) of (month) ...., (year).........., at (specify time) in (specify place), being at large on an undertaking [OR recognizance] given to [OR entered into before] C.D., a justice [OR judge], did fail without lawful excuse to comply with a condition of that undertaking [OR recognizance (OR a direction ordered under s. 515(12) or s. 522(2.1) prohibiting communication with a witness or other person)] directed by C.D., to wit: (specify the particulars of the offence), contrary to s. 145(3) of the Criminal Code of Canada.

Section 145(4) Failure to appear or to comply with summons

A.B., on the..........(day) of (month) ...., (year).........., at (specify time) in (specify place), having being served with a summons,

..........did fail without lawful excuse to appear at the time and place stated therein for the purposes of the Identification of Criminals Act, to wit: (specify the particulars of the offence), contrary to s. 145(4) of the Criminal Code of Canada.

..........did fail without lawful excuse to attend at court in accordance therewith, to wit: (specify the particulars of the offence), contrary to s. 145(4) of the Criminal Code of Canada.

Section 145(5) Failure to appear or to comply with appearance notice or promise to appear

A.B., on the..........(day) of (month) ...., (year).........., at (specify time) in (specify place), having been named in an appearance notice [OR a promise to appear OR a recognizance entered into before C.D., an officer in charge], that was confirmed by E.F., a justice, under s. 508,

..........did fail without lawful excuse to appear at the time and place stated therein for the purposes of the Identification of Criminals Act, to wit: (specify the particulars of the offence), contrary to s. 145(5) of the Criminal Code of Canada.

..........did fail without lawful excuse to attend court in accordance therewith, to wit: (specify the particulars of the offence), contrary to s. 145(5) of the Criminal Code of Canada.

Section 145(5.1) Failure to comply with conditions of an undertaking

A.B., on the ....(day) of (month) ...., (year).........., at (specify time) in (specify place),

..........did fail without lawful excuse to comply with a condition of an undertaking entered into pursuant to s. 499(2) [OR s. 503(2.1)], to wit: (specify the particulars of the offence), contrary to s. 145(5) of the Criminal Code of Canada.

Section 146 Permitting or assisting escape

A.B., on the..........(day) of (month) ...., (year).........., at (specify time) in (specify place),

..........did permit C.D., a person who A.B. had in lawful custody, to escape such custody by failing to perform a legal duty, to wit: (specify the particulars of the offence), contrary to s. 146(a) of the Criminal Code of Canada.

..........did convey [OR cause to be conveyed] into a prison a (specify the thing conveyed), with intent to facilitate the escape of C.D., a person imprisoned therein, to wit: (specify the particulars of the offence), contrary to s. 146(b) of the Criminal Code of Canada.

..........did direct [OR procure], under colour of pretended authority, the discharge of C.D., a prisoner who was not entitled to be discharged, to wit: (specify the particulars of the offence), contrary to s. 146(c) of the Criminal Code of Canada.

Section 147 Rescue or permitting escape

A.B., on the..........(day) of (month) ...., (year).........., at (specify time) in (specify place),

..........did rescue C.D. in escaping [OR in attempting to escape] from lawful custody, to wit: (specify the particulars of the offence), contrary to s. 147(a) of the Criminal Code of Canada.

..........did assist C.D. in escaping [OR in attempting to escape] from lawful custody, to wit: (specify the particulars of the offence), contrary to s. 147(a) of the Criminal Code of Canada.

..........did wilfully permit C.D., a person his [OR her] in lawful custody to escape, to wit: (specify the particulars of the offence), contrary to s. 147(b) of the Criminal Code of Canada.

..........being an officer of [OR an employee in] a prison, did lawfully permit C.D. to escape from lawful custody therein, to wit: (specify the particulars of the offence), contrary to s. 147(c) of the Criminal Code of Canada.

Part V — Sexual Offences, Public Morals and Disorderly Conduct

Section 151 Sexual interference

A.B., on the..........(day) of (month) ...., (year).........., at (specify time) in (specify place), for a sexual purpose, did touch, directly [OR indirectly] with [specify a part of the body of A.B. OR an object] (specify a part of the body) of C.D., a person under the age of 14 years, to wit: (specify the particulars of the offence), contrary to s. 151 of the Criminal Code of Canada.

Section 152 Invitation to sexual touching

A.B., on the..........(day) of (month) ...., (year).........., at (specify time) in (specify place), for a sexual purpose, did invite [OR counsel OR incite] C.D., a person under the age of 14 years, to touch directly [OR indirectly] the body of A.B. [OR E.F.] with (specify a part of the body of A.B. or E.F.or an object), to wit: (specify the particulars of the offence), contrary to s. 152 of the Criminal Code of Canada.

Section 153(1) Sexual exploitation

A.B., on the..........(day) of (month) ...., (year).........., at (specify time) in (specify place), being in a position of trust [OR authority] towards C.D., a young person [OR being a person with whom C.D., a young person, was in a relationship of dependency], for a sexual purpose.

..........did touch, directly [OR indirectly] (specify), the body of C.D. with (specify a part of the body of A.B. or an object), to wit: (specify the particulars of the offence), contrary to s. 153(1)(b) of the Criminal Code of Canada.

..........did invite [OR counsel OR incite] C.D., to touch directly [OR indirectly] (specify), the body of A.B. [OR C.D.] with (specify a part of the body OR an object), to wit: (specify the particulars of the offence), contrary to s. 153(1)(b) of the Criminal Code of Canada.

Section 153.1 Sexual exploitation of person with a disability

A.B., on the..........(day) of (month) ...., (year).........., at (specify time) in (specify place),

..........being in a position of trust [OR authority] towards C.D., a person with a mental [OR physical] disability without the consent of C.D. and for a sexual purpose, did counsel [OR incite] C.D. to touch directly [OR indirectly] with (specify a part of C.D.'s body OR an object) the body of A.B. [OR C.D. OR E.F.], to wit: (specify the particulars of the offence), contrary to s. 153.1 of the Criminal Code of Canada.

..........being a person with whom C.D., a person with a mental [OR physical] disability was in a relationship of dependency, without the consent of C.D. and for a sexual purpose, did counsel [OR incite] C.D. to touch directly [OR indirectly] with (specify a part of C.D.'s body OR an object) the body of A.B. [OR C.D. OR E.F.], to wit: (specify the particulars of the offence), contrary to s. 153.1 of the Criminal Code of Canada.

Section 155(1) Incest

A.B., on the..........(day) of (month) ...., (year).........., at (specify time) in (specify place), knowing that C.D. was by blood relationship his [OR her] parent [OR child OR brother OR sister OR grandparent OR grandchild] had sexual intercourse with C.D. and did thereby commit incest, to wit: (specify the particulars of the offence), contrary to s. 155(1) of the Criminal Code of Canada.

Section 159(1) Anal intercourse

A.B., on the..........(day) of (month) ...., (year).........., at (specify time) in (specify place), did engage in an act of anal intercourse with C.D., to wit: (specify the particulars of the offence), contrary to s. 159(1) of the Criminal Code of Canada.

Section 160(2) Compulsion to commit bestiality

A.B., on the..........(day) of (month) ...., (year).........., at (specify time) in (specify place), did compel C.D. to commit bestiality with (specify the animal), to wit: (specify the particulars of the offence), contrary to s. 159(1) of the Criminal Code of Canada.

Section 160(3) Bestiality in presence of or by child

A.B., on the..........(day) of (month) ...., (year).........., at (specify time) in (specify place),

..........did commit bestiality with (specify the animal) in the presence of C.D., a person who was under the age of 14 years, to wit: (specify the particulars of the offence), contrary to s. 160(3) of the Criminal Code of Canada.

..........did incite C.D., a person under the age of 14 years, to commit bestiality with (specify the animal), to wit: (specify the particulars of the offence), contrary to s. 160(3) of the Criminal Code of Canada.

Section 161(4) Order of prohibition regarding children

A.B., on the..........(day) of (month) ...., (year).........., at (specify time) in (specify place), being bound by an order of prohibition (specify the particulars of the order), did not comply with the order, to wit: (specify the particulars of the offence), contrary to s. 161(4) of the Criminal Code of Canada.

Section 163(1)(a) Making, printing, publishing, distributing, circulating or having in possession obscene matter

A.B., on the..........(day) of (month) ...., (year).........., at (specify time) in (specify place), did make [OR print OR publish OR distribute OR circulate OR have in his (OR her) possession for the purpose of publication (OR distribution OR circulation)] obscene written matter [OR an obscene picture OR an obscene model OR an obscene phonograph record OR (specify any other obscene thing)], to wit: (specify the particulars of the offence), contrary to s. 163(1)(a) of the Criminal Code of Canada.

Section 163(1)(b) Offences in connection with crime comics

A.B., on the..........(day) of (month) ...., (year).........., at (specify time) in (specify place),

..........did make [OR print OR publish OR distribute OR sell] a crime comic, to wit: (specify the particulars of the offence), contrary to s. 163(1)(b) of the Criminal Code of Canada.

..........did have in his [OR her] possession for the purpose of publication [OR distribution OR circulation] a crime comic, to wit: (specify the particulars of the offence), contrary to s. 163(1)(b) of the Criminal Code of Canada.

Section 163(2)(a) Selling, exposing to public view or having in possession obscene matter

A.B., on the..........(day) of (month) ...., (year).........., at (specify time) in (specify place), knowingly and without lawful justification or excuse, did sell [OR expose to public view OR have in his [OR her] possession for the purpose of sale], obscene written matter [OR an obscene picture OR an obscene model OR an obscene phonograph record OR (specify any other obscene thing)], to wit: (specify the particulars of the offence), contrary to s. 163(2)(a) of the Criminal Code of Canada.

Section 163(2)(b) Exhibiting disgusting objects or indecent show

A.B., on the..........(day) of (month) ...., (year).........., at (specify time) in (specify place), knowingly and without lawful justification or excuse, did publicly exhibit a disgusting object [OR an indecent show], to wit: (specify the particulars of the offence), contrary to s. 163(2)(b) of the Criminal Code of Canada.

Section 163(2)(c) Advertising means of causing abortion or miscarriage

A.B., on the..........(day) of (month) ...., (year).........., at (specify time) in (specify place), did knowingly without lawful justification or excuse, offer to sell [OR advertise OR publish an advertisement of OR have for sale OR have for disposal] means [OR instructions OR medicine OR a drug OR an article] intended [OR represented] as a method of causing an abortion [OR miscarriage], to wit: (specify the particulars of the offence), contrary to s. 163(2) of the Criminal Code of Canada.

Section 163(2)(d) Advertising means of restoring sexual virility or curing venereal disease

A.B., on the..........(day) of (month) ...., (year).........., at (specify time) in (specify place), knowingly and without lawful excuse, did advertise [OR publish an advertisement] of means [OR instructions OR medicine OR a drug OR an article] intended [OR represented] as a method for restoring sexual virility [OR curing venereal diseases OR curing diseases of the generative organs], to wit: (specify the particulars of the offence), contrary to s. 163(2) of the Criminal Code of Canada.

Section 163.1(2) Making, printing, publishing or possessing for purposes of publication

A.B., on the..........(day) of (month) ...., (year).........., at (specify time) in (specify place), knowingly, did make [OR print OR publish OR possess for the purpose of publication] child pornography, to wit: (specify the particulars of the offence), contrary to s. 163.1(2) of the Criminal Code of Canada.

Section 163.1(3) Importing, distributing, selling or possessing for purpose of distribution or sale

A.B., on the..........(day) of (month) ...., (year).........., at (specify time) in (specify place), did import [OR distribute OR sell OR possess for the purpose of distribution or sale] child pornography, to wit: (specify the particulars of the offence), contrary to s. 163.1(3) of the Criminal Code of Canada.

Section 163.1(4) Possession of child pornography

A.B., on the..........(day) of (month) ...., (year).........., at (specify time) in (specify place), did possess child pornography, to wit: (specify the particulars of the offence), contrary to s. 163.1(4) of the Criminal Code of Canada.

Section 165 Tied sales

A.B., on the..........(day) of (month) ...., (year).........., at (specify time) in (specify place), did refuse to sell [OR supply] to C.D., copies of a publication for the reason only that C.D. refused to purchase [OR acquire] from A.B. copies of any other publication that C.D. was apprehensive might be obscene [OR a crime comic], to wit: (specify the particulars of the offence), contrary to s. 165 of the Criminal Code of Canada.

Section 167(1) Presenting or giving immoral theatrical performance

A.B., on the..........(day) of (month) ...., (year).........., at (specify time) in (specify place), being the lessee [OR manager OR agent OR person in charge] of a theatre, did present [OR give OR allow to be presented OR allow to be given] therein an immoral [OR indecent OR obscene] performance [OR entertainment OR representation] to wit: (specify the particulars of the offence), contrary to s. 167(1) of the Criminal Code of Canada.

Section 167(2) Taking part or appearing in immoral theatrical performance

A.B., on the..........(day) of (month) ...., (year).........., at (specify time) in (specify place), did take part [OR appear] as an actor [OR a performer OR an assistant], in an immoral [OR indecent OR obscene] performance [OR entertainment OR representation] in a theatre, to wit: (specify the particulars of the offence), contrary to s. 167(2) of the Criminal Code of Canada.

Section 168 Mailing obscene matter

A.B., on the..........(day) of (month) ...., (year).........., at (specify time) in (specify place), did make use of the mails for the purpose of transmitting [OR delivering] (specify the thing transmitted or delivered), that was obscene [OR indecent OR immoral OR scurrilous], to wit: (specify the particulars of the offence), contrary to s. 168 of the Criminal Code of Canada.

Section 170 Parent or guardian procuring sexual activity

A.B., on the..........(day) of (month) ...., (year).........., at (specify time) in (specify place), being the parent [OR guardian] of C.D., a person under the age of 18 years, did procure C.D. to engage in prohibited sexual activity with E.F., to wit: (specify the particulars of the offence), contrary to s. 170 of the Criminal Code of Canada.

Section 171 Householder permitting sexual activity

A.B., on the..........(day) of (month) ...., (year).........., at (specify time) in (specify place), being the owner [OR the occupier OR the manager OR a person having control of premises OR a person assisting in the management (OR control)], of premises knowingly did permit C.D., a person under the age of 18 years to resort to [OR to be in OR to be upon] the premises for the purpose of engaging in prohibited sexual activity with E.F., to wit: (specify the particulars of the offence), contrary to s. 171 of the Criminal Code of Canada.

Section 172(1) Corrupting children

A.B., on the..........(day) of (month) ...., (year).........., at (specify time) in (specify place), while in the home of C.D., a child, did participate in adultery [OR sexual immorality OR did indulge in habitual drunkenness (OR specify any other form of vice)] and thereby endangered the morals of C.D. [OR rendered the home an unfit place for C.D. to be in], to wit: (specify the particulars of the offence), contrary to s. 172(1) of the Criminal Code of Canada.

Section 173(1) Indecent acts

A.B., on the..........(day) of (month) ...., (year).........., at (specify time) in (specify place), wilfully

..........did an indecent act in a public place in the presence of C.D., to wit: (specify the particulars of the offence), contrary to s. 173(1)(a) of the Criminal Code of Canada.

..........did an indecent act with intent thereby to insult or offend C.D., to wit: (specify the particulars of the offence), contrary to s. 173(1)(b) of the Criminal Code of Canada.

Section 173(2) Exposure

A.B., on the..........(day) of (month) ...., (year).........., at (specify time) in (specify place), for a sexual purpose did expose his [OR her] genital organs to C.D., a person under the age of 14 years, to wit: (specify the particulars of the offence), contrary to s. 173(2) of the Criminal Code of Canada.

Section 174(1) Nudity

A.B., on the..........(day) of (month) ...., (year).........., at (specify time) in (specify place), without lawful excuse,

..........was nude in a public place, to wit: (specify the particulars of the offence), contrary to s. 174(1)(a) of the Criminal Code of Canada.

..........was nude and exposed to public view while on private property, to wit: (specify the particulars of the offence), contrary to s. 174(1)(b) of the Criminal Code of Canada.

Section 175(1)(a) Causing a disturbance

A.B., on the..........(day) of (month) ...., (year).........., at (specify time) in (specify place), not being in a dwelling-house, did cause a disturbance in [OR near] a public place by fighting [OR screaming OR shouting OR swearing OR singing OR using insulting language OR using obscene language OR impeding C.D. OR molesting C.D. OR being drunk], to wit: (specify the particulars of the offence), contrary to s. 175(1)(a) of the Criminal Code of Canada.

Section 175(1)(b) Indecent exhibition

A.B., on the..........(day) of (month) ...., (year).........., at (specify time) in (specify place), did openly expose [OR exhibit] an indecent exhibition in a public place, to wit: (specify the particulars of the offence), contrary to s. 175(1)(b) of the Criminal Code of Canada.

Section 175(1)(c) Loitering and obstructing

A.B., on the..........(day) of (month) ...., (year).........., at (specify time) in (specify place), did loiter in a public place and did obstruct C.D., a person who was there, to wit: (specify the particulars of the offence), contrary to s. 175(1)(c) of the Criminal Code of Canada.

Section 175(1)(d) Disturbing the occupants of a dwelling-house

A.B., on the..........(day) of (month) ...., (year).........., at (specify time) in (specify place), did disturb the peace and quiet of C.D., the occupant of a dwelling-house,

..........by discharging firearms [OR by disorderly conduct] in a public place, to wit: (specify the particulars of the offence), contrary to s. 175(1)(d) of the Criminal Code of Canada.

..........in a particular building [OR structure] in which A.B. was not himself [OR herself] an occupant, by discharging a firearm [OR by disorderly conduct] in a part of the building [OR structure] to which other occupants of dwelling-houses in the building [OR structure] have access, to wit: (specify the particulars of the offence), contrary to s. 175(1)(d) of the Criminal Code of Canada.

Section 176(1) Obstructing officiating clergyman

A.B., on the..........(day) of (month) ...., (year).........., at (specify time) in (specify place),

..........by threats [OR force] unlawfully did obstruct [OR prevent OR endeavour to obstruct OR endeavour to prevent] C.D., a clergyman [OR minister] from celebrating divine service [OR from performing a function in connection with his (OR her) calling], to wit: (specify the particulars of the offence), contrary to s. 176(1)(a) of the Criminal Code of Canada.

..........knowing that C.D., a clergyman [OR minister] was about to perform [OR was on his (OR her) way to perform OR was returning from the performance of] divine service [OR from a function in connection with his (OR her) calling], did assault [OR offer violence to OR arrest upon a civil process OR arrest under the pretence of executing a civil process] C.D., to wit: (specify the particulars of the offence), contrary to s. 176(1)(b) of the Criminal Code of Canada.

Section 176(2), (3) Disturbing religious worship

A.B., on the..........(day) of (month) ...., (year).........., at (specify time) in (specify place),

..........did wilfully disturb [OR interrupt] an assemblage of persons meeting for religious worship [OR for a moral purpose OR for a social purpose OR for a benevolent purpose], to wit: (specify the particulars of the offence), contrary to s. 176(2) of the Criminal Code of Canada.

..........being at [OR near] a meeting for religious worship [OR for a moral purpose OR for a social purpose OR for a benevolent purpose], by (specify action), disturbed the order [OR solemnity] of the meeting, to wit: (specify the particulars of the offence), contrary to s. 176(3) of the Criminal Code of Canada.

Section 177 Trespassing at night

A.B., on the..........(day) of (month) ...., (year).........., at (specify time) in (specify place), without lawful excuse, did loiter [OR prowl] at night upon the property of C.D. near the dwelling-house situated on that property, to wit: (specify the particulars of the offence), contrary to s. 177 of the Criminal Code of Canada.

Section 178 Stink or stench bombs

A.B., on the..........(day) of (month) ...., (year).........., at (specify time) in (specify place), not being a peace officer engaged in the discharge of his [OR her] duty, did have in his [OR her] possession in a public place [OR did deposit OR throw OR inject OR cause to be deposited (OR thrown OR injected) in (OR into OR near) (specify any place)]

..........an offensive volatile substance that was likely to harm [OR inconvenience OR discommode OR cause discomfort to] C.D. [OR to cause damage to property], to wit: (specify the particulars of the offence), contrary to s. 178 of the Criminal Code of Canada.

..........a stink bomb [OR stench bomb OR a device from which such substance is capable of being liberated], to wit: (specify the particulars of the offence), contrary to s. 178 of the Criminal Code of Canada.

Section 179(1)(a) Supporting oneself by gaming or crime and committing vagrancy

A.B., on the..........(day) of (month) ...., (year).........., at (specify time) in (specify place), having no lawful profession or calling by which to maintain himself [OR herself], did support himself [OR herself] in whole [OR in part] by gaming [OR crime], and did thereby commit vagrancy, to wit: (specify the particulars of the offence), contrary to s. 179(1)(a) of the Criminal Code of Canada.

Section 179(1)(b) Person convicted of sexual offence and committing vagrancy

A.B., on the..........(day) of (month) ...., (year).........., at (specify time) in (specify place), having been convicted of the offence of (specify an offence mentioned in s. 179(1)(b)), was found loitering in [OR near] a school ground [OR playground OR public park OR bathing area], and did thereby commit vagrancy, to wit: (specify the particulars of the offence), contrary to s. 179(1)(b) of the Criminal Code of Canada.

Section 180 Common nuisance

A.B., on the..........(day) of (month) ...., (year).........., at (specify time) in (specify place),

..........did commit a common nuisance by (specify how the common nuisance was committed) and did thereby endanger the lives [OR safety OR health] of the public, to wit: (specify the particulars of the offence), contrary to s. 180 of the Criminal Code of Canada.

..........did commit a common nuisance by (specify how the common nuisance was committed) and did thereby cause physical injury to C.D., to wit: (specify the particulars of the offence), contrary to s. 180 of the Criminal Code of Canada.

Section 181 Spreading false news

A.B., on the..........(day) of (month) ...., (year).........., at (specify time) in (specify place), wilfully did publish a statement [OR tale OR news] that A.B. knew was false and that did cause [OR was likely to cause] injury [OR mischief] to a public interest, to wit: (specify the particulars of the offence), contrary to s. 181 of the Criminal Code of Canada.

Section 182 Neglect of or indignity to dead human body

A.B., on the..........(day) of (month) ...., (year).........., at (specify time) in (specify place),

..........did without lawful excuse, neglect to perform a duty imposed upon A.B. by law [OR undertaken by A.B.] with reference to a dead human body [OR human remains], to wit: (specify the particulars of the offence), contrary to s. 182(a) of the Criminal Code of Canada.

..........did improperly [OR indecently] interfere with [OR offer an indignity to] a dead human body [OR human remains], to wit: (specify the particulars of the offence), contrary to s. 182(b) of the Criminal Code of Canada.

Part VI — Invasion of Privacy

Section 184(1) Interception of private communication

A.B., on the..........(day) of (month) ...., (year).........., at (specify time) in (specify place), by means of an electro-magnetic [OR an acoustic OR a mechanical OR (specify other device)] device, did wilfully intercept a private communication, to wit: (specify the particulars of the offence), contrary to s. 184(1) of the Criminal Code of Canada.

Section 184.5(1) Interception of radio-based telephone communication

A.B., on the..........(day) of (month) ...., (year).........., at (specify time) in (specify place), maliciously [OR for gain], did intercept by means of a electro-magnetic [OR acoustic OR mechanical OR specify other type of device] device, a radio-based telephone communication, while C.D., the originator of the communication [OR the person intended by E.F., the originator of the communication to receive it] was in Canada, to wit: (specify the particulars of the offence), contrary to s. 184.5(1) of the Criminal Code of Canada.

Section 191(1) Possession of devices for interception

A.B., on the..........(day) of (month) ...., (year).........., at (specify time) in (specify place), did possess [OR sell OR purchase] an electro-magnetic [OR an acoustic OR a mechanical OR (specify other type of device)] device, knowing that the design thereof did render it primarily useful for surreptitious interception of private communications, to wit: (specify the particulars of the offence), contrary to s. 191(1) of the Criminal Code of Canada.

Section 193(1) Disclosure of information from private communication

A.B., on the..........(day) of (month) ...., (year).........., at (specify time) in (specify place), wilfully did use [OR disclose OR disclose the existence of] a private communication [OR a part of a private communication OR the substance (OR meaning OR purport) of a private communication] that had been intercepted by means of an electro-magnetic [OR an acoustic OR a mechanical OR (specify other type of device) device], without the consent, express or implied, of C.D., the originator of the private communication [OR E.F., the person intended by C.D. to receive it], to wit: (specify the particulars of the offence), contrary to s. 193(1) of the Criminal Code of Canada.

Section 193.1(1) Disclosure of information received from interception of radio-based telephone communication

A.B., on the..........(day) of (month) ...., (year).........., at (specify time) in (specify place), without the express [OR implied] consent of A.B., the originator of the communication [OR E.F., the person intended by the originator of the communication] wilfully did use [OR disclose OR disclose the existence] of a radio-based telephone communication that was intercepted by means of an electromagnetic [OR acoustic OR mechanical OR (specify other type of device)], to wit: (specify the particulars of the offence), contrary to s. 193.1(1) of the Criminal Code of Canada.

Part VII — Disorderly Houses, Gaming and Betting

Section 201(1) Keeping a gaming house or betting house

A.B., on the..........(day) of (month) ...., (year).........., at (specify time) in (specify place), did keep a common gaming house [OR common betting house], to wit: (specify the particulars of the offence), contrary to s. 201(1) of the Criminal Code of Canada.

Section 201(2)(a) Found in gaming house or betting house

A.B., on the..........(day) of (month) ...., (year).........., at (specify time) in (specify place), was found, without lawful excuse, in a common gaming [OR betting] house, to wit: (specify the particulars of the offence), contrary to s. 201(2) of the Criminal Code of Canada.

Section 201(2)(b) Allowing premises to be used as gaming house or betting house

A.B., on the..........(day) of (month) ...., (year).........., at (specify time) in (specify place), being the owner [OR landlord OR lessor OR tenant OR occupier OR agent] of (specify the place), did knowingly permit such place to be let [OR used] for the purposes of a common gaming [OR betting] house, to wit: (specify the particulars of the offence), contrary to s. 201(2)(b) of the Criminal Code of Canada.

Section 202(1) Betting, pool-making and book-making

A.B., on the..........(day) of (month) ...., (year).........., at (specify time) in (specify place),

..........did use [OR knowingly allow to be used], a place under his [OR her] control, for the purpose of recording bets [OR registering bets OR selling a pool], to wit: (specify the particulars of the offence), contrary to s. 202(1)(a) of the Criminal Code of Canada.

..........did import [OR make OR buy OR sell OR rent OR lease OR hire OR keep OR exhibit OR employ OR knowingly allow to be kept (OR exhibited OR employed)] a device [OR apparatus] for the purpose of recording bets [OR registering bets OR selling a pool], to wit: (specify the particulars of the offence), contrary to s. 202(1)(b) of the Criminal Code of Canada.

..........did import [OR make OR buy OR sell OR rent OR lease OR hire OR keep OR exhibit OR employ OR knowingly allow to be kept (OR exhibited OR employed)] a machine [OR device] for gambling [OR betting] to wit: (specify the particulars of the offence), contrary to s. 202(1)(b) of the Criminal Code of Canada.

..........did have under his [OR her] control money in the amount of — [OR (specify other property)] relating to a transaction that is an offence under s. 202 of the Criminal Code, to wit: (specify the particulars of the offence), contrary to s. 202(1)(c) of the Criminal Code of Canada.

..........did record bets [OR register bets OR sell a pool], to wit: (specify the particulars of the offence), contrary to s. 202(1)(d) of the Criminal Code of Canada.

..........did engage in pool-selling [OR book-making OR in the business (OR occupation) of betting], to wit: (specify the particulars of the offence), contrary to s. 202(1)(e) of the Criminal Code of Canada.

..........did make an agreement for the purchase [OR sale] of betting [OR gaming] privileges, to wit: (specify the particulars of the offence), contrary to s. 202(1)(e) of the Criminal Code of Canada.

..........did make an agreement for the purchase [OR sale] of information that is intended to assist in book-making [OR pool-selling OR betting], to wit: (specify the particulars of the offence), contrary to s. 202(1)(e) of the Criminal Code of Canada.

..........did print [OR provide OR offer to print (OR provide)] information intended for use in connection with book-making [OR pool-selling OR betting] on a horse-race [OR fight OR game OR (specify a sport)] that has [OR has not yet] taken place in [OR outside] Canada, to wit: (specify the particulars of the offence), contrary to s. 202(1)(f) of the Criminal Code of Canada.

..........did import [OR bring] into Canada information [OR writing] that was intended [OR was likely] to promote [OR to be of use in] gambling [OR book-making OR pool-selling OR betting] upon a horse-race [OR fight OR game OR (specify a sport)], to wit: (specify the particulars of the offence), contrary to s. 202(1)(g) of the Criminal Code of Canada.

..........did advertise [OR print OR publish OR exhibit OR post up OR give notice of] an offer [OR invitation OR inducement] to be on [OR guess OR foretell] the results of a contest [OR a result of (OR contingency relating to) a contest], to wit: (specify the particulars of the offence), contrary to s. 202(1)(h) of the Criminal Code of Canada.

..........did wilfully and knowingly send [OR transmit OR deliver OR receive] a message by radio [OR telegraph OR telephone OR mail OR express] that conveyed information relating to book-making [OR pool-selling OR betting OR wagering], to wit: (specify the particulars of the offence), contrary to s. 202(1)(i) of the Criminal Code of Canada.

..........did wilfully and knowingly send [OR transmit OR deliver OR receive] a message by radio [OR telegraph OR telephone OR mail OR express] that conveyed information that was intended to assist in book-making [OR pool-selling OR betting

OR wagering], to wit: (specify the particulars of the offence), contrary to s. 202(1)(i) of the Criminal Code of Canada.

..........did aid [OR assist] in the committing of an offence under s. 202 of the Criminal Code of Canada, to wit: (specify the particulars of the offence), contrary to s. 202(1)(j) of the Criminal Code of Canada.

Section 203 Placing bets on behalf of others

A.B., on the..........(day) of (month) ...., (year).........., at (specify time) in (specify place),

..........did place [OR offer to place OR agree to place] a bet on behalf of C.D. for a consideration paid [OR to be paid] by [OR on behalf of] C.D., to wit: (specify the particulars of the offence), contrary to s. 203(a) of the Criminal Code of Canada.

..........did engage in the business [OR practice] of placing [OR of agreeing to place] bets on behalf of C.D., to wit: (specify the particulars of the offence) contrary to s. 203(b) of the Criminal Code of Canada.

..........did hold himself [OR herself] out [OR allow himself (OR herself) to be held out] as engaging in the business [OR practice] of placing [OR of agreeing to place] bets on behalf of C.D., to wit: (specify the particulars of the offence), contrary to s. 203(c) of the Criminal Code of Canada.

Section 204(10) Pari-mutuel betting

A.B., on the..........(day) of (month) ...., (year).........., at (specify time) in (specify place), did contravene [OR fail to comply with] (specify provisions of s. 204 (pari-mutuel betting)), to wit: (specify the particulars of the offence), contrary to s. 204(10)) of the Criminal Code of Canada.

Section 204(10) Violation or non-compliance with race-track regulations

A.B., on the..........(day) of (month) ...., (year).........., at (specify time) in (specify place), did contravene [OR fail to comply with] (specify a regulation made under s. 204 (race-track regulations)), to wit: (specify the particulars of the offence), contrary to s. 204(10) of the Criminal Code of Canada.

Section 206, 207 Lotteries and games of chance prohibited by law

A.B., on the..........(day) of (month) ...., (year).........., at (specify time) in (specify place),

..........did make [OR print OR advertise OR publish OR cause (OR procure) to be made (OR printed OR advertised OR published)] a proposal [OR scheme OR plan] for advancing [OR lending OR giving OR selling OR disposing of] property by lots [OR cards OR tickets OR a mode of chance)], to wit: (specify the particulars of the offence), contrary to s. 206(1)(a) of the Criminal Code of Canada.

..........did sell [OR barter OR exchange OR dispose of OR cause (OR procure OR aid OR assist in), the sale (OR barter OR exchange OR disposal of OR offer for sale OR offer for barter OR offer for exchange)] a lot [OR card OR ticket OR (specify other means OR device)] for advancing [OR lending OR giving OR selling OR otherwise disposing of] property by lots [OR tickets OR (specify a mode of chance)] to wit: (specify the particulars of the offence), contrary to s. 206(1)(b) of the Criminal Code of Canada.

..........knowingly, did send [OR transmit OR mail OR ship OR deliver OR allow to be sent (OR transmitted OR mailed OR shipped OR delivered) OR accept for carriage OR transport OR convey] (specify an article) that was used [OR intended for use] in carrying out a device [OR proposal OR scheme OR plan] for advancing [OR lending OR giving OR selling OR disposing of] (specify property) by (specify a mode of chance), to wit: (specify the particulars of the offence), contrary to s. 206(1)(c) of the Criminal Code of Canada.

..........did conduct [OR manage] a scheme [OR contrivance OR operation] for the purpose of determining who [OR the holders of what lots (OR tickets OR numbers OR chances)] were the winners of (specify property) so proposed to be advanced [OR lent OR given OR sold OR disposed of], to wit: (specify the particulars of the offence), contrary to s. 206(1)(d) of the Criminal Code of Canada

..........did conduct [OR manage OR was a party to] a scheme [OR contrivance OR operation] by which a C.D. became entitled under the scheme [OR contrivance OR operation] on payment of any sum of money [OR the giving of any valuable security OR by obligating himself (OR herself) to pay any sum of money (OR give any valuable security)] to receive from A.B., the person conducting the scheme [OR contrivance OR operation] [OR from E.F.] a larger sum of money [OR amount of valuable security] than the sum [OR amount] paid [OR given OR to be paid (OR given)] by reason of the fact that E.F. and G.H. have paid [OR given OR obligated themselves to pay (OR give)] a sum of money [OR valuable security] under the scheme [OR contrivance OR operation], to wit: (specify the particulars of the offence), contrary to s. 206(1)(e) of the Criminal Code of Canada.

..........did dispose of goods [OR wares OR merchandise] by a game of chance [OR a game of mixed chance and skill] in which C.D., the contestant [OR competitor] paid money [OR (specify other valuable consideration)], to wit: (specify the particulars of the offence), contrary to s. 206(1)(f) of the Criminal Code of Canada

..........did induce C.D. to stake [OR hazard] money [OR other valuable property (OR specify other thing)] on the result of a dice game [OR three-card monte OR punch board OR coin table OR on the operation of a wheel of fortune], to wit: (specify the particulars of the offence), contrary to s. 206(1)(g) of the Criminal Code of Canada.

..........for valuable consideration, did carry on [OR play OR offer to carry on (OR play) OR employ C.D. to carry on (OR play)], in a public place [OR a place to which the public had access], the game of three-card monte, to wit: (specify the particulars of the offence), contrary to s. 206(1)(h) of the Criminal Code of Canada.

..........did receive bets on the outcome of a game of three-card monte, to wit: (specify the particulars of the offence), contrary to s. 206(1)(i) of the Criminal Code of Canada.

..........being the owner of a place, did permit C.D. to play the game of three-card monte therein, to wit: (specify the particulars of the offence), contrary to s. 206(1)(j) of the Criminal Code of Canada.

..........did buy [OR take OR receive] (specify a lot OR ticket OR other device mentioned in s. 206(1) of the Criminal Code), to wit: (specify the particulars of the offence), contrary to s. 206(4) of the Criminal Code of Canada.

Section 207 Lottery Schemes

A.B., on the ....(day) of (month) ...., (year).........., at (specify time) in (specify place),

..........for the purposes of a lottery scheme, did (specify a thing that was not authorized by pursuant to a provision of s. 207 of the Criminal Code) in the case of the conduct [OR management OR operation] of that lottery scheme, to wit: (specify the particulars of the offence), contrary to s. 207(3) of the Criminal Code of Canada.

..........for the purposes of a lottery scheme, did (specify anything that was not authorized by pursuant to a provision of s. 207 of the Criminal Code), in the course of participating in that lottery scheme, to wit: (specify the particulars of the offence), contrary to s. 207(3) of the Criminal Code of Canada.

Section 209 Cheating at play

A.B., on the..........(day) of (month) ...., (year).........., at (specify time) in (specify place), with intent to defraud C.D., did cheat while playing a game [OR in holding the stakes for a game OR in betting], to wit: (specify the particulars of the offence), contrary to s. 209 of the Criminal Code of Canada.

Section 210(1) Keeping common bawdy-house

A.B., on the..........(day) of (month) ...., (year).........., at (specify time) in (specify place), did keep a common bawdy-house, to wit: (specify the particulars of the offence), contrary to s. 210(1) of the Criminal Code of Canada.

Section 210(2)(a), (b) Being an inmate or being found in a common bawdy-house

A.B., on the..........(day) of (month) ...., (year).........., at (specify time) in (specify place),

..........was an inmate of a common bawdy-house, to wit: (specify the particulars of the offence), contrary to s. 210(2)(a) of the Criminal Code of Canada.

..........was found, without lawful excuse, in a common bawdy-house, to wit: (specify the particulars of the offence), contrary to s. 210(2)(b) of the Criminal Code of Canada.

Section 210(2)(c) Having charge or control of place used for common bawdy-house

A.B., on the..........(day) of (month) ...., (year).........., at (specify time) in (specify place), being the owner [OR landlord OR lessor OR tenant OR occupier OR agent OR having charge or control] of (specify the place) did knowingly permit the place [OR part of the place], to be let [OR used] for the purposes of a common bawdy-house, to wit: (specify the particulars of the offence), contrary to s. 210(2)(c) of the Criminal Code of Canada.

Forms of Charges

Section 211 Transporting person to bawdy-house

A.B., on the..........(day) of (month) ...., (year).........., at (specify time) in (specify place), did knowingly take [OR transport OR direct OR offer to take OR offer to transport OR offer to direct] C.D. to a common bawdy-house, to wit: (specify the particulars of the offence), contrary to s. 211 of the Criminal Code of Canada.

Section 212(1) Procuring offences

A.B., on the..........(day) of (month) ...., (year).........., at (specify time) in (specify place),

..........did procure [OR attempt to procure OR solicit] C.D., to have illicit sexual intercourse with E.F., to wit: (specify the particulars of the offence), contrary to s. 212(1)(a) of the Criminal Code of Canada.

..........did inveigle [OR entice] C.D., a person who is not a prostitute, to a common bawdy-house for the purpose of illicit sexual intercourse [OR prostitution], to wit: (specify the particulars of the offence), contrary to s. 212(1)(b) of the Criminal Code of Canada.

..........did knowingly conceal C.D. in a common bawdy-house, to wit: (specify the particulars of the offence), contrary to s. 212(1)(c) of the Criminal Code of Canada.

..........did procure [OR attempt to procure] C.D. to become a prostitute, to wit: (specify the particulars of the offence), contrary to s. 212(1)(d) of the Criminal code of Canada.

..........did procure [OR attempt to procure] C.D. to leave the usual place of abode of that person with intent that C.D. become an inmate [OR frequenter] of a common bawdy-house, to wit: (specify the particulars of the offence), contrary to s. 212(1)(e) of the Criminal Code of Canada.

..........did direct C.D. [OR cause C.D. to be directed OR take C.D. OR cause C.D. to be taken] to a common bawdy-house on his [OR her] arrival in Canada, to wit: (specify the particulars of the offence), contrary to s. 212(1)(f) of the Criminal Code of Canada.

..........did procure C.D. to enter [OR leave] Canada, for the purpose of prostitution, to wit: (specify the particulars of the offence), contrary to s. 212(1)(g) of the Criminal Code of Canada.

..........for the purpose of gain, did exercise control [OR direction OR influence] over the movements of C.D. in such a manner as to show that A.B. was aiding [OR abetting OR compelling] C.D. to engage in [OR carry on] prostitution with E.F. [OR generally], to wit: (specify the particulars of the offence), contrary to s. 212(1)(h) of the Criminal Code of Canada.

..........did apply to C.D. [OR administer to C.D. OR cause C.D. to take] a drug [OR intoxicating liquor OR (specify a matter OR thing)] with intent to stupefy [OR overpower] C.D. in order thereby to enable E.F. to have illicit sexual intercourse with C.D., to wit: (specify the particulars of the offence), contrary to s. 212(1)(i) of the Criminal Code of Canada.

Section 212(1)(j) Living on avails of prostitution

A.B., on the..........(day) of (month) ...., (year).........., at (specify time) in (specify place), did live wholly [OR in part] on the avails of prostitution of C.D., to wit: (specify the particulars of the offence), contrary to s. 212(1)(j) of the Criminal Code of Canada.

Section 212(2) Living on the avails of prostitution of a person under the age of eighteen years

A.B., on the..........(day) of (month) ...., (year).........., at (specify time) in (specify place), did live wholly [OR in part] on the avails of prostitution of C.D., a person under the age of 18 years, to wit: (specify the particulars of the offence), contrary to s. 212(1) of the Criminal Code of Canada.

Section 212(2.1) Aggravated offence in relation to living on the avails of a person under 18 years

A.B., on the..........(day) of (month) ...., (year).........., at (specify time) in (specify place), did live wholly [OR in part] on the avails of prostitution by C.D., a person under the age of 18 years and, for the purpose of profit, did aid [OR abet OR counsel OR compel] C.D. to engage in [OR carry on] prostitution with E.F. and did use [OR threaten to use OR attempt to use] violence [OR intimidation OR coercion] with C.D., to wit: (specify the particulars to the offence), contrary to s. 212(2.1) of the Criminal Code of Canada.

Section 212(4) Offence in relation to juvenile prostitution

A.B., on the..........(day) of (month) ...., (year).........., at (specify time) in (specify place), did obtain [OR attempt to obtain] for consideration the sexual services of C.D., a person who was under the age of 18 years [OR a person that A.B. believed was under the age of 18 years], to wit: (specify the particulars of the offence), contrary to s. 212(4) of the Criminal Code of Canada.

Section 213(1) Offence in relation to prostitution

A.B., on the..........(day) of (month) ...., (year).........., at (specify time) in (specify place),

..........did stop a motor vehicle [OR attempt to stop a motor vehicle] in a public place [OR in a place open to public view] for the purpose of engaging in prostitution [OR of obtaining the sexual services of a prostitute], to wit: (specify the particulars of the offence), contrary to s. 213(1) of the Criminal Code of Canada.

..........did impede the free flow of pedestrian [OR vehicular] traffic in a public place [OR a place open to public view] from premises adjacent to that place, for the purpose of engaging in prostitution [OR of obtaining the sexual services of a prostitute], to wit: (specify the particulars of the offence), contrary to s. 213(b) of the Criminal Code of Canada.

..........did impede the ingress to [OR egress from] a public place [OR a place open to public view] from premises adjacent to that place, for the purpose of engaging in prostitution [OR of obtaining the sexual services of a prostitute], to wit: (specify the particulars of the offence), contrary to s. 213(b) of the Criminal Code of Canada.

..........stopped [OR attempted to stop OR communicated with OR attempted to communicate with] C.D. in a public place [OR a place open to public view] for the purpose of engaging in prostitution [OR of obtaining the sexual services of a prostitute], to wit: (specify the particulars of the offence), contrary to s. 213(c) of the Criminal Code of Canada.

Part VIII — Offences Against the Person and Reputation

Section 215 Parent, foster parent, guardian or head of family failing in duties

A.B., on the..........(day) of (month) ...., (year).........., at (specify time) in (specify place), being the parent of C.D. [OR the foster parent of C.D., OR the guardian of C.D., OR the head of a family of which C.D. was a member], without lawful excuse

.... did fail to provide the necessaries of life to C.D., a child under the age of 16 years, who was in destitute or necessitous circumstances, to wit: (specify the particulars of the offence), contrary to s. 215 of the Criminal Code of Canada.

.... did fail to provide the necessaries of life to C.D., a child under the age of 16 years, thereby endangering the life of C.D. [OR causing the health of C.D. to be endangered permanently], to wit: (specify the particulars of the offence contrary to s. 215 of the Criminal Code of Canada.

Section 215(2)(a) Married person failing in duties

A.B., on the..........(day) of (month) ...., (year).........., at (specify time) in (specify place), being married to C.D., without lawful excuse

..........did fail to provide the necessaries of life to C.D., who was in destitute or necessitous circumstances, to wit: (specify the particulars of the offence), contrary to s. 215 of the Criminal Code of Canada.

..........did fail to provide the necessaries of life to C.D., thereby endangering the life of C.D. [OR causing the health of C.D. to be endangered permanently], to wit: (specify the particulars of the offence) contrary to s. 215 of the Criminal Code of Canada.

Section 215(2)(b) Person under the charge of another person failing in duties

A.B., on the..........(day) of (month) ...., (year).........., at (specify time) in (specify place), being under a legal duty to provide the necessaries of life to C.D., a person in his [OR her] charge unable to withdraw from that charge and unable to provide himself [OR herself] with the necessaries of life, did fail to perform that duty thereby endangering the life of C.D. [OR causing OR being likely to cause permanent injury to the health of C.D.], to wit: (specify the particulars of the offence, contrary to s. 215(2)(b) of the Criminal Code of Canada.

Section 218 Abandoning child

A.B., on the..........(day) of (month) ...., (year).........., at (specify time) in (specify place), unlawfully

..........did abandon [OR expose] C.D., a child under the age of 10 years, so that the life of C.D. was endangered [OR was likely to be endangered], to wit: (specify the particulars of the offence), contrary to s. 218 of the Criminal Code of Canada.

..........did abandon [OR expose] C.D., a child under the age of 10 years, so that the health of C.D. was permanently injured [OR was likely to be permanently injured], to wit: (specify the particulars of the offence), contrary to s. 218 of the Criminal Code of Canada.

Section 220 Causing death by criminal negligence

A.B., on the..........(day) of (month) ...., (year).........., at (specify time) in (specify place), by criminal negligence, did cause death to C.D., to wit: (specify the particulars of the offence), contrary to s. 220 of the Criminal Code of Canada.

Section 221 Causing bodily harm by criminal negligence

A.B., on the..........(day) of (month) ...., (year).........., at (specify time) in (specify place), by criminal negligence, did cause bodily harm to C.D., to wit: (specify the particulars of the offence), contrary to s. 221 of the Criminal Code of Canada.

Section 235(1) Murder

A.B., on the..........(day) of (month) ...., (year).........., at (specify time) in (specify place), did cause the death of C.D. and thereby commit murder in the first degree [OR murder in the second degree], to wit: (specify the particulars of the offence), contrary to s. 235(1) of the Criminal Code of Canada.

Section 236 Manslaughter

A.B., on the..........(day) of (month) ...., (year).........., at (specify time) in (specify place), did cause the death of C.D. and thereby commit manslaughter, to wit: (specify the particulars of the offence), contrary to s. 236 of the Criminal Code of Canada.

Section 237 Infanticide

A.B., on the..........(day) of (month) ...., (year).........., at (specify time) in (specify place), being a female person, did commit infanticide, to wit: (specify the particulars of the offence), contrary to s. 237 of the Criminal Code of Canada.

Section 238(1) Killing unborn child in act of birth

A.B., on the..........(day) of (month) ...., (year).........., at (specify time) in (specify place), did cause the death, in the act of birth, of a child that had not become a human being in such a manner that if the child were a human being, A.B. would be guilty of murder, to wit: (specify the particulars of the offence), contrary to s. 238(1) of the Criminal Code of Canada.

Section 239 Attempt to commit murder by any means

A.B., on the..........(day) of (month) ...., (year).........., at (specify time) in (specify place), did attempt to cause the death of C.D. and thereby commit murder, to wit:

(specify the particulars of the offence), contrary to s. 239 of the Criminal Code of Canada.

Section 240 Accessary after the fact to murder

A.B., on the..........(day) of (month) ...., (year).........., at (specify time) in (specify place), was an accessory after the fact to murder, to wit: (specify the particulars of the offence), contrary to s. 240 of the Criminal Code of Canada.

Section 241 Counselling or aiding suicide

A.B., on the..........(day) of (month) ...., (year).........., at (specify time) in (specify place),

..........did counsel C.D. to commit suicide, to wit: (specify the particulars of the offence), contrary to s. 241 (a) of the Criminal Code of Canada.

..........did aid [OR abet] C.D. to commit suicide, to wit: (specify the particulars of the offence), contrary to s. 241(b) of the Criminal Code of Canada.

Section 242 Neglect in childbirth

A.B., on the..........(day) of (month) ...., (year).........., at (specify time) in (specify place), being a pregnant female person about to be delivered, did fail to make provision for reasonable assistance in respect of her delivery, with intent that her child should not live [OR with intent to conceal the birth of the child], resulting in permanent injury to her child [OR resulting in the death of her child] before [OR during OR a short time after] birth, to wit: (specify the particulars of the offence), contrary to s. 242 of the Criminal Code of Canada.

Section 243 Concealing dead body of child

A.B., on the..........(day) of (month) ...., (year).........., at (specify time) in (specify place), did dispose of the dead body of the child of A.B. [OR C.D.] with intent to conceal the fact that A.B. [OR C.D.] had been delivered of it, to wit: (specify the particulars of the offence), contrary to s. 243 of the Criminal Code of Canada.

Section 244 Discharging a firearm

A.B., on the..........(day) of (month) ...., (year).........., at (specify time) in (specify place), with intent to wound [OR maim OR disfigure OR endanger the life of OR prevent the arrest (OR detention) of] C.D., did discharge a firearm at C.D. [OR E.F.], to wit: (specify the particulars of the offence), contrary to s. 244 of the Criminal Code of Canada.

Section 244.1 Discharging an air gun with intent

A.B., on the..........(day) of (month) ...., (year).........., at (specify time) in (specify place), with intent to wound [OR maim OR disfigure OR endanger the life of OR prevent the arrest (OR detention) of] C.D., did discharge an air gun [OR air pistol OR compressed gas gun or compressed gas pistol] at C.D. [OR E.F.], to wit: specify the particulars of the offence), contrary to s. 244.1 of the Criminal Code of Canada.

Section 245 Administering poison or other destructive or noxious thing

A.B., on the..........(day) of (month) ...., (year).........., at (specify time) in (specify place), did administer to C.D. [OR cause to be administered to C.D. OR cause C.D. to take] poison [OR specify a destructive OR noxious thing] with intent thereby to endanger the life of [OR cause bodily harm to OR grieve OR annoy] C.D., to wit: (specify the particulars of the offence), contrary to s. 245 of the Criminal Code of Canada.

Section 246 Overcoming resistance to commission of offence

A.B., on the..........(day) of (month) ...., (year).........., at (specify time) in (specify place), with intent to enable [OR assist] himself [OR herself OR E.F.] to commit the indictable offence of (specify),

..........did attempt to choke [OR suffocate OR strangle] C.D., to wit: (specify the particulars of the offence), contrary to s. 246(a) of the Criminal Code of Canada.

..........did attempt to render C.D. insensible [OR unconscious OR incapable of resistance] by a means calculated to choke [OR suffocate OR strangle] C.D., to wit: (specify the particulars of the offence), contrary to s. 246(a) of the Criminal Code of Canada.

..........did administer [OR cause to be administered OR attempt to administer] to C.D., (specify a stupefying OR overpowering drug OR matter OR thing), to wit: (specify the particulars of the offence), contrary to s. 246(b) of the Criminal Code of Canada.

..........did cause [OR attempt to cause] C.D. to take (specify a stupefying OR overpowering drug OR matter OR thing) to wit: (specify the particulars of the offence), contrary to s. 246(b) of the Criminal Code of Canada.

Section 247(1) Traps likely to cause bodily harm

A.B., on the..........(day) of (month) ...., (year).........., at (specify time) in (specify place), with intent to cause the death of [OR bodily harm to] C.D. [OR C.D. and E.F.], did set [OR place OR cause to be set (OR placed)] a trap [OR (specify some device likely to cause death or bodily harm to persons)] that was likely to cause death or bodily harm to C.D. [OR C.D. and E.F.], to wit: (specify the particulars of the offence), contrary to s. 247(1) of the Criminal Code of Canada.

Section 248 Interfering with transportation facilities

A.B., on the..........(day) of (month) ...., (year).........., at (specify time) in (specify place), with intent to endanger the safety of C.D.,

..........did place a (specify the thing placed) upon property that was used for [or in connection with] the transportation of persons [OR goods] by land [OR water OR air], that was likely to cause the death of [OR bodily harm to] C.D. [OR E.F.], to wit: (specify the particulars of the offence), contrary to s. 248 of the Criminal Code of Canada.

..........did (specify the thing done) to property that was used for [OR in connection with] the transportation of persons [OR goods] by land [OR water OR air], that was likely to cause the death of [OR bodily harm to] C.D. [OR E.F.], to wit: (specify the particulars of the offence), contrary to s. 248 of the Criminal Code of Canada.

Section 249(1)(a) Dangerous operation of motor vehicle

A.B., on the..........(day) of (month) ...., (year).........., at (specify time) in (specify place), did drive [OR operate] a motor vehicle in a manner dangerous to the public, to wit: specify the particulars of the offence), contrary to s. 249(1)(a) of the Criminal Code of Canada.

Section 249(1)(b) Dangerous operation of vessel, water skis, surf-board

A.B., on the..........(day) of (month) ...., (year).........., at (specify time) in (specify place),

..........did operate [OR navigate] a vessel in a manner dangerous to the public, to wit: (specify the particulars of the offence), contrary to s. 249(1)(b) of the Criminal Code of Canada.

..........did operate water skis [OR a surf-board] in a manner dangerous to the public, to wit: (specify the particulars of the offence), contrary to s. 249(1)(b) of the Criminal Code of Canada.

Section 249(1)(c) Dangerous operation of aircraft

A.B., on the..........(day) of (month) ...., (year).........., at (specify time) in (specify place), did operate an aircraft in a manner dangerous to the public, to wit: (specify the particulars of the offence), contrary to s. 249(1)(c) of the Criminal Code of Canada.

Section 249(1)(d) Dangerous operation of railway equipment

A.B., on the..........(day) of (month) ...., (year).........., at (specify time) in (specify place), did operate railway equipment in a manner dangerous to the public, to wit: (specify the particulars of the offence), contrary to s. 249(1)(d) of the Criminal Code of Canada.

Section 249(3) Dangerous operation of a vessel, water skis, surf-board causing bodily harm

A.B., on the..........(day) of (month) ...., (year).........., at (specify time) in (specify place),

..........did operate [OR navigate] a vessel in a manner dangerous to the public, thereby causing bodily harm to C.D., to wit: (specify the particulars of the offence), contrary to s. 249(3) of the Criminal Code of Canada.

..........did operate water skis [OR a surf-board] in a manner dangerous to the public, thereby causing bodily harm to C.D., to wit: (specify the particulars of the offence), contrary to s. 249(3) of the Criminal Code of Canada.

Section 249(3) Dangerous driving causing bodily harm

A.B., on the..........(day) of (month) ...., (year).........., at (specify time) in (specify place), did drive [OR operate] a motor vehicle in a manner dangerous to the public, thereby causing bodily harm to C.D., to wit: (specify the particulars of the offence), contrary to s. 249(3) of the Criminal Code of Canada.

Section 249(3) Dangerous operation of aircraft causing bodily harm

A.B., on the..........(day) of (month) ...., (year).........., at (specify time) in (specify place), did operate an aircraft in a manner dangerous to the public, thereby causing bodily harm to C.D., to wit: (specify the particulars of the offence), contrary to s. 249(3) of the Criminal Code of Canada.

Section 249(3) Dangerous operation of railway equipment causing bodily harm

A.B., on the..........(day) of (month) ...., (year).........., at (specify time) in (specify place), did operate railway equipment in a manner dangerous to the public, thereby causing bodily harm to C.D., to wit: (specify the particulars of the offence), contrary to s. 249(3) of the Criminal Code of Canada.

Section 249(4) Dangerous operation of vessel, water skis, surf-board causing death

A.B., on the..........(day) of (month) ...., (year).........., at (specify time) in (specify place),

..........did operate [OR navigate] a vessel in a manner dangerous to the public, thereby causing the death of C.D., to wit: (specify the particulars of the offence), contrary to s. 249(4) of the Criminal Code of Canada.

..........did operate water skis [OR a surf-board] in a manner dangerous to the public, thereby causing the death of C.D., to wit: (specify the particulars of the offence), contrary to s. 249(4) of the Criminal Code of Canada.

Section 249(4) Dangerous driving causing death

A.B., on the..........(day) of (month) ...., (year).........., at (specify time) in (specify place), did drive [OR operate] a motor vehicle in a manner dangerous to the public, thereby causing the death of C.D., to wit: (specify the particulars of the offence), contrary to s. 249(4) of the Criminal Code of Canada.

Section 249(4) Dangerous operation of aircraft causing death

A.B., on the..........(day) of (month) ...., (year).........., at (specify time) in (specify place), did operate an aircraft in a manner dangerous to the public, thereby causing the death of C.D., to wit: (specify the particulars of the offence), contrary to s. 249(4) of the Criminal Code of Canada.

Section 249(4) Dangerous operation of railway equipment causing death

A.B., on the..........(day) of (month) ...., (year).........., at (specify time) in (specify place), did operate railway equipment in a manner dangerous to the public thereby causing the death of C.D., to wit: (specify the particulars of the offence), contrary to s. 249(4) of the Criminal Code of Canada.

Section 250(1) Failure to keep watch on person towed by vessel

A.B., on the..........(day) of (month) ...., (year).........., at (specify time) in (specify place), did operate [OR navigate] a vessel while towing a person on water skis, at which time there was not on board such vessel another responsible person keeping watch on the person being towed, to wit: (specify the particulars of the offence), contrary to s. 250(1) of the Criminal Code of Canada.

Section 250(2) Towing person after dark by vessel

A.B., on the..........(day) of (month) ...., (year).........., at (specify time) in (specify place), did operate [OR navigate] a vessel while towing a person on water skis, during the period from one hour after sunset to sunrise, to wit: (specify the particulars of the offence), contrary to s. 250(2) of the Criminal Code of Canada.

Section 251(1)(a) Unseaworthy vessel

A.B., on the..........(day) of (month) ...., (year).........., at (specify time) in (specify place), knowingly did send [OR being the master did take] a vessel that was registered [OR licensed OR for which an identification number has been issued] pursuant to (specify the Act of Parliament) and that was unseaworthy, on a voyage from (specify a place in Canada) to (specify other place in or out of Canada) [OR on a voyage (specify a place on the inland waters of the United States) to (specify a place in Canada)] and thereby endangered the life of C.D., to wit: (specify the particulars of the offence), contrary to s. 251(1)(a) of the Criminal Code of Canada.

Section 251(1)(b) Unsafe aircraft

A.B., on the..........(day) of (month) ...., (year).........., at (specify time) in (specify place), did knowingly send an aircraft on a flight [OR did knowingly operate an aircraft], that was not fit and safe for flight, thereby endangering the life of C.D., to wit: (specify the particulars of the offence), contrary to s. 251(1)(b) of the Criminal Code of Canada.

Section 252(1) Failing to stop aircraft at scene of accident

A.B., on the..........(day) of (month) ...., (year).........., at (specify time) in (specify place), having the care [OR charge OR control] of an aircraft that was involved in an accident with C.D. [OR a vehicle (OR a vessel OR an aircraft) in the charge of C.D.], with intent to escape civil or criminal liability, did fail to stop his [OR her] aircraft and give his [OR her] name and address [and offer assistance to C.D. (OR C.D. and E.F.), a person who was injured in the accident], to wit: (specify the particulars of the offence), contrary to s. 252(1) of the Criminal Code of Canada.

Section 251(1) Failing to stop vehicle at scene of accident

A.B., on the..........(day) of (month) ...., (year).........., at (specify time) in (specify place), having the care [OR charge OR control] of a vehicle that was involved in an accident with C.D. [OR a vehicle in the charge of C.D. OR cattle in the charge of C.D.], with intent to escape civil or criminal liability, did fail to stop his [OR her] vehicle and give his [OR her] name and address [and offer assistance to C.D. (OR

C.D. and E.F.), who was (OR were) injured in the accident], to wit: (specify the particulars of the offence), contrary to s. 252(1) of the Criminal Code of Canada.

Section 252(1) Failure to stop vessel at scene of accident

A.B., on the..........(day) of (month) ...., (year).........., at (specify time) in (specify place), having the care [OR charge OR control] of a vessel that was involved in an accident with C.D. [OR a vehicle (OR a vessel OR an aircraft) in the charge of C.D.], with intent to escape civil or criminal liability, did fail to stop his [OR her] vessel and give his [OR her] name and address [and offer assistance to C.D. (OR C.D. and E.F.), who was injured (OR were) in the accident], to wit: (specify the particulars of the offence), contrary to s. 252(1) of the Criminal Code of Canada.

Section 253 Operation of aircraft while impaired or with more than 80 mg of alcohol in blood

A.B., on the..........(day) of (month) ...., (year).........., at (specify time) in (specify place),

..........while his [OR her] ability to operate an aircraft was impaired by alcohol [OR a drug], did operate [OR assist in the operation of OR have the care or control of] an aircraft, to wit: specify the particulars of the offence), contrary to s. 253 of the Criminal Code of Canada.

..........did operate [OR assist in the operation of OR have the care or control of] an aircraft, having consumed alcohol in such a quantity that the concentration thereof in the blood of A.B. exceeded 80 mg. of alcohol in 100 ml. of blood, to wit: (specify the particulars of the offence), contrary to s. 253 of the Criminal Code of Canada.

Section 253 Operation of motor vehicle while impaired or with more than 80 ml. of alcohol in blood

A.B., on the..........(day) of (month) ...., (year).........., at (specify time) in (specify place),

..........while his [OR her] ability to operate a motor vehicle was impaired by alcohol [OR a drug], did operate [OR have the care or control of] a motor vehicle, to wit: (specify the particulars of the offence), contrary to s. 253 of the Criminal Code of Canada.

..........did operate [OR have the care or control of] a motor vehicle, having consumed alcohol in such a quantity that the concentration thereof in the blood of A.B. exceeded 80 ml. of alcohol in 100 ml. of blood, to wit: (specify the particulars of the offence), contrary to s. 253 of the Criminal Code of Canada.

Section 253 Operation of vessel while impaired or with more than 80 ml. of alcohol in blood

A.B., on the..........(day) of (month) ...., (year).........., at (specify time) in (specify place),

..........while his [OR her] ability to operate a vessel was impaired by alcohol [OR a drug], did operate [OR have the care or control of] a vessel, to wit: (specify the particulars of the offence), contrary to s. 253 of the Criminal Code of Canada.

..........did operate [OR have the care or control of] a vessel, having consumed alcohol in such a quantity that the concentration thereof in the blood of A.B. exceeded 80 mgs. of alcohol in 100 ml. of blood, to wit: (specify the particulars of the offence), contrary to s. 253 of the Criminal Code of Canada.

Section 253 Operation of railway equipment while impaired or with more than 80 mg. of alcohol in blood

A.B., on the..........(day) of (month) ...., (year).........., at (specify time) in (specify place),

..........while his [OR her] ability to operate railway equipment was impaired by alcohol [OR a drug], did operate [OR assist in the operation of OR have the care or control of] railway equipment, to wit: (specify the particulars of the offence), contrary to s. 253 of the Criminal Code of Canada.

..........did operate [OR assist in the operation of OR have the care or control of] railway equipment, having consumed alcohol in such a quantity that the concentration thereof in the blood of A.B. exceeded 80 mg. of alcohol in 100 ml. of blood, to wit: (specify the particulars of the offence), contrary to s. 253 of the Criminal Code of Canada.

Section 254(5) Failure or refusal to provide sample

A.B., on the..........(day) of (month) ...., (year).........., at (specify time) in (specify place), without reasonable excuse, did fail [OR refuse] to comply with a demand made to A.B. by C.D., a peace officer, under s. 254(2) [OR s. 254(3)] of the Criminal Code, to wit: (specify the particulars of the offence), contrary to s. 254(5) of the Criminal Code of Canada.

Section 255(2) Impaired operation of aircraft causing bodily harm

A.B., on the..........(day) of (month) ...., (year).........., at (specify time) in (specify place), while his [OR her] ability to operate an aircraft was impaired by alcohol [OR a drug], did operate [OR assist in the operation of OR have the care or control of] an aircraft, thereby causing bodily harm to C.D., to wit: (specify the particulars of the offence), contrary to s. 255(2) of the Criminal Code of Canada.

Section 255(2) Impaired operation of motor vehicle causing bodily harm

A.B., on the..........(day) of (month) ...., (year).........., at (specify time) in (specify place), while his [OR her] ability to operate a motor vehicle was impaired by alcohol [OR a drug], did operate [OR have the care or control of] a motor vehicle, thereby causing bodily harm to C.D., to wit: (specify the particulars of the offence), contrary to s. 255(2) of the Criminal Code of Canada.

Section 255(2) Impaired operation of vessel causing bodily harm

A.B., on the..........(day) of (month) ...., (year).........., at (specify time) in (specify place), while his [OR her] ability to operate a vessel was impaired by alcohol [OR a drug], did operate [OR have the care or control of] a vessel, thereby causing bodily harm to C.D., to wit: (specify the particulars of the offence), contrary to s. 255(2) of the Criminal Code of Canada.

Section 255(2) Impaired operation of railway equipment causing bodily harm

A.B., on the..........(day) of (month) ...., (year).........., at (specify time) in (specify place), while his [OR her] ability to operate railway equipment was impaired by alcohol [OR a drug], did operate [OR have the care or control of] railway equipment, thereby causing bodily harm to C.D., to wit: (specify the particulars of the offence), contrary to s. 255(2) of the Criminal Code of Canada.

Section 255(3) Impaired operation of aircraft causing death

A.B., on the..........(day) of (month) ...., (year).........., at (specify time) in (specify place), while his [OR her] ability to operate an aircraft was impaired by alcohol [OR a drug], did operate [OR assist in the operation of OR have the care or control of] an aircraft, thereby causing the death of C.D. to wit: (specify the particulars of the offence), contrary to s. 255(3) of the Criminal Code of Canada.

Section 255(3) Impaired operation of motor vehicle causing death

A.B., on the..........(day) of (month) ...., (year).........., at (specify time) in (specify place), while his [OR her] ability to operate a motor vehicle was impaired by alcohol [OR a drug], did operate [OR have the care or control of] a motor vehicle, thereby causing the death of C.D., to wit: (specify the particulars of the offence), contrary to s. 255(3) of the Criminal Code of Canada.

Section 255(3) Impaired operation of vessel causing death

A.B., on the..........(day) of (month) ...., (year).........., at (specify time) in (specify place), while his [OR her] ability to operate a vessel was impaired by alcohol [OR a drug], did operate [OR have the care or control of] a vessel, thereby causing the death of C.D., to wit: (specify the particulars of the offence), contrary to s. 255(3) of the Criminal Code of Canada.

Section 255(3) Impaired operation of railway equipment causing death

A.B., on the..........(day) of (month) ...., (year).........., at (specify time) in (specify place), while his [OR her] ability to operate railway equipment was impaired by alcohol [OR a drug], did operate [OR have the care or control of] railway equipment, thereby causing the death of C.D., to wit: (specify the particulars of the offence), contrary to s. 255(3) of the Criminal Code of Canada.

Section 259(4) Operation of aircraft while disqualified

A.B., on the..........(day) of (month) ...., (year).........., at (specify time) in (specify place), did operate an aircraft in Canada while A.B. was disqualified from doing so, to wit: (specify the particulars of the offence), contrary to s. 259(4) of the Criminal Code of Canada.

Section 259(4) Operation of motor vehicle while disqualified

A.B., on the..........(day) of (month) ...., (year).........., at (specify time) in (specify place), did operate a motor vehicle in Canada while A.B. was disqualified from doing so, to wit: (specify the particulars of the offence), contrary to s. 259(4) of the Criminal Code of Canada.

Section 259(4) Operation of vessel while disqualified

A.B., on the.......... day of ...., 19.........., at (specify time) in (specify place), did operate a vessel in Canada while A.B. was disqualified from doing so, to wit: (specify the particulars of the offence), contrary to s. 259(4) of the Criminal Code of Canada.

Section 259(4) Operation of railway equipment while disqualified

A.B., on the..........(day) of (month) ...., (year).........., at (specify time) in (specify place), did operate railway equipment in Canada while A.B. was disqualified from doing so, to wit: (specify the particulars of the offence), contrary to s. 259(4) of the Criminal Code of Canada.

Section 262 Impeding attempt to save life

A.B., on the..........(day) of (month) ...., (year).........., at (specify time) in (specify place),

..........did prevent [OR impede OR attempt to prevent OR attempt to impede] C.D., who was attempting to save his [OR her] own life, to wit: (specify the particulars of the offence), contrary to s. 262(a) of the Criminal Code of Canada.

..........without reasonable cause, did prevent [OR impede OR attempt to prevent OR attempt to impede] C.D., who was attempting to save the life of E.F., to wit: (specify the particulars of the offence), contrary to s. 262(b) of the Criminal Code of Canada.

Section 263(1) Opening in ice

A.B., on the..........(day) of (month) ...., (year).........., at (specify time) in (specify place), did make [OR cause to be made] an opening in ice frequented by [OR open to] the public and failed to perform his [OR her] legal duty to guard it in a manner adequate to prevent persons from falling in by accident and to warn persons that the opening existed, to wit: (specify the particulars of the offence), contrary to s. 263(1) of the Criminal Code of Canada.

Section 263(3) Excavation

A.B., on the..........(day) of (month) ...., (year).........., at (specify time) in (specify place), failed to perform the legal duty that arises on leaving an excavation on land that A.B. owned [OR on land of which A.B. had charge (OR supervision)], to guard it in a manner that was adequate to prevent persons from falling in by accident and to warn them that the excavation existed, to wit: (specify the particulars of the offence), contrary to s. 263(3) of the Criminal Code of Canada.

Section 264(3) Criminal harassment

A.B., on the..........(day) of (month) ...., (year).........., at (specify time) in (specify place), without lawful authority and knowing that C.D. was harassed [OR reckless as to whether C.D. was harassed], did engage in conduct consisting of repeatedly following C.D. from place to place [OR anyone known to C.D. OR repeatedly communicating with C.D., either directly or indirectly, (OR anyone known to them) OR besetting (OR watching) the dwelling-house (OR place) where the other person (OR anyone known to them) resides (OR works OR carries on business OR happens to be) OR engaging in threatening conduct directed at C.D. (OR any member of the family of C.D.)], that causes C.D. reasonably in all the circumstances, to fear for their safety [OR the safety of anyone known to them], to wit: (specify the particulars of the offence), contrary to s. 264(3) of the Criminal Code of Canada.

Section 264.1(1)(a) and (2) Uttering threats relating to persons

A.B., on the..........(day) of (month) ...., (year).........., at (specify time) in (specify place), did knowingly utter [OR convey OR cause C.D. to receive] a threat to cause death [OR bodily harm] to C.D. [OR E.F.], to wit: (specify the particulars of the offence), contrary to s. 264.1(1)(a) and (2) of the Criminal Code of Canada.

Section 264.1(1)(b) and (3) Uttering threats relating to property

A.B., on the..........(day) of (month) ...., (year).........., at (specify time) in (specify place), did knowingly utter [OR convey OR cause C.D. to receive] a threat to burn [OR destroy OR damage] real [OR personal] property, to wit: (specify the particulars of the offence), contrary to s. 264.1(1)(b) and (3) of the Criminal Code of Canada.

Section 264.1(1)(c) and (3) Uttering threats relating to animals

A.B., on the..........(day) of (month) ...., (year).........., at (specify time) in (specify place), did knowingly utter [OR convey OR cause C.D. to receive] a threat to [OR poison OR injure] an animal [OR a bird] belonging to C.D. [OR E.F.], to wit: (specify the particulars of the offence), contrary to s. 264.1(1)(c) and (3) of the Criminal Code of Canada.

Section 266 Assault

A.B., on the..........(day) of (month) ...., (year).........., at (specify time) in (specify place), did commit an assault on C.D., to wit: (specify the particulars of the offence), contrary to s. 266 of the Criminal Code of Canada.

Section 267(a) Assault with a weapon

A.B., on the..........(day) of (month) ...., (year).........., at (specify time) in (specify place), while committing an assault on C.D., did carry [OR use OR threaten to use] a weapon [OR an imitation of a weapon], to wit: (specify the particulars of the offence), contrary to s. 267(a) of the Criminal Code of Canada.

Section 267(b) Assault causing bodily harm

A.B., on the..........(day) of (month) ...., (year).........., at (specify time) in (specify place), while committing an assault against C.D., did cause bodily harm to C.D., to wit: (specify the particulars of the offence), contrary to s. 267(b) of the Criminal Code of Canada.

Section 268(2) Aggravated assault

A.B., on the..........(day) of (month) ...., (year).........., at (specify time) in (specify place), did wound [OR maim OR disfigure OR endanger the life of] C.D. and thereby commit an aggravated assault to wit: (specify the particulars of the offence), contrary to s. 268(2) of the Criminal Code of Canada.

Section 269 Unlawfully causing bodily harm

A.B., on the..........(day) of (month) ...., (year).........., at (specify time) in (specify place), did unlawfully cause bodily harm to C.D., to wit: (specify the particulars of the offence), contrary to s. 269 of the Criminal Code of Canada.

Section 269.1 (1) Torture

A.B., being an official [OR being a person acting at the instigation of or with the consent or acquiescence of C.D., an official], on or about the .... day of ...., 19.........., at the.......... of ...., in the said (territorial division), did inflict torture on E.F., to wit: (specify the particulars of the offence), contrary to s. 269.1(1) of the Criminal Code of Canada.

Section 270(1)(a) Assaulting a public officer or a peace officer

A.B., on the..........(day) of (month) ...., (year).........., at (specify time) in (specify place), did assault C.D., a public officer [OR peace officer OR person acting in aid of E.F., a public (OR peace) officer], engaged in the execution of his [OR her] duty, to wit: (specify the particulars of the offence), contrary to s. 270(1)(a) of the Criminal Code of Canada.

Section 270(1)(b) Assault with intent to resist arrest

A.B., on the..........(day) of (month) ...., (year).........., at (specify time) in (specify place), did assault C.D., with intent to resist [OR prevent] the lawful arrest [OR detention] of A.B. [OR E.F.], to wit: (specify the particulars of the offence), contrary to s. 270(1)(b) of the Criminal Code of Canada.

Section 270(1)(c)(i) Assault during execution of process or making a distress or seizure

A.B., on the..........(day) of (month) ...., (year).........., at (specify time) in (specify place),

..........did assault C.D., a person engaged in the lawful execution of a process against the lands [OR goods] of A.B. [OR E.F.], to wit: (specify the particulars of the assault as well as the particulars of the process being lawfully executed), contrary to s. 270(1)(c)(i) of the Criminal Code of Canada.

..........did assault C.D., a person engaged in making a lawful distress [OR seizure], to wit: (specify the particulars of the assault as well as the particulars of the lawful distress or seizure), contrary to s. 270(1)(c)(i) of the Criminal Code of Canada.

Section 270(1)(c)(ii) Assault with intent to rescue thing taken under lawful process

A.B., on the..........(day) of (month) ...., (year).........., at (specify time) in (specify place), did assault C.D., with intent to rescue property that had been taken under a lawful process [OR distress OR seizure], to wit: (specify the particulars of the offence), contrary to s. 270(1)(c)(ii) of the Criminal Code of Canada.

Section 271(1) Sexual assault

A.B., on the..........(day) of (month) ...., (year).........., at (specify time) in (specify place), did commit a sexual assault on C.D., to wit: (specify the particulars of the offence), contrary to s. 271(1) of the Criminal Code of Canada.

Section 272(a) Sexual assault with a weapon

A.B., on the..........(day) of (month) ...., (year).........., at (specify time) in (specify place), while committing a sexual assault on C.D., did carry [OR use OR threaten to use] a weapon [OR an imitation of a weapon], to wit: (specify the particulars of the offence), contrary to s. 272(a) of the Criminal Code of Canada.

Section 272(b) Sexual assault with threats to a third party

A.B., on the..........(day) of (month) ...., (year).........., at (specify time) in (specify place), while committing a sexual assault on C.D., did threaten to cause bodily harm to E.F., to wit: (specify the particulars of the offence), contrary to s. 272(b) of the Criminal Code of Canada.

Section 272(c) Sexual assault causing bodily harm

A.B., on the..........(day) of (month) ...., (year).........., at (specify time) in (specify place), while committing a sexual assault on C.D., did cause bodily harm to C.D., to wit: (specify the particulars of the offence), contrary to s. 272(c) of the Criminal Code of Canada.

Section 272(d) Sexual assault — party to the offence

A.B., on the..........(day) of (month) ...., (year).........., at (specify time) in (specify place), was a party to the commission of a sexual assault on C.D. by E.F., to wit: (specify the particulars of the offence), contrary to s. 272(d) of the Criminal Code of Canada.

Section 273(2) Aggravated sexual assault

A.B., on the..........(day) of (month) ...., (year).........., at (specify time) in (specify place), did commit an aggravated assault on C.D., to wit: (specify the particulars of the offence), contrary to s. 273(2) of the Criminal Code of Canada.

Forms of Charges

Section 273.3(1) Removal of child from Canada

A.B., on the..........(day) of (month) ...., (year).........., at (specify time) in (specify place),

..........did (specify act done), for the purpose of removing from Canada C.D., a person ordinarily resident in Canada and under 14 years of age, with the intention of committing an act outside Canada that if it were committed in Canada would be an offence under s. 151 (sexual interference) [OR s. 152 (invitation to sexual touching) OR s. 160(3) (bestiality in presence of or by a child) OR s. 173(2) (exposure)] of the Criminal Code, to wit: (specify the particulars of the offence), contrary to s. 273.3(1)(a) of the Criminal Code of Canada.

..........did (specify act done), for the purpose of removing from Canada C.D., a person ordinarily resident in Canada, over 14 years of age and under 18 years of age, with the intention of committing an act outside Canada that if it were committed in Canada would be an offence under s. 153 (sexual exploitation) of the Criminal Code, to wit: (specify the particulars of the offence), contrary to s. 273.3(1)(b) of the Criminal Code of Canada.

..........did (specify act done), for the purpose of removing from Canada C.D., a person ordinarily resident in Canada and under 18 years of age, with the intention of committing an act outside Canada that if it were committed in Canada would be an offence under s. 155 (incest) [OR s. 159 (anal intercourse) OR s. 160(2) (compulsion to commit bestiality) OR s. 170 (parent or guardian procuring sexual activity) OR s. 171 (householder permitting sexual activity) OR s. 267 (assault) OR s. 269 (unlawfully causing bodily harm) OR s. 272 (sexual assault) OR s. 273 (aggravated sexual assault)] of the Criminal Code, to wit: (specify the particulars of the offence), contrary to s. 273.3(1)(c) of the Criminal Code of Canada.

Section 276.3(2) Publishing evidence of sexual activity

A.B., on the..........(day) of (month) ...., (year).........., at (specify time) in (specify place),

..........did publish in a newspaper [OR in a broadcast] the contents of an application made under s. 276.3, to wit: (specify the particulars of the offence), contrary to s. 276.3(2)(a) of the Criminal Code of Canada.

..........did publish in a newspaper [OR in a broadcast] evidence taken [OR the information given OR the representations made] at an application under s. 276.1 [OR at a hearing under s. 276.2], to wit: (specify the particulars of the offence), contrary to s. 276.3(2)(b) of the Criminal Code of Canada.

..........did publish in a newspaper [OR in a broadcast] the decision of the judge [OR provincial court judge OR justice] under s. 276.1(4), without an order permitting publication, to wit: (specify the particulars of the offence), contrary to s. 276.3(2)(c) of the Criminal Code of Canada.

..........did publish in a newspaper [OR in a broadcast] the determination made and the reasons provided under s. 276.2, without a determination that evidence is admissible [OR without an order] permitting publication, to wit: (specify the particulars of the offence), contrary to s. 276.3(2)(d) of the Criminal Code of Canada.

Section 278.9(2) Publication regarding production of records in sexual offence proceedings

A.B., on the..........(day) of (month) ...., (year).........., at (specify time) in (specify place),

..........did publish in a newspaper [OR in a broadcast] the contents of an application made under s. 278.3, to wit: (specify the particulars of the offence), contrary to s. 278.9(a) of the Criminal Code of Canada.

..........did publish in a newspaper [OR in a broadcast] evidence taken [OR information given OR submissions made] at a hearing under s. 278.4(1) [OR s. 278.6(2)], to wit: (specify the particulars of the offence), contrary to s. 278.9(b) of the Criminal Code of Canada.

..........did publish in a newspaper, [OR in a broadcast] the determination of a judge pursuant to s. 278.5(1) [OR s. 278.7(1)] and the reasons provided pursuant to s. 278.8, without an order of the judge permitting publication, to wit: (specify the particulars of the offence), contrary to s. 278.9(2)(c) of the Criminal Code of Canada.

Section 279(1) Kidnapping

A.B., on the..........(day) of (month) ...., (year).........., at (specify time) in (specify place),

..........did kidnap C.D. with intent to cause C.D. to be confined [OR imprisoned] against his [OR her] will, to wit: (specify the particulars of the offence), contrary to s. 279(1)(a) of the Criminal Code of Canada.

..........did kidnap C.D. with intent to cause C.D. to be unlawfully sent or transported out of Canada against his [OR her] will, to wit: (specify the particulars of the offence), contrary to s. 279(1)(b) of the Criminal Code of Canada.

..........did kidnap C.D. with intent to hold C.D. to ransom [OR to service] against his [OR her] will, to wit: (specify the particulars of the offence), contrary to s. 279(1)(c) of the Criminal Code of Canada.

Section 279(2) Forcible confinement

A.B., on the..........(day) of (month) ...., (year).........., at (specify time) in (specify place), did without lawful authority confine [OR imprison OR forcibly seize] C.D., to wit: (specify the particulars of the offence), contrary to s. 279(2) of the Criminal Code of Canada.

Section 279.1(2) Hostage taking

A.B., on the..........(day) of (month) ...., (year).........., at (specify time) in (specify place),

..........did confine [OR imprison OR forcibly seize OR detain] C.D. and did utter [OR convey OR cause a person to receive] a threat that the death of [OR bodily harm to] C.D. would be caused, with intent to induce (specify an act or omission) as a condition of the release of C.D., to wit: (specify the particulars of the offence), contrary to s. 279.1(2) of the Criminal Code of Canada.

..........did confine [OR imprison OR forcibly seize OR detain] C.D. and did utter [OR convey OR cause a person to receive] a threat that the confinement [OR imprisonment OR detention] of C.D. would be continued, with intent to induce (specify an act or omission) as a condition of the release of C.D., to wit: (specify the particulars of the offence), contrary to s. 279.1(2) of the Criminal Code of Canada.

Section 280 Abduction of person under sixteen

A.B., on the..........(day) of (month) ...., (year).........., at (specify time) in (specify place), did without lawful authority take [OR cause to be taken] C.D., an unmarried person under the age of 16 years, out of the possession of and against the will of E.F., her [OR his] father [OR mother OR guardian OR (specify other person)] then having the lawful care or charge of her [OR him], to wit: (specify the particulars of the offence), contrary to s. 280 of the Criminal Code of Canada.

Section 281 Abduction of person under fourteen

A.B., not being the parent, guardian or person having the lawful care or charge of C.D., a person under the age of 14 years, on or about the..........of ...., 19.........., at the .... of ...., in the said (territorial division), did unlawfully take [OR entice away OR conceal OR detain OR receive OR harbour] C.D. with intent to deprive E.F., the parent [OR guardian OR person having the lawful care or charge] of C.D., of the possession of C.D., to wit: (specify the particulars of the offence), contrary to s. 281 of the Criminal Code of Canada.

Section 282 Abduction in contravention of custody order

A.B., on the..........(day) of (month) ...., (year).........., at (specify time) in (specify place), being the parent, guardian or person having the lawful care or charge of C.D., a person under the age of 14 years, did take [OR entice away OR conceal OR detain OR receive OR harbour] C.D. in contravention of the custody provisions of a custody order in relation to C.D. made by (specify the name of the court) at (specify the location of the court) on (specify the date that the order was made), with intent to deprive E.F., the parent [OR guardian OR person having the lawful care or charge] of C.D., of the possession of C.D., to wit: (specify the particulars of the offence), contrary to s. 282 of the Criminal Code of Canada.

Section 283 Abduction where no custody order

A.B., on the..........(day) of (month) ...., (year).........., at (specify time) in (specify place), being the parent, guardian or person having the lawful care or charge of C.D., a person under the age of 14 years, did unlawfully take [OR entice away OR conceal OR detain OR receive OR harbour] C.D., with intent to deprive E.F., the parent [OR guardian OR person who has the lawful care or charge of] C.D., of the possession of C.D., to wit: (specify the particulars of the offence), contrary to s. 283 ofthe Criminal Code of Canada.

Section 288 Supplying noxious things for purposes of miscarriage

A.B., on the..........(day) of (month) ...., (year).........., at (specify time) in (specify place), did unlawfully supply [OR procure] (specify a drug OR noxious thing OR instrument) to [OR for] C.D., knowing it was intended to be used [OR employed] to procure the miscarriage of C.D. [OR E.F.], a female person, to wit: (specify the particulars of the offence), contrary to s. 288 of the Criminal Code of Canada.

Section 291(1)(a) Bigamy

A.B., on the..........(day) of (month) ...., (year).........., at (specify time) in (specify place),

..........being married [OR knowing C.D. to be then married] did go through a form of marriage with C.D., and did thereby commit bigamy, to wit: (specify the particulars of the offence), contrary to s. 291(1) of the Criminal Code of Canada.

..........on the same day [OR simultaneously] did go through a form of marriage with C.D. and E.F., and did thereby commit bigamy, to wit: (specify the particulars of the offence), contrary to s. 291(1) of the Criminal Code of Canada.

Section 291(1)(b) Leaving Canada to commit bigamy

A.B., on the..........(day) of (month) ...., (year).........., at (specify time) in (specify place), being a Canadian citizen resident in Canada, left Canada with intent and

..........being married [OR knowing that C.D. is married], did go through a form of marriage with C.D., and did thereby commit bigamy, to wit: (specify the particulars of the offence), contrary to s. 291(1) of the Criminal Code.

..........on the same day [OR simultaneously] did go through a form of marriage with C.D. and E.F., and did thereby commit bigamy, to wit: (specify the particulars of the offence), contrary to s. 291(1) of the Criminal Code.

Section 292(1) Feigned marriage

A.B., on the..........(day) of (month) ...., (year).........., at (specify time) in (specify place), did procure a feigned marriage to be performed between himself [OR herself] and C.D., [OR did assist E.F. in procuring a feigned marriage between E.F. and C.D.], to wit: (specify the particulars of the offence), contrary to s. 292(1) of the Criminal Code of Canada.

Section 292(1) Procuring feigned marriage

A.B., on the..........(day) of (month) ...., (year).........., at (specify time) in (specify place), procured [OR knowingly aided in procuring] a feigned marriage between A.B. and C.D., to wit: (specify the particulars of the offence), contrary to s. 292(1) of the Criminal Code of Canada.

Section 293(1)(a) Practising or agreeing to practise polygamy

A.B., on the..........(day) of (month) ...., (year).........., at (specify time) in (specify place), did practise [OR enter into OR agrees to practise OR agrees to enter into] a form of polygamy [OR a conjugal union with more than one person at the same time], to wit: (specify the particulars of the offence), contrary to s. 293 of the Criminal Code of Canada.

Section 293(1)(b) Party to the offence of polygamy

A.B., on the..........(day) of (month) ...., (year).........., at (specify time) in (specify place), celebrated [OR assisted OR was a party to] a rite [OR ceremony OR contract OR consent] that purports to sanction a form of polygamy [OR a conjugal union with more than one person at the same time], to wit: (specify the particulars of the offence), contrary to s. 293 of the Criminal Code of Canada.

Section 294 Pretending to solemnize marriage

A.B., on the..........(day) of (month) ...., (year).........., at (specify time) in (specify place),

..........without lawful authority did solemnize [OR pretend to solemnize] a marriage between C.D. and E.F., to wit: (specify the particulars of the offence), contrary to s. 294(a) of the Criminal Code of Canada.

..........then knowing that C.D. was not lawfully authorized to solemnize a marriage, did procure C.D. to solemnize a marriage between E.F. and G.H., to wit: (specify the particulars of the offence), contrary to s. 294(b) of the Criminal Code of Canada.

Section 295 Solemnizing a marriage contrary to law

A.B., on the..........(day) of (month) ...., (year).........., at (specify time) in (specify place), being lawfully authorized to solemnize marriage, knowingly and wilfully, did solemnize a marriage in contravention of the laws of the province of (specify the province) in which the marriage was solemnized), to wit: (specify the particulars of the offence), contrary to s. 295 of the Criminal Code of Canada.

Section 296(1) Publishing a blasphemous libel

A.B., on the..........(day) of (month) ...., (year).........., at (specify time) in (specify place), did publish a blasphemous libel, to wit: (specify the particulars of the offence), contrary to s. 296(1) of the Criminal Code of Canada.

Section 300 Publishing a defamatory libel known to be false

A.B., on the..........(day) of (month) ...., (year).........., at (specify time) in (specify place), did publish a defamatory libel that A.B. knew was false, to wit: (specify the particulars of the offence), contrary to s. 300 of the Criminal Code of Canada.

Section 301 Publishing a defamatory libel

A.B., on the..........(day) of (month) ...., (year).........., at (specify time) in (specify place), did publish a defamatory libel, to wit: (specify the particulars of the offence), contrary to s. 301 of the Criminal Code of Canada.

Section 302(1) and (2) Extortion by libel

A.B., on the..........(day) of (month) ...., (year).........., at (specify time) in (specify place),

..........with intent to extort money from C.D. [OR to induce C.D. to confer on (OR procure for) E.F. an appointment (OR office of profit OR trust)] did publish [OR threaten to publish OR offer to abstain from publishing (OR prevent the publication of)] a defamatory libel, to wit: (specify the particulars of the offence), contrary to s. 302(2) of the Criminal Code of Canada.

..........as the result of the refusal of C.D. to permit money to be extorted [OR to confer (OR procure) an appointment (OR office of profit OR trust)] did publish [OR threaten to publish] a defamatory libel, to wit: (specify the particulars of the offence), contrary to s. 302(2) of the Criminal Code of Canada.

Section 318(1) Advocating genocide

A.B., on the..........(day) of (month) ...., (year).........., at (specify time) in (specify place), did advocate [OR promote] genocide, to wit: (specify the particulars of the offence), contrary to s. 318(1) of the Criminal Code of Canada.

Section 319(1) Public incitement of hatred

A.B., on the..........(day) of (month) ...., (year).........., at (specify time) in (specify place), in a public place, did by communicating statements incite hatred against (specify an identifiable group) where such incitement was likely to lead to a breach of the peace, to wit: (specify the particulars of the offence), contrary to s. 319(1) of the Criminal Code of Canada.

Section 319(2) Wilful promotion of hatred

A.B., on the..........(day) of (month) ...., (year).........., at (specify time) in (specify place), did by communicating statements wilfully promote hatred against (specify an identifiable group), to wit: (specify the particulars of the offence), contrary to s. 319(2) of the Criminal Code of Canada.

Part IX — Offence Against Rights of Property

Section 324 and 327 Instrument or device to obtain telecommunication service without payment

A.B., on the..........(day) of (month) ...., (year).........., at (specify time) in (specify place), did manufacture [OR possess Or sell OR offer for sale OR distribute] an instrument [OR device OR component of an instrument OR component of a device] the design of which renders it primarily useful for obtaining the use of a telecommunication service [OR facility], under circumstances that gave rise to a reasonable inference that the device had been used [OR was intended to be used OR had been intended to be used] to obtain the use of any telecommunication service [OR facility] without payment of a lawful charge therefor, to wit: (specify the particulars of the offence), contrary to s. 327 of the Criminal Code of Canada.

Section 334 Theft

A.B., on the..........(day) of (month) ...., (year).........., at (specify time) in (specify place), did steal (specify what) of the value of (specify the value in dollars), the property of C.D., to wit: (specify the particulars of the offence), contrary to s. 334 of the Criminal Code of Canada.

Section 334 and 326(1)(a) Theft of electricity or gas

A.B., on the..........(day) of (month) ...., (year).........., at (specify time) in (specify place), did fraudulently [OR maliciously OR without colour of right] abstract [OR consume OR use] electricity [OR gas] and did thereby commit theft, to wit: (specify the particulars of the offence), contrary to s. 334 of the Criminal Code of Canada.

Section 334 and 326(1)(b) Theft of telecommunications

A.B., on the..........(day) of (month) ...., (year).........., at (specify time) in (specify place), did fraudulently [OR maliciously OR without colour of right] use a telecommunication facility [OR obtain a telecommunication service], to wit: (specify the particulars of the offence), and did thereby commit theft contrary to s. 334 of the Criminal Code of Canada.

Section 334 and 324 — Theft by bailee of things under seizure

A.B., on the..........(day) of (month) ...., (year).........., at (specify time) in (specify place), being a bailee of (specify thing) that was under lawful seizure by C.D., a peace officer [OR public officer] in the execution of the duties of his [OR her] office and being obliged by law [OR agreement] to produce and deliver it to C.D. [OR to E.F., a person entitled thereto] at a certain time and place [OR on demand], did steal it by not producing and delivering it in accordance with his [OR her] obligation, to wit: (specify the particulars of the offence), contrary to s. 334 of the Criminal Code of Canada.

Section 334 and 329(2) Theft by husband or wife

A.B., on the..........(day) of (month) ...., (year).........., at (specify time) in (specify place), with the intention to desert [OR on deserting OR while living apart from] C.D., the wife [OR husband] of A.B., did fraudulently take [OR convert] (specify what was taken or converted), the property of C.D., to wit: (specify the particulars of the offence), and did thereby commit theft, contrary to s. 334 of the Criminal Code of Canada.

Section 334 and 329(3) Assisting theft by husband or wife

A.B., on the..........(day) of (month) ...., (year).........., at (specify time) in (specify place),

..........during the cohabitation of C.D. and E.F., a husband and wife, knowingly did assist C.D. (OR E.F.) in dealing with the property of E.F. [OR C.D.], in a manner that would have been theft if C.D. and E.F. were not married, to wit: (specify the particulars of the offence), and did thereby commit theft, contrary to s. 334 of the Criminal Code of Canada.

..........during the cohabitation of C.D. and E.F., a husband and wife, knowingly did receive from C.D. [OR E.F.] (specify what was received) that is by law the property of E.F. [OR C.D.] and had been obtained from E.F. [OR C.D.] by dealing with it in a manner that would have been theft if C.D. and E.F. were not married, to wit: (specify the particulars of the offence), and did thereby commit theft, contrary to s. 334 of the Criminal Code of Canada.

Section 334 and 331 Theft by person holding power of attorney

A.B., on the..........(day) of (month) ...., (year).........., at (specify time) in (specify place), being entrusted solely [OR jointly with C.D.], with a power of attorney for the sale [OR mortgage OR pledge OR other disposition of real (OR personal) property] did fraudulently sell [OR mortgage OR pledge OR otherwise dispose of] the property [OR any part of it] [OR fraudulently did convert the proceeds of a sale (OR mortgage OR pledge OR other disposition) of the property (OR any part of the proceeds) to a purpose other than that for which A.B. was entrusted by the power of attorney], to wit: (specify the particulars of the offence), contrary to s. 334 of the Criminal Code of Canada.

Section 334 and 330(1) Theft by person required to account

A.B., on the..........(day) of (month) ...., (year).........., at (specify time) in (specify place), did receive (specify what was received) from C.D. on terms that required A.B. to account for it [OR pay it OR pay the proceeds of it OR pay a part of the proceeds of it] to C.D. [OR E.F.] and did fraudulently fail to account for it [OR pay it OR pay the proceeds of it OR pay a part of the proceeds of it] accordingly, to wit: (specify the particulars of the offence), contrary to s. 334 of the Criminal Code of Canada.

Section 334 and 332(1) Misappropriation of money held under direction

A.B., on the..........(day) of (month) ...., (year).........., at (specify time) in (specify place), having received, solely [or jointly with another person], money [OR valuable security OR a power of attorney for the sale of real (OR personal) property] with a direction that the money [OR a part of it OR the proceeds (OR a part of the proceeds) of the security (or the property)] shall be applied to a purpose [OR paid to C.D., a person] specified in the direction, fraudulently and contrary to the direction did apply to another purpose [OR pay to E.F.] the money [OR proceeds OR part of the money (OR proceeds)], to wit: (specify the particulars of the offence), contrary to s. 334 of the Criminal Code of Canada.

Section 335 Taking motor vehicle or vessel without consent

A.B., on the..........(day) of (month) ...., (year).........., at (specify time) in (specify place),

..........did take a motor vehicle [OR vessel] without the consent of C.D., the owner of a motor vehicle [OR vessel], with intent to drive [OR use OR navigate OR operate] to wit: (specify the particulars of the offence), contrary to s. 335 of the Criminal Code of Canada.

..........did take a motor vehicle [OR vessel] without the consent of C.D., the owner of the motor vehicle [OR vessel], with intent to cause it to be driven [OR used OR navigated OR operated], to wit: (specify the particulars of the offence), contrary to s. 335 of the Criminal Code of Canada.

Section 336 Criminal breach of trust

A.B., on the..........(day) of (month) ...., (year).........., at (specify time) in (specify place), being a trustee of (specify anything) for the use [OR benefit], whether in whole or in part, of C.D. [OR for a public (OR charitable) purpose] with intent to defraud and in contravention of his [OR her] trust, did convert that thing [OR any part of it] to a use that was not authorized by the trust, to wit: (specify the particulars of the offence), contrary to s. 336 of the Criminal Code of Canada.

Section 337 Public servant refusing to deliver property

A.B., on the..........(day) of (month) ...., (year).........., at (specify time) in (specify place), being [OR having been] employed in the service of Her Majesty in right of Canada [OR in right of a province OR in the service of a municipality] and entrusted by virtue of that employment with the receipt [OR custody OR management OR control] of (specify anything) did refuse [OR fail] to deliver it to C.D., a person who was authorized to demand it and did demand it, to wit: (specify the particulars of the offence), contrary to s. 337 of the Criminal Code of Canada.

Section 338(1) Fraudulently taking cattle or defacing brand

A.B., on the..........(day) of (month) ...., (year).........., at (specify time) in (specify place),

..........without the consent of C.D., did fraudulently take [OR hold OR keep in his (OR her) possession OR conceal OR receive OR appropriate OR purchase OR sell] cattle owned by C.D. that were found astray, to wit: (specify the particulars of the offence), contrary to s. 338(1)(a) of the Criminal Code of Canada.

..........without the consent of C.D., did fraudulently, in whole or in part, obliterate [OR alter OR deface] a brand [OR mark] on cattle owned by C.D., to wit: (specify the particulars of the offence), contrary to s. 338(1)(b) of the Criminal Code of Canada.

..........without the consent of C.D., did fraudulently, in whole or in part, make a false [OR counterfeit] brand [OR mark] on cattle owned by C.D., to wit: (specify the particulars of the offence), contrary to s. 338(1)(b) of the Criminal Code of Canada.

Section 338(2) Theft of cattle

A.B., on the..........(day) of (month) ...., (year).........., at (specify time) in (specify place), did commit theft of cattle, to wit: (specify the particulars of the offence), contrary to s. 338(2) of the Criminal Code of Canada.

Section 339(1) Lumber and lumbering equipment

A.B., on the..........(day) of (month) ...., (year).........., at (specify time) in (specify place), without the consent of the owner

..........fraudulently did take [OR hold OR keep in his (OR her) possession OR conceal OR receive OR appropriate OR purchase OR sell] lumber [OR lumbering equipment] that was found adrift [OR cast ashore OR lying] on [OR embedded in] the bed [OR bottom OR on the bank OR beach] of a river [OR stream OR lake] in Canada [OR in the harbours (OR the coastal waters) of Canada], to wit: (specify the particulars of the offence), contrary to s. 339(1)(a) of the Criminal Code of Canada.

..........did remove [OR alter OR obliterate OR deface] a mark [OR number] on lumber [OR lumbering equipment] that was found adrift [OR cast ashore OR lying] on [OR embedded in] the bed [OR bottom OR on the bank OR beach] of a river [OR stream OR lake] in Canada [OR in the harbours (OR the coastal waters) of Canada], to wit: (specify the particulars of the offence), contrary to s. 339(1)(b) of the Criminal Code of Canada.

..........did refuse to deliver up to C.D. the owner [OR to E.F., the person in charge thereof on behalf of the owner OR to a person authorized by the owner to receive it] lumber [OR lumbering equipment] that was found adrift [OR cast ashore OR lying] on [OR embedded in] the bed [OR bottom OR on the bank OR beach] of a river [OR stream OR lake] in Canada [OR in the harbours (OR the coastal waters) of Canada], to wit: (specify the particulars of the offence), contrary to s. 339(1)(c) of the Criminal Code of Canada.

Section 339(2) Dealing in marked lumbering equipment

A.B., on the..........(day) of (month) ...., (year).........., at (specify time) in (specify place), being a dealer in second-hand goods, did trade in [OR traffic in OR have in his (OR her) possession for sale (OR traffic)] lumbering equipment that was marked with a mark [OR brand OR registered timber mark OR name OR initials] of C.D., without the written consent of C.D., to wit: (specify the particulars of the offence), contrary to s. 339(2) of the Criminal Code of Canada.

Section 340 Destroying documents of title

A.B., on the..........(day) of (month) ...., (year).........., at (specify time) in (specify place), for a fraudulent purpose, did destroy [OR cancel OR conceal OR obliterate] a document of title to goods [OR a document of title to lands OR a valuable security OR a testamentary instrument OR a judicial (OR official) document], to wit: (specify the particulars of the offence), contrary to s. 340 of the Criminal Code of Canada.

Section 341 Fraudulent concealment

A.B., on the..........(day) of (month) ...., (year).........., at (specify time) in (specify place), for a fraudulent purpose, did take [OR obtain OR remove OR conceal] (specify the thing), to wit: (specify the particulars of the offence), contrary to s. 341 of the Criminal Code of Canada.

Section 342.1(1) Unauthorized use of computer

A.B., on the..........(day) of (month) ...., (year).........., at (specify time) in (specify place), fraudulently and without colour of right

..........directly [OR indirectly] did obtain, a computer service, to wit: (specify the particulars of the offence), contrary to s. 342.1(1)(a) of the Criminal Code of Canada.

..........by means of an electro-magnetic [OR acoustic OR mechanical OR (specify other type of device)] device, directly [OR indirectly], did intercept [OR cause to be intercepted], a function of a computer system, to wit: (specify the particulars of the offence), contrary to s. 342.1(2)(b) of the Criminal Code of Canada.

Section 342.2(1) Possession of device to obtain computer service

A.B., on the..........(day) of (month) ...., (year).........., at (specify time) in (specify place), without lawful justification or excuse, did make [OR possess OR sell OR offer for sale OR distribute] (specify the thing), an instrument [OR device OR component of an instrument OR component of a device] designed to be useful for committing (specify an offence under s. 342.1 of the Criminal Code), under circumstances that give rise to the inference that it had been used [OR is intended to be used OR was intended to be used] to commit such an offence, to wit: (specify the particulars of the offence), contrary to s. 342.2(1) of the Criminal Code.

Section 342(1) Credit card offences

A.B., on the..........(day) of (month) ...., (year).........., at (specify time) in (specify place),

..........did steal a credit card, to wit: (specify the particulars of the offence), contrary to s. 342(1)(a) of the Criminal Code of Canada.

..........did forge [OR falsify] a credit card, to wit: (specify the particulars of the offence), contrary to s. 342(1)(b) of the Criminal Code of Canada.

..........did have in his (OR her) possession [OR use OR deal] with a credit card that A.B. knew was obtained by the commission in Canada of an offence [OR by an act (OR omission) that, if it had occurred in Canada, would have constituted an offence], to wit: (specify the particulars of the offence), contrary to s. 342(1)(c) of the Criminal Code of Canada.

..........did use a credit card that A.B. knew had been revoked [OR cancelled], contrary to s. 342(1)(d) of the Criminal Code of Canada.

Section 342.01 Instruments for forging or falsifying credit cards

A.B., on the..........(day) of (month) ...., (year).........., at (specify time) in (specify place), without lawful justification or excuse, did make [OR repair OR buy OR sell OR export from Canada OR import into Canada OR possess] (specify), an instrument [OR a device OR an apparatus OR material OR thing] that A.B. knew had been used [OR was adapted for use OR was intended for use] in forging [OR falsifying] a credit card, to wit: (specify the particulars of the offence), contrary to s. 342.01 of the Criminal Code of Canada.

Section 343 and 344 Robbery

A.B., on the..........(day) of (month) ...., (year).........., at (specify time) in (specify place),

..........did steal (specify the thing stolen) from C.D., and for the purpose of extorting what was stolen [OR to prevent resistance to the stealing OR to overcome resistance to the stealing] used violence [OR threats of violence] to C.D. [OR to the property of C.D.], and did thereby commit robbery, to wit: (specify the particulars of the offence), contrary to s. 343(a) and s. 344 of the Criminal Code of Canada.

..........did steal (specify the thing stolen) from C.D., and at the same time [OR immediately before OR immediately thereafter] did wound [OR beat OR strike OR use personal violence to] C.D., and did thereby commit robbery, to wit: (specify the particulars of the offence), contrary to s. 343(b) and s. 344 of the Criminal Code of Canada.

..........did assault C.D. with intent to steal from C.D., and did thereby commit robbery, to wit: (specify the particulars of the offence), contrary to s. 343(d) and s. 344 of the Criminal Code of Canada.

..........did rob C.D. of (specify the thing), to wit: (specify the particulars of the offence), contrary to s. 344 of the Criminal Code of Canada.

Section 345 Stopping mail with intent to rob or search

A.B., on the..........(day) of (month) ...., (year).........., at (specify time) in (specify place), did stop a mail conveyance with the intent to rob [OR search] it, to wit: (specify the particulars of the offence), contrary to s. 345 of the Criminal Code of Canada.

Section 346(1.1) Extortion

A.B., on the..........(day) of (month) ...., (year).........., at (specify time) in (specify place), without reasonable justification or excuse and with intent to obtain (specify the thing sought to be obtained), by threats [OR accusations OR menaces OR violence] did induce [OR attempt to induce] C.D., the person threatened [OR the person accused OR the person menaced OR the person to whom violence was shown OR (specify any other person)], to do [OR cause to be done] (specify the thing done or caused to be done), to wit: (specify the particulars of the offence), contrary to s. 346(1.1) of the Criminal Code of Canada.

Section 347(1) Criminal interest rates

A.B., on the..........(day) of (month) ...., (year).........., at (specify time) in (specify place),

..........did enter into an agreement [OR arrangement] to receive interest at a criminal rate, to wit: (specify the particulars of the offence), contrary to s. 347(1)(a) of the Criminal Code of Canada.

..........did receive a payment [OR partial payment] of interest at a criminal rate, to wit: (specify the particulars of the offence), contrary to s. 347(1)(b) of the Criminal Code of Canada.

Section 348(1)(a) Breaking and entering with intent

A.B., on the..........(day) of (month) ...., (year).........., at (specify time) in (specify place), did break and enter (specify a place) with intent to commit therein the indictable offence of (specify the indictable offence), to wit: (specify the particulars of the break-in and entry), contrary to s. 348(1)(a) of the Criminal Code of Canada.

Section 348(1)(b) Breaking and entering and committing offence

A.B., on the..........(day) of (month) ...., (year).........., at (specify time) in (specify place), did break and enter (specify a place) and did commit therein the indictable offence of (specify the indictable offence committed), to wit: (specify the particulars of the break-in and entry), contrary to s. 348(1)(b) of the Criminal Code of Canada.

Section 348(1)(c) Breaking out

A.B., on the..........(day) of (month) ...., (year).........., at (specify time) in (specify place),

..........did break out of (specify a place) after having committed therein the indictable offence of (specify the indictable offence committed), to wit: (specify the particulars of the breaking-out), contrary to s. 348(1)(c) of the Criminal Code of Canada.

..........did break out of (specify a place) after having entered the place with the intention to commit therein the indictable offence of (specify the indictable offence), to wit: (specify the particulars of the breaking-out), contrary to s. 348(1)(c) of the Criminal Code of Canada.

Section 349(1) Being unlawfully in dwelling-house

A.B., on the..........(day) of (month) ...., (year).........., at (specify time) in (specify place), without lawful excuse, did enter [OR was in] the dwelling-house of C.D. with intent to commit therein the indictable offence of (specify the indictable offence), to wit: (specify the particulars of the offence), contrary to s. 349(1) of the Criminal Code of Canada.

Section 351(1) Possession of break-in instrument

A.B., on the..........(day) of (month) ...., (year).........., at (specify time) in (specify place), without lawful excuse, did have in his [OR her] possession an instrument suitable for breaking into a place [OR motor vehicle OR vault OR safe] under circumstances that gave rise to a reasonable inference that the instrument had been used [OR was intended to be used OR had been intended to be used] for breaking into (specify a place) [OR a motor vehicle OR a vault OR a safe], to wit: (specify the particulars of the offence), contrary to s. 351(1) of the Criminal Code of Canada.

Section 351(2) Being in disguise

A.B., on the..........(day) of (month) ...., (year).........., at (specify time) in (specify place), with intent to commit the indictable offence of (specify the indictable offence),

..........did have his [OR her] face masked [OR coloured], to wit: (specify the particulars of the offence), contrary to s. 351(2) of the Criminal Code of Canada.

..........was disguised, to wit: (specify the particulars of the offence), contrary to s. 351(2) of the Criminal Code of Canada.

Section 352 Possession of instruments for breaking into coin-operated device or currency exchange device

A.B., on the..........(day) of (month) ...., (year).........., at (specify time) in (specify place),

..........did have in his [OR her] possession an instrument suitable for breaking into a currency exchange device under circumstances that gave rise to a reasonable inference that the instrument had been used [OR was (OR had been) intended to be used] for breaking into a currency exchange device, to wit: (specify the particulars of the offence), contrary to s. 352 of the Criminal Code of Canada.

..........did have in his [OR her] possession an instrument suitable for breaking into a coin-operated device under circumstances that gave rise to a reasonable inference that the instrument had been used [OR was (OR had been) intended to be used] for breaking into a coin-operated device, to wit: (specify the particulars of the offence), contrary to s. 352 of the Criminal Code of Canada.

Section 353(1) Automobile master keys

A.B., on the..........(day) of (month) ...., (year).........., at (specify time) in (specify place),

..........did sell [OR offer for sale OR advertise] in the Province of (specify), an automobile master key without the authority of a licence issued by the Attorney General of that Province, to wit: (specify the particulars of the offence), contrary to s. 353(1) of the Criminal Code of Canada.

..........did purchase [OR have in his [OR her] possession] in the Province of (specify), an automobile master key without the authority of a licence issued by the Attorney General of that Province, to wit: (specify the particulars of the offence), contrary to s. 353(1) of the Criminal Code of Canada.

Section 353(4) Records of sales of automobile master keys

A.B., on the..........(day) of (month) ...., (year).........., at (specify time) in (specify place),

..........did fail to keep a record of the transaction showing the name and address of the purchaser and the particulars of the licence issued to the purchaser as described in s. 353(1)(b) of the Criminal Code of Canada, contrary to s. 353(3) of the Criminal Code.

..........did fail to produce for inspection at the request of C.D., a peace officer, the record of that transaction required by law to be kept by anyone who sells an automobile master key, to wit: (specify the particulars of the offence), contrary to s. 353(4) of the Criminal Code of Canada.

Section 354(1) Possession of property obtained by crime

A.B., on the..........(day) of (month) ...., (year).........., at (specify time) in (specify place), did have in his [OR her] possession (specify the property or thing or proceeds of any property or thing) of a value of more than [OR less than] $5,000, knowing that it was [OR they were] obtained by [OR derived directly from or indirectly derived from] the commission in Canada of an offence punishable by indictment [OR an act (OR omission) that, if it had occurred in Canada, would have constituted an offence punishable by indictment] to wit: (specify the particulars of the offence), contrary to s. 354(1) of the Criminal Code of Canada.

Section 356(1)(a) Theft from mail

A.B., on the..........(day) of (month) ...., (year).........., at (specify time) in (specify place),

..........did steal (specify the thing stolen) that had been sent by post, after it had been deposited at a post office and before it was delivered, to wit: (specify the particulars of the offence), contrary to s. 356(1)(a) of the Criminal Code of Canada.

..........did steal a bag [OR sack OR container OR covering] in which mail is conveyed, to wit: (specify the particulars of the offence), contrary to s. 356(1)(a) of the Criminal Code of Canada.

..........did steal a key suited to a lock adopted for use by the Canada Post Office, to wit: (specify the particulars of the offence), contrary to s. 356(1)(a) of the Criminal Code of Canada.

Section 356(1)(b) Possession of stolen mail

A.B., on the..........(day) of (month) ...., (year).........., at (specify time) in (specify place), did have in his possession (specify the thing in possession), a thing in respect of which A.B. knew that an offence had been committed under s. 356(1)(a) of the Criminal Code, to wit: (specify the particulars of the offence), contrary to s. 356(1)(b) of the Criminal Code of Canada.

Section 357 Bringing into Canada property obtained by crime

A.B., on the..........(day) of (month) ...., (year).........., at (specify time) in (specify place), did bring into [OR have in] Canada (specify the thing) that A.B. had obtained outside Canada by an act that if it had been committed in Canada, would have been an offence under s. 354 of the Criminal Code [OR an offence under s. 342 of the Criminal Code OR the offence of theft] to wit: (specify the particulars of the offence), contrary to s. 357 of the Criminal Code of Canada.

Section 362(1)(a) Obtaining anything by false pretences that may be the object of theft

A.B., on the..........(day) of (month) ...., (year).........., at (specify time) in (specify place), by a false pretence did obtain [OR cause to be delivered to C.D.] (specify the thing in respect of which the offence of theft may be committed), to wit: (specify the particulars of the offence), contrary to s. 362(1)(a) of the Criminal Code of Canada.

Section 362(1)(b) Obtaining credit by false pretences or fraud

A.B., on the..........(day) of (month) ...., (year).........., at (specify time) in (specify place), did obtain credit by false pretence [OR fraud] to wit: (specify the particulars of the offence), contrary to s. 362(1)(b) of the Criminal Code of Canada.

Section 362(1) False statement in writing

A.B., on the..........(day) of (month) ...., (year).........., at (specify time) in (specify place),

..........knowingly, did make [OR cause to be made], directly [OR indirectly], a false statement in writing with intent that it should be relied on with respect to the financial condition [OR means OR ability to pay] of A.B. [OR E.F. (OR firm OR corporation) that A.B. was interested in (OR that A.B. acts for)] for the purpose of procuring in any form whatever, whether for his [OR her] benefit [OR the benefit of E.F. (OR firm OR corporation)], the delivery of personal property [OR the payment of money OR the making of a loan OR the grant (OR extension) of credit OR the discount of an account receivable OR the making (OR accepting OR discounting OR endorsing) of a bill of exchange (OR cheque OR draft OR promissory note)], to wit: (specify the particular of the offence), contrary to s. 362(1)(c) of the Criminal Code of Canada.

..........knowing that a false statement in writing had been made with respect to the financial condition [OR means OR ability to pay] of A.B. [OR E.F. (OR firm or corporation) that A.B. was interested in (OR that A.B. acts for)] on the faith of that statement did procure the delivery of personal property [OR the payment of money OR the making of a loan OR the grant (OR extension) of credit OR the discount of an account receivable OR the making (OR accepting OR discounting OR endorsing) of a bill of exchange (OR cheque OR draft OR promissory note)] whether for his [OR her] benefit [OR for the benefit of E.F. (OR firm OR corporation)], to wit: (specify the particulars of the offence), contrary to s. 362(1)(d) of the Criminal Code of Canada.

Section 363(a) Obtaining execution of valuable security by fraud

A.B., on the..........(day) of (month) ...., (year).........., at (specify time) in (specify place), with intent to defraud [OR injure] C.D., by a false pretense did cause [OR induce] C.D. to execute [OR make OR accept OR endorse OR destroy] the whole of [OR a part of] a valuable security, to wit: (specify the particulars of the offence), contrary to s. 363(a) of the Criminal Code of Canada.

Section 364(1) Fraudulently obtaining food and lodging

A.B., on the..........(day) of (month) ...., (year).........., at (specify time) in (specify place), did fraudulently obtain food [OR beverage OR accommodation] at a place that is in the business of providing it, to wit: (specify the particulars of the offence), contrary to s. 364(1) of the Criminal Code of Canada.

Section 365 Witchcraft and fortune-telling

A.B., on the..........(day) of (month) ...., (year).........., at (specify time) in (specify place),

..........fraudulently did pretend to use [OR to exercise] witchcraft [OR sorcery OR an enchantment OR a conjuration], to wit: (specify the particulars of the offence), contrary to s. 365(a) of the Criminal Code of Canada.

..........fraudulently did undertake, for a consideration, to tell fortunes, to wit: (specify the particulars of the offence), contrary to s. 365(b) of the Criminal Code of Canada.

..........did pretend from his [OR her] skill in [OR knowledge of] an occult [OR crafty] science to discover where [OR in what manner] (specify a thing), that was supposed to have been stolen [OR lost], may be found, to wit: (specify the particulars of the offence), contrary to s. 365(c) of the Criminal Code of Canada.

Section 366(1)(a) Forgery

A.B., on the..........(day) of (month) ...., (year).........., at (specify time) in (specify place), did make a false document, knowing it to be false, with intent that it should be acted on [OR used] as genuine, to the prejudice of C.D., and did thereby commit forgery, to wit: (specify the particulars of the offence), contrary to s. 366(1)(a) of the Criminal Code of Canada.

Section 368(1) Uttering forged document

A.B., on the..........(day) of (month) ...., (year).........., at (specify time) in (specify place), knowing that a document was forged, did use it [OR deal with it OR act upon it OR cause C.D. (OR attempt to cause C.D.) to use it (OR deal with it OR act upon it)] as if it were genuine, to wit: (specify the particulars of the offence including a description of the document), contrary to s. 368(1) of the Criminal Code of Canada.

Section 369(a) Forgery of exchequer bill paper, revenue paper and bank note paper

A.B., on the..........(day) of (month) ...., (year).........., at (specify time) in (specify place), without lawful authority [OR excuse], did make [OR use OR knowingly have in his possession] exchequer bill paper [OR revenue paper OR paper that it used to make bank notes OR paper that is intended to resemble such paper], to wit: (specify the particulars of the offence), contrary to s. 369(a) of the Criminal Code of Canada.

Section 369(b) Instrument, writing or material adapted and intended to be used in forgery

A.B., on the..........(day) of (month) ...., (year).........., at (specify time) in (specify place), without lawful authority [OR excuse], did make [OR offer OR dispose of OR knowingly have in his possession] plate [OR die OR machinery OR instrument OR other writing (OR material)] that was adapted and intended to be used to commit forgery to wit: (specify the particulars of the offence), contrary to s. 369(b) of the Criminal Code of Canada.

Section 369(c) Forgery of seal of public body or authority

AA.B., on the..........(day) of (month) ...., (year).........., at (specify time) in (specify place), without lawful authority [OR excuse], did make [OR reproduce OR use] a public seal of Canada [OR (specify the province) OR the seal of (specify a public body OR authority) in Canada (OR of a court of law)], to wit: (specify the particulars of the offence), contrary to s. 369(1) of the Criminal Code of Canada.

Section 370 Counterfeit proclamation, order, regulation or appointment

A.B., on the..........(day) of (month) ...., (year).........., at (specify time) in (specify place), knowingly,

..........did print a proclamation [OR notice thereof] and did cause it falsely to purport to have been printed by the Queen's Printer for Canada [OR the Queen's Printer for (specify the province)], to wit: (specify the particulars of the offence), contrary to s. 370 of the Criminal Code of Canada.

..........did tender in evidence a copy of a proclamation [OR order OR regulation OR appointment] that falsely did purport to have been printed by the Queen's Printer for Canada [OR the Queen's Printer for (specify the province)], to wit: (specify the particulars of the offence), contrary to s. 370 of the Criminal Code of Canada.

Section 371 Telegram, cablegram or radio message in false name

A.B., on the..........(day) of (month) ...., (year).........., at (specify time) in (specify place), with intent to defraud, did cause [OR procure] a telegram [OR cablegram OR radio message] to be sent [OR delivered as being sent] by the authority of C.D. knowing that it was not sent by his [OR her] authority and with intent that the message should be acted on as being sent by his [OR her] authority, to wit: (specify the particulars of the offence), contrary to s. 371 of the Criminal Code of Canada.

Section 372(1) False messages

A.B., on the..........(day) of (month) ...., (year).........., at (specify time) in (specify place), with intent to injure [OR alarm] C.D., did convey [OR cause (OR procure) to be conveyed] by letter [OR telegram OR telephone OR cable OR radio OR otherwise], information that A.B. knew was false, to wit: (specify the particulars of the offence), contrary to s. 372(1) of the Criminal Code of Canada.

Section 372(2) Indecent telephone calls

A.B., on the..........(day) of (month) ...., (year).........., at (specify time) in (specify place), with intent to alarm [OR annoy] C.D., did make any indecent telephone call to C.D., to wit: (specify the particulars of the offence), contrary to s. 372(2) of the Criminal Code of Canada.

Section 372(3) Harassing telephone calls

A.B., on the..........(day) of (month) ...., (year).........., at (specify time) in (specify place), without lawful excuse, and with intent to harass C.D., did make [OR cause to be made] repeated telephone calls to C.D., to wit: (specify the particulars of the offence), contrary to s. 372(3) of the Criminal Code of Canada.

Section 374 Drawing or using documents without authority

A.B., on the..........(day) of (month) ...., (year).........., at (specify time) in (specify place),

..........with intent to defraud and without lawful authority, did make [OR execute OR draw OR sign OR accept OR endorse] a document in the name [OR on the account] of C.D. by procuration [OR specify otherwise], to wit: (specify the particulars of the offence), contrary to s. 374(a) of the Criminal Code of Canada.

..........did make use of [OR utter] a document, knowing that it had been made [OR executed OR signed OR accepted OR endorsed] with intent to defraud and without lawful authority in the name [OR on the account] of C.D. by procuration [OR specify otherwise], to wit: (specify the particulars of the offence), contrary to s. 374(b) of the Criminal Code of Canada.

Section 375 Obtaining anything by instrument based on forged document

A.B., on the..........(day) of (month) ...., (year).........., at (specify time) in (specify place),did demand [OR receive OR obtain] anything [OR did cause (OR procure) anything to be delivered (OR paid) to C.D.] under [OR on OR by] virtue of any instrument issued under the authority of law knowing that it was based on a forged document, to wit: (specify the particulars of the offence), contrary to s. 375 of the Criminal Code of Canada.

Section 376(1) Counterfeiting stamp

AA.B., on the..........(day) of (month) ...., (year).........., at (specify time) in (specify place),

..........fraudulently, did use [OR mutilate OR affix OR remove OR counterfeit] a stamp [OR a part of a stamp], to wit: (specify the particulars of the offence), contrary to s. 376(1)(b) of the Criminal Code of Canada.

..........knowingly and without lawful excuse, had in his [OR her] possession a counterfeit stamp [OR a stamp that had been fraudulently mutilated OR (specify a thing) bearing a stamp of which a part had been fraudulently erased (OR removed OR concealed)], to wit: (specify the particulars of the offence), contrary to s. 376(1)(b) of the Criminal Code of Canada.

..........without lawful excuse, did make [OR knowingly have in his possession] a die [OR an instrument] that was capable of making the impression of a stamp [OR part thereof], to wit: contrary to s. 376(1)(c) of the Criminal Code of Canada.

Section 376(2) Counterfeiting mark

A.B., on the..........(day) of (month) ...., (year).........., at (specify time) in (specify place), without lawful authority, did make a mark [OR did sell (OR expose for sale OR have in his [OR her] possession) a counterfeit mark OR did affix a mark to anything that was required by law to be marked (OR branded OR sealed OR wrapped) other than the thing to which the mark was originally affixed (OR was intended to be affixed) OR did affix a counterfeit mark to anything that was required by law to be marked (OR branded OR sealed OR wrapped)], to wit: (specify the particulars of the offence), contrary to s. 376(2) of the Criminal Code of Canada.

Section 377 Damaging documents

AA.B., on the..........(day) of (month) ...., (year).........., at (specify time) in (specify place), unlawfully,

..........did destroy [OR deface OR injure] a register [OR part of a register] of birth [OR baptism OR marriages OR deaths OR burials] that was required [OR authorized] by law to be kept in Canada [OR a copy (OR any part of a copy) of such a register that was required by law to be transmitted to a registrar (OR other officer)], to wit: (specify the particulars of the offence), contrary to s. 377(1)(a) of the Criminal Code of Canada.

..........did insert [OR cause to be inserted] in a register [OR part of a register] of birth [OR baptism OR marriages OR deaths OR burials] that was required [OR authorized] by law to be kept in Canada [OR a copy (OR any part of a copy) of such a register that was required by law to be transmitted to a registrar (OR other officer)], an entry that he knew was false of any matter relating to a birth [OR baptism OR marriage OR death OR burial] [OR did erase any material part from that register (OR copy)], to wit: (specify the particulars of the offence), contrary to s. 377(1)(b) of the Criminal Code of Canada.

..........did destroy [OR damage OR obliterate OR cause to be destroyed (OR damaged OR obliterated)] an election document, to wit: (specify the particulars of the offence), contrary to s. 377(1)(c) of the Criminal Code of Canada.

..........did make [OR cause to be made] an erasure [OR alteration OR interlineation] in [OR on] an election document, to wit: (specify the particulars of the offence), contrary to s. 377(1)(d) of the Criminal Code of Canada.

Section 378 False certified copies

A.B., on the..........(day) of (month) ...., (year).........., at (specify time) in (specify place),

..........being authorized [OR required] by law to make [OR issue] a certified copy of [OR extract from OR certificate in respect of] a register [OR record OR document], knowingly, did make [OR issue] a false certified copy [OR extract OR certificate], to wit: (specify the particulars of the offence), contrary to s. 378(a) of the Criminal Code of Canada.

..........not being authorized [OR required] by law to make [OR issue a certified copy of [OR extract from OR certificate in respect of] a register [OR record OR document], fraudulently, did make [OR issue] a copy [OR extract OR certificate] that purported to be certified as authorized [OR required] by law, to wit: (specify the particulars of the offence), contrary to s. 378(b) of the Criminal Code of Canada.

Section 378(c) False certificate or declaration

A.B., on the..........(day) of (month) ...., (year).........., at (specify time) in (specify place), being authorized [OR required] by law to make a certificate [OR declaration] concerning particular required for the purpose of making entries in a register [OR record OR document], knowingly and falsely, did make the certificate [OR declaration], to wit: (specify the particulars of the offence), contrary to s. 378(c) of the Criminal Code of Canada.

Part X — Fraudulent Transactions Relating to Contracts and Trade

Section 380(1) Fraud

A.B., on the..........(day) of (month) ...., (year).........., at (specify time) in (specify place), by deceit [OR by falsehood OR by fraudulent means], did defraud the public [OR C.D.] of property [OR of money OR of a valuable security], to wit: (specify the particulars of the offence), contrary to s. 380(1) of the Criminal Code of Canada.

Section 380(2) Frauds affecting public market price

A.B., on the..........(day) of (month) ...., (year).........., at (specify time) in (specify place), by deceit [OR by falsehood OR by fraudulent means], with intent to defraud, did affect the public market price of stocks [OR shares OR merchandise OR (specify a thing that was offered for sale to the public)], to wit: (specify the particulars of the offence), contrary to s. 380(2) of the Criminal Code of Canada.

Section 381 Using mails to defraud

A.B., on the..........(day) of (month) ...., (year).........., at (specify time) in (specify place), did make use of the mails for the purpose of transmitting [OR delivering] letters [OR circulars] concerning schemes devised [OR intended] to deceive the public [OR to defraud the public OR for the purpose of obtaining money under false pretences], to wit: (specify the particulars of the offence), contrary to s. 381 of the Criminal Code of Canada.

Section 382 Fraudulent manipulation of stock exchange transactions

A.B., on the..........(day) of (month) ...., (year).........., at (specify time) in (specify place), through the facility of a stock exchange [OR curb market OR other market], with intent to create a false [OR misleading] appearance of active public trading in a security [OR with intent to create a false (OR misleading) appearance with respect to the market price of a security], did effect a transaction in the security that involved no change in the beneficial ownership thereof [OR did enter an order for the purchase of the security knowing that an order of substantially the same size at substantially the same time and at substantially the same price for the sale of the security had been (OR would be) entered by (OR for) the same (OR different) persons OR did enter an order for the sale of the security knowing that an order of substantially the same size at substantially the same time and at substantially the same price for the purchase of the security had been (OR would be) entered by (OR for) the same (OR different) persons], to wit: (specify the particulars of the offence), contrary to s. 382 of the Criminal Code of Canada.

Section 383(1) Gaming in stocks or merchandise

A.B., on the..........(day) of (month) ...., (year).........., at (specify time) in (specify place), with intent to make gain [OR profit] by the rise [OR fall] in price of the stock of an incorporated [OR unincorporated] company [OR undertaking], in [OR outside] Canada, [OR of any goods (OR wares OR merchandise)], did make [OR sign OR authorize to be made (OR signed)] any contract [OR agreement], oral or written, purporting to be for the purchase [OR sale] of shares of stock [OR goods OR wares OR merchandise] without the bona fide intention of acquiring the shares [OR goods OR wares or merchandise] [OR of selling them] [OR did make (OR sign OR authorize to be made (OR signed)) a contract (OR agreement), oral or written, purporting to be for the sale (OR purchase) of shares of stock (OR goods OR wares OR merchandise) in respect of which no delivery of the things sold (OR purchased) was made (OR received) and without the bona fide intention of making (OR receiving) delivery thereof], to wit: (specify the particulars of the offence), to wit: (specify the particulars of the offence), contrary to s. 383(1) of the Criminal Code of Canada.

Section 384 Broker reducing stock by selling for his own account

A.B., on the..........(day) of (month) ...., (year).........., at (specify time) in (specify place), being an individual [OR a member (OR an employee) of a partnership OR a director (OR officer OR an employee) of a corporation] where A.B. [OR the partnership OR corporation] is employed as a broker by any customer to buy and carry on margin any shares of an incorporated [OR unincorporated] company [OR undertaking], in [OR out of] Canada, thereafter did sell [OR cause to be sold] shares of the company [OR undertaking] for any account in which A.B. [OR his (OR her) firm (OR a partner thereof) OR the corporation (OR a director thereof)] had a direct [OR indirect] interest, if the effect of the sale was, otherwise than unintentionally, to reduce the amount of those shares in the hands of the broker [OR under his (OR her) control in the ordinary course of business] below the amount of those shares that the broker should be carrying for all customers, to wit: (specify the particulars of the offence), contrary to s. 384 of the Criminal Code of Canada.

Section 385(1) Fraudulent concealment of title documents

A.B., on the..........(day) of (month) ...., (year).........., at (specify time) in (specify place), being a vendor [OR mortgagor] of property [OR of a chose in action] [OR being a solicitor for (OR agent of) a vendor (OR mortgagor) of property (OR a chose in action)] was served with a written demand for an abstract of title by [OR on behalf of] the purchaser [OR mortgagee] before the completion of the purchase [OR mortgage], and with intent to defraud and for the purpose of inducing the purchaser [OR mortgagee] to accept the title offered [OR produced] to him [OR her], did conceal from him [OR her] any settlement [OR deed OR will OR other instrument] material to the title [OR any encumbrance on the title] [OR did falsify any pedigree on which the title depended], to wit: (specify the particulars of the offence), contrary to s. 385(1) of the Criminal Code of Canada.

Section 386 Fraudulent registration of title

A.B., on the..........(day) of (month) ...., (year).........., at (specify time) in (specify place), as principal [OR agent] in a proceeding to register title to real property [OR in a transaction relating to real property that was (OR was proposed) to be registered], knowingly and with intent to deceive, did make a material false statement [OR representation] [OR did suppress (OR conceal) from a judge (OR registrar OR any person employed by (OR assisting) the registrar) a material document (OR fact OR matter OR information OR was privy to anything just mentioned)], to wit: (specify the particulars of the offence), contrary to s. 386 of the Criminal Code of Canada.

Section 387 Fraudulent sale of real property

A.B., on the..........(day) of (month) ...., (year).........., at (specify time) in (specify place), knowing of an unregistered prior sale [OR of an existing unregistered grant OR mortgage OR hypothec OR privilege OR encumbrance] of [OR on] real prop-

erty, fraudulently did sell the property [OR part thereof], to wit: (specify the particulars of the offence), contrary to s. 387 of the Criminal Code of Canada.

Section 388 Misleading receipt

A.B., on the..........(day) of (month) ...., (year).........., at (specify time) in (specify
place), wilfully

..........with intent to mislead [OR injure OR defraud] C.D., whether or not C.D. was
known to A.B., did give C.D. (specify a thing in writing) that purported to be a
receipt for [OR an acknowledgment of] property that had been delivered to [OR
received by] A.B. before the property referred to in the purported receipt [OR ac-
knowledgment] had been delivered to [OR received by] A.B., to wit: (specify the
particulars of the offence), contrary to s. 388(a) of the Criminal Code of Canada.

..........did accept [OR transmit OR use] such purported receipt [OR acknowledg-
ment] in s. 388(a), to wit: (specify the particulars of the offence), contrary to s.
388(b) of the Criminal Code of Canada.

Section 389(1) Fraudulent disposal of goods on which money advanced

A.B., on the..........(day) of (month) ...., (year).........., at (specify time) in (specify
place),

..........having shipped [OR delivered] to C.D., the keeper of a warehouse [OR to a
factor OR agent OR carrier] anything on which E.F., the consignee thereof had advanced money [OR had given valuable security], with intent to deceive [OR defraud
OR injure] the consignee, thereafter did dispose of it in a manner that was different
from and inconsistent with the agreement that had been made in that behalf between
A.B. and the consignee, to wit: (specify the particulars of the offence), contrary to s.
389(1)(a) of the Criminal Code of Canada.

..........knowingly and wilfully, did aid [OR assist] C.D. to make a disposition of
(specify any thing mentioned in s. 389(1)(a) of the Criminal Code) for the purpose
of deceiving [OR defrauding OR injuring] the consignee, to wit: (specify the particulars of the offence), contrary to s. 389(1)(b) of the Criminal Code of Canada.

Section 390 Fraudulent receipts under Bank Act

A.B., on the..........(day) of (month) ...., (year).........., at (specify time) in (specify
place), wilfully,

..........did make a false statement in a receipt [OR certificate OR acknowledgment]
for a thing that might be used for a purpose mentioned in the Bank Act, to wit:
(specify the particulars of the offence), contrary to s. 390(a) of the Criminal Code of
Canada.

..........after giving to C.D. [OR after C.D. employed by A.B. to his (OR her) knowledge has given to E.F. OR after obtaining and endorsing (OR assigning) to E.F.] a
receipt [OR certificate OR acknowledgment] for anything that might be used for a
purpose mentioned in the Bank Act, without the consent in writing of the holder
[OR endorsee] [OR without the production and delivery of the receipt (OR certificate OR acknowledgment)] did alienate [OR part with OR did not deliver to the
holder (OR owner)] the property mentioned in the receipt [OR certificate OR ac-

knowledgment], to wit: (specify the particulars of the offence), contrary to s. 390(b) of the Criminal Code of Canada.

Section 392 Disposal of property to defraud creditors

A.B., on the..........(day) of (month) ...., (year).........., at (specify time) in (specify place),

..........with intent to defraud his [OR her] creditors did make [OR cause to be made] a gift [OR conveyance OR assignment OR sale OR transfer OR delivery] of his [OR her] property [OR did remove (OR conceal OR dispose of) any of his (OR her) property], to wit: (specify the particulars of the offence), contrary to s. 392(a) of the Criminal Code of Canada.

..........with intent that C.D. should defraud his [OR her] creditors, did receive property by means of [OR in relation to] which such an offence had been committed, to wit: (specify the particulars of the offence), contrary to s. 392(b) of the Criminal Code of Canada.

Section 393 Fraud in relation to fares

A.B., on the..........(day) of (month) ...., (year).........., at (specify time) in (specify place),

..........whose duty it was to collect a fare [OR toll OR ticket OR admission] wilfully did fail to collect it [OR did collect less than the proper amount payable in respect thereof OR did accept to collect it (OR for collecting less than the proper amount payable in respect thereof)], to wit: (specify the particulars of the offence), contrary to s. 393(1) of the Criminal Code of Canada.

..........did give [OR offer] valuable consideration to C.D., a person whose duty it was to collect a fare [OR toll OR ticket OR admission fee], for failing to collect it [OR for collecting an amount less than the amount payable in respect thereof], to wit: (specify the particulars of the offence), contrary to s. 393(2) of the Criminal Code of Canada.

Section 393(3) Fraudulently obtaining transportation

A.B., on the..........(day) of (month) ...., (year).........., at (specify time) in (specify place), by any false pretence [OR fraud] unlawfully did obtain transportation by land [OR water OR air], to wit: (specify the particulars of the offence), contrary to s. 393(3) of the Criminal Code of Canada.

Section 394(1) Fraud in relation to minerals

A.B., on the..........(day) of (month) ...., (year).........., at (specify time) in (specify place),

..........being the holder of a lease [OR licence] issued under (specify an Act relating to the mining of precious metals) [OR by the owner of land that was supposed to contain precious metals], by a fraudulent device [OR contrivance], did defraud [OR attempt to defraud] C.D. of precious metals [OR money] payable [OR reserved] by the lease [OR licence] [OR did fraudulently conceal (OR make a false statement with respect to) the amount of precious metals procured by A.B.], to wit: (specify the particulars of the offence), contrary to s. 394(1)(a) of the Criminal Code of Canada.

..........did sell [OR purchase] a rock [OR mineral OR other substance] that contained precious metals [OR unsmelted (OR untreated OR unmanufactured OR partly smelted OR partly treated OR partly manufactured) precious metals] without establishing that A.B. was the owner [OR agent of the owner OR was acting under lawful authority], to wit: (specify the particulars of the offence), contrary to s. 394(1)(b) of the Criminal Code of Canada.

..........had in his possession [OR knowingly had upon his premises], a rock [OR mineral] of a value of 55¢ per kilogram [OR more] [OR any mica of a value of 15¢ per kilogram (OR more) OR any precious metals] that there were reasonable grounds to believe had been stolen [OR had been dealt with contrary to s. 394], without establishing that A.B. was lawfully in possession thereof, to wit: (specify the particulars of the offence), contrary to s. 394(1)(c) of the Criminal Code of Canada.

Section 396(1) Fraud in relation to mines

A.B., on the..........(day) of (month) ...., (year).........., at (specify time) in (specify place),

..........did add anything to [OR remove anything from] any existing [OR prospective] mine [OR mining claim OR oil well] with a fraudulent intent to affect the result of an assay [OR a test OR a valuation] that had been made [OR was to be made] with respect to the mine [OR mining claim OR oil well], to wit: (specify the particulars of the offence), contrary to s. 396(1)(a) of the Criminal Code of Canada.

..........did add anything to [OR remove anything from OR tamper with] a sample [OR material] that had been taken [OR was being (OR was about to be) taken] from a existing [OR prospective] mine [OR mining claim OR oil well] for the purpose of being assayed [OR tested OR otherwise valued] with a fraudulent intent to affect the result of the assay [OR test OR valuation], to wit: (specify the particulars of the offence), contrary to s. 396(1)(b) of the Criminal Code of Canada.

Section 397(1) Falsification of book, paper, writing, valuable security or document

A.B., on the..........(day) of (month) ...., (year).........., at (specify time) in (specify place),

..........with intent to defraud, did destroy [OR mutilate OR alter OR falsify OR made a false entry in] a book [OR a paper OR a writing OR a valuable security OR a document], to wit: (specify the particulars of the offence), contrary to s. 397(1)(a) of the Criminal Code of Canada.

..........with intent to defraud, did omit a material particular from [OR alter a material particular in] a book [OR a paper OR a writing OR a valuable security OR a document], to wit: (specify the particulars of the offence), contrary to s. 397(1)(b) of the Criminal Code of Canada.

Section 397(2) Being privy to the falsification of a book, paper, writing, valuable security or document

A.B., on the..........(day) of (month) ...., (year).........., at (specify time) in (specify place), with intent to defraud A.B.'s creditors

..........was privy to the destruction of [OR mutilation of OR alteration of OR falsification of OR making of a false entry in] (specify a book OR a paper OR a writing OR a valuable security OR a document), to wit: (specify the particulars of the offence), contrary to s. 397(2) of the Criminal Code of Canada.

..........was privy to the omission of a material particular from [OR alteration of a material particular in] (specify a book OR a paper OR a writing OR a valuable security OR a document), to wit: (specify the particulars of the offence), contrary to s. 397(2) of the Criminal Code of Canada.

Section 398 Falsification of employment record

A.B., on the..........(day) of (month) ...., (year).........., at (specify time) in (specify place), with intent to deceive, did falsify an employment record by (specify the means), to wit: (specify the particulars of the offence), contrary to s. 398 of the Criminal Code of Canada.

Section 399 Falsification of statement or return of public officer

A.B., on the..........(day) of (month) ...., (year).........., at (specify time) in (specify place), being entrusted with the receipt [OR custody OR management] of any part of the public statement [OR return] of any sum of money collected by A.B. [OR entrusted to his (OR her) care] [OR any balance of money in his hands (OR under his (OR her) control)], to wit: (specify the particulars of the offence), contrary to s. 399 of the Criminal Code of Canada.

Section 400(1) Falsification of prospectus

A.B., on the..........(day) of (month) ...., (year).........., at (specify time) in (specify place), did make [OR circulate OR publish] a written [OR oral] prospectus [OR statement OR an account], that A.B. knew was false in a material particular with intent to induce C.D. and E.F., to become shareholders [OR partners] in a company [OR to deceive (OR defraud) the members (OR shareholder OR creditors), of a company OR to induce C.D. to entrust (OR advance) a thing to a company OR to induce C.D. to enter into a security for the benefit of a company], to wit: (specify the particulars of the offence), contrary to s. 400(1) of the Criminal Code of Canada.

Section 401(1) Obtaining carriage by false billing

A.B., on the..........(day) of (month) ...., (year).........., at (specify time) in (specify place), by means of a false [OR misleading] representation, knowingly did obtain [OR attempt to obtain] the carriage of (specify a thing) by C.D. into a country [OR province OR district OR other place], where the importation [OR transportation] of it was, in the circumstances of the case, unlawful, to wit: (specify the particulars of the offence), contrary to s. 401(1) of the Criminal Code of Canada.

Section 402(1) Trader or businessman failing to keep accounts

A.B., on the..........(day) of (month) ...., (year).........., at (specify time) in (specify place), being a trader [OR in business], was indebted in an amount exceeding $1,000 and was unable to pay his [OR her] creditors in full and had not kept books of account that, in the ordinary course of the trade [OR business] in which A.B. was engaged, were necessary to exhibit [OR explain] his [OR her] transactions, to wit: (specify the particulars of the offence), contrary to s. 402(1) of the Criminal Code of Canada.

Section 403 Personation with intent to gain property or advantage or cause disadvantage

A.B., on the..........(day) of (month) ...., (year).........., at (specify time) in (specify place),

..........did fraudulently personate C.D., with intent to gain advantage for himself [OR herself OR E.F.], to wit: (specify the particulars of the offence), contrary to s. 403(a) of the Criminal Code of Canada.

..........did fraudulently personate C.D., with intent to obtain property [OR an interest in property], to wit: (specify the particulars of the offence), contrary to s. 403(b) of the Criminal Code of Canada.

..........did fraudulently personate C.D., with intent to cause disadvantage to C.D. [OR to E.F.], to wit: (specify the particulars of the offence), contrary to s. 403(c) of the Criminal Code of Canada.

Section 404 Personation at an examination

A.B., on the..........(day) of (month) ...., (year).........., at (specify time) in (specify place),

..........falsely, with intent to gain advantage for himself [OR herself OR C.D.], did personate C.D., a candidate at a competitive [OR a qualifying] examination held under the authority of law [OR in connection with a university (OR a college OR a school)], to wit: (specify the particulars of the offence), contrary to s. 404 of the Criminal Code of Canada.

..........did knowingly avail himself of the results of the personation of himself [OR herself OR C.D.], a candidate at a competitive [OR a qualifying] examination held under the authority of law [OR in connection with a university (OR a college OR a school)], to wit: (specify the particulars of the offence), contrary to s. 404 of the Criminal Code of Canada.

Section 405 Acknowledging instrument in false name

A.B., on the..........(day) of (month) ...., (year).........., at (specify time) in (specify place), without lawful authority or excuse, did acknowledge, in the name of C.D., before a court [OR a judge OR (specify another person authorized to receive the acknowledgment)] a recognizance of bail [OR a confession of judgment OR a consent to judgment OR a judgment OR a deed OR (specify other instrument)], to wit: (specify the particulars of the offence), contrary to s. 405 of the Criminal Code of Canada.

Forms of Charges

Section 407 Forging a trade-mark

A.B., on the..........(day) of (month) ...., (year).........., at (specify time) in (specify place), with intent to deceive [OR defraud] the public [OR a person (whether ascertained or not)], did forge a trade-mark, to wit: (specify the particulars of the offence), contrary to s. 407 of the Criminal Code of Canada.

Section 408 Passing off

A.B., on the..........(day) of (month) ...., (year).........., at (specify time) in (specify place),

..........with intent to deceive [OR defraud] the public [OR C.D.], did pass off other wares [OR services] as and for those ordered [OR required], to wit: (specify the particulars of the offence), contrary to s. 408(a) of the Criminal Code of Canada.

..........with intent to deceive or defraud the public [OR C.D.], did make use, in association with wares [OR with services] of a description that was false in a material aspect as to the kind [OR the quality OR the quantity OR the composition OR the geographical origin OR the mode of manufacture OR the mode of production OR the mode of performance] of such wares [OR services], to wit: (specify the particulars of the offence), contrary to s. 408(b) of the Criminal Code of Canada.

Section 409(1) Possession of instruments for forging trade-mark

A.B., on the..........(day) of (month) ...., (year).........., at (specify time) in (specify place), did make [OR have in his [OR her] possession OR dispose of] a die [OR a block OR a machine OR (specify some other instrument)], designed [OR intended] to be used in forging a trade mark, to wit: (specify the particulars of the offence), contrary to s. 409(1) of the Criminal Code of Canada.

Section 410(a) Defacing, concealing or removing trade-mark

A.B., on the..........(day) of (month) ...., (year).........., at (specify time) in (specify place), with intent to deceive [OR to defraud], did deface [OR conceal OR remove] a trade mark [OR the name of C.D. from (specify the thing) without the consent of C.D.], to wit: (specify the particulars of the offence), contrary to s. 410(a) of the Criminal Code of Canada.

Section 410(b) Using bottle or siphon bearing trade-mark

A.B., on the..........(day) of (month) ...., (year).........., at (specify time) in (specify place), being a manufacturer [OR dealer OR trader OR bottler] with intent to deceive [OR defraud], did fill any bottle [OR siphon] that bore the trade-mark [OR name] of C.D. without the consent of that C.D. with a beverage [OR milk OR by-product of milk OR specify other liquid commodity] for the purpose of sale [OR traffic], to wit: (specify the particulars of the offence), contrary to s. 410(b) of the Criminal Code of Canada.

Section 411 Reconditioned goods

A.B., on the..........(day) of (month) ...., (year).........., at (specify time) in (specify place), did sell [OR expose (OR have in his [OR her] possession) for sale OR ad-

Forms of Charges

vertise for sale] goods that had been used [OR reconditioned OR remade] and that bore the trade-mark [OR the trade-name] of A.B. without making full disclosure that the goods had been reconditioned [OR rebuilt OR remade] for sale and that they were not in the condition in which they were originally made [OR produced], to wit: (specify the particulars of the offence), contrary to s. 411 of the Criminal Code of Canada.

Section 413 Falsely claiming royal warrant

A.B., on the..........(day) of (month) ...., (year).........., at (specify time) in (specify place), did falsely represent that goods were made by A.B., a person holding a royal warrant [OR for the service of Her Majesty (OR a member of the Royal Family OR a public department)], to wit: (specify the particulars of the offence), contrary to s. 413 of the Criminal Code of Canada.

Section 415 Offences in relation to wreck

A.B., on the..........(day) of (month) ...., (year).........., at (specify time) in (specify place),

..........did secrete a wreck [OR deface (OR obliterate) the marks on a wreck OR use any means to disguise (OR conceal) the fact that anything is a wreck OR in any manner conceal the character of a wreck] from C.D., a person entitled to inquire into the wreck, to wit: (specify the particulars of the offence), contrary to s. 415(a) of the Criminal Code of Canada.

..........did receive a wreck, knowing that it was a wreck, from C.D., a person other than the owner thereof [OR a receiver of the wreck] and did not within 48 hours thereafter inform the receiver of the wreck, to wit: (specify the particulars of the offence), contrary to s. 415(b) of the Criminal Code of Canada.

..........did offer a wreck for sale [OR otherwise deal with it] knowing that it was a wreck and not having a lawful authority to sell [OR deal with] it, to wit: (specify the particulars of the offence), contrary to s. 415(c) of the Criminal Code of Canada.

..........did keep a wreck in his [OR her] possession knowing that it was a wreck without lawful authority, to keep it for any time longer than the time reasonably necessary to deliver it to the receiver of the wreck, to wit: (specify the particulars of the offence), contrary to s. 415(d) of the Criminal Code of Canada.

..........did board a vessel that was wrecked [OR stranded OR in distress] against the will of C.D., the master, unless A.B. was a receiver of the wreck [OR a person acting under orders of a receiver of the wreck], to wit: (specify the particulars of the offence), contrary to s. 415(e) of the Criminal Code of Canada.

Section 417(1) Applying or removing marks without authority

A.B., on the..........(day) of (month) ...., (year).........., at (specify time) in (specify place),

..........without lawful authority, did apply a distinguishing mark to (specify the thing), to wit: (specify the particulars of the offence), contrary to s. 417(1)(a) of the Criminal Code of Canada.

..........with intent to conceal the property of Her Majesty in public stores, did remove [OR destroy OR obliterate] a distinguishing mark in whole [OR in part], to wit: (specify the particulars of the offence), contrary to s. 417(1)(b) of the Criminal Code of Canada.

Section 417(2) Unlawful transactions in public stores

A.B., on the..........(day) of (month) ...., (year).........., at (specify time) in (specify place), without lawful authority, did receive [OR possess OR keep OR sell OR deliver public stores that A.B. knew bore a distinguishing mark, to wit: (specify the particulars of the offence), contrary to s. 417(2) of the Criminal Code of Canada.

Section 418(1) Selling defective stores to the government

A.B., on the..........(day) of (month) ...., (year).........., at (specify time) in (specify place),

..........did knowingly sell [OR deliver] to Her Majesty defective stores, to wit: (specify the particulars of the offence), contrary to s. 418(1) of the Criminal Code of Canada.

..........did commit an act of fraud upon Her Majesty [OR an officer in Her Majesty's service] in connection with the sale [OR lease OR delivery OR manufacture] of certain stores, to wit: (specify the particulars of the offence), contrary to s. 418(1) of the Criminal Code of Canada.

Section 418(2) Being a party to the selling of defective stores to the government

A.B., on the..........(day) of (month) ...., (year).........., at (specify time) in (specify place),

..........being a director [OR an officer OR an agent OR an employee] of (specify the corporation) that did commit, by fraud, the offence of selling defective stores to the government, knowingly did take part in the fraud, to wit: (specify the particulars of the offence), contrary to s. 418(2)(a) of the Criminal Code of Canada.

..........being a director [OR an officer OR an agent OR an employee] of (specify the corporation) that did commit, by fraud, the offence of selling defective stores to the government, did know [OR had reason to suspect] that the fraud was being committed [OR had been (OR was about to be) committed] and did not inform the responsible government [OR a department thereof] of Her Majesty, to wit: (specify the particulars of the offence), contrary to s. 418(2)(b) of the Criminal Code of Canada.

Section 419 Unlawful use of military uniforms or certificates

A.B., on the..........(day) of (month) ...., (year).........., at (specify time) in (specify place), without lawful authority,

..........did wear a uniform of the Canadian Forces [OR specify other naval OR army OR air force OR a uniform that was so similar to the uniform of any of those forces that it was likely to be mistaken therefor], to wit: (specify the particulars of the offence), contrary to s. 419(a) of the Criminal Code of Canada.

..........did wear a distinctive mark relating to wound received [OR service performed] in war [OR a military medal (OR ribbon OR badge OR chevron OR any decoration OR order) that was awarded for war services OR any imitation thereof OR any mark (OR device OR thing) that was likely to be mistaken for any such mark (OR medal OR ribbon OR badge OR chevron OR decoration OR order)], to wit: (specify the particulars of the offence), contrary to s. 419(b) of the Criminal Code of Canada.

..........did have in his [OR her] possession a certificate of discharge [OR certificate of release OR statement of service OR identity card] from the Canadian Forces [OR specify other naval (OR army OR air) force] that had not been issued to and does not belong to him, to wit: (specify the particulars of the offence), contrary to s. 419(c) of the Criminal Code of Canada.

..........did have in his [OR her] possession a commission [OR warrant OR a certificate of discharge OR certificate of release OR statement of service OR identity card] issued to A.B., an officer [OR a person] in [OR who has been in] the Canadian Forces [OR specify other naval (OR army OR air) force] that contained any alteration that was not verified by the initials of the officer who issued it [OR by the initials of an officer thereto lawfully authorized], to wit: (specify the particulars of the offence), contrary to s. 419(d) of the Criminal Code of Canada.

Section 420(1) Buying military stores from members of Canadian Forces or from deserter

A.B., on the..........(day) of (month) ...., (year).........., at (specify time) in (specify place), did buy [OR receive OR detain] from C.D., a member of the Canadian Forces [OR a deserter OR an absentee without leave therefrom] military stores that were owned by Her Majesty [OR for which the member (OR deserter OR absentee without leave) was accountable to Her Majesty] to wit: (specify the particulars of the offence), contrary to s. 420(1) of the Criminal Code of Canada.

Section 422(1) Breach of contract endangering human life

A.B., on the..........(day) of (month) ...., (year).........., at (specify time) in (specify place), wilfully did break a contract knowing [OR having reasonable cause to believe] that the probable consequences of doing so would be to endanger human life [OR to cause bodily injury OR to expose valuable property to destruction (OR to serious injury) OR to deprive the inhabitants of a city (OR a place OR part of a city OR part of a place) wholly (OR to a great extent) of their supply of light (OR power OR gas OR water) OR to delay (OR prevent) the running of a locomotive engine (OR tender OR freight train OR passenger train OR car) on a railway that was a common carrier], to wit: (specify the particulars of the offence), contrary to s. 422(1) of the Criminal Code of Canada.

Section 423(1)(a) Intimidation of a person

A.B., on the..........(day) of (month) ...., (year).........., at (specify time) in (specify place), wrongfully and without lawful authority, for the purpose of compelling C.D. to abstain from (specify a thing that C.D. had a lawful right to do), did use violence [OR threats of violence] to C.D. [OR to the wife of C.D. OR to the children of

C.D.], to wit: (specify the particulars of the offence), contrary to s. 423(1)(a) of the Criminal Code of Canada.

Section 424 Threatening to commit offence against internationally protected person

A.B., on the..........(day) of (month) ...., (year).........., at (specify time) in (specify place),

..........did threaten to commit an offence under s. 431 of the Criminal Code, to wit: (specify the particulars of the offence), contrary to s. 424 of the Criminal Code of Canada.

..........did threaten to commit an offence under s. 235 [OR s. 266 OR s. 279 OR s. 279.1] of the Criminal Code against C.D., an internationally protected person, to wit: (specify the particulars of the offence), contrary to s. 424 of the Criminal Code of Canada.

Section 425(a) Refusing to employ trade union members

A.B., on the..........(day) of (month) ...., (year).........., at (specify time) in (specify place), being an employer [OR the agent of C.D., an employer] wrongfully and without lawful authority refused to employ E.F. [OR dismissed E.F. from his employment] for the reason only that the said E.F. was a member of a lawful trade union [OR a lawful association (OR combination) of workmen (OR employees)] formed for the purpose of advancing, in a lawful manner, their interests and organized for their protection in the regulation of wages and conditions of work, to wit: (specify the particulars of the offence), contrary to s. 425(a) of the Criminal Code of Canada.

Section 425(b) Intimidation of employees

A.B., on the..........(day) of (month) ...., (year).........., at (specify time) in (specify place), being an employer [OR the agent of C.D. an employer] wrongfully and without lawful authority did seek by intimidation [OR by threat of loss of position (OR employment) OR by causing actual loss of position (OR employment) OR by threatening (OR imposing) a pecuniary penalty] to compel E.F. and F.G., workmen [OR employees], in the employ of C.D., to abstain from belonging to a trade union [OR an association (OR combination) of workmen (OR employees)] to which they had a lawful right to belong, to wit: (specify the particulars of the offence), contrary to s. 425(b) of the Criminal Code of Canada.

Section 425(c) Employer conspiring to refuse to employ or intimidate

A.B., on the..........(day) of (month) ...., (year).........., at (specify time) in (specify place),

..........being an employer [OR the agent of an employer], wrongfully and without lawful authority, did conspire [OR combine OR agree OR arrange] with C.D., another employer [OR his agent], to refuse to employ [OR to dismiss from his employment] E.F., for the reason only that E.F. was a member of a lawful trade union [OR of a lawful association (OR combination) of workmen] formed for the purpose of advancing, in a lawful manner, their interests and organized for their protection in the regulation of wages and conditions of work, to wit: (specify the particulars of the offence), contrary to s. 425(c) of the Criminal Code of Canada.

..........being an employer [OR the agent of an employer], wrongfully and without lawful authority, did conspire [OR combine OR agree OR arrange] with C.D., another employer [OR his agent], by intimidation [OR threat of loss of position (OR employment) OR by causing actual loss of position (OR employment) OR by threatening (OR imposing) any pecuniary penalty] did seek to compel workmen [OR employees] to abstain from belonging to a trade union [OR association OR combination] to which they had a lawful right to belong, to wit: (specify the particulars of the offence), contrary to s. 425(c) of the Criminal Code of Canada.

Section 426 Secret commission

A.B., on the..........(day) of (month) ...., (year).........., at (specify time) in (specify place),

..........corruptly, did give [OR offer OR agree to give (OR offer)] to C.D., an agent [OR being an agent did demand (OR accept OR offer (OR agree) to accept) from C.D.] a reward [OR advantage OR benefit of any kind] as consideration for doing [OR forbearing to do OR for having done (OR forborne to do)] any act relating to the affairs [OR business] of E.F., his [OR her] principal [OR as consideration for showing (OR forbearing to show) favour (OR disfavour) to a person with relation to the affairs (OR business) of his [OR her] principal] to wit: (specify the particulars of the offence), contrary to s. 426(1)(a) of the Criminal Code of Canada.

..........with intent to deceive C.D., a principal, did give to E.F., an agent of that principal [OR being an agent, with intent to deceive his [OR her] principal, did use] a receipt [OR an account OR other writing] in which the principal had an interest and that contained any statement that was false [OR erroneous OR defective] in any material particular and that was intended to mislead the principal, to wit: (specify the particulars of the offence), contrary to s. 426(1)(b) of the Criminal Code of Canada.

..........knowingly, was privy to the commission of such offence mentioned in s. 426(1) of the Criminal Code, to wit: (specify the particulars of the offence), contrary to s. 426(2) of the Criminal Code of Canada.

Section 427(1) Issuing trading stamps

A.B., on the..........(day) of (month) ...., (year).........., at (specify time) in (specify place), by himself [OR by herself OR by C.D., his (OR her) employee, OR by C.D., his (OR her) agent] directly [OR indirectly] did issue [OR give OR sell OR dispose of OR offer to issue OR offer to sell OR offer to dispose of] trading stamps to E.F., a merchant [OR dealer in goods] for use in his (OR her) business, to wit: (specify the particulars of the offence), contrary to s. 427(1) of the Criminal Code of Canada.

Section 427(2) Giving trading stamps to purchaser of goods

A.B., on the..........(day) of (month) ...., (year).........., at (specify time) in (specify place), being a merchant [OR a dealer in goods] by himself [OR by herself OR by C.D., his (OR her) employee, OR by C.D., his (OR her) agent] directly [OR indirectly] did give [OR dispose of OR offer to dispose of] trading stamps to E.F., a person who purchased goods from him, to wit: (specify the particulars of the offence), contrary to s. 427(2) of the Criminal Code of Canada.

Part XI — Wilful and Forbidden Acts in Respect of Certain Property

Section 430(1.1) Mischief in relation to data

A.B., on the..........(day) of (month) ...., (year).........., at (specify time) in (specify place), wilfully, did destroy [OR alter] data [OR did render data meaningless (OR useless OR ineffective) OR did obstruct (OR interrupt OR interfere with) the lawful use of data OR did obstruct (OR interrupt OR interfere with C.D. in the lawful use of data OR did deny access to data to C.D. who was entitled to access thereto], to wit: (specify the particulars of the offence), contrary to s. 430(1.1) of the Criminal Code of Canada.

Section 430(2) Mischief causing danger to life

A.B., on the..........(day) of (month) ...., (year).........., at (specify time) in (specify place), wilfully did destroy [OR damage] property [OR render property dangerous (OR useless OR inoperative OR ineffective) OR obstruct (OR interrupt OR interfere with) the lawful use (OR enjoyment OR operation) of property OR obstruct (OR interfere with or interrupt) C.D. in the lawful use (OR enjoyment OR operation) of property], and thereby commit mischief that caused actual danger to life, to wit: (specify the particulars of the offence), contrary to s. 430(2) of the Criminal Code of Canada.

Section 430(3) Mischief in relation to testamentary instrument

A.B., on the..........(day) of (month) ...., (year).........., at (specify time) in (specify place), did commit mischief in relation to a testamentary instrument, to wit: (specify the particulars of the offence), contrary to s. 430(3) of the Criminal Code of Canada.

Section 430(3) Mischief in relation to property worth more than $5,000

A.B., on the..........(day) of (month) ...., (year).........., at (specify time) in (specify place), did commit mischief in relation to property the value of which exceeded $5,000, to wit: (specify the particulars of the offence), contrary to s. 430(3) of the Criminal Code of Canada.

Section 430(4) Mischief in relation to other property

A.B., on the..........(day) of (month) ...., (year).........., at (specify time) in (specify place), did commit mischief in relation to (specify property other than property that was a testamentary instrument OR the value of which exceeds $5,000), to wit: (specify the particulars of the offence contrary to s. 430(4) of the Criminal Code of Canada.

Section 430(5.1) Acts or omissions likely to cause mischief

A.B., on the..........(day) of (month) ...., (year).........., at (specify time) in (specify place), wilfully did an act [OR wilfully did omit to do an act] that it was his [OR her] duty to do and that act [OR omission] was likely to constitute mischief causing actual danger to life [OR was likely to constitute mischief in relation to property (OR data)], to wit: (specify the particulars of the offence), contrary to s. 430(5.1) of the Criminal Code of Canada.

Section 431 Attack on premises, residence or transport of international protected person

A.B., on the..........(day) of (month) ...., (year).........., at (specify time) in (specify place), did commit an attack on the official premises [OR private accommodation OR means of transport] of C.D., an internationally protected person that was likely to endanger the life [OR liberty] of C.D., to wit: (specify the particulars of the offence), contrary to s. 431 of the Criminal Code of Canada.

Section 433(a) Arson with disregard for human life

A.B., on the..........(day) of (month) ...., (year).........., at (specify time) in (specify place), intentionally [OR recklessly] did cause damage by fire [OR explosion] to property, where A.B. knew that [OR was reckless with respect to whether] the property was inhabited [OR occupied], to wit: (specify the particulars of the offence), contrary to s. 433(a) of the Criminal Code of Canada.

Section 433(b) Arson causing bodily harm

A.B., on the..........(day) of (month) ...., (year).........., at (specify time) in (specify place), intentionally [OR recklessly] did cause damage by fire [OR explosion] to property where the fire [OR explosion] causes bodily harm to C.D., to wit: (specify the particulars of the offence), contrary to s. 433(b) of the Criminal Code of Canada.

Section 434 Arson with damage to property

A.B., on the..........(day) of (month) ...., (year).........., at (specify time) in (specify place), did intentionally [OR recklessly] cause damage by fire [OR explosion] to property not wholly owned by A.B., to wit: (specify the particulars of the offence), contrary to s. 434 of the Criminal Code of Canada.

Section 434.1 Arson of own property

A.B., on the..........(day) of (month) ...., (year).........., at (specify time) in (specify place), did intentionally [OR recklessly] cause damage by fire [OR explosion] to property owned in whole [OR in part] by A.B. thereby threatening the health [OR safety OR property] of C.D., to wit: (specify the particulars of the offence), contrary to s. 434.1 of the Criminal Code of Canada.

Section 435(1) Arson for fraudulent purpose

A.B., on the..........(day) of (month) ...., (year).........., at (specify time) in (specify place), did with intent to defraud C.D. cause damage by fire [OR explosion] to property, to wit: (specify the particulars of the offence), contrary to s. 435(1) of the Criminal Code of Canada.

Section 436(1) Arson due to negligence

A.B., on the..........(day) of (month) ...., (year).........., at (specify time) in (specify place), being the owner [OR part owner OR person in control] of (specify property owned or controlled), did cause a fire [OR explosion] in the said property, as a result of a marked departure from the standard of care that a reasonably prudent person would use to prevent or control the spread of fires [OR explosions], that caused bodily harm to C.D. [OR damage to property], to wit: (specify the particulars of the offence), contrary to s. 436(1) of the Criminal Code of Canada.

Section 436.1 Possession of incendiary material

A.B., on the..........(day) of (month) ...., (year).........., at (specify time) in (specify place), did have in his possession incendiary material [OR an incendiary device OR an explosive substance] for the purpose of committing an offence under s. 433 [OR s. 434 OR s. 435 OR s. 436] of the Criminal Code, to wit: (specify the particulars of the offence), contrary to s. 436.1 of the Criminal Code of Canada.

Section 437 False alarm of fire

A.B., on the..........(day) of (month) ...., (year).........., at (specify time) in (specify place), wilfully and without reasonable cause, did not make [OR circulate OR cause to be made OR cause to be circulated] an alarm of fire by outcry [OR ringing bells OR using a fire alarm (OR telephone OR telegraph) OR (specify other manner in which the alarm was made)], to wit: (specify the particulars of the offence), contrary to s. 437 of the Criminal Code of Canada.

Section 438(1) Preventing or impeding the saving of a vessel

A.B., on the..........(day) of (month) ...., (year).........., at (specify time) in (specify place), wilfully

..........did prevent or impede [OR wilfully did endeavour to prevent or impede] the saving of a vessel that was wrecked [OR stranded OR abandoned OR in distress], to wit: (specify the particulars of the offence), contrary to s. 438(1)(a) of the Criminal Code of Canada.

..........did prevent or impede [OR wilfully did endeavour to prevent or impede] C.D., a person who attempted to save a vessel that was wrecked [OR stranded OR abandoned OR in distress], to wit: (specify the particulars of the offence), contrary to s. 438(1)(b) of the Criminal Code of Canada.

Section 438(2) Preventing or impeding the saving of wreck

A.B., on the..........(day) of (month) ...., (year).........., at (specify time) in (specify place), wilfully did prevent or impede [OR wilfully did endeavour to prevent or impede] the saving of a wreck, to wit: (specify the particulars of the offence), contrary to s. 438(2) of the Criminal Code of Canada.

Section 439(1) Making fast a vessel or boat to a marine signal

A.B., on the..........(day) of (month) ...., (year).........., at (specify time) in (specify place), did make fast a vessel [OR boat] to a signal [OR buoy OR (specify other sea-mark)] that was used for purposes of navigation, to wit: (specify the particulars of the offence), contrary to s. 439(1) of the Criminal Code of Canada.

Section 439(2) Altering, removing or concealing marine signal

A.B., on the..........(day) of (month) ...., (year).........., at (specify time) in (specify place), wilfully did alter [OR remove OR conceal] a signal [OR buoy OR specify other sea-mark] that was used for the purposes of navigation, to wit: (specify the particulars of the offence), contrary to s. 439(2) of the Criminal Code of Canada.

Section 440 Public harbours

A.B., on the..........(day) of (month) ...., (year).........., at (specify time) in (specify place), wilfully and without the written permission of the Minister of Transport did remove a stone [OR wood OR earth OR other material] that formed a natural bar necessary to the existence of a public harbour [OR that forms a natural protection to such a bar], to wit: (specify the particulars of the offence), contrary to s. 440 of the Criminal Code of Canada.

Section 441 Demolishing or damaging building

AA.B., on the..........(day) of (month) ...., (year).........., at (specify time) in (specify place), wilfully and to the prejudice of a mortgagee [OR an owner]

..........did pull down [OR demolish OR remove all (OR any part) of a dwelling-house (OR other building)] of which he was in possession [OR occupation], to wit: (specify the particulars of the offence), contrary to s. 441 of the Criminal Code of Canada.

..........did sever from the freehold any fixture fixed therein [OR thereto], to wit: (specify the particulars of the offence), contrary to s. 441 of the Criminal Code of Canada.

Section 442 Interfering with boundary lines of land

A.B., on the..........(day) of (month) ...., (year).........., at (specify time) in (specify place), wilfully did pull down [OR deface OR alter OR remove] anything planted [OR set up] as the boundary line [OR part of the boundary line] of land, to wit: (specify the particulars of the offence), contrary to s. 442 of the Criminal Code of Canada.

Section 443(1)(a) Interfering with international, provincial, county or municipal boundary line

A.B., on the..........(day) of (month) ...., (year).........., at (specify time) in (specify place), wilfully did pull down [OR deface OR alter OR remove] a boundary mark lawfully placed to mark an international [OR provincial OR county OR municipal] boundary, to wit: (specify the particulars of the offence), contrary to s. 443(1)(a) of the Criminal Code of Canada.

Section 443(1)(b) Interfering with boundary marks placed by land surveyors

A.B., on the..........(day) of (month) ...., (year).........., at (specify time) in (specify place), wilfully did pull down [OR deface OR alter OR remove] a boundary mark lawfully placed by a land surveyor to mark any limit [OR boundary OR angle of a concession OR range OR lot OR parcel of land], to wit: (specify the particulars of the offence), contrary to s. 443(1)(b) of the Criminal Code of Canada.

Section 444 Injuring or endangering cattle

A.B., on the..........(day) of (month) ...., (year).........., at (specify time) in (specify place), wilfully

..........did kill [OR maim OR wound OR poison OR injure] certain cattle, to wit: (specify the particulars of the offence), contrary to s. 444(a) of the Criminal Code of Canada.

..........did place poison in such a position as to be easily consumed by certain cattle, to wit: (specify the particulars of the offence), contrary to s. 444(b) of the Criminal Code of Canada.

Section 445 Injuring or endangering animals other than cattle

A.B., on the..........(day) of (month) ...., (year).........., at (specify time) in (specify place), wilfully and without lawful excuse

..........did kill [OR maim OR wound OR poison OR injure] a dog [OR a bird OR (specify animal other than cattle)], that was kept for a lawful purpose to wit: (specify the particulars of the offence), contrary to s. 445(a) of the Criminal Code of Canada.

..........did place poison in such a position as to be easily consumed by dogs [OR birds OR (specify animals other than cattle)] that were kept for a lawful purpose, to wit: (specify the particulars of the offence), contrary to s. 445(b) of the Criminal Code of Canada.

Section 446(1) Cruelty to animals

A.B., on the..........(day) of (month) ...., (year).........., at (specify time) in (specify place),

..........did wilfully cause [OR being the owner, did wilfully permit to be caused] unneccessary pain [OR suffering OR injury] to a bird [OR an animal], to wit: (specify the particulars of the offence), contrary to s. 446(1)(a) of the Criminal Code of Canada.

..........by wilful neglect did cause damage [OR injury] to animals [OR birds] while they were being driven [OR conveyed], to wit: (specify the particulars of the offence), contrary to s. 446(1)(b) of the Criminal Code of Canada.

..........being the owner [OR the person having the custody or control] of a domestic animal [OR bird OR an animal OR a bird wild by nature that was in captivity] did abandon it in distress [OR wilfully neglect (OR fail) to provide suitable and adequate food and water and shelter and care for such animal (OR bird)], to wit: (specify the particulars of the offence), contrary to s. 446(1)(c) of the Criminal Code of Canada.

..........did encourage [OR aid OR assist] at the fighting [OR baiting] of an animal [OR bird], to wit: (specify the particulars of the offence), contrary to s. 446(1)(d) of the Criminal Code of Canada.

..........did wilfully and without reasonable excuse, administer [OR being the the owner thereof did permit to be administered] a poisonous [OR an injurious] drug [OR substance] to a domestic animal [OR bird OR an animal OR a bird wild by nature that was kept in captivity], to wit: (specify the particulars of the offence), contrary to s. 446(1)(e) of the Criminal Code of Canada.

..........did promote [OR arrange OR conduct OR assist in OR receive money for OR take part in] any meeting [OR competition OR exhibition OR pastime OR practice OR display OR event] at [OR in the course of] which captive birds were liberated by hand [OR trap OR contrivance OR (specify other means)] for the purpose of being shot while they were liberated, to wit: (specify the particulars of the offence), contrary to s. 446(1)(f) of the Criminal Code of Canada.

..........being the owner [OR occupier OR person in charge] of (specify the premises) did permit the said [OR part of the said] premises to be used for any meeting [OR competition OR exhibition OR pastime OR practice OR display OR event] at [OR in the course of] which captive birds were liberated for the purpose of being shot while they were liberated, to wit: (specify the particulars of the offence), contrary to s. 446(1)(g) of the Criminal Code of Canada.

Section 446(1)(d) Assisting at cock fight

A.B., on the..........(day) of (month) ...., (year).........., at (specify time) in (specify place),did encourage [OR aid OR assist at] the fighting [OR baiting] of animals [OR birds], to wit: (specify the particulars of the offence), contrary to s. 446(1)(d) of the Criminal Code of Canada.

Section 446(6) Owning or having custody of animal or bird while prohibited

A.B., on the..........(day) of (month) ...., (year).........., at (specify time) in (specify place), did own [OR have the custody (OR control) of an animal [OR bird] while prohibited from doing so by an order of the court made under s. 446(5) of the Criminal Code, to wit: (specify the particulars of the offence), contrary to s. 446(6) of the Criminal Code of Canada.

Section 447(1) Keeping cockpit

A.B., on the..........(day) of (month) ...., (year).........., at (specify time) in (specify place),

..........did build [OR make OR maintain OR keep] a cockpit on premises that A.B. owned [OR occupied], to wit: (specify the particulars of the offence), contrary to s. 447(1) of the Criminal Code of Canada.

..........did allow a cockpit to be built [OR made OR maintained OR kept] on premises that A.B. owned [OR occupied] to wit: (specify the particulars of the offence), contrary to s. 447(1) of the Criminal Code of Canada.

Part XII — Offences Relating to Currency

Section 449 Making counterfeit money

A.B., on the..........(day) of (month) ...., (year).........., at (specify time) in (specify place), did make [OR begin to make] counterfeit money, to wit: (specify the particulars of the offence), contrary to s. 449 of the Criminal Code of Canada.

Section 450 Possession of counterfeit money

A.B., on the..........(day) of (month) ...., (year).........., at (specify time) in (specify place), without lawful justification or excuse,

..........did buy [OR receive OR offer to buy OR offer to receive] counterfeit money, to wit: (specify the particulars of the offence), contrary to s. 450(a) of the Criminal Code of Canada.

..........did have in his [OR her] custody [OR did have in his [OR her] possession] counterfeit money, to wit: (specify the particulars of the offence), contrary to s. 450(b) of the Criminal Code of Canada.

..........did introduce into Canada counterfeit money, to wit: (specify the particulars of the offence), contrary to s. 450(c) of the Criminal Code of Canada.

Section 451 Possession of filings or clippings

A.B., on the..........(day) of (month) ...., (year).........., at (specify time) in (specify place), without lawful justification or excuse, did have in his [OR her] custody or possession gold [OR silver] filings [OR clippings OR bullion OR in dust OR in solution OR (specify)], produced or obtained by impairing [OR diminishing OR lightening] a current gold [OR silver] coin, knowing that it has been so produced [OR obtained], to wit: (specify the particulars of the offence), contrary to s. 451 of the Criminal Code of Canada.

Section 452 Uttering or exporting counterfeit money

A.B., on the..........(day) of (month) ...., (year).........., at (specify time) in (specify place), without lawful justification or excuse,

..........did utter [OR offer to utter OR use as if it were genuine] counterfeit money, to wit: (specify the particulars of the offence), contrary to s. 452(a) of the Criminal Code of Canada.

..........did export [OR send OR take] counterfeit money out of Canada, to wit: (specify the particulars of the offence), contrary to s. 452(b) of the Criminal Code of Canada.

Section 453 Fraudulently uttering coins

A.B., on the..........(day) of (month) ...., (year).........., at (specify time) in (specify place), with intent to defraud, knowingly

..........did utter a coin that was not current, to wit: (specify the particulars of the offence), contrary to s. 453(a) of the Criminal Code of Canada.

..........did utter a piece of metal [OR mixed metals] that resembles in size [OR figure OR colour] a current coin for which it was uttered, to wit: (specify the particulars of the offence), contrary to s. 453(b) of the Criminal Code of Canada.

Section 454 Slugs and tokens

A.B., on the..........(day) of (month) ...., (year).........., at (specify time) in (specify place), without lawful justification or excuse, did manufacture [OR produce OR sell OR have in his (OR her) possession] (specify the thing), that was intended to be fraudulently used in substitution for a coin [OR token of value] that a coin [OR token-operated] device was designed to receive, to wit: (specify the particulars of the offence), contrary to s. 454 of the Criminal Code of Canada.

Section 455 Clipping or uttering clipped coins

A.B., on the..........(day) of (month) ...., (year).........., at (specify time) in (specify place),

..........did impair [OR diminish OR lighten] a current gold [OR silver] coin with intent that it should pass for a current gold [OR silver] coin, to wit: (specify the particulars of the offence), contrary to s. 455(a) of the Criminal Code of Canada.

..........did utter a current gold [OR silver] coin, knowing that it had been impaired [OR diminished OR lightened] with intent to pass for a current gold [OR silver] coin, to wit: (specify the particulars of the offence), contrary to s. 455(b) of the Criminal Code of Canada.

Section 456 Defacing current coin or uttering defaced coin

A.B., on the..........(day) of (month) ...., (year).........., at (specify time) in (specify place), did deface a current coin [OR utter a current coin that had been defaced], to wit: (specify the particulars of the offence), contrary to s. 456 of the Criminal Code of Canada.

Section 457(1) Making or distributing likeness of bank note or security, including by electronic or computer-assisted means

A.B., on the..........(day) of (month) ...., (year).........., at (specify time) in (specify place), did make [OR publish OR print OR execute OR issue OR distribute OR circulate] (specify anything) in the likeness of a current bank-note [OR an obligation OR a security] of (specify a government or bank), to wit: (specify the particulars of the offence), contrary to s. 457(1) of the Criminal Code of Canada.

Section 458 Making, having or dealing in instruments for counterfeiting

A.B., on the..........(day) of (month) ...., (year).........., at (specify time) in (specify place), without lawful justification or excuse, did make [OR repair OR begin to make OR begin to repair OR proceed to make OR proceed to repair OR buy OR sell OR have in his (OR her) custody OR have in his (OR her) possession] a machine [OR an engine OR a tool OR an instrument OR material OR a thing] that A.B. knew had been used [OR that A.B. knew was adapted and intended for use] in making counterfeit money [OR counterfeit tokens of value], to wit: (specify the particulars of the offence), contrary to s. 458 of the Criminal Code of Canada.

Section 459 Conveying instruments for coining or metals out of mint

A.B., on the..........(day) of (month) ...., (year).........., at (specify time) in (specify place), without lawful justification or excuse, knowingly

..........did convey out of Her Majesty's mints in Canada, a machine [OR part of a machine OR an engine OR part of an engine OR a tool OR a part of a tool OR an instrument OR part of an instrument OR material OR thing] used or employed in connection with the manufacture of coins, to wit: (specify the particulars of the offence), contrary to s. 459(a) [OR (b)] of the Criminal Code of Canada.

..........did convey out of Her Majesty's mints in Canada, coin [OR bullion OR metal OR a mixture of metals], to wit: specify the particulars of the offence), contrary to s. 459(c) of the Criminal Code of Canada.

Section 460(1)(a) Advertising counterfeit money or tokens of value

A.B., on the..........(day) of (month) ...., (year).........., at (specify time) in (specify place),

..........did by an advertisement [OR a writing] offer to sell [OR procure OR dispose of] counterfeit money [OR counterfeit tokens of value], to wit: (specify the particulars of the offence), contrary to s. 460(1)(a) of the Criminal Code of Canada.

..........did by an advertisement [OR a writing] offer to give information with respect to the manner in which [OR the means by which] counterfeit money [OR counterfeit tokens of value] may be sold [OR procured OR disposed of], to wit: (specify the particulars of the offence), contrary to s. 460(1)(a) of the Criminal Code of Canada.

Section 460(1)(b) Trafficking or dealing in counterfeit money or tokens of value

A.B., on the..........(day) of (month) ...., (year).........., at (specify time) in (specify place),

..........did purchase [OR obtain OR negotiate OR deal with] counterfeit tokens of value, to wit: (specify the particulars of the offence), contrary to s. 460(1)(b) of the Criminal Code of Canada.

..........did offer to negotiate with a view to purchasing [OR obtaining] counterfeit tokens of value, to wit: (specify the particulars of the offence), contrary to s. 460(1)(b) of the Criminal Code of Canada.

Part XII.1 — Instruments and Literature for Illicit Drug Use

Section 462.2 Instruments or literature for illicit drug use

A.B., on the..........(day) of (month) ...., (year).........., at (specify time) in (specify place), did import into Canada [OR export from Canada OR manufacture OR promote OR sell] (specify), an instrument [OR literature], for illicit drug use, to wit: (specify the particulars of the offence), contrary to s. 462.2 of the Criminal Code of Canada.

Part XII.2 — Proceeds of Crime

Section 462.31 Laundering proceeds of crime

A.B., on the..........(day) of (month) ...., (year).........., at (specify time) in (specify place), did use [OR transfer the possession of OR send (OR deliver) to C.D. (OR specify a place) OR transport OR alter OR dispose of OR otherwise deal with], property [OR proceeds of property] with intent to conceal [OR convert] that property [OR those proceeds] and knowing that all [OR a part] of that property [OR of those proceeds] was obtained [OR derived] directly [OR indirectly] as a result of the commission in Canada of an enterprise crime offence [OR a designated drug offence OR an act (OR omission) that, if it had occurred in Canada, would have constituted an enterprise crime offence (OR a designated drug offence)], to wit: (specify the particulars of the offence), contrary to s. 462.31 of the Criminal Code of Canada.

Part XIII — Attempts, Conspiracies, Accessories

Section 463 Attempts

A.B., on the..........(day) of (month) ...., (year).........., at (specify time) in (specify place), did attempt to (specify the particulars using form of charge for the offence attempted).

Section 463 Accessory after the fact

A.B., on the..........(day) of (month) ...., (year).........., at (specify time) in (specify place), knowing that C.D. had been a party to the offence of (specify the offence to which C.D. had been a party), did receive [OR comfort OR assist] C.D. for the purpose of enabling C.D. to escape, to wit: (specify the particulars of the offence), contrary to s. 463 of the Criminal Code of Canada.

Section 464 Counselling commission of offence which is not committed

A.B., on the..........(day) of (month) ...., (year).........., at (specify time) in (specify place), did counsel C.D. to commit the offence of (specify the offence), to wit: (specify the particulars of the offence), contrary to s. 464 of the Criminal Code of Canada.

Section 465(1)(a) Conspiracy to commit murder

A.B., on the..........(day) of (month) ...., (year).........., at (specify time) in (specify place), did conspire with C.D. to commit murder [OR to cause E.F. to be murdered], to wit: (specify the particulars of the offence), contrary to s. 465(1)(a) of the Criminal Code of Canada.

Section 465(1)(b) Conspiracy to prosecute innocent person

A.B., on the..........(day) of (month) ...., (year).........., at (specify time) in (specify place), did conspire with C.D. to prosecute E.F. for an alleged offence, knowing that E.F. did not commit that offence, to wit: (specify the particulars of the offence), contrary to s. 465(1)(b) of the Criminal Code of Canada.

Section 465(1)(c) Conspiracy to commit an indictable offence

A.B., on the..........(day) of (month) ...., (year).........., at (specify time) in (specify place), did conspire with C.D. to commit the indictable offence of (specify the indictable offence), to wit: (specify the particulars of the offence), contrary to s. 465(1)(c) of the Criminal Code of Canada.

Section 465(1)(d) Conspiracy to commit an offence punishable on summary conviction

A.B., on the..........(day) of (month) ...., (year).........., at (specify time) in (specify place), did conspire with C.D. to commit the offence of (specify the offence punishable on summary conviction), such offence being punishable on summary conviction, to wit: (specify the particulars of the offence), contrary to s. 465(1)(d) of the Criminal Code of Canada.

Section 467.1 Participation in criminal organization

A.B., on the..........(day) of (month) ...., (year).........., at (specify time) in (specify place),

..........did participate in [OR substantially contribute to] the activities of a criminal organization knowing that C.D. [OR C.D. and E.F.], who were members of the organization, did engage in the commission of a series of indictable offences within the preceding five years, to wit: (specify the particulars of the offence), contrary to s. 467.1(a) of the Criminal Code of Canada.

..........was a party to the commission of an indictable offence for the benefit of [OR at the direction of OR in association with] a criminal organization, to wit: (specify the particulars of the offence including a reference to the indictable offence to which A.B. was a party), contrary to s. 467.1(b) of the Criminal Code of Canada.

Part XV — Special Procedure and Powers

Section 487.08(1) and (3) Failure to observe limitations on the use of results of forensic DNA analysis

A.B., on the..........(day) of (month) ...., (year).........., at (specify time) in (specify place), did use the results of forensic DNA analysis of a bodily substance, for a purpose not authorized by the warrant by which it was obtained, to wit: (specify the particulars of the offence), contrary to s. 487.08(3) of the Criminal Code of Canada.

Section 487.08(1) and (3) Failure to observe limitations on use of bodily substances obtained for forensic DNA analysis

A.B., on the..........(day) of (month) ...., (year).........., at (specify time) in (specify place), did use (specify the bodily substance) that was obtained in the execution of a warrant for an unauthorized purpose, to wit: (specify a manner of use other than in the course of an investigation of the designated offence for the purpose of forensic DNA analysis), contrary to s. 487.08(3) of the Criminal Code of Canada.

Section 490.8(9) Failure to comply with restraint order

A.B., on the..........(day) of (month) ...., (year).........., at (specify time) in (specify place), did act in contravention of [OR did fail to comply with] a restraint order in respect of offence-related property that had been served on him [OR her], to wit: (specify the particulars of the offence), contrary to s. 490.8(9) of the Criminal Code of Canada.

Part XVIII — Procedure on Preliminary Inquiry

Section 542(2) Publishing report of admission or confession tendered at preliminary inquiry

A.B., on the..........(day) of (month) ...., (year).........., at (specify time) in (specify place), did publish in (specify a newspaper broadcast) a report that an admission [OR confession] was tendered in evidence at a preliminary inquiry [OR a report of the nature of such admission (OR confession) so tendered in evidence] without the accused having been discharged [OR the accused having been committed for trial, the trial having ended], to wit: (specify the particulars of the offence), contrary to s. 542(2) of the Criminal Code of Canada.

Part XXIII — Sentencing

Section 733.1(1) Breach of probation order

A.B., on the..........(day) of (month) ...., (year).........., at (specify time) in (specify place), being a person bound by a probation order made (specify where and when the order was made), without reasonable excuse did fail [OR refuse] to comply with that order, to wit: (specify the particulars of the offence), contrary to s. 740(1) of the Criminal Code of Canada.

Part XXVII — Summary Convictions

Section 810 and 811 Breach of recognizance where injury or damage feared

A.B., on the..........(day) of (month) ...., (year).........., at (specify time) in (specify place),

..........being bound by a recognizance that was entered into because A.B. did utter certain words [OR do such things] so as to cause fear on the part of C.D. that A.B. would cause personal injury to C.D. [OR the spouse of C.D. OR the children of C.D.], did commit a breach of the recognizance, to wit: (specify the particulars of the offence), contrary to s. 811 of the Criminal Code of Canada.

..........being bound by a recognizance that was entered into because A.B. did utter certain words [OR do such things] so as to cause fear on the part of C.D. that A.B. will damage the property of C.D., did commit a breach of the recognizance, to wit: (specify the particulars of the offence), contrary to s. 811 of the Criminal Code of Canada.

Section 810.1 and 811 Breach of recognizance where fear of sexual violence

A.B., on the..........(day) of (month) ...., (year).........., at (specify time) in (specify place), being bound by a recognizance that was entered into because A.B. did utter certain words [OR do such things] so as to cause fear on the part of C.D. that A.B. would commit an offence under s. 151 [OR s. 152, s. 155, s. 159, s. 160(2), s. 160(3), s. 170, s. 171, s. 173(2), s. 271, s. 272, or s. 273], in respect of one or more persons who were under the age of 14 years, did commit a breach of the recognizance, to wit: (specify the particulars of the offence), contrary to s. 811 of the Criminal Code of Canada.

Section 810.01 and 811 Breach of recognizance where fear of criminal organization offence

A.B., on the..........(day) of (month) ...., (year).........., at (specify time) in (specify place), being bound by a recognizance that was entered into by A.B., because there were reasonable grounds to believe that A.B. would commit a criminal organization offence, did breach the recognizance, to wit: (specify the particulars of the offence), contrary to s. 811 of the Criminal Code of Canada.

Section 810.02 and 811 Breach of recognizance where fear of serious personal injury offence

A.B., on the..........(day) of (month) ...., (year).........., at (specify time) in (specify place), being bound by a recognizance that was entered into by A.B., because there were reasonable grounds to believe that A.B. would commit a serious personal injury offence, did breach the recognizance, to wit: (specify the particulars of the offence), contrary to s. 811 of the Criminal Code of Canada.

Controlled Drugs and Substances Act

Section 4(1) Possession of controlled substance

A.B., on the..........(day) of (month) ...., (year).........., at (specify time) in (specify place), did have in his [OR her] possession (specify a substance included in Schedule I, II, III, or IV), a controlled substance, without being authorized by the Controlled Drugs and Substances Act Regulations, to wit: (specify the particulars of the offence), contrary to s. 4(1) of the Controlled Drugs and Substances Act.

Section 4(2)(a) Obtaining controlled substance

A.B., on the..........(day) of (month) ...., (year).........., at (specify time) in (specify place), did seek [OR obtain](specify a substance included in Schedule I, II, III, or IV) a controlled substance, from C.D., a medical [OR dental OR veterinary] practitioner, without disclosing to C.D. the particulars relating to the acquisition by A.B. of every controlled substance, or of every authorization to obtain a controlled substance, from any practitioner in the preceding 30 days, to wit: (specify the particulars of the offence), contrary to s. 4(2)(a) of the Controlled Drugs and Substances Act.

Section 4(2)(b) Obtaining authorization to obtain a controlled substance

A.B., on the..........(day) of (month) ...., (year).........., at (specify time) in (specify place), did seek [OR obtain] an authorization to obtain a (specify a particular substance included in Schedules I, II, III, or IV), a controlled substance, from C.D., a medical [OR dental OR veterinary] professional, without disclosing to C.D. the particulars relating to the acquisition of A.B. of every controlled substance, or of every authorization to obtain a controlled substance, from any practitioner in the preceding 30 days, to wit: (specify the particulars of the offence), contrary to s. 4(2)(a) of the Controlled Drugs and Substances Act.

Section 5(1) Trafficking in controlled substance

A.B., on the..........(day) of (month) ...., (year).........., at (specify time) in (specify place),

..........did traffic in (specify a controlled substance included in Schedule I, II, III, or IV), a controlled substance, to wit: (specify the particulars of the offence), contrary to s. 5(1) of the Controlled Drugs and Substances Act.

..........did traffic in a substance represented [OR held out] to be a controlled substance, to wit: (specify the particulars of the offence), contrary to s. 5(1) of the Controlled Drugs and Substances Act.

Section 5(2) Possession for purpose of trafficking

A.B., on the..........(day) of (month) ...., (year).........., at (specify time) in (specify place), did possess (specify a substance included in Schedule I, II, III, or IV), a controlled substance, for the purpose of trafficking, to wit: (specify the particulars of the offence), contrary to s. 5(2) of the Controlled Drugs and Substances Act.

Section 6(1) Importing and Exporting

A.B., on the..........(day) of (month) ...., (year).........., at (specify time) in (specify place), did import into Canada [OR export from Canada](specify a substance included in Schedule I, II, III, IV, V, or VI), a controlled substance without authorization, to wit: (specify the particulars of the offence), contrary to s. 6(1) of the Controlled Drugs and Substances Act.

Section 6(2) Possession for the purpose of exporting

A.B., on the..........(day) of (month) ...., (year).........., at (specify time) in (specify place), did possess (specify a substance included in Schedule I, II, III, IV, V, or VI), a controlled substance, for the purpose of exporting it from Canada, without authorization, to wit: (specify the particulars of the offence), contrary to s. 6(2) of the Controlled Drugs and Substances Act.

Section 7(1) Production of substance

A.B., on the..........(day) of (month) ...., (year).........., at (specify time) in (specify place), did produce (specify substance in Schedule I, II, III, or IV), a controlled substance, without authorization to wit: (specify the particulars of the offence), contrary to s. 7(1) of the Controlled Drugs and Substances Act.

Section 8(1) Possession of property obtained by certain offences

A.B., on the..........(day) of (month) ...., (year).........., at (specify time) in (specify place),

..........did have in his [OR her] possession (specify particular property or proceeds of property), knowing that all [OR part] of it was obtained [OR derived] directly [OR indirectly], as a result of the commission of an offence in Canada under the Controlled Drugs and Substances Act, to wit: (specify the particulars of the offence), contrary to s. 8(1)(a) of the Controlled Drugs and Substances Act.

..........did have in his [OR her] possession (specify particular property or proceeds of property), knowing that all [OR part] of it was obtained [OR derived] directly [OR indirectly], as a result of an act [OR omission] that would have constituted an offence under the Controlled Drugs and Substances Act if it had occurred in Canada, to wit: (specify the particulars of the offence), contrary to s. 8(1)(b) of the Controlled Drugs and Substances Act.

..........did have in his [OR her] possession (specify particular property or proceeds of property), knowing that all [OR part] of it was obtained [OR derived] directly [OR indirectly], as the result of a conspiracy to commit [OR an attempt to commit OR being an accessory after the fact in relation to OR counselling in relation to] an offence under the Controlled Drugs and Substances Act, to wit: (specify the particulars of the offence), contrary to s. 8(1)(c) of the Controlled Drugs and Substances Act.

Firearms Act

Section 106(1) False statements to procure a licence, registration certificate or authorization

A.B., on the..........(day) of (month) ...., (year).........., at (specify time) in (specify place), for the purpose of procuring a licence [OR a registration certificate OR an authorization] for A.B., knowingly made a false misleading statement [OR failed to disclose relevant information], to wit: (specify the particulars of the offence), contrary to s. 106(1) of the Firearms Act.

Section 106(2) False statements to procure a customs confirmation

A.B., on the..........(day) of (month) ...., (year).........., at (specify time) in (specify place), for the purpose of procuring the confirmation of (specify document), by C.D., a customs officer, for A.B. [OR E.F.], knowingly made a false or misleading statement [OR failed to disclose relevant information], to wit: (specify the particulars of the offence), contrary to s. 106(2) of the the Firearms Act.

Section 107 Tampering with a licence, registration certificate, authorization or confirmation

A.B., on the..........(day) of (month) ...., (year).........., at (specify time) in (specify place), without lawful excuse, altered [OR defaced or falsified] a licence [OR registration certificate OR authorization OR confirmation], to wit: (specify the particulars of the offence), contrary to s. 107 of the Firearms Act.

Section 108 Unauthorized use of ammunition

A.B., on the..........(day) of (month) ...., (year).........., at (specify time) in (specify place), did possess ammunition without holding a licence under which the business is permitted to possess ammunition, to wit: (specify the particulars of the offence), contrary to s. 108 of the Firearms Act.

Section 29(1) Operating a shooting club or shooting range without approval

A.B., on the..........(day) of (month) ...., (year).........., at (specify time) in (specify place), operated a shooting club [OR a shooting range] without the approval of the Minister of (specify designated provincial Ministry), to wit: (specify the particulars of the offence), contrary to s. 29(1) of the Firearms Act.

Section 110 Contravention of conditions of a licence, registration certificate or authorization

A.B., on the..........(day) of (month) ...., (year).........., at (specify time) in (specify place), without lawful excuse, contravened a condition of a licence [OR registration certificate OR authorization] held by A.B., that required A.B. to (specify condition), to wit: (specify the particulars of the offence), contrary to s. 110 of the Firearms Act.

Section 112(1) Possession of unregistered firearm

A.B., on the..........(day) of (month) ...., (year).........., at (specify time) in (specify place), possessed a firearm without holding a registration certificate, to wit: (specify the particulars of the offence), contrary to s. 112(1) of the Firearms Act.

Section 113 Non-compliance with demand to produce a firearm

A.B., on the..........(day) of (month) ...., (year).........., at (specify time) in (specify place), without reasonable excuse, failed to comply with a lawful demand made by C.D., an inspector, pursuant to s. 105 of the Firearms Act, to wit: (specify the particulars of the offence), contrary to s. 113 of the Firearms Act.

Section 114 Failure to deliver up a revoked licence, certificate or authorization to a peace officer or firearms officer

A.B., on the..........(day) of (month) ...., (year).........., at (specify time) in (specify place), being the holder of a revoked licence [OR registration certificate OR authorization] did not deliver it up to a peace officer or firearms officer without delay after revocation, to wit: (specify the particulars of the offence), contrary to s. 114 of the Firearms Act.

Section 103 Failure to assist inspectors

A.B., on the..........(day) of (month) ...., (year).........., at (specify time) in (specify place), being the owner of [OR person in charge of OR person found in] (specify place), failed to give to C.D., an inspector, all reasonable assistance to enable C.D. to carry out an inspection and exercise a lawful power [OR failed to give C.D., an inspector, required information], to wit: (specify the particulars of the offence), contrary to s. 103 of the Firearms Act.

INDEX

Canadian Bill of Rights, *CBR*; Criminal Code, *CC*; Constitution Act, *CA*; Controlled Drugs and Substances Act, *CDA*; Criminal Records Act, *CRA*; Canada Evidence Act, *CEA*; Extradition Act, R.S.C. 1985, *EA*; Extradition Act, S.C. 1999, *EXA*; Firearms Act, *FA*; Food and Drugs Act, *FDA*; Identification of Criminals Act, *ICA*; Interpretation Act, *IA*; Motor Vehicle Transport Act, 1987, *MVTA*; Narcotic Control Act, *NCA*; Young Offenders Act, *YOA*

Index

Index